CURIOSITIES

OF DISCARDED

POPULAR CUSTOMS

AND OF

RITES, CEREMONIES, OBSERVANCES, AND MISCELLANEOUS ANTIQUITIES

BY

WILLIAM S. WALSH

AUTHOR OF "HANDY-BOOK OF LITERARY CURIOSITIES"

ILLUSTRATED

PHILADELPHIA
J. B. LIPPINCOTT COMPANY
LONDON : 6 HENRIETTA STREET, COVENT GARDEN
1898

REPUBLISHED BY GALE RESEARCH COMPANY, BOOK TOWER, DETROIT, 1966

Library of Congress Catalog Card Number 66-23951

PREFACE.

THE series of books of which this is the second is designed rather to be a supplement to the encyclopædias than to be of an encyclopedic character in itself. That is to say, it is the strange and out-of-the-way things usually left out of current works of reference which form the staple of this book, as of its predecessor.

The book is largely a compilation. I have been greatly indebted to the antiquarian writers who have gone before. Bourne, Brand, Hone, and Chambers have been placed under contribution. Thiselton Dyer's "British Popular Customs" (1891) and P. H. Ditchfield's "Old English Customs Extant at the Present Time" (1897) have proved especially valuable among the more modern authorities. To all these I cordially give my thanks. I must also call attention to that very remarkable French work by B. Picart, "Cérémonies et Coutumes religieuses de tous les Peuples" (1723), because it has furnished many of the most striking and unique of the illustrations to this book.

A word about Barnaby Googe's translation of Naogeorgus, from which many excerpts have been made, will not prove out of place. Naogeorgus was the assumed name of Thomas Kirchmayer, a German of the time of the Reformation, whose "Popish Kingdom, or Reign of Antichrist," was originally published in Latin. Googe's translation into English appeared in 1570. A new edition, by C. R. Hope, was published in 1880. The book, it must be remembered, though many antiquarians have failed so to remember, deals with the Germany and not the England of Catholic times.

W. S. W.

CURIOSITIES

OF

POPULAR CUSTOMS.

A.

Ab, Fast of, or **Black Fast.** The most mournful day in the Jewish calendar. It occurs on the ninth day of the fifth month, Ab,—a month which corresponds roughly with the end of July and the beginning of August. This is the anniversary of the two destructions of Jerusalem, the first by Nebuchadnezzar, which resulted in the Babylonish Captivity, the second by Titus, when the Jewish nation was dispersed over the face of the earth. The fast is observed scrupulously from sunset of the eighth day of Ab until nightfall of the ninth. The synagogues are darkened so that the light of the sun cannot penetrate within, only a few dim candles are lit, the ornaments are all removed, and the ark is stripped of its curtain. The service consists of readings from the book of Lamentations, and dirges describing the destruction of Jerusalem and the dispersion of its people, all conducted in a low and melancholy key.

Adam's Peak, or **Samanala,** a holy mountain in Ceylon. According to Mohammedan legend, Adam after the fall was taken by an angel to the top of this mountain, whence a panorama of all the ills that should afflict mankind was unrolled before him. His foot left an impress on the solid rock which is still shown to visitors, while his tears formed the lake from which pilgrims still drink. The Buddhists have their own legend of the Sripada, or Sacred Footstep, according to which Buddha, ascending to heaven, left the impression where last he touched the earth on the highest point of Samanala. The Brahmins, the Mohammedans, and the Chinese have differing legends, and for more than two thousand years all have worshipped in their own way round the gigantic footprint. The latter is a flat rocky basin, five and a quarter feet by two and a half feet, on the top of a huge boulder, in which only a very active imagination, aided by a lively faith, can see the likeness to a human foot. The boulder is covered with a wooden shrine of slender columns, which is open on all sides to the wild winds that rage there, and is sheltered only by a roof with shady, overhanging eaves, from which hang down two ancient bells. Although the shrine offers but slight resistance to the elements, the winds which blow and beat about that sacred summit are so strong and wild that it has to be secured in its place by great chains, which pass over it and are fastened to the living rock below. To perform a pilgrimage to this shrine and to lay an offering upon it is to a Buddhist what a visit to Mecca is to a Mohammedan. The favorite months are April and May, but all the year round a steady stream of devotees flows hither. The devotions of the pilgrims, who are usually clad in spotless white, consist of low bowings and prayers before Sripada, gifts of flowers and incense, burning of candles, ringing of small bells, and presents to the priests of rice and of gold and silver coins. Rags of old clothes are also considered a worthy sacrifice, and the words "Sadu, Sadu," corresponding to our "Amen, Amen," are often repeated. Tradition asserts that the iron chains fastened to the walls of rock to give the pilgrims safety along the precipices were placed there by Alexander.

Adam's Tomb. This is pointed out in a chamber of the church of the Holy Sepulchre in Jerusalem. Mark Twain's apostrophe at the tomb is one of the most famous bits in his "Innocents Abroad:" "The tomb of Adam! how touching it was, here in a land of strangers, far away from home and friends! True, he was a blood-relation; though a distant one, still a relation! The unerring instinct of nature thrilled its recognition. The fountain of my filial affection was stirred to its profoundest depths, and I gave way to tumultuous emotion. I leaned upon a pillar and burst into tears. I deem it no shame to have wept over the grave of my poor dead relative. Let him who would sneer at my emotion close this volume. Noble old man—he did not live to see his child; and I—I—I, alas! did not live to see him. Weighed down by sorrow and disappointment, he died before I was born—six thousand brief summers before I was born. But let us try to bear it with fortitude. Let us trust he is better off where he is. Let us take comfort in the thought that his loss is our eternal gain."

Adrian, St. His festival, together with that of his wife, St. Natalia, occurs September 8, the anniversary of the translation of his relics to Rome. He was anciently commemorated on March 4, his death-day. The greatest military saint next to St. George, he is especially reverenced in Flanders, Germany, and the north of France as the patron of soldiers and a protector against the plague. In Flanders he is also the patron of brewers. Adrian was one of the Prætorian Guards of the Emperor Galerius Maximian. While superintending the torture of thirty-four Christians, he was converted at sight of their fortitude and devotion, and, publicly confessing his faith, was thrown into prison. His wife Natalia was in secret a Christian, and greatly did she rejoice at the news. Disguised as a man, she obtained admittance to his cell and exhorted him to endure to the end. The next day Adrian's limbs were struck off on an anvil, and he was beheaded, March 4, 306. Natalia held him and sustained him in his sufferings, and before the final blow could be given by the headsman he expired in her arms. St. Adrian is usually represented armed, with an anvil in his hands or at his feet. His relics were conveyed to Constantinople, thence to Rome, afterwards into Flanders, and found a final resting-place in the abbey of St. Adrian, founded in 1088 at Geersburg in Belgium by Baldwin VI., Earl of Flanders. But Raulcourt in the same country claims to possess a complete body, all save an arm. Ghent has another, entirely complete. The jaw and half an arm are shown at Cologne, another part of an arm at Prague, a head at Bologna, and various fragments at Douai and at the cathedral of Bruges.

Adriatic, Marriage of the. (It. *Sposalizio del Adriatico.*) A solemn ceremony anciently performed in the Venice of the

MARRIAGE OF THE ADRIATIC.
(From an old print.)

Doges on Ascension Day. It was instituted in 1177 by Pope Alexander III. in commemoration of a great naval victory won by the Venetians over the hostile fleet of Frederick Barbarossa at Istria. Giving the Doge, Vitale Michieli II., a ring from his own finger, the Pontiff instructed him and his successors on every coming Ascension Day to cast a similar ring into the Adriatic, promising that the bride so espoused should be as dutiful as a wife to her husband. The initial ceremony was performed on Ascension Day in that year. The state gondola known as the Bucentaur, manned by forty rowers, and gorgeously appointed, left the Piazza di San Marco and proceeded slowly towards the isle of Lido. In its wake followed gondolas, barges, sailing-vessels, and galleys, occupied by persons of rank, with minstrels and other attendants. Arriving off the island, the Doge first poured holy water into the sea. Then he took the ring from his finger and dropped it into the bosom of the Adriatic, saying, "We espouse thee, O Sea, in token of our just and perpetual dominion." Solemn mass was attended by all the celebrants and spectators at the church of St. Nicholas on the isle of Lido, and the festivities were rounded out to an epicurean end by a sumptuous banquet at the ducal palace. After the invention of gunpowder a salute of guns was fired as the signal for the gondolas and their train to start from St. Mark's Square. (See DART, THROWING OF THE.)

Advent. A preparation for Christmas, as Lent is a preparation for Easter. In one form or another it is recognized by the Roman, Greek, Lutheran, and Anglican Churches. It is impossible to fix the exact time when the season began to be observed. A canon of a Council at Saragossa, in 380, forbade the faithful to absent themselves from the church services during the three weeks from December 17 to the Epiphany; this is perhaps the earliest trace on record of the observance of Advent. In the fifth century it was closely assimilated to Lent, being kept as a fast of forty days,—*i.e.*, from Martinmas (November 11) to Christmas Eve. Later the length of the season was limited, and in the ninth century it was made to begin, as it now does, with the Sunday nearest to the feast of St. Andrew (November 30), whether before or after that day, so that in all cases the season of Advent shall contain the uniform number of four Sundays. In the Greek Church, however, it contains six Sundays.

Besides being a preparation for Christmas, Advent has another significance in the Roman Church, as the beginning of the ecclesiastical year. Before the sixth century that beginning was Easter, both in the West and in the East. The reason for the change was that the Jewish ecclesiastical year also began about Easter, and the Christians sought to differentiate themselves as much as possible from the Jews.

Since the curtailing of the season the ancient austerities also have been greatly relaxed, until at present only the Fridays in Advent are fast-days. But no marriages are celebrated during the season. Special devotions are enjoined upon the faithful. The purple hue of penance is the only color used in the services of Advent, except on the feasts of saints. The organ is silenced until the third Sunday in Advent, when it again finds its voice, to indicate that the assured expectation of a Redeemer has tempered mourning. In the Episcopal Church the services appointed for the Advent season bear particularly upon the coming of the Lord.

Popular custom has marked this season with quaint and peculiar observances. In the department of Eure-et-Loire in Normandy every farmer fixes upon some day in Advent for the purpose of exorcising such animals as prove injurious to his crops. He furnishes his younger children with prepared flambeaux, well dried in the oven. If he have no children his neighbors lend him theirs, for only young and innocent children can command certain injurious animals to withdraw from his lands. After twelve years of age children are unfit to perform the office of exorcists. These little people run over the country like so many spirits, set fire to bundles of hay, flourish their torches among the branches of the trees, burn the straw placed underneath, and continually cry out,—

> Mice, caterpillars, and moles,
> Get out, get out of my field;
> I will burn your beard and bones:
> Trees and shrubs
> Give me bushels of apples.

Accidents might be supposed to arise from this lawless assembly of juvenile torch-bearers; but their fire is believed to burn only vermin. Such at least is the opinion of the simple inhabitants of Eure-et-Loire.

In Italy the Advent season is duly celebrated, especially in Rome. One custom is worth referring to. In the last days of Advent the Calabrian *pifferari*, or bagpipe-players, enter Rome, and are to be seen in every street saluting the shrines of the Virgin Mother with their wild music, under the traditional notion of soothing her until the birth-time of her infant at the approaching Christmas. They also stop in front of carpenter-shops, out of respect to St. Joseph, who was a carpenter by trade.

The *pifferari* play a pipe very similar in form and sound to the bagpipes of the Highlanders. "Just before Christmas," says Lady Morgan, "they descend from the mountains to Naples and Rome, in order to play before the pictures of the Virgin and Child," which are common in every Italian town, and abound in the

cities. Raphael's picture of the Nativity has a shepherd standing at the door playing upon his pipes. This is in accordance
with Italian tradition, which holds that the bagpipe was the
favorite instrument of the Virgin Mary, and that the shepherds
played on it when they visited the Saviour.

Aubanus tells us that in Franconia, on each of the three
Thursdays preceding Christmas, it was customary for young
boys and girls to go from house to house, knocking at the doors,
singing their Christmas carols and wishing a happy New Year.
In return they received gifts of pears, apples, nuts, or money.
Barnaby Googe also refers to this custom, in his paraphrase of
Naogeorgus's " Popish Kingdom :"

> Three weekes before the day whereon was borne the Lorde of Grace,
> And on the Thursdays boyes and gyrles do runne in every place,
> And bounce and beat at every doore, with blowes and lustie snaps,
> And crie the Advent of the Lord, not borne as yet perhaps,
> And wishing to the neighbours all, that in the houses dwell,
> A happy year, and everything to spring and prosper well :
> Here have they peares, and plumbs, and pence, each man gives willinglie,
> For these three nightes are always thought unfortunate to bee :
> Wherein they are afrayde of sprites, and cankred witches spight,
> And dreadfull devils blacke and grim, that then have chiefest might.

At this season, also, rustic young girls attempted to divine the
names of their husbands that should be. Barnaby says,— .

> In these same dayes yong, wanton gyrles that meete for marriage bee,
> Doe search to know the names of them that shall their husbands bee.
> Foure onyons, five, or eight, they take, and make in every one
> Such names as they do fansie most and best do thinke upon.
> Thus neere the chimney them they set, and that same onyon than,
> That first doth sproute, doth surely beare the name of their good man.

They also endeavor to divine the character of the "good man"
by going at night to the wood-stack and drawing out the first
stick that the hand meets :

> Which if it streight and even be, and have no knots at all,
> A gentle husband then they thinke shall surely to them fall ;
> But if it fowle and crooked be, and knottie here and there,
> A crabbed, churlish husband then they earnestly do feare.

For all these wicked doings Barnaby goes on to blame the
" Papistes,"

> Who rather had the people should obey their foolish lust,
> Than truly God to know, and in him here alone to trust.

An English custom which is extinct save in remote interior
parishes is more directly traceable to the "Papistes." This is
the custom of carrying about Advent Images—two dolls dressed

up to represent the Saviour and the Virgin Mary—by poor women in the week before Christmas. A halfpenny is expected from every person to whom these are exhibited. Bad luck will follow to him who refuses. (See VESSEL-CUP.)

Afra, St., patroness of Augsburg, Germany. Her feast on August 5 is especially honored in this her native city. Legend asserts that she was originally a courtesan, who with her three handmaidens, Digna, Eunomia, and Eutropia, led a dissolute life during the reign of Diocletian. A priest named Narcissus, fleeing from persecution, took shelter in her house in ignorance of its character. He converted and baptized her and her companions, and she aided him to escape. For this offence she was imprisoned, and when she confessed the faith she was burnt alive, August 7, 304. All the members of her household also suffered martyrdom on the same day. But for some reason St. Afra and her companions are commemorated on August 5. Her relics are supposed to have been discovered in 955 by St. Ulfric. They now repose in the church of SS. Ulfric and Afra in Augsburg.

Agape, pl. **Agapæ.** (Gr. ἀγάπη, "love.") The love-feast of the ancient Christians, when all the members of a congregation, even the master and his slaves, met together at a common meal, celebrating the Eucharist, as brethren and sisters of the same family. The Agape therefore was a social symbol of the equality and solidarity of all Christendom, hallowed and sealed by the eucharistic sacrifice. Here all gave and received the kiss of peace (*q. v.*), and here communications from other congregations were received and read. The Agape dates from apostolic times, for it is mentioned in Jude 12 and described at some length in I. Corinthians xi. 23. But even in St. Paul's day its liability to abuse was recognized. As each congregation grew larger and more diverse in its membership, social differences began to assert themselves. The Agapæ lost their original significance. They either became distinctively the entertainments of the rich, where luxury was encouraged, or sank down into a kind of poor-house institution. Finally the third Council of Carthage (A.D. 391) decreed that the Eucharist should be taken fasting, and thereby separated the Agape from the celebration of the Eucharist. Towards the end of the fourth century the Council of Laodicea forbade "eating in the house of the Lord;" but from the fact that the Synod in Trullo (A.D. 692) had to repeat this prohibition it is evident that the practice died hard. From the complaints of St. Augustine it would seem that in his time the custom still survived of permitting communion once a year—viz., Holy Thursday—to those who had just partaken of Agape.

Agatha, St. The festival of this saint occurs on February 5, and is specially honored in Malta and in Catania, Sicily, of which places she is the patroness. She is generally held to be a native of Catania, though Palermo disputes the honor. Quintianus, whom Decius had made King of Sicily, laid siege to her virtue, and because she repulsed him ordered her to be bound and beaten and her bosom to be torn with shears. But at midnight St. Peter descended into her dungeon and healed her. Then Quintianus ordered her to the stake. No sooner was the torch applied than an earthquake broke out, and the citizens forced Quintianus to rescue her from the flames. She was cast back into prison, and God took her to himself (February 5, 251). A year after her death the volcano of Mt. Etna burst into flame. The fire had nearly reached the city, when its progress was arrested by the veil of St. Agatha, which some of the inhabitants had placed upon the top of a pole and borne out in procession; and all the heathen were converted by this miracle and received baptism. St. Agatha is a patroness against fire and all diseases of the breast. She is represented with the palm in one hand and in the other a salver on which is the female breast.

Most of the saint's relics are preserved at Catania in a church dedicated to her which Gregory the Great purged from the Arian impiety, and which was rebuilt in 460. The same Pope sent some of her bones to the monastery of St. Stephen, in the island of Capri.

The distinguishing feature of the festival at Catania is a pony-race, closely analogous to the Barberi (*q. v.*) of the Roman Carnival. It is thus described by an eye-witness : "The ponies destined for the contest have no riders; but, by means of wax, ribbons are firmly attached to their backs; and to these again are appended bladders, and weighted pieces of wood, armed with sharp spikes; the noise of the one, and the pain inflicted by the other, being amply sufficient to urge to exertion animals much better qualified to resist the effect of either than the horse. At the firing of a signal gun they are turned loose from one extremity of the street; and amidst the shouts of the populace which lines it on both sides, they make what haste they can to the other. Here I discovered to my great surprise, sitting in the open air, under a canopy of crimson, arrayed in robes of office a good deal resembling those of our barristers, the members of the senate, with their intendente or president. The business of these first magistrates of the city, decked out in all their paraphernalia, and attended by drummers, fifers, and musketeers, was to declare the winner among half a dozen jades, the best of which was not worth ten pounds. It was difficult to suppress a smile on seeing one of the parties rise, discuss the matter with the rest of the

bench, and, not without much action and emphasis and delibera-
tion, deliver the *senatus consultum* to the expectant crowd. The
mottoes on the canopy might have been selected for the purposes
of burlesque: ' *Invictas supero,*' ' *Catana Regum,*' ' *Tutrix Castigo
Rebellis.*' " (REV. JOHN JAMES BLUNT: *Vestiges of Ancient Manners and Customs discoverable in Modern Italy and Sicily,* London,
1823.)

A curious ceremony on St. Agatha's Day still survives at
Biddenham, England, and possibly other remote rural parishes.
Shortly before noon a procession of villagers, carrying a white
rabbit decorated with scarlet ribbons, passes through the village,
singing a hymn in honor of St. Agatha. Maids old and young
who meet the procession point at the rabbit with the first two
fingers of the right hand, saying,—

> Gustin, Gustin, lacks a bier!
> Maidens, maidens, bury him here.

The custom is said to date from the year of the first Crusade.

Agnes, St. One of the four great virgin martyrs of the
Latin Church. Her festival occurs on January 21, the reputed
anniversary of her martyrdom. St. Agnes was born a Christian, and at a very early age had vowed herself to virginity.
When only thirteen she was sought in marriage by the son of the
prefect Sempronius. She refused him, saying she was already
affianced to one whom she dearly loved, meaning Jesus. The
young man fell sick of disappointed love, and Sempronius, learning his secret, besought the maiden to take pity on the unhappy
youth. But Agnes answered as before that she was already
affianced. When Sempronius inquired her meaning and learned
that she was a Christian, he rejoiced, for he knew she was in his
power. He commanded her to become a vestal virgin, and on
her refusal he had her taken to a house of infamy to be exposed
to outrage. The soldiers stripped her of her raiment, but her
hair became as a veil, covering her whole body, and those who
looked upon her were filled with fear. When they had left her
to herself, she prayed that she might not be dishonored, and a
shining white garment descended into the room. She put it
on, rejoicing. Soon afterwards the son of Sempronius entered,
thinking that now she must be subdued, but the light from the
garment struck him blind, and he fell down in convulsions.
Agnes was moved to compassion by the tears of his relations,
and through her prayers he was healed. Then Sempronius would
fain have released her, but the multitude cried out that she was
a sorceress, and clamored for her death. She was bound to a
stake. The fire consumed her executioners, but would not hurt

her. At last a soldier climbed the pile and killed her with his
sword. The day of her martyrdom is given as January 21, 304.
She was buried by the Christians in the Via Nomentana, and her
tomb became their place of assembly for devotion. At first the
pagans sought to drive them away by hurling stones at them,
but, having struck a maiden named Emerantiane, lightning
darted out of the skies and killed many of the assailants. Thereafter they suffered the Christians to assemble in peace around
the tomb, and there on the eighth day after her death the
virgin appeared to them, surrounded by other holy martyrs
and with a spotless lamb by her side, and assured them of her
happiness. It is on this account that St. Agnes is represented
with a lamb by her side. She is usually clothed in white, with
the palm of martyrdom in her hand.

Constantine built a church in her honor over the reputed spot
of her burial. It was repaired by Pope Honorius in the seventh
century, and was enriched with her relics (still preserved here
in a rich silver shrine) by Pope Paul V., in whose time they were
discovered under the floor of the church. The edifice is of Byzantine architecture, with galleries high up near the roof, and an
altar turned towards the apse instead of facing the nave.

In Catholic countries it was once usual to bless a lamb on St.
Agnes' Day, no doubt a recrudescence under Christian forms of
the ancient Roman custom of invoking upon sheep the blessing
of Pales, the goddess of sheepfolds and pastures. The lamb,
gayly decorated, was first led through the streets by a holiday-
making crowd. A more special celebration of this kind is still
practised at Rome, when every year on St Agnes' Day two
chosen lambs, of undoubted virginity, are blessed by the Pope
in the church of St. Agnes after pontifical high mass. These
are carefully guarded until shearing-time, when their wool is
woven by nuns into the pallium (*q. v.*) worn by the Pope and the
primates of the Church.

This ceremony is mentioned by Naogeorgus:

> For in St. Agnes' church upon this day while masse they sing,
> Two lambes as white as snowe, the Nonnes do yearely use to bring:
> And when the Agnus chaunted is, upon the aultar hie
> (For in this thing there hidden is a solemne mysterie),
> They offer them. The servaunts of the Pope, when this is done,
> Do put them into pasture good till shearing time be come.
> Then other wooll they mingle with these holy fleeces twaine,
> Whereof, being sponne and drest, are made the Pals of passing gaine.
> (*The Popish Kingdom*, translated by Barnaby Googe.)

In Jephson's "Manners, etc., of France and Italy" is a poetical epistle dated from Rome, 14th February, 1793, certifying
the use of this ceremony at that time:

Where each pretty *Ba*-lamb most gaily appears,
With ribands stuck round on its tail and its ears;
On gold-fringed cushions they're stretch'd out to eat,
And piously *ba*, and to church music bleat;
Yet to me they seem'd crying—alack, and alas!
What's all this white damask to daisies and grass!
Then they're brought to the Pope, and with transport they're kiss'd,
And receive consecration from Sanctity's fist:
To chaste Nuns he consigns them, instead of their dams,
And orders the friars to keep them from rams.

About 1850 the Pope and his retinue, while enjoying a slight refection in a hall adjoining the church, just after the ceremony, were suddenly precipitated through the rotten floor into a cellar beneath. Almost all escaped unhurt, which was certainly a remarkable occurrence, and was commemorated in after-years by a fresco of marvellous ugliness and very small skill, painted on the remaining wall of the former cellar. It is now enclosed within a portico looking into the court in front of the church, and, if a credit to Roman feeling, is no less a disgrace to modern Roman art.

The eve of St. Agnes' feast is not to be despised as a period of prophetic promise for maidens in search of a husband. An ancient method of divination, mentioned by Aubrey in his "Miscellanies," directs that "upon St. Agnes' Night you take a row of pins, and pull out every one, one after another, saying a Pater Noster, sticking a pin in your sleeve, and you will dream of him or her you shall marry." A more elaborate method was for a maiden to leave her home and go to a strange locality. When she retired to sleep that night she was to take her right-leg stocking and knit the left garter around it, saying the while,—

I knit this knot, this knot I knit,
To know the thing I know not yet,
That I may see
The man that shall my husband be,
Not in his best or worst array,
But what he weareth every day;
That I to-morrow may him ken
From among all other men.

At the conclusion of these words she was to lie down on her back with her hands under her head, and her future spouse would surely appear in a dream and salute her with a kiss. In all cases the charm was rendered more certain if the maiden went supperless to bed. Thus Burton, in "The Anatomy of Melancholy," speaks of "maids fasting on St. Agnes' Eve, to know who shall be their first husband." It is John Keats who has made the superstitions of this vigil ever memorable in literature by founding upon them his exquisite poem of "St. Agnes' Eve."

> They told her how, upon St. Agnes' Eve,
> Young virgins might have visions of delight,
> And soft adorings from their loves receive
> Upon the honeyed middle of the night,
> If ceremonies due they did aright;
> As, supperless to bed they must retire,
> And couch supine their beauties lily-white;
> Nor look behind, nor sideways, but require
> Of Heaven with upward eyes for all that they desire.

Another dream-charm for St. Agnes' Eve was to take a sprig of rosemary and another of thyme and sprinkle them thrice with water, then place one in each shoe, and stand shoe and sprig on each side of the bed, repeating,—

> St. Agnes, that's to lovers kind,
> Come ease the trouble of my mind.

In the northern parts of Scotland the lads and lasses used to meet together on St. Agnes' Eve at midnight. One by one would then go into a cornfield and throw grain on the soil. After this all said the following rhyme:

> Agnes sweet and Agnes fair,
> Hither, hither, now repair;
> Bonny Agnes, let me see
> The lad [or lass] who is to marry me.

On their return home it was expected that each would see in a mirror the shadow of the destined bride or bridegroom.

Agnus Dei. (Lat., "Lamb of God.") A prayer based on John i. 29, "Lamb of God, who takest away the sins of the world, have mercy on us," which was introduced into the mass by Pope Sergius I. in 680. The name is also applied to heart-shaped wax medallions bearing the figure of a lamb, which are made from the remains of the Paschal candle (*q. v.*), and solemnly blessed by the Pope on the Thursday after Easter, in the first and seventh year of his pontificate. From Amalarius we learn that in the ninth century the Agnus Dei's were made of wax and oil by the Archdeacon of Rome, blessed by the Pope, and distributed to the people during the octave of Easter. An Agnus Dei said to have belonged to Charlemagne is among the treasures of the cathedral of Aix-la-Chapelle.

Aïssaoua. An exhibition of immunity from pain given by the Aïssaoui, members of a Mohammedan sect which was founded in the fifteenth century by Sidi Mohammed-ben-Aissa. The latter was a marabout prophet who lived a holy life near Mequinez, in Morocco, aroused the jealousy of the Sultan Moulaï-Ismaïl by his increasing influence, and was driven out with his wives and children and those of his disciples who were faithful enough to follow him into exile. Sustenance failed them on the way, and when his hungry followers asked for food the saint bade them eat poison, if they could find nothing else, and himself set about searching among the stones for scorpions and serpents, which they devoured without harm. So runs the legend. To this day the Aïssaoui, it is pretended, have the power to resist the poison of venomous beasts in themselves, and to cure its effects in others. Not only this, but they claim immunity from physical harm and an absolute insensibility to pain of all kinds. The members of the confraternity nowadays exhibit their powers of endurance to native audiences, or are even willing to turn an honest penny, at times, by giving a special show to Europeans. William H. Carpenter, in the *New York Evening Post* for January 12, 1896, describes an Aïssaoua that he witnessed in Algiers. He tells how the performers gathered around a charcoal fire burning in a brazier. One of them drew out a red-hot iron and licked it with his tongue. He then placed a burning coal between his teeth and fanned it by his breath into a white heat. Another snatched an iron rod with a ball on one end from the fire, and after winding one of his eyelids around it until the eyeball was completely exposed, he thrust its point in behind the eye, which was forced far out on his cheek. It was held there for a moment, when it was withdrawn, and the eye released, which was then rubbed vigorously a few times with the balled end of the rod. Another let a live scorpion fasten its fangs into the inside of his cheek, where it hung suspended for some time before he chewed and ate it. Another balanced himself across the edge of a bare sword on his naked stomach while a comrade sprang violently upon his back and stood there. Still another took a burning wisp of hay and passed it all over his body and then wound up the performance by pulling out of the fire the balled instrument already described and jabbing it repeatedly into the pit of his stomach. " How much of the exhibition was real," says Mr. Carpenter, " and how much pure sleight of hand, I have no means of knowing. A critical analysis of the performance came later, and it was then for the first time remembered that there had been no sign of blood, not even the slightest, from beginning to end ; no mark of any kind had been left by the sword ; and the fire of the blazing wisp had not even singed the man's garments, over which it had inadvertently been passed. The man whose stomach was so ruthlessly assaulted apparently had the worst part to play of all, for there were indubitably a number of black and blue scars which plainly bespoke previous experiences."

Aix-la-Chapelle, Great Relics of. The relics distinctively so known are four in number,—viz., the tunic of the Blessed Virgin, the swaddling-clothes of the infant Jesus, the cloth that encircled the loins of Jesus on the cross, and the cloth in which the head of St. John the Baptist was enveloped after his decapitation. Their exposition in the cathedral of Aix-la-Chapelle every seven years from the 10th to the 24th of July is one of the most famous ceremonies of Catholicity, and draws to Aix enormous crowds of pilgrims. The tunic of the Virgin is yellowish in color, five feet and a half in length, and three feet and a quarter in circumference. A very small amount of decoration is to be found upon it, and a small piece of the cloth has been torn out. The swaddling-clothes of the infant Jesus are folded thrice in double folds. Ribbons are the sole decoration, which border them in the fashion of a collar. They are brownish yellow, loosely woven. The linen of St. John the Baptist is of fine texture, folded and bound with red ribbons. It is stained with blood. The linen cloth which was bound about Christ's loins upon the cross is of a heavy texture, folded, and showing great blood-stains. It is folded in triangular shape, having a length of four feet two and a half inches and a width of four feet ten inches.

According to the legend, when Charlemagne had finished building the church of Our Lady in Aix-la-Chapelle he set himself to the collecting of these relics from Rome, Constantinople, and Jerusalem, and secured in addition a number of lesser ones, among which may be mentioned the girdle of Christ, which is sealed at the ends with the seal of the Emperor Constantine ; a small piece of the cord with which Christ was bound during the flagellation; the girdle of the Virgin; a bit of the sponge which was offered to Christ on the cross; a lock of hair from the head of St. Bartholomew; two of St. Thomas the Apostle's teeth; one of the arms of the old Simeon; a fragment of the cross, which was given to Charlemagne by Pope Leo III., and which he bore continually on his person ; a tooth of St. Catherine; the point of a nail with which Christ was attached to the cross; a bit of the rod which served in the mocking of Christ; a lock of hair from the head of St. John the Baptist; a bust in gilded silver of Charlemagne, in which is enclosed the emperor's skull; and, in a reliquary shaped like an arm, the right arm of Charlemagne, presented by Louis XI., King of France, in 1481.

The septennial exhibition dates from the ninth century, and

remains practically the same that it was from its origin. Every
morning at ten o'clock the relics are brought out by the priests
to a lofty balcony on the exterior of the church and there exposed to the veneration of the crowd gathered outside in the
square. Later (from one to eight P.M.) the church is thrown
open to pilgrims. The relics are arranged on various altars, but
at stated times are carried around by the priests for the laity to
kiss. The last day of the exposition is distinguished by a procession in the streets, in which the Great Relics are borne in
their superb shrines by the canons of the cathedral. The date
of the last ceremony was 1895.

The Antiquary for November, 1888, translates from the Roman
Catholic *Germania* this description of the manner in which these
famous relics are stored away after their exposure in the cathedral: " The relics were first placed in silk wrappers, the gown
of the Mother of God being enveloped in white, the swaddling-
clothes of Christ in yellow, His loin-cloth in red, and the cloth
on which rested the head of John the Baptist was carried in pale
pink silk. After this each relic was wrapped up in a cloth richly
embroidered with real pearls, the four cloths being presents which
in 1629 the Infanta Isabella Clara Eugénie of Spain offered at
the sacred shrines. Next, each relic was put in a special pocket
closed with buttons, another cloth was wrapped round them, and
a cover of tissue-paper, the color of which corresponded to that
of the silk wrapper. Each parcel was then tied up with silk
ribbons, the ends of which were sealed with the seal of the
relics. Then a torchlight procession accompanied them to the
Hungarian chapel, and they were deposited in the large ' Mary's
shrine.' The iron lid was screwed on, the padlock filled with lead,
and the key to it crushed to powder before the eyes of the spectators. A Te Deum was sung, and the solemn procession returned to the upper regions to sign a paper in which it is stated
that the sealed relics had once again been enclosed in the secret
parts of the minster."

Alb. (Lat. *alba,* " white.") A long tunic or vestment of white
linen worn by the Roman priest at mass. While donning it he
prays, " Make me white, O Lord, and cleanse me." It differs
from the Anglican surplice in fitting closer and in being encircled
with a girdle. The alb is a modification of the tunic or under-
garment of the Greeks and Romans. It first appears in Church
history as the distinctive robe of the newly baptized, worn until
the Sunday after Easter, White-Sunday (Whitsunday). By the
fourth century it had become a special part of the ecclesiastical
garment. A canon of the fourth Council of Carthage, 398,
orders deacons to use the alb " only at the time of the oblation

or of reading." The Council of Narbonne in 589 forbade deacons, subdeacons, or lectores to put off the alb until after mass.
But it seems that for a long time after the alb was worn in daily
life as well as at the altar, for we read of a bishop of Soissons in
889 forbidding an ecclesiastic to use at mass the same alb that
he wore at home.

Alban, St. His festival is June 22. As the first English saint
and martyr, he was highly venerated in pre-Reformation times in
England. The Abbot of St. Alban's in Hertfordshire had precedence over all others. Born in Verulam, St. Alban was converted
by a priest who had sought refuge with him against persecution.
St. Alban donned his guest's robes, and delivered himself up to
the soldiers in pursuit. When the fraud was discovered, he confessed himself a Christian, and was tortured and beheaded, June
22, 303. To reach the place of execution it was necessary to
cross the river Coln, but, the bridge being insufficient for the
vast multitude of spectators, St. Alban said a prayer, the waters
were divided, and all went over dry-shod. At the place of execution he prayed for water, and a spring gushed out. Hence his
attribute, besides the sword, is a fountain of water.

The present town of St. Albans is built upon the scene of the
martyrdom. In the time of Constantine, according to Bede, a
large church was erected on the very spot, and was rendered
illustrious by frequent miracles. The pagon Saxons destroyed
it, but Offa, King of the Mercians, raised another in 793 with a
great monastery. In mediæval times the shrine of St. Alban's
was a popular place of pilgrimage. "Our island for many ages,"
says Alban Butler, "had recourse to St. Alban as its glorious
protomartyr and powerful patron with God, and acknowledged
many great favors received from God, through his intercession.
By it St. Germanus procured a triumph without Christian blood
and gained a complete victory both over the spiritual and corporal enemies of this country."

About the year 900 the Danes sacked the abbey and carried
off the bones of the martyr to a convent at Owensee. But a
holy man named Egwin obtained admittance by stratagem to
the latter convent and surreptitiously returned the remains to
St. Alban's, where numerous miracles attested the saint's approval of the pious theft. When the Danes next ravaged the
country, Ælfric, the eleventh abbot, concealed the true relics in
a cavity in the walls of the church, and as a further precaution
sent a bogus body to the monastery at Ely. On the departure
of the Danes Ælfric reclaimed the counterfeit, but the wily monks
at Ely sent him a counterfeit of the counterfeit. The true relics
were then brought from their hiding-place and deposited in a

shrine. Straightway the monks of Ely publicly proclaimed the artifice they had practised and declared that the only genuine saint was in their possession. For a century the "true bones" were exhibited both at St. Alban's and at Ely, until the Pope sent three bishops to Ely to inquire into the matter, when the monks acknowledged that they had been outwitted.

The shrine stood near the centre of St. Alban's Chapel. According to contemporary chroniclers, it was a glorious work, rich in gold and precious stones and cunning workmanship. It was shown only on high holidays, being on other occasions covered with an operculum worked by cords and pulleys. On the suppression of the monastery by Henry VIII. in 1539, the shrine with its contents disappeared. There is a legend that it found its way to the church of St. Mauritius in Cologne, where indeed the shrine of St. Albinus is still exhibited. But Albinus and Alban were two different saints. In 1872, in the course of certain restorations, an immense quantity of carved fragments was found, evidently the remnants of the shrine destroyed by the fury of an iconoclastic mob. As soon as the general plan was made out, the work of rebuilding was commenced, and continued with amazing patience until the whole was put together as it now stands in the site it occupied for centuries, and in a more perfect condition than even the more famous shrine of St. Edward at Westminster.

Ale, Church and **College.** In mediæval England, festivals at which ale was the chief item of refreshment were celebrated both in parishes and in universities, and hence were known as Church or College Ales. The ecclesiastical custom, as Strutt points out ("Sports and Pastimes," Chatto & Windus's ed., p. 471), originated from the wakes (*q. v.*). The churchwardens and other chief parish officers, observing the latter festival to be more popular than any others, rightly conceived that by establishing similar institutions within the church limits they might draw together a large concourse of people and annually collect from them such sums of money as would be a great easement to the parish rates. The meeting was held in the churchyard or in some barn near the church, and took on something of a picnic character, as every man brought what victuals he could spare. The ale, which had been brewed good and strong for the occasion, was sold by the churchwardens, who retained the profits as a fund to keep the church in repairs, or to be distributed in alms to the poor.

To modern temperance ideas it is somewhat surprising to come upon an inscription like the following on a church gallery, as actually occurs at Sygate, in Norfolk:

God speed the plough
And give us good ale enow. . . .
Be merry and glade,
With good ale was this work made.

In some instances the inhabitants of one or more parishes were mulcted in a certain sum to provide the ale for the day. Among the Dodsworth MSS. (Bid. Bob., vol. 148, folio 97) is preserved an ancient stipulation, couched in the following terms: "The parishioners of Elverton and those of Okebrook in Derbyshire agree jointly to brew four ales, and every ale of one quarter of malt, between this and the feast of Saint John the Baptist next comming, and every inhabitant of the said town of Okebrook shall be at the several ales; and every husband and his wife shall pay two pence, and every cottager one penny. And the inhabitants of Elverton shall have and receive all the profits comming of the said ales, to the use and behoof of the church of Elverton; and the inhabitants of Elverton shall brew eight ales betwixt this and the feast of Saint John, at which ales the inhabitants of Okebrook shall come and pay as before rehearsed; and if any be away one ale, he is to pay at t'oder ale for both."

In Sir Richard Worsley's "History of the Isle of Wight," p. 210, speaking of the parish of Whitwell, he tells us that there is a lease in the parish chest, dated 1574, "of a house called the church house, held by the inhabitants of Whitwell, parishioners of Gatcombe, of the Lord of the manor, and demised by them to John Brode, in which is the following proviso: Provided always, that, if the Quarter shall need at any time to make a Quarter-Ale, or Church-Ale, for the maintenance of the chapel, that it shall be lawful for them to have the use of the said house, with all the rooms, both above and beneath, during their Ale." It appears from a Sermon made at Blandford Forum, 1570, by William Kethe, that it was the custom at that time for the Church Ales to be kept upon the Sabbath-day; which holy day, says our author, "the multitude call their revelyng day, which day is spent in bulbeatings, beare-beatings, bowlings, dicyng, cardyng, daunsynges, and drunkenness, in so much, as men could not keepe their servauntes from lyinge out of theyre own houses the same Sabbath-day at night."

In course of time the word ale not only grew to be the generic designation for these feasts, but entered into the names of other merrymakings, such as Gyst-ale, Lammas-ale, Leet-ale, and even Bride-ale or Bridal. Celebrated at first on Sundays, without regard to the season, they gradually grew to be limited first to Easter, Christmas, and Whitsuntide, and eventually to the latter holiday alone. Hence the Whitsun-ales were the last remnant of the custom, and in spite of Puritan opposition these have or until recently did have local survivals in England.

Audrey mentions this custom as continuing to his grandfather's time, and speaks approvingly of it, remarking that in his own parish "there were no poor rates; the Whitsun ale did the business. . . . All things [at the festival] were civil and without scandal." The abuse of such festivities is often denounced, but the most sober and religious persons of the vicinity never appear to have objected to the fact of the brewing and sale of the beer. Even the Puritans of the seventeenth century had no special quarrel with the beverages vended on these occasions; they merely denounced "church ales" in the same company with Maypoles, stage plays, and all other amusements. Prynne himself was certainly no abstainer; for he records that during his imprisonment he took few regular meals, "rarely dined," but every three or four hours "munched a manchet and refreshed his exhausted spirits" with a cup of ale brought by his servant.

In 1597 a certain Puritanic minister of Redbourne inveighed thus against the Whitsun-ales: "These are in their origin bad; they are shamefully abused, having in them piping and dancing, and Maid Marian coming into the church at the time of prayer to move laughter with kissing in the church, and they justly deserve to be called profane, riotous and disorderly." (*Antiquary*, vol. xiii. p. 183.)

In the "Virgins' complaint for the loss of their sweethearts by these present wars, and their now long solitude, and keeping their virginities against their wills," presented to the House of Commons in the "names and behalfes" of all damsels both country and city, January 29, 1632–3, by sundry virgins of the city of London, occurs the following mention of church ales: "since the departure of the lusty young gentlemen courtiers and cavaliers, and the ablest 'prentices and handsome journeymen with whom we had used to walk to Islington and Pimlico to eat cakes and drink Christian-ale on holy days."

"At present," says Douce, quoting from Rudder, "the Whitsun-ales are conducted in the following manner. Two persons are chosen, previously to the meeting, to be lord and lady of the ale, who dress as suitably as they can to the character they assume. A large empty barn, or some such building, is provided for the lord's hall, and fitted up with seats to accommodate the company. Here they assemble to dance and regale in the best manner their circumstances and the place will afford; and each young fellow treats his girl with a ribbon or favor. The lord and lady honor the hall with their presence, attended by the steward, sword-bearer, purse-bearer, and mace-bearer, with their several badges or ensigns of office. They have likewise a train-bearer or page, and a fool or jester, drest in a party-colored jacket, whose ribaldry and gesticulation contribute not a little to the entertainment of some part of the company. The lord's music, consisting of a pipe and tabor, is employed to conduct the dance. Some people think this custom is a commemoration of the ancient *Drink-lean*, a day of festivity formerly observed by the tenants and vassals of the lord of the fee within his manor; the memory of which, on account of the jollity of those meetings, the people have thus preserved ever since. The glossaries inform us that this Drink-lean was a contribution of tenants towards a potation or *Ale* provided to entertain the lord or his steward."

Dunkin in his "History of Bicester" (1816) gives a curious account of a survival in his day and at that place of the Whitsun-ale: "A barn, the scene of the festivities, is called a hall, two of the principal male and female characters are dubbed lord and lady, and others bear the name of my lord's waiting-man and my lady's waiting-maid. A treasurer, who carries a tin box before him, a set of morris dancers, a Merry Andrew to clear the ring for dancing in, form the remainder of the group, and these, fantastically dressed and decorated with ribbons, dance or parade among the spectators. The barn doors are ornamented with an owl or monkey, who bear the appropriate names of my lord's parrot and my lady's lapdog, and to miscall any of them, or accept of my lord's cake and ale which are carried about in profusion and offered to all comers, subjects the offending party to a forfeiture of sixpence, for which, however, he is treated to a ride on my lord's gelding [a fantastic hobby-horse carried on men's shoulders], if a man, before my lady, or if a lady, before my lord, who of course considers himself entitled to a salute; but if this honor is declined, for an additional sixpence the forfeiting party is privileged to enter my lord's hall, and is entertained with cake and ale. By the sums collected in this manner, together with those arising from the voluntary visits of parties to the hall, the expenses of the entertainment, which are very considerable, are defrayed, and oftentimes the surplus is applied to charitable purposes. A few years ago a funeral pall, for the use of the poor, was purchased in this way. A towering Maypole erected some time before Whitsuntide serves to announce the amusement to the neighboring villages, and the crowds which usually attend attract great numbers of those itinerant traders who attend markets and fairs, so that the festival may be considered one of the most entertaining in the country. At the neighboring village of Kirtlington is a similar amusement held annually on Lammas day, and thence denominated a Lamb Ale."

Colleges in former times used to brew their own ale and hold festivities known as College Ales. The ales of Brasenose and

Magdalen Colleges at Oxford were especially famous, the poems connected with the Brasenose celebrations being among the best of bibulous songs. In one of them occurs this theory of evolution :

> A Grand Cross of " Malta" one night at a ball
> Fell in love with and married Hoppetta the Tall,
> Hoppetta, the bitterest, best of her sex,
> By whom he had issue the first Double X.
> Three others were born by this marriage : a girl,
> Transparent as amber and precious as pearl ;
> Then a son twice as strong as a porter or scout,
> And another as " spruce" as his brother was " stout."
>
> Double X, like his sister, is brilliant and clear ;
> Like his mother, though bitter, by no means severe ;
> Like his father, not small, and, resembling each brother,
> Joins the spirit of one to the strength of the other.

An ale of unusual strength is still brewed at Oxford, called Chancellor's Ale. Sixteen bushels of malt are used to the barrel. Two wineglassfuls will intoxicate most people. It is kept in oak bell-shaped casks, and is never tapped until it is two years old. Some of the casks have been in use for half a century, but "Chancellor ale" is used only at high table, when a man takes very high honors. On such or other extra-special occasions the dean will grant an order for a pint of this liquor, the largest quantity ever allowed at a time.

Allan Day. A great children's festival celebrated on the nearest Saturday to Halloween in Penzance and St. Ives, both in Cornwall County, England. The fruiterers then display in their windows very large apples, known locally as " Allan" apples. The eating of them is supposed to bring good luck. The girls and boys put them under their pillows at night, expecting to dream of their future husband or wife. The fulfilment of the dream depends upon the silence observed before eating the apple next morning. The full ritual involves rising before dawn and sitting under a tree clad in the night-dress only and then partaking of the apple. The future consort ought then to make his or her appearance. Moreover, if the sitter experiences no cold, the same immunity from cold will continue throughout the winter. (DITCHFIELD, p. 171.)

All Saints' Day. November 1, the eve of All Souls' Day. The Greek Church so early as the fourth century kept a feast of all martyrs and saints on the first Sunday of Pentecost. The object of this day was in its inception probably to do honor in bulk to all the lesser saints who could not have a feast specially set apart for them, as well as to all holy men and martyrs whose record had not survived. A sermon of St. Chrysostom's delivered on this feast is still extant. In the West All Saints' Day was introduced by Pope Boniface IV. in the seventh century on the occasion of the conversion of the Roman Pantheon into a Christian church dedicated to the Virgin and all the martyrs. The anniversary of this event was kept on May 13. But when Gregory III., about November 1, 731, consecrated a chapel in St. Peter's Church in honor of all the saints, the date of the feast of All Saints was shifted, and it has ever since been November 1. From about the middle of the ninth century its observance became general throughout the West. The festival has been retained by the Anglican Church. A correspondent of the *Gentleman's Magazine* (1788, vol. lviii. p. 602) alludes to a custom prevailing among English Roman Catholics of illuminating some of their grounds on All Saints' Night, the eve of All Souls', by bearing around them bundles of straw or other fit material kindled into a blaze. This ceremony is called a Tinley, and is an emblematical lighting of souls out of purgatory.

In Austria it is the faith of the peasantry (and even some of higher position) that on All Souls' Eve, at midnight, any one visiting the cemetery will see a procession of the dead drawing after them those who are to die during the coming year. There is a gloomy drama founded on it, which is still acted on every All Souls' Eve in the people's theatre at Vienna. It is called "The Miller and his Child." The miller has a lovely daughter, the daughter a lover: the miller obstinately opposes the marriage. After some years of despair the youth goes to the churchyard at midnight and sees the spectral train, and following it the cruel miller. The miller, then, will die during the year. The drama might have passed at this point from the graveyard to the marriage bells; but it would never be allowed in Austria that young people should be so encouraged to look forward cheerfully to the demise of parents, however cruel; and therefore the youth sees following close to the miller—himself. In the course of the year the poor girl loses both father and lover. During the performance of this drama the audience is generally bathed in tears, some persons sobbing painfully. It is evidently no fiction to them; and it is impossible not to believe that the heaping of their friends' graves with wreaths next day is in part due to the surviving belief that the dead have some awful power over the living, which is generally exerted for evil.

All Souls' Day. A festival of the Roman Catholic Church (November 2) distinguished by solemn commemoration of and prayer for all the souls in purgatory. The mass said on that day is always the mass of the dead, and priests are obliged to recite in private the matins and lauds from the office of the dead. This solemnity owes its origin to the Abbot Odilon of Cluny, who instituted it for all the monasteries of his congregation in the year 998. Some authorities see traces of at least a local celebration of this day before Odilon's time. With the Greeks Saturday was a day of special prayer for the dead, particularly the Saturday before Lent and the one before Pentecost.

The observance of All Souls' Day after its establishment was deemed of such importance that in the event of its falling on Sunday it was ordered not to be postponed till Monday, as happens with some other festivals, but to take place on the previous Saturday, so that the souls in purgatory should not have the ministrations in their behalf unnecessarily postponed. Thus All Saints' and All Souls' Days were occasionally celebrated together.

In ancient times it was customary for criers dressed in black to parade the streets, ringing a bell of mournful sound and calling on all good Christians to remember the poor souls in purgatory and join in prayer for their relief. In Southern Italy, notably in Salerno, there was another ancient custom, which was put an end to in the fifteenth century because it was thought to savor of paganism. Every family used to spread a table abundantly for the regalement of the souls of its dead members on their way from purgatory. All then spent the day at church, leaving the house open, and if any of the food remained on the table when they came back it was an ill omen. Curiously enough, large numbers of thieves used to resort to the city at this time, and there was seldom any of the food left to presage evil. A story strangely like this is told in the Apocryphal book of Bel and the Dragon.

All Souls' Day is a natural corollary to its predecessor All Saints' Day (November 1). That is a day dedicated specially to all the faithful dead who have achieved paradise. This is a day dedicated specially to the faithful dead who still remain in purgatory. Nevertheless, like most Christian festivals, it is a rehabilitation of a pagan feast. Days specially set apart for ceremonies in honor of the dead are common to humanity. Even in China and in Japan there is a feast of the dead, known best under the alternative name of Feast of Lanterns. What is more to the point, the very dates of November 1 and November 2 were the dates on which our Druidical ancestors celebrated their festivals of the dead. It was then that the god Samhan was held to pass judgment upon the souls of the defunct. (See HALLOWEEN and DECORATION DAY.)

All Souls' Day possesses a peculiar sanctity for all who have ever felt the poetry which underlies the services of the Catholic Church. In the toil and moil of life we too easily forget the dead, or remember them only with a sense of loss instead of gratitude. Hence it seems well that once in the year an opportunity should be afforded for dwelling on them in a different way, for recalling all that endeared them to us, which often means all that has lent our past life its emotional value, for drawing close to them in the spiritual bonds which according to the Catholic Church are not severed by death, and for offering them that pious meed of prayer which, the same authority guarantees, will shorten their stay in purgatory and open out to them the sooner the final glory and peace of paradise.

In nothing does the strange contrast of feeling appear more strongly than in the different ways in which this day is celebrated in countries or districts which are equally Roman Catholic in their profession of faith. In all, the religious services are substantially the same ; masses for the dead are read, the " Dies Iræ" is sung, and the prayer " Eternal rest grant them, O Lord, and let perpetual life shine upon them," rises from thousands of hearts as well as lips. But outside the church nothing can be more unlike than the bearing of the worshippers.

In France the Jour des Morts, as it is generally known, is a decorous, pathetic, and beautiful occasion among all believers. For two or three weeks before the day arrives the shop-windows and the news-venders' kiosks are laden with wreaths and garlands of immortelles, some in their natural color, some dyed blue, pink, or purple. On All Saints' the people stream to the cemeteries. Thousands of people, thousands of wreaths. The cemeteries are one mass of brilliant color, of moving throngs, for not even the remotest corner of the potter's field is neglected. Above the dust of the pauper as well as of the prince is left some token of remembrance. Pains are taken that no graves of friends and relatives are neglected, lest their spirits should have their feelings hurt during their visit by perceiving this neglect. The children, especially, are encouraged to delight in the thought of pleasing the little dead brother, sister, or friend by making the tiny mounds that mark their resting-places gay and bright-looking.

The higher classes behave with the quietude and self-restraint of well-bred people everywhere. But down among the common people are manifested the emotions of the heart, sad remembrance, reawakened grief, love outlasting its object.

It is true that even into the midst of this pathetic ceremony the Parisians sometimes manage to obtrude politics. On November 2, 1868, a strange scene was enacted in the cemetery of Montmartre. The Empire was then at the height of its unpopularity. A large number of its enemies came bearing flowers to seek for the tomb of Alphonse Baudin, the representative of the people who had died at the barricades on December 2, 1851. For seventeen years this tomb had been reported lost. But thousands of eager searchers soon located it, and it was covered with a pyramid of immortelles and other flowers. Revolutionary speeches were made, and there were some conflicts with the police. Next morning some of the liberal journals opened a subscription-list for a monument to Baudin. But the movement was stopped by the Imperial government, and several of the editors were fined.

Scenes of this sort, however, are infrequent, and occur only among unbelievers. Now contrast the Frenchman with the Southern Italian.

Nothing can be more gruesome, incongruous, and flippant—to the Northern mind—than the All Souls' celebrations in Naples. The *Saturday Review* of January 7, 1888, gives an account of these which is as true to-day as it was then :

"In Naples All Souls' Day is regarded as a holiday, and the visit of the families to the churchyard for the purpose of decorating the graves degenerates into a pleasure-party. Metal garlands are chiefly used for the purpose ; and, though they are more durable, they hardly possess the charm of real leaves and flowers. They may, however, be regarded as symbolic of the behavior, if not always of the feelings, of those who offer them. On the way to the cemetery a decent sobriety is observed, and the various families usually remain separate ; but on the return general sociability and mirth are the rule. The roadside is lined with inns, which are better filled on this than any other day in the year ; and from all of them the sound of singing and dancing may be heard. Indeed, it is by no means uncommon for a young Neapolitan to say to a friend, 'We are going to visit our mother's grave to-morrow, and on our way back we shall stop at such or such an inn ;' which means, If you like to come there, you can dance with my sister. To an Englishman no celebration of the day seems a better thing. If we forget our dead, we do not make their memory the excuse for a jollification.

"It is not, however, in this point alone that a difference of sentiment exists. The whole way in which the Neapolitans treat the bodies of the dead fills us with disgust. To exhume a corpse a year or two after it has been buried, to have the skeleton taken to pieces and the bones carefully cleaned, would seem to us a wanton outrage ; the wealthy Neapolitan who neglects to have this done for his kindred is regarded as heartless. To carry about the prepared bones of a pet child, and to place them in a sealed casket on the drawing-room mantel-piece, seems to us simply shocking; in Southern Italy it has been regarded as a most pathetic expression of sorrow. But the height of what appears to us grotesque horror has been reached by a widower, who has the embalmed corpse of his wife dressed anew once a year in fresh and gorgeous apparel, and seizes the opportunity to present it with a new ring or bracelet.

"In the villages, too, where the day is observed with a certain seriousness, grotesque incidents are apt to mar, for the stranger at least, the sense of mournful calm which the religious services excite. In one of the churches of Ravello, for example, a disgusting effigy is placed before the high altar, instead of the shrouded structure in which, during the funeral service, the coffin is placed. The very skill with which it is made renders it the more repulsive. The fallen cheeks and livid hue are rendered with what seems, in the half-light, a frightful realism; and it is clad in the court dress of some former century, in a suit embroidered with gold, red stockings, and pointed shoes. Or is it perhaps a real mummy? The writer did not pause to inquire. In fact, the South Italian seems to be utterly destitute of the feeling which prompts us to conceal as far as possible, even from our imaginations, all that is revolting in death."

In France the Jour des Morts is kept utterly distinct from La Toussaint, or All Saints' Day, which occurs on November 1. This is also true of Italy. But in many other European Catholic countries the decorating of graves begins on All Saints' Day, either because it is looked upon as the Eve of All Souls', or from the pious and complimentary hope that the dead in whom the celebrant is interested may have already passed out of the penitential flames of purgatory into the company of the blessed. In a Catholic Alpine village, as soon as the mass has been heard on All Saints', the women of the family busy themselves with weaving wreaths of evergreens, into which any flowers that are still hardy enough to blossom are eagerly worked. In the afternoon these are carried to the churchyard and laid upon the graves with almost silent reverence; and in the evening a lamp is placed at the foot of the last resting-place of every departed friend. At such a time the cemetery is a strange sight, with the garlands, the lights, and the groups of mourners kneeling, often in the snow.

Almanac Day (November 22). Formerly this was a notable occasion at Stationers' Hall, London. The Stationers' Company originally enjoyed a monopoly of the printing of books. Even after this privilege had been withdrawn from them they claimed the exclusive right of issuing almanacs. Not till 1775 was this claim successfully contested by one Thomas Carnan, a bookseller in St. Paul's Churchyard. But for long afterwards, despite their loss of what they considered a vested right, the almanacs of the Stationers' Company continued to be the standard publications in this sort, the most popular and the most eagerly sought for. Knight's "London" (1841) thus describes the scene on Almanac Day in Stationers' Hall: "All over the long tables that extend through the hall, which is of considerable size, and piled up in tall heaps on the floor, are canvas bales or bags innumerable. This is the 22d of November. The doors are locked as yet, but will be opened presently for a novel scene. The clock strikes, wide asunder start the gates, and in they come, a whole army of porters, darting hither and thither, and seizing the said bags, in many instances as big as themselves. Before we can well understand what is the matter, men and bags have alike vanished—the hall is clear; another hour or two, and the contents of the latter will be flying along railways, east, west, north, and south. . . . Yes, they are all almanacs: those bags contain nothing but almanacs." Even now on November 22 in some of the byways of London the cry once so familiar in all the principal streets, "Almanacs for the ensuing year!" is occasionally heard from peripatetic peddlers. The Stationers' Company still keep up the old practice of sending an early copy of each of their almanacs to the Archbishop of Canterbury on publication-day. This custom originated in the early part of the eighteenth century, while Edward Tenison was archbishop. A near relative of his was Master of the Stationers' Company. On one Lord Mayor's Day the latter, who had achieved the dignity of Alderman, was awaiting in the civic barge at Westminster Stairs the return of the Mayor from Westminster Hall. As time hung heavy, he and his fellow-aldermen rowed over to Lambeth Palace to call on Cousin Edward, who hospitably entertained them with a pint of wine apiece and the watermen with hot spiced ale and bread and cheese. This grew into a settled custom year by year, until the abolition of the Mayor's procession by water, and year by year the archiepiscopal hospitality was acknowledged by the Stationers' Company by presenting His Grace with copies of their several almanacs as soon as published.

Almohada. (Sp., "Pillow.") A ceremony at the court of Madrid which dates back to the reign of Charles V. It consists in conferring the rank of grandee upon members of the Spanish nobility. It is thus described by an eye-witness in October, 1888, the only Almohada which has been held during the reign of

Alfonso XIII.: " On the afternoon of the appointed day the grandees who happened to be residing at the time in the city assembled in the small throne-room of the palace and took their seats on carved stools upholstered with crimson velvet cushions, which were ranged on either side of the room at right angles with the throne, the gentlemen being on the right and the ladies on the left thereof. Punctually at three o'clock the queen regent made her entry in state, accompanied by her sisters-in-law and attended by the proud Duchess of Fernan-Nuñez, her Camarera-Mayor, or Grand Mistress of the Robes, by the Duke of Medina-Sidonia, who is her Mayordomo-Mayor, or Grand Marshal of the Court, and by other great officers of her household. As soon as she' had taken her seat on the throne she turned to the right and the left with a slight inclination of her head, and, addressing the grandees present, exclaimed, ' Be seated.' A moment afterwards the folding doors at the farther end of the room were thrown open, and, preceded by a chamberlain and conducted by the two grandees appointed to act as sponsors, the postulant for admission to the grandezza made his appearance, and, after bowing profoundly three times,—once on entering the royal presence, once on reaching the centre of the room, and once on approaching the throne,—stood still and awaited her majesty's orders. A stool and crimson velvet cushion having been brought and placed on the lowest step of the royal dais, the queen commanded that the candidate should be seated, which he did with another low obeisance. Christina then addressed a few complimentary words to him, recalling the services rendered by his family to the dynasty in times gone by, and, after extending her hand to be kissed, signified her desire that he should assume his place among his peers. Retiring backward from the royal presence, he was, in the first place, conducted by his sponsors to the side of the hall occupied by the ladies of grandee rank, to whom he made a low bow, and then to that of the men, whom he saluted in a similar manner. He thereupon put his hat on his head, his example being instantaneously followed by every grandee present, and all remained covered until, his stool and cushion having been removed from the steps of the throne and placed beside those of his peers, the newly elected grandee had seated himself thereon. The object which the grandees have in view in putting on their hats during this portion of the ceremony is to perpetuate and to assert their ancient and traditional privilege of remaining covered in the presence of royalty. It is they alone who represent the old blue blood of Spain and from whose number the great officers of the royal household are almost exclusively selected. A grandee and a grandesse are daily in attendance on the monarch as chamberlain and as lady-in-waiting, and almost as many nobiliary quarterings are required for admission to the grandezza as to the sovereign Order of Knighthood of Malta."

Altar. (Lat. *altare*, " an altar," from *altus*, "high.") A place or object for sacrifice, adoration, or other priestly office. The earliest altars were turf mounds, large flat-topped stones, or other rude elevations, natural or artificial. When temples came to be built, altars were generally made of stone, marble, or metal. Greek and Roman altars were circular, square, or triangular in form, and were highly ornamented. In the Jewish worship two altars were used, the altar of burnt-offering and the altar of incense. Both were made of shittim wood, the first overlaid with brazen plates and the latter with gold. In the primitive Christian Church the altar was usually of wood. But during the persecutions the tombs of martyrs in the Catacombs were used as altars. Hence the Catholic Church requires that the altar must either consist of stone or contain an altar stone large enough for the sacred vessels to stand upon. Hence also its general likeness in form to a sarcophagus. The altar stone is consecrated by the bishop or a specially licensed abbot, who anoints it with chrism, and frequently seals up certain relics in a small cavity made for the purpose. Such relics were at one time absolutely necessary. The east end of a church, where possible, is the preferable position, so that worshippers may face towards the east, as a reminder of Christ, " the Dayspring and the Resurrection." Here undoubtedly is a reminiscence of the sun-worship which was the primitive cult of our Aryan ancestors. Both Greeks and Romans turned their faces to the east when praying. Originally there was one altar in each church dedicated to the patron saint. But as other relics than those of the patron were added to a church, special altars were raised and consecrated to them. In the Reformed Churches only one altar is used. The zeal of the early Reformers frequently carried them so far as to abolish the altar entirely. In Switzerland it was replaced by a plain communion-table, and in Holland and Scotland even this communion-table was not tolerated except when communion was actually celebrated.

Amable, St. (died 475). One of the early apostles of Christianity in France. He is the patron of Riom, France, where his festival, June 11, is celebrated with a curious ceremonial that attracts large crowds from the neighboring peasantry. A procession is formed in which the most important feature is a wax wheel several feet in diameter decorated with ribbons. This is borne in the air by the priests, who from time to time make it turn on its axle, to the great edification of the faithful. The wheel, it appears, is made by the churchwardens from a thread of wax which is coiled into a circular form. The thread is just long enough to measure around the town of Riom. It is evident, therefore, that this is a survival of wheel-worship (see WHEEL OF FIRE) transferred from the time of the summer solstice to the festival of the patron saint. We may also surmise that originally the wheel was carried round the town, so as to protect it from all evil influences, as is done to this day in the burning of the Clavie at Burghead. By some curious mutation, however, the wax thread of the length of the circuit was substituted. The wheel is now carried to the neighboring village of Marsat, where it is received by the priests of the chapel of Notre-Dame as an offering to the honor of the blessed Virgin Mary, mother of Jesus. Another wheel, made by the peasants of flowers, also capable of revolving on its axis, is carried in the procession.

Ambrose, St. The festival of this saint is celebrated on December 7, the day on which he was ordained bishop. It is especially observed in Milan, of which city he is the patron saint.

He was one of the four Latin Fathers of the Church. He was born at Treves in Gaul. It is related that when an infant a swarm of bees alighted on his mouth without doing him any harm, thus indicating his future eloquence. The same story, it will be remembered, was told of Plato and of Archilochus. Ambrose studied at Rome and then removed to Milan. Shortly after, the bishop of that city died, and a great dispute arose between the Catholics and the Arians as to who should succeed him. Ambrose pacified the disputants by his eloquence. Then a child's voice was heard crying, "Ambrose shall be bishop;" and although he protested, saying that he had not even been baptized, the whole assembly took up the cry, his objections were overruled, the ceremony of baptism was performed on the spot, and eight days afterwards he was consecrated bishop. He threw his whole soul into the performance of his duties, allowing no respect of persons to interfere with them. On one occasion the Emperor Theodosius, after having been guilty of a general massacre of the insurgents in Thessalonica, presented himself to worship in the cathedral, but St. Ambrose sternly refused him admittance until he had performed public penance for his sin. In 387 he founded the church now known as the basilica of Sant' Ambrogio Maggiore at Milan, which he dedicated to all the saints. At the consecration of this church the relics of SS. Gervasius and Protasius were miraculously revealed to him. Many other wonderful things are recorded about this saint. On one occasion a heretic who came to scoff at his preaching saw an angel standing by his side and prompting him, and was at once converted to the truth. At another time, while celebrating mass, he fell into a trance and beheld the burial of St. Martin of Tours, then taking place in France. When he was on his death-bed, the Bishop of Vercelli, who was attending him, fell asleep, but an angel awoke him in time to administer the last sacraments, and then all present beheld St. Ambrose carried up to heaven in the arms of angels. This was on April 4, 397. He is represented as

ST. AMBROSE ENTHRONED.
(From a German print of the fifteenth century.)

a mitred bishop with a crosier. Sometimes a beehive is at his feet, but his usual attribute is a knotted scourge with three thongs.

The body of St. Ambrose was originally interred near the relics of SS. Gervasius and Protasius in the basilica of St. Ambrose, Milan. It now reposes in a vault under the high altar. "God," says Alban Butler, "was pleased to honor him by manifesting that through his intercession he protected the state against the idolaters." He instances the case of Radagæsus,

King of the Goths, who in 450 invaded Italy, swearing to sacrifice all the Romans before his gods. He quotes from Tillemont: " Radagæsus besieged Florence. This city was reduced to the utmost straits, when St. Ambrose, who had once retired thither (and who had now been dead nine years), appeared to a person of the house where he had lodged, and promised him that the city should be delivered from the enemy on the next day. The man told it to the inhabitants, who took courage and resumed the hopes which they had quite lost, and on the next day came Stilicho with his army. Paulinus, who relates this, learned it from a lady who lived at Florence." Stilicho, it will be remembered, won a complete victory, and captured Radagæsus and his two sons and put them to death.

Amen Corner. A spot in Paternoster Row, London. Prior to the Reformation an annual procession to St. Paul's Cathedral used to be performed on Corpus Christi Day. Mustering at the end of Cheapside, the clergy there commenced the chanting of the Our Father, or Paternoster, through the whole length of the street, hence called Paternoster Row, so timing themselves that the Amen would be reached at Amen Corner. Then began the Ave Maria as they turned down Ave Maria Lane. After crossing Ludgate Hill they chanted the Credo in Creed Lane. It appears from Stow's " London" that the amen to the creed, and hence the end of the chanting, was pronounced in Amen Lane, which he says " is lately added to" Creed Lane. Amen Lane, however, no longer exists.

Ampulla. The old Roman, and still the ecclesiastical, name for a vial or bottle of peculiar semiglobular shape, usually with two handles. The Romans kept their wine in ampullæ of glass or earthenware, as also the oil with which they anointed themselves after bathing. In modern ecclesiastical usage the term is applied to the vessels holding the sacramental wine and water, and to the cruets of precious metal holding the consecrated oil or chrism used in extreme unction, at the coronation of kings, and in other functions. The name and the thing are retained in the English coronation service. Among the regalia preserved in the Tower of London is the golden ampulla in the form of an eagle, richly chased, which is said to have been made expressly for the coronation of Charles II.

The anointing was a peculiarly sacred ceremony, used in the earliest time only for the kings of England, France, Jerusalem, and Sicily. Subsequently the kings of Scotland obtained the privilege of anointing by special grant from the Pope. The English kings were anointed, not with holy oil, but with a specially prepared cream, which was consecrated by the primate, or by some bishop deputed by him, and the custom continued after the Reformation. Thus the cream used for anointing Charles I. was consecrated by Laud, then Bishop of St. David's.

In France, the sacred ampulla (*la sainte ampoule*) containing the balm with which the kings were anointed was kept in the tomb of St. Remy in the cathedral of Rheims. According to legend, a legend much younger than the pretended fact it commemorates, this ampulla was brought down from heaven by a dove, in answer to the prayer of St. Remy, to serve at the baptism and coronation of King Clovis in 496. Neither St. Remy himself, however, nor any of his contemporaries mentions the miracle, which appears to have been a ninth-century invention. The ampulla was always used at the coronation of French kings down to Charles X. It was a glass vial forty-one millimetres high, with an aperture sixteen millimetres in circumference, filled with a compound of oil and balm " thick and slab," which in the end had become solidified and of a reddish-brown color. At the ceremony of coronation the High Prior of St. Remy hung the rich shrine that contained it about his neck, and by means of a gold needle scooped out a particle which he placed upon the monarch's brow.

The legend goes on to say that there was such a relation between the holy vial and the life of the reigning king that the bulk of the ointment it contained diminished if his health happened to be impaired. In 1793 the revolutionists under Ruhl, then appointed commissioner in the department of Marne, broke this relic to pieces in the public square of Rheims. But it is said that the Abbé Seraine, curé of St. Remy, secreted a part of the contents in a crystal vessel which was providentially discovered in time for the coronation of Charles X. in 1825. This is still preserved in a silver gilt shrine in Rheims Cathedral, the revolutionists of 1848 contemptuously allowing it to remain in its ancient tabernacle.

Amuck or **Amok.** A species of semi-voluntary insanity which is peculiar to the Malays of the Indian Archipelago. The curious feature about it is that, though the result of a momentary passion, it seems to depend, in the Malay's mind, on a belief that to run amok is, under certain circumstances, the right thing to do. The circumstance may be any accident or sorrow which overwhelms a man with uncontrollable emotion. His grief then takes the form of violent and indiscriminate anger against the whole human race. With drawn kris he rushes out to slay or be slain. His frenzied appearance proclaims his condition. " Amok! Amok!" shriek the people, as they trample over each other in their hurry to save their lives. The alarm spreads far and wide. The hand of every Malay springs to the twisted band of his sheath, to draw forth the dagger that hangs by his side; the police clutch their weapons; the Europeans seize their guns; every eye, every nerve, is strained for the coming peril. "Amok! Amok!"—a wild shriek, a groan, a cry for mercy, and on rushes the maniac with the bloody kris in his hand, striking right and left, heedless of friend or foe. He is pursued by a number of people armed with spears, daggers, knives, guns, and clubs, who grow as madly excited as the wild creature they chase. Brandishing his ruddy blade, the ghastly Malay, perhaps himself gashed with cuts and riddled with bullets, dashes along in his fury, marking his course with his own blood and that of fresh victims. And so he goes on and on till he falls from some shot, or sinks from exhaustion, to be despatched by the ready daggers of his chasers. Or perhaps, cut off and hemmed in, the amok-runner, dripping with blood, stands at bay in some house or against a wall, glaring with bloodshot eyes, and, holding out his stained kris, defies any one to approach. Then the police bring into use a huge short-pronged pitchfork, with which they are provided in the Straits Settlement, deftly thrusting at him till he is caught by the throat, pinned to the wall, and held there by powerful arms. His kris having been wrested from him, he is quickly pinioned, and, if he does not die of his wounds, is tried and executed by native or British laws.

The nearest thing in nature to a Malay running amok is the conduct of an elephant who goes "must." Both do all the violent injury in their power without notice or warning. Neither is usually spared when he returns to a calmer frame of mind, by way of seeing whether his reformation will endure or whether he will relapse.

Andisop. Train tells us in his "History of the Isle of Man" (1845, vol. ii. p. 127) that the fiddlers go round from house to house in the latter part of the night for two or three weeks before Christmas, playing a tune called the Andisop. On their way they stop before particular houses, wish the inmates individually good-morning, call the hour, then report the state of the weather, and, after receiving a small gratuity, move on to the next halting-place.

Andrew, St., the Apostle, patron of Scotland and of Russia. His feast is celebrated on November 30, the reputed day of his death. Scripture informs us that he was the son of Jonas, a fisherman of Bethsaida in Galilee, and the brother of Simon

Peter. A disciple of John the Baptist, he followed Jesus upon the Baptist's pointing him out with the words "Behold the Lamb of God!" (John i. 35–40.) Andrew introduced his brother to Jesus, a circumstance which has invested him with special eminence. They abode a day with the Saviour, and subsequently accompanied him to the marriage at Cana, after which they returned to their trade as fishermen. Some months later, Jesus, meeting them while they were fishing, called them to him, promising to make them fishers of men. Thereupon they left their nets and followed him. (Matt. iv. 19, 20.) After the Ascension there is no further scriptural mention of St. Andrew, but tradition assigns Scythia, Greece, and Thrace as the scenes of his missionary labors, and asserts that he was martyred at Patræ, in Achaia, on November 30, A.D. 70. The Roman pro-

MARTYRDOM OF ST. ANDREW.
(From an old print.)

consul, it is said, angered because he had converted his wife Maximilla, caused him to be first flogged and then crucified. The cross upon which he suffered was of the form called decussate,—*i.e.*, shaped like the letter X. To this day a cross of that kind is called by his name. He was fastened to it by cords instead of nails, to produce a lingering death by hunger and thirst. The legend goes on to say that Maximilla caused the body to be decently interred, and that for many years manna came out from his tomb, together with a fragrant oil, and when these were abundant the crops for that season were good, but if not the crops also were scanty. The Emperor Constantine removed the body to Constantinople and placed it in a church consecrated to the Twelve Apostles. Thirty years after the death of Constantine, in 368, a Greek monk named Regulus, or Rule, conveyed the body to Scotland, and reburied it on the eastern coast of Fife, where he built a church, and here afterwards arose the city and cathedral of St. Andrew. In the mediæval chap-book entitled "The Seven Champions of Christendom," which is purely a secular performance, full of astounding anachronisms, a different legend is told. After performing prodigies of valor in Thrace, St. Andrew is represented as coming to Scotland, then "a rude and heathenish country, where the common sort of people inhabited." Although the king and the nobility welcomed him, the people put him secretly to death ; whereat the king, greatly incensed, raised a power of his best resolved knights of war, and put every one to the sword, man, woman, and child, that in any manner had consented to the champion's martyrdom. So only Christian believers were left in Scotland. Subsequently the king appointed a monastery to be built on the place where St. Andrew died.

The cross upon which St. Andrew was crucified is one of the most precious relics of the church of St. Victor (*q. v.*) in Marseilles. It was brought from Patmos by the Burgondes, whose king took Marseilles about the year 400 and deposited this relic in St. Victor. Fearing its profanation during an invasion of the Saracens, St. Eusebia, the abbess, hid it in a place known only to herself and her martyred companions. Lost for some centuries, it was supposed to have been seized by the infidels, until, after having at three different times during mass a vision of its place of concealment, the pious Hugues de Glacius searched the spot indicated, and, amid a heap of rubbish, found the sacred wood.

From time immemorial St. Andrew has been the patron of Scotland. His day, which is also known as Andrys Day, Androiss Mess, and Andermess, is made the occasion of banquets, not only at home, but wherever in foreign ports enough Scotsmen can be mustered to partake of the festivity. In London a procession of Scots used to be held, a singed sheep's head being borne in the van. The use of sheep's head, boiled, baked, or singed, began in the village of Duddington, a mile or so out from Edinburgh, whither the citizens of the metropolis were wont to resort on summer days for gastronomic purposes. It is supposed that the custom arose from the practice of slaughtering for the market the sheep fed on the neighboring hill. The carcasses were sent to town, the head, etc., being left to be consumed in the place. In the parish of Eastling, in Kent, England, the yearly diversion of squirrel-hunting took place on St. Andrew's Day. Peasants and laborers would assemble together armed with guns, clubs, poles, and other weapons, and under pretence of hunting squirrels would parade through the woods and grounds with loud shoutings and kill every species of game, squirrels, hares, pheasants, or partridges, that came in their way, doing much injury to trees and hedges, and finally ending the day with a carousal at the ale-houses.

Luther in his "Table-Talk" describes how on the evening of

the feast of St. Andrew the young maids in Germany would strip themselves naked and utter the following prayer: " Deus, Deus meus, o Sancte Andrea, effice ut bonum pium acquiram virum; hodie mihi ostende qualis sit cui me in uxorem ducere debet" ("God, my God, O·Saint Andrew, bring it about that I may obtain a good affectionate husband; show me to-day what manner of man it is that shall lead me to the altar"). Probably there is an allusion to this custom in "The Popish Kingdom" of Naogeorgus, thus translated by Barnaby Googe:

> To Andrew all the lovers and the lustie wooers come,
> Beleeving through his aid and certaine ceremonies done
> (While as to him they presentes bring, and conjure all the night)
> To have good lucke, and to obtaine their chiefe and sweete delight.

A somewhat analogous ceremony is practised in England on St. Agnes' Eve (*q. v.*).

A pretty German superstition that still survives locally on St. Andrew's Day is the following:

To learn which of the persons present love each other, or will one day be united, a vessel with pure water is set on the table, and there are placed, to float upon the water, little cups of silver-foil, inscribed with the names of those whose fortune is to be determined. If a youth's cup advances to a maiden's, or a maiden's to a youth's, it is worth while to note which makes the chief advances; and if they eventually cling together, they will be sweethearts. But little cups must also be set floating marked as priests; and it is only when the youth and the maid coming together get a priest between them that they can look forward with any certainty to marriage.

Angelus. The name given to the Catholic practice of re-citing at morning, noon, and evening three Hail Marys, together with sentences and a collect expressive of rejoicing trust in the mystery of the Incarnation. The first sentence of the collect begins, "Angelus Domini nuntiavit Mariæ" ("The angel of the Lord announced unto Mary"). Hence the name of the devotion. In Catholic countries a bell called the Angelus rings at the several hours six A.M., twelve M., and six P.M. The evening Angelus had the earliest origin. Introduced by Pope John XXII. in 1326, he ordered that the church bells should sound at the hour of curfew and that parishioners at this bell-stroke should, on bended knees, repeat three times the angel's salutation to the Virgin Mary, thus gaining ten days' indulgence. In 1369 it was ordained that at dawn (*in aurora diei*) there should be three bell-strokes, and that whoever hearing said three aves and as many paternosters should obtain twenty days' indulgence. In

1472 Louis XI. ordered the Angelus to be repeated three times a day, and obtained a papal decree that whoever obeyed the order should thereby acquire three hundred additional days of indulgence. This threefold daily Angelus had also been recommended as early as 1423 in Mainz and Cologne, in Breslau in 1416, etc. It has continued, with only slight modification in the order of the prayers, up to the present day. Millet's famous picture represents the evening Angelus.

Anne, St., mother of the Virgin. She is commemorated on July 26, the reputed anniversary of her death. The patroness of Canada, her famous shrine in the church of St. Anne, at the little village of Beaupré, about twenty miles below Quebec, is the Lourdes of the New World, attracting pilgrims from all parts not only of Canada but also of the United States.

St. Anne, according to the legend, was the wife of Joachim, a devout and wealthy man. For a long time the couple were childless. Therefore when Joachim on a certain feast-day appeared at the temple his offering was refused by the high-priest. And he went away into the wilderness and fasted forty days. Meanwhile Anne also bewailed her childlessness. And while she was praying an angel appeared and told her that her prayer was answered. Another angel appeared to Joachim with the same message. The two met at the Golden Gate. And when her time came Anne brought forth a daughter, whom she called Mary.

The body of St. Anne was found in the time of Charlemagne, at Apte, in France. A miracle revealed its abiding-place. A boy born dumb suddenly spoke, saying, " Here lies the body of Anne, mother of the Blessed Virgin Mary." This discovery is commemorated by a yearly festival at Apte. To account for the presence of the relics at that place the legend current at Apte says that St. Paul dug St. Anne out of her grave in the Valley of Jehoshaphat, and, carrying her to Rome, gave her to St. Clement, who made a present of her bones to St. Auspicius, Bishop of Apte. There are other legends about these relics, and in fact there are other bodies or parts of bodies all claiming to be genuine. There is a second head of St. Anne at Chartres, brought from the East in the twelfth century by Louis, Count of Blois; a third at Bologna, given by Henry VI. of England to Nicholas Albegarti; a fourth at Düren, in Germany, brought from the Holy Land in 1212; a fifth at Castelbona, in Sicily, brought from Lorraine by John de Hieac about A.D. 1468. The arms and legs of this saint are relatively very much more numerous than her heads. A noted relic, " a most miraculous and odoriferous relic" (JOHN COMNENUS: *The Pilgrim's Guide to the Holy Moun-*

tain, Venice, 1701), is kept in a silver case set with precious stones in the church of St. Anne at Mount Athos, Greece. This is the left foot of the saint. If the traveller is anxious to see this relic, the monks, having first lighted candles and put on their full canonicals, will draw forth the ghastly and shrunken limb, which they devoutly kiss.

The special Canadian devotion to the saint began when the original church was built at Beaupré. The legend runs that in 1650 or 1651, that is, in the very infancy of the French colony in Canada, some Breton sailors, caught in a storm, vowed that if the good St. Anne would but bring them safely to land they would build her a sanctuary on the spot where their feet first touched land. The prayer was granted, the vow was kept. A small wooden church was erected. Some years later a little child was thrice favored with a heavenly vision near this building, and on her third appearance the Virgin commanded the little one to tell the people that they should build her a larger church on that spot.

The governor of the colony, M. Aillebout, commenced with his own hands the pious work, and laid the first stone in 1658, and a *habitant* of the place, Louis Guimont, sorely afflicted with rheumatism, came, grinning with pain, to lay three stones in the foundation, in honor, probably, of St. Anne, St. Joachim, and their daughter the Virgin. Instantly he was cured of his rheumatism. That was but the beginning of a long course of miracles, continued more than two and a quarter centuries already, and still continuing.

Since 1666, pilgrimages have been frequent to St. Anne de Beaupré. On the 30th of March of that year the Marquis de Tracey, governor of the colony, went there to return thanks to St. Anne for the preservation at sea of the ship which had brought him from France and had been nearly wrecked, and in August following he again visited the shrine, this time accompanied by Monsignor de Laval, first Bishop of Quebec, and presented it with the celebrated painting of St. Anne by Le Brun which hangs over the richly adorned high altar, while a rich chasuble, embroidered in gold, was presented to the church by Anne of Austria, the queen mother of Louis XIV., who had worked it with her own hands.

In 1668 the shrine was enriched by a relic which was nothing less than a fragment of a finger of St. Anne. This is still retained and carefully preserved. Its exposition, save on St. Anne's Day, is a favor rarely vouchsafed even to the faithful.

It was long the custom of all ships returning from voyages to anchor here and honor Canada's patroness by a broadside.

In the number of its pilgrims St. Anne de Beaupré compares

favorably with Loretto, Notre Dame de Lourdes, and Paray-le-Monial. Under the French *régime* the whole shore was frequently covered with the wigwams of Indian converts, who had paddled their birch-bark canoes from the farthest wilds of Canada. The more fervent would crawl on their knees from the shore to the altar.

Ever since that period there has been a steady increase in the volume of pilgrims to St. Anne. In one recent year forty thousand visited the shrine between June and October. The average yearly number of pilgrims is from seventy-five thousand to one hundred thousand. They come from all parts of the United States and Canada, and, as they are of various origins, they speak a variety of languages. The Redemptorist Fathers in charge of the church preach in English, French, German, Spanish, Flemish, Italian, and Russian, as the occasion demands.

The proprietor of the new railroad to Beaupré has not failed to secure for it a character thoroughly in accord with its mission. On the day of its opening to travel Cardinal Taschereau blessed both road and rolling stock, the ceremony of the benediction being as interesting as it was novel, including the sprinkling of engines, cars, and track with holy water, and the offering up of prayers for the protection of all that travel by the railway, for those that direct it, "that they may be directed in the way of God's commandments," and for the passengers, "that, as the Ethiopian eunuch was accorded grace while seated on his car, so may they obtain eternal joys when their journey of life shall come to an end."

The handsome new church of La Bonne Ste.-Anne was commenced in 1850, has cost from two hundred thousand dollars to a quarter of a million, and has been raised by the Pope to the dignity of a basilica. It is surrounded by a number of magnificent lateral chapels, each the gift of a Canadian diocese. In front of the chancel is a splendid statue of St. Anne.

At intervals along the road there are small chapels, which are used but once annually, when the shrines enclosed are exposed to receive the votive offerings of processionists winding with stately chant along the dusty highway upon St. Anne's Day.

There are numerous rude *ex-voto* pictures in the church, representing marvellous deliverances of ships in peril through the aid of St. Anne, though by far the most interesting features of the sanctuary are the massive tiers of crutches, sticks, and splints and other peculiar contrivances for strengthening structural weaknesses, which have been joyfully cast aside by those who suddenly found that they no longer required them. There is a very large collection of spectacles and eye-glasses, indicative of the benefits derived at the shrine by those who had previously suffered from weak or defective vision, while a long row of tobacco-pipes and another of snuff-boxes testify to the power of the saint in curing the habits that called for their former use. A few bracelets illustrate the power of St. Anne in curing the vanity that is principally illustrated in the inordinate display of jewelry. No wonder that St. Anne has been specially designated the patroness of Canada, though it has been ecclesiastically provided that this is to be without prejudice to the office of St. Joseph as its patron.

New York City boasts a famous relic of this saint,—a wrist-bone taken from an arm possessed by the Benedictine monastery at Rome. The manner of its arrival here is as follows. The growing devotion to the shrine of St. Anne at Beaupré had led the Cardinal Archbishop of Quebec in 1892 to send Monsignor Marquis, prothonotary apostolic, on a journey to Rome seeking for some larger and more important relic of the saint than was in possession of the church. Pope Leo was pleased to accord a gracious hearing to the ambassador, and, in accordance with a papal request, the wrist of St. Anne was given to him by the abbot of the Benedictine monastery. It was placed in a small casket of bronze, lined with gold, and having a glass top, through which the relic could be seen. On his way to Canada Monsignor Marquis stopped over in New York and permitted the exhibition and veneration of the relic at the church of St. Jean Baptiste. Such crowds flocked to the shrine, so many miracles were wrought in the way of cures, such was the interest which it awakened among the Roman Catholic clergy and people of New York, that the good Monsignor was loath to remove it. The relic is brought out when sick people want to see it, and the priest touches the patient with the glass case. There are a number of prayers and much penance in connection with the ceremony, and the cure, when it is effected, is, of course, due to faith. This, the most famous relic in the country, is watched with the most jealous care, especially in view of the many attempts that have been made to steal it. There is another but a very minute relic preserved in the church of St. Anne in New York City. (See also AURAY, PARDON OF.)

Anniversary Week. The name formerly given in New York to the week beginning with the last Monday in May. This is the week in which the Quakers hold their annual meetings, and it gradually became the habit for other religionists, as well as for political and social agitators and benevolent societies of all sorts, to descend upon New York at the same period. " It was a week of great interest and excitement," writes George W. Curtis, "and, while the newspapers sneered and cheered at many a word spoken, the impulse given to public opinion was prodigious. The meetings were of all kinds: religious, charitable, and reformatory, from the most conservative and 'respectable'—meetings with which no well-ordered citizen was unwilling to have his name associated—to those which were alleged to be composed mainly of lunatics, fanatics, and long-haired fools, association with which was supposed to brand a man as deficient in common sense. The missionary meetings, those of the established charities and philanthropic enterprises, had always a full attendance and an ample flow of well-regulated oratory." (*Harper's Magazine*, vol. lv. p. 463.)

But the seeker of excitement was supposed to find more fun at the " radical" assemblies, and especially at the meetings of the Abolitionists and Women's Rights advocates. Of these the papers published the most exaggerated and ludicrous reports or caricatures.

Now all is changed. Mr. Curtis mourns that even in his time " the glory of anniversary week, in New York at least, is gone. Except to those interested members of the societies, those to whom 'meetings' of any kind are a delight, its return is scarcely known. The great public is unaware of the old festival, and the venerable joke of the return of the Quakers, who bring to town the rain of May, sleeps undisturbed. The 'anniversaries' are becoming almost as obsolete in memory as the figures of the clergymen upon Broadway, which even the Easy Chair can recall, walking to church in the sunny Sunday morning in all the flowing pomp of robes, their black silk gowns floating around them in the breeze as they moved." The venerable joke to which reference is made is not dead, however. Here is how it was revived so recently as May 27, 1896, in the editorial columns of the *New York Herald :*

" It may be that within the memory of some octogenarian a Quaker meeting has been held without any accompanying downpour. But if any eighty-year-older dares to make the assertion, we shall boldly declare that he has reached that period of mental decrepitude when he draws his facts from his imagination."

Annunciation, Feast of the (known locally in England as **Lady Day of March**). The anniversary of the day when the angel Gabriel announced to the Virgin the mystery of the Incarnation.

As it was necessary to place the Annunciation nine months before the Nativity, it follows that it was not until December 25 had been fixed on for Christmas that March 25 was decided on for the Annunciation. But the feast itself dates from earlier times, since St. Athanasius makes mention of it in one of his sermons.

It is obvious that March 25 may happen in Lent. An ordinance of the patriarch Nicephorus, however, allowed the Lenten fast to be broken if the Annunciation happened to fall on the Thursday or Friday of Holy Week. Hence the Council of Toledo in 656, to preserve the integrity of Lent, ordered the transference of the feast to the week preceding Christmas. Some of the Eastern Churches still follow this decree, but the Syrians have fixed the date on December 1, and the Armenians on the 5th of January, while in the Latin Church it has resumed its more logical place in the ecclesiastical calendar. Nevertheless, if it should fall in the Easter fortnight, its celebration is postponed until the second Monday following the festival.

In Rome in the early part of the century the day used to be celebrated with great pomp and splendor. We read that the windows were hung with crimson and yellow silk draperies and occupied by females in most gorgeous attire, while the churches were patrolled by the Pope's horse-guards in their splendid full-dress uniforms, all of whom wore in their caps a sprig of myrtle as a sign of rejoicing. Before the service a procession appeared, preceded by another detachment of the guards mounted on black chargers, who rode forward to clear the way to the sound of trumpets and the beating of drums. This martial array was followed by a bareheaded priest on a white mule, bearing the host in a gold cup, at the sight of which everybody prostrated himself. The Pope used formerly to ride on the white mule himself, and all the cardinals used to follow him in their magnificent robes of state, but, as the eminentissimi were for the most part not very eminent horsemen, they were generally fastened on, lest they should tumble off.

Misson in his " Voyage d'Italie" has described another ceremony which was in use in his day at the Papal chapel of the Minerva, whither the Pope and the Sacred College used to proceed on horseback on the feast of the Annunciation. "After the Pope has said high mass, a number of young girls confess and communicate. Then these girls, who are dressed in white serge, and enveloped like phantoms in a piece of cloth which covers their heads, leaving only a little orifice for one eye, enter two by two into the choir, where all the cardinals are assembled, and prostrate themselves at the feet of the Pope. An officer appointed for the purpose stands by, holding a basin full of little bags of white cloth. These ·enclose a bank-note either of fifty shillings for those who choose marriage or of one hundred shillings for those who prefer the convent. Each girl having humbly declared her choice, her bag is handed out. She kisses it in receiving it, makes a profound obeisance, and turns away to give place to the others. The future nuns are distinguished by a garland of flowers which crowns their virginity. They hold the honorable rank in the procession."

In England the term Lady Day (more properly Our Lady's Day) is applied to four other festivals,—namely, February 2, or Candlemas, July 2, or the Visitation, to commemorate the visit paid by the Virgin Mary to her cousin Elisabeth (instituted by Pope Urban VI. in 1383), September 8, or the Nativity, and December 8, or the Conception.

Lady Day of March has always been very highly observed in England. The Synod of Worcester, A.D. 1240, by one of its canons forbade all servile work upon it, and this was afterwards confirmed by various provincial and diocesan councils in all respects except agricultural labor.

Gyst-ales (see ALES) were frequently held on this day. At St. Albans in Hertfordshire it is still the custom to sell a species of buns known as Pope Ladies (*q. v.*). Popular tradition still predicts public misfortune if Lady Day falls on Easter Sunday. The mediæval couplet runs,—

> When our Lady falls in our Lord's lap,
> Then England beware of great mishap.

No less than thirteen saints figure in the calendar on this day; among these two ladies, St. Dula and St. Ida, one Irishman, St. Cammin, Abbot of Iniskeltra, and two Englishmen, St. Alfwolf, Bishop of Sherborne, and St. William, the child-martyr of Norwich.

In England, besides its religious importance, which has been greatly minimized since the Reformation, Lady Day has for centuries preserved its fiscal significance as the first quarter-day in the year for rents and other payments. The pay-days in England have been arbitrarily fixed on Lady Day, Midsummer Day, Michaelmas Day, and Christmas. Why? Nobody has been able to explain, unless it be that, arriving, as they do, near the end of each quarter, such important days are better as reminders of duty to landlords than any ordinary 30th or 31st of the month would be likely to be. In England and Ireland alone have they this importance, for Scotland has quarter-days of her own. There the legal dates are Whitsunday (May 15) and Martinmas (November 11), the conventional terms Candlemas (February 2) and Lammas (August 1) making up the quarter-days.

Anselm, St., Archbishop of Canterbury. Born in Piedmont in 1033, he entered the monastic state at Bec, France, in 1060, and in 1093 succeeded his friend Lanfranc in the archiepiscopate of Canterbury. He died April 21, 1109. The anniversary of that date is celebrated as his festival.

St. Anselm was one of the most powerful mediæval advocates
of the supremacy of Church over State, and did much to establish the Papal authority in England against the recalcitrance

SEAL OF ST. ANSELM.
(From Stanley's "Memorials of Canterbury.")

of King William Rufus and King Henry I. He was buried
in his own cathedral, and many miracles were reported at his
shrine.

Anthony, St., hermit (251–356), the originator of the monastic idea in Christianity. His day in the Catholic calendar is
January 17. He is the great misogynist of the Church. He
regarded the whole sex with profound mistrust, a mistrust not
untinged with fear; for, although always on the alert, he seems
to have been never quite sure what trick they might be up to
next. That they were, for the most part, the devil's closest and
most unscrupulous allies was a point about which he personally
had very little doubt. Again and again in the course of his life
he proved clearly what he thought of them and their ways; he
would refuse to look on them or hold parley with them; and the
burden of much of his teaching was, lions are less to be feared

than women. He was, in fact, the organizer and leader of the first anti-women crusade; and it was part of his regular propaganda to insist that there could be neither peace on earth nor good will among men unless the whole feminine tribe were boycotted. Evidently he had no great faith in the resisting powers of his fellows; for the lesson he most impressed upon them was that in dealing with women their only chance of safety lay in

ST. ANTHONY AND THE DEVIL.
(From an old print reproduced in Wright's "Caricature.")

flight. Yet, strange to say, in spite of the suspicion with which he regarded them, and of the contumely with which he sometimes treated them, St. Anthony seems always to have been very popular among the ladies. No matter whose altar goes undecked, his is sure of its due meed of flowers, especially on his fête-day.

Born in Alexandria, Anthony inherited great wealth from his parents, who died when he was eighteen years old. But he gave it all to the poor, and retired to the desert with a small company of hermits, who lived in community, though in separate cells. Here his austerities attracted the special enmity of Satan. Evil spirits spread delicious fruit before him, and, assuming the forms of lovely women, tempted him to sin. When they found they could not enmesh him in this way, they fell upon him and overwhelmed him with hideous sights and sounds. But in the midst of these horrors a great light shone from heaven, and Christ's voice was heard, calming and comforting him. Then Anthony knew that the arch-fiend had been baffled. He sought another retreat in the ruins of an old castle on the Rhine. Here he shut himself up and saw no one for twenty years. When he emerged, great multitudes came to hear him preach, and such was the force of his words and his example that no less than five thousand hermits were at one time assembled around him in caves and tombs. Now, when the saint had reached the great age of ninety and had passed nearly seventy-five years in the desert, he began to be puffed up with pride at the thought that no one had lived in solitude and self-denial so long as he. But a voice told him that there was one Paul who had lived as a hermit for ninety years. Anthony went in search of Paul, and found him in a cavern. While the two were engaged in deep converse, there came a raven carrying a loaf in its beak, and Paul explained that for ninety years this raven had daily brought him half a loaf, but now for Anthony's sake the portion was doubled. After they had eaten, Paul told Anthony that he had come in time to receive his last breath. And he prayed him go and fetch a cloak to bury him in. And Anthony on his return heard heavenly music and saw the spirit of Paul winging its way to heaven. He wrapped the body in the cloak, and then two lions came out of the desert and dug the grave in which Anthony buried him. Fourteen years after, Anthony died, at the age of one hundred and five. This saint has been a favorite subject for painters of all schools. He wears the monk's garb and cowl, and his attributes are various: a crutch denotes his old age and feebleness; a bell shows his power in exorcising evil spirits, for after his victory over the arch-fiend he was held in great terror by all the powers of hell; and the aspergus, or rod for sprinkling holy water, conveys the same idea. A hog represents the sensuality and gluttony over which he triumphed. Flames of fire also are often placed near him, to indicate that he is a patron against fire of all sorts, natural and supernatural.

Anthony's body, according to his instructions, was buried secretly on his mountain retreat by two of his disciples. About the year 561, according to Bollandus, it was discovered, and with great solemnity translated first to Alexandria and then to Constantinople. In the year 1070 the Emperor of Constantinople presented the relics to Joselin, a nobleman of Dauphiné, who brought them back with him and deposited them in the church of La Motte St.-Didier in Vienne, France, then a Benedictine priory belonging to the abbey of Mont-Majour near Arles, but now an independent abbey of regular canons of St. Anthony.

Bollandus mentions a number of miracles wrought at his shrine. None was more memorable than the sudden stopping of the plague known as the Sacred Fire, wrought through the saint's intercession when it was raging violently in France and other parts of Europe.

This was in the year 1089. The plague has been popularly known as St. Anthony's fire ever since. Its more scientific name is erysipelas. "Public prayers and processions," says Alban Butler, "were ordered against this scourge. At length it pleased God to grant many miraculous cures of this dreadful distemper, to those who implored his mercy through the intercession of St. Anthony, especially before his relics. The church in which they were deposited was resorted to by great numbers of pilgrims, and his patronage was implored over the whole kingdom against this disease. A nobleman near Vienne, named Gaston, and his son Girond, devoted themselves and their estate to found and serve an hospital near this priory, for the benefit of the poor that were afflicted with this distemper; seven others joined them in their charitable attendance on the sick, whence a confraternity of laymen who served this hospital took its rise, and continued till Boniface VIII. converted the Benedictine priory into an abbey, which he bestowed on these hospitaller brothers, and, giving them the religious rule of regular canons of St. Austin, declared the abbot general of this new order, called Regular Canons of St. Antony."

Anthony of Padua, St., patron of that city and of animals. His festival is celebrated on June 13, the anniversary of his death, which took place in Padua in 1231. A Portuguese by birth, his youthful imagination became so inflamed by the story of the devotion and sufferings of the Franciscan friars that he joined St. Francis in Italy and was enrolled in the order. He is a favorite subject with the Italian painters, who represent him in the Franciscan habit, his attributes being the book and lily, and a flame of fire in his hand or on his breast. He is said to have performed many miracles, the most famous being that of his preaching to the fishes. When the inhabitants of Rimini stopped their ears and refused to listen to the saint, he repaired to the sea-shore and called upon the fish to hearken to him. "And, truly, it was a marvellous thing to see, how an infinite number of fishes, great and little, lifted their heads above water and listened attentively to the sermon."

Pope Gregory IX. canonized the saint in 1232, the year after his death. In 1263 a large church was built in Padua for his order, and his remains were translated into it. The flesh had all been consumed save only the tongue, which was found incorrupt, as red and fresh as in life. According to Butler, St. Bonaventure, who was among the witnesses, took it up in his hands, kissed it devoutly, and, bathing it with tears, poured out these words: "O blessed tongue, that didst always praise God, and hast been the cause that an infinite number learned to praise him: now it appears how precious thou art before Him who framed thee to be employed in so excellent and high a function." The tongue is now kept separately in a silver case. The sarcophagus of the saint is unusually rich, the costly lamps that hang before it being presents from various cities.

At Rome the great celebration of St. Anthony's Day is at the Franciscan church dedicated to him. Pope, cardinals, nobles, and commoners send thither their horses and mules, as well as saddles and harness, and the animals and their trappings are aspersed and blessed in the name of the saint.

In the Balearic Islands donkeys and horses are similarly blessed on St. Anthony's Day. In Palma and Mahon, the capitals respectively of the islands of Majorca and Minorca, the ceremony is one which half the population turns out to witness. The priest, in his surplice, takes up his position in the doorway of one of the houses in a principal thoroughfare. Beside him is placed a table, on which are set a bowl of holy water and a large plate for offerings. Servants or owners ride past on the quadrupeds, reining up for a moment to receive the blessing and sprinkling and deposit a copper in the plate. The popular belief is that the sprinkling of holy water will keep the devil out of the beast for at least a year, when the ceremony should be renewed on the next anniversary of St. Anthony's Day.

For some inexplicable reason St. Anthony of Padua is regarded as the special patron of the careless, at least of such of them as lose their possessions. Throughout France, Spain, and Italy prayers are straightway raised to him whenever anything goes astray, no matter whether a child, a sheep, or a thimble. Not so very long ago, at a school within fifty miles of Paris, some sixty children and their teachers were discovered, at the very hour, too, when they ought to have been working out sums, rending the air with supplications to St. Anthony to find for them some book they had lost. The sous-préfet was scandalized when he heard of the affair, and threatened to report it to Paris, but the townsfolk to a man supported the teachers, and, after all, the book was certainly found.

Antigonus of Antwerp. A monstrous figure, nearly forty feet in height, preserved in the city hall of Antwerp and brought out on great occasions to be paraded through the streets. (See GIANTS.) A door in the pedestal on which he sits gives access through a stairway to the interior of the giant's body as far up as the shoulders, beneath which a platform is constructed. Here stands a man during the processions, working the colossal head backward and forward by means of a winch.

ANTIGONUS.

According to legend, Antigonus was a giant who anciently intrenched himself on the river Scheldt where may still be seen the ruins of the old castle of Antwerp and there extorted heavy tolls from all travellers, cutting off the hands of such as would not or could not accede to his request. The hands he threw into the river. Hence, the legend adds, the origin of the word Antwerp (Hantwerpen, or Hand-tossing). Finally, through the agency of Prince Brabo (*q. v.*), Antigonus was slain and the city relieved. This legend is incorporated in the arms of Antwerp, which consists of a castle with three towers argent, surmounted by two hands.

In the processions the figure of Antigonus is preceded by two men, arrayed in the livery of the citizen, carrying severed hands as a trophy. In old times it was found necessary to lower the lanterns and remove the chains or ropes by which they were suspended, in all streets through which the figure passed. It always takes part in processions to honor the arrival of kings and potentates within the city.

Apollonia, St., the patroness against toothache and all diseases of the teeth. Her day is February 9. She was born in Alexandria, of heathen parents. When she became a convert to Christianity, her father handed her over to the authorities. They bound her to a column, drew her teeth out one by one with pincers, and then burned her, February 9, A.D. 250. Her attributes are a pair of pincers with a tooth. Sometimes a golden tooth is suspended on her neck-chain. The major part of her relics are preserved in the church of St. Apollonia at Rome, her head at Santa Maria Transtiberina, her arms in St. Lawrence outside the walls, parts of her jaw in St. Basil's, and other relics are in the Jesuit church at Antwerp, in St. Augustine's at Brussels, in the Jesuit church at Mechlin, in St. Cross at Liége, and in several churches at Cologne. These relics consist in some cases of a tooth only or a splinter of bone.

Apprentices' Feast. In the seventeenth century the apprentices of the city of London held an annual feast at Saddlers' Hall on August 4. In Noorthouck's "History of London" it is recorded that Charles II. sent to this feast a brace of bucks, that his natural son the Duke of Grafton officiated as one of the stewards, and that a number of his courtiers dined with the apprentices.

April. The fourth month of the modern year, and the first month of spring. In the ancient Albanian calendar, which

APRIL FEASTING.
(From an eleventh-century MS.)

divided the year into ten months of irregular length, April, with thirty-six days, stood first. In the calendar of Romulus it had thirty days, and was the second month. Numa's twelve-month calendar assigned it the fourth place, with twenty-nine days; and so it remained till Julius Cæsar's reformation of the calendar, when it recovered its quota of thirty days, which it has ever since retained. (See CALENDAR.)

The name has been a subject of considerable etymological guess-work. It has been supposed to come from *aperio,* "I open," as marking the time when buds of trees and flowers begin to open. But, inasmuch as all the other months are named after divinities or supposititious demigods, and as the Romans always looked upon April as being under the peculiar tutelage of Venus, it seems not impossible that Aprilis was originally Aphrilis, from Aphrodite, the Greek name of Venus.

Among the Anglo-Saxons the month was known as Oster-monath, whence our word Easter is sometimes imagined to have been derived.

Proverbial philosophy looks benignly upon April. The staccato rains which form its chief peculiarity are welcomed:

> April showers
> Bring May flowers.

Even something more emphatic than a shower is productive of good:

> An April flood
> Carries away the frog and his brood.

Nor is there any harm in wind:

> When April blows his horn
> 'Tis good for both hay and corn.

April Fool Day, or **All Fools' Day.** The First of April, when it is an almost universal custom throughout Christendom to play more or less amiably asinine tricks upon one's neighbor. Of the origin of this custom nothing positive is known. True, there be antiquaries of a peculiarly sanguine and sapient type who have evolved explanations that have all the rich humor of other "origins" invented by people destitute of humor. Believe these, and you will look on April fooling as well-nigh coeval with the race.

One speculator gravely goes back to Noah and the Ark. The April fool custom, says the *London Public Advertiser* of March 13, 1769, arose from "the mistake of Noah sending the dove out of the ark before the water had abated, on the first day of the month among the Hebrews which answers to our first of April, and to perpetuate the memory of this deliverance it was thought proper, whoever forgot so remarkable a circumstance, to punish them by sending them upon some sleeveless errand similar to that ineffectual message upon which the bird was sent by the patriarch."

Another refers it to the time of Christ, arguing that as the Passion of our Saviour took place about this time of the year, and as the Jews sent Christ backward and forward to mock and torment him,—*i.e.*, from Annas to Caiaphas, from Caiaphas to Pilate, from Pilate to Herod, and from Herod back again to Pilate,— this ridiculous or rather impious custom took its rise thence, by which we send about from one place to another such persons as we think proper objects of our ridicule. Further confirmation is sought in the French name for an April fool, " poisson d'Avril," on the theory that this poisson is a corruption of " passion."

Such an explanation would be unpleasant enough, but, luckily, it has not a leg to stand on. All Fools' Day is at once far older and far younger than the time of Christ,—older if looked upon as a day set apart for merriment at the expense of one's neighbor, younger if the merriment be specially associated with the 1st of April. As to the term " poisson d'Avril," it means exactly what it says, an " April fish,"—*i.e.*, a young fish, and therefore a fish easily caught,—much as in English we use the words " gudgeon" and " sucker."

The most plausible conjecture is that which ascribes the origin of the custom to France. This nation took the lead over all Christendom in commencing the New Year on January 1 instead of March 25. Before the change was made the merry-making culminated on the octave of the feast, April 1, when visits were paid and gifts bestowed. With the adoption of the reformed calendar in 1564, New Year's Day was carried back to January 1, and only pretended gifts and mock ceremonial visits were made on April 1, with the view of making fools of those who had forgotten the change of date. The custom once started was kept up after its origin had been forgotten. Its continuance was helped on by the fact that it appeals to an integral part of human nature which has asserted itself at all times and in all countries.

In character, though not in point of time, All Fools' Day corresponds with the Roman Saturnalia, when Caius and Manlius and the rest of the us's bent their classic wits to the task of fooling one the other, and with the mediæval Feast of Fools, when the pre-Renaissance intellect battened in all sorts of absurdities. But the nearest and most startling analogy, not only in kind, but almost in actual date, was and is the Feast of Huli, in Hindostan. The last day of this feast is March 31, when the chief diversion is to send people on errands and expeditions that are to end in disappointment for the sendee and merriment for the sender and his friends. " They carry the joke so far," says Colonel Pearce in his " Asiatic Researches," " as to send letters making appointments in the names of persons it is known must be absent from their houses at the time fixed upon, and the laugh is always in proportion to the trouble given."

It is not impossible that the English borrowed their April fooling from the French. For, in spite of all antiquarian guesses, the custom does not seem to have had any existence in Great Britain until about the beginning of the eighteenth century. The earliest literary allusion to it is by Addison in the "Spectator," where he scornfully tells how "a neighbor of mine, who is a haberdasher by trade, and a very shallow, conceited fellow, makes his boast that for these ten years consecutively he has not made less than a hundred Fools. My landlady had a falling out with him about a fortnight ago for sending every one of her children upon a sleeveless errand, as she terms it. Her eldest son went to buy a halfpenny's worth of inkle at a shoemaker's; the eldest daughter was despatched half a mile to see a monster; and, in short, the whole family of innocent children made April Fools. Nay, my landlady herself did not escape him."

Yet, though the great Addison did not approve of April fooling, the greater Swift seems to have condescended to custom. In his "Journal to Stella," March 31, 1713, he tells how he, Dr. Arbuthnot, and Lady Masham spent an amusing evening "in contriving a lie for the morrow." The scheme was that the august trio should, through their servants, circulate a report that one Noble, who had been hanged a few days previous, had come to life again and was now to be seen in the flesh as a guest of the Black Swan in Holborn. Thus mine host would have his hands full with an influx of curious visitors. Next day, however, Swift records that his colleagues did not come up to their agreement, and thus the scheme had failed.

What are known as "sleeveless" errands have always been a special favorite on this day in England. Endless is the joy if a rustic can be found so simple as to apply at the village bookstore for a "History of Eve's Grandmother," at the grocer's for a pint of pigeon's milk, at the cobbler's for strap oil. The latter was a prime favorite. The cobbler, if he were up to the game, would promptly give the innocent customer the strap with no oil to moisten it. It is curious to find that all these jests were practised over a century and a half ago. So early as 1728 we find them thus recorded in "Poor Robin's Almanac:"

> No sooner doth St. All-fools' morn approach,
> But waggs, ere Phebus mount his gilded coach,
> In sholes assemble to employ their sense,
> In sending fools to get intelligence;
> One seeks hen's teeth, in farthest part of th' town;
> Another pigeon's milk; a third a gown
> From strolling cobler's stall, left there by chance;
> Thus lead the giddy tribe a merry dance.
> And to reward them for their harmless toil,
> The cobler 'noints their limbs with stirrup oil.
> Thus by contriver's inadvertent jest,
> One fool expos'd makes pastime for the rest.

Not yet has the habit disappeared of leaving a valuable-looking package in a public place, nor the trick, devised by a refinement of strategy to meet a refinement of perspicacity, of making the package heavy and hard, so that he who contemptuously kicks it aside may come to grief no less surely than he who trustingly picks it up. Still does the small boy take delight in calling to the passing dude to look to his coat-tails, when he may find them with a piece of paper pinned thereon, or may not, in either case being saluted as an April fool.

In Scotland, that proverbial land of " wut" and humor, an exquisite bit of foolery is as popular as it was a century ago. This is called Hunting the Gowk. Gowk, originally a cuckoo, means by extension a fool, a simpleton. The trick is for Wag No. 1 to send his victim to Wag No. 2, at some distance, with a letter containing such words as these:

> This is the first of Aprile,
> Hunt the gowk another mile.

No. 2 then says that he is not the person sought, or that he cannot do what the letter asks, and advises the messenger to go to somebody else, some distance farther on. The third sends him to a fourth, and so on, till the victim suspects the trick, or is told of it by some kindly Sandy.

In the words of " Poor Robin's Almanac,"—

> It is a thing to be disputed,
> Which is the greatest fool reputed,
> The man who innocently went
> Or he that him designedly sent?

These pleasantries are not unknown in America, where street urchins also find great comfort in placing a brick under an old hat on the sidewalk for the passer-by to kick at with disastrous effect on his toes, or to put a purse with a string attached to it in the same public place and jerk it away if the unwary seek to grasp it. A hot iron carelessly laid where it may be picked up—and dropped—is also a favorite implement with juvenile jesters.

Many a paterfamilias on rising in the morning finds that the legs of his trousers have been turned into a *mare clausum* by the cunning adjustment of prohibitory pins. At the breakfast he is hailed with the information that " there is something on your face, papa!" and after ineffectual efforts to wipe it off is told with wild shrieks of juvenile laughter that that something is his nose, with the further information that he is an April fool for his trouble.

Being a kindly man and a good father, he does not explain to his progeny that the uproarious jest is one which he himself had practised in the days of his nonage upon his equally complacent parent.

April Fool candy, made of gun-cotton plentifully spiced with Cayenne pepper, coated with sugar, and appetizingly colored, is sold in American candy- and toy-shops for juvenile use on this day.

The story is told, though of doubtful authenticity, how Francis, Duke of Lorraine, and his wife escaped from captivity at Nantes one April 1. Dressed as peasants, they started off boldly to pass the sentries. Some one, detecting their disguise, ran ahead and warned the guards. The latter laughed in derision, however, and shouted back, knowingly, " Poisson d'Avril !" and thus the pretended peasants made good their escape.

Another French story bears an excellent moral. A lady stole a watch from a friend's house, as an April joke. and, still as an April joke, sent the police all over the town. When at last it was located and the jester cried, " Poisson d'Avril !" the magistrate continued the merry bit of drollery by informing the lady that she would have to go to jail until the ensuing 1st of April as a poisson d'Avril! A Daniel come to judgment!

So recently as 1860 some gay spirits in London put their heads together and perpetrated a successful and notorious piece of foolery on the wholesale plan. Towards the latter part of March many well-known persons received through the post the following invitation card, bearing the stamp of an inverted sixpence on one of the corners for official effect:

"Tower of London—Admit Bearer and Friend to view annual ceremony of Washing the White Lions on Sunday, April 1, 1860. Admittance only at White Gate.

"It is particularly requested that no gratuities be given to wardens or attendants."

The ruse worked so well that a succession of cabs rattled around Tower Hill all the morning, much to the disturbance of the customary peace of the Sabbath, in vain attempts to discover the White Gate.

Arbor Day. In most of the States of the Union, and in portions of Canada. a fixed day on which the citizens, the magistrates, the school-children, and others plant trees and shrubs along roadsides and in other suitable places. It is a movable festival, varying according to climate, though usually falling in April or May, and in the United States is appointed either by the legislature or the governor acting under legislative authority. The pioneer State in the movement was Nebraska. The pioneer mover was J. Sterling Morton, afterwards Secretary of Agriculture during President Cleveland's second term. In 1872 he was a member of the Nebraska State Board of Agriculture, and he offered a resolution setting apart April 10 of that year as "tree-planting day." There were some members of the Board who contended for the name "Sylvan Day," but Mr. Morton talked them out of this title. The resolution as finally adopted recommended that the people throughout the State plant trees on the day named, and offered, in the name of the Board, a prize of one hundred dollars to the agricultural society of that county which should plant properly the largest number of trees. To the person planting the largest number of trees a farm library worth twenty-five dollars was offered. The Board requested the newspapers to keep this resolution before their readers, and the newspapers responded so generously that more than one million trees were planted throughout Nebraska on the first Arbor Day.

Next year the day was observed with increased interest, and in 1874 the governor officially proclaimed the second Wednesday of April as Arbor Day for Nebraska. The day was named thus by proclamation until 1885, when the legislature designated April 22 as Arbor Day and a holiday. Since that time a provision has been inserted in the Constitution of Nebraska declaring that "the increased value of lands, by reason of live fences, fruit and forest trees grown and cultivated thereon, shall not be taken into account in the assessment thereof." In addition to this, Nebraska has enacted many statutory provisions touching upon the planting of trees. One directs the corporate authorities of cities and towns to cause shade-trees to be planted along the streets, and empowers the authorities to make additional assessments for taxation upon lands benefited by such planting. Another section of the law provides for the planting of trees not more than twenty feet apart upon each side of one-fourth of the streets in every city and village of Nebraska. Most persons acquainted with the needs of really valuable shade-trees realize that such trees should be planted a good deal farther apart than the distance thus indicated by law.

One result of all this legislation, and of the premiums offered each year by the State Board of Agriculture, has been the astonishing prosperity of nurserymen in Nebraska. In the first sixteen years after Arbor Day was instituted there were more than three hundred and fifty million trees and vines planted in Nebraska, and the observance of the day is still kept up with interest.

In 1876 Michigan and Minnesota followed suit, and like action was soon taken in other States. In 1887 the Education Department of Ontario ordered that the first Friday in May should be set apart by the trustees of every rural school and incorporated village for planting shade-trees and making flower-beds in the school-grounds.

New York did not fall in line until 1888, when on April 30 the following act was approved by the governor :

SECTION 1. The Friday following the first day of May in each year shall hereafter be known throughout this State as Arbor Day.

§ 2. It shall be the duty of the authorities of every public school in this State, to assemble the scholars in their charge on that day in the school building, or elsewhere, as they may deem proper, and to provide for and conduct, under the general supervision of the city superintendent or the school commissioner, or other chief officers having the general oversight of the public schools in each city or district, such exercises as shall tend to encourage the planting, protection and preservation of trees and shrubs, and an acquaintance with the best methods to be adopted to accomplish such results.

§ 3. The State Superintendent of Public Instruction shall have power to prescribe from time to time, in writing, a course of exercises and instruction in the subjects hereinbefore mentioned, which shall be adopted and observed by the public school authorities on Arbor Day, and upon receipt of copies of such course, sufficient in number to supply all the schools under their supervision, the school commissioner or city superintendent aforesaid shall promptly provide each of the schools under his or their charge with a copy, and cause it to be adopted and observed.

By a popular vote the pupils of the State schools of New York decided that the white elm was the tree and the rose the flower of the State. They are therefore called upon to do all in their power to increase the number of both by planting them on Arbor Day. With this object in view, Central Park and the big pleasure-grounds in the upper part of the city are thrown open to them. Small parties of tree planters start from most of the up-town schools in the afternoon, and go to some nook chosen by the Park Commissioners to add their tribute to the day. Songs are sung during the planting, and the teachers tell the pupils all about the tree they have planted, how it will grow, and how grateful its shade will be to future generations. A luncheon spread in the open concludes the ceremonies. Arbor Day has been imitated by Spain. (See Feast of the TREE.)

Arthur's Oon. A supposititious Roman relic which formerly existed on the Carron in Stirlingshire, Scotland. Alexander Gordon has preserved its appearance in his " Itinerarium Septentrionale." It was a diminutive building, twenty-two feet in height, with an outer circumference of some ninety feet, and an arched door about nine feet high, the whole crowned with a dome having a circular opening. It became a fruitful subject for antiquarian speculation. In dimensions and structure it was acknowledged that it bore some resemblance to the curious beehive houses to be found in some of the ancient Irish burial-grounds, but these are of the roughest handiwork, while the accurately hewn and nicely adjusted stones of Arthur's Oon suggested Roman artisanship. The etymologist jumped in with a guess that Arthur's Oon was a contraction for Arthur's Oven, as if it were the circular baking-place where that hospitable prince appropriately prepared the viands consumed at his round table. But the general run of antiquaries from a very early period preferred to believe in the Roman origin. The not always reliable Nennius tells us as explicitly as possible that Carausius built on the banks of the Carron a round house of polished stone as a triumphal arch in memory of his victory, while he rebuilt the wall between the Forth and the Clyde and fortified it with seven castles. The ever unreliable Hector Boece is not less specific in stating that it was raised by Vespasian in honor of his predecessor Claudius, and that it covers the ashes of the distinguished officer Aulus Plautius. Hector mentions some other little particulars, which, if true, are decidedly to the point,—as that in his day the effigy of a Roman eagle was visible cut in the pavement, and that there stood within the building a stone sacrificial altar. Sir Robert Sibbald, the naturalist and historian, probably having his imagination heightened by this statement, declared that with a lighted link he could trace the outline of an eagle's head, and that he could also trace something extremely like the figure of a Victory. Moreover, he saw certain letters which, with a diffidence unprecedented and unimitated in the antiquarian world, he declared to be to him (Sir Robert) quite unintelligible.

Thus Arthur's Oon had become accepted as one of the wonders of Scotland, when the proprietor of the estate in which it stood, not having the fear of the antiquarian world before his eyes, but desiring some good hewn stone for the purpose of flagging a mill-dam, and believing that he could do what he liked with his own, took Arthur's Oon to pieces. The mill-dam which he built was carried off by a flood,—a just judgment, as it was deemed, on its sacrilegious owner; and the hewn stones of Arthur's Oon have for over a century been buried in silt, or tossed about and rounded by the water of the stream. The antiquaries were loud in their wail, and propagated their indignant grief far around. Posterity took up the cry. "We remember," says *Blackwood's Magazine* for November, 1853, "that, when the representative of the original victim stood for a Scottish constituency after the passing of the Reform Bill, it was stated against him, with mysterious emphasis, that he was the descendant of the destroyer of Arthur's Oon; and we saw the whole delinquency specifically described as a sort of celebrated crime in the work of a German historian, published within the past five years."

Artillery Day. In the early part of the nineteenth century this was a festival celebrated in Boston within the week after the announcement of the election of a new governor. The day the announcement was made was known as Nigger 'Lection Day (*q. v.*), because on that day blacks as well as whites were allowed to throng the Boston Common to buy gingerbread and drink beer. On Artillery Day the Ancient and Honorable Artillery held a formal parade, and chose its new officers, who received with much ceremony, out of doors, their new commissions from the new governor. Negroes were strictly debarred from its high privileges and pleasures. In 1817 a negro boy named William Read, enraged at this restriction, blew up a ship called the Canton Packet in Boston harbor. For years it was a standing taunt of white boys in Boston to negroes,—

> Who blew up the ship?
> Nigger. Why for?
> 'Cause he couldn't go to 'lection
> And shake pawpaw.

Pawpaw was a gambling game which was played on the Common with four sea-shells of the *Cyprœa moneta*.

Arval, or **Avril.** (Dan. *arveöl*, "a wake," "a funeral feast.") In the northern parts of England a feast or entertainment at funerals. After the interment, the relations first, and then their attendants, throw upon the grave sprigs of bay, rosemary, or other odoriferous evergreens, which have previously been distributed among them. The company then adjourn to a neighboring public house, where they are severally presented with a cake and a glass of ale, which refreshment is called an arval.

Asaruf, Al. (Arabic, "The Sacred Relic.") The name given by Mohammedans to a hair of either the beard or the moustache of the Prophet, or to his footprint. The most famous of the Al Asarufs (a hair of the beard) is exhibited in the great mosque at Delhi; another is in a mosque in Cashmere.

Ascension Day, or **Holy Thursday,** is celebrated on the fortieth day after Easter Sunday in honor of the ascension of the Messiah into heaven forty days after his resurrection. It is one of the oldest festivals of the Church. St. Augustine says that in his day it had been kept from time immemorial, and he attributes its institution to the apostles. Gregory of Tours mentions a procession which used to be held on this day, in

memory of that which the apostles made from Jerusalem to
Bethany and the Mount of Olives. It was also the custom in
ancient Catholic days to bless the bread and new fruits in the
mass of this day. In Catholic churches the paschal candle is
removed from the altar and extinguished after the Gospel at
high mass, the rite symbolizing Christ's departure from the
apostles.

Naogeorgus, in "The Popish Kingdom," as rendered by Barnaby Googe, thus satirically describes some of the scenes which
characterized Ascension Day in mediæval times:

> Then comes the day when Christ ascended to his Father's seate,
> Which day they also celebrate with store of drink and meate.
> Then every man some bird must eate, I know not to what ende,
> And after dinner all to church they come and there attende.
> The blocke that on the aultar still till then was seen to stande,
> Is drawn up hie above the roofe by ropes and force of hande:
> The priests about it round do stande, and chant it to the skie,
> For all these men's religion great in singing most doth lie.
> Then out of hande the dreadfull shape of Sathan downe they throwe
> Oft times, with fire burning bright and dasht asunder tho.
> The boyes with greedie eyes do watch and on him straight they fall,
> And beat him sore with rods and breake him into pieces small.
> This done, they wafers downe do cast, and singing cakes the while,
> With papers round amongst them put the children to beguile.
> With laughter great are all things done: and from the beames they let
> Great streams of water downe to fall on whom they mean to wet.
> And thus this solemn holiday and hie renowned feast,
> And all their whole devotion here, is ended with a jeast.

In the Anglican Church it is the only weekday, save Christmas, for which there is provided a special preface to the communion. On this day, or on one of the three days preceding
(known as Rogation days), was performed the old English
custom of beating the bounds. Lysons also mentions the practices on this day of "rush-bearing, of hanging up white gloves
and garlands of roses in the churches at the funerals of young
maidens, of foot-ball plays, and of well-dressing" (*q. v.*).

Many English towns have or have had their own local observances on Ascension Day. In Nantwich the Blessing of the
Brine was then performed. Pennant describes this custom in
his "Tour from Chester to London" (1811, p. 40): "A very
ancient pit called the Old Brine was also held in great veneration, and till within these few years was annually on this festival
decked with flowers and garlands and was encircled by a jovial
band of young people, celebrating the day with song and dance."
A correspondent of *The Gentleman's Magazine* (1787, vol. lvii.
p. 718) calls attention to a custom in many villages of Exeter
to "hail the Lamb" on Ascension morn. "That the figure of a

lamb actually appears in the east upon this morning is the popular persuasion ; and so deeply is it rooted that it has frequently
resisted (even in intelligent minds) the force of the strongest
argument." Brand in his " Popular Antiquities" mentions the
smock-race on Ascension Day, run by young country wenches
in the north of England. The prize was a fine Holland chemise,
usually decorated with ribbons. In Nottinghamshire it is believed that an egg laid on Ascension Day if placed in the roof
of a house will ward off fire, lightning, and other calamities.

The men in the slate-quarries of Northern Wales have a
curious superstition that if they work on Ascension Day a fatal
accident will happen to one of their number. "Some years
ago," says *Notes and Queries*, Seventh Series, vol. ii. p. 232, " an
attempt was made to break down this superstition, and for two
years the managers succeeded in inducing the men to work as
usual. Strange to relate, however, a fatal accident occurred each
year, and this naturally tended to increase the dislike of the
superstitious to work on that day."

Ascension Day at Etretat, near Havre, is marked by a singular religious ceremony peculiar to this ancient town of Normandy. Two centuries ago a small river flowed down the narrow
valley that here breaks the continuity of the high chalk cliffs
between Havre and Dieppe. A violent storm from the northwest on Ascension Day, 1690, sent the sea far up this gully, and
submerged the little fishing-town which nestled on its steep
slopes. When they receded, the waves left behind them a memorial in the shape of a shingle bank, which has served ever
since as a bulwark against further incursions. On every recurring Ascension Day morning a solemn procession walks from the
church of Etretat to the beach. First comes a beadle in cocked
hat, red stockings, and red small clothes and a profusion of gold
lace, then the children of the infant schools marshalled by the
Sisters of Charity, next a troop of young girls dressed in white,
behind them weather-beaten tars carrying a banner with the
inscription " Aïmons-nous, aidons-nous," then a gold crucifix,
followed by the clergy in gorgeous vestments and the church
officials, and last of all the curé in his richly embroidered
chasuble.

After chanting some prayers on the beach, the curé takes the
crucifix from the hands of one of the acolytes and holds it forward so that the handle may dip into the incoming waves. Then
with the holy water brush he sprinkles the sea, making the sign
of the cross over it. This being done, the blessing is pronounced,
the band strikes up a march, and the procession returns to church
to finish the mass. The military band takes an important part
in this mass, and the effect of the brass instruments is very

grand in the echoing walls of the old Norman church. An illustration of this ceremony may be found in the *London Graphic* of May 28, 1892.

In dogal Venice Ascension Day was chosen for the great festival of the Doge's marriage to the Adriatic.

At Rome the paschal candle is extinguished after the Gospel, to show the faithful that Christ on this day left the earth to shine in heaven. The altar is adorned with flowers, images, and relics. The priests and assistants on this occasion resume their white vestments. The benediction given by the Pope on this day is one of the three solemn benedictions of the Church. Formerly the benediction was preceded by a solemn excommunication of heretics and infidels.

Ascot, Royal. Ascot Heath is a race-course in Berkshire, England, some twenty-nine miles to the southwest of London. The races which are held here early in June are usually attended by the royal family in semi-state. Hence the title Royal Ascot. Hence also the fact that of all occasions of out-door sport these are the most patrician and fashionable. There is evidence that Queen Anne instituted the meetings on August 6, 1711, though the common supposition is that they originated in 1727 with William, Duke of Cumberland, uncle to George III. But they did not attain any great prestige until the memorable race for the Oakland Stakes in June, 1791, won by the Prince of Wales, afterwards George IV. Thereafter George III. never missed a race. He ran horses there, he gave prizes, and he instituted the Royal Processions from Windsor Castle, six miles away, which are still a feature of the meeting on Tuesday and Thursday of Ascot week. The Master of the Buckhounds leads the way on a handsome steed; behind him are the servants of the hunt, in scarlet-and-green liveries, and then the carriages. To each of these are four horses ridden by postilions in scarlet, and a brave showing the whole makes. The carriages are open landaus, and have two footmen sitting behind. The Prince and Princess of Wales are always in the first landau, with some other English or foreign royal person, and loud cheers greet them as they drive up the course and into the enclosure. The next two or three carriages also have royalties in them, and the last two or three the suite, outriders in scarlet being between each carriage.

Ash Wednesday. The first day of Lent in our modern observance. The name has a general reference to the penitential sackcloth and ashes so frequently spoken of in the Old Testament, but a more special one to a peculiar rite in the Roman

Church. Before the commencement of mass the congregation
approach and kneel at the altar rails, and the priest puts ashes
on the forehead of each, saying, " Memento, homo, quia pulvis
es, et in pulverem reverteris" (" Remember, man, that thou art
dust, and unto dust thou shalt return"). The ashes are obtained
by burning the palm branches consecrated in the church on the
Palm Sunday of the year previous.

ASH WEDNESDAY.
(From Picart.)

Originally the administration of the ashes was made only to
public penitents. These had to appear barefooted and in penitential garb before the church door on the first day of Lent.
There their penances were imposed upon them. Then they were
admitted into the church and brought before the bishop. He
put ashes on their heads, and to the words already quoted added,
" age pœnitentiam ut habeas vitam æternam" (" do penance that
thou mayest have eternal life"). Then he addressed them a
few words of exhortation, at the end of which they were solemnly excluded from the church. Gradually it came to be the
custom for friends and relatives to manifest their humility and
affection by joining the penitents, expressing a similar contri-
tion in their outward guise and offering their foreheads for the
ashes. The numbers of these self-condemned penitents grew in

time to be so large that at last the administration of ashes was extended to the whole congregation and the rite took its present form.

Nor was Ash Wednesday always included within the Lenten period. In the fifth and sixth centuries Lent began with the succeeding Sunday, lasting for six weeks, which (omitting Sundays) would be thirty-six days. At what time Ash Wednesday and the three following days were added to the fast is not precisely known, but it was certainly before 714, as a capitulary of the church of Toulon of that date describes the Lenten usage as identical with our own. The reason for the change is readily intelligible. The addition of these four days makes the fast (omitting Sundays) exactly forty days in duration, and therefore accords with the fasts of Moses and Elias, and especially the fast of the Saviour.

In Protestant Churches the Lenten sermons generally begin on Ash Wednesday, but a special service is held only in the English Church. Even here, however, the use of ashes has been discontinued since shortly after the Reformation, as being a "vain show," and the only memorial of the original character of the day is in the reading of the curses denounced against impenitent sinners, when the people are directed to repeat an Amen at the end of each malediction. This was not always so, however, for in an original black-letter proclamation, dated 26 February, 30 Henry VIII., concerning rites and ceremonies to be retained in the Church of England, we read, " On Ashe Wenisday it shall be declared, that these ashes be gyven to put every Christen man in remembrance of penaunce at the beginning."

Naogeorgus gives a burlesque account of the Ash Wednesday solemnities in his day :

The Wednesday next, a solemn day, to church they early go,
To sponge out all the foolish deedes by them committed so ;
They money give, and on their heddes the Prieste doth ashes laye,
And with his holy water washeth all their sinnes away :
In woondrous sort against the veniall sinnes doth profite this,
Yet here no stay of madnesse now, nor ende of follie is,
With mirth to dinner straight they go, and to their woonted play,
And on their deuills shapes they put, and sprightish fonde araye.
Some sort there are that mourning go, with lantarnes in their hande,
While in the day time Titan bright, amid the skies doth stande :
And seeke their Shroftide Bachanal, still crying every where,
Where are our feastes become ? alas the cruell fastes appere.
Some beare about a herring on a staffe, and lowde doe rore,
Herrings, herrings, stincking herrings, puddings now no more.
And hereto joyne they foolish playes, and doltish dogrell rimes,
And what beside they can invent, belonging to the times.
Some others beare upon a staffe their fellowes horsed hie,
And carie them unto some ponde, or running river nie,

That what so of their foolish feast, doth in them yet remayne,
May underneth the floud be plungde, and wash't away againe.
Some children doe intise with nuttes, and peares abrode to play,
And singing through the towne they go, before them all the way.
In some place all the youthful flocke, with minstrels doe repaire,
And out of every house they plucke the girles, and maydens fayre,
And them to plough they straightways put, with whip one doth them hit,
Another holds the plough in hande ; the Minstrell here doth sit
Amidde the same, and drounken songes with gaping mouth, he sings,
Whome foloweth one that sowes out sande, or ashes fondly flings.
When thus they through the streetes have plaide, the man that guideth all,
Doth drive both plough and maydens through some ponde or river small :
And dabbled all with durt, and wringing wette as they may bee,
To supper calles, and after that to daunsing lustilee.

Aubanus corroborates the last folly described. "There is a strange custom," he says, "used in many places of Germany upon Ash Wednesday, for then the young youth get all the maids together, which have practised daunciug all the year before, and carrying them in a cart or tumbrell (which they draw themselves instead of horses) and a minstrell standing atop of it playing all the way, they draw them into some lake or river, and there wash them well favouredly."

The Jack-o'-Lent made its first appearance on Ash Wednesday. This was a ragged scarecrow-like effigy, used as a symbol or personification of Lent, and carried around in processions to be shied at with sticks as a sort of burlesque of the sport of throwing at cocks practised on Shrove Tuesday.

A singular custom came to an abrupt end in the reign of George I. During the Lenten season it had long been customary for an officer of the royal household, known as the King's Cock Crower, to crow the hour every night within the precincts of the palace, instead of leaving it to the watchmen to proclaim it. On the first Ash Wednesday after the Hanoverian succession, just as the Prince of Wales, subsequently George II., sat down to supper, this officer made his appearance and emitted ten shrill crows. The astonished prince, thinking some insult was intended, jumped up to resent it, and was with difficulty calmed by an explanation. "From that period," says Brady, " we find no further account of the exertion of the imitative powers of this important officer, but the court has been left to the voice of reason and conscience to remind them of their errors, and not to that of a cock, whose clarion called back Peter to repentance, which this fantastical and silly ceremóny was meant to typify."

In rural France the peasantry on Ash Wednesday used to carry around an effigy supposed to be a personification of good cheer, and collected money for its funeral, inasmuch as this day was the burial of good living. After sundry absurd mummeries, the corpse was deposited in the earth. (See SARDINE, BURIAL OF THE.)

Ashton Fagot. A huge fagot composed of sticks or branches of ash, securely bound together with ash bands or withes, which is burned on Christmas Eve in lieu of the Yule-log (*q. v.*) in Devonshire and Somersetshire, England. Sometimes it is placed in the grate; but, as grates are not common there, it is more usually burned on the floor. A crowd of merrymakers gather around it, to whom a quart of cider is served upon the bursting of every band. As the timber is green and elastic, each band generally bursts open with a smart report, which is greeted with loud calls for the cider. The men who make up the fagot take care to put as many bands around it as possible, to insure a goodly supply of cider. A poem written in 1795 thus refers to the fagot, bands, and cider:

> The pond'rous ashen faggot from the yard
> The jolly farmer to his crowded hall
> Conveys with speed; where, on the rising flames
> (Already fed with store of massy brands),
> It blazes soon; nine bandages it bears,
> And as they each disjoin (so custom wills),
> A mighty jug of sparkling cyder's brought,
> With brandy mixt to elevate the guests.

The brands were originally saved, that they might serve to relight the Christmas fire the following year:

> With the last year's brand
> Light the new blocks.

There is a superstition that misfortune will follow in any house where the fagot is not burned. It is common to hear the claim that the fagot has been burned in this or that house for so many centuries.

At Taunton there used to be an annual "Ash Fagot ball." The fagot was bound with three withes, which were severally chosen to represent them by the young people present,—the first withe that broke in the fire signifying that they who selected it would be the first to be married.

Ass, Feast of the. A burlesque ceremony (a sort of variant of the Feast of FOOLS, *q. v.*) once highly popular in Northern France, in which priests and congregation joined to parody the services of the Church. It seems to have been instituted in good faith, and without any intentional irreverence, in part perhaps as a means of attracting the godless and the ignorant to church through their sense of humor. But eventually it degenerated into scurrilous indecency. In the fifteenth century it was prohibited by ecclesiastical authority, but in many localities was not fully suppressed until much later. The *Festum Asinorum* was variously celebrated in various cities. In Rouen it occurred shortly before Christmas, and consisted in the representation of a little farce in whose principal scene Balaam's ass (a priest concealed between the legs of an ass) appeared before the altar of the cathedral and predicted the early coming of Christ. In Beauvais the feast was far more elaborate. It was celebrated on Circumcision Day (January 1). Before the beginning of vespers an ass richly caparisoned, sometimes riderless, sometimes with a maiden on its back, was led up to the principal door of the church. Two criers chanted in a loud voice the following Latin verses :

> Lux hodie, lux lætitiæ! me judice, tristis
> Quisquis erit, revomendus erit solemnibus istis.
>
> Læta volunt, quicunque colunt asinaria festa.
> Sunt hodie procul invidiæ, procul omnia mœsta.

("Light to-day, the light of joy! Believe me, whoever is sad shall be cast out from these solemnities. Those who celebrate the feast of the Ass wish only gayety. Far from here to-day the sentiment of envy, far from here all that is sad.")

Two canons then conducted the ass (the rider, if any, having dismounted) to a table, where a celebrant called the prechantre opened the ceremonies by chanting a burlesque ditty beginning,—

> Orientis partibus
> Adventavit asinus,
> Pulcher et fortissimus,
> Sarcinis aptissimus.
> Hez! sire ane! Hez!
>
> Hic in collibus Sichem
> Jam nutritus sub Reuben,
> Transiit per Jordanem,
> Saliit in Bethlehem.
> Hez! sire ane! Hez!
>
> ("From the Orient
> Comes an ass,
> Beautiful and strong,
> Able for burdens.
> Hey! master Ass! Hey!
>
> In the hills of Sichem
> Brought up under Reuben,
> He crossed the Jordan,
> And leaped into Bethlehem.
> Hey! master Ass! Hey!")

The congregation all joined in the chorus as a response. Vespers were then read. But into the services were introduced fragments of other offices, joyful and sad, bits of prose and verse, an olio, in short, of sacred and profane literature. At intervals the ass was given to eat and drink. Finally clergy and people danced around him with loud imitations of braying. Then the congregation was led into the street by the prechantre, preceded by an enormous lantern. Booths had been fitted up before the church, where ribald farces were performed. There were more songs and dances, at the end of which the prechantre was deluged with water. The occasion wound up with a midnight mass, a burlesque of the regular mass, as the vespers had been of regular vespers. At its conclusion the priest brayed thrice instead of saying, " Ite missa est," and the people answered, " Hin han," in lieu of " Deo gratias." (See also PALM SUNDAY.)

Assumption of the Blessed Virgin. A festival celebrated by the Catholic Church on August 15. Butler asserts that it was established before the sixth century. According to tradition, the Blessed Virgin, after the death of her son, lived under the care of St. John, and died at Jerusalem, where her empty tomb was shown to pilgrims in the seventh century. Her body was believed to have been preserved from corruption and united to her soul in the kingdom of heaven. It is true that there is no distinct assertion of the corporal assumption in the prayers of the feast, nor is that corporal assumption a necessary article of faith, but that the Catholic Church encourages the belief is apparent from the fact that among the lessons used during the octave is a passage from St. John Damascene in which the legend of the Assumption is given in detail. And this is the legend. When the Virgin Mary had reached the age of seventy-three she was stricken with mortal sickness. The apostles, miraculously summoned from all parts of the earth, surrounded her death-bed, all save Thomas, who was late as usual. The latter, arriving after the funeral, gained permission to have the tomb opened, in order that he might once more gaze upon the features of the mother of the Redeemer. When, lo ! a miracle ! The body had disappeared, leaving behind it only a bunch of lilies. Another legend relates that Mary was taken up bodily into heaven in the actual presence of the apostles.

Bishop Hall tells us in the " Triumphs of Rome" that upon this day it was customary to implore blessings upon herbs, plants, roots, and fruits. It is to this that Naogeorgus alludes :

The blessed Virgin Marie's feast hath here his place and time,
Wherein, departing from the earth, she did the heavens clime ;

Great bundles then of hearbes to church, the people fast doe beare,
The which against all hurtfull things, the priest doth hallow theare.
Thus kindle they and nourish still the peoples wickednesse,
And vainly make them to believe, whatsoever they expresse:
For sundrie witchcrafts by these hearbes are wrought and divers charmes,
And cast into the fire, are thought to drive away all harmes,
And every painefull griefe from man, or beast, for to expell,
Far otherwise than nature or the worde of God doth tell.

(*The Popish Kingdom*, trans. by BARNABY GOOGE.)

In many parts of Catholic Europe the festival of the Assumption is celebrated with great splendor and pageantry. Howell tells us that in his day it was kept under the name of Bara at Messina in Sicily: "An immense machine of about fifty feet high is constructed to represent heaven; and in the midst is placed a young female personating the Virgin, with an image of Jesus in her right hand; round the Virgin twelve little children turn vertically, representing so many seraphim, and below them twelve children turn horizontally, as cherubim; lower down in the machine a sun turns vertically, with a child at the extremity of each of the four principal radii of his circle, who ascend and descend with his rotation, yet always in an erect posture; and still lower, within seven feet of the ground, are placed twelve boys, who turn horizontally around the principal figure, exhibiting thereby the Twelve Apostles. All are assembled to witness the decease and assumption of the Virgin. The machine is drawn through the main streets, and families regard it as a favor to have their children admitted to the divine exhibition, though the little ones do not seem to appreciate the honor of being apostles, cherubim, and seraphim."

In France the festival assumed a national character when Louis XIII. chose this day to place his kingdom under the patronage of the Blessed Virgin, asking her to intercede for him that he might obtain from heaven the gift of a dauphin. Napoleon I. and afterwards Napoleon III. re-established the feast as a national one. Napoleon I., indeed, is said to have changed the real date of his birthday to make it coincide with the feast of the Assumption.

Athanasius, St. The festival of this saint is celebrated on May 2, the anniversary of his death (373), as likewise of the translation of his remains to St. Sophia. The Greeks, however, who nevertheless celebrate on the date of the translation, place his death on January 18. Athanasius is one of the four Greek Fathers of the Church, and the author of the creed which bears his name. An Alexandrian and a pupil of St. Anthony, he devoted himself first to worldly learning, but, being converted, he turned his studies into religious channels and became one of the greatest theologians of his day. At the Council of Nice in 325 he stood forth as the opponent of Arius, earning for himself the title of the "Father of Orthodoxy." He became Bishop of Alexandria, and spent his whole life in conflict with the Arians, achieving a final victory only at the cost of exile and other hardships. He was bishop forty-six years, twenty of which were spent in exile. He was originally buried in Alexandria, but the remains were translated to the church of St. Sophia in Constantinople.

Athos, Mount. One of the three tongues of the Chalcidian peninsula on the Ægean Sea. The entire peninsula, as well as the mount itself, is generally known as the Holy Mountain (Gr. ῞Αγιον ῎Ορος; It. *Monte Santo*), from the great number of monasteries and chapels of the Greek faith with which it is covered. There are twenty of the convents, most of which were founded during the Byzantine Empire, and some of them trace their origin to the time of Constantine the Great. St. Helena is traditionally reputed to have been the first founder of convents on Mount Athos. The spot is visited periodically by pilgrims from Russia, Servia, Bulgaria, Greece, Asia Minor, and all other "orthodox" communities. The society owe the privileges which they enjoy under the Turks to the fact that before the fall of Constantinople they submitted to Mohammed II., who gave them his protection and guaranteed their privileges, which favor his successors have continued. The community maintains an armed guard of forty or fifty Christian soldiers. The only Mohammedan allowed to reside within the peninsula is one Turkish officer, who is the means of communication between the Sultan and the monks. Even he cannot have a woman in his house; all female animals of whatever species are rigidly excluded.

AUGUST. HARVESTING.

August. The eighth month in the modern calendar. In the old Roman calendar it was originally the sixth month, and was hence known as Sextilis. It then consisted of twenty-nine days. Julius Cæsar's reformed calendar extended it to thirty days.

Augustus added still another day to it, which he took from February, and renamed it in his own honor. He chose August rather than his birth-month of September because in the first place it came immediately after the month named in honor of his great prototype, Julius Cæsar, and in the second because it had proved itself a propitious season in his life.

August, Twelfth of. In England this day marks the beginning of the shooting season. For days if not weeks previous the minds of a large mass of the titled and wealthy classes are occupied, to the exclusion of almost everything else, in preparations for the moors. The game-keepers on every great estate send down to London bulletins as to the condition of the birds. Parliament invariably adjourns just before this date, for if it did not both houses would be left without a quorum.

Something of the excitement attending the occasion may be understood from an excellent article in *Harper's Magazine*, vol. xlvii. p. 567, 1873. The writer, an American, had been invited by an English nobleman to visit him at his manor-house for two weeks' shooting. The letter of invitation concluded as follows:

" Don't fail to come on Saturday, as all my guests will arrive on that day, and we shall take the field at eight o'clock on Monday morning [Monday being the 12th]. This game-killing is a sort of solemn duty with us squires; we go through it in the usual sad manner of Englishmen enjoying themselves; indeed, a real game-keeping squire, who lives for nothing else (and there are many of this class), is one of the curious creations of modern civilization. But it is amusing enough for a time, and I have no doubt that you will enjoy it. . . . My house is 1300 feet above the level of the sea, and we shoot over ground going up to 2200 feet. Some of our scenery is considered to be among the finest in England."

The invited guest found the trains all late and crowded with gentlemen bound for the moors of England, Ireland, and Scotland, accompanied by their servants, dogs, guns, and huge piles of baggage, including ample supplies of solid and liquid ammunition. Nevertheless the journey was safely accomplished.

"Punctually at seven on Monday, the 12th of August, the valet entered, threw aside the heavy curtains of my chamber windows, and, while I was taking my morning bath, laid out my shooting-suit, and announced breakfast at half-past seven. At eight o'clock we were driven down to the game-keeper's, and, selecting six dogs from the kennel, we started for the moor, where we were that day to open the campaign of 1872, followed in another vehicle by the six game-keepers and dogs. Reaching our shooting-ground, a distance of five miles from the manor-house, we were divided into parties of two each, accompanied by the same number of pointers and keepers carrying the game-bags, each squad taking by agreement different directions, with the understanding that we were to meet at the appointed rendez-vous for lunch at one o'clock. Our guns being loaded, and each gentleman carrying fifty rounds in his pouch, and the pointers enfranchised from their couples, the three parties separated, and took off their several ways, the dogs bounding and barking around us with joy."

It is pleasant to chronicle that in the shooting that followed the American did his share of the killing. The rendezvous for lunch was kept, and promptly at two the party separated again and set out in the same order as before on the various routes assigned by the chief game-keeper.

"With an instinct and training that obey the slightest word or wave of the hand, the dogs again range over the moors, and again are soon heard the *fusilados* from hill, valley, and moun-tain-side. After a capital afternoon's shooting we again assemble at half-past six at a farm-yard, where the carriage is in waiting for us. As each party came in, the bags were emptied, and the result of the day's sport was spread out before us, the grouse being placed in lines of twenty, with the hares and snipe in the rear, and summing up as follows: two hundred and sixty-four grouse, seven hares, and eight snipe. After seeing the game placed in large baskets, and resigning our guns to the attend-ants, we were driven to the hall. . . .

"At the front door we were met by servants and slippers, which latter were a pleasant exchange for our wet and heavy shooting-boots. Going to our rooms to dress for dinner (after receiving our letters, which arrived during the afternoon of each day, together with the London morning papers), I found a hot bath prepared for me, and my evening dress laid out in an artistic manner by the servant assigned to my service. Descending to the drawing-room at eight o'clock, we proceeded to dinner. And such a dinner! 'Twould have tempted a dyspeptic anchorite, while our nine hours of hard walking and 'carrying weight,' as the Country Parson says, had given us tremendous appetites, that would have served as sauce and seasoning for even such soldiers' fare as was served out to us at Vicksburg.

"The following morning I was called as before, my shooting-suit laid out for me, and my evening dress placed carefully in the armoire. After breakfast Lord —— desired us to write the address on parchment tags lying on his desk of any friends to whom we desired to send some grouse. This done, the steward received orders to attach them to little hampers containing six brace of birds each, and have them forwarded to their various destinations by that day's trains, the charges being prepaid. All being prepared for a start, our boots, which had been carefully dried during the night and oiled, were brought out and put on, and we were, as before, driven to the game-keeper's to select dogs for the day, when we proceeded to fresh shooting-grounds, on a different portion of the estate from where we had been the previous day,—the attendants following in a carry-all drawn by two horses, and bringing with them the dogs and shooting paraphernalia, including the guns, cleaned and oiled, like the boots, every night.

"The succeeding days of the week were substantially repetitions of the first, and it is therefore unnecessary to describe them.

"On Saturday guests who had been invited for a week took their departure, others arriving the same evening and the following Monday morning to occupy their places. All of my readers may not possibly know that in England persons are usually invited to a country-house for a certain period, and at the expiration of the time are expected to take their departure, other guests having been previously asked to occupy their rooms. You may be invited to come on a stated day and spend a week: if you arrive behind the time fixed, you simply curtail by so many days the period that you are expected to remain."

Augustalia or **Augustales, Ludi.** Ancient games in honor of Augustus celebrated in Rome and other parts of the Roman Empire. After the battle of Actium a quinquennial festival was instituted at Rome, and the birthday of Augustus, as well as the day on which the victory was announced at Rome, was regarded as a festival day. Quinquennial games were also instituted in the provinces. On the return of Augustus from Greece to Rome in B.C. 19 the day on which he returned was made a festival and called Augustalia.

The formal recognition of the games was made at the beginning of the reign of Tiberius. They were exhibited annually in the Circus. In Naples the Augustalia were celebrated with great splendor every fifth year. They consisted of gymnastic and musical contests, and lasted for several days. They were also celebrated at Alexandria, and at numerous other places throughout the Roman Empire.

Augustine or **Austin, St.,** patron of theologians and learned men. His day is August 28. Though not converted until his thirty-third year, he became one of the greatest names in the Church. He died Bishop of Hippo, in A.D. 430. His usual attribute in Christian art is a flaming heart, symbolizing the ardor of his piety. Sometimes it is transfixed by a sword, to express the poignancy of his repentance for having delayed his conversion, in spite of the prayers of St. Monica, his mother. Occasionally he is represented with only a pen and a book.

The saint was buried in the church of St. Stephen at Hippo, but according to Bede his body was fifty years later taken to Sardinia by the bishops whom Huneric had banished. They remained in that island till Luitprand, the pious and magnificent king of the Lombards, purchased them from the Saracens. He placed them in a coffin of lead enclosed in another of silver, and that again within a coffin of marble, and hid the whole under a brick wall in the church of St. Peter in Pavia. Here they were discovered in the year 1695. Pope Benedict XIII. declared them to be authentic in 1728. On account of its possession of this treasure, the church of St. Peter changed its name to St. Augustine. The relics have since been translated to the cathedral. Some portions were in 1837 given to the diocese of Algiers and placed on the ruined site of Hippo.

Another famous saint of the same name was the apostle to England sent over by Pope Gregory the Great in the year 596. He converted King Ethelbert of Kent, and so introduced Christianity into the island. This saint's festival is celebrated on May 26, the anniversary of his death in 604. His body, after several translations, found its last resting-place in a marble tomb in the cathedral at Canterbury. His head was put into a rich shrine ornamented with gold and precious stones in the year 1221. All the shrines in the cathedral were broken up at the time of the Reformation, and their contents were destroyed.

Auray, Pardon of. A famous festival celebrated at Auray in Brittany in honor of St. Anne, mother of the Blessed Virgin. on July 25 and 26, the eve and the day of her feast. The legend runs that in 1623 the saint appeared to a peasant named Yves Nicolazie and directed him to induce good Christians to rebuild her chapel at Auray, which had been in ruins for nearly ten centuries. Nicolazie's pastor thought him crazed, but his bishop patronized him. Soon after a broken effigy of wood was found in a field, and, being identified as St. Anne's, attracted pilgrims from far and near, who left behind them offerings sufficient to build a chapel in which the relic might be enshrined. This, together with a holy well adjoining, and a scala santa, or sacred staircase, by which the chapel was reached, became the resort of the most numerous and remarkable pilgrimages in Brittany, which have been lent additional prestige through the attendance of such pious and exemplary Christians as Louis XIV. and Louis Napoleon, besides an innumerable multitude of other kings, queens, dukes, countesses, and burgesses and peasantry without end. It is stated that as many as eighty thousand have been known to assemble at St. Anne at a single festival.

Hence the church at Auray has come to be known as the milch-cow of the Bishop of Vannes (in whose diocese it lies), such being the wealth it brings into his coffers.

Even before July 25 the pilgrims begin to pour into the village. They come on foot and on horseback, in carts and in all manner of strange vehicles, in steamboats down the river Auray, in railway carriages by the Chemin de Fer de l'Ouest. They come singly and in companies. Sometimes an entire family will make the journey, the weak and aged supported by the young and stalwart, the mother, mayhap, carrying her new-born babe. The inhabitants of the Isle Dieu are not deterred by the sixty leagues which they have to traverse from paying their annual homage to St. Anne. Sailors, also, in pursuance of some vow made in time of peril, will flock hither, bareheaded and barefooted, from any point of the coast where they have landed or been cast ashore.

No household can prosper, no ships be safe at sea, nor crops or cattle thrive, unless once a year the people for miles around come to burn their candles at St. Anne's shrine.

By the morning of the 25th a vast crowd has gathered in the open square near the church of St. Anne. Some congregate around the miraculous well, drinking of its healing waters or washing their hands, feet, and faces in its basins; others find a temporary repose on the ground or on the steps of the neighboring amphitheatre; while the more indefatigable make the round of the chapel walls, or of the cloistered galleries of the church, bareheaded and with lighted tapers in their hands, or climb up the scala santa on their knees to kiss the statues in the chapel. The latter is a small edifice, open to the air and surmounted by a cupola, which is approached on all sides by the sacred stairway.

In the afternoon a procession of male pilgrims is formed, who move solemnly around the town, headed by the priests. The green-and-gold vestments of the latter, the white robes and crimson sashes of the acolytes, the quaint costumes of the peasantry enlivened with beads, medals, and other gewgaws, the lighted tapers, the silver crucifixes, the flags and banners carried high in air, the fanfare of the band, the chanting of the litanies, make up a memorable sight. The surging crowds press as near as they can, leaving only a narrow lane for the return to the scala santa. When this is reached, the priests and their attendants crowd upon the steps, and the Bishop of Vannes or some other dignitary, mounting to the platform, addresses the crowd.

Beginning at four o'clock on the morning of the 26th, continuous masses are said in the church, and crowds pour in and out incessantly. Meanwhile outside in the square a thriving business is done by the booths, which dispense toys, rosaries, medals, and statuettes of St. Anne. Women cook fish and galettes (cakes), itinerant venders hawk gigantic wax candles, peep-shows and games attract the more volatile, and families gather in the cafés or the open fields.

Whit Monday is the occasion of another pilgrimage, of less importance, yet that attracts its hundreds to the other's thousands. This is the date chosen by the sailors of the commune of Arzon, at the extremity of the peninsula of Rhins, to fulfil a vow made by their fathers during a naval combat with the Dutch. They embark with their wives and children, at Port Navalo, on board luggers with red sails, having at the head of the flotilla a richly decked vessel, in which are the clergy of the parish in charge of a massive silver crucifix.

Auriesville. The shrine of Our Lady of Martyrs in this New York village, commemorating the spot where, in the early missionary days, Jesuit priests and others suffered for the faith, has earned it the title of the American Lourdes. Here the League of the Five Nations of the Iroquois Indians formerly held sway over the country between the Mohawk and Genesee rivers. Auriesville is situated on the left bank of the Mohawk. On August 14, 1642, the Jesuit father Isaac Jogues, his attendants René Goupil and William Couture, and several Christian Hurons, were brought here and underwent a long series of indignities and tortures. René was finally killed on September 29. The others were allowed to escape. In 1644 Father Jogues established here the Mission of the Martyrs, where on October 18, 1646, he was tortured and slain by the Mohawks. The thirty-eight years that followed his martyrdom were eventful to the Mission. Many priests and Christian laymen were tortured here to make an Indian holiday. Among the Indian converts the most famous was the Iroquois maiden Catherine Tegakwitha (1656–1680), "the Lily of the Mohawk," who after laboring for the conversion of her fellow-Indians was forced to flee to Caughnawaga, near Montreal, where her remains are kept to this day as a precious treasure by her own Indian people. At the beginning of the year 1684 the missions among the Mohawks were abandoned, on account of the French and English wars. In 1884, just two centuries later, nearly the whole site of the ancient village, ten acres in all, came into the possession of the Society of Jesus. A small octagonal chapel, large enough for an altar, a priest, and his servers, was built on the brow of the hill, —where once was the Indian torture-platform,—the gilt cross that surmounts it being visible far down the valley. A glass plate in the front door enables visitors to pray in sight of the altar during the seasons when the oratory is closed. Pilgrimages have been made to this shrine every year since 1885 during the months of July and August. In August a daily mass is said in the chapel by one of the Jesuit fathers. The feast of the Assumption, August 15, and its eve, which is the anniversary of the first public torture of Father Jogues and Goupil, are the days which draw the largest number of pilgrims. Many miraculous cures have been reported at the shrine.

At the twenty-seventh private session of the Third Plenary Council of Baltimore the committee on new business reported the petition of the fathers of the Society of Jesus to the Holy See for the introduction of the cause of the beatification of Father Jogues, René Goupil, and Catherine Tegakwitha. The council unanimously subscribed to the postulate.

Austerlitz, La Sainte. The colloquial name under which the anniversary of the battle of Austerlitz, December 2 (1805), is celebrated at the military schools in France. At the college of St.-Cyr the cadets all join a torchlight parade, singing the Saint-Cyrienne:

> Noble galette, que ton nom
> Soit immortel dans notre histoire;
> Qu'il soit embelli par la gloire
> D'une vaillante promotion!

The whole ends by a magnificent pyrotechnic display on the parade-ground. In the bedrooms afterwards the cadets indulge in a mimic attack upon the plateau of Stratzen, mattresses serving as barricades and pillows as weapons, and it is needless to say that the height is always successfully stormed.

Azan. (Arabic, "Announcement.") The Mohammedan call or summons to public prayer proclaimed by the Muezzin, or crier,—in small mosques from the side of the building or at the door, and in large mosques from the minaret. The words of the call are as follows: "God is most great! (*four times.*) I testify that there is no God but God! (*twice.*) I testify that Mohammed is the apostle of God! (*twice.*) Come to prayer! (*twice.*) Come to salvation! (*twice.*) God is most great! (*twice.*) There is no God but God!"

At the early morning Azan, after the words "Come to salvation!" are added, "Prayer is better than sleep! Prayer is better than sleep!"

When the Azan is recited it is usual for every one in hearing to respond to each call. The first three responses are a mere repetition of the words of the Muezzin. To the cry "Come to prayer!" the response is, "I have no power nor strength but from God the most High and Great;" to the "Come to salvation!" "What God willeth will be; what he willeth not will not be."

The recital of the Azan must be listened to with great reverence. If a person be walking at the time, he should stand still; if reclining, sit up. The Muezzin, a paid official of the mosque, must stand with his face towards Mecca and the points of his forefingers in his ears. Four classes of people are debarred from becoming Muezzins,—the unclean, the intemperate, the insane, and the female. The Azan was established by Mohammed himself, and tradition has invented the following legend: While the matter was under discussion a certain Abdullah dreamed that he met a man in green raiment carrying a bell. Abdullah sought to buy it, saying it would do well for bringing together the assembly of the faithful. "I will show thee a better way," replied the stranger: "let a crier cry aloud, 'God is most great,' etc." Waking from his sleep, Abdullah sought the presence of Mohammed, and related to him his dream.

All lovers of poetry will remember Edwin Arnold's lines beginning

> He who died at Azan sends
> This to comfort all his friends.

B.

Babylas, St. (237-250). A bishop of Antioch, who was martyred in the Decian persecution. In the Eastern Church his festival is September 4, in the Western, January 24. Historically he is famous for compelling the Emperor Philip, on a visit to Antioch, to take his place among the penitents and undergo penance for the murder of Gordian, as a condition precedent to his reinstatement in church membership. In legend he is still more famous for that his relics are said to have silenced the revived oracle of Apollo during the reign of Julian the Apostate. Julian, furious, ordered the relics to be removed. On that very night the temple and statue of Apollo were destroyed by lightning.

Bacon. As is well known, swine were held unclean animals by the Jews, and their flesh was forbidden by Moses. This taboo is still kept up. Hence our English forefathers loved to show their abhorrence of Judaism by eating a gammon of bacon on Easter, the day on which Christ was triumphant over his enemies. The custom is not extinct in some rural localities. But even in classic times bacon had a certain religious significance. Robert Bell, in "Shakespeare's Puck and his Folk-Lore," cites a passage in point from Spence's "Polymetis:" "Alba Longa is the place where Æneas met the white sow and thirty pigs; and here was a very fine flitch of bacon kept in the chief temple, even in Augustus's time, I find recorded in that excellent historian, Dionysius Halicarnassus."

In Tettan and Temme's "Volksagen" (1837) it is said, "A mighty deity of the heathen Prussians was Percunnos. An eternal fire was kept burning before him, fed by oak billets. He was the god of thunder and fertility, and he was therefore invoked for rain and fair weather, and in thunderstorms the flitch of bacon (*Speckseite*) was offered to him. Even now, when it thunders, the boor in Prussia takes a flitch of bacon on his shoulder, and goes with his head uncovered out of the house, and carries it into the fields, and exclaims, 'O God, fall not on my fields, and I will give thee this flitch.' When the storm is passed he takes the bacon home and consumes it with his household as a sacrifice."

It is probably as the reward and symbol of fertility that a flitch of bacon used anciently to be presented to any married couple who, after a certain period of wedded life, could swear that they had never regretted taking the step. The most notable instance of this ceremony was at the priory of Dunmow (*q. v.*).

Baddeley Cake. The eating of the Baddeley cake, or, as it is sometimes facetiously called, St. Baddeley's Cake, is an annual ceremony performed at the greenroom of Drury Lane Theatre in London on the evening of the 6th of January. Its history is as follows. Robert Baddeley, originally a cook, afterwards a valet, and lastly an actor, died in 1794, and by will set apart one hundred pounds as a fund whose income should be used to furnish a cake and a bowl of punch every Twelfth-Night to the Drury Lane greenroom, which by long custom had been annually given over on that night to feasting and merriment.

Baddeley's bequest has been faithfully carried out, with the exception of one provision, that whenever the cake was eaten some commemoration should be made of his conjugal infelicity. In his lifetime his wife was better known than himself. She sang well and danced charmingly, was beautiful and vivacious, and was said to have been the cause of more duels than any other woman of her time. Baddeley himself was an indifferent actor, though noteworthy in histrionic annals as the original Moses in "The School for Scandal."

The present proprietor of Drury Lane has added a few hundred pounds of his own to the Baddeley gift, increased the bill of fare so that it includes a large number of delicacies, and reserved the privilege of inviting distinguished outsiders, both lay and professional, to join in the ceremonials. The *pièce de résistance* is still the large, round white cake, with red and green icing in the centre, which is known as St. Baddeley's Cake, and no guest goes away without securing a portion of it.

Badrinath. A peak of the main Himalayan range, in the Northwestern Provinces of India, 22,901 feet above the sea. A shrine of Vishnu stands on one of its shoulders at a height of 10,400 feet, about fifty-six miles northeast of Serinagur. This temple overhangs a sacred tank, which is supplied from a thermal spring.

The annual number of pilgrims to the shrine is about fifteen thousand; and every twelfth year, when the Kumbh Melah is celebrated there, the number rises to fifty thousand. Adoration of the idol, liberal fees to the attendant Brahmins, and ablution in the sacred tank, in which both sexes bathe indiscriminately, are believed to be efficacious in cleansing from past offences. The officiating priests are Brahmins from the Deccan, of which caste there are no women at Badrinath, so that they cannot marry; but they are a very profligate set.

Bairam or Beiram. The name of two Mohammedan feasts. The lesser Bairam, being celebrated at the termination of the great fast of Ramadan (*q. v.*), is to that extent the analogue of the Christian Easter. Then the Moslem world puts on its new clothes and comes out and rejoices over the return of sumptuary liberty. Visits and presents are exchanged. In Constantinople bands of music parade the streets, and the boats in the Bosporus are decorated with flags. In the palace of Dolma-baktche the Sultan receives his friends after worshipping at the mosque. He takes his seat on the throne in the centre of the vast audience-room. The grand vizier is received first. He presses to his forehead a broad scarf or veil which is attached to the throne, and then bows low and withdraws. The Sheik-ul-Islam makes a feint at doing the same. But, being almost as high as the Sultan in religious rank, that sublime gentleman interrupts him and bows to him instead. The festivities are generally protracted over three days.

The second or greater Bairam, known also as the Feast of the Sacrifices, is celebrated seventy days later. This is the culminating ceremony of the pilgrimage to Mecca, but it has an individual significance as a commemoration of the willingness of Abraham to offer up his son Ishmael (not Isaac, as stated in the Bible). The Moslem story runs thus: After the foundation of Mecca by Abraham, God commanded him to prepare a feast. The patriarch asked what the Lord would have served for the occasion, and the answer was, "Offer up thy son Ishmael." So Abraham placed Ishmael on his back with his head towards the black stone. But the patriarch's hand trembled, and the knife dropped out of it. Thereupon Ishmael told him to cover his eyes with the end of his turban and strike blindfolded. Abraham obeyed, and striking felt the blood gush forth from the victim. "God is great!" he cried. But, lo! when he unbound his eyes, a dying ram lay at his feet, which the archangel Gabriel had substituted for Ishmael. In memory of this deliverance of the patriarch's son, from whom Mohammed and his followers claimed descent, sacrifices of goats and sheep are offered by all who can afford them. These animals it is believed will reappear after death to help the souls of the offerers across the bridge that leads to paradise. Hence the richer Moslems, in a spirit of altruistic charity, frequently supply their more indigent brethren with victims to sacrifice.

Balaam's Ass Sunday. In Gloucestershire this was the name formerly given to the second Sunday after Easter, when the story of Balaam was read in the lesson for the day. *Notes and Queries* (Seventh Series, vol. v. p. 426) mentions Randwich Church, near Stroud, and Hawkesbury Church, near Chipping-Sodbury, as places where this custom survived up to the middle of the nineteenth century, and suggests that this was probably a relic from the days of Miracle Plays.

Bambino, Il (It., "The Babe"), or, as it is frequently called, **Il Santissimo Bambino** ("The Most Holy Babe"). A figure of the child Jesus in the Franciscan church of Ara Cœli at Rome. It is reputed to heal the sick and to possess other miraculous virtues. The festival of the Bambino, which occurs on EPIPHANY (January 6), is a gorgeous spectacle, and is attended by the faithful in Rome and the peasants for miles around. The Bambino, loaded with jewels, is placed in a presepio, or manger, and all day long the people pass in an endless procession before the stolid features and unblinking eyes, beseeching some favor,—health for themselves or for a loved one, a successful number in the lottery, the safe return of a friend from afar, or the fulfilment of any desire, serious or trivial.

The same church of Ara Cœli used to be the scene of a curious performance on Christmas. Opposite the lifelike representation of the stable of Bethlehem, called the PRESEPIO, was placed a tribune, or palco, on which a number of baby orators successively took their places and preached, or recited little speeches prepared beforehand descriptive of the birth of our Lord and his early childhood.

The Bambino often goes out to attend the sick, especially women in childbirth, being driven from door to door in a large tan-colored coach floating a vermilion flag. Two monks act as its attendants. The fees paid for its presence at the sick-bed are always large, and in case of recovery the gratuitous offerings subsequently made are frequently magnificent.

There are several legends of its miraculous powers. Once when it was left over-night in a house it returned next morning of its own volition, and all the bells in the churches and convents rang out a merry peal of salutation without any human aid. On another occasion a woman desiring the Bambino to stay with her longer than was necessary had a false image made, which she sent back to the church in its stead. The true Bambino was so indignant that on its own little bare feet it went back to the church. When an astonished monk opened the door it strode straight past him to its accustomed niche.

It is said the image was carved at Jerusalem by a Franciscan monk out of a piece of wood from the Mount of Olives. Though possessed of great skill in carving, this monk was not an adept in the use of pigments. In despair he resorted to fasting and prayer. He fell into a deep sleep, and when he awoke he found the little olive-wood image tinted a beautiful flesh color. Now, it is well known that St. Luke is the chosen painter to the Holy Family, and it was instantly surmised that this was his work. The monk decided to send it to the church of Ara Cœli, and, although the vessel that bore it suffered shipwreck on the way, the Bambino itself was washed safe ashore at Leghorn, whence it was sent to Rome.

There are similar images known as Bambinos in Catholic churches elsewhere. In England the most notable are preserved in the Trappist monasteries at Kensington, Staplehill in Dorset, and Mount St. Bernard in Leicestershire. The ceremony of the Adoration of the Bambino is performed here on Christmas morning. As soon as the midnight of Christmas Eve has passed and the holy day has arrived, the monastery bells ring joyfully out, and all the monks arise to attend early service in the convent chapel. Mass is celebrated, and as soon as the host is returned to the tabernacle the officiating priest lifts a cloth and discloses the Bambino,—a little swathed waxen doll, whose wrappings leave exposed a tiny face and a pair of feet. The priest raises the Bambino and faces the bowed monks. The priests and monks circle round in procession from the front, and, passing up, halt for a moment before the waxen image. Then, kneeling down, they reverently kiss the face and hands, cross themselves, and pass on. This ceremony is performed only by the Trappist monks, and only at the Christmas season.

Banian or Banyan Days. In the British navy there were at first two days and afterwards one day in the week on which no allowance of meat was made to the crew. These have now been abolished, but the term is still applied among sailors generally to days of poor fare. It is possibly derived from banian, the East Indian fig, as a general symbol of vegetarian fare, but a more likely suggestion is that it comes from the merchants and traders of the Banian sect, who scrupulously avoid the use of flesh meat and confine themselves to an ascetic diet.

Bank Holiday. In Great Britain a weekday specially fixed by law, whereon parties to negotiable paper are exempted from the obligation of presentment, payment, etc. The banks therefore, as well as the government offices, are closed on such a day, and business establishments of all sorts usually follow suit. It was Sir John Lubbock who was mainly instrumental in securing the passage of the bank holiday law in 1871, the days named being, in England and Ireland, Easter Monday, Whit Monday, the first Monday in August, and the 26th of December (Boxing Day); in Scotland, New Year's Day, the first Monday in May, the first Monday in August, and Christmas Day. At the August bank holiday it has now become well-nigh universal for employers to close their shops or offices on the preceding Saturday also, so as to give their employees a three days' outing.

The effect of the bank holiday law on all negotiable paper falling due on such a day is that it is made payable on the next following secular day, whereas paper falling due on Sunday is payable the preceding Saturday.

Banners, Feast of. (Japanese, *Nobori-no-Sekku.*) A Japanese holiday in honor of male children, celebrated on the fifth day of the fifth month, which in the Europeanized calendar of Japan is now May 5. On every house that can boast of a male child is affixed a pole of bamboo, and floating therefrom are one or more gaudy fish made of paper. The exact number is determined by the number of boys in the household. The wind, blowing into the mouths of the fish, inflates them and makes them writhe and wriggle with a curiously lifelike motion. The fish are supposed to be carp, which in Japan are recognized symbols of health and long life. Other staffs support paper pennons of every color, while banners blazoned with heraldic devices float in the wind. Boys of all ages appear in the street in gala attire, some having little sabres in their belts, some bearing on their shoulders huge swords of wood, gayly painted and decorated, and others carrying miniature banners.

Baptism. In the earliest days of the Christian Church those who were admitted into it by baptism were necessarily not infants, but adolescent or adult converts. These previously underwent a course of religious instruction, generally for two years. They were called during their pupilage "catechumens," a name afterwards applied to all infants before baptism. When such candidates were judged worthy to be received within the pale of the Church, their names were inscribed at the beginning of Lent on a list of the competent or "illuminated." On Easter or Pentecost Eve they were baptized, by three solemn immersions in honor of the Trinity, the first of the right side, the second of the left, and the third of the face. But, as the Arians found in this triple immersion an argument in favor of plurality of natures in the Godhead, Pope Gregory by a letter addressed to St. Leander of Seville ordained that in Spain, the then stronghold of Arianism, only one immersion should be practised. This prescription was preserved and applied to the Church universal by the sixth canon of the Council of Toledo in 633. The triple immersion was, however, persisted in in Ireland to the twelfth century. Infants were thus baptized by their fathers, or indeed by any other person at hand, either in water or in milk; but the custom was abolished in 1172 by the Council of Cashel.

The baptistery of the early church was one of the *exedræ,* or out-buildings, and consisted of a porch or anteroom, where adult converts made their confession of faith, and an inner room, where the actual baptism took place. Thus it continued till the sixth century, when baptisteries began to be taken into the church itself. The font was always of wood or stone. Indeed, we find the provincial council held in Scotland in 1225 prescribing those materials as the only ones to be used. The Church in all ages discouraged private baptism. By the fifty-fifth canon of the same council, the water which had been used to baptize a child out of church was to be thrown into the fire, or carried immediately to the parish baptistery, that it might be em᷑   . for no other purpose; in like manner, the vessel which au .eld it was to be either burnt or consecrated for church use. For many centuries superstitious virtues were attributed to water which had been used for baptism. The blind bathed their eyes in it, in the hope of regaining their sight. It was said to "drown the devil" and to purify those who had recourse to it.

Baptism was by the early Church strictly forbidden during

Lent, and every baptistery was closed during the fast and sealed up with the seal of the church.

Christening fees originated at an early date. At first bisho‚ s and those who had aided in the ceremony of baptism were entertained at a feast. This was afterwards commuted to an actual payment of money.

Both were afterwards forbidden. The forty-eighth canon of the Council of Elvira, held in 303, prohibits the leaving of money in the fonts, "that the ministers of the Church may not appear to sell that which it is their duty to give gratuitously." This rule was, however, as little observed in the Middle Ages as it has been since. Strype says that in 1560 it was enjoined by the heads of the Church that "to avoid contention, let the curate have the value of the 'chrisom,' not under fourpence, and above as they can agree, and as the state of the parents may require." The chrisom was the white cloth placed by the minister upon the head of a child which had been newly anointed with chrism, or hallowed ointment composed of oil and balm, always used after baptism. The gift of this cloth was usually made by the mother at the time of churching. To show how enduring such customs are, even after the occasion for them has passed away, we need only quote a passage from Morant's "Essex:" "In Denton Church there has been a custom, time out of mind, at the churching of a woman, for her to give a white cambric handkerchief to the minister as an offering." The same custom is kept up in Kent, as may be seen in Lewis's History of the Isle of Thanet.

In the county of Durham it is an old custom to give fruit cake and cheese to the first person met on the way to the church by a christening party. *The Antiquary* for February, 1886, tells this story: "At Hexham a few Sundays ago some Wesleyan Sunday-school scholars met a christening party on Gilesgate Bank, and one of the women shouted to the foremost boy, 'Here, hinny, is some cheese and cake for you.' Some of the youngsters were much amused, and a division of the two slices of fruit loaf and its complement of cheese quickly took place."

In Protestant churches the godmother holds the child until it is taken by the cleric; in Catholic churches the child is held by the godfather over the font and the godmother takes it by the feet and holds them towards the west. The priest puts a lighted taper in the godfather's hand and the chrisom cloth over the child's head.

Though baptism in its regenerative symbolism is unknown to non-Christians, there are in many parts of the world peculiar ceremonies attached to the giving of a name to a child.

"Unless the father be very poor indeed,"—writes Mrs. Bishop

in her "Journeys in Persia and Kurdistan,"—"he makes a feast
for his friends on an auspicious day and invites the village
mollahs. Sweetmeats are solemnly eaten after the guests have
assembled. Then the infant, stiffened and mummied in its
swaddling clothes, is brought in and laid on the floor by one of
the mollahs. Five names are written on five slips of paper,
which are placed between the leaves of the Koran, or under
the edge of the carpet. The first chapter of the Koran is then
read. One of the slips is drawn at random, and a mollah takes
up the child and pronounces in its ear the name found upon it,
after which he places the paper on its clothes." This lottery-
like proceeding over, the relations and friends give the babe
presents according to their means,—a custom obviously analogous to our christening gifts. "Thereafter," continues Mrs.
Bishop, "it is called by the name it has received. Among men's
names there is a preponderance of those taken from the Old
Testament, among which Ibrahim, Ismail, Suleiman, Yusuf, and
Moussa are prominent. Abdullah, Mahmoud, Hassan, Raouf,
Baba Houssein, Imam, are also common, and many names have
the suffix of Ali among the Shiahs. Fatmeh is a woman's name,
but girl-children usually receive the name of some flower or bird
or fascinating quality of disposition or person."

The incident of laying the child on the floor brings to mind
the custom of the Japanese in the performance of this function.
Mrs. C. M. Sawley, writing in the *Asiatic Monthly*, tells us that
when a Japanese baby boy is a hundred days old he is carried to
the priest's house in the Shinto temple, and there receives a
compound name, from the family name and that of his guardian.
"This guardian is generally the dearest friend of the family,
and his duty is to watch over the child's future career. The dual
name insures the bond of union between them. The priest writes
down the name and gives it to the child to keep in his prayer-bag,
as the sponsor's name has to be remembered continually before
the household shrine. When prayers have been said over the
child, he is placed on the floor and allowed for the first time to
wander at his own sweet will whithersoever he chooses. Towards
whichever cardinal point he turns, so will his future be influenced." The Gohei, or sacred slips of paper, are held over
the boy's head to propitiate the ancestral spirits so that they
will induce him to turn in the right direction. Two fans are
then presented to him, which in after-years will be exchanged
for swords.

In China the ceremony of naming the baby is accompanied by
the shaving of all its hair. If it is a boy his relations and
friends are invited to a feast the day his head is shaved, and
many of them bring a present; in some parts of the country

the present is always a silver plate, on which is engraved, " Long life, honors, and happiness." On this day the baby gets its name, but it does not keep it all its life : so this first name is called the milk name. A girl is generally called by her milk name till she marries ; but a boy gets a new name the first day he goes to school.

Among the Parsees fire and water are both used in the naming ceremony. When a child is born, a priest waits on the parents at their own house, and, after he has made a note of the hour, moment, and circumstances of the child's introduction to the world, he calculates its nativity. He then consults the father and mother about a name, and, that point being settled, he pronounces the choice in the presence of the assembled friends. The child is washed, or dipped into a tub of water, and subsequently taken to the church, where it is held for a few moments over a fire.

A curious analogue of the Parsee ceremony existed in Scotland, where it was once a common usage and still has its local survivals. After baptism the child was put into a clean basket, over which a cloth had previously been spread. Bread and cheese were laid upon the cloth, and the whole arrangement was then moved three times successively round the iron crook which hangs over the fire for the purpose of supporting the pot when water is boiled or victuals are prepared. The import of the proceeding is clearly shown in the words repeated three times, " Let the flame consume thee now or never."

Barbara, St., patron of Ferrara, Mantua, and Guastalla ; also of fortifications and fire-arms, as well as of armorers and gunsmiths. She is invoked as a protector against lightning and explosions. The festival of this saint, December 4, is celebrated in Southern France and Southern Germany as the beginning of the Christmas season. Her relics are very numerous, especially in Germany. But her legends, which are widely discrepant, are not accepted as authoritative by careful Catholic hagiologists. The very date of her death is as arbitrary as the fixing of the place where she suffered. But December 4, A.D. 235, is the most favored date, and Heliopolis is as plausible a locality as Tuscany or Nicomedia, which are alternatively suggested. Legends generally agree that her father, whose name was Dioscorus, shut her up in a high tower lest she should attract suitors by her beauty. Somehow a trusty servant of Origen penetrated her seclusion, instructed her in Christianity, and baptized her. Her father proposed to make a bath-room in the tower, and she requested that three windows should be introduced, in honor of the three windows through which the soul receives light, the Father, the Son, and the Holy Ghost. Then her father knew that she was a Christian, and he carried her to a mountain where he himself beheaded her. Immediately a great tempest arose, and the lightning consumed the father.

In Southern France the women in every house fill two and sometimes three plates with wheat or lentils, and then stand them in the warm ashes of the fireplace or on a sunny window-ledge to germinate. According as St. Barbara's grain grows well or ill, the harvest of the coming year will be good or bad. At what is known as the Great Supper on Christmas Eve the table is decorated with the growing grain as a symbol of the harvest that is to be.

In Servia the peasants on the eve of this saint's feast boil all sorts of grain together in the same pot, which they leave near the fire during the night. The next morning they carefully observe on which side the boiling has most swelled the grain, and on this indication they sow the fields which extend in that direction.

Barbecue. (From Sp. *barbacoa*, an attempt to transliterate a native Haytien term for a wooden framework supporting meat or fish to be smoked or dried over a fire.) In its most popular modern signification, a large social or political entertainment in the open air, at which sheep or oxen are roasted whole and all the feasting is conducted on a Gargantuan scale.

Georgia is probably the native home of the barbecue, but it spread thence to most of the Southern and Southwestern States, and has even invaded some of the Northern ones. Georgia, however, still retains its supremacy as the Barbecue State. "The barbecue is to Georgia," says D. Allen Willey, in the *Home-Maker's Magazine* for December, 1896, "what the clam-bake is to Rhode Island, what a roast-beef dinner is to our English cousins, what canvas-back duck is to the Marylander, and what a pork-and-beans supper is to the Bostonian. The barbecue has done much for Georgia. It has played its part in politics, in social gatherings, in the entertainment of strangers, and in festivities generally. It has come to be a necessary part of all kinds of social functions, and the man who has visited Georgia and come away without a sample of barbecue viands is indeed to be commiserated.

"The genius who prepared the first barbecue is unknown, although there are a dozen theories offered as to its origin. Get into a country store and sit on the cracker-box by the side of two or three Georgia 'colonels' and 'majors,' and they will tell any number of tales about how their ancestors bought their estates from the Indians and to close up the bargain gave the 'noble red men' a barbecue, consisting of venison and sweetened hoe-cake, followed by plenty of imported rum and other 'fire-waters.' One thing is clear, and that is that game constituted the meat cooked in the barbecue of fifty years ago. As deer, bear, and other animals became scarce, oxen, sheep, and pigs took their places. The variety of viands increased until the barbecue of to-day may contain fish, beef, mutton, pork, vegetables, and fowls. It depends much on the liberality of the givers and the number invited to participate. The popularity of this kind of entertainment is so great that it is enjoyed in cities as well as towns. Even in the wire-grass country, where possibly the white farmers live two or three miles apart, a half-dozen families will get together on a holiday, or some one's birthday, perhaps, kill a sheep or a pig, and have a barbecue. During the Atlanta Exposition a daily barbecue, at which three or four hundred persons were fed at once, was a feature.

" As an aid to political campaigns, the barbecue exerts a powerful influence. Many a man has been elected senator, or governor, or Congressman from this State by a majority secured largely through votes gained at barbecues. A canvass for the governorship of Georgia is not considered completed without a series of these affairs, sometimes one in every county, given just before election, to which every one is invited."

In other Southern and Western States the barbecue plays its part in the political game; and it is not entirely unknown in New York. It was first introduced into that State in the Presidential campaign of 1876 by Republican managers, and the example so set has since been followed occasionally by members of both the great parties.

On the morning of Wednesday, October 18, 1876, two huge oxen were paraded through the cities of New York and Brooklyn and then taken to Myrtle Park in the latter city.

There they were killed in the afternoon. By eleven in the evening one weighing nine hundred and eighty-three pounds was on the spit and in process of roasting over a coke fire. Though less picturesque than the old-fashioned pit, with its wood fire, its forked flames, and occasionally its superabundant smoke, this was found to be an improvement as a cooking apparatus. The coke fire was placed in two large iron pans, ranged parallel to the spit, but not directly under the carcass, the heat being thrown on that by a peaked roof of the same metal stretched over the spit and about two feet from it. Between the two fires was a long dripping-pan, from which the meat was frequently basted with its own fat. The first ox was declared done at eight o'clock on Thursday morning (October 20), and was taken off to cool, while the other, over one thousand pounds in weight, took its place upon the spit. Even at that early hour some hundred or more curious citizens were on the ground, and the number kept steadily increasing until by noon over a thousand had arrived. The barbecue was then declared opened. All present were invited to a share of the ox which had been roasted during the morning. This had been cut up and with the aid of eight hundred loaves of bread turned into sandwiches. So great was the public demand that in twenty minutes the only vestiges left were the skeleton and such fragments as were unfit for food. The other ox was served up at night. Upwards of fifty thousand people in all participated in the exercises. Five speakers, at as many stands, simultaneously addressed audiences of thousands, while thousands more amused themselves in various ways in the grounds.

Barberi, The. Until very recently this was the crowning sport of the Carnival in Rome, preserving even down to our time

THE START OF THE BARBERI.

that element of cruelty which has been all through the ages one of the distinguishing features of the Romans' taste in pleasure. The Barberi (so called because in old times the finest coursers of Barbary were used for this purpose) were in the latter days some half-dozen horses of small value. They were taken to an appointed spot at the head of the Corso, where heated bits of iron and twisted wire were driven into their flesh and their haunches bedecked with spiked balls and flags. Maddened with pain, they were then allowed to dash riderless down the Corso, with a reckless indifference to their own safety and that of the dense masses of people who choked the sidewalks, until stopped at the end of a mile by employees who held carpets in front of them. The owner of the winner bore off a prize banner.

Formerly these races excited the greatest emulation among the noblest houses in Rome, and the winners would hang up the prize banners in their private chapels. Thus from the middle of the seventeenth to the middle of the eighteenth century we find all the most aristocratic names in Rome on the list of winners. In 1788, however, Goethe tells us, the horse-races were no longer confined to the aristocracy, but the middle and lower classes also took part in them: "The great men are parsimonious; they hold aloof from the proceedings." Finally they were entirely abandoned by the patrician to the plebeian. (See AGATHA, ST.)

Barnabas, St., one of the patrons of Milan. His feast is on the day of his nativity, June 11. This unusual selection of a birthday in lieu of a death-day was partly due to the fact that he was not commemorated in either the East or the West until late. Florus of Lyons first introduced the name of St. Barnabas in the Western martyrology. Radulph de Rivo, in the beginning of the fifteenth century, speaks of the feast of the saint as being generally observed then, but Paul III. was the first to allow proper lessons in the Breviary of Cardinal Quiñones for this day. The Abyssinian Church commemorates St. Barnabas on December 17. He was not one of the original twelve apostles, although he is styled an apostle by Luke (Acts xiv. 13). He accompanied Paul on his missions to the Jews and Gentiles, and tradition asserts that he carried the gospel to Milan. He is said to have been stoned to death by a heathen mob in Cyprus.

Mark and other Christians buried him near the site of his martyrdom. More than four centuries later, in the time of the Emperor Zeno, his relics were found and removed to Constantinople, a stately church being erected over them and dedicated in his honor. It is said that the saint's skeleton arms clasped across his breast a copy of the Gospel according to St. Matthew, written in Hebrew by St. Barnabas himself. On the occupation of Cyprus by the Saracens in the seventh century, the head and some other relics of the saint are said to have been translated to Milan. The translation of these relics to a new shrine was made in 1521, and an annual festival instituted to commemorate it, to which the Pope attached an indulgence of a hundred years.

Toulouse, however, claims to be in possession of rival relics in the church of St. Saturninus. May 27 is the feast of the Invention of these to Toulouse. Saussaye in his "Gallican Martyrology" says, "the head is now exposed there to veneration, apart from the body, which reposes in its own shrine." This head was examined and verified in 1807 by Clement de Barbazan, Vicar-General. It is still at Toulouse. Other heads are in the church of Edna in Bergamo, in the cathedral at Genoa, in the Jesuit church at Naples, and at Andechs in Bavaria. Fragments of the same head are in Prague, Cremona, and Pavia.

In England the feast of St. Barnabas is sometimes known as Barnabee's Day. It was usual in some churches to decorate the altars with garlands of flowers. In Hesket, an extensive parish of Cumberlandshire, England, the Court of Inglewood Forest is held annually on June 11 in the open air. The suitors assemble by the highway-side at a place marked only by an ancient thorn, where the annual dues to the lord of the forest, compositions for improvements, etc., are paid; and a jury for the whole jurisdiction is chosen from among the inhabitants of twenty mesne manors who attend on this spot.

Barring Out. An obsolescent practice among British schoolboys of excluding the school-master from the proper scene of his labors by barricading the doors and windows and holding the place in a state of siege until the master acceded to their demands. The time chosen was during the Christmas season in some places and at Shrove Tuesday in others. The understanding was that if the boys could keep their teacher on the outside of the academy door for the full term of three days, the deposed dignitary was bound by custom to enter into a capitulation with the youngsters, and to grant to them certain demands relating to the number of holidays for the ensuing year, to the allotment of the hours of study and recreation, and to other important points connected with the economy of the establishment. On the other hand, if the pupils failed in holding the school-house against their assailants for the period of three days, the master admittedly had a right to dictate his own terms in all those matters which have been mentioned. He obtained also the momentous right of castigating at will the actors in the rebellion,—a labor which they always took care to save him, in cases where they were successful, by making that point the subject of a very explicit condition in the act of capitulation. This document, it may be observed, was commonly drawn up in

a formal and most diplomatic style, securities for the fulfilment
of all its stipulations being provided on both sides, and signatures affixed by the master and the scholars, or by plenipoten-
tiaries appointed by the latter for the purpose. The "high
contracting parties" were then at peace for the year.

The grave and gentle Addison is said to have been the leader
in a barring out during his school-days at Lichfield, *circa* 1684,
and to have displayed a degree of disorderly daring scarcely intelligible in the future "parson in a tie-wig."

Ditchfield reports that the custom still prevails in Cumberland. "A few years ago," he says, "the Dalston School Board
received a letter from the master, requesting that the school
might close on the Thursday before Christmas instead of the
Friday, on the ground that the 'old barbarous custom of barring
out' the school-master might no longer be resorted to. If the
school were opened on the Friday the master was of opinion
that the children might possibly be persuaded by outsiders to
make an attempt to bar him out, and would then have to suffer
a large amount of severe castigation. The school accordingly
closed on the Thursday, much to the regret of the chairman and
others, who would like to have witnessed the repetition of so
ancient a custom."

Bartholomew, St., the Apostle, whose day is celebrated on
August 24, is variously represented as the son of Prince Ptolo-
mæus and of a simple husbandman. His name means "son of a
drawer of water." Tradition says that on the dispersion of the
apostles he travelled as far as India, entering pagan temples and
imposing silence upon the oracles, curing the possessed and converting mighty princes. On his return through Armenia he was
flayed alive and then crucified. His bones were dispersed by
the heathen, but a monk, informed by a vision, gathered them
together at night-time, when they shone like fire, and carried
them to Benevento, where they still repose. Another legend
asserts that the relics were transferred to Rome. His attribute
is a large knife, in addition to which he sometimes carries his
own skin on his arm. At the abbey of Croyland, in Lincolnshire, England, there used to be a distribution of knives to all
comers on the saint's day. But the custom grew to be so
financially onerous that it was abolished in the time of Edward
IV. by Abbot John de Wisbech. In the parish of Dorrington
in the same county the maidens would go in procession on St.
Bartholomew's Day to a small chapel whose floor they strewed
with rushes. Thence they proceeded to a piece of land called
the Play-Garths, where they were joined by most of the inhabitants of the place, and the remainder of the day was passed in

rural sports. It was a custom in olden time for the scholars of various schools to meet upon this day and hold debates and discussions. The practice remained long in vogue in Yorkshire, but has now disappeared. There was also held formerly, in London, a celebrated fair, which bore the name of Bartholomew, but it became so debased in its character that it was at last put down.

A popular English distich alludes to the insetting of chilly evenings at about this period :

> St. Bartholomew
> Brings the cold dew.

But, as the feast happens just forty days after St. Swithin's, the good Bartholomew is looked upon as the deliverer from the quarantine of rain that is due if St. Swithin's be rainy :

> St. Bartlemy's mantle wipes dry
> All the tears that St Swithin can cry.

Of course it often happens that after a showery August the rain clears off towards the end of the month preparatory to a sunshiny September. The verification of the proverb is eagerly looked for in still other phrases : "As Bartholomew's Day, so the whole autumn," and, again,

> If the 24th of August be fair and clear,
> Then hope for a prosperous autumn that year.

The Massacre of St. Bartholomew, which has cast a bloody stain upon the feast, took place on the eve of St. Bartholomew in 1572. Charles IX. of France, Catherine de Médicis the queen mother, the Duke of Anjou, and the Guises, had determined upon the extermination of the Huguenots. The slaughter was to be indiscriminate; the Princes of Condé and Navarre were the only Protestants to be spared. Charles, in a moment of compassion, endeavored to persuade the young Count de la Rochefoucault to remain that night in the Louvre, but without success. Everything had been arranged. Suddenly, deep in the night, a pistol was fired; the tocsin of St.-Germain sounded the assault, and the Duke of Guise and his band of wretches rushed upon the defenceless Protestants. Guise made for the abode of the noble old Admiral Coligny, crying, "To death! to death!" but he did not dare to meet the admiral face to face. Brême, one of his German guards, ascended the stairs, and found a venerable old man engaged in his devotions. "Art thou Coligny?" demanded the assassin. "I am," replied the admiral: "young man, respect my gray hairs." Brême thrust his sword through the helpless old man, crying to those below, " He is done for !" To satisfy the remorseless Guise, the body of the admiral was flung into the street. Thus perished Coligny, one of the noblest and purest men of that day. Over ten thousand Protestants are said to have been slain that night in Paris alone, five hundred of whom were men of rank. Great numbers also fell in the provinces. But Catholic historians contend that the number has been greatly exaggerated.

Basil the Great, St. (328–380). The second in rank in the Greek Church, and the founder of the Basilicans, the only monastic order known in that Church. His festival is celebrated in the Western Church on June 14, the day of his ordination, but in the Eastern on January 1, his death-day. He was a great preacher and a great theologian, but, fearing for his humility, retired to the desert as a hermit. In 370 he became Bishop of Cæsarea. He disobeyed the orders of the Emperor Valens to use the Arian rites. The Emperor threatened him even with death, but to no avail. Then Valens determined to awe the prelate into submission. He came in great pomp with his court and soldiers to church on the feast of the Epiphany. But Basil would not notice him even when he came to the altar with his oblation. Valens swooned and fell into the arms of an attendant. Baffled again and again, he finally suffered Basil to go his own way. Some of the relics of the saint are said to be preserved at Bruges, brought thither in 1187.

Bathilda, St. (Fr. *Bathilde, Baldochide,* or *Bauteur.*) The wife of Clovis III., King of France, and after his death regent of the kingdom. Her festival is celebrated in France on January 30, the anniversary of her death (about A.D. 680), but is named on the 26th in the Roman Martyrology. She founded many churches and religious houses, especially the great abbey of Corbie in Picardy, and the church of the Holy Cross at Chelles, near Paris, where she is buried in a rich silver shrine. Le Bœuf in his " Histoire du Diocèse de Paris" asserts that six nuns were cured of inveterate distempers, attended with frequent fits of convulsions, by touching the relics of St. Bathilde, when her shrine was opened on July 13, 1631.

Bavo or **Bavon, St.** (589–653), patron of Ghent in Flanders, and of Haarlem in Holland. His festival is celebrated on the anniversary of his death, October 1. His name in the world was Allowin. He was a profligate nobleman, but the death of his wife and the preaching of St. Amandus converted him. The remainder of his life he spent in various cells and huts constructed by himself in the woods adjoining the monastery of St. Peter in Ghent. His conversion was followed by that of sixty of his fellow-nobles, who founded the church of St. Bavo at Ghent, where his relics remained until the church was torn down to give place to a citadel, when they were transferred to St. John's Church, which was re-named in his honor and is now the cathedral of Ghent. An arm of St. Bavo is kept in a silver case at Haarlem in the church which bears his name.

Bee, Bees, or Bega, St. A saint whose name is commemorated in the abbey in Cumberland known by any one of these three names, and who appears in the Latin calendar on September 6, probably her death-day. Legend asserts that she was the daughter of an Irish king who on the eve of her wedding to a son of the King of Norway escaped by night to preserve her vows of virginity, and lived for many years in a cell which she built for herself near the site of the abbey. This was towards the close of the seventh century. She was celebrated during her lifetime for her austerity and charity, the latter leading her, during the building of her monastery, to prepare with her own hands the food of the masons and to wait upon them in their workshops, hastening from place to place like a bee laden with honey. She remained down to the Middle Ages the patroness of the laborious and often oppressed population of the district. A bracelet said to have been given to her by an angel was regarded as a sacred relic, and petty tyrants against whom there was no other defence were made to swear upon it, in the belief that a perjury committed on so sacred a pledge could not pass unpunished.

Bee Customs. A superstition which prevails in rural England and New England, and also in parts of Europe, is that bees will either fly away or die on the occasion of a death in the family unless some one knock at their hive and tell them of it. In some places the hives are further put into mourning, or, again, a bit of the funeral biscuit is offered to the bees. Whittier's poem " Telling the Bees" is founded on this custom :

> Under the garden wall,
> Forward and back,
> Went drearily singing the chore-girl small,
> Draping each hive with a shred of black.
>
>   *   *   *   *   *   *   *
>
> And the song she was singing ever since
> In my ear sounds on :
> " Stay at home, pretty bees, fly not hence!
> Mistress Mary is dead and gone!"

In some places bees are formally invited to funerals. Another custom of the same sort is mentioned in this paragraph from the *London Argus* of September 13, 1790: " A superstitious custom prevails at every funeral in Devon of turning round the bee-hives that belonged to the deceased, if he had any, and that at the moment the corpse is carried out of the house."

At a funeral some time since, at Collumpton, in Devonshire, England, of a rich old farmer, just as the corpse was placed in the hearse, and the horsemen, to a large number, were drawn up in order for the procession of the funeral, a person called out, " Turn the bees !" when a servant, who had no knowledge of such a custom, instead of turning the hives round, lifted them up and then laid them down on their sides. The bees, thus hastily in-vaded, instantly attacked and fastened on the horses and their riders. It was in vain they galloped off: the bees as precipitately followed, and left their stings as marks of their indignation. A general confusion took place, attended with loss of hats, wigs, etc., and the corpse during the conflict was left unattended; nor was it till after a considerable time that the funeral attendants could be rallied in order to proceed to the interment of their deceased friend.

As good order is so strikingly exhibited in the government of the bees for the bees and by the bees, it seems not inappropriate that in Egyptian hieroglyphics the bee should represent royalty and that in later times it should have become the symbol of the French Empire. In France the royal mantle and standard were thickly sewn with golden bees, and in the tomb of Childeric in 1653 there were discovered three hundred bees made from the same precious metal.

In Roman Catholic days in England, and even occasionally in rural parishes in America, it used to be a custom to place in the centre of a hive of bees a small piece of the sacred wafer sur-reptitiously carried away from the communion. This was called the " little God Almighty," and was supposed to insure the bees from all harm and to increase their power of honey-making. The custom was denounced by the Church. Hawker, in his " Echoes from Old Cornwall," tells how the bees, to rebuke the irreverence of their owner, raised a shrine around the sacred bread, to show

> How holier hearts than his may beat
> Beneath the bold blasphemer's feet.
> (*A Legend of the Hive.*)

In England it is considered unlucky to buy or sell bees; they must be given, and the donee in return makes a gift of a bushel of corn, a small pig, or other equivalent. Stolen bees will not thrive, but pine away and die by degrees. It is even unlucky for a swarm of bees to settle on strange premises, unless they are subsequently claimed by the owner. When bees die, or even when they remove or go away from their hives, there will be a death in the owner's family.

In Virgil we find the story that Jupiter endowed the bee with its marvellous intelligence because when as an infant he lay concealed from his father's search in the Cretan cave bees fed him with honey. The Cretans themselves came to his aid by dancing around the babe and rattling brazen cymbals to drown the cries that might have betrayed him. To this latter legend is traced the still extant custom of pursuing swarms of bees with the clangor of keys on pans and kettles in order to induce them to settle down. Pliny argues that because this clatter is always made when bees swarm, therefore they must be gifted with the sense of hearing, which is rather curious logic. In "Tusser Redivivus" (1744) is a paragraph with considerably more good sense: "The tinkling after them with a warming-pan, frying-pan, or kettle is of good use to let the neighbors know you have a swarm in the air, which you claim wherever it alights, but I believe of very little purpose to the reclaiming of the bees, who are thought to delight in no noise but their own."

Bells. In the larger sense of the word, bells are of unknown antiquity. From the very earliest ages we hear of metal instruments that yielded musical notes when struck by metal wands or clappers, and the names of such instruments are usually translated as bells. But it is doubtful, for example, whether the golden bells described in Exodus xxviii. 33–35 as part of the apparel of Aaron were anything but jangling ornaments of some sort worn by the high-priest. The same doubt hangs around the tintinnabulating Egyptian instruments which were used to announce the sacred feasts of Osiris. Nevertheless small bronze bells were found by Layard in the palace of Nimroud in Nineveh. Bell-like also in the modern sense were many of the percussion instruments that we find described by classical authors, from the *tintinnabulum*, and the *petasus*, or hat-shaped bell, which invited the ancient Greeks to the fish-market and the Romans to their public baths; the *codon*, with which the Greek sentinels were kept awake, and which was the prototype of the signal which our bell-wether carries around its neck; the *nola*, which was appended to the necks of pet dogs and the feet of pet birds; the *campana*, the first turret-bell; the *Dodonœi lebetes*, or caldrons of Dodona, by means of which, according to Strabo, the oracles were sometimes conveyed; down to the *squilla*, of which Hieronymus seems to have known nothing save that it was a smaller tintinnabulum.

Large bells appear to have originated in China. Tradition asserts that popular justice bells were in use there in every large town long before the birth of Christ. These were fixed to the wall above the head of the prince or governor. A rope a mile or so in length was attached to each, and laid so temptingly along the main thoroughfare that the humblest sufferer from injustice seldom hesitated to tug at it. As soon as the bell sounded, the governor sent for the petitioner, and " serious business, craving quick despatch," met with instant and honest recognition. And even above the head of the Emperor himself there was such a noisy friend to the people, but he who rang it without sufficient cause—and His Celestial Majesty was often difficult to please in this particular—was switched in a very lively manner.

Bells were unused by the early Christians. During the heathen persecutions it was of course impossible to call the faithful by any signal which would have attracted public notice. After Constantine's time, monastic communities used to signify the hour of prayer by blowing a trumpet, or by rapping with a hammer at the cells of the monks. The invention of church-bells is often ascribed to Bishop Paulinus of Nola in Campania, who died in 431. From his native town and district came, it is urged, the Latin names for a bell, *nola* and *campana*, the latter still surviving in Italy. But more cautious historians think that it was only the facile etymologies which suggested the ascription of the invention to the bishop; for in his extant writings no mention of bells is made; and it is quite certain that the terms *nola* and *campana* are of a date anterior to the time of Paulinus.

Whoever the inventor, church-bells had come into use in some parts of Europe before the seventh century. It was the bells of St. Stephen's Church in Sens whose clangor frightened away the besieging army of Clotaire II. in the year 610. Bede mentions their existence in England in his day. It has been asserted that they were unknown to the Eastern Christians until the ninth century, when Duke Ursus of Venice sent twelve great bells as a present to the Byzantine Emperor Michael, who erected a belfry for them at the church of St. Sophia. In the East, however, their general introduction was checked by the spread of Islam, the Mohammedans forbidding their use even to the Christians, partly from a kind of superstitious dread, and partly because they might be used as signals for revolt.

In the Western Church, bells, like other church furniture, were solemnly consecrated before being taken into use. This custom still continues in Catholic countries. It is ecclesiastically known as " blessing the bell," though it is more popularly called " the baptism of the bell," a title by which the office is mentioned

as early as the tenth century. The bishop washes the bell with
holy water, signs it with the oil of the sick outside and with chrism
inside, and lastly places it under the thurible with burning incense. He prays repeatedly that the sound of the bell may
avail to summon the faithful, to excite their devotion, to drive

BAPTISM OF A BELL.
(From Picart.)

away storms, and to terrify evil spirits. Thus consecrated, bells
become spiritual things, and cannot be rung without the consent
of the ecclesiastical authorities.

It is not only large bells to be hung in steeples, but also the
smaller hand-bells rung at the elevation of the host (a practice
introduced about the twelfth century) and in other churchly
functions, which are thus baptized.

This ceremony was prohibited in England at the time of the
Reformation, and was frequently burlesqued by a rabid No-
Popery rabble, which would seize upon a new bell, turn it upside
down, fill it with wine, and baptize it amid bacchanalian revels.
In recent times, however, the bishops of Oxford, Salisbury, and
other sees have set the example of dedicating the bells of their
churches with a simple form of prayer.

The church-bell had its civic as well as its religious uses. It summoned the soldiers to arms, it sounded the alarm in fire or tumult. Often the chief bell in the cathedral belonged not to the cathedral chapter, but to the town, and the rights of the burghers were jealously guarded against ecclesiastical encroachment. He who commanded the bell commanded the town, for at a moment's notice its sound could rally and concentrate his adherents. Hence a conqueror commonly acknowledged the political importance of bells by melting them down; and the cannon of the conquered was in turn melted down to be used in the suppression of revolts.

Other civil uses of bells may be briefly indicated. The curfew (*q. v.*) was rung at or about eight o'clock to command the extinguishment of all lights. At Strasburg the Holy Ghost Bell, dating from 1375, is rung when two fires are seen in the town at once. The recall or storm bell warns travellers in the plain of storms coming from the Vosges Mountains. The Thor or gate bell, for closing and opening the gates of the city, has been cast three times (1618, 1641, and 1651).

The inscriptions on old European bells are full of curious antiquarian interest. Most common of all is that which Schiller has used as the motto of his most famous lyric, "The Song of the Bell:"

> Vivos voco; mortuos plango; fulgura frango.

("I call the living; I mourn the dead; I break the lightning.")

This is frequently expanded into the less epigrammatic form,—

> Laudo Deum verum, plebem voco, conjugo clerum;
> Defunctos ploro, pestem fugo, festa decoro;
> Funera plango, fulgura frango, Sabbata pango;
> Excito centos, dissipo ventos, paco cruentos.

("I praise the true God, I summon the people, I assemble the clergy; I mourn the dead, I put the plague to flight, I grace the feast; I wail at the funeral, I abate the lightning, I proclaim the Sabbath; I arouse the indolent, I disperse the winds, I appease the revengeful.")

Very old and very common is the following:

> Gaudemus gaudentibus,
> Dolemus dolentibus.

("We rejoice with the joyous, we sorrow with the sorrowing.")

And this:

> I to the church the living call,
> And to the grave do summon all.

In many of the old spires of English churches are found painted or written, in old English script, "Laws of the Belfry."

There is no more curious example extant than the following, dated 1627, which is found in St. John's Church, Chester:

> You ringers all observe these orders well,
> He forfiets 12 pence who turns ore a bell:
> And he y^t ringes with either spur or hatt
> His 6 pence certainely shall pay for y^t,
> And he that spoil or doth disturbe a peale
> Shall pay his 4 pence or a cann of ale;
> And he that is harde to curse or sweare
> Shall pay his 12 pence and forbeare.
> These customs elsewhere now are used
> Lest bells and ringers be abused.
> You gallants, then, y^t on purpose come to ring
> See that you coyne alonge with you doth bringe;
> And further also if y^t you ring here
> You must ring truly with hande and eare
> Or else your forfiets surely pay
> Full speedily, and that without delay.
> Our laws are old, y^y are not new,
> The sextone looketh for his due.

Avignon, the famous city in the south of France which during the period of the Papal expatriation from Rome—1305–1377— was the residence of seven successive Popes, has always been especially famous for its bells. It was the *ville sonnante*, the "ringing city," of Rabelais. In its palmy days it had three hundred bells, which were always ringing the offices of the Church. Specially famous was the silver bell at the cathedral, which even after the return of the Papal court to Rome would ring out of its own volition to announce the accession or death of a Pope, in the latter case tolling without cessation for the space of twenty-four hours:

> Then pealed the note of a silver bell,
> And the great city her breath did draw
> Quick, and the gunners paused in awe,
> Waiting some portent; for they know
> The silver bell sends never so
> From that high tower its single tone
> Save when a Pope ascends a throne,
> Or haply when Death calls for him.
> (MISTRAL: *Calendau*.)

But such automatic action was necessarily rare, and for ordinary occasions the bells, like all others, required the services of bell-ringers, who became exceptionally proficient in their art. These men were famous also for the personal affection which they felt for their metal-tongued *protégées*, almost as if they were sentient beings. An old ringer of St. Agricol, for example, is said to have gone up to his bell to kiss it and bestow on it a thousand terms of endearment. And when once the bell of the White Penitents was temporarily interdicted, the peasant who was used to ringing it ascended the tower, and, leaning against his beloved bell, gave vent to his grief in sobbing and wailing, which, reverberated by the sonorous metal, was heard all over the city and far across the plain, and there he died, heart-broken, still clinging to his bell.

The largest if not the most famous bell in the world is the "great bell of Moscow," or Czar Kolokol ("emperor of bells"). Its weight is about 440,000 pounds, and its cost in simple bell-material is estimated at about $300,000, to which, it is said, $1,000,000 was added in precious jewels, plate, etc., by the nobles at the time of casting. This bell is about twenty-one feet in height and twenty-two feet in diameter. It was cast by the Empress Anne in 1733 from the metal of a gigantic predecessor which had been greatly damaged. The beams which held it were destroyed by fire in 1734, and it fell and broke. Another story is that it was cracked in the furnace and was never hung at all. It remained in the earth until raised by the Emperor Nicholas in 1836. It is now consecrated as a chapel, and through the opening of the break two men can pass at the same time.

There is another monstrous bell in the cathedral, weighing 120,000 pounds. This is the largest in the world in actual use. It is rung three times a year, when all the other bells are silent. Its sound is like the roaring of distant thunder. In the same tower are several other bells, some weighing many tons.

The "great bell of China" in Pekin weighs 120,000 pounds, is fourteen feet in height and twelve feet in diameter. In Nankin there is a bell, now fallen to the ground, weighing 50,000 pounds.

A bell in Vienna weighs 40,000 pounds, and in Olmutz there is one of equal weight. A bell in Rouen, France, weighs 36,000 pounds. The largest bell in England is the Westminster bell, "Big Ben," weighing 30,000 pounds. A bell of the like weight is in Erfurt, Germany.

The largest bell on the American continent is at Montreal, in the cathedral, and weighs 25,000 pounds. One in Notre-Dame, Paris, also weighs 25,000 pounds. St. Peter's, at Rome, weighs 17,500 pounds, and "Great Tom" at Oxford, England, weighs 17,000 pounds. The "Jacqueline," of Paris, cast in 1400, weighs 15,000 pounds, "Great Tom" at Lincoln, England, weighs 12,000 pounds, and St. Paul's, of London, 11,500 pounds.

The Independence Hall bell at Boston was cast in 1876 at the Meneely Foundry, and weighs 13,000 pounds. The famous "Liberty Bell," of Philadelphia, was cast in 1751. This is the bell which in July, 1776, rang out the announcement of the adoption of the Declaration of Independence. It was subsequently broken when ringing a fire-alarm. It is now suspended by a chain of thirteen links from the ceiling in the hall of the State-House in Philadelphia.

Bells were currently believed to calm storms, to avert lightning, to disperse pestilences, to extinguish fires, to exorcise demons, and to drive away enemies. Among the superstitious uses recorded to have taken place in Old St. Paul's Church in London was the "ringinge the hallowed belle in great tempests or lightnings."

Church-bells were and in some Catholic countries still are tolled for the dying, or those who are passing out of the world. Hence they were known as passing bells (*q. v.*). The custom of tolling bells slowly and solemnly after deaths and before funerals is still common in England.

Of the varied uses in times past and present of small bells only a few can be chronicled here. The custom of hanging bells on the necks of horses and cattle, in use among the Romans, still survives, especially in Switzerland. In Italy they are often made of baked earth; these have a very sweet sound, and cost but a penny. The bells are useful in the dark, or when the animals that wear them have strayed out of sight. Hunting-hawks were formerly supplied with small bells to aid recovery. The attaching of small spherical bells or crotals to driving- and sleighing horses is common in many parts of Europe and America. The crotals so used are often identical with those found in British graves, which were suspended on the spears of warriors. The dustman's bell survives in some rural localities in England. So does the bell of the town crier, or bellman. The five-o'clock postman, with his hand-bell to collect letters, went out when the present postal system came in. On the other hand, the muffin-bell, the railway-bell, the dock-bell, the stage-bell, and the half-hour bells at sea, still survive. The hanging of bells in private houses, to be rung by means of wires from the different apartments, is a comparatively modern innovation, dating from the reign of George I., but even this is rapidly disappearing in favor of the electric bell system, where the pushing of a small knob or button arouses a current of electricity that sets a small hammer in motion. Other new applications of the same principle are revolutionizing ancient methods everywhere. Nevertheless the whole of civilized life is still, as formerly, set to bell-music in one shape or another.

Benares. The Holy City of India, and the Mecca of Hindoo pilgrims. It has been described as a labyrinth of lofty alleys, rich with shrines and minarets and balconies and carved oriels to which the sacred apes cling by hundreds. These apes have a temple specially devoted to them, but are allowed to roam the streets at will, together with the holy bulls. The traveller can hardly make his way through the press of holy mendicants and these not less holy animals. Broad and stately flights of steps, known as ghats, descend from these swarming haunts to the bathing-places along the Ganges, which are worn every day by an innumerable crowd of worshippers, who believe that they can expiate all the sins of the flesh by dipping their faces or their bodies into the filthy but sacrosanct waters.

Every believer who can afford the expense brings his dying relatives to Benares, so that the soul may take its flight from the vantage ground of the Sacred City, which is held to be sixty thousand miles nearer heaven than any other locality on earth. Should the patient unexpectedly show signs of recovery, it is whispered that his mouth is filled with sacred mud and the end is hastened. He must not lose the opportune place and moment for a heavenward flight. Indeed, a dying person who has once been brought to the sacred banks of the Ganges can never be taken home alive; therefore it would be awkward, expensive, and inconvenient to allow him to defeat the obvious intentions of Providence. Yet sometimes filial love triumphs over all other considerations. Stories are occasionally told of devoted sons who, after bringing their sick mothers or fathers to Benares, have witnessed their recovery and have built little houses upon the banks of the river and settled therein, so that the convalescents might await their end and die at their leisure.

It is for the same reason of propinquity to heaven that Hindoos come from all parts of India bearing the bodies of their dead to be cremated on the burning-ghats that line the Ganges. Each ghat has some fifteen or twenty hollow places scooped in the soil, each about six feet long and two feet wide. Here the funeral pyres are built of wood and straw. The bodies are placed upon them. The nearest relative lights the fire, and in two hours nothing is left but a heap of ashes, which are carefully swept up and thrown into the Ganges.

Poor people who cannot afford to burn their relatives light a little wisp of straw, blacken their faces with it, and, if possible, throw the bodies surreptitiously into the Ganges. This practice is now forbidden by law, and the sight of floating bodies on the sacred river is not so common as it used to be a dozen years ago.

Hindoo theology teaches that after the body has been burned the parts are all mystically joined together in the spirit-world and must march through a river of mire and blood. A real material cow given to a Brahmin will, however, greatly expedite the journey. Next the soul comes to ground paved with fiery hot copper. A gift of shoes to the Brahmin will help the soul to pass over without blistering its poor feet. Next comes a road full of spikes, but a bed-spread presented to the same kind gentleman will obviate any necessity for the spirit to sit upon these spikes. Here the Brahminic ingenuity fails, or perhaps the Brahminic avarice is satisfied, and the spirit is allowed to get along as best it can for the rest of the journey.

In Benares there are not fewer than from twenty to twenty-five thousand Brahmins, or high-caste Hindoos. They have control over the temples, the sacred wells, streams, and reservoirs, and other holy places about the city. They superintend the worship of the people, and give directions respecting the numberless ceremonies which are performed. Every sacred spot has some peculiarity connected with it; and it is of great moment that no punctilio should be omitted. They receive the offerings, the alms, the public dinners, and the good things which devout Hindoos are ever willing to bestow. Some of them are termed Sons of the Ganges, and are chiefly found on the banks of that stream, aiding the devotions of the numerous worshippers daily resorting thither.

Devotees and pilgrims, separated or in crowds, enter or depart from the city constantly throughout the year, especially on occasions of great festivals. They come from all parts of India. Many carry with them the sacred water of the Ganges in small bottles hermetically sealed, placed in baskets hanging from the extremities of poles which they bear upon their shoulders. (See PRADAKSHINA.)

Benedict, St. (Fr. *Benoît;* It. *Benedetto;* Sp. *Benito*), founder, patriarch, and first abbot of the order of Benedictines. Born at Norcia, in Spoleto, in 480, he died at Monte Casino, March 21, 543, and is commemorated on his death-day. He became a hermit at fifteen at Subiaco, then a wilderness. But he was greatly tempted by memories of his student life in Rome, especially of a beautiful woman he had seen there, insomuch that he flung himself into a thicket of briers, wherein he rolled himself until he was torn and bleeding. At the monastery of Subiaco to this day roses said to have been propagated from these briers are shown. The fame of his sanctity brought many other hermits around him, who lived in huts and caves, until at length Benedict, for the sake of order, commanded them to build twelve monasteries. In each he placed twelve monks. Later he withdrew to Monte Casino, where he founded the monastery which has always been regarded as the parent of all others of the

Benedictine order. Here he promulgated the rules of that order. He was at last seized with fever, and ordered his grave to be dug; after standing on the edge of it in silent contemplation, he was borne by his disciples to the altar of the church, and after receiving the last sacrament there died.

Bernard of Clairvaux, St. (1091–1153), founder of the abbey of Clairvaux in France, and one of the Fathers of the Church. He is commemorated on August 20, his death-day. He preached the second Crusade, was the adversary of Abelard and of Arnold of Brescia, and a great authority in law as in religion. Owing to his special championship of the Virgin Mary, she is reported to have visited him twice: once when, ill and unable to write, she restored him by her presence; and again when she moistened his lips with the milk from her bosom and made his eloquence irresistible. His attributes are the demon fettered behind him, three mitres at his feet, as emblems of three bishoprics which he refused, and the beehive, as a symbol of eloquence. He was buried before Our Lady's altar in Clairvaux, and numerous miracles performed at his shrine caused Alexander III. to canonize him in 1165.

Bernard of Menthon, St. (923–1008). The founder of the hospitals for travellers across the Alpine passes known as "The Great St. Bernard" and "The Little St. Bernard," where some of the regular canons of St. Augustine have for nine centuries ministered charity and offered guidance to distressed travellers lost in the snows. He is commemorated in the calendar on June 15, the day of his burial. He was Archdeacon of Aosta, and for forty years was engaged on missions among the mountaineers. His observations of the hardships which Alpine travellers had to undergo suggested to him the idea of erecting places of refuge for them. He died at Novara on May 28, 1008

A clever woman traveller has recorded in the *New York Tribune* her impressions of the Hospice St. Bernard as it now appears:

"One of the joys of my childhood was to contemplate with wide-open eyes, night and morning, as I lay tucked up in my little cot, an etching which hung above it, and which represented the rescue of two unfortunate travellers half buried in eternal snows, by a couple of magnificent, huge St. Bernard dogs. My young imagination conjured up mountain disasters ceaselessly, and then I took a solemn resolution to become, when I grew older, a distinguished Alpine climber. Life decided otherwise for me, and, although I have always retained my love for the mountains and have spent many summers in the Tyrol, the Alps, the Pyrenees, etc., my celebrity as a professional mountaineer is yet to be born. Nevertheless, some time ago, returning from Italy to Austria *via* Switzerland, I decided to go and investigate for myself whether my childhood's admiration, the great St. Bernard dog, was truly as majestic as he is painted when seen in his native haunts and exercising his charitable and heroic mission.

"The winter was almost over, but still the ascent of the snow-covered giant was by no means an easy task. The Mont St. Bernard is anything but easily accessible, but still, thanks to the adroitness of the guides, we at last reached the refuge of 'la Cantine de Proz,' a spot from which one can plainly see the ancient monastery, looking grim and forbidding in its shroud of snow and ice. I gazed with delight upon this scene, and so great was my eagerness to reach the goal of my ambitions that I urged my guides to proceed without delay. Much to my astonishment, and also, I confess, to my utter disgust, they explained to me, in that hideous mixture of *patois*, vile French, and viler German, which is the idiom of Wilhelm Tell's fatherland, that they had just telephoned to the abbot there yonder, in order to obtain further reinforcements before attempting to cross the last 'col' or pass, a peculiarly dangerous one.

"Telephone! My amazement was so great that I stared helplessly and silently at my companions. Could I have misunderstood their vernacular? Telephone, from the pure, unsullied, frozen summits of this proud peak! But no, I had not mistaken the import of their words, for here behind me I suddenly heard the familiar and exasperating tinkling of the telephone bell, followed by the yet more exasperating 'Hullo! Hullo!' which one finds acclimatized from Benares to Yokohama, San Francisco, Melbourne, Teheran, or wherever else the invention has penetrated. I may call the impression which I then received my first disappointment, one, by the bye, which was speedily capped by several more. Resigned for the time being, I sat down on a bench before the glowing stove to await the coming of the good monks' forces, and, after a space of time which seemed long, a small procession of brown-robed figures, headed by three or four enormous dogs, appeared in view. Little attention did I grant to the saintly men, but the dogs!—the sweet-tempered, noble, kind-hearted dogs! I literally flung myself out of the door to meet them, and, with that impulsiveness which has already cost me so many needless troubles, I flung my arms about the neck of the first one I reached. There was a low, vicious growl, a snap of the mighty jaws, a contemptuous toss of the massive head, and had it not been for the timely interference of a portly monk I should not only have stood there unmercifully reproved but also cruelly bitten. So much for the kind-heartedness of the great St. Bernard breed, for, as my rescuer explained to me in melodious Italian, the animals realize that they are required only to save the lives of those perishing in the snow, and that when they have done this occasionally they do not see the need of showing any further amiability toward the human race. He added mournfully that, anyhow, the dogs are degenerating, and that they are very reluctant to go out on their life-saving expeditions, quite unlike their sires, for they were all fire and flame for the good cause. Disappointment number two having thus been inflicted upon me, I resumed my voyage a wiser if a sadder woman.

"The road was arduous, snow was falling, and the wind howled piteously over the vast frozen slopes; moreover, I was so tired that I felt like lying down in the snow and pretending to be on the point of death in order to test the one remaining virtue of the dogs who bounded in front of us. The sample which I had had of their sweetness of behavior, however, encouraged me so little to throw myself on their tender mercies that I reconsidered my plan and faced the icy wind with renewed energy.

"I was expected, in spite of the lateness of the hour, and the reception I met with touched me much. All that warmth, hot wine, palatable food, and a grateful shelter from the outer blasts of the weather could do for me was accomplished, and that in so simple and charming a way that my heart was immediately won. There, at least, was no disappointment; the great granite hearth whereon crackled and blazed enormous pine logs, the white-bearded abbot who ministered in so kindly a way to my wants, the solemn hush overspreading the entire rambling pile of building, interrupted alone by an intermittent burst of chanting which was wafted toward us as the inside door of the neighboring chapel opened and closed, were all as I had pictured them to be.

"The St. Bernard monks belong to the Augustinian order, but do not resemble those of their brothers who live in the plains. Amiable, learned, devoid of all intolerance, they remind one, with their serious, weather-beaten countenances, of sailors used to braving the elements and being ever on the alert for some catastrophe of nature. A great peace surrounded us in our mountain fastness, and a right pleasant evening did we spend, the venerable abbot telling me all about the monastery which he loves so well. I learned that since the year 960, when St. Bernard had founded this place of refuge for those lost in the snow and ice of this, one of the most dangerous portions of the European Alps, a record had been kept by the worthy monks of all the lives saved. At the end of the sixteenth century this record was transcribed in Latin on the parchment pages of some old missal-like volumes, which are of the greatest interest, and to this day the practice is faithfully kept up. Rather gruesome is it to find that the corpses of the victims who have succumbed in precipices, crevices, or avalanches, or from mere exhaustion and snow-sickness, have been preserved, not under-ground, for there is hardly any earth on the rocks of St. Bernard, but in two caves, one being now reserved for Catholics, while the other, as the abbot said, is tenanted by Protestants and other infidels.

"The next morning I was taken to see this mortuary ice-house, which contains the stiffened corpses of many of Napoleon's brave soldiers, gaunt grenadiers, even now half covered by the snow which caused their death during the dreadful crossing of the Alps in the train of Europe's greatest general. The sight is not a pretty one, and for many a night I dreamed of the row of rigid corpses I had gazed upon there.

"Far more to my taste was the museum contained in one wing of the monastery. This museum is filled with the relics discovered in the ruins of the temple of Jupiter, which once stood on the edge of the tiny lake stretching its sheet of ice a hundred yards from the portals of the holy edifice devoted to the rescue of Christian souls and bodies. The ancient Romans certainly built this temple to meet the same purpose as did St. Bernard the monastery bearing his name. It was used as a refuge for travelling soldiers, and the excavations undertaken by the Italian government brought to light a considerable amount of riches, including two thousand five hundred pieces of gold and silver, dating back as far as Julius Cæsar, some magnificently jewelled *ex votos*, and a statue of Jupiter which is a marvel of sculpture.

"Filled with enthusiasm at what I had seen, I was stepping back toward the refectory of the monks, where breakfast was awaiting us, when I was startled by a sharp, clicking sound. Peering out of the gloom which filled the narrow stone passage I was traversing, I caught sight of a rubicund monk, who, in a small cell-like room, was seated before a typewriter, rattling away for dear life!

"'Enough! Enough!' I almost cried, as I fled toward the main hall. Julius Cæsar, Roman coins, frozen corpses, kindly abbot, vicious dogs, telephone, and typewriters, made up a miscellaneous jumble in my head which threatened to turn me crazy. 'Oh, dear!' thought I, after having bidden my adieus to the entire congregation and deposited my offerings in the alms-box of the chapel,—the only remuneration one is permitted to give for all one has received at the hands of the Augustinian monks, —'is there not one corner left in this wretched world of ours where one can forget for once that one is unfortunate enough to live at the latter end of the nineteenth century, and must one be pursued to the very topmost peaks of the Alps by all the modern improvements ?' "

Bible Orchard.   A piece of land in the parish of St. Ives, Hants, England, which has a curious history.   Dr. Robert Wilde, who died in August, 1678, bequeathed fifty pounds, the yearly interest of which was to be expended in the purchase of six Bibles, not exceeding the price of seven shillings and sixpence each, which should be "cast for by dice" on the communion-table in the church of St. Ives on the last Thursday in May by six boys and six girls of the town.   Hence the day is locally known as Bible Thursday.   The capital sum was invested in what is now known as Bible Orchard.   The legacy also provided for the payment of ten shillings yearly to the vicar for preaching a sermon on the occasion "commending the excellency, the perfection, and divine authority of the Holy Scriptures."   This singular custom has been observed every year, with the exception that the dice-throwing now takes place on a table erected at the chancel steps, the bishop of the diocese having decided in 1880 that the communion-table was not the proper place for a raffle.

Biddenden Cakes.   In the parish of Biddenden, Kent, England, there still exists an endowment of unknown date.   On Easter Sunday some six hundred so-called Biddenden cakes are distributed among parishioners who attended the afternoon services at the church, and in addition some three hundred loaves of bread, each of three and a half pounds weight, and each accompanied by a pound and a half of cheese.   The endowment is charged upon an estate known as the Bread and Cheese lands, which, according to the best authorities, were some centuries ago left to the parish for this purpose by two maiden ladies of the name of Preston.   The Biddenden cakes are impressed with the figures of two females standing closely side by side in such fashion that they appear to be bound together like the Siamese Twins.   On this hint tradition has founded a curious and circumstantial story.   It has rebaptized the ladies under the names of Mary and Elizabeth Chalkhurst, and asserts that they were in fact joined by a ligature at birth and lived just thirty years, when the death of one was followed in a few hours by the death of the other.   The whole story is minutely told in a sort of hand-bill still printed and sold on the spot, entitled "A Short but Concise Account of Elizabeth and Mary Chalkhurst."   It may be mentioned in passing that a similar story is related of two females whose figures appear in the pavement of Norton St. Philip Church in Somersetshire.   Hasted in his "History of

Kent" (1798) has examined the Biddenden myth, and decides that it arose simply from the rude impression on the cakes, which had been printed in this manner only within the preceding fifty years.

Birthday. The celebration of the anniversary of an individual's birth, though customary among the ancients, was originally frowned upon by the Christians. Nor was this to be wondered at. To the early followers of Christ the world was a hard and cruel one. They were oppressed and persecuted and martyred alike by Jews and by pagans. It was no benefit to them to be born. Death was the true deliverance. To die was to pass from a life of sorrow and humiliation into endless glory. Moreover, birth was in its very essence a degradation, inasmuch as it implied an assumption of that heritage of original sin which Adam has bequeathed to all his descendants. Thus, Origen, in a homily on Leviticus xii. 2, assures his hearers that "none of the saints can be found who ever held a feast or a banquet upon his birthday, or rejoiced on the day when his son or his daughter was born. But sinners rejoice and make merry on such days. For we find in the Old Testament that Pharaoh, King of Egypt, celebrated his birthday with a feast, and that Herod, in the New Testament, did the same. But the saints not only neglect to mark the day of their birth with festivity, but also, filled with the Holy Ghost, they curse this day, after the example of Job and Jeremiah and David."

It was not the birthdays but the death-days of the saints that were made the occasions of the Church festivals in their honor. Nevertheless the term birthday was applied by the early Church to these festivals. "When you hear of a birthday of saints, brethren," says Peter Chrysologus, "do not think that that is spoken of in which they are born of earth, in the flesh, but that in which they are born from earth into heaven, from labor to rest, from temptations to repose, from torments to delights not fluctuating, but strong and stable and eternal, from the derision of the world to a crown of glory. Such are the birthdays of the martyrs that we celebrate."

While such was the temper of the leading teachers in the Church, it is only natural that the Christians thought little even of the immaculate birth of Christ or the equally immaculate birth of the Virgin Mary. Indeed, it was not till the fourth and ninth centuries respectively that even the dates of these events were agreed upon. Not that this was the universal and unbroken condition of thought and feeling in the Church during the first three centuries. "There were some men in advance of their age," says the Rev. Henry J. Vandyke in *Harper's Maga-*

zine for December, 1885, " who had learned to think of the whole life of Christ in its unity as a life for and with man, crowned by His vicarious death and resurrection. Irenæus in particular is worthy of special mention and enduring honor as the first of the Fathers to bring out the unfolding of all the stages of human life in Jesus Christ; and, even though he had never written another word than this, he deserves to be immortal in the memory of the Church for having said, ' The Son of God became a child among the children in order that childhood might be made holy.' *

" This sentence holds the heart of Christmas. But it was not until long after it was uttered, it was not until the latter half of the fourth century, that the Church at large began to feel and to unfold its meaning. Then it was that she emerged from the storm of persecution into the sunshine of imperial favor. Then she saw that she had a work to do here on earth in the cleansing and adorning of human life with the beauty of holiness. Then she realized that patient suffering and faithful death were not the only duties of the Christian, but that, following God in love, it was possible to begin in this world the purity and peace of heaven. Then she began to feel the wondrous significance of the living entrance of the Son of God into the life of man, and His perfect pattern of holiness in every human relation. Then she passed from the lower conception of a church saved out of the world, to the higher conception of a world to be saved through the ministry of the church, a natural year to be transformed by reverent devotion and wholesome piety into the Christian year, a redeeming life as well as an atoning death of Christ, to be preserved in living remembrance by the perpetual commemoration of its chief events. Then it was that, opening her heart to the humanity of religion, she began to draw near to the humanity of Jesus, and to seek with eager interest for the day of His birth, that she might make it holy."

With the celebration of Christ's Nativity returned the celebration of the nativities of ordinary mortals.

Black-Letter Days. Minor holidays and saints' days whose names appear in black instead of red letters in the calendar. (See Red-Letter Days.) In the English (reformed) calendar the black-letter days were retained in some cases because the person commemorated was a public benefactor or a national hero, in

---

* Compare Ruskin : " From the moment when the spirit of Christianity had been entirely interpreted to the Western races, the sanctity of womanhood worshipped in the Madonna, and the sanctity of childhood in union with that of Christ, became the light of every honest hearth and the joy of every pure and chastened soul."

others because the day marked some civil date of importance. A few have entered into the common speech of England, as Hilary term, Martinmas summer, etc.

Black Monday. In English history this title is given specifically to Easter Monday, the 14th of April, 1360, on which day Edward III. "with his hoast lay before the Citty of Paris, which day was full darke of mist and haile and so bitter cold that many men dyed on their horses with cold; wherefore unto this day it hath beene called the Blacke Munday." (*Stow's Annals*, p. 264.) By extension the term was also applied to every Easter Monday. It is used in this sense by Shakespeare: "Then it was not for nothing that my nose fell a-bleeding on Black Monday last." (*Merchant of Venice*, ii. 5, 25.) But at present Black Monday is generally understood in England in its application to the first Monday after the long vacation, when school-boys return to their studies. The term was appropriate enough in those earlier unhappy times when learning was considered a thing that could be whacked in from above or spanked in from below, and only scant attention was paid to the creature comforts of the victims. These times are rather pleasantly recalled in an article on "Black Monday" contributed to Dickens's *Household Words*, vol. vi. p. 569 (1853). A few paragraphs may be quoted:

"Cases do now, I believe, frequently occur in which the pains of school are more than counterbalanced by its pleasures; in such cases degenerate boys fly in the face of the poet, and go willingly to school, abolishing the due observance of the ancient institution of Black Monday. I am for due observance of all fasts and festivals, and feel quite sure that there is no better reason why Gunpowder Treason should be celebrated than why Black Monday should never be forgot.

"There may be many who keep the day dull now, I don't deny that I believe there *are* many; but in my younger days the proper celebration of it was a rule absolute, and there were no exceptions. The eve of Black Monday used to be kept on Saturday, when the school-box was packed. We then used to get out our books with solemn faces. They were not done with yet, we felt; ere long they would give plague to us, and the first day of plague would be the day most fitly called, on the same principle that gave a title to the Black Assizes, Black Monday.

"Another penance undergone by school-boys of the last generation, that ought not to be shirked by boys in this, was the great washing of feet and heads upon Black Monday Eve, the Saturday night previous. Sunday intervened always as a day of quiet rest. We were to go so clean to school that our legs on that last Saturday night were parboiled, and our heads were scrubbed so that the skin felt to be coming off about our ears. This penance was the more acutely felt as we knew well that when we got to school on Black Monday evening our heads would be again raked severely with a small-toothed comb. On the Sunday before Black Monday was the Feast of Uncles, when we would take care to go and say good-by to any relative who had not paid his nephew's tax for the half-year then to commence. Before getting into bed on Sunday night, we always counted up our shillings and half-crowns, and put the money into a big purse made by a little sweetheart with blue eyes and fairy feet, then put the purse into a pocket of the new and strong school trousers that lay, neatly folded by a mother's hand, ready for wear next morning, on a chair by the bedside. Then we got into bed, and lay awake so long that we caught the mother's face over our own attempting a sly kiss at the grown people's bed-time; then we fell asleep. We dressed next morning, hurriedly roused by candle-light, in frost and cold, were made to swallow eggs and toast and ham and boiling coffee, and rolled off in a hackney-coach through dark and snowy streets to the Swan with Two Necks, Lad Lane. From that place we were booked—or I was booked, for it will be seen that I have slipped insensibly from generalities into a recollection of my individual experience —from that place I was booked outside to Millstone."

But with the descent from the general to the particular the article loses its value for the purposes of this compilation.

Black Rod. The name given to the official who carries messages from royalty to the Houses of Parliament. He presents a picturesque appearance in his black tunic lavishly slashed with gold embroidery, knee-breeches, silk stockings, and silver-buckled shoes; but neither the sword that dangles by his side nor the short eponymic rod of black ivory with gold knob which he carries in his right hand throws about him a sufficiently aggressive dignity to explain the time-honored reception which always greets him in the House of Commons. As he walks along the lobby that lies between the chamber of the Lords and the chamber of the Commons, his approach is heralded by an iron-throated usher shouting, "Black Rod! Way for Black Rod!" But the moment that stentorian cry reaches the ears of the sergeant-at-arms in the House of Commons he springs from his chair, close to the main entrance to the chamber, and, rushing to the open door behind him, closes it with a most inhospitable bang, right in the face of Black Rod, and securely locks and bolts it. The sergeant-at-arms then peers out into the lobby through a grated peep-hole, with a wooden slot, fixed in the stout oak door. Presently three faint knocks are heard at the door. They are administered by Black Rod. The petitionary appeal of this soft, humble "rat-a-tat-tat" no one could resist; and so, at a nod from the Speaker, the doors are flung open by the sergeant-at-arms, and in walks the royal messenger.

Blaise, St. (Lat. *Blasius ;* It. *Biagio*), patron of Ragusa, also of wool-combers and against diseases of the throat. The Roman Church celebrates his martyrdom on February 3, the Greek on February 11. He was Bishop of Sebaste, in Cappadocia, but spent most of his time in retirement on a hill not far from the city, where wild beasts used to come for his blessing. During the persecution of the Christians under Licinius he was seized and taken before the governor. On the way a woman besought the saint to relieve her child, who was choking from a bone in its throat. He laid his hand on the child's throat and prayed, and it was healed. After being tortured by having his flesh torn with wool-combers' irons, St. Blaise was beheaded (A.D. 316).

In England the saint was specially popular before the Reformation. The Council of Oxford, A.D. 1222, prohibited servile labor on his feast. Its observance in England was marked by curious ceremonies. Among others, a taper used to be offered at high mass; and it was until lately the custom in many parts of England to light bonfires on the hills on St. Blaise's Night. These usages are sometimes referred to a pun on his name (Blaise = blaze); but this seems erroneous, as they are not peculiar to England. In some parts of Germany St. Blaise's Day is known as Little Candlemas Day, from the bonfires that it was usual to kindle on that night, or perhaps from the candles offered in the churches. Googe's translation of " The Popish Kingdom" has these lines :

> Then followeth good Sir Blaze, who doth a waxen candell give,
> And holy water to his men, whereby they safely live.
> I divers barrels oft have seene, drawne out of water cleare,
> Through one small blessed bone of this same Martyr heare,
> And caryed thence to other townes and cities farre away,
> Ech superstition doth require such earnest kinde of play.

Minsheu, in his Dictionary, under the word " Hocke-tide," speaks of " St. Blaze his day, about Candlemasse, when country women goe about and make good cheere, and if they finde any of their neighbour women a spinning that day, they burne and make a blaze of fire of the distaffe, and thereof called S. Blaze his day."

Which shows that a bad pun has immortal life.

Both in Germany and in the United States special services are held in the Catholic churches on St. Blaise's Day, when the throats of people suffering from bronchial or pulmonary troubles are blessed. Candles are frequently brought to church by the patients, which after receiving the priestly benediction are supposed to have certain sanctifying and hygienic qualities.

Reginald Scot, in his " Discovery of Witchcraft," ed. 1665, p. 137, gives us a charm used in the Roman Church upon St. Blaise's Day, that will fetch a thorn out of any place of one's body, a bone out of the throat, etc., to wit, " Call upon God, and remember St. Blaise." An ancient receipt "for a stoppage in the throat" was the following: "Hold the diseased party by the throat, and pronounce these words, Blaise, the martyr and servant of Jesus Christ, commands thee to pass up and down."

In England the wool-combers still acknowledge St. Blaise as their patron. The flourishing communities engaged in this business in Bradford and other English towns are accustomed to hold a jubilee on the 3d of February every seventh year in honor of Jason of the Golden Fleece and St. Blaise. At one time the festival was conducted with immense state and ceremony. The following was the order of the singular procession on this day: The masters on horseback, with each a white sliver; the masters' sons on horseback; their colors; the apprentices on horseback, in their uniforms; music; mummers representing the king and queen, the royal family, their guards and attendants; Jason and the golden fleece; attendants; Bishop Blaise and his chaplain; their attendants; shepherd and shepherdess; shepherd's swains, attendants, etc.; foremen and wool-sorters on horseback; combers' colors; wool-combers, two and two, with ornamented caps, wool wigs, and various colored slivers. See a further account in Hone's " Every Day Book," i. 210.

In Greek art St. Blaise is painted as an old man with a pointed beard. In the West he appears in the vestments of a bishop, with an iron comb of the sort used by wool-combers.

Blarney Stone. A famous piece of rock in Blarney Castle, near Cork, Ireland. Father Prout calls it the palladium of Ireland, and humorously sums up the various legends concerning it, —namely, that it was brought over by the Phœnician colony said to have peopled the island; that the Syrians and Carthaginians, long its custodians, gave rise to the expression *Punica fides Syriosque bilingues* from their labial devotion to the stone. He adds that some Carthaginian adventurers, enamored of the relic, stole it and carried it off to Minorca, and afterwards, driven by a storm into Cork harbor, deposited it near the present spot.

Everybody knows that to kiss the Blarney Stone is to secure a fluent, flattering, but not over-sincere tongue.

Every Irishman south of the Liffey is popularly supposed to

have enjoyed the renowned osculation, and, moreover, to have taken a dip in the Shannon, that makes perfect the quality of impudence, or, as the natives euphemistically express it, civil courage. The origin of the superstition about the stone is told in numberless traditions. Crofton Croker states—and this is the most plausible of all the stories—that in 1602, when the Spaniards were urging the Irish chieftains to harass the English, one Cormach M'Dermod Carthy, who held the castle, had concluded an armistice with the Lord President on condition of surrendering it to an English garrison. Carthy put off his lordship day after day with fair promises and false pretexts, until the latter became the laughing-stock of Elizabeth's ministers, and the former's honeyed and delusive speeches were stamped with the title of Blarney.

The custodians of the castle all seem to have taken advantage of the properties of the stone confided to their care. It is a well-known trick of theirs to regulate their choice of the particular stone which shall for the nonce be passed off upon the traveller, according to the latter's willingness and capacity to climb. If he is old or feeble, they will inform him that the stone has been knocked down by some indecent blayguard, and now lies near the front door. But if he is young, vigorous, and alert, they will tell him the truth, that it is situated at the northern angle of the massive donjon, about one hundred and twenty-five feet from the ground, and that to reach it with one's lips requires that one should be held over the parapet by one's heels. The stone bears the inscription, now very dim, " Cormach MacCarthy fortis me fieri facit, A.D. 1446."

Blood and Blood Vengeance. In the forms of civilization that preceded our own, and in some existing modern races of lower type, there appear traces of a sense of wrong attaching to any form of bloodshed whatever, whether of fair battle or of base treachery, and calling for the purifying influences of expiation and cleansing. In South Africa, for instance, the Basuto returning from war proceeds with all his arms to the nearest stream, to purify not only his own person but his javelins and his battle-axe. The Zulu, too, practises ablutions on the same occasion, and the Bechuana warrior wears a rude kind of necklace, to remind him of the expiation due from him to the slain and to disperse the dreams that might otherwise trouble him and perhaps even drive him to die of remorse. The same feelings may be detected in ancient times. The Macedonians had a peculiar form of sacrificatory purification, which consisted in cutting a dog in half and leading the whole army, arrayed in full armor, between the two parts. As the Bœotians had the same custom, it was probably for the same reason. At Rome, for the same purpose, a sheep, a bull, and a pig or a boar were every year led three times round the army and then sacrificed to Mars. In Jewish history the prohibition to King David to build the temple was expressly connected with the blood he had shed in battle. In old Greek mythology Theseus held himself unfit, without expiation, to be admitted to the mysteries of Ceres, though the blood that stained his hands was only that of thieves and robbers. And in the same spirit Hector refused to make a libation to the gods before he had purified his hands after battle. " With unwashen hands," he said, " to pour out sparkling wine to Zeus I dare not, nor is it ever the custom for one soiled with the blood and dust of battle to offer prayers to the god whose seat is in the clouds."

Blood-Covenant. A rite by which two persons absorb each the other's blood, either by drinking or by transfusion to the veins, whereby they become bound to each other in even a closer connection than that of brotherhood. It prevails in many countries, civilized and uncivilized, and may be traced back to extreme antiquity. It existed in the rites and literature of the ancient Egyptians, and is frequently alluded to in the Bible. Dr. H. Clay Trumbull, who has made a scientific examination of the subject, holds that its origin is in the universally dominative primitive convictions that the blood is the life; that the heart, as the blood-fountain, is the very soul of every personality; that blood-transfer is soul-transfer; that blood-sharing, human or divine-human, secures an interunion of natures; and that a union of the human nature with the divine is the highest ultimate attainment reached out after by the most primitive as well as by the most enlightened mind of humanity. With savage and barbarous peoples the rite lies at the foundations of cannibalism; it is the motive of sacrifices, in which the animal is offered to the god as a substitute for the human blood. In one form the drops of blood were put in wine or other draughts and drunken; then the wine was drunken without the actual presence of the blood; whence we have the use of wine in pledges of friendship and in marriage. Among the Jews it is symbolized in circumcision; among Christians, in the use of wine in the sacrament.

Blood of Christ. Many cities profess to possess as a relic some portion of the actual blood of Christ. St. Louis brought particles to Paris which he had received from the Emperor of Constantinople. Readers of Chaucer will remember " the blode of Crist that it is in Hayles." This is probably the same mentioned by Matthew Paris as brought to England from Jerusalem in the middle of the thirteenth century. The church of St. John Lateran in Rome, the Imperial Monastery at Weingarten, a church in Mantua, and the Chapel of the Precious Blood in Bruges, all put forward similar claims. The two latter are considered the best authenticated. The relic of Mantua is supposed to have been preserved by Longinus the centurion. It reposes in a silver shrine attributed to Benvenuto Cellini. The precious blood at Bruges, which is one of the most famous of all the city's possessions, is reputed to have been collected from the wounds by Joseph of Arimathea and Nicodemus when they took down the body from the cross. It was brought to Bruges by Thierry of Alsace, Count of Flanders, in 1147. He had received it from his brother-in-law, Baldwin III., King of Jerusalem.

Against these legends, however, must be put the opinion of St. Thomas Aquinas that all the particles of blood which Christ shed

HENRY III. CARRYING THE PRECIOUS BLOOD TO WESTMINSTER.
(From a drawing by Matthew Paris.)

in his passion were reassumed by him in his resurrection, " and that the blood which is kept in some churches as relics did not flow from Christ's side, but is said to have flowed miraculously from some image of Christ when struck." Benedict XIV., on the other hand, admits the possibility that some particles of Christ's blood may not have been reassumed and may remain as relics. In this case they are not reunited to the Godhead, and it would be the crime of idolatry to give them divine worship.

The feast of the Precious Blood was instituted and fixed for the first Sunday of July by Pius IX. after his return from Gaeta. There were already a mass and an office for the Friday after the fourth Sunday in Lent, but they were permitted only for certain places.

Nearly six centuries ago, however, the extraordinary devotion paid to the relic in Bruges by the inhabitants and visitors had induced the ecclesiastical and civil authorities to institute a solemn procession in which it should be borne in the streets. The first ceremony was performed on May 3, 1311.

A Confraternity of the Precious Blood, consisting of thirty members, with a provost and four chaplains, was established to guard it at all times. That confraternity still exists, though it has unfortunately discarded the picturesque costume of mediæval times.

It would be impossible to describe the vicissitudes and dangers to which the relic has been exposed. One legendary episode, however, is sufficiently curious to record. Philip van Artevelde marched on Bruges with five thousand men on May 2, 1382, and encamped outside the city. The procession, which at that time followed a route less protected than at present, was proceeding on its way, when an irregular band of armed burghers rushed out of the gates to attack the men of Ghent, and unintentionally threw the procession into confusion. The clergy stood their ground for a time, but were ultimately affected with the prevailing panic and took to flight. The bearer of the sacred relic, also losing his head, cast about him how he could save the treasure, and, finding no other means, threw the crystal phial into the canal which bounds the Béguinage.

The inhabitants, having recovered from their groundless alarm, became inconsolable for the loss of their relic; they conjectured that the men of Ghent must have carried it off, and the misadventure seemed to them to presage further calamities. One day a nun of the Béguinage who had gone to draw water saw some glittering object at the bottom of the canal. With the help of her superior the object was easily drawn out, and was found to be the lost relic. The news was received with extraordinary enthusiasm, and the Béguinage was besieged by enormous crowds eager to bear their treasure back to its own chapel with special pomp. This incident is the alleged cause of certain privileges still enjoyed by the Béguines, and is represented in an ancient picture in the church of their settlement.

In 1578 the Calvinists distinguished themselves in a manner equalled afterwards only by the sans-culottes of 1792. When reading the accounts of their depredations in Bruges, especially upon the Chapel of the Sacred Blood, the most persistent Protestant may well shudder. Happily, the relic was carried off and hidden by the provost Malvenda in his own house. The people to this day hold in special respect those houses which at different times have afforded an asylum to their beloved treasure. In 1792 the French entered Bruges and completed the havoc begun by the Calvinists. The adventures through which the relic passed read like some mediæval romance, and the devotion and care bestowed on it by the confraternity excite the most sympathetic interest. It was not until May 2, 1819, that it was restored to its former resting-place and exposed for the veneration of the faithful.

The solemn ceremonies were again established, and have been continued without interruption up to the present day. The pro- cession, though stripped of much of its ancient splendor, is ma- terially the same; and the enthusiasm surrounding it is not less marked than it was six hundred years ago.

A correspondent of the *Saturday Review* describes the proces- sion as he saw it in 1893. This being the jubilee year of the Bishop of Bruges, it was a doubly important occasion. Five members of the Belgian hierarchy, including the Cardinal Arch- bishop of Malines, were present. "The graceful costume of the seminaries, societies, and guilds of Bruges; the gorgeous crim- son vestments of the priests; the choristers, in scarlet cassocks, swinging the heavy silver censers and chanting as they slowly marched before the Sacred Blood, formed a most imposing spec- tacle. Gayly painted or richly vested images of the patron saints of Bruges, borne on litters, were followed or preceded by children carrying the emblems of their martyrdom and led by a boy or girl dressed to represent the saint in life. Two little boys, representing St. John the Baptist and the child Jesus, at- tracted particular attention; and a man in a purple robe, as Christ bearing the cross, was an impressive figure. The long procession, with its many tapers and brilliant banners, winding through the streets of the old city, crossing and recrossing the canals, presented an imposing spectacle. The official presence of civil and military persons marked its unique character as the great civic and popular as well as the most solemn religious cere- mony of Flanders. After the procession the benediction was given by the cardinal archbishop from an altar erected in the open air, in the Place du Bourg, and in front of the Chapel of the Sacred Blood."

The blood is contained in a crystal cylinder, closed at each end by a golden crown: when the relic is exposed, this cylinder is fastened to a silver chain hanging round a priest's neck. The shrine in which the reliquary is carried is of very elaborate gold and silver workmanship, made by Jean Crabbe, a goldsmith of the city, in 1617. It consists of a hexagonal base covered by a baldacchino which is supported by six slender fluted pillars; within stands the shrine proper, a coffer surmounted by a crucifix and figures of the Blessed Virgin and St. John; above the cru- cifix hangs the enamelled crown presented by Mary of Burgundy and worn by her on state occasions; upon the baldacchino are three open, domed niches, also resting on little columns, containing the figures of the Saviour, St. Donat, and St. Basil; the centre niche is itself surmounted by a fourth, in which is an image of the Madonna and Child; above this, again, is the symbolic pelican feeding her young. The figures are of solid gold, the rest of the shrine being of silver gilt and thickly incrusted with precious stones.

Blood Tax in the Pyrenees.

There is a vague tradition that some time in the thirteenth century, in the high pasturelands of Arlas, in the Pyrenees, some shepherds of the valley of Roncal, in Navarre, were murdered by shepherds of the valley of Bareton, in Béarn. One is shown on an upland lawn on French soil stones that are said to cover the graves of the victims, and the story lives on in a *chanson* still sung in the canton of the Baretonnais. In consequence of this massacre, the Baretonnais were condemned in perpetuity to the payment of a tax to the Roncalais, and this they accepted apparently as an alternative, or possibly as an end, to a vendetta. The tax has been paid during the last six or seven hundred years. The extraordinary thing is that it survived the Revolution.

The scene of the ceremony is the Pierre de St.-Martin, a frontier stone remote from roads and villages under the Pic d'Arlas.

A correspondent of the London *Pall Mall Gazette* thus describes the celebration in 1896: " By nine o'clock in the morning a company of about one hundred and fifty had assembled, including the sous-préfet of the Basses-Pyrénées, who attended, however, merely as a spectator, the curé of one of the Baretonnais villages and his vicaire, and some *gardes des montagnes* and *douaniers*. The Spaniards were the last to appear, heralding their approach by musket-shots, and on their arrival the business of the day began.

" The two peoples drew up in line on either side of the frontier stone in their respective territories. Immediately opposite the stone was the alcade of Isaba, wearing a black coat edged with crimson, with a hood and long false sleeves, and round his neck a large white pleated collar, the whole costume dating from 1600. He carried a black baton tipped with silver, the wand of his office as chief-justice of the court. He was attended by a notary and supported by the alcades of Urzainqui, Garde, and Ustarroz,— the other villages of the Roncal concerned,—habited in long, full-skirted, black, eighteenth-century collarless coats, long waistcoats, and the usual broad violet waistbands, knee-breeches, and black stockings of the Navarrese. A number of their followers were armed, and stood to attention with their guns loaded. A herald by the side of the President carried a javelin to which was attached a crimson streamer,—a sign of just revenge. On the other side it must be confessed that the French presented a less imposing appearance. They wore their blue blouses and Béarnaise caps, and here and there were some in the red-striped waistcoats said to be peculiar to the Baretonnais. The maires of Arette, Lanne, Aramits, and Issor were to be distinguished only by their tricolor scarfs, which they wore round their waists over their blouses. (It was noticeable, by the way, that the national colors were not displayed on the Spanish side.) The French herald carried a javelin bearing a white streamer,—sign of the pacific intentions of those for whom he acted, all of whom were unarmed.

"The order of proceedings is fixed by a document bearing the date of 1375. The President, the alcade of Isaba, speaking in Spanish, demanded of the French if they desired peace. The maires replied, 'Yes,' in the same language. Their herald then advanced and laid his javelin on the top of the stone in line with the frontier. The Spanish herald then drove his lance into French soil close to the stone, the two lances thus forming a cross. One of the French maires then placed his right hand on the section of the cross on the stone, then an alcade his hand on the Frenchman's, and so on in order, the alcade of Isaba's hand being the last. Then on the pile of hands the latter rested the baton of justice, and all took the oath of peace. The President then cried three times, '*Paz davans*' ('Peace henceforth'), and at this signal the Spaniards discharged their pieces over the heads of the Frenchmen, and consequently in the direction of France. Then followed *l'impôt du sang*. Originally the payment was three white mares, but, these being difficult to procure, the Baretonnais were allowed to substitute three heifers of a particular color and breed. Six or seven of these creatures had been brought. The Spanish veterinary, having taken the oath by placing his right thumb on the top of his baton that he would deal fairly, proceeded to examine the animals. One of the three first offered was rejected, and this gave rise to a very lively dispute before the alcade, who, it may be observed, with his shaven face, serious judicial air, and perfect self-command, acted his part to perfection. Unmoved, apparently, by the display of feeling on both sides, he listened to all, spoke little, but apparently to the point, and succeeded finally in quelling the storm. The affair of the animals (which were valued at about six pounds each) having been settled, and an account of it drawn up by the notary, it was asked if the compact between the two valleys had been observed during the past year, and if any one wished to speak. No one replying, the alcade then presented his baton to the two Spanish and to the two French *gardes des montagnes*, who, placing their right thumbs on it, swore as representatives to observe the convention. The notary then obtained the signatures of the alcades and maires to his procès-verbal for lodgement among the archives of the Roncalais. This closed the proceedings, and the assembly broke up."

Boar's Head, Bringing in the. In mediæval England it was customary to commence all great Christmas feasts by the solemn ceremony of bringing in the boar's head as the initial dish. The master-cook, preceded by trumpeters and other musicians, and followed by huntsmen with boar-spears and drawn falchions and pages carrying mustard, bore the smoking head aloft on a silver platter, which he deposited at the head of the table. The head was garnished and garlanded with rosemary and laurel, and a lemon was placed between its grinning chops. Holinshed tells us that in the year 1170 upon the day of the young prince's coronation King Henry II. " served his son at the table as server, bringing up the boar's head with trumpets before it, according to the manner." (*Chronicles*, iii. 76.)

The custom goes back to pre-Christian days. The Druids killed a boar at the winter solstice and offered its head in sacrifice to Freya, the goddess of peace and plenty, who was supposed to ride upon a boar with golden bristles. Hence it was not unusual even in Christian times to gild the head. The very lemon placed in the boar's mouth was a Norse symbol of plenty. An orange or an apple was sometimes substituted. The common practice in England of eating sucking pig at Christmas has the same origin.

Queen Victoria has retained the old custom. Her Christmas dinner at Osborne House or Windsor has for over fifty years consisted of a baron of beef and woodcock pie,—historic dishes, —while the bringing in of the boar's head is performed with all the ancient ceremony.

In many of the public schools and universities the boar's head is still retained as the great dish of the Christmas banquet. At these institutions every diner rises and joins in the " Boar's Song," which has been sung for centuries. The words are set " to the common chant of the prose version of the psalms in cathedrals." They run as follows:

A CAROL BRYNGYNG IN THE BOAR'S HEAD.

Caput apri defero
Reddens laudes Domino.

The bore's head in hande bring I,
With garlandes gay and rosemary,
I pray you all synge merely,
Qui estis in convivio.

The bore's head I understande,
Is the chefe servyce in this lande
Loke wherer it be fande
    Servite cum cantico.

Be gladde, lords, both more and lasse,
    For this hath ordayned our stewarde
To cheer you all this Christmasse,
    The bore's head with mustarde.

This carol is contained in Wynkyn de Worde's collection of
"Christmasse Carolles" (1521), but is there given as an old song.
Here is another carol which was anciently very popular:

ANCIENT BOAR'S HEAD CANTICLE.

In die natiuitat.

Nowell, nowell, nowell, nowell,
    Tydyng' gode y thynke to telle.
The borys hede that we bryng here,
Betokeneth a prince without pere,
Ys born this day to bye v'dere.
            Nowell, etc.

A bore ys a souverayn beste,
And acceptab(l)e in eu'ry feste,
So mote thys lorde be to moste and leste.
            Nowell, etc.

This borys hede we bring with song,
In worchyp of hym that thus sprang
Of a virgine to redresse all wrong.
            Nowell, etc.

Queen's College, Oxford, is especially famous for its continued
retention of the Boar's Head ceremonial. The method as practised for five centuries is as follows: A large boar's head, weighing between sixty and seventy pounds, surmounted by a cross,
and wreathed with gilded sprays of laurel and bay, mistletoe and
rosemary, with small banners surrounding, is brought into the hall
by three bearers, whose entry is announced by trumpets. A procession of the Provost and Fellows precedes the entry of the
boar's head. The bearers are accompanied by the precentors,
who chant the "Caput apri defero," the Latin refrain being joined
in by the company.

There is a local legend to explain the institution of the ceremony. Some five hundred years ago, so the story runs, a student
of the college wandering near Shotover Hill in deep study of
Aristotle was attacked by a wild boar. Having no other means
of defence, he shoved his book down the animal's throat, exclaim-

ing, "Græcum est!" The sage choked the savage, and his head was brought home in triumph by the student.

Hone in his "Every Day Book" (1827, vol. ii. p. 1649) tells us that the lessee of the tithes at Hornchurch in Essex, which is attached to New College, Oxford, supplies every Christmas Day a boar's head, dressed and garnished with bay-leaves, etc. In the afternoon it is carried in procession into the mill-field adjoining the churchyard, where it is wrestled for, and afterwards feasted upon at one of the public houses by the rustic conqueror and his friends, with all the merriment peculiar to the season.

A paragraph quoted by Thiselton Dyer (" British Customs," p. 479) from the *Daily News* of January 5, 1852, shows that the custom still survived at that date : " By ancient charter or usage in Horn Church a boar's head is wrestled for in a field adjoining the church, a boar, the property of the parish, having been slaughtered for the purpose. The boar's head, elevated on a pole and decorated with ribbons, was brought into the ring when the competitors entered, and the prize was awarded."

Boat Sunday. In Kent, England, the Sunday (usually in December) preceding the departure of the fishermen for the herring-fisheries. All their friends from the neighboring villages attend the morning services to bid them farewell. When later in the week the men start upon their expedition, they send a piece of sea-beef on shore from each boat to such of their friends at the public houses as they wish "weel beea." This occasions "a bit of a supper," at which those who are going away and those who remain enjoy good cheer heightened by mutual good will. (COLE: *History and Antiquities of Filey,* 1828, p. 143.)

Bobolition Day. Bobolition was the negro attempt at pronouncing "abolition," and was gleefully seized upon by the enemies of the Abolition movement. During the early part of the nineteenth century the negroes of Boston observed the 14th of July to commemorate the introduction of measures for the abolition of the slave-trade. Hence it was derisively called Bobolition Day, and the orderly convention of black men that annually assembled to do honor to the occasion was greeted with a fusillade of rotten fruit and eggs and much jesting abuse. A correspondent of the New York *Nation* writes that he remembers having seen the word at least as early as 1824 "on a broad sheet containing what purported to be an account of a bobolition celebration at Boston, July 14. At the top of the broad sheet was a grotesque procession of negroes." At one of these

Bobolition Day celebrations the famous Malapropian toast was seriously given in honor of the newly elected governor: "Governor Brooks—May the mantelpiece of Caleb Strong fall on the head of his distinguished predecessor."

Bodhi-druma. (Hindoo, "Tree of Understanding.") A big tree of the peepul tribe in Gaya, India, still pointed out as the identical tree under which Buddha accomplished the "meditation of perfection" by which he achieved Nirvâna. It is more usually known to Europeans as the Bo-tree, a general term extended also to its offshoots. The earliest record of the original tree is that preserved in the Chinese Hwen-Thsang's narrative (about A.D. 637). He found it surrounded by an oblong walled enclosure of brick, some twenty feet in height and five hundred paces in circuit and girdled with umbrageous trees. In the centre of this enclosure stood the Diamond Throne, dating from the foundation of the world. When all the world quaked, this throne alone was unmoved, and seated on it all the Buddhas of past ages had achieved the divine climax of wisdom and power. And there, immovable, it still remained; only since the degeneracy of this latter Kalpa sand and soil had spread over the precious adamant, and it was no longer visible. Above its site, however, still grew the tree, which had undergone many vicissitudes, but survived them all. According to the legend, the leaves did not fall either in summer or in autumn, but the tree suddenly denuded itself and as suddenly assumed an entirely new leafage on the anniversary of the day of Buddha's Nirvâna. Every year on this day, kings, ministers, and magistrates assembled around this tree, watered it with milk, illuminated it with lanterns, and withdrew after gathering the leaves which had fallen.

Other Bo-trees said to have been propagated from slips of the great original are extant. A very famous one is in the sacred city of Anarajapoora, in Ceylon, reputed to have been planted in B.C. 228. Its leaves are carried away as treasures by pilgrims, but it is too sacred to be touched with a knife: hence they are gathered only when they fall.

A famous tree connected with Buddha-worship is that preserved in front of the lamasery of Kunbum, in Northeastern Thibet, near the sources of China's Yellow River. It is a variety of the elder, and on its leaves and bark are indelibly inscribed by no earthly hand, the Lamas say, sacred formulæ and images. Father Huc first described this tree to Europeans. He made no attempt to solve the mystery. Later travellers have made various guesses, as that some insect works indistinct tracings in which the faithful read what they choose. But the latest of all,

M. Edouard Blanc, insists that the figures are unmistakable and are an evident artifice of human hands. The fraud, he says, has been handed down from one generation of Lamas to another. They sell the leaves to pilgrims, claiming for them rare medicinal virtues.

Bodmin Riding. A festival kept until recently at Bodmin, in Cornwall, Wales, on the Sunday and Monday following St. Thomas's Day (July 7). In the preceding October an anticipatory puncheon of ale had been brewed and bottled. On Sunday morning two young men representing the "wardens" bore these bottles in baskets around the town, attended by a band of fifes and drums and sometimes other instruments. Pausing before the house of every leading citizen, the crier shouted the salutation, "To the people of this house a prosperous morning, long life, and a merry riding." Then the musicians struck up the riding-tune, and the householder was solicited to taste the ale. He responded by taking in a bottle and paying such sum as his means or his humor dictated. Monday morning a procession was formed,—all who could afford it riding on a horse or an ass,—and proceeded first to the Priory, to receive two large garlands of flowers fixed on staves, and then through the principal streets to the Town End. Here the festivities were formally organized. Wrestling, foot-races, jumping in sacks, and other games were practised. A curious kind of mock trial was also one of the features. A Lord of Misrule was appointed. Before him was dragged any unpopular person so unlucky as to be captured, to answer to a charge of felony. Inculpatory evidence was furnished by any breach of good manners, negligence of attire, or other accident in his bearing or appearance. The trial was conducted with much gravity, sentence was pronounced, and the culprit was hurried off to receive his punishment, which consisted " in some ungracious prank or other, more to the scorn than hurt of the party condemned" (CAREW: *Survey of Cornwall*, 1811, p. 296), and usually concluded by his being dragged through the mire of Halgaver. The latter name " signifieth the goat's moor, and such a place it is, lying a little without the town, and very full of quagmires." (*Ibid.*) To this day " Take him before the Mayor of Halgaver" and " Present him in Halgaver Court" are Cornish sayings.

Bœuf Gras. (Fr., " Fat Ox.") The fête or procession of the Fat Ox is the culminating Carnival festivity celebrated by the butchers of Paris on Mardi-Gras, or Shrove Tuesday (*q. v.*). Comparative mythologists trace the origin of the custom from the processions in honor of the bull Apis among the Egyptians, though similar ceremonies in ancient Greece and Rome were celebrated at the equinox of spring, when the sun enters the sign Taurus, at which oxen or bulls were sacrificed. But a more immediate ancestry may be found in the similar ceremonies

BŒUF GRAS OF 1827.
(From the official programme.)

among the ancient Gauls, who likewise had a special cult for this zodiacal sign and dressed the ox up for the occasion in an ecclesiastical stole. As Christianity penetrated Gaul, the sacrifice of the ox lost its importance and its sacred character, as well as its periodic recurrence. Under Charles V. it had become a mere occasional recreation, in which all classes joined. In course of time a rivalry sprang up among the butchers as to who should furnish the ox, and eventually the guild of butchers took the matter under their charge and raised the necessary funds. The procession, celebrated so early as 1512, is commemorated in a contemporary stained-glass window presented by the master-butchers of Bar-sur-Seine. Two butchers, in holiday attire, lead the ox by means of a scarf wrapped around its neck; preceding them are two apprentices playing musical instruments, while children shout and dance around them.

The modern date of the procession was not fixed until the introduction of the Carnival into France under Louis XIV., when it was permanently settled on as the day before Ash Wednesday.

A memorable procession was that of 1739. It started from l'Apport, Paris. The ox was crowned with a garland of leaves, and his shoulders were covered with tapestry. On his back sat a naked child, decorated with a huge scarf of blue ribbon and carrying a gilded sceptre in one hand, a drawn sword in the other. The child was known as the King of the Butchers.

Fifteen butcher-boys dressed in red and white formed the ox's escort. Two led him by his horns, after the fashion of the ancient sacrificers. Other butchers and their apprentices preceded and followed, all playing on viols, fifes, and drums. The procession not only paraded the streets of Paris, but also invaded the houses of various magistrates, who gave gifts of money to the celebrants. The President not happening to be at home, the Bœuf Gras was led up the steps of the Palace of Justice, and, after being presented to the official who in his red robe was sitting on the judges' bench, was led back again into the streets. The festivities on this occasion began on Monday and lasted until Ash Wednesday.

The Revolution put a temporary end to the Carnival and to the Bœuf Gras. In 1805 Napoleon restored both by an ordinance dated February 23. The ox was usually paraded through the streets during the last three days of the Carnival. The little King of the Butchers was transformed into a Cupid carrying a quiver of arrows and a torch. The escort consisted of butcher-boys disguised as mythological and historical characters. Royalty itself deigned to review the parade from the windows and balconies of the Tuileries.

The choice of the ox itself became a matter of anticipatory public interest. Rival butchers competed as to who should submit the fattest, sleekest, and largest candidate. A jury of twelve expert butchers was appointed. Their decision was based upon height, breadth, weight, and general comeliness. Here is how the choice made in 1846 was announced on the programme for that year: "On the 12th of February, 1846, in the midst of an immense crowd, took place the competition for the choice of the Fat Ox which according to ancient custom is to do the honors of the Carnival. At midday, 1607 oxen were exhibited in the great fair-grounds. The jury selected from them such as best fulfilled the triple conditions of strength, stature, and adiposity. Then the oxen thus selected were led to the court of the slaughter-house at Caisse de Poissy. Here the jury rendered its final verdict, which declared that Dagobert, five and a half years old, belonging to M. Cornet, of Caen, worthy successor to his father, was the unanimous choice for the Carnival of 1846. Dagobert in bulk has no rival save the elephant of the Jardin des Plantes. He weighs five kilos more than Père Goriot, the Bœuf Gras of 1845." From 1848 to 1851 the procession was suspended, mainly for monetary reasons. In the latter year Arnault of the Hippodrome assumed all the expenses of a revival. After 1855 there was an increase in the number and gorgeousness of the paraders, and eventually not one but several Fat Oxen took part, and the procession became one of the most brilliant popular fêtes under the Second Empire. Like many other things, however, it was dropped on account of the disasters of 1870, and was not revived until 1893.

"The revival," says the correspondent of the *New York Sun,* writing from Paris on February 18, "was on a grand scale. Three oxen were provided, and the festivities were spread over three days, the Sunday, Monday, and Tuesday before Ash Wednesday brought in Lent. This time the procession was organized not by the butchers alone, but by the Food Syndicate, whose president is M. Marquély, a well-known restaurant owner, assisted by M. Zidler, the manager of two Parisian music-halls. In the procession were seventeen carriages, drawn by ninety-two horses, fourteen floats, each with six horses, one hundred and seventy-eight horsemen in costumes, and seven hundred mummers on foot.

"No expense was spared. It is even said that the actual cost was more than double the original estimate. While some idea may be formed of the magnificence of the procession, no words can picture the animation of the great crowd shut in between the high houses of the boulevards, over twenty-five miles long, its enthusiasm, good humor, and extreme politeness, which on those days even affected the policemen. They were seen smiling at the showers of confetti, and even throwing them back occasionally without roughness."

At Marseilles the Fat Ox is paraded through the streets not on Mardi-Gras, but on the eve and the day of Corpus Christi. Ruffi's' "History of Marseilles" refers the origin of the custom to the fourteenth century. The Confraternity of the Holy Sacrament, wishing to feast the poor on the day which they particularly honored, bought a huge ox and marched it through the poorer quarters of the town as at once an advertisement and an invitation. The procession gave so much pleasure that it was kept up annually. Various superstitions grew around it. Old women were careful to make children kiss the ox as a preservative against sickness, everybody clamored to get some small portion of the meat as an emblem of luck, and whenever the ox paused before a house to attend to any of the functions of nature the inmates were envied for the fortunate omen.

Bona Dea. (Lat., "The Good Goddess.") An ancient Roman festival in honor of the goddess Maia, celebrated May 1. The word Maia is derived from the month in which her chief festival was celebrated. On this occasion the Romans seem to have recognized the secret, mysterious forces of nature. The cult of the goddess belonged especially to women. Besides the regular festival on May 1, mysterious rites in honor of the Bona

Dea were performed by women during the early part of December. These mysteries were celebrated by the Roman women with great solemnity. They were held in the night, and in the house either of the consul or the prætor, who on this occasion must be absent from his home, for no male was allowed to be present. When Cicero was consul, B.C. 63, the celebration took place at his house on the night of December 3. It will be remembered that on this day Cicero had made the speech which is known as his third oration against Catiline, describing to the people the capture of the conspirators. When the assembly was dismissed, the people accompanied him home, as was usual, but, his house being occupied by the women, he was obliged to go to a friend's house to spend the night. Here he sat deliberating with a few of his trusted counsellors what disposition should be made of the prisoners, when a message came hastily from his wife Terentia that an auspicious sign had occurred in the mysteries, at which he should take courage. The fire upon the altar had blazed up with great brilliancy, and when the women were terrified, the Vestal Virgins, who had the direction of this festival, at once interpreted the event as a good omen, and urged Terentia to send word to her husband to that effect.

The next year, B.C. 62, the mysteries were celebrated in the house of Cæsar, who was prætor. Having lately been elected Pontifex Maximus, he occupied the public residence which belonged to this officer,—the *regia*, or palace. This was on the Sacred Way, adjoining the residence of the Vestal Virgins, to whom this house was afterwards given by Augustus when he became Pontifex Maximus. A young nobleman of profligate character, named Publius Clodius, by an understanding with Cæsar's wife Pompeia, contrived to steal into the building in the dress of a harp-player; for the mysteries were celebrated to the sound of musical instruments. But one of the slaves of the household, undertaking to ask him some questions, detected him by his voice, and called Cæsar's mother, Aurelia, who at once suspended the rites, when the women speedily drove the offender out of the house. It was the greatest scandal in the history of the republic. Clodius escaped punishment,—it was believed, by bribery. Cæsar at once divorced his wife, not assuming that she was guilty, but asserting that Cæsar's wife must be above suspicion.

Boniface, St. (680–755). The "Apostle to Germany," one of the greatest missionaries of the Church in the eighth century. He is commemorated on his death-day, June 5. His real name was Winfred, and he was a native of Devonshire, England. Ordained a priest at thirty years of age, he resolved to become

a missionary to those parts of Germany which were still idolatrous. At Fulda he founded the celebrated abbey, and he left
other ecclesiastical monuments to himself in Bavaria, Thuringia,
Saxony, etc. Gregory III. made him Archbishop and Primate
of Germany. He was massacred in Friesland by a band of
pagans who had sworn to take his life. He always carried in
his bosom a copy of the "De Bono Mortis" of St. Ambrose.
This copy, stained with his blood, was long preserved as a sacred
relic in the monastery at Fulda, where he was buried. A portion
of his skull is still kept there. At Dochum was long shown
another part of his skull, together with his cape and chasuble.
Other relics are at Louvain, Mechlin, Cologne, Bruges, Prague,
Eichfeld, and Erfurt.

Bounds, Beating the. A Protestant survival of the ancient
Catholic custom of processions on the Rogation Days (*q. v.*).
The processions, which originated in Gaul and were brought
over to England by St. Augustine, used to be performed with
great pomp. As every parish came to have its own procession,
which could not transgress the limits of that parish, the ceremony gradually and insensibly drew to itself some of the still
more ancient pagan practices of the Terminalia (*q. v.*), or Feast
of Boundaries. The lord of the manor in country places, or the
highest member of the parochial clergy in cities, led the way,
followed by surpliced ecclesiastics bearing crosses, and public
officials and other prominent parishioners with hand-bells, banners, and staves. They perambulated round the parish singing
rogations or litanies, stopping at crosses, forming crosses on the
ground, "saying or singing gospels to the corn," and allowing
"drinkings and good cheer." But good cheer did not mean
meat, inasmuch as the Rogation days were fasts, or at least days
of abstinence.

If the parish contained a fine oak-tree, the gospel was read
here, the tree receiving the name of Gospel Oak. In most
places a representation of the evil one, in the form of a dragon,
was a part of the procession. As often as a pause was made
for prayer the dragon was taken to a place quite out of earshot,
and left there until the procession moved on again. Hence
many rural parishes even to this day have their Dragon's Rock
or Dragon's Well, denoting the place where the dragon reposed
at prayer-time or where it was kicked, stoned, buffeted, and
finally pulled to pieces by the processionists at the close of the
third day's rogation.

The Reformation did not abolish the processions, though it
altered their character, and eventually transferred them to
Ascension Day itself. The Book of Common Prayer still enjoins

such part of the ancient ceremony as relates to the perambulating of the circuit of parishes, conformably to the regulation made in the reign of Queen Elizabeth. "The people shall once a year, at the time accustomed," says the injunction of that sovereign, "with the curate and substantial men of the parish, walk about the parishes as they were accustomed, and at their return to church make their common prayers ; provided that the curate in the said common perambulations, as heretofore in the days of Rogations, at certain convenient places, shall admonish the people to give thanks to God, in the beholding of God's benefits, for the increase and abundance of his fruits upon the face of the earth, with the saying of Psalm civ., *Benedic, anima mea,* etc. ; at which time also the same minister shall inculcate this and such like sentences, ' Cursed be he which translateth the bounds and dales of his neighbour,' or such other words of prayer as shall be hereafter appointed."

The religious sentiment gradually died out of these parochial perambulations, and they degenerated into colossal junketings. The traditional usage of always following in the old track gave them at certain stages of their progress a blithesome steeple-chase aspect. If a canal, for example, had been cut through the old boundaries, some of the perambulators had to cross it, either by swimming or in boats. So if a house had been erected over the line the procession claimed the right to pass through it. Chambers's " Book of Days" tells of a house in Buckinghamshire which had an oven traversing the line. It was customary in the perambulations to put a boy into the recess, to preserve the integrity of the procession. Now boys everywhere looked on Beating the Bounds as a more elaborate game of Follow my Leader. The boys in this Buckinghamshire parish used to be ambitious of the honor of invading the oven. They settled their claims by lot as they approached the house. On one occasion the perambulators found the oven heated up, baking bread. There was a cry from the juvenile members, " Tom Smith is the boy to go into the oven." Tom Smith uttered a wild shriek and made off as fast as his legs would carry him. Another boy was asked to climb over the roof of the oven, and thus the boundary line was deemed to be sufficiently maintained.

On another occasion, in London, a nobleman's carriage happened to be standing across the boundary line. His lordship was paying a visit in the opposite house. The coachman was requested to move out of the way. He refused until his master should tell him to move. The churchwarden calmly opened one door of the carriage and passed through the other, followed by the rest of the procession.

" Hone's Year Book" gives a rather humorous account of a

man who being asked whether such a stream were a boundary replies, " Ees, that 'tis, I'm sure o't, by the same token that I were tossed into 't, and paddled about there like a water-rat, till I were hafe dead."

Sometimes the boys in the procession were whipped as they reached the boundaries, to impress their exact location upon plastic youth. At other times they were "bumped;" *i.e.*, the senior perambulators took hold of them by the shoulders and the heels and bumped what might be called the southern façade of the juvenile body against the landmark. Not only boys but strangers were frequently seized upon for the purpose. So recently as January 10, 1830, the *London Observer* recorded the trial of a case brought by an angler against the parishioners of Walthamstow parish. On the preceding Ascension Day he had been found angling in the Lea. The parishioners bethought them that to bump a stranger would produce an independent witness of parish boundary. But he relished neither the practice nor the reason for it. and the jury so far agreed with him that they rendered a verdict of fifty pounds damages.

In several parishes in London the bounds are still beaten on Ascension Day. Men and boys make the tour of the parish limits, beating the landmarks with peeled willow rods.

At Marlborough, in Devonshire, the mayor and the town-councillors perform the function ; and it is on record that on one occasion within the present century the mayor himself was thoroughly ducked during his progress, in order to insure his remembering a certain bit of the river boundary.

" In beating the bounds of the city of Oxford," says Ditch-field, " it is necessary for the mayor and corporation to take a boat and go on the river. A few years ago we read that ' the mayor and others were upset,' and later on the boat capsized. Perhaps this ducking was in lieu of bumping." (" Old English Customs," p. 116.)

On Ascension Day, says Mackenzie in his " History of Newcastle" (1827, vol. ii. p. 744), every year the mayor and burgesses of Newcastle survey the boundaries of the river Tyne. This annual festive expedition starts at the Mansion-House Quay, and proceeds to or near the place in the sea called Sparhawk, and returns up the river to the utmost limits of the corporation at Hedivin Streams. They are accompanied by the brethren of the Trinity House and the river jury in their barges.

The bounds of the parish of St. Mary's, Leicester, are beaten every three years. The procession is composed of the vicar, churchwardens, and other officials, and two or three hundred boys. Formerly at one spot in the route a hole was dug, and any newly appointed parish officer was seized and his head placed in the hole, while his body was thumped with a shovel. A feast was held, and various sports followed, such as racing, bobbing for apples in buckets of water, etc.; but these have been discontinued.

At Lichfield on Ascension Day the choristers of the cathedral deck the houses and street-lamps in the parish of the Close with elm boughs. After the midday service the clergy and choir start in procession from the cathedral, properly vested, the boys carrying small pieces of elm, and go round the boundaries of the parish, making a halt at eight stations where wells exist or are said to have existed. At each of these stations the Gospel for the day is said by one of the priest-vicars in turn, followed by the singing of one verse of Psalm civ. or c. On re-entering the cathedral by the northwest door, the verse "Oh, enter then his gates with praise" is sung, and the company gather round the font, where the blessing is given, and the boys throw down their boughs. On the same day the sacrist gives a bun to every unconfirmed child in the parish. (DITCHFIELD: *Old English Customs.*)

A queer variation of the custom is observed in Leighton Buzzard, in accordance with the will of a London merchant, who founded ten almshouses in the town and who died in 1646. The trustees, accompanied by the town crier and a band of boys carrying green boughs, beat the boundaries of the parish, stopping at the properties from whose incomes the charities are supported. At all these places one boy stands on his head while the will is read. After the procession plum rolls are given to the boys. Until recently a half-pint of beer was given, but this has been suppressed, rolls being distributed to all the school-children instead. In the evening the trustees, the town crier, and the inmates of the almshouses dine together.

In Scotland a similar ceremony is known as the Riding of the MARCHES (*q. v.*).

Boy-Bishop. One of the most curious observances of the mediæval Church, mingling the sacred with the profane and seriousness with burlesque, was the election of a boy-bishop. The origin of the custom is not clearly understood, but it is known to have existed from the thirteenth century, both in England and on the Continent. On December 5, the eve of the festival of St. Nicholas, patron of children, all the boys who sang in the choir or served at the altar met in every parish church, cathedral, and nobleman's chapel, and elected from among their number a bishop and his prebendaries, or, as they were alternatively called, "a Nicholas and his clerks." These remained in office until Holy Innocents' Day, December 28. During this time, with the knowledge and sanction of his elders, the boy-bishop exercised nearly if not quite the whole of the episcopal functions, saying mass and vespers, giving benedictions, preaching sermons, going on visitations, occasionally filling up vacancies, and if he died during the time being buried with episcopal honors. Moreover, these pseudo-clergy, arrayed in their vestments, perambulated the neighborhood and demanded from passers-by and householders some small money tribute, which was known as the Bishop's Subsidy. Royalty itself deigned to be amused with the burlesque ritual of the mimic prelate. In the year 1299 we find Edward I., on his way to Scotland, permitting one of these boy-bishops to say vespers before him on the 7th of December, the day after St. Nicholas's Day, in his chapel at Hetton, near Newcastle-upon-Tyne, and making a considerable present to the said bishop and certain other boys that came and sang with him on the occasion. What was the custom in the houses of the nobles may be learned from the "Northumberland Household Book," which tells us that "My lord useth and accustomyth to gyfe yerly, upon Saynt Nicolas-Even, if he kepe chapell for Saynt Nicolas, to the master of his childeren of his chapell, for one of the childeren of his chapell, yerely, vi$^{s.}$ viii$^{d.}$; and if Saynt Nicolas com owt of the towne wher my lord lyeth, and my lord kepe no chapell, than to have yerely iii$^{s.}$ iiij$^{d.}$"

The fun grew faster and more furious in the last days of the juvenile episcopacy. Towards the end of evensong on December 27 the little Nicholas and his clerks, arrayed in their copes, bearing lighted tapers, and singing the words of the Apocalypse (chap. xiv.), " Centum quadraginta," walked in procession from the choir to the altar of the Blessed Trinity, which the boy-bishop incensed; afterwards they all sang the anthem, and he recited the prayer commemorative of the Holy Innocents. Going back into the choir, these boys took possession of the upper canons' stalls, and those dignitaries themselves had to serve in the boys' place, and carry the candles, the thurible, and the book, like acolytes, thurifers, and lower clerks. Standing on high, wearing his mitre, and holding his pastoral staff in his left hand, the boy-bishop gave a solemn benediction to all present, and, while making the sign of the cross over the kneeling crowd, said,—

Crucis signo vos consigno; vestra sit tuitio,
Quos nos emit et redemit suæ carnis pretio.

The next day, the feast itself of Holy Innocents, the boy-bishop preached a sermon, which had been written for him, probably by some distinguished prelate. Thus, one from the pen of Erasmus, "Concio de Puero Jesu," spoken by a boy of St. Paul's School, London, is still preserved.

The Reformers looked askance at all these and similar "mummeries," and in 1542 Cranmer issued a sweeping proclamation against them : "Whereas heretofore dyverse and many superstitions and childysshe observations have been used, and yet to this day are observed and kept in many and sondry parties of this realm, as upon Sainte Nicolas, Sainte Catheryne, Sainte Clement, the Holy Innocentes, and such like ; children be strangelye decked and apparelid to counterfaite priestes, byshoppes, and women ; and so ledde with songes and daunces from house to house, bleassing the people, and gatherynge of monye, and boyes doo singe masse and preache in the pulpitt . . . the Kyng's majestie willith and commaundeth that from henceforth all suche superstitions be loste and clyerlye exstinguished."

Queen Mary restored the ceremonial which her father had abrogated. Strype in his " Ecclesiastical Memorials" informs us that in 1556 on the 5th day of December " St. Nicholas, that is, a boy habited like a bishop *in pontificalibus*, went abroad in most parts of London, singing after the old fashion, and was received by many ignorant but well-disposed people into their houses, and had as much good cheer as ever was wont to be had before, at least in many places."

With the final establishment of Protestantism in England the pastime of the boy-bishop disappeared; but the well-known festivity of the Eton Montem appears to have originated in and been a continuance under another form of the mediæval custom.

Brabo or **Brabon of Brussels.** A gigantic figure which, with that of his wife Sumniana, is preserved in the City Hall of Brussels and takes part in all the parades and processions held on the feast of St. Gudula and other important occasions. (See GIANTS, PROCESSIONS OF.) According to local tradition, Servius Brabo was one of the generals of Julius Cæsar, married to a niece of the latter. He was likewise the first Duke of Brabant and the first Marquis of Antwerp. This last dignity he assumed after encouraging seven young men from Antwerp to kill Antigonus (*q. v.*), a giant who was terrorizing Antwerp. Brabo, from whom descended a long line of dukes and likewise the brothers Aymon and Pepin of Landen, perished at Rome with Julius Cæsar. The legend is probably a distorted summary of many popular fictions.

Bread, Holy. (Fr. *pain bénit ;* Lat. *panis benedictus.*) The distribution of holy bread is a Catholic rite entirely distinct from the administration of the communion, yet the two are frequently confounded together by Protestant travellers. In England before the Reformation the distribution used to take place every Sunday after the principal mass. Probably this was the custom all through the Western Church. At present the ceremony is only occasional. The holy bread has nothing sacramental in its nature. It is ordinary leavened bread, cut into small pieces, blessed, and given to the people after the manner of the love-feasts of the early Church, as a symbol of the fellowship and

DISTRIBUTING THE BLESSED BREAD.
(From Picart.)

brotherly love which should exist among all who are of the same household of faith. In some cases we have evidence that the rich and powerful among the English relieved the parishioners from the burden of providing the holy bread by taking it upon themselves. Thus, on Palm Sunday in 1361, the then head of the great house of Berkeley offered to Our Blessed Lady in Berkeley Church a pound of virgin wax, "*pro candela caritatis*," and a bushel of fine wheat, "*pro pane benedicto*," an offering which was continued for many generations.

The distribution of holy bread does not seem to have been discontinued at once on the change of religion, for one of the rubrics at the end of the communion office in the Prayer Book of 1549 provides that "In such chapels annexed, where the people hath not been accustomed to pay any holy bread, there they must

either make some charitable provision for the bearing of the
charges of the communion, or else (for receiving the same) resort
to their parish church."

It appears from Foxe's "Acts and Monuments," ed. 1861, vol.
vii. p. 461, that Latimer reluctantly permitted the use of holy
water and holy bread in his diocese, because, his historian explains, the days were then "so dangerous and variable that he
could not in all things do what he would." With the Protestant
settlement under Elizabeth, holy bread, which had been restored
by Queen Mary, seems to have entirely disappeared from the
Anglican Church.

Many legends are preserved of miracles performed by the
saints with holy bread. A fragment of a holy loaf blessed
by St. Cuthbert cured an officer of King Egfrid's court of a
dangerous sickness. St. Bernard of Clairvaux used the holy
bread with great efficacy in at least two cases. Laymen sometimes brought the bread home with them and used it as a charm
against the bite of mad dogs, and as a destroyer of rats.

It has furnished the French with certain figures of speech.
A well-merited disgrace is spoken of as *pain bénit*, and there is
the idiom "C'est pain bénit que d'escroquer un avare," which
Chambaud renders, "'Tis nuts to one to cheat a covetous man."
(EDWARD PEACOCK, in *The Antiquary*, vol. xvii. p. 191.)

Brides of Venice. It was an ancient usage among the
Venetians for twelve poor virgins, endowed by the state, to be
united to their lovers, every year, on St. Mary's Eve, in the
church of St. Peter the Apostle at Olivolo. These virgins were
styled "the Brides of Venice," and upon the auspicious day
aforementioned the relatives and friends of the betrothed assembled on the island of Olivolo, laden with presents for the happy
couples. During the reign of Pietro Sanudo II. the corsairs of
Trieste, who were acquainted with the annual custom, resolved
to profit by the unarmed state of the joyful train and to ravish
the "Brides of Venice." The pirates concealed themselves in
an uninhabited portion of Olivolo, and when the bridal procession had entered the church they quitted their hiding-place,
forced their way into the church, tore the terrified maidens from
the foot of the altar, bore them to their vessels, and set sail for
Trieste. The Doge, followed by the injured lovers, summoned
the people to arms, and gave chase in a few vessels belonging to
the corporation of Trunk-Makers, who occupied a quarter in
the parish of Santa Maria Formosa, and who offered their ships
to the Doge and his companions. The pirates were overtaken
and destroyed, and the "brides" were borne back in triumph to
Olivolo, where great festivities celebrated their return. To

commemorate this event, a solemn procession of young virgins, attended by the Doge and the clergy, paid a visit in each succeeding year to the parish of Santa Maria Formosa, where they were hospitably received by the Trunk-Makers. The heavy reverses which were terminated by the battle of Chioggia led to a discontinuation of the custom for a while, but it was afterwards renewed.

Bridget or **Bride, St.** (450–521), patroness of Ireland, called also **Thaumaturga,** or the "wonder-worker." Her festival is celebrated on the reputed anniversary of her death, February 1. Born at Fouchard, in the county of Louth, the illegitimate child of an Irishman named Dulbach, she early took the veil at the hands of St. Mel, a disciple of St. Patrick, and retired into a cell at Kildare,—*i.e.,* "the cell of the oak." Here she was soon joined by so numerous a community that she was compelled to separate the members into distinct bodies and to build nunneries for them in different parts of the country, all of which acknowledged her as their mother and foundress. To these scanty historical particulars legend has added a mass of fables.

St. Bridget's body was interred at the church of Kildare, where her nuns for many years honored her memory by keeping a fire forever burning. Hence the church was known as the House of Fire, until in 1220 the Archbishop of Dublin, "to take away all occasion of superstition," ordered the fire to be extinguished. Long before this the body had been translated to Downpatrick. Here, in 1185, it was found in a triple vault with the bodies of St. Patrick and St. Columba. The Pope's legate caused all these relics to be translated, in the presence of fifteen bishops and an immense concourse of clergy, nobility, and people, to a more honorable place in the cathedral of Down. This was destroyed by Henry VIII. St. Bridget's head, however, was saved by some of the clergy and carried to Neustadt in Austria. In 1587 the Emperor Rudolf II. gave it to the church of the Jesuits at Lisbon.

Bruno, St., the founder of the Carthusian order of monks. His feast is celebrated on the anniversary of his death, October 6 (1101). A member of the noble family of d'Hartenfaust, he was born at Cologne about 1035. Embracing the clerical life, he first became famous as the opponent of Manasses, who in 1067 obtained the archbishopric of Rheims by simoniacal methods and whose life had become a public scandal. At the Council held in Autun in 1077 he and two other canons openly accused the archbishop, who was suspended by the Papal legate, but for a period was able to defy the rulers of the Church and to drive his accusers from their homes. They took refuge in the castle of the Count de Ronci, where they remained until the following year.

And now at length the indignation of the populace did what the rulers of the Church could not do, for in 1079 the people of Rheims drove the unworthy archbishop out of their city; he retired to the court of the King of Germany, and died there outside the pale of the Church.

It is according to the Carthusian tradition that Bruno, shortly after these events, was the witness of a miracle: this was nothing less than the resurrection of Raymond, a learned doctor of Paris, over whose body the funeral service was being read in the church of Notre-Dame. In the middle of the service, says the legend, Raymond rose upon the bier and called out, in terrifying tones, "I am justly accused," again, "I am judged," and again, "I am condemned." The tradition continues that Bruno was so profoundly impressed by this occurrence that he determined to spend the rest of his life in solitude, that he might by prayer and penance bring peace to his soul. The story was at one period widely believed, for it found a place in the Roman breviary, but it has not even that substratum of fact which the severest critic can discover in some alleged miracles of the Middle Ages; for a long time, indeed, the best ecclesiastical writers have rejected it, and Urban VIII. wisely expunged it from the breviary. In a letter of which the text has been preserved, Bruno himself, writing to his friend Ralph le Vert, at that time Church-provost and subsequently Archbishop of Rheims, suggests a far simpler explanation of the whole matter: his own heart's longings were more powerful than the doctor and the miracle.

In 1084 Bruno at last carried out the dream of his life, and with six companions founded his first oratory at Chartreuse, not far from the spot where the first great monastery of the order followed in 1137. This monastery, as well as those built to replace it in later times (several of which were destroyed by fire), has been known as La Grande Chartreuse, and has always been recognized by Carthusians as the mother-house of their order. Bruno himself died at another monastery which he founded at Calabria. His body is in the church of St. Stephen at Torre, but portions of his bones have been distributed among different churches of the order. A part of his jaw, with two teeth, is at the Grande Chartreuse.

In 1514, four centuries after Bruno's death, Pope Leo X. authorized the Carthusians to make use of a special office in honor of their founder; this was regarded as equivalent to beatification; but Bruno was not canonized until 1623, during the pontificate of Gregory XV.

The Carthusian is one of the austerest of monastic orders. The original rules as recorded by contemporaries enjoined absolute silence save on Sundays at dinner, and total abstinence from flesh meat, a rule not relaxed even in case of sickness. On Tuesdays and Saturdays they ate nothing but vegetables; Mondays, Thursdays, and Fridays, only brown bread. On Sundays and holidays they feasted on bread and cheese, and added fish if these were presented to them. Meagre as their meals were, they ate only once a day, save on Sundays and holidays. A hair shirt was worn next to the skin, and next to the hair shirt nothing save their white robes crowned with white hoods. Their whole heads are shaven. One custom is peculiar to the order. Once a week the convent gates are opened and all the solitaries go forth in twos for a walk among the mountains, through the forests, or over the flowery meadows.

Buddha, Sacred Tooth of. There are no fewer than twelve dental relics of Gautama Buddha enshrined in India, and seven in China. Far the most famous of all is the one preserved in the Dalada Malagawa, or great temple of the Sacred Tooth, in Kandy, Ceylon. It is the aim of every good Buddhist to make a pilgrimage hither at least once in his lifetime. Innumerable Buddhist royalties have enriched the shrine with costly gifts. When the Portuguese occupied the island, the Roman Catholic priests, recognizing what a centre of Buddhism the temple was, seized the sacred tooth and took it on board one of the Portuguese ships, where it was placed in a mortar, pounded to dust by the Archbishop of Goa himself, and then cast into the river. But all without avail. The particles came together again, and next day the Buddhist priests found the relic, sound and whole as ever, reposing within a lotos-leaf. It was carefully replaced in the sanctuary of the temple, where it still remains. Only at rare intervals, when ready money becomes necessary for the support of the many priests, is the relic exhibited. These occasions attract immense crowds of pilgrims. Generous donors are granted a prolonged stare, smaller donors are allowed to look and move on, while the rest, whose offerings are insignificant, but who are admitted on the principle that "mony a mickle maks a muckle," are hurried past.

All that the visitor can do at ordinary times is to stare through an iron grating at a huge silver-gilt bell-shaped shrine. This encloses six other shrines of pure gold of decreasing sizes, one placed within the other. Each is full of jewels and idols. The last and smallest contains the sacred tooth. Burrows describes the latter as an "oblong piece of discolored ivory, tapering to a point, and about one and one-fourth inches in length, and half an inch in diameter at the base. It is not in the least like a human tooth, and more resembles that of a crocodile or large pig."

Bunker Hill Day, also known jocularly and colloquially as Boston's Fourth of July. The anniversary of the battle of Bunker Hill (fought on June 17, 1775), which is celebrated with great pomp throughout Massachusetts. In Boston itself the centre of the commemoration is the monument on Bunker Hill.

It is only necessary briefly to sum up the story of the battle. Enough that the yeomanry of Charlestown and the Boston suburbs took up their position within a rough extemporized fortification on Bunker Hill, in defiance of the British army; that at one o'clock of the afternoon of June 17 the red-coats landed in good order at Moulton's Point, and immediately formed in three lines, while the barges returned to Boston for more troops, who arrived at three; that the British, some three thousand strong, advanced upon the American works; that they were driven back with fearful slaughter; that they advanced again, with the flames of the burning town to veil their movements, and were again repulsed; that they rallied again with reinforcements against the Americans, who were not only worn down with labor and fasting, but out of ammunition; and at about five o'clock, after this bloody conflict of an hour and a half with raw volunteers, these picked soldiers of the British army took possession of the hill, with more than a thousand dead and wounded as the price of their victory, among these two hundred and twenty-six being among the killed. The Americans had one hundred and forty killed, two hundred and seventy-one wounded, and thirty captured, or four hundred and forty-one in all, in a force probably not exceeding fifteen hundred men actually engaged. The British had less than four thousand men engaged on the field, according to Richard Frothingham's excellent history of the battle, but he apparently does not include the sailors and gunners in the British ships who were so active in the fight, and who killed the first American in the fort.

In 1794 the Freemasons of Charlestown built a monument of brick and wood, twenty-five feet high, upon the summit of the hill. This was replaced in 1825, the semi-centennial of the battle, by a massive obelisk two hundred and twenty-one feet high and thirty feet square, the corner-stone being laid on Bunker Hill Day in that year amid a concourse of fifty thousand people. The presence of La Fayette as the guest of the occasion and of Daniel Webster as its orator made this one of the great events in American civic history. Webster's oration (together with the oration that he delivered on Bunker Hill Day in 1843) is ranked among his most masterly performances, and would alone serve to immortalize the occasion. The centennial jubilee of the battle was another memorable event, celebrated June 17, 1875, at which Judge Charles Devens delivered a notable address.

Burns Festival. A celebration in honor of the birthday (January 25) of Robert Burns (1759–1796), the great lyric poet

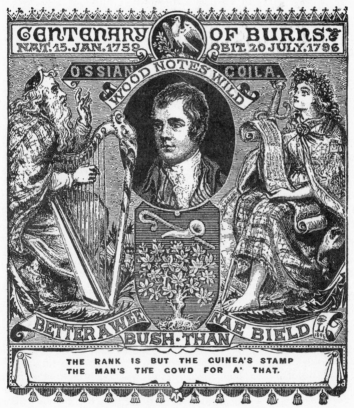

PROGRAMME OF THE BURNS FESTIVAL, 1896.
(Designed by John Leighton, F.S.A.)

of Scotland, is annually held in most of the large Scotch cities, but especially at his native city of Ayr. *Blackwood's Magazine* for September, 1844, gives a long account of the earliest celebration of this sort.

It is curious to note that Burns himself had jocularly anticipated this. In a letter to his early patron Gavin Hamilton in 1786 he says, " For my own affairs I am in a fair way of becoming as eminent as Thomas à Kempis or John Bunyan, and you may expect henceforth to see my birthday inscribed among the wonderful events in the Poor Robin and Aberdeen Almanacks, along with the Black-Monday and the Battle of Bothwell Bridge." But even in his most burlesque mood he could not have exaggerated the interest which greeted the centennial anniversary of his birth in 1859, when celebrations were held not only in every town in Scotland, but wherever English is spoken,—in the United States, in Canada, in Victoria, in Calcutta, in Hong-Kong, in Natal. He could not even as a joke have anticipated that a great festival would be held at the Crystal Palace, Sydenham, nor that a perfect flood of Burnsiana should have inundated the literary world. The centenary of his death was celebrated with equal pomp on July 20, 1896.

Butchers' Leap. (Ger. *Metzgersprung.*) A festival celebrated once every three years by the butchers of Munich on Fasching Montag (the Monday before Lent), in commemoration of the manner in which their predecessors aided the coopers (see COOPERS' DANCE) in suppressing the after-effects of the plague of 1517. This was simply by leaping into the public fountain, to prove to the people that the water was harmless.

The butchers begin the day by attending high mass at St. Peter's Church, close to the Marienplatz, where the fountain is situated. Then they form themselves into solemn procession. First come the musicians, on foot, followed by a baker's dozen of chubby boys, sons of the master-butchers, ranging in age from four to six years, elaborately tricked out in green and scarlet, and mounted on their fathers' great dray-horses, whose bridles are held by the fathers themselves, the latter in dress-coats and white gloves, carrying enormous bouquets in their hands. Then ride ten butchers' apprentices (the leapers of the day), in scarlet jackets and green hats, followed by another detachment of master-butchers, on foot. Last of all walk two men in scarlet jackets and flower-adorned hats, bearing aloft on their shoulders two huge silver flagons, hung over with large silver medals, coins, and chains. These flagons are of great antiquity and belong to the butchers' guild. In this manner the procession marches in succession to the various royal palaces. Entering at each, they present bouquets and tender a loving-cup to be passed around among the princes and their families.

By four o'clock in the afternoon the round of royalty has been made, and everything is ready for the Leap. The ten apprentices, their scarlet and gold exchanged for sheepskin garments all hung over with party-colored calves' tails, range themselves round the stone edge of the fountain, ready for the plunge. A master-butcher puts them through a series of questions: as to what they want; if they know what an honor it is to belong to the ancient, most loyal and honorable guild of butchers; if they are ready and willing to prove their courage and show themselves worthy of the privilege they ask, etc.; to all of which they answer in proper formula. Then a basket containing wine and a number of small glasses is brought, and the master-butcher, having filled a glass for each of the shaggy apprentices and one for himself, tells them to drink to the health of H. R. H. the Prince Regent. A loud " *Lebe hoch !*" rings out; the eleven glasses are emptied at the same moment, and thrown into the fountain. More than fifty times this toasting is repeated (fortunately the glasses are very small, and the wine not of the strongest quality), until the health of every member of the royal family of Bavaria, young and old, is drunk, besides that of the ministers, mayors, and principal authorities of Munich.

Then the master-butcher, giving the nearest apprentice a sounding blow on the shoulder, tells him and his companions to do their duty; which they do by jumping, all ten, into the fountain, at the same time, with a tremendous splash, and there floundering about. Several baskets of apples and nuts are emptied out into the small space round the fountain, which has been kept clear by the police and soldiers from the invasion of the crowd.

Then begins the tug of war. The youngsters in the crowd commence pushing and squeezing themselves through, scrambling and fighting for the apples and nuts, while the ten monsters in the fountain, catching up the little blue-and white buckets there ready to hand, dash the water with a will over the shrieking urchins, who, fleeing one moment before the deluge, return the next, impelled by their overwhelming desire for the apples and nuts, only to rush screaming away again as another drenching shower greets their hardihood.

After this has continued about ten or fifteen minutes, and the space round the fountain is converted into a lake on which floats the débris of the apples and nuts, the newly-made butchers come out of their bath, dripping like so many waterdogs; a white cloth is tied round their necks, over which are hung a quantity of silver medals as reward for their prowess, and the *Metzgersprung* is over. (*Catholic World*, December, 1896, p. 313.)

Butchers' Serenade. A sort of London Charivari (*pace* **Mr.** Punch) anciently performed by the metropolitan butchers. These made a point of attending in front of the house where a marriage party was in progress. Each had a cleaver and a marrow-bone, and by striking these instruments together they produced a rude sort of music which was expected to draw forth gratuities from the wedding guests. The group sometimes consisted of four, but eight was considered the right complement. The cleaver of each being ground to the production of a single note, a full band produced a complete octave, and if well trained the effect was not unlike that of a peal of bells. When this serenade occurred in the evening the men would be dressed in clean blue aprons and wear an enormous wedding favor of white paper in their hats. The men of Clare Market were reputed to be the best performers. It cannot be added that the appearance of the serenaders was always hailed with joy by the serenaded, but it was the delight of the street-boys, who frequently joined in the music with tin canisters filled with pebbles. Hogarth in the Marriage of the Industrious Apprentice preserves what was no unusual spectacle in his time, the arrival of the butcher serenaders, who in the exercise of their ancient right push aside the legitimate musicians that had been engaged for the occasion. Such affrays frequently led to broken heads and the intervention of the police. (See CHARIVARI.)

Byzant, Bezant, Besant, or **Byzantine.** A coin of pure gold, so named from having been first struck at Byzantium (Constantinople) in the reign of the Emperor Constantine the Great. These coins, or the gold circles representing them (for they sometimes bore no impression), were introduced into Europe by the Crusaders, and became current from the ninth century downward. In England they continued to circulate till they were superseded by the noble of Edward III. (1327–1347), and varied in value from fifteen pounds, when first introduced, down to a sovereign, and finally to nine shillings four and one-half pence. Owing to the association of the byzant with the Crusades,—it was the coin in which the higher class of soldiers that bore the cross were paid,—it acquired a sort of sacred character. This accounts for the frequency of its appearance on heraldic shields. Three byzants became the badge of the Medici family, and were thence adopted as the national arms of Lombardy. The Lombards became the first bankers or professional money-lenders in England, and hence we have the three byzants or balls now employed as the sign for a pawnbroker. The offering of gold made by the English sovereigns at the altar on receiving communion, and on other occasions, was called their byzant, and amounted to fifteen pounds; and this sum the monarch continued to present down to 1752. Sometimes, in a more generous or penitent mood, his offering was a wedge of gold of the value of thirty pounds. In the historical chronicle of the *Gentleman's Magazine* for January 1, 1752, we find the following: " Was a great court at St. James's to compliment his Majesty and the royal family, but, on account of the mourning for the Queen of Denmark (his Majestie's daughter), his Majesty did not go to the royal chapel to offer the byzant." Camden, in his " Remains," article " Money," says that " a great piece of gold valued at fifteen pounds, which the King offereth on high festival days, is yet called a Byzantine, which was anciently a piece of money coined by the Emperors of Constantinople; but afterwards there were two, purposely made for the king and queen, with the resemblance of the Trinity, inscribed, ' *In honorem Sanctæ Trinitatis,*' and on the other side a figure of the Virgin Mary, with the inscription, ' *In honorem Sanctæ Mariæ Virginis.*' " Byzants of this character continued to be used till the first year of James I., who had new coins cast—one for the king and one for the queen—with different inscriptions. A writer in 1779 says, " It is a very common idea (though not at the present strictly true) that our kings offer on New Year's Day a byzant, or wedge of gold. Whatever may have been the ancient custom, the present royal offering, whenever the king communicates at the altar, is five guineas." He adds, " There is no offering on New Year's Day, but that made for the king by the lord chamberlain on Twelfth Day is a box containing three purses, wherein are separately contained leaf-gold, frankincense, and myrrh, in imitation of the offerings of the Magi." The latter custom is still kept up by the British sovereign on the feast of the Epiphany (*q. v.*).

The town of Shaftesbury, in Dorsetshire, England, stands upon the brow of a lofty hill, and till a comparatively recent period its inhabitants had to depend for their water-supply on the little village of Enmore Green, which lies below it in the valley. Now, the burgesses of Shaftesbury were frequently in the habit of paying the lord of the manor of Enmore a stated sum annually—not improbably an actual byzant—for the water-privilege conceded them. But in process of time the byzant became commuted into a different form, viz., into that of a " trophy," the presentation of which constituted a formal acknowledgment of obligation and indebtedness yearly made by the mayor and town council of Shaftesbury to the lord of Enmore. On the morning of each Rogation Monday the town authorities, leading burgesses, etc., went in solemn state and procession to Enmore Green, where they were met by the

steward of the manor. The mayor then formally presented the
"trophy" to him, along with a calf's head (uncooked), a gallon
of ale, two penny loaves, and a pair of gloves edged with gold
lace, craving, at the same time, permission to use the wells as
of old times. The steward, like a prudent man, retained the
comestibles, ale, and gloves, but returned the "trophy" to the
good people of Shaftesbury. Leave was granted to use the
wells, and the ceremony, of course, wound up with a dinner.

The "trophy," or byzant, which gave name to the festival, was
constructed of ribbons and peacock feathers, attached to a large
wooden frame, around which were hung jewels, coins, and
medals, lent for the occasion by the gentry of the districts.
From a quotation in Brand's "Popular Antiquities," *s. v.* "Parochial Perambulations in Rogation Week," it would seem that the
trophy was anciently called the Prize Besom (or Broom); and it
may be that Bezant in this connection is a corruption of Besom.

Latterly the festival degenerated, and, on the town falling
into the hands of the Superior of Enmore in 1830 and being
consolidated therewith, the ceremony was discontinued.

C.

Cader Idris. (Welsh, "Chair of Idris.")   Tennyson refers
to this chair in "Geraint and Enid:"

> And when Geraint
> Beheld her first in field, awaiting him,
> He felt, were she the prize of bodily force,
> Himself beyond the rest pushing could move
> The chair of Idris.

On the summit of Cader Idris, a mountain-peak in Merioneth-
shire, Wales, there is a hollow, couch-like excavation, and this is
called the "Chair of Idris." The mountain is situated in what
was supposed to have been King Arthur's territory. It was a
tradition among the Welsh bards that whoever should pass the
night upon this seat would be found the next morning either
dead, mad, or endowed with supernatural powers. This tradition is alluded to in Mrs. Hemans's poem "The Rock of Cader-
Idris."

Idris figures in Welsh tradition as a prince, a magician, and an
astronomer. All authorities agree, however, upon his giant-like
proportions. In the "Lake of the Three Pebbles" near the base
of the mountain are three large blocks of stone which the giant
is said to have shaken out of one of his boots.

Calendar. (From the Latin word *Kalendæ*, or "Calends.") The standard by which aggregations of human beings agree to measure the years, months, and days. Every Protestant and Roman Catholic nation now accepts what is known as the Gregorian calendar, the most nearly accurate ever devised by the wit of man. Japan has recently followed suit. But the Greek Church adheres to the Julian calendar, and the Jews, Mohammedans, and Chinese have each a different calendar, which will be considered in turn.

As every one knows, the earth revolves round its axis, and also travels round the sun, the one revolution causing the alternation of day and night, the other that of the seasons. From the earliest times men have made use of both these series of changes as a means of reckoning time, and had there been a simple numerical relation between them there need never have been any trouble.

Unfortunately this is not the case. The number of revolutions which the earth makes when it goes once round the sun, instead of being a whole number, is a number and a fraction; or, in other words, the earth goes round the sun in three hundred and sixty-five days, five hours, forty-eight minutes, and forty-six seconds, or 365.2422 days. This was not discovered in a day. Various guesses were made at the proper length of the year, and calendars were drawn up in accordance with them.

The primeval system of reckoning time was based on the moon's changes, as is shown in our word "month." By the ruling of the moon months were reckoned with either twenty-nine or thirty days. Soon the recurrence of the seasons suggested the year. But now great difficulty was experienced in fitting the right number of days into a month, and the right number of months into a year. One of the earliest means devised was that in use among the Egyptians. By their arrangement the year was made up of the seasons, and included three hundred and sixty-five days, with twelve months of thirty days each. To fill out the lack arising from this system of months, five supplementary days were added at the end of the year.

The Jews reckoned their year as composed of twelve lunar months of twenty-nine and thirty days alternately, and the resulting discrepancy was relieved by the occasional introduction of a thirteenth month. The Syrians, Macedonians, and kindred peoples generally followed the Jewish method. In pursuing this reckoning seven years in a cycle of nineteen have this intercalary month, and the number of days in any year varies from three hundred and fifty-three to three hundred and eighty-five.

The ancient Greeks made their year to consist of twelve really lunar months, but Solon in 594 B.C. made a law for the Athenians that the months should comprise twenty-nine and thirty days, with the addition of an intercalary period occasionally. Afterwards three times in eight years a month of thirty days was added, by which means the average length of each year was made to be three hundred and sixty-four and one-fourth days. Ancient Rome had but ten months in the year, but in the time of its kings the lunar year was introduced, numbering three hundred and fifty-five days in the twelve months, an occasional intercalary month being employed to make the necessary rectification. The whole matter was left to the College of the Pontifices, or priests who superintended the state religion. Theirs was the duty to watch the seasons and see when an intercalation was needed, and thus keep the year balanced. Unfortunately, the Pontifices were politicians first and priests afterwards. Their judgment as to the necessity of intercalation was governed largely by the consideration whether to lengthen or shorten the year would accommodate a friend or gratify a grudge. At last the year was so thoroughly out of joint that Cicero speaks of being delayed by the equinoctial storm in October.

This was the condition of things when Cæsar, being Pontifex Maximus and thus having the official direction of the calendar, undertook a permanent reform. He consulted with Sosigenes, an Egyptian astronomer. Basing his calculations upon the assumption that the year is just three hundred and sixty-five days and six hours long, he provided three years of three hundred and sixty-five days followed by one of three hundred and sixty-six. (See LEAP-YEAR.) If the earth had any respect for round numbers, this arrangement would have been unimpeachable. But in point of fact its solar revolution is performed in just about eleven minutes less time than Cæsar had imagined. Consequently the Julian calendar made the year eleven minutes too long, the error amounting to a day in one hundred and twenty-eight years. In the course of the centuries the equinox gradually receded towards the beginning of the year.

Now, the equinox was an important date in the Catholic Church. The Council of Nice, which had assembled in 325 A.D., ordered, among other matters, that Easter should be celebrated on the first Sunday after the full moon next following the vernal equinox. This was a guide to other Church festivals. Advent Sunday, Ascension Day, Whitsuntide, Trinity Sunday, the forty days of Lent, the Ember days, the Rogation days, and others, depended upon Easter. They had become, in the course of ages, fasts and festivals intermingled with the daily concerns of life. Planting and harvesting, dairy-work and sheep-shearing, felling of timber and salving of kine, brewing ale, preparing conserves, curing meats, housing garden-stuffs, distilling domestic spirits, and drying medicinal herbs grew during the Dark Ages into superstitious connection with certain holy days. But as every revolving year failed to bring the earth quite back to the same point in the ecliptic, the sun that warmed, the stars that were supposed to vivify, and the elements that nourished the sown seed grew slack in their work. The value of old traditions decreased. Calculations failed. Farmers believed the seasons to be changing. In the fifteenth century nine days of variation had taken place, and the gap was constantly widening.

At last Pope Gregory XIII. effected a new reformation of the calendar, in a bull dated March 1, 1582.

To restore the civil year to a correspondence with the astronomical, he ordered that the 5th of October, 1582, should be called the 15th. To prevent the intrusion of the same errors in the measurement of time in future ages, and to secure the recurrence of the festivals of the Church at the same period of the year, he further decreed that every year whose number is not divisible by four shall consist of three hundred and sixty-five days; every year which is so divisible, but not divisible by one hundred, of three hundred and sixty-six days; every year divisible by one hundred, but not by four hundred, of three hundred and sixty-five; and every year divisible by four hundred, of three hundred and sixty-six. A more perfect correspondence of the civil and astronomical years will probably never be obtained. In the preparation of this rule every source of disagreement is estimated, and as far as possible corrected. The allowance of an extra day every fourth year is indeed a small excess; but this is not allowed to accumulate, for at the commencement of every century the centennial year is not to consist of three hundred and sixty six days, or, in other words, is not to be counted a leap-year, unless its number can be divided by four hundred. Thus, the year 1600 was a leap-year, and the year 2000 will be the same; but the years 1700 and 1800 contained, and the year 1900 will contain, only three hundred and sixty-five days.

Pope Gregory's correction gives an average year of 365.2425 days, or twenty-six seconds longer than the true year. These odd seconds will amount to a whole year in 3323 years, and it has been proposed to allow for this error by providing that the year 4000 and all its multiples shall be common years. But this would be pedantic foresight, and it is unnecessary to discuss the question whether the year 4000 ought or ought not to be a leap-year. In ages yet to come, when the friction of the tides shall have so retarded the rotation of the earth that three hundred and sixty-five days will make a year, leap-years will be unnecessary. But that is a still remoter contingency, and in the

11

mean time Pope Gregory's calendar is likely to remain in its present form.

And now an extraordinary bit of bigotry must be recorded. The Gregorian calendar, exacted by necessity, founded upon science, recommended by common sense, and universal in benefit, was at first accepted only in Catholic countries. In the Protestant states of Germany the Julian calendar was retained until 1700, and the Gregorian in its entirety was not received until 1774. In Denmark and Sweden the reformed calendar was accepted in 1700. Scotland adopted it in 1600. But England held out until 1751. It was then enacted that eleven days should be omitted after the 2d of September, 1752, so that the ensuing day should be the 14th. The enactment was not carried out without bitter popular opposition. Many honest Protestants imagined that they were defrauded by some Papistical or devilish ingenuity of the days omitted from the calendar. "Give us back our eleven days," was a cry with which many an unpopular statesman was greeted. Russia, Greece, and the smaller states, such as Servia, belonging to the Greek Church, are the only countries now adhering to the Julian calendar, which is known as Old Style, frequently abbreviated to O. S., while the Gregorian is New Style, or N. S.

At present—since 1800 was a leap-year according to Old Style and a common year according to New Style—there is a difference of twelve days between the styles. The resultant inconveniences in Russia and Greece are very great. Letters to foreign countries, orders for shipments, times of departure for steamers and sailing-vessels, news from abroad, advertisements of the holding of international fairs, and one knows not what besides, must all bear two dates,—Old Style and New. The mariner cannot read the nautical almanac, nor the merchant accept a draft from abroad, nor the broker determine foreign exchanges, without having two dates at hand. Advices cannot be understood, bills of lading cannot be made effective, telegrams cannot be comprehended, without an extra labor, small in each instance, but large in the aggregate, which the Julian calendar in Russia imposes. "Does he mean Old Style or New?" is a question asked in St. Petersburg and Moscow thousands of times in a day.

The calendar underwent some fantastic changes at the time of the French Revolution. The Convention charged its Committee of Public Instruction to mark the new era on which France seemed to be entering by creating a new calendar, which should be purely civil. The excuse was that it had degenerated into a sort of record of saints' days and served chiefly to mark the festivals of the Catholic Church. The new system was presented and adopted in the autumn of 1793, or just at the period of the Terror, with the exception of the names of the months, which as first reported by the committee bore such fantastic names as Jeu de Paume ("ball-playing"), Niveau ("level"), Bastile, Bonnet, Pique ("pike"), etc. The Assembly preferred to call the months first, second, third, etc., after the present manner of the Quakers. The weeks, which represented no natural divisions of time, but served only to perpetuate the superstitions of ancient astrologers, were suppressed, and the month was divided into three decades or fractions of ten days each. The year was divided into twelve months of thirty days each, and kept in its proper relation to the seasons by five days added in ordinary years and six every leap-year. It was proposed that the days should be divided into ten parts, a change that could not be conveniently made at the moment, since it would have rendered necessary the entire remodelling of every clock in France. The new system, being dated backward, went into operation on September 22, 1792, which was the year 1 of the new epoch, but the first year was only three months long, the second beginning on January 1, 1793. Great inconvenience resulted immediately from its practical use. For instance, it was found necessary to employ such phrases as the following : " The first day of the first decade of the first month of the first year of the republic," for which it appeared that life was far too brief, especially when the Terror was beginning to count its victims by the thousand. So the poet Fabre d'Eglantine was charged with the task of finding more suitable names for the months and days. The system of the new almanac-maker was based on nature itself,—that is, nature as seen in the north of France,—and it was intended to serve as a manual of labor and rural instruction for the present.

Here is the calendar as reformed on this educational basis :

Vendémiaire (Vintage), September 22 to October 21.
Brumaire (Foggy), October 22 to November 20.
Frimaire (Sleety), November 21 to December 20.
Nivose (Snowy), December 21 to January 19.
Pluviose (Rainy), January 20 to February 18.
Ventose (Windy), February 19 to March 20.
Germinal (Budding), March 21 to April 19.
Floréal (Flowery), April 20 to May 19.
Prairial (Pasture), May 20 to June 18.
Messidor (Harvest), June 19 to July 18.
Thermidor (Heat), July 19 to August 17.
Fructidor (Fruit), August 18 to September 16.

The system of the decade was not changed, but each day received a name according to its number, as Primidi ("first day"), Duodi ("second day"), etc. One extra day was called Sans-Culottides, to honor the new aristocracy of the common people. They formed half a decade of festal days in which Virtue, Genius. Labor, Opinion, and Rewards were to be celebrated. Nothing can give an idea better than this almanac of the peculiarly unpractical character of the French of that epoch called upon to govern so suddenly after so many ages of absolute servitude. This republican almanac was in use until the year 1806,—that is, nearly twelve years and three months,—when Bonaparte, partly as a compliment to the Papal court, which he desired to conciliate, put an end to it and restored the Gregorian calendar. The change was accomplished in the form of a law proposed to the senate by the government orators, and had the effect of replacing things just where they were at the beginning of 1793. This event occurred in the month Nivose of the so-called year 14, which had lasted but one hundred days, as the year 1 had had an existence of but three months. Such an absurdity as this effort to revolutionize the almanac can never occur again, the inconvenience of a special calendar for a single nation being recognized.

To Auguste Comte we owe the pregnant idea of a calendar for the race, in which every day should recall to us the name of a predecessor memorable in some one of the varied departments of human activity, the whole forming a record of our progress towards civilization intended to rouse gratitude and stimulate effort.

The Jewish calendar is dated from the creation, which is considered to have taken place 3750 years and 3 months before the commencement of the Christian era. The year is luni-solar, and may be ordinary or embolismic. An ordinary year has twelve lunar months, each of twenty-nine or thirty days; an embolismic year has thirteen. Thus, the duration of the ordinary year is three hundred and fifty-four days, and that of the embolismic is three hundred and eighty-four days. In either case it is sometimes made a day more or a day less in order that certain festivals may fall upon proper days of the week for their due observance. The names of the months are Tisri, Hesvan, Kislev, Tebet, Sebat, Adar (with Veadar in embolismic years), Nisan, Yiar, Sivan, Tamuz, Ab, Elul. The New Year, 1st Tisri, occurs anywhere between September 5 and October 5 of our computation.

The Mohammedan calendar is dated from the flight of Mohammed from Mecca to Medina, which was in the night of July 15–16, 622. The years always consist of twelve lunar months. They are partitioned into cycles of thirty years, nineteen of which are common years of three hundred and fifty-four days each; the other eleven are intercalary years having an additional day appended to the last month. The mean length of the year is therefore three hundred and fifty-four days, eight hours, and forty-eight minutes. No attempt is made to square the calendar with the astronomical year, so that the months retrograde through all the seasons in about thirty-two and one-half years. The first day of Muharram is New Year, but it may of course occur in midwinter or in midsummer or at any intervening period.

The Hindoo year began with the new moon preceding the beginning of the solar year, and when two lunar months began within the same solar month the first one was intercalated. If no lunar month began in a particular solar month, the year lost an ordinary month, but two intermediate months were added. Each Hindoo month had a particular name, and the new moons served to fix the beginnings of the months and years. The Hindoo years began with zero, the first year counting as 0, the second as 1, and so on. These were arranged in cycles of sixty years. The Hindoos reckoned their time by "ages," and these were divided into periods. The first age, sometimes called the age of gold and sometimes the age of innocence, was supposed to be 1,728,000 years; the second age, an age of silver, 1,296,000 years; the third age, 864,000 years. The present age is the Kali yuga, or the age of iron; only 4985 years of it have passed, but its total duration is supposed to be 432,000 years.

Some idea of the enormous length of the Hindoo calendar can be gained from the following. The length of a patriarchate is seventy-one maha yugas, or 306,720,000 years, to which is added a twilight period of 1,728,000 years, making in all 308,448,000 years. Fourteen of these patriarchates, augmented by a dawn of 1,728,000 years, give 4,320,000,000 years, which form a Kalpa, or the æon of Hindoo chronology. Now, a Kalpa is only a day in the life of Brahma, whose nights are also of the same duration. Brahma lives a hundred years of three hundred and sixty days and three hundred and sixty nights. Accordingly it is figured that the present epoch is the Kali yuga of the twenty-seventh grand age of the seventh patriarchate of the first æon of the second half of the life of Brahma, who is now in his 155,521,972,848,985th spring. But we should remember that the whole life of Brahma is only a little longer than a single wink of the great god Siva's eye!

The Chinese civil year is regulated by the moon, and from the time of the Han dynasty, two centuries before Christ, has begun with the first day of that moon, during the course of which the sun enters their sign of the zodiac corresponding to our sign Pisces. They have also an astronomical year which is solar, and for the adjustment of these solar and lunar years employ a system similar to our leap-year plan, except that instead of an intercalary day every fourth year, as in the Gregorian calendar, they insert an intercalary month occurring alternately every third and second year in periods of nineteen. The year, therefore, contains thirteen or twelve months according as it has or has not an intercalary one. A month has either twenty-nine or thirty days, the number of days being intended to correspond to the number of days which the moon takes to make the revolution around the earth. A *month*, indeed, means one *moon*, the same Chinese character being used to indicate both. So, too, the number used to indicate the age of the moon at any time denotes also the day of the month; thus, there is always a full moon on the 15th, no moon on the 1st, etc. Consequently the moon always presents the same appearance on the same day in any month from year to year. This plan is particularly convenient for farmers and sailors, whose memory is thus materially assisted in remembering the changes of moon and tides. The era used by the Chinese in their histories is, next to that of the Jews, the oldest employed by any nation, as for over four thousand years they have for chronological purposes made use of a series of daily, monthly, and yearly cycles of sixty. Each day, month, and year has its own name in its cycle, and by compounding these names a single one is made to express the date employed. A new cycle began in 1864. But the common events of every-day life among the Chinese have during these last twenty centuries been dated from the year of the accession of the reigning emperor. Some particular name, usually that of the new sovereign, is given by official proclamation to each reign, the years being numbered 1, 2, 3, 4, etc. A record of these eras is kept, called a Catalogue of the Nienh-hao.

Candle, Sale by. An old method of conducting an auction, which has its most frequent survival in France. In sales of importance the affair is placed in the hands of a notary, who for the time being becomes an auctioneer. The auctioneer is provided with a number of small wax tapers, each capable of burning about five minutes. As soon as a bid is made, one of these tapers is placed in full view of all interested parties and lighted. If before the flame expires another bid is offered, it is immediately extinguished and a fresh taper placed in its stead, and so on until one flickers and dies out of itself, when the last bid becomes irrevocable. This simple plan prevents all contention among rival bidders, and affords a reasonable time for reflection before making a higher offer than the one preceding. By this means, too, the auctioneer is prevented from exercising undue influence upon the bidders or hastily accepting the bid of a favorite.

The custom of selling by candle was once prevalent in England. Pepys refers in his Diary to this in the following extract (September 3, 1662): "After dinner we met and sold the Waymouth, Successe, and Fellowship hulks, when pleasant to see how backward men are at first to bid; and yet, when the candle is going out, how they bawl and dispute afterwards who bid the most first. And here I observed one man cunninger than the rest, that was sure to bid the last man, and to carry it; and inquiring the reason, he told me that just as the flame goes out the smoke descends, which is a thing I never observed before; and by that he do know the instant when to bid last."

A few local survivals of the custom in England are noted by Mr. Ditchfield :

"At Aldermaston, Berks, land is let by means of a lighted candle. The villagers assemble in the school room on the occasion of the letting of the 'Church Acre,' a piece of meadowland which was bequeathed some centuries ago to the vicar and churchwardens of the parish for the expenses of the church. The custom is as follows. A candle is lighted, and one inch below the flame is duly measured off, at which point a pin is inserted. The bidding then commences, and continues till the inch of candle is consumed and the pin drops out. Every three years this ancient ceremony is performed. At Tatworth, near Chard, a sale by lighted candle takes place every year, and at Chedzoy the 'Church Acre' is let every twenty-one years by this means. The land belonging to the parish charities in the village of Corby, near Kettering, is let every eight years by the sale of candle, and the procedure is similar to that which has already been described. Also in Warwickshire, where old customs die hard, the grazing rights upon the roadside and on the common lands at Warton, near Polesworth, have been annually let by the same means. This custom has been observed since the time of George III., when an old Act of Parliament was passed directing that the herbage should be sold by candle-light, and that the last bidder when the flame had burned itself out should be the purchaser. The surveyor presides at the auction, and produces an old book containing the record of the annual lettings since the year 1815. An ordinary candle is then cut into five equal portions, about half an inch high, one for each lot."

At Bremen a long-established custom was discontinued with the end of 1893. Every Friday afternoon, in a room in the old Exchange, a judge and his secretary took their seats, attended by a crier and a servant dressed in a flame-colored coat, and supplied with a box of tiny matches, each of which was intended to burn for one minute. At a given signal a candle was lighted, and the bidding began. At each bid the burning candle was extinguished and a new one lighted, and the property was disposed of only when the candle burned itself out before the receipt of a fresh bid had been announced by the crier.

Candlemas Day, known also as **The Purification of the Blessed Virgin, Christ's Presentation at The Temple,** and colloquially in England as **The Wives' Feast.** A festival

CANDLEMAS PROCESSION IN ROME.
(From Picart.)

celebrated in the Anglican, Roman, and Greek Churches on February 2. This, being the fortieth day after the birth of Christ, was the day on which, according to Levitical rules, the purification of the mother and the presentation of the son should occur. (See CHURCHING OF WOMEN.) The institution of the festival is attributed to Pope Gelasius, in the latter part of the fifth century In many of its details it shows itself to be a Christianization of the pagan Februalia celebrated in ancient Rome at about the same period. In fact, this is expressly acknowledged by Pope Innocent XII. in the course of a sermon: "Why do we in this feast carry candles? Because the Gentiles dedicated the month of February to the infernal gods, and as at the beginning of it Pluto stole Proserpine, and her mother Ceres sought her in the night with lighted candles, so they, at the beginning of this month, walked about the city with lighted candles. Because the holy fathers could not extirpate this custom, they ordained that Christians should carry about candles in honor of the Blessed Virgin; and thus what was done before to the honor of Ceres is now done to the honor of the Virgin." In the Eastern Church the festival was adopted by the Emperor Justinian in 542 under the name of 'Υπαπαντή, or "meeting," because Simeon and Anna the prophetess met in the temple at the presentation of Christ. (Luke ii.) The keynote of the festival in the Greek Church is formed by these words of Simeon addressed to the infant Christ, "A light to lighten the Gentiles, and the glory of thy people Israel." In the West the Virgin came to be the most important figure of the day, and the words of Simeon, "Yea, a sword shall pierce through thine own soul also," were taken to denote the first of her seven sorrows, which were often represented in a matter-of-fact way as seven swords in the heart of the Mater Dolorosa.

The special services of the day among Roman Catholics consist of a blessing of candles by the priests and a distribution of them to the congregation, by which they are afterwards carried lighted in solemn procession.

Before the downfall of the Papacy, the Pope used to officiate at this festival in the chapel of the Quirinal. When he had blessed the candles he distributed them with his own hand among those in the church, each of whom, going singly up to him, knelt to receive it. The cardinals went first; then followed bishops, canons, priors, abbots, priests, and others, down to the sacristans and humblest officers of the Church. Then the candles were lighted, the Pope was seated in his chair and carried in procession, with the chanting of hymns, around the ante-chapel; the throne was stripped of its splendid hangings, the Pope and cardinals took off their gold and crimson robes, and the usual mass of the morning was sung.

It appears that in England, in Catholic times, a meaning was attached to the size of the candles and the manner in which they burned during the procession; that, moreover, the reserved parts of the candles were deemed to possess a strong supernatural virtue.

Candlemas in the Middle Ages was the favorite time for the ceremony among Christian mothers analogous to the Mosaic presentation in the temple. Hence came the custom of bearing candles for those services at other times of the year. In England, however, men were not particularly attentive to the pious custom, for it is recorded that " Men seldom offer candles at women's churchynges saving our Ladie's, but reason it is that she have some preferement;" and, even though she did have some preferment, the English before the Reformation were inclined to find fault because they were not allowed to eat flesh every Saturday with joy and pardon in honor of the Virgin, as was done in Flanders, saying, " the Pope is not so good to us," and drawing the conclusion that there was as good reason for them to eat flesh with the Flemish " as that we shuld bear our Candel to her Churchinge at Candlemas with theym as they doe."

With the Reformation there came a reaction against the high honor paid the Virgin. John Bale in 1554 complained that it was a Romish error " to beare their Candels soberly and to offer them to the Saintes, not of God's makynge, but the Carvers and Paynters," and in the thirtieth year of his reign Henry VIII. issued a proclamation, saying, " On Candelmas Daye it shall be declared that the bearynge of Candels is done in the memorie of Christe, the spirituall lyghte whom Simeon dyd prophecye, as it is redde in the Churche that daye." This brought the festival back to the old Greek meaning. In the most ancient pictures and mosaics Simeon is the figure of importance, as the type of those who recognized and embraced the Messiah, and his song, the " Nunc Dimittis," furnished one of the names by which the day was known.

On Candlemas Eve all Christmas greens must be taken down. Herrick has this little poem on the subject :

A Ceremony upon Candlemas Eve.

Down with the Rosemary, and so
Down with the Baies and Mistletoe ;
Down with the Holly, Ivie, all
Wherewith ye drest the Christmas Hall ;
That so the superstitious find
Not one least branch there left behind,
For look, how many leaves there be
Neglected there, Maids, trust to me,
So many Goblins you shall see.

He also alludes to the reservation of part of the candles or torches, as calculated to have the effect of protecting from mischief :

Kindle the Christmas brand, and then
   Till sunset let it burn,
Which quenched, then lay it up again,
   Till Christmas next return

Part must be kept, wherewith to teend
   The Christmas log next year ;
And where 'tis safely kept, the fiend
   Can do no mischief there.

Candlemas is everywhere a great day for weather prognostications. But these prognostications, like dreams, go by contraries, fine weather on Candlemas foretelling a succession of unseasonably cold days and necessarily a failure of the crops, while foul weather on that day is a sure promise of a bright spring, with a summer to match. Numerous popular rhymes in England and Scotland embody this superstition :

> If Candlemas Day be dry and fair,
> The half o' winter's to come and mair ;
> If Candlemas Day be wet and foul,
> The half o' winter's gane at Yule.

> If Candlemas Day be fair and bright,
> Winter will have another flight ; .
> But if it be dark with clouds and rain,
> Winter is gone, and will not come again.

> The hind had as lief see
>   His wife on the bier
> As that Candlemas Day
>   Should be pleasant and clear.

" The Country Almanac" in 1676 came out with this version of the story :

> Foul weather is no news; hail, rain, and snow
> Are now expected, and esteem'd no woe ;
> Nay, 'tis an omen bad, the yeomen say,
> If Phœbus shows his face the second day.

Though they expected foul weather, still the yeomen thought that by that time the worst of the winter was past, and they had the proverb,—

> When Candlemas Day is come and gone,
> The snow lies on a hot stone.

In Germany there are two proverbial expressions on this subject : " The shepherd would rather see the wolf enter his stable on Candlemas Day than the sun." " The badger peeps out of his hole on Candlemas Day, and when he finds snow walks abroad ; but if he sees the sun shining he draws back into his hole."

The Germans have brought over with them to America the superstition about the badger. But as the badger, even in its distinctly American variety, is little known east of the Mississippi River, the fable has been transferred from its shoulders to those of the woodchuck, or ground-hog. Farmers in the Middle States give the name of Ground-Hog Day to Candlemas. They will tell you that it is the day whereon the ground-hog awakens from his hibernating slumber, stretches himself, and comes out of his hole to look for his shadow. If he finds it,—that is to say, if the sun be shining out of a clear sky so that the woodchuck casts a shadow,—he hurries back to his hole and to sleep again, knowing that it is but a temporary meteorological change, which must speedily be followed by a renewal of wintry severity. But if the sky be overcast and the sun obscured, and the day be cold and cheerless, and the ground-hog casts no shadow, then he exults and disports himself, and counts his slumbers at an end, for he knows that winter also is at its end.

The following rhymes, common in the rural parts of New England, may be contrasted with the similar versified proverbs of Old England and Scotland, in regard to the prophetic quality of Candlemas weather :

> As far as the sun shines out on Candlemas Day,
> So far will the snow blow in before May ;
> As far as the snow blows in on Candlemas Day,
> So far will the sun shine out before May.

The ground-hog was not the only medium to foretell the future on Candlemas. According to Martin, in his " Description of the Western Islands," the Hebrideans observed this custom : "The mistress and servants of each family take a sheaf of oats and dress it up in women's apparel, put it in a large basket, and lay a wooden club by it, and this they call ' Briid's Bed ;' and then the mistress and servants cry three times, ' Briid is come ! Briid is welcome !' This they do just before going to bed, and when they rise in the morning they look among the ashes, expecting to see the impression of Briid's club there, which if they do they reckon it a true presage of a good crop and prosperous year, and the contrary they take as a bad omen." Briid may be a corruption of Bridget, whose day occurs on the eve of Candlemas.

There is a custom of old standing in Scotland in connection with Candlemas Day. On that day it is, or lately was, the universal practice for children attending school to make small presents of money to their teachers. The master sits at his desk or table, exchanging for the moment his usual authoritative look for one of bland civility, and each child goes up in turn and lays his offering before him, the sum being generally proportioned to the abilities of the parents. Sixpence and a shilling are the common sums in most schools, but some give half and whole crowns, and even more. The boy and girl who give most are respectively styled king and queen. The children being then dismissed for a holiday proceed along the streets in a confused procession, carrying the king and queen in state. In some schools it used to be customary for the teacher, on the conclusion of the offerings, to make a bowl of punch and regale each urchin with a glass and a biscuit. The latter part of the day was usually devoted to what was called the Candlemas bleeze, or blaze,— namely, the burning of any piece of furze which might exist in their neighborhood.

Another old custom in Scotland on Candlemas Day was to hold a foot-ball match. On one occasion, not long ago, when the sport took place in Jedburgh, the contending parties, after a struggle of two hours in the streets, transferred the contention to the bed of the river Jed, and there fought it out amid a scene of fearful splash and dabblement, to the infinite amusement of a multitude looking on from the bridge.

Candles, Use of. A candle (Lat. *candeo,* " I burn") was originally made of wax, and wax candles are still used in the religious ceremonies of the Roman, English, and Greek Churches. An old legend of non-ecclesiastical origin asserts that bees derive their origin from Paradise, and are especially blessed by the Almighty; therefore mass ought not to be performed without the aid of the wax derived from these favored creatures. St. Luke (Acts xx. 7, 8) mentions the great number of lamps which burned in the upper chamber while St. Paul "continued his speech until midnight." The fact that Christian assemblies during the ages of persecution were held before dawn made a similar employment of lights necessary. Moreover, the early Christians, familiar as they were with the Old Testament symbolism, in connection with the candlestick in the tabernacle and the temple, doubtless attached similar significance to the lights which they burned during the sacred mysteries. This conjecture is confirmed by the fact that the Church of the fourth century still continued the religious use of lights when they were no longer needed to dispel the darkness. "Throughout the churches of the East," says Jerome, writing against Vigilantius, "lights are kindled when the Gospel is to be read, although the sun is shining, not indeed to drive away the darkness, but as a sign of spiritual joy." A similar custom prevailed in the West. The mediæval author of the "Micrologus" writes, "According to the Roman order, we never celebrate mass without lights, . . . using them as a type of that light without which even in midday we grope as in the night."

According to the present Catholic usage, mass cannot be celebrated without candles of pure wax and of white color, save at masses for the dead, when candles of yellow wax are to be substituted. Two candles must be lighted at a low mass, unless the mass be said for the convent or the parish, or on one of the greater solemnities, when four may be used. Six candles are lighted at high mass, seven at a bishop's mass. No less than twelve candles must be lighted at Benediction of the Blessed Sacrament, or six if Benediction be given with a pyx. Candles must also be lighted when communion is given either in a church or in a private house, and one lighted candle is required at extreme unction. The use of candles at funerals dates back to the fourth century.

There are many instances during the Middle Ages of persons having a candle made, as a special devotion, of the same height or the same weight as themselves. Erasmus gibes at this in the " Colloquies," where a Zealander is represented during a storm as promising to St. Christopher a wax candle as large as the saint's statue in the great church in Paris.

Louisa Costello in " A Summer among the Bocages," i. 341, tells of the custom of presenting a very large candle to St. Sebastian at his church on the Loire. It was placed in a boat instead of a mast, and was borne with infinite ceremony to the church.

In some parts of Ireland it was usual on Christmas Eve to burn a large candle which no one was permitted to snuff except those who bore the name of Mary.

There was at one time in England a due called wax-shot or wax-scot, a gift of wax candles presented to churches three times a year. What were called wax-rolls were pieces or cakes of wax, flat circular disks, presented to churches, for the use of which they were made into candles or tapers. Mr. Toulmin Smith has published some interesting researches on this subject gathered from the " Original Ordinances of more than One Hundred Early English Guilds," compiled by order of a Parliament held at Cambridge in the time of Richard II.

Wax candles, or wax to make into candles, are frequently mentioned in the records, sometimes as presentations to churches, abbeys, and convents, sometimes as forfeits or penalties. The Guild of St. Katherine, Aldersgate, prescribed that five round tapers of wax, of the weight of twenty pounds, were to burn on high feast days to the honor of God, of the Virgin Mary, of St. Katherine and all saints, and to be used to light round the body of a dead brother, and in his funeral procession. The wardens of St. Botolph's Guild, Norwich, stated in their return that they had in hand twenty-six shillings and eightpence for the maintenance of a light. The Guild of St. George in the same city had in hand forty shillings for the support of a light and the making of an image. In relation to St. Katherine's Guild, another in old Norwich, " of the chattel of the guild shall there be two candles of wax, of sixteen pounds weight, about the body of the dead," whenever any brother or sister departed this life. The Guild of Young Scholars at Lynn was established

chiefly to maintain an image of St. William, standing in a tabernacle in the church of St. Margaret, with six tapers of wax burning on festival days. The Guild of St. Elene at Beverley kept
three wax lights burning every Sunday and feast day, in honor
of St. Elene; while at the morning mass of Christmas Day thirteen wax lights were burned. There must have been a goodly
amount of wax consumed on the Feast of Candlemas by the
Guild of St. Mary at Beverley; for the brethren got up a pageant,
in which two youths representing angels carried a chandelier or
compound candlestick containing twenty-four thick wax lights,
and the other members each carried a wax light. In the Guild
of the Resurrection of Our Lord, at Lincoln, at the funeral rites
of a brother, thirteen wax lights were burned in four stands. In
the Guild of St. Katherine at Stamford a fine of one pound of
wax, plus twopence, was imposed on any member absent from
the guild feast; and, as the feast itself was valued at twopence
per head, the absentee paid for a dinner which he did not eat,
besides losing a pound of wax.

Wax lights were indispensable accompaniments to the other
adornments of the royal palace, the feudal castle, and the baronial mansion of the olden time. In the Wardrobe Accounts
of Edward IV., somewhat less than four centuries ago, there
is a curious entry to the following effect: "William Whyte,
tallough-chaundeller, for iij dosen and ix lb. of p's candell, for to
light when the king's highness and goode grace on a nyght come
unto his sayd grete warderobe, and at other divers tymes." From
other entries it appears that p's was sometimes spelled peris,
sometimes pares, sometimes parys: it is believed that the lights
so used were called Paris candles. In that singular forerunner
of our modern books of etiquette called the "Boke of Curtasye,"
written about the same period as the Wardrobe Accounts above
adverted to, there is distinct mention of wax candles and Paris
candles, but without any notification as to the materials whereof
the latter were made:

> In chambre no lyght ther shalle be brent
> But of wax, thereto yf ye take tent:
> In halle at soper schalle candels brenne
> Of Parys, therein that alle men kenne.

Here we are told of wax candles in the chamber and Paris
candles in the hall, the former probably more delicate and costly
than the latter.

In Paris, the police commissary of the district of St.-Germain-
l'Auxerrois receives annually a present of ten pounds of candles
from the Chamber of Notaries. "The origin of this observance
dates a long way back. It arose out of a dispute between the

police commissary of the Châtelet and the Corporation of Notaries. The duty of the former was to hold a lighted candle at
the door of the chamber as the legal gentlemen were entering it,
and on one occasion the commissary complained that it was
unfair for the expense of the candles to fall upon him, contending
that he ought rather to receive an indemnity for his services.
He gained his point, and from that time forward the commissary
was given three hundred pounds of wax annually. In the course
of time the three hundred pounds of wax have gradually melted
away and dwindled, till at the present day the ancient custom
has come down to the gift of a ten-pound box of composite
candles. Very likely it will not be long before the offering of
this substitute for the original gift will be dropped." (*London
Standard*, 1891.)

Canonization. An act of the Pope whereby he decrees, after
a regular form of inquiry, that a deceased servant of God be
enrolled among the saints and commended to the veneration and
invocation of all Catholics. The idea which underlies canonization is one closely connected with the doctrine of the Communion
of Saints, and has existed from a very early period in the Church,
when the persecuted Christians were wont to collect and preserve with reverence and affection the remains of those who had
suffered for their faith. And there appears, from what St.
Jerome tells us, to have been, long before any regular practice
of invocation was established, a prevalent belief that the souls
of these martyrs hovered about the place where their bodies were
laid and were there somehow brought into contact with the living. The departed were believed still to take an interest in their
old friends and the affairs of their earthly home, and to exercise,
through their intercession, a beneficent influence over them. At
the beginning popular admiration enjoyed, unchecked, the privilege of canonization. A saint became a saint by acclamation.
That was the beginning of canonization, though the name itself
was of subsequent growth. Gradually, as these local and other
cults came to multiply beyond measure, the Popes assumed to
themselves the sole prerogative of advancing claimants to the
successive ranks of Beatitude and Sanctity. The canonized
saints thenceforth held no merely local or precarious dignity;
they were presented in solemn bulls and with rites of imposing
splendor to the general homage of Christendom. Of course there
were some saints, like the early martyrs, the four "great Doctors" respectively of East and West, and some other conspicuous
bishops, confessors, and founders of religious orders, who may be
called the saints of the universal Christian world. But down to
the tenth century the popular voice, with the sanction of the

bishop, was held to be sufficient authority for conferring the honor. After that time the sanction of the Pope was required, though bishops still for a time retained their initiative. The first recorded canonization by Papal authority was that of Ulrich, Bishop of Augsburg, raised to that honor by a bull of John XV. in 993 at the request of Liutolf, Ulrich's immediate successor in the see, who had, however, already established public veneration for him in his own diocese. Pope John explained in an epistle that this usage was introduced in order that by honoring martyrs and confessors we may worship Him of whom they testified, and, being conscious of our own imperfections, seek the aid of their merits and prayers at the throne of God. But it was not until two centuries later that the prerogative was assigned exclusively to the Holy See by constitutions first of Alexander III. and then of Innocent III. The canonization of St. Gaultier of Pontoise by the Archbishop of Rouen in 1153 is the latest example of such an act being accomplished by any lower authority. Innocent III. finally announced that the decision in such matters appertained exclusively to the legitimate successor of St. Peter. The first canonization solemnized with anything like the present ritual pomp was that of St. Francis of Assisi, in 1228. It was not till fifty years later that the regular process, since developed into a minute and searching investigation of each individual case, was first exemplified in the canonization of St. Raymond of Pennafort.

The process begins with an appeal for canonization supported by the bishop of the diocese wherein the potential saint resided. This appeal must be made at Rome in the presence of a *promotor fidei*, better known as the *advocatus diaboli*, or devil's advocate, whose duty it is to detect flaws either in the character of the candidate or in the evidence adduced. If the inquiry be satisfactory and the eminent virtue of the candidate be certified by miracles duly authenticated, he is elevated first to the rank of Blessed, an act which is known as Beatification, and finally, after some years have elapsed, during which at least two new miracles have established the justice of the first verdict, three successive congregations are convened, at the third of which the Pope presides and the public are admitted; the Papal consent is given, and a day fixed for the canonization to take place at St. Peter's. On that day a mass is said in honor of the new saint, his statue is unveiled, and his place in the calendar is announced.

Caravaggio. This little village in Lombardy, half-way between Milan and Cremona, famous in art as the birthplace of the painters Caravaggio, jumped into a new sort of fame in 1882 as the scene of apparitions of the Virgin in the church of the

Madonna. The manifestations continued sporadically for several years. They are thus described by a correspondent of the London *Court Journal* writing in 1883 : " Every day, at noon, the vision of the Virgin Mary rises from a dark recess behind one of the pillars of the aisle, and the struggles of the thousands of eager devotees to catch a glimpse of the apparition are most extraordinary. The shrieks and screams of the victims who are knocked down and trampled on amid the confusion are appalling. Those who cannot approach near enough to the shrine throw handfuls of copper coin against the iron grating which encloses it, and the shock of the metallic sound, amid the deep monotonous intoning of the priests, seems to produce a frenzy in the crowd, many of whom rush wildly about, shrieking and tearing their hair, and treading without mercy on the limbs of the paralytics outstretched on the pavement. The simple village church, which is capable of containing only a few hundred people, is made to hold ten thousand, who, although packed, suffocating, perspiring, and trembling beneath the stifling atmosphere, yet continue to howl out their invocations. Outside, on the piazza, the scene is still more astounding. Around the fountain stand groups of devotees of every grade of life. The paralytic, with the maimed and crippled, are laid on the bare stones under a burning sun, and in due time are lifted into the fountain, while others, filling their little tin mugs with water, drink greedily, without heed of the pollution it has undergone from the sick who have been immersed therein. When the dismal howlings of the pilgrims within the church announce the appearance of the misty vapor which precedes the apparition of the Virgin, the whole crowd fall to the ground, and literally shriek forth the litany composed for the occasion. The cripples fall back upon the pavement, the tin mugs are left to float upon the fountain, and the litany is succeeded by a dead silence."

Carmentalia.   An ancient Roman festival celebrated on the 11th of January.

Carmenta, or Carmentis, was an ancient goddess of Latium, whose name points to prophetic powers, being of the same root as *carmen,* " song ;" the early oracles were all expressed in verse. The goddess is sometimes identified as the mother of Evander, who came to Latium from Arcadia and is said to have brought with him a knowledge of the arts, and the Latin alphabetical characters as distinguished from the Etruscan.

A second festival, on the 15th, participated in chiefly by women, recognized two Carmentes, Porrima and Postverta, whose names were sometimes interpreted as referring to knowledge of both past and future. Of this goddess little is said in historical times, when the primitive Latin worship was obscured by a crowd of Grecian and Oriental deities; but she must have held a leading place in early times, for she had a special priest, the Flamen Carmentalis, and the gate near which her altar stood—just at the foot of the Capitoline, between it and the river—was called Carmentalis. Plutarch says that some supposed Carmenta to be one of the Fates who presided over the birth of men. The Greek title of the goddess was Themis. Into her chapel it was not permitted to carry any part of a dead animal,—for example, anything made of leather. It is related that the famous Marcus Popillius, in the time of the Samnite wars,—the first plebeian who ever obtained the honor of a triumph,—was flamen of Carmentis. When one day he was performing a sacrifice, clad in the *læna*, or priestly robe, a tumult arose in the city. Popillius then hastily left the sacrifice, clad as he was, made his way to the assembly, and calmed the tumult by his authority and eloquence. In memory of this, from the *læna* or robe which he wore, the people gave him the name of *Lænas*, which was borne by his descendants; for it was quite out of order to address the people in any robe but the toga, the distinctive costume of a Roman citizen.

Carnival. (From the Latin words *carne vale*, "farewell meat.") A period of feasting, license, and merrymaking immediately preceding Lent, to make up in anticipation for the gloom and abstinence of the forty days of penance. Strictly the Carnival begins at Twelfth Day, but only the latter days are termed High Carnival, when the public festivities wax fast and furious, culminating in the revelry of Shrove Tuesday. Like the Christmas mummeries, it has its roots in the pagan Saturnalia (*q. v.*). The northern nations of Europe concerned themselves most with Christmas, the southern with the Carnival; and the latter season now retains its hold only in Catholic localities.

In ancient times the Carnival was emphatically the season for banquets. And these banquets, again, were the scenes of certain rash and romantic vows, made by the lords of the feast and their friends, and called vows of the swan, peacock, heron, pheasant, etc., according to the bird which the principal swearer happened to prefer. The ceremonies with which the oath was made were always fantastic. Sometimes the bird was produced living, but more frequently it formed the crowning dish. It was brought into the banquet-hall when excitement ran highest, and always with striking parade. The creature itself was profusely ornamented with jewels, a trumpet-blast announced its approach, a herald in all the pomp of his costume preceded it, and a body of knights, squires, and pages attended it; in short, it was accorded all the stately ceremonial of a sovereign prince when visiting an equal. The bird, living or dead, having been presented to the host, the latter stood up, and, laying his hand upon it, pledged himself to perform some remarkable feat before the year was out, in honor of it and the ladies. For the most part these vows

ROMAN CARNIVAL IN 1861.

evaporated harmlessly. At times, however, the results were serious. One made by Edward III. led to the battle of Crécy; another—by which Henry V. pledged himself to traverse France from sea to sea with banners spread—produced the dangerous march that closed so gloriously at Agincourt; and a third by a Duke of Burgundy sent his heir, John the Fearless,—he who was afterwards murdered at Montereau,—to meet the Turk at the fatal battle of Nicopolis.

Mere feasting was but a portion of a Carnival banquet. Through its whole course the guests were entertained by music, juggling tricks, athletic feats, the wit and folly of jesters, and pieces of show called *entremets*. Of these the last two were most popular. The Chancellor l'Hôpital has described in choice Latin how a jester could enliven a banquet. "Covering himself with the skin of a fox, and bedaubing his face with flour, he went through the satyr's dance, in which he imitated the silly movements of a clown at a village fête. Improving as he went on, he perched himself on the end of a stick, and, grasping it between his knees, spun round and round like a top. Many of the pages and valets attempted to imitate this portion of the performance, but they all tumbled down, to the amusement of the company." Polished society in those days, it is clear, was not fastidious.

The *entremets* consisted in the introduction of the model of a ship, castle, or rock, elaborately decorated, and in the performance of its tenants. The latter represented fiends, fairies, Turks, damsels, knights-errant, necromancers, etc. The apparatus was wheeled into the hall with what a quaint writer terms "an fair hurley-burley of minstrelsie," and the tenants, jumping out, danced, sang songs, made complimentary speeches, imitated the evolutions of a battle, or enacted a classic legend in dumb show. They then returned to their receptacle, which was wheeled out again in the midst of a deafening flourish of trumpets. Not infrequently the cumbrous machinery broke down, and the model stuck fast in some particularly inconvenient spot. In such cases guests and actors united to trundle the thing out by main force,—a sequel in which there was always more good fun than in the performance itself.

After the banquet came the ballet,—a matter in which everything sacred and profane was reduced to a dance. It was designed by the universal genius of the court, assisted by all the talent he could press into the service; it was rehearsed for months previous to the grand exhibition; the performers were all of gentle birth; and not the least of its attractions was the splendor of the dresses and the scenery. The Duke of Ossuna, Viceroy of Naples 1616–20, was a great master of the art of giving ballets. In one of these the actresses—twelve beauties of high rank—were provided with every article of their superb array at his expense. The whole cost amounted to seven thousand two hundred ducats, or three thousand dollars apiece. The Jenkins of the viceregal court went into ecstasies over the results. Taking a liberty denied to his successors, he described the undergarments of the twelve as of white satin fringed with gold lace. Their petticoats, which he takes care to let us know were not too lengthy, consisted of the same material, and were similarly fringed. They wore crowns of white satin and silver, ornamented with heron-plumes, and their trains of silver brocade hung over their left arms. Thus garbed, they executed a torch dance, which was enthusiastically applauded.

Of all Carnival entertainments decidedly the first in point of taste was one given by Mazarin. After a repast which Mademoiselle d'Orléans pronounced " no less elegant than abundant," the cardinal led his guests—all the leading courtiers—into a gallery full of beautiful toys and glittering trifles of every description. There were ornaments from China and Japan, rare shawls from India, chandeliers of crystal, mirrors, tables, cabinets, silver goblets, gloves, ribbons, lace, fans, etc., enough to stock a dozen fancy warehouses. The ladies were delighted with the spectacle, especially when their host handed each of them a ticket for a lottery which was held a few days after and wherein every one drew a prize, until the gallery was emptied of its pretty store. It is stated that the whole affair cost Mazarin a sum equal to one hundred and fifty thousand dollars.

Not the least singular of the scenes which marked the Carnival of the past were its processions. They were moral, mythic, historic, politic, and comic, according to the taste of those who got them up. A specimen of these processions, whose exact character it would be difficult to determine, was exhibited in Paris during the supremacy of the League by the Walloon soldiers of the Spanish garrison. It was called the Mask of the Patience of Job. One of the Walloons representing the "good man Job" was mounted on an ass, whose tail he held instead of a bridle. In front of him went a crowd of musicians playing with all their might, and after him followed some hundreds of his comrades, naked to the waist, and painted like so many Indians about to take to the war-path. Close behind Job came two soldiers, got up to represent, the one the wife of the patriarch, and the other the evil spirit. And between the three was maintained a conversation which grossly parodied those recorded in the Bible. This farce was interrupted from time to time in order that the "good man Job" might bestow his blessing—a choice piece of low ribaldry—on the spectators.

A mask of another order—perhaps the most striking ever witnessed—was exhibited at Florence during the Carnival of 1512, the Medici being then in exile. The night had already closed round, and the streets were thronged with merrymakers, when a low, deep, wailing sound was heard in the distance. Every one paused and listened. The strange sound drew nearer, and. as it did so, the " Miserere," chanted by many voices, fell clearly on the ear. While the listeners were still wondering, a procession came in view, like a river of fire, for every member thereof carried a lighted torch. The concentrated blaze rendered the torch-bearers strangely distinct, and the spectators shuddered, for every one wore a snow-white death's-head mask over an inky shroud. It seemed as if the grave had released its dead to share in this particular Carnival. The thrilling interest of the scene increased as the procession streamed along. In its centre was a cart, drawn by four oxen, whose sides were grim with pale crosses, skulls, and bones painted on a jet-black ground, and from the roof six black banners, similarly blazoned, streamed to the ground. On a pedestal in the centre of that roof stood the figure of Death, with a scythe in his hand, the light streaming through his hollow skull and empty ribs and glancing on his bleached bones; and at the feet of Death lay six half-opened sepulchres, in which were seen six dead bodies, partly decayed. Immediately behind the car rode a troop of skeletons, mounted on miserable horses, whose sable trappings were embroidered with pale crosses and symbols of the grave; and each ghastly cavalier was attended by four squires, ghastly as himself, carrying a blazing torch in one hand, and a black banner, sown with white crosses and bleaching bones, in the other. Suddenly a long, piercing trumpet-blast pealed. The spectators shrank, and thought of the last judgment. At the call the dreary procession ceased its chant and came to a dead halt. Then the sepulchres on the car flew open, and the dead within, springing to their feet, burst into a dismal song, one of whose verses ran as follows:

> Morti siam', come vedete;
> Cosi morti, vedrem' voi:
> Fummo gia, come voi siete,
> Voi sarete, come noi.

> (" Dead we are, as ye may see,
> Dead like us ye soon shall be:
> Once ourselves were just as ye,
> Soon yourselves shall be as we.")

At the close of this song the trumpet rang again. Then the dead sank back into their sepulchres, the maskers resumed their chant, and the spectre march moved on.

But the usual character of Florentine Carnival processions was not so lugubrious. Such subjects as the triumphs of Bacchus and Silenus or other mythic and allegoric groups were far more popular. All these were produced in the most sumptuous manner. The greatest painters were employed in designing them, the greatest poets wrote the verses for the occasion.

During the period of religious excitement produced by the preaching of Savonarola the procession assumed a scriptural tone. In every street Shrove Tuesday beheld a repetition of the patriarch David and his Israelites dancing around the ark. And as they danced they sang a fantastic hymn with the following refrain :

> We dance and sing and prance and fling,
> 'Tis grace that makes us glad :
> No greater bliss can be than his
> Who piously goes mad, goes mad !
> Then let us all go mad.

And mad they went accordingly. The whole city joined in the madness. No better proof can be given than the sacrifice which closed the Carnival of 1496. In answer to the demands of peripatetic enthusiasts, fine gentlemen and fair ladies surrendered all their "vanities," their dresses, their jewelry, their lewd paintings and lewd books, their musical and gambling instruments, their padding, false hair, and rouge. Of the motley heap a vast bonfire was made in the Piazza della Signoria, and around it capered the mighty multitude, chanting its frantic chorus.

The Italian monk was not the only reformer who turned the doings of the Carnival to account. At Wittenberg the Shrove Tuesday of 1521 was signalized by a parody on the Papal procession through the Eternal City, which gave the Germans of that quarter an opportunity of manifesting their anti-Roman sentiments. And on the Shrove Tuesday of 1522 a street-show exhibited at Berne, which satirized all the officials of the older Church, from the Pope down to the sexton, did much towards effecting the triumph of the Reformation in the sovereign canton.

The Carnival was always remarkable for its rude sports. Cockfighting, bear-baiting, and other species of animal torture were then allowed full swing. (See SHROVE TUESDAY.)

It was also a chosen season for practical jesting. At a Carnival ball in the Louvre, Charles IX. once secretly let loose ten of the most skilful pickpockets in Paris, giving them full leave to steal whatever they could, and threatening them with punishment only if they were detected. Then he looked on in great glee as they plundered lord and lady alike, his delight at every dexterous theft being increased by the dismay of the despoiled upon missing their jewels, their girdles, their fans, their swords, or their comfit-boxes.

Grimmer was the prank played by his predecessor Louis XI. All round the old tiger's den, Plessis-les-Tours, stretched a wood, and from nearly every tree of it dangled a dead body ; for Louis was terribly ready with capital punishment, and he never allowed the remains of such victims as died by strangulation to be removed. On Shrove Tuesday night Louis commanded his guards to rouse up the neighboring villagers and hurry them to the castle. There he had already provided music, and, while his fiddlers played, he compelled each of his unwilling guests to take a gibbeted corpse as partner and dance before it until dawn. Nor did he forget to arrange the couples. There were many there who had husbands, sweethearts, and relatives among the dead, and good King Louis did not allow friends and relatives to be separated at his nice ball.

Atrocious as was the jest of Louis XI., it was hardly more so than many others which the chroniclers record of the great seigneurs of the olden time. Among the few of these that will bear quoting should be classed the feudal custom of causing every plebeian bride to dance an unseemly dance and to sing a ludicrous song in the church porch, and before the lord of the manor, within a year of her wedding. The ceremony for the most part took place during the Carnival. We find that it was observed in France so late as 1620. We have now under our eyes the report of a judgment of that date, which terminated a suit that had lasted for nine years, by deciding which of the rival seigneurs was entitled to preside at the "*chansons.*"

Rome has always been the head-quarters of the Carnival. It holds its pre-eminence even in these days when there, as elsewhere, the custom is in its decadence. In the Middle Ages the Corso was the scene of grand tournaments and stately pageants. The palaces glittered with jewelled cloths, and their owners, in festal raiment, crowded the tapestried balconies to pelt their friends, neighbors, or sweethearts in the streets below. Although the people took their part as spectators and jostled and jested with one another in a struggling mass in the Corso, it was eminently a feast provided for them by the aristocracy. The people had little more to do with the active part of it than the rank and file of the Achæans and Trojans had to do with the Homeric battles, for much money had to be spent upon it. To-day all is changed. The patrician and the grandee have gone out. Il Popolo Romano has come in. The Corso now is its playground. The Carnival, once the sport of Popes and cardinals, the plaything of princes, is now the people's peculiar festival, their holiday of mirth. Fashionable Romans disdain it, since the plebeian is in possession. Only those modern Goths and Vandals, the tourists, come to see the sport.

Nor do they go unrewarded. Even in its decadence a Roman Carnival is well worth seeing, as a pleasant bit of low comedy. In the Corso the crowds swarm up and down, the masks and dominos among them lighting up the grim palaces, whose balconies, decorated with flowers and ribbons, and crowded with spectators of many nationalities, flash back an answering light. On the last three days, including Shrove Tuesday, war breaks out between the streets and the balconies, the missiles being showers of confetti (*q. v.*), hard lime pellets of the size of a hailstone and quite as hard, and coriandoli, or small bonbons. Battles of Flowers (*q. v.*) are also a feature.

The Carnival ends in a blaze of light. As night descends on Shrove Tuesday every masker lights the *moccoletto*, or wax taper, with which he has provided himself, and parades through the streets seeking to blow out his neighbor's and retain his own light.

The same general features are found in other Italian cities, save of course in Venice, where an exceptional environment produces exceptional effects. A procession of gondolas and boats along the Grand Canal, all brilliantly decorated and filled with maskers, public dances in the Piazza of St. Mark, illuminated at night for the purpose, and in the Ridotto, the ancient hall of the Venetian dancers, feasting in private houses, grand balls in the palaces of the nobility, and splendid receptions at the official residences,—these occupy the full measure of the time from Epiphany to Ash Wednesday. On Shrove Tuesday the ceremony of burying King Carnival (*q. v.*) is performed.

For a score of years back Nice has been famous for its Carnival parades, in which King Carnival also appears. The Battle of Flowers was long a unique feature here, but it has been caught up and appropriated by other places.

Spain still enters into the spirit of the Carnival with naïve earnestness. Madrid in especial gives itself up entirely to the enjoyment of the hour. The Corso lasts for four days, beginning on the last Sunday before Lent. From noon until night the great drive is crowded with a double line of carriages, and between this double line are the landaus of those who have paid for the privilege of driving up and down free from the law of the road.

A great variety of fantastic costumes are worn. All liberties are pardoned to the maskers. They jump in and out of the coaches, and dart about the drive. Turks, prophets, kings, monks, devils, and a variety of other characters may be seen wandering about in the festive throng. A democratic spirit prevails everywhere. A duke may wander about in the dress of a chimney-sweep, while a store clerk by his side may be decked in the garb of a prince. A duchess may be hailed by her first name by a peasant, and may accept bonbons from his hand with no loss of dignity.

The gayety waxes fast and furious before it is finally quenched in the gloom of Lent. Ash Wednesday is a day of merriment, then three days of gloom follow, and on Sunday the Carnival has a resurrection, and the gayest ball of the year takes place at the Opera. After this ball Lent begins in earnest, and sackcloth and ashes succeed the brilliant costumes of the Carnival.

In France the festivities are confined almost entirely to the Shrove Tuesday or Mardi-Gras procession of the Bœuf Gras (*q. v.*) and to certain student revelries. In Belgium, in Germany, and in almost all other European countries and their dependencies where the Catholic religion retains any hold, a more or less dim survival from the past still flits through a ghost-like existence.

In Russia the week before Lent is given up to Carnival gaye-ties. The Russians have no Ash Wednesday. With them Car-nival begins and ends on Sunday. These eight days are crammed full of performances,—national plays, native and foreign operas, dramatized folk-tales, ballets,—some given in the regular theatres and others in huge temporary barn-like structures run up for the occasion in the public squares.

There is out-door amusement in plenty. Coasting down ice hills, riding in merry-go-rounds, feasting on the pancakes, ginger-bread, sunflower-seed, and other dainties offered at sidewalk stalls, or drinking tea from the huge samovars that stand hissing in the snow,—such are the recreations of the open-air revellers who parade the streets in masks and dominos or in their mere Sunday best.

The New Orleans Carnival has been growing steadily since its establishment in 1830, and is now one of the most brilliant of the public and social festivities in the United States. A dozen organizations, most of them secret societies, join to give *éclat* to its last days, especially to the Monday and Tuesday before Lent. The most important of these are the Rex, Momus, Proteus, and Comus associations.

At sunset on Monday, bells, trumpets, whistles, and human throats join in tumultuous din to welcome the announcement that his Majesty Rex is approaching his well-loved city. At this signal flags fly, and thousands of men, women, and children spring as by magic from the banquettes. All are brimful of curiosity to see the sovereign with his escort land at the foot of Canal Street, visit the City Hall, receive the keys and homage from the mayor, and then disappear till the morrow. By ten o'clock on Tuesday morning (Mardi-Gras) every available inch of space along the route of the procession is occupied. Finally a mighty shout goes up, and far in the distance is heard the steady march of the on-coming parade with the lilting notes of the king's own band. It was for the Russian Grand Duke Alexis that Rex first rode in his regal costume at the head of a body of Arabic troops. This was in 1872, when all the day maskers were first united in a procession. The experiment was a success, and Rex became an established favorite. The festivities in his honor close with a ball at Artillery Hall. But the Rex organization already noted is only one of a dozen, each of which contributes its share to the festivities. Rex is not the only king, nor is his queen the only queen. There are other royalties, whose subjects, although not so numerous, are more powerful. The organization of the Mystic Krewe of Comus is the oldest of them all, and its parade, which takes place after nightfall, is the most gorgeous.

FIGURES IN THE NEW ORLEANS CARNIVAL BALL.

In 1857, coming apparently from nowhere and known to no one, appeared the Mystic Krewe of Comus in a fantastic night parade made up of gorgeous floats manned by masked revellers. No one knew who the maskers were, and no one admitted that he belonged to the organization. Every year since then, except during the war, Comus has paraded and given his ball on the night of Shrove Tuesday, and in some respects his Krewe is the most interesting of all the Carnival companies.

In the first place, Comus outdoes them all in mystery, and mystery is at a premium in these affairs. If you should ask a man to get you an invitation to the Comus ball, he would perhaps say that " he thought he knew a man" who might be able to get it for him. He never would hint that he himself was a member of the organization, even though he might be at the very head of it. The men who belong to the various organizations are not known to the general public, and they are not supposed to be known to any one outside of the limits of the membership.

The people who go to the ball, the very queen herself and her maids of honor, are not informed of the identity of the king. They all guess, but the completeness of the disguise may be imagined from the statement of a woman who knows the men who have filled the royal throne for several years. She said that she had heard a great many guesses as to the identity of the king, but she never had heard a correct one. So the people go on from year to year, bowing to one king after another, and never knowing who these kings are. As for the men who are the kings, they seem to be just as anxious to keep up the game of blindman's-buff as anybody is. They never tell about "when I was king of Comus."

The queen is not masked. In fact, no one is masked except the men who have taken part in the parade. There are no women in the parade, all female characters being represented by men. A woman wearing a mask would not be admitted to the hall.

Carnival, King. A burlesque potentate, the lineal descendant of the Abbot of Unreason and the Lord of Misrule, who in some localities represents the Carnival as elsewhere Santa Claus represents Christmas. But, as Santa Claus is a myth, King Carnival is usually an effigy. In this form he makes his most famous appearances at Venice and at Nice, and has recently been introduced into Rome, Paris, and other places. A flesh and blood King Carnival, however, better known as Rex, is annually named in New Orleans, to conduct the more popular of the festivities. This is purely an American innovation.

In Venice, where King Carnival was born, he is born again every year only to die. He does not put in an appearance until the afternoon of Shrove Tuesday, and then at the end of a few hours of vicarious gayety is laid on the funeral pyre. The procession in his honor forms at the gardens of Napoleon : he himself, a straw effigy richly dressed and stuffed with fireworks, is placed in a splendid palanquin which is borne on the shoulders of a score or so of maskers. An army of attendants follow him, an array of caricature and personification,—troops of devils, troops of sprites, troops of outlandish creatures with heads of bears, hogs, wolves, and bulls, hunchbacks and deformities, some unnaturally large, others unnaturally tall or crooked, still others elegantly and artistically attired in expensive masks and vestments, bespeaking their position among the higher classes. When the procession reaches the Piazza of St. Mark it stops there. Dancing and revelry are conducted before the kingly throne. As midnight approaches, a change occurs in the appearance of his majesty. His hair is powdered white, his festive robe and sceptre are exchanged for a long white sheet or pall, his hands are pinioned upon his breast. The richly decked car has become an execution-block and a bier. Slowly and solemnly it is escorted to the Molo, and there, upon the spot where were executed the state criminals of the old republic, King Carnival's palanquin is set on fire and he and it are consumed together.

An eye-witness of the Venetian Carnival of 1868, when the ceremony was at its best, thus describes the final scene:

" As the great clock of St. Mark was striking the midnight hour, the band ceased playing, and scarcely a sound was heard in all that immense crowd. A moment of silence and darkness intervened, and then a small light was seen to issue from one corner of the high palanquin, which soon broke into a varicolored blaze of different hues, according to the various hidden compounds ignited; then a rocket shot up from the same framework, and Roman candles threw out their soft, beautiful balls of fire, while fiery serpents sprang out in every direction from the same hidden source, whence issued every variety of pyrotechnic fires. The flames now spread to every part of the palanquin, igniting fiery wheels, circles, and all manner of figures, giving to many of them an automatic movement quite magical in appearance. The fire now surged in waves over the bier and around the ghastly figure of the doomed monarch, who stood immovable amid his dissolving glory,—his very throne proving, like many another, to be a mine of destructive elements to its possessor. Finally the discharge of rockets became so rapid and so noisy, as they leaped into the dark vault overhead with startling screeches and long trails of fire, that the crowd who had been so attracted by the milder discharges of fireworks at the beginning of the exhibition became terrified, swayed back, very willing to retreat from so close a proximity to what appeared to be, as it was in fact, an infernal machine. The flames now reached the sacred person of the fated king, and, climbing up his gaunt limbs, ignited innumerable fireworks concealed in his legs and body, wrapping his pale visage in a blaze, and, communicating with his combustible brain, caused the whole figure to burst into a thousand fragments with a deafening explosion, ending in a brilliant coruscation of light in the national colors. Thus died King Carnival, amid one of the finest and most wonderful automatic pyrotechnical displays imaginable." (*Galaxy*, February, 1869.)

In Greece the people on Shrove Tuesday take a block of wood and dress it in old clothes to represent a very fat but armless and legless personage. This is dubbed the Carnival. A rough bier is made of four sticks of wood fastened together with ropes, whereon the Carnival is placed, and half a dozen young men bear this on their shoulders to the tomb, preceded by a company of others who, hand in hand and some ten abreast, dance and sing ribald songs. The effigy is paraded through the streets of town or village, every passer-by and every householder being solicited for alms, and is then taken out into some open space and buried with a burlesque of the rites of the Church.

KING CARNIVAL II. OF PARIS. (1897.)

The King Carnival of Nice was first introduced into the festivities in 1872. He makes his annual appearance on the second Sunday before Shrove Tuesday, takes his place in the parade on that day, stops at the Casino, where the keys of the city are delivered to him with a florid speech by the mayor, and is escorted to his throne, there to remain for ten days, the monarch of all he surveys. When his brief reign is over he is dethroned and burned amid the same rejoicings as those which had originally welcomed him.

This King Carnival is a huge effigy. Of recent times it has been usual to make every year add to his stature, so as to retain a record of his actual age. In 1897, for example, being then twenty-five years old, he was twenty-five feet high. But it is improbable that he will rise much higher. Every year also the king takes on different accoutrements, but always he is meant to be representative of the times. When the bicycle fever first broke out he was a gigantic bicyclist, in 1896 he was perched on an automobile carriage, etc.

In 1896 the Parisians introduced a king into their Carnival festivities, which is an obvious importation from Nice. King Carnival II. made his due appearance in 1897.

The burial of King Carnival has a curious affiliation with the more ancient rite of the Burial of the Sardine (*q. v.*), and is no doubt a collateral descendant of the latter.

Carols. Joyous songs for festive occasions, and specifically for Christmas. They were anciently accompanied by dancing.

In an old vocabulary of A.D. 1440, *Caral* is defined as *Songe;* in John Palsgrave's work of A.D. 1530, as *Chanson de Noël.* The word comes directly from the Middle English *carolen,* "to sing joyously." The earliest carol in English, known under that name, is the production of Dame Berners, Prioress of St. Albans in the fourteenth century, entitled "A Carolle of Huntynge." This is printed on the last leaf of Wynkyn de Worde's collection of Christmas carols, A.D. 1521, and the first verse, modernized, runs thus :

> As I came by a green forest side,
> I met with a forester that bade me abide,
> Whey go bet, hey go bet, hey go how,
> We shall have sport and game enow.

Milton uses the word "carol" to express a devotional hymn :

> A quire
> Of squadron'd angels hear his carol sung.

And that distinguished light of the English Church, Bishop Jeremy Taylor, speaks of the angels' song on the morning of the Nativity as the first Christmas carol : "As soon as these blessed choristers had sung their Christmas carol, and taught the Church a hymn to put into her offices forever," etc.

According to Durandus, it was customary in early days for bishops to sing with their clergy in the episcopal houses on the feast of the Nativity : "In Natali prælati cum suis clericis ludant, vel in domibus episcopalibus."

When the Mystery and Morality Plays were in vogue as a

means of religious instruction and were represented in churches, monasteries, and nunneries, carols grew in favor, since they were to the olden play what the music between the acts is to the modern drama. Companies of singers were retained to appear before the stage and divert the audience with carols and other songs, and thus the dreary time of waiting while a new scene was in preparation was passed agreeably to the people,—so agreeably, in fact, that there was frequently no little disturbance created by the rivalry between the singers and the players, each party striving for more time. The people, fond of joining in with the chorus, sometimes espoused the cause of the singers, and on one occasion, in Chester, during the progress of a miracle play, the stage was wrecked, the properties and dresses of the performers were destroyed, and the players severely beaten by a musical mob, who fancied their favorite carol-singers were ill-treated by the managers of the play.

Difficulties of this kind were, it seems, not infrequent in England, France, and Germany during the thirteenth and fourteenth centuries, the result being that, to obviate all danger of a disturbance, the carol-singing was incorporated in the play and the singers were actors as well as musicians. They had their accompaniments also, for many churches had portable organs, carried by a strap thrown over the shoulder of the performer, who with one hand worked the bellows of the instrument and with the other played the melody of the hymn. Thus accoutred, the organist led the procession, the singers following him to and fro on the stage, and sometimes the parade was continued through the streets, the people falling in line and joining in the hymn.

Not all the Christmas carols, however, were religious in their nature. Many were lively secular airs, some wedded to words that were anything but devotional. Dancing was quite as much a part of the Christmas entertainment as singing, and the same tune often served both purposes. Convivial songs, songs of pleasantry, love-songs, even merry ballads of questionable propriety, were used at this season, and in one of Pepys's curious volumes he gives a list of tunes that were sung at a social gathering he visited, and in mentioning them he seems especially impressed by one. All the people in a dancing set on the floor sang a verse, then the instruments played the same tune, while all danced during the interlude, then sang again.

Of all the carols, either religious or secular, which have come down to us from the past, the most abidingly popular is the one beginning

> God rest you, merry gentlemen,
> Let nothing you dismay,
> For Jesus Christ in Bethlehem
> Was born upon this day.

Dickens in the " Carol" puts this old rhyme into the mouth of Scrooge's unlucky caller on Christmas Eve, who, the reader will remember, had a narrow escape from the mahogany ruler in the hands of the irate old miser. It is still sung in England by choruses of men and boys on their annual rounds in the evening and far into the night before the great holiday.

Carol-singing on Christmas Eve is also as much in vogue in the east end of London as ever it was a century or two ago. The elder members of the various church choirs and the Sunday-school children always parade the streets after midnight on Christmas Eve, singing outside the dwelling-houses of the more influential parishioners. They are usually invited into the houses they visit, and regaled with tea, coffee, and hot toast.

In some of the cathedral churches of England carol-singing is kept up as a part of the service, the choristers singing a Christmas carol at the door, in some parts of the nave, or on one of the towers. In one church in Kent a carol is sung every Christmas morning, the choristers standing around a particular slab in the floor which covers the remains of an old lady who during the reign of Elizabeth made a bequest to provide the church choir with a Christmas dinner in consideration of this mark of respect shown her memory. Such instances of the perpetuation of the custom, are, however, rare.

Catherine, St., patron saint of Venice, of philosophy and belles-lettres, of maidens, and against diseases of the tongue. Her father, Castio, King of Egypt, died when she was fourteen, and she succeeded to the throne. Urged by her subjects to marry, she replied that her husband must have four gifts : he must be so nobly born that all would worship him ; so great that he would not be indebted to her for being made a king; so beautiful that angels should desire to see him ; and so benign as to forgive all offences. Then her subjects despaired, for they knew of no such man. But the Virgin Mary appeared in a vision to a hermit named Alexandria, and bade him tell Catherine that her son was the husband she desired. The hermit gave Catherine pictures of Mary and Jesus. And gazing on his face she loved him, and could think of nothing else, and her studies became dull to her. One night she dreamed that angels bore her to his presence, but he turned away, saying, " She is not fair enough for me." Waking she wept. and besought the hermit to tell her how she might make herself worthy ; and he, finding that she was a heathen, taught her the Christian faith, and baptized her. That night the Virgin and Son appeared to her, and Mary presented her to Jesus, saying, " Lo, she hath been baptized, and I myself am her godmother." Then Jesus smiled on her, and was betrothed to her, and, waking, she found a ring upon her finger. From that time she despised all worldly things. Soon after Maximin came to Alexandria and persecuted the Christians. Then Catherine went to the temple and held an argument with the tyrant and confounded him. He ordered fifty learned men

ST. CATHERINE.
(From a mediæval manuscript.)

to come from all parts of the world to dispute with her, but she converted them all. Maximin in a great rage condemned them to the stake, and Catherine stood by and comforted them while they were burning. The Emperor fell in love with her beauty, and when she would not yield her virtue cast her into a dungeon. But angels ministered to her; and when, twelve days after, the Empress and her hundred attendants opened the dungeon, a bright light filled the whole place. The Empress and two hundred heathen were converted by the sight. Maximin put them all to death, and Catherine, having indignantly refused his offer of marriage, was bound between four spiked wheels, which turning in opposite directions would rend her to pieces. But fire came down from heaven and consumed the wheels, and three thousand persons were killed by flying pieces. Then Catherine was scourged and beheaded. Angels bore her body to Mount

Sinai. She is represented as richly dressed, and her attribute is the wheel, either whole or broken. She has also the martyr's palm, the royal crown, and a book, symbolical of her learning.

The convent of St. Catherine, situated in a valley on the slope of Mount Sinai, was founded by the Emperor Justinian in the sixth century. A marble sarcophagus contains the supposed relics of St. Catherine. Of these the skeleton of the hand, covered with rings and jewels, is exhibited to pilgrims and visitors.

> St. Cathern favors learned men, and gives them wisdom high,
> And teacheth to resolve the doubts, and always giveth aid
> Unto the scolding sophister, to make his reason staid.

So runs Barnaby Googe's translation of "The Popish Kingdom." The same authority asks,—

> What should I tell what sophisters on Cathern's day devise?
> Or else the superstitious joyes that maisters exercise.

But it was mainly as the patron of spinsters and an aid to matrimony that St. Catherine was courted. So late as 1730 La Motte in his "Essay on Poetry and Painting," p. 126, says, "St. Catherine is esteemed in the Church of Rome as the saint and patroness of the spinsters; and her holiday is observed, not in Popish countries only, but even in many places in this nation: young women meeting on the 25th of November and making merry together. which they call Catherning."

A correspondent of the *Athenæum*, October 31, 1840, recalls the custom in Worcestershire, when he was a boy, of going a-Cattaring, in honor of St. Catherine and of St. Clement: "About this season of the year," he says, "the children of the cottagers used to go round to the neighboring farm-houses, to beg apples and beer, for a festival on the above saints' days. The apples were roasted on a string before the fire, stuck thickly over with cloves, and allowed to fall into a vessel beneath. There were set verses for the occasion, which were sung, in a not unmusical chant, in the manner of carol-singing. I can only recollect the first few lines:

> Catt'n and Clement comes year by year.
> Some of your apples and some of your beer;
> Some for Peter, some for Paul,
> Some for Him who made us all.
> Peter was a good old man,
> For his sake give us some:
> Some of the best, and none of the worst,
> And God will send your souls to roost.

I well remember it always concluded with—

> Up with the ladder and down with the can,
> Give me red apples and I'll begone;

the ladder alluding to the store of apples generally kept in a loft or somewhere at the top of the house; and the can, doubtless, to the same going down into the cellar for the beer."

E. Gulson has this paragraph in *Notes and Queries:*

"At a recent meeting of the Archæological Institution, in Dorset, a party visited the little Norman Chapel of St. Catherine at Milton Abbey, when the Rev. C. W. Bingham told us of the legend. On a certain day in the year the young women used to go up to St. Catherine's Chapel, where they made use of the following prayer:

> A husband, St. Catherine;
> A handsome one, St. Catherine;
> A rich one, St. Catherine;
> A nice one, St. Catherine;
> And soon, St. Catherine.

"Mr. Beresford Hope, who at these gatherings is always equal to any emergency, modestly proposed that all the gentlemen and married ladies should retire from the chapel, so as to afford the young ladies present the opportunity of using so desirable a prayer."

Catherine of Siena, St., patroness of that Italian city. She lived in the fourteenth century, and was a woman of great energy and influence in her time. It is certain that she procured the return of Pope Gregory XI. from Avignon to Rome, and had a voice in many important affairs of state. The house where she was born is in one of the poorest and dirtiest parts of the city, now, as anciently, the fullers' quarter, for St. Catherine was the daughter of a dyer and fuller. It is near the old fountain of Fontebranda, which Dante mentions. Very little of the saint's original dwelling remains, except the chamber, and within is the cell which she inhabited. The latter is a little room about seven feet by six, lighted only by the door which communicates with the outer chamber. The brick floor is protected by a wooden covering, with a plate of glass inserted above the stone which formed St. Catherine's pillow. There is no furniture, and no ornament save a crucifix. But the rest of the house is converted into oratories gaudily decorated, with a few fine frescos representing the life of St. Catherine, and the miraculous crucifix from which she is said to have received the *stigmata*. A fine fresco by Sodoma, in one of the chapels of the church of San Domenico, represents her as swooning beneath the heavenly visitation. She is supported in the arms of two nuns, and the divinely given wounds are seen in her hands.

Cattino, Sacro. (It., " Sacred Dish.") A once famous relic, still kept in the church of St. Lawrence in Genoa, which used to be reverenced as the emerald dish given by the Queen of Sheba to King Solomon and afterwards preserved in the temple. Tradition likewise asserted that from this dish Christ ate the Last Supper. Found among the spoils of Cæsarea on the capture of that town by the combined armies of Genoa and Pisa in 1101, the Genoese took the " Sacro Cattino" for their share of the booty, leaving to the Pisans the entire mass of filthy lucre. It was brought to Genoa, where it continued to be held in such veneration that twelve nobles were appointed to guard the tabernacle which contained it, each a month in turn. It was exhibited but once a year to the adoration of the crowd. Then a priest held it aloft by a cord, while its twelve guardians formed a circle around. In 1476 a law was enacted condemning to death whoever touched the holy emerald with any substance whatever. Unless the booty at Cæsarea was very large, the Genoese did not make a bad investment in their emerald, for within fifty years the Jews lent them four millions of francs on its security. In 1809, among the other valuables borrowed of Italy by Napoleon, it travelled to Paris, where it remained until 1815, when it was restored without difficulty, broken, and ascertained to be glass. It is still preserved on account of its souvenirs, and as a curious ancient dish; but Genoa has lost, in losing her belief in the relic, a capital of nearly a million of dollars.

Cecilia, St., patron of music, and especially of sacred music. Honored in both the Eastern and Western Churches, she is counted as one of the four great Virgins of the Latin Church, and is named along with only a few others in the canon of the mass. Her festival is celebrated on November 22, the reputed date of her martyrdom.

Authentic history has nothing to say about her. Legends are plentiful. The most familiar makes her a native of Rome, of noble parentage. Converted early to Christianity, she took a vow of perpetual virginity. But she was forced by her parents to marry a pagan, Valerian. On the wedding night she took him into her confidence and told him that she had a guardian angel in perpetual attendance. He asked to see the angel, and she promised that the vision should be revealed to him if he became a Christian. So he sought out St. Urban, the Pope, and was baptized. Then his eyes were opened. The angel extended to the pair two crowns of roses and lilies, which he had brought from paradise and which were invisible save to believers. But their fragrance could not be concealed. It attracted the attention of Valerian's brother Tibertius, who was himself converted. These three wrought many good deeds and wonders. Persecution followed. Valerian and Tibertius, with an officer named Maximus whom they had converted, were put to death. Their feast is commemorated on April 14. Subsequently Cecilia herself was brought before the wicked prefect Almachius and condemned to death in a hot bath. But her life was miraculously preserved. Then the headsman was called in, but the three strokes allowed by the law failed to do their work; the half-beheaded martyr lived three days among her friends, and then died, bequeathing her house to Urban for a church. The date of her martyrdom is usually given as A.D. 230, which would place it within the reign of Alexander Severus, who was not a persecutor. But others substitute the year 180, which would be the time of Marcus Aurelius.

It is certain, however, that there was a church dedicated to St. Cecilia which had fallen into decay in 821. Pope Paschal I. rebuilt it in that year. During the progress of the work the saint, it is said, appeared to him in a vision and told him where her body lay in the cemetery of Calixtus. He proceeded to the spot and found it, clothed in a robe of gold tissue, with linen cloths at the feet, dipped in her blood. With her were found the bodies of Valerian, Tibertius, and Maximus. All these, together with the relics of Popes Urban and Lucius, lying in the adjoining cemetery of Pretextatus, were translated to St. Cecilia's Church, which is to-day known as Santa Cecilia in Trastevere, or St. Cecilia beyond the Tiber.

When the church was again rebuilt in 1599 the body was again found, in a marvellous state of preservation, and the sculptor Stefano Maderno made it the model for his celebrated recumbent statue which now surmounts the tomb of the Virgin Martyr.

Alban Butler explains that St. Cecilia has been accepted as the patron of church music " from her assiduity in singing the divine praises, in which, according to her Acts, she often joins instrumental music with vocal." But Herder asserts that the choice came from the misunderstanding of a passage in these Acts or legends. No saint, he says, ever came to renown more innocently than Cecilia; for instead of being described as a musician she is said to have turned away from worldly music, to sing in her heart only. The passage in question, important in several connections, narrates that on the day of her marriage, *et cantantibus organis illa in corde suo solo domino decantabat, dicens, Fiat Domine cor meum et corpus meum immaculatum ut non fundar :* or, in Caxton's translation, " and she heeryng the organes makyng melodye she sange in hir herte onelye to God sayeng O Lord I beseche the that myn herte and body may be undefowled so that I may not be confounded."

It is quite certain that the earlier artists did not depict her with musical instruments, neither in the rude drawings of the sixth or seventh century in the Catacombs, nor in the great mosaic in her church at Rome, dating from about 817, nor in the series of frescos of about the same date, nor in Cimabue's picture of nearly five centuries later. The earliest important representation is in the magnificent wing of Van Eyck's Ghent altar-piece, now in the Berlin Museum, painted about 1435, if this be a saint, and not merely an angel, as some critics hold. Nearly a hundred years later, in 1513, came Raphael's famous picture now preserved in Bologna. The moment chosen is that characterized by the passage from the legend already quoted. At the saint's feet lie the disregarded instruments of secular music, the flute, violin, etc., while in her hands is a small portable organ; but she does not play it, being rapt in ecstasy as she sees through the opened heavens a beautiful choir and hears their song. Raphael in his first drawing put instruments into the hands of the heavenly musicians, but the idea of the choir is far finer. After Raphael's came other pictures of the saint as musician or patron. In the seventeenth century, following the opening of the tomb in 1599, many painters were busy with the subject, especially Domenichino, who was in Rome during the enthusiastic period of the re-entombment.

It must be remembered that during this period of two centuries the science and art of music were making great strides; ideas of harmony were growing up as the organs were slowly improved, so that chords were endurable; but how far those were from modern ideas will be suggested by recalling the fact that Palestrina was not born till after Raphael's death. This growing art, whose most conspicuous usefulness and triumph were thus far in sacred song, deserved a patron saint quite as truly as the heathen arts of whose uses every one was now hearing, thanks to the revival of classical learning. And so, when a choice had once been made, men everywhere accepted it eagerly. In a French town early in the sixteenth century an association of musicians was put by the magistrate under the patronage of St. Cecilia, instead of St. Job's, as they had requested; and in later times countless musical societies and some journals have borne her name. In Evreux, France, in 1571, musical festivals were inaugurated, with contests and prizes for compositions, and continued for some years. In England the celebrations of the saint's day, beginning in 1683, carried on pretty regularly for twenty years and intermittently in the next century, were opened by religious services in some church, and then the company adjourned to a hall for the further exercises. These included an ode on some subject relating to music, the music itself to which the ode was sung being written by some composer of eminence. The words were likewise written by poets of temporary and sometimes immortal repute. The most famous of all are Dryden's two odes. The first was written for the London celebration of 1687, and was set to music by Draghi.

Dryden's second ode, entitled " Alexander's Feast, or the Power of Music," is one of the best known poems in the language: it was written for the festival of 1697, with music by Clarke; later, Handel gave it a more fitting setting. Taine calls it "an admirable trumpet-blast, in which metre and sound impress upon the nerves the emotions of the mind; a masterpiece of rapture and of art, which Victor Hugo alone has come up to."

Addison's "Song for St. Cecilia's Day at Oxford" was written for the celebration in 1692, when he was only twenty years old. It is mainly an apostrophe to the saint to attend the celebration and assist her "vocal sons of harmony."

Alexander Pope must not be left out of this short list, although it has been severely said that he wrote "in praise of an art of the principles of which he was ignorant, while to its effects he was insensible." His ode for the London festival of 1717, written, however, in 1708, has some fine lines, but is far inferior to Dryden's. (*New York Evening Post*, November 21, 1896. See also Butler, Baring-Gould, Mrs. Jameson, etc.)

The empty shrine of St. Cecilia in the Catacombs of St. Calixtus is an object of special worship on the feast-day of the Virgin Martyr. On that occasion only the catacomb chapel is thrown open, and masses are said there in quick succession from early dawn till noon. A correspondent of the *Baltimore Sun* writing from Rome under date of November 22, 1895, gives this account of the celebration in that year:

"It may be said that the majority of travellers and tourists at present visiting Rome might be met with here in this cemetery of Calixtus, crowding the chapel of St. Cecilia and the galleries and corridors near it, and attending with silent awe to the ceremonies held here on this her feast-day beside the empty tomb of that popular saint. Year by year the crowds that throng this spot increase, and the decoration of the place becomes more elaborate.

"This shrine, which once held the body of St. Cecilia, is a rudely shaped, spacious cave, cut beneath the soil, at the entrance to the catacomb, and it is to-day turned into a bower of beauty by the profusion of flowers with which it is decorated. From the conical-shaped *lucernario*, or air-aperture, admitting faintly the pale rays of sunlight, great long festoons of odoriferous box branches, interwoven with pale pink and flaming red roses, droop in graceful outlines. The walls are of the crude tufa,—the volcanic stone of the soil around here,—and resemble the sides of a quarry. To-day, the feast of St. Cecilia, they are almost hidden behind wreaths harmoniously interwoven of chrysanthemum and narcissus and nasturtium and tiny ferns. In the great cavity, or niche, opening into the wall on a level with the floor the flowers are most profuse. This was the spot where the remains of Cecilia were entombed. Here stood the huge marble sarcophagus, and within it the coffin of cypress wood in which she lay, just as she died. Lights and flowers—the choicest flowers of all—render this rude niche a fair shrine. And in the centre of it is a tiny statuette, in alabaster, copied after the renowned statue by Stefano Maderno, which lies beneath the high altar in the church of St. Cecilia in Trastevere, in Rome, at the very spot to which her remains were transferred in the ninth century.

"Very few saints have been so popular with artists as Cecilia. On the rude wall, quite close to the place of her empty tomb, an early artist's loving hand has depicted his ideal of what she might resemble. The method of painting and other considerations known or observed by archæologists lead them to the conclusion that this work of art should be attributed to the seventh century. It is in fresco, and occupies the place of a mosaic demolished at an earlier period. Some of the tiny cubes of mosaic are still to be seen inserted in the wall around this fresco. The picture is that of a young woman standing in a garden of flowers, tall red roses blooming on each side of her. The face is beautiful; clear brown eyes, under high arched brows, look out calmly at the spectator.

"Her rich golden hair, amid which large pearls gleam, is but a shade darker than the yellow nimbus which encircles her head. A crimson tunic, bound at the neck with many rows of pearls and other jewels in rich settings, covers the body and is gathered in at the waist by a cincture set with large pearls. The arms, enclosed in sleeves tight at the wrists, are held wide open, in that attitude of prayer so frequently met with in the catacomb figures known as Orantes.

"For those who take an interest in the marvellous history of early Christian Rome, or who are touched by the charming associations of Cecilia with music, to-day's visitation of the catacomb, where her remains were placed after her martyrdom, is a memorable event. Many hundreds of strangers from far-away lands crowded these narrow passages, with the numberless empty graves on either hand, where the darkness was dispersed by the many lighted candles placed in wooden sconces at intervals along the walls."

Century, End of. When does a century end? When does a new one begin? This question agitated all the civilized world at the end of the eighteenth century. It is again disturbing it at the end of the nineteenth.

The London *Times* in August, 1896, makes this contribution to the question:

"Let us suppose a person to be writing a letter some eighteen months after the birth of Christ. How will he date his letter? Will he write, say, July 10, year 1, or July 10, year 2? If he writes the former, he will consistently hold that the next century begins January 1, 1900; if he writes the latter, he will hold that it begins January 1, 1901. The first view is based on the theory that the time specified is one year, six months, and nine days (and some hours, to be exact) after the birth of our Lord. The second view is based on the theory that the time specified is the second year, sixth month, and tenth day after the same event. According to the first view, February 10, 1896, means 1896 years, one month, nine days (and some hours) after the birth of Christ, and we are consequently in the 1897th year. According to the second view, February 10, 1896, means the 1896th year, second month, and tenth day, and we are consequently in the 1896th year. According to the first view, the number of the year is a cardinal number; according to the second view, it is an ordinal number. Both of these methods can conceivably be maintained, and, as stated above, both are in use. If we write a letter in the afternoon and wish to specify the exact time, we date, *e.g.*, 4.30 P.M., which means four hours and thirty minutes after twelve o'clock. There we use a cardinal number. We might equally well write 'in the fifth hour,' but as a fact we do not so write. Again, in walking, as soon as you reach the tenth milestone from a given starting-place you have completed ten miles. So when a boy is twelve years old we say he is in his thirteenth year, and he does not have to wait another year before getting into his teens. All these calculations are based on the reasonable ground that in concrete reckonings of time and space we do not begin with 1, but with 0, and that there is the same space between 0 and 1 as there is between 1 and 2. The question then is, When we write 1896 are we using a cardinal or an ordinal number? It is clear that if we are using a cardinal number the last day of the century is December 31, 1899, while if we are using an ordinal number the last day of the century is December 31, 1900."

The *Times* concluded in favor of December 31, 1900. Here are its reasons:

"(1) In English we use the ordinal number in the day of the month; we say 1st, 2d, 3d, etc., and not 1, 2, 3, etc. The name of the month also is equivalent to an ordinal number, because by

February, *e.g.*, we mean the second month. It would thus be illogical to suppose that the year is a cardinal number when the month and day are ordinal. (2) If we turn the year into Latin, it is an ordinal number,—viz., anno millesimo nonagesimo sexto. If it is objected that the Latin number may be ordinal and yet the English be cardinal, the obvious reply is that by this number the Latin means the same year as we mean by 1896, and not what we mean by 1895. (3) The parallel tables of years made by chronologists in comparing one system of dating with another make 1 B.C. followed immediately by 1 A.D. Thus, in Zumpt's 'Annales' (to take a well-known book) the year of Rome (A.U.C.) 753 corresponds with B.C. 1, and the next year, 754, with A.D. 1. And this is, of course, not an arbitrary calculation of Zumpt, but he is merely carrying on the accepted mode of reckoning. Strictly speaking, A.D. (Anno Domini) is applicable only to this mode of dating, for if a cardinal number is used it should be P.C. (post Christum). On the whole, we may consider we are tolerably safe in holding that the next century begins on January 1, 1901, though great names may be quoted on the other side."

Cerealia, or Feast of Ceres. An ancient Roman festival, lasting from the 12th to the 19th of April, or, according to some authorities, from the 7th to the 14th. This festival was celebrated in honor of Ceres, whose wanderings in search of her lost daughter Proserpine were represented by women, clothed in white, running about with lighted torches. As the foreign Megalesia was especially appropriated by the nobles, so the festival of the Roman goddess of agriculture belonged peculiarly to the plebeians; they feasted one another at this time, as the nobles had done in the former festival. This was, indeed, a time of the greatest hilarity and merriment, and for this reason the celebration of the Cerealia was omitted in times of public mourning, and it was regarded as a great breach of propriety when on one occasion the gladiatorial shows were given instead of the Circensian games which properly belonged to the festival. The last day, the 19th, was the great festival of the year for the common people. They crowded in the Circus or race-course, where nuts and other trifles were thrown among them; and, besides the horse-races, it was the practice to set foxes loose in the Circus with lighted torches tied to their tails,—a symbol, it is thought, of the red blight or rust that burns up the corn.

Both the Megalesia and the Cerealia were, like many other festivals, originally celebrated for only one day; and when the Cerealia were extended over an entire week they were made to embrace the ancient festival of the Fordicidia, when a sacrifice was made to Tellus, goddess of the earth.

Chalitzah or **Halitza.** (From the Jewish word *halitz*, "to loosen," "to detach.") A Jewish ceremony which is fully described in the twenty-fifth chapter of Deuteronomy. "If brethren dwell together," says verse 5, "and one of them die, and have no child, the wife of the dead shall not marry without unto a stranger: her husband's brother shall go in unto her, and take her to him to wife, and perform the duty of a husband's brother unto her." The first-born of this marriage, the text goes on to explain, shall be named after the dead brother and be treated as his heir. But if the living brother refuse, he must submit to the Chalitzah : "Then shall his brother's wife come unto him in the presence of the elders, and loose his shoe from off his foot, and spit in his face, and shall answer and say, 'So shall it be done unto that man that will not build up his brother's house.'" The loosening of the recalcitrant brother's shoe was a symbol that the widow took away in public court his right to her and to the possessions of the deceased. It will be remembered that anciently the possession of property was claimed by planting the foot upon it, and its sale was consummated by the original owner's taking off his shoe and handing it to the new proprietor. Among the orthodox Jews the ceremony of the Chalitzah is still practised even in America. But in 1869 a Rabbinical convention of the Reformed Jews declared that brother-in-law and sister-in-law were within the prohibited degrees of kindred, and that the entire custom which involved the Chalitzah was out of date.

Champion of England. At the coronation of an English sovereign it was long usual for a man in armor to make his appearance on horseback just as the second course had been served at the royal banquet in Westminster Hall. A herald proclaimed that if anybody dared to deny that the recently crowned monarch was not the lawful king of England "here was a champion that would fight with him." At these words the champion would fling down his gauntlet. This ceremony was thrice repeated. No one answering after the third defiance, the champion found his way to the king's table, where his majesty drank to him and presented him with the gilt cup to keep as his own. By prescriptive right the perquisites of this important functionary were "one of the king's great coursers, with the saddle, harness, and trappings of cloth of gold; one of the king's best suits of armor, with cases of cloth of gold; and all other things belonging to the king's body when he goes into mortal battle; and the gold cup in which the king drinks to him, with its cover." The arms provided for the royal champion at the coronation of King James II. in 1685 are very particularly enumerated : " A complete suit of white armor, a pair of gauntlets, a sword and hanger, a case of rich pistols, an oval shield with the champion's arms painted on it, and a gilded lance fringed about the handles. Also a field saddle of crimson velvet with breastplate and other caparisons for the horse, richly laden with gold and silver, a plume of red, white, and blue feathers, consisting of eighteen falls and a heron's top, another plume for the horse's head, and trumpet banners with the champion's own arms depicted on them." All this magnificence was the lawful fee of the champion, with the understanding, however, that certain compensation money would be allowed upon re-delivery of the property to the Master of the Royal Armory for the time being.

The office is a very ancient one, and is popularly supposed to have been brought to England by William the Conqueror. It was originally vested in the Marmion family, said to have been hereditary champions to the Dukes of Normandy long prior to the Conquest, and later became one of the privileges that went with their feudal manor of Scrivelsby, Lincolnshire. Upon the death without male issue of Philip de Marmion during the reign of Edward II., the manor of Scrivelsby became the property of his younger daughter. By marriage with her heiress, Margaret, Sir John Dymoke acquired the estate and the hereditary office, and duly performed the duties of champion at the coronation of Richard II. Estate and office still remain in the Dymoke family. At the coronation of King William IV., however, and of Queen Victoria, the public banquet of the sovereign in Westminster Hall was dispensed with, as well as the services of the champion, in 1841 the then head of the Dymoke house being rewarded with a baronetcy in return for waiving his claim. The last appearance of the champion, therefore, was at the coronation of King George IV., on July 19, 1821. Walpole, writing to George Montagu, says, " The champion acted his part admirably, and dashed down his gauntlet with proud defiance. His associates, Lord Effingham, Lord Talbot, and the Duke of Bedford, were woful. Lord Talbot [the Lord High Steward] piqued himself on backing his horse down the hall and not turning its tail towards the king; but he had taken such pains to drill it to that duty that it entered backwards; and at his retreat the spectators clapped. A terrible indecorum, but suitable to such Bartholomew Fair doings."

There is no lack of stories setting forth the acceptance of the champion's challenge. Myths of this sort are associated with every eighteenth-century coronation that took place while a Pretender existed. Usually it is a woman who pushes her way through the crowd, takes up the champion's gauntlet, and leaves her own glove in its place. Sometimes the woman is described as old and infirm and supported by crutches, and at other times as young and beautiful. One version makes the Pretender himself, disguised in female attire, accomplish the daring feat. Sir Walter Scott in "Redgauntlet," it may be remembered, avails himself of this curious legend. Obedient to the command of her uncle, Redgauntlet, Lilias, the heroine of the novel, on the third sounding of the champion's challenge rushes through the crowd, a lane being opened for her as though by word of command, picks up the "parader's gage," and leaves another in lieu thereof.

Chantry. (Lat. *capellania;* Fr. *chapellenie.*) The old English name for an endowment of land or other revenues which were to be used for the maintenance of a priest to say a daily mass for the souls of the founder and his family or other benefactors. By extension the name came to be applied to the chapel, aisle, or part of an aisle in a church set apart for the offering of such masses.

Chantries formed the chief means of livelihood of thousands of priests during the Middle Ages. The salary was seldom more than seven or eight pounds a year. Very rarely the priest had a little house and garden, but, as a rule, he had nothing better than a two-roomed hut, often with no fireplace beyond a space on the ground on which he burnt some dried turf, and with no chimney except a hole in the roof. A bench and a bed-stead were usually his entire furniture. This, however, was the case only where he held no other office and did not belong to a religious order. Although his duties were sometimes confined to his daily mass, he was often bound to act as village school-master, or even as master of the town grammar-school. Where the chantry priest said his mass in a cathedral, or in a collegiate, parochial, or other church where the divine office was sung, by the law of the English Church he was bound to assist at these services, which entailed some three or four hours in choir during the course of the day. Some foundations of chantries obliged the priest to act as a librarian. The celebrated Whittington, lord mayor of London, who established a library in the city, also founded a chantry, binding the priest to act as librarian.

These were necessarily men of education; but there are reasons for believing that many chantry priests were put through a very simple course of theology, and were taught only Latin enough to enable them to say their mass and their office. Very few of them had permission to preach, or faculties for hearing confessions. Sometimes, however, chantries were given to parish priests or their curates, and at other times to monas-teries. A large number of chantries were attached to cathedrals, and very many were founded by bishops and ecclesiastics. There were nearly one hundred chantries at St. Paul's Cathedral alone; but some that were insufficiently endowed were united, and at the dissolution there were only fifty-four priests saying mass daily in the cathedral.

Chantries were dissolved by Henry VIII. in 1545 and 1547, although he was inconsistently anxious to take a personal and selfish advantage of their possible benefits, as he willed that masses should be said for his own soul "forever," enjoining all his "heirs and successors who should be kings of this realm, as they would answer before Almighty God at the dreadful day of judgment," to carry out this bequest.

Chanuckah, or **Hunuka.** (Heb., "Feast of Lights;" known also as the Feast of Dedication.) A Jewish festival commencing on the 23d day of Kislev and commemorating the recapture of the temple and city of Jerusalem by the Maccabees. In the summer of 165 B.C. the forces of the Maccabees met a large army of the Syrians and vanquished them at Bethzur. After the triumph Maccabeus with his army entered Jerusalem, only to find the sacred city a place of desolation. The temple was deserted and defiled by heathen altars, the gates had been thrown down, and the sacred places desecrated. The pious work of purification was begun, and on the 25th of Kislev, 165 B.C., it was finished. The temple was once more consecrated, and the perpetual light, which Antiochus had quenched, was lighted. A jar of sacred oil, sealed with the ring of the high-priest, and sufficient for one day's consumption, was discovered just when it was wanted. Miraculously enough, it lasted for eight days. According to Jewish tradition, it was then decreed that every year the eight days beginning with the 25th of Kislev should be celebrated as a festival to commemorate the event.

Among orthodox Jews the home celebration of Chanuckah takes this form. On the first night two waxen tapers are lighted, one as a torch, the other to symbolize the first day of the feast. On the second night after sundown a second taper is lighted, and so on successively until on the eighth night there are eight tapers, exclusive of the torch. A modern innovation is to start with a lighted taper for every member of the household, increasing the number by one every night. These tapers remain lighted until they burn out, and are not renewed. The inner meaning of the observance is the increasing strength of spiritual light and truth. In the Jewish synagogues there are prayers twice a day, at sunrise and at sunset. No fast or mourning is allowed during the eight days of the festival.

The week prior to its commencement is given up to the preparation of the wax tapers. These are made of genuine beeswax. The head of the family softens the yellow wax in hot water so that he can manipulate it, and moulds it into the form of tapers around pieces of twine. These candles are not so smooth and pretty as the store candles, but they are odd and quaint, and seem more appropriate to the ceremonies which accompany the lighting of them. These consist of the chanting of verses of praise. The verses are repeated by each male, and begin as follows:

"Blessed art thou, Lord our God, King of the world, who hast sanctified us with thy commandments, and enjoined upon us to light the lamps of the Feast of the Dedication."

The Jewish month of Kislev corresponds roughly with our December. Hence the 25th of Kislev may and sometimes does fall on the 25th of December, or at least our Christmas Day may be included in the week of Chanuckah. There are some Jews who have departed from the customs of their fathers sufficiently to buy the colored wax tapers which Christians use on their Christmas-trees, but your real orthodox Jew would look with horror upon the use of such candles. In his eyes it would be sacrilege. These candles are made of a composition by the hands of Gentiles. Possibly—the thought is almost too horrible to dwell upon—the composition may contain lard, the fat of the beast which is most repugnant of all animals to the Jew.

The coincidence of dates has led to some confusion between Christmas and Chanuckah in the minds of the less instructed Jews, and it is the aim of the orthodox rabbi to keep constant guard against the Christian innovations which are only too likely to enter into the Hebrew ceremonial.

Charivari (in local American usage frequently corrupted into **Chivaree** or **Shivaree**). A French word of uncertain origin, but probably onomatopoetic or imitative, signifying a mock serenade with horns, kettles, saucepans, etc. In France serenades of this sort were formerly inflicted upon newly married couples and upon persons who had made themselves socially or politically unpopular. The charivari still survives in spots through the provinces. The French inhabitants of Louisiana and of Canada brought the custom to America, and through them it was pretty generally distributed over the United States, where it is not yet altogether extinct. The same sort of concert in Germany is called Katzenmusik ("cats' music"), and in England Rough-music.

The chivaree was originally extended both in this country and in France to all bridal couples, but more recently was limited to widows or widowers who remarried too hastily, to couples in whom an unusual disparity of age existed, or to such other unions as were either ridiculous or unpopular. Cases of notorious domestic infelicity or infidelity called forth similar expres-

A CHARIVARI IN THE MIDDLE AGES.
(From Wright's " Caricature and Grotesque.")

sions of neighborly disapproval. In mediæval times in many European countries a wife who beat her husband was placed upon a donkey, with her back to its head, its tail was grasped by the lickspittle spouse who had allowed himself to be trounced, and thus they paraded through the streets, greeted with shouts and cries and beatings of tin pans. It is not impossible that here was the germ idea of the charivari. Nor was it everywhere entirely superseded by the latter. So recently as 1867 the *Courrier de l'Ain* (quoted *sub voce* in La Rousse's Encyclopædia) had this paragraph : " On January 22, in the little village of Turgon, a commune of Druillat, a large mob met together. Upon a large cart whereto a pair of horses were harnessed sat sundry individuals representing a court of justice, all in appropriate costumes : a president in a toque and a red gown, five judges in robes made of women's dresses or window-curtains, an officer of the public ministry dubbed Procureur de la Cornaillerie, two lawyers, a jury, two policemen, and two witnesses. Before the solemn tribunal came a husband and wife, represented by two other persons. The first was accused of having received, the second of having given, sundry blows from a broomstick. In front of a cart was a float whereon was the effigy of an ass, and on this ass, seated with his face to the tail, was a man bearing on his head the horns of a stag and in his hands a distaff which he was pretending to spin." A mock judgment was just about to be delivered, when a party of genuine policemen burst on the scene and brought the actors before the real justice, who fined them forty sous apiece.

At the beginning of the seventeenth century charivaris were forbidden by the Council of Tours under pain of excommunication. The French parliament also thundered against "the tumults known as charivaris practised before the houses of those who remarried." But neither Church nor State could put an end to the custom.

On the 31st of July, 1751, the eve of the feast of St. Peter in Vinculis, whom the Parisian cobblers had taken as their patron, a number of charcoal-burners determined to amuse themselves at the expense of such of their fellows as had married aged widows, and with this object to present them with bouquets amid a fanfare of musical instruments. The pretence was that these unfortunates ought to acknowledge the same patron as the cobblers, who dealt in second-hand leather. So they took two donkeys which they adorned with the implements of their trade and especially with old pieces of leather, old shoes, and pendent ox-feet. Each was ridden by a mummer similarly ornamented. A procession of charcoal-burners followed, walking two by two. All were grotesquely accoutred in similar taste. The first cobbler before whose house they stopped received them good-humoredly and opened beer for them. The next took the affair as an insult to himself and his fellow-cobblers. He informed the syndic of the guild, the cobblers gathered in force and mobbed the procession, the two riders were thrown into prison, and the courts punished them for inciting to riot.

Even so late as January, 1862, a troop of students of the Latin Quarter, having done their sibilatory best to damn Edmond About's play of " Gaetana" at the Odéon Theatre, marched to his house and celebrated a charivari under his windows.

Alice T. Chase, in *American Notes and Queries*, vol. i. p. 263, has some interesting notes on the American shivaree. " Twenty years ago," she says (she is writing in September, 1888), " it may be safely said, there were very few hamlets or rural communities of any size, from Pennsylvania west through the central belt of States, where the custom was not known and more or less frequently practised. Whether it ever gained much hold in Michigan, Wisconsin, and the northern States of the West, I cannot say, but I do know that it was most prevalent in Ohio, Indiana, and

Illinois, and that in some instances colonies from these States transplanted it into Kansas and Nebraska. That it still prevails in many districts, I could bring abundant evidence. You speak of the custom as being French in its origin, as its name unquestionably is. I thought that we owed it to the class known as 'Pennsylvania Dutch,' a class made up of diligent and sober citizens, but altogether illiterate and unappreciative of the refinements of civilized life. The 'shivaree' is described at length in Eggleston's 'The End of the World.' I know of no other writer who has ever tried to convert its unpleasant vulgarity into dramatic effect. It was a compliment extended to every married couple on their nuptial night, and consisted of a serenade made up of beating tin pans, blowing horns, ringing cow-bells, playing horse-fiddles, caterwauling, and, in fine, of the use of every disagreeable sound possible to make night hideous. This noise was kept up often for hours, or until the bridegroom made his appearance and 'treated' the crowd. It was of no use for this luckless individual to attempt to wear out the crowd by an obstinate refusal to appear. In that case the outside company would grow riotous, would hurl stones and fire blank cartridges through the windows, and after them, perhaps, dead cats and rotten eggs. Nor was it of any use for a couple to have the ceremony performed earlier in the day and start immediately on their bridal tour; the 'shivaree' would and did keep, and was served up to them in all its unadulterated nastiness immediately upon their return. Of course the actors in the 'shivaree' business were mainly young men and boys. The older men of the community protested against it, and all respectable women utterly loathed it. But protests were of no avail, nor was it of any use to send a constable around the next morning with warrants to arrest the ringleaders. When brought before the judge they were simply dismissed with a trifling fine, and were quite ready to repeat the performance with emphasis on the occasion of the next wedding. The fact was, the young men, having few diversions in their quiet life, enjoyed these 'sprees,' and no one had moral courage enough to interfere and forbid their amusement. The decadence of this rough form of sport may be ascribed first to the general diffusion of education and civilized customs that has been going on of late years, and, secondly, to the great tendency of population toward cities. This latter fact has acted in two ways: it has taken the ringleaders away from the rural communities, causing the custom there to die a natural death, and these characters have not been able to transplant their amusement to their new abodes, since there they come under the supervision of police officers, whose business it is to interfere with such infractions of the peace. The 'shivaree' custom was unquestionably a survival of semi-barbaric times; the curious point to note is how nearly this barbarous custom touches our advanced civilization of the present day."

The natural result of the chivaree in many remote parts of the United States has been to increase the number of secret marriages. No one can be blamed for reticence which avoids this harrowing experience. A correspondent of the *New York Evening Post* (February 6, 1897, p. 13) finds in the mountains of the Southern States " a general concealment of proposed connubiality and nuptial intent. It may be generally known that Zeb is ' keeping regular company' with Lize. Suddenly the town will be apprised of the fact that ' Zeb and Lize done got married last night.' This constitutes what might be called an anticipated surprise.

"A man who was doing some work for me came to me one day at noon, and asked permission to be absent until ' quartering time,' half-past three o'clock. He said nothing to me or to his associates of his purpose. He returned promptly on time, to announce, in a casual and indifferent manner, that during his absence he had been married, and, with the little furniture possessed by the pair, had settled in a cabin of his own. Again and again have I seen the same plan followed in other cases."

Charlemagne, St., Festival of. (Fr. *Fête de St. Charlemagne,* or, colloquially, *La Sainte Charlemagne.*) The title under which the death-day of the Emperor Charlemagne is celebrated in all the higher French educational institutions. Charlemagne was born April 2, 742, and died January 28, 814. Of course his canonization is merely a jocular and scholastic one. But he took a great interest in educational matters, and is the reputed founder of the Paris University. It may be added, however, as a curious coincidence, that Charlemagne was actually raised to saintship by one of the antipopes.

On La Sainte Charlemagne all the students who have obtained the first place in their class once, or the second place twice, are invited to a grand breakfast, which is presided over by the principal, and at which all the professors assist. At dessert the principal makes an address. Then the scholars recite poems composed by them for the occasion. Formerly these were in Latin. Since the middle of the nineteenth century they have been in French. In 1896 another change was introduced, which Francisque Sarcey thus bemoans in the pages of the *Cosmopolitan Magazine* for April, 1896:

"Up to this time it had always been the custom, when the breakfast of the pupils was ended, that all the personnel of the college should sit down to table, in their turn, and that the feast should begin over again for the professors. It was naturally out of the funds of the Institute that the expenses of the repast—which was of the most modest kind, indeed—were defrayed. But the university is not rich, and the Minister of Public Instruction, with a view to economizing the educational fund, decided in his wisdom that this year the professors, after making the tour of the tables at which the students were celebrating the feast of the saint, should return to their homes to eat their breakfasts there.

"Between ourselves, I do not believe that the professors regretted this measure. The breakfast, at a set price, was generally indifferent; and the professors have so many opportunities every day of seeing and conversing with one another that the pleasure of sitting at the same table together to drink champagne at three francs a bottle was for them a very slight one. I know some of them who thanked the minister in their hearts for his niggardliness, which freed them from this extra duty.

"But we, who regard the matter from another point of view, —a less selfish and a more general one,—cannot see without regret this first attack upon an ancient custom which contributed to the lustre and glory of the university.

"You cannot conceive how in former times this fête of Charlemagne excited the minds and kindled the imaginations of all the students. To have one's St. Charlemagne, as they used to say in those days, was a sign that one was the first, or one of the first, in his class. It was a great honor, ardently desired. At the breakfast, which had been anticipated with joyful eagerness, the professors looked on with an indulgent eye while the gayety became more and more boisterous; and they were ready to excuse all the pranks played by the young people under the exhilarating influence of the wine.

"I shall never forget how, after leaving one of these love-feasts in company with Edmond About, who was a little intoxicated by the champagne, the talking, and the shouting, he and I went into the bursar's garden, in which there was a large basin where goldfish were darting about. Using our handkerchiefs as nets, we caught several of the poor little fishes and made ourselves a glorious dish of fried fish.

"In the evening,—this was also a traditional custom,—as it was a holiday, the boys made appointments with one another to meet at the Théâtre Français, whose manager they had requested to give a play appropriate for the occasion. They filled the house from top to bottom; they applauded vociferously; but if by chance any actor appeared who failed to please them, he was greeted with such a crowing of cocks and roaring of wild beasts as might make nature tremble.

" I greatly fear that the measure adopted by the minister, no doubt with good intention, has dealt a fatal blow to this ancient custom, which had already begun to fall into decadence. Now it is the professors who have lost their part in it; soon it will be the students."

Charles, St. King Charles I. of England is held by High Church authorities to be the only saint officially enrolled in her calendar by the Church of England since the Reformation. The anniversary of the date on which he was beheaded by order of Cromwell and the Long Parliament (January 30, 1649) is celebrated by a mass. The vespers of a martyr are sung on the preceding evening.

The ritualists hold that King Charles I. laid down his life as a martyr for the Church of England. The argument, briefly stated, is that if Charles had consented to the abolition of Episcopacy by the Puritan Parliament his life would have been spared.

This argument, of course, rejects the more common belief that in fighting for his bishops Charles was fighting for his kingdom. " No Bishop! No King!" was the programme of the Puritans. The ritualists will not allow that any alloy of selfishness entered into the motives of Charles I.

Accepting their argument, it is obvious that Charles deserved to be canonized. But the ritualists go further. They insist that he was actually canonized, and by the only authority within the Episcopal Church which is empowered to do so,—*i.e.*, by Convocation. They acknowledge that this is the only instance in which Convocation has ever exercised the power, but they assert that the power itself is, has been, and always will be resident within the Church, through its representative, Convocation. Their presentation of the case is full of curious ecclesiastical interest.

On May 29, 1660, eleven years after the martyrdom of Charles I., his son rode back into power as King Charles II. Early next year Convocation—the clergy, Lords, and Commons—united with Charles II. in appointing a special service of prayer with fasting " to be used yearly on the 30th of January, being the day of the martyrdom of the blessed King Charles the First." On the Prayer Book calendar the name of " King Charles, Martyr," was entered at January 30. The prayer applying specially to the new martyr ran as follows :

" O Lord, we offer unto Thee all praise and thanks for the glory of Thy grace that shined forth in Thine anointed, our sovereign, King Charles, and we beseech Thee to give us all grace by a careful, studious imitation of this Thy blessed saint and martyr, and all other saints and martyrs that have gone before us, that we may be made worthy to receive benefits by their prayers, which they, in communion with the church catholic, offer up unto Thee for that part of it here militant, through Thy Son, our blessed Saviour, Jesus Christ. Amen."

Here, then, are the documents in the case: Convocation characterized the death of Charles as a "martyrdom;" it caused him to be enrolled in the calendar as "King Charles, Martyr;" it set aside a special day for his commemoration, that day being, as was the old custom of the Catholic Church, the death-day and not the birthday; and it sanctioned a prayer in which King Charles was spoken of as God's "blessed saint and martyr." Nothing can be clearer than that Convocation, by the legitimate exercise of a function which it can legitimately claim, enrolled King Charles I. in the calendar of its saints and martyrs,—in other words, canonized him.

The Rev. John Keble, who wrote that once popular series of hymns, "The Christian Year," was evidently of this opinion. His hymn for January 30 begins as follows:

> Our own, our Royal Saint,—
> True son of our dear mother, early taught
> With her to worship, and for her to die,
> Nursed in her aisles to more than kingly thought,—
> Oft in her solemn hours we dream thee nigh.

Nor was there wanting the confirmation of miracles to show that heaven approved of the honors showered upon one of its favorite sons. A handkerchief which had been dipped in his blood at the execution was found to have antitoxine qualities. Pilgrims who visited the tomb of the martyr in St. George's Chapel at Windsor, where he was buried by permission of Oliver Cromwell, testified that they had been relieved of scrofula, or king's evil. For more than a century after the Restoration strict tories and Church of England men kept the 30th of January as a day of fasting and humiliation.

The first Lord Holland used to relate that during the lifetime of his father, Sir Stephen Fox, upon the return of every 30th of January the wainscot of the house was hung with black, and no meal of any sort was permitted until after midnight. This attempt at rendering the day melancholy by fasting had a directly contrary effect on the children; for the housekeeper, fearing that they might suffer through so long an abstinence from food, used to give the little folks clandestinely as many comfits and sweetmeats as they could eat. Thus Sir Stephen's intended fast was turned into a juvenile feast. (*Correspondence of C. J. Fox*, edited by Earl Russell.)

There were others also among their adult contemporaries who
brought revelry into the day of mourning, and did so of malice
prepense. For there were certain enemies of the Church of
England and admirers of Cromwell, who formed themselves
into a secret society called the Calves'-Head Club which met
every 30th of January to rejoice over the death of the Martyr-
King. Little is known about the early history of this organization. That little is to be gleaned from an anonymous pamphlet
of no great credibility entitled "The Secret History of the
Calves'-Head Club, or the Republicans Unmasked" (second
edition, 1703). The author asserts that "a certain active Whig"
had informed him "that Milton and other creatures of the
Commonwealth had instituted this club (as he was informed) in
opposition to Bishop Juxon, Dr. Sanderson, Dr. Hammond, and
other divines of the Church of England, who met privately
every 30th of January, and, though it was under the time of
the usurpation, had compiled a private form of service of the
day, not much different from what we now find in the Liturgy."
In the eighth edition, published in 1713, are added some particulars as to the manner in which the day was spent: "Their bill
of fare was a large dish of calves' heads, dressed several ways,
by which they represented the king, and his friends who had
suffered in his cause ; a large pike with a small one in his mouth,
as an emblem of tyranny ; a large cod's head, by which they
pretended to represent the person of the king singly ; a boar's
head, with an apple in its mouth, to represent the king. . . .
After the repast was over, one of the elders presented an Eikon
Basilike, which was with great solemnity burned upon the table."
Several thanksgiving songs or anthems are included, with the
information that they were sung at the anniversary meetings
in 1693–97. Here are a few agreeable references to Charles I.
from the 1696 anthem:

> This monarch wore a peaked beard
>   And seem'd a doughty hero,
> As Dioclesian innocent,
>   And merciful as Nero.

> The Church's darling implement,
>   And scourge of all the people,
> He swore he'd make each mother's son
>   Adore their idol steeple ;

> But they, perceiving his designs,
>   Grew plaguy shy and jealous,
> And timely chopt his calves' head off,
>   And sent him to his fellows.

The first note of public opposition to the anniversary as a
church festival was sounded in March, 1772, by Mr. Montague.

He led an attempt in the House of Commons to repeal so much of the Act of 12 Charles II. c. 30 as related to the ordering the 30th of January to be kept as a day of fasting and humiliation. Mr. Montague declared his motive to be the abolition of any absurdity from Church as well as State. He said that he saw great and solid reasons for abolishing the observance of that day by the Church, and hoped he should not be deemed to be speaking too harshly if he should brand the prescribed service with the name of impiety, particularly in those parts where Charles I. is likened to the Saviour of mankind. On a division, there being for the motion 97, and against it 125, it was lost by a majority of 27.

On the very second day of her reign, Queen Victoria, taking advantage of the addition to the Prayer Book of a special service " to be recited on the twentieth of June, being the anniversary of·the beginning of the Present Glorious Reign," promulgated the following order:

" Our will and pleasure is that these four forms of prayer and service made for the fifth of November, the thirtieth of January, the twenty-ninth of May, and the twentieth of June, be forthwith printed and published and annexed to the book of Common Prayer and liturgy of the United Church of England and Ireland, to be said yearly on the said days in all cathedrals and collegiate churches and chapels, in all chapels of colleges and halls within our universities of Oxford, Cambridge, and Dublin, and of our colleges of Eton and Winchester, and in all parish churches and chapels within those parts of our United Kingdom called England and Ireland.

" Given at our court at Kensington, the twenty-first day of June, 1837, in the first year of our reign.

" By Her Majesty's command.   J. Russell."

Thus it is seen that one of the very first acts of Queen Victoria was to republish and declare the " Martyrdom of King Charles the First," and, as the head of the Established Church, to enjoin the use of this service, as appropriate for the anniversary of his death.

A little over two decades later the opposition to the festival finally triumphed. At the meeting of Convocation in 1857 Dr. Milman, Dean of St. Paul's, expressed doubts as to the propriety in the present day of the special services for King Charles's Martyrdom, the Gunpowder Treason, and the Restoration. His views were supported by Dr. Martin, chancellor of the diocese of Exeter. In 1858 Lord Stanhope brought the matter before the House of Lords, moving an address to the queen on the subject. It was then stated that great objection to the ser-

vices prevailed, and that many clergymen, including the dean
and chapter of Canterbury Cathedral, refused to read them, and
already omitted them, without waiting for royal or parliamentary sanction to the course they adopted. Lord Stanhope was
supported by the Archbishop of Canterbury, the Bishops of
London and Oxford, the Earl of Derby, and other peers on both
sides of the House. A similar address was voted by the House
of Commons.

On January 17, 1859, Queen Victoria took matters into her
own hands and issued a royal warrant abolishing the three services. But it was perceived that, these services being appointed
by Acts of Parliament, clergymen might feel embarrassed by the
abolition being only the result of a royal warrant. A short Act
of Parliament was therefore introduced and passed the same
session, repealing the objectionable statutes. The services were
accordingly removed from the Prayer Book.

Not yet do the High Churchmen yield. Charles's removal
from the calendar was effected not by Convocation, or the clergy,
Lords, and Commons combined, but by Queen Victoria and the
House of Commons alone. It was, therefore, they contend,
illegal and of no effect. January 30 is still devoted rightfully
to the commemoration of St. Charles's martyrdom, they say,
and unless the removal from the calendar is sanctioned by Convocation, an unlikely contingency, King Charles, Martyr, is entitled to the commemoration decreed to him by Convocation in
1661.

In 1894 the Hon. Mrs. Greville Nugent founded the Society of
King Charles the Martyr, which numbers among its members
many persons of rank and influence. The prospectus sets forth
that the object of the society is " intercessory prayer for the
defence of the Church of England against the attacks of her
enemies," and continues,—

" The society is emphatically non-political. It is to the Church
in her spiritual aspect—the kingdom that is not of this world—
that its attention is principally directed, though it is prepared
also to resist anything that may tend to impair the usefulness
of the Church in the world. Those who join the society do not,
however, pledge themselves to more than the weekly use of the
annexed prayers (the first of which, being adapted from the
Eikon Basiliké, may be regarded as the words of King Charles
himself), and to the observance in some way of the 30th of January, the day of the king's death (which will be the anniversary
of the society), especially by attending, when possible, in any
church where they have been revived, the services formerly appointed for the day in the Book of Common Prayer."

It is proposed to establish the society in all parts of the globe where the Episcopal Church exists, and nowhere is membership to conflict with the existing form of government.

There are four churches in England dedicated to King Charles the Martyr. In New York city the church of St. Mary the Virgin and in Philadelphia the Church of the Evangelists celebrate the annual return of the martyrdom. A devotional picture of the saint was solemnly unveiled in 1896 in the Philadelphia church in the presence of Rt. Rev. William Stevens Perry, D.D., Bishop of Iowa and Historiographer of the American Church, who delivered a glowing panegyric, and of numerous prominent Anglican ecclesiastics. The day was celebrated with equal pomp in London. At the Anglican Church of St. Margaret Pattens a solemn eucharist was celebrated. The altar and sacrarium were vested in crimson and gold, the altar being ablaze with tapers, while the rest of the church was darkened. Around the altar were hung banners, one having a portrait of King Charles bearing the martyr's palm-branch, with the words "Sanctus Carolus, Rex et Martyr," embroidered in gold. The celebrant was attired in a crimson chasuble embroidered with silver, and was attended by a number of acolytes in scarlet cassocks and small caps. A choir sang, the anthem being "Be thou faithful unto death." The service was read from Laud's Book of Common Prayer, that ultimately cost Charles his head. The congregation was dressed in mourning and wore white Stuart roses. It included the Order of the White Rose, the Order of St. Germain, the Jacobite Club, the Legitimist Club, the Thames Valley Legitimists, the Society of King Charles the Martyr, and other Stuart organizations. In the evening there was a choral service, the clergy and choir marching round the church in procession with the banners. A great many wreaths of magnificent flowers, the inscriptions on which had first been examined by the government officials, were hung about King Charles's statue in Trafalgar Square. One was inscribed "Remember," another, "I go from a corruptible to an incorruptible crown." A Scottish society sent a wreath tied with a tartan silk ribbon, with the legend "In memory of the great-grandson of King Charles I., Charles Edward, died January 31, 1788. Wha wadna follow thee, King of the Hieland heart, bonnie Prince Charlie?" The Legitimist Club attached to a laurel wreath a long prayer, beseeching that the guilt of the king's innocent blood might not be laid to the people of the land.

The vault in which King Charles's coffin is interred was last opened in 1813, on the occasion of the funeral of the Duchess of Brunswick, the sister of George III. Before the reclosing of the vault search was made for the coffin of King Charles, in the presence of the Prince Regent. When found it was partially opened. Sir Henry Halford, one of the witnesses, published in the same year "An account of what appeared on opening the coffin of King Charles I." (1813), from which it appears that the body was found in good condition among the gums and resins employed to preserve it: "At length the whole face was disengaged from its covering. The complexion of the skin was dark and discolored. The forehead and temples had lost little or nothing of their muscular substance; the cartilage of the nose was gone; but the left eye in the first moment of exposure was open and full, though it vanished almost immediately, and the pointed beard was perfect. The shape of the face was a long oval; many of the teeth remained. . . . When the head had been entirely disengaged from the attachments which confined it, it was found to be loose, and without any difficulty was taken up and held to view. . . . The back part of the scalp was perfect, and had a remarkably fresh appearance; the pores of the skin being more distinct, as they usually are when soaked in moisture; and the tendons and filaments of the neck were of considerable substance and firmness. The hair was thick at the back part of the head, and in appearance nearly black. . . . On holding up the head to examine the place of separation from the body, the muscles of the neck had evidently retracted themselves; and the fourth cervical vertebra was found to be cut through its substance transversely, leaving the surfaces of the divided portions perfectly smooth and even."

Byron, it may be noted, has some virulent lines "On the occasion of his Royal Highness the Prince Regent being seen standing between the coffins of Henry VIII. and Charles I. in the royal vault at Windsor :"

> Famed for contemptuous breach of sacred ties,
> By headless Charles see heartless Henry lies;
> Between them stands another sceptred thing—
> It moves, it reigns—in all but name, a king:
> Charles to his people, Henry to his wife,
> In him the double tyrant starts to life:
> Justice and Death have mixed their dust in vain,
> Each royal vampire wakes to life again.
> Ah, what can tombs avail! since these disgorge
> The blood and dust of both—to mould a George!

Robert Southey enters in his "Common-Place Book," "I find in a newspaper, 'The sheet in which Charles's head was received is preserved with the communion plate in the church at Ashburnham, and his watch also. The blood with which the sheet was covered is now almost black.'" The entry is without date: the newspaper quoted was probably very old. In the *Scots Magazine* for October, 1743, occurs the following: "*Died*, The Hon.

Bertram Ashburnham. He bequeathed to the clerk of the parish of Ashburnham and his successors forever the watch which King Charles I. had in his pocket at the time of his death, and the shirt he then wore, which has some drops of blood on it. And they are deposited in the vestry of the said church." A correspondent of *Notes and Queries* (1854), quoting the above, inquires concerning the relics. He obtains no satisfactory reply beyond a reference to Horsfield's "Sussex" (1835), wherein may be read that " in the chancel of Ashburnham Church are kept, in a glass case, lined with red velvet, some relics of the unfortunate Charles I. These consist of the shirt with ruffled wrists (on which are a few faint traces of blood) in which he was beheaded ; his watch, which at the place of execution he gave to Mr. John Ashburnham ; his white silk drawers ; and the sheet that was thrown over the body after the execution. These articles have certainly been carefully preserved. •Long were they treasured up as precious relics, fit only to be gazed upon by the devotees of the *Icon Basilike*. At length, however, the charm was broken by Bertram Ashburnham, Esq., who in 1743 bequeathed them to the clerk of the parish and his successors forever, to be exhibited as great curiosities." Mr. Horsfield adds, in a note, that " the superstitious of the last, and even of the present, age have occasionally resorted to these relics for the cure of the king's evil." An objection has been taken to the watch alleged to have been given to Mr. Ashburnham, by reason of the absence of any proof that Mr. Ashburnham was near the king on the morning of the execution : certainly he was not upon the scaffold.

The difficulty in the way of acknowledging the genuineness of many of these royal relics arises from the fact that the owners invariably maintain that they were given away by the king on the scaffold. To accept all these statements would be to look upon Charles as a sort of gallows-bird Santa Claus distributing an infinite number of rings, watches, Bibles, prayer-books, and even backgammon-boards and sets of bed-hangings.

Undoubtedly he did have a fondness for accumulating watches and clocks, many of which, though they did not all accompany him to the scaffold, are still extant. In Sir Thomas Herbert's " Memoirs of the Last Two Years of the Reign of that Unparalleled Prince of ever blessed Memory, King Charles I." (1702) appears a particular account of the various gifts presented by the king immediately before his execution. His gold watch was confided to Herbert—who, with Bishop Juxon, was in almost sole attendance upon the king after his trial—to be delivered to the Duchess of Richmond. A small silver watch that hung by his bedside was carried by Herbert towards the place of execution. While passing through the garden into the park the king "asked Mr. Herbert the hour of the day, and taking the clock into his hand gave it to him and said, 'Keep this in memory of me,' which Mr. Herbert kept to his dying day." This watch descended as an heirloom to William Townley Mitford in 1865. In Brayley and Britton's "Description of Cheshire" mention is made of another watch at Vale Royal, the residence of Lord Delamere, which it was stated had also belonged to King Charles, and was given by him to Bishop Juxon on the scaffold. This watch had come into the Cholmondeley family by an intermarriage with the Cowpers of Overleigh, near Chester, who were related to the Juxon family.

The king's Prayer Book is now in the possession of the Evelyn family, of Wotton Park, near Dorking, descendants of the great John Evelyn. The royal Bible was given by the king to Sir Thomas Herbert. In the margin of the book "he had with his own hand written many annotations and quotations, and he charged that the same should be given to the prince so soon as he returned." Herbert's account differs from the usual narrative, in which the Bible is bestowed by the king upon Bishop Juxon. In that prelate's hands he also deposited his George of the Order of the Garter, diamond, and seals, to be transmitted to his eldest son. The word "Remember" was presumed to have reference to this charge. The Parliament, however, prohibited Juxon's so dealing with the George. A pearl which he always wore in his ear, as may be noticed in his portrait on horseback by Vandyck, was taken out after his death, and (in Walpole's time) was in the collection of the Duchess of Portland, attested by the handwriting of his daughter the Princess of Orange, and was given to the Earl of Portland by King William. In another account there is a little variation: "Charles wore pearl ear-rings, and the day before his execution took one of great value from his ear and gave it to Juxon in charge for his daughter the Princess Royal."

Cherries, Feast of. A holiday occasion, now well-nigh obsolete, which for centuries was observed in Hamburg, Germany, in the early summer, by processions of little children, all dressed in white, who passed through the streets, each one bearing in the right hand a bunch of cherries. The custom was said to celebrate an event in the siege of Hamburg by the Hussite warrior Procopius the Great in 1432. He invested the city with his army and waited for the inhabitants to be starved into surrender. In this dilemma somebody proposed that an attempt be made to soften the hearts of the enemy by sending out the city's children to ask for food and mercy. The plan was carried out, and the surprise of the outlying hosts may be guessed when they saw the gates of the city open to let forth, not armed soldiers with helmets and swords, but a long line of children. Every one of this strange army was dressed in white, the elder ones leading the way, and the tiny toddlers holding their hands trustfully, wondering what it all meant, but showing no fear. When the rough soldiers outside heard the pattering of the little feet and saw the white-robed innocent throng surrounding their tents, they thought of their own children at home, and felt only love and kindness for their little visitors. They looked around for something to give them, and, as the trees of the great orchards in which they lay encamped were heavy with their burden of cherries, the soldiers broke off big branches of the fruit and gave one to every child and sent the little ones back to their parents with a message of peace and good will. So the city was saved by the children.

Cherry Feast, or **Cherry Fair.** Festivals which are still held in Worcester and some other parts of England in the cherry-orchards, and " are almost always," says Halliwell Phillipps, " the resort for lovers and the gay portion of the lower classes." Hence they " may appropriately retain their significant type of the uncertainty and vanity of things of this world." His allusion is to Gower's lines in the " Confessio Amantis," book vi. :

> Sometime I draw unto memoire
> How sorwe may nought ever last,
> And so cometh hope in atte last
> When I none other fodé know,
> And that endureth but a throw,
> Right as it were a chery fest.

Chester Cup. An annual race run in the first week in May on the race-course in Chester known as the Roodee or Roodeye, an equivalent of Rood-Isle, because before the modern improvements the course was surrounded by water. The cup is the final survival through many changes of the mediæval Chester Mysteries. These were performed on Shrove Tuesday. The festivities then consisted not only of the Mystery Plays themselves, full of quaint yet not intentionally irreverent burlesques of scriptural episodes, but also of sundry " lawdable exercises," including homages offered to or by the various guilds.

Conspicuous among these were two which constitute the remote originals of the Chester cup. All persons married within the past year " did offer unto the Companye of Drapers in homage a ball of salte, of the quantitie of a boule, profitable for few uses or purposes." This ball of salt was afterwards changed into a silver arrow, a meet prize for archers, and contended for by them on the Roodee, the pleasant meadow which served in winter for the pasture of cows, in summer as a recreation-ground for the good citizens.

The saddlers' old homage to the drapers is thus set forth: "Also whereas the company and occupation of the Sadlers within the cittie of Chester did yearely by custom, time out of the memory of man, did the same day (Shrove Tuesday), hower, and place, before the said mayor unto the Companye of Drapers in Chester, did offer, upon the truncheon of a staffe or speare, a certain homage, called the Sadlers' ball, being a ball of salte of the bignes of a bowle, which was profitable for few uses and purposes as it was, the which ball the said Drapers did cast up among the throunge, to get it who could, in which throunge much hurt was done. The said mayor and aldermen with consent of the drapers aforesaid did alter and change: that in place thereof the said Company of Sadlers should offer before the mayor unto the Drapers a bell of silver, the which bell was ordained also to the reward for that horse which with speede running there should run before all others, and then presentlye should be given the same day and place." Thus the race was instituted, and in due time, through the influence of the Puritan wave which overwhelmed England in the hundred years ending with the Restoration, the pagan associations of Shrove Tuesday were got rid of by transferring the horse-race to St. George's Day. By 1609 we find that the drapers and saddlers have vanished into night, and the contest on the Roodee becomes St. George's race. The change was due somewhat to the public spirit of Mr. Robert Ambrye, ironmonger, sometime sheriff of Chester, who at his own cost offered three silver bells, the first and second best to be given to the first and second horses in the initial race, the third bell to be contested for separately in another race.

St. George's races were celebrated with great pomp and ceremony. The programme of the civic march to the Roodee is minutely given in the Harleian MSS. First marched men in ivy, with black hair and beards "very owgly to behoulde," with garlands and clubs. The duty of these "salvage men"—favorite characters in all masques and mummings—was to scatter fireworks abroad to make "way for the rest of the showe:" doubtless an effectual method of getting through a crowd. Following these came St. George on horseback, with his attendants; then Fame, also on horseback, with a trumpet and an oration ready prepared for delivery. Next came Mercury, "to descend from above in a cloude, his winges and all other matters in pompe and heavenlie musicke with him, and after his oration spoken to ryde on horsebacke with the musicke before him." Then followed one called Chester, "with an oration and drums," and others bearing the arms of the king, and of the Prince of Wales, Earl of Chester. Close behind these rode the prize-bearers. The Cestrian population at the commencement of the seventeenth century must have had a tremendous appetite for speech-making, for Peace, Plenty, Envy, and Love all delivered their orations before the mayor and his brethren in their best apparel of scarlet.

A further change was effected in 1623 by Mr. John Brereton, the mayor, who substituted a single bell, of more value than all the former ones put together, which was "to be runne for on St. George's Day forever."

Why and when St. George's Day, like Shrove Tuesday, was abandoned for the first week in May, or under what circumstances the bell was changed for a silver cup, there is no evidence to show; in fact, a strange darkness hangs over the Roodee from Mayor Brereton's time. The rectification of the calendar is perhaps the best explanation of the former fact, as the first week in May comes very near old St. George's Day.

Chicago Day. The anniversary of the great fire in Chicago (1871) is celebrated in that city on October 9. "There has been of late years," says *Harper's Weekly* for October 24, 1896, "a growing tendency to make it a civic holiday, and its observance has been conducted upon an increasingly elaborate scale. This year is the twenty-fifth since the devastation of the city, and the celebration was carried out upon a scale far beyond anything hitherto attempted." It will be remembered that this was in the very thick of the McKinley-Bryan Presidential campaign. It was inevitable, therefore, that the celebration should have a political coloring. Both parties put forth their best efforts to make display of their strength. The great day parade, in which about seventy thousand citizens took part, was a sound money demonstration of the most impressive sort. The business portion of the city was given up to it, and all vehicles were excluded from the streets, as in Paris on the Jour de la République. The advocates of repudiation made no attempt to take part in this parade, but tried to offset its effect by the organization of a sort of silver side-show in the evening. A procession of about twelve thousand people was formed, and made all the noise it could, but the anticlimax was too obvious.

Christmas. The reputed anniversary of the birth of Jesus Christ, December 25, and as such one of the greatest festivals of the Protestant, Catholic, and Greek Churches. It is essentially a day of thanksgiving and rejoicing,—a day of good cheer. Though Christians celebrate it as a Christian festival, though to them it is the anniversary of the most solemn event in all history, the meeting of heaven and earth in the birth of the God-Man, the festivities that mark the epoch are part of the universal history of the race. In pagan Rome and Greece, in the days of the Teutonic barbarians, in the remote times of ancient Egyptian civilization, in the infancy of the race East and West and North and South, the period of the winter solstice was ever a period of rejoicing and festivity. Even the Puritanism of the Anglo-Saxon has not been equal to the task of defending Yule-tide from a triumphant inroad of pagan rites and customs, so that the evangelical churchman who is shocked to see flowers decorating the sanctuaries at Easter would be sorry to miss the scarlet berries that hang there at Christmas, so that even austerest lovers of the plain-song tolerate and even welcome " quips and cranks and wreathed smiles" in their Christmas carols, so that joviality and merrymaking are the order of the day at Christmas banquets,—a joviality sanctified and made glorious by good will to all men. Yet the holly and the mistletoe are a survival of ancient Druidical worship, the Christmas carol is a new birth, purified and exalted, of the hymns of the Saturnalia, the Christmas banquet itself is a reminiscence of the feasts given in honor of ancient gods and goddesses, when, as Cato said of the analogous feasts in imperial Rome, commemorating the birth of Cybele, the prospect that drew one thither was "not so much the pleasure of eating and of drinking as that of finding one's self among his friends and of conversing with them." Nay, the very idea of the Child-God, which gives its meaning to the Feast of the Nativity, was prefigured and foretold not only in the vaticinations of sibyl, seer, and prophet, but in the infant gods of the Greek. the Egyptian, the Hindoo, and the Buddhist, which in different ways showed the rude efforts of the earlier races to grasp the idea of a perfect human child who is also God.

Great as the feast is, however, nobody knows anything definite about its origin, nobody knows who first celebrated it, or when or where or how. And nobody even knows if December 25 be indeed the right anniversary of Christ's nativity.

This anomaly arises from the habit of the early Christians to look upon the celebration of birthdays as heathenish. The birthday of the Lord himself was not excepted. But after the triumph of Christianity the old prejudice died out ; and then the date of the Saviour's birth became a matter of ecclesiastical investigation. St. John Chrysostom, writing in 386, relates that

St. Cyril at the request of Julius (Bishop or Pope of Rome from 337 to 352) made a strict inquiry as to the exact date. Cyril reported that the Western Churches had always held it to be December 25. It is true that other communities of Christians preferred other dates. In many Eastern Churches the 6th of January had been fixed on as the anniversary not only of the birth of Christ, but of his manifestation to the Gentiles. (See EPIPHANY.) April 20, May 20, March 29, and September 29 were respectively accepted by small minorities. In short, as St. Clement says, the matter was very uncertain.

Nevertheless it appears that Pope Julius was so far satisfied with the report of Cyril that somewhere about the middle of the fourth century he established the festival at Rome on December 25. Before the end of the century that date had been accepted by all the nations of Christendom. This acceptance was facilitated by the fact that it is the date of the winter solstice,—the turning-point of the year, when winter, having reached its apogee, must begin to decline again towards spring,—when for unnumbered ages before the Christian era pagan Europe through all its tribes and nations had been accustomed to celebrate its chief festival.

Now, it was always the aim of the early Church to reconcile heathen converts to the new faith by the adoption of all the more harmless features of their festivities and ceremonials. With Christmas the Church had a hard task. Though it aimed only to retain the pagan forms, it found it could not restrain the pagan spirit. In spite of clerical protests and papal anathemas, in spite of the condemnation of the wise and the sane, Christmas in the early days frequently reproduced all the worst orgies, the debaucheries and indecencies, of the Bacchanalia and the Saturnalia. The clergy themselves were whirled into the vortex. A special celebration called the Feast of Fools was instituted,—as learned doctors explained,—with a view that " the folly which is natural to and born with us might exhale at least once a year." The intention was excellent. But in practice the liberty so accorded speedily degenerated into license. The Council of Auxerre was moved to inquire into the matter. A Flemish divine rose and declared that the festival was an excellent thing and quite as acceptable to God as that of the Immaculate Conception. There was great applause among his like-minded brethren. Then Gerson, the most noted theologian of the day, made a counter-sensation by retorting that " if all the devils in hell had put their heads together to devise a feast that should utterly scandalize Christianity, they could not have improved upon this one."

If even among the clergy heathen traditions so strenuously survived, what better could be expected from the laity? The wild revels, indeed, of the Christmas period in olden times almost stagger belief. Obscenity, drunkenness, blasphemy,—nothing came amiss. License was carried to the fullest extent of licentiousness.

Memorable as an illustration of the manners of the French court was a catastrophe that occurred in Paris in 1393. Riot and disorder had run wild all through the Christmas festivities. But the court was not yet satisfied. Then Sir Hugonin de Guisay, most reckless among all the reckless spirits of the period, suggested that as an excuse for prolonging the merriment a marriage should be arranged between two of the court attendants. This was eagerly agreed upon. Sir Hugonin assumed the leadership, a post for which he was well fitted. He was loved and admired by the disorderly as much as he was hated and feared by the orderly. Among other pleasant traits, he was fond of exercising his wit upon tradesmen and mechanics, whom he would accost in the street, prick with his spurs, and compel to creep on all fours and bark like curs before he released them. Such were the traits which endeared him to the courtiers of His Most Gracious Majesty and Christian King of France. The marriage passed off in a blaze of glory with an accompaniment of attendant Gargantuan pleasantry. At the height of the ceremonies Sir Hugonin quietly withdrew with the king and four other wild ones, scions of the noblest houses in France. With a pot of tar and a quantity of tow the six conspirators were speedily changed into very fair imitations of the dancing bears then very common in mountebanks' booths. A mask completed the transformation. Five were then bound together with a silken rope. The sixth, the king himself, led them into the hall. Their appearance created a general stir. "Who are they?" was the cry. Nobody knew. At this moment entered the wildest of all the wild Dukes of Orleans. "Who are they?" he echoed between hiccoughs. "Well, we'll soon find out." Seizing a brand from one of the torch-bearers ranged along the wall, he staggered forward. Some gentlemen essayed to stay him. But he was obstinate and quarrelsome. Main force could not be thought of against a prince of the blood. He was given his way. He thrust his torch under the chin of the nearest of the maskers. The tow caught fire. In a moment the whole group was in flames. The young Duchess of Berri seized the king and enveloped him in her ample robe. Thus he was saved. Another masker, the Lord of Nantouillet, noted for strength and agility, rent the silken rope with a wrench of his strong teeth, pitched himself like a flaming comet through the first window, and dived into a cistern in the court, whence he emerged black and smoking, but almost unhurt. As for the other four, they whirled hither and thither through the horrified mob, struggling with one another, fighting with the flames, cursing, shrieking with pain. Women fainted by scores. Men who had never faltered in a hundred fights sickened at the hideous spectacle. All Paris was roused by the uproar, and gathered, an excited mob, about the palace. At last the flames burnt out. The four maskers lay, a black and writhing heap, on the floor. One was a mere cinder. A second survived till daybreak. A third died at noon the next day. The fourth—no other than Sir Hugonin himself—survived for three days, while all Paris rejoiced over his agonies. " Bark, dog, bark !" was the cry with which the citizens saluted his charred and mangled corpse, when it was at last borne to the grave.

But why dwell on only one side of the picture ? In the coarser days of our ancestors riot and revelry did indeed go hand in hand, but the revelry was of a lusty, vigorous, and hearty sort unknown to these quieter times which have eliminated the riot. As we read of the great feats performed by these heroes of the trencher and the tankard, by these adepts in all out-door sports, the Gargantuan good nature of the season impresses us more than the cruelty, gluttony, and drunkenness which were apt to sully it. A race of jolly giants must needs give and take harder blows than their pygmy descendants.

Merrie old England was the soil in which Merrie Christmas took its firmest root. Even in Anglo-Saxon days we hear of Alfred holding high revelry in December, 878, so that he allowed the Danes to surprise him, cut his army to pieces, and send him a fugitive. The court revelries increased in splendor after the Conquest. Christmas, it must be remembered, was not then a single day of sport. It had its preliminary novena which began December 16, and it ended on January 6, or Twelfth-Night. All this period was devoted to holiday-making.

It was a democratic festival. All classes mixed in its merrymakings. Hospitality was universal. An English country gentleman of the fifteenth and sixteenth centuries held open house. With daybreak on Christmas morning the tenants and neighbors thronged into the hall. The ale was broached. Blackjacks and Cheshire cheese, with toast and sugar and nutmeg, went plentifully round. The Hackin, or great sausage, must be boiled at daybreak, and if it failed to be ready two young men took the cook by the arm and ran her around the market-place till she was ashamed of her laziness.

The women also had their privileges. In some places in Oxfordshire it was the right of every maid-servant to ask the man for ivy to dress the house withal, and if the man refused or forgot, the maid stole a pair of his breeches and nailed them to the gate in the yard or highway. In other places a refusal to comply with such a request debarred the man from the privilege of the mistletoe.

The gentlemen went to early service in the church and returned to breakfast on brawn and mustard and malmsey. Mustard is your great provoker of a noble thirst. Brawn was a dish of great antiquity, made from the flesh of large boars which lived in a half-wild state and when put to fatten were strapped and belted tight around the body, so as to make the flesh dense and brawny.

With the rise of Puritanism the very existence of Christmas was threatened. Even the harmless good cheer of that season was looked upon as pagan, or, what was worse, Popish. "Into what a stupendous *height* of more than pagan impiety," cried Prynne in his "Histrio-Mastix," "have we not now *degenerated!*" Prynne's rhetoric, it will be seen, is not without an unconscious charm of humor. He complained that the England of his day could not celebrate Christmas or any other festival "without drinking, roaring, healthing, dicing, carding, dancing, masques and stage-plays . . . which Turkes and Infidels would abhor to practise."

Puritanism brought over with it in the Mayflower the anti-Christmas feeling to New England. So early as 1621 Governor Bradford was called upon to administer a rebuke to "certain lusty yonge men" who had just come over in the little ship Fortune. "On ye day called Christmas-day," says William Bradford, "ye Govr caled them out to worke (as was used), but ye most of this new company excused themselves and said it went against their consciences to worke on ye day. So ye Govr tould them that if they made it mater of conscience, he would spare them till they were better informed. So he led away ye rest, and left them; but when they came home at noone from their worke, he found them in ye streete at play, openly: some pitching ye barr, and some at stoole-ball and such like sports. So he went to them and tooke away their implements, and tould them that it was against his conscience that they should play and others worke. If they made ye keeping of it matter of devotion, let them kepe their houses, but ther should be no gameing or revelling in ye streets. Since which time nothing hath been atempted that way, at least openly."

In England the feeling culminated in 1643, when the Roundhead Parliament abolished the observance of saints' days and "the three grand festivals" of Christmas, Easter, and Whitsuntide, "any law, statute, custom, constitution, or canon to the contrary in any wise notwithstanding." The king protested.

But he was answered. In London, nevertheless, there was an alarming disposition to observe Christmas. The mob attacked those who by opening their shops flouted the holiday. In several counties the disorder was threatening. But Parliament adopted strong measures, and during the twelve years in which the great festivals were discountenanced there was no further tumult, and the observance of Christmas as a general holiday ceased.

The General Court of Massachusetts followed the example of the English Parliament in 1659 when it enacted that " anybody who is found observing, by abstinence from labor, feasting, or any other way, any such day as Christmas day, shall pay for every such offence five shillings."

The restoration of English royalty brought about the restoration of the English Christmas. It was not till 1681, however, that Massachusetts repealed the ordinance of 1659. But the repeal was bitter to old Puritanism, which kept up an ever attenuating protest even down to the early part of the present century. (See THANKSGIVING. Also see BOAR'S HEAD; CAROLS; MISTLETOE; MISRULE, LORD OF; WAITS; YULE-LOG, etc., for special Christmas festivities.)

There are many superstitions connected with the coming of Christmas itself. To the cock have from time immemorial been attributed unwonted energy and sagacity at that season. Even now in England it is common to hear one say, when the cock crows in the stillness of the November and December nights, " The cock is crowing for Christmas." He is supposed to do this for the purpose of scaring off the evil spirits from the holy season.

The bees are said to sing, the cattle to kneel, in honor of the manger, and the sheep to go in procession in commemoration of the visit of the angel to the shepherds.

Howison in his " Sketches of Upper Canada" relates that on one moonlit Christmas Eve he saw an Indian creeping cautiously through the woods. In response to an inquiry, he said, " Me watch to see deer kneel. Christmas night all deer kneel and look up to Great Spirit."

In the German Alps it is believed that the cattle have the gift of language on Christmas Eve. But it is a sin to attempt to play the eavesdropper upon them. An Alpine story is told of a farmer's servant who did not believe that the cattle could speak, and, to make sure, he hid in his master's stable on Christmas Eve and listened. When the clock struck twelve he was surprised at what he heard. " We shall have hard work to do this day week," said one horse. " Yes; the farmer's servant is heavy," answered the other horse. " And the way to the churchyard is long and steep," said the first. The servant was buried that day week.

An English writer says that two countrymen who watched the cattle in the barns reported that two only knelt, but they fell upon their knees with a groan almost human. His informants were much angered that he received this story with incredulity.

These well-known lines from " Hamlet" recognize these super-stitions :

> Some say that ever 'gainst that season comes,
> Wherein our Saviour's birth is celebrated,
> The bird of dawning singeth all night long ;
> And then, they say, no spirit can walk abroad ;
> The nights are wholesome ; then no planets strike,
> No fairy takes, nor witch hath power to charm,
> So hallowed and so gracious is that time.

The salmon was a great Christmas favorite, and Sandys mentions a Monmouthshire tradition to the effect that on every Christmas Day, in the morning only, a large salmon appeared in the adjoining river, showed himself openly, and permitted himself to be taken and handled ; but it would have been the greatest impiety to capture him.

Meteorological superstitions are embodied in the following verses :

> Now take heed, every man,
> That English understand can,
> If that Christmas day fall
> Upon Friday, know well all
> That winter season shall be easy,
> Save great winds aloft shall fly ;
> The summer also shall be dry
> And right seasonable, I say.
> Beasts and sheep shall thrive right well,
> But other victuals shall fail ;
> What child that day is born
> Great and rich he shall be of corn.

> If Christmas day on Monday be,
> A great winter that year you'll see,
> And full of winds, both loud and shrill ;
> But, in summer, truth to tell,
> High winds shall there be and strong,
> Full of tempests lasting long,
> While battles they shall multiply,
> And great plenty of beasts shall die.

It has been pointed out that this latter direful prophecy was fulfilled in 1866, following the Christmas of 1865, which fell upon Monday.

In some places, as in Suabia, it is customary for maidens, in-quisitive as to their prospective lovers, to draw a stick of wood out of a heap to see whether he will be long or short, crooked or straight. At other times they will pour melted lead into cold water, and from the figures formed will prognosticate the trade or profession of the future husband. If they imagine they see a plane, or a last, or a pair of shears, it signifies that he is to be a carpenter, or shoemaker, or tailor; while a hammer or a pickaxe indicates a smith or a common laborer. The maidens of Pfullingen, when they wish to ascertain which of them will first become a wife, form a circle, and place in their midst a blindfolded gander, and the one to whom he goes first will soon be a bride; while the Tyrolese peasants, on the "knocking nights," listen at the baking-ovens, and if they hear music it signifies an early wedding, but if the ringing of bells, it fore-bodes the death of the listener. Among many others, a favorite method of forecasting the future is to sit upon the floor and throw one's shoe with the foot over the shoulder, and then to predict from the position it assumes what is about to happen.

In Poland, and elsewhere, it is believed that on Christmas night the heavens are opened and the scene of Jacob's ladder is re-enacted, but it is permitted only to the saints to see it. Throughout Northern Germany the tables are spread and lights left burning during the entire night, that the Virgin Mary and the angel who passes when everybody sleeps may find some-thing to eat. In certain parts of Austria they put candles in the windows, that the Christ-Child may not stumble in passing through the village. There is also a wide-spread opinion that a pack of wolves, which were no other than wicked men trans-formed into wolves, committed great havoc upon Christmas night. Taking advantage of this superstition, it was not un-usual for rogues disguised in wolf-skins to attack honest people, rifle their houses, sack their cellars, and drink or steal all their beer. As a specific charm, no doubt, against these wolfish depredations, it was customary in Austria, up to a recent date, after high mass on Christmas night, to sing in a particular tone, to the sound of the large bell, the chapter of the generation of Jesus Christ.

In Germany the decoration of the house begins as early as the morning of the 24th. One room, from which all save "die Mutter" is rigidly excluded, contains the Christmas-tree and all the presents, set in a shining row upon the table. Greens are hung from window and door, and garlands upon the walls. Upon the dining-table a great cold supper is spread. Family and guests begin to gather at five o'clock. The children's eyes are glued to the sliding doors, which are presently to open and disclose the tree. Six o'clock,—a bell rings. Back swings the portal, and there it stands, resplendent with lights and tinsel. The children pounce upon it, and are with difficulty held back while the presents are taken down from the branches and distributed. Everybody kisses everybody else, and for two or three hours the cares of life are forgotten. Then the late supper and to bed. Thus the German Christmas is well over before the day itself arrives. The family arise late on the morning of the 25th. The day is spent in paying and receiving visits, at which the children compare presents. In the evening there is a dance, with much music and much merriment.

Christmas Eve is a fête in Paris, and the Grand Boulevard possesses a character distinctive of the occasion. Late in the evening the cafés become crowded, and the café-restaurants that are to keep open all night for the Christmas "réveillon" begin to arrange their tables, many of which have been engaged in advance. The "réveillon," or Christmas Eve supper at midnight, is more important to the Frenchman than the Christmas dinner, and the indulgence in it may somewhat account for the general atmosphere of almost gloomy abstinence that seems to hang over Paris on Christmas Day. Oysters represent the favorite first course, and any one interested in statistics may like to know that half a million dozen oysters were sold at the Halles on Christmas Eve in 1896, and of écrevisse, that appetizing crawfish, sixty thousand represents the number consumed during the "réveillon." Impecunious clerks and reckless Latin Quarter students go dinnerless, in the first instance a week beforehand, and in the second often a month afterwards, that they may partake of a proper "réveillon" in a restaurant that is usually closed to them by apparent bars of gold. The thoroughly up-to-date Parisian divides his Christmas supper into many courses, taking each at a different place, and perhaps reaching home for the last cup of coffee, served in place of the "petit déjeuner."

In the rural life of Russia Christmas Eve is an important event. At sunset young and old assemble in the principal street of the village, and, forming in a procession, visit the houses of the resident nobleman, the mayor, and other village dignitaries, where they sing carols and receive coppers in return. This part of the ceremonies is called Kolenda, which means begging for money or presents. A masquerade follows, in which the adults transform themselves into imitation cows, pigs, goats, and other animals, in remembrance of the Nativity in the manger.

As soon as the evening star appears above the horizon, a colatzia, or supper, is served. A long table is covered with straw. Over this a cloth is laid, on which the samovar is placed, together with fish prepared in various ways, and different kinds of cakes. The feast begins by dividing the blessed wafer, a small portion of which is given to each person present. This is a sacred rite in which none dare refuse to participate. The head of each family is given his share first. The remaining members are served according to their ages, the little children, of course, being left till the last.

At the conclusion of the evening-star celebration, a majority of the peasants proceed to the house of the nobleman whom they first visited, where an immense tree has been prepared for them. This tree is laden with inexpensive presents of various kinds. If the nobleman has any young children, he supplies them with quantities of small coin, which they distribute among the peasant guests.

In no land is Christmas more generally celebrated than in Scandinavia. Peace and good will is the order of the season. The courts are closed, old quarrels are adjusted, and feuds are forgotten. A pretty symbol of the spirit that reigns is the Yule-night practice of placing in a row every pair of shoes in each household, typifying that during the year the family will live together in peace and harmony.

Scandinavia is especially the land of the Yule-log, of Christmas stories and legends of Thor and Odin. Then is the time for skating, sledging, dancing, and a general frolic. It is customary for every member of the family to take a bath on the afternoon preceding Christmas, and oftentimes it is the only thorough bath that is received during the year. When the eve comes, the Bible is read in nearly every household and family service is held. In many villages candles are left burning in the windows all night, to give light to Kristine, who brings the gifts. It is also the custom to set a cake of meal out in the snow as a Christmas offering. The birds of the air are thought of, and a sheaf of wheat is placed on a pole in front of each house to provide them with food.

On Christmas evening are the usual games. They are more than likely to be interrupted by a knock at the door and the entrance of four or five boys dressed in white. One carries a colored star-shaped lantern, and another an ornamented glass box containing two dolls, representing the Virgin and Child. The boys chant a carol or two, and after partaking of refreshments are dismissed, to continue their journey to the next house. The games are likely to be interrupted again by the coming of another band of merrymakers. This time it is masked performers, wearing tattered uniforms decked with tinsel, and carrying wooden swords. They perform tricks and pantomime, and go through a mock military review. These performances are always enjoyed, and the performers never go away from a house empty-handed. The festivities do not close until a late hour.

From the frozen North, of the midnight sun, to the evergreen South, of perpetual summer, is a long journey, but in all the distance there is found no land where the Christmas festival is not celebrated.

A Christmas celebration in Peru has peculiar features. In the cities, and more especially in Lima, there are bewildering scenes of activity on Christmas Eve. The streets and squares are crowded with a gayly dressed people. Droves of asses are to be seen in every direction, laden with fruits, boughs from the mountains, liquors, and other merchandise. Ice-stalls, provided with chairs and benches, are crowded by the perspiring pleasure-seekers, who find ice necessary on sultry Christmas.

As night approaches, the streets are packed with a noisy people, and joke and jest and merry pranks become the rule. These are participated in mostly by strangely attired persons in masks. Music of guitars, clattering castanets, and pebbles rattling in gourds fill the air with mingled discordant sounds. No door is closed. There are music and dancing and the distribution of gifts in every house. All are welcome to enter. Strangers are sure of a hearty welcome, and to be a foreigner is to have a double claim on hospitality and to receive a double welcome. All ceremony and restraint are absent. In many houses the love of the Christmas drama is shown by theatrical representations of the Nativity, with the same characters as are seen the world over.

Suddenly the scene changes. The curtain falls on the play, the music and dancing cease, and the people go from their homes. The midnight bell at the cathedral has summoned all to mass. The houses and streets are nearly deserted, while the churches, with their decorations and blazing tapers, are thronged. Worshippers are kneeling before the many shrines that line their walls, and wherever they can find a place where one of the many waxen images of the saints is displayed. With the organ's peal, and the entering of the richly vested priests and plainly attired monks, begins the celebration of the mass.

Again on Christmas morning the streets are crowded and the markets are thronged, but at nine o'clock the churches are again filled. After the services come the feast and the games and the sports. Of all the sports, bull-fighting is the favorite, and the Christmas fight is generally the best of the season, as eight or ten bulls are frequently killed on that day, besides several horses, and not infrequently one or two of the fighting-men. In this sport the women appear to take more enthusiastic pleasure than the men.

When night comes there is a grand procession, headed by the priests and monks, who are followed by the soldiers and people. All are gayly dressed, and many in fantastic costumes and masks. Banners, flags, streaming ribbons, and green boughs are carried, and music fills the air. In the midst of the procession there is held aloft the figure of the Madonna bearing in her arms the Holy Child. After a long march the procession returns to the cathedral, there disbands, and the Christmas Day celebration is at an end.

The ante-bellum period in the Southern States was signalized by a special celebration at Christmas-tide, handed down from those English folk, gentle and simple, who first peopled Virginia and the Carolinas, and whose descendants have spread over the face of the country south of Mason and Dixon's line.

"There's no such thing as real Christmas now," sigh elder folk, white and black, whose memories run back to the gay, good days of slavery. Then, in truth, it was a two weeks' saturnalia. No master who respected himself, or hoped to keep the respect of his neighbors, dreamed of asking his black people to do more in the month of December than kill hogs and get up a big Christmas wood-pile.

When the hauling was finished, a dozen axes flew, chopping it in lengths for the big-throated open fireplaces. By and by there was a procession of stout fellows with a log or a turn of small sticks on the shoulder, setting up great piles of firewood beside all the doors. After every exit to the great house was duly surrounded, the back piazzas filled, and chips banked high in the saddle-room, great sticks and small began to be heaped at the cabin doors. By the time they were all fully furnished the mountain of a wood-pile was sensibly smaller, though far from exhausted. Usually this came to pass about midday of December 24.

To the mass of slaves their masters' concerns were as much a matter of interest and of pride as they were to those affected by them. Besides, the darky is a born gossip, likewise a born detective. The shrewdest match-making mamma was not quicker to detect serious intentions in a promising young man visitor. Where there were young ladies in the great house the young man visitor was mighty plentiful about Christmas-time. He came from far and near,—often across three counties. He rode a high-stepping horse, and was nice in the matter of equipage. Often he brought along his own black boy, likewise mounted, and carrying behind him fat, bulging saddle-bags stuffed with his master's wardrobe. For the young man came to stay at least the week,—most likely the fortnight, unless he "got the sack" from the object of his affections and so rode away in a furious huff.

Often, too, the old negroes went visiting on their own account. No time like Christmas for a trip back to old Marster's or to see the sister or brother who had been given to some other branch of the family and so lived maybe twenty miles away. Duly mounted, tricked out in Sunday best, with all sorts of queer bundles dangling here and there, and a carpet-bag fat to bursting swung at the horn of the saddle, Black Daddy and Black Mammy rode a-Christmasing, and at the journey's end were as welcome to whites as to blacks.

Nightfall brought swarms of visitors, both to house and kitchen. Very often there was a dance in both as soon as it was fairly dark. In every cabin there were laughter, singing, and good cheer. In many of them revelry went on through the night. The dancing lasted maybe to one o'clock ; after that there was singing to the accompaniment of a gourd banjo, with, a little later, tale-telling in the light of the waning fire.

The pious among the slaves sang and prayed the night through. But their piety did not take the form of a prohibition sentiment. With a psalm yet hot in the mouth they were as ready as their fellows to troop up to the great house at daylight and drink their share of Christmas eggnog. Small blame to them, either, since the eggnog of those days was a mighty seductive thing to any who had a nice taste in drinks.

Christmas Card. Legitimately, a piece of card-board of any handy size, breathing pictorial and verbal benevolence in every variety of tone from the religious to the comic, which is sent to a friend or relative on Christmas. At present the term has been enlarged so as to include almanacs and even pamphlets illuminated with gay colors and obscured with maudlin prose and doggerel verse that has no earthly connection with the season.

The Christmas card is the legitimate descendant of the " school pieces" or " Christmas pieces" which were popular from the beginning to the middle of the nineteenth century. These were sheets of writing-paper, sometimes surrounded with those hideous and elaborate pen-flourishes forming birds, scrolls, etc., to which writing-masters still have an unnatural and inexplicable attachment, and sometimes headed with copperplate engravings, plain or colored. They were used by school-boys at the approach of the holidays for carefully written letters exploiting the progress they had made in composition and chirography.

A publisher writing to *Notes and Queries* in 1871 (Fourth Series, vi. 462) tells us that some thirty years previous the sale of these was very considerable. " My father published some thirty different subjects (a new one every year, one of the old ones being let go out of print). There were also three other publishers of them. The order to print used to average about five hundred of each kind, but double of the Life of Our Saviour. Most of the subjects were those of the Old Testament. I only recollect four subjects not sacred. Printing at home, we generally commenced the printing in August from the copperplates, as they had to be colored by hand. They sold, retail, at sixpence each, and we used to supply them to the trade at thirty shillings per gross and to schools at three shillings sixpence per dozen. Charity boys were large purchasers of these pieces, and at Christmas time used to take them round their parish to show and at the same time solicit a trifle."

The Christmas card proper had a tentative origin in 1846. Mr. Joseph Cundall, a London artist, lays claim to being the publisher of the first one. He acknowledges, however, that the idea was another's. " The first Christmas card ever published," he wrote in the London *Times* of January 2, 1884, " was issued by me in the usual way, in the year 1846, at the office of Felix Summerly's Home Treasury, 12 Old Bond St. Mr. Henry Cole (afterwards Sir Henry) originated the idea. The drawing was made by J. C. Horsley, R.A., it was printed in lithography by Mr. Jobbins of Warwick Court, Holborn, and colored by hand. Many copies were sold, but possibly not more than one thousand. It was of the usual size of a lady's card."

Not until 1862, however, did the custom obtain any foothold. Then experiments were made with cards of the size of an ordinary *carte de visite* inscribed simply " A Merry Christmas" and " A Happy New Year." After that there came to be added robins and holly branches, embossed figures and landscapes. " I have the original designs before me now," wrote " Luke Limner," or John Leighton, to the London *Publishers' Circular*, December 31, 1883; " they were produced by Goodall & Son. Seeing a growing want, and the great sale obtained abroad, this house produced (1868) a Little Red Riding-Hood, a Hermit and his Cell, and many other subjects in which snow and the robin played a part."

The Christmas card has some advantages. It is an inexpensive method of exchanging Christmas remembrances between people of moderate means. But it has been degenerating into something akin to a nuisance. It is a real inconvenience to business-men to find their correspondence interrupted by the flood of cards which chokes the mail-bag through the Christmas season, and even to people of leisure it is an annoyance. Moreover, in this case the actual annoyance is aggravated by a feeling of sentimental injury. If the Christmas card were an honest tribute of regard or admiration, we might be content to tolerate it as a well-meaning nuisance; but it is felt at best to be a threadbare convention, and it is often little better than an impudent fraud. It frequently serves as a cheap and unworthy substitute for the turkey, the Stilton, the barrel of oysters, or even the check, in which the healthier benevolence of former days found expression at Christmas time. It comes upon us in the specious guise of a letter; but in this respect it shares all the reprehensible peculiarities of the whited sepulchre. The new woman may cherish a fine scorn for social frivolities; the old woman, however (if she happens to be a young one), is not cast in the same heroic mould, and grievous is her disappointment when the stiff envelope disgorges a simpering Christmas card, instead of, as she had fondly hoped, "a ball."

Even from an artistic point of view the Christmas card is not free from reproach, since the imagination of the artist in its search for the beautiful has somewhat unduly neglected the appropriate. The traditional robin in a snow-storm is more or less in keeping with the associations of the season, and he is still to be found among Christmas cards, but in steadily decreasing numbers. His place is being taken by summer seas, winding rivers, spring lawns, and other similar suggestions of the past and the future which tend to make the average man profoundly discontented with the immediate present.

Christmas-Tree. Many countries have their popular legends claiming for them the honor of having given the Christmas-tree to the world. Though of no historical value, these have their antiquarian interest.

A Scandinavian myth of great antiquity speaks of a "service-tree" sprung from the blood-drenched soil where two lovers had been killed by violence. At certain nights in the Christmas season mysterious lights were seen flaming in its branches, that no wind could extinguish.

The French have their legend as well. In a romance of the thirteenth century the hero finds a gigantic tree whose branches are covered with burning candles, some standing erect, the others upside down, and on the top the vision of a child with a halo around his curly head. The knight asked the Pope for an explanation, who declared that the tree undoubtedly represented mankind, the child the Saviour, and the candles good and bad human beings.

Wolfram von Eschenbach, the famous minstrel, sings of a prevailing custom of welcoming guests with branches ornamented with burning candles.

One tale bestows the honor upon Martin Luther. One Christmas Eve, travelling alone over the snow-covered country, the sky, with its thousands of glittering stars, made such a deep impression upon the Reformer that after arriving at home he tried to explain it to his wife and children. Suddenly an idea suggested itself to him. He went into the garden, cut off a little fir-tree, dragged it into the nursery, put some candles on its branches, and lighted them.

One of the most popular of German engravings represents Martin Luther sitting in the bosom of his family with a lighted Christmas-tree on the table before him.

An older German legend makes St. Winfrid the inventor of the idea. In the midst of a crowd of converts he hewed down a giant oak which had formerly been the object of their Druidic worship.

"Then the sole wonder in Winfrid's life came to pass. For, as the bright blade circled above his head, and the flakes of wood flew from the deepening gash in the body of the tree, a whirling wind passed over the forest. It gripped the oak from its foundations. Backward it fell like a tower, groaning as it split asunder in four pieces. But just behind it, and unharmed by the ruin, stood a young fir-tree, pointing a green spire towards the stars.

"Winfrid let the axe drop, and turned to speak to the people.

"'This little tree, a young child of the forest, shall be your holy tree to-night. It is the wood of peace, for your houses are built of the fir. It is the sign of an endless life, for its leaves are ever green. See how it points upward to heaven. Let this be called the tree of the Christ-child; gather about it, not in the wild wood, but in your own homes; there it will shelter no deeds of blood, but loving gifts and rites of kindness.'"

But, myths aside, the history of the Christmas-tree is difficult to trace. It may have some remote connection with the great tree Yggdrasil of Norse mythology. It may be a revival of the pine-trees in the Roman Saturnalia which were decorated with images of Bacchus, as described by Virgil in the Georgics:

> In jolly hymns they praise the god of wine,
> Whose earthen images adorn the pine,
> And these are hung on high in honor of the vine.
> *(Dryden's translation.)*

Two other suggestions are offered by Sir George Birdswood in the *Asiatic Quarterly Review* (vol. i. pp. 19–20). "It has been explained," he says, "as being derived from the ancient Egyptian practice of decking houses at the time of the winter solstice with branches of the date-palm, the symbol of life triumphant over death, and therefore of perennial life in the renewal of each bounteous year; and the supporters of these suggestions point to the fact that pyramids of green paper, covered all over with wreaths and festoons of flowers and strings of sweetmeats, are often substituted in Germany for the Christmas-tree.

" But similar pyramids, together with similar trees, the latter usually altogether artificial, and often constructed of the costliest materials, even of gems and gold, are carried about at marriage ceremonies in India and at many festivals, such as the Huli, or annual festival of the vernal equinox. These pyramids represent Mount Meru and the earth, and the trees, the Kalpadrama, or Tree of Ages, and the fragrant Parijata, the tree of every perfect gift, which grew on the slopes of Mount Meru ; and in their enlarged sense they symbolize the splendor of the outstretched heavens, as of a tree, laden with golden fruit, deep-rooted in the earth. Both pyramids and trees are also phallic emblems of life, individual, terrestrial, and celestial. Therefore, if a relationship exists between the Egyptian practice of decking houses at the winter solstice with branches of the date-palm, and the German and English custom of using gift-bearing and brilliantly illuminated evergreen trees, which are nearly always firs, as a Christmas decoration, it is most probably due to collateral rather than to direct descent; and this is indicated by the Egyptians having regarded the date-palm not only as an emblem of immortality, but also of the starlit firmament."

The suggestion as to collateral rather than direct descent is eminently plausible. The legends already quoted show that even in mediæval times there was a tradition of holiness investing an illuminated tree which made it mystically appropriate to the season of the winter solstice,—*i.e.*, the season which Christianity had recently redeemed from paganism by making it the birth-time of Christ. These traditions may have been strongly influenced by the fact that about this time the Jews celebrated their feast of Chanuckah (*q. v.*), or Lights, also known as the Feast of the Dedication. Lighted candles are a feature of the Jewish feast. Innumerable lights must therefore have been twinkling in every Jewish house in Bethlehem and Nazareth at about the reputed time of the Saviour's birth. It is worthy of note that the German name for Christmas is Weihnacht, the Night of Dedication, and that the Greeks call Christmas the Feast of Lights.

These vague traditions merging together finally led to the permanent establishment of the Christmas-tree. As a regular institution, however, it can be traced back only to the sixteenth century. During the Middle Ages it suddenly appears in Strassburg. A valuable authentic manuscript of 1608, by a Strassburg burgher, now in a private collection in Friedberg, Hesse, describes the tree as a feature of the Christmas season. The manuscript of a book entitled "The Milk of Catechism," by the Strassburg theologian Dannhauer, mentions the same subject in a similar way. For two hundred years the fashion maintained itself along the Rhine, when suddenly, at the beginning of this century, it spread all over Germany, and fifty years later had conquered Christendom.

The first description of a Christmas-tree in modern literature is to be found in "The Nut-Cracker," a fairy-tale, by Fouqué and Hoffmann.

In 1830 the Christmas-tree was introduced by Queen Caroline into Munich. At the same time it beat its path through Bohemia into Hungary, where it became fashionable among the Magyar aristocracy.

In 1840 the Duchess Helena of Orleans brought it to the Tuileries. Empress Eugénie also patronized it, but by the middle class it was still considered an intruder of Alsatian origin. In 1860 the German residents of Paris could procure a Christmas-tree only with the greatest difficulty. However, nine years later the trees were regularly sold in the market. In 1870 the German army celebrated Christmas in the church of Notre-Dame, and to-day Paris uses fifty thousand trees each year, of which only about one-fourth part are bought by Swiss, Germans, and Alsatians. The French plant the entire tree, with its root in a tub, so as to be able to preserve the tree until New Year, when it is "plundered."

It was the marriage of Queen Victoria to a German prince which led to the introduction of the German custom into England. But a Christmas-tree, or something like it, is known to have played an important part in a Christmas pageant given in honor of Henry VIII., and Greville's Memoirs under date of December 29, 1829, mentions that "on Christmas the Princess Lieven got up a little fête such as is customary all over Germany. Three trees, in great pots, were put upon a long table covered with pink linen ; each tree was illuminated with three circular tiers of colored wax candles,—blue, green, red, and white. Before each tree was displayed a quantity of toys, gloves, pocket-handkerchiefs, workboxes, books, and various articles,—presents made to the owner of the tree. It was very pretty. Here it was only for the children ; in Germany the custom extended to persons of all ages."

In America the German emigrant brought the tree with him, and it was soon taken up by all classes.

A modern writer describes how a Christmas-tree is set up for all the children of the neighborhood in the great hall of an English country squire's house. At nightfall on Christmas Eve the children, marshalled by the vicar and the village school-mistress, made their way to the hall, where they took their appointed places. The Christmas-tree had been drawn back into the bay-windows, and was hidden by the sheet now hung up for the magic lantern. "The squire was the showman, who expounded the successive men and beasts, ships and comets, and their eccentric performances, with appropriate comic gravity. The children listened in admiring silence, which now and then broke into a half-suppressed murmur of delight, especially when the rat ran into the mouth of the old gentleman asleep in his bed, and continued to repeat the feat over and over again. Then the last disk of light upon the sheet disappeared, and was succeeded by the twinkling of minute lights behind. There was breathless expectation; the sheet was drawn back, and the tree in all its glory was brought into the middle of the hall. The murmur of half-suppressed delight came again from the rows of children, some of whom saw the fairy scene for the first time, while to others the renewal of the pleasure was perhaps even greater than its first awaking; and one little one whispered, in an awe-subdued voice, ' I think it is like heaven.' On the very top shoot stood an angel, with a Union Jack in one hand and a lighted red taper in the other ; on every branch were like tapers of red, blue, yellow, white, and green, skilfully fixed and counterpoised so that they should not set fire to the tree, nor to the smaller toys and trinkets hung upon the branches. All round the foot of the tree, and on a table near, were the larger toys for the children and the more useful presents for their elders. Behind was the gardener, with a bucket of water and a garden-syringe,—happily not to be needed. These fruits of the magic tree had already been labelled with the name of a boy or girl, children of the farmers or the cottagers, or the squire's grandchildren. Each name was called out in succession, and the hall soon resounded with joyful voices intermingled with the sound of the crackers which were drawn with exclamations of surprised triumph : paper caps, and aprons, and bonnets, and mottoes in the most execrable verse that ever wit of man has devised. There was a due quota of penny whistles, trumpets, and accordions. The oranges and bonbons from the tree were followed by slices of cake from the table, till the hands and arms of every child were laden and overladen. Then they gathered round the dismantled tree with its tapering lights and sang Hark the herald angels. This was followed by God save the Queen, and then the procession re-formed, and the happy little ones went home in the moonlight." (*Atlantic Monthly*, December, 1894.)

Chrysanthemums, Feast of. (Japanese, *Kiku-no-Sekku*.) A Japanese holiday celebrated on the ninth day of the ninth month, or towards the end of October in our calendar, and therefore at a season when the kiku, or chrysanthemum, is almost the only flower in full bloom. A cheerful and gayly dressed multitude streams out to visit the places devoted to its cultivation and sale.

At all the family repasts during the day the leaves of chrysan-themum flowers are scattered over the cups of tea. It is be-lieved that libations so prepared have the power of prolonging life and strength.

Churching of Women. This is a survival of the Jewish rite of purification after childbirth from ceremonial uncleanness. It is not enjoined as matter of obligation by either the Roman or the English Church, but is recommended as a pious and laudable custom. In the Roman ritual the woman, wearing a veil, kneels at the door of the church, holding a lighted candle with holy water. The priest sprinkles her, and, having recited the 23d Psalm, puts the end of his stole in her hand and leads her into the church, saying, " Come into the temple of God. Adore the Son of the blessed Virgin Mary, who has given thee fruitfulness in child-bearing." The woman then advances to the altar and kneels before it, while the priest, having said a prayer of thanks-giving, blesses her, and again sprinkles her with holy water in the form of a cross. The rite is given only to women who have borne children in wedlock.

In England after the Reformation the place where the woman must kneel was shifted to the altar rails. The office was not used for unmarried women till they had done their penance, and even then could take place only on a Sunday or holy-day. These re-strictions have been abolished; but it is required of a cleric that he satisfy himself of the woman's penitence.

The idea of uncleanness attached to pregnancy is ancient and wide-spread. It took curious forms in England. Thus, in Ellis's " Historical Letters," Third Series, ii. 226, occurs the following: " There is a certain superstitious opinion and usage among women, which is that in case a woman go with child she may christen (that is, be sponsor to) no other man's child as long as she is in that case." In 1880 a woman with child refused to take an oath at a police court,—probably an unreasoning survival of the same thought. (*Notes and Queries*, Sixth Series, iii. 48.)

Churruk Poojah. (Swinging Festival.) An out-door relig-ious fête celebrated in honor of the goddess Kali by the Hindoos in many parts of India. The main feature is the swinging in the air of self-immolated victims on iron hooks depending from a cross beam, which in its turn seesaws across the top of a huge upright pole. The hooks are passed into about two and a half inches of the skin and flesh of the back. They are fastened by ropes to the end of the cross-pole, lowered by tilting for the purpose. Then the victim is lifted up into the air, the body fairly hanging by the hooks without any auxiliary support, and made to gyrate in wide circles. The victims generally remain up, swinging about, for fifteen or twenty minutes, but they are lowered at any time on their making a sign. Instances sometimes occur in which the flesh and muscles of the back give way, and the devotee is dashed to the ground with fatal violence. Accidents are rare, however. In many cases the saints are "old hands," who perform this rite from motives of gain and reputation, and who go through their martyrdom with great cheerfulness and self-satisfaction. But in many other cases they are novices, who offer themselves in fulfilment of a vow made to Siva or his spouse Kali.

Seldom do even novices wince when the hooks are fastened, and the subsequent swinging in the air is invariably borne with composure, often with enthusiasm. Sometimes the devotee smokes his pipe while whirling in his lofty gyrations. It is usual for the devotee to take up with him fruits and flowers in his girdle, which he throws down to the crowd, who,—especially the female portion,—laughing and shouting with delight, rush eagerly to catch them in their hands or in umbrellas inverted to receive them. Sterile women are especially anxious to obtain the fruit scattered by these devotees of Siva, as a means of wiping away their reproach ; and wealthy childless ladies frequently send their servants to the festival to procure some of the auspicious fruit for their mistresses to eat.

A writer in *Household Words*, v. 506, describes a Churruk Poojah which he witnessed some time in the early fifties. The spot was an extensive valley in the neighborhood of one of the leading cities of Bengal. Far as the eye could reach, it teemed with human life. Thousands flocked from many a point and pressed to where the gaudy flags and beating drums told of the approaching Poojah. Here a number of bamboo and leaf sheds had been erected, where amusements of various sorts were in progress or preparation. But what fixed his eye were "several huge poles standing at a great height, with ropes and some apparatus attached to them, the use of which I knew from report alone." Report was speedily to be confirmed by experience. A young and pretty girl was the first victim. " It appeared that her husband had, months since, gone upon some distant dangerous journey, and that, being long absent, and rumors raised in the native bazaar of his death, she, the anxious wife, had vowed to Siva, the protector of life, to undergo self-torture on his next festival if her loved husband's life should be spared. He had returned, and now, mighty in faith and love, this simple-minded, single-hearted creature gave up herself to pain such as the stoutest of our sex or race might shrink from. She sat looking fondly on her little infant as it lay asleep in the arms of an old nurse, all unconscious of the mother's sacrifice, and, turning her eyes from that to her husband, who stood near in a wild, excited state, she gave the signal that she was ready. The stout-limbed, burly-bodied husband rushed like a tiger at such of the crowd as attempted to press too near the sacrificial girl; he had a staff in his hand, and with it played such a tune on bare and turbaned

CHURRUK POOJAH IN A BENGAL VILLAGE.

heads and ebony shoulders as brought down many an angry malediction on the player. The nurse with the infant moved farther away among the crowd of admiring spectators. Two or three persons, men and women, pressed forward to adjust the horrid-looking hooks. Was it possible, I thought, that those huge instruments of torture, heavy enough to hold an elephant, were to be forced into the flesh of that gentle girl! I felt sick as I saw the poor child stretched upon her face, and first one and then the other of those ugly, crooked pieces of iron forced slowly through the flesh and below the muscles of her back. They lifted her up, and as I watched her I saw big drops of perspiration starting from her forehead; her small eyes seemed closed at first, and, for the moment, I fancied she had fainted; but as they raised her to her feet and then quickly drew her up in the air high above us, hanging by those two horrid hooks, I saw her looking down quite placidly. She sought her husband out, and, seeing him watching her eagerly, gave him a smile, and, waving her little hands, drew from her bosom small pieces of the sacred cocoanut and flung them amidst the gazing crowd. To scramble for and obtain one of these precious fragments was deemed a fortunate thing, for they were supposed to contain all sorts of charmed powers.

"And now the Poojah was fairly commenced. The ropes which carried the iron hooks were so arranged that by pulling one end—which passed over the top of the pole—it swung round a plate of iron which set in motion the other ropes holding the hooks and the living operator. Two men seized on this rope, and soon the poor girl was in rapid flight over the heads of the crowd, who cheered her on by a variety of wild cries, and shouts, and songs. Not that she seemed to need encouragement; her eyes were still bent towards her husband; I almost fancied she smiled as she caught his eye. There was no sign of pain, or shrinking, or yielding: she bore it as many a hero of the old world would have been proud to have done, scattering beneath her flowers and fruit among the busy throng.

"I felt as though a heavy weight were off my mind when I perceived the whirling motion of the ropes first to slacken, and then to cease, and finally the girl, all bleeding, relieved from the cruel torture. They laid her on a mat beneath some shady trees: the women gave her a draught of cool water in a cocoanut-shell. But her thoughts were not upon herself: she looked anxiously around, and could not be satisfied until her husband sat beside her and their little swarthy infant was placed within her arms. The only care her deep and open wounds received was to have them rubbed with a little turmeric powder and covered with the fresh tender leaf of a banana."

Another votary was an aged mother, whose prayers (she believed) had saved the life of her son. The vow had been made, and the deliverance effected, eleven years before; but the poor people had never been able till then to incur the expenses of the offering to the god and the feast with which these solemnities are always closed. With the utmost heroism this aged woman endured the whole, shouting aloud with the spectators, and scattering her flowers with flurried enthusiasm. Her son, a man of thirty years, was present, and in a state of greater excitement than his mother, to whom he paid the most anxious attention, and to whose devotion he evidently believed he owed the continuance of his life.

Other victims, of all ages and both sexes, followed, and bore their self-chosen tortures with similar equanimity. The British government has made several attempts to suppress the Churruk Poojah, but so recently as 1893 an artist correspondent of the *Illustrated London News* forwarded an illustrated description to that paper of a festival of this sort witnessed in the neighborhood of Calcutta.

Circumcision.
According to Genesis xvii. 9–14, God gave Abraham the command to circumcise every male child on the eighth day after birth, "and it shall be a token of the covenant betwixt me and you." Christian commentators look upon this rite as a token that through the shedding of the blood of the future Redeemer remission of the original sin inherited from Adam could alone be obtained. It also signified that the Jews were cut off and separate from all other nations. By circumcision a Jew became a party to the covenant, was consecrated to the service of God, and agreed to accept his revelation and obey his commandments. In other words, this outward sign admitted him to true knowledge of God, true worship of God, and true obedience to God's moral law. But, inasmuch as it pointed to the coming of Christ, it was abolished with his advent and its place was taken by baptism, which also is a sign of covenant with God, admitting to true worship, true knowledge, and true obedience. But baptism is more than circumcision; it is more than a mere covenant; it is a sacrament, whereby supernatural power, or grace, is given to the child to enable it to carry out the covenant. Christ submitted to circumcision, not because he had inherited the sin of Adam, or needed grace, but because he came to fulfil all righteousness, to accomplish the law, and for the letter to give the spirit.

By the Jews circumcision is still practised with all the ancient ceremonies. Sometimes when the child is ill or weak it is deferred beyond the eight days mentioned in the law. A godmother brings the child to the place and carries it back again. But neither she nor any other woman is admitted to the ceremony. The place may be a private house as well as the synagogue. The godmother delivers the infant at the door to the godfather, and when borne within it is greeted with cries of "Baruc Habba!" or "Welcome!" The Mohel, or Circumciser, is waiting among a circle of male friends. In a dish are all the necessaries,—a razor, astringent powder, rags, cotton, and oil of roses. The operation over, the Mohel takes a cup of wine, blesses it once, and then repeats a second benediction for the child, who now receives the name chosen for him.

The 128th Psalm is now repeated, and then the child is handed back to the godmother.

Among the Mohammedans circumcision is practised, but not until the boy is old enough to make his own profession of faith. It was a legacy from the pre-Mohammedan Arabs, who are said to have learned it from the Ishmaelites, the descendants of the son of Hagar. The custom is also derived from the Jews by the Egyptians, Colchians, Phœnicians, and Ethiopians, but rather as a method of promoting health and warding off certain diseases than as a religious rite.

In the "Romance of Lady Burton's Life" a rather amusing paragraph is quoted from a letter written from Damascus:

"We went to every kind of ceremony, whether it was a circumcision, or a wedding, or a funeral, or a dervish dance, or anything that was going on; and we mixed with all classes, and religions, and races, and tongues. I remember my first invitation was to a grand *fête* to celebrate the circumcision of a youth about ten years of age. He was very pretty, and was dressed in gorgeous garments covered with jewelry. Singing, dancing, and feasting went on for about three days. The ceremony took place quite publicly. There was a loud clang of music and firing of guns to drown the boy's cries, and with one stroke of a circular knife the operation was finished in a second. The part cut off was then handed round on a silver salver, as if to force all present to attest that the rite had been performed. I felt quite sick, and English modesty overpowered curiosity, and I could not look. Later on, when I grew more used to Eastern ways, I was forced to accept the compliment paid to the highest rank, and a great compliment to me as a Christian, to hold the boy in my arms whilst the ceremony was being performed. It was rather curious at first to be asked to a circumcision, as one might be asked to a christening in England or a 'small and early.'"

Clavie, Burning of the. A curious semi-jocular ceremony, a relic of some ancient pagan rite, celebrated on the 11th of January (the last day of the year, Old Style) in the fishing town of Burghead, situated on the south shore of Moray Firth, Morayshire, Scotland. The headland on which Burghead is situated was for ages held by the marauding Norsemen, even after their final overthrow by Malcolm II. in 1010. Before the Norsemen set foot upon it, it is believed to have been held by the Romans, and to have been the northernmost point reached in Britain by the conquerors of the world.

On the evening of the 11th of January all the fishermen of the village assemble about dusk and proceed to some shop, where they demand a strong empty barrel. This is usually surrendered at once, but, if refused, it is taken by force. Another barrel, for breaking up, and a quantity of tar, are procured in the same way. A hole about four inches in diameter is made in the bottom of the stronger barrel, through which a stone pole five feet in length is inserted. The barrel is filled with tar and set on fire. The remaining barrel is then broken up, and stave after stave is thrown into the bonfire. The Clavie, burning fiercely, is now shouldered by one of the fishermen, who rushes along one of the streets, followed by the crowd. At the end of the street he is relieved by another fisherman. In this way every street in the village is gone through, the Clavie being replenished from time to time. Formerly the procession visited all the fishing-boats, but this has been discontinued for some time. When the procession has passed through the village, the Clavie is deposited on the top of a little mound called the Durie. This mound is interesting as being a portion of the ancient fortifications, spared probably for use in this particular ceremony. On this mound the present proprietor (1897) has erected a small round column, with a cavity in the centre for the admission of the fire end of the pole. Here the Clavie is left to burn far into the night. It is then broken up and the embers are scattered. The people rush upon the pieces. Every fragment is carefully gathered up and carried home to be preserved as a charm against witchcraft. At one time superstition invested the whole proceedings with all the solemnity of a religious rite. The whole fishing population joined in it as an act necessary to the welfare of the little community during the year about to commence.

No landsman can take part in the programme. Even strange fishermen are forbidden to participate. About 1830 a colony of fishermen from Campbelltown (Inverness-shire) settled in Burghead. After a few years' residence they were allowed to accompany the procession. The strangers grew and multiplied until they became almost as numerous as the Burgheaders. Feeling their strength, they decided that it would be more in accordance with the fitness of things if the Clavie were burnt on the evening of the 31st of December instead of the 11th of January. The innovation was fiercely resisted, and after a protracted struggle the strangers had to succumb. A curious superstition connected with the ceremony is that should any one fall in the rush along the streets it is a sign that he will never be present at another Clavie-burning. So sure are they of this, that should the Clavie-bearer for the time fall, another at once seizes the fiery mass, and, without waiting for the fallen man to rise, the crowd rushes onward, at the imminent risk of trampling him under foot.

This remnant of paganism, now slowly dying out in the lone village of Burghead, was once common throughout Scotland. Some say that it is of Scandinavian origin, and others that it is purely Celtic. There is no authority for either statement. The ceremony was probably performed by both races. It is certain that in the beginning of the last century the kirk-session of Inveravon forbade the " heathenish custom" and took steps to put it down. A minute to that effect is recorded in the session-books.

Inveravon is a parish in the Highlands of Banffshire, where probably the foot of Norseman never trod, thus showing that the ceremony was practised by the Highlanders.

It is believed that the mysterious rite was originated for the purpose of frightening witches. No doubt the belief in it among the fishermen degenerated into something like that; but the origin of the Clavie lies deeper. The use of a stone hammer instead of an iron one in constructing the Clavie is by some held as indicating that the ceremony was in existence in the stone age. The Clavie, in short, appears to be the remnant of a religious belief, and is probably connected with fire-worship. (*Notes and Queries*, Second Series, vol. ix. pp. 38, 106, 169, 269; *Book of Days*, vol. ii. pp. 789–791. See also JOHN THE BAPTIST, ST.)

Clebach's Fountain. A holy well in the southern slope of Cruachan, near Roscommon, Ireland. The legend is that St. Patrick met here the two daughters of King Leoghaire, Fedelm and Ethna, as they came from the royal palace of Rath Cruachan to bathe in the fountain. The maidens wondered at sight of the venerable stranger, surrounded by his monks, and they questioned him eagerly as to who he was, and whence he came, and what king he served. When Patrick told the lofty message that he bore, the grace of God touched the hearts of the maidens, so that they believed and were baptized in the waters of the fountain, which the saint blessed for the purpose. They begged for the eucharistic bread, and after it was given them they prayed that they might be united to their spouse and king forever. And the flush of health left their cheek, and they calmly sank to sleep in death. Their bodies were laid side by side at Clebach's fountain, which became one of the holy wells of Erin, famous for the miracles that were wrought by its waters.

Clement, St., patron of farriers and blacksmiths. Little authentic is known about him, but ecclesiastical tradition represents him as a blacksmith who was converted to Christianity in the reign of Domitian, became Bishop of Rome, and was martyred November 23, A.D. 100, by being bound to an anchor and cast into the sea. Hence the anchor is his attribute in art. The church of St. Clement Danes in London had formerly an anchor for a vane, the parish boundaries are still indicated by an anchor, while the beadles bear an anchor on their staves and buttons.

Popular English myth has added some astonishing details to this saint's legend. He is represented as the son of St. Catherine, as the first founder of brass, iron, and steel from the ore, and as the first man who ever shoed a horse. It is added that he was crowned king of all trades by Alfred.

His festival on November 23 is still celebrated in rural England by the children in what is known as Clemmening, which consists in a house-to-house quest for gratuities of apples. Formerly this was the custom of the blacksmiths, who added beer or wine to their desiderata. Hence the bibulous survival in the following doggerel which the children of Staffordshire sing during their rounds :

> Clemany ! Clemany ! Clemany mine !
> A good red apple and a pint of wine,
> Some of your mutton and some of your veal,
> If it is good, pray give me a deal ;
> If it is not, pray give me some salt.
> Butler, butler, fill your bowl ;
> If thou fill'st it of the best,
> The Lord'll send your soul to rest ;
> If thou fill'st it of the small,
> Down goes butler, bowl and all.
> Pray, good mistress, send to me
> One for Peter, one for Paul,
> One for Him who made us all :
> Apple, pear, plum, or cherry,
> Any good thing to make us merry ;
> A bouncing buck and a velvet chair,
> Clement comes but once a year ;
> Off with the pot and on with the pan,
> A good red apple and I'll be gone.
> > (*Notes and Queries*, First Series, vol. viii. p. 618.)

Owing to the proximity of St. Clement's feast to that of his "mother" (November 25), Catterning and Clemmening are often merged into one ceremony which spreads over three days. In Sussex the children sing this rhyme :

> Cattern and Clemen be here, here, here,
> Give us your apples and give us your beer.
> One for Peter, two for Paul,
> Three for Him who made us all.
> Clemen was a good man,
> Cattern was his mother :
> Give us your best,
> And not your worst,
> And God will give your soul good rest.

The blacksmiths in England still celebrate St. Clement's Day locally by dressing up an effigy or one of their own number in a long cloak, an oakum wig, a long white beard, and a mask. This figure, known as Old Clem, is placed in a chair with a wooden anvil in front of him and in his hands a pair of tongs and a wooden hammer. Sometimes he is merely made the subject of toasts and the presiding officer of the merrymakings. At other times he is taken round on an eleemosynary quest.

Such a procession, with a live Old Clem at its head, was cele-brated as late as 1826 (see " Every Day Book," vol. i. p. 1501) by the blacksmiths' apprentices of the dock-yard at Woolwich. The Old Clem of the occasion was made to recite the following speech :

"I am the real St. Clement, the first founder of brass, iron, and steel, from the ore. I have been to Mount Etna, where the god Vulcan first built his forge, and forged the armor and thunder-bolts for the god Jupiter. I have been through the deserts of Arabia; through Asia, Africa, and America; through the city of Pongrove, through the town of Jipmingo, and all the north-ern parts of Scotland. I arrived in London on the 23d of No-vember, and came down to his Majesty's dock-yard at Wool-wich to see how all the gentleman Vulcans came on there. I found them all hard at work, and wish to leave them well on the 24th."

Old Clem's memory is still kept green in many of the govern-ment dock-yards by mumming and feasting. The master-black-smiths often give their employees a wayz-goose, a leg of pork stuffed with sage and onions, on this day. The Brighton Rail-way Company's smiths hold an annual supper at White Horse Inn. The anvils used to be fired with gunpowder, but this part of the ceremonial has now been discontinued.

Coat, Holy. This is the general name given to certain relics which are said to have been garments worn by Christ during his earthly life. The most famous of these is the Holy Coat pre-served at Trier, or Treves, in Germany, claimed to be the seam-less garment for which the Roman soldiers cast lots during the crucifixion. It is a tunic about five feet long, cut narrow at the shoulders and gradually widening towards the knees. It is woven in one piece without seams. The material is supposed to be linen, but its great age prevents any exact examination. It is enclosed in an outer casing of purple and gold cloth, supposed to have been added some time in the seventh century in order to preserve the relic. Many miracles are claimed to have been performed by this robe, and it is said still to possess great merit.

Its history for the last seven hundred years is clear enough. But darkness shrouds the story of the relic prior to the twelfth century. The Church relies for proof of its authenticity upon a tradition that it was one of a chest-full of relics sent as a gift to the church at Treves by the Empress Helena to celebrate the conversion to Christianity of her son the Emperor Constantine. She herself had found the coat while on her pilgrimage to Jeru-salem in search of the true Cross (see CROSS, INVENTION OF THE). The cathedral in which it is now housed was built A.D. 550 on the site (still according to legend) of an ancient Roman palace which was the birthplace of St. Helena. The legend goes on to say that in the ninth century the Holy Coat was concealed from the Normans in a crypt of the cathedral. There it remained forgotten until 1196, when it was rediscovered and placed in the high altar. Just about here authentic history supersedes legend. In 1512 Leo X. ordered that the coat should be exposed to the veneration of the faithful. The multitudes who flocked to see it

ST. HELENA AND THE HOLY COAT.

were so great that the Pope decided on a public exposition every seven years. But the disturbances that followed the Reformation prevented the regular observance of this great religious festival, and during the seventeenth and eighteenth centuries the coat was deposited for safety in the castle of Ehrenbreitstein, on the Rhine. In 1810, with the permission of Napoleon, the Bishop of Treves, Mgr. Mannay, brought the sacred relic back to his own city, and, in spite of the confusion of the times, a multitude of pilgrims, numbering over two hundred thousand, visited Treves to celebrate this joyful restoration. In granting the desired permission, Napoleon added the characteristic condition that " the working of miracles was to be forbidden." Hence a revival of the famous epigram,—

De par le Roi, défense à Dieu
De faire miracle en ce lieu.

In 1844 a still more successful exposition of the Holy Coat took place.

Since the Middle Ages no such pilgrimage had been known, and no mediæval shrine could have attracted the same number of people in the same space of time,—from August 18 to October 6,—for it is said that one million five hundred thousand devotees visited the high altar on which the coat was placed. They came from all quarters, many from long distances, travelling on foot, preceded by their village priests and by surpliced boys bearing banners. All the inns and lodging-houses of the town were crammed, and not a vacant room which the owners were willing to let could be had after the first week for either love or money. But it was summer, and there was little hardship in sleeping on staircases, in outhouses, or even in the streets and squares, with the pilgrim wallets for pillows. Every morning at early dawn the eager sight-seers took up their posts by the cathedral doors, until a line of more than a mile in length was formed, so that it was difficult for any save the head of the procession to reach the coat much under three hours. The heat, dust, and fatigue exhausted many, who fainted by the way, while the pent-up excitement of others gave way to hysteria as they made their oblations before the sacred object.

There being no Napoleon to forbid miracles, they broke out with great violence. The most noteworthy case was that of a young woman, the Countess of Droste Vischering, who approached the altar on crutches, one of her legs having been contracted by a scrofulous swelling of the knee, and after praying before the relic succeeded in bringing her foot to the floor and walking out of the cathedral, though her leg had been bent at an angle of nearly forty-five degrees for years. Naturally, so astounding a case caused a commotion in medical as well as religious circles. The miraculous nature, as well as the permanency, of the cure was disputed. It was an excellent subject for scientific inquiry, but none was made. A month after the sensational scene in the cathedral a physician certified that the improvement miraculously begun (it was not claimed that she was instantaneously cured, but only that through the relic she had received the power to stretch the contracted member) was still in progress. Then the countess, who was a grand-niece of the Bishop of

17

Cologne, whose cathedral is also rich in relics, entered a cloister, and the world heard nothing more of her except that she performed the duties of a Sister of Mercy. She and her story live in a Commersbuch of the German students in a ballad beginning,—

> Freifrau von Droste Vischering,
> Vi va Vischering,
> Zum Heil'gen Rock nach Triere ging,
> Tri tra Triere ging.

The scenes of 1844 were repeated and magnified in 1891, when the Holy Coat was once more exposed to public adoration. The ceremonies began on August 20, and lasted six weeks. They opened in an impressive manner. "After the provost had read the protocol of the last locking-up of the relic last year," writes a correspondent of the London *Standard,* "the cathedral architect and two other gentlemen opened the high altar and broke large masses of stone out of it with heavy crowbars. A box about two metres long was then lifted out and opened, and a long document and a smaller box, covered with leather, were taken out. The latter was opened, when a third box, of metal closed with six seals and containing the sacred garment, came to light. On this third box lay another document. Bishop Korum then threw a red cloth over the third box, and bore it himself, assisted by the provost, to the treasure-chamber, where it was opened after the seals had been examined and found intact. The bishop then took out the sacred garment, which was enveloped in blue, red, and white silk wrappers. These the bishop removed, and then spread out the coat on the table. He then read the passage in St. John's Gospel referring to the coat, and then admitted the persons invited to see it. Nobody, however, was allowed to touch it, this privilege being reserved for the bishop alone."

The relic was exhibited in its full length and breadth, hanging in an oaken shrine, lined with white silk, open in front, and draped with costly silk, adorned with braid and tassels of gold. On the main spire of the cathedral had been erected a large flag-staff, from which, during the exposition of the relic, there floated a flag with a red cross on a white ground. A thousand citizens of Treves watched beside the relic during the exposition.

The Berlin correspondent of the *New York Herald* cabled as follows under date of August 20, 1891: "The garment known as the Holy Coat was exposed to view this morning in the cathedral at Treves. Two Knights of Malta in full costume, with drawn swords in their hands, stood on either side of the shrine enclosing the Holy Coat case, which was surrounded by tall lighted candlesticks and surmounted by a large gold cross.

There was an impressive scene in the sanctuary. Over a hundred priests assisted in the pontifical high mass which followed the unveiling of the Coat. The cathedral was richly decorated for the occasion, and was packed to the doors with people. The white surplices of the choir, the gorgeous vestments of the priests, the scarlet uniforms of the Knights of Malta, the countless lights flickering in every nook and corner, the prismatic rays filtering through the old windows, the strange congregation composed of people of many nations and all walks of life, formed a picture not often seen. Bishop Korum during the course of his address earnestly urged the faithful to unite in revering the garment from which power and virtue proceed. The nave of the cathedral was then cleared, so as to enable the municipal authorities and the parochial societies to march up to the shrine of the Holy Coat and venerate that relic. Treves is overflowing with pilgrims and with visitors. The streets are filled with processions of all descriptions, and sacred banners, crosses, and lighted candles are to be seen on all sides. During the whole time the Holy Coat is on exhibition about twenty excursion trains a day will arrive at Treves, a very great number for a Continental city, and a large temporary railroad station has been built for the pilgrims; but in order that the town may not be overcrowded the different bands of pilgrims, led by their priests, will only be permitted to remain one night in town. Arriving, say, in the evening, they will march the next morning in procession to the cathedral, and must leave town the same evening, in order to make way for other religious bodies of people."

Next to the relic at Treves the most famous of all Holy Coats is that at Argenteuil. This also claims to be the seamless garment of Christ. Legend traces it back to the Roman soldier who won it by lot. The record declares that it was bought from this soldier and guarded vigilantly in various countries till it came into the possession of the Empress Irene, who sent it to Charlemagne. The latter presented it to his daughter Theodrada, Abbess of Argenteuil.

This coat is about five feet long by three and a half feet wide. The left sleeve is missing, and a large piece has been taken from the left side. The garment is hand-woven, and is of camels' hair. It lies in a casket, and has a reddish tone like that of a dried rose. Every afternoon from Ascension Day to Whit Monday the shrine in which the relic is kept is carried in procession through the Argenteuil church. The garment is exhibited in its entirety only at rare intervals, as it is placed under seal by the Bishop of Versailles, in whose diocese Argenteuil is. He alone has authority, with the sanction of the Pope, to open the casket. In the year 1862 Pope Pius IX. secured a small fragment of the garment, and the other two small pieces were cut off at the same time. These pieces are in two small caskets which the faithful are allowed to kiss while kneeling at the altar. It is said that the relic has recently been examined with a microscope, and that traces of what was believed to be blood were found on it. Miraculous cures are alleged to have been effected by means of this relic. Lord Clifford's eldest son, the Count de Damas, and the Marquis of Harcourt, are among those said to have been cured.

"The Holy Coat of Argenteuil has recently been submitted by the Bishop of Versailles to a close examination at the hands of experts of the Gobelins Factory. They report that the cloth is a sort of bunting, the texture of which is not close, but soft and light. The warp and weft are of exactly the same thickness and nature. The garment has been woven on a loom of the most primitive kind. The raw material of the texture is fine wool. They found a complete identity, both as to raw material and manufacture, in the fabric examined and in the ancient fabrics found in Christian tombs of the second and third centuries of our era. Samples of the coat were also submitted to several distinguished chemists, who report that the stains in them were produced by human blood. From all the circumstances of the analysis they presume this blood to be very ancient." (*Antiquary*, December, 1893.) A paper contributed by Emile Gautier to the *New Science Review* (New York) for October, 1894, gives further particulars.

Other coats said to have belonged to Christ are preserved at Moscow, Venice, and other places. The pious Catholic explains their existence by saying that Christ probably had several garments during the thirty-three years of his life. Therefore they may all be genuine. As to the question which is the seamless coat gambled for by the soldiers, the majority of Catholics will cast their vote for the relic at Treves.

Coat of Mohammed. This Mohammedan counterpart to the Holy Coat of Treves is preserved at Constantinople in the shrine of Eski-Serai, and is exhibited to the adoration of the faithful twice in every hundred years. The last exposition was in 1896. The Holy Coat of Mohammed, according to tradition, was presented by the Prophet to a Yemen dervish, Was-ul-Karani, as a token of gratitude for his services in discovering the use and preparation of coffee. It is a kind of chukva, or robe, with flowing sleeves somewhat similar to Western dressing-gowns, which is worn in the Levant by those whom foreigners are accustomed to designate as Turks of the old school. It is needless to add that its color is green,—the hue above all others sacred to the

Prophet. The extent to which the garment is venerated by all true believers may be estimated from the fact that the most cherished title of the Sultan is Hadum-ul-Haremeen, or guardian of the holy relic. The coat was brought to Constantinople by the Sultan Selim I., along with the keys of the holy cities of Mecca and Medina, from Cairo, where all had been preserved until that time in the keeping of the Caliphs. The shrine in which it was placed by Sultan Selim, and where it has remained ever since until this day, is within the precincts of the Imperial Treasury at Gulchane.

The last exposition of the Prophet's coat was made in 1895. The Sultan left his palace in company with old Osman Ghazi Pasha, the hero of Plevna. Alighting at the Bab-ul-Saida, or Sublime Porte, he, with his own hands, unlocked, by means of a massive golden key, the silver grating or cage which protects the Holy of Holies from intrusion by the profane. With another key of the same precious metal he proceeded to open a huge cupboard or box composed of the purest and most massive gold, and to extract therefrom a bundle, which he placed on a silver table of great beauty. One by one the Sultan then removed the forty outer cloths in which the Holy Coat was wrapped up, until the last but one was reached. The latter consists of some thin, transparent kind of gauze, and is left intact. For no mortal eye may behold nor human lips touch the sacred relic unshrouded. Reverently, and with every token of the utmost veneration, the Sultan bent and kissed the dingy-looking bundle, his example being followed by the Sheik-ul-Islam, the Grand Vizier, and the various chief dignitaries of the realm according to their rank, during which time verses of the Koran were chanted by the ulema.

Subsequently all the men withdrew, and, under the guidance of his highness Yaver Aga, the grand eunuch of the imperial seraglio, the Valide Sultana, or mother empress, along with the various wives of the monarch and princesses of the family, appeared upon the scene and likewise paid their respects to the Holy Coat. As soon as they had closed their devotions and departed, the Sultan carefully wrapped up the bundle again in the nine-and-thirty wrappers which he had removed, after which he replaced it in its gold cupboard, locked it, as well as its silver cage or grating, and returned to his palace at Yildiz Kiosk between a double line of troops, who kept a path open through the vast multitude of people for the imperial procession. In the evening the Sultan sent to all those who had been present at this ceremony small white cambric handkerchiefs with the verses of the Koran embroidered on them, which had been specially consecrated at Mecca for the purpose.

Besides this, splendid presents were made by the Padishah to the Sheik-ul-Islam, the primate of the Turkish Church, and also to Yaver Aga, a coal-black and gigantic negro, who is addressed as " Your Highness" and ranks with the Grand Vizier and bears the title of " Dar ul Sadr Aghassi," which rendered in English means " he whose post is behind the door of the sanctuary of bliss." The Grand Vizier and the ministers also received tokens of imperial good will in the shape of jewelry and decorations.

Cocoanut Day. A Hindoo festival celebrating the conciliation of land and sea. It is thus described by the *Times of India*, September, 1896 :

" Cocoanut Day—the conciliation of Neptune—has just been celebrated in India. God Neptune is a most important deity, and it is always advisable to keep him in good humor. There is no saying otherwise how his friend Varuna may blow the monsoons. The cocoanut day, of course, marks the subsidence of god Neptune's playfulness, when the hoary deity made some fun by leading the ' floating palace' of the humans a nice little dance on his frisky waves.

" We set about god Neptune's propitiation in right royal style. Brahmins, of course, come in as the pivot of the affair. We all of us—unless we are too old, or sickly, or lame, or too much engrossed in self-admiration—repair to the sea-shore, taking with us a lot of materials of worship, as an offering to the water-deity. We move some distance into the water; the Brahmin stands in the middle and recites hymns; and we, surrounding him, respectfully offer our cocoanuts, and flowers, and milk, and sugar-candy, and fragrant powders, to the sea-god. One supreme honor still remains behind, and we render it. We make lights, and wave them before the pacified divinity. Most of us formerly used to throw the cocoanuts right into the sea, but, as the Brahmins took them up and made them their own, we now, in order to save trouble to the holy men, give them straight into their hands.

" In Kurrachee and other ports they throw the cocoanuts into the sea, where Mussulman boat-people get hold of them and sell them later to the Bunnias in the bazaar, whence they come back to us as edibles. These Mohammedan boat-wallahs are expert swimmers; and though the little Arab fellows at Aden and Port Said, we are told, perform some marvellous feats of diving, in bringing up silver coin thrown to them, their Moslem confrères of the Indian ports are not less expert in personal navigation. Once our offerings to the deity are made, it matters not to whom they go. So it is perfectly indifferent to us whether the Brahmin youngsters eat the cocoanuts or Moslem boat-people collect them in boatfuls.

"There is no particular reason why cocoanuts, of all nuts, should be offered to the water-deity. Any other fruits too may be offered. Only the cocoanut is the tropical fruit *par excellence*, and, as it is pre-eminently 'watery,' we imagine god Neptune may just fancy it better. But we do not simply give the cocoanuts to the Brahmins: we accompany them with some money present. Nothing can be given to the Brahmins unless her majesty's coin accompanies the gift. But they eminently deserve it, on some occasions. In ceremonies in which ablutions or any sort of 'water-taking' comes in, we do the thing and pass on. But the Brahmins remain constantly in the water, ministering to every succeeding batch,—which means standing several hours together in wet. And yet they never develop bronchitis. I suppose it is a case of adaptation to the spiritual environment."

Collop Monday. The Monday before Shrove Tuesday, so called because, says Hone, "it was the last day of flesh-eating before Lent, and our forefathers cut their flesh meat into collops, or steaks, for salting and hanging up until Lent was over." Polydore Virgil says of this season "that it sprang from the feasts of Bacchus, which were formerly celebrated in Rome at the same period." Collop Monday, therefore, may be only an adaptation from the heathen. In confirmation it may be added that at this period the Eton boys write verses to Bacchus.

Verses are still written and put up on this day, but the young poets are not confined to eulogiums on the god of wine. Nevertheless the day still retains its old name of Bacchus. In Cornwall the day is termed Hall Monday. About the dusk of the evening it is the custom for boys, and in some cases for those who are above the age of boys, to prowl about the streets with short clubs, and to knock loudly at every door, running off to escape detection on the slightest sign of a motion within. If, however, no attention be excited, and especially if any article be discovered negligently exposed or carelessly guarded, then the things are carried away, and on the following morning are discovered displayed in some conspicuous place, to expose the disgraceful want of vigilance supposed to characterize the owner. The time when this is practised is called " Nickanan night ;" and the individuals concerned are supposed to represent some imps of darkness who take advantage of unguarded moments.

On the following evening (Shrove Tuesday) the clubs are again in requisition ; but on this occasion the blows on the door keep time to the following chant :

Nicka, nicka, nan;
Give me some pancake, and then I'll be gone.
But if you give me none,
I'll throw a great stone,
And down your doors shall come.
  (*Report of the Royal Institution of Cornwall for* 1842:
          Notes and Queries, First Series, vol. xii. p. 297.)

In the neighborhood of Bridestow, Okehampton, England, the children go round to the different houses in the parish on this day, generally by twos and threes, and chant the following verses, by way of extracting from the inmates sundry contributions of eggs, flour, butter, halfpence, etc., to furnish out the Tuesday's feast:

Lent Crock, give a pancake,
Or a fritter, for my labor,
Or a dish of flour, or a piece of bread,
Or what you please to render.
I see by the latch
There's something to catch;
I see by the string
There's a good dame within.
Trap, trapping throw,
Give me my mumps, and I'll be go [gone].

The above is the most popular version, and the one indigenous to the place; but there is another set, which was introduced some years ago by a late school-mistress, who was a native of another part of the country, where her version was customary:

Shrovetide is nigh at hand,
And we are come a-shroving;
Pray, dame, give something,
An apple, or a dumpling,
Or a piece of crumple cheese,
Of your own making,
Or a piece of pancake.
Trip, trapping throw,
Give me my mumps, and I'll be go.

This custom existed also in the neighborhood of Salisbury. (*Notes and Queries*, First Series, vol. v. p. 77; *Popular Antiquities*, 1849, vol. i. p. 62.)

Columban, St. (543–615.) A famous Irish saint, a native of Leinster, who about 595 with twelve brother monks travelled into France, founded the monasteries of Luxeuil and Fontaine, was banished by King Theodore (ostensibly because his views on mooted points of faith did not agree with those of the Frank-

ish Church, but really because of the freedom he used in repri-
manding that prince for his libertinism), and finally retired into
Italy, where he founded a religious house at Bobbio, near Naples.
At the latter place he died on November 21, 615, which is the
date on which he is commemorated.

A small fragment of the original tomb of St. Columban, with
its inscription, still remains in the church dedicated to the saint
at Bobbio. The body itself was removed from its original grave
in 1482, and placed in a new marble shrine beneath the altar in
the midst of the crypt or subterranean church at Bobbio. But
the entire body of the saint was not suffered to remain there.
In accordance with a custom that prevailed in the latter part of
the Middle Ages, the head or skull was in 1514 detached and
placed in a beautifully wrought silver shrine that takes the
form of a mitred bust. It is now kept in the sacristy of the
church that bears his name. Other relics of the saint kept in
the same sacristy are wooden cups, a little bell, and a knife, the
latter of such virtue that bread cut with it is never liable to corruption or putrescence, " and if women eat this bread when
nursing it causes an abundance of milk, and moreover has great
efficacy against the bites of mad dogs and against fevers."
(MARGARET STOKES: *Six Months in the Apennines.*) Miss Stokes
adds a full account of the hermitage of La Spanna, near Bobbio,
where, on the summit of a cliff, is a hand-print in the rock, said
to have been marked by the impression of the palm (*spanna*) of
St. Columban's hand, which is still believed to possess healing
virtues for sufferers who place their palms upon it.

Commencement. In English and American colleges, the
day when degrees are conferred, the day when the graduating
classes commence bachelors (or lawyers, or doctors, or what not).
The term is now extended to academies and primary schools of
all grades. In the mediæval universities graduation was simply
the conferring of a qualification and right to teach (or, in the
case of law and medicine, to practise).

Commencement, then, existed at first for those taking what
are now called the higher degrees, and was the time when young
men ceased to be pupils and commenced to teach. The bachelor's degree marking the end of the trivium, or preparatory
course, was first given at Paris ; and it seems that the bachelors
were required to serve an apprenticeship at teaching, as a part
of their preparation for the master's degree. The student having performed the requirements of the trivium, he was named a
bachelor by the masters of that subject, and had now the right
to wear a round cap, and not only the right, but the obligation,
to teach freshmen. He was then said *incipere in artibus* (" to

commence in arts"). Hence, even when extended to the graduation of bachelors, Commencement still carried the implication
of commencing to teach. The requirement that all graduates
should serve as teachers was gradually relaxed, till teaching was
made entirely optional, and Commencement came to be, as at
present, simply the occasion when degrees of all grades were
conferred.

"There is no season more delightful than Commencement.
Every year that long, sparkling billow of youth breaks upon the
shore of manhood, and each successive wave is as fresh and beautiful as all its predecessors. The president of a college annually
confronting the graduating class, under the same circumstance
of summer and roses, with the same associations, the same tender
recollections, the same eager and proud anticipations, must feel
himself to be a perpetual youth ; and if he gives a blessing to
the class, not less does the class leave with him its benediction.
His attitude, indeed, is that of Mentor, but he must feel that his
counsel springs from experience, and, being addressed to those
who have experience yet to gain, it is, after all, a kind of fairy
lore, a singing in an unknown tongue.

" But there has gathered around Commencement a multitude
of delightful occasions all related to scholarly sympathy and
association, and taking precedence even of the especial function
of the season. The class-day exercises of the graduating class,
the reunions of alumni, with their orations and dinners, the social
festivals of the Greek-letter societies, from that of the venerable
Alpha or Phi Beta Kappa down to the very last Omega of the
mystic characters. and all these held at the chapter houses or
rooms, for a day or two preceding Commencement Day itself,
with every form of literary exercise and social entertainment in
the most enchanting moment of the year, combine to throw a
spell of June romance over young and susceptible hearts, which
is not only delightful, but permanent, and gives to the Commencement season a singular power." (GEORGE W. CURTIS.)

Commercial Day. On December 19, 1895, a banquet was
held at Delmonico's in New York by three hundred of its prominent citizens, under the auspices of the *Commercial List and
Price Current*, to celebrate not only the centenary of the publication of this the oldest commercial paper in the country, but
also that of the passage of the treaty of amity, commerce, and
navigation between Great Britain and the United States which
led directly to the founding of the newspaper on December 19,
1795. At that banquet it was determined that the 19th of December should henceforth be denominated Commercial Day and
should be celebrated by an annual banquet of the leading mer-

chants and business-men of New York, in honor of the commercial treaty.

The treaty itself, however, it should be borne in mind, has no direct connection with the day. The treaty had been negotiated by John Jay, of New York, who had been sent over for the purpose by Washington as Envoy Extraordinary of the United States, was ratified by the Senate, and formally approved by the President.

The treaty secured to the United States freedom on the seas, privilege to trade with Great Britain, the withdrawal of all British posts from our territories, and a policy of non-interference by the mother-country in affairs concerning the United States.

The confidence it inspired in the business world by its recognition of this country as a treaty power, and the immediate advantages it brought to American commerce, are shown in the fact that the foreign trade of the United States almost doubled in the single year following its making. But unfortunately it was arranged at a time when the American people were smarting under a sense of bitter wrong inflicted by Great Britain. Hence its many advantages were not at first fully appreciated. Political partisanship attacked it blindly, and the great party then clamoring for an alliance with France denounced it fiercely. In its support the calmer counsels of such statesmen as Washington and Hamilton, representing the conservative and substantial elements of the nation, finally prevailed, and the treaty was adopted. Time has too fully demonstrated the wisdom of this measure to make necessary a discussion of the long-since refuted arguments by which its consummation was opposed. The era it ushered in was for the nation one of progress and prosperity unprecedented.

Confetti. This is an Italian word signifying, literally, "confectionery," and as such entirely applicable to the small hard bonbons which were formerly exchanged as missiles during the Carnival. These bonbons are now, however, known as *coriandoli*, and the term *confetti* is applied to their cheaper and therefore more popular substitutes,—hard lime pellets of the size of a hailstone and quite as hard,—which are carried around in a bag by maskers and thrown with a tin ladle. Originally the confetti were done up in paper, to mitigate the sting of their impact, but this mercy is seldom observed at present. The custom has passed over to Paris, and is especially practised at the fêtes of Mi-Carême (Mid-Lent, *q. v.*) and Mardi-Gras (Shrove Tuesday, *q. v.*). But there only the paper and the name confetti are retained. The hard missiles have been eliminated. French confetti (the name is properly plural, like macaroni) are made out of thin paper of all colors, cut into pieces of the size of a leather tack head.

Miss Constance Fenimore Woolson, in an article in *Harper's Magazine*, has given a pleasant description of the manner in which confetti-throwing is practised during the Roman Carnival:

" In watching some of the more dexterous throwers about me," she says, " I was amused to see what a test of organization and temperament confetti-throwing could resolve itself into. Across the way was a young Russian lady who in the fury of her attacks had warmed into the excitement of a Bacchante. There was an English girl next her, whose pure fresh face, timid but accurate shots, and calm sobriety of demeanor were as typical of her nationality as a Du Maurier drawing. On our own balcony there was such a spirit of jollity and vivacious enjoyment in the sport as make the American girl the ideal of a man's responsiveness in fun. The crowd below, despite its *canaille* character, was now full of enchanting Italian gayety. There were laughter and mirth, and quick return charges of confetti fire; there were young French art students filling their bags with shot, and young German officers bringing Von Moltke's tactics to bear on their tin-ladle throwing. Even Romans themselves, much as they may scorn Carnival sports, cannot resist this last riot of mimic fighting. Italian officers, at least, are men before they are Romans, too much men not to try their luck before the battery of discriminating eyes. For the hail of confetti is to be taken as something personal and complimentary. Its intensity is in proportion to the attraction of the object. A whitewashed coat and battered hat are to be looked upon as proofs of the sincerest flattery.

" Few features of the fun are more amusing to watch than the flirtations that grow out of it. On the balcony on my right there was a young Italian whose admirable shooting announced him an expert. His fire had been at first indiscriminate in its aim, hitting the Neapolitan model in the head as unerringly as he had pelted a pretty contadina in the nose. But soon his practised eye discovered a target worthy of his skill. Half hidden behind the scarlet curtains draping a box directly opposite was the figure of a beautiful young woman, whose nationality betrayed itself in the dusky glory of her dark eyes and the childlike *naïveté* with which she abandoned herself to the enjoyment of the scene. She was quite unprotected. Her wire mask lay in her lap, her dipper beside it, and behind her huge feather fan she was laughing heartily at some of the nonsense before her. With the aim of true science my young neighbor covered the beauty with a shower like hail. She, with the quickness of the

Italian temperament to take fire, dropped her fan, seized her dipper, and, seeing then what manner of man her antagonist was, loaded it to the full, and returned a shot as effective as his own. For the next half-hour the fight went on, the most serious damage resulting from the now equally active interchange of glances. There is nothing more characteristic of the Carnival season than these swiftly born mimic fights, beneath the artifice of which there as suddenly leaps into life the flashing fire of a flirtation."

Compare the Roman custom with the more *chic* and gracious confetti-throwing of the French as described by a correspondent of the Louisville *Courier-Journal* writing from Paris under date of March 18, 1896. "Confetti," he says, "are thrown on you to make you beautiful, and before a fête is over you are very beautiful indeed, both inside and out, as confetti get down your back, and when you disrobe at night there is a shower of confetti, and, behold, the inside of your undershirt is like a flower-garden in the spring, and the bottoms of your shoes shine darkly with confetti, and you wonder whether you will have to go to a doctor to-morrow to have that piece of confetti taken out of your eye, and whether confetti are digestible, and try to swallow that papery dryness at the bottom of your throat. The French all delight to make strangers beautiful first. Every one has a handful of confetti for the American, and so you warm with the pretty compliment, and a red eye and a dry throat are nothing, for you see the stars and stripes waving in a shower of confetti thrown by the French people.

"Generally there are three days of confetti-throwing before Lent begins. This year more confetti were thrown than ever before. It was estimated by one of the daily papers that one million five hundred thousand pounds were sold the three days preceding Lent. The price of confetti varies. On the fashionable boulevards where the rich walk, the price is from thirty to forty cents a pound. In the poorer quarters they sell for from fifteen to thirty cents a pound. The last day the price generally goes up ten cents a pound everywhere. Striking an average of twenty cents a pound, three hundred thousand dollars was spent in three days to make people beautiful.

"Confetti were introduced in Paris five years ago. They came out at a ball at the Moulin Rouge. A little cupful cost two sous, and none were thrown in the streets that year. The confetti were such a success that a great deal was manufactured the next year, and the price came down, and the poor could buy confetti and give the rich back handful for handful. Since then each year the streets have been covered with a deeper and deeper layer of confetti. Until this year it was the custom when the confetti were an inch deep in the streets to grab up handfuls and throw them. The authorities ordered this stopped, because dust was mixed with the confetti and dust will not make one beautiful. Mainly on account of this order, the confetti were much deeper this year than before. In the Boulevard des Italiens they were five inches deep the last night of the fêtes. Walking was more fatiguing than in six inches of snow.

"At Mi-Carême and Mardi-Gras there is a parade, and the people all come out to see it, and when it has passed right then begins the difference between France and the United States. In America the whole show is over, and the people go home wondering whether it was really worth waiting an hour after the advertised time to see. In France the parade is just an incident, and the real fun and confetti-throwing begin after the parade has gone by. Every one buys a sack of confetti and starts out looking for those whom they make beautiful. The men throw at the women, and the women at the men. A pretty woman is soon covered with confetti, a handsome man too. Many a battle takes place. A woman receives a handful of confetti in her face and looks and sees around her innocent-looking men, all with their hands down. She looks closer, and detects a smile under the black moustache of the young man in the gray overcoat. A second later that young man's face is full of confetti, and before he can defend himself another handful blinds him. The young woman thinks she has won, and passes on, but before she has taken four steps a hand from behind douses her face in confetti. She turns, and there is that young man in the gray overcoat, daring her to come on. She goes down into her sack of confetti, and tries to get hold of enough to bury that young man, who, when struck, utters a cry as if his heart was pierced, and flies, and the young woman, flushed with success, pursues him. He turns suddenly and finds her unprepared and empties his whole sack of confetti in her face. Before she has recovered her breath he has bought another sack of confetti and emptied that on her, and unless she confesses herself beaten in a contest where it is most winning and womanly to be weakest, he may buy out the whole stock of the confetti market.

"No one must get angry, for that is impolite, and impoliteness is shocking on a fête-day in Paris. Here is the reprimand which a young woman received who did not smile and say 'thank you' when a young man got the best of her. At first the young woman had the upper hand in the confetti-throwing, and it was great fun. However, the young woman did not have overcoat-pockets, and her confetti soon gave out. But she did have an umbrella, and, rushing out of the dense cloud of confetti, she gave the young man a poke in the ribs. The crowd indignantly interfered at once, telling her that she was no proper young woman. The umbrella had dropped from her hands. A man picked it up, and, opening it and raising it above his head, said that an umbrella was to keep off the sun and rain. ' See,' he said, pointing to the end of the handle, 'this is not sharp, and cannot be used effectively as a sword,' and, bowing low, he returned the umbrella to her. Then the crowd told her to go home and to learn how to behave herself before she came out on another fête-day.

"The shopkeepers have fun with one another. One loads up with confetti and rushes into his neighbor's store and rushes out again, leaving behind him a man in a cloud of confetti. Later the compliment is returned, and several such visits back and forth are made during the day. A party of men and women enter the café, and from their innocent bearing one would never suspect that they are on mischief bent. There is a signal, and with a 'Vive la République' enthusiasm the men and women blow off confetti as if they were so much pent-up steam. The patron is surrounded, and becomes the middle of a pillar of confetti. Such visits explain why they say in Paris that you find confetti in your soup a month after a fête. The policemen are a favorite mark for confetti, and they must stand all day and receive gusts of confetti in their faces, followed by mischievous ripples of laughter from women, with never the pleasure of throwing a handful in return. The children have a great time with confetti. From the beginning to the end of a fête the children and the confetti are so mixed that when a mother wants her child she feels around in the confetti until her hand rests on a head. If the head is that of her own child and not that of her neighbor's child, she leads the young one home. Many houses in Paris have balconies. Those who live in the apartments come out on the balconies and have battles with a street-full of people for spectators, who have a cheer for the woman whenever she gives the man a blinding handful. Others who live in upper stories sift confetti on the crowds, with a sackful now and then for one that interests them."

Consualia. An ancient Roman festival, celebrated on August 21, in honor of the god Consus. This festival was supposed to be the precursor of the Ludi Circenses, and was celebrated annually in the Circus by the symbolical ceremony of uncovering an altar dedicated to the god, which was buried in the earth. Romulus was considered as the founder of the festival, and was said to have discovered an altar upon the spot where this ceremony took place. The festival was associated with the tradition of the rape of the Sabine women, by which it was believed that the founders of Rome procured wives for themselves, by violence, from the neighboring Sabines. The Sabines, it was related, had come to Rome to see the spectacle; and their hosts, in the midst of the games, seized upon the Sabine maidens and carried them to their homes. The tradition assumes the existence of the games at this early epoch. They were celebrated, under the direction of the Pontifices, with chariot- and horse-races; and it was a holiday for animals as well as men, horses and asses being allowed to rest, and being adorned with garlands. Who this god Consus was, the ancients themselves did not know. He was generally identified with the equestrian Poseidon, or Neptune of the Greeks; but there was nothing in his cult that reminds of Neptune.

Contribution-Box in Churches. The contribution-box is an American invention, or, rather, a gradual evolution. In the early colonial days no contribution was taken up in the churches, but the support of the minister and his family depended upon the gifts of the people. Cord-wood and pumpkins, fresh pork and dried apples, were given in sufficient abundance to keep the preacher from season to season. But as the Church advanced a demand arose which could not be satisfied by these merely bucolic contributions. One could not, for instance, send mission-aries abroad on a capital of pork and potatoes. Then it was voted to " pass around the hat," but, as the colonial hat was not considered dignified enough for that purpose, one of the tithing-men conceived the idea of substituting the old-fashioned warm-ing-pan. With this the collector could stand at the door of the square, box-like pews and gather in all the shekels with ease, the coin as it dropped in the brass warming-pan gauging the generosity of the giver. It may have been some of the thriftier members of the congregation who decided that the warming pan was too noisy and clamored for an improvement. In answer to this appeal came the corn-popper, whose wire meshes served to deaden the noise. This was used until the rise of an artistic sense called for something more æsthetic as well as more con-venient in the handling. So at length was invented the modern contribution-box, the long handled square box with which the vigilant deacon can reach to the extreme end of the pew. These were not lined until the old complaint about the attendant noise caused them to be lined with some soft material, the Methodists and Baptists generally using flannel and the Presbyterians and Congregationalists preferring velvet. These boxes are still ex-tensively used throughout the country towns. As the offertory is usually accompanied by a selection from the choir, the accom-paniment of jingling coins adds greatly to the service.

Coopers' Dance. (Ger. *Schäfflertanz.*) A curious ceremony performed by the coopers of Munich, Bavaria, every seven years, during the last days of the Carnival, and ending on Shrove Tuesday. According to popular tradition, the custom originated in the year 1517, when Munich was ravaged by a terrible plague. Desolation and despair reigned. Fear took possession of the citizens, so that even when the plague began to abate they durst not open their windows or doors or leave their houses, fearing that the air and the water were tainted with the disease. Finally the master coopers and the master-butchers put their heads together and decided to reassure their unfortunate fellow-citizens by public shows and amusements. So one day the whole town was startled by a procession marching to the sound of merry music. First came the coopers, dressed in bright red jackets and waving fresh green garlands in time with the music, while they called to the people to open their doors and windows and come out in the open air. Then followed the butchers, also dressed in bright costumes and mounted on their dray-horses. Curiosity and excitement overcame fear. The people rushed out and followed the procession to the market-place. There the coopers danced in a circle, whilst the butchers' apprentices leaped into the fountain to prove that the water was innocuous. Thus was public confidence once more restored.

Since that period the coopers once every seven years dance their Schäfflertanz in commemoration of the event, and once every three years the butchers' apprentices perform the Butchers' Leap.

The last time the Coopers' Dance was performed was in 1893. A contributor to the *Catholic World* (December, 1896) who was an eye-witness gives an account here condensed. He was fortunate enough to obtain a place at a window of the palace of Prince Ludwig Ferdinand in the Wittelsbacherplatz. This was one of the palaces visited by the coopers. They perform before the royal palace for the prince regent, and before the houses of all the other princes in turn. They also dance opposite the Rathhaus, and the houses of the ministers and principal magnates of Munich. But they must keep in Munich; outside the limits of the city they are not allowed to roam. They receive twenty-five dollars from each royal personage before whose palace they dance, and from ministers, etc., never less than fifteen dollars. The festivities as witnessed from Prince Ludwig Ferdinand's windows in 1893 were but a repetition of what happened before the other houses.

"The Schäffler, about twenty young men, came marching up the platz, dressed in close fitting scarlet jackets trimmed with silver lace, black velvet knee-breeches, white stockings, and buckled shoes; they had little, short leather aprons, one corner tucked back, tied round the waist with a broad crimson silk sash, the gold-fringed ends of which hung down at one side. On their heads they wore green velvet turned-up caps, adorned with a tuft of blue and white feathers, and carried large half-arches of fresh box-trees in their hands. The musicians followed with fife and drum, and another scarlet-coated individual, who bore a black and yellow banner (the colors of Munich), with the coopers' arms—a beer-barrel, with hammer and nails—painted on it. At the end of the procession walked a harlequin (*Hanswurst*), clearing the way with a long pole, striped with blue and white, with a ball and cross at the top.

" The musicians stood at one side, while the dancers arranged themselves in a circle in the centre of the platz, opposite the palace. The performance began by their all dancing round in a ring, each holding one end of his own and his neighbor's arch in his right hand, while his left was placed jauntily at his side. The harlequin stood with his pole in the centre of the ring, and the Schäffler wound in and out, out and in, in intricate mazes; but little by little, out of the seemingly hopeless confusion, they formed with their green arches a huge royal crown of which the centre was the harlequin's cross and ball. The next figure was an arbor, then a monster beer-barrel round which the performers danced, while they tapped it with little hammers, keeping time with the music. Then followed a variety of figures, all ingeniously formed out of the verdant arches.

"The figures finished, the harlequin brought forward a gay-looking little barrel, painted blue and white, and two hoops, also blue and white, with three holes in each, in which were placed three small glasses of wine. One of the Schäffler jumped lightly upon the barrel and began to swing about the hoops from one hand to the other, over his head and under his knees, in time with the music, without spilling a drop of the wine. He then took out one of the glasses, and, having handed the hoops to the harlequin, who emptied the others by throwing the contents on the ground, he drank ' *Lebe hoch !*' to Prince Ludwig Ferdinand. The swinging of hoops and drinking were continued until the health of the eight members of the royal family present had been drunk. After each toast the empty glass was tossed over the drinker's shoulder and caught behind by the harlequin in his cap. Then the dancers marched gayly away as they had come. The Schäfflertanz will be seen no more in this century. When its seven years come round again it will be 1900."

Copacabana, Nuestra Señora de. (Sp., "Our Lady of Copacabana.") One of the most famous shrines in South Amer-

ica. The sacred city (*ciudad bendita*) of Copacabana is a large
and rambling town on the peninsula of the same name in
Bolivia. It lies within the neighborhood of the sacred islands
of the ancient Incas, and was a holy spot long before the advent
of Christianity. Its chief edifice is the splendid church containing the miraculous image of Our Lady of Copacabana. This
stands in the *camarin*, a large room behind the great altar, admission to which among the natives must be prefaced by confession and the payment of a small sum of money. The former
condition is not exacted from heretical visitors. All round the
walls are ranged votive offerings, from the diamond hilted sword
and gold-mounted pistols of General Santa Cruz and the jewels
of his wife, to little rude representations in silver of arms,
legs, hearts, and eyes, deposited here by grateful Indians and
whites as emblematic tokens of the cures wrought by Nuestra
Señora.

She herself stands in an alcove, behind a heavy curtain of
embroidered velvet, and shut off from too close approach by a
stout silver railing. At stated times the curtain is rolled back
and she stands revealed to sight. She is a wooden image
scarce three feet high, elaborately dressed in gay satins and
loaded with gold and jewels. Her head is a mere mite in comparison with the blazing crown which it supports. The legend
runs that the image was carved in 1582 by Tito Yupanqui, a
lineal descendant of the ruling Incas, who had no previous instruction in art, but who was inspired by the Virgin. Our Lady
even favored him with a special sitting, so that the portrait is
celestially guaranteed to be accurate.

Little wooden crosses are hung around the neck of Nuestra
Señora, and, having thus become imbued with special virtues,
are distributed to pilgrims. As many as thirty thousand devotees have been known to visit the shrine in a single season,
coming from all parts of Catholic America, and even occasionally
from Spain or Portugal.

Copacabana—the word in ancient Peruvian means a precious
stone that gives vision—derives its name more immediately
from an idol carved of blue stone which lent sanctity and fame
to the spot in the days of the Incas. This idol was buried by
the Indians after the arrival of the Spaniards, but was subsequently disinterred by the latter and broken in pieces. The
temples of which the early writers speak have disappeared and
left only few and unsatisfactory traces. Yet in the suburbs of
the town near the cemetery are found a number of niches,
steps, and what appear to be seats, cut in the rocks, which
may have had some connection with the ancient worship.

The Catholics have raised a number of subsidiary shrines

along the approaches to Copacabana, in which pilgrims through prayer and penance prepare themselves to encounter the greater sanctities that await them in the sacred village.

Corn-Dance. An ancient festival among the Indians of North America, which is still kept up, especially among the Senecas of New York. It is held at the coming of the harvest season (about the end of August) as a sort of thanksgiving to the Great Spirit for the return of the crops. The date of the festival is usually announced by a carrier, fantastically dressed, with painted face and bespattered hair, who rides from house to house all over the reservation. At the appointed time the entire tribe gather at their council-house, where the materials of the feast have been prepared. The braves sit at one end of the hall, the squaws at the other. The ceremonies open with speeches delivered by the elders. Then follows a banquet. Huge caldrons filled with choice Indian delicacies—dog-meat, cabbage, succotash, etc.—are placed on the floor. Behind the kettles stand officers of the nation. As each member of the assembly comes up, carrying a tin pail or a wooden dish, he or she is helped to a portion from each of the kettles. Then all retire to the shade of near-by trees and bushes to dispose of the eatables. When sated, they fall back in a sleep which lasts nearly all the afternoon. As evening approaches, the feasters again gather in the council-house for the dance. The musicians are seated on benches in the centre of the room. The instruments are horns or shells filled with shot, and drums made by stretching a hide over a hoop. The drums produce a dull booming sound, and the horns give out a sharper rattling noise. The dance is led by an elder of the tribe, and is a sort of exaggerated cake-walk, except that grotesqueness rather than grace seems to be aimed at in the movements. All the men and women form in a circle about the players and follow exactly with limbs and body the movements of the leader. At first the circle moves very slowly in a sedate and stately march, but as the musicians get warmed up to their work they rise from their seats and sway their own bodies in unison with those of the dancers. The time becomes faster and faster. The leader begins to execute grotesque figures, throwing out his arms and legs and at every few steps emitting a yell, and all the time is faithfully imitated by his followers. The movement of the circle becomes more and more rapid until the whole line is whirling at a dizzy speed. Often men and women sink exhausted, but the line continues until the leader gives the signal to stop. After a short rest another number follows, and the dance is continued until late at night.

Corn-Shucking or **Husking-Bee.** The harvesting or " husk-ing" of corn which occurs in late October or early November is one of the most popular festivals in rural America from Maine to Florida. The stalks are cut in full fruit and stacked in the fields to mature, after which they are carried into a large barn, where all the lads and lasses of the neighborhood are already assembled; here they strip the ears from the parent stem, and, removing the outer sheaths, cast them into open bins, to be further selected and " shucked" before they are finally garnered. Several days are occupied in this way, and many are the jests and merry the laughter while dexterous fingers tear apart the sheaths and bright eyes look expectantly at each concealed ear as it comes to light; for he or she who first finds a red ear of corn is made king or queen of the revels that follow. When all the ears are stripped and lie heaped together in open bins, and the red ear has been proclaimed, a procession is formed, headed by the farmer and his wife, who walk in triumph followed by all their hands, leading the victorious maid carrying her patent of royalty—the red ear—in her hand, from the " huskins" barn to another large granary which has been effectively decorated with green boughs and corn-ears. At one end stands the throne, and the rough plank floor has been plentifully strewn with sawdust. Here the ceremony of crowning takes place, and the subsequent enthronement. The throne is usually some treasured old chair, high-backed, and so tall in the seat as to be approached only by a companion footstool or " cricket," carved very resplendently about the legs.

A corn dinner may follow. On each guest's plate lies a small napkin, spread cornerwise, and beside it are tiny cruets of salt and pepper, and a small plate holding a roll of fresh butter. Ears of corn, white and smoking hot, are served up. Then come corn fritters, succotash, roasted corn, corn cooked in cream, hunks of corn bread, and heaping plates of corn cakes. Toasts are given and drunk in cider, or light wines, or punch, or may-hap champagne. Then follow dances and other revels, and the party is at an end.

Such are the corn-shuckings of the present. But in the old slavery days there was an added element of picturesqueness in the festival as practised in the Southern States. An excellent reminiscent interview on these ante-bellum glories held with an ex-slaveholder by a *New York Sun* reporter appeared in that paper for November 11, 1895, whence the following paragraphs are quoted :

" My father owned about three hundred negroes, and as I was the oldest boy of course I was known on the plantation as ' young marster.' The event of the year down in the negro ' quarters' was the corn-shuckin', and when corn-shuckin' time came they were permitted to invite their friends on the neighboring plantations, and would go miles and miles to attend one of these frolics. The season is just at hand for them now. Yes, boys, it's corn-shuckin' time in Dixie, and I wish I was there. I can see the woods, all crimson and brown and gold, and the blue haze of Indian summer over it all, and I can hear the birds as they stop over on their way to the far South.

"As soon as a corn-shuckin' was talked about, all the darkies would begin to sing,—

> "Ha, ha, ha, you and me,
> Little brown jug, don't I love thee!

They all knew that the little brown jug would be on hand. When the night of the shuckin' arrived, the darkies poured in from every direction. They travelled paths in those days and took near cuts, and they had signals by which to let each other know that they were on the way. Most plantations had a bugler who owned an old wooden bugle five or six feet long. These bugles were made generally of poplar wood coated with tar and kept under water for several days. Soaking it kept the instrument from shrinking, and gave it a resonant sound which could be heard for miles on a clear night. The bugles were carried to the corn-shuckin's, and the coming darkies would blow and blow, and be answered by the bugler at the corn-pile, and as he did so he would say, ' Dar's the niggers comin' from Byers's plantation,' ' Dar dey is from Elliott's.' As they drew nearer to the pile of corn the bugle-blowers would stop and give way to quill- or reed-blowers. A set of from three to seven reeds of different sizes and lengths were always on hand, and those darkies could play any tune they'd ever heard on 'em by shifting 'em across their lips. The roads and paths would resound with the weird music of the quill-blowers as they came in from many directions. They used these instruments, too, in going to their wives' houses at night. You know, fellows, the darkies had right smart intuitive sense about some things. They preferred to have a wife on some other man's plantation than their marster's, and would only visit her on Wednesday and Saturday nights. You could hear them going and coming, blowing their quills for all they were worth.

"The corn was divided into two piles as big as a house, and two captains were appointed. Each chose sides, just as the captains in spellin'-matches do, and then the fun began. There was always whiskey enough to please 'em, and not enough for any drunkenness. A man was entitled to sample the jug every time he found a red ear of corn, and also to kiss any dusky damsel that he fancied. It was astonishing how many red ears some of 'em managed to find, and very funny to see how anxious the young wenches were for the red ears to come to light. The young marster was always on hand to see that the drams were given out judiciously, and to see that all got a taste. The side which shucked out their pile first got the prize, and it was usually plug tobacco. While the shuckin' was going on the darkies would sing, talk, and dance. A leader would mount on top of one pile of corn and call, and all would join in the chorus. The leader at every corn-shuckin' I ever attended began, 'I will start the holler,' and the crowd yelled the response, 'Bugleloo!'

> " I will start the holler!
>   Bugleloo!
> I will start the holler!
>   Bugleloo!
> Oh, doan' yer hear my holler?
>   Bugleloo!
> Massa's got er bugler,
>   Bugleloo!   ·
> A ten-cent bugle,
>   Bugleloo!

"There were about fifty stanzas to this song, or else the leader improvised as he went on, and he would call until the crowd grew thoroughly sick and wanted a change. They brought him down by throwing ears of corn at him. Sometimes a fellow that was very much stuck on his voice would mount to call, and it took devilish rough treatment to get him down. Then another caller would take the lead. He would probably 'hist' a religious tune, such as—

> " Lord, I can't stay away.
> Lord, I can't stay away;
> Lord, I can't stay away.

And the crowd, with groanings and moanings, would half sing, half chant,—

> "Oh, I mus' come to jedgment to stan' my trial:
> Oh, I mus' come to jedgment to stan' my trial!
>   I can't stay away.

The leader again called,—

> " Lord, I can't stay away;
> Lord, I can't stay away.
> Oh, my God, gwine ter rain down brimstone an' fire,
>   I can't stay away.
> Gwine ter walk on dat glass all mingled wid fire,
>   I can't stay away;
> Lord, I can't stay away;
> Lord, I can't stay away;

I'm gwine ter jine dat heav'nly choir,
    I can't stay away.
John says he seed forty an' fo' thousan';
    I can't stay away.
Jesus is comin' wid forty an' fo' thousan';
    I can't stay away.

"At the end of each verse the crowd would join in with the chorus, swaying their bodies and nodding their heads in time to the music. Their dreadful earnestness in singing of the judgment and brimstone could only arise from a profound belief in such things. Many of the girls and women would clear away a space and pat and dance. The night would wear on, and as the pile of unshucked corn grew smaller and smaller the spirits of the darkies would rise. They hate work, even when mixed with fun, and as the corn-pile disappeared the crowd would yell,—

"Lookin' fur de las' year,
    Bang-a-ma-lango!
Lookin'.fur de las' year,
    Bang-a-ma-lango!
Roun' up de co'n, boys,
    Bang-a-ma-lango!
Roun' up de co'n, boys,
    Bang-a-ma-lango!

"They always say 'year' for ear, and as the last one was shucked there was a mighty rush and scramble. Three or four strapping bucks would lift the young marster to their shoulders and the crowd would fall in line behind. Then they would march three times around the 'big house,' as the marster's house was always called, singing as they marched, coming to a halt at the tables under the trees, where they were sure of finding a feast of good things. A beef and a mutton were always killed for a corn-shuckin' supper, and then there was an abundance of bacon and cabbage, sweet and Irish potatoes, stewed pumpkin, fruit pies, and pecks and pecks of ginger-cakes and biscuits, and gallons of molasses. Darkies 'jes' naterally love coffee,' as they say themselves, and every one had as much as he or she wanted in corn-shuckin' time. It was served in bowls. They would eat awhile and then rest and eat again. And while they were resting some would pat and sing, play the jewsharp or quills, while others pulled ears and danced. Others would wrestle and box, and the old men and women would settle themselves about the numerous fat-pine bonfires and talk about 'ole marse and ole missy an' young marster,' or sing the old negro melodies that they love so well. Ah, they felt as grand and as free as they've ever felt since, boys, and such music as they made! There has never been anything like it since, and there never will be anything to take its place. The old slaves are dying with the old Confeds that fought to keep them. Already ' ole marster an' ole missy' and Mammy Liza and Daddy Hannibal have passed away, and it is almost time for young marster and the young darkies to go, too. I want to go back, boys. I want to go back to one more corn-shuckin' in the cotton-growin' section ; all made up of darkies. I don't want to go to one where the crowd is mixed, part black and part white. Do you know, I'd like to feel that I was the young marster once more. You can have all the tickets to hear Melba, Nordica, and Eames, and the De Rezskes and Paderewski, if you'll just let me hear the blowin' of the bugles and quills and the old corn-shuckin' songs; but what's the matter with us all taking a pull at the little brown jug before we go back to work ?"

Coronation Stone. A rough block of stone preserved in Westminster Abbey, inside an oaken chair, known as the Coronation Chair, chair and stone alike being looked upon with singular veneration by the English people. It is in this chair that every English sovereign, from Edward I. to Queen Victoria, has been inaugurated. Only once has it been moved out of the Abbey. When Cromwell was installed as Lord Protector in Westminster Hall, he was placed in the chair, which had been transferred there for the purpose. The early history of the Coronation Stone is involved in obscurity. It is certain that it was brought from Scone, in Scotland, to Westminster by Edward I., who built for it the chair that still contains it. It is also certain that Scone, as far back as the tenth century, was the place where the Scottish kings were inaugurated by being placed in " the royal chair of stone," and it is very likely, therefore, that this shapeless block was a portion of the chair and was brought over by Edward as a trophy of victory. Further than this authentic history says nothing. But, dating from about the fourteenth century, strange legends began to cluster around the stone, and were gradually wrought into a consistent narrative. English chroniclers gravely asserted that it was the pillow upon which Jacob slept at Bethel, and which his descendants had carried to Egypt. A Scottish fable stepped in to afford an explanation how it had been translated to Northern latitudes. It seems that a Greek, named Gathelus, had married Scota, a daughter of Pharaoh, and after the destruction of the Egyptians in the Red Sea had fled with her and the remnant who had escaped drowning along the north coast of Africa, and, crossing the Straits of Gibraltar, had founded a kingdom at Brigantium, now Compostella. His royal seat, and that of his successors, was a stone, fashioned like a chair and known as the " Stone of

Destiny," which, wherever it was found, promised sovereignty to the Scots, the descendants of the eponymic Scota. Just here Scotch and English traditions were neatly welded together by identifying the Stone of Destiny with Jacob's pillow and supposing that it had been brought by Gathelus from Egypt. Simon Breck, a descendant from Gathelus, carried the chair with him from Spain to Ireland, and was crowned in it as king of that country. After having been used for the coronation of a long series of Irish kings, it was transferred to Scotland by Fergus, the Irish king who subdued that country, and remained there till it fell into the hands of the English Edward.

Now, it happens that the Irish, too, had their Coronation Stone, their Stone of Destiny, the Lia Fail of Tara, which also had a legendary history connecting it with the East. Nothing could be more flattering to their national pride than to imagine that the English Coronation Stone was in effect their own Lia Fail, and that the long line of English monarchs who have been inaugurated upon it were mere upstarts, mere creatures of yesterday, in comparison with the illustrious dynasty of ancient Irish kings who took their seat upon the same stone in the heroic ages. By the dropping of inconvenient details the Irish legend, therefore, was merged into the Scotch, and it was held to be the Lia Fail that Fergus had taken over to Scotland, in spite of the fact that the Lia Fail was never removed from Tara, but remains there to this day. It may be mentioned, further, that the Coronation Stone has been examined by geologists, who agree in describing it as a block of old red sandstone, similar in all respects to the sandstone found in the neighborhood of Scone, and that it is quite impossible it should have come from the rocky formations of either Tara, Bethel, or Egypt. The whole matter is thus summed up by Mr. Skene, in the concluding paragraph of his essay on the Coronation Stone:

"It was the custom of Celtic tribes to inaugurate their kings on a sacred stone, supposed to symbolize the monarchy. The Irish kings were inaugurated on the Lia Fail, which never was anywhere but at Tara, the ' *sedes principalis*' of Ireland ; and the kings in Scotland, first of the Pictish monarchy and afterwards of the Scottish kingdom which succeeded it, were inaugurated on this stone, which never was anywhere but at Scone, the ' *sedes principalis*' both of the Pictish and Scottish kingdoms."

When a sovereign is to be crowned the coronation chair is carried around the screen and placed in the sacrarium before the altar. A robe of cloth of gold and ermine is thrown over it. A companion chair as nearly like it as possible was provided when at the coronation of William and Mary it was necessary that two thrones of equal importance be employed. Although the chairs are of nearly the same size, the seat of the newer one is quite four inches higher than the old. For William was a short man and Mary a tall woman; hence the seat of the chair in which he was to sit had to be made high enough to bring his head on a level with that of the queen.

Cut boldly in the solid oak seat, in scrawling letters such as a school-boy might make with his knife, is the legend " P. Abbott slept in this chair Jan. 4, 1801." P. Abbott, in fact, was a West-minster School boy, and a tradition, which there is every reason to believe is true, tells that he made a wager with a school-mate that he dare stay in the Abbey all night, alone. In order to win his wager he hid in some corner of the old building until the doors were locked for the night, and thus was left alone there. Fearing, however, that when morning came the boy with whom he had made the bet would disbelieve his statement that he had won it, he determined to leave some proof of the fact, and so spent the hours of the early morning in carving on the coronation chair the sentence which even now, nearly a century after, bears witness for him.

Corpus Christi. (Lat., "Body of Christ." Known also in France as *Fête-Dieu,* and in Germany as the *Frohnleichnamsfest.*) One of the greatest festivals of the Catholic Church, held on the Thursday after Whitsunday in memory of the institution of the eucharist and in honor of the doctrine of transubstantiation. Logically it should have been celebrated on Holy or Maundy Thursday, the anniversary of the Lord's Supper. But the Church at that season is occupied with the consideration of the mournful aspects of the Passion, and a joyous festival would have jarred upon the tone of mind so produced. The doctrine of transubstantiation was formally adopted at the Lateran Council in 1215. It was immediately felt that it should be made the occasion of a great holy-day. None felt this need more acutely than a certain religious of Liége named Juliana. No wonder, therefore, that a vision should have appeared to her. She saw the moon fully illuminated, with the exception of one dark spot, and was told that this dark spot referred to the lack in the Church of a festival in honor of the Transubstantiation. When in 1230 she became prioress of her order she urged upon the local ecclesiastical authorities the appointment of such a festival. In 1246 Robert, Bishop of Liége, acceded to her wishes, and the Thursday after Whitsunday became known through his diocese as Corpus Christi Day. An office for the day was compiled by Juliana. For almost a score of years the feast remained a local one. In 1261 a former archdeacon of Liége became Pope, under the name of Urban IV. Juliana was then dead, but a holy woman named Eve, who had been in her confidence and who knew of the friendship that had existed between Juliana and the new Pope, induced Henry, then bishop of Liége, to petition Urban IV. for the celebration of the feast throughout the Church. The Pope had not quite made up his mind, when a miracle that occurred in Bolsena in 1264 precipitated his assent. A priest celebrating mass spilt a drop of the communion wine after consecration. He strove to conceal the accident by covering the place on which it fell with the corporal. Suddenly the corporal was covered with red spots in the shape of a host. The corporal is still preserved at the neighboring town of Orvieto, where the Pope was then temporarily holding his court. Another account (embalmed in a famous picture by Raphael in the Vatican) makes a drop of blood appear upon the consecrated host to convince the doubting priest of the truth of the doctrine of transubstantiation. Both accounts, however, agree that the miracle led the Pope to delay the institution of the feast no longer. He therefore published a bull commanding its celebration throughout the Church. But as he died shortly afterwards it is possible that the bull was never published (no mention of Corpus Christi being found in Durandus, who lived twenty-two years after Urban), although it is pretty well established that Urban himself and the Roman Court celebrated the festival. The office which is still used was composed by St. Thomas Aquinas at the bidding of Urban IV. Clement V. in the Council of Vienne confirmed Urban's constitution, and succeeding Popes promoted the devotion to Corpus Christi by grants of indulgences ranging from forty to one hundred days.

The carrying of the Blessed Sacrament in procession on this festival has been almost from the first a recognized part of the ceremonial, if it was not, as some Catholic authorities believe, actually appointed by Urban IV. But it is borrowed from a still older procession of the same sort which had been instituted by Louis VIII. in 1226 on the feast of the Exaltation of the Cross (*q. v.*) in the city of Avignon, and which to this day is celebrated by the Gray Penitents of that city.

In mediæval times the Corpus Christi procession was celebrated throughout Christendom with much picturesque detail. Naogeorgus in his " Popish Kingdom" has left us a vivid description of the ceremonial as practised in Germany. First came a priest attired as St. John the Baptist, pointing backward to another who bore the silver pyx wherein was enshrined the eucharist. The arms of this second ecclesiastic were upheld by two of the wealthiest and most influential of the citizens, while four others bore a silken canopy over the pyx,—

least that some filthie thing
Should fall from hie, or some mad birde her doung thereon should fling.

Two angels walking beside the canopy cast flowers upon the pyx. Then followed St. Ursula and St. George. A float representing hell came next,

wherein there doth appere
A wondrous sort of damned sprites, with foule and fearful looke.

Then came St. Christopher bearing the infant Christ upon his shoulders, St. Sebastian transfixed with numerous arrows, St. Catherine with her wheel, and St. Barbara with her " singing cake."

And sundry other pageants played, in worship of this bread,
That please the foolish people well : what should I stand upon
Their banners, crosses, candlesticks, and reliques many on,
Their cups and carved images, that priestes with countenance hie,
Or rude and common people beare about full solemnie ?
The common ways with boughes are strawde and every street beside
And to the walls and windowes all are boughes and branches tied.
The monkes in every place do roame, the nonnes abrode are sent,
The priestes and schoolmen lowd do rore, some use the instrument.
The straunger passing through the streete, upon his knees doe fall :
And earnestly upon this bread, as on his God, doth call.
For why, they count it for their Lorde, and that he doth not take
The form of flesh, but nature now of breade that we do bake.
A number great of armed men here all this while doe stande,
To looke that no disorder be, nor any filching hande :
For all the church goodes out are brought, which certainly would bee
A bootie good, if every man might have his libertie.

The Blessed Sacrament was exposed in the churches for eight days, a custom still kept up. In the interim the St. John of the procession, carrying the consecrated host in a bag slung around his neck and accompanied by the peasantry bearing crosses and banners, passed from field to field, reading texts from the gospel in each, all which was held to protect the crop from storm and blight.

In old Catholic England the Corpus Christi processions were largely participated in by the various guilds of each city. York was especially celebrated for the splendor of these shows. Hargrove in his " History of York," 1818, vol. ii. p. 494, tells us that they consisted of a solemn procession, in remembrance of the Sacrament of the Body of Christ, the symbolic representation being borne in a shrine. Every trade in the city was obliged to furnish a pageant at its own expense, and join the procession, and each individual had to personify some particular passage in the Old or New Testament, and to repeat some poetry on the occasion. The whole was preceded by a great number of lighted torches, and a multitude of priests in their proper habits; after which followed the mayor and citizens, surrounded by an immense concourse of spectators. Commencing at the great gate of the priory of the Holy Trinity, they proceeded to the cathedral church and thence to St. Leonard's Hospital, where they left the sacrament. There are several public orders yet remaining in the old register of the city relative to the regulation of this ceremony; and indulgences were granted from the Pope to those who contributed to the relief of the fraternity, or who observed the annual ceremony in the most devout manner, particularly if they personally attended from the country. In York the custom was not abolished until 1584.

Corpus Christi Day was formerly celebrated at Dublin with high veneration. In the Chain-book of the City of Dublin are several entries to that purpose. We are told that there was a grand procession, in which the glovers were to represent Adam and Eve, with an angel bearing a sword before them. " The corrisees (perhaps curriers) were to represent Cain and Abel, with an altar and their offering. Mariners and vintners, Noah and the persons in his Ark, apparelled in the habit of carpenters and salmon-takers. The weavers personated Abraham and Isaac, with their offering and altar. The smiths represented Pharaoh with his host. The skinners, the camell with the children of Israel, etc." (See Harris, " History of Dublin," 1766, p. 147.)

In the " Royal Entertainment of the Earle of Nottingham, sent Ambassador from his Majestie to the King of Spaine," 1605, p. 12, it is stated that on Corpus Christi Day, "the greatest day of account in Spaine in all the yeare," at Valladolid, where the court was, " the king went a procession with all the apostles very richly, and eight giants, foure men and foure women, and the cheefe was named Gog-magog."

It was usual in earlier times to conclude the day with Mystery Plays, in which the chief characters of the procession made their appearance. The Cotton MS., Vesp. D. viii., contains a collection of dramas in old English verse (of the fifteenth century) relating principally to the history of the New Testament. Sir William Dugdale mentions this manuscript under the name of " Ludus Corporis Christi," or " Ludus Coventriæ," and adds, " I have been told by some people, who in their younger years were eye-witnesses of these pageants so acted, that the yearly confluence of people to see that shew was extraordinary great, and yielded no small advantage to this city." (See " Antiquities of Warwickshire," p. 116.) It appears by the latter end of the prologue that these plays or interludes were played not only in

Coventry, but in other towns and places upon occasion. This MS. was edited by Mr. Halliwell in 1841 for the Shakespeare Society. The elder Heywood thus alludes to the devil as a character in these mysteries:

> For as good happe wolde have it chaunce,
> Thys devyll and I were of olde acqueyntaunce;
> For oft in the play of Corpus Christi
> He hath played the devyll at Coventry.

In most Catholic countries the Corpus Christi processions still parade through the streets, though without the attendant mummers of the old days. The pyx is carried by an ecclesiastic under a canopy, as of yore, and is followed by the citizens bearing candles. Appropriate hymns and psalms are sung, among them the "Pange lingua gloriosi Corporis mysterium," known in "Hymns Ancient and Modern" as "Now my tongue, the mystery telling." But in Protestant countries the Catholics confine their processions to the church itself, or at the most it debouches from the front door, and, passing through the church-yard, re-enters by the door of the sacristy.

In the gala times of the Papacy the Corpus Christi procession around the colonnade of St. Peter's Square was one of the most gorgeous functions of the year; and it still retains a semblance of its former glory.

In Spain especially and in the colonies founded by Spain it is the greatest ecclesiastical holiday of the year. Work is abso-lutely suspended, and the entire population dons its holiday garb. In the cities the host is carried in solemn procession through the principal streets, attended by the highest local magnates (even royalty itself, as in Madrid), civic and military officials in fresh bright uniforms, and a vast array of ecclesiastics in gorgeous stoles and chasubles. A vanguard of silver bell ringers announces the coming of the host. "As the superb structure of filigree gold goes by, a movement of reverent wor-ship vibrates through the crowd. Forgetful of silks and broad-cloth and gossip, they fall on their knees in one party-colored mass, and bowing their heads and beating their breasts they mutter their mechanical prayers." (JOHN HAY: *Castilian Days*.)

A unique Corpus Christi ceremonial, performed at the cathe-dral of Seville, is known as the dances of the sixes (*las danzas de los seises*). An eye-witness thus describes it in the *Rosary Magazine* for July, 1897:

"We reached the cathedral at an early hour in the evening. There were other visitors, like ourselves, anxious for an advan-tageous point from which to observe the dance. We secured positions very near the railing of the chapel. Quite a time had elapsed when the clerics and canons, followed by the cardinal-archbishop, filed into the sanctuary. The canons seated themselves, some to the right, others to the left of the altar, and the cardinal-archbishop occupied what appeared to be a desk, rather than a throne. Very soon the organ back of the altar was intoned, and the singers, all men, stationed themselves in an adjoining alcove. Twelve boys (whence the Spaniards say, ' *Las danzas de los seises*,' dances of the sixes),—choir-boys,—equal in size and apparently in age, placed themselves in two groups of six each in the space left them in the sanctuary immediately in front of the Blessed Sacrament, which was exposed. These boys were dressed as royal pages, and their rich apparel suggested the idea that they were sons of nobles. In their hats were long feathers, which waved gracefully as they made their obeisance before the Blessed Sacrament. They sang a strophe so harmoniously that it excited devotion throughout the immense gathering, where all was quiet and recollected. The refrain was accompanied by the organ, and the boys danced to its melody with wonderful grace, beating time with castanets, to which their movements responded so perfectly that music, dance, and song produced complete harmony. As they moved backward and forward, they apparently mingled in confusion, yet there was an elegance and a regularity in their motions which proved the art and beauty of movement and manifested the fact that dance is to the Spaniard what music is to the Italian,—a national trait.

" Suddenly the boys stood again in line, but now facing each other, six on each side. Several times they resumed this position, singing each time a strophe, and dancing to the music of the chorus."

The custom comes down from immemorial times, and, though the Spanish authorities have frequently protested against it, Rome has allowed it to continue.

Vienna runs a close second with Madrid in its celebration of the Corpus Christi processions. Every shop and place of business is closed. The Emperor of Austria in person takes his place in a procession, falling into the ranks behind the clergy, followed by the court, the ministers, the municipal authorities. and the trade guilds. There are waving plumes, caparisoned horses, with all the noble Hungarian body-guard glittering in their mediæval trappings. There are benedictions and genuflections at the successive stations; and as the crosses and the sacred symbols are held on high, the people drop devoutly on their knees in the mud or the dust.

A pretty custom at Aix in Savoy is described by a contributor to *All the Year Round* for August 31, 1878. The Fête-Dieu procession there consisted mainly of little children,—" atoms of two and three years old, just able to creep, in robes of glistening gold, each carrying a golden flower, or a wheat-ear, a star, or a palm. Some tiny children, with careful mothers, added a parasol for the sun. The parasols marred the effect of the rich robes and glossy childish curls, so well combed out and frizzed down the little backs, and the flower garlands placed on the innocent little heads.

" What is so delightful about the golden children is that there are so many of them. The gravity and indifference with which they step out is surprising. Were these little children fresh from the courts of heaven? and was this Fête-Dieu but an echo of the pageants at which they had so lately figured in paradise? Who can tell?

" Seeing these miraculously steady golden babies so adapted to their work, I was by no means amazed to behold a fat fair child, —three years old, perhaps,—of a most comfortable aspect, file by alone, its flaxen curls set with a crown of big spiked thorns, its innocent, chubby little face bespattered with daubs of red paint, a dark-colored cross lying on one shoulder. Nor was I amazed, either, to see this little personage followed by another infant, stripped to its waist, wearing a strip of white curly lamb-skin over one little shining shoulder, leaving the other bare. A pilgrim's flask dangled on its lamb-skin skirt, and a toy lamb, on red wooden rollers, was tucked under one tiny arm. Not at all surprised was I, I assure you, nor was the child. St. John had a miraculous gift of gravity, and a swing in his walk, quite delightful to behold, as emblematic of the desert. The easy contempt with which he treated that toy lamb on red rollers under his arm was perfect. St. John was a very pretty child, about four, and appeared as an old and practised hand repeating a well-known performance."

Corpus Christi in mediæval times was everywhere and nowadays in all Latin countries is emphatically a Feast of Flowers. The Diocesan Synod of Worms, for example, held in 1610, among other decrees relating to the celebration of Corpus Christi, enacted that boys wearing wreaths on their heads should walk in the processions appointed for the day. And Serarius in his elaborate treatise is at great pains not only to lay down the rules for the due solemnization of the Corpus Christi processions in the diocese of Mayence, with clergy and laymen, girls and boys, all wearing wreaths and garlands composed of roses and various other flowers, and oak and ivy; but he also defends the use of wreaths against the mockery of some and the condemnation of others who, far from considering it a fes-

19

tive and joyful rite giving glory and honor to God,—which he maintained it was,—cried it down on account of its long-standing connection with the licentious and idolatrous usages of paganism ; and he naïvely concludes his lengthy argument with the somewhat utilitarian plea that " the wreaths serve another purpose than the honor and glory of God : they protect the head from the rays of the sun, which at the time is scorching hot ;" but even this, he exultingly adds, " may be referred to the end set forth above, for as all walked bareheaded in honor of Christ, so likewise for His glory they ought in a measure to consult the interests of their bodily health. Where is the harm ? Is it not rather a praiseworthy act thus to combine prudence with religion and piety ?" The whole city of Mayence on this occasion, he says, was made one single temple ; the walls, the houses, every place available for decoration, was ornamented with flowers and foliage ; and all the roadways were strewed with them. Even the Emperor wore a floral crown at such times ; for we learn from Sarnelli's letters that Ferdinand the Second used to take part in the solemnity " sola florea redimitus corolla."

The same practice was, moreover, general in France and Italy. Indeed, wherever the festival of Corpus Christi was kept flowers were in great request. In the Roman Ritual edited by Catalani at the command of Benedict XIV. it is strictly enjoined that each of the laymen bearing the baldacchino on Corpus Christi Day should be crowned with wreaths of flowers ; that boys walking two and two with garlands on their heads should scatter rose-leaves before the Blessed Sacrament ; that men carrying lamps should likewise wear roses twined round their heads ; and that the other boys and girls of the procession should also have wreaths.

The little village of Genzano near Rome and Villa Orotava in Teneriffe are especially famous for the flower-carpets which are there spread all over the streets where the Corpus Christi processions pass. Andersen in the "Improvisatore" has given a charming description of the Genzano celebration. In that village the church stands on rising ground, with two converging streets starting from its very doors. The procession of monks and clergy, school-children and confraternities, issues down one of these avenues and returns by the other, walking all the time on a thick carpet of flowers. These are for the most part wild flowers, skilfully formed into tapestry patterns of strange accuracy, each house on the street being, by immemorial custom, bound to design and perfect a square corresponding to its own line of frontage. The armorial bearings of the lords of the soil, of the cardinal bishop of the diocese, and of the Holy See, figure very often in this marvellous carpet.

Fanciful patterns of all kinds abound, and this broad strip of novel tapestry is guarded on each side by "railings" of box wreaths hung in festoons. A narrow space is left on either side for the spectators, of whom there are hundreds, some from Rome and many from the surrounding villages.

The flower-carpets at Villa Orotava are even more elaborate. For weeks before the great day, flowers of all kinds are assiduously collected in baskets from the inexhaustible gardens round about. After these have been sorted, according to color, they are torn to pieces and converted into opulent heaps of fragrant petals.

At dawn on the morning of the fiesta, moulds of wood and carpet are placed in position; and, later, the baskets of petals are brought forward by scores of willing workers. Then, patiently and skilfully, the practised artists begin to fill in the designs with glowing petals. The background—the full width of each street excepting the footpaths—is usually of an effective dark green composed of chopped heather. As a rule, one design runs the whole length of a street, carried out in many combinations of color.

FLOWER-CARPET AT VILLA OROTAVA.

But every new street introduces a new design.

The street-corners are adorned with larger and more ambitious pictures, and several houses are noted for their own individual efforts. When all the coloring is deftly fitted in, the moulds are withdrawn, leaving the streets carpeted with many-colored flowers. The whole is then carefully sprinkled with water, so as to keep it fresh until the procession shall come and tread it out of existence.

"Presently the entire pageant comes into view,—white-robed boys, priests in splendid vestments, and serried lines of chanting, crimson-robed 'Brothers of the Lord.' At this moment the different effects of color are very striking, as the procession moves through the flower-carpeted street. Seen from above, the red kerchiefs which cover the women's heads form a glowing mass, rivalling the wide spread petals in variety, if not in beauty, of coloring.

" But the procession has faded in the distance now ; the band strikes up a march, and the crowd surges into its wake. Coachmen rush off by side-streets to get their vehicles, and then one realizes, swiftly, the full extent of the floral holocaust. Nothing remains but a scattered, pitiful covering of bruised petals, from which a faint perfume is wafted up appealingly to those who have witnessed the strange scene." (W. N. REID, in *The Strand Magazine*, December, 1896.)

Cracknut Sunday. The Sunday before Michaelmas Day was so known in Kingston-upon-Thames, for on that day the congregation, old and young alike, attended church with their pockets stuffed with nuts, which they cracked during the service, the noise at times becoming so loud that the reading or sermon had to be suspended. The practice was with much difficulty suppressed about the end of the last century. The association of nuts with Michaelmas is a prevalent one. It may be remembered that Dr. Primrose's parishioners, retaining "the primeval simplicity of manners," among their other simple customs " religiously cracked nuts on Michaelmas Eve."

Creeling the Bridegroom. A rather indelicate pastime once very common in Scotland, and not yet entirely extinct. It is most commonly practised just after a marriage. Early next morning a party of young men, including the most intimate friends of the happy man, provide themselves with a " creel" or wicker basket full of stones and take their station outside the door of the bridal chamber. Here they await the coming forth of the bridegroom, who, according to the rules of the game, must perform the ceremony of ablution in the waters of a running brook. This he attempts by a dart past his sentinels. Should the stream be at a distance, the chase thither is highly amusing. Not unfrequently, however, he eludes his wary friends by making his escape through a window or over the roof. Should all his attempts fail and the luckless wight be caught, the creel is then fastened firmly on his back, where it remains till the bride appears and declares that she has no cause of complaint against him, whereupon she is allowed to take it off. In some parts of Scotland creeling is done by wholesale.

Once a year, or oftener, according to circumstances, all the men who have been married within the last twelve months or so are creeled. This consists in having a large basket of the breadth of a man's back attached by a rope to the victim's shoulders. He has to run with all his speed from his own house to that of his next new-married neighbor. He is pursued by the unmarried men, who endeavor to fill his basket with stones. The wife following, armed with a knife, strives to relieve her husband of his burden by cutting the rope which attaches the basket to his person.

In 1876 the marriage of Miss Whitelaw to Mr. Arthur St. Quintin Forbes took place in the parish church, Athelstaneford. According to a report in the *Glasgow Weekly Herald*, September 9, 1876, " After the marriage ceremony was performed by the father of the bride it was stated that the newly-married pair left on their marriage trip in the afternoon, the bridegroom having first to go through the ancient custom of bearing the creel."

Crispin and Crispinian, Sts., patrons of shoemakers. Their festival is celebrated on October 25, the anniversary of the translation of their remains to Rome in the ninth century. At Osnabrück, in Westphalia, the anniversary of an earlier translation is kept on June 20. In the Anglican reformed calendar St. Crispin appears alone.

Crispin and Crispinian are said to have been brothers, natives of Rome, who came to Soissons to preach the gospel and supported themselves by shoemaking. In 284 Maximinus Hercules visited Soissons. Hating Christians, he caused the two brothers to be cast into prison. An abbey called Saint-Crépin-en-Chaie (*in cavea*) is said to mark the spot where they were immured. The prefect of Gaul, Rictiovarus, was charged with their execution. He had a hard time of it. First he ordered splinters of wood to be thrust between their nails and the quick. But the splinters flew out and stabbed their tormentors, killing several. Millstones were tied around the brothers' necks and they were cast into the river Aisne. They swam across, bearing the millstones with them. Boiling lead was poured in vain over the indomitable shoemakers, and they were plunged into a bubbling caldron of pitch, oil, and fat. They emerged, refreshed. Rictiovarus, in disgust, pitched himself into the caldron and perished there. Then the martyrs, seeing their chief persecutor disposed of, placidly yielded their necks to the sword, and their heads were struck off without difficulty.

The bodies of the martyrs are said to have been buried in Soissons where afterwards stood the church of St.-Crépin-le-Petit. It is customary at Soissons at Rogations for the procession to halt before the house No. 14 Rue de la Congrégation, which occupies the site of this old chapel, and there to chant an antiphon and collect of Saints Crispin and Crispinian. Charlemagne in the eighth century translated the main portion of the relics to Osnabrück, and in the ninth century these were taken to Rome and buried in the church of St. Lawrence. Nevertheless the church at Soissons exhibited during the Middle Ages, if not all the bones of the martyrs, at least a considerable number of them. These were scattered and lost during the Revolution, save only a portion of the skull, a thigh-bone, and some bony splinters. Other relics are at Fulda.

According to a Kentish tradition, the bodies of the martyrs were cast into the sea by their persecutors and were washed ashore at Romney Marsh in that county.

In France a cobbler's kit of tools was known as his Saint-Crépin. The bootjack was St. Crispin's stole, the awl St. Crispin's lance. Of a person too tightly booted it is said that he is "in the prison of St. Crispin." Formerly the cobblers worked at night with a large spherical bottle full of water between them and their candle or lamp. This was known as St. Crispin's lamp, and its invention was attributed to Crispin himself.

French cobblers from the Middle Ages down to recent times celebrated the feast of SS. Crispin and Crispinian with much pomp. They were roused in the morning by the bells of the church dedicated to their patron or containing a chapel so dedicated, whither they repaired in procession in the wake of a great crucifix and a monster wax candle. At Bourges the master-cobblers who absented themselves without a legitimate excuse were fined a pound of wax, to be delivered at the chapel. After high mass had been heard, the paraders returned in similar order to sit down to a monster banquet, where the affairs of the guild were discussed. All this disappeared with the Revolution. In Troyes the confraternity of St. Crispin was reorganized in 1820 and established an annual festival which was celebrated in the church of St. Urban on the Monday following the 25th of October. The staff which is raffled off for the benefit of the guild is still borne to the church with great pomp. In other places St. Crispin is no longer commemorated.

Up to 1870, however, the shoemakers of Moncontour met together at a tavern and walked in pairs to the church, where holy bread was distributed to them at the mass and formed the chief feature of the subsequent banquet at the tavern. Street Arabs used to follow them, crying.—

> To-day is Monday,
>   My friend.
> The shoemakers dress up
> To visit St. Crispin,
>   My friend,
> Who used to work in his shirt.

The children still sing this song, which remains the sole relic of the festival.

In Provence there is a legend that on the day when St. Crispin's feast was first celebrated by the shoemakers their patron was so pleased that he asked God to allow the best of them a glimpse of paradise. The Almighty consented, and St. Crispin lowered from heaven a long ladder garnished with peas. But the best men held back through humility, and the vainglorious ones scaled the miraculous ladder. Now, it happened that when they arrived the feast of St. Peter was being celebrated in the upper regions, with Peter himself as the officiating minister at high mass. St. Paul had been left in charge of the gates. As the eager mob pressed upward, St. Peter had just reached the *Sursum corda*, which St. Paul, being slightly deaf since his fall on the way to Damascus, misunderstood as *Zou sus la cordo!* So he cut the cord. The shoemakers fell to earth, and though God, who is good, would not allow them to be killed, many were badly hurt. And that is how it happens that so many shoemakers are cripples or hunchbacks.

In England St. Crispin's Day has an additional significance as the anniversary of the battle of Agincourt (1415). Shakespeare's lines will occur readily to memory :

> This day is called the feast of Crispian :
> He that outlives this day and comes safe home
> Will stand a-tiptoe when this day is named,
> And rouse him at the name of Crispian.
> He that shall live this day and see old age
> Will yearly on the vigil feast his friends,
> And say, To-morrow is St. Crispian.
>
> *   *   *   *   *   *   *
>
> And Crispin Crispian shall ne'er go by,
> From this day to the ending of the world,
> But we in it shall be remembered.
>
> (*Henry V.*, Act iv. Sc. 3.)

These lines show that St. Crispin's Day had been honored even before Agincourt. But the victory gave it an additional impetus, so that it survived after every other trade festival had died out. The custom was for the brethren of the craft to march in a great procession with banners and music, while various characters representing King Crispin and his court were sustained by different members. The processions at Edinburgh and Stirling were especially elaborate. At the former place the mock king was dressed in a very fair imitation of the royal robes, while at the latter both Houses of Parliament followed the pseudo-monarch, as well as officers and men-at-arms without number. In London, during the mayoralty of Sir Simon Eyre, who had once been a shoemaker, an imitation king of the City followed very closely upon the heels of the imitation monarch in the shoemakers' annual procession, and ever afterwards the lord mayor was generally represented. The procession over, a dinner invariably took place, and the day closed with a dance, led off by the workman who had played the part of king.

The last survival of the ancient procession is mentioned in *Notes and Queries*, First Series, vol. vi. p. 243, as occurring at the town of Hexham, in Northumberland: "The shoemakers of the town meet and dine by previous arrangements at some tavern; a King Crispin, queen, prince, and princess, elected from members of their fraternity of families, being present. They afterwards form in grand procession (the ladies and their attendants excepted), and parade the streets with banners, music, etc., the royal party and suite gayly dressed in character. In the evening they reassemble for dancing and other festivities. To his majesty and consort, and their royal highnesses the prince and princess (the latter usually a pretty girl), due regal homage is paid during that day."

At one time the cordwainers of Newcastle celebrated the festival of St. Crispin by holding a coronation of their patron saint in the court of the Freemen's Hospital at the West-gate, and afterwards walking in procession through the principal streets of the town. This caricature show produced much laughter and mirth. (MACKENZIE: *History of Newcastle*, 1827, vol. i. p. 88.)

In the parishes of Cuckfield and Hurstpierpoint, in Sussex, St. Crispin's Day is kept with much rejoicing. The boys go round asking for money in the name of St. Crispin, bonfires are lighted, and it passes off very much in the same way as the 5th of November. It appears from an inscription on a monument to one of the ancient family of Bunell, in the parish church of Cuckfield, that a Sir John Bunell attended Henry V. to France in the year 1415 with one ship, twenty men-at-arms, and forty archers, and it is probable that the observance of this day in that neighborhood is connected with that fact. (*Notes and Queries*, First Series, vol. v. p. 30.)

At Tenby, in Wales, it was customary on the eve of St. Crispin's Day to make an effigy of the saint and suspend it from the steeple or some other elevated place. In the morning it was formally cut down and carried in procession throughout the town. In front of the doors of each member of the craft the procession halted, when a document purporting to be the last will and testament of the saint was read, and in pursuance thereof some article of dress was left as a memento of the noisy visit. At length, when nothing remained to be distributed, the padding which formed the body of the effigy was made into a football, and kicked about by the crowd till they were tired. As a sort of revenge for the treatment of St. Crispin, his followers hung up on St. Clement's Day the effigy of a carpenter, which was treated in a similar way.

Cross. (Lat. *Crux;* Fr. *Croix;* It. *Croce.*) No symbol, either in art or in religion, is so universal as the cross. It appears twice in our alphabet, as the letter T and the letter X. It is worn by priests on their sacrificial robes, by distinguished laymen as a sign of distinction on occasions of state, and by male and female nonentities as taste may direct. It is graven on eucharistic vessels, embroidered on altar-cloths, and cut in relief on tombs and monuments. Some of the greatest churches and cathedrals of Christendom are fashioned in its shape. In European countries it is common to see large crosses erected in public places. The famous Charing (chère reine) Cross, in London, derives its name from the fact that it was one of the places at which King Edward I. set up a cross to mark where the body of his Queen Eleanor rested during the progress of the funeral cortége to Westminster.

Yet it is a mistake to suppose that the cross has only a Christian history.

It was used as a religious symbol by the aborigines of North and South America, as well as by the most ancient nations of the Old World. Prescott tells us that the Spaniards found the cross as an object of worship in the temples of Mexico. Researches in Central America and Peru prove that it was used in the same way by the inhabitants of those countries. Dr. Brinton, in "Myths of the New World," informs us that the Indians regard the cross as a mystic emblem of the four cardinal points of the compass.

The ancient Phœnicians, Persians, Assyrians, and Brahmins looked upon the cross as a holy symbol, as is abundantly shown by the numerous hieroglyphics and other pictorial representations on their monumental remains. Osiris by the cross gave light eternal to the spirits of the just, beneath the cross the Muysca mothers laid their babes, trusting by that sign to secure them from the power of the evil spirits, and with that symbol to protect them the Etruscans, the ancient people of Northern Italy, calmly laid them down to die.

The Thau of the Jews and the Tau of the Greeks, whence came the T of the Roman alphabet, were held to be not merely letters, but sacred symbols, on account of their being suggested by a cross.

Among the Scandinavians Thor was the thunder, and the

hammer was his symbol. It was with this hammer that Thor crushed the head of the great Mitgard serpent; that he destroyed the giants; that he restored to life the dead goats, which ever after drew his car; that he consecrated the pyre of Baldur. This hammer was a cross. In Iceland the cross of Thor is still used as a magical sign 'in connection with storms of wind and rain. Longfellow tells us how King Olaf kept Christmas at Drontheim:

> O'er his drinking-horn the sign
> He made of the Cross Divine,
>   As he drank, and muttered his prayers;
> But the Berserks evermore
> Made the sign of the Hammer of Thor
>   Over theirs.

Neither King Olaf nor his Berserkers, nor, indeed, Longfellow himself, seem to have realized that the two symbols were identical.

Comparative mythologists draw various deductions from these remarkable facts. Let us, however, appeal to a man who is not only a comparative mythologist, but a Christian priest. "For my own part," says the Rev. S. Baring-Gould, "I see no difficulty in believing that the cross formed a portion of the primeval religion, traces of which exist over the whole world, among every people; that trust in the cross was a part of the ancient faith which taught men to believe in a Trinity, in a war in heaven, a paradise from which man fell, a Flood and a Babel, a faith which was deeply impressed with a conviction that a Virgin should conceive and bear a Son, that the dragon's head should be bruised, and that through shedding of blood should come remission. The use of the cross as a symbol of life and regeneration through water is as widely spread over the world as the belief in the ark of Noah. Maybe the shadow of the cross was cast further back into the night of ages, and fell on a wider range of country, than we are aware of."

It was only natural that the early and mediæval Christians, finding the cross a symbol of life among the nations of antiquity, should look curiously into the Old Testament to see whether there were not foreshadowings in it of " the wood whereby righteousness cometh." Nor was their search unrewarded. In Isaac bearing the wood of the sacrifice they saw prefigured both Christ and the cross. They saw the cross in Moses with arms expanded on the Mount, in the pole with transverse bars upon which was wreathed the brazen serpent, in the two sticks gathered by the widow of Sarepta. But plainest of all they read it in Ezekiel ix. 4, 6 : "Go through the midst of the city, through the midst of Jerusalem, and set a mark upon the foreheads of the men" that are to be saved from destruction by the sword. The word here rendered "mark" is in the Vulgate "signa thau." The Thau was the old Hebrew character, shaped like a cross, which was regarded as the sign of life, felicity, and safety.

Yet the cross was not always a symbol of honor. Among the Phœnicians and Syrians, and later among the Romans, it was a punishment inflicted on slaves, robbers, assassins, and rebels,—among which last Jesus was reckoned, on account of his proclaiming himself King, or Messiah. The person sentenced to this punishment was stripped of his clothes, except a covering around the loins. In a state of nudity he was beaten with whips. Such was the severity of this flagellation that numbers died of it. Jesus was crowned with thorns, and was made the subject of mockery; but insults of this kind were not common. In this instance they were owing to the petulance of the Roman soldiers.

The criminal, having been beaten, was condemned to the further suffering of carrying the cross to the place of punishment, which was commonly a hill near the public highway and out of the city. The place of crucifixion at Jerusalem was a hill to the northwest of the city. The cross, otherwise called the "post,"—the unpropitious or ominous tree,—consisted of a piece of wood erected perpendicularly, and intersected by another one at right angles near the top. The crime for which the culprit suffered was inscribed on the transverse piece, near the top of the perpendicular one. There is no mention made by the ancient writers of anything on which the feet of the crucified person rested. It is known, however, that near the base of the perpendicular beam there projected a piece of wood, on which he sat, and which answered as a support to the body,—since the weight of the latter might have otherwise torn the hands by the nails driven through them.

The cross, when driven firmly in the ground, rarely exceeded ten feet in height. The victim was elevated, and his hands were bound by a rope around the transverse beam and nailed through the palm. His feet were also nailed. He thus remained fastened until death ended his sufferings. While he exhibited any signs of life he was watched by guards; but they left him when it appeared that he was dead. If there was no prospect that the victim would die on the day of execution, the executioners hastened the end by kindling a fire at the foot of the cross, so as to suffocate him with smoke; or by letting loose upon him wild beasts; or occasionally, when in particular haste, by breaking his bones upon the cross with a mallet, as upon an anvil. It was at one time customary to offer the criminal, before the commencement of his sufferings, a medicated drink, compounded of wine and myrrh. The object of this was to produce intoxication, and thereby to lessen the suffering.

Crucifixion was not only the most ignominious, but by far the most cruel, mode of punishment. The victim sometimes lived until the seventh day. The thieves who were executed at the same time with our Saviour were broken with mallets on the same day; and in order to ascertain the condition of Jesus a lance was thrust in his side, but no signs of life appeared.

ANCIENT ROMAN CARICATURE OF THE CROSS.

There is preserved in the museum of the Collegio Romano at Rome a curious caricature which was found in the ruins of the ancient pædagogium for the imperial pages. This is a mock crucifix roughly scratched with a stylus. It was probably the work of some page, done to deride a Christian comrade. It represents a man with the head of an ass hanging on a cross, and to the left another figure in an attitude of adoration. A superscription runs Ἀλεξαμενος σεβετε Θεον. The Greek is a trifle shaky (σεβετε should be σεβεται), but the obvious meaning is " Alexamenos worships God." The character of the letters indicates that the caricature dates from the early part of the third century. Thus it is evident that even at that early period pagan Rome identified the cross with Christianity.

Cicero says the very name of the cross should be removed afar " not only from the body, but from the thoughts, the eyes, the ears, of Roman citizens, for of all these things, not only the actual occurrence and endurance, but the very contingency and expectation, nay, the mention itself, are unworthy of a Roman citizen and a free man." Hence the force of St. Paul's frequent allusions to the humiliation which Christ endured when he suffered death upon the cross.

It was precisely this idea which made the early Christians seize upon the cross as the emblem of their faith. That which had been the symbol of shame now became their glory. The instrument of Christ's passion, by his death upon it, became hallowed for all time. The mediæval Christians, desiring to see the cross identified still more closely with the Jewish Church, inserted a legend to supplement the Old Testament.

The story runs that Seth received from the angels three seeds of the forbidden tree which he saw standing, though blasted, upon the spot where sin had been first committed. Taking the seeds away with him, he put them in the mouth of the dead Adam, and so buried them. The young trees that grew from them, on the grave of Adam in Hebron, were carefully tended by Abraham, Moses, and David. After they were removed to Jerusalem the Psalms were composed beneath them, and finally they slowly grew together and formed a single giant tree. This tree was felled by the order of Solomon, in order that it might be preserved forever as a beam in the temple. The plan failed, however, for the carpenters found they could not manage the mighty beam.

When they raised it to its intended position they found it too long; then they sawed it, and it proved too short; they spliced it, but to no purpose, they could not make it fit. This was taken as a sign that it was intended for some other purpose, and they laid it aside in the temple. On one occasion it was improperly made use of as a seat by a woman named Maximella, and she was at once enveloped in flames. She invoked the aid of Christ, and was driven from the city and stoned to death. In the course of its eventful history the beam became a bridge over Cedron, and, being then thrown into the stream of Bethesda, it gave to the waters healing virtues. Finally from it was made the cross of Christ. After the crucifixion it was buried in Calvary, and exhumed three centuries later by the Empress Helena, the mother of Constantine, who was miraculously directed to the spot where it lay. (See CROSS, INVENTION OF THE.)

Cross, Exaltation of the. A festival now celebrated on September 14 by the Latin and Greek Churches. In England it was known as Holy Cross or Holy Rood Day. Like the feast of the Invention, it was removed at the Reformation, and remains only as a black-letter day. As such, with the Invention, it first reappeared in Queen Elizabeth's Calendar of 1561, and is again found in King James's Prayer Book of 1604. It was instituted in ancient times in memory of the miraculous apparition which Constantine saw as he was preparing to fight against Maxentius (October 26, 312). He beheld in the daylight a luminous cross in the heavens with the Greek inscription 'Ἐν τούτῳ νίκα ("Conquer by this"), or, as the more familiar Latin freely translates it, *In hoc signo vinces* ("By this sign thou shalt conquer").

Eusebius, who is not always trustworthy, assures us that he had heard the story related on oath by Constantine himself. (*Vita Constantii*, i. 28.) Thomassin suggests that Constantine himself instituted the feast. (*Traité des Festes*, ii. 124.) The day was kept with greater solemnity after 629. The 14th of September in that year marked the conclusion of a series of festivals in honor of the true cross. In order to understand these it is necessary briefly to recapitulate the events that immediately preceded.

In June, 614, then, the Persian Emperor Chosroes captured and plundered Jerusalem. The churches, even that of the Holy Sepulchre, were burnt, and among other precious relics carried away was that portion of the true cross which had been left there by St. Helena. Only the sponge with which the soldiers gave our Saviour vinegar to drink, and the lance which pierced his side, were saved from the wreck and sent to Constantinople for safe-keeping. The sacred sponge was exposed to the view of the faithful in St. Sophia's Church on the Feast of the Exaltation of the Cross in that year, and on the 26th of October a similar exposition was made of the lance. Then Heraclius declared war against Chosroes, and after many years of varying success finally cut the Persian army to pieces at Nineveh, December 12, 627. The fragment of the true cross was recovered and brought to Constantinople in the spring of 629. Heraclius in person restored it to Jerusalem. He would fain have carried it upon his own shoulders into the city with the utmost pomp, but stopped suddenly at the entrance, and found that he was not able to go forward. The patriarch Zachary, who walked by his side, suggested to him that this pomp seemed not agreeable to the humble appearance which Christ made when he bore his cross through the streets of that city. The Emperor accepted the reproof. He laid aside his purple and his crown, put on mean clothes, went along barefoot with the procession, and devoutly replaced the cross where it stood before. It still continued in the case in which it had been carried away, and the patriarch and clergy, finding the seals whole, opened the case with the key, venerated it, and showed it to the people. Many miraculous cures are reported to have followed. (BUTLER : *Lives of the Saints*, under date September 14.)

On his return to Constantinople the Emperor paid due honors to that portion of the cross which was preserved there. The festivities closed on September 14. Thereafter similar ceremonies were performed every year. Butler quotes from the Emperor Constantine Porphyrogenitus ("De Ceremoniis Aulæ Constantinopolitanæ," edition of 1751, Leipsic, folio II. ch. xxii. p. 74) as follows:

"About seven days before the 1st of August the holy cross was taken out of the holy treasury in which it was kept with other precious relics and rich holy vessels, betwixt the third and the sixth ode of matins then singing. It was laid on the ground, that the protopapa, or chief priest of the palace, might anoint it all over with balsam and precious perfumes. Then it was set up in the church of the palace of Our Lady of the Pharos, exposed to the veneration of the people. After matins the clergy of the palace assembled before it, singing hymns in praise of the cross. The chief priest then took up the cross on his head, and, attended by the clergy and others in procession, carried it through the golden hall, before the oratory of St. Basil, placed it to be venerated by all the senate; then proceeded to the palace of Daphne and exposed it in the church of St. Stephen. On the 28th of July the priests began to carry the cross through all the streets and to all the houses, and afterwards round the walls of the city, that by the devotion of the people and their united prayers God would, through the cross and merits of his Son, bless and protect the city and all its inhabitants. On the 13th of September it was brought back to the palace and placed on a rich throne in the golden hall, where the clergy sung the hymns in praise of the cross during its exaltation there. It was afterward carried through all the apartments of the palace, and then deposited in the chapel of St. Theodorus. In the evening it was delivered back to the keeper of the sacred treasure. Next morning it was carefully cleansed by the protopapa and the keeper, and again deposited in the rich case in the treasury."

A famous procession of the Blessed Sacrament was instituted in Avignon on the Feast of the Exaltation of the Cross a century before the similar processions on Corpus Christi Day were appointed generally by the Church. This was in the year 1226. France was in the throes of the Albigensian war. The Albigenses held possession of Avignon. Louis VIII. besieged the town, and took it on September 8. By way of atoning for the heretical desecration of the Catholic churches, he ordered a general procession of the Corpus Domini on the feast of the Exaltation. The Bishop of Avignon bore down the holy sacrament from the church of the Doms, and the king himself, clad in sackcloth and girded with a rope, his head bare and a torch in his hand, took part in the procession, attended by Cardinal St. Angelo, the papal legate, and the whole court, as well as the magistrates and chief men of the city, all in penitential garments. With torches and incense and solemn invocation they traversed the entire city and went to the small church of the Holy Cross, then without the walls, where a few devout people were in the habit of assembling every Friday in honor of the Passion. The bishop placed the host in a stone niche at the side of the altar, and left it exposed to the veneration of the people, but veiled, after the custom of that time. The king visited the church daily during his stay in the city, and his example was followed by multitudes.

This devotion induced the papal legate to authorize the continued exposition of the Blessed Sacrament, and he ordered the citizens, by way of reparation for giving countenance to the Albigenses, to visit the church every Friday for a year and there recite the Seven Penitential Psalms. This gave rise to the order of the Gray Penitents, the oldest company of the kind in the Church,—the one at Rome not being established till twenty years later. They constituted a kind of body-guard that took turns, day and night, to watch and pray before the Divine Host. They wore the sackcloth tunic to which the pious king had given consecration, and met in a body every Friday for special exercises of devotion and penance, and on account of their frequent scourgings were often called the *Battus de la Croix*. (See SEPARATION OF THE WATERS.)

The exposition of the host in the church of the Holy Cross, at first intended only to be temporary, was prolonged from time to time, and finally became perpetual, and has been continued to our day—that is, for six hundred and sixty years—without any other interruption than that caused by the French Revolution and the First Empire.

Cross, Invention or **Discovery of the.** A festival celebrated by the Latin and Greek Churches on May 3, because on or about that day in the year 326 St. Helena, mother of Constantine the Great, is reputed to have discovered the cross on which Christ suffered. The story runs that the venerable lady, visiting the Holy Land in her seventy-ninth year, was guided to the site of Calvary by an aged Jew who had treasured up the local traditions which the anti-Christian animosity of the heathen conquerors of Jerusalem had failed entirely to obliterate. On excavation at a considerable depth three crosses were found, and with them, but lying apart by itself, was the title placed by Pilate's command on the cross of Christ. The problem now presented itself, which was that cross? It was solved through the instrumentality of Macarius, Bishop of Jerusalem. He suggested that the three crosses be carried to the bedside of an invalid woman in the city, not doubting but that Christ's cross would be discovered by its healing powers. The crosses were applied singly to the patient, who was immediately and perfectly recovered by the touch of one of them, the other two having been tried without effect. The greater part of the cross, so vindicated, was deposited in a church built on the spot of the Invention. Here it was enshrined in a splendid silver case. The remainder Helena took to her son in Constantinople, whence a portion was sent by Constantine to Rome.

The first mention of the Invention, without any mention, however, of St. Helena's share in it, is by St. Cyril of Jerusalem, about the year 350. From this it is evident that the cross was exhibited at Jerusalem when St. Cyril was a priest. The next authority is St. Ambrose, Archbishop of Milan, who in a funeral sermon on the Emperor Theodosius in 395 gives St. Helena the credit of the discovery. As we go later the story is amplified and all the details are given with wonderful minuteness.

But Eusebius, who lived at the time when the cross is said to have been found, and who in his Life of Constantine mentions St. Helena's visit to Palestine, has not a word about the Invention. What makes it more extraordinary is that Eusebius was present in 335 at the dedication of the Church of the Resurrection, and has described the ceremonies, but is still silent about the cross. Further, a pilgrim named Burdigala who visited Jerusalem in 333 has left behind him a minute record of all extant Christian relics, again with no word about the cross; so that it is evident it could not have been shown in 333. Constantine died in 337: so the finding of the cross must have occurred between 333 and 337, if we accept St. Cyril's word for it that the finding occurred in the reign of that emperor. But St. Helena was in Jerusalem in 326. Thus stands the case. Any definite conclusion is impossible.

Both in Constantinople and in Rome churches were built expressly to receive so precious a relic. The former was known as the Basilica of the Holy Cross; the latter, the church of Santa Croce, still stands, and retains the relic which gave it its name. A festival to commemorate the Invention soon followed, Rome taking the lead in the fifth century, but it is not quite certain whether the date selected, May 3, was the anniversary of the Invention itself, or of the dedication of Santa Croce, or of Constantine's vision. Then came pilgrimages undertaken in order to obtain a sight of the cross. Lastly fragments of the sacred wood were sold at high prices to wealthy purchasers, it having been discovered that the wood exercised a power of miraculous self-multiplication, "ut detrimenta non sentiret, et quasi intacta permaneret." (Paulinus, *Ep. XI. ad Lev.*) St. Cyril of Jerusalem, twenty-five years after the discovery, affirmed that pieces of the cross were spread all over the earth, and compares this marvel to the miraculous feeding of five thousand men, as recorded in the Gospel.

In A.D. 637 Jerusalem was reconquered by the Saracens, and nothing has since been heard of the fragment of the cross that had been left there. In the thirteenth century during the reign of St. Louis what remained of the portion taken by Helena to Constantinople was removed to Paris, and is still preserved in the Sainte-Chapelle. Sergius I. is said to have placed a portion of the cross in a silver box in St. Peter's Cathedral about 690. A reputed relic of the true cross was kept in the Tower of London as late as the reign of James I.

The enemies of the Roman Church have made merry at the self-multiplying powers of the cross, which Paulinus and Cyril accepted as marvels not to be questioned. " To be short," says Calvin, " if a man would gather together all that hath been found of this cross, there would be enough to freight a great ship." Swift repeats and expands the jest.

On the other hand, M. Rohault de Fleury, who calculates that the total volume of the wood of the original cross must have been somewhere about 178,000,000 cubic millimetres, has made a list of all the relics in Europe and Asia of which he can find any record, and the sum of their measurements amounts to only 3,941,975 cubic millimetres,—a very small portion indeed of any cross that could sustain a man.

Of places where relics of the Holy Cross have accumulated, Mount Athos stands pre-eminent with a total volume of 878,360 cubic millimetres; then Rome, with 537,587 ; Brussels, 516,090 ; Venice, 445,582 ; Ghent, 436,450 ; Paris, 237,731.

All England can boast of but 30,516 cubic millimetres, of which 8287 belong to Lord Petrie in two pieces. At St. Mary's, York, is a pectoral cross of the tenth century which contains two fragments.

In the United States there is not an authenticated relic of the cross as large as half a lead-pencil, and there are many so minute as to be visible only through the aid of a microscope. The church of St. Francis Xavier in New York has a fragment which is exposed for veneration on Easter Sunday, as is the custom in European churches. Another fragment at the cathedral is shown on Good Friday. This relic is in a crystal and gold casket set with precious stones, and forms the centre of a handsome altar cross. The French church of St. John the Baptist in East Seventy-Sixth Street also possesses a relic of the cross.

Every church which is the custodian of a portion of the cross is also in possession of a document bearing the seal of the Vatican and testifying to the authenticity of the relic. The relic itself is most carefully sealed in an air-tight receptacle. If the seals were once broken the relics would lose their historical value, as identification would thenceforth be impossible.

Nevertheless M. de Fleury had an opportunity of microscopically examining some of the larger fragments through the glass which encloses them, and he comes to the conclusion that the wood was either pine, or something closely allied to it.

With Catholics this ought to settle a matter that has been much disputed. Wise theologians and simple country-folk have held many and various opinions as to the material of the cross. From Anselm, Aquinas, and others, we learn that the upright beam was made of the "immortal cedar;" the cross-beam, of cypress; the piece on which the inscription was written, of olive; and the piece for the feet, of palm: hence the line

> Ligna crucis palma, cedrus, cupressus, oliva.

Sir John Mandeville's account of the legend differs from this. He says the piece athwart was made of "victorious palm;" the tablet, of "peaceful olive;" the trunk, of the tree of which Adam had eaten; and the stock, of cedar. Some versions say that it was made of fir, pine, and box; others, of cypress, cedar, pine, and box; one names cedar for the support of the feet, cypress for the body, palm for the hands, and olive for the title. Southey, in his "Common-Place Book" and "Omniana," says that the four kinds of wood were symbolical of the four quarters of the globe, or all mankind. Some affirm that the cross was made entirely of the stately oak. Chaucer, speaking of the Blessed Virgin, says,—

> Benigne braunchlet of the pine tree.

Popular superstition in many countries favors the idea that it was made of the elder-tree; therefore, although fuel may be scarce and these sticks plentiful, the poor people will not burn them. In Scotland the elder is called the bourtree, and the following rhyme is indicative of peasant beliefs:

> Bourtree, bourtree, crooked rung,
> Never straight and never strong,
> Ever bush and never tree,
> Since our Lord was nailed on thee.

Chambers's "Book of Days" records an instance of the belief that a person is perfectly safe under the shelter of an elder-tree during a thunderstorm, as the lightning never strikes the tree of which the cross was made. Experience has taught that this is a fallacy, although many curious exceptional instances are recorded. James Napier, in his "Folk-Lore of the Northern Counties of England," tells us of a peculiar custom. The elder is planted in the form of a cross upon a newly-made grave, and if it blooms it is a sure sign that the soul of the dead person is happy. Dyer, in his "English Folk-Lore," says that the most common belief in England is that the cross was made of the aspen (*Populus tremula*), the leaves having trembled ever since at the recollection of their guilt. Another legend is that all the trees shivered at the crucifixion except the aspen, which has been doomed to quiver ever since. An extract from Mrs. Hemans's "Wood Walk and Hymn" is worthy of quotation here as illustrating the first idea:

> FATHER. Hast thou heard, my boy,
> The peasant's legend of that quivering tree?
> CHILD. No, father; doth he say the fairies dance
> Amidst its branches?
> FATHER. Oh, a cause more deep,
> More solemn far, the rustic doth assign
> To the strange restlessness of those wan leaves.
> The Cross he deems, the blessed Cross, whereon
> The meek Redeemer bowed his head to death,
> Was formed of aspen wood;' and since that hour
> Through all its race the pale tree hath sent down
> A thrilling consciousness, a secret awe,
> Making them tremulous, when not a breeze
> Disturbs the airy thistle-down or shakes
> The light lines from the shining gossamer.

In Ulster the aspen is called "quiggenepsy,"—*i.e.*, "quaking aspen." In support of these beliefs the aspen still flourishes near Jerusalem. In the west of England there is a tradition that the cross was formed of the mistletoe, which before that event used to be a fine forest tree, but has since been doomed to lead a parasitical existence. The gypsies believe that it was made of the ash-tree. In Cheshire the *Arum maculatum* is called "Gethsemane," because it is said to have been growing at the foot of the cross, and to have received some drops of blood on its petals.

In Scotland it was formerly believed that the dwarf birch is stunted in growth because from it were fashioned the rods with which Christ was scourged.

The title in Hebrew, Greek, and Latin is said to have been found by St. Helena with the cross. It was brought to Rome and deposited in the basilica of Santa Croce. It is said to have been hidden in the time of Valentinian lest it should be stolen by the Goths; but it was seen in or about 570 by Antoninus Martyr, after whose time it disappeared, to be discovered again built up in an arch near the roof, enclosed in a leaden box, on the cover of which these words were engraved: "Hic est titulus veræ crucis." It was found to be a little board about a hand's breadth and a half, much decayed, covered with a partially legible inscription in Latin and Greek, the writing being from right to left, Hebrew fashion. A line of writing has been broken off the upper part, but parts of a few letters which remain may have been those of the Hebrew title.

The nails used at the crucifixion, the crown of thorns, and the lance which pierced Christ's side were all included in the Invention. All have their own legendary history.

One of the original four nails is said to have been thrown by the Empress Helena into the Adriatic during a storm, which it instantly quelled. A second, after having been placed either in his crown or his helmet by Constantine, somehow found its way in a mutilated state to the church of Santa Croce in Rome. The two others were made into a bit by Constantine, whose possession is disputed by Milan and Carpentras. But Mr. John Ashton, in his book on "The Legendary History of the Cross," enumerates no fewer than thirty-two of these nails in twenty-nine towns, including three at Venice, two at Rome, a point at Compiègne, and the famous Iron Crown preserved at Monza, which is a circlet of gold "indebted for its name of 'Iron' to a thin band of that metal" within. The crown is too small to be actually worn; but Charlemagne was crowned with it in 774, and "Napoleon did not think himself King of Italy until he had placed this precious diadem on his head in 1805."

Butler explains that "some multiplication of these relics has sprung from the filings of that precious relic put into another nail made like it, or at least from like nails which have touched it." He points out that the true nail in Santa Croce has been manifestly filed, and is now without a point.

Cross, Sign of the. In the Roman and Greek Churches it is customary for the faithful to make the sign of the cross by manual gesture on various public and private occasions, as before and after prayer, and in conferring baptism, blessing, etc. The most usual form of this rite, practised by the clergy and laity alike, is to place the thumb or the forefinger on the forehead, saying, "In the name of the Father;" on the breast, saying, "and of the Son;" on the left shoulder, saying, "and of the Holy Ghost;" and lastly on the right shoulder, with the concluding word, "Amen." The sign is also made in the air by the officiating clergyman at baptisms, at the consecration of the emblems in the mass, and at blessings, always in the direction of the object of the ceremonial. St. Basil refers the custom to apostolic times, and it is certain that it was a familiar one by the beginning of the third century, for Tertullian says, "At every step and motion, when we go in and out, when we dress or put on our shoes, at the baths, at the table, when lights are brought, when we go to bed, when we sit down, whatever it is which occupies us, we mark the forehead with the sign of the cross." (*De Coron. Mil.*, iii.) In the Roman Church the sign is usually made with the thumb, in the Greek Church with the forefinger, and among the Armenians and the Raskolnik with index and middle fingers. In the Lutheran Church the custom of making the sign of the cross was retained to a limited extent at the Reformation. In the Church of England it is only prescribed to be used in baptism, but it is used by some at holy communion, as well as privately, its object being " to remind a Christian of his profession."

A very similar rite is practised by the higher Lamas of Thibet before commencing any devotional exercises. " The Lama gently touches his forehead either with the finger or with the bell, uttering the mystic OM ; then he touches the top of his chest, uttering AH ; then the epigastrium (pit of the stomach), uttering HUM, and some Lamas add SYA-HA, while others complete the cross by touching the left shoulder, uttering DAM and then YAM. It is alleged that the object of these manipulations is to concentrate the parts of the Sattva, namely, the body, speech, and mind, upon the image or divinity which he is about to commune with." (WADDALL : *The Buddhism of Thibet.*)

The sign of the cross made by gesture is entitled the *crux usualis*. But when the sign is actually impressed on some material, as with a pen on a piece of paper, it becomes a *crux exemplata*, which is a name common to all representations of the cross, whether written, painted, or sculptured. In the fifth century it became customary to apply a cross mark at the beginning of treaties, diplomatic notes, etc., in lieu of the customary invocation of the name of God, and at the end, beside the name of the signer, as a token of trustworthiness. Ecclesiastics always used it in this way, and the primates of the Church still continue the practice. The Greek Emperor used a red cross before his name in signing; the Byzantine princes, a green; the English kings, a golden.

Crossing the Line, *i.e.*, either the equator or the Arctic circle, was formerly the occasion, not only among merchant vessels and men-of-war, but also among whalers, for curious ceremonies that are now well-nigh obsolete. The details of the performance varied even among the ships of the same waters, but it always took the form of some tribute to Neptune exacted from such of the officers, passengers, or crew as had never before crossed the line in question. Captain Marryat, in " Frank Mildmay," gives a description which covers all the essential points. He represents the ship as being hailed from the supposed depths of the sea the evening before the line is to be reached, and the captain is given the compliments of Neptune and asked to muster his novices for the sea-lord's inspection. The next day the ship is hove to at the proper moment, and Neptune, with his dear Amphitrite and suite, comes on board over the bow, or through a bridle-port, if the weather permits. "Neptune appears," writes Marryat, "preceded by a young man dandily dressed in tights and riding on a car made of a gun-carriage drawn by six nearly naked blacks, spotted with yellow paint. He has a long beard of oakum, an iron crown on his head, and carries a trident with a small dolphin between its prongs. His attendants consist of a secretary, with quills of the sea fowl; a surgeon, with lancet and pill-box; a barber, with a huge wooden razor, with its blade made of an iron hoop; and a barber's mate, with a tub for a shaving-box. Amphitrite, wearing a woman's night-cap with sea-weed ribbons on her head, and bearing an albicore on a harpoon, carries a ship's boy in her lap as a baby, with a marlinspike to cut his teeth on. She is attended by three men dressed as nymphs, with curry-combs, mirrors, and pots of paint. The sheep-pen, lined with canvas and filled with water, has already been prepared. The victim, seated on a platform laid over it, is blindfolded, then shaved by the barber, and finally plunged backward into the water. Officers escape by paying a fine in money or rum."

To this day it is the roughest sort of rough man-handling, but it is a short shrift for those who take it good-naturedly, and, like bear-baiting, affords great amusement to the spectators.

Cucking-Stool. This is sometimes confounded with the ducking-stool, but was entirely dissimilar. Its exact construction cannot be explained in these pages. Let it suffice to say that it was a seat of even flagitious indelicacy upon which offending females were exposed at their own doors or in some public place as a means of putting upon them the last degree of ignominy. The cucking-stool, in fact, was analogous to the *Sedes Stercoraria* in which a new Pope was formerly placed during the installation ceremonies, to remind him that he was human.

Curfew. (Fr. *Couvre-feu.*) A bell tolled at evening as a signal to the inhabitants to cover fires, extinguish lights, and retire to rest. It is erroneously said to have been instituted in England by William the Conqueror as an arbitrary bit of tyranny, and the nursery historian has waxed sentimental over the wrongs of the conquered Saxon, and conjured up pictures that must be balm to the down-trodden Celt. Even Thomson tells us,—

The shivering wretches at the curfew sound
Dejected sunk into their sordid beds.

But the couvre-feu was known before William's time, both in England and on the Continent. He did, indeed, issue an edict on the subject, and, although this edict may incidentally have helped to put down the Saxon beer-clubs, which were hotbeds of political conspiracies, its primary aim was as a precaution against fire. That danger was an ever-present one in those days of chimneyless wooden houses.

The ancient city ordinances of London abound in stringent fire regulations. None of them, however, was more effective than the "cover-fire" bell, which as far back as the time of King Alfred was rung in certain places in England. William's edict rendered compulsory an ancient custom. But it was a wise legislative act, and not a bit of arbitrary tyranny. We find plenty of early traces of the custom or its equivalent, as, for instance, the blowing of a horn at the market-place in Continental Europe.

It is a curious instance of the conservative tendency of the rural mind in England that the custom of ringing the curfew should have so long survived its original significance.

Curfew is still religiously tolled in many hundreds of towns and villages, either all the year round or—which is still more usual—from September to April. No part of the kingdom can claim it as a special proof of its adherence to a primitive simplicity. Geographically considered, its survivals are by no means uninstructive. It tolls from the Isle of Wight in the south through Kent and Surrey, Middlesex, Suffolk, Norfolk, Lincoln, York, Durham, and Northumberland, and even across the border, in the Scotch lowlands. And it can be traced again through Cumberland and Lancashire, Cheshire, Derbyshire, Stafford, Notts, Leicestershire, Worcestershire, Shropshire, Hertfordshire, Monmouthshire, down to Devon and Dorset.

It is, in short, perpetuated all over the kingdom. Here and there it has become identified with local customs. At Newcastle, until it was discontinued, it was the signal for shutting the shops. At Durham, again (where it is tolled at nine o'clock), it heralds the closing of the college gates; while in many Cheshire and Yorkshire villages it has for hundreds of years warned farmers to lock up their cattle for the night. The almost universal hour at which it is tolled is eight o'clock in the evening, although here and there it is rung instead at seven and nine o'clock. In some places, too, there is a morning curfew,—a curious variation. At Stow, for instance, it is, or was lately, rung as early as four o'clock in the morning, and at Tamworth at the more seasonable hour of six o'clock. At Waltham in the Wolds, again, a grateful farmer, who was lost in the snow and found his way home by its sound, left a field to endow a five o'clock curfew forever.

The facts, indeed, plainly show that the custom has kept its hold on the popular sympathies through all the ages. The Pilgrims and the Puritans brought it over with them to New England, where the curfew bell is still rung in many towns and villages. In the "Bells of Lynn" Longfellow appeals to the "curfew of the setting sun" as heard at Nahant, and other allusions are freely found in our native poets.

Nay, so firmly has the curfew intrenched itself in parts of New England that in 1894 there was a popular uprising at the old seaport town of Portsmouth, New Hampshire, when the more progressive residents sought to abolish the ringing of the bell of the North Church at nine o'clock every night. This bell rang when General Washington stopped over-night in the town, and also when Daniel Webster was reading cases in a law office there. It had sent generations to bed. Should it be silent now? "No!" cried the old-timers, as they rose in their wrath and kept on ringing it.

It was about the same time that the curfew habit spread to the West, and, later, to the South. It started at Stillwater, Minnesota, and by July, 1895, about twenty other towns in that State had passed curfew ordinances. Not only that, but other towns in Oregon, Washington, Idaho, South Dakota, Nebraska, Kansas, Michigan, Missouri, Indiana, and Georgia had followed the leader.

The general principle of the curfew ordinances is the same wherever they have been adopted, but the ordinances differ in details. The idea is to provide that children under a certain age, varying in different towns from eighteen down to fifteen years, shall not be on the streets of the town after a stated time, ranging from half-past seven P.M. to nine P.M., unless accompanied by a lawful guardian. The penalty for violation of the ordinance also varies in different towns.

Throughout Minnesota children under sixteen years of age are required to be at home by nine o'clock at night, or very soon after. Curfew is sounded by tolling nine strokes on the fire-bell of the town. Any child found on the streets after that hour unaccompanied by a guardian may be arrested, and for the first offence taken home to his parents and cautioned. If arrested a second time, a fine of from three to ten dollars, or imprisonment of from three to ten days in jail, at the discretion of the magistrate, is the penalty.

In most other Western States the curfew rings earlier than in Minnesota. Usually it is rung at either eight or half-past eight o'clock. Warrensburg, Missouri, rings the curfew at half-past seven P.M. Topeka, Kansas, puts the age-limit at sixteen years; Wallace, Idaho, puts it at fifteen years. Chanute, Kansas, requires children to be off the streets as early as seven o'clock. Way Cross, Georgia, permits children to be abroad until ten o'clock. A unique addition to the curfew ordinance at Pierce, Nebraska, makes it unlawful for any boy when spoken to to return other than a civil answer.

Custom of the Country. The name popularly given to a custom said to have flourished in France, Scotland, and England during the feudal ages which gave to the lord of the manor the right to deflower the daughters of his vassals upon their marriage night. Aubrey De Vere alludes to this right in his play of "St. Thomas of Canterbury :"

> Customs !   Customs !
> Custom was that which to the lord of the soil
> Yielded the virgin one day wedded.

Beaumarchais, with an abuse of dramatic license, makes the custom an episode of his play "The Marriage of Figaro," though it certainly never existed in Spain. A comic opera, "Le Droit du Seigneur," produced half a century ago at the Opéra Comique at Paris, is still occasionally played. There is also a well-known picture of the same name by Jules Garnier. A wedding party has just left the church, and the lord is leading away the unwilling bride. Two monks are striving to reconcile the groom to the inevitable : one of them holds up three fingers, possibly to signify the number of days that must elapse before his bride will be restored to him. Literature, art, and the drama have combined to impress upon the mind the existence of this custom. Yet the real historical evidence is not convincing. It is possible that such a right may have been asserted by some semi-savage lord here and there, but that it ever existed as a recognized and established custom is highly incredible. Louis Veuillot, in "Le Droit du Seigneur au Moyen-Age" ("The Right of the Lord in the Middle Ages"), published in 1854, treats the subject exhaustively, and comes to the above conclusion. There was indeed a Droit du Seigneur, or *jus primæ noctis*, but the Seigneur in question was the Lord in heaven, and the jus, established by the Council of Carthage in 398, ordained that out of respect for the nuptial benediction, and for the greater glory of God, a newly married couple should remain continent on their wedding night. Later, in conformity with the advice given by the archangel Raphael to the son of Tobit (Tobit vi. 16–22), the precept was extended to three days immediately following the marriage.

According to several rituals of the fifteenth century, more especially at Liége, Limoges, and Bordeaux, the *jus primœ noctis* seems to have been in force up to that time, but by the sixteenth century it had come to be a mere religious counsel. It is possible that the myth, if myth indeed it be, arose from a misinterpretation of the Latin words *jus primœ noctis.*

A curious reversal of this custom is quoted by Lagrize in his " Histoire du Droit dans les Pyrénées" (1868). He finds his authority in a charter of 1330. When the Seigneur de Sadirac married, his vassal, the Seigneur de Brorden, was bound to meet the bride at the boundary of his lands, accompanied by his tenants. There the vassal was to dismount from his horse, to salute the lady, assist her to alight, kiss her, and strip her of all her clothes to the chemise, keeping them as his perquisite. If he politely vouchsafed to lend her the garments until she reached her home, the ceremony of disrobing her might be postponed until then, but the spoils still belonged to him.

Cuthbert, St., patron saint of Durham, England, and of its cathedral. The anniversary of his death, March 20, was a great festival in the early English Church, which commemorated also the 4th of September as the anniversary of the translation of his body to Durham. Originally a shepherd boy in the valley of the Lauder, a vision which he saw, while tending his flocks, of St. Aidan's soul being received into paradise, induced him to enter the neighboring monastery of Old Melrose. As an evangelist he shares with King Oswald and St. Aidan the honor of the conversion of Northeastern England. He became prior of Melrose, then was for twelve years a simple monk at Lindisfarne, and for nine years an austere hermit in a rude hut on House Island, one of the Farne group, then Bishop of Hexham, and in 685 Bishop of Lindisfarne. Two years later he resigned his bishopric and returned to his hut on House Island, where he died March 20, 687.

By his own desire, he was buried in the monastery of St. Peter in Lindisfarne. Many miracles were reported at the tomb, and Cuthbert's fame grew even greater after death than before. Bede relates that in 698 the monks disinterred his body and found it uncorrupted. It was put in a fresh coffin, which contained also the skull of St. Oswald, and placed in the ground. In 875 the monks fleeing before an invasion of the Danes carried the sacred relics with them, and for many years wandered with them from place to place throughout Northumbria and Southern Scotland, everywhere willingly supported by the faithful, until finally in 883 they reached Durham. Here St. Cuthbert caused his coffin to remain immovable for three days, and then made known his wish to be sepultured where the cathedral now stands. The first church was built of wood, but at the end of four years this was replaced by one of stone. In 1104 the present cathedral had sufficiently advanced towards completion to allow of the reinterment of the saint in a magnificent shrine, which shared with that of St. Edward at Westminster and St. Thomas at Canterbury the homage of England.

This shrine, we are told, was of green marble, partly gilt, and so rich in offerings and jewels that it was allowed to be one of the most sumptuous in England. In the base were worked four seats where cripples and invalids might get rest and healing. Over the shrine waved the famous banner of St. Cuthbert, crimson and green, with a square of white velvet in the centre, and within the square a sacred relic, the corporal-cloth wherewith St. Cuthbert used to cover the chalice when he said mass. This banner was at the battle of Brankenfield in Henry the Eighth's time, and brought home with it the royal banner of Scotland, and many Scottish noblemen's banners, which were hung in the feretory. This consecrated standard was thought by north-country people to be one of the most magnificent relics in England, and was carried out only on great processions, such as Easter Day, Ascension Day, Whitsunday, Corpus Christi Day, and St. Cuthbert's Day.

The corporal-cloth which the banner of St. Cuthbert contained was that which the night before the battle of Nevill's Cross Prior Fossour had been commanded in a vision to mount on a spear and carry to the Red Hills to abide the battle on the morrow. The great victory that followed, and the death of seven Scottish earls and fifteen thousand Scotchmen, were naturally attributed to St. Cuthbert and his corporale, and in this battle was taken that famous Scottish relic, the black rood of Scotland, a silver cross miraculously brought by a deer to a Scotch king who was hunting. The sacred banner is said to have been contemptuously burnt by the French wife of that sacrilegious dean, Whittingham.

At the west end of the shrine stood an altar for mass to be said on St. Cuthbert's Day, when the prior and all the brethren kept open house in the fratry. At this feast they used to draw up the gilt and painted wooden cover of the shrine with a rope whence depended six silver bells which "made a goodly sound."

Anciently no women were allowed to approach the shrine. A blue line of stone in the floor of the nave still marks the limit beyond which they dared not go.

Nor was any tomb save that of St. Cuthbert tolerated within the church until the first exception was made in 1310 in favor of Bishop Anthony Bek. A tradition (which architectural evidence proves false, but which is significant none the less) says that even his body might not be carried through the church, and that a breach was made in the chapel wall to admit it.

In 1542, at the time of the dissolution of the monasteries under Henry VIII., the shrine was destroyed, and the tomb broken open. "They found many goodly and valuable jewels, especially one precious stone, which was of value sufficient to redeem a prince. After the spoil of ornaments and jewels, they approached near to the saint's body, expecting nothing but dust and ashes; but, perceiving the chest he lay in strongly bound with iron, the goldsmith with a smith's great forge-hammer broke it open, when they found him lying whole, uncorrupt, with his face bare, and his beard of a fortnight's growth, and all the vestments about him, as he was accustomed to say mass, and his metwand of gold lying by him."

The marvel was reported to the king, who, more lenient than in the case of the rival saints Thomas à Becket and Edward the Confessor, ordered the body to be returned to the prior. The latter buried it beneath the place where the shrine had stood.

In 1827 the tomb was again opened. In it were found the coffin made in 1542, within this the successive fragments of two other coffins answering to the dates of the two interments in 698 and 1104, and then an entire skeleton wrapped in the rags of once-rich robes, and a second skull, obviously that of St. Oswald. The bones were piously replaced. Fragments of the episcopal garments, together with a comb and other relics found in the coffin, are now shown in the cathedral library. A sapphire ring, one of the spoils wrested from the tomb by the officers of Henry VIII., passed after a series of adventures to the monastery of English canonesses at Paris, which also preserves a tooth of St. Cuthbert.

Cwnstree. In Wales an ordeal through which a shrewish wife was obliged to pass if in the course of a connubial tiff she struck her husband with any unaccustomed weapon, as, for example, a pair of tongs. *Per contra,* a poker was a recognized implement of domestic warfare. Husband and wife were both represented by attorneys in a special court (their personal appearance there being disallowed), which was usually held in the town court. When a verdict of guilty had been returned by a proper jury of twelve good men and true, the sentence of death was passed by the judge. An effigy of the woman was then conveyed to a gibbet below the town hall clock, and, after being hanged, was fired at until completely destroyed by the crowd. It is said that the custom did much towards preventing family quarrels.

D.

Dance of Torches, Royal.   A distinctive feature at all weddings in the royal house of Prussia. After the bridal couple have been pronounced man and wife, the musicians are placed on the solid silver stage of the White Hall in the royal palace of Berlin, and the couple, preceded by six ministers of state and six lieutenant-generals, two by two, all holding white torches, make the tour of the hall, saluting the company as they go. The bride then gives her hand to the Emperor, he in turn to the Queen-mother, the bridegroom extends his to the Empress, and she in turn to the best man. The princes and princesses, following, lead up the dance in like professional manner. After the dance follows the distribution of the bride's garter among the guests. In place of the real garter, however, are substituted pieces of silk, three inches long, woven in the colors of the bride's hose, stamped with her monogram, and fringed with silver.

Dart, Throwing of the.   A ceremony performed triennially on the first Thursday of September in Cork Harbor, Ireland. By virtue of a clause in the city's charter, the mayor of Cork is constituted Admiral of the Port, but every three years he must claim jurisdiction over it by throwing a dart into the sea. The weapon is generally made of mahogany tipped and winged with bronze. At two o'clock in the afternoon the members of the Cork Town Council embark on board a steam-vessel, attended by all the civic officers and the band of the Cork civic artillery. A number of ladies also attend. The steamer proceeds out to sea until she reaches an imaginary line between Poor Head and Cork Head, which is supposed to be the maritime boundary of the borough. Here the mayor dons his official robes and proceeds, attended by the mace and sword-bearer, the city treasurer, and the town clerk, all wearing their official robes, to the prow of the vessel, whence he launches his javelin into the water, thereby asserting his authority as lord high admiral of the port. The affair winds up with a banquet in the evening at the mayor's house. The entire ceremony has a remarkable analogy to the Marriage of the Adriatic (*q. v.*) which was anciently performed by the Doges of Venice. A similar custom also once existed in Dublin, where it was called " Riding the Fringes" (franchises), in which the lord mayor and corporation, after riding round the inland boundaries of the borough, halted at a point on the shore near Bullock, whence the lord mayor hurled a dart into the sea, the spot where it fell marking the limit of the maritime jurisdiction. (See also BOUNDS, BEATING THE.)

David, St. (446–549), patron of Wales. The anniversary of his death on March 1 is celebrated by Welshmen wherever a sufficient number are congregated in any part of the world. Welsh legends relate many marvels of this saint, as that he was a descendant of the Virgin Mary in the eighteenth generation, and also an uncle of King Arthur, that an angel foretold his birth thirty years before it happened, that another angel accompanied him through life and administered to all his wants, that when he was baptized by Alicas, Bishop of Munster, at Porthclaes, a spring miraculously bubbled up for the purpose (it is still reverenced as a holy well), and that when he preached, the ground beneath his feet rose to form a natural pulpit. But in fact his ·life and work were sufficiently notable without these accretions of myth. He was a great preacher and controversialist, and as Archbishop of Carleon and Primate of Wales an able organizer and disciplinarian. The uncompromising enemy of Pelagianism, he succeeded in stamping out that heresy in Wales. St. David transferred the archiepiscopate from Carleon to Menevia, now St. David's. Here he was buried, but in 964 his body was transferred to Glastonbury. It was destroyed when Henry VIII. dismantled that abbey. The empty shrine still stands in the choir of St. David's Cathedral. In the front of it are four quatrefoil apertures, through which pious votaries deposited their offerings, which the monks secured in strong iron boxes behind.

Pope Calixtus, who canonized the saint in 1120, declared that two visits to St. David's were as good as one visit to Rome, according to the old monkish lines,—

> Meneviam pete bis, Romam procedere si vis ;
> Æqua tibi merces redditur hic et ibi :
> Roma semel quantum, bis dat Menevia tantum.

Among those who made the pilgrimage to St. David's shrine were William I., Henry II., and Edward I. and his queen Eleanor, if the local tradition is worthy of belief.

Various reasons are assigned by the Welsh for wearing the leek on his anniversary. The most usual legend runs that in a great battle against the Saxons where St. David led his people on to victory he caused them to wear leeks in their hats to distinguish them from the enemy. Nevertheless the Welsh themselves have another and more humorous legend. Wales in early days was troubled by orang-outangs, who proved too much for the inhabitants. So they sent over for assistance to England. But when the English arrived they found it difficult to tell orang-outangs from their Welsh neighbors, and at last, after numerous disastrous mistakes, asked the latter to wear a leek in their hats as a distinguishing mark.

Shakespeare in his play of Henry V., Act iv. Sc. 7, seems to imply that the custom originated at Crécy or Poitiers. Fluellen, addressing the monarch, says,—

"Your grandfather of famous memory, an't please your majesty, and your great uncle Edward, the plack prince of Wales, as I have read in the chronicles, fought a most prave pattle here in France.

"*K. Hen.* They did, Fluellen.

"*Flu.* Your majesty says very true : if your majesty is remembered of it, the Welshmen did goot service in a garden where leeks did grow, wearing leeks in their Monmouth caps; which, your majesty knows, to this hour is an honorable padge of the service; and I do believe your majesty takes no scorn to wear the leek upon St. Tavy's day."

This allusion by Fluellen to the Welsh having worn the leek in a battle under the Black Prince really proves nothing save that when Shakespeare wrote Welshmen wore leeks. In the same play the well-remembered Fluellen's enforcement of Pistol to eat the leek he had ridiculed further establishes the wearing as a common usage in Shakespeare's time.

Is it not sufficient to hold that the leek became the national insignia of the Welsh because it was their favorite vegetable? As far back as we can trace his domestic history, Taffy and the leek are inseparable. Caxton's "Description of Wales" has these lines :

> They have gruell to potage,
> And leekes kynde to companage.

And again :

> Atte meete, and after eke,
> Her solace is salt and leeke.

Worlidge says, "I have seen the greater part of a garden there stowed with leeks, and parts of the remainder with onions and garlic."

The observance of St. David's Day was long countenanced by royalty in England. Even economical Henry VII. could disburse two pounds "To the Walshemen towardes their feste" (*Med. Ævi Kalend.*, vol. i. p. 268) in 1494, and among the household expenses of the Princess Mary for 1544 is an entry of fifteen shillings to the Yeomen of the King's Guard for bringing a leek to Her Grace on St. David's Day. William III. always joined his Welsh subjects in wearing a leek on this day, witness the following paragraph in *The Flying Post*, 1699: "Yesterday being St. David's Day, the King, according to custom, wore a leek in honor of the ancient Britons, the same being presented to him by the sergeant-porter whose place it is, and for which he claims the clothes His Majesty wore that day; the courtiers in imitation of His Majesty wore leeks also."

Gilt leeks are now worn in the hat or carried in procession by the Welsh branches of charitable societies on the saint's day, and every mantel-piece in the principality is decorated with the genuine vegetable.

It appears to have been at one time customary in England for effigies of Welshmen to be burned on this day. These effigies were known as Taffies. Pepys has the following entry in his Diary, under the date of March 1, 1667: "In Mark Lane I do observe (it being St. David's Day) the picture of a man dressed like a Welshman, hanging by the neck upon one of the poles that stand out at the top of the merchants' houses, in full proportion: and very handsomely done, which is one of the oddest sights I have seen, a good while." The custom was not extinct in the middle of the eighteenth century:

> But it would make a stranger laugh
> To see the English hang poor Taff:
> A pair of breeches and a coat,
> Hat, shoes, and stockings, and what not,
> All stuffed with hay to represent
> The Cambrian hero thereby meant:
> With sword sometimes three inches broad,
> And other armor made of wood,
> They drag hur to some publick tree,
> And hang hur up in effigy.

The goat has by time honored custom been attached to the regiment of the Royal Welsh (23d) Fusiliers, and the following extract, taken from the *Graphic* (No. 171, March 8, 1873), shows how St. David's Day is observed by the officers and men of this regiment:

"The drum-major, as well as every man in the regiment, wears a leek in his busby; the goat is dressed with rosettes and ribbons of red and blue. The officers have a party, and the drum-major, accompanied by the goat, marches round the table after dinner, carrying a plate of leeks, of which he offers one to each officer or guest who has never eaten one before, and who is bound to eat it up, standing on his chair, with one foot on the table, while a drummer beats a roll behind his chair. All the toasts given are coupled with the name of St. David, nor is the memory of Toby Purcell forgotten. This worthy was gazetted major of the regiment when it was first raised, and was killed in the battle of the Boyne."

Dead, Festival of the (Japanese, *Bon Matsuri*), in Japan. This is celebrated from the 13th to the 15th of July. Foreigners often call it the Feast of Lanterns, from the lanterns which form a prominent feature in the celebration. It is believed that on these days the dead come back and mingle with their relations. Early on the morning of the 13th offerings of fruit and vegetables are laid upon the altars in churches and the little shrines before which the morning and evening prayers are said in every believing home. Clear water is sprinkled from time to time, and tea is poured out every hour for the viewless visitors. So for three days the dead are feasted. At sunset pine torches are kindled to guide their steps, and lanterns are suspended over houses and tombs.

On the third night the ghostly visitants are supposed to return to their abodes, and all the living can do is to speed them on their journey. Little boats, barely a foot in length, are launched on canal, river, or lake, each with a miniature lantern glowing at the prow and incense burning at the stern, and so they are allowed to float down to the sea. A recent law, however, has forbidden the launching of these *shoryobuni,* or "boats of the blessed ghosts," in the large seaport towns, owing to the danger to the shipping. There is some analogy both in the object of the feast and in the lighting of the lanterns with the Christian feast of All Souls. (See ALL SOULS' DAY, and HALLOWEEN.)

Dead, Festival of the Unforgotten. (Chinese, *Ching Ming Chieh.*) The Chinese All Souls' Day. Ancestor-worship is the

FESTIVAL OF THE UNFORGOTTEN DEAD.
(By a Chinese artist.)

most prominent feature of the Chinese religion. It was sanctioned by Confucius. Like the ancient Egyptians, the Chinese hold that every person has three souls. At death, one soul goes into the unseen world, the second remains with the body in the tomb, the third takes up its abode in the ancestral tablet, which is the holiest thing in the household. This tablet is simply a narrow piece of wood, about a foot long, two or three inches wide, and half an inch thick, set in a low pedestal, and on one side are inscribed the ancestral names. The eldest son has charge of the tablet and its worship. It is placed in the main hall of the house, offerings are presented before it, and incense is burned to it every day. The son regards this tablet as in very truth the abode of a personality which is far more to him for weal or woe than all the gods of the empire. The gods are to be feared and their favor is to be propitiated; but ancestors are loved and their needs in the spirit-world are generously supplied. Food is offered daily before the tablet, in order to satisfy the hunger of the spirit, while paper money, suits of paper clothes, and paper figures representing men-servants and maid-servants are burnt to ashes,—the idea being that thus sublimated they pass without difficulty to the souls in the regions of the blest.

Twice in the year—the first time in the third month, when also, as we learn from the Gospels, it was customary to sweep and gar-nish the tombs in the neighborhood of Jerusalem, and again in the seventh—the males of every family of standing betake them-selves to the graveyards, and, having cleansed and embellished the tombs, offer sacrifices of food and burn paper representations before an altar in front of the graves. Each worshipper bows re-peatedly with his head to the ground, as though in the presence of a deity, and brings his devotions to an end by pouring libations of wine over the altar and firing volleys of crackers to drive to a dis-tance any evil spirits that may be lurking in the neighborhood. But there are other evil spirits in the company of the deceased, who, being beyond the reach of the sound of fireworks, have to be propitiated. Lepers and beggars are believed to haunt the eter-nal regions, and, as these might become annoyingly clamorous if the offerings and presents were confined to the deceased alone, food, consisting of small cakes, and offerings of paper money are presented to them. But even these do not exhaust the unseen powers which have to be propitiated in order to secure the undis-turbed repose of the dead. " To leave out of count the local deity would be almost to invite the disturbance of the genial influences secured by the position of the tomb. Three dishes of food, three cups of wine, three incense-sticks, two candles, and three packets of paper money are supposed to satisfy his wants, and these are readily offered at his shrine. When the service is over and the spiritual essence of the food offered has been consumed by the spirits, the worshippers gather round the altar and partake of the more material portion of the viands. This is but a prelude to a subsequent feast, which is held in the ancestral hall of the clan." (PROF. R. K. DOUGLASS, in *Good Words* for January, 1895.)

In Formosa the feast in honor of the dead was differently conducted. The food was tied row upon row on great cone-like structures of bamboo poles, from five to ten feet in diameter at the base, and sometimes fifty or sixty feet high.

When the spirits had consumed the spiritual part, the carnal became the property of a vast mob that always assembled on the grounds. A gong gave the signal for the latter to rush in. " Scarcely had the first stroke fallen," says George Leslie Mackay, speaking of a Seventh Moon Feast he had witnessed at Bang-Kah, " when that whole scene was one mass of arms and legs and tongues. Screaming, cursing, howling, like demons of the pit, they all joined in the onset. A rush was made for the cones, and those nearest seized the supports and pulled now this way, now that. The huge, heavily laden structures began to sway from side to side until with a crash one after another fell into the crowd, crushing their way to the ground. Then it was every man for himself. In one wild scramble, groaning and yelling all the while, trampling on those who had lost their footing or were smothered by the falling cones, fighting and tearing one another like mad dogs, they all made for the coveted food. It was a very bedlam, and the wildness of the scene was enhanced by the irregular explosion of the fire-crackers and the death-groan of some one worsted in the fray. As each secured what he could carry, he tried to extricate himself from the mob, holding fast to the treasures for which he had fought, and one of the less successful in the outskirts of the crowd would fain plunder him. Escaping the mob, he hurried to his home, expecting every moment to be attacked by those who thought it easier to waylay and rob the solitary spoilsman than to join in the general scramble in the plain."

These barbarities were abolished in 1894 by the Chinese governor, Lin Ming Chuan.

December. Like the three preceding months, December derives its name from the place which it held in the old Roman

DECEMBER. THRESHING AND WINNOWING.
(From an eleventh-century MS.)

calendar, which divided the year into ten months, December (the tenth) being the last. The ancient Saxons called this the *Wintermonath*, or Winter Month, but after their conversion to Christianity they changed the name to *Halig Monath*, or Holy Month, in honor of the Christmas anniversary on the 25th.

For the same reason the modern Germans style it alternatively *Christmonat.*

At Craig-Madden, in Stirlingshire, there is a triangular hole beneath the Druidic stones. Persons who crawl through this hole avoid the danger of dying childless. Probably these are the last extant survivals in the British Isles of the numerous rock-crevices which in the Middle Ages were held to bestow blessings of various sorts upon those who resolutely squeezed through them.

An interesting coincidence pointed out by Forbes-Leslie and Miss C. F. Gordon-Cumming is that crevices which superstition has dowered with similar attributes are not uncommon in India. Hindoo pilgrims from all parts of the empire throng to the temple of Malabar Point, at Bombay, where the priests assure them that by squeezing through a narrow opening between two great rocks they will leave their sins behind them and will also insure having descendants to perform their funeral rites. Analogous also was the ancient superstition which gave a ritual value to all manner of perforated stones, some so large that people could pass through them, some so small that they were worn as amulets, or tied to the key of the stable-door to prevent the witches from riding the horses at night.

Declan, St. The festival, or, as it is better known, the patern, of this saint is celebrated at Ardmore, Ireland, on July 24. On that day and on the Sundays immediately preceding and following it, the country-people flock into the village, which, decorated with booths and stands, has the appearance of a fair. The ruined church and holy well of St. Declan, half-way between the village and Ardmore Head, are visited, as well as the cell near the old cathedral and round tower, said to be the tomb of the saint. But the most famous custom—that of passing under the St. Declan Stone—has been discouraged by the Church authorities, and is now practised only by strangers. This holy rock stands in Ardmore Bay, whither it is said to have been wafted over the ocean from Rome, at the time when the saint was building his church, bearing on its top a large bell for the church tower and vestments for the saint himself. It rests on a number of smaller stones. At low water it is not difficult for men and women to pass under it by stretching themselves full length on face and stomach and squeezing or dragging through with a motion somewhat like swimming. Once on the other side, the devotees proceeded on bare knees over a number of little rocks round again to the place of entrance, until they had passed under the stone three times.

St. Declan, according to the hagiologists, was the first bishop of Ardmore in Ireland. Baptized by St. Colman, he preached the gospel in that country some time before the arrival of St. Patrick.

Decoration or Memorial Day. In most of the Northern States of the Union May 30 is set apart by statute as a day for decorating the graves of the soldiers who fell in the civil war, for holding military parades, and for listening to an oration by some famous orator appointed for the occasion. The origin of the observance was thus told by Chauncey M. Depew in a famous Decoration Day address made in the Metropolitan Opera-

DECORATION DAY PARADE.

House in New York on May 30, 1879: " When the war was over in the South, where under warmer skies and with more poetic temperaments symbols and emblems are better understood than in the practical North, the widows, mothers, and children of the Confederate dead went out and strewed their graves with flowers; at many places the women scattered them impartially also over the unknown and unmarked resting-places of the Union soldiers. As the news of this touching tribute flashed over the North it roused, as nothing else could have done, national amity and love and allayed sectional animosity and passion. . . . Thus out of sorrows common alike to North and South came this beautiful custom." But its growth was a gradual one. There was no general celebration and no settled date until, in 1868, General John A. Logan, commander-in-chief of the Grand Army of the Republic, issued an order that on May 30 of that year every post, from East to West, should engage in fitting ceremonies and scatter tokens of respect over the resting-places of their comrades in arms. Later the Legislatures took up the matter, until at present (1897) it is a legal holiday in the following States and Territories: Arizona, California, Colorado, Connecticut, Delaware, District of Columbia, Illinois, Indiana, Iowa, Kentucky, Maine, Maryland, Massachusetts, Michigan, Minnesota, Missouri, Montana, Nebraska, New Hampshire, New Jersey, New York, North Dakota, Ohio, Oklahoma, Oregon, Pennsylvania, Rhode Island, South Dakota, Tennessee, Utah, Vermont, Washington, Wisconsin, and Wyoming. In Kansas and Nevada, which have no statutory holidays, it is universally observed. It is also celebrated by Grand Army men and others on all the battle-fields of the South where National cemeteries have been established for the Federal dead.

Decoration Day is a sort of lay All Souls' Day. "Decoration Day," says the *Illustrated American* for June 21, 1890, " is not merely a holiday in the modern acceptation of the word; it realizes its etymological significance as a holy day. It is our All Saints' Day, sacred to the memory of the glorified dead who consecrated themselves to their country, were baptized in blood, were beatified and canonized as martyrs for the right. It is well that, in the hurry and press of our times, when the higher soul within us is choked and stifled by the more sordid cares of the hour, by the selfish struggle for place and pelf, we should pause for a period to dwell upon the memory of the illustrious dead who gave their lives for their country, and who typify that higher and truer Americanism which lies within us still, dormant and latent indeed, yet ready to spring again to the surface whenever the needs of the country issue a new call to arms. It is well that we should do them honor which honors ourselves in the doing. But it is well, also, that we should remember what was their true mission and their higher success: that they fought not through enmity to a gallant and mistaken foe, but through love for the Union, which recognized no North and no South. That Union they have restored, and union means peace, harmony, mutual good will. If they had merely pinned together with bayonets the two divided sections of the country, they had fought and bled and fallen in vain. Northern hatred for the South, Southern hatred for the North, is disloyalty, is treason indeed to the Union which they re-established. A few political 'leaders'—'leaders' who are far in the rear of public sentiment —have sought to make political capital out of the fact that Southerners cherish the memory of the heroes who fought on their side, and have raised statues to commemorate them. But we who remember with pride the achievements of our soldiers are proud to acknowledge that they had foemen worthy of their steel, and that a common country gave birth to both. The arbitrament of the sword has settled forever the questions over which no other tribunal had jurisdiction, and the nation went through the throes of a civil war for the benefit of North and South alike."

Not only is Decoration Day allied to the Christian All Souls' Day, but through and behind All Souls' Day to various pagan rituals.

Among the Greeks and Romans flowers were intimately associated with the honors paid to the dead. When a Greek died, the nearest female relatives assembled to perform the last offices, which were concluded by crowning the head with flowers. In addition to this, the Romans sometimes covered the couch on which the dead body lay with leaves and flowers. It was likewise a universal custom for the relatives and friends of one just dead, especially if the deceased was young, to carry wreaths of flowers to the house or place of burial of such a one. At the Χοαί, the ceremony at the grave, libations of milk, honey, water, and wine, and offerings of flowers and olives, were made; and after burial the grave was constantly crowned and adorned with wreaths. Moreover, the springing of flowers from the tomb of the dead was welcomed as an earnest of their happiness; and it was the universal wish that the tombstones of departed friends might be light to them, and that a perpetual springtide of all kinds of sweet flowers might encircle their graves.

More closely analogous to the modern Decoration Day and All Souls' Day are the ancient Parentalia (*q. v.*). The Romans were strict in their observance of them; and even the hateful Caracalla, when he visited Achilles' grave, laid garlands of flowers upon it. And when he himself died, to the great joy of his people, some were found who for a long time afterwards decked his tomb with spring and summer flowers: "Non defuerunt, qui per longum tempus vernis æstivisque floribus tumulum ejus ornarint." And Antony dying begged to have roses scattered on his tomb:

> Manibus est imis rosa grata, et grata sepulchris,
> Et rosa flos florum.

So too Ovid, writing from the land of his exile, prayed his wife, "But do you perform the funeral rites for me when dead, and offer chaplets wet with your tears. Although the fire shall have changed my body into ashes, yet the sad dust will be sensible of your pious affection."

Dedication Festival. The anniversary of the consecration of a church. In Catholic countries it is observed as a feast of

the highest rank. It must not be confounded with a patron day
(*q. v.*), which is the feast of the patron saint in whose honor the
church is dedicated. The mass and office for the anniversary of
the dedication exist by themselves, are of singular beauty, and
have nothing to do with the patronal feast. At the time of the
actual consecration the bishop may fix a day other than the
actual anniversary for the feast of the dedication, in all future
times ; but after the consecration Papal permission is required
to change the day.

   Deisul, or **Deasil.** A custom, now almost extinct, but once
very prevalent, in the Scotch Highlands. It consisted in going
three times around a person or an object in a rightwise direction,
—that is, keeping that person or object always on the right side.
This was considered, and is considered all over the world, as the
sunwise direction. To perform the circuit in this manner was
to bring down a blessing, to perform it in the opposite manner,
or, as the Celtic word ran, widdershins, or withershins, was to
invoke a curse. Witches were said to approach sacred places
and advance towards the demons whom they served in widdershins fashion. This was in opposition to what at one time must
have been an established religious duty.—*i.e.*, to perform all acts
in accordance with the sun's apparent motion. It was sunwise
that the Celts approached a consecrated place, and all their religious processions moved in that direction. Martin in his " Description of the Western Islands of Scotland" (1703) mentions
the common practice of carrying fires deasil or sunwise around
persons or property in order to preserve them from any malignant influence. For the same reason boatmen rowed their boats
round sunwise before proceeding in the direct course. To insure
happiness in marriage the bride was conducted deasil towards
her future spouse, and it was in the same manner that a corpse
was conveyed to the grave or funeral pyre. On Martin's arrival
in the island of Rona, one of the inhabitants gave him a blessing,
at the same time going round him sunwise. Lachlan Shaw testifies to a continuance of these ceremonies at the end of the
eighteenth century in the Lowland district of Moray. He mentions witnessing " Deas soil" processions made round the churches
at marriages. churchings of women, and burials ; as well as processions with lighted torches made in like manner around the
corn-fields, in order to obtain a blessing on the crops. (*History
of Moray.*)
   In short, while this custom of deisul endured among the Highlanders there seem to have been few events in their lives at
which it was not performed. But the most common rite was
that whose object was to call down blessings upon an individual

by making a sunwise circuit around him. Scott affords numerous instances in his novels. The old woman in "The Two Drovers" asks permission to "walk the deasil" around Robin Oig, "that you may go safe out into the foreign land, and come safe home." Sir Walter explains that "it consists in the person who made the deasil walking three times round the person who is the object of the ceremony, taking care to move according to the course of the sun." Again, he describes how the Highland doctor came when Waverley had been wounded : "He observed great ceremony in approaching Edward, and, though our hero was writhing with pain, would not proceed to any operation which might assuage it until he had perambulated his couch three times, moving from east to west, according to the course of the sun. This, which was called making the deasil, both the leech and his assistants seemed to consider as a matter of the last importance to the accomplishment of a cure." (*Waverley,* chap. xxiv.) And in a note he adds, "To go round a person in the opposite direction, or *withershins,* is unlucky, and a sort of incantation." Dr. Macleod also records that when a boy in the Highlands the parishioners all came to his father's manse on New Year's Day and performed deisul round the house to bring good luck to the minister and his family for the ensuing year.

Miss Constance F. Gordon-Cumming has recorded some survivals of the deisul rite even in our own times. One is at Kilbar, in the isle of Barra, where on St. Barr's Day (September 25) all the Roman Catholic population attend mass in the chapel at Borve in honor of their titular saint, and then ride across the island to Kilbar, the ancient burial-place of the McNeils, where they march thrice round the ruins to secure luck for the island in the coming year. Another is at Inverness. A long hill, looking not unlike a boat turned upside down, and known as the Fairies' Hill, was some years ago made into a modern cemetery, with winding walks leading to the graves. It so chanced that the turn in the principal path went sunwise, but the portion of the cemetery in which the poor were buried could be reached by a shorter cut. At first this route was taken, but it was observed that this path turned in the opposite direction to what is sunwise, and this raised such an outcry that the poor are now taken by the longer way, to save them from the dire results of being carried "withershins" to the grave. (*From the Hebrides to the Himalayas,* vol. i. p. 210.)

A quaint survival in the very heart of English civilization is that of "passing the bottle sunwise" at table, which is insisted upon by all good topers. Perhaps another may be found in the well-nigh universal gambler's habit of turning a chair or walking round it in order to bring about a change of luck. It may be noted that this turning is always sunwise. In Ireland when any one falls he springs up and turns about three times to the right.

The custom of deisul is at least as old as the sixth century. William Reeves in his "Life of St. Columba," p. clxiii, refers to the famous relic known as the Cathach, a copy of the Psalms in the saint's own handwriting, richly bound in silver and gold, and quotes from O'Donnell: "If it be sent thrice rightwise round the army when they are going to battle, they will return safe with victory; and it is on the breast of a coward or a cleric, who is to the best of his power free from mortal sin, that the Cathach should be, when brought round the army." This story takes the deisul as a rite back at least to the times of St. Columba, and it is probably much older than that period. Mr. William Simpson in his admirable book on "The Buddhist Praying-Wheel," to which indebtedness for most of these references is here acknowledged, sees a close analogy between the deisul and the Hindoo rite of Pradakshina, and refers both back to a common origin, sun-worship.

Denis, St. (Lat. *Dionysius;* It. *Dionisio* or *Dionigi*), patron saint of France. His festival is celebrated on October 9. St. Denis is said to be the apostle of France and the first bishop of Paris. Among the many traditions about him it is difficult to arrive at any certain information. The legend which confuses St. Denis, Bishop of Paris in the third century, with Dionysius the Areopagite, is so universally represented in art that it must be related. Dionysius was an Athenian philosopher who went to Egypt to study astrology. While there, it is related, he was much perplexed by the sudden darkening of the world which took place during the crucifixion. On his return to Athens he heard St. Paul preach, and was converted. He travelled to Jerusalem to visit the Virgin Mary, and in some letters he is said to have left an account of her death and burial. He next travelled to Rome, where he beheld the martyrdom of St. Paul, and from thence was sent by St. Clement to preach in France, where he made many converts. After his arrival in Paris, according to the legend, he was called Denis. A more probable account is that St. Denis came to Paris about the year 250. He was brought with two priests before the Roman governor, and all three were beheaded. The bodies were left for wild beasts to devour, but legend asserts that St. Denis arose, and, taking his head in his hands, walked for two miles to the place now called Montmartre. The relics of the three martyrs were translated to the Abbey of St. Denis in the reign of Dagobert. The name of St. Denis was the war-cry of the French armies, and the oriflamme, the standard of France, was consecrated at his tomb. His particular attribute in art is the severed head.

Derby Day. The second and most important day of the great Spring Meeting at Epsom, in Surrey, England, which begins with the first Tuesday after Trinity Sunday. Derby Day itself thus always falls on Wednesday. It is then that the famous Derby stakes are contended for. These consist of fifty guineas each entry. When the first Derby was, run for, there were only thirty-six entries (with twenty-five pounds forfeit in case of non-starters); but the number of subscribers is now so large that the value of the stakes sometimes amounts to six thousand pounds.

Epsom may lay claim to be the first of English race-courses. So early as 1663 Pepys records in his Diary that he was prevented by an important sitting of the House of Lords from attending " some famous horse-races" on Banstead Downs, part and parcel of the Epsom range. This was a year or two before Charles II. had set about establishing the meeting at Newmarket.

But the Derby stakes and Derby Day are of later origin. About the middle of the last century a certain Captain Burgoyne (who afterwards, as General Burgoyne, was to surrender to the American forces at Saratoga) made a clandestine marriage with a daughter of the then Earl of Derby, which was eventually recognized by the family. He purchased a little house at Epsom,—some say it was at the time an ale-house,—and, having altered and improved it, called it " The Oaks." Here he resided for some time, and eventually he sold the property to a relative in the person of the eleventh Earl of Derby. This noble lord was the one who took as his second wife the famous Miss Eliza Farren, known to the theatrical world as the finest Lady Teazle that ever stepped upon the stage. Lord Derby seems to have taken a fancy to Epsom, and he founded in 1779 an annual race, to be known as the Oaks stakes, after his residence, and a year later the Derby stakes, which have made the family name famous in every part of the civilized world.

Lord Beaconsfield, as everybody will remember, called the Derby stakes the Blue Ribbon of the turf. To win them is to be for the moment the foremost man in all England. While still an undergraduate, Lord Rosebery announced that he had three ambitions,—to marry the richest woman in England, to become prime minister, and to win the Derby. The first he achieved very early by his union with a daughter of the Rothschilds, whilst the last and culminating glory was thrust upon him at almost the very moment that he had achieved the second.

Derby Day, in fact, is the national holiday of England. It comes at the very apogee of the season. The proximity of Epsom to London makes the Downs easily accessible. Hence royalty, Parliament, the aristocracy, the middle classes, and the mob flock thither by rail and in all sorts of conveyances, from the four-in-hand drag to the one-horse shay. A vast stock of pigeon pie is baked for the occasion, and gallons of wine and spirits are bought and consumed. Hence the more elegant among sporting writers are fond of calling it the Epsom Carnival and the Saturnalia on the Downs.

The scenes that characterize Derby Day before, during, and after the race are sufficiently amusing. The procession of con-

ANNOUNCING THE DERBY WINNER.

veyances along the high-road is itself motley and various. When the huge crowds of pilgrims have at length arrived at the scene, "they find the ring a cloud of dust, a very pandemonium of shouts and yells. Books are opened; heavy bets are laid; and, as the satin-coated heroes of the day are led into the paddock, the odds chop and change about in bewildering fashion. Roaring and pencilling go on apace; the course is cleared; and then, after the canter, the noise redoubles as the favorite is observed to go 'like a bird,' or 'a lion,' to step along with sweeping stride, or to go 'short and stilty.' Murmurs, shouts, and deep-drawn breaths proclaim the various false starts until the flag drops, the bell rings, and eyes—some bright enough, others reddened with excitement—watch the turn into the great light-green ribbon which stretches from Tottenham Corner to the winning-post. Then the shouts recommence, never to cease until the mighty steeds, ' clothed in thunder,' pass the winning-post. Then hats fly high in air, and everybody drinks, and drinks deeply,—the winners for joy, the losers to drown their grief. Among the vulgar everybody eats also. Lobsters, chickens, and pigeon pies disappear with fearful rapidity; champagne-corks fly aloft; and the gathering puts on the appearance of a gigantic picnic, continued, with intervals of amusements proper to the hour, till the last race is run and holiday London streams back to its bed.

" Thus far all has gone merrily enough. The national holiday has been a great success. Money-making and losing, eating and drinking,—especially drinking,—have occupied at least a quarter of a million of people from early morning till far into the night. Perhaps it is as well not to remain on the course till the last of the flushed and excited crowd have driven townward, and left the downs to the nomad population, whose tents are pitched there for the nonce, for the spectacle then presented is apt to awaken other emotions than those of joy. As the moon rises over the grand stand,—staring over the deserted race-course with its empty boxes, like the ghosts of departed fortunes,—queer sights may be seen on the downs. Out of the drinking-booths, towards the wagons and the tent carts posted in the neighborhood, reel strange figures, caricatures of humanity, hiccuping snatches of the ribald songs which have shocked ears polite during the day. Like the spoilers of the slain on the battle-field, hover other loathsome objects picking up eagerly the waifs and strays, the crumbs which have dropped from the Derby luncheon. The policeman's lantern turned on hedge and ditch reveals shapeless masses of presumedly human origin crouched down in drunken sleep. It is better, perhaps, not to see the last of the Derby. Let us, therefore, hie back to town, in spite of the dust and noise, and observe the 'fun of the road.' Is it funny to mark the faces pale with fatigue or flushed with strong drink? Is there anything particularly sportive and light-hearted in the practice of flinging dolls and pin-cushions, bags of flour, rotten eggs, or china dogs, at one another? Perhaps it is, if the spectator have taken care to drink himself up or down to the Derby level; but otherwise the scene is as coarse and uninviting as a Dutch fair,—a fit theme for Teniers or Jan Steen. It is not wise to tarry by the wayside. The 'fun of the road,' if not ready, is rough enough in all conscience, but it is edifying when compared with the scenes in tavern-gardens by the road. As night creeps on, the most riotous members of the long pro-

cession to London wax tired of shouting and yelling, the last
bottle of champagne is drunk, and the cold butt-end of the last
cigar drops from parched lips into the dust of the road, unheeded by the bloodshot eyes now closed in feverish slumber.
A few case-hardened roysterers, those who have done their
spiriting gently in the earlier part of the day, 'stay' better, and
wake the echoes of the quiet streets, as they drive homewards,
after a last halt at Cremorne, with shouts of laughter, and
snatches of 'Tommy make room for your uncle.' " (*All the Year
Round,* June 3, 1876.)

Dervishes. It is usually said that what the monkish orders
are to the Catholic religion the dervishes are to the Mohammedan. This is true in a broad and general way, but, like all
general statements, it has its qualifications. The Catholic monks
are under the discipline and supervision of the Church ; they
are bound to accept its dogmas and to yield implicit submission
to the Pope acting through their superiors. The dervishes, on
the other hand, hold themselves in many ways independent of
the Sultan, and even of some doctrines of the Mohammedan
faith. They do not recognize the legal exposition of the Koran,
nor acknowledge the authority of any other than their spiritual
chief, or of Allah himself speaking directly to them. They even
set at naught the teachings of the Koran in regard to spirituous
liquors, and during their public performances often drink wine
or brandy to stimulate their flagging energies.

There are other particulars, however, in which they resemble
the Catholic monks. They live in monasteries. They take vows
of poverty, chastity, and obedience, although the second of these
vows is occasionally so far relaxed as to allow certain individuals among them to go out from their monasteries and marry.
But even the few benedicts must pass at least two nights every
week within the convent walls. Like the mendicant friars, they
support themselves by begging from door to door. The very
name dervish indicates this. It comes from a Persian word
meaning " door-sill."

An alternative name by which they are known is Mevelavites,
from their founder, Mevelava. This venerable gentleman flourished in the thirteenth century. He was a poet of some eminence, but was mainly distinguished for his acrobatic feats. It
is recorded that on one memorable occasion he spun round and
round like a sacrosanct humming-top for fourteen days at a
stretch. No wonder that at the close of this extraordinary performance he fell into an ecstasy and had visions in which Allah
revealed his wishes concerning the settlement of the order. The
modern dervishes strive in their poor little *fin-de-siècle* manner

to imitate their great protagonist. But the best they can do is to whirl around for an hour or so every Tuesday and Friday to the accompaniment of flutes and tambourines. The flute is especially esteemed by them, inasmuch as its use was sanctified by Jacob and other shepherds of the Old Testament.

These bi-weekly séances are public, and constitute one of the "sights" to visitors in the East. Fanatical as they are, the people witness them with the deepest earnestness. Some years back a fearful tumult was raised in Cairo because in the middle of the spinning one of the dervishes stopped short and declared that a European was laughing at them. The person gifted with this too abundant sense of humor narrowly escaped being torn to pieces by the mob.

The dervishes are divided into two classes, the whirlers, or dancers, and the howlers. The former are many of them persons of high rank. But if they do not go beyond the first stage they may fill all requirements by saying a few prayers at home and wearing for a few minutes every day the sacred white cap or "tag." If, however, they aim at the attainment of the full dignity, they must undergo a novitiate of hard labor for a thousand and one days. During this probationary period they have to submit to the additional indignity of being styled "jackals." When the term has expired the jackal emerges into a full-fledged Mevelavite. In token of this he receives a woollen belt, with its cabalistic "stone of contentment," the tag, the ear-rings shaped like the horseshoe of Ali, and the rosary with the ninety-nine names of God.

In the public services the dancers wear high hats without a rim, and short skirts which stand out at right angles to their bodies as they whirl around upon the left heel, ring within ring, without touching one another, their hands outstretched, their eyes fixed ecstatically, all the time quietly but closely watched by the sheik. They keep up this extraordinary performance, with brief intervals of rest, for an hour.

Meanwhile the howling dervishes are not idle. These wear white felt hats and long gowns encircled by a belt in which are two or three big stones. Over their shoulders is a mantle edged with green. They sway themselves backward and forward, either in line or a ring, shouting the name of Allah ever faster and louder as the music gets more uproarious, until the whole sounds like the baying of multitudinous hounds; then two or three make a dive at the bare walls, striking them again and again with their heads until somebody seizes the frenzied fanatics and lays them, just breathing, on their backs. Running daggers through the cheeks is still done, though rarely, but the mystery remains how they escape all injury, and how the butting of the head against marble walls leaves any brains. It must be that the excitement sustains the system,—that fervor of feeling makes up for the injury done to the frame.

In their daily life the dervishes practise the utmost austerities. They go about almost naked, and fast every Thursday from sunrise until sunset, besides the ordinary fast of Ramadan.

Besides the members of the regular orders, there are many dervishes in the Mohammedan world who wander about and support themselves and even acquire considerable wealth from the voluntary contributions of the faithful. They cure diseases or drive away evil spirits by incantations, charm snakes, or perform feats of legerdemain and other kinds of more or less conscious imposture.

It is in Egypt and Hindostan that the extreme degrees of squalor, fraud, and also of self-mortification are found among the peripatetic dervishes. Some spend their lives in absolute nakedness, their bodies smeared with wood-ash, their unkempt hair twisted into a turban ; some roll head over heels for hundreds of miles; some spend hours in contemplating the tips of their noses in eighty-four different postures.

Discovery Day. This is celebrated on October 21 in commemoration of the discovery by Columbus of the island of San Salvador in 1492. This was the first revelation of the existence of the New World to the Old. Columbus sailed from Spain on Friday, August 3 (Old Style), 1492, at eight o'clock in the morning. He was in command of three ships, the Santa Maria, the Pinta, and the Niña, carrying in all one hundred and twenty men. Various discouragements attended the voyage, but on September 18, while bearing to the southwest, many birds were seen, indicating the neighborhood of land, and on October 11 a cane, a log of wood, a stick wrought with iron, a board, and a stake covered with dog-roses were fished up. At ten o'clock at night Columbus saw and pointed out a light ahead. At two o'clock on the morning of the 12th land was sighted. This proved to be an island, which Columbus named San Salvador. He landed in the morning, bearing the royal banner of Spain, which he planted into the soil. The above dates are all Old Style. To make them correspond with the modern calendar nine days should be added. Discovery Day is not a general holiday in the United States, but is celebrated locally with speeches and appropriate festivities. The 21st of October, 1892, however, as the fourth centennial of the discovery, and in recognition of the fact that it preluded the great World's Fair at Chicago (which had been postponed from the centennial year to 1893), was by authority of Congress recommended to the people of the United

22

States by President Benjamin Harrison in a proclamation issued on July 21 of that year as a day to be observed throughout the United States " by public demonstration and by suitable exercises in their schools and other places of assembly." The proclamation was honored in nearly every State, and the day was kept as a general holiday. The Board of Managers of the World's Fair dedicated their buildings on that day. But the New York celebration had been already fixed for the 12th, and this could not be changed without calling an extra session of the Legislature. Hence New York's celebration preceded that of the rest of the nation.

Distaff's Day, St., or Rock Day. This name was in ancient England given to the 7th of January, which, following as it did Twelfth Night, or Epiphany, the conclusion of the Christmas season, was the date at which women were expected to resume the rock or distaff, as well as other household duties. The hired men postponed their definitive resumption of work until Plough Monday (*q. v.*), the first Monday after Twelfth Night, which frequently left a lee-way of several days, in which they amused themselves by playing pranks upon the maids, such as setting their flax or tow a-burning. In requital, the maids soused the men from the water-pails.

> Partly work and partly play
> You must on St. Distaff's Day.
> From the plough soon free the team,
> Then come home and fother them ;
> Bring in pails of water then,
> Let the maids bewash the men.
> Give St. Distaff all the right :
> Then bid Christmas sport good-night,
> And next morrow every one
> To his own vocation.

Doed-Koecks. (Dutch, meaning literally "dead-cakes.") A sort of cookies served in old New York to the attendants at funerals. Alice Morse Earle, in "Colonial Days in Old New York," cites an old receipt for their manufacture: "Fourteen pounds of flour, six pounds of sugar, five pounds of butter, one quart of water, two teaspoonfuls of pearlash, two teaspoonfuls of salt, one ounce of caraway seed. Cut in thick slices four inches in diameter." Sometimes the cakes were marked with the initials of the deceased. Friends and acquaintances frequently carried them home to retain them for years as mementos of the occasion. In Albany, a well-known bakery made a specialty of these cakes; but they were frequently of domestic manufacture. Families of extra good breeding sometimes sent a couple of the cakes, with a bottle of wine and a pair of gloves, as a summons to the funeral.

Burial-cakes were not unknown in England, and, indeed, they are still baked in Lincolnshire and Cumberland, to be served at funerals. So late as 1748 they are advertised by a Philadelphia baker.

Dog-Days. According to the ordinary computation, these begin on July 3 and continue to August 11. They derive their name from the heliacal rising and setting of Sirius, the dog-star, and properly should be made to conform thereto in the calendar.

The heliacal rising means the time when the star, after being practically in conjunction with the sun and invisible, emerges from the light so as to be visible in the morning before sunrise.

We must look to Egypt for the origin of the observance of these days. The rising of Tayout, Sihor, or Sirius coincided in ancient times with the summer solstice and the overflowing of the Nile ; and, as the latter was the source of the fertility of Egypt, the period was regarded as sacred, and the influence of the dog-star was deemed peculiarly auspicious. The superstitious feelings generated in Egypt with regard to the dog-days gradually spread throughout the world, and made themselves felt like many other ancient superstitions. But, while the rising of the dog-star was the harbinger of plenty and prosperity to the Egyptian, it was just the reverse to the Roman, who looked upon the dog-days as unfortunate and even prejudicial to life, coming as they did in the most unhealthy period of the year. The dog-days are still talked about, not only in Europe but in America ; but it does not require Gassendi's grave argument to convince people that the dog-star cannot possibly exercise any good or bad influence upon the earth. Popular prejudices linger a long time even after light has begun to break. To this day many sensible persons believe that the weather is affected by the moon, and that equinoctial storms attend the sun's imaginary passage across an imaginary line. Yet the fixed stars combined do affect the earth. They are original sources of light and heat ; their force is identical with that of the sun, and they daguerrotype themselves. Without the additional heat furnished by the fixed stars the sun would not render the earth habitable. Sirius is a sun superior to Sol himself ; but, individually, he can but give a name to the dog-days.

Doggett's Coat and Badge. A trophy annually rowed for, August 1, on the Thames between London Bridge and Chelsea, against the tide, by six young watermen whose apprenticeship comes to an end on that day. The trophy is provided out of a fund left for the purpose by Thomas Doggett (1670–1721), a famous comedian and zealous Whig, to commemorate " the happy accession to the throne" of George I. on August 1, 1714. The first race was run in 1716.

Colley Cibber describes Doggett as a most original actor. He borrowed from none, though he was imitated by many. He was, in stage parlance, an excellent dresser; the least article of whatever habit he wore seemed in some degree to speak and mark the special humor he represented at the time. He could with great exactness paint his face to resemble any age, from manhood to extreme senility, which led Sir Godfrey Kneller to say that Doggett excelled him in his own art; for he could only copy nature from the original before him, while the actor could vary his face at will and yet always preserve a true resemblance.

Doggett wrote one comedy, " The Country Wake," 1696, 4to, in which he played the leading character; and Steele. in the *Spectator*, No. 502, pays this high tribute to the excellence of the performance: " There is something so miraculously pleasant in Doggett's acting the awkward triumph and comic sorrow of *Hob*, in different circumstances, that I shall not be able to stay away whenever it is acted." And from the *Spectator*, No. 446, by Addison, we gather that Doggett excelled in grave or elderly men, knights and baronets, country squires, and justices of the quorum. Congreve was a great admirer of Doggett, and wrote for him the characters of Fondlewife in " The Old Bachelor" and Ben the Sailor in " Love for Love ;" the latter the earliest humorous and natural personation of the English sailor on our stage.

Doggett grew rich, and became a member of the Fishmongers' Company. He died September 22, 1721, at Eltham, in Kent, where his remains are interred. He had continued to give the coat-and-badge prize yearly ; and he bequeathed a sum of money, the interest of which was to be appropriated to the same purpose annually forever on August 1 ; and, with the minute attention to costume which distinguished him as an actor as well as in political principle, he directed that the color of the coat should be *orange*, and the White Horse of Hanover badge should be adhered to. The Fishmongers' Company have very properly taken charge of the bequest. They view the boats to be rowed a short time previous to August 1, when they hold a court to start the watermen ; and the coat and badge are presented to the winner after a banquet given at Fishmongers' Hall in the evening. The Company have also added four money prizes. Incidentally, by providing a well-equipped and fully provisioned steamer to follow the race, it keeps alive the interest of the public, or of a part of it, in the pleasantest possible manner, and each year the race makes an agreeable little stir in the thronged waterway from the Pool to Pimlico.

Thus has the old comedian had his memory kept green by the annual rowing for the Coat and Badge; the Hanoverian succession may have been commemorated by observances more pretentious than the river prize, but certainly not with more sincerity. In the water-side parishes the name of Doggett became a sort of household word; and some fifteen years after the player's decease there were written upon a window-pane in a house at Lambeth the following lines:

> Tom Doggett, the greatest sly droll in his parts,
> In acting was certain a master of arts;
> A monument left,—no herald is fuller,—
> His praise is sung yearly by many a sculler.
> Ten thousand years hence, if the world lasts so long,
> Tom Doggett will still be the theme of their song,
> When old Noll with great Louis and Bourbon are forgot,
> And when numberless kings in oblivion shall rot.

Dog-Whip Day. A curious custom of whipping dogs on certain anniversaries has existed in many parts of England. In York the occasion used to be St. Luke's Day (October 18), hence known as Dog-Whip Day, when school-boys took delight in thrashing all dogs that were found on the streets. Tradition explains that once in Catholic days a priest accidentally dropped the eucharist while celebrating mass on this festival. It was snapped up and eaten by a dog. The dog was promptly killed, and all its brethren were doomed to a periodical flagellation in memory of the sacrilege. The same custom also existed at Manchester on the first day of Acres Fair, which was held about the same time. In Hull the 10th of October was selected. Every boy procured a whip for the unlucky dogs found running in the streets. This custom dates back to the fairs which were formerly held on October 11 in Hull. The good monks in the monasteries were wont to provide liberally for the poor wayfarers who tramped it to the fair. On one occasion, on the eve of the fair, a dog found its way into the monasterial larder and made off with a good-sized joint. But he was intercepted by a crowd of suppliants at the gate, who beat him soundly and rescued the meat. Hence it grew to be the custom to beat off any dog who appeared in the streets on the day before the fair, and the custom survived among the boys of Hull until the advent of the new police.

Dog-Whippers. Church officials who in mediæval times went about during the time of public worship to drive out any stray dogs that might have happened within the church, and also incidentally to keep the congregation awake. The dog-whipper was especially useful in the rural districts, where the parish was extensive, and some of the worshippers from solitary farm-houses, living miles away from the church, would bring their dogs with them to the Sunday services. So long as the dog crouched under his master's seat he was allowed to remain undisturbed, but if he entered into any altercation with his fellows, the dog-whipper bore down upon the canine rioters and reduced them to silence. In city churches dogs were not allowed at all. The dog-whipper's usual instrument consisted of a long ash stick to which was fastened a thong of leather three feet long. But he often combined with this duty that of slug-gard-waking, and for that purpose was armed with a rousing-stick (*q. v.*). Not a few people in bygone ages felt it a duty to leave part of their worldly wealth to pay dog-whippers and slug-gard-wakers. At Claverley, Shropshire, one Richard Dovey, in the year 1659, left certain property near the church on condition that eight shillings per year be paid out of the rent to a poor man to awaken sleepers in the church and to drive out dogs. At Chislet, Kent, is a piece of land known as " Dog-Whipper's Marsh," from which a payment of ten shillings a year was to be devoted to paying for the services of keeping order in the church during the time of public worship. Other instances may be found in Andrews's " Curiosities of the Church," p. 173.

The Antiquary for August, 1886, has the following note : " Amongst the officials of Exeter Cathedral, until a few years ago, was the dog-whipper, whose duty was to keep dogs out of the building. On his death the office, having become a sinecure, was abolished. His widow has since been employed as care-taker at the prebendal house in the cloisters, but was a few days ago provided with one of the Dingham free cottages, of which charity the dean is a leading trustee. The office of dog-whipper formerly existed in many large churches, but the late function-ary at Exeter Cathedral was the last survivor of his order."

Dole. This word comes from the same root as the verb " to deal." and means a portion of money, food, or other things dealt out in charity. In early Christian times, as St. Chrysostom assures us, " doles were used at funerals to procure the rest of the soul of the deceased, that he might find his judge propitious." In time the amount and quantity of such doles came to be spe-cially described and appointed in the will of the dying person. At first these were distributed among the actual attendants at the funeral. Thus, in 1399, Eleanor, Duchess of Gloucester, ap-pointed that fifteen poor men should bear torches at her funeral, " each having a gown and hood lined with white, breeches of blue

cloth, shoes, and a shirt, and twenty pounds amongst them."
Again, in 1428, Thomas, Lord Poyning, prescribed that twelve
poor men should bear torches at his funeral, and each was to
receive a gown of black cloth and twelve pence in money; and
in 1423 twenty-eight poor men who attended the funeral of
Andrew, Lord Windsor, were rewarded with a frieze gown and
sixpence each.

Later doles were appointed to be sent to the homes of the
inhabitants of the village in which the donor had died. The
practice was sometimes to bequeath it by will, but, whether so
specified or not, the ceremony was seldom omitted. A small loaf
was sent to every person, without any distinction of age or
circumstances, and not to receive it was a mark of particular
disrespect.

The final evolution of this custom came in the custom of leaving money or lands the interest or rent of which was annually
to be devoted to some form of charity, usually, but not always,
at the tomb or in the church where the donor was buried. Thus,
William Robinson, who died at Hull on October 8, 1708, left
sufficient money to purchase a dozen loaves of bread, costing a
shilling each, to be given to twelve poor widows at his grave
every Christmas Day. In the churchyard of Kildale, Yorkshire,
is a tomb bearing the following inscription: "Here lyeth the
body of Joseph Dunn, who dyed ye 10th day of March 1716 aged
82 years. He left to ye poor of Kildale xx.s.; of Commondale
xx.s.; of Danby xx.s.; of Westerdale xx.s. to be paid upon his
gravestone by equal portions on ye 1st May and ye 11th November for ever."

Lenten doles were frequent in the Catholic past. John Thake,
in a will drawn up in 1537, left his property with the condition
that a barrel of white herrings and a cade of red herrings be
given to the poor of Clavering, Essex, to help them tide over the
austerities of the fast. Similar bequests were left by Richard
Stevenson, of Dronfield, Derbyshire, and David Salter, of Farnham
Royal, Bucks, the latter adding the annual sum of two shillings
to be laid out in the purchase of a pair of kid gloves for the parson on the first Sunday in Lent.

Every year in the crypt beneath St. Peter's Church, Walworth,
London, a Christmas dinner is given to three hundred poor people of the district. No one may be invited who is under sixty
years of age, and both sexes are eligible for the treat. The dark,
arched crypt of a London church is a curious place for a Christmas feast, but by means of holly, evergreen, bunting, and a good
supply of lamps the place is made to look pleasant and cheery.
Tables are arranged up and down under the arches, and on these
a plentiful supply of roast beef, plum pudding, and other Christ-

mas fare is placed. The dinner is unique in that it is cooked in the church.

There is an ancient payment made by the chamberlain of the corporation of Stafford of an annual sum of money, generally six shillings, at Christmas, for the purchasing of plums, to be distributed among the inhabitants of certain old houses in the liberty of Forebridge. The origin of this payment is ascribed by general reputation to the bounty of some individual who heard from some poor children a complaint on Christmas Day that they had no plums for a pudding; and it is reported that he counted the houses then in the place and made provision for the supply of a pound of plums for each house. The money received is laid out in plums, which are divided into equal quantities, and made up into parcels, one for each of the houses, fifteen or sixteen in number, entitled by the established usage to receive a portion, without reference to the circumstances of the inhabitants. (*Old English Customs and Charities,* p. 5.)

Peter Symonds, a London mercer, by his will, dated 1586, left a sum of money for a sermon to be preached on Good Friday in the church of All-Hallows, Lombard Street, at the close whereof sixty scholars of Christ's Hospital are to be presented with a bunch of raisins and a bright penny. He further left property for purchasing sixty loaves of bread to be given on Whitsunday to poor persons on his grave in Liverpool Street. The railway now covers the site of his tomb, and the bread is distributed in front of the school-room in Bishopsgate churchyard. Symonds likewise left several charities to his natal city of Winchester, and directed that " Leave was to be obtained from the bishop or the dean to place his picture in the body of the cathedral, with a small table before it, on which were to be placed twelve penny loaves of good wheaten bread, which immediately after the service were to be given to twelve poor persons at the will of the mayor, except on one Sunday, in each quarter, when the bishop or dean was to nominate the recipients."

A pilgrim's dole of bread and ale is offered to all wayfarers at the Hospital of St. Cross at Winchester. This is said to have been established by William of Wykeham. Emerson when in England paid a visit to the hospital, claimed and received the victuals, and cited the incident as a curious proof of the stability of English institutions.

The washing of Molly Grime was the object of a curious bequest whose conditions were observed until 1832. Molly Grime was the current name for a tomb in the parish church of Glentham, Lincolnshire. Seven old maids of the parish received annually a small sum for washing this tomb with water brought annually from Newell Well.

A notable charity left by Robert Dove in 1705, and still in the custody of the vicar of St. Sepulchre's Church in London, directed that a bell shall be tolled previous to every execution at Newgate.

The sexton appeared in Newgate at midnight on the eve of the execution to deliver the following cheerful and beautiful exhortation:

> Ye prisoners that are within
> For your wickedness and sin,
> Watch all and pray ; the hour is drawing near,
> That ye before the Almighty must appear.
> Examine well yourselves, in time repent,
> That you may not to eternal flames be sent.
> And when St. Sepulchre's bell to-morrow tolls,
> The Lord above have mercy on your souls.

Doubtless Mr. Dove was the author of this literary gem, and deemed that his legacy of fifty pounds bought a cheap immortality for them.

During the days of slavery doles were frequently left whose interest was to be expended in the redemption of English slaves. The Belton charity, and the Alicia, Duchess Dudley's bequest, are the most famous of them. Both are now diverted to other uses.

Money has frequently been left for the benefit of servant-maids, the interest to be thrown for with dice by a certain number of selected candidates. This was the method adopted at Guildford according to the will of John How, made in 1674, and at Reading, under the wills of John Kendrick and John Blagrave. The throwing of dice has, however, now been discontinued.

One of the strangest of strange bequests is that of John Knill, who died in 1811 and had a building called Knill's Mausoleum erected near St. Ives. He left sundry bequests of a useful nature, but ordered that every five years five pounds should be divided among the girls, not exceeding ten years of age, who should between ten and twelve o'clock in the forenoon of St. James's Day dance for a quarter of an hour at least on the ground near the mausoleum, and after the dance sing Psalm C. of the old version to "the fine old tune" to which the same was then sung in St. Ives Church. He provided also white ribbons for breast-knots for the girls and a cockade for the fiddler, and gave other evidences of vanity and eccentricity.

Charities have been founded and still exist for the preaching of sermons on the defeat of the Spanish Armada, the discovery of the Gunpowder Plot, the victories of Nelson at the Nile and

Trafalgar, the victories of Wellington, the commemoration of the accession of George IV., and other national events. There are also bequests for the encouragement of matrimony and horse racing, providing portions for poor maids, catechising children, buying Bibles, for repeating the Lord's Prayer, Apostles' Creed, and Ten Commandments, strewing the church with rushes, to awaken sleepers and whip dogs out of church, to dress graves with flowers, to plant rose-trees in churchyards, to promote peace and good will among neighbors, and to achieve many other desirable and excellent objects.

Figs and ale were provided for the poor scholars of the Free School in Giggleswick on St. Gregory's Day by the will of William Clapham in 1603, and at Harlington, Middlesex, the ringers received a leg of pork for ringing on November 5. White peas, rye, oatmeal, malt, barley, appear in other bequests. A small piece of land, called Petticoat Hole, at Stockton, Yorkshire, is held subject to an ancient custom of providing a petticoat for a poor woman of Stockton. In the same county there is an ancient payment of three shillings fourpence as the value of a pound of pepper due from the occupier of a farm at Yapham for taking care of the parson's horse, which he is bound to do whenever the parson goes there to do duty.

The most famous dole in the United States is that which is designated in the register of Trinity Church, New York, as the "Leake Dole of Bread." John Leake was a millionaire and philanthropist who in 1792 left one thousand pounds to Trinity Church "to be laid out, in the annual income, in sixpenny wheaten loaves of bread and distributed every Sabbath morning after divine service, to such poor as shall appear most deserving." The wish has been faithfully carried out, with one exception. About 1855 the distribution station was transferred from Trinity Church to the vestibule of old St. John's at 46 Varick Street, and the weekly day of distribution from Sunday to Saturday Every Saturday morning, between seven and eight o'clock, sixty-seven loaves are distributed.

Dolls, Festival of. (Japanese, *Hina-no-Sekku.*) A Japanese festival, specially dedicated to girls, and celebrated on the third day of the third month, which in our calendar may correspond with the middle or last day of April. As the sakura-trees, which are somewhat similar to our peach-trees, burst into bloom at this period, Europeans have named this the festival of peach-flowers. On this day girls and women array themselves in holiday attire. The mothers adorn the chamber of state with blossoming sakura boughs, and arrange therein an exhibition of all the dolls which their daughters have received. The children prepare a banquet for them, which is eaten by the grown folks in the evening after the dolls are supposed to have had a surfeit.

Dominic, St. (It. *Domenico;* Fr. *Dominique;* Sp. *Domingo*), founder of the order of Dominicans, or Preaching Friars. His festival is celebrated August 4. St. Dominic was born in 1170 at Calahorra in Old Castile. He was of noble parentage. At his baptism, legend says, a star descended from heaven to crown his brow. He studied at Valencia, and joined the order of St. Augustine at an early age. He went to France and preached against the Albigenses, making many converts. It was in consequence of the danger which seemed to threaten the Church that St. Dominic founded a religious order whose chief business it should be to preach the gospel, convert heretics, and defend and disseminate the faith. This is known as the order of Dominicans. In 1218 St. Dominic was commissioned by the Pope to reform the nunneries at Rome. He made a new rule, which was adopted, and from this originated the order of Dominican nuns. He died at Bologna in 1221, and was canonized by Gregory IX. in 1234. Legend says that his portrait was brought from heaven by St. Catherine and Mary Magdalene to a convent of Dominican nuns. His remains lie at Bologna in a splendid shrine in the church of his order. Legends attribute many miracles to him. It is related that once when at the monastery of St. Sabina in Rome there was not sufficient food. St. Dominic made all the brothers sit at the table, and blessed what food there was; immediately two angels appeared, bringing bread and wine. His attributes in art are a dog by his side, a star on or above his head, a lily in one hand, and a book in the other.

Doorga, Festival of. One of the greatest of Hindoo poojahs, or feasts. Doorga is the name under which the goddess Kali is worshipped as the female principle in creation. Her special festival in autumn consists of three days of great rejoicing wound up by one of ceremonial lamentation. All business is suspended throughout India, the houses of the wealthy Hindoos are at night splendidly illuminated and thrown open to visitors of all kinds, and numerous buffaloes, sheep, goats, and other animals are sacrificed in the temples; and after all the animals have been slain the multitude daub their bodies with the mud and gore, and indulge in bacchanalian and lascivious dances. For Doorga is then believed to be married, and these dances are meant to entice her to the propagation of children, who are to fight with and overcome the evil spirits who injure mankind. An image of the goddess made of straw and clay and profusely decorated is the centre of all the worship. It is supposed to be animated by the divine spirit until the fourth day, when nothing remains but to consign it to some sacred river or lake. Borne on the shoulders of stout porters, the idol is paraded through the streets with great pomp. The neighborhood resounds with music and singing. The acclamations of the worshippers are heard above the din. At length, arrived at the water, the image with all its trappings and tinsel ornaments is cast into the waters, the poor subsequently vying with one another in rifling the goddess of her decorations. On returning from the immersion the priest sprinkles the votaries with holy water and offers them his benedictions. They embrace with enthusiasm, and usually wind up the festivities with draughts of a solution of hemp leaves, which produces a slight intoxication.

Dough-Day. (From *dough*, a slang term for money.) A semi-humorous name applied in New York and other States of the Union to the Thursday, Friday, and Saturday of the second week before election. These were the days for the distribution of campaign funds from head-quarters to the workers in every county. Until that time the rural leaders lived and worked on expectations. On the appointed days they swarmed down from the counties, each with a gripsack, to carry back the cash for rewards to the faithful.

The word "money" has always been carefully avoided by shrewd leaders. It has a bad sound to the public, they say. Some unknown politician adopted the word "dough" as meaning campaign cash, and it stuck. From it grew the appellation of "bake-shop" for the treasurer's office, and "dough-day" for the welcome time of distribution.

The general adoption of the Australian or secret ballot system has done away with Dough-Day, because it has restricted the possibilities of bribery, to which purpose the "dough" was chiefly applied.

Dragon-Boats, Feast of. The story runs that in about the fourth century before Christ one Ku-Yuan, minister of the State of Tsu, was disgraced and deposed on account of his virtuous persistence in pointing out the evil doings of his master. Thereupon he published a poetical lament in which he reiterated his charges, and forthwith drowned himself in the Milo River, despite the efforts of an eye-witness, a fisherman, who launched his boat to save him. Ever since on the anniversary of the suicide the fisherman's attempt at rescue has been commemorated by a procession of dragon-boats over the inland waters of China. Each of these boats is owned by a clan, and the occasion has now become the excuse for a boatmen's holiday. The processions of the past have developed into races between rival clans. The boats, which are from fifty to a hundred feet long, are built more or less in the form of dragons. The rowers may number between fifty and sixty, and they are timed by a drummer in the centre, who beats his instrument faster and faster as the fun grows furious. In the bow stands a man who with one hand waves a flag while with the other he goes through the dumb show of casting rice upon the waves as a method of appeasing the evil spirits who would otherwise wreak their malevolence upon a drowning man.

FEAST OF DRAGON-BOATS.
(By a Chinese artist.)

Sometimes prizes are awarded to the winners; but the decisions of the judges in close cases often create more tumult and quarrelling than even those of the American baseball umpire.

Ducking-Stool. An instrument for the punishment of scolds and other unquiet women. It was much in use among the chivalric inhabitants of Great Britain, and occasionally in other countries of Europe, during the sixteenth and seventeenth centuries, and had a sporadic survival even into the nineteenth. There were two kinds of ducking-stools. One was merely a strong chair into which the offender was securely fastened and then exposed at her own door or in some public place, as the market or the town gates. The other and more popular was a chair affixed to the end of a plank or depending from a cross-beam, and was used for ducking the culprit in a contiguous pond or stream. The exact antiquity of this method of correction, as well as its origin, whether in England or on the Continent, is uncertain. But it undoubtedly dates from Anglo-Saxon times, as it is mentioned in the Doomsday Survey in the account of the city of Chester. So late as 1809 Jenny Pipes was carried about Leominster in a ducking-stool and then immersed in the Lug, near Kenwater Bridge, at the instance of the magistrates. Sarah Leeke of the same town would have been served similarly in 1817 if the river had not just then been too low, luckily for her. These are the latest instances on record. Though

usually consecrated to the correction of shrews, the ducking-
stool was occasionally occupied by brewers of undrinkable beer,
bakers of bad bread, and millers who pilfered wheat. That its
use sometimes proved fatal is not to be wondered at. In 1731
its remedial efficacy was tried, by order of the mayor of Nottingham, on a courtesan of that place, with the result that she
died soon afterwards. A chap-book of uncertain date tells its
story on the title-page: "Strange and Wonderful Relation of
the Old Woman who was drowned at Ratcliff Highway a fortnight ago."

There is an old tradition of a Gloucestershire scold whose
obstinate disposition defied the ducking-stool.

After the first sousing in the village horse-pond, her husband
exclaimed, "Molly! Molly! Woot thee promise I never to scold
at I again?"

As soon as Molly recovered her breath, she replied in a thun-
dering voice of moroseness, "No, I won't do nothing o' th'
zort!"

Molly had another souse, and the husband met with the same
acrimonious response to his anxious interrogations. The sousing was repeated; but Molly continued to be obdurate and con-
tumacious.

"You may drown I," shouted Molly, "but I wool never give in."

They did not run the risk of drowning Molly, but released
her, for the husband was convinced that she would "rather
drown than refuse to wag her red rag at un" whenever she felt
inclined to do so. It did not cure Molly. She became as great
a scold as ever she had been before her public sousing.

Some years after that critical punishment, the lord of the
manor met John at a court-leet, and inquired, " Well, John, how
does Molly get on now with her scolding?"

"Oh, squire, her be pretty nearly cured on't."

"Did the ducking-stool do that business?"

"Oh, no; I let her jaw on as long as her liked. I ged her no
back answers. I zot quiet and blowed me bacca, and her soon
dropt her scolding and be now as good a woman as they be
made."

Dumb-Cake. A cake famous in English folk-lore whose con-
stituents may vary with different seasons, so long as the essential of perfect silence during the making and the baking be maintained. Thus prepared, it is invaluable for matrimonial divina-
tions. Its greatest efficacy is on Halloween, St. John's Eve, and
St. Faith's Eve, but it also has been put to a successful test on the
eves of St. Agnes, St. Valentine, and St. Mark. The Halloween
cake is generally made of an eggshell-full of salt, an eggshell-

full of wheat meal, and an eggshell-full of barley meal. Any number of young women may join in the concoction. The meal must be made into a dough without the aid of spring water. Every one of the company rolls it up, and spreads it thin and broad, and then, at some distance from the others, marks the initials of her name with a large new pin towards the end of the cake. The cake is then set before the fire, and each person sits down in a chair as far distant from the fire as the room will admit, not speaking a single word all the time. This must be done soon after eleven at night; and between that and twelve o'clock each person must turn the cake once, and in a few minutes after the clock strikes twelve the husband of her who is first to be married will appear, and lay his hand on that part of the cake which is marked with her name. Silence must be strictly preserved throughout this operation.

The eating of the dumb-cake on St. Mark's Eve as practised in Northamptonshire is attended with all sorts of somnolent results. The number of the party never exceeds three; they meet in silence to make the cake, and as soon as the clock strikes twelve they each break a portion off to eat, and when done they walk up to bed backward without speaking a word, for if one speaks the spell is broken. Those that are to be married see the likeness of their sweethearts hurrying after them, as if wishing to catch them before they get into bed; but the maids being apprised of this beforehand (by the cautions of old women who have tried it) take care to unpin their clothes before they start, and are ready to slip into bed before they are caught by the pursuing shadow. If nothing is seen, the desired token may be a knocking at the doors, or a rustling in the house, as soon as they have retired. To be convinced that it comes from nothing else but the desired cause, they are always particular in turning out the cats and dogs before the ceremony begins. Those that are to die unmarried neither see nor hear anything; but they have terrible dreams, which are sure to be of newly-made graves, winding-sheets, and churchyards, and of rings that will fit no finger, or which, if they do, crumble into dust as soon as put on. There is another dumb ceremony, of eating the yolk of an egg in silence and then filling the shell with salt, when the sweetheart is sure to make his visit in some way or other before morning. (*Every Day Book*, vol. i. p. 523.)

On St. John's Eve, likewise, the party of girls must number three, and absolute silence must prevail through the whole of the operation.

> Two make it,
> Two bake it,
> Two break it.

At midnight each maid eats a portion of the cake and takes a portion in her hand, walks to bed backward, and sleeps with the dumb cake under her pillow. Of course she sees plainly in her dreams her future husband. On St. Faith's Day, though the number of participants is the same, the custom somewhat varies; the cake must be made of spring water, flour, sugar, and salt. The cake must be turned three times by each person during the baking. It is then divided into long strips and passed three times through a wedding-ring borrowed from a woman who has been married at least seven years. All this in silence; but as the husband-hunter eats her dumb-cake she says,—

> O good St. Faith, be kind to-night
> And bring to me my heart's delight,
> Let me my future husband view,
> And be my vision chaste and true.

Then all three maids get into bed together, with the wedding-ring tied to the head of the bed. Three widows can also try this charm.

In the "Journal of the Young Lady of Virginia" we find the gay group of young Southern beauties, with much fear and trembling, eating the "dum-cake" in Mr. Washington's house.

Dunmow Flitch. At the church of Dunmow, in Essex County, England, a flitch of bacon used to be given to any married couple who after a twelvemonth of matrimony would come forward and make oath that during that time they had lived in perfect harmony and fidelity. The origin of the custom is lost in the mists of antiquity. By some it is dubiously referred to Robert Fitzwalter, a favorite of King John, who revived the Dunmow Priory at the beginning of the thirteenth century; but it seems quite as likely that the good fathers themselves, rejoicing in their celibacy, instituted the custom as a jest upon their less fortunate fellows. The earliest recorded case of the awarding of the flitch is in 1445, when Richard Wright, of Bradbury, Norfolk, a laborer, claimed and obtained it. But that there had been earlier cases of similar success is clearly evidenced by many references in early English literature, the first being in the "Vision of Piers Plowman," about 1362.

The passage, translated from its primitive tongue, reads,—

> Many a couple since the Pestilence
> Have plighted them together;
> The fruit that they bring forth
> Is foul words,
> In jealousy without happiness,
> And quarrelling in bed;

> They have no children but strife,
> And slapping between them;
> And though they go to Dunmow
> (Unless the devil help!)
> To follow after the Flitch,
> They never obtain it;
> And unless they both are perjured,
> They lose the Bacon.

Though it is clear from this that both husband and wife had to take the oath, antiquaries hold that during the fifteenth and sixteenth centuries it became customary to present the flitch to the husband alone, as the reward of patience. They cite in evidence Chaucer's " Wife of Bath," who relates how she treated her husbands, and says,—

> The bacoun was not fet for hem, I trowe,
> That som men han in Essex at Dunmowe.

But by the end of the sixteenth century the original custom had re-established itself, with the following additional cere-monies. A jury of six bachelors and six maidens was empan-elled. Before them came the competing couple, who were forced to kneel on two sharp-pointed stones and assent to this metrical oath :

> You shall swear by custom of confession
> That you ne'er made nuptial transgression ;
> Nor since you were married man and wife,
> By household brawls or contentious strife,
> Or otherwise at bed or at board
> Offended each other in deed or in word,
> Or in a twelvemonth and a day
> Repented not in thought any way,
> Or since the parish clerk said amen
> Wished yourselves unmarried again,
> But continued true in thought and desire
> As when you joined hands in the quire.

The jury was not satisfied with the mere taking of the oath. Witnesses were questioned and tests applied. Few indeed went scathless through the ordeal.

An amusing incident is related of a couple who were on the very point of receiving the prize, when, as a final test, the flitch was suspended at the top of a greased pole, and the happy hus-band was bidden by the jury to climb there and get it. The worthy fellow hesitated, and then frankly explained that he had his best clothes on, which if he should spoil, his wife would scold him soundly. He was told to be off, as a fraud, matri-monial and porcine.

If the couple proved successful, the flitch was finally awarded with these words :

23

> Since to these conditions without any fear
> Of your own accord you do freely declare,
> A whole flitch of bacon you shall receive,
> And bear it hence with love and good leave:
> For this is our custom at Dunmow, well known,
> Though the pleasure is ours, the bacon's your own.

Thrifty couples took full advantage of the freedom conveyed in the latter clause, by selling slices of the bacon at good prices to the crowd of merrymakers present.

The custom seems to have lapsed and been revived from time to time at considerable intervals until 1762, when John and Susan Gilder, having applied for the flitch, found admission refused. Next year the lord of the manor removed the symbolical "swearing stones" upon which the couple knelt to take the oath.

Nothing more was heard of the flitch till February 11, 1841, when it was rumored that the lord of the manor offered the flitch to the queen and prince consort, who had then been married a year and a day. It is said to have been declined. In 1851, Mr. and Mrs. Hurrell having applied, the lord of the manor pleaded desuetude, and the villagers supplied the flitch. This awakened the interest, amid which Ainsworth's novel "The Flitch of Bacon" appeared, which book led to a meeting at Dunmow and a correspondence with the novelist, who consented to co-operate in a formal revival of the custom and to pay for the flitch on the occasion. The result was the celebrated festival of July 19, 1855. But the popular interest could not be re-awakened, and though in 1857, in 1876, in 1877, and in 1880 the flitch was again contested for, the contemporary reports tell us that "the attendance was poor and the true joyous spirit was absent."

The custom of awarding a prize of this sort for wedded faithfulness is not peculiar to Dunmow. For a century the abbots of St. Meleine, in Bretagne, gave a like trophy. The idea was known in Vienna, where, beneath the Red Tower, a flitch of bacon used to hang, beneath which were the following lines:

> Befind' sich irgend hir ein Mann
> Der mit den Wahrheit sprecken kann,
> Dass ihm sine Heurath nischt gerowe,
> Und fürcht' sich nischt vor sine Frowe,
> Der mag desen Backen herunter howe.

> (" Is there to be found a married man
> That in verity declare can
> That his marriage him doth not rue,
> That he has no fear of his wife for a shrew,
> He may this bacon for himself down hew.")

The manor of Whichmore, in Stafford, was in the time of Edward III. granted by the Earls of Lancaster to Sir Philip de Somerville on condition that he should maintain and sustain one bacon flyke to be given to every man or woman after the day and year of their marriage were past who could take this oath: "Hear ye, Sir Philip de Somerville, Lord of Whichmore, mayntener and gyver of this baconne, that I, A, sithe I wedded B, my wyfe, and sythe I hadd hyr in my keepyng and at my wylle by a yere and a day after our marryage, I wo'd not haue chaunged for none other, farer ne fowler, rycher ne pourer, ne for none other descended of greater lyneage, slepyng ne wekyng, at noo tyme. And yf the said B were sole, and I sole, I wolde take hyr to be my wyfe before all the wymen in the worlde, of what condicions soever they be, goode or evylle, so helpe me God and his sayntis, and thys fleshe and all fleshes." This was for a tenure, and in remembrance of it a piece of wood in the form of a flitch of bacon hangs in the new mansion, the estate being no longer in possession of the Somervilles. (See also Bacon.)

Dusserah Festival. One of the greatest annual events among the Hindoos, celebrated in honor of the goddess Kali. The sacrifice of a bullock is the chief feature. The Brahmin priests begin by burning incense and making offerings to the goddess. The victim is then led to the stake, a man throwing water from a jar on its neck until it is tied up and held in position for the death-stroke. Two men pull the beast forward by ropes attached to the horns, and two others behind pull in the opposite direction with ropes which are passed round the neck. A Goorkha then advances with a razor-edged "kookrie" and severs the head at a blow. The sacrifice is completed by the burning of incense.

Duwalee Festival. A Hindoo celebration marking the close of the mercantile year, when those engaged in commerce carefully cleanse and decorate the exteriors of their houses, and at night there is a universal illumination. "The city then appears like a creation of the fire-king, the view from the water affording the most superb and remarkable spectacle imaginable. The outlines of the whole city are marked in streams of fire; and the coruscations of light shoot up into the dark-blue sky above, and tremble in long undulations on the rippling waves below."

E.

Easter. The Sunday on which Christian Churches commemorate the resurrection of Christ. The name, which is in use only among the English- and German-speaking peoples, is derived, in all probability, from that of a goddess of the heathen Saxons, Ostara, Osterr, or Eastre. She was the personification of the East, of the morning, of the spring. The month of April was dedicated to her, and was called *Eastermonath* among the Saxons and Angles, and is still known in Germany as *Ostermonat*. Her worship struck deep root in Northern Germany, was carried to England by the Saxons, and still survives in some obscure customs in feasts to celebrate the return of the spring.

Non-Teutonic nations cling to the Semitic word derived from the Aramaic word *pesach*, "to pass by," which has been translated into English as Passover (*q. v.*). Thus the Spanish say *Pascua*, the French *Pâques*, and the Italians *Pasqua*. Nevertheless the Scandinavians say *Paaske*, and the Dutch *Paasch*. In England the Semitic form survives in many terms applicable to the season, as pass-flower, paschal lamb or pass-lamb, and pasch, pace, or pase eggs. (See PASCH EGG.) These terms remind us that our Christian festival is the successor to the Jewish Passover, while the word Easter carries us back through the Saxons to the more ancient celebrations which from the earliest ages of man have expressed the universal outburst of rejoicing over the reawakening of nature after the long sleep of winter.

In the early Church Easter was identical in date with the Passover, as in fact the two festivals are identical in their root. But the opposition of the Christians to the Jews led to a change. The records of the Nicæan Council of A.D. 325 show that this opposition was most acute. The very call for the Council breathed hostility against the Jews and those Christians who celebrated Easter on the day on which the Jews kept passover. These Christians were called Quartodecimanians, because they celebrated Easter on the 14th day of Nisan, the first month of the Jewish year. But the opposition to the Quartodecimanians of Asia was more zealous than intelligent; for the artificial day chosen for Easter fell occasionally, as in 1805 and in 1825, on the 14th day of the Jewish Nisan, and the Christian Fathers, while bitterly opposed to the Jews, adopted without hesitation the Jewish mode of reckoning time by lunations. To make the matter worse, these lunations do not tally with the facts of astronomy. The result is that Easter calculations are so extraordinarily difficult as to lead to occasional mistakes, like that of 1818, when Easter was kept on the wrong day.

It was determined, in the first place, that Easter must invariably fall on the first Sunday after the fourteenth day of the moon
that happens to be reigning at the time of the vernal equinox.
Then it was declared that the date of the equinox should be arbitrarily made March 21, although the equinox really comes sometimes a little earlier or a little later than the 21st. For example,
suppose the equinox moon is just fourteen days old on the 21st
of March and that this day falls on Saturday; then the next day,
Sunday, would fill the condition noted above, and consequently
be Easter. The festival may thus be as early as March 22 or as
late as April 25. In 1761 and 1818, Easter fell on March 22, but
neither in this nor in the following century will this be the case.
In 1913, however, it will fall on March 23, as it did in 1845 and
1856. The latest Easters in this century and the twentieth are
April 25, in 1886 and 1943. When the right day for Easter is
finally found, it determines a long series of ecclesiastical days,
from Ash Wednesday to Trinity Sunday.

The Christian Easter was originally a sort of thanksgiving
observance lasting eight days. This conformed somewhat to
the length of time devoted by pagans to their spring festivities,
and approached the duration of the Jewish paschal observances.
The eight-day period was afterwards cut down to three days, after
that to two, and finally it became, as we have it now, a single
day commemorative of the resurrection.

It was the invariable policy of the early Church to give a
Christian significance to such of the extant pagan ceremonies as
could not be rooted out. In the case of Easter the conversion
was peculiarly easy. Joy at the rising of the natural sun, and
at the awakening of nature from the death of winter, became
joy at the rising of the Sun of righteousness, at the resurrection of Christ from the grave. Some of the pagan observances
which took place about the 1st of May were also shifted to correspond with the celebration of Easter. Many new features were
added. It was a time of exuberant joy. Gregory of Nyssa
draws a vivid picture of the joyous crowds who, by their dress
(a feature still preserved) and their devout attendance at church,
sought to do honor to the festival. All labor ceased, all trades
were suspended. It was a favorite time for baptism, the law
courts were closed, alms were given to the poor, slaves were
freed. Easter Sunday became known as *Dominica gaudii* ("Sunday of joy"). In the reaction from the austerities of Lent,
people gave themselves up to enjoyment, popular sports, dances,
and farcical entertainments. In some places the clergy, to increase the mirth, recited from the pulpit humorous stories and
legends for the purpose of exciting the *risus Paschalis*, or "Easter
smile." Monks and clerics used to have regular games of ball in

church, and in England the winners received tansy cakes as prizes. Feasts were served in churches, till the consequent excesses and disorders became past endurance. People exchanged the Easter kiss and the salutation "Christ is risen," to which the reply was made, "He is risen indeed,"—a custom kept up to this day in some parts of the world.

In England there was a custom in the thirteenth century of seizing all ecclesiastics who walked abroad between Easter and Pentecost (because the apostles were seized by the Jews after Christ's Passion) and making them purchase their liberty by money.

One of the oldest and most wide-spread of Easter superstitions is that which makes the sun participate in the general felicity by dancing in the heavens. Sir John Suckling wrote, in "The Bride,"—

> But, oh, she dances such a way,
> No sun upon an Easter Day
> Is half so fine a sight.

The question whether the sun really did dance was solemnly discussed and combated by grave old scholars, who took the trouble to demonstrate, by irrefutable arguments and at great length, that while the sun might sometimes shine more brightly on Easter morning than on another, it was simply by accident, and that in any event there was no dancing and could be none. " In some parts of England they call it the lamb playing," wrote one, " which they look for, as soon as the sun rises, in some clear spring or water, and is nothing but the pretty reflection it makes from the water, which they may find at any time, if the sun rise clear and they themselves early and unprejudiced with fancy." The question was definitively settled by the sun himself, thus, in doggerel, in "The British Apollo," in 1708 :

> Q.— Old wives, Phœbus, say
> That on Easter Day
> To the music o' th' spheres you do caper ;
> If the fact, sir, be true.
> Pray let's the cause know,
> When you have any room in your paper.

> A.— The old wives get merry
> With spiced ale and sherry
> On Easter, which makes them romance ;
> And whilst in a rout
> Their brains whirl about,
> They fancy we caper and dance.

This idea of the sun dancing on Easter Day may easily be traced back to heathen customs, when the spectators themselves danced at a festival in honor of the sun, after the vernal equinox.

Devonshire maidens still get up early on Easter morning to see not only the dancing sun, but also a lamb and a flag in the centre of its disk.

In Scotland the sun was even more active, for there it was expected to whirl round like a mill-wheel and give three leaps. One way of looking at the sun's unusual feat was to watch for its reflection in a pond or a pail of water, when any movement on the surface would materially strengthen the illusion. In a similar way, the credulous would be deceived by the morning vapor, through which the rising sun would appear to flicker.

Other superstitions have clustered round this festival, some of which still linger on. It is considered by many unlucky to omit wearing new clothes on Easter Day, and in East Yorkshire young people go to the nearest market town to buy some new article of dress or personal ornament, as otherwise they believe that birds—notably rooks or "crakes"—will spoil their clothes. To see a lamb on first looking out of the window on Easter morning is a good omen, especially if its head be turned in the direction of the house; but it is not so fortunate if it be lying down or looking the other way. It must be remembered, however, that to meet a lamb at any time is lucky, as, according to the popular notion, the devil can take any other form than that of a lamb or a dove.

If the wind is in the east on Easter Day, it is regarded in some places as a wise plan to draw water and wash in it, as by this means one will avoid the various ill effects from the east wind throughout the remaining months of the year. The same superstition exists on the Continent. Thus, in the neighborhood of Mecklenburg, on Easter morning the maid-servants fetch Easter water, or on the evening preceding spread out linen clothes in the garden, and in the morning wash themselves with the dew, rain, or snow that may have fallen on them. This is said to be a preservative against illness for the whole year. In Sachsenburg the peasants ride their horses into the water to ward off sickness from them. The Easter water, how-ever, has virtue only when while drawing it the wind is due east. Much importance is attached to rain falling on Easter Day, for, according to an old proverb,—

> A good deal of rain on Easter Day
> Gives a crop of good grass, but little good hay.

Again, if the sun shines on Easter morning it will, we are told, shine on Whitsunday. A Sussex piece of weather-lore goes further, and tells us that if the sun shines on Easter Day it will shine a little every day all the year round; while there is a corresponding notion that if it rains it will rain a little, if only a few drops, every day during the ensuing year.

A curious custom, called "sugar-cupping," was formerly kept up on Easter Day at the Dripping Torr, near Tideswell, in Derbyshire. The young people assembled at the Torr, each provided with a cup and a small quantity of sugar or honey, and, having caught the required supply of water, they mixed the sugar with it, and then drank it, meantime repeating a doggerel verse.

A singular ceremony formerly prevailed at Lostwithiel, in Cornwall, on Easter Day. The freeholders of the town and manor having met together, either in person or their deputies, one among them, each in his turn, gayly attired, with a sceptre in his hand, a crown on his head, and a sword borne before him, and attended by all the rest on horseback, rode through the principal streets in solemn state to the church. At the church-yard the officiating minister met him, and then conducted him to the church to hear divine service. On leaving the church he repaired, with the same pomp and retinue, to a house previously prepared for his reception. Here a feast, suited to the dignity he had assumed, awaited him and his suite, at the conclusion of which the prince was disrobed, and so the ceremony ended. This custom, it is said, originated in the actual appearance of the prince, who resided at Restormel Castle, in former ages. On the removal of royalty this mimic grandeur stepped forth as its shadowy representative, and continued for many generations as a memorial to posterity of the princely magnificence with which Lostwithiel had formerly been honored.

Such is the explanation given by Hitchens in his "History of Cornwall" (1824, vol. i. p. **717**). But in truth the appearance of a symbolical Easter King was frequent at this season in continental Europe. There is in confirmation the old story of Charles V., who while riding through a village in his Spanish kingdom was met by a peasant attired in the fantastic robes of the Paschal monarch, with a tin crown upon his head and a spit for a truncheon. Not knowing who the rider was, the peasant commanded him to doff his hat. "My good friend," responded the Emperor, as he complied with the request, "I wish you joy in your new office : you will find it a troublesome one, I can assure you."

Until recently an immemorial custom called "chipping the block" was observed at University College, Oxford. A block in the form of a long wooden pole, decorated with flowers and ever-greens, was placed outside the door of the hall, leaning against the wall of the buttery opposite. After dinner on Easter Day the college cook and his attendant, dressed in white paper caps and white jackets, took their stand on either side of the block, each bearing a pewter dish, one supporting a blunt chopping-axe from the kitchen, the other in readiness for the fees expected on the occasion. As the members of the college came out of the hall, each took the axe and struck the block with it, and then placed in the pewter dish the usual fee to the cook. According to one tradition mentioned by Mr. Henderson, any one who could chop the block in two was entitled to lay claim to all the college estates.

In Rome Easter Sunday is celebrated with elaborate ceremonies; though since the fall of the temporal power these have been shorn of much of their magnificence. The day is ushered in by the firing of cannon from the castle of St. Angelo, and about seven o'clock carriages with ladies and gentlemen are beginning to pour towards St. Peter's. That magnificent basilica is richly decorated for the occasion, the altars are freshly ornamented, and the lights around the tomb and figure of St. Peter are blazing after their temporary extinction on Good Friday. Formerly the Pope officiated this day at mass in St. Peter's. From a hall in an adjoining palace of the Vatican he was borne into the church. Seated in his Sedia Gestatoria, his vestments blazed with gold; on his head he wore the tiara, a tall round gilded cap representing a triple crown, understood to signify spiritual power, temporal power, and the union of both. Beside him were borne the *flabelli*, or large fans, composed of ostrich feathers, in which were set the eye-like parts of peacocks' feathers, to signify the eyes or vigilance of the Church. Over him was carried a silk canopy richly fringed. Thus he was escorted to his throne, which stands far back in the distance behind the altar. Lining the avenue from it to the shrine of the apostles stood the Noble Guards in full uniform, a living hedge of athletic men. The tribunes built up in the transepts contained all those official persons whose duty it was to be present on this occasion, and all wore uniform. The ladies were in black, and their long lace veils, which were *de rigueur* in their costume for the ceremonies, lent a softening tone to the bright splendor of the uniforms and colored robes of office. The crown of the whole great pageant, however, was the unrivalled Papal choir, which now outdid itself in its magnificently calm rendering of the solemn church chant. At the elevation of the sacred host, the word of command was rung out in a clarion-like voice by one of the officers, and the military in the body of the church all presented arms as they suddenly dropped on one knee. The Noble Guards drew their swords and lifted them up in a bristling hedge of steel, while they also were on their knees ; and from the lofty tribune under the dome issued the sound of the silver trumpets, the only instrumental music allowed during the Papal functions. Again at the moment of the communion the same evolutions were gone through, save that the trumpets no longer sounded, and that in perfect silence a cardinal bore the consecrated host to the foot of the Papal throne, where the Pontiff knelt to receive it.

No sooner was the mass over than the Pope was with the same ceremony and to the sound of music borne back through the crowded church to the balcony over the central doorway. There, rising from his chair of state and turning first to the east and then to the west, he pronounced a benediction, with indulgence and absolution. The crowd was most dense immediately under the balcony at which the Pope appeared, for there papers were thrown down containing a copy of the prayers that had been uttered, and ordinarily there was a scramble to catch them.

"At night," says a spectator of the ancient glories, "civic festivities follow the religious pageant of the morning. St. Peter's is illuminated by means of hundreds of thousands of tiny oil lamps, whose white gleam has given the name of 'silver illumination' to this part of the show. These lamps are placed at short intervals along every prominent line and curve of the colossal building, and produce an effect as of a fairy architect's plan. After about half an hour, a gun suddenly booms from the castle of St. Angelo, and the 'silver' is changed almost instantaneously to a 'golden' illumination. This magical effect is produced by the sudden kindling of large hanging pans full of resinous matter, also disposed along the architectural lines and curves of the basilica, and completely outshining in their strong, fiery glare the more delicate radiance of the little lamps. One man has no more than two or three of these pans to attend to, so that it is easy for him to fire them all almost simultaneously. The numberless dark figures moving aloft with cat-like agility among the massive shadows of the basilica are plainly visible to those stationed in the balconies of the piazza ; but a far more satisfactory way of seeing the illumination is to go to the Monte Pincio, at the opposite side of the town ; the great dome of fire stands out in weird magnificence against the sky, and the sudden change, of which no human agency can be seen at that distance, has in consequence a proportionately enhanced effect upon the imagination."

All this is now changed. It is the cardinal arch-priest who says mass in St. Peter's. The Pope himself officiates at a private mass in the Consistory within the Vatican palace. It needs what in Yankee is called "a pull" to obtain an invitation. The costume required is full dress for men spectators and a Spanish mantilla thrown over the dress for women. The ceremony begins at eight o'clock. Two prelates assist the Pope.

A ceremony which survives in many of the Spanish-American countries is thus described by a traveller who witnessed it in Cuba:

"At the great cathedral was drawn up an escort of troops. Soon comes forth a full-sized wax figure of the Saviour, with open wounds, standing upon a platform or pedestal, highly decorated, and borne upon the heads of men who are shielded from the public gaze by a deep curtain, reaching nearly to the ground. With music playing, the procession, with priests, crosses, candles, etc., moved slowly along the street.

"Soon appeared, coming in an opposite direction, a full-sized figure of Mary Magdalene, borne on the shoulders of four priests. It approaches the image of the Saviour, until a seeming recognition takes place, when it turns suddenly round, and, by the peculiar running motion of the priests, the image appears to run very hard up the street, with her long curls shaking in wild confusion. She meets the image of the Virgin Mary, and tells her of the resurrection, when they both return down the street, the Virgin Mary being in advance.

"When the Virgin Mary arrives near the Saviour, by the sudden motion of the forward bearers each figure is made to bow to the other several times, and they all proceed onward to the church from which the two Marys were taken. Both images of the Marys are dressed very gaudily. The dress of the Virgin Mary was of yellow satin, trimmed with gold, and she had a crown upon her head. Mary Magdalene was dressed in blue.

"After entering the church, the troops fired a *feu-de-joie*, and slowly the crowd of wondering spectators dispersed."

Midnight mass is said in churches of the Greek faith. A contributor to the *National Review* thus describes the ceremony as he witnessed it in the cathedral at Tiflis:

"The service commences in the dull gloom, for, with the exception of a few lights upon and in the vicinity of the altar, the church is unlit. But this gloom tends to heighten the effect of the group of richly-robed and mitred priests that throng the steps, chanting in turn with the choir of unaccompanied boys' and men's voices the music of the service. In contrast to the group about the altar steps was the dark heaving crowd, half hidden in the filmy clouds of the incense and the dusk of the building. At length, as midnight approached, the priests and choir filed down the church and left the building by the main entrance, one or two alone remaining within. Then, as a rocket without gave the sign of midnight, a loud knocking commenced at the door, which was repeated several times. On the gate being opened, the priests and choir hurried in, crying out again and again, 'Christ is risen! Christ is risen!' Each bore in his hand a lighted taper, from which the nearer members of the crowd lit their own, passing the flame from candle to candle, for every one in the building bore a taper. It took but a minute to change the entire scene, and as the priests made their way to the altar, swinging their censers as they went, the gloom of the church disappeared, and the building was lit by thousands upon thousands of candles; where, before, the dusk had prevented one seeing either the church or the crowd, every picture and detail of the decoration of the building and every figure in it became distinct. The seething mass of humanity took form and shape, and where, before, one recognized only dark figures in an incense-laden twilight, one recognized now the officers of the government, in uniforms bespangled with orders, accompanied by their wives and daughters."

The celebration of Easter in the United States is now an established practice. New England was the last section to adopt a festival upon which the settlers of Puritan Massachusetts looked with particular abhorrence. Some of the States, like Virginia and Louisiana, have always kept Easter after a fashion, and so have certain denominations, like the Catholics, the Anglicans, and the Lutherans. But fifty years ago these denominations were neither strong nor popular in this country, and the influence of Virginia and Louisiana upon the manners of the American people was not great.

It is impossible to name the exact time when Easter began to commend itself to many people and many Churches that had looked upon the Christian festival as a Catholic or quasi-Catholic error. It appears that about the time of the war the Presbyterians began to preach Easter sermons and to adorn their churches with Easter flowers. These churches seem to have followed the example set to them by their sister societies. It had been customary to embellish the sanctuary with flowers, and the war period made it natural for many people to remember with special fervor the Christian lesson of the resurrection. The movement thus begun was aided by the season in which the older Churches celebrated the resurrection of Christ, while all nature proclaimed the revival of spring, its flowers and its hopes. Even now, however, it is in the cities rather than in the country that Easter is most generally celebrated.

By a singular coincidence, polite society and the Churches have entered upon a quiet agreement to make Easter a marked day. When Lent begins, society gives up dancing-parties, and all ladies, who choose, may rest from their social labors. This period of comparative quiet ends on Easter Day. On that day the spring season of society begins, and young women appear for the first time in their spring bonnets. Milliners, caterers, dress-makers, and flower-dealers understand this law of the social world. Latterly the manufacturers and dealers in Easter cards have developed a taste both novel and popular. Indeed, American Easter cards have fairly outstripped the English article ; and the American consumption of these pretty commodities exceeds that of England.

Easter Hare. In Germany the Easter hare is almost as im-portant a figure in nursery lore as the Christmas St. Nicholas. Children are taught to believe that if they are good and mind their parents and are truthful and kind to one another, a white hare will steal into the house on Easter Eve, when everybody is asleep, and secrete any number of beautifully colored eggs in odd corners for the good little children.

When the housewife comes in from her marketing on the fateful evening, the " kinderkins" do not see the heaps of eggs in the basket. They can think of nothing but the white hare. Has Maya been naughty ? Has Hans been good ? Those are the questions that agitate their little minds all through the even-ing meal.

Soon afterwards they are tucked nicely in bed, but not to sleep. They are watching for the white hare. Meanwhile the house-wife is in the kitchen boiling the eggs in many gay patterns of cheap print cloth, which ultimately leaves them decked in all the hues of the rainbow. There are blue eggs, green eggs, and red eggs, and eggs that are all three colors, and more besides.

When the eggs are all nicely done the parents take them and hide them away in various corners where they cannot easily be found. Then perhaps the chuckling couple go around the corner to a beer-saloon to enjoy the music and drink beer. Sometimes in the midst of the music and the clink of mugs they think of the kinderkins at home listening for the white hare, and they laugh and are happy.

It is almost dawn before the children fall asleep. When they awake it is broad daylight and Easter morning. How about the white hare? Has anybody seen it ? The mother is certain she heard a noise. The father is not quite sure whether they have been good enough or not. When they are dressed he leads them all over the house in search of the eggs left by the white hare. They are nowhere to be found. Alas ! they have been bad chil-dren. Just then, over in a dark corner, the father spies a gor-geous red egg. How the children shout as they carry the prize into the light. What a marvellous egg it is ! Then more and more are found, until there can be no possible doubt that the wonderful white hare thinks them very good children.

The connection between Easter and the hare springs from the latter's connection with the moon. Easter, inasmuch as its date depends upon the moon, is in a sense a lunar holiday. Now, from very ancient times the hare has been a symbol for the moon. There are many reasons for this. A few only need be given. The hare is a nocturnal animal, and comes out at night to feed. The female carries her young for a month, thus representing the lunar cycle. Both hare and moon were thought to have the power of changing their sex. The new moon was masculine, the waning moon feminine. The superstition about the hare is mentioned by Pliny, Archelaus, and others. It is crystallized in the lines of Beaumont and Fletcher (" Faithless Shepherdess," Act III.),—

> Hares that yearly sexes change,
> Proteus, altering oft and strange,
> Hecate with shapes three,
> Let this maiden changed be.

Here again we have the hare in close connection with Hecate, or the moon.

But a more important reason for the identification of the hare with the moon lay in the fact that its young are born with their eyes open, unlike rabbits, which are born blind. The name of the hare in Egyptian was *un*, which means "open," "to open," " the opener." Now, the moon was the open-eyed watcher of the skies at night, and the hare, born with open eyes, was fabled never to close them ; hence the old Latin expression *somnus leporinus* and the identification of the open-eyed hare with the full moon. The old principle of cure by sympathies led to the prescription in the early English folk-lore of the brains and eyes of the hare as a cure for somnolency.

The Egyptian *un* meant not only "hare" and "open," but " period," and for this reason the hare became the type of periodicity, both human and lunar, and in the character of opener was associated with the opening of the new year at Easter, as well as with the beginning of a new life in the youth and maiden. Hence the hare became connected in the popular mind with the paschal eggs, broken to signify the opening of the year.

Even in America we may see in the confectioners' windows the hare (or rather a rabbit) wheeling his barrow full of eggs or drawing one large one as a sort of triumphal chariot. In some parts of Europe the Easter eggs are made up into cakes in the shape of hares, and the little children are told that babies are found in the form of hares.

Among English popular customs celebrating Easter are many traces of the hare myth. In Warwickshire, at Coleshill, if the young men of the parish can catch a hare and bring it to the parson before ten o'clock in the morning of Easter Monday (the moon-day), he is bound to give them a calf's head, one hundred eggs, and a groat, the calf's head being probably a survival of the worship of Baal, or the sun, as the Golden Calf.

The Leicester custom of hunting the hare is also in point. On Easter Monday the mayor and the city officials, in their scarlet robes, used to go to Black-Annis' Bower Close for the ostensible purpose of hunting a hare. But, as there were no hares to be hunted at this season, a feeble compromise was effected by trailing a dead cat soaked in anise-seed water before a pack of hounds, amid the shouts of the spectators. Although this form of drag-hunting has long been discontinued, an annual fair held in the neighborhood preserved until recently many traces of the Leicester Hare Hunt.

Most curious of all is the Hallaton Hare Scramble and Bottle-Kicking which occurs annually on Easter Monday. C. J. Billson, in "County Folk-Lore, Leicestershire and Rutland" (1895), tells us that "at a remote period," unidentifiable to modern antiquaries, a piece of land was bequeathed to the rector, conditionally that he provided annually two hare pies, a quantity of ale, and two dozen penny loaves, to be scrambled for on each succeeding Easter Monday at the rising ground called Hare-Pie Bank, about a quarter of a mile south of the village of Hallaton. Of course, hares being out of season at this time of the year, pies of mutton, veal, and bacon are substituted. A benevolent rector of the last century made an effort to have the funds applied to a better use; but the village wags were equal to the occasion, and raised the cry, and chalked on his walls and door, as well as on the church, "No pie, no parson, and a job for the glazier." Other subsequent efforts alike failed. "Easter Monday at Hallaton is the great carnival of the year. The two benefit societies hold their anniversary at the 'Royal Oak' and the 'Fox Inn,' and bands accompany the processions to the parish church, where the 'club sermon' is preached. After dinner at the inns, a deputation is sent to the rectory for the 'pies and beer,' and then the procession is formed in the following order:

"Two men abreast, carrying two sacks with the pies cut up.

"Three men abreast, carrying aloft a bottle each; two of these are filled with beer; they are ordinary field wood bottles, but without the usual mouth, iron-hooped all over, with a hole left for drinking from; the third is a dummy. Occasionally a hare is carried, in a sitting posture, mounted on the top of a pole.

"The procession increases greatly in numbers as it approaches Hare-Pie Bank, where the pies are pitched out of the sack and scrambled for. The spectators amuse themselves by throwing the contents of the pies at each other. Then follows the well-known 'Hallaton bottle-kicking.' One of the large bottles containing ale is thrown into the circular hollow on the mound, and the 'Medbourne men,' or other villagers who care to join in the sport, try to wrest the bottle from the Hallatonian grasp. A fierce contest then ensues, in comparison with which a foot-ball scrimmage is mere child's play. It is useless to describe the battle that ensues, the Hallatonians striving to kick the bottle to their boundary-line over the brook adjoining the village, while their opponents endeavor to convey it towards the Medbourne boundary. The victors, of course, claim the contents of the bottle. Then 'the dummy' is fought for with unabated zest, for the Hallaton people boast that this has never been wrested from them. The third bottle is taken in triumph to the market-cross and its contents drunk with accustomed honors. The bottles are carefully kept from year to year, and those now in use have done duty for more than thirty years."

The Easter hare myth has reached America. Here, however, as in other countries where the hare is scarce or unknown, it has been transformed into its near relation the rabbit. Perhaps this was originally due to the confectioners, who are rarely experts in natural history.

Another form of the hare myth is the curious superstition among the negroes as to the talismanic virtues of the left hind foot of a graveyard rabbit killed in the dark of the moon.

Easter Monday and **Tuesday.** In England and Ireland Easter Monday is a holiday (see BANK HOLIDAY), and on the continent of Europe the following day is also a popular holiday. The curious custom of heaving or lifting on Easter holidays still survives in some parts of England. In imitation of the sun, supposed to rise on Easter morning in three leaps, the men lift the women on Easter Monday and the women return the compliment on Easter Tuesday, the victim being lifted three times, and then kissed and let off for a consideration. The lifting is sometimes done by means of a chair, sometimes by the lifters joining their hands at the wrist so as to improvise a seat, upon which the person to be lifted is placed, and at other times less decorously by the lifters taking hold of the victim by the arms and legs. The custom is an old one, as appears from a record in the Tower entitled "Liber Contrarotulatoris Hospicii," referring to an event in the eighteenth year of the reign of Edward I. (1290). On the Easter Monday seven of Queen Eleonora's ladies unceremoniously invaded Longshanks's chamber, and, seizing their majestic master, proceeded to heave him in his chair till he was glad to pay a fine of fourteen pounds to regain his liberty.

Brand in his "Popular Antiquities" quotes a correspondent who under date of 1799 gives a graphic description of a heaving to which he was subjected in Shrewsbury. "I was sitting alone," he says, "last Easter Tuesday at breakfast at the Talbot in Shrewsbury, when I was surprised by the entrance of all the female servants of the house handing in an arm-chair, lined with white, and decorated with ribbons and favors of different colors. I asked them what they wanted. Their answer was, they came to *heave* me. It was the custom of the place on that morning, and they hoped I would take a seat in their chair. It was impossible not to comply with a request very modestly made, and to a set of nymphs in their best apparel, and several of them under twenty. I wished to see all the ceremony, and seated myself accordingly. The group then lifted me from the ground, turned the chair about, and I had the felicity of a salute from each. I told them I supposed there was a fee due upon the occasion, and was answered in the affirmative; and, having satisfied the damsels in this respect, they withdrew to *heave* others. At this time I had never heard of such a custom; but, on inquiry, I found that on Easter Monday, between nine and twelve, the men heave the women in the same manner as on the Tuesday, between the same hours, the women heave the men. I will not offer any conjecture on the ground of the custom, because I have nothing like data to go upon; but if you should happen to have heard anything satisfactory respecting it, I should be highly gratified by your mentioning it."

A Warwickshire correspondent in a later edition of the same book (1849) adds this note:

"The women's heaving day was the most amusing. Many a time have I passed along the streets inhabited by the lower orders of people, and seen parties of jolly matrons assembled round tables on which stood a foaming tankard of ale. There they sat in all the pride of absolute sovereignty, and woe to the luckless man that dared to invade their prerogatives! as sure as he was seen he was pursued, as sure as he was pursued he was taken, and as sure as he was taken he was heaved and kissed, and compelled to pay sixpence for 'leave and license' to depart."

No one, no matter what his age or dignity, could escape. Chambers's "Book of Days," vol. i. p. 425, tells an amusing story in point:

A grave clergyman who happened to be passing through a town in Lancashire on an Easter Tuesday, and having to stay an hour or two at an inn, was astonished by three or four lusty women rushing into his room, exclaiming they had "come to lift him." "To lift me!" repeated the amazed divine; "what can you mean?" "Why, your reverence, we've come to lift you, 'cause it's Easter Tuesday." "Lift me because it's Easter Tuesday! I don't understand you. Is there any such custom here?" "Yes, to be sure; why, don't you know? All us women was lifted yesterday, and us lifts the men to-day in turn. And, in course, it's our rights and duties to lift 'em." After a little further parley, the reverend traveller compromised with his fair visitors for half a crown, and thus escaped the dreaded compliment.

Variants of the custom exist, or used to exist, in certain parts of England and Wales. Thus, in many Yorkshire villages the young men on Easter Sunday used to take off the young girls' buckles, and on the Easter Monday the young men's shoes and buckles were taken off by the young women. On the Wednesday they were redeemed by little pecuniary forfeits, out of which an entertainment called a *Tansy Cake* was provided, and the jollity concluded with dancing. At Ripon, where this custom also prevailed, it is reported that no traveller could pass the town without being stopped, and, if a horseman, having his spurs taken away, unless redeemed by a little money, which was the only means to get them returned.

Cole in his "History of Filey" (1828, p. 136) mentions a similar custom as practised in that place. He says the young men seize the shoes of the females, collecting as many as they can, and on the following day the girls retaliate by getting the men's hats, which are to be redeemed on a subsequent evening, when both parties assemble at one of the inns and partake of a rural repast. (*Gentleman's Magazine*, 1790, vol. lx. p. 719.)

Durand tells us that on Easter Tuesday wives used to beat their husbands, on the day following the husbands their wives. The Hocktide (*q. v.*) customs were remotely analogous to these of Easter.

That all had a root in some common custom in the remote past is evident from the fact that similar rites are not unknown in Germany. Thus, at Warth the boys go about flogging the girls on Easter Monday, in return for which the boys must give them fish and potatoes on Easter Tuesday and provide the music for a general dance.

A custom called "clipping the church" was kept up in Warwickshire on Easter Monday until the beginning of the nineteenth century. It was performed by the children of the different charity schools, who at a certain hour flocked together for the purpose. The first comers placed themselves hand in hand with their backs against the church, and were joined by their companions, who gradually increased in number, till at last the chain was of sufficient length to surround the sacred edifice. As soon as the hand of the last of the train had grasped that of the first, the party broke up, and walked in procession to the other church (for in those days Birmingham boasted of but two churches), where the ceremony was repeated. (*Hone's Every Day Book*, vol. i. p. 431.)

In the days of the temporal power of the Papacy the girandola, or monster exhibition of fireworks, took place on Easter Monday on the slope of the Pincian Hill in Rome. A covered tribune opposite the ascent to the Pincio, divided into boxes and stretching the whole length of the Piazza del Popolo, was reserved for official personages. The piazza itself was crowded with a surging crowd arrayed in all sorts of picturesque garbs. " It is impossible," says Lady Blanche Murphy in the *Galaxy* for April, 1873, " to give an idea of the scale on which these fireworks were offered gratis as a public spectacle to the people by the Papal government, and it was certainly a scale which would dwarf and shame the most elaborate exhibition of pyrotechnics in any other capital. Foremost in the programme was always some stately architectural device. One year we had a view of Pompeii, with its delicate temples and Grecian columns rising gracefully one behind the other, the whole flooded with quivering light, and looking like the realization of a classic dream, while in the piazza below the band of the Papal chasseurs played the march out of 'Tone,' an opera founded on Bulwer's 'Last Days of Pompeii.' Another year the architectural device was a grand temple, more graceful than St. Peter's and more perfect than St. Paul's (London), its dome uplifted like a great fiery bell, in perfect proportion with the rest of the airy building. Turning to the programme, I found it was a representation of Michael Angelo's original plan of St. Peter's, now preserved in the Vatican Library."

An ancient custom still observed by the boys of Christ's Hospital, London, on Easter Tuesday, is that of paying a visit to the Mansion House to receive from the lord mayor what are known as the Easter Bobs. The ceremony annually attracts a good deal of public attention, as the boys march " in fours" through the streets of the City to the Mansion House, where they are forthwith regaled with two buns apiece. Thus fortified, they file before the lord mayor, who, from sundry piles of new money on the table before him, presents each " Grecian" with a sovereign, and all the other boys, according to their standing, with coins of lesser value. Before they retire, the boys have a glass of lemonade. At one time the alternative of sherry was permitted. This form of " local option," however, has been abolished.

After the ceremony the lord mayor and the rest of the civic authorities, in the customary state, accompany the boys to Christ Church, Newgate Street, where a sermon is preached. This sermon still retains the name of the second Spital sermon,

EASTER BOBS AT THE MANSION HOUSE.

although the first, which used to be preached on Easter Monday, has been discontinued.

In the Tyrol a peculiar bit of drollery similar to our April fool custom is practised on Easter Tuesday. The bauer awakes in the morning to find his manure-heap carefully laden on a cart and hoisted onto his roof, along with ploughs, flails, harrows, and other farming-utensils. The milkmaid seeks her pails in vain, for they are lying in the trough of the village pump, with the churn to keep them company. The church is completely barricaded with wagons, benches, doors, fagots, etc. Mich'l misses his new pipe, and neighbor Jos'l his brindled cow; but the latter's absence is easily accounted for when the priest's good old housekeeper goes into the garden to water the lettuces. She might have saved herself the trouble, for the brindled cow has made short work with the vegetables. It may easily be conceived that the sufferers are not choice in their language towards the perpetrators of the mischief; but there the matter rests. No harm is done, and the missing goods and chattels are soon recovered by their rightful owners.

Easter Sepulchre. A stone or wooden structure more common in the ancient churches of the Roman faith than in the modern. In general design it resembled a tomb, and usually stood on the north side of the chancel. Though in use only two days in the year. it was frequently adorned with a wealth of paintings, sculptures, and bas-reliefs. Easter sepulchres were especially popular in Catholic England, and more or less mutilated remains are still extant in some of the great cathedrals and churches.

On Maundy Thursday it is still the Roman custom for the priest celebrating mass to consecrate three hosts, one for reception that day, another for use on Good Friday, and still another to be shut up in the pyx, or, where the church contains an Easter sepulchre, to be buried therein on Good Friday. Often the crucifix exposed for adoration on Good Friday accompanies it. In many places numerous candles are lighted, and a continual succession of watchers stand by the sepulchre or other receptacle until the dawn of Easter Day. Then crucifix and host are once more removed to the altar, and the church re-echoes with joyous praise.

In a curious work entitled "The Ancient Rites and Monuments of the Monastical and Cathedral Church of Durham," collected from ancient monasteries about the time of the suppression, and published by J. D. (J. Davies) of Kidwelly in 1672, there is a minute account of a Good Friday ceremonial of this sort as celebrated at Durham Cathedral. Its value is enhanced by the fact that the book was probably written by one who had acted as a participant. "Within the church of Durham, upon Good Friday, there was a marvellous solemn service, in which service time, after the Passion was sung, two of the ancient monks took a goodly large crucifix, all of gold, of the picture of our Saviour Christ, nayled upon the cross. . . . The service being ended, the said two monks carried the cross to the sepulchre with great reverence, which sepulchre was set up in the morning on the north side of the quire, nigh the high altar, before the service time, and they did lay it within the said sepulchre with great devotion, with another picture of our Saviour Christ, in whose Breast they did enclose, with great reverence, the most holy and blessed Sacrament of the Altar, censing and praying unto it upon their knees, a great space; and setting two lighted tapers before it, which did burn till Easter Day in the morning, at which time it was taken forth. . . . There was very solemn service betwixt three and four of the clock in the morning, in honor of the Resurrection, where two of the eldest monks in the quire came to the sepulchre, set up upon Good Fryday, after the Passion, all covered with red velvet embroidered with gold, and did then cense it, either of the monks, with a pair of silver censers, sitting on their knees before the sepulchre. Then they, both rising, came to the sepulchre. out of which, with great reverence, they took a marvellous beautiful image of our Saviour, representing the Resurrection, with a cross in his hand, and on the breast was enclosed, in most bright crystal, the Holy Sacrament of the Altar, through which crystal the Blessed Host was conspicuous to the beholders. Then after the elevation of the said picture carried by the said two monks, upon a fair velvet cushion, all embroidered, singing the anthem of *Christus Resurgens*, they brought it to the high altar."

Elsewhere in England, as well as on the Continent, it was often the custom to wash the cross, after its adoration on Good Friday, with wine and water. The ablution was given to the priest and people to drink, in memory of the blood and water which flowed from the side of the crucified Redeemer. After washing, the cross was carried to the sepulchre, thence to be triumphantly taken to the high altar on Easter morning, the choir meanwhile singing the anthem "Surrexit Dominus."

Both usages, the burial of the host and of the cross, were practised in Rouen in 1079. They have local survivals in Catholic Europe, but the name sepulchre is not always given to the place of temporary deposit. (See GOOD FRIDAY.)

The Greek Church celebrates a somewhat similar ceremony.. Upon Good Friday evening a procession starts from every church, headed by a military band playing a funeral march, priests, choristers, and others following immediately after it, chanting a melancholy dirge during all the intervals of military music. Then comes an effigy of the Saviour borne upon a bier (or sometimes only a painting upon white satin), as if going to burial. As the dead are always carried in Greece in an unclosed coffin, with the body exposed to view, so the effigy is carried low by slings, that all may see it. Members of the several congregations in great numbers follow it, bearing lighted tapers, and thus they perambulate the streets, only stopping at the corners of some of the principal thoroughfares for the reading of certain prayers and for singing low, monotonous chants.

In the Church of the Holy Sepulchre at Jerusalem the Greeks on Good Friday bear in procession, in lieu of the image, a piece of brocade embroidered with a representation of the body of our Saviour, which is placed in the tomb, and after a short repose there is brought out again and carried into the Greek chapel.

Edmund, St., King and Martyr. His festival is celebrated on the day of his death, November 20. Son of the King of Saxony, he was chosen by Offa, King of East Anglia, to succeed him, and landed in England in 856. After a peaceful reign of fifteen years his kingdom was invaded by the Danes, and he was defeated in the battle of Hoxne. He was offered life and liberty if he would abjure his faith, but he refused, whereupon he was bound by the Danes to a tree, shot with arrows, and finally beheaded (November 20, 870). Legend says that when the

Christians who had hidden came forth to bury the king his head could not be found, till at last it was discovered guarded by a wolf, who allowed them to take it and followed it to the burial. Being placed on the body, it united instantly. A great church and monastery were built over the shrine of the saint, and the town about was called Bury St. Edmunds, a name it still retains. During a Danish war in 1010 the bones of St. Edmund were borne to London, and legend has it that as the relics passed through Cripplegate the lame were restored to the use of their limbs. The body was taken back to Bury St. Edmunds in 1013. The shrine of St. Edmund is memorable as the place where the English barons banded together to obtain Magna Charta from King John.

Edward, St., King and Martyr (962–978). His festival is celebrated on his death-day, March 18. When only thirteen years of age he succeeded his father Edgar on the throne of England, despite the opposition of his step-mother Elfrida, the late king's widow, who had formed a party in favor of her own son, Ethelred. Under the guidance of St. Dunstan, he ruled well, but only for three years. One day he was out hunting in the neighborhood of Corfe Castle, in Dorsetshire, Queen Elfrida's residence. He stopped there for refreshment, and while drinking was treacherously stabbed,—it is said, by order of his step-mother. She had him buried without any royal honors at Wareham. Many miracles are said to have been performed at his grave. Two years later his body was removed, with much pomp, to King Alfred's minster at Shaftesbury. The title of Martyr was given to him partly on account of his unjust and cruel murder, and partly because of the favor he had won from the monks and clergy.

Edward the Confessor, St. (1004–1066), King of England. He was canonized by Pope Alexander III. in 1161. His festival was first kept on his death-day, January 5, but later was transferred to October 13, in honor of the solemn translation of his body performed in 1163 by Thomas à Becket in the presence of Henry II. The National Council of Oxford in 1222 ordered this feast to be kept in England as a holy day.

King Edward succeeded his half-brother Hardicanute on the English throne in 1042. Shortly after his accession he married Edith, daughter of Earl Godwin, who proved an unruly subject and a refractory father-in-law. But in the end Edward triumphed over all opposition, rather by winning gentleness than by any great strength of character. He relieved his subjects of the Danish tax. Legend explains that after gathering a large part of it he saw the devil dancing upon the receipts, and so decided that it was unholy. He founded Westminster Abbey in 1049, and was the first to be buried there, as he died the year after its consecration. His wife Edith was subsequently buried with him. Both declared that though married they had respected each other's virginity. Hence the Church has always looked upon the couple as models of saintly purity. He reposes in a noble mausoleum which was substituted by Henry II. for the plain sarcophagus in which the body was originally deposited.

Edward was the first English king to touch scrofulous sores and swellings. (See TOUCHING.) Many came to him, and every one who asserted that he was healed was rewarded with a gold medal. On his death-bed the king gave his ring to the Abbot of Westminster, who kept it as a precious relic and found that it cured the falling sickness. Subsequently it passed to the chapel of Havering (so called from this very possession), near Rumford, in Essex. This had been one of his hunting-seats. His successors on the English throne used to bless rings on Good Friday against cramp and falling sickness. Out of respect to the memory of St. Edward, the kings of England have always kept up the custom at their coronation of putting on his dalmatic and maniple as part of the royal robes. The crown itself still bears his name, though a new one was long since substituted.

On October 13, 1885, a curious scene was enacted before St. Edward's shrine in Westminster Abbey, which proved the precedent for similar ones afterwards. A large congregation had been present at the high mass said by Cardinal Manning in the Catholic church of St. Edward. The sermon was for the most part a consideration of the probabilities of the return of the English nation to the Roman Catholic faith. At its close a pilgrimage was organized in furtherance of this object to the shrine of the Confessor. At the request of the cardinal, the appearance of a demonstration was avoided as far as possible, but the sudden inroad of the band of devotees indulging in adoration at the tomb of the historic saint excited general curiosity. The vergers and authorities of the Abbey did not interfere with the visitors, who finally retired in good order, but the question of the propriety of the affair was immediately taken into consideration by the dean and chapter. It was decided, however, to take no action in the matter.

Effigy, Burning or Hanging in. In modern times, even in the most civilized countries, the hanging or burning of a figure made out of straw or wood, dressed up to imitate some unpopular personage, is a favorite method of expressing the scorn and loathing of a mob. Many Presidents, generals, and politicians in the

United States have been the objects of this form of contumely. Two remarkable examples of the annual recurrence for centuries of this vicarious punishment are afforded in the burning of Guy Fawkes (*q. v.*) in England, and of Judas (*q. v.*) in Portuguese countries. Benedict Arnold was treated in the same way in Philadelphia and New York for many successive years after the Revolution as a part of the Fourth of July festivities. Giant Pope in the seventeenth and eighteenth centuries used to be burned on the anniversary of the accession of Queen Elizabeth in England. The custom is a survival from a more brutal superstition of ancient and mediæval times, that the individual whose effigy was offered up suffered pain or death in his own proper person as a result.

BURNING BENEDICT ARNOLD IN EFFIGY.
(From an old Philadelphia print.)

Among the Greeks, as we learn from Theocritus, the sorcerers killed their enemies by magic rites performed over an effigy of the person who had offended them.

Virgil's lines, too, will be remembered, where not death but love is to be obtained through the mediation of the clay and wax images :

> As fire this image hardens, made of clay,
> And this of wax with fire consumes away,
> Such let the soul of cruel Daphnis be,
> Hard to the rest of women, soft to me.

In the days of witchcraft persecution one of the most frequent charges was that the witches made waxen images of their enemies which they melted before a fire and so caused the dissolution of the originals.

In Japan the effigy is still regarded as a means of punishment to faithless lovers.

"The maiden who is jilted," we are told by Mr. A. B. Mitford, in "Tales of Old Japan," "rises at two o'clock in the morning, dresses herself in white, and carries a little straw figure—the effigy of the faithless one—to the sacred grove around some Shintô shrine. The trees are supposed to be under the special protection of the god to whom the shrine is dedicated, and any injury done to them arouses him to vengeance. Taking the effigy in her left hand, and hammer in the right, she sacrilegiously nails the figure to one of the holy trees, praying the god to slay the traitorous youth, and vowing that if he grant her prayer she will pull out the nails which offend the god by wounding his consecrated tree. Night after night she strikes in two or more nails, believing that every nail will shorten her unfaithful lover's life, because the god will be sure at the last, in order to save his tree, to strike the young man dead."

In France, up to the time of the first Revolution, execution by effigy was a solemn legal institution. M. Bourcher d'Argis, an assistant of Diderot and D'Alembert in the "Encyclopédie," tries to find an explanation of this in the custom which Plutarch mentions of substituting an effigy for the person to be sacrificed at a triumph.

In France, at the time of Louis VI., in the beginning of the twelfth century, punishment by effigy was exercised in the case of Thomas de Marne, who was a foe of the bishops and condemned by the monarch for high treason. The Ordonnance Criminelle of 1670 permitted punishment by effigy only when the criminal was condemned to death. When the criminal was condemned to the galleys, perpetual banishment, the lash, or the wheel, and took to flight, his name and crime were to be written on a card and set up in some public place as a warning to the people and as a means of disgracing him. This is analogous to the Greek punishment of the *stele*. Under the same ordonnance, if a criminal condemned to death managed to make his escape, his effigy was delivered into the prison, the executioner entered the cell with his escort and the apparatus of punishment, and the figure was led to the place of punishment and solemnly executed. It is possible that under this law there was a provision that there should be but one effigy, although prior to this date, in the year 1639, the Duke of La Valette, who was condemned to the block, was beheaded in three different cities, Paris, Bordeaux, and Bayonne, on the same day. The criminal, meanwhile, was safe in England.

At the time of the Revolution the legal punishment by effigy was abolished, but the burning and hanging of representations of objects of popular hatred continued. In Rheims, for instance, in 1793, the Pope, the "coalesced tyrants," and La Fayette were all burned together in effigy at the Revolution Feast.

In the Low Countries the same custom of popular vengeance prevailed, and Catholic and Protestant burned each other in effigy with fierce theologic zeal. The confessor of Charles V. was convicted of heresy by the Inquisition, but died before sentence could be pronounced upon him, and his crime was punished by a burning of his doll counterfeit.

In England, on the first anniversary of Restoration Day, which celebrated the restoration of the monarchy and of the Church, there was great activity in effigy-punishment. The *Kingdom's Intelligencer* and the *Mercurius Publicus* announce that on the 29th of May, 1661, at Bury St. Edmund's, the common hangman led the effigy of the courageous and eccentric Parliamentarian chaplain, Hugh Peters, followed by the entire populace, and the common beadle whipped it through the streets. At Halesworth, Oliver Cromwell was pilloried in effigy and afterwards burned in a bonfire of five hundred fagots. At Exeter "a counterfeit of the Covenanter" was drawn to the gibbet " on a poor jade." At Reading the Covenant itself was incarcerated as soon as condemned by Parliament, and kept in prison until the 29th of May, when it was dragged through the streets by a rope and burned in the market-place.

So late as 1756, at Gateshead, Sunderland, Shields, and Newcastle, in England, the luckless Admiral Byng was hanged and burned in effigy. In the last-named place the figure was drawn through the streets on a donkey, with the legend, "This is the villain that would not fight;" after which it was hanged on a gallows, mutilated, and finally burned.

In the time of Louis XV. the Princess of Monaco was a lady who loved much and many. But among the many her own husband was not included. She would not even live with the latter, preferring the artificial delights of Versailles to the natural beauties of Monaco. He nevertheless kept himself informed about her goings-on, and found a solace in erecting gibbets all around his principality whereon he hanged effigies of his wife's lovers. The principality was small (though larger then than it is now), and the number of courtiers who enjoyed the favors of the prince's flighty spouse was very great: so that finally the gibbeted effigies formed a continuous line all along the frontier.

Famous are the wax effigies preserved in Westminster Abbey in a little oratory above the Islip chapel. These are mementos of a strange old-time ceremony. Long ago, when some great personage died, it was the custom to model a representation of the deceased, dressed as in life, which was carried in the funeral procession. After the burial the effigy was set up in church as a temporary monument. One odd feature of the practice was that during the time that the effigy was on exhibition it was customary to affix to it, by means of paste or pins, short poems or epitaphs complimentary to the person represented. In the case of a sovereign the statue was usually left in position for a month only, though after Charles II. died his wax figure stood for two centuries over his tomb in the chapel of Henry VII., and was the only monument he had.

The royal effigies in Westminster date back to the fourteenth century; but all the oldest ones are so mutilated and defaced that they are not shown. Many of them were of wood, and have been wantonly stripped of the rich garments which they wore. About a dozen of the later figures are still preserved, each standing stiffly in a glass case by itself, and, decked as they are in faded silk and tarnished tinsel, they form so startling a contrast to their stately marble successors on the tombs below that it seems as if the coming up of this one short flight of steps had translated the visitor from the consecrated atmosphere of the Abbey into the vulgar air of Madame Tussaud's establishment.

The oldest figure is that of Charles II. It is dressed in the blue and red velvet robes of the Garter, trimmed with superb old point lace. By his side, in another case, is the figure of General Monk, clad in armor. The head of the figure is now bare, but it originally wore the famous cap mentioned in the "Ingoldsby Legends:"

I thought on Naseby, Marston Moor, and Worcester's crowning fight,
When on mine ear a sound there fell, it filled me with affright,
As thus in low, unearthly tones I heard a voice begin:
"This here's the cap of Gen'ral Monk! Sir, please put summat in."

In the last century the vergers, when showing these figures to visitors, came to use this cap as a gentle hint that their none too large wages might be acceptably increased by a small coin dropped into it. Goldsmith, who has recorded an account of his visit to the Abbey, says of this cap, in an account of a conversation with the verger who was his guide, "'Pray, friend, what might this cap have cost originally?' 'That, sir,' says he, 'I don't know; but this cap is all the wages I have for my trouble.'"

The two latest figures, those of the Earl of Chatham and Admiral Nelson, were unquestionably put in by the officers of the Abbey merely for show purposes, to increase the attractiveness of the exhibit. That of Lord Nelson is interesting from the fact that it is dressed in a suit of clothes which the admiral once wore. There seems good reason to believe this to be true, since when Maclise borrowed the figure as a model while he was painting his famous painting "The Death of Nelson" he found attached to the lining of the hat the eye-patch without which the admiral, who was blind in one eye, never appeared.

Einsiedeln, Black Virgin of. A miraculous image of the Virgin, whose shrine in the church at Einsiedeln, Switzerland, attracts a vast concourse of pilgrims on the great annual festival of September 14. The founder of Einsiedeln (literally, "a hermitage") was St. Meinrad, Count of Sulgen (797–861), a Hohenzollern, and an ancestor of the present Emperor of Germany. Studious, pious, and gentle, he shrank from the world, and passed from one cloister to another, and finally, as an "einsiedler" or hermit, retired to a little hut built for him by a pious lady on a lonely peak of the Etzelberg. Driven thence by the increasing number of those who sought his advice and help, he retreated to the then wild forests of the Finsterwald, and made his cell where now the great church and convent stand, risen in abundant harvest from the little seed of good. Here he received in solemn gift from Hildegarde, foundress and abbess of the great Zurich convent, and daughter of King Louis, the grandson of Charlemagne, a sacred image of the Virgin and Child, which from the ninth century to the present day has reigned at Einsiedeln.

On September 14, 861, he was murdered in his cell by two robbers seeking for imaginary treasures. Tracked by two ravens which the saint had kept, the assassins were detected, and were tried and executed at Zurich, where, in memory of this miracle, long stood the Raven's Hotel, now the Hotel Bilharz. The thousandth anniversary of the saint's death was celebrated with great pomp at Einsiedeln in 1861.

A convent was founded here in the year 900. Gradually, too, a great church rose above and enclosed the little chapel with the sacred image. In 948 Conrad, Bishop of Constance, came, with an immense train of priests and nobles, to consecrate the finished building. At midnight before September 14, the day fixed for the ceremony, he went to the church to spend the early hours in prayer; but at the door he was stayed by the sound of heavenly music, and, looking in, beheld a multitude of angels going through all the forms of consecration. In the Virgin's chapel he saw our Lord officiating in priestly dress, surrounded and assisted by saints; before the altar stood the Blessed Virgin, robed in light. The vision faded with the dawn; but Conrad, spellbound, knelt in the same spot till midday, in spite of entreaties to begin the service. Then he told what he had seen; but they held it for a dream, and urged him to proceed to the consecration. As he at last did so, a voice spoke from above, thrice repeating, "Brother, stay; the chapel is consecrated by

God." Then, with reverence, they forbore their persuasions, and Conrad consecrated only the great church which stood over the chapel.

Such is the legend of the " Engelweihe." Sixteen years later Conrad went, with the Emperor Otho I., to Rome, and laid before Leo VIII. the question whether the chapel should receive regular consecration. This, after consultation with many bishops, the Pope decided against, acknowledging as valid the miraculous work of the angels.

Great, after this, were the glories of Einsiedeln. Emperors and kings sent rich gifts and made over land. Abbot Gregory, nephew of the English King Alfred, and brother-in-law of Otho the Great, was created a prince of the Empire, which dignity, by a further decree of Rudolph of Hapsburg, descended to his suc cessors ; they are prince-abbots to the present day. Distinguished pilgrims flocked to Einsiedeln. Otho the Great was there in 965, the Emperor Sigismund in 1417, Ferdinand III. in 1442 ; St. Nicholas came in 1480, St. Charles Borromeo in 1576. The visitors' list is nine centuries long, and rich in the names of princes. Marie Louise came in 1814 ; Queen Hortense came year by year, and hither brought her son Louis to receive his first communion. The Bourbon princes came in 1859, the Orleans in 1863. The Catholic members of the Hohenzollern family visit frequently the foundation of their holy ancestor St. Meinrad.

Yet, for all these royal favors, Einsiedeln has had times of trouble. Many times has it been robbed or burnt in the conflicts of the adjacent cantons. Worst of all, the French army came there in 1798, and, after their unfailing habit in those days, carried off all they could, and burnt the rest. Even the sacred image they packed up and sent home ; but the monks, forewarned of the coming danger, had hidden away the true Virgin, and it was a counterfeit which travelled to Paris. The real image wandered long, into various graves : buried first at Alpthal, then at Häggenegg, next it travelled across the Rhine to Bludenz, then by sea to Trieste, later to Bludenz again. In some places where it had been concealed the peasants built chapels to commemorate the fact. At length, in 1802, it was brought back in triumph to its ancient home.

Since that time the pilgrimages have been kept up uninterruptedly. Baedeker estimates that the pilgrims who come from Switzerland, Bavaria, Suabia, Baden, and Alsace number about one hundred and fifty thousand annually. Strangely enough, few tourists visit the place, though it lies in the most frequented part of Switzerland. A writer in *Macmillan's Magazine* who was present at the great September festival in 1891 says that his own party comprised the only English present. His admirable description of the scene is here condensed:

"The Platz, where the ceremonies of the day were to take place, was a space like in shape and size to Trafalgar Square, though rather larger, and, like Trafalgar Square, slanting down-hill. At the upper side stand the long lines of the convent, straight and monotonous, and in their centre the church, double-towered, of immense size but no very beautiful design. In front of these the ground is raised to form a level terrace, which is approached in the centre by a broad flight of steps, and under the brow of which arcades are built stretching down to right and left in a broad semicircle. At the lower side the Platz is bounded by a line of hotels. As we saw the scene, on a bright cloudless day, it was very attractive. The pilgrims were everywhere,—clustered round the arcades, swarming up and down the steps, leaning over the balustrades at the terrace edge. And, lest the word 'pilgrim' should suggest 'travel-stained garments' and 'sorrowful countenances,' it must be added that they looked a well-contented set of holiday-makers; though, as they were Swiss, without much vivacity or personal beauty. There were traces of picturesque costume among the women. The men were, as usual, soberly dressed.

"A large fountain is in the centre of the Platz, whence, by fourteen separate spouts, water flows out and splashes on the pavement round. The legend is that from one of these our Lord once drank, but which one is not known: so we saw the more devout among the pilgrims gravely going all round and drinking from every spout in succession. One old man had a ginger-beer bottle, which he was gradually filling up with a few drops from each of the fourteen spouts.

"We went on to the church, and found it very big and gaudily bright. The side aisles were, as usual, occupied with numerous chapels; and for this high festival the relics were exposed on every altar. There, through a glass side in every coffin, we saw the withered bodies of saints and martyrs, wreathed about with strings of beads, flowers, and gilt ornaments; the outline of the features traced in pearls, rings put on the fingers, a crown on the head, and the instrument of martyrdom laid in the clinched hand.

"Standing in the centre of the nave, facing the west door, was the famous angel-consecrated chapel, crowded about with pilgrims. It was made of black marble, and, like a great bird-cage, shut in behind, and partly at the sides, and wired round the front with iron rails, through which, as through prison-bars, we saw the lighted altar, and above 'Maria Einsiedeln' herself, so swathed and sunk in cloth of gold, lace, and satin that only the faces of the Virgin and Child were visible; all jet black, as it apparently behooves ancient and sacred images to be. The rest of the tiny edifice was wreathed with paper flowers and covered with scarlet and white inscriptions in German,—pious rhymes mostly, about the angel-consecration.

"As it grew dusk, the aspect of the church was very strange. Each chapel was besieged by a little crowd: women swaying to and fro, as they passed the rosary beads through their slow fingers; some few ecstatic, kneeling with outstretched arms; some in groups, a large family or party of friends, were making the round of the chapels, pausing to repeat at each their monotonous rote of prayers. The sacred chapel was pressed on from all sides; hundreds of votive offerings were strung on the iron bars, long rows of lighted tapers were stuck on the ledge below, and pilgrims knelt all round, while old women, asleep from sheer fatigue, rested their heads against its walls. Nor was there the usual silence of Roman Catholic churches, for the low hum of praying voices was rising like a storm, in a strange, monotonous, wordless way, coming one hardly knew whence or how, and beating all on one wailing note.

"We saw them begin to illuminate the church. It was a curious effect when, at the end of the long dark vista, a brilliant fiery cross glided slowly up from the ground and hung suspended over the high altar. Outside, when all was complete, the scene was one hard to describe, harder still to forget. Every available place was illuminated uniformly with small, clear oil-lamps. With their soft golden lustre, the lower line of every window in the long convent façade was traced out, displaying the rare beauty of a great concerted illumination, falling in regular ordered lines. The church porch was very brilliant, massed round with lamps, and surmounted by the sacred monogram and a large cross. Moreover, the arcades, the hotels below, and all the houses within sight were traced with the same lustrous golden lines; and high on the hills a large brilliant cross seemed in the darkness to float in the air. In the lower right-hand part of the Platz was a great altar. Behind stood an illuminated transparent picture of the Madonna, and above this a smaller sketch of angels' heads; the golden-tinted lamps surrounded both with a deep border, tracing out arches and pillars of light. The altar was raised on steps covered with scarlet cloth; it faced the cathedral with all the wide stretch of the Platz between, and seemed to wait, as the multitude of people were waiting, for what was to come.

"Inside the church there was now scarcely standing-room. The gallery was traced round with lamps. Behind the choir-screen all was brilliant light, figures moving to and fro, clouds of incense floating up, dimming the gorgeous vestments of the officiating priests, broken pieces of chant caught up and answered by an organ at the further end of the church. Last came the solemn elevation of the host; and then the gates were opened, and slowly down the centre of the church moved the long-expected procession. First the chanting choristers with lighted tapers ; next the bishops, priests, visitors, a hundred or more; and then, under a splendid canopy, in trailing robes stiff with gold, came the prince-abbot, bearing in a high jewelled chalice the consecrated host; and, as he passed, all fell on their knees or bowed to the very ground.

" I wish, and hopelessly wish, I could describe the scene on the Platz. It was a perfect summer night, with neither moon nor cloud, and the dark dome of the sky seemed to quiver with the multitude of the stars. The convent and the church, the arcades and the hotels, all were sketched out with long, brilliant lines of light; the great cross on the distant hill, with no visible standing-point, looked like a new wonder of the heavens. On every side, silent and bareheaded, some ten thousand people were waiting; and what they waited for was coming,—a long procession with glimmering lines of tapers slowly moving out from the church doors, across the terrace, down the steps, then curving round towards the illuminated altar. As the abbot came out of the church, the low chant of the choristers was caught up by a sudden burst of military music; as he passed down, the close-pressing lines of people knelt on both sides. He came to the altar, and there prayed, under the starlit sky, with bishops, in vestments only less gorgeous than his own, grouped round him. In the balcony of a house near was a picturesque band of priests with various instruments, and of choristers who accompanied the service with some beautiful mass-music; the effect was heightened by the soft, distant tones of a hidden organ, which filled every interval. As if to leave no emotion untouched, one was startled now and then by the sudden thunder of cannon from the hills behind. The climax came when the music was hushed, and, amid such silence that his every tone was heard, the prince-abbot turned round to the people, and, three times raising the host on high, three times blessed them in the Holy Name, while three times, as he paused between, the tolling sound of the cannon shook the air, and the whole multitude knelt on the ground, as if a sudden gentle wind were passing over a field and bending every blade of grass.

" Then the procession was formed again, and made its way back to the church."

Eisteddfod. (Welsh, " a session," " a sitting." The plural is *Eisteddfodan.*) A national congress of Welsh bards and musicians, whose objects are to encourage the music, poetry, and general literature of Wales, to sustain ancient customs and traditions, and to foster a patriotic spirit. The institution in its modern form dates from the time of Owain ap Maxen Wledig, chief sovereign of the Britons at the close of the fourth century. But it did not receive its modern name until about the twelfth century. A congress of this sort held in the sixth century under the auspices of Maelgwn Gwynedd, Prince of North Wales, is especially noted in early Welsh history on account of a trick played by that wily potentate. He had undertaken to prove the superiority of vocal over instrumental music. So he offered a reward to such bards and minstrels as should swim over the Conway. Of course the minstrels found on arriving at the opposite shore that the strings of their harps were hopelessly out of tune, while the vocal cords of the bards were uninjured.

The Eisteddfodan of the early and middle ages were held every three years. No one could be accounted a bard unless he had passed with approval through an Eisteddfod; nothing could be accounted poetry save under its rules. Bard and harpist were sternly differentiated; the two professions could not be united in one man. But these high standards could not be maintained forever. Gradually abuses crept in. By the time of Queen Elizabeth they had become intolerable. From a royal proclamation issued in her reign it appears that "expert mynstrells and musicons" had grown so scarce, and sham "Rithmors and Barthes" so plentiful, that the whole tribe were summoned to appear on a certain day "to shew forth their learnings" before "such expert men in ye faculte of Welsh musick as shall be thought convenient." Those found unworthy were to be commanded "that they returne to some honest labor such as they be most apte unto, upon pain to be taken as sturdie vagabonds." As a result of this proclamation the bardic congresses were discontinued for about two hundred years. They were revived in the eighteenth century with great and lasting enthusiasm. At present the national Eisteddfodan are held annually, alternately in North and in South Wales. They are under the patronage of the highest in the land, beginning with the sovereign, and the judges are sought for among the most distinguished and competent in their respective departments.

The modern Eisteddfod has a very wide scope. It includes competitions in poetry, prose essay, fiction, and translation, and in the composition and performance of music. The prizes range from two hundred and fifty pounds to one pound. In the United States the Eisteddfod is almost exclusively a musical festival. A few recitations are always on the programme, but the poem and the essay rarely find a place there.

Welsh-Americans who wish to attain the rank of bard must send their work to Wales. If a sufficient number are found deserving of honors, and if they are unable to cross the ocean to receive them, a commission of bards comes over here and bestows the bardic accolade. The attendant ceremonies are performed in a circle of stones. A book of runes is read aloud, an ancient sword is laid upon the shoulders of the kneeling candidate, and a bit of blue ribbon (the nineteenth-century survival of the blue robe with which the bard was anciently invested) is presented to him, to be tied in a knot in his button-hole.

Elephant, Lord White. An elephant of uniform white, or rather gray, which is honored in Burmah as a minister of state of semi-divine attributes. He has a palace or state apartment, with a humbler every-day residence, and sheds for the vulgar herd of the same species, and brick godowns in which the state carriages and golden litters are stowed away. He is a regular "estate of the realm," having a woon or minister of his own, four gold umbrellas,—the white umbrellas which are peculiar to royalty,—with a suite of attendants said to be thirty in number. Like many other sinecurists and "estates of the realm," he does not seem to flourish much under his dignities, but would doubt-less be a happier elephant if he could exchange his palace and his umbrellas for coverts, forests, and overhanging trees. The possession of a white elephant is a sort of ensign of universal sovereignty, and the discovery of one is hailed as a good and happy omen for a reign. The slightest blemish, however,—a few black hairs in the tail, or some such matter,—at once mars its claims to sanctity.

Elizabeth's Day, Queen. The 17th of November, as the anniversary of the accession of the Virgin Queen to the English throne (1558), was formerly celebrated in England as emphati-cally a Protestant holiday. The custom appears to have begun in the twelfth year of her reign (1570), and to have been kept up intermittently for over a century,—whenever the anti-Popery sentiment proved particularly rampant. Eventually it was merged into Guy Fawkes's Day, which had borrowed some of its characteristics. The main feature of the day was a procession of mummers bearing an effigy of the Pope in a chair of state, behind which stood a masker dressed as the devil, who lavished affectionate caresses upon His Holiness. In Queen Anne's time an effigy of the Pretender was added to that of the Pope. The festivities wound up by the burning of the effigy or effigies amid great rejoicings.

During the reigns of James I. and Charles I. the close proximity of Guy Fawkes's Day, on November 5, caused the suspension of the Pope-burnings, but in the years 1679–1681, when the murder of Sir Edmund Berry Godfrey and the pretended discovery by Titus Oates of the Popish Plot had aroused a frenzy of excitement, they were revived as a welcome opportunity for reduplication of Protestant zeal. A rare pamphlet, "London's Defiance to Rome," quoted in Chambers's "Book of Days," vol. ii. p. 588, describes "the magnificent procession and solemn burning of the Pope at Temple Bar, November 17, 1679." We learn that "the bells generally about the town began to ring about three o'clock in the morning;" but the great procession was deferred till night, when "the whole was attended with one hundred and fifty flambeaus and lights, by order; but so many more came in volunteers, as made up some thousands. . . . At the approach of evening (all things being in readiness), the solemn procession began, setting forth from Moorgate, and so passing first to Aldgate, and thence through Leadenhall Street, by the Royal Exchange, through Cheapside, and so to Temple Bar. Never were the balconies, windows, and houses more numerously lined, or the streets closer thronged, with multitudes of people, all expressing their abhorrence of popery with continued shouts and exclamations, so that 'tis modestly computed that, in the whole progress, there could not be fewer than two hundred thousand spectators." The way was cleared by six pioneers in caps and red waistcoats, followed by a bell-man bearing his lantern and staff, and ringing his bell, crying out all the way in a loud but dolesome voice, "Remember Justice Godfrey!" He was followed by a man on horseback, dressed like a Jesuit, carrying a dead body before him, "representing Justice Godfrey, in like manner as he was carried by the assassins to Primrose Hill." It will be remembered that Godfrey was a London magistrate, before whom Titus Oates had made his first deposition. He was found murdered in the fields at the back of Primrose Hill with a sword run through his body to make it appear that by falling upon it intentionally he had committed suicide. But wounds in other parts of his person, and undeniable marks of strangulation, testified to the fact that he had been murdered, and it required only a slight stretch of the Protestant imagination to conjure up pictures of monks and priests as his assassins.

Another performer in the procession was habited as a priest, "giving pardons very plentifully to all those that should murder Protestants, and proclaiming it meritorious." He was followed by a train of other priests, and "six Jesuits with bloody daggers;" then, by way of relief, came "a consort of wind-musick." This was succeeded by a long array of Catholic church dignitaries, ending with "the Pope, in a lofty glorious pageant, representing a chair of state, covered with scarlet, richly embroidered and fringed, and bedecked with golden balls and crosses." At his feet were two boys with censers, " at his back his holiness's privy-councillor (the degraded seraphim, *Anglicé*, the devil), frequently caressing, hugging, and whispering him, and ofttimes instructing him aloud to destroy his majesty, to forge a Protestant plot, and to fire the city again, to which purpose he held an infernal torch in his hand." When the procession reached the foot of Chancery Lane, in Fleet Street, it came to a stop; " then, having entertained the thronging spectators for some time with the ingenious fireworks, a vast bonfire being prepared just over against the Inner Temple gate, his holiness, after some compliments and reluctances, was decently toppled from all his grandeur into the impartial flames; the crafty devil leaving his infallibilityship in the lurch, and laughing as heartily at his deserved ignominious end as subtle Jesuits do at the ruin of bigoted lay Catholics whom they have themselves drawn in." This concluding feat was greeted by " a prodigious shout, that might be heard far beyond Somerset House," where Queen Catherine was lodged at that time; but the ultra-Protestant author of this pamphlet, anxious to make the most of the public lungs, declares " 'twas believed the echo, by continued reverberations before it ceased, reached Scotland, France, and even Rome itself, damping them all with a dreadful astonishment."

This show proved so immensely popular that it was reproduced in succeeding years, with additional political pageantry.

In 1683, however, it was suppressed through royal influence brought to bear upon the mayor, who was a mere creature of Charles II. during the temporary suppression of the City charter. " Thus ended these Diavolarias," comments Roger North.

Not yet, however, had they received their final quietus. During the excitement caused in Queen Anne's reign by the claims of the High Church party under Dr. Sacheverell and the fear of the Pretender, sporadic efforts were made for the revival of the pageants. Effigies of the Pope, the Pretender, and the devil were in fact publicly burnt, although the vigilance of the police prevented the general observance of the day which was planned in 1711 and again in 1713. These minor celebrations are alluded to in an epigram by one Bishop, quoted in Sir Henry Ellis's notes to Brand's " Popular Antiquities :"

QUÆRE PEREGRINUM.

Three strangers blaze amidst a bonfire's revel :
The Pope, and the Pretender, and the Devil.
Three strangers hate our faith, and faith's defender :
The Devil, and the Pope, and the Pretender

> Three strangers will be strangers long, we hope :
> The Devil, and the Pretender, and the Pope.
> Thus, in three rhymes, three strangers dance the hay :
> And he that chooses to dance after them may.

A correspondent of *Notes and Queries* (First Series, vol. iv. p. 345) says that when he was at Christ's Hospital a curious custom prevailed on Queen Elizabeth's Day : "Two or more boys would take one against whom they had any spite or grudge, and, having lifted him by the arms and legs, would bump him on the hard stones of the cloisters." He believes that the bumpee represented the Pope or one of his emissaries, and the bumpers stout and loyal Protestants. (See STONE OF INFAMY for an analogous Italian ceremony with a totally different meaning.)

Elizabeth of Hungary, St. (It. *Elisabeta de Ungheria ;* Sp. *Isabel.*) Her festival is celebrated on November 19, the anniversary of her death. St. Elizabeth (1207–1231) was the daughter of Alexander II., King of Hungary. Being betrothed at the age of four years to Louis, son of the Landgrave of Thuringia, she was sent to that court to be brought up. When she was nine years old the landgrave died, and the government passed to his wife during the minority of Louis. The landgravine disliked Elizabeth and treated her with contumely. When Louis was twenty years of age the nuptials took place. But her accession to royal rank did not swerve her from the life of asceticism and good works to which she had vowed herself. Legend asserts that once as she was proceeding to a state banquet a beggar appealed to her charity and she took off her royal mantle and gave it to him. Just as she was confessing to her husband what she had done, her maid came bearing her mantle, which was found hanging in her wardrobe. The legend has it that the beggar was Christ himself. On another occasion, it is related, St. Elizabeth found a poor leprous child, and took it in her arms and laid it in her own bed. The landgravine was enraged, and called Louis to see, but when the latter came he found instead of a leper a radiant infant who smiled on him and vanished. These legends are obvious variants of the more famous miracle of the Roses.

At one season there was a great scarcity of crops throughout the land, and caution and economy in the use of the royal stores had been advised even in the palace. Elizabeth could not bear to know of unrelieved suffering among her people ; so, by close economy in her own wants, she managed to furnish food for many others. On one occasion a very pressing case of necessity reached her ; and, not wishing to encourage her servants in disobedience to the general command, she started alone on her errand of mercy, with some lighter articles of food concealed in the folds of her dress. Just as she reached the foot of the stairs, however, she met her husband, with several gentlemen, returning from the chase. Astonished to see his wife alone and thus burdened, he asked her to show him what she was carrying; but as she held her dress in terror to her breast, he gently disengaged her hands, and, behold, "·it was filled with white and red roses, the most beautiful he ever saw."

In Thuringia to this day there is a species of rose that is universally cultivated by the poorest peasant as well as the richest landholder; and if anybody asks of them a question as to its origin, the answer is, "Oh, that is the rose of the dear St. Elizabeth, our former queen, and was grown from one of the sprigs given to her by the angels."

In 1226 Louis set out with Frederick Barbarossa for the Holy Land, but died on the way. His brother Henry seized the government, and drove Elizabeth from the palace. She found a shelter for her children, and supported herself by spinning wool. When the knights who had accompanied Louis returned they dethroned Henry, and made Elizabeth's son, Herman, landgrave. The city of Marburg was bestowed on Elizabeth. She parted with her children in order to devote herself entirely to the religious life, and bound herself to observe the third rule of St. Francis. She died November 19, 1231, in the twenty-fourth year of her age. She was canonized by Gregory IX. in 1235. Her relics were translated to Marburg in 1236, where they were enshrined in the church of St. Elizabeth. Philip, Landgrave of Hesse, during the Reformation, removed the relics and buried them in some secret spot. The Carmelites of Brussels claim to have some of the bones of the saint, and some more are exhibited in a shrine at Hanover. Many stories are current of remarkable cures effected through the invocation of this saint, and the nuns of the third order of St. Francis chose her for their patroness, being sometimes known as "the nuns of St. Elizabeth." There are many pictures of this saint, the most celebrated of which is one by Murillo for the church of La Caritad at Seville.

Elmo, St. (An Italian corruption, through *Sant' Ermo*, of the name of **St. Erasmus.**) An Italian bishop of the reign of Domitian and Maximin. History has little to say of him, but the hagiologies assert that he suffered a cruel martyrdom on the wheel, June 2, A.D. 304. His death has been a favorite subject with artists, Poussin's repulsive yet powerful picture in the Vatican and Hans Burgkhmair's equally unpleasant one in Munich being the most famous. St. Erasmus, or St. Elmo, has from time immemorial been invoked by sailors on the Mediterranean in time of storms, and the electrical appearances known as St. Elmo's fire are held to be signs of his beneficent interference. These appearances are most frequently seen in southern climates during thunder-storms, and take the form of stars or brushes of light at the tops of masts, spires, or other pointed objects. The phenomenon was familiar to the Greeks, who when the light was double styled the twin flames Castor and Pollux. The general superstition that one light is unlucky and two are lucky may be traceable to this identification with the Dioscuri. When it appears on the deck, however, instead of at the mast-head, it is less welcome, and assumes something of the characteristic of a corpse-candle.

Bartolommeo Crescentio says it was called St. Elmo's light because of its reflections on the helms of the soldiers,—which only shows that Bartolommeo was a pre-scientific etymologist. Varenius, a Dutch writer, knew all about it in the spirit of your more modern man of science. It was produced by "some sulphurous and bituminous matter which, being beaten down by the agitation of the air, is kindled and gathered as butter is gathered by the agitation of cream." But other authorities were equally sure that it came from "thin, clammy vapors rising from the salt seas and ugly slime."

In modern Greece (and this is curious, considering the old Dioscuri belief) it appears to have a wholly evil significance, but you can get rid of it there by pulling the tail of a pig. Sometimes each light had a name,—St. Elmo for the first, and St. Nicholas and St. Anne for the second and third. The Chinese, with their usual perversity, reverse the European rule about St. Elmo. With us, as long as the light is aloft it is a good sign and when it descends it is an evil. Those who go down to the sea in junks hold the exact contrary.

Eloy, St. (Lat. *Eligius;* Eng. *Loo;* It. *Alò* or *Lò, Eligio*), patron saint of Bologna, Dunkerque, and Noyon, and of goldsmiths and all other metal-workers (A.D. 588–659). His festival is celebrated on December 1, the anniversary of his death.

St. Eloy was born at the village of Châtelat, two leagues from Limoges. He learned the trade of a goldsmith, and evinced such talent that he received a commission to make a golden throne set with pearls for King Clotaire II. Out of the materials given him Eloy made two thrones instead of one, which so pleased the king that Eloy was intrusted with affairs of state. Dagobert, successor to King Clotaire, made Eloy Master of the Mint, and later he was made Bishop of Noyon and Tournay. He was remarkable for his eloquence, and was sent to preach in Belgium. By some he is held to have been the first to carry the gospel to

Sweden and Denmark. Legend relates of him, as of St. Dunstan, that he seized the devil by the nose with a pair of red-hot pincers. One of the miracles attributed to this saint is represented in the exterior of Or San Michele at Florence. A horse being brought to him to be shod, which was possessed by the devil, he cut off the horse's leg and put on the shoe; then he made the sign of the cross and replaced the leg.

When St. Eloy fell ill of his last sickness, the queen Bathildes set out from Paris with a numerous retinue, but did not arrive at Noyon until the morning after his death. She would have taken the body to her monastery at Chelles, but desisted at the earnest request of the saint's flock. The body was thereupon deposited in the church of St. Lupus of Troyes, soon after called St. Eligius's, and later translated to the cathedral of St. Eloy at Dunkerque. Queen Bathildes placed a *repa* or small canopy of gold and silver over his tomb, and as it shone very brightly it was covered in Lent with a linen cloth bordered with silk. It is reported that a certain liquor which dropped from this cloth cured various distempers. The head of St. Eloy is in the parish church of St. André at Chelles. Other relics are at the cathedral at Bruges, the church of St. Martin at Tournay, and the church of St. Pierre at Douai. In the cathedral at Paris an arm of the saint is preserved. In art he is represented as a farrier with a horse's leg in his hand.

Emancipation Day. This was formerly a great festival among the colored people of several of the Atlantic and contiguous States in the Union, and was celebrated on August 15. The event which it commemorated was not the issuing of the Emancipation proclamation by Abraham Lincoln (September 22. 1862), but the earlier emancipation of the slaves in the British West Indies. The act of abolition was presented on behalf of the government by Lord Stanley on August 28, 1833 ; it was passed by Parliament on August 1, 1834, and the proclamation was made on August 15 of the same year. There have been no celebrations of Emancipation Day since the death (*circa* 1875) of Abe Trower, a colored man in the employ of Messrs. Robbins, of Fulton Market, through whose efforts the event was commemorated each August by a grand picnic at Myrtle Avenue Park, Brooklyn, that gave the cue to colored people in many of the neighboring States.

Ember Days, known in the ecclesiastical calendar as *quattuor tempora,* because these fasting days recur in each quarter of the year. The name may come from the Anglo-Saxon *ymbren,* a "revolution" or "circuit," or may be a corruption of the Latin *quattuor tempora.* The Dutch *quatertemper,* German *quatember,* and Danish *kvatember* exhibit the process of the corruption. The Ember Days are recognized by both the Roman and the Anglican Church. The Book of Common Prayer defines them as "days of fasting, on which the Church requires such a measure of abstinence as is more especially suited to extraordinary acts and exercises of devotion." They occur on the Wednesday, Friday, and Saturday after the first Sunday in Lent, and after the feasts of Pentecost, of the Exaltation of the Cross, and of St. Lucy. The Ember Days were certainly observed in Rome in the time of St. Augustine of Hippo. St. Leo ascribes to them an apostolic origin. As the synagogue regularly observed four fasts in the year,—in the fourth, fifth, seventh, and tenth months,—it seems not impossible that the apostles should have handed down the Jewish custom to the Church. The fasts were introduced into England by its apostle St. Augustine at the end of the sixth century. At first the weeks in which the Ember Days occur were not definitely fixed, and even in the eleventh century a German council speaks of the Ember fast as *jejunium incertum*. According to ancient custom in the Roman Church the clergy are ordained only on the Saturdays of the Ember weeks, and in the Anglican on the Sundays following. Hence the Ember Days are especially a period of preparation for candidates for holy orders.

Emeric, St. The eldest son of St. Stephen of Hungary, commemorated in the calendar on the anniversary of his death, November 4, when he was prematurely cut off in the lifetime of his father. He is associated with the latter in the veneration of the Hungarians. His celebrity popularized his name, which in the Italianized form of Amerigo was conferred upon the navigator Vespucci; and, as the name of America is generally derived from Amerigo, St. Emeric may be looked upon as the eponymic patron of America.

Emmet, Robert. The birthday of this ill-fated Irish patriot is celebrated in Ireland and (mainly under the auspices of the Clan-na-Gael) in New York, Chicago, and other American cities. Born March 4, 1778, in Dublin, Emmet in 1803 planned an unsuccessful insurrection, and escaped to the Wicklow Mountains. Returning for a last interview with his sweetheart, Sarah Curran (daughter of the famous John Philpot Curran, and heroine of Moore's song " She is far from the Land" and of Irving's story "The Broken Heart"), he was arrested, put on trial on September 19, 1803, condemned to death, and hanged on the following day. Just before receiving sentence he delivered a speech full of the most noble and pathetic eloquence, which is still a favorite for recitation.

In 1896 a double celebration was held in New York at the Grand Central Palace under the auspices of the Clan-na-Gael and at Cooper Union under the auspices of the Irish Nationalists and Irish National Alliance. The orator of the occasion at the first was W. Bourke Cockran, at the second John E. Fitzgerald. The first regiment of Irish volunteers and the members of the 69th Regiment took part in the celebrations, as usual.

England, Conquest of. This event, which was secured by the battle of Hastings, fought on October 14, 1066, between William, Duke of Normandy, and Harold, King of the Saxons, is celebrated annually at Falaise, the birthplace of the Conqueror, on September 28,—that being the anniversary of the latter's landing on English soil. A writer in *Once a Week* for November 6, 1875, gives this picture of the festivities as he witnessed them in that year :

"I happened last September to be at Falaise, in Normandy. At the station I was met by an immense crowd. William the Conqueror had landed in England, and it was certain that we should all be vanquished. A hundred blue blouses were shouting at the ticket-receiver to know the last train. The young princes looked very well in an open cart. Arlette was not there, her washing days were over, and Count Robert was dead. No, I have not got a copper for the poor this time. Hotel prices risen? Never mind ; get into the omnibus *du Grand Cerf ;* give up your luggage-ticket to the *conducteur* before you are hustled to pieces, and drive on. Flags on both sides, fir-trees, suddenly transplanted and lining the streets, sound of drums, trumpets, and shouting. What is it all about?

"I arrive at the 'grand stage.' All heads on both sides out of the window. William the Conqueror has just come by ; after him went a very large ship with fine green calico waves, and oars very much in everybody's way, knights in chain armor, seated uneasily on oppressed and recalcitrant horses, and historical personages mixed up with all sorts of posterity.

"This is too much ! For once I am indifferent to the price of rooms. I fling my travelling bag to the garçon, bolt out of the omnibus with an umbrella,—I don't happen to have a halberd about me,—and, shouting the daring war-cry of ' *Sauve qui peut !*' which strikes terror into the breasts of all the Norman apple-women on the road, I rush down a by-lane in order to intercept the procession before it gets to the Place de la Mairie. But just in time. A row of horses' tails, wriggling and tossing behind the unaccustomed chain armor, show me plainly that the pageant has arrived before me. The ship, full of armed men, reels perilously in front of me and stops. The drums and trumpets cease.

The cavalcade becomes unmanageable. Carts, with counts and young princes, and Norman dukes, in flowing silk and velvet, and coats of mail, are met astray in all directions. It is clear the game is over, and the reign of long-restrained confusion has set in.

"I get a good footing on a curb-stone, collar a terrific and truculent Norman, and ask after William the Conqueror. He tells me that Britain is a small island; that the Channel is a trackless and well-nigh unnavigable ocean; but that Duke William, having entered a big pasteboard ship, soon mastered both, shot Harold, and set himself down on his throne. Hence consumption of cakes and ale, immense slaughter of fat oxen, collections for the poor, illuminations at night, and band, admission 1 fr."

Engracia, St. (from the Latin *Encratis* or *Encratides*), was the daughter of Ont Camerus, to whom the Romans had given the city of Norba Cæsarea, in Spain. She was brought up a Christian, and while still a young girl was betrothed to a governor on the Gallic side of the Pyrenees and sent to him with suitable escort. Their way lay through Cæsarea Augusta, the modern Saragossa, where the governor, Publius Dacianus, one of the bloodiest ministers of the tenth persecution, was at that time endeavoring to extirpate Christianity. Engracia visited him for the purpose of remonstrating on his cruelty. When Dacianus learned that she was a Christian he seized her and had her put to the torture. Some accounts make her survive the rack, but the favorite legend represents her as having fallen a victim to torture. Angels are said to have descended at her death and to have officiated at her funeral, bearing tapers and thuribles and singing hymns of triumph. During the Moorish captivity her relics disappeared, but they were discovered in 1389, during the excavations necessitated by the rebuilding of an old church dedicated to the martyrs of Saragossa. Seventy years afterwards Juan II. declared that by St. Engracia's intercession he was cured of a complaint in his eyes,—in consequence of which he resolved to enlarge the church and build a monastery adjoining it and dedicate the whole to St. Engracia. He began the work, but died before completing it, leaving that charge by will to his son, Ferdinand, the Catholic King, who continued the building, but it was not finished till the reign of Charles V.

Epiphany. (Gr. ἐπιφάνεια, "manifestation," "appearance.") A festival celebrated on January 6, the twelfth day after Christmas, hence known popularly in England as Twelfth Night. It is the anniversary of three different occasions whereon Christ manifested his glory: (1) in his adoration in the manger by the three Wise Men from the East, or Magi; (2) in his baptism, when a voice from heaven proclaimed him the Son of God; (3) in the marriage at Cana, when he began his miracles by changing water into wine.

The word Epiphany, being Greek, establishes the fact that this festival is of Eastern origin, and in fact in the Greek Church it has always been held the most important next to Easter. The first mention of it occurs in the year 200, in the writings of Clement of Alexandria. In the fourth century we find that in Gaul it was kept as a separate festival from Christmas. There is no doubt that in the early days the story of the Wise Men did not receive the prominence, in the different instances in which Christ manifested himself to the world, that it has now. Indeed, it appears from St. Gregory Nazianzen that the baptism of Christ was the chief event commemorated on the Epiphany. Hence, probably, the alternative Greek name for the feast, " the holy day of lights" (ἡ ἁγία τῶν φώτων ἡμέρα), which refers to the " illumination" of baptism, or possibly to an ancient tradition that at Christ's baptism lights appeared on the Jordan. However, the Breviary hymn for the day, composed by Prudentius in the fourth century, proves that the threefold commemoration on the Epiphany is ancient in the West.

In course of time the incident of the Wise Men's visit came to be looked upon as typical of the extension of the gospel to the Gentile world, and consequently as of preponderant importance to all of Gentile race. By the twelfth century romantic additions had been made to the simple Biblical narrative. The unnamed Wise Men had risen to specific regal rank as Caspar or Jaspar, King of Tarsus, the land of myrrh, Melchior, King of Arabia, where the land is ruddy with gold, and Balthasar, King of Saba, where frankincense flows from the trees. (See WISE MEN OF THE EAST.) When they beheld the star of Bethlehem they gathered together their retinue and set out on their journey. They reached Jerusalem and interviewed Herod, who was greatly impressed with their story. Then as they went out towards Bethlehem they came across an old woman who was cleaning her house. She asked them whither they were going. And when they told her she besought them to tarry until she had finished her task, and she would accompany them. They answered that they could not wait, and bade her follow after them. When she had finished she did strive to do so. But they were lost to sight; and ever since that day she has been wandering about the earth seeking for the child Jesus. And on the eve of Epiphany, according to Russian and Italian folk-lore, she comes down the chimneys of the houses, leaving gifts for the little ones, in imitation of the kings' fine gifts to the infant Christ, and hoping against hope that she may find Him whom she still seeks. In

THE STAR OF BETHLEHEM.
(From Wright's " Caricature and Grotesque.")

Italy she is known to this day as the Befana (a corruption of Epiphania), and in Russia as the Baboushka.

In the Greek Church, however, Christ's baptism is the most important event commemorated in the ceremonial of the day. Solemn baptism was given on the vigil of the Epiphany. At the present day among the Oriental sects it is usual for the clergy to bless the rivers at this time, the devout plunging into the icy waters, at imminent pulmonary risk. (See JORDAN, FÊTE OF THE.)

In memory of the Magi's offerings, it is even to this day the custom for the British sovereign to make gifts of gold, frankincense, and myrrh in the Chapel Royal, St. James. For many centuries this was done by the sovereign himself. George III., however, was the last king who appeared in person. Now the offerings are presented by two officers of the Lord Chamberlain, attended by the Yeomen of the Guard, while the offertory sentences are being read; the representatives of royalty bring up three purses and lay them on the alms-dish held by the celebrant, who presents them on the altar.

The Twelfth Cake was another long-established feature of the day, not only in England, but in France. This cake contained hidden within it a bean or a silver penny. At the family gathering around it, the cake was divided by lot, and whoever got the piece containing the bean was accepted as king.

A correspondent in the *Universal Magazine* for 1774 thus describes the method at that date of drawing for King and Queen of Twelfth Night. The ceremony of the cake and the bean had been outgrown in England. "I went to a friend's house in the country to partake of some of those innocent pleasures that constitute a merry Christmas. I did not return till I had been present at drawing King and Queen and eaten a slice of the Twelfth Cake, made by the fair hands of my good friend's consort. After tea, yesterday, a noble cake was produced, and two bowls, containing the fortunate chances for the different sexes. Our host filled up the tickets; the whole company, except the King and Queen, were to be ministers of state, maids of honor, or ladies of the bedchamber. Our kind host and hostess, whether by design or accident, became King and Queen. According to Twelfth Day law, each party is to support their character till midnight."

Hone in his "Every Day Book," vol. i. p. 51, describes the drawing as it was conducted in 1823: "First, buy your cake. Then, before your visitors arrive, buy your characters, each of which should have a pleasant verse beneath. Next, look at your invitation list and count the number of ladies you expect; and afterwards the number of gentlemen. Then take as many female characters as you have invited ladies; fold them up, exactly of the same size, and number each on the back, taking care to make the king No. 1 and the queen No. 2. Then prepare and number the gentlemen's characters. Cause tea and coffee to be handed to your visitors as they drop in. When all are assembled, and tea over, put as many ladies' characters in a reticule as there are ladies present; next, put the gentlemen's characters in a hat. Then call a gentleman to carry the reticule to the ladies, as they sit, from which each lady is to draw one ticket, and to preserve it unopened. Select a lady to bear the hat to the gentlemen for the same purpose. There will be one ticket left in the reticule and another in the hat, which the lady and gentleman who carried each is to interchange, as having fallen to each. Next arrange your visitors according to their numbers,—the king No. 1, the queen No. 2, and so on. The king is then to recite the verse on his ticket, then the queen the verse on hers, and so the characters are to proceed in numerical order. This done, let the cake and refreshments go round, and hey! for merriment!"

On Twelfth Day, 1563, Mary Queen of Scots celebrated the pastime of the King of the Bean at Holyrood, but with a queen instead of a king. The lot fell to the real queen's attendant, Mary Fleming, and the mistress arrayed the servant in her own robes and jewels. The English resident, Randolph, who was in love with Mary Beton, another of the queen's maids of honor, wrote in excited terms about this festival to the Earl of Leicester. "Happy was it," says he, "unto this realm that her reign endured no longer. Two such sights in one state in so good accord I believe was never seen, as to behold two worthy queens possess without envy one kingdom, both upon a day. I leave the rest to your lordship to be judged of. My pen staggereth, my hand faileth further to write."

The Twelfth Night festivities in old England were of a riotous sort. The nobility amused themselves by blowing up pasteboard castles and letting claret flow like blood out of a stag made of paste. Pasteboard castles were bombarded from a pasteboard ship, with cannon, in the midst of which the company pelted one another with egg-shells filled with rose-water; and large pies were made, filled with live frogs, which hopped out upon some curious person lifting up the lid. At court gaming was a costly feature. Evelyn records that on Twelfth Night, 1662, according to custom, his majesty (Charles II.) opened the revels of that night by throwing the dice himself in the Privy Chamber, where was a table set on purpose, and lost his hundred pounds. (The year before he had won fifteen hundred pounds.) The ladies also played very deep. Evelyn came away when the Duke of Ormond had won about one thousand pounds, and left them still at passage, cards, etc., at other tables.

Among the lower orders also the day was given up to revelry; and among them this has had a greater tenacity of life. In London, where the pastry-cook shops and confectioners' stalls with their Twelfth cakes were the great attraction, the boys of the street used to delight in nailing the coat-tails of spectators to the window-frames, or in pinning them together. Sometimes eight or ten persons found themselves thus connected. The dexterity of the nail-driving was so quick and sure that a single blow seldom failed of doing the business effectually. Withdrawal of the nail without a proper instrument was out of the question, and consequently the person nailed was forced either to leave part of his coat as a cognizance of his attachment, or quit the spot with a hole in it. At every nailing and pinning shouts of laughter arose from the perpetrators; yet it often happened to one who turned and smiled at the duress of another that he also found himself nailed. Efforts at extrication increased mirth; nor was the presence of a constable, who was usually employed to attend and preserve free " ingress, egress, and regress," sufficiently awful to deter the offender. (*Every Day Book*, vol. i. p. 50.)

Up to a comparatively recent date itinerant minstrels with bowls of lambs' wool would appear in the rural parts of England on the eve of the Epiphany. (See WASSAIL.) In Staffordshire the star that led the Magi was represented by a lighted hill-fire. Seemingly in connection with this, though it is not easy to trace the train of ideas, are the customs that still prevail

on the borders of Gloucestershire and Herefordshire. At Paunt-
ley, near Newent, the men of a farm would assemble in a field
sown with wheat, and, after making twelve fires of straw in a
row, would, standing round one much larger than the rest, drink
a glass of cider to the master's health. Then, returning to the
farm-house, they were regaled on cakes soaked in cider.

The same ceremony went on on the other side of the boundary
line of the counties, with a little more drinking, hallooing, and
chorusing round the fires. At the supper afterwards there was a
plum-cake with a hole in the middle which the bailiff (or head
of the oxen) took to the wain-house. There the master pledged
the best ox in a curious toast, the company following his example
with all the other oxen, addressing each by name. The cake
was placed on the ox's horn. If the ox, when tickled, tossed it off
backward, the cake fell to the mistress ; if forward, to the bailiff.

A kindred recognition of the twelve lights of the world, the
apostles, and the Saviour in their midst, was customary in West-
meath in the seventeenth century ; and so much of the custom
as concerns the ox and the health-drinking formula seems also
to have been in use at Tretire, near the Wye-side, the ox's toss
arbitrating between the boys and the men as to the ownership
of the cake.

A curious custom obtained at the Isle of Man in olden days,
when the Christmas festivities were kept up throughout the whole
twelve days and every parish hired a fiddler at the public charge.
On Twelfth Day the fiddler would lay his head in the lap of one
of the girls, and then a third person would ask whom such and
such a maid would marry, and the fiddler had to predict, and
whatever he said was regarded as oracular, even though he
coupled a pair who detested each other. This was called cutting
off the fiddler's head, as from that night he was dead until the
following Christmas.

In France, where it probably originated, the Twelfth Night
cake still survives. It is known there as La Galette du Roi
("the king's cake"). This cake is generally made of pastry,
and baked in a round sheet like a pie. The size of the cake depends upon the number of persons in the company. In former
times a broad bean was baked in the cake, but now a small china
doll is substituted for the bean. The cake is the last course in
the dinner. One of the youngest people at the table is asked to
say to whom each piece shall be given. This creates a little
excitement, and all watch breathlessly to see who gets the
doll. The person who gets it is king or queen, and immediately
chooses a king or queen for a partner. As soon as the king and
queen are announced they are under the constant observation of
the other members of the party, and whatever they do is imme-

26

diately commented upon. In a short time there is a perfect uproar: "The king drinks," "The queen speaks," "The queen laughs," etc. This is kept up for a long time; then there are games, music, and dancing.

In many parts of France, Belgium, and Holland processions of children tramp through the streets bearing a large paper star illuminated from within by a candle.

As already noted, the Baboushka in Russia and the Befana in Italy are the respective representatives of our Santa Claus, performing their functions on the eve of the Epiphany in lieu of Christmas Eve. Italian children carefully hang their clothes with empty pockets around the hearth, and the Befana fills them with confectionery and other presents if they have been good, and with charcoal ashes or birch rods if they have been bad. In Florence a procession of the Befana used to be held on the eve of Epiphany. She was personified by a colossal puppet representing a sorceress in flowing garments, the figure being so contrived as to appear taller or shorter at the pleasure of the bearer, whose person was concealed by the draperies. This monstrous effigy frightened the children by looking in the open windows of the houses. She

TWELFTH NIGHT PROCESSION IN HOLLAND.
(From Picart.)

was borne through the principal streets of Florence, preceded by a burning broom, as a reminder of the work of sweeping which she refused to abandon for the sake of the infant Christ, and followed by a torchlight procession beating drums and blowing long glass trumpets. Finally she was thrown from a bridge into the Arno, amid the acclamations of the multitude. The glass trumpets are still a discordant element in the Epiphany celebration. It is also customary for the Florentine shops to blossom out at Epiphany with puppets representing the Magi, amid which the grinning blackamoor face of Balthasar is especially conspicuous.

At Rome the special fun of Epiphany Eve is found in the Piazza Romana, where the din grows fast and furious at night-fall. Story describes it as almost deafening. "The object of every one is to make as much noise as possible, and every kind of instrument for this purpose is sold at the toy-booths. There are drums beating, tambourines thumping and jingling, pipes squeaking, watchmen's rattles clacking, penny trumpets and tin horns shrilling, the sharpest whistles shrieking, and mingling with these are heard the din of voices, screams of laughter, and the confused burr and buzz of a great crowd. Companies of people are marching together in platoons, or piercing through the crowd in long files, and dancing and blowing like mad on their instruments. It is a perfect witches' Sabbath."

In Milan the feast of the Wise Men is observed with great parade and flourish. Three kings, brilliantly dressed and mounted on beautiful horses which are gayly accoutred, attended by showy pages and escorted by a large guard and followed by throngs of people, march through the streets. In front of the procession is borne a gold star, carried on a tall mast. The march is continued until the manger is found, when the gifts are presented to the infant Christ.

In Spain also Epiphany is the great holiday for the children. Here, however, it is not the Befana nor the Baboushka, but one of the three kings—no less a person, indeed, than Balthasar—who is the purveyor of gifts. He is always represented as a blackamoor, and as such he survives in Spanish legend. On the eve of the Epiphany the children leave their shoes and boots out in some convenient spot near the chimney, to find them laden with gifts in the morning.

Another curious ceremony which exists in Spain on the eve of the Epiphany is similar to one that in England and France was practised on the eve of St. Valentine's (*q. v.*).

"In the burgher society of Castile," says John Hay, "each little social circle comes together in a house agreed upon. They take mottoes of gilded paper and write on each the name of some one of the company. The names of the ladies are thrown into one urn, and those of the cavaliers into another, and they are drawn out by pairs. These couples are thus condemned by fortune to intimacy during the year. The gentleman is always to be at the order of the dame, and to serve her faithfully in every knightly fashion. He has all the duties and none of the privileges of a lover, unless it be the joy of those who stand and wait."

The same authority tells us that the eve of the Epiphany is celebrated in Madrid by a bit of practical joking known as "the Kings." A crowd of men of the lower orders, playing on discordant horns and thumping drums, surround the first simple fellow who happens to pass and persuade him that he must join them in the search for the Magi, who are expected to enter the city by one of the gates that night. Over the yokel's head they throw a mule-collar to which dozens of bells are attached. He is then made to carry a ladder through the streets, and first at one gate and then at another is commanded to halt and climb up to see if the kings are anywhere in sight. Sometimes when he reaches the top he is allowed to fall, at the risk of a broken head or limb. But if he escapes injury the exquisite jest is kept up until suspicion supplants faith in the mind of the neophyte, and the farce is over.

Charles V. instituted in Spain the custom for the reigning sovereign to offer three gold chalices on Epiphany. Each chalice is worth about three hundred ducats. A piece of gold is placed in one, incense in the second, and myrrh in the third. After the offering one of these chalices is sent to the sacristy of St. Lawrence in the Escorial, and the other two to such churches or monasteries as the king may designate.

Epulum Jovis in Capitolio. An ancient Roman festival in honor of Jupiter, celebrated on the 13th of November. This festival took the form of a luxurious banquet which was held in the Capitol under the direction of a special board of seven, known as Epulones, and was participated in by the entire Senate. The statues of the three Capitoline deities, Jupiter, Juno, and Minerva, were taken down upon this occasion and allowed to participate in the feast. Their hair was arranged, a mirror being held up before them, that they might satisfy themselves as to their looks, their bodies were anointed, and their cheeks were colored with vermilion, and then they were placed at the table, —Jupiter reclining on a couch, after the manner of men, the goddesses erect in chairs, which was thought the proper attitude for women.

At this feast it happened once that the greatest Roman general of his time, Scipio Africanus, and Tiberius Gracchus, a young man of great promise, sat side by side. They had for a long time been unfriendly, but Gracchus on this day had spoken in the Senate in defence of Scipio's brother, and the two enemies were reconciled. In token of the reconciliation, Scipio betrothed his younger daughter to Gracchus; and when he returned home at night and informed his wife that he had promised her in marriage, she remonstrated, saying that, even if it were to Tiberius Gracchus, the mother of the girl ought to have been consulted. The maiden thus summarily disposed of was Cornelia, mother of the Gracchi, and her sons were the famous tribunes, Tiberius and Caius Gracchus.

Eric, St. (or **St. Henry**), patron saint of Sweden, whose festival on the anniversary of his death, May 18, is still celebrated
as a national holiday, was an historical character, King of Sweden
and of Norway, the ninth of the name. He was a Christian, and
built numerous churches. He attempted an unsuccessful crusade against the Finns, and then wisely turned his attention to
domestic legislation. He compiled a code of laws from the ancient constitutions of the nation, and " St. Eric's Law" was long
spoken of in Sweden with that kind of reverence with which
the laws of St. Edward the Confessor were regarded by the
English people under the rule of the foreign Normans. He was
slain in battle on Ascension Day, 1151. He was in church when
news was brought him that Magnus of Denmark had landed on
the coast and was marching against him. He said, calmly, " Let
us at least finish the sacrifice; the rest of the festival I shall
keep elsewhere." When the mass was ended, he went forth at
the head of his guards, and fell after a brave defence. His tomb
remains to this day at Upsal, undefiled. The title of saint was
given him by a popular and national canonization, and was afterwards confirmed by the Church. He is also known as " the
Pious" and " the Legislator."

Escalade. The great annual festival of Geneva, held on December 11 and 12. It keeps alive the memory of the repulse of
a sudden and secret assault on the city by its hereditary enemies the Savoyards.

During the night of the 11th of December, 1602, large forces
marched from their several strongholds in Savoy, crossed the
river Arve, and began to scale the town walls. At the moment
the alarm was given, the citizens sprang from their beds and
rushed out in the scantiest of attire, and proceeded to repel the
attack. Some of the enemy had actually got into the town,
but, thanks to the narrow, tortuous streets and their absolute
darkness, had lost their way, and were soon overcome. Those
climbing the walls were driven back, the women, who had also
hastened to take part in the defence, pouring hot soup and water
down on their heads. By noon of the 12th the Savoyards were
completely routed and driven back into the fastnesses of their
own country.

" Ever since then," writes Percy Gordon in the *New York
Evening Post* for February 15, 1896, " Geneva has celebrated the
11th and 12th of December with unfailing regularity; and to-
day, nearly three hundred years later, the time of the Escalade,
as it is called, is observed with a hilarity which shows no signs
of having spent itself. Men, women, and children, after dark of
the 11th and 12th, dress up in the most ludicrous of costumes,

putting on the absurd Carnival masks, and walk the principal streets, throwing confetti at each other and the passers-by, until midnight, when the older folk adjourn to the Kursaal to indulge until morning in the dance and frolic of a masquerade ball. Woe to all unsuspecting foreigners who venture on the streets without costume! It is a traditional privilege of the gallants to kiss any woman caught on the streets unmasked. Last year an American gentleman escorted three pretty American ladies to see the sights, unconscious, of course, of this tradition. The little party was soon surrounded by a laughing crowd of maskers, who caught hands and danced around them, enjoying their confusion, until one bolder than the rest caught and kissed the prettiest of the three, when they all swung off with a merry laugh to go and annoy other unwary sight-seers. During this season very little work of any kind is done, of course. It is, in fact, the Genevese Thanksgiving Day, when, as with us, turkeys are fattened and killed, and the individual members of the various families gather, when they can, round the common ancestral boards. In the confectioners' shops are chocolate bonbons in the shape of little iron pots with lids on which are stamped the date 1602 and that of the current year. These little dainties serve to keep alive the incident of the patriotic soup-pouring by the women of the besieged city. It is indeed a merry time for all."

Ethelreda, St., also called **St. Audrey.** Her festival is celebrated on October 17, the anniversary of the translation of her relics in 695. St. Ethelreda was a princess of East Anglia. Her kinsmen forced her to marry Tombert, King of the Gervii, and after his death Egfrid, King of Northumbria. But she retained her virginity with both. After twelve years, with the consent of Egfrid she withdrew to the convent of Coldingham. Later Egfrid wished her back and tried to drag her from her retreat, but Ethelreda fled to a rock, since called St. Ebb's Head. Her husband pursued her, and legend says that the tide suddenly rose and rendered the rock inaccessible. Egfrid gave up the chase and married another wife. Ethelreda crossed the Humber, and had a dream in which she thought that, having stuck her staff in the ground, it put forth branches and blossomed into a large tree. Shortly afterwards she founded the cathedral and monastery of Ely, on the island of that name, and was the first abbess. She died June 23, 679. She made a dying request that she should be buried with the other sisters without any mark of distinction, but in 695 Sexburga, her sister, who had succeeded as abbess, ordered her relics to be enclosed in a stone monument. In 1106 Robert of Ely had the relics removed to the cathedral church of Ely. Her shrine perished during the Reformation. It is related that four hundred years after her death a wicked man repented and vowed to serve God in the monastery of Ely. On his way thither he was taken and imprisoned for his crimes, but on his invoking St. Ethelreda she appeared in the night with St. Benedict and liberated him.

Eucharist. (From the Pauline word *eucharistia*, "thanksgiving.") The name given to the consecrated bread used in the communion services. To Catholics it is also known as the host (Lat. *hostia*, "a victim"). With them it takes the form of a circular wafer made of unleavened wheat. They claim to follow the use of Christ himself, for leavened bread could not have been employed at the paschal supper. But their own authorities differ as to the ancient Christian usage. Perhaps Bona is right in his opinion that, whereas the Greeks have always used leavened bread, the Latins in the early ages used either leavened or unleavened bread according to convenience, and that the use of the latter was not obligatory among them till the tenth century. As Catholics believe that the host after consecration becomes the actual body of Christ, they guard it with the most anxious reverence. "We are full of anxiety," says Tertullian, "lest anything of our chalice and bread should fall to the ground." Severe penalties were imposed, both in the East and in the West, upon the ministers of the altar, if through their negligence any accident happened to the Blessed Sacrament. Catholics are obliged to pay to the eucharist, present on the altar, reserved in the tabernacle, or carried in procession, that supreme worship which is due to God alone. "The eucharist," says the Council of Trent, "is not the less to be adored because Christ instituted it in order that it might be received; for we believe that that same God is present in it of whom the eternal Father, bringing him into the world, said, 'Let all the angels of God adore him;' that God whom the Magi adored falling down before him ; who, finally, was adored by the apostles in Galilee, as the Scripture bears witness."

It was on account of this reverence due to the host that the devil-worshippers of France and other antichristian and Jewish societies have always been reputed anxious to secure the consecrated wafers in order to inflict indignities upon them. So recently as 1894, it is asserted, two ciboria, containing one hundred consecrated hosts, were carried off by an old woman from the cathedral of Notre-Dame under circumstances which indicated that the vessels were not the objects of the larceny. Similar depredations are said to have increased in an extraordinary manner during recent years, and have occurred in all parts of

France. No less than thirteen churches belonging to the diocese of Orleans were despoiled in the space of twelve months.

Alleged miracles of the host bleeding when profanely lacerated by malevolent Jews, to whom in the Middle Ages was ascribed a fatal fascination for meddling with the Christian eucharist, have been chronicled at Paris in 1290 ; at Deckendorf in Bavaria, 1337 ; at Brussels, 1369 ; at Posen, 1399 ; at Nivelles, Brabant, 1405 ; and at Brandenburg, 1510. In most cases, with incredible obstinacy, the son of Israel denied his guilt, and was delivered over to the authorities to be burned. His possessions were confiscated ; his wife and children were either converted or killed.

In the Paris case the accused, a Jew named Johnathas, was alleged to have craftily obtained the host from a poor woman whose goods he held in pawn. He first stabbed it with a knife, when it bled profusely, and then he successively placed it in the fire, whence it leaped out, and in a pot of boiling water, where it assumed in miniature the appearance of the crucified Saviour. Ultimately it was rescued by a pious woman and adored by multitudes. Many Jews were converted by it. Johnathas was burned alive. Clementina, second wife of Louis le Hutin, by her will (1328) left a bequest of ten Parisian pounds to the convent in Paris where God was boiled ("où Dieu fut bouliz"). (See *Notes and Queries*, Eighth Series, vol. ix. p. 269.)

In the " Secret Archives of the Vatican," 133, Epist. 294, the same authority found " a long, interesting, and possibly yet unpublished letter" from Benedict XII., dated Avignon, August 29, 1338, to Albert, Duke of Austria, written in response to the duke's inquiry how he should proceed concerning a case where a bleeding host had been discovered at the doors of a Hebrew's house. The Pope wisely and humanely refers to instances of similar happenings where the evidence was of a doubtful nature, and suggests that certain evil-minded laics may have done the thing.

There is still preserved at Dijon a consecrated host sent to Philip III., Duke of Burgundy, by Eugenius IV. This was stained with blood, it was alleged, by reason of having been repeatedly struck by the knife of an unbeliever. Many miracles have been ascribed to it, its own incorruptibility heading the list.

In Orvieto, Italy, is preserved a corporal cloth which is said to have been splashed with blood while a doubting priest was officiating at mass. (See CORPUS CHRISTI.)

Physicians have suggested that the *bacillus prodigiosus* is responsible for these stories of bleeding hosts. It forms red or pink patches not only upon bread, but also upon cooked meat and fish. In 1843 it became almost an epidemic in Paris, where it grew more especially on the bread made in military barracks. (See *Woodhead's Bacteria and their Products*, 1891.)

Euphemia, St. (patroness of Chalcedon, and one of the chief martyrs of the Greek Church). Her festival, celebrated on September 16, is a holiday over almost all the East. She was martyred near Byzantium about 307. After being cruelly tortured, she was cast first into a den of lions, who licked her feet and refused to do her any violence, and then into the fire, which would not burn her: so she was finally despatched with a sword. Within a century after her death many churches were dedicated to her, both East and West. The most famous was in Chalcedon, which contained her relics. Here in 451 was held the fourth general Council, that condemned Eutyches. The fathers who took part attributed to the intercession of the saint much of the credit for the happy issue of that affair. Her shrine became so popular that for the convenience of pilgrims the relics were transferred to St. Sophia in Constantinople. In 813 Leo the Iconoclast ordered them to be thrown into the sea, but the sea gave them back again, and the faithful concealed them until after Leo's death. They are now preserved at Syllebria, on the Propontine shore. A small portion is also possessed by the church of the Sorbonne at Paris.

Another St. Euphemia was abbess of the monastery of St. Victor in Marseilles. During an irruption of the Saracens she and her virgins all suffered martyrdom, after having first cut off their lips and noses to render themselves physically distasteful to the heathen invaders.

Evacuation Day. A holiday celebrated in New York city on November 25, in commemoration of the day in 1783 when the British soldiers, who had still held possession of the city, finally evacuated it and left America to her new destiny. The war of the Revolution practically closed with the surrender of Cornwallis at Yorktown in October, 1781. It is true that neither side relaxed its vigilance, but neither attempted serious aggressive operations. Six months after Yorktown came the first acknowledgment from England that she had seen the beginning of the end.

Wilmington, North Carolina, was evacuated in May, 1782, Savannah in June, Charleston in December. These steps were significant and most acceptable to that war-worn section of the country, but they were not final. The abandonment of the South did not certainly foreshadow England's intentions.

With the opening of 1783 matters took a definite shape. All doubts were soon removed. There was to be a final peace, based upon the absolute independence of the American States, with all their material claims to rights and territory recognized and accepted by Great Britain. The great news reached America officially in March, and on the 19th of April following Washington proclaimed to the army the cessation of hostilities. The war was over. What remained to be done of a military nature was, for the Americans, the adjustment of the soldiers' pay and discharge of the greater part of them from the service, and, for the British, the settlement of claims according to treaty, the disposition of Tories, the gathering up of paraphernalia, and final departure.

At the time of the peace announcement the enemy occupied but two points on the coast of the thirteen States,—New York and the mouth of the Penobscot. The latter post they had held since 1779 as a protection for English settlers and refugees, and to secure a valuable lumber region. New York had been in British hands since September 15, 1776. It had ever since been their head-quarters and base of operations.

There were many and vexatious delays, but finally at eight o'clock on November 25, 1783, the American troops under Washington marched into the city, and by noon the last guards of the English had evacuated it. The last boat-load of Britishers presumably carried away the British flag that had so long waved from Fort George at the Battery. The Continentals hoisted in its place the flag of the thirteen States and saluted it with thirteen rounds fired from John Bull's guns.

Up to the middle of the nineteenth century Evacuation Day was one of the greatest of New York's holidays. But its close proximity to Thanksgiving led to its gradual fading away before the more national celebration. Nowadays it is marked only by a parade of the Old Guard of New York down to the Battery, where a flag-raising is held on the old site of Fort George. The person who raises the flag has always been a lineal descendant of the sailor-boy who raised it in 1783.

Eve, Even, or **Vigil.** In their present acceptation these words apply to the whole day which precedes a feast. Originally Christians were in the habit of keeping vigils, *i.e.*, watchings, on the evenings prior to certain festivals, and by extraordinary devotions preparing for the better celebration of the feast on the following day. The words eve or even and vigil thus grew to be almost synonymous. By the ninth century or thereabouts the practice of fasting on vigils, at first a voluntary devotion, had grown to be obligatory. The eves of Christmas and Easter were considered the most important during the year, and the midnight mass on the first date is a relic of the old custom. But none of the festivals which occur between Christmas and Candlemas nor between Easter and Whitsuntide is preceded by a vigil, the period being regarded as one of joy and not proper for fasting. Hence the familiar New Year's Eve is, ecclesiastically, a misnomer. The feast of Michaelmas and All Angels as commemorating the bliss of heaven is also without a vigil, as is that of St. Luke because preceded by the feast of St. Ethelreda.

Eve, Tomb of. The Arabs assert that Eve's tomb is at Jiddah, the seaport of Mecca. The temple, with a palm growing out of the solid stone roof (a curiosity which is of itself the wonder of the Orient), is supposed to mark the last resting-place of the first woman. According to Arabian tradition, Eve measured over two hundred feet in height. Her tomb, in a graveyard surrounded with high white walls, which has not been opened for a single interment for over a thousand years, is the shrine of thousands of devoted Ishmaelites, who make a pilgrimage to the spot once every seven years. It is hemmed in on all sides by the tombs of departed sheiks and other worthies who have lived out their days in that region of scorching sun and burning sands. Once each year, on June 3, which is, according to Arabian legends, the anniversary of the death of Abel, the doors of the temple forming a canopy over this supposed tomb of our first mother remain open all night, in spite of the keeper's efforts to close them. Terrible cries of anguish are said to be emitted thence, as though the memory of the first known tragedy still haunted the remains which blind superstition believes to be deposited there.

Excommunication. The formal exclusion of a person from religious communion and privileges. Excommunication, often with very severe consequences, was practised in various ways by the ancient Greeks, Romans, and Jews. It is still in use among Mohammedans. In the early Christian Church it consisted simply in the exclusion of an offending member from fellowship by some formal action. This is still the practice among most Protestant denominations. As the power of the Church increased, excommunication became more complicated in method and severe in effect. In the Roman and related Churches excommunication may be either partial or total, temporary or perpetual. By the partial, or *excommunicatio minor*, the culprit is merely excluded from the sacraments; by the total, or *excommunicatio major*, he is excluded from the mass, from all intercourse with Christians, from ecclesiastical jurisdiction, and from burial in consecrated ground. Bell, book, and candle are the three instruments em-

ployed in the formal ceremony of excommunication. The ringing of the bell apprises the faithful within the church of what is

CEREMONY OF EXCOMMUNICATION.
(From Picart.)

about to happen, the sentence is read out of the book, and the
lighted candle is then extinguished to denote the spiritual darkness in which the excommunicated person must for the future
abide.

Expectation of the Confinement of Our Lady. A
Catholic festival celebrated on December 18 in many churches of
France and Spain, and generally among the Cistercian, Dominican, Franciscan, and Carmelite monastic orders.   The festival
was ordered by the tenth Council of Toledo, in 654, in the time
of King Rechaswinth, because the feast of the Annunciation
generally falls in Lent, when the Church is engaged on other
solemnities, and cannot celebrate that mystery with the application it deserves.   In France the day often goes by the name of
" Notre-Dame de l'O," because on it begins the antiphon " O
Sapientia," the first of the eight Greater Antiphons, all beginning with O.   Similarly in England, though the Reformed Church
does not recognize the festival, the day is known as " O Sapientia."

F.

Fair. An assemblage of men and women, gathered together at periodical intervals, primarily for the purpose of traffic and barter, but also for affording an outlet for the exuberant animal forces which are characteristic of the populace of most nations. It would seem, indeed, that the holiday idea preceded the work-day. The origin of fairs was in ancient Egypt. When the annual overflow of the Nile converted the lower level of its valley into a watery waste, the entire population would crowd in barges to the various festivals held in the principal towns or in the neighborhood of the great temples. Bustle and activity prevailed here, products and manufactures found a ready market, priests played lucratively upon popular superstition, and mummers and fakirs found ready gratuities. This periodical flocking to the great festivals, with the attendant mingling of traffic and amusement, still survives among the Hindoos and other Asiatic races. The Greeks and Romans had their fairs also, when labor and law-pleadings were for the nonce suspended.

In the Middle Ages fairs sprang up in Europe just as they had done in Egypt. They were the result of the gatherings of pilgrims to sacred places at fixed seasons. Those sacred places were often in the country, remote from houses of public entertainment, and thus tents were pitched and stalls set up for the lodging and refection of worshippers. Tradesmen naturally flocked hither to dispose of their wares. The priors were entitled to certain tolls, and to render the festivals more attractive they speedily introduced various amusements. Indeed, it was at such places that the best entertainment was to be found which was within men's reach in the Middle Ages. The fairs were frequented by lords and princes. Those of Beaucaire, Frankfort, and Leipsic amused the nobles of Normandy and Germany; the great fairs of England—Bartholomew Fair, Greenwich Fair, Peterborough Fair, and Edmonton Fair—attracted royalty itself.

Thus the fair was originally bound to the life of the nation by the three ties of religion, trade, and pleasure. But the time came when the tie of religion was loosened: then it was a place for trade and pleasure. A few more generations having lived and waned, trade was no longer bound to it. The nation still grew, and at last broke from it even as a pleasure-place.

The history of Bartholomew Fair is in essentials if not in details the history of all English fairs.

The old priory and church of St. Bartholomew in Smithfield were founded in March, 1123, by one Rayer, who had been jester to Henry I. He had not forgotten his juggling tricks when he became an abbot. The numerous miracles performed at the shrine were even by many of his contemporaries regarded as the result of Rayer's ingenuity. From the time of the establishment of his priory a fair had begun to be held in the graveyard and open space before it on St. Bartholomew's Day. Thus in the beginning we have a fair full of worshippers, among whom were the sick and maimed, praying for health about its altar; a graveyard full of traders loudly magnifying their wares; and a place of jesting and edification where women and men caroused together, where the minstrel and the story-teller and the tumbler gathered knots about them, where the young men bowled at nine-pins, while the clerks and friars peeped at the young maids, where mounted knights and ladies curveted and ambled, where oxen lowed, horses neighed, and sheep bleated among their purchasers, where great shouts of laughter answered to the ho! ho! of the devil on the stage, while a band of pipers and guitar-beaters added music to the din.

After the Reformation the priory went down, but the fair continued. Lord Rich, the man who helped to rack Anne Askew, bought the priory and all its rights for £1064. The Reformed Church took no notice of the fair, but it was supported by municipal patronage. The lord mayor, sheriffs, and aldermen, going to Smithfield in a procession, opened the fair with a solemn proclamation; and after they had drunk a cup of ale, the sports and business commenced.

The license of the Restoration extended the fair from a three days' market to a fortnight's riot of amusement.

In 1697 the lord mayor on St. Bartholomew's Day published an ordinance recorded in the *Postman* "for the suppression of vicious practices in Bartholomew Fair, as obscene, lascivious, and scandalous plays. comedies, and farces. unlawful games and interludes, drunkenness. etc., strictly charging all constables and other officers to use their utmost diligence in persecuting the same." In 1698 a Frenchman, Monsieur Sorbière, visiting London, says, " I was at Bartholomew Fair. It consists mostly of toy-shops, also fiacres and pictures, ribbon-shops, no books; many shops of confectioners, where any woman may be commodiously treated. Knavery is here in perfection, dexterous cutpurses and pick-pockets. I went to see the dancing on the ropes, which was admirable. Coming out, I met a man that would have took off my hat, but I secured it. and was going to draw my sword, crying out, ' Begar! damn'd rogue! morbleu!' etc., when on a sudden I had a hundred people about me, crying, ' Here, monsieur, see *Jephthah's Rash Vow*,' ' Here, monsieur, see *The Tall Dutch-woman;*' ' See *The Tiger*,' says another; ' See *The Horse and No Horse*, whose tail stands where his head should do;' ' See the

German Artist, monsieur;' 'See *The Siege of Namur,* monsieur;' so that betwixt rudeness and civility I was forced to get into a fiacre, and, with an air of haste and a full trot, got home to my lodgings."

In 1701 Bartholomew Fair was presented as a nuisance by the Grand Jury of London, and in 1750 it was reduced to its original three days. In consequence of the alteration of the calendar in 1752, the fair in the following year was, for the first time, proclaimed on September 3.

A few years later things had come to this, that "by every thief living in London Bartholomew Fair was regarded as an annual performance for his benefit." Decency could hardly venture there; and the deterioration of the shows is proved by the fact that nearly all of them charged but a penny for admission. At the beginning of the nineteenth century a favorite amusement of the assembled blackguards was to surround some respectable woman and tear her clothes off her back.

In 1849 Bartholomew Fair contained only a dozen gingerbread-stalls. In 1850 the lord mayor, quietly walking to Smithfield, proclaimed the fair for the last time. In 1855 the form of proclamation, done for the last five times by deputy, ceased to be observed. The single relic of the great fair is an annual fee of three shillings and sixpence paid by the city to the rector of St. Bartholomew the Great. And thus passed away an observance which had its day, and which served its end, and which died out naturally when its day was over.

In the earlier days all the great fairs were almost identical in their main features. Yet in course of time as the fairs lost their usefulness they developed picturesque idiosyncrasies. Edmonton Statute Fair, for example, became the most profoundly useless of them all. It was a combination of three fairs in one, all "unmixed," says Mr. R. H. Horne, "with the sale of pigs, cattle, or 'baser matter;' nothing of the least utility or permanent value was to be found there, everything being of the most ostentatious gorgeous finery, gilt and painted trumpery, and grotesque absurdity." Of course he is speaking of the fair as it appeared in his own boyhood. Of Greenwich Fair the same authority reports that it had many striking peculiarities, besides the usual number of large shows. First there was the noble old hospital and the frequent presence of old pensioners in their quaint old-fashioned sombre uniform of navy blue, with the three-cornered cocked hat, knee-breeches, and square-toed shoes with huge plated buckles. The other great feature was the "Crown and Anchor" booth, which, varying its size at different fairs, invariably put forth its utmost magnitude and its fullest splendors for Greenwich Fair.

"The Crown and Anchor booth was so long that a full band played for dances at the top, by the bar, another at the bottom of the booth, and a third in the centre; and though they often played different dances, different airs to suit, and in different keys, you could only hear the music of your own dance, the predominant accompaniment to each being the measured muffled thunders of the boots of the fair-going Londoners. At these high moments it may be supposed that the fun was too fast and furious for the gentler beings of creation,—of course with some rather conspicuous exceptions." The last great specialty was the roll down Greenwich Hill. "Many persons at home as well as abroad have never seen that celebrated hill, never rolled down it, and some, perhaps, may not even have heard of it. But a word or two will suffice to make them in some degree aware of the pleasure they have lost. A number of fair-going young people of both sexes—but most commonly lovers or brothers and sisters—seated themselves on the top of this steep and beautifully green hill, and, beginning to roll down slowly, they pres-

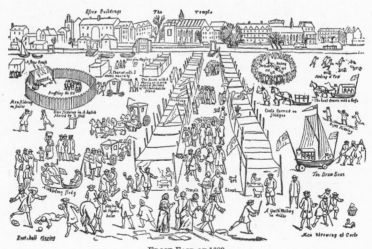

FROST FAIR OF 1683.
(From a contemporary print.)

ently found that the rolling became quicker and quicker,—that they had no power to govern their rapidity, still less to stop; and they invariably rolled to the bottom. It didn't agree with everybody."

Peterborough Market Fair was celebrated for only one peculiarity, its immense quantities of woodwork for farming operations. There you might see piles on piles of axe-, hoe-, fork-, rake-, and spade-handles; also handles for smiths' and carpenters' hammers; also tires and spokes for cart-wheels, window-frames, wheelbarrows, and dense arrays of field-gates, hurdles, and fences.

The London frost fairs which resulted from the occasional freezing over of the river Thames had a character and individuality of their own. One of the most remarkable of these was that held in the winter of 1683–4, when the frost lasted without a moment's cessation from early in December to February 4. The Thames was congealed into a solid mass of ice, eleven inches in thickness. A new city sprang into existence on the river. A contemporaneous print has the following legend:

"A WONDERFUL FAIR, or a FAIR OF WONDERS; being a new and true Illustration and Description of the several things acted and done on the river Thames in the time of the terrible frost, which began at the beginning of December, 1683–4, and continued till the 4th of February, and held on with such violence that men and beasts, coaches and sledges, went common thereon. There was also a street of boothes, built from the Temple to South-wark, where was sold all sorts of goods; there likewise were bulls baited, a fox hunted, and an ox roasted whole, and many other strange things, as the Mapp and Description doth plainly shew."

This fair was known as the Blanket Fair, from the fact that the booths were formed of blankets, a fact celebrated in a doggerel ballad of the day which anticipates a famous conceit of Goldsmith's:

> Like Babel, this fair's not built with brick or stone,
> Though here, I believe, is a great confusion.
> Now blankets are forced a double duty to pay,
> As beds all the night, and for houses all day.

The booths supplied every conceivable kind of commodity, such as goldsmiths' work, books, toys, cutlery, ornaments, and refreshments, for which they charged exorbitant prices, a fact the rhyming historians of the scene have not failed duly to chronicle:

> And such a fair I never yet came near,
> Where shop-rents were so cheap and goods so dear.

Llandaff has the greatest fair in Wales. Tradition dates its origin back to the first century of the Christian era. At the most prosperous period of its career it was prolonged for many days. Monks and laymen flocked to it from many miles around. Llandaff churchyard was one scene of buying and selling, in tents and booths. Nowadays booths are not set up in the

churchyard, but they occupy the streets of the decayed cathedral city, even to the very walls of the bishop's palace. This
fair legally commences on Whit Monday, which is the greatest
of Welsh feasts, and lasts until Wednesday. But in point of fact
the revels commence with Whitsunday.

No cries of hawkers rend the air, but a thriving trade is done
in oranges, nuts, and gingerbread, all the same. Keepers of
shows surreptitiously take pence and pass people quietly into
their tents to see the African serpents, the wax-works, and the
rest. As the hours pass, matters grow worse. After dusk, the
beer begins to flow, and with the falling darkness the license
becomes greater. At midnight there are uncountable crowds
on the scene. The following morning the fair ostensibly begins;
before noon it is roaring with bustle; Punch and Judy squeak;
hawkers howl; exhibitors of curiosities bawl at the highest
pitch of their voices. There are curiosities enough here,—fat
women, living skeletons, wax-works, pygmies, giants, performing
dogs and monkeys, an endless array of idle and profitless diversions. Merry-go-rounds whirl their laughing, shrieking freight
through the air,—" warranted to make you sea-sick for a penny."
Shooting-galleries, and even perambulating photograph-galleries,
are there.

The pre-eminently great fair in Ireland was that held at Don-
nybrook, a village a few miles outside of Dublin. The familiar
song which makes the " shillelah" the all-in-all of the fair belongs
to a traditionary period. " A few fights and broken heads," says
Mr. Horne, " inseparable from *all* English as well as Irish fairs,
of course always took place, but the crowd was too dense to
allow of much damage being done. There was not only no
room for ' science,' but no room to strike a blow of a real kind
from the shoulder and ' using the toes.' We saw no blood
flow."

The fair, as to its great shows and booths, was held in a large
hollow or basin of green ground, on descending into which you
found the immediate skirtings occupied by a set of very little,
very low-roofed, tomb-like booths, where a busy trade was carried on in fried potatoes, fried sausages, and oysters, cold and
scalloped. But what amused Mr. Horne most were the scenes
in the village itself.

" The houses were all very small, the largest generally rising
no higher than one floor above the ground-floor rooms, and every
house being entirely appropriated to the use of the fair-coming
people. The rooms below were devoted to whiskey-drinking,
songs, jokes, politeness, and courtship, with a jig in the middle;
and very much the same, but with more elaborate and constant
dancing, in the rooms above. Every house presented the same

In every land, O,
The land that ere we go,
With Hal-an-tow, etc.,
And we were up, etc.

As for St. George, O,
St. George he was a knight, O,
Of all the kings in Christendom,
King George is the right, O.
In every land, O,
The land that ere we go
With Hal-an-tow, etc.

God bless Aunt Mary Moses,
With all her power and might, O;
And send us peace in merry England,
Both day and night, O.

At nine o'clock the revellers appear before the grammar-school and demand a holiday for the school-boys, after which they collect money from house to house. They then *fadé* into the country (*fadé* being an old English word for "go"), and about the middle of the day return with flowers and oak branches in their hats and caps, and spend the rest of the day until dusk in dancing through the streets to the sound of the fiddle, playing the "Furry tune," and thread the houses as they choose,—claiming a right to go through any person's house, in at one door and out of the other.

This goes on through countless houses, and through whole streets. Whenever the head of the procession emerges it is received with roars of delight; whenever the tail of the procession disappears it is followed by numerous adherents, who join on, and begin dancing too.

It was formerly the custom for the resident gentry to follow suit in the afternoon, beginning by visiting some farm-house in the neighborhood, whence, after regaling themselves with syllabubs, they returned, after the fashion of the vulgar, to the town, dancing as briskly the *fadé* dance, and entering the houses as unceremoniously. In later times a select party only made their progress through the streets very late in the evening, and, having quickly vanished from the scene, reappeared in the ball-room of the Angel Inn, where they danced until supper, and then returned home. At present, however, Furry Day is observed only among the lower classes, and even among them has lost much of its ancient spirit.

The meaning and derivation of the word Furry are not easy to determine. Polwhele in his "History of Cornwall" (1826, vol. ii. p. 41) suggested its origin in *fer*, a "fair," and buttressed this opinion with the second line of the "furry" song,—

> They both are gone to the fair, O.

Fusi-Jama. The sacred mountain of Japan. The glory of the regular, pure white cone, rising from the plain, and towering king-like over the petty hills scattered to the right and left, has been sung by Japanese poets, and limned by Japanese artists, from time immemorial. Well-omened is the house so situated as to command a view of the mountain; fortunate the man who can

FIRST SIGHT OF FUSI-JAMA.
(From a Japanese sketch.)

show, among his household treasures, the duly signed certificate of his having made its arduous ascent. Scarcely a screen or a tray or a lacquered bowl exists on which the well-known shape of the mountain is not portrayed. Ignorant rustics cannot be convinced that there are spots in the world whence the cone cannot be descried. To the citizen of Yedo it is a barometer, a protective genius, a sight to amaze the foreign visitor; to the peasant it is a something so sublime and grand as not to be spoken of without reverence.

To make a pilgrimage hither is the desire of all devout Japanese and the accomplishment of most. The pilgrims find shelter for the night in a number of rude stone huts. Immediately before sunrise they all kneel among the rough cinder-heaps and watch for the moment when the sun-goddess appears upon the far-distant horizon; prayers and litanies are chanted, and then the circuit of the crater is begun. This is a toilsome march of three miles, over ashes, crags, and lava of many different colors; and it is done sunwise, with the right hand to the centre.

Some of the pilgrims make a second circuit lower down the

mountain, where the line of vegetation begins. This is a much longer march than the other, the circumference being about twelve miles, and the path is over masses of volcanic ash and heaps of lava.

G.

Gayant, Fête de. A festival celebrated annually at Douai, France, from the 8th to the 11th of July. Its distinguishing feature is the procession, on two out of the four days, of Sire de Gayant and his family through the gayly decorated streets of the town. Gayant is a figure twenty-five feet high made of wicker-work. Resplendently clad in mediæval armor, with nodding plumes in his helmet and a mighty mace in his hand, he is down to his hips of the most masculine fibre. But the exigencies of processional duties require that he must have no legs, and that his lower half should be covered by a petticoat descending from his thigh-pieces and his apron of chain mail to the ground, so as to conceal the nine men who move the figure from within.

He heads the procession. Around him madly prance mummers mounted on hobby-horses, who make all the foolish noise they can. Behind him comes his goodly consort Marie Cagenon, another wicker toy, twenty-two feet high, in brocaded gown, with stomacher and farthingale, and a huge fan held before her face. Their three children follow,—Jacquot, in troubadour costume, Mlle. Fillon, in plain Renaissance gown, and the baby of the family, Mlle. Thérèse, otherwise known as Little Binbin, a mere mite of eight feet, wearing a round cap and a white pinafore, and running hither and thither in mad childish glee. She is the special favorite of the children of Douai, who clamor to be held up in their fathers' arms to kiss her cheeks. The interesting family is accompanied by allegorical or saintly personages who vary in identity from year to year. St. Michael slaying the dragon, the seven deadly sins, the cardinal virtues, demons, buffoons, and fantastic animals may be among them. During the intervals of the processions rural fun-making of all sorts goes on. Greased poles hung with fluttering prizes tempt the unwary, gayly decorated boats run races in the Scarpe, archers contend for prizes in the Place St.-Amé, concerts break out in the most unexpected places. The Chant de Gayant is sung, played, and danced. This song was composed in 1775 by a certain Lajoye, a dancing-master in a grenadier regiment stationed at Douai, and is always wildly applauded.

GAYANT AND HIS FAMILY.

The origin of the Fête de Gayant has been a puzzle to many antiquarians. The Church claims him as identical with St. Maurand, the patron of Douai. As for madame and the children (questionable encumbrances upon celibate saintship), it insists that the Gayant of the procession was a single man until 1665, when the good people of Douai abruptly ended his bachelorhood, the three children being born triplets of varying ages in 1715. Etymologists have made sad havoc with his name, tracing it to the Greek γῆ, "the earth," and heaven knows what other sources. But the common-sense view accepts Gayant simply as the Spanish *gigante*, "a giant," that and many other words being preserved in the local patois of Flanders as a reminiscence of the Spanish dominion.

The facts of the case as seen by common sense are somewhat as follows. In the year 1479 a feast and an accompanying procession were instituted in the city as a memorial of the repulse of Louis XI., who had laid siege to Douai in that year. In this pageant St. Maurand's image was probably a prominent feature. When Charles V. came into control of Flanders as part of his imperial heritage, he sought to graft Spanish innovations upon ancient Flemish customs. Hence he introduced some features of the Spanish pageant known as the Procession of the Giants (*q. v.*) into the yearly festival with which the city celebrated its victory over Louis XI. By the time the Spaniards were finally driven from the soil, the Sire de Gayant, owing to his conspicuous size, had entirely superseded the saint who had been the original patron of the festival, and, his peninsular paternity having been forgotten, he retained his place in popular favor.

As the procession became more and more secularized the Church grew more and more shocked at the license that accompanied it, and in 1770 the Bishop of Arras obtained from Louis XV. a decree of suppression. The clamorous discontent of the populace resulted in the rescinding of the decree nine years later. The opposition of the godly was at an end. But a new opposition of the ungodly began in 1792 with the triumph of the Revolution. Gayant and his family were dethroned for the Goddess of Reason and Liberty. Neither heaven nor hell, however, could prevail against the gallant Sire de Gayant. In 1801 the whole family were resurrected, although they had to pay a necessary tribute to contemporary modes of thought and dress by donning the costume of the Republic. Even in this guise the peasantry who flocked from all sides to applaud the reappearance of their grandfather, as they had come to call him, went into wild raptures of recognition. It was a sort of family fête. Then in 1821 an awful thing happened. Grandfather fell to pieces! His family were all more or less damaged. A complete restoration was decided upon. The modern puppets are the result of this restoration, which was tenderly and reverently planned and carried out by M. Vallet, professor of drawing in the village school.

Genevieve, St., patroness of Paris. Her festival on January 3, the anniversary of her death, was formerly celebrated with great pomp at the church of St. Genevieve in Paris. But since that church was secularized under the present republic and renamed the Pantheon, the celebration of the feast has been transferred to St. Etienne du Mont. Beginning on January 3, it closes with the end of the octave on the 11th.

St. Genevieve was a shepherdess, born at Nanterre, now almost a suburb of Paris, about 422. Christianity was at that time accepted by only a small proportion of the Franks. As the legend runs, she was very pious from her infancy, and St. Germain, passing through the then tiny village, consecrated her to religious work. From that time she worked miracles. Her mother, in a fit of temper boxing her ears, became blind, and Genevieve, by her prayers and by bathing the closed eyes with the water of the well in front of the house, restored the lost sight. The well became sacred, and during a famine she is said to have made nourishing soup of its waters for the starving peasants. The well still flows in front of the chapel at Nanterre that marks the site of Genevieve's home, and pilgrims still flock to it. On the death of her parents the maiden went to Paris, and before she was twenty she had become famous through her power of effecting cures by the use of herbs. Soon the word "sorceress" began to be whispered around. There is little doubt what would have been her fate if St. Germain had not come forward as her protector.

Later, when Attila, King of the Huns, threatened Paris, Genevieve exhorted the people not to fly, prophesying that Heaven would protect them. And when, in truth, the enemy withdrew without striking a blow, the people believed that the miracle had been wrought by her supplications.

As soon as order was restored, Genevieve established the first convent in France, on the spot now occupied by the Lycée Henri IV. In 456, when Childeric besieged Paris, and famine came on, Genevieve did her utmost to alleviate the suffering, and fitted out a boat in which she procured provision from Troyes. After Paris was taken she became the friend and adviser of the conqueror, gaining many concessions for the vanquished. She converted Clovis, the son and successor of Childeric, and instigated him to build the first Christian church in France, on the site now occupied by St. Etienne du Mont, which succeeded it in the sixteenth century. In this church Clovis himself, St. Clotilde, his wife, and Genevieve were subsequently buried. Genevieve's death is placed in the year 511. In 845, on the occasion of a Norman invasion, her relics were removed to Athis, then successively to Draveil, where a tooth is still preserved, and to Marizy, and finally in 855 were returned to Paris. When the church of St. Genevieve was built in that city the relics were enshrined there in a tomb ornamented with gold. There they remained, an object of universal veneration, until the outbreak of the Revolution, when the tomb was broken open, the gold was carried to the mints, and the relics were publicly burned. Nevertheless it is claimed that some of the bones were saved, and placed in the church of St. Etienne du Mont.

During the centuries prior to the Revolution many miracles were reported to have been wrought by the relics of the saint and through her intercession. Especially famous is the miracle "des Ardens," or of the burning fever. In 1129, during the reign of Louis VI., a pestilential fever swept off many thousands in Paris. To stem the plague the relics of St. Genevieve were carried in solemn procession to Notre-Dame. Many of the sick, it is said, were cured by touching the shrine, and the plague disappeared in a few days. An annual festival in commemoration of this miracle was ordered by Pope Innocent II. to take place on the 26th of November.

During the Middle Ages, in short, if any misfortune threatened France,—plague, famine, inundation, or invasion,—the people straightway had recourse to St. Genevieve. Eighty times in all her bones were carried through the streets in solemn procession, with priests burning incense in their honor, and laymen scattering flowers before them and prostrating themselves with wild prayers for help as the cortége passed.

In those weary, hopeless days in 1871, when in Paris famine was doing a more deadly work even than the Prussians, men and women who had never before uttered a prayer joined eagerly in the common supplication to the patron saint:

"St. Genevieve, thou who by thy prayers didst save our city from the hordes of Attila, save us now from the hordes of his descendants."

And when the news came that General Faidherbe had won a battle on the fête of St. Genevieve, the man who had dared to say that it was not by the help of the saint would have stood a fair chance of being lynched, in some parts of Paris. When happier days came, however, St. Genevieve was as usual quietly thrust into the background, there to remain until some fresh misfortune to the land brings her again to the fore.

But to the Catholic minority in Paris St. Genevieve's Day with its octave is still a great occasion, as is evidenced in the following from the *New York Tribune* of January 24, 1897:

"PARIS, January 11.—There is closing to-day the interesting ceremony that takes place annually in the Paris church of St. Etienne du Mont. For these nine days of the fête the usually deserted square in front of the church is filled with booths, where chaplets, images, and mementos of all kinds are sold, with crowds of the curious or reverent hurrying to and from the church, with the sick and the crippled who have come here with the same spirit with which they go to Lourdes, with priests and nuns and the pious not only of Paris but of the surrounding villages, for cart-loads of pilgrims arrive every morning from the country.

"The scene outside of the church has more of a fête-day air than a religious aspect, and there is a strong spirit of ' marchandering.' The gamins of the street run about demanding 'sous,' for which the bundles of paper prayers they carry present an excuse. The pilgrims, who are laden with rosaries, sacred images, and medals confided to their care by less fortunate neighbors,— or often with a robe or bundle of bandages for the sick that are to be blessed at the shrine,—eat their frugal luncheons on the curb-stones, and are the best, if most careful, patrons of the booths. They buy little silver rings and charms, souvenirs of the fête, for daughter or niece at home, and these become a part of the bundle that rests for one moment on the relics of the saint exposed for this week in the interior of the church.

"The interior of the church is not large, but it is majestic and harmonious, and is curiously divided by a gallery reached by winding stone stairways. On the right is the chapel, with its altar and gilt Gothic shrine of the saint, about and over which innumerable candles are burning. On this occasion one side of the tomb is opened, and a priest stands there to receive whatever offerings may be handed him, to place them for a moment on the relics before handing them back, and to give a blessing if asked for while the recipient puts a two-sou piece in the plate before him. Most of the crowd, kept severely in line by the officials, hand the priest large bundles, of which the interior is only to be conjectured, and have also candles, which, passing behind the tomb, they either light themselves and place on one of the tiny spikes provided, or hand to a small boy if the candle is sufficiently large to be placed in the front of the tomb. Familiarity with his office may have destroyed the small boy's sense of the dignity befitting it, for at times, when the ranks grow thin, he may be seen rearranging the tapers to suit his own ideas or to blow out one to hold it as far as possible from a lighted one and yet have it catch fire.

"The church during these nine days is draped with pale blue and gold banners, and services commence early in the morning and continue until late in the evening ; indeed, the chairs and prie-dieus are no sooner emptied of one congregation than they are filled by another."

George, St., patron of England, also of Germany and Venice and of soldiers and armorers. His festival is celebrated on April 23, the supposed anniversary of his martyrdom.

The legends about this saint are numerous and inconsistent,

but the generally accepted story is as follows. He was born in Cappadocia in the third century. Setting out in search of adventures, he reached a city (sometimes given as Selene in Libya, sometimes as Berytus in Syria), to find it greatly annoyed by a terrible dragon, which, unless it had a virgin to devour every day, emitted a pestiferous and death-dealing stench. The lot had fallen to the king's daughter (Cleodolinda and Sabra are her most usual names) to be made a meal of, and St. George met her on the way to her doom. Learning the story, he at once gave battle to the dragon, and with the aid of his good sword Ascalon he soon pinned it to the ground. Then he bound the monster with the girdle of the princess, and in this way it was led into the town. Seeing that many would have fled at the sight, St. George called out to them not to be afraid, but to trust in the Lord who had aided him, and be baptized in the faith, and the animal would be slain before their eyes. And as many as twenty thousand were baptized. Then the saint drew his sword and slew the dragon. Some of the legends make him marry the princess. All agree, however, that he was martyred under the Emperor Dacian. He was first submitted to various tortures, but through miraculous intervention they all proved incapable of hurting him. He was then taken to assist at the heathen sacrifices in the temple, and crowds came to witness his humiliation, but a flash of lightning from heaven destroyed the temple, and with it many of his enemies. Finally, on April 23, A.D. 303, he was beheaded. The worship of St. George began in the East, where he was known as the Great Martyr. By the Western Church he was comparatively ignored until the time of Godfrey de Bouillon, who found his intercession to be of great value in military matters. When Richard I. departed for the Crusades, he placed his country under the protection of this saint, who has ever since been the patron of England. Popular English legend, however, was not satisfied with so prosaic an origin of the patronship, and it therefore represents that when Robert, Duke of Normandy (son of William the Conqueror), was besieging Antioch, and the Saracens had come to the town's relief, St. George suddenly made his appearance with a numerous army, coming down the hills all in white with a red cross on his banner, and put the infidels to flight.

In the church of the convent of Zoographos on Mount Athos, in Greece, is a miraculous picture of St. George, which conveyed itself from Palestine without human aid, like the sacred house of Loretto. The monks declare it to have been painted by the divine will, and not by the hands of men, whence the monastery was dedicated to the Zoographos, or Painter. There is a small hole near the eyes of the picture which is thus explained. Once on a time a free-thinking bishop from Constantinople, doubting the divine origin of the picture, derisively thrust his finger through it, and was unable to withdraw it, so that at length he was forced to cut it off.

The remains of the saint are said to rest in a church at Lydda, still extant, which was built over them by the Emperor Justinian.

Gibbon has sought, but not very successfully, to identify St. George with an infamous army contractor, named George of Cappadocia, who became a champion of the Arians and died in 361.

Edward III. dedicated St. George's Chapel, Windsor, to him in 1348, and made him patron of the new order of the Garter. In the first Prayer Book of Edward VI. St. George's Day was a red-letter day, and in many parts of Christendom it is still a high day. In England the date has additional interest from the fact that it was at once the birth- and the death-day of Shakespeare, and the death-day of Wordsworth. Furthermore, the death of Cervantes was exactly coincident with that of Shakespeare, April 23, 1616.

As a battle-cry we have frequent evidence of the use of St. George's name in Shakespeare and other dramatists. Richard III. exclaims,—

> Our ancient word of courage, fair St. George,
> Inspires us with the spleen of fiery dragons!

And Richmond cries,—

> Sound drums and trumpets boldly and cheerfully,
> God and St. George! Richmond and victory!

In Marlowe's "Edward II." twice occurs the cry,—

> St. George for England and the right!

Similar examples could be indefinitely accumulated. It is sufficient to add that in many old documents even prior to the reign of Henry VII. appear royal ordinances commending the use of St. George's cross and St. George's battle-cry to all English soldiers serving abroad.

The people learned to love the name which had so often nerved the arms of their soldiers to victory, and the feast of St. George became one of the greatest anniversaries of the year in England. Bedford in "Henry VI." says,—

> Bonfires in France forthwith I am to make,
> To keep our great St. George's Feast withal.

Henry VII. was especially devoted to St. George. History relates how Elizabeth of York, his queen, attended the pageant of St. George on Garter Day clad in crimson velvet, and mounted on a palfrey of which the housings were white, ornamented with red roses.

In the reign of Edward VI. the holding of the chapter of the Garter was transferred from St. George's Day to Whitsunday. In the first year of the reign of Queen Mary, however, the enactment was reversed, and since that date (1553) the chapter has been annually held on the 23d of April, the original feast-day, in commemoration of the martyrdom of George the soldier saint.

The king's spurs became the fee of the choristers at Windsor on installations and feasts on St. George's Day. In the " Privy Purse Expenses of Henry VII." is an entry under the year 1495 :

" Oct. 1. At Windesor. To the children for the spoures."

A similar disbursement occurs thrice in the Privy Purse Expenses of Henry VIII. in 1530. (*Med. Ævi Kalend.*, vol. i. p. 214.)

Strype, in his " Ecclesiastical Memorials" (1822, vol. iii. pt. ii. p. 3), says, "April 23rd [1557], being St. George's Day, the King's grace went a procession at Whitehall, through the hall, and round about the court hard by the gate, certain of the Knights of the Garter accompanying him, viz., the Lord Mountagu, the Lord Admiral St. Anthony St. Leger, the Lord Cobham, the Lord Dacre, Sir Thomas Cheyne, the Lord Paget, the Earl of Pembroke, the Earl of Arundel, the Lord Treasurer, and Secretary Petre, in a robe of crimson velvet, with the garter embroidered on his shoulder (as Chancellor of the Garter). One bare a rod of black, and a doctor the book of records. Then went all the heralds, and then the Lord Talbot bare the sword, and after him the sergeant-at-arms. And then came the king, the Queen's grace looking out of a window beside the court on the garden side. And the bishop of Winchester did execute the mass, wearing his mitre. The same afternoon were chosen three Knights of the Garter, viz., the Lord Fitz-Water, the deputy of Ireland; Lord Grey of Wilton, deputy of Guynes; and Sir Robert Rochester, comptroller of the Queen's house. After, the duke of Muscovia (as that ambassador was usually termed) came through the hall and the guard stood on a row, in their rich coats, with halberts; and so passed up to the Queen's chamber, with divers aldermen and merchants. And after came down again to the chapel to evensong, to see the ceremonies. And immediately came the king (the Lord Strange bearing the sword), and the Knights of the Garter, to evensong, which done, they went all up to the chamber of presence.   After came the ambassador, and took his barge to London."

At Leicester a great annual pageant called the " Riding of the George" was held.   The town observed strict holiday.   All business was suspended, and the evening closed on the sports of the day with feasting and revelry.

In Dublin, probably as a gentle reminder of the supremacy of England, the pageant of St. George was ordered to be religiously observed, with the result of making the day annually notable for disturbances and riots that filled the jails with misdemeanants and the city with broken heads.

So late as the beginning of the nineteenth century it was customary for gentlemen to wear blue coats with dragon buttons on this festival.   George IV. changed the celebration of his birthday from August 12 to St. George's Day, and the festival was marked in London by the annual procession of mail-coaches from Lombard Street to Millbank and back, the drivers and guards brilliant in new uniforms, decked with huge bouquets and rosettes, and the vehicles gorgeous with new paint and burnished metal-work.   In some villages of Kent the custom still survives for boys mounted on hobby-horses to go through a burlesque imitation of the old pageants of St. George and the Dragon. But, with these exceptions, the celebration of the anniversary of her patron saint has died out of England.

In Derbyshire, however, his memory is still celebrated on Christmas Day by mummers or guisers who go from house to house and perform a play of St. George.   They are dressed up in character and decorated with ribbons, tinsel, and other finery. On being admitted into the house their performance is commenced by St. George:

> I am St. George, the noble champion bold,
> And with my glittering sword
> I've won three crowns of gold ;
> It's I who fought the fiery dragon,
> And brought it to the slaughter ;
> And so I won fair Sabra,
> The king of Egypt's daughter.
> —Seven have I won, but married none,
> And bear my glory all alone,
> —With *my* Sword in my hand,
> Who dare against me stand ?
> I swear I'll cut him down
> With my victorious brand.

A champion is soon found in the person of Slasher, who accepts the challenge.   St. George then replies in a neat speech, when they sing, shake hands, and fight with their wooden swords, and Slasher is slain. The King then enters, saying, " I am the King of England, the greatest man alive," and, after walking round the dead body, calls for " Sir Guy, one of the chiefest men in the world's wonder," who shows his wonderful courage and prowess in calling for a doctor. The doctor, on making his appearance, gives a long and quaint account of his birth, parentage, education, and travels, whilst perambulating around the fallen Slasher, and ends his oration by saying,—

> Here, take a little out of my bottle,
> And put it down thy throttle.

The dead man is thus cured, and, having received the advice of " Rise, Jack, and fight again," the play is ended. (*Journal of the Archæological Association*, 1852, vol. vii. p. 206.)

There was a famous story once current at Rome that on St. George's Day a meditation used to be read out in the chapel of the English College there, divided into three parts or points, which ran as follows :

" Point I. Let us consider that we know very little indeed about St. George." After due time had been given for a devout apprehension of this fundamental verity, there followed

" Point II. Let us consider that the little we do know is very doubtful." To say nothing of the somewhat Hibernian method of conveying this supplementary information, it does seem hard that when there was so little to begin with, that little should not have been left alone. But, to clinch matters by excluding once for all any illusory anticipations of future enlightenment, the meditation closed with a third and last point :

" Let us consider that it is quite certain we shall never know anything more about St. George."

Under the Empire in Brazil the great festival of the year was St. George's Day. Royalty itself joined in the procession which was the feature of the occasion. " I once saw the late Emperor Dom Pedro II. traverse the main street of Rio de Janeiro on foot, with his noble head bared to the noonday sun, while just in front of him, fastened to the saddle (in which it was with difficulty held upright by two assistants), reeled helplessly to and fro, amid the unconcealed laughter of even its nominal worshippers themselves, the overgrown doll that represented São Jorge." (*Harper's Young People*, vol. xiv. p. 167.)

On the eve of St. George's Day the Servian women gather fresh leaves and flowers, which they throw into water set in motion by a windmill. Next day or on the feast itself they bathe in the water made fragrant by their springtide offerings.

Giants, Procession of the. A bit of mummery once very popular in England, Spain, and Flanders. Into the latter land it was introduced by the Emperor Charles V. from Spain. Yet Spain now boasts of only one survival, at Barcelona, while 'in that part of modern Belgium and France which once was Flanders almost every city has its communal giants,—colossal effigies which with their colossal consorts or attendants are carried about the streets on certain days. Each has its own name, its own legend, and its own festival. Antwerp has its ANTIGONUS, Brussels its BRABO, Douai its GAYANT, scores of other cities their own legendary monstrosities. These are fashioned in many ways and attired in still more various costumes, ranging from the Roman, as at Antwerp, to the court dress of the last century, as at Brussels. Sometimes they are formed of osier, as at Douai, sometimes carved elaborately in wood, as at Antwerp. But all are so constructed that their lower robes hang around their feet so as to conceal the motive power, a dozen or so of stout fellows who now and then set down their burdens and emerge from the draperies to breathe.

These men are experts in their line, for the movements of each giant should be in keeping with his character. An ogre giant, for example, must have a firm and defiant port, while the motions of a funny giant must be funny.

On solemn occasions of national importance, such as the entries of sovereigns into cities, centenary celebrations, religious or secular, and the like, there is a reunion of giants. They are lent by the corporations of each town to swell the public shows. Such an occasion was the centenary of St. Rombaud at Malines, that of St. Macaire at Mons, and especially the World's Fair held in Brussels in 1890. On July 13 of that year more than two hundred colossal figures, representing nearly fifty cities, took part in a procession through the streets of Brussels. Even the town of Tarascon, in France, had been induced to send on its famous Tarasque, the dragon which St. Martha tamed into innocuousness and which furnishes the only approximation in Southern France to the Hispano-Flemish mummeries. (See MARTHA, ST.)

The procession of the giants in Barcelona occurs on Corpus Christi Day. A dozen enormously tall figures, representing scriptural and legendary men and women,—the Cid, Santiago, etc.,— dressed in ancient costumes, promenade the streets.

Around these giants dance dozens of bronze-faced men in female garb, and behind them march troops of children arrayed as angels. The child at the head of the angelic host is usually the son or the daughter of one of the richest merchants of the city; the dainty little body has wings made of tulle fastened upon card-board. Sometimes a bevy of children ranged around some sweet-faced woman represent angels grouped around the Madonna. Then follow long rows of pupils of religious societies, the officials of the city, carrying wax tapers in their hands; and finally, escorted by military bands and surrounded by priests and soldiers, the throne of one of the earliest of canonized Catalonian kings,—a golden chair richly chased, encrusted with jewels and heaped with flowers.

If Antwerp has its Antigonus, London has its Gog and Magog, whose representations still stand in (they do not adorn) the old Guildhall of London. These are taken down to form part of the Lord Mayor's show. Formerly they figured with other giants and with monstrous dragons in the popular processions on Midsummer Eve, May-Day, and Shrovetide. The original images were made of wicker and pasteboard, so that they were easy to move; but the London fire destroyed one set, the rats subsequently ate up the entrails of another, and the modern ones are wooden counterparts. The Puritans under Cromwell succeeded in breaking up the processions of giants, and, though they had a temporary revival under Charles II., they finally languished and died.

Among the relics of this ancient pastime is the Tailors' Giant still preserved at Salisbury,—the last of the old English perambulating giants. A pasteboard head crowned with tow hair is fitted on a framework of lath and hoops. A person could walk inside and carry the figure, being himself completely concealed by the drapery of colored chintz, bordered with red and purple and trimmed with yellow fringe. A gold-laced cocked hat was placed on the head, a pipe in the mouth, and a branch of artificial laurel in the right hand. Thus accoutred, he won the facile applause of the spectators.

No mere giant, however, could quite satisfy the mediæval English love for the grotesque. Various monstrous devices were added, the most popular of all being the dragon. At Norwich this emblem survived in the mayoralty processions until so late as 1832. It was composed of canvas stretched over a framework of wood. The outside was painted of a sea-green color, with gilt scales and a crimson mane tied in fantastic knots about the tail. The body was five feet in length, but the neck and head could be elongated three feet and a half, and could also be turned in any direction at the will of the bearer.

The feeling expressed in the scriptural verse "There were giants in those days" seems to have been universal with primitive men. Most nations of the world have traditions of ancestors heroic in size as well as courage. Moslem and Rabbinical legends place the size of Adam and Eve at a hundred feet and more.

The Hindoos have a tradition of a giant race who bestrode elephants as we do horses. The Greek heroes at the siege of Troy threw stones at their enemies which the strongest of their descendants could not move. Homer and Virgil speak of the men of their own day as mere dwarfs in comparison with those elder heroes of whom they sang.

When Queen Elizabeth visited Kenilworth Castle, in 1575, there were six gigantic figures, eight feet in height, standing guard over the castle gate. "By this dumb show," explains a contemporary writer, "it was meant that in the days of King Arthur men were of that stature, so that the Castle of Kenilworth should still seem to be kept by King Arthur's heirs and their servants."

Giles, St. (Lat. *Ægidius;* Ital. *Sant' Egidio;* Fr. *Saint Gilles;* Sp. *San Gil*), patron saint of Edinburgh, and of tinkers, cripples, and beggars. His festival is celebrated on September 1, the reputed anniversary of his death. St. Giles was born in Athens about 640, and came to Gaul, where he became abbot of a monastery in Arles. Some miracles which he performed, one of which was healing a sick man by throwing his cloak over him, gave him so much fame that, fearing for his humility, he withdrew to a solitary cave near Nismes, where he spent the remainder of his days in prayer and mortification. Legend says that he was fed by a hind, and that one day the hind was wounded by the King of France, or, according to other accounts, by the King of the Goths. The king in pursuing the hind came upon the saint in his retreat. He tried in vain to persuade the saint to return with him to his court. It is said that many miracles were worked at his cave, and the spot became so sacred that a monastery was built there which was called after the saint. The church still remains upon the spot, and is an extraordinary remnant of the Middle Ages. Queen Matilda dedicated a hospital which she founded outside of London to St. Giles, and the name now belongs to an extensive parish. The cathedral at Edinburgh is named after St. Giles. His attribute in art is a wounded hind.

The relics of St. Giles are preserved at St. Saturninus in Toulouse. On St. Giles's Day in Valencia it is the custom to bless a sprig of fennel.

In Belgium the tinkers' apprentices parade through the streets of the cities under the leadership of two of their number, one wearing a kind of shako surmounted by a plume, while the other bears upon a little wooden platform with a long handle a statue of the saint, surrounded with flowers. From the platform depend spoons, pots, and other household utensils.

In this guise they stop at the houses of their various patrons and demand some small gratuity.

TINKERS' PARADE ON ST. GILES'S DAY.
(From a Belgian lithograph.)

Girdle (It. *Cintola*) **of the Blessed Virgin.** A famous relic in the cathedral at Prato, exhibited from the pulpit on all the great festivals of the Virgin. The legend runs that Doubting Thomas, true to his name, refused to believe in the Virgin's Assumption into heaven, as he had refused to believe in the Saviour's Ascension. But when the grave was opened he found it empty; and the Virgin, pitying the weakness of his faith, let down her girdle to him from heaven to remove all further doubts from his mind. This girdle remained for centuries in the Holy Land. In the eleventh century one Michele dei Dogamari, a pilgrim from Prato, fell in love with the daughter of the priest who possessed the girdle. Marrying the lady, he received the relic as her dowry, brought it with him to Prato, and on his death-bed delivered it to a priest on condition that it should be preserved forever in the cathedral of his native city.

Glastonbury Thorn. A species of thorn (*Cratægus præcox*) which flourishes in Glastonbury and other portions of England as well as Europe, but which is especially associated with its eponymic city through an ancient legend. The original thorn is asserted to have been the walking-staff of St. Joseph of Arimathea, who, after Christ's death, came over to England and settled at Glastonbury. In what was afterwards the church-yard of Glastonbury Abbey he stuck his staff into the ground. It immediately took root and put forth leaves, and on the day following, which happened to be Christmas Eve, was covered all over with snow-white blossoms. On every recurring Christmas Eve it continued thus to bloom for a long series of years, great numbers of people visiting it annually to witness the miracle. During the time of the civil wars this bush was destroyed, but several trees which are descended from it by cuttings still survive in Glastonbury and are believed to retain its characteristics. One of them, of rather scanty growth, occupies the site of the original thorn, on the summit of Weary-All Hill. Another, a much finer specimen, stands on private premises near the entrance of a house that faces the abbot's kitchen.

When the change of calendar was effected in 1752 a vast concourse of people assembled on Christmas Eve, New Style, to watch the famous thorn, "but, to their great disappointment, there was no appearance of its blowing, which made them watch it narrowly the 5th of January, the Christmas Eve, Old Style, when it blowed as usual." (*Gentleman's Magazine*, January, 1753.) A similar refusal to blossom on the new date was observed in a shoot of the Glastonbury Thorn in Buckinghamshire, where thousands of spectators with lights and lanterns had assembled to see it. Thereupon the people declared that the 25th of December, New Style, was not the true Christmas, and refused to observe it as such, most of all as the white thorn continued to blossom on the 5th of January as usual. (*Ibid.*) To put an end to the dispute, the clergy of the neighborhood issued an order that both days, Old Style and New, were to be similarly kept.

The thorn superstition is not yet extinct. A writer in *Notes and Queries* (Third Series, ix. 33) says, " A friend of mine met a girl on Old Christmas Day in a village of North Somerset, who told him that she was going to see the Christmas Thorn in blossom. He accompanied her to an orchard, where he found a tree, propagated from the celebrated Glastonbury Thorn, and gathered from it several sprigs in blossom. Afterwards the girl's mother informed him that it had formerly been the custom for the youth of both sexes to assemble under the tree at midnight on Christmas Eve, in order to hear the bursting of the buds into flower; and, she added, ' as they comed out you could hear 'em haffer' (crackle)."

Until the time of King Charles I. it was customary in England at Christmas time to proceed in solemn state and present the king and queen with a flowering branch of the Glastonbury Thorn.

In point of fact, though the thorn does usually put forth blossoms at about the advent of New Year, a mild season will make it blossom even before Christmas.

Aubrey mentions an oak in the New Forest that was a rival of the Glastonbury Thorn, inasmuch as " it putteth forth young leaves on Christmas Day, for about a week at that time of the year. Old Mr. Hastings was wont to send a basketful of them to King Charles I. I have seen of them several Christmases brought to my father. But Mr. Perkins, who lives in the New Forest, says that there are two other oaks besides that which breed green buds after Christmas Day (pollards also), but not constantly."

Godfathers and **Godmothers,** known also as **Sponsors** (Lat. *spondeo,* " I promise") and **Sureties.** There seem to have been sponsors at the baptismal font in very early Christian times, and it is said they were first appointed by Hyginus, Bishop of Rome, in 154. There was at first only one sponsor for each catechumen, who was chosen from the deacons and deaconesses. Catechumens, heretics, and penitents, and subsequently monks and nuns, were excluded from the office. At first it was not uncommon for parents to stand as sponsors, but this was forbidden in the ninth century, though the privilege was subsequently restored by the English Church.

The number of sponsors for each child was prescribed by the fourth canon of the Council of York, in 1196, to be *no more* than three persons, two males and one female for a boy, and two females and one male for a girl,—a rule which is still preserved in the English Church. In the Roman Church it is not necessary to have more than one godparent, though there are sometimes more. By little and little, large presents were looked for from sponsors, not only to the child but to its mother; the result was that there grew to be a great difficulty in procuring persons to undertake so expensive an office. Indeed, it sometimes happened that fraudulent parents had a child baptized thrice, for the sake of the godfather's gifts. To remedy these evils, a council held at L'Isle, in Provence, in 1288, ordered that thenceforth nothing was to be given to the baptized but a white robe. This prescription appears to have been kept for ages. Stow, in his "Chronicle of King James's Reign," says, "At this time, and for many ages, it was not the use and custom (as now it is) for godfathers and godmothers to give plate at the baptism of children, but only to give *christening shirts*, with little bands and cuffs, wrought either with silk or blue thread, the best of them edged with a small lace of silk and gold." Cups and spoons have, however, stood their ground as favorite presents to babies on such occasions ever since. "Apostle spoons"—so called because a figure of one of the apostles was chased on the handle of each—were anciently given, opulent sponsors presenting the whole twelve. Those in middling circumstances gave four, and the poorer sort contented themselves with the gift of one, exhibiting the figure of any saint, in honor of whom the child received its name.

Shakespeare in "Henry VIII." makes the king say when Cranmer professes himself unworthy to be sponsor to the young princess,—

> Come, come, my lord, you'd spare your spoons.

Davenant's comedy of "The Wits" (1639) has these lines:

> My pendants, cascanets, and rings,
> My christening caudle-cups and spoons,
> Are dissolved into that lump.

The coral and bells is an old invention for baptismal presents. Coral was anciently considered an amulet against fascination and evil spirits.

Godchildren were placed not only in a state of pupilage with their sureties, but also in the position of relations. A sort of relationship was established even between the godfathers and godmothers, insomuch that marriage between any such parties was forbidden under pain of severe punishment. This injunction, like many others, had, it appears, been sufficiently disobeyed to warrant a special canon (twelfth) of the Council of Compiègne, held so early as 757, which enforced the separation of all those sponsors and godchildren of both sexes who had intermarried, and the Church refused the rites of marriage to the women so separated.

In the English Church the prohibition does not now exist, though there is still extant a popular saying that "those who meet at the font shall not meet at the altar."

Godiva's Procession, Lady. A famous pageant which for two centuries has been intermittently celebrated at Coventry, England, on August 2. The leading figures in it are Lady Godiva and Peeping Tom. A local legend, part history and part myth, is cited in explanation of the custom.

Matthew of Westminster, who flourished about 1300–1310, first set down the episode as sober history, but failed to make a place for "Peeping Tom." He says,—

"This Countess (Godiva), devoutly anxious to free the city of Coventry from a grievous and base thraldom, often besought the Count, her husband, that he would, for the love of the Holy Trinity and the Sacred Mother of God, liberate it from such servitude. But he rebuked her for vainly demanding a thing so injurious to himself, and forbade her to move further therein. Yet she, out of her womanly pertinacity, continued to press the matter, insomuch that she obtained this answer from him : 'Ascend,' he said, 'thy horse naked, and pass thus through the city, from one end of it to the other, in sight of the people, and on thy return thou shalt obtain thy request.' Upon which she returned, 'And should I be willing to do this, wilt thou give me leave?' 'I will,' he responded. Then the Countess Godiva, beloved of God, ascended her horse naked, loosing her long hair, which clothed her entire body except her snow-white legs, and having performed the journey, seen by none, returned with joy to her husband, who, regarding it as a miracle, thereupon granted Coventry a Charter of Freedom, confirming it with his seal."

Everybody will remember Tennyson's lesson which incorporates a later addition to the myth :

> Then she rode forth, clothed on with chastity;
> *   *   *   *   *   *   *
> And one low churl, compact of thankless earth,
> The fatal byword of all years to come,
> Boring a little auger hole in fear,
> Peeped—but his eyes before they had their will
> Were shrivelled into darkness in his head,
> And dropt before him. So the Powers who wait
> On noble deeds cancel a sense misused.

How or when this "one low churl, compact of thankless earth," was first made the horrid antithesis of Lady Godiva's noble sacrifice, or why the honest vocation of a tailor was called upon to supply a culprit, no man can tell. But Coventry has accepted him as a fact. Effigies of Peeping Tom are countless here,—in stone, in wood, in delft, in porcelain, in wax; while the very school-boys are eternally testing new jack-knives upon grotesque imitations of the repulsive object. "The thing leers at you from niches above ancient buildings; seems to crane its lecherous head from the cornices of new and old hotels; shows its horse-like teeth from among shop-window trifles, and haunts and pursues you until you are startled to see its lineaments reproduced in the faces of tramps and beldames in shadowy quarters of the musty old town. Truly the Peeping Tom you will find everywhere in Coventry is a dreadful travesty upon the human form and face. They have put his trunk and chest in armor. He is made a man of arms as well as of shears, with a military cocked hat decked with a huge rosette. His face is wide, square, and white. The eyes are Brobdingnagian in size and possess a leer both sanctimonious and repulsively suggestive. His bearded chin looks likes the mirage of a savage flame. And the mouth, as wide as a cow's, discloses a ghastly row of gravestone teeth." (EDWARD L. WAKEMAN, in *New York Sun*, October 18, 1891.)

But if this luckless wight is merely a popular embodiment of evil as opposed to good, Lady Godiva at least was an historical personage. She was sister to Thorald, Sheriff of Lincolnshire, and wife of Leofric, or Lorich, Earl of Mercia, a favorite of Edward the Confessor, and in his time at the head of various great state transactions. Both history and tradition unite in honoring Lady Godiva with the possession of unusual piety, goodness, and beauty. The devout pair certainly founded a great monastery for Benedictine monks, which attained enormous wealth and splendor, suffered strange vicissitudes, passed into silence and decay, and left massive vestiges of its remains on the banks of the river here. Leofric died at Bromley, Staffordshire, but was buried in one porch of the monastery at Coventry, while his wife, who at her death gave a "rich chain of precious stones to be put around the neck of the Blessed Virgin's image, so that those who came of devotion thither should say as many prayers as there were several gems within," received burial in the other. It is incontestably true that the citizens of Coventry, when Leofric's vassals, did receive, through Lady Godiva's efforts with her grim warrior husband, some sort of manumission from servile tenure. Not only do ancient records prove this, but also the memorial window which stood in the south transept of

Trinity Church up to the fifteenth century, and contained a picture of Lady Godiva and Leofric, the latter holding in his right hand a charter bearing the following inscription :

> I, Lorich, for love of thee
> Doe make Coventry tol-free.

From the year 1217, when Coventry Fair was chartered by Henry III., the town of Coventry had been famous for the Mystery Plays performed there at the Corpus Christi season. They were an important source of attraction to the fair. Most popular of all was the play of Adam and Eve, in which our first parents appeared in a state of paradisiacal nudity. The destruction of the monasteries and the discontinuance of the Mysteries proved a heavy blow to the wealth and trade of Coventry. Its population was reduced by over twelve thousand, and its fair was not well attended. The inhabitants had sufficient reason to mourn that the clothesless Eve no longer exhibited herself annually among them. There is reason to believe that for a time they sought to revive the attraction in a pageant in which Eve perambulated the streets on horseback.

Then the wave of Puritanism involved all festivities and pageants in a common ruin. For nearly a century the pageant at Coventry was discontinued. Coventry still went downward. Its fair had lost its fame as an emporium of commerce. Even the Restoration did not improve matters much. Under these circumstances, the authorities hit upon the idea of reviving the pageant, and the licentious period of Charles II. enabled them to do so. The revival occurred in 1678. Mayor and corporation had always been in the habit of going through the streets and proclaiming the opening of the fair, but they were on this occasion accompanied by the trading companies of the city displaying flags. Boys fancifully dressed as pages took the part of the angels in the old Corpus Christi pageants, and in the heart of the procession a naked woman bestrode a horse. But she was no longer known as Eve. She was now the Lady Godiva. The local legend explained everything.

From year to year until the beginning of the eighteenth century the nude Godiva allured to Coventry the numerous descendants of Peeping Tom in Warwickshire. Then she fell into disfavor, and reappeared only at irregular intervals until the early part of the nineteenth century, when she made way for a new Lady Godiva, got up more in accordance with nineteenth-century prejudices and clad in close-fitting cambric without a skirt, relieved by a variety of ornaments and a splendid gauze scarf suspended from her long flowing hair. For many succeeding years a Godiva of this sort compromised the rival demands of the people on the one hand and of the prudes and parsons on the other. But the compromise was not effected without bitter annual quarrels, and every now and then the show has been suspended.

In 1887 the Lady Godiva procession had dwindled down to nothingness, and for four years thereafter it was suffered to lapse. On August 2, 1892, it was revived by the working people, mainly for commercial reasons, and it was successful in attracting a large concourse of people. *The Antiquary* for September, 1892, informs us that it recalled much of Dugdale's description of its predecessors. "There were the pageants very large and high, placed upon wheels, and drawn to all the eminent parts of the city for the better advantage of the spectators. Those of the bricklayers, the carpenters, and the Druids were especially successful. The dresses of the foresters, too, were bright. There were companies of various friendly societies and trades associations, though how far these latter are the descendants or representatives of the Craft Guilds we know not. Lady Godiva herself was a gruesome failure. She appeared neither as she did on the famous occasion when she rode forth clothed on with chastity only, nor as she presumably did at normal and less momentous times. In fact, she had simply stepped from the stage of nineteenth-century burlesque. The other historic personages represented were dressed with some attempt at accuracy. It was altogether a curious blending of the modern and the mediæval. There was the feudal knight in silken masquerade. The chimney-pot hats of the committee followed in close proximity behind St. George of England. Brass bands blatantly heralded 'the lady champion swimmer' who was for the nonce 'the woman of a thousand summers back.' But, most incongruously congruous of all, in the early part of the procession came a car advertising tubular bells, at its close rolled a vehicle setting forth the merits of Bolus's pills."

Going in State. In England this is the name given to a triumphal procession in which civic or regal dignitaries form the central glory. The mayor of London, for example, goes in state on the occasion of his inauguration on every successive November 9. But the most important ceremonial of this sort is when the reigning sovereign goes from Buckingham Palace to the cathedral of St. Paul's to render thanks for some signal benefit accorded by the Almighty to the royal family or the royal dominions. About the earliest occasion of this sort on an important scale was when Henry IV. in 1399 went to St. Paul's to offer up prayers on his accession to the throne. Henry VI.

followed the example of his predecessor, and Henry VII., after the defeat of Lambert Simnel, went on two successive days in solemn procession to return thanks to God. But one of the grandest processions to the church of St. Paul was when, on Sunday, the 21st of May, 1514, Henry VIII. went to receive the sword and cap of maintenance which the Pope had sent him as Defender of the Faith. The crowd on this occasion was estimated as numbering over thirty thousand people.

The next grand occasion was when Queen Elizabeth went, in magnificent splendor, on the 24th of November, 1588, to old St. Paul's. She was seated in a kind of triumphal chariot, drawn by two white horses, and was received at the door of the church by the Bishop of London, the dean, and fifty other clergymen, habited in superb copes. On entering the church the queen kneeled, pronounced a prayer, and then proceeded to her seat, under a canopy, in the choir, when the Litany was chanted. After that she was conducted to a closet, prepared for the occasion in the north wall of the church, "where," says an historian of the occasion, "shame to our effeminacy, she remained exposed to the wintry blasts of November during the space of time which Pierce, Bishop of Salisbury, occupied in delivering a sermon."

Several of these thanksgiving services took place in the reign of Queen Anne. Scarcely an important victory was gained in this reign—when important victories were by no means infrequent—but what the pious queen proceeded in solemn state to return thanks to the Almighty for the divine favor. One of the grandest of these occasions, perhaps, was on the 12th of November, 1702, after the brilliant successes of Marlborough in the Low Countries and the destruction of the Spanish fleet in the harbor of Vigo by the Duke of Ormond and Sir George Rooke. Dean Milman, in his "Annals of St. Paul's," says that the Council declared that the cathedral being for that day the queen's Chapel Royal, the seats were to be disposed of and all the arrangements made by the Lord Chamberlain. The queen's throne, as in the House of Lords of that day, was about three feet higher than the floor of the choir, covered with a Persian carpet, and surmounted by a canopy fifteen feet high. There was, according to the proclamation, an arm-chair on the throne, and a desk for the queen's book, covered with crimson velvet, richly embroidered and fringed with gold, with a cushion of the same. The two Houses of Parliament assisted at the ceremony, the Lords being seated in the area or body of the choir, the Speaker of the House of Commons in a seat next to the Lord Bishop of London, in the middle of the south side of the choir, and the members in the stalls and galleries on each side.

In the procession to the cathedral the House of Commons led the way. At eight o'clock they went to St. James's Palace, then along Pall-Mall, and so to the cathedral, where they took their places. The Lords met at ten, and formed into procession, preceded by the officers of the House, masters in chancery, judges, peers under age, then barons, bishops, viscounts, earls, dukes, the great officers of state, the archbishops, and the Keeper of the Great Seal. In that order they proceeded to the cathedral, and took their seats till the arrival of the queen, the organ in the interval playing voluntaries. At eleven o'clock the queen entered her carriage at St. James's. At Temple Bar she was received by the lord mayor, sheriffs, and aldermen, on horseback.

Then the lord mayor surrendered the sword, prefacing the ceremony with a brief speech. It was immediately returned by the queen, and the lord mayor carried it before her to the church. On her arrival at the west door her majesty was met by the peers and principal officers of state, and conducted along the nave to her throne. Then followed divine service, and a sermon of about half an hour's duration from the old Whig Bishop of Exeter, Sir Jonathan Trelawney. The queen led the way back. The Tower guns, those on the river, and those in St. James's Park were fired three times: once, as the queen left St. James's; next, when the *Te Deum* was chanted; and, lastly, on the queen's return to the palace.

This procession was taken as the established model for all subsequent occasions of the same sort; and when George III. went in state to St. Paul's, on the 23d of April, 1789, after his recovery from a dangerous illness, the form of the ceremony was, in the main, similar to that just described.

Blackwood's Magazine for March, 1842, gives a description of a pageant of this sort in the early days of Queen Victoria:

"First come, trotting slowly, a detachment of Life Guards clearing the way—their sabres glisten in the air—their bearskin caps flout the sky—ladies are in raptures—such divine men, such lovely coats, beautiful swords—fascinating mustaches—handsome horses; and then the officer, covered with gold lace—divine, love-inspiring man!—tremble now, ye unwhiskered beaux, for the affections of your fair ones, and assure yourselves, that however your belles may regard you, at this moment that dear delightful officer is the god of their idolatry; and whatever sweet smiles they may condescendingly bestow on you, 'tis of that Adonis of the household troops they are thinking all the while. But the ladies have no time to fall desperately in love, for the beef-eaters appear—remarkable old files, in the fashion of the days of Elizabeth, with embroidered frocks, and little porringer velvet caps, bedizened with red and white ribbon, halberts over their shoulders, tottering and shambling along, like pilgrims of the unboiled peas;—next following, behold several preliminary carriages and four, containing lovely ladies of the bedchamber, in lappets and diamonds, and fair-faced, elegant gentlemen of the *ditto*, in blue embroidered coats, and elegantly fitting primrose tights:—a little pretty-faced page, in a military uniform, lolls carelessly in the lap of a lovely lady, like a sucking Mars nurtured by one of the Graces ; next, in a carriage and six splendid bays, comes the Master of the Horse, a grand and awe-inspiring personage ; after him, in a carriage with half a dozen beautiful blacks, the gracious-looking Mistress of the Robes ; and *then*, heralded by another squadron of horse, moves past us, more slowly than the rest, a pale, fair form, of youthful grace and beauty, her brow encircled by a diadem, and thoughtful, as if the weight of that glittering but uneasy burden pressed upon the brain ; each heart, as she passes, is upon each lip, and a burst of enthusiasm heralds the youthful Monarch in her triumphant way. A cloud of horse closes the procession, but unheeded and unremembered ; we turn away, oppressed with the weight of reflection that crowds upon us, contemplating the form of her upon whose dominions the sun never sets, and whose sovereignty a hundred millions of human beings cheerfully obey; whose councils influence, directly or indirectly, the interests of the civilized world."

In February, 1872, Queen Victoria went in state to offer public thanks at St. Paul's for the recovery of the Prince of Wales from a dangerous illness.

Golden Rose. Once a year at the utmost, on the fourth Sunday in Lent (known theologically as Lætare Sunday, but more popularly as Mothering Sunday), a golden rose is blessed by the Pope, to be afterwards sent off as a mark of approval to Catholic members of royal or noble families, either male or female, to great generals, to noted churches and sanctuaries, to illustrious Catholic cities or republics. But often no one is considered worthy of the honor, and then it is laid away in the Vatican and brought out again the next year.

Originally the Golden Rose was a single flower of wrought gold, colored red ; afterwards the golden petals were decked with rubies and other gems; finally the form adopted was that of a branch, bearing leaves, thorns, and buds, and a full-blown rose at the top, all of pure gold. The branch is put in a decorated flower-pot, which has engraved on its pedestal the arms and name of the Pope who blessed and bestowed the gift. Its intrinsic value was formerly very great, but economical reasons have caused the later Popes to dispense with the splendid ruby that used to be attached as a bud to the chief flower, and with the other precious stones with which the branch was laden. The vase, once of gold, is now silver gilt. Pope Clement IX. sent a rose to the Queen of France which weighed eight pounds and was valued at eight thousand francs.

Popular opinion dates the observance of this custom from the year 1049, under the pontificate of Leo IX. There is now every reason to suppose that he was not the originator ; but it was this Pope who, wishing to establish his right of patronage over the monastery of the Holy Cross in Alsace, decreed that the abbess should supply the Golden Rose every year, ready made, or two ounces of gold with which to supply the goldsmith. And this mandate naturally connected his name with the emblem in such a way as to give the impression that he was something more than a mere imitator of his predecessors.

In the eleventh century, according to Mabillon, the Pope sang mass on Lætare Sunday in the basilica of Santa Croce in Gerusalemme, holding the rose in his hand during the Gospel, and while preaching a sermon of which, as it were, the flower afforded the text. The rose was presented before the mass to the Holy Father, in his room, by a chamberlain, together with balm and musk In many a Roman *Ordo*, and in briefs and other documents of an early date, constant mention is made of the rose and of its usage, but nowhere mention of its being blessed. The first to mention the ceremony of blessing the rose is Agostino Patrizio, master of ceremonies to Pope Innocent VIII., in his work printed at Venice in 1488. It may have been Nicholas V. who first blessed the rose. The Pope was crowned on Lætare Sunday, and went, riding on a milk-white steed, to take possession of his cathedral at the Lateran, holding in his hand the precious rose. The blessing always now takes place at the high mass on Mid-Lent Sunday. The rose is placed between two lighted tapers on a table in the sacristy, and is presented by the youngest cleric of the Pope's household to the Pope on his way to the Sistine Chapel. The Holy Father, in alb and stole, after placing incense in a thurible held by the senior cardinal priest present, reads a special prayer for the occasion, and places the scents in the rose, which he blesses and incenses. The rose is then carried before the Pope to the altar at which his Holiness celebrates mass, where it remains until the Holy Sacrifice is over, when it is taken away to the pontifical treasury.

Originally it seems to have been the custom to present the golden rose to the Prefect of Rome after the latter had led the Pope's horses by a golden bridle to the doors of the Lateran basilica and aided his Holiness to dismount. But the distribution of the gift soon became broadened, and it was bestowed both upon persons and places.

It is an old superstition that the Golden Rose brings ill luck to its owner. People cite the instances of Joanna of Sicily, the first Rose Queen, made so by Urban VI., who was dethroned and strangled by her nephew, Gonsalvo de Córdova, the Great Captain, who died in disgrace; the Queen of Naples, wife of King Bomba, the Empress Josephine, Isabella herself, and other high dignitaries, who shortly after the reception of the Golden Rose met with death or misfortune. So when, in 1889, Pope Leo singled out Dona Isabella of Brazil for this honor, her countrymen predicted that evil would befall her or her family, and, in fact, before the news was out Dom Pedro was dethroned and she was no longer the heiress to a sceptre.

It has been stated that the Golden Rose was sent to two American ladies, Mrs. William T. Sherman and Miss Mary Caldwell, whose gift of three hundred thousand dollars to the Catholic University at Washington would certainly be worthy of such an acknowledgment. But, in fact, these ladies received formal tokens of Papal approval, but not the Golden Rose. The rule has never been broken which requires that the Golden Rose shall be presented to no individuals outside of royalty and the nobility.

Good Friday. The Friday in Holy Week, instituted in commemoration of Christ's crucifixion. It probably received this name from the good things which he gained for us by his suffering and death. A plausible alternative etymology, however, would make it a corruption of Goddes or God's Friday. Among the Saxons it was called Long Friday, probably on account of the long fasts and offices used on this day.

From the first ages of the Church the commemoration of Christ's sufferings has been kept as a day of strictest fasting and humiliation. The Fourth Council in 633 severely rebuked all those who fasted only up to three P.M., and shut them out from participation in the Paschal communion.

Much of this early austerity is remitted, but the day is still one of strict fast and mourning. In the Roman Church the officiating clergy appear in black garments, the altar is stripped, the candles are not lighted. After a short pause the altar is covered with white cloths. Passages from the Old and New Testaments are read and prayers are recited. Mass cannot be consecrated on this day, but the priest receives a host consecrated on Holy Thursday. A special feature of the day is the Adoration of the Cross. After mass the crucifix is divested of the black with which it had been covered, and is kissed by the clergy and people while four hymns are sung.

In the Latin countries this Adoration of the Cross is a far more elaborate ceremony. A huge crucifix or a wax image of Christ rests on a cushion on the floor for all to kiss. In many places the effigy is buried in the afternoon with solemn rites in an Easter sepulchre (*q. v.*), there to remain until the dawn of Easter Sunday, when it is returned to the church. The Easter sepulchre is sometimes a temporary and sometimes a permanent adjunct to the church. In Rome the ceremony is far more simple. The eucharistic body of Christ, blessed on Holy Thursday, is borne in a silver monstrance by the Pope and the cardinals in procession from the Sistine Chapel into that of St. Paul. There the host is deposited in a glittering shrine of crystal which towers up to the ceiling and is so placed as to appear bathed in light while the rest of the chapel is in darkness. For the remainder of Thursday and the beginning of Friday it is exposed to the veneration of the faithful.

In Munich and Vienna the ceremony is the most elaborate in Europe. An effigy of Christ is placed on a bier covered with a white veil, and borne in procession round the interior of the church. First come the choristers in their white robes, then priests in black and white, with the bier in their centre, then a long train of men, followed by another long train of women, all in black, and all bearing lighted tapers. Thus slowly proceeding round the church, the figure is laid in the sepulchre.

This is usually an imitation cave under the altar. Artificial rocks surround the opening, a small lamp is suspended over the corpse, and a row of tiny lamps burn upon the ground in front, not unlike footlights, save that each burns behind a small globe filled with colored liquids, green, blue, crimson, and yellow, after the fashion of the ornamental bottles in drug-stores. The altar above is transformed into a very mountain of plants and flowers, blooming in pots which are artfully concealed or beautifully decorated. Lights are disposed everywhere on the altar. Figures of angels in fluttering robes of pale pink and white, and with very yellow hair and very pink cheeks, crown the mountain-top.

Tall orange-trees in tubs, laurels, and cedars stand in groups on either hand. "To complete the general idea, you must imagine the rest of the church darkened, with daylight struggling through blinded windows, and through the doorways, as the heavy doors swing ever to and fro to admit the entrance and the departure of the restless crowd. Imagine, also, a dense multitude circulating through all these churches, and only stationary before the sepulchre; and, above the shuffle of feet and the murmur of prayers or adoration, fitful, plaintive strains of music, moaning through the gloom, and the sonorous voices of the

ADORATION OF THE CROSS AT ST. PETER'S.

PILGRIMS CLIMBING FUSI-JAMA.
(From a Japanese sketch.)

priests chanting their solemn dirge. Such, with slight variations, was the scene in the Munich churches throughout this
Good Friday." (*Household Words.*)

A famous procession of the Dead Christ occurs triennially at
the little village of San Domino near Florence, Italy. In *The
Churchman* for April 10, 1897, Miss Edith R. Crosby thus describes the procession as she had seen it on the Good Friday
of 1896: "Heralded by the eager buzz and murmur of the expectant people, a half-dozen Roman soldiers came galloping up
the narrow street, raising a cloud of dust about them; their costumes of red and blue, and much tinsel, probably borrowed from
some provincial theatre company. Behind them, in martial step,
came a really fine military band, with muffled drums, playing a
heart-breaking funeral march, which hushed the spectators and
prepared their impressionable spirits for what was coming.
After the band came a company of young village girls, in black,
with long black veils, and holding huge burning tapers; then
little boys, in white, carrying the emblems of the Passion and
Crucifixion,—the scarlet robe, the scourges and chains, the dice,
the spear, a large stuffed cock, and banners inscribed with the seven
words. Then, quite alone, bearing herself with the instinctive
theatrical grace of the Italians, a tiny girl, as an angel, dressed
in pink, with white wings, and curly hair, holding the great gilt
cup steadily in her little hands. After her walked old men in
sackcloth. Then another band playing a dirge. Then all the
priests of the village and environs, in their holiday vestments,
and behind them, after a solemn pause, with much swinging of
incense, the huge catafalque, rolling silently through the clear
starlit and lamplit night, bearing the life-size figure of the *Gesù
Morte*, the dead Jesus, extended under a heavy baldaquin of
black and silver. By the time that it reached us, the solemn
music, the slow-stepping procession, the tense expectancy of the
crowd, and the hallowing influence of the night, had so worked
upon our imagination that all seemed terribly real, and terribly
sad, and as the dead Jesus was borne past us, His pale, calm face
turned towards us, and all around us fell upon their knees, bareheaded, we bent our heads, and knelt with them.

"But a moment later the spell was broken by a tasteless
statue of the Virgin, which followed the catafalque, dressed in
deep mourning, and holding a lace handkerchief to her streaming eyes. Behind her came contadine representing the women
of the crucifixion; among others, Mary, with her hair down her
back, and her alabaster box of ointment in her hand. Another
band and a few more Roman soldiers finished the procession."

Similar celebrations occur in the Greek Church, both in Greece
and in Russia. On Holy Thursday a prostrate image of Christ

on the cross is brought out by the priest and laid in the middle of the church. The devout—usually more women and children than men—then come forward and kiss the hands and feet of the image. When leaving the church each one is expected to leave a coin on one of the holy disks, for which he receives a blessing in return.

On Good Friday evening there is a service called the Epitaphion,—a kind of funeral service in memory of the mourning and sorrow at the burial of Christ. Then the image of Christ is placed on a bier and borne in solemn procession through the streets. Crowds of people take part, all carrying lighted candles.

The military band with muffled drums plays a dead march, and at intervals the people cross themselves before a large wooden cross carried at the head of the procession.

In Catholic England Good Friday was the day upon which the king blessed certain rings and thereby was supposed to endow them with a miraculous power of curing cramps. The service which attended the blessing of those cramp-rings was so original that it deserves description. The king and his suite would proceed in state to the palace chapel, upon the floor of which rested a crucifix upon a silken cushion, and in front of which was spread a rich carpet. The king would creep along the carpet to the crucifix,—as a token of absolute humility,—his "almoner" creeping after him. Having reached the crucifix, he would there bless the cramp-rings, which were deposited in a silver basin. After this was done, the queen and her ladies-in-waiting entered the chapel and also crept to the cross. This completed the ceremony, and the rings had been transformed into the most potent remedial agents. The custom probably arose from the miraculous properties accredited to Edward the Confessor's ring, which was kept in Westminster Abbey for a long time.

In London, and all over England (not, however, in Scotland), the morning of Good Friday is ushered in with a universal cry of " Hot cross buns!" A parcel of them appears on every breakfast-table. The hot cross bun is rather a small bun, more than usually spiced, and having its brown sugary surface marked with a cross. The ear of every person who has ever dwelt in England is familiar with the cry of the street bun-venders. Usually it runs as follows :

> One a penny, buns,
> Two a penny, buns,
> One a penny, two a penny,
> Hot cross buns!

There are many variants, however, the following being an instance :

> One a penny, two a penny,
>   Hot cross buns.
> If you have no daughters,
>   Give them to your sons;
> But if you have none of these merry little elves,
> Then you may keep them all for yourselves.

Men, women, and children used to be early astir to supply the general demand, carrying large baskets covered with flannel and white cloth to keep their fresh wares warm. For a century and a half Chelsea was famous for its buns. Swift mentions the "rare Chelsea buns" in his "Journal to Stella," in 1712. These were made and sold at the Old Chelsea Bun-House, in Jews' Row, a single-story building, with a colonnade projecting over the foot-pavement. It was a great meeting-place on Good Friday mornings, sometimes as many as fifty thousand persons calling for buns, two hundred and forty thousand of which have been sold in a single day.

A rival bun-house arose, and competition became fierce, especially in the reign of George III., when royalty itself deigned to visit Chelsea to partake of these delicacies.

The history of the cross bun goes back to the time of Cecrops, and to the *liba* offered to Astarte, and thence can be traced upward through the Jewish passover cakes, and the eucharistic bread, or cross-marked wafers, mentioned in St. Chrysostom's Liturgy. So that the Good Friday bun has antiquity and tradition to recommend it; and, indeed, its very name of *bun* is but the oblique *boun*, from *bous*, the sacred ox, the semblance of whose horns was stamped upon the cake. There, too, they also did duty for the horns of Astarte, in which word some philologists affect to trace a connection with Easter. The substitution by the Greeks of the cross-mark in place of the horn-mark would seem to have chiefly been for the easier division of the round bun into four equal parts. Such cross-marked buns were found at Herculaneum.

The original home of the English custom, where it is still chiefly observed, is Cambridgeshire and Hertfordshire. There the old Roman roads, the Icknield Street and the Armynge Street, crossed. There stood in Roman times the altar of Diana of the Crossways, to whom the Romans offered their sacred cakes.

In many parts a small loaf of bread is baked on the morning of Good Friday and then put by till the same anniversary in the ensuing year. This bread is not intended to be eaten, but to be used as a medicine, and the mode of administering it is by grating a small portion of it into water and forming a sort of panada. It is believed to be good for many disorders, but particularly for diarrhœa, for which it is considered a sovereign remedy. Some years ago a cottager lamented that her poor neighbor must certainly die of this complaint, because she had already given her two doses of Good Friday bread without any benefit. (BRAND: *Popular Antiquities*, 1849, vol. i. p. 155; see *Notes and Queries*, Third Series, vol. iii. pp. 262, 263.)

Every Good Friday a large crowd gathers at St. Bartholomew's Church in London (which all through the remainder of the year is practically deserted) to witness a performance that is anything but agreeable,—namely, twenty-one aged women bending down on the floor to pick up twenty-one sixpences. Some time before the Great Fire, but exactly when is not known, a lady bequeathed property to have twenty-one sixpences laid upon her grave-stone in St. Bartholomew's Church, which were to be picked up and severally owned by the same number of aged widow women. The grave-stone was to be in the floor; and the lady was so particular as to provide that any widow who from infirmities could not, or from pride would not, stoop down to procure a sixpence, should not have it. The name of the testatrix and the actual place of her burial are now forgotten, as all the records of the period were destroyed in the Great Fire. Nevertheless the sixpences are picked up from the floor by the most aged women that can still bend the stiffening hinges of their limbs.

At the church of All Hallows a sermon is preached every Good Friday, in accordance with the direction in the will of Peter Symonds, dated 1587, to the youngest boys of the Blue-Coat School, after which sixty new pennies and sixty packets of raisins are distributed among them. Under the same will the children of Langbourn Ward Schools who help in the choir, and the children of the Sunday-school, receive each a bun, and various sums of new money, ranging from one penny to one shilling, besides the poor of the parish, on whom it bestowed one shilling each and a loaf. The money used to be given away over the tomb of the donor, until the railway in Liverpool Street effaced the spot.

The custom of skipping the rope on Good Friday still exists at Brighton, though it is rapidly falling into disuse. It is generally practised with a long rope, from six to ten adults skipping at one rope. Formerly the entire fishing community used to engage in this amusement during the whole day, which was thence known as Long-Rope Day. In nearly all the Sussex villages marbles are played on Good Friday by both boys and men.

At Guildford, Surrey, many people flock to St. Martha's Hill. Formerly they used to spend the day in singing and dancing; but this part of the festivities is no longer retained. St. Martha's

Church on this spot is an old pilgrim church whither the faithful used to go when they were on their way to the shrine of St. Thomas of Canterbury. But Martha's Hill is said to be a corruption of Martyr's Hill. Doubtless the visit of the Guildford folk is a relic of some ancient religious ceremony or pilgrimage.

In Spain the señoras appear in the streets in funeral garb. No colors are worn. Even the *jeunesse dorée* are in black from hat to boots, with jet studs and sleeve-buttons. Fashionable ladies sit within the church doors and beg in the name of charity and earn large sums for the poor.

The hanging or burning of Judas in effigy is celebrated on Good Friday or Holy Saturday in Portuguese countries.

Many are the quaint and often grotesque rites observed in other countries on this the anniversary of Christ's Passion. There is the Mystery Play at Monaco, with its night procession. The countless candles and torches, the fantastic costumes of the participants, the minor, monotonous chanting of the priests, all combine—canopied as they are with the starlit heavens—to cast a poetic spell about the scene, hiding the grotesqueness of its mummeries and bringing out only its beauties. Lastly, there is the procession of penitents in the Sicilian city of Palermo. Masked with a hood, which only contains two holes to see through, crowned with a garland of thorns, and wearing a rope noose around their necks, which also is tied around their clasped hands, thus do the penitents parade through the streets, marshalled by priests or monks.

Gorsedd. A mystic ceremony which usually precedes the opening of an Eisteddfod (*q. v.*). It is performed in an open space. In the centre of this is a huge stone, the " Maen Llog," surrounded by a circle, thirty feet in diameter, of other stones, supposed to represent the signs of the zodiac. On the outside of the eastern portion of the circle three more stones are placed, in such a position as regards the Gorsedd stone that lines drawn from it to them will indicate the rising of the sun at the summer and winter solstices and the vernal and autumnal equinoxes respectively. To this Gorsedd stone moves a curious and picturesque procession of bards, druids, and ovates, or candidates for higher orders. The first are dressed in blue, to indicate their celestial aspirations, the second in white, as a symbol of great purity, the third in green, to represent the grass of the field, which is typical of growth and progress. One of the bards carries a sword by its point, to show that he is a man of peace and would prefer to turn the weapon against himself rather than against any other person. On arriving at the circle, a prayer, said to have been composed thirteen hundred years ago, is recited, and then

the Gorsedd is declared to be opened, and the business of conferring degrees on the bards and ovates is proceeded with. Then
follows the Eisteddfod. This is thrown open to the general
public which is not initiated into the mysteries of bardism.

OPENING CEREMONIES AT A GORSEDD.

Gregory the Great, St. His festival is celebrated on March
12, the anniversary of his death.

St. Gregory was the son of a Roman senator, and was born in
540. He was prætor of Rome for twelve years, but later he
turned his house into a monastery and hospital, and lived in a
cell there as a Benedictine monk. On the death of Pope Pelagius,
Gregory was elected to succeed him. During his popedom he
convened many synods and endeavored to restore the discipline
of the Church. He rearranged the liturgy and introduced the
style of chanting still called Gregorian. Legends relate many
miracles performed by this saint, and tell of heavenly messengers
that appeared to him. One legend relates that he gave many
alms to a beggar who came and besought him again and again
until Gregory gave him his last possession, a silver bowl given
to him by his mother. Years afterwards when he became Pope
he daily entertained twelve poor men at his table; but one night
he beheld thirteen, though his steward could see only twelve.
Gregory inquired of the thirteenth man who he was. "I am
the beggar," was the reply, "whom thou didst relieve; but my
name is Wonderful, and through me thou shalt obtain whatsoever thou askest of God." John the Deacon, secretary to St.
Gregory, has left an account in which he declares that he has
seen the Holy Spirit in the shape of a dove perched upon the
shoulder of St. Gregory as he wrote. This explains why the

dove is so often an attribute of St. Gregory in art. St. Gregory died in 604, and his remains were laid in the Vatican church. In 826 the remains were translated to Soissons and placed in the monastery of St. Medard. The head was placed in the abbey of St. Pierre-le-Vif, at Sens, and a bone was given to Rome at the request of Urban VIII. in 1628. The Council of Clif, or Cloveshore, in 747 commanded that the feast of St. Gregory be observed as a holy-day in all the monasteries of England. The Council of Oxford in 1222 extended the holy-day to the whole kingdom.

The feast was formerly observed as a holiday in all the rural schools in the baronies of Forth and Baigy (the Strongbonian Colony) in the county of Wexford, Ireland. The manner of observance was this. The children for some days previous brought contributions, according to the means and liberality of their parents, consisting of money, bread, butter, cream, etc., and delivered them to the teacher. On the morning of the joyous day the children repaired to the school-house in holiday dress, where the teacher had everything prepared for the festivity, the simple temple of learning decorated with the richest flowers within his means of obtaining, and the presence of two or more kind-hearted females to do the honors and duties of the tea-table to the happy juveniles. A "king" and a "queen" were nominated, who, of course, took the seat of honor, and the proud and busy teacher was everywhere all attention to his little pupils. The day passed off in hilarity and innocent enjoyment, and the competitive system of free offerings left, generally, something pleasing to tell for some days in the pockets and humble cupboard of the teacher. This custom prevailed until after the beginning of the present century.

Guadalupe, Our Lady of. (Sp. *Nuestra Señora de Guadalupe.*) A famous picture of the Virgin, preserved in the collegiate church of Guadalupe, a little town three and a half miles north of Mexico. The number of pilgrims, singly and in bands, that resort to this shrine entitles Guadalupe to the designation of the American Lourdes. Special ceremonies are celebrated on the 12th of every month, but the great festival of the year is on December 12, the anniversary of the first appearance of the picture, when the Indians from far and near assemble in vast troops to do honor to their patroness, huge crowds standing on the eve of the feast through the night at the church doors, so as to gain entrance in the morning. Other devotees on their knees make the ascent of the neighboring steep of Tepayacac. Nor are Indians alone attracted hither. Dainty dames in Spanish mantillas are jostled by frowsy drabs from Cuautitlan, dudes from the Paseo find themselves cheek by jowl with half-clad muleteers, fashionable broughams compete for place with ramshackle hackney-coaches.

The pontifical high mass begins at twelve o'clock, and when it is well under way, beggars, decked out in the bizarre garniture of olden days, with plumes of feathers and gaudy masks, dance their barbaric reels in the middle of the church.

The legend runs that in the year 1531 an Indian convert, baptized under the name of Juan Diego, was thrice blessed with a vision of the Virgin Mary, who bade him make known to the Bishop of Mexico that she desired a church to be built on the spot where she had appeared, and that she would be a kind and loving mother to the poor Indians and to all who should invoke her aid. But when the bishop, doubting, requested the attestation of some sign or miracle, the Virgin on the third day bade Juan fill his *tilma*, or homespun blanket, with flowers. And when he took the flower-laden tilma to the bishop and opened it out before him, lo! it was found that the flowers, though visible to the eye, were not palpable to the touch, and moreover that a marvellous picture was limned upon the blanket in colors which partook of no earthly quality and with an art no human hand could equal. And this picture was the portrait of the Holy Virgin as she had appeared to Juan. The sign was accepted, the church was built, the picture was hung up within the church. And there it has remained ever since during all the successive enlargements from the original chapel to the present imposing edifice, save that at the time of the terrible floods of 1629, when the ordinary road-bed was submerged, the archbishop and his attendants went by boat, in solemn pilgrimage, to Guadalupe, and transferred the venerated picture to his cathedral. Here it was visited by immense crowds of devotees, day by day, until the waters subsided. By common acclamation relief from the total destruction which threatened Mexico was attributed to Our Lady of Guadalupe.

"After that period," says Archbishop Corrigan of New York, in an article in *The Seminary* for December, 1895, "devotion to Our Lady of Guadalupe spread so rapidly throughout the entire kingdom that it would be worse than useless to adduce proofs to establish its universality. At this day you can hardly enter a shop in the city of Mexico without finding a lamp burning before a picture of Our Lady of Guadalupe. You can hardly enter a church without seeing an altar erected in her honor. Indeed, the Provincial Council of Antequera or Oaxaca specially ordains that no church be built in the entire province without its special altar in honor of Our Lady of Guadalupe. Every diocese in Mexico dedicates the 12th of every month to Our Lady of Guadalupe, and every year sends thousands of devout pilgrims to her shrine. When the patriot priest, Hidalgo, who is called the Washington of Mexico, began the fight for independence in 1810, his standard and his battle-cry were 'Our Lady of Guadalupe.' The revolution itself, although it despoiled every other church in Mexico, has ever respected this shrine of Our Lady. In one word, the Virgin of Guadalupe has taken such hold on the Mexican people that to attempt to dislodge her from their affections would be to tear out their hearts by the roots."

Archbishop Corrigan was one of the twenty-two foreign prelates who, with the forty-three bishops of Mexico, and fifty thousand pilgrims of all ranks, were present at the coronation of the Blessed Virgin of Guadalupe on October 12, 1895. The crown, which is of gold, sparkling with precious stones, and valued at twenty-five thousand dollars, was lifted up to a level with the head in the picture.

A number of interesting details are given by Archbishop Corrigan in the article already quoted from.

"The material," he says, "on which the image is formed is a coarse product of the maguey plant, such as is still used by the Indians for their wraps and for other domestic purposes. The image is painted on this rough canvas, without any sizing or preparation. In fact, the canvas is transparent, the same image showing on both sides. At various times the picture has been examined by a committee of experts composed of distinguished artists and of scientific men, and they have deposed under oath that they could not account either for its production or for its preservation. The image exhibits peculiar characteristics of painting in oil, in water-color, in distemper, and in relief. In fact, these four dissimilar kinds of painting are discernible in different portions of the same canvas ; and, in addition to this, the gilding, which appears in the stars embroidered on the garment of Our Lady and in the texture of the robe itself, as well as in the rays of light which issue from the figure, is not applied according to any known process, and seems rather to have been woven into the fibre than painted on it.

"Apart from the curious commingling of dissimilar kinds of painting on the same canvas, there is this other peculiarity about the picture, that for years it was exposed, without any covering, not only to the smoke of censers and innumerable candles, but to the damp air, charged with saltpetre, which continually arises from the neighboring lakes and marshes, and which affects and corrodes the hardest substances ; and yet, after a period of more than three hundred and sixty years, this product of the maguey plant, which ought to have perished long ago, is still in a state of perfect preservation. This is the more remarkable, because experiments have been tried in the same locality with similar material, but with very different results. An able artist, Don Rafael Gutierrez, took a fine tilma, September 12, 1789, and painted on it a fac-simile of Our Lady of Guadalupe. When finished, it was protected by a glass cover and placed in the neighboring chapel, Del Pocito. The result was that before eight years elapsed it was so discolored and disfigured by the fumes of the saltpetre that it was necessary to withdraw it from public view and relegate it to the sacristy.

" The great proof of the authenticity of the apparitions," the archbishop continues, " is the constant and uninterrupted tradition, bearing all the marks of credibility, accepted by all classes of people, and extending from the days of Juan Diego to our own time. This tradition has been twice officially examined and approved by the Holy See. Only last year, after a long and most searching examination, Pope Leo XIII. granted a new office and mass in honor of Our Lady of Guadalupe, by letters dated March 6, 1894. In 1754, Pope Benedict XIV. had already granted a similar favor, although the text relating to the apparition was not so explicit. In fact, hardly a Pontiff has sat on the throne of Peter during the past two hundred and fifty years who has not accorded special favors to the sanctuary at Guadalupe." (See also REMEDIOS.)

Guadalupe, Virgin of. Long before the advent of the Mexican Lady of Guadalupe, the mother-country of Spain had a famous image of the Virgin, still preserved in the Jeronymite convent at Guadalupe in Estremadura. It was discovered in 1330 by one Giles, a cow-keeper of Cáceres, and somehow it turned out to have been carved by St. Luke, to have been given to San Leandro, the Gothic uprooter of Arianism, by Gregory the Great, and to have been miraculously preserved during the six centuries of Moorish invasion. A hermitage was built on the spot. In 1340 Alonzo XI. raised a chapel which Juan I. in 1389 converted into a convent subject to the Pope alone. For ages this was one of the richest and most frequented shrines in Europe. Cortes made a special cult of this image, hence the recurrence of the name in Mexico. His first act on his return in 1538 was a pilgrimage to the convent, where he and his followers worshipped for the space of nine days, offering at the altar the *spolia opima* of their strangely achieved wealth. At present the convent is degraded into a barrack, but the splendid chapel and the image have escaped.

Gudula, St. (Flemish, *Goole*), patron saint of Brussels. Her festival is celebrated on January 8, the anniversary of her burial.

Gudula was born about the middle of the seventh century, in Brabant. She was of noble parentage, and her relative St. Gertrude was her sponsor and took charge of her early education. She devoted herself from childhood to a religious life. The castle of her father, Count Witger, was two miles from the little village of Moorsel, where there was an oratory dedicated to the Saviour. Thither went Gudula at cock-crow every morning to her devotions, taking a maid with her to carry her lantern.

It is related that on one occasion the Evil One put out this lantern, but Gudula knelt by the roadway and prayed, and the lantern was miraculously relighted. She devoted her entire revenue to the poor, and when she died all the people followed her body to the grave. She was buried on the 8th of January, 712, according to general opinion, at the village of Hanum, near Relegham. On the morning after her burial a poplar that stood at the foot of her tomb burst into leaf in spite of the season. The body of the saint was transported successively to Nivelles, Ums, and Maubeuge, through fear of the Normans. It was afterwards laid in the oratory at Moorsel. Charlemagne built a monastery in honor of St. Gudula in Moorsel, but this was destroyed by the Normans.

The remains of the saint were finally taken from Moorsel to Brussels in 978. Since 1047 a magnificent church, known as St. Gudula's, has perpetuated her memory, and here the saint is enshrined.

In art she is represented with a lantern, which an angel is kindling.

Guernica, Tree of. Close to the town of Guernica in Biscay, Spain, is the so-called tree of the Basque Liberties. Formerly the Lords of Biscay took their oaths on a stone bench placed at its foot. At present the general juntas are inaugurated here and are continued in the adjoining church of Santa Maria la Antigua. It is perpetuated like the Euskarian family, and is succeeded by its scions, the tree which is to substitute the present one having been planted in 1880. The present tree was thirty years old when, in 1811, its predecessor fell down under the weight of some three centuries. Several patriotic songs have been dedicated to the tree. Rousseau sent it his blessing, and Tallien saluted it in the midst of the French Convention.

Guingamp, Pardon of. Next to the Pardon of St. Anne of Auray (see AURAY), this is the most notable of all the Breton Pardons, or festivals. It begins on the Saturday preceding the first Sunday in July.

According to the local historians, its origin can be traced back to a remote antiquity. Save during the interregnum of the Revolution, it has always attracted an immense crowd of pilgrims. But not until the sixteenth century was the image known as Notre-Dame de Bon Secours, " Our Lady of Good Help" (the object of all this homage), invested with a crown by the Pope, thenceforth assuming a rank to which she had not previously been entitled. By sunrise on the morning of Saturday the narrow winding streets of the old town of Guingamp are crowded with pilgrims, come to perform their devotions at the shrine of Notre-Dame de Bon Secours, and to take part in the evening procession in her honor. This is the distinctive feature of the day. It is held after vespers, and is thus described by George M. Towle in *Harper's Magazine*, vol. xlii. p. 39:

" The church, which is brilliantly lit up, is crowded in every part. The service terminated, precisely at nine o'clock the bells begin to chime, and then to toll a monotonous peal, while most of the houses in the town are being illuminated, and the head of the procession—composed of men and women mingled together indiscriminately, the half-wild-looking Bas-Breton every now and then alternating with some charming-looking demoiselle whose toilet is after the latest mode—is seen descending the flight of steps in front of the north door of the church, preceded by a priest bearing the cross. A troop of cavalry, stationed immediately opposite, salutes the sacred symbol; and for a quarter of an hour pilgrims, all with lighted tapers in their hands, and the men with their heads bare, continue descending the steps in double file. While these are passing out at the north door, another detachment of pilgrims, also in double file, and similarly provided with lighted tapers, is leaving the church by the west. The two detachments proceed in opposite directions—the one moving toward the upper, the other to the lower end of the town. At the expiration of the quarter of an hour just spoken of, the ornamental portion of the procession is seen to emerge from the north door of the church, consisting, first of all, of some young and rather pretty girls, robed entirely in white, and carrying the silk-embroidered banner of the Virgin; then more girls and banners, followed by the members of various female religious communities, in the costumes of their order, bearing their respective banners; next come several small gilt statuettes, carried on handsome stands, one of which represents St. Fiacre, the patron saint of the gardeners, and another St. Joseph, the patron saint of the carpenters. Then follow richly gilt baskets containing various relics, borne by and surrounded by priests; a gold bust, with a long forked beard; a wax figure of a dead child in white, her head wreathed with lilies, lying on a purple cushion covered with a crimson pall, and preceded and followed by banners innumerable. Then a number of men and boys dressed up to represent sailors, and bearing a couple of models of men-of-war of the old school, and a huge gilt anchor; then some of the youths of the college, accompanied by their band; next a number of men with banners and large ornamental open-work lanterns; then the *sapeurs pompiers* and their band; and, finally, a body of priests in rich vestments. The two detachments of pilgrims eventually join themselves together, and the procession, composed by this time of at least ten thousand people, passes up the main street of the town and round the large triangular place where the fountain is situated, chanting all the while. Here three tall poles have been erected, surrounded by banners in honor of the Virgin, and having immense piles of fagots stacked at their base. While the procession is moving round this open space in the direction of the church, these stacks of fagots are set fire to one after the other, filling the air above with fiery sparks, as the ground is already thronged below with lighted tapers, and throwing out such intense heat in their immediate proximity as to cause pilgrims and spectators alike to struggle to escape from it. Such are the aspects of a Breton Pilgrimage or Pardon as seen at Guingamp."

Guy Fawkes's Day. The anniversary of the discovery of the Gunpowder Plot on November 5, 1605, still celebrated in England and her colonies. The conspirators in this plot were all English Catholics of gentle lineage and good position who bloodied their delicate fingers to no end. Hence with a natural and pardonable injustice the entire Catholic party was held responsible for their acts, and the 5th of November has been utilized for a Protestant and anti-Catholic demonstration, borrowing many features from the celebrations on Queen Elizabeth's Day (*q. v.*).

When James VI. of Scotland became James I. of England the Catholics in the latter country had cherished hopes that the penalties imposed against their religion by Queen Elizabeth would be remitted or minimized. And indeed the new monarch began his reign in a mild and tolerant spirit. But he found Parliament arrayed against him. .His pecuniary necessities obliged him to court the good will of the Commons by putting afresh into execution the penal laws against papists. The most odious severities were revived. The fanaticism of persecution bred the fanaticism of retaliation. Hence the Gunpowder Plot, for blowing up at once the King, Lords, and Commons, originated by Robert Catesby, a Catholic gentleman of good family who, doubly an apostate, had found himself back in the Church of his birth after once being a Protestant convert, and had drawn into his plans Thomas Winter, Guido or Guy Fawkes, and several others. In a secluded house in Lambeth, oaths of secrecy were taken, and the communion was administered by a Jesuit named Father Gerard, who, however, does not appear to have been taken into the plot. The next step was to hire a house near the building where Parliament formerly met, with the view of blowing the legislature into the air by carrying a mine through the wall. But when they came to pierce the walls of the Parliament House they found the task beyond their powers, especially as all were gentlemen unused to manual labor. One day, while at work, they heard a rumbling noise over their heads. Fear seized them that they had been discovered. Guy Fawkes, going out to in-

GUY FAWKES.
(From the English Prayer Book of 1607.)

quire, returned with the news that the disturbance had been caused by a coal-dealer who was moving out from a cellar he had rented below the House of Lords. Forthwith the conspirators saw their opportunity. Hiring the cellar from the outgoing dealer, they placed therein thirty-six barrels of gunpowder. These they covered up with coal and fagots of wood. By May, 1605, the preparations were all completed. The conspirators separated until the time to strike had arrived. This was finally determined to be the 5th of November, when the king in person was to open Parliament. In some way, about which historians differ, the plot was discovered. At two o'clock in the morning of November 5, a party of soldiers under command of Sir Thomas Knyvett, a Westminster magistrate, visited the cellar and arrested Guy Fawkes, the man who was to have fired the train that should explode the gunpowder, and who was at his post with a dark lantern in his hand. He was interrogated by the king and council, and shut up in the Tower. Meanwhile the other conspirators, all save Tresham, fled from London in an effort to reach Dunsmore Heath in Warwickshire, where other Catholics under Sir Edmund Digby had agreed to join them in an insurrection should the plot prove successful. Pursued by the civil and military authorities, some of them were overtaken at the mansion of Holbeach, on the borders of Staffordshire. Resisting arrest, four, including Catesby, were slain. But seven others were captured here and in other places. These, with their accomplice Guy Fawkes, were put to the torture, tried, and finally executed at the west end of St. Paul's Churchyard on January 30 and 31, 1606. All the hideous ceremonies attending the deaths of traitors were honored in the observance.

It was in January of the same year that the British Parliament appointed the 5th of November as "a holiday for ever in thankfulness to God for our deliverance and detestation of the Papists." A special service for this day formed part of the ritual of the English Book of Common Prayer until 1859, when an ordinance of the Queen in Council abolished it, together with the service for the Martyrdom of Charles I. and the Restoration of Charles II. (See CHARLES, ST.) At the opening of every session of Parliament even to this day the initial ceremony is the marching of the Yeomen of the Guards through the vaults under the Houses in search of gunpowder. It would be impossible, of course, to get any gunpowder into the basement. Even granting the possibility, it could not be discovered by merely strolling through the cellars. Such, however, is the British love for crystallized custom that it has even been humorously conjectured whether had the Gunpowder Plot succeeded it would have been necessary to blow up the Houses every session because a precedent had been established.

Guy Fawkes's Day is now almost entirely abandoned to the juvenile population of England. Even so late as 1847 the author of the anonymous booklet "Sports, Pastimes, and Customs of London" complains that its old-time glory has departed. "Originally," he says, "the burning of Guy Fawkes in effigy was a ceremony much in vogue, especially among the lower classes, but it is now confined chiefly to school-boys, and even with them it is not so popular as in days gone by. Formerly the burning of 'a good guy' was a scene of uproar perhaps unknown to the present day. The bonfire, for example, in Lincoln's Inn Fields was conducted on a very grand scale. It was made at the Great Queen Street corner, immediately opposite Newcastle House. Fuel came all day long in carts properly guarded against surprise. Old people have recollected when upwards of two hundred cart-loads were brought to make and feed this bonfire, and more than thirty ' guys' were burnt upon gibbets between eight and twelve o'clock at night.

" The butchers of Clare Market, also, were accustomed to celebrate this anniversary in a somewhat peculiar style; one of their body, personating Guy Fawkes, being seated in a cart, with a prayer-book in his hand, and a priest, executioner, etc., attending, was drawn through the streets, as if going to the place of execution ; while a select party, with marrow-bones and cleavers, led the way, and others solicited money from the inhabitants and spectators. The sums thus obtained were spent at night in jollity and carousing."

In all parts of England it is still customary for boys to dress up an effigy of Guy Fawkes, parade it in a chair through the streets, and at nightfall burn it with strident enjoyment in a huge bonfire. The effigy's face is formed of a huge comic mask crowned with a paper fool's cap, it wears such cast-off clothes as are obtainable, in one hand it carries a dark lantern and in the other a bunch of matches. The procession visits successively the different houses in the neighborhood, reciting before each certain time-honored rhymes which vary with the locality. In London they run as follows :

> Remember, remember
> The fifth of November,
> The Gunpowder treason and plot;
> There is no reason
> Why the Gunpowder treason
> Should ever be forgot!

Numerous variations and additions are made in different parts of the country. Thus, in Islip, Oxfordshire, the following lines, as quoted by Sir Henry Ellis in his edition of Brand's " Popular Antiquities," are chanted :

> The fifth of November,
> Since I can remember,
> Gunpowder treason and plot:
> This is the day that God did prevent,
> To blow up his king and parliament.
> A stick and a stake,
> For Victoria's sake ;

> If you won't give me one,
> I'll take two :
> The better for me,
> And the worse for you.

The following song, according to the same authority, is used in some parts of the north of England :

> Hollo, boys, hollo, boys,
>   Let the bells ring ;
> Hollo, boys, hollo, boys,
>   God save the queen.
>
> Pray to remember
> The fifth of November,
>   Gunpowder treason and plot,
> When the king and his train
> Had nearly been slain,
>   Therefore it shall not be forgot.
>
> Guy Fawkes, Guy Fawkes,
>   And his companions,
> Strove to blow all England up ;
> But God's mercy did prevent,
> And saved our king and his Parliament.
> Happy was the man,
>   And happy was the day,
> That caught Guy,
>   Going to his play,
> With a dark lanthorn,
> And a brimstone match,
> Ready for the prime to touch.
>
> As I was going through the dark entry,
>   I spied the devil.
>   Stand back ! stand back !
> Queen Mary's daughter,
> Put your hand in your pocket
> And give us some money,
> To kindle our bonfire.
>   Huzza !   Huzza !

That final eleemosynary plea was never forgotten. When not put into metrical form, it took such prosaic shape as " Please remember Guy," or " Please to remember the bonfire."

Sometimes Guy Fawkes's day is taken advantage of to parade the effigy of any unpopular personage of the day. Thus, during the ferment occasioned by the " Papal Aggression" in 1850 Cardinal Wiseman, newly appointed Archbishop of Westminster by the Pope, was substituted for Guy Fawkes, and solemnly burnt in London amid No Popery demonstrations. In 1857 a similar honor was accorded to Nana Sahib, whose atrocities at Cawnpore in the previous month of July had excited a cry of horror throughout the civilized world. The opportunity also is frequently seized by many of that numerous class in London who live by their wits to earn a few pence by parading through the streets, on the 5th of November, gigantic figures of the leading celebrities of the day. These are sometimes rather ingeniously got up, and the curiosity of the passer-by who stops to look at them is generally taxed with the contribution of a copper.

In *Notes and Queries*, Second Series, vol. iv. p. 368, is the following entry: " A very old custom prevails in the West Riding of Yorkshire, of preparing, against the anniversary of Gunpowder Plot, a kind of oatmeal gingerbread, if it may be so called, and of religiously partaking of the same on this day and subsequently. The local name of the delicacy is *Parkin*, and it is usually seen in the form of massive loaves, substantial cakes, or bannocks."

Blount in his " Fragmenta Antiquitatis" (Beckwith, 1815, p. 565) gives the following account of a custom observed at Doncaster. He says at this place on the 5th of November, yearly, whether it happens on a Sunday or any other day in the week, the town waits play for some time on the top of the church steeple, at the time when the congregation are coming out of the church from morning service, the tune of " God Save the King." This has been done for fourscore years at least, and very possibly ever since the 5th of November has been a festival, except that formerly the tune played was " Britons, strike home." The waits always receive from the churchwardens sixpence apiece for this service.

The celebration of Guy Fawkes's Day was brought over from England to America by the early colonists, and still has local survivals in several of the original thirteen States. In New York, the code known as the Duke's Laws, given to the province in 1665, ordered that every minister should on November 5 preach a sermon commemorative of the English deliverance from Guy Fawkes and his Gunpowder Plot.

The *New York Gazette* of November 7, 1737, affords a glimpse of how the festival was celebrated at that time: " Saturday last, being the fifth of November, it was observed here in memory of that horrid and Treasonable Popish Gun-Powder Plot to blow up and destroy King, Lords, and Commons, and the Gentlemen of his Majesty's Council. The Assembly and Corporation and other the principal Gentlemen and Merchants of this City waited upon his Honor the Lieutenant-Governor at Fort George, where the Royal Healths were drunk, as usual, under the discharge of the Cannon, and at the Night the City was illuminated." All through the English provinces bonfires were burned, volleys were fired, effigies were carried in procession, and mummers and maskers singing No Popery songs importuned passers-by for a gratuity. Giant Pope came in time to be substituted for Guy Fawkes, and the 5th of November was known as Pope Day. Under this name it survives in Newburyport, Massachusetts, and Portsmouth, New Hampshire. In Newcastle, New Hampshire, it is corrupted into Pork Night. In other New England towns fires are still lighted on the 5th of November by boys who know not what they commemorate. In New York and Brooklyn there is a feeble and divided survival of Pope Day sports in the bonfires kindled on election night, and in the bedraggled parades of begging child maskers on Thanksgiving Day.

Gyst-Ale, or **Guising.** An annual festival formerly celebrated in Lancashire in the spring, probably about Lady Day, when manorial rents were due. It has been surmised that the term is an allusion to the attendant gyst or hire for the privilege of selling ale and other refreshments during the festivals held on the payment of the rents of the manor. But a plausible etymon derives the word gyst from *geste,* "an act," "a sport," while guising is but another form of disguising,—*i.e.*, masquerading. Cf. *guisards*, the Scotch for mummers.

These gyst-ales, or guisings, once ranked among the principal festivals of Lancashire, and large sums of money were subscribed by all ranks of society in order that they might be celebrated with becoming splendor. The lord of the manor, the vicar of the parish, the farmer, and the operative severally announced the sums they intended to give, and when the treasurer exclaimed, " A largesse," the crowd demanded, " From whom ?" and then due proclamation was made of the sum subscribed. The real amount, however, was seldom named, but it was announced that " Lord Johnson," or some other equally distinguished person, had contributed " a portion of ten thousand pounds" towards the expenses of the feast.

After the subscription lists were closed, an immense garland was prepared, which contained abundance of every flower in season, interspersed with a profusion of evergreens and ribbons of every shade and pattern. The framework of this garland was made of wood, to which hooks were affixed, and on these was suspended a large collection of watches, jewels, and silver articles borrowed from the richer residents in the town. On the day of the gyst this garland was borne through the principal streets and thoroughfares, attended by crowds of townspeople dressed in their best attire. These were formed into a procession by a master of the ceremonies, locally termed the King. Another principal attendant was the Fool, dressed in a grotesque cap, a hideous grinning mask, a long tail hanging behind him, and a bell with which he commanded attention when announcements were to be made. In an early period of these guisings the fool was usually mounted on a hobby-horse, and indulged in grotesque pranks as he passed along: hence we obtained the term "hob-riding," and more recently the proverbial expression of "riding one's hobby to death." (HARLAND AND WILKINSON: *Legends and Traditions of Lancashire*, 1873, p. 86.)

H.

Hachette, Joan. (Fr. *Jeanne Hachette.*) A French heroine who distinguished herself at the siege of Beauvais, France, in 1472, and in whose honor an annual festival is held in that city on July 6. Charles the Bold of Burgundy, revolting against Louis XI., had thrown himself against the town. The adult male population and many of the women and children gathered upon the ramparts and with muskets and stones beat off the assault. Most noticeable among the women was Joan Laisne, afterwards nicknamed Hachette, from the axe which she effect-ually wielded in the struggle. A Burgundian sought to plant his standard in a breach. Joan killed him, and, capturing the flag, bore it in triumph to the chapel of St. Angadrème, patroness of Beauvais. Charles the Bold, surprised by so stout a resistance, raised the siege, and a few days later Louis XI. entered the town in triumph.

That monarch decreed that to honor the valor of Beauvais an annual procession should be held on the festival of St. Angadrème, wherein the women should take precedence of the men. The flag which Joan had seized has always been brought out of the church to take part in this procession, and little by little her fame has dominated that of even the patroness of the city, so that the festival is known as the Fête Jeanne Hachette. On July 6, 1851, a bronze statue of the heroine was unveiled in the public square, amid great solemnities.

On the eve of the festival a salvo of artillery announces the coming event. In the morning mass is celebrated at the cathe-dral, and at its close the Rosière named for the occasion is crowned by the mayor. In the afternoon at three o'clock occurs the procession. It consists of two wings, the civil and the reli-gious, the former starting from the city hall, the latter from the cathedral. Both meet in front of the statue of Joan Hachette. Here the body of young girls dressed in white and crowned with flowers, who follow the clergy in the religious wing, are intrusted with the duty of firing off, turn and turn about, the salute of one hundred guns which forms part of the traditional usage.

Halloween or **All Hallow Even** (also known locally as **Nutcrack Night** and **Snapapple Night**). The name given to the night of October 31, as the eve or vigil of All Saints' or All Hallows Day (November 1). Of all nights in the year this is the one upon which supernatural influences most prevail. The spirits of the dead wander abroad, together with witches, devils, and mischief-making elves, and in some cases the spirits of living persons have the temporary power to leave their bodies and join the ghostly crew. Children born on this day preserve through their youth the power to converse with these airy visitants. But often the latter reveal themselves to ordinary folk, to advise or warn them. Hence it is the night of all nights for divination. Impartially weighed against the others, it is the very best time of the whole year for discovering just what sort of husband or wife one is to be blessed withal.

Halloween is a curious recrudescence of classic mythology, Druidic beliefs, and Christian superstitions. On November 1 the Romans had a feast to Pomona, the goddess of fruits and seeds, and it was then that the stores laid up in the summer for use in the winter were opened. Hence the appropriateness of the use of nuts and apples at this time. November 1 or thereabouts was also the great autumn festival to the sun which the Druids celebrated in thanksgiving for their harvest. Now, the Druids believed in transmigration, and taught that on the eve of this festival Saman, the Lord of Death, called together the wicked souls that within the last twelve months had been condemned to occupy the bodies of animals. But Saman might be propitiated through the priests by means of gifts and incantations to mitigate his sentences.

November was also one of the quaternary periods when the Druids lighted their bonfires in honor of Baal. (See MAY-DAY.) The custom was kept up in many portions of Great Britain until a comparatively recent period. Wales was especially tenacious of it, and the observances which marked the November fire may be held to have descended directly from the Druids.

Each family used to make its own fire, and as it was dying out each member would throw a white stone into it, the stones being marked for future identification. Then all said their prayers and went to bed, and in the morning they tried to find all the stones again. If any stone was missing it betokened that the owner of it would die within a year. Some superstitions are pretty and picturesque and attractive; this was one of the many which were cruel as well as picturesque. It would take but a slight accident to cause a fright that might be actually dangerous to a superstitious person, and it would not be hard for an enemy of such a person to cause that fright by stealing his stone from the fire.

These fires in Wales were commonly followed by feasting on nuts, apples, and parsnips, and by the games of which something will be said presently. Sometimes nuts were thrown into the fires, in the belief that they indicated prosperity to those who threw them if they burned well and the reverse if they simply smouldered and turned black. There were fires also in Scotland, and there, in some parts of the country at least, the ashes were carefully raked into a circle and just within this the stones were placed, one for each person present. If in the morning any of these appeared to have been disturbed, it betokened death. Sometimes it was the custom to make large torches by binding combustible material to the tops of poles and to bear them blazing about the village, lighting new ones as often as the old were burned out. Fires were also used at different times and places on All Saints' Night, which is the eve of All Souls' Day, and on All Souls' Day itself, the 2d of November. In these cases the fires were regarded as typical of immortality, and were thought to be efficacious, as an outward and visible sign at least, for lighting souls from purgatory.

But if anything were wanting to prove the Druidic origin of many of the Halloween observances it would be found in the fact that in some parts of Ireland October 31 was known as Oidhche Shamhna, or Vigil of Saman. Vallancey's "Collectanea de Rebus Hibernicis" tells us that on this night the peasants in Ireland assemble with sticks and clubs, "going from house to house, collecting money, breadcake, butter, cheese, eggs, etc., for

the feast, repeating verses in honor of the solemnity, demanding preparations for the festival in the name of St. Columb Kill, desiring them to lay aside the fatted calf and to bring forth the black sheep. The good women are employed in making the griddle-cake and candles; these last are sent from house to house in the vicinity, and are lighted up on the (Saman) next day, before which they pray, or are supposed to pray, for the departed soul of the donor. Every house abounds in the best viands they can afford: apples and nuts are devoured in abundance; the nut-shells are burnt, and from the ashes many strange things are foretold; cabbages are torn up by the root; hemp-seed is sown by the maidens, and they believe that if they look back they will see the apparition of the man intended for their future spouse; they hang a smock before the fire, on the close of the feast, and sit up all night, concealed in a corner of the room, convinced that his apparition will come down the chimney and turn the smock; they throw a ball of yarn out of the window, and wind it on the reel within, convinced that if they repeat the Pater Noster backwards, and look at the ball of yarn without, they will then also see his sith or apparition; they dip for apples in a tub of water, and endeavor to bring one up in the mouth; they suspend a cord with a cross-stick, with apples at one point, and candles lighted at the other, and endeavor to

catch the apple, while it is in a circular motion, in the mouth." Vallancey sagely concludes that these superstitious practices, the remains of Druidism, will never be eradicated while the name of Saman is permitted to remain.

In the island of Lewis the name Shamhna, or Saman, seems to have been corrupted to Shony. Martin talks with considerable disgust of "an ancient custom here to sacrifice to a sea-god, called Shony, at Hallowtide." The inhabitants, it seems, used to gather to the church of St. Mulvay, at night, each family bringing provisions, and also furnishing a peck of malt, which was brewed into ale. One who was chosen for the purpose waded into the sea up to his middle and poured out a cup of ale, calling on Shony to favor the people through the coming year. "At his return to land they all went to church, where there was a candle burning upon the altar: and then standing silent for a little time, one of them gave a signal, at which the candle was put out, and immediately all of them went to the fields, where they fell a-drinking their ale, and spent the remainder of the night in dancing and singing." He adds, "The ministers in Lewis told me they spent several years before they could persuade the vulgar natives to abandon this ridiculous piece of superstition."

If in the word Saman the Irish preserve a distinct evidence of Druidism, on the other hand in the drink called "Lambs-wool" they equally confess the Roman intermixture. Lambs-wool is made by bruising roasted apples and mixing them with ale or sometimes with milk. The *Gentleman's Magazine* for May, 1784, says "this is a constant ingredient at a merrymaking on Holy Eve." Now, Vallancey makes a shrewd etymological guess when he says, "The first day of November was dedicated to the angel presiding over fruits, seeds, etc., and was therefore named La Mas Ubhal,—that is, the day of the apple fruit,—and being pronounced Lamasool, the English have corrupted the name to Lambs-wool." The "angel presiding over fruits, seeds, etc.," was obviously a reminiscence of Pomona.

It may be interesting to record a few of the Halloween customs which are now practically extinct.

A curious little book called "The Festyvall" (1511) mentions a custom obsolete even at that time. "We rede," it says, "in olde tyme good people wolde on All halowen daye bake brade and dele it for all crysten soules." Yet bread or cake in one form or other was locally associated with Halloween until a far more recent period. Indeed, even at the present moment it is said that the women of Ripon, Yorkshire, on this night make a cake for every one in the family, so that it is popularly known as Cake Night. In Warwickshire and elsewhere seed-cake was an accompaniment of Halloween, as indicating the end of wheat seedtime. This custom seems to have been general in the time of Thomas Tusser:

> Wife, some time this weeke, if the wether hold cleere,
> An end of wheat-sowing we make for this yeare.
> Remember you, therefore, though I do it not,
> The Seed-Cake, the Pasties, and Furmentie-pot.
> (*Five Hundred Points of Good Husbandry*, 1580.)

Aubrey says that in his time in Shropshire and elsewhere there was set upon the board at All Hallows Eve a high heap of Soul-cakes, about the bigness of twopenny cakes, lying one upon another, like the picture of the shewbread in the old Bibles. Every visitor was expected to take one. "There is an old rhyme or saying," he adds,—"A Soule-cake, a Soule-cake, have mercy on all Christen soules for a Soule-cake."

Tollet in a note in his Variorum Shakespeare to the "Two Gentlemen of Verona" (Act ii. Sc. 2) says, "It is worth remarking that on All Saints' Day the poor people in Staffordshire, and perhaps in other country places, go from parish to parish *a-soul-*

ing, as they call it,—*i.e.*, begging and puling (or singing small, as Bailey's Dictionary explains puling) for Soul Cakes, or any good thing to make them merry. This custom is mentioned by Peck, and seems a remnant of Popish superstition to pray for departed souls, particularly those of friends."

Another Popish practice was summarily stopped by the Reformation. This was the custom of ringing bells at this season for all Christian souls.

In the draught of a letter which King Henry VIII. was to send to Cranmer "against superstitious practices" (BURNET: *Hist. Ref.*, 1683), "the Vigil and ringing of bells all the night long upon Allhallow Day at night" are directed to be abolished; and the said Vigil to have no watching or ringing. And in the appendix to Strype's "Annals of the Reformation" the following injunction, made early in the reign of Queen Elizabeth, occurs: "That the superfluous ringing of bels, and the superstitious ringing of bells at Allhallowntide, and at Al Souls' Day, with the two nights next before and after, be prohibited."

In the Churchwardens' Accounts of the parish of Heybridge, near Malden, in Essex, under A.D. 1517 are the following items:

"Imprimis, payed for frankyncense agense Hollowmasse, 0*l*. 0*s*. 1*d*.

"Item, payed to Andrew Elyott, of Maldon, for newe mendynge of the third bell knappell agenste Hallowmasse, 0*l*. 1*s*. 8*d*.

"Item, payed to John Gidney, of Maldon, for a new bell rope agenste Hallowmasse, 0*l*. 0*s*. 8*d*."

Among articles to be inquired of within the archdeaconry of Yorke by the churchwardens and sworn men, between the years 1630 and 1640, one is, " Whether there be any within your parish or chappelry that use to ring bells superstitiously upon any abrogated holiday, or the eves thereof."

Everybody is familiar with Burns's famous poem " Halloween," which gives a panoramic insight into the customs of Old Scotia on this night of mirth and mystery. Perhaps no influence has done more than this to preserve and spread these observances among English-speaking folk. All of them are based on immemorial custom.

But what was once a ceremony of belief has now become a thing of sport, of welcome sport in a day of such serious thought and work and sense of responsibility that any excuse for sport should be laid hold of; so that now its observances are all a jest which young people play upon themselves, not in the least believing in the consequences, only half hoping there may be something in it, and saying to themselves that stranger things have happened.

So they practise matrimonial vaticinations of all sorts. Most common of all and most intimately associated with the season is the roasting of nuts. These are placed together on the bar of the grate side by side in pairs, and named for supposed lovers. If a nut burns quietly and brightly it indicates sincerity of affection. If it cracks and jumps it tells of unfaithfulness, while if the nuts burn together the youth and maid so indicated will be married.

> These glowing nuts are emblems true
> Of what in human life we view.
> The ill-matched couple fret and fume,
> And thus in strife themselves consume,
> Or from each other wildly start,
> And with a noise forever part.
> But see the happy, happy pair,
> Of genuine love and truth sincere:
> With natural fondness while they burn,
> Still to each other kindly turn,
> And as the vital sparks decay,
> Together gently sink away,
> Till, life's fierce ordeal being past,
> Their mingled ashes rest at last.
>
> (CHARLES GRAYDON: *Poems*, Dublin, 1801.)

Or perchance two hazel-nuts are thrown into the hot coals by a maiden. She secretly gives a lover's name to each. If one of the nuts bursts, then that lover is unfaithful; but if it burns with a steady glow until it becomes ashes, she knows that her lover's faith is true. Sometimes it happens, but not often, that both nuts will burn steadily, and then is the maiden's heart sore perplexed.

Burns's stanza on this subject is as pretty as any in his poem:

> Jean slips in twa, wi' tentie e'e;
> Wha 'twas she wadna tell;
> But this is Jock and this is me,
> She says in to hersel;
> He bleez'd owre her, an' she owre him,
> As they wad never mair part;
> Till, 'fuff'! he started up the lum,
> An' Jean had e'en a sair heart
> To see't that night.

Gay has also some pretty lines about a girl who proved her lover in this way:

> Two hazel-nuts I threw into the flame,
> And to each nut I gave a sweetheart's name;
> This with the loudest bounce me sore amazed,
> That in a flame of brightest color blazed;

> As blazed the nut, so may thy passion grow,
> For 'twas thy nut that did so brightly glow!

Next to nuts in importance come apples.

Endless are the methods of extracting from these fruit either fun or prophecy.   What greater fun can there be when you are at the right age and in the right mood, than ducking for apples? These apples are set afloat in a tub of water.   They must be caught with the teeth, and the hands must not be used at all. The surest way to get an apple, it is said, is to force it to the bottom of the tub, and there hold it close while it is caught by the teeth.   Any other way is hard to manage and uncertain

of result.   Another trick is to suspend a stick by a string tied in the middle.   An apple is placed at one end and a lighted candle at the other.   The stick is then whirled around, and the purpose is to catch the apple with the teeth and not to catch the candle.

And as to prophecy, any maiden may find out at least the first letter of the name of her future husband by peeling a pippin, taking the paring by one end in her fingers, swinging it three times about her head, and then letting it drop.   The pippin-paring thus dropped will surely fall in the shape of the initial of his name, as she will readily see, though the rest of the company, not having quite so discerning eyes as hers, may not.

It is said to help among the witches wonderfully to repeat these North of England lines while swinging the paring about the head:

> I pare this pippin round and round again,
> My sweetheart's name to flourish on the plain:
> I fling the unbroken paring o'er my head,
> My sweetheart's letter on the ground is read.

Two cut apple-seeds stuck on the lids of the eyes help one immensely on Halloween in determining which of two lovers is the more desirable. All that is necessary is to name the apple-seeds after the lovers, respectively, and that which drops from the eye first points to him whose love is not adhesive. The advantage of this spell is that a body may help the Fates along, if they seem undecided, by winking.

The hemp-seed divination is known both to the United States and to Britain. The experimenter must go out alone and unper-ceived with a handful of hemp-seed, which he must sow on the ground, dragging after him anything that may be convenient by way of a harrow. He must then say, "Hemp-seed, I sow thee, hemp-seed, I sow thee: and him or her that is to be my true love come after me and pou thee." If he then looks over his left shoulder, he ought to see a likeness of his future sweetheart pulling the seed which he has sowed. If he sees nobody, he may conclude that he is never to marry, or that there is some mistake in the experiment. A trial very like this may be made on Midsummer Eve.

If a girl would see her husband by an Irish method, here it is. Let her throw a ball of yarn out of the window, holding the end of the thread, and then rewind it, at the same time saying the Pater Noster backward. Watching the ball of yarn with-out, she will see the desired apparition. Burns shows that the Scottish form of this test was more solemn. He says nothing of the Pater Noster, but he says that the yarn must be blue, and that the experimenter must go out to a lime-kiln and throw the ball therein; then, when the rewinding is nearly finished, some-thing will hold the thread. To the question, "Wha hauds?" the name of the future husband will be returned in answer. Of course it is understood that this or any of the other methods of divination of this night may be used with equal effect by a man or a woman.

Wet the sleeve of a shirt and hang it on a chair before the fire, as if to dry. Then go to bed, but do not go to sleep, only watch. At about midnight you may confidently expect to see your spouse that is to be enter the room and turn the drying garment. If you do not see him, it must be because you allow yourself to drop asleep, if only for a minute, and so miss him when he comes. Burns adds to the difficulty of this trial, and therefore to its probable success if carried out rightly, by re-quiring that the shirt shall be wet in a spring or rivulet running towards the south at a point where three lairds' lands meet. It is the left sleeve that must be wet. This, also, is a test which may be tried equally well at midsummer.

Numerous are the other ways in which the beatific vision of the future spouse may be conjured up. Lovers set three dishes on the floor, one empty, one with clean water, and one with foul water, and then approaching blindfolded dip their hands at random : they who dip in the empty one shall remain unmarried, and they who dip in the foul shall get one that is widowed, and they who dip in the clean shall be joined to a virgin. Or all alone they eat an apple before a mirror, feeling creepy as they look over the shoulder in the glass for the face of the sweetheart or spouse to be ; or they go down the cellar stairs with a candle in one hand and a mirror in the other, for the same expected vision. Or they winnow in the dark three measures of nothing, simply with empty mimicry of winnowing, whereupon the face is to appear ; or they pull the dead stalk from the garden, and judge by the earth clinging to the roots whether or not the lover has gold and gear ; or they drop the yolk of an egg in water, and take heed of the indications concerning a lover's trade and tools, be they pen or be they spade.

But the mysterious rites of Halloween are not complete when the merrymaking is done and "good-night" is said. Each young lady, in order to complete the charms of the night, on reaching her home must pluck two roses with long stems, naming one for herself and the other for her lover. She must then go directly to her sleeping-room without speaking to any one, and, kneeling beside her bed, must twine together the stems of the two roses and repeat the following lines, gazing meanwhile intently upon the lover's rose :

> Twine, twine, and intertwine,
> Let my love be wholly mine.
> If his heart be kind and true,
> Deeper grow his rose's hue.

If her swain be faithful, the color of the rose will grow darker and more intense.

The moment has at last arrived for the final and, to many, the most convincing and satisfactory test as to the identity of the maid's lover if she is still in doubt. A glass of water, in which a small sliver of wood has been placed, must stand on a small table by her bedside. In the night she will dream of falling from a bridge into a river ; but scarcely will she touch the water when her future husband, whose face she can plainly see, will jump in and rescue her.

A noteworthy circumstance in the Scottish observance of the night which has not been largely followed elsewhere is the extraordinary and varied use to which cabbage, or kail, is put in the traditions and merrymaking of the occasion. Kail brose, or cabbage broth, is inseparable from the Scotch Halloween feast. Mischievous boys push the pith from the stalk, fill the cavity with tow which they set on fire, and then through the keyholes of houses of folk who have given them offence blow darts of flame a yard in length. If on Halloween a farmer's or crofter's kail-yard still contains ungathered cabbages, the boys and girls of the neighborhood descend upon it *en masse*, and the entire crop is harvested in five minutes' time and thumped against the owner's doors, which rattle as though pounded by a thunderous tempest. In some shires at the "pulling of the kail" the youths of both sexes go into the kail-yard blindfolded and in pairs, holding each other's hands. They each pull the first "runt" or stalk they find, not being permitted to make selection. All thus gathered are carried back to the house for inspection. The straightness or crookedness, leanness or fatness, and other peculiarities of the stalks are indicative of the general appearance of their future husbands or wives, while the taste of the pith, whether sweet, bitter, or vapid, forecasts their disposition and character. But the most singular of all beliefs in Scotland regarding the cabbage-stalk is confined to the minds of very young children, though it is so peculiarly a tender delusion that the guidwife holds it in respect to her dying day. The idea is universal among the little folks in the Land o' Cakes that where a new brother or sister appears in the household it has come, through fairy aid, from the roots of the cabbage-stalk. So that when all the bairns of Scotland are singing,—

> This is the nicht o' Halloween,
> When a' the witchie micht be seen ;
> Some o' them black, some o' them green,
> Some o' them like a turkey bean,—

however mad and merry all their games, they never lay their joy-weary heads upon their pillows until with their own hands they have laid generous piles of "kail runts" against door-sill and window-ledge, so that the gracious and kindly fairies of blessed Halloween night shall set free at least one baby soul from the roots and mould, and the household shall not fail of welcoming another tiny bairn within the coming year.

The following extract is taken from the *Guardian* (November 11, 1874): "Halloween was duly celebrated at Balmoral Castle. Preparations had been made days beforehand, and farmers and others for miles around were present. When darkness set in, the celebration began, and her majesty and the Princess Beatrice, each bearing a large torch, drove out in an open phaeton. A procession formed of the tenants and servants on the estates followed, all carrying huge torches lighted. They walked through the grounds and round the castle, and the scene as the procession moved onwards was very weird and striking. When it had arrived in front of the castle, an immense bonfire, composed of old boxes, packing cases, and other materials, stored up during the year for the occasion, was set fire to. When the flames were at their brightest, a figure dressed as a hobgoblin appeared on the scene, drawing a car surrounded by a number of fairies carrying long spears, the car containing the effigy of a witch. A circle having been formed by the torch-bearers, the presiding elf tossed the figure of the witch into the fire, where it was speedily consumed. This cremation over, reels were begun, and were danced with great vigor to the stirring strains of Willie Ross, her majesty's piper."

A custom that prevails in Ireland and Scotland, and that is religiously followed in the United States by the people of those countries, has to do with the character of the evening meal. A dish, largely made up of mashed parsnips and potatoes and chopped onions, is served as the principal item on the bill of fare. It is called "call-cannon," though why it is thus designated only these people understand. A deep bowl filled to the brim with the food is placed in the middle of the table. Somewhere in the bowl is a gold ring, and in the centre is a deep well filled with melted butter. Portions are distributed to each person, and the one who finds the ring is certain to be married within a year, unless already married, in which event good luck will follow the finder.

A loaf-cake is often made and in it are placed a ring and a key. The former signifies marriage, the latter a journey, and the finder of either must accept the inevitable.

In the United States it is to be regretted that the spirit of rowdyism has in a measure superseded the kindly old customs. In towns and villages gangs of hoodlums throng the streets, ringing the door-bells or wrenching the handles from their sockets, and taking gates from off their hinges. In Washington the boys carry flour in a bag. Care is taken to have the web of the bags so worn that a slight blow will release a generous supply of the white powder. The bags are long and narrow, and are handled as if they were slung-shots. These the boys use upon one another as well as upon non-belligerent passers-by.

Handsel Monday. The first Monday in the year. This is a great holiday among the peasantry and the children generally in Scotland, being especially devoted to the giving and receiving of presents, or, in the Scotch vocabulary, handsels. The young visit their seniors in expectation of some remembrance, and postmen, scavengers, and newspaper-carriers look for the equivalent of what in England are known as Christmas-boxes. In the remoter rural regions Auld Handsel Monday—*i.e.*, Handsel Monday, Old Style, or the first Monday after the 12th of January—

is the day usually held. On this occasion it was the ancient custom for farmers to treat all their servants to a liberal breakfast of roast and boiled, with ale, whiskey, and cake, after which the guests spent the day in visiting among their friends. It was also moving day in old Scotland, and the date when new engagements were entered into with servants and farm-hands.

Hangman's Stone. There are numerous large boulders in different parts of England and the United States which have received the name of "Hangman's Stone," in consequence of a legend which attaches much the same story to each. There were two fields in the parish of Foremark, Derbyshire, called the Great and the Little Hangman's Stone, from the boulders which they contained. In the former there was a stone five or six feet high, with an indentation running across the top of it. This peculiar mark was explained by the tradition that once upon a time a thief, having stolen a sheep, placed his booty on the top of the stone while he rested, but it slipped off, and strangled the man with the rope which tied the sheep to his back, the indentation being made by the friction of the rope passing back and forth in the struggles of the dying man to extricate himself.

At a picturesque angle in the road between Sheffield and Barnsby, and about three miles south of the latter place, there is a toll-bar called "Hangman's Stone Bar." Attached to this title is the usual legend of a sheep-stealer being strangled by the kicking animal which he had slung across his shoulders, and which pulled him backward as he tried to climb over the stone wall with his spoil. Here no one particular stone is marked with evidence of the struggle, but the Jehu of the now extinct Barnsby mail always used to tell the story to any inquiring passenger who happened to be one of the "five at top" on his quaint four-in-hand.

At the end of Lamber Moor, on the roadside between Haverford West and Little Haven, in the county of Pembroke, there is a stone about four feet high, called "Hang Davy Stone," connected with which is the same legend, only in this case the unfortunate's name has survived. There is also, about five miles from Sidmouth, on the road to Colyton, on the right-hand side, near Bovey House, another boulder which bears this ominous appellation.

In Westcote's "View of Devonshire in 1630" mention is made of the fact that the parish of Tatchcomb is separated from Combmartin by a long row of boundary stones, one of which is distinguished as the "Hangman's Stone," for the same reason that has been given before. And only a few years ago there was still to be seen, near the boundary of Littlebury parish in Essex, another large stone which bore this same name and history. This was subsequently removed to the private garden of a Mr. Gibson of Saffron Walden.

North Essex abounds in these strange boulders, and quantities of them may be seen along the roadside. The general impression is that they have been disinterred in by-gone times and left near the spot where they were discovered.

Hangman's Stones occur also on the road between Brighton and New Haven; and the most famous instance of all is the one recorded in Potter's "Charwood," where the death of the deer-stealer John of Oxley is rehearsed in verse, under the title of "The Legend of the Hangman's Stone:"

> One shaft he drew on his well-tried yew,
>   And a gallant hart lay dead ;
> He tied its legs, and he hoisted his prize,
>   And he toiled over Lubcloud brow—
> He reached the tall stone standing out and alone,
>   Standing there as it standeth now ;
> With his back to the stone, he rested his load,
>   And he chuckled with glee to think
> That the rest of his way on the down-hill lay,
>   And his wife would have spied the strong drink.
>
> *   *   *   *   *   *   *
>
> A swineherd was passing o'er great Ive's Head,
>   When he noticed a motionless man ;
> He shouted in vain,—no reply could he gain,—
>   So down to the gray stone he ran.
> All was clear: there was Oxley on one side the stone,
>   On the other the down-hanging deer;
> The burden had slipped, and his neck it had nipped ;
>   He was hanged by his prize: all was clear.

It is a curious fact that a tale almost identical with the tradition attached to the Hangman's Stones is related of a pig-stealer and a stile, in Craven. "Swine Harry" is the name of a field on the side of Pinnow, a hill in Tothersdale, in Craven. It is said that a native of the valley was once crossing the field at the dead of night with a pig which he had stolen from a neighboring farm-yard. He led the obstinate animal by a rope which was tied to its leg and noosed at the other end, which he held in his hand. On coming to a ladder-stile, being a very stout man, and wishing to have both hands at liberty, but not liking to release the pig, he transferred the rope from his hands to his neck. But when he reached the top step, his feet slipped, the pig pulled hard on the other side, the noose tightened, and the next morning he was found dead.

The fatal character which seems to distinguish these boulders is not satisfactorily accounted for. It may be that they are remnants of the devil's missiles; for he is known to have utilized such large boulders in many of his encounters with the early inhabitants. In the German popular tales the devil is frequently made to step into the place of the giants. Like them, he has his abode in rocks, and hurls stones in which the impression of his fingers or other members is often to be seen; and, according to tradition, compacts are made with him for the building of churches.

Hara-Kiri. (Japanese, from *hara*, "the belly," and *kiri*, "cutting," "cut.") The official suicide by disembowelling formerly practised in Japan by daimios and members of the military class, either voluntarily, to avoid surviving some personal or family disgrace, or by instigation of the Mikado as a punishment for crime. In the latter case the act was performed with punctilious ceremonial in the presence of witnesses. The moment the suicide had ripped open his abdomen with his dirk his head was struck off by his *kaishaku*, or second, usually a kinsman, or at least a friend of his own rank. Japanese gentlemen were trained to look upon the hara-kiri as an honorable expiation of crime or blotting out of obloquy. If the offence had been heinous, and such as might otherwise have involved the ruin of the whole family, the Mikado in his clemency usually confiscated only half the property and returned the other half to the heir; if the offence were trivial, the property was inherited intact by the heir and the family was exonerated. In all cases where the criminal disembowelled himself of his own accord without condemnation and without investigation, inasmuch as he was no longer able to defend himself, the offence was considered as non-proven, and the property was not confiscated.

It was customary for the Mikado, when hara-kiri had been determined upon, and the culprit happened to be of very high rank, to send him a jewelled sword wherewith to operate upon himself. This custom was put to a severe test on one occasion when the Mikado had been grievously hurt by the words and conduct of a high court official. The man was an old and very valued servant of the crown, but his crime was unpardonable. Next day, therefore, an officer brought him the fatal sword, a magnificent weapon, with a blade inlaid with gold and a handle incrusted with diamonds, together with a sympathetic intimation that his early death would be regarded as a benefit to the empire in general and to the Mikado in particular. The culprit received the sword with all proper respect, but as soon as the emissary had departed, the wily Japanese—in whose mind European habits of thought had evidently taken firm root—walked down to the quay, went on board a mail steamer that was bound for Havre, and upon reaching Paris incontinently sold his sword of honor for six thousand pounds.

Hara-kiri is often misspelled hari-kari and harri-karri, and is alternatively known as the Happy Despatch. It was established in Japan in the days of the Ashi-Kaga dynasty (A.D. 1336–1568). Japanese authorities estimate that at one time no less than fifteen hundred of these suicides occurred annually. The custom was abolished in 1868.

The only Europeans who ever witnessed an execution by hara-kiri were A. B. Mitford and six fellow-diplomats, who were all invited to be present at the execution of Taki Zenzaburo in 1867. He was an officer of the Mikado who had given the order to fire upon the foreign settlements at Hiogo during the civil war against the Tycoon and had thereby almost brought down the vengeance of Europe upon the Mikado. The ceremony took place at half-past ten o'clock at night in the temple of Seikukuji, at Hiogo.

"It was an imposing scene," says Mr. Mitford,—"a large hall with a high roof supported by dark pillars of wood. From the ceiling hung a profusion of those huge gilt lamps and ornaments peculiar to Buddhist temples. In front of the high altar, where the floor, covered with beautiful white mats, is raised some three or four inches from the ground, was laid a rug of scarlet felt. Tall candles placed at regular intervals gave out a dim mysterious light, just sufficient to let all the proceedings be seen. The seven Japanese took their places on the left of the raised floor, the seven foreigners on the right. No other person was present.

"After an interval of a few minutes of anxious suspense, Taki Zenzaburo, a stalwart man thirty-two years of age, with a noble air, walked into the hall attired in his dress of ceremony, with the peculiar hempen cloth wings which are worn on great occasions. He was accompanied by a *kaishaku* and three officers, who wore the *zimbaori*, or war surcoat with gold-tissue facings.

"With the *kaishaku* on his left hand, Taki Zenzaburo advanced slowly towards the Japanese witnesses, and the two bowed before them, then drawing near to the foreigners they saluted us in the same way, perhaps even with more deference: in each case the salutation was ceremoniously returned. Slowly, and with great dignity, the condemned man mounted onto the raised floor, prostrated himself before the high altar twice, and seated himself on the felt carpet with his back to the high altar, the *kaishaku* crouching on his left-hand side. One of the three attendant officers then came forward bearing a stand of the kind used in temples for offerings, on which, wrapped in paper, lay the *wakizashi*, the short sword or dirk of the Japanese, nine inches and a half in length, with a point and an edge as sharp as a razor's. This he handed, prostrating himself, to the condemned man, who received it reverently, raising it to his head with both hands, and placed it in front of himself.

"After another profound obeisance, Taki Zenzaburo, in a voice which betrayed just so much emotion and hesitation as might be expected from a man who is making a painful confession, but with no sign of fear either in his face or manner, spoke as follows:

"'I, and I alone, unwarrantably gave the order to fire on the foreigners at Kobé, and again as they tried to escape. For this crime I disembowel myself, and I beg you who are present to do me the honor of witnessing the act.'

"Bowing once more, the speaker allowed his upper garments to slip down to his girdle, and remained naked to the waist. Carefully, according to custom, he tucked his sleeves under his knees to prevent himself from falling backward, for a noble Japanese gentleman should die falling forward. Deliberately, with a steady hand, he took the dirk that lay before him; he looked at it wistfully, almost affectionately; for a moment he seemed to collect his thoughts for the last time, and then, stabbing himself below the waist on the left-hand side, he drew it slowly across to the right side, and, turning the dirk in the wound, gave a slight cut upward. During the sickeningly painful operation he never moved a muscle of his face. When he drew out the dirk he leaned forward and stretched out his neck; an expression of pain for the first time crossed his face, but he uttered no sound. At that moment the *kaishaku*, who, still crouching by his side, had been keenly watching his every movement, sprang to his feet, poised his sword for a second in the air; there was a flash, a heavy, ugly thud, a crashing fall; with one blow the head had been severed from the body.

"A dead silence followed, broken only by the hideous noise of the blood gushing out of the inert heap before us, which but a moment before had been a brave and chivalrous man. It was horrible.

"The *kaishaku* made a low bow, wiped his sword, and retired from the raised floor; and the stained dirk was solemnly borne away, a bloody proof of the execution.

"The two representatives of the Mikado then left their places, and, crossing over to where the foreign witnesses sat, called us to witness that the sentence of death upon Taki Zenzaburo had been faithfully carried out. The ceremony being at an end, we left the temple."

Mr. Mitford tells some stories of extraordinary heroism displayed in the hara-kiri which had been related to him. The case of a young fellow only twenty years old deserves mention as a marvellous instance of determination. Not content with giving himself the one necessary cut, he slashed himself thrice horizontally and twice vertically. Then he stabbed himself in the throat until the dirk protruded on the other side, with its sharp edge to the front; setting his teeth in one supreme effort, he drove the knife forward with both hands through his throat, and fell dead.

When the Tycoon, beaten on every side, had fled ignominiously to Yeddo, a member of his second council went to him and said, "Sir, the only way for you now to retrieve the honor of the family of Tokugawa is to disembowel yourself; and to prove to you that I am sincere and disinterested in what I say, I am here ready to disembowel myself with you." The Tycoon flew into a great rage, saying that he would listen to no such nonsense, and left the room. His faithful retainer, to prove his honesty, retired to another part of the castle and solemnly performed the hara-kiri.

One of the great scenes in the play of " Chiushingura," the most popular of Japanese dramas, is that which represents the hara-kiri of Yenya Hanguwan, chief of the Forty-Seven Ronins, after the defeat of his followers.

Harvest Customs. From early times the ingathering of the harvest has afforded occasion for revelry and thanksgiving. When the Jews inhabited Palestine the festival of Pentecost embraced a thanksgiving for a bountiful harvest ; but, as the wheat is not gathered in Northern Europe or America at the time of Pentecost, flowers take the place of the first-fruits in the synagogues. The Romans had their Cerealia, or feasts in honor of Ceres. The Druids celebrated their harvest festival on November 1, the Japanese and Chinese each celebrate one at the close of their year. The American Thanksgiving is an acknowledgment of the blessings of the year in general and the bounties of the harvest in particular. In pre-Reformation times in England Lammas-Day was marked by the presentation of a loaf made of new wheat in the churches by every member of the congregation. Afterwards the feast of Ingathering or Harvest-Home, known in Scotland as the Kern, was a peculiarly secular method of celebrating the close of the harvest. This still has its local survivals, although they are fast passing away before the modern innovation of a general harvest festival for the whole parish, to which all the farmers are expected to contribute, and which their laborers may freely attend. This festival is commenced with a special service in the village church, beautifully decorated for the occasion with fruit and flowers, followed by a dinner in a tent or in some building sufficiently large, and continued with rural sports, and sometimes includes a tea-drinking for the women.

Nevertheless, as Canon Atkinson says, we cannot even yet use the past tense in speaking of the old harvest-home. " In the northern part of Northumberland," writes Henderson in his " Folk-Lore of North England" (1879), " the festival takes place at the close of the reaping, not the ingathering. When the sickle is laid down and the last sheaf of corn set on end, it is said that they have ' got the kern.' The reapers announce the fact by loud shouting, and an image crowned with wheat-ears and dressed in a white frock and colored ribbons is hoisted on a pole by the tallest and strongest men of the party. All circle round this ' kern-baby' or harvest-queen and proceed to the barn, where they set the image on high, and proceed to do justice to the harvest-supper." In some places "this nodding sheaf, the symbol of the god," is quite small, fashioned with much care and neatness, and plaited with wonderful skill; in others it is large and cumbersome, taking a strong man's strength to bear it.

In Scotland it is called "the maiden," and is dressed like a doll. It is preserved in the farm-house above the chimney-piece. The youngest girl in the harvest-field is supposed to have the privilege of cutting "the maiden." Its head is formed of ears of oats ; a broad blue ribbon is tied in a bow round the neck, and a skirt of paper completes the costume of "the maiden." In the northeast of Scotland the last sheaf is known as the " clyack," or "cailleach" (old woman), and is dressed up and made to look as much like an old woman as possible. It has a white cap, a dress, a little shawl over the shoulders, fastened with a sprig of heather, an apron turned up to form a pocket, which is stuffed with bread and cheese, and a sickle is stuck in the string of the apron at the back. At the harvest feast the cailleach is placed at the head of the table, the company drink to her, and in the evening the lads dance with her.

The manner of escorting the last load to the barn varied in different places. In many parts of England it was borne in a wagon known as the hock-cart. A pipe and tabor went merrily sounding in front, and the reapers, male and female, tripped around in a hand-in-hand ring, shouting and singing. Herrick's description shows how ancient is this custom :

> Come forth, my Lord, to see the cart
> Drest up with all the country art.
> The horses, mares and frisking fillies
> Clad all in linen white as lilies.
> The harvest swains and wenches bound
> For joy, to see the hock-cart crown'd.

> About the cart heare how the rout
> Of rural younglings raise the shout;
> Pressing before, some coming after,
> Those with a shout, and these with laughter.
> Some blesse the cart; some kisse the sheaves;
> Some prank them up with oaken leaves:
> Some crosse the fill-horse; some with great
> Devotion stroak the home-borne wheat;
> While other rusticks, lesse attent
> To prayers than to merryment,
> Run after with their breeches rent.

In some provinces it was a favorite practical joke to lay an ambuscade along the road, and from the vantage-point of some tree or hill to drench the hock-party with water.

An old song with many variants still survives at the bearing home of the last load. Its usual form runs as follows:

> Harvest home! harvest home!
> We've ploughed, we've sowed,
> We've reaped, we've mowed,
> We've brought home every load.
> Hip, hip, hip, harvest-home!

Here is a glimpse of an East Anglian custom:

"The sun is setting behind the old windmill as we cross the field of stubble; from a group of harvesters comes a woman who, with a low courtesy, asks us for 'largess.' As we pass along we hear merry shouts and cheering, and presently round the corner of the road comes a fine team of horses, mounted by two lads dressed in the garb of women, while the wagon is filled with the last load of corn, and merry youths and maidens ride above it. The wagon stops, and the riders give us three cheers, and then on they go to the village green amidst much laughter and bright songs."

The custom is known locally as "Hallering Largess," and has been described as a certain rhythmic chant, rendered with action and gesture, and followed by a certain number of shouts, in return for gifts. When they have received the offering they shout thrice the words "Halloo, largess," which may be a corruption of *à la largesse.* The ritual appears to be as follows. The laborers gather in front of the house, and form a ring by joining hands. They bow their heads very low towards the centre of the circle and give utterance to a low deep mutter, saying, "Hoo-Hoo-Hoo;" then they jerk their heads backward and utter a shrill shriek of "Ah! Ah!" repeated several times. The Lord of the Largess, the leader of the band, then cries, "Holla, largess," which is echoed by the company, and thus the performance ends, a very interesting survival of old usages.

In Herefordshire a final handful of grain was left uncut. But it was tied up and erected under the name of a *mare*, and the reapers then, one after another, threw their sickles at it, to cut it down. The successful individual called out, " I have her!" " What have you?" cried the rest. " A mare, a mare, a mare!" he replied. " What will you do with her?" was then asked. " We'll send her to John Snooks," or whatever other name, referring to some neighboring farmer who had not yet got all his grain cut down.

This piece of rustic pleasantry was called " Crying the Mare." It is very curious to learn that there used to be a similar practice in so remote a district as the Isle of Skye. A farmer having got his harvest completed, the last cut handful was sent, under the name of Goabbir Bhacagh (" the Cripple Goat"), to the next farmer who was still at work upon his crops, it being of course necessary for the bearer to take some care that, on delivery, he should be able instantly to take to his heels and escape the punishment otherwise sure to befall him.

" In the southeastern part of Shropshire," says the Rev. C. H. Hartshorne in his " Salopia Antiqua," p. 498, " the ceremony is performed with a slight variation. The last few stalks of the wheat are left standing; all the reapers throw their sickles, and he who cuts it off cries, ' I have her, I have her, I have her!' on which the rustic mirth begins; and it is practised in a manner very similar in Devonshire. The latest farmer in the neighborhood, whose reapers therefore cannot send her to any other person, is said to keep her all the winter. This rural ceremony, which is fast wearing away, evidently refers to the time when, our country lying all open in common fields, and the corn consequently exposed to the depredations of the wild mares, the season at which it was secured from their ravages was a time of rejoicing, and of exulting over a tardier neighbor."

Mr. Bray describes the same custom as practised in Devonshire, and the chief peculiarity in that instance is that the last handful of the standing grain is called the Nack. On this being cut, the reapers assemble round it, calling at the top of their voices, " Arnack, arnack, arnack! we have'n, we have'n, we have'n," and the firkin is then handed round; after which the party goes home dancing and shouting.

Clarke in his Travels (1812) gives this account of a harvest-home festival in Cambridge :

" At the Hawkie, as it is called, or Harvest-Home, I have seen a clown dressed in woman's clothes, having his face painted, his head decorated with ears of corn, and bearing about with him other emblems of Ceres, carried in a wagon, with great pomp and loud shouts, through the streets, the horses being covered with white sheets; and, when I inquired the meaning of the ceremony, was answered by the people that 'they were drawing the Harvest Queen.'" (Vol. ii. p. 229.)

At harvest suppers in Dumfriesshire and Lincolnshire "the old sow," or "Paiky," used to make her appearance. This curious animal was nothing more nor less than two men dressed up in sacks to personate the visiting quadruped. The head was filled with cuttings from a furze-bush. The animal pranced around before the supper, pricking every one it approached. "I used to be very much afraid of it when I was a child," says a correspondent of *Notes and Queries*, Eighth Series, ix. 128. "That was a part of the harvest supper I never could like."

In some parts of Scotland a similar figure seems to have been called "Auld Glenae," as witness the lines in a poem on "Harvest-Home" published in *Blackwood's Magazine* for June, 1821:

> But tumbling, rolling, sprawling on his way,
> Comes in the straw-clad masker, "Auld Glenae;"
> A lengthen'd pole adorns his better paw,
> Well swathed with ribbons, and well wrapp'd with straw.
> Like shaggy bear he heaves his limbs along,
> And drives, and leaps, and bustles through the throng;
> Tries every art the younger folks to "scar,"
> And only joins the reel, the sport to mar;
> Trips up the dancer in his figure pace,
> And thrusts his stubble presence in each face;
> With Lizy foots the droll duett away,
> And capers to the tune of "Auld Glenae,"
> Then winds his bunchy arms her waist about,
> And bears aloft the farmer's daughter out;
> "And wha can this be now?" each damsel cries;
> "What can he want wi' Lizy?" each replies.
> "Aweel," rejoins a third, "she's nae great prize!"

A rural celebration akin to the English, and known as the Fête of the Big Sheaf, survived until recently in Canada and closed the harvest season among the *habitans* in the neighborhood of Bay St. Paul. The last sheaf, made large, was put on the last cart-load of grain as an emblem of abundance; the lads and lasses, decorated with ears of grain, walked on each side of the load, and sang some of their national songs on the way to the house.

"According to the usual ceremony," says the author of an article on "The Canadian Habitant" in *Harper's Monthly*, vol. lxvii. p. 389, "the master of the house sits in a large arm-chair at the head of the room, and awaits with a joyful and contented air the arrival of his people. These soon come trooping in, led by the eldest son, who carries in one hand a fine sheaf of wheat all decorated with ribbons, and in the other hand a decanter and a glass. He advances to the master of the house, gives him the sheaf, wishes him as good a harvest every year of his life, and pours him out a glass of brandy. The old gentleman thanks him, and drinks off the glass. Then the son goes round the room and serves the company; after which they pass to the next room for supper, composed of mutton, milk, and pancakes with maple sugar. After supper the decanter and glass go their rounds again, and then the young man who presented the sheaf asks his father to sing a song. Songs, dances, and other amusements close the festival.

" As this pretty ceremony fell into disuse some years ago, the priest of one of the parishes on the south shore of the St. Lawrence took it under his own patronage, and made it a Church festival by carrying the Big Sheaf into the choir of the church and saying mass over it. But even this duller rite is now seldom witnessed: the farmers instead pay the priest to say a mass as thanks for the harvest."

Hassan and Hussein. Two Imams or saints of Persia, the sons of Fatima, the daughter of Mohammed, and of Ali, his bosom friend and successor. Their tragic deaths are commemorated, on the tenth day of the Mussulman month of Mouharem, in Persia and in all cities where a Persian colony exists, by a religious ceremony the mystic rites and sanguinary ferocity of which are almost without a parallel.

When the office of Caliph became vacant through the assassination of Ali in 660, Hassan as the nearest heir was murdered by Yezzid, son of Muhavijeh, who usurped the throne. Hussein fled to Medina, and twenty years later led a revolt of the Kyuffeh tribes. At the hour of need, however, his allies forsook him, and Hussein, with only forty foot and thirty horse, was forced to meet Yezzid at the head of four thousand men. After a terrific contest the little band was cut to pieces, Hussein falling last of all, pierced with thirty-two wounds.

His head was severed from his body and conveyed to Yezzid, by whom it was received with savage exultation. "It was observed that a light streamed upward from the lifeless head and extended towards the heavens, white doves hovering round." The body was buried at Kerbela, which city has ever since been regarded with the utmost veneration and reverence by all Persians and Shiahs, large numbers of whom annually visit the mausoleum of the martyred saint. Kerbela has been and still is the favorite burial-ground of the Persians, their remains being transported thither from all parts of the world.

A sort of Passion Play is the leading feature of the festival of Hassan and Hussein. At Constantinople, where there is a large Persian colony, this is performed at night in a large square surrounded by houses and shops, planted with trees and crowded with people. Edwin C. De Leon, who was American consul to Constantinople for many years, thus describes the ceremony in *The Epoch*, New York:

" Shortly after we were seated we heard wild shouts and clamors outside, and presently saw a band of wild-looking men bearing aloft flaming *maschallahs*. They entered in marching time, and announced the approach of a numerous procession of ' the Faithful.' In they poured, preceded by the Persian priests, lugubriously chanting with nasal melody a kind of funeral song, reciting the tragic death of Hassan and Hussein, with maledictions on their assassin, Yezzid, doomed to an immortality of infamy. Then suddenly appeared at the termination of the chant a ghostly-looking crew of men, clad in long white robes, with uncovered heads and naked swords in their hands. These men numbered many hundreds, and were termed Nazirs,—a Persian name signifying those consecrated to God, being dedicated by their parents from infancy to observe the ceremonial and the fasts commemorating the deaths of Hassan and Hussein. They flourished their naked swords, clashed them wildly together, and occasionally turned the points on themselves or their companions, gashing heads, faces, and breasts until the blood flowed and discolored their white robes. They then dragged each other by the hand, passed round and round, hoarsely reciting mourning hymns, with wild invocations of the names of the martyrs, Hussein and Hassan. These men looked really like demons under the red glare of the torches borne by their companions, who to the number of several thousands passed in after the singers, often wiping the bloody brows of the fanatics.

" The horror of this fearful scene was magnified by the dull, thumping sound made by the self-flagellations of another band of fanatics who accompanied the swordsmen. These men belabored their broad backs with scourges made of iron chains, the blows resounding with a sickening sound. The secretaries told us that the backs of these men, from the annual repetition of this scourging, and from their daily habit of carrying heavy burdens, as hamals or porters, were actually more like iron than flesh.

" After the Nazirs came a typical procession of the flight of the martyrs' families, with the tents, the banners and household goods, and even the children perched upon horses which formed part of the show. Wild wailings of ' Oh, Hassan! Oh, Hussein !' accompanied these, as though the incidents commemorated had occurred not six hundred years but six hours ago.

" One of the most curious and at the same time one of the

most repulsive features of the spectacle was the appearance in the procession, with the fanatical Nazirs, of a large school of boys, of from ten to fourteen years of age, some of whom gashed themselves with knives and were thus prepared for fanaticism. Then the fanatical assemblage withdrew through the arch of the gate, but distant shouts and wild wailing from without warned us that the performance was not yet quite at an end.

"For more than two hours this wild work went on, until the final round of the exhausted Nazirs was made, when they stopped just in front of the Ambassador's loge and the priests pronounced a prayer, first for the Shah of Persia, next for the Sultan, and lastly for the Ambassador. After this the procession drifted out to the outer gate, and passed away under the still stars."

See also "Letters from Turkey," by Mrs. Max Müller (1897), most of which had previously appeared in *Longmans' Magazine,* "The Tenth of Mouharem," by Fuad Bey, in *London Society,* and Matthew Arnold's essay "A Persian Passion Play."

Hatred, Our Lady of. (Fr. *Notre-Dame de la Haine.*) The name popularly given to a church in Tréguier, Brittany. Souvestre in his "Derniers Bretons," vol. i. p. 92, tells us that hither come at even-tide young people tired of the surveillance of their elders, old men envious of the prosperity of their neighbors, wives chafing under the despotism of their husbands, each praying for the death of the object of their hate. Three Aves, devoutly repeated, will bring about this death within the twelve-month. Similarly Laisnel de la Salle tells us ("Croyances et Légendes du Centre de la France," 1875, i. 332) that there exists in the neighborhood of Argent, in the department of Cher, a spring consecrated to St. Mauvais ("St. Wicked"), near to which wretches come and pray who wish the death of an enemy, of a rival in love, of a relation standing between them and an inheritance, etc. The Basques recommend their enemies to St. Séquaire in order to have them dried up. These are all undoubtedly survivals under other forms of pagan superstitions. They recall the various Hindoo deities who are always ready to assist their devotees each time they have an evil passion to gratify.

Heart-Burial. In popular parlance, in poetry, and even in philosophy, the human heart has ever been deemed the seat of affection, of passion, of courage, and of conscience,—even of life itself. Small wonder, therefore, that it has been considered as a votive gift peculiarly sacred. And this feeling has led to many instances of the burial of the heart apart from the place where the ashes of the body might repose.

The very name of Richard Cœur de Lion, or Lion-Heart,

embodies this traditionary feeling. It is only meet, therefore, that his heart should have been looked upon as being the most important portion of his physical self. Our sense of appropriateness is gratified by the historical anecdote that when he fell beneath Gourdon's arrow at the siege of Chalus the gallant heart which, in its greatness and mercy, inspired him to forgive and even to reward the luckless archer was, after his death, preserved in a casket in the treasury of that splendid cathedral which William the Conqueror built at Rouen.

History and song have alike made us familiar with the last wish of Robert Bruce, the heroic King of Scotland, when, after two years of peace and contemplation, he died in the north of Cardross. He desired that in part fulfilment of a vow he had made to march to Jerusalem, a purpose which the incessant war with England baffled, his heart should be laid in the church of the Holy Sepulchre, and on his death-bed he besought his old friend and faithful brother soldier, the good Sir James Douglas, to undertake that which was then a most arduous journey, and be the bearer of the relic.

It is a matter of history how Douglas departed on this errand with a train of knights, and, choosing to land on the Spanish coast, heard that Alfonso of Leon and Castile was at war with Osman, the Moorish King of Granada. In the true spirit of the age, he could not resist the temptation of striking a blow for the Christian faith, and so joined the Spaniards. He led their van upon the plain of Theba, near the Andalusian frontier. In a silver casket at his neck he bore the heart of Bruce, which rashly and repeatedly he cast before him amid the Moors, crying,—

"Now pass on as ye were wont, and Douglas, as of old, will follow thee or die."

And there he fell, together with Sir William Sinclair of Roslyn, Sir Robert and Sir Walter Logan of Restalrig, and others. Bruce's heart, instead of being taken to Jerusalem, was brought home by Sir Simon of Lee, and deposited in Melrose Abbey.

On October 5, 1318, was killed near Dundalk, Ireland, Edward, brother to King Robert Bruce. In 1613 another Lord Edward Bruce was killed in a duel and his body buried at Bergen, in Holland, where he died. A family tradition averred that his heart had been brought back to Scotland and interred in a certain churchyard. In 1806 a search for the relic was undertaken. Two flat stones curiously fastened together with iron were disinterred, and out of curiosity separated. In a cavity between them was found a heart-shaped silver case with the engraved arms of Lord Edward. Opening this, a heart was found within, embalmed in a brownish liquid.

Of all the treasured hearts of the heroic or illustrious dead, none perhaps ever underwent so many marvellous adventures as that of James, Marquis of Montrose, who was executed by the Scottish Puritans in 1650. His body was interred like that of a common criminal by the side of a road leading to Edinburgh. His niece, the Lady Napier, had it disinterred long enough to take therefrom the heart, which she enclosed in a steel box and sent to the second Duke of Montrose, who was then an exile. But it was lost on the way, and not till years afterwards was it discovered in the collection of a Flemish virtuoso. Restored to the Napiers, it was taken to India by a member of the family, was stolen by a Madrassa chief, who deemed it a powerful amulet and wore it suspended from a string around his neck, was once more regained by its owner, and was finally and irretrievably lost by her in France during the troublous times of the Revolution.

The last ceremonial burial of a heart in England was that of Paul Whitehead, in 1775. In his youth he had been secretary to the infamous Monks of Medmenham Club. It is interesting to know that Whitehead's old age was respectable, and that he was esteemed as a benevolent and exemplary old gentleman. His heart was buried with military honors on Lord Despencer's place in a mausoleum built out of funds left for the purpose by that George Bubb Dodington, Lord Melcombe, whose "Memoirs" afford one of the most wonderful of all pictures of English society.

The heart was not only a symbol of honor but also of dishonor in England. Formerly the executioner of a traitor was required to remove the body from the gallows before life was extinct and pluck out the heart, exhibiting it to the people with the words " Here is the heart of a traitor." Anthony à Wood reports that the severed head of Sir Kenelm Digby opened its ghastly lips and answered, "Thou liest!" Lord Bacon reports that two or three persons were reported to have spoken two or three words under similar circumstances.

Heart-burial was as frequent on the Continent as in England. The body of Louis IX. after his death at Carthage in 1270 is related to have been boiled in wine and water in order to preserve it for transportation, and it was then shipped by Charles of Anjou (I.) to Sicily. Here the flesh and viscera were deposited in the Benedictine abbey of Monreale, near Palermo. The heart and the bones remained, by desire of the soldiers, in the camp. Later, his son Philip (le Hardi) having carried them, and those of his brother Tristan, into Italy, they were brought to Paris in 1271. On March 21 of that year the bones, reduced to ashes, were deposited temporarily in Notre-Dame, whence they were presently borne in state to the Benedictine abbey of St. Denis, and at each spot by the way where the bearers paused, seven in number, Philip subsequently caused a cross to be raised.

Charles of Anjou dying at Foggia in 1285, his heart was sent to Angers, while his body was entombed in San Gennaro, at Naples. His viscera remained in the Duomo at Foggia.

Philip III. (le Hardi) died of pestilence, at Perpignan, October 5, 1285. His flesh was buried at Narbonne. His bones were transferred to St. Denis. His heart was given by Philip IV. (le Bel) to the Dominicans of Paris.

In Austria since the thirteenth century every dead Hapsburg has had his or her heart removed and buried apart from the body. In the Capuchin chapel on the Neumarkt, Vienna, placed in a vault beneath the ground, there are one hundred and thirteen coffins, containing all that remains of the royal Hapsburgs who have ruled over the destinies of Austria, and there are one hundred and fifty-two vases of crystal mounted in gold, each containing the heart of one of these rulers and of others whose bodies rest elsewhere.

When the body of the Emperor Napoleon was prepared for burial at St. Helena in May, 1821, the heart was removed by a medical officer, who kept it all night in his own room and under his own eye in a wineglass. The noise of the crystal breaking aroused him, not from sleep, but rather from a waking doze, and he started forward to see the heart in the clutches of a huge brown rat, which was dragging it across the floor to a hole. One story runs that he rescued it, but there is a gruesome tradition that it had been so gnawed and bitten as to be unrecognizable, and that the doctor was fain to substitute the heart of a sheep, which he soldered up in a silver urn filled with spirits and placed in the coffin.

It is a strange thought that the heart of a sheep, proverbially one of the most timid of animals, should be handed down to posterity as that of one of the most ruthless and most indomitable human beings who ever lived!

In 1894 the heart of Louis XVII., the unfortunate Dauphin who died a victim of the cruelty of Simon the Cobbler, was handed over with much ceremony to Don Carlos, the Pretender to the French throne. For years the heart was in possession of M. Edouard Dumont, who inherited it from his mother, who in her turn received it from M. Gabriel Pelletin, the son of the doctor who performed the autopsy on the body of the royal lad. The different possessors of the relic, which had an eventful history, had made various attempts to hand it over to the Bourbon family, but circumstances had always frustrated their efforts until 1894, when the relic was at last intrusted to Don Carlos. The heart, enclosed in a glass case ornamented with fleurs-de-lis, was handed by M. Dumont to the Comte de Mialle, who received it on bended knee and swore that he would send it to the "King" Don Carlos. This vow he fulfilled through the agency of M. Pascal and the Comte de Marichalar, who conveyed it direct to Don Carlos at Venice. The latter placed it in the chapel of the palace of Frohsdorf.

In 1895 the heart of the patriot Kosciusko was formally presented to the Polish Museum in Rapperschwyll, on Lake Zurich, in Switzerland. This museum is unique, and it is in many ways one of the most interesting of all the depositories of patriotic relics. Founded by Count Stanislas Plater, an exile from the country which he loved, it stands to-day as an eloquent protest against an historical iniquity.

The hero's body lies buried at Cracow; his heart was handed over to the friend of his declining years, M. de Zeltner, and later passed, a revered heirloom, into the noble house of Morosini, on the occasion of the marriage of Kosciusko's goddaughter, Mlle. de Zeltner, to Count Morosini. It was then placed for safe-keeping in the chapel in Vezio, near Lugano. The heirs of Count Morosini recognized that the relic could find no fitter resting-place than the Rapperschwyll Museum.

A great ceremony greeted the occasion. Delegates from the Poles of Galicia, including the President and municipal authorities of Cracow, also Polish delegates from Posen, Prussia, and from the United States, were present. Eulogies of the patriot were delivered by Polish orators, and the whole affair went off in a blaze of glory.

Helena, St. The first wife of Constantius, one of the colleagues of the Emperor Maximin, and the mother of Constantine the Great. Her festival is celebrated on the reputed date of her death, August 18 (328). Little is known with any historical certainty of the details of her life. Traditions vary. One account makes her the daughter of a British prince named Coel (the mythical original of the King Cole of the nursery ballad). The local mythology of Treves represents her as of a patrician family in that city, and adds that after her marriage she presented to the church her magnificent house, which was turned into the present cathedral. Indeed, she is associated with almost everything else that is striking or splendid in the city of Treves. The imperial palace was built by her; the villa at Euren was her country-seat, and children playing by the fountain of the Roman villa have seen her seated beneath the waters, wearing a golden crown. The monument of the Secundini at Igel was erected to commemorate her marriage. In the city library is still preserved the *Codex Aureus,* a superbly bound and illuminated manuscript of the Gospels, which was presented to the abbey of St. Maximin by Ada, the sister of Charlemagne, but in the legend this is the work of Helena's pious and skilful fingers. She it was who presented to the cathedral the holy coat without seam, which has of late years played so prominent a part in Prussian politics.

There is a better founded story that she was the daughter of an innkeeper, either in Gaul or in Bithynia. In any case she was probably of humble parentage, and not at first admitted to the status of a full wife of the noble young soldier Constantius, though there is no doubt from the fact of her subsequent divorce, when her husband was raised to the purple in 292 and married to Maximin's step-daughter Theodora, that she did eventually become so, perhaps upon the birth of her only son, the future Emperor, in 274. Nothing further is known of her till her son's succession in 306 to the Empire, when it is probable that she was invested with all the dignity befitting the Emperor's mother. At all events, there is the direct evidence of coins still extant to support the statement of Eusebius that she received the title of Augusta from Constantine, together with other honors. The same historian says that she was converted to Christianity by her son. In about the year 326, when nearly eighty years of age, she undertook her famous pilgrimage to Palestine and Jerusalem, which did so much to revive men's interest in and reverence for these sacred localities and their remains and associations. (See CROSS, DISCOVERY OF THE; LORETTO, HOLY HOUSE OF; SEPULCHRE OF CHRIST.) Her death probably took place somewhere on the return journey. Her body was brought with great pomp to Constantinople, and was buried there with splendor in the church of the Holy Apostles, lately erected in his new capital by Constantine. This is one legend. By some it is supposed that she died near Rome and was buried there. Among her relics that have survived are a head at Treves, some bones in the Vatican, and others at Lisbon, and at Altrelle, near Rheims.

Her memory was perpetuated in the names of two cities, Helenopolis and Helenopontus. Eventually, in 1164, she received the honor of canonization by Pope Alexander III., in consideration of the many miracles attributed to her.

In Yorkshire, England, St. Helen's Day is celebrated on **May** 2, possibly because that is the eve of the Invention of the Cross. It is alternatively known as Rowan-Tree Day, because of the custom for some member of every household to go out in search of a rowan-tree, from which he gathers a supply of branches. Returning by a different route from that by which he left home, he sticks the twigs over every door of the house, where they are scrupulously left until they fall out of themselves. " A piece is also always borne about by many in their pockets or purses, as a prophylactic against witching. Not so very long since, either, the farmers used to have whip-stocks of rowan-tree wood,—rowan-tree gads they were called,—and it was held that, thus supplied, they were safe against having their draught fixed or their horses made restive by a witch. If ever a draught came to a stand-still,—there being in such cases no rowan-tree gad in the driver's hands, of course,—then the nearest witchwood-tree was resorted to, and a stick cut to flog the horses on with, to the discomfiture of the malevolent witch who had caused the stoppage." (ATKINSON: *Cleveland Glossary*, p. 417.)

Henry of Bavaria, St. (the Emperor Henry II. of Germany, 972–1024), patron of Bavaria. His festival is July 15, the day after the anniversary of his death.

A splendid benefactor of the Papacy, at the time when it had reached one of its greatest crises through the rival claims of Popes and Antipopes, he confirmed the extensive donations of the sovereignty of Rome and the exarchate of Ravenna made to it by his predecessors, Pepin, Charlemagne, and Otho I. The diploma was delivered on the occasion of Henry's triumphal visit to Rome in 1014, when he was crowned Emperor by Pope Benedict VIII. He had declared for Benedict in opposition to the Antipope, Gregory VI. For the protection of Christendom, and especially of the Holy See, he returned to Italy in 1022 and led an army against the combined power of the Saracens and Greeks, whom he drove out of the country. His health, always feeble, now rapidly declined, and he died July 14, 1024.

He had reigned twenty-two years from his election and ten years and five months from his coronation at Rome. He was buried with great pomp in the cathedral at Bamberg, in Bavaria, which he had himself built and dedicated to St. Peter. At Bamberg likewise he had founded a rich episcopal see, which was placed under the immediate jurisdiction of the Pope, and to which he left by will all his treasures and his magnificent allodial possessions. So great a number of miracles were reported at his shrine that he was canonized by Eugenius III. in 1152.

His wife, St. Cunegunde, who was canonized later, is also one of the patrons of Bavaria. The imperial couple lived in perpetual chastity, to which they had bound themselves by a vow. It happened that the Empress was falsely accused of incontinency, but she cleared herself by an oath and by the ordeal of walking barefoot over twelve red-hot ploughshares without injury. Her husband severely condemned himself for having lent an ear to her accusers, and in his last illness recommended her to her relations, declaring that he left her an untouched virgin.

In 1499–1513 was erected the highly ornate sarcophagus of SS. Henry and Cunegunde in the nave of the Bamberg Cathedral, Tilman Riemenschneider being the sculptor. Effigies of the royal couple repose on the top, and scenes from their lives are sculptured in relief on the sides of the monument. Their skulls are preserved in the treasury of the cathedral.

Herring, Procession of the. (Fr. *La Procession du Hareng.*) A curious ceremony which in the sixteenth century took place in the church of St. Remi, at Rheims. On the Wednesday of Holy Week, after the tenebræ had been chanted, all the clergy of the cathedral went to perform the stations of the cross at St. Remi. Preceded by the crucifix, every one of the reverend canons, who were arranged in double file as in ordinary processions, trailed after him a herring attached to a string. The effort of each was to step upon the herring belonging to his neighbor in front, and to save his own from the foot of his neighbor in the rear.

Hilary, St., patron saint of Parma. His festival is celebrated January 14, though his death is usually ascribed to January 13 (368), and in some very ancient martyrologies to November 1. Butler refers the festival to "some translation of his relics." St. Hilary was born in Poitiers, in Gaul. His parents were pagans, but he was converted to Christianity. He was married before his conversion, and had a daughter, but from the time of his ordination he lived in continence. He was chosen Bishop of Poitiers about the year 353. He opposed the Arians with all his power, and in 356 he was banished on this account by the Emperor Constantius. Going to Phrygia, and afterwards to Italy, he kept up a constant warfare against the Arians. He returned to Gaul and died at Poitiers. A brilliant celestial light is said to have filled his chamber at the time of his death. Many miracles are said to have been wrought at his tomb. His remains were translated in the ninth century from Poitiers to the abbey of St. Denis, near Paris. The story that his relics were burned at Poitiers by the Huguenots in 1567 is held by Butler to refer only to some portion of the dust remaining in his tomb. The cathedral of Parma contains some of his relics.

In English jurisprudence the name of this saint is commemorated in Hilary term, one of the four terms of the Courts of Law, which begins on January 11 and ends on the Wednesday before Easter. On the first day of the term it is a very old custom for the judges to breakfast with the Lord Chancellor at Lincoln's Inn and drive down with him in their respective carriages to Westminster Hall. The proceedings on arriving at the hall, however, have been greatly curtailed. Formerly the sergeants used to assemble, in their robes, in front of the Court of Common Pleas, and were formally saluted by each of the judges in order with " How d'ye do, brother?—I wish you a good term ;" but since the exclusive right of the sergeants to practise in the Common Pleas has been abolished this custom has been discontinued. At present the judges only walk up Westminster Hall in procession, and make formal bows to the assembled barristers on taking their seats upon the bench.

At Oxford College Hilary term commences on January 14 and ends on the Saturday before Palm Sunday.

Hilda's Tower. The genius of Hawthorne has given a new name to the famous mediæval tower in Rome which is locally called La Torre della Scimia ("The Ape's Tower"). Legend relates that a baby, carried away by an ape, and borne to the top of the battlements, was restored in safety to its parents, in consequence of a vow which they made that they would cause a lamp to burn nightly, forever, before an image of the Virgin, upon the summit. This building is known as Hilda's Tower, from the connection it has in Hawthorne's " Marble Faun," under the chapter entitled "The Virgin's Shrine."

Hiring Fair, known also as **Statute Fair.** A peculiar institution which still lingers in Wales and also to a less degree in Yorkshire, Derbyshire, and Lincolnshire, in England. From time immemorial the custom has been to hold these fairs in every important centre of a farming district, their sole purpose being to bring servants and masters together. To them troop men and maidens in vast numbers, on fun and profit both intent. To them also troop the farmers, in search of the human toilers on their farms for the coming year. Sometimes, and originally always, these hiring-fairs were held on Martinmas Day, known as the servants' saint's day. At present the hiring fair is not confined to that day, but is held on different days in different towns, usually in either October or November.

Men and maids stood in rows, the males together and the females together, while masters and mistresses walked down the lines and selected those whom they considered suitable. The men in Cumberland who desired to be hired stood with straws in their mouths, as indicated in the old couplet,—

> Suin at Carel [Carlisle] I stuid wid a strae i' my mooth,
> And they tuik me, nae doubt, for a promisin' youth.

In Lincolnshire the bargain is closed by the giving and taking of the fessen- or fasten-penny. This is usually a shilling. It is the accepted sign that the contract between the employer and employed is closed for a twelve-month. The farm-servant who has once accepted the fessen-penny and entered upon his situation may not, in fact, discharge himself under the twelve-month.

The night of the fair is given up to riotous amusement, in which drunkenness plays a prominent part.

Hock or **Hoke Day.** A former holiday in England, which still has some faint local survivals, and which was usually cele brated on the Tuesday following the second Sunday after Easter. In many places, however, Monday as well as Tuesday was devoted to the characteristic pastime of Hocktide, which was known as Binding; hence Binding Monday and Binding Tuesday were alternative titles. On Monday the women bound the men, and *vice versa* on Tuesday. Binding consisted in stretching a rope across the highways and catching in the toils wayfarers of the appointed sex, who were not released until they had given some small sum to be laid out in pious uses. Numerous ancient parish registers contain records of money thus gathered. So late as 1559 the following entry occurs in St. Mary's parish register:

> Hoctyde money, the mens gatheryng, iiijs.
> The womens, xijs.

One of the uses of the money collected at Hocktide was the repairing of the parish church. Various etymologies have been suggested for the word *hock* or *hoke*, but none is entirely satisfactory.

The custom, which became obsolete in the beginning of the eighteenth century, can be traced under this name as far back as the thirteenth century, but it probably dates from an earlier period, and may even be a survival from Anglo-Saxon times, when the offerings subsequently devoted to church uses may have been meant for some one of the pagan gods. There is a striking analogy between this custom and that of lifting (*q. v.*) on Easter Monday. At Coventry there was a play or pageant attached to the ceremony known as the Old Coventry Play of Hock Tuesday. This was revived for the benefit of Queen Elizabeth as part of the festivities attending her visit to Kenilworth in July, 1575. It represented a series of combats between the Danes and the Saxons, in which the former were twice triumphant, but were finally overcome by the appearance of the Saxon women, who took many of them captive and led them in triumph past the royal throne. The regular performance had been suppressed soon after the Reformation, on account of the riot and disorder which it frequently occasioned. It has been surmised from the evidence of the play that Hocktide was originally instituted to commemorate the massacre of the Danes on St. Brice's Day, A.D. 1002 (but St. Brice's Day, unfortunately for this conjecture, is November 13), or the rejoicings which followed the death of Hardicanute, the expulsion of•the Danish invaders, and the accession of Edward the Confessor. It is probable, however, that these explanations were invented in Christian times after the pagan origin of the feast had been forgotten.

Some singular Hocktide customs survive in Hungerford, Berkshire. They are connected with the charter whereby the commons hold the rights of fishing, shooting, and pasturage of cattle on the lands bequeathed to the town by John o' Gaunt, Duke of Lancaster, in 1399. A "watercress supper" at the hotel of "John o' Gaunt" inaugurates the festivities on Hock Monday. Besides the eponymic herb, black broth, macaroni, Welsh rabbit, and salad are served, accompanied by bowls of punch. Early on the morrow, which is known as Tuth Day, the town crier blows from the balcony of the town hall an ancient horn, the gift of John o' Gaunt. The Hocktide Court assembles, and the commoners are summoned to appear and "save their commons" for the ensuing year. Then the tuth or tutti men proceed to the high constable's residence, to receive the emblems of their office. These are long poles, wreathed around with tutties or posies of flowers and gaudy ribbons. The first duty of these officials of a day (who are usually substantial tradesmen of the borough) is to visit the various schools and ask a holiday for the children, then to call at each house and demand a coin from the men and a kiss from the women, presenting every member of the household with an orange. The collection of pennies is a simple matter, and the majority of the women submit gracefully to ancient usage. But the haughtier dames are apt to retreat behind bolts and bars until the tutti men have departed. A troop of children expectant of oranges follow the tutti men through the streets, which are for several hours kept alive by joyous shouts and huzzas. At the Three Swans a luncheon is given by the high constable, during the progress of which the boys and girls scramble for pennies and oranges thrown to them from the windows. The Hocktide proceedings are brought to a close by the constable, feoffers, and other officers attending service in the parish church. (DITCHFIELD, pp. 90–92; DYER, pp. 188–192.)

Hodening. A custom which prevails in Wales, and locally in Kent, Lancashire, and other English counties, at various dates during the Christmas and New Year seasons, and seems to be a survival of the Hobby-horse once rampant at Christmas-time. A horse's skull, or sometimes a wooden imitation, is dressed up

with ribbons, and supported on a pole by a man who is concealed
under a large white cloth. By pulling a string tied to the lower
jaw he keeps up a loud snapping noise. In Wales a party of
young men grotesquely habited and ringing hand-bells accompany him on Christmas Eve in a house-to-house procession. At
every door they sing some extempore verses requesting admittance, and are in turn answered by those within, until one party
or the other is at a loss for a reply. If the processioners fail
they move away baffled, but if they win in this poetical tournament they are rewarded with beer and cakes and perhaps money.
Another feature of the fun which has its pecuniary attractions
is for the horse to pursue and bite such well-to-do wayfarer as
may happen to be met on the way, and refuse to release him save
on payment of a fine. In Wales the horse's head is called Mari
Lwyd. A contributor to the *Church Times* of January 23, 1891,
gives this description of a hodening in Kent: "When I was a
lad, about forty-five years since, it was always the custom, on
Christmas Eve, with the male farm-servants from every farm in
our parish of Hoath, and neighboring parishes of Herne and
Chislet, to go round in the evening from house to house with the
hoodining horse, which consisted of the imitation of a horse's
head made of wood, life-size, fixed on a stick about the length
of a broom-handle. The lower jaw of the head was made to
open with hinges; a hole was made through the roof of the
mouth, then another through the forehead, coming out by the
throat; through this was passed a cord attached to the lower jaw,
which, when pulled by the cord at the throat, caused it to close
and open; on the lower jaw large-headed hobnails were driven
in to form the teeth. The strongest of the lads was selected for
the horse; he stooped, and made as long a back as he could, supporting himself by the stick carrying the head; then he was
covered with a horse-cloth, and one of his companions mounted
his back. The horse had a bridle and reins. Then commenced
the kicking, rearing, jumping, etc., and the banging together of
the teeth." There was no singing by the accompanying paraders.
They simply by ringing or knocking at the houses on their way
summoned the inmates to the doors and begged a gratuity. "I
have seen some of the wooden heads carved out quite hollow in
the throat part, and two holes bored through the forehead to
form the eyes. The lad who played the horse would hold a
lighted candle in the hollow, and you can imagine how horrible
it was to any one who opened the door to see such a thing close
to his eyes." The same authority adds that the custom had been
kept up to within three or four years of the date of his writing.

In the "Penitential" of Archbishop Theodore (died 690) penances are ordained for "any who, on the Kalends of January,

clothe themselves with the skins of cattle and carry heads of animals." The practice is condemned as being *dæmoniacum.* It is noticeable that at the ancient Scandinavian sacrifices performed at the time of the winter solstice the horse was a frequent victim in the offerings to Odin for martial success, as the hog was the chosen animal in the offerings to Freya for a fruitful year. It has therefore been suggested that hodening is a corruption of Odining and is a relic of Scandinavian mythology.

There is a wide-spread superstition that were-wolves, or men who have been changed into wolves, meet together at certain places on Christmas night and there " do so rage with wonderful fierceness both against mankind and other creatures that are not fierce by nature, that the inhabitants of that country suffer more hurt from them than ever they do from the true natural wolves " Such are the words of Olaus Magnus, who further describes how these were-wolves go into cellars and drink up all the mead and beer they can find, " wherein they differ from the natural and true wolves."

When the Prince of Wales was in India he was present at a wild dance performed by a party of Lamas at Jummu. Mr. William Simpson, in his " Buddhist Praying-Wheel," p. 31, quotes an account given in the *Indian Public Opinion and Panjab Times,* January, 1876. The dancers came along "jumping and dancing in the most outrageous costumes. One man carried an incense-vessel, held in his hands with chains identically as it is carried ih a Roman Catholic church. One man had a hat in color and shape resembling the comb of a cock, but most of them had huge wide-brimmed hats surmounted by tridents and all sorts of things like vanes and weathercocks, from which long strips of colored silk hung down behind. The costumes were purely Chinese, the body of their dresses being similar to that worn by mandarins, only that they had capes, aprons, and tags and rags of all kinds hanging upon them, which flew out as the dancers went round in their uncouth gambols. After dancing in a circle for a short time, going round with the right shoulder to the centre, which is the same turn as the praying-wheel goes round, they retired, and very quickly came back again. The large broad-brimmed hats were wanting, and all the dancers had the heads of animals exactly like what we see in a pantomime; there were ox-heads, boar-heads, elephant-heads, also large grinning and laughing heads, painted in all tints. The jumping and whirling round was the same each time they changed their head-dresses. We were led to understand that symbolism was expressed in the costumes, the heads, and in all the various parts of this uncouth performance, but its meaning was not at all clear to our Western ideas."

Holiday. This is an obvious corruption of holy day,—*i.e.*, a day set apart by the Church in honor of some important event or saintly personage associated with the date. In the latter case it is the death-day and not the birthday that is usually commemorated. The Catholic Church distinguishes holidays into those of obligation and those not of obligation. In the former case the faithful must attend mass, and as far as possible should refrain from worldly pursuits. But a certain latitude is allowed in Protestant countries, where cessation from business would entail serious individual loss. In Catholic countries the multiplicity of holidays is frequently attended with civic embarrassments, and the government has frequently interfered to curb sacerdotal zeal. The same thing has happened in India. So numerous were the Hindoo holidays that at one time the British found it difficult to get the natives in their employ to give their services for more than two hundred days in the year. It was an indolent pleasure-seeking, however, rather than the exactions of their religion, which made so many blank days in the working year; and a government inquiry into the subject, with a subsequent threat of dismissal, enabled the Hindoo officials materially to curb their passion for devotional exercises. From seventy or eighty the "red-letter days" have now fallen to less than twenty; the great *poojahs* ("worships") are limited to two or three; and it is only upon the occasion of the Doorga festival—called the Dusserah in Western India—that several days of entire absence from public duties are permitted.

In America every individual State has its legal holidays, which are enforced by statute. But each State is left to its own devices in this matter. Properly speaking, national holidays do not exist, although there are several holidays, as Christmas, the Fourth of July, and Thanksgiving, which are now observed by all the States. But they derive their sanction from State and not from national authority.

The English indulge in very few periodical glorifications. The anniversary of Waterloo was kept during the life of the Duke of Wellington strictly as a private gathering, and there is not a single event in their prolific history which they celebrate by national jubilation. Political feasts and fasts have had no vitality except when associated with party struggles, and even in this sense they are becoming obsolete. A few obstinate Orangemen glorify themselves very absurdly on the anniversary of the battle of the Boyne, Guy Fawkes still amuses children on the 5th of November, but the questionable memories of Stuart triumphs and the annual remembrance of the great revolution had died out of the minds of men long before it was determined to obliterate them from the pages of the Prayer Book.

As to saints' days, they were abolished at the Reformation, when Merrie England at the bidding of the Puritans gave up holidays altogether. The restoration of the Stuart family brought with it the restoration of Christmas and Good Friday, and eventually Easter Monday, Whit Monday, and Boxing Day crept back into the popular calendar as at least partial holidays. But bankers and merchants could not close on the latter days, because they were bound during business hours to meet all claims legally made upon them, nor could they allow their employees to leave. As a matter of fact, no commercial offices recognized any week-day holidays save only Christmas and Good Friday. Thus stood matters when Sir John Lubbock in 1865 was invited to stand as a Liberal candidate for West Kent. "I naturally asked myself," he says, "what I should do if I were elected, and one of the reasons which influenced me was the hope of securing, on behalf of our people, a few days for rest and recreation. The holidays already in existence were all of religious origin. It is remarkable that the Bank Holidays created by the Act of 1871 were the first ever instituted by any Legislature for the purposes of rest and enjoyment." (See BANK HOLIDAYS.)

Holly Bussing. An ancient custom still surviving at Netherwitton, in Northumberland, England. The lads and lasses of the village and vicinity meet on Easter Tuesday, and, accompanied by the parish clerk and a fiddler (this dual capacity is often combined in one individual), proceed to the wood to get holly, with which some decorate a stone across the stands in the village, while others "bob around" to the tune of "Speed the Plough" or "Birnie Bouzle." (DYER: *British Popular Customs*, p. 180.)

Holy Saturday. The Saturday before Easter. In Catholic churches the ceremonies begin early in the morning with the striking of the new fire struck from the flint. This custom is comparatively recent. It would appear that in some churches a daily blessing was given to the fire struck for the kindling of the lamps. About the year 1100 this benediction was reserved exclusively for Holy Saturday, the fire being considered an appropriate image of the Light of light rising again like the sun in his strength. From this fire a three-stemmed candle, affixed to a reed, is lighted and carried up the church by a deacon, who three times chants the words "Lumen Christi." The same symbol reappears in the Paschal candle (*q. v.*), which is blessed by the deacon on this day. Then occurs the blessing of the baptismal font, a reminiscence of the time in the ancient Church

BAPTISM OF A JEWISH CHILD ON HOLY SATURDAY.

when the catechumens were presented to the bishop for baptism
on Holy Saturday and the vigil of Pentecost. At Rome this
day is especially chosen for the baptism of converted Jews, and
the ceremony of baptizing a Jewish child in the church of St.
John Lateran is especially formal and imposing.

At Rome the houses of the faithful are annually blessed on
Holy Saturday. The curé or a priest of the parish in a beretta
and white surplice, a prayer book in his hand, and preceded by a
little choir-boy who carries the holy water and the aspersory,
walks through the streets, entering shops and houses for the
purpose of sprinkling them. He is rewarded by some slight

DEPOSITING THE SACRAMENT.
(From Picart.)

money offering from the faithful who consent to have the ceremony performed. In the old days of the temporal power he did
not wait for this consent.

A remarkable variant of this custom, evidently a survival of
Catholic usage, was practised on New Year's eves at Tenby in
Wales up to the middle of the eighteenth century. Crowds of
boys and girls used to visit each house, carrying with them a cup
of water and a sprig of box-wood with which they besprinkled
not only the inmates but also the furniture of the rooms, accompanying the operation with the following singular rhyme:

Here we bring new water from the well so clear,
For to worship God with this happy New Year;
Sing levy dew, sing levy dew, the water and the wine,
With seven bright gold wires, and bugles that do shine;
Sing reign of fair maid, with gold upon her toe,
Open you the west door and turn the old year go;
Sing reign of fair maid, with gold upon her chin,
Open you the east door and let the new year in.

The term levy dew is sometimes interpreted as the French "levez Dieu," but more plausibly as the Welsh "llef i Dduw," —a cry to God.

In the middle parts of Ireland great preparations are made on Holy Saturday for the finishing of Lent. Many a fat hen and dainty piece of bacon is put into the pot, by the cotter's wife, about eight or nine o'clock, and woe be to the person who should taste it before the cock crows. At twelve is heard the clapping of hands, and the joyous laugh, mixed with an Irish phrase which signifies "out with the Lent." All is merriment for a few hours, when they retire, and rise about four o'clock to see the sun dance in honor of the resurrection. This custom is not confined to the humble laborer and his family, but is scrupulously observed by many highly respectable and wealthy families. (BRAND: *Popular Antiquities*, 1849, vol. i. p. 161.)

Honoratus, St. (Fr. *Honoré*), patron of bakers. His festival is celebrated on his death-day, May 16. He was Bishop of Amiens in the seventh century. In 1204 a collegiate church was built in his honor at Paris by a private gentleman named Renold Cherins, which became very famous.

A representation of St. Honoré, clad in his episcopal robes, with the crosier in his left hand and in his right an oven-peel bearing three loaves of bread, appears on the ancient banners of the Bakers' Guild in Paris. His festival was solemnly celebrated by a procession of bakers and their apprentices, accompanied by girls in white dresses, to the church of the Trinity, in Paris, where they heard high mass. Subsequently they wound up the day with a dinner and a ball.

Hood, Throwing the. An annual sport performed on January 6 at Haxey, in Lincolnshire. It is said to have been instituted many centuries ago by a female member of the house of Mowbray, who were once considered the greatest folk in that part of the country. One Christmas Day as she was riding over the Meeres to the village church a gale of wind blew off her hood. Twelve farming men quit their work in the field and ran to gather up the hood. The lady found so much amusement in the scene that she forbade her own attendants to join in the pursuit. When the hood was at length recaptured and placed on the lady's head, she cordially thanked the men, gave them each some money, and promised that forty acres of land should be devoted to the annual sport of throwing up a hood for capture on Christmas Day. The land is still known as the hoodlands, and even after the change in the calendar the sport has continued to be celebrated on Old Christmas Day, or January 6. By the terms of the gift twelve men should fight for the possession of a hood thrown up in the air. They should be clothed in a uniform of scarlet jerkins and velvet caps.

Folklore for December, 1896, quotes an account of the game as it was played that year, from the pen of Mr. C. C. Bell, a resident of the island of Axholme. "The hood," he says, "is now kept up by subscription, or rather by begging. The boggans go round the parish and neighborhood for a week or a fortnight before the date, and collect what they can. This year, I believe, they got thirty or forty shillings. The boggans were originally twelve in number, but have now dwindled down to four or five. There is also 'My Lord' and a Fool. The company are called together at two P.M. by the ringing of the church bells, the place of assembly being the green close by the churchyard. Here there is a stone, round which the people group themselves. On Monday My Lord with his fool and the boggans arrived on the scene at two-fifty. The fool was dressed in a suit of old sailing, stitched all over with threads of gayly-colored cloth. He carried the hoods under his arm, and a stout staff with a rabbit-skin slung to the end of it. The fool was hoisted on the stone by My Lord, and the boggans grouped themselves close round. They were dressed in short red smocks, with their caps grotesquely decorated. The fool then opened the proceedings by a speech. Formerly this was a great feature, being made the occasion of a good deal of topical wit and satire, but it is now a very tame affair, lasting only a couple of minutes, and consisting of a few traditionary phrases. It ran something like this :

" ' Now, good folks, this is Haxa' Hood. We've killed two bullocks and a half, but the other half we had to leave running about field : we can fetch it if it's wanted. Remember it's

> Hoose agin hoose, toon agin toon,
> And if you meet a man knock him doon.'

This was all, the verses being clearly a most essential feature. They were much applauded, and at their conclusion the fool jumped down, and My Lord led the way to the open field behind the church. It is his part to throw the hood, or, rather, hoods, for there are six of them, one, I suppose, for each of the principal hamlets round. The first five were of sacking, and these are, I understand, made every year as wanted, but the last, the hood *par excellence*, is of leather, and is kept from year to year. The object is to carry them off the field away from the boggans. If any of these can get hold of them, or even touch them, they have to be given up and carried back to My Lord. For every one carried off the field the boggans forfeit half a crown, which is spent in beer, doubtless by the men of the particular hamlet who have carried off the hood. There are certain wards—it may be a tree or a building—showing the limits of the field, and when one of these is reached the hood is struck against it and is then out of the boggans' domain. This is termed ' wyking' the hood. This goes on with the different hoods in turn until four o'clock, when the leather hood (*the* hood) is thrown up, and for this there is a great struggle, chiefly between the men of Haxey and those of Westwoodside,—that is to say, really between the customers of the public houses there,—each trying to get it to his favorite house. The publican at the successful house stands beer,—I do not know whether there is any stated amount,—and the game ends usually in a drunken spree."

In conclusion, Mr. Bell adds, it was the custom until recently to "smoke" the fool over a straw fire on the morning after the hood. " He was suspended above the fire and swung backward and forward over it until almost suffocated, then allowed to drop into the smouldering straw, which was well wetted, and to scramble out when he could."

Horn Dance. A curious survival from mediæval times which is still celebrated during the September "wakes" at Abbots Bromley, a village on the borders of Needwood Forest in Staffordshire. Six or seven quaintly dressed fellows, each wearing a deer's skull with antlers, caper through the streets, urged on in their gyrations by another individual "wearing" a property-horse made of wood and cloth. This horseman carries a whip, with which he keeps the dancers moving energetically, whilst a sportsman with a bow and arrow takes make-believe shots at the excited "deer." In former time, a pot full of cakes and ale was an appanage of the dance, and contributions towards church repairs were levied on all spectators. The horn dance then took place on certain Sunday mornings at the main entrance to the parish church ; the present date is the Monday after Wakes Sunday, which is the Sunday next to September 4. The horns are the property of the vicar during his incumbency, and are kept, with the hobby-horse frame, the bow and arrow, and the curious old pot for collecting money, in the church tower. The horns have been examined by Dr. Cox and pronounced to be reindeer horns. The hobby-horse is of the familiar pattern used in the hobby-horse and hodening sports of the past; *i.e.*, its under jaw is worked by a string, so that it "clacks" against the upper jaw in time with the step.

Dr. Plot, in his "Natural History of Staffordshire," 1686, p. 434, mentions this custom, which seems then to have been in temporary abeyance, doubtless owing to the civil wars.

The dance, according to his account, took place "within memory" during the Christmas holidays, and the stag's horns were painted with the arms of the chief families of the town. Some traces of the paint still remain. "To the Hobby-Horse Dance,"

HORN DANCE.

he says, "there also belonged a pot, which was kept by Turnes by four or five of the chief of the Town, whom they call'd Reeves, who provided cakes and ale to put in this pot." It was then, probably, shared as a loving-cup among the spectators. Every well-disposed householder contributed a penny apiece for himself and his family; and with the levy thus made, together with the contributions of "forraigners that come to see it," were defrayed, first, the cost of the cakes and ale, then the expense of the repairs of the church and the support of the poor. Tradition says that when the money collected was used for these public purposes the dance was performed in the churchyard on Sunday after service. Now the ·dancers have the proceeds for themselves. (See *Folklore*, vol. vii. (1896) p. 381.)

Hospital Saturday, Hospital Sunday. The last Saturday and the last Sunday in December are so denominated in London and in New York because in most of the churches and synagogues those days are devoted to the taking up of special contributions for the metropolitan hospitals. In New York the idea of making a special appeal at the close of every year in behalf of the hospitals was first suggested in 1873. It was not, however, original in this country. It has been in successful operation in England for many years, until now about fifteen hundred churches of various denominations, as well as Jewish synagogues, take up collections for the hospitals. In St. Paul's Cathedral and Westminster Abbey, in London, services are continued throughout the day, with a collection at each service. The queen is the patron of the movement, and the lord mayor of London is the treasurer. Last year the total contributions in London amounted to about a quarter of a million dollars, against $58,208.29 contributed from all sources in New York, which, perhaps, may be regarded as a fair showing for the latter when its size, compared with that of London, is taken into account.

The movement in New York is under the patronage of the Hospital Saturday and Sunday Association, which divides the contributions received among thirty-eight hospitals on the basis of the free work performed by them in behalf of the suffering poor through the year.

Hubert of Liége, St., patron saint of the chase and of dogs. Though hagiologists name May 30, 727, as the date of his death, his festival is celebrated on November 3, "probably on account of some translation," says Butler. Not impossibly, however, it is due to the fact that the beginning of November is the natural opening of the hunting season. All that is known of St. Hubert as a matter of history is that he was born in the latter half of the seventh century, that he succeeded his master, St. Lambert, as Bishop of Maestricht, that he removed the seat of the see to Liége, that he labored with great success for the evangelization of the heathen population of the Ardennes, and that he died a natural death about 727.

Legend makes him begin life as a nobleman at the court of Theodoric III., passionately addicted, among other worldly amusements, to the chase. On a certain Good Friday, as he was profanely engaged in his favorite amusement, the crucified Saviour appeared to him between the horns of the stag and commanded him to forsake the vanities of the world and devote himself to the service of God.

Legend, supplemented by some historical evidence, adds that his body was conveyed to Liége and deposited in the collegiate church of St. Peter. In 825 it was translated to the Benedictine abbey of Audain (since called St. Hubert's) in the Ardennes, on the frontiers of the duchy of Luxembourg.

St. Hubert's Day is the formal commencement of the hunting season in France, as the first Monday in November is in England. In many of the rural churches of France St. Hubert's mass is celebrated on this occasion. All the hunting dogs in the neighborhood are brought to the church. Low mass is said, and then the priest solemnly makes his way down through the aisle into the yard. A piqueur toots a jolly fanfare. At this familiar sound the pack tears pell-mell out of the chapel, and in obedience to a word from the keeper rallies around the priest, who thereupon blesses and breaks the sacred cake, which is a sovereign antidote against madness, and administers it to the brutes, together with a priestly pat between the ears. Then huntsmen, villagers, spectators, and dogs are included in a general blessing, and away go the huntsmen and the pack, anointed with the oil of righteousness, ready for the slaughter of as many of God's creatures as they can run to their death.

The association of St. Hubert with the chase accounts for his being invoked for protection from rabies, this being one of the perils to which huntsmen were especially liable. A document written about the year 1100 records a miraculous cure of hydrophobia wrought through the intercession of the saint, and the terms in which it is mentioned show that at that time the custom of seeking his aid in cases of this disease was already well established. The cure was effected by inserting under the skin of the patient a thread from St. Hubert's stole; and this mode of treatment has continued to be practised down to the present day.

This operation, however, is resorted to only in what are considered extreme cases; that is to say, when there is no reason to doubt that the dog by which the patient has been bitten was really mad, and when the bite has drawn blood. In other cases the priests in charge of St. Hubert's shrine are empowered to grant what is called a "respite" (*répit*), which secures the patient against hydrophobia for a specified period varying from forty days to ninety-nine years. The "respite" for forty days may also be given by any person who has himself undergone the operation of the "incision." It is to be remarked that the use of ordinary means of healing, in addition to those of a supernatural kind, is rather encouraged than otherwise, and that the patient who avails himself of either the "incision" or the "respite" is required to submit to certain judicious regulations with regard to his diet and to his general manner of life. Some even of M. Pasteur's patients are said to have made themselves doubly secure by undergoing the "incision" after having been treated by the Parisian *savant*.

Mad dogs are known in literature as early as Homer (Iliad, viii. 299). Ælian says that if a stone which a dog has bitten be put in the wine at a banquet it will madden the guests. As the origin of rabies was, and is, unknown, early science attributed it to a "worm," which may have been short for microbe, but more probably was only the magical worm of folk-medicine. The worm was in the tongue or the tail of the dog; hence the practice of "worming" it (*éverement* or *éverration*). The usual remedy was "a hair of the dog that bit you" reduced to ashes. Gubernatis mentions a cure in which the wound given by the dog is covered with wolf-skin, perhaps as a magical counter-irritant. Pliny has a wondrous tale of a Roman matron, mother of a Prætorian, who was advised, in a dream, to send her son the root of a dog-rose. The Guards were in Spain, where the dog-rose root reached the man just when he had been bitten by a mad dog. He was about going mad when the dog-rose reached him; he drank a decoction of it, and recovered. *Similia similibus curantur.* In Crete it was usual to take mad dogs, and people bitten by mad dogs, to the temple of Artemis at Rocca. The sufferers were made to eat a fish provocative of thirst. Modern myth-mongers suppose that Diana, a favorite goddess in Gaul, survived long in the woodlands,—

> Échevelée à travers la clairière
> Diane court dans la noire forêt,—

and that St. Hubert succeeded to her divine power of healing rabies. The legendary book " Les Miracles de Saint-Hubert" was written between 1087 and 1106. From this work we learn that the first-fruits of the chase had long been offered to St. Hubert, as of old to Diana. He had long, moreover, been in the habit of curing rabies by means of a thread of gold from the sacred stole worked by the Virgin herself and given to the saint in a vision.

Professor John W. Hales has plausibly suggested, in the *Athenæum*, an identification of Old Mother Hubbard of the nursery rhyme with St. Hubert. That Hubbard is a corruption of Hubert is evident enough. The story of Mother Hubbard with her care for the dog may be a sort of parody of the legend of the dog-saint Hubert, possibly a Protestant mockery of it, composed when the belief in saints and their powers was rapidly decaying, or decayed, the title "Mother" being given in a contemptuous sense, just as we style a certain kind of man an "old woman." Mother Hubbard is a good old soul, but all her canine anxieties and efforts are quite futile; her dog is none the better for her patronage. And so, it is by no means unlikely, in her person the saint is derided. Old Mother Hubbard seems to have been a familiar figure in the days of Spenser, for in his " Prosopopoia, or Mother Hubberds Tale," he merely introduces her as the teller of the story of the fox and the ape and how they went swindling together, without deeming it necessary to enter into any explanation as to who she was. To mention her honored name was apparently enough. Her great reputation made any fuller record unnecessary.

Hugh, St. There are two saints of this name, both venerated in Lincoln, England. The first (1140–1200) became Bishop of Lincoln in 1186, and enlarged the cathedral. He died in London, and his body arrived at the gate of Lincoln just as John and Malcolm of Scotland entered the city. The two kings, eager to honor so holy a corpse, at once set their shoulders to the bier and bore it to the cathedral, where it was buried near the altar of St. John the Baptist. Bishop Hugh was canonized at Rome in 1220, and sixty years later his bones were placed in a gold shrine, which disappeared at the Reformation, when zeal and theft ran high. Bishop Fuller afterwards erected a plain altar-tomb over the good man's grave.

A monument standing in the south aisle of the choir of Lincoln Cathedral is traditionally believed to have been the tomb of little Sir or Saint Hugh, a child found murdered at Lincoln in 1225, and vulgarly supposed to have been crucified by some cruel and blasphemous Jews in derision of our Saviour's sufferings. There were many ballads written about this supposed crime, the best of which commences,—

> The bonny boys of merry Lincoln
> Were playing at the ball ;
> And with them stood the sweet Sir Hugh,
> The flower among them all.

Chaucer at once seized on so recent a miracle, and introduced "Young Hew of Lincoln" into his Prioress's story. Bishop Percy, with less than his usual acumen, mistook "Mirryland Toun" for Mailand, Milan, and concluded the whole to be of Italian origin. The story may, after all, be a true one, for Matthew Paris, who was living at the time, relates it circumstantially. Mr. Lethieullier in the *Archæologia* cites two records, one of which was a commission from the king (Henry III.) to seize for the king's use the houses belonging to those Jews who were hanged at Lincoln for crucifying a child. According to Matthew Paris, the boy, eight years old, was tortured for ten days before a large council of Jews, in contempt of Christianity. They scourged him with rods, spat in his face, mutilated his nose, ears, and lips, and on the tenth day they crucified him, and, while he hung on the cross, pierced his side with a spear. The body was found in a pit or draw-well in the house of a Jew, named Joppin, which the boy had been seen to enter. Joppin, being promised pardon, confessed the crime, and avowed that such murders were committed nearly every year by his nation. Notwithstanding the promise of pardon, the Jew was tied to the tail of a horse and dragged to the gallows, and eventually eighteen of the richest and most distinguished Jews in Lincoln were hanged for sharing in the murder, and many more sent as hostages to the Tower of London. Herd and Jamieson both give variations of this once popular ballad. In 1736, when Lethieullier visited Lincoln Cathedral, he was shown a painted statuette of a boy which was erroneously supposed to have formed part of " Bishop Hugh's" tomb. There were bleeding wounds marked on the hands, feet, and side, and the antiquary conjectures that the shrine given in Stukeley's " Itinerarium Curiosum" was the real tomb of Sir Hugh.

Little Hugh's name appears in the Calendar of Saints on August 27, although his death seems to have occurred at about the time of the feast of St. Peter and St. Paul, June 29.

Besides this boy many other Christian children are said to have suffered martyrdom at the hands of the Jews, who made a practice of sacrificing them at the Paschal season. There is the famous case of Richard of Pontoise in 1182, which led to the expulsion of the Jews from France, and that of William of Norwich in 1137. The shrine of St. William in the Wood, built where his body was found, was long an object of pious pilgrimage.

The Jews, we are told, never buried their victims after a sacrifice, because of a law which forbade their so dealing with Christians. Consequently their crimes rarely went undiscovered. Heaven itself was interested in seeing that they should not, for when the Jews sought at least to hide the bodies in a well or thicket a miraculous light revealed their whereabouts.

Sir Richard Burton leans to the view that there is some truth in these hideous stories. And when one reads the more hideous stories of Jewish persecution in the Middle Ages, more hideous because more frequent and more unprovoked, one's only regret is that in lieu of innocent children the Jews did not seize some burly monarch or prelate and give him a taste of his own medicine.

I.

Ignatius Loyola, St., founder of the order of Jesuits. His festival is celebrated on the day of his death, July 3.

St. Ignatius Loyola was of a noble Spanish family, and was

born in Biscay in 1491. He was brought up at the court of Ferdinand and Isabella, and spent the early years of his life amid the pleasures of the court and in fighting in the army of Ferdinand. A long illness caused by a wound turned his mind towards religion, and on his recovery he retired to Manresa, where he gave himself up to penance and meditation.

It is related that he went nearly mad from doubt, but was comforted by heavenly visions. He spent several years in theological study, and then went to Paris, where he became a pupil of St. Francis Xavier. He founded a community which, in addition to the usual vows of poverty, chastity, and obedience, bound themselves to unreserved obedience to the Pope. The order was called the Society of Jesus. It was three years before St. Ignatius obtained the confirmation of this order, of which he was the first general. Many miracles of healing the sick and casting out devils are attributed to him. He had the satisfaction of seeing his order grow and flourish in many countries. He died in 1556, and was buried in a church at Rome, but in 1597 his relics were removed to the Jesuit church of the Gesù, of which Cardinal Farnese had laid the corner-stone in 1568. He was canonized by Gregory XV in 1622.

A miraculous picture of St. Ignatius is preserved at Munebrega, a village of Aragon, Spain. The tradition runs that a stranger appeared in January, 1623, before the ecclesiastical authorities and offered to paint the portrait of St. Ignatius. He was left alone in the studio. A few hours later the picture was finished and the artist had disappeared. Obviously he was an angel. Later in the year, on April 21, a copious sweat flowed for four hours from under the right arm of the picture. It was neither blood nor water, but some wholly unknown liquid. The prodigy was repeated a fortnight afterwards. Since that time the chapel of St. Ignatius, where the picture is housed, has been one of the most renowned shrines in all Spain. Miraculous cures and other wonders are of continual occurrence among the pilgrims who resort thither.

Immaculate Conception of the Virgin Mary. A festival celebrated by the Catholic Church on December 8. In the Anglican reformed calendar it appears as "The Conception of the B. V. Mary," which was the original title in the mediæval Church everywhere. The doctrine of the Immaculate Conception, though long held as a pious belief, was not authoritatively proclaimed as an article of faith until 1854. This doctrine in brief is that the Blessed Virgin was conceived in the womb of Anna her mother without the stain of original sin inherited by the rest of humanity from Adam.

The Greek Emperor Manuel Comnenus (died 1180), in a Novella quoted by Balsamon, mentions the feast of the Blessed Virgin's Conception as one to be observed by the people on December 9. This is the date on which the festival is still celebrated in the Greek Church.

England is said to have been the first among the countries of Western Europe to keep this feast. Its introduction there is attributed to St. Anselm. At first it was left free to the people to observe it or not, but a Synod of London in 1287 enjoined it as a holiday of obligation. From England the celebration seems to have passed to Normandy, and then south to Lyons. St. Bernard reproved the canons of that city for introducing a custom which had not the sanction of the Roman Church. St. Buonaventura (died 1274) speaks of the feast as established, but says he does not dare either to approve or disapprove it. (Lib. iii., Sententiæ, d. iii., qu. l.) It is certain, however, that the feast had established itself in the calendar of the Roman Church before the middle of the fourteenth century. Sixtus IV., towards the close of the fifteenth century, sanctioned an office and mass proper to the day, for which, however, a new office was substituted by Pius V. Clement XI. made the day a holiday of obligation, which it has remained ever since in the Catholic Church. Meanwhile the doctrine of the Immaculate Conception had been quietly gaining headway among Catholic theologians. The controversy had begun so early as the twelfth century, when the weight of opinion was against the theory. Duns Scotus, who died in 1308, seems to have inaugurated a general change to the affirmative.

A rare illustrated pamphlet, published in 1470, and entitled "Defensorium inviolatæ perpetuæque virginitatis Mariæ," sums up all the mediæval arguments on this subject, and enforces them by appropriate illustrations. Thus, it asks, "If the companions of Diomedes were turned into birds, why should not God wish that his mother should be a maid?"

Why not, indeed? The point, obvious enough, is made dazzlingly clear by an elegant wood-cut representing the companions of Diomedes, after their metamorphosis, hopping cheerfully about the rocks in front of a mediæval castle not much larger than themselves.

The matter gave rise to keen discussion at Trent, and, though most of the bishops held the doctrine, the Council contented itself with a declaration that in defining the truth that the whole human race fell under original sin it did not intend to include in the decree "the blessed and immaculate Virgin Mary." Successive Popes intimated their approval of the doctrine, though they did not bind it upon the consciences of the faithful. Benedict XIV., writing about the middle of the eighteenth century, sums up the whole state of the question in his day thus: "The Church inclines to the opinion of the Immaculate Conception; but the Apostolic See has not yet defined it as an article of faith."

A PICTORIAL ARGUMENT.

So matters stood when, in February, 1849, Pius IX. wrote from Gaeta to the bishops of the Catholic Church asking for their opinions on the subject. The Italian, Portuguese, and Spanish bishops, about four hundred and ninety in number, were nearly unanimous in their wish for the definition. But many bishops in France, Germany, and Switzerland hesitated, some because they did not accept the doctrine, others because they held its promulgation to be temporarily inexpedient. Nearly six years later the question was closed. On December 8, 1854, Pius IX., in the presence of more than two hundred bishops, issued his solemn definition that the immaculate conception of Mary was a truth contained in the original teachings of the apostles, and an article of faith. Since then the feast has been officially known as that of the "Immaculate Conception of the Blessed Virgin Mary."

Indian Summer. The name given by Americans to the short but surpassingly beautiful season in the latter part of autumn. A similar spell of fine weather is noticed in other countries also, and frequently compared to the halcyon period of the Greeks, so that Shakespeare could pointedly say, "Expect Saint Martin's Summer, halcyon days" (*Henry VI.*, Part I.,

Act I., Scene 2, line 131), in allusion to the season of which he elsewhere says,—

> Farewell thou latter spring,
> Farewell all hallown summer.　(*Henry IV.*)

In England the season derived its name of St. Martin's or Martinmas Summer from the fact that it commonly begins there about November 11, St. Martin's Day; on the Continent it is called Summer Close and " L'été de St.-Martin," with an ungallant double meaning, which allows the term to be applied to ladies of advancing years. It may be that there is an association of the same idea, though less delicately expressed, in the German " der alte Weibersommer," while in Chili it is called St. John's Summer. In the United States this season generally begins in November, though the period varies within a month. It is characterized by fair but not brilliant weather; the air is smoky and hazy, perfectly still and moist, and the sun shines dimly, but softly and sweetly, through an atmosphere that some call copper-colored, and others golden, in accordance with their power of poetical perception. The name of Indian summer is differently explained. Rev. James Freeman derives it from the fact that the Indians are particularly fond of it, regarding it as a special gift of their favorite god, the god of the Southwest, who sends the soft southwest winds, and to whom they go after death. Daniel Webster said that the early settlers gave that name to the season because they ascribed its peculiar features, the heat and the haze, to the burning of the prairies by the Indians at that time. Mr. Kercheval, however, gives a more plausible explanation : " It sometimes happened that after the apparent onset of winter the weather became warm, the smoky time commenced, and lasted for a considerable number of days. This was the Indian summer, because it afforded the Indians—who during the severe winter never made any incursions into the settlements—another opportunity of visiting them with their destructive warfare. The melting of the snow saddened every countenance, and the genial warmth of the sun chilled every heart with horror. The apprehension of another visit from the Indians, and of being driven back to the detested fort, was painful in the highest degree." (Schele de Vere : *Americanisms.*)

Innocents' Day, Holy (in England more popularly known as **Childermas**). A festival celebrated in the Latin Church on December 28, and in the Greek Church on December 29 (O. S.), in commemoration of the babes slaughtered by order of King Herod to insure the killing of the infant Christ. From very early times these children were looked upon as martyrs. Irenæus

(iii. 16, 4) and St. Augustine (" De Symbolo ad Catech.," lib. iii.) assert this clearly. But it is less certain when the feast began to be kept. In the earlier times it appears to have been bound up with the Epiphany. Pope Leo I. in almost all his sermons on the Epiphany refers to the Innocents. However, a separate festival of the Holy Innocents is mentioned in the Calendar of Carthage issued at the end of the fifth century.

In Rome meat was anciently forbidden on this day, and it was observed with mourning. Micrologus gives this reason : " With right are the sufferings of the Holy Innocents attended with less festivity than the celebration of other saints, for, though they were crowned with martyrdom, they went at once, not into Paradise, but into Limbo." They had to wait till Christ at his ascension opened the gates of heaven. Skulls of these children were among the relics shown at Paris in Notre-Dame, at St. Denis, and in the church of the Augustinians at Limoges.

In the Middle Ages it was usual for children to keep a time of festivity in honor of the Holy Innocents which lasted from St. Stephen's Day to the octave of the Epiphany. Boys used to sit in the canons' stalls; one of them, vested with the episcopal robes, gave his blessing pontifically. (See BOY-BISHOP.) The Council of Basle condemned the extravagances of this celebration, which in some places deteriorated into the still more heinous mockeries of the Feast of Fools (*q. v.*). But a Feast of Children is still innocently observed in some monasteries and convents.

In consequence probably of the horror attaching to the atrocious act of Herod, Childermas was always looked upon as an unlucky day. No one who could avoid it entered upon any undertaking, began any work, or, especially, got married, on this day. Louis XI. shunned any discussion of state or social matters, and was exasperated beyond measure if any subject of the sort were introduced, on Childermas. The coronation of Edward IV., which had been set for a Sunday, was postponed to Monday when it was found that Sunday fell on December 28. Chambers's " Book of Days" informs us that " to the present hour we understand that the housewives in Cornwall and probably also in other parts of the country refrain scrupulously from scouring or scrubbing on Innocents' Day." It was, moreover, not considered lucky upon this day to put on new clothes or pare the nails. At various places in Gloucestershire, Somersetshire, and Worcestershire it is still customary to ring a muffled peal on this anniversary. At Norton in the latter county the muffled peal for the slaughter of the Innocents is followed by an unmuffled peal of joy for the deliverance of the Infant Christ. (*Notes and Queries*, First Series, vol. viii. p. 617.)

In Northamptonshire this festival was called " Dyzemas Day."

Miss Baker, in her "Glossary of Northamptonshire Words" (1854, vol. i. p. 207), says she was told by a sexagenarian on the southern side of the county that within his remembrance this day was kept as sacred as the Sabbath, and it was considered particularly unlucky to commence any undertaking, or even to wash, on the same day of the week throughout the year on which the anniversary of this day last fell, and it was commonly said, "What is begun on Dyzemas Day will never be finished."

The source of the ill omened *Dyzemas* has not been settled : its origin has been suggested from Greek *dus*, and *mass*, as being expressive of misfortune, evil, peril, in allusion to the massacre of the Innocents. A correspondent of *Notes and Queries* (Second Series, vol. iii. pp. 289, 495) asks if it has not reference to the name Desmas, given to one of the thieves crucified with our Lord,—universal tradition seeming to attach Desmas to the penitent and Gestas (or Yesmas) to the impenitent thief. And if the local tradition has any reference to these names, it would seem as if Desmas was the name of ill omen. It has also been suggested that Dyzemas Day is tithe day : in Portuguese, *dizimas, dizimos,* "tenths," "tithes ;" in law Latin, *decimœ,* the same.

The Irish call this *La croasta na bliana,* "the cross day of the year," and *Diar dasin darg,* or "blood Thursday." On this day they will not warp thread nor permit it to be warped, and they declare that any undertaking must prove unlucky. In the county of Clare a dismal legend is current concerning a white thornbush growing on an island in Lake Turlough between the parishes of Quin and Tulla. The bush is known as the Scagh an Earla, "the earl's bush." A suit of clothes made on Cross day was put on a child, who straightway died. A second and a third child to whom it was given also died. Then the parents put the clothes at high tide on the Scagh an Earla, and when the waters fell, the clothes were found full of dead eels. Many similar legends are extant as to the fatality attending anything begun on the cross day of the year. (*Notes and Queries,* Fourth Series, vol. xii. p. 185.)

In mediæval England the juvenile members of the family used to be reminded of the dismal character of the day by a sound whipping administered in bed. This custom endured so late as the seventeenth century, for it is mentioned by Gregory: "It hath been a custom, and yet is elsewhere, to whip up the children upon Innocents' Day morning, that the memorie of this murther might stick the closer; and, in a moderate proportion, to act over the crueltie again in kind." Gregory also states another custom, on the authority of an old ritual belonging to the abbey of Oseney, communicated to him by his friend Dr. Gerard Langbain, the provost of Queen's College, Oxford, from which it appears that at the church of Oseney "they were wont to bring out, upon this day, the foot of a child prepared after their fashion, and put upon with red and black colors, as to signify the dismal part of the day. They put this up in a chest in the vestry, ready to be produced at the time, and to be solemnly carried about the church to be adored by the people." (*Episcopus Puerorum in Die Innocentium*, 1684, p. 113.)

So far as the whipping was concerned, it might be avoided by the children taking care to rise betimes before their elders; and in fact the whole affair eventually resolved itself into a frolic, in which the lively and active, who managed to be first astir, amused themselves at the expense of the sluggards by awaking them with a sound drubbing administered in bed. It is noteworthy that in Wales on St. Stephen's Day, December 26, everybody has long been privileged to whip another person's legs with holly, and this is often reciprocally done until the blood streams down.

Theologians are fond of pointing out that in the three successive anniversaries, St. Stephen's Day on the 26th, St. John the Evangelist's Day on the 27th, and Innocents' Day on the 28th of December, are comprehended three descriptions of martyrdom, all of which have their peculiar efficacy, though differing in degree. In the death of St. Stephen an example is furnished of the highest class of martyrdom,—that is to say, both in *will* and in *deed;* St. John the Evangelist, who gave practical evidence of his readiness to suffer death for the cause of Christ, though, through miraculous interposition, he was saved from actually doing so, is an instance of the second description of martyrdom, —in *will* though not in *deed;* and the slaughter of the Innocents affords an instance of martyrdom in *deed* and not in *will*, these unfortunate children having lost their lives, though involuntarily, on account of the Saviour, and it being therefore considered "that God supplied the defects of their will by his own acceptance of the sacrifice."

Isidore the Ploughman, St. (Sp. *Isidro el Labrado;* It. *Isidoro Agricola*), patron of farmers and of Madrid, where his shrine in the church of St. Andrew is an object of enthusiastic devotion.

The festival of the saint, May 15, the anniversary of his death, is the most notable of all the holidays of Madrid. Then the town puts on its gayest array. The walls of the houses are lined with tapestries and colored curtains, flags and banners stream in the air, the church bells ring, and a procession winds through the streets with military band and cross and lights and song of clergy. The objective point of the procession and of all good citizens for miles around is the hermitage of the saint on the banks of the Manzanares, where they spend the entire day in noisy frolic. The little church stands on a bare brown hill. All about it is an extemporized village, consisting half of restaurants and half of toy-shops. In these shops are kept little earthen pig-bells, whose ringing scares away the thunder, and artificial roses with glass handles terminating in a whistle. Thousands of whistles are sold and are blown cheerily all day long. In the intervals of tooting crowds stream into the oratory of the church to kiss a glass-covered relic of the saint which is held in the hands of an ecclesiastical attendant. For this privilege they drop a penny into a saucer proffered by an acolyte, who follows at the heels of the relic-keeper as he makes the rounds of the worshippers.

.St. Isidore was born in Madrid about 1110. A day-laborer in the employment of Don Juan de Vargas, who owned a farm outside the city, Isidore was pious, hard-working, and faithful. Yet he could not escape the tongue of slander. A jealous fellow-servant accused him to his master of coming late to his work in the morning. So De Vargas rose one morning before daybreak and hid himself, to see if Isidore were remiss in his work. He was indeed a few minutes late, for with the first dawn in the east he had gone to church. When he returned and put his hand to the plough De Vargas stepped forth to rebuke him. But, lo! in the field was a second plough, drawn by white oxen, urged on by an angel. Up the field and down again went the strange team, cutting a clean furrow and cutting it rapidly. On De Vargas's approach the vision disappeared. Then he questioned Isidore as to who were his assistants. "Sir," replied Isidore, in surprise, "I work alone, and know of none save God, to whom I look for aid." This convinced De Vargas that he was faithful, and thereafter he admitted the saint to his full confidence. The story of the angel who helped Isidore with his ploughing spread through the country and excited the respectful wonder of all who would fain have transferred their daily toil to celestial shoulders. For that is exactly the sort of saintship that every Spaniard would love to attain.

Isidore died on May 15, 1170. His remains were buried in the yard of St. Andrew's Church, in Madrid, which he had attended daily throughout his life. Angels came by night and took up the body and reburied it in the church itself. Then all the bells rang out untouched by human hands.

The body is now preserved in the bishop's chapel, and Butler informs us that "during these five hundred years" it "remains entire and fresh, being honored by a succession of miracles down to the present day."

In desperate cases of sufficient rank the doctors were wont to throw up the sponge and send for Isidore's urn, and, the drugging having ceased, the noble patient frequently recovered.

One of the best authenticated of these miracles was the healing of King Philip III., who fell sick at Casambios del Monte while returning from Madrid. The king's sickness was so serious that his physicians despaired of saving his life. As a last resort a "solemn procession" of ecclesiastical, civil, and military dignitaries took the shrine of Isidore from Madrid and bore it to where the king lay. As the shrine was lifted from its resting-place the king's fever left him, and as the shrine was brought nearer to him he became better. When it was placed beside his bed Philip was cured. The next year Isidore's body was placed in a new shrine of cunning design, which cost sixteen hundred ducats.

As the patron of farmers, Isidore is specially invoked in periods of prolonged drought, and when the case becomes desperate his body is paraded through the streets in solemn procession from the church to his hermitage and back again. The last time this was done, in May, 1896, rain was vouchsafed at once; and this prompt and gracious affability won for the saint a greater devotion than ever.

Isidore was canonized on March 12, 1622, on the same day as Ignatius Loyola, Philip Neri, Francis Xavier, and Theresa. The event was made one of great rejoicing in Madrid. A poetical tournament, still celebrated in the literary annals of Spain, was held in the saint's honor. Lope de Vega wrote two sacred dramas, or Mystery Plays, about the saint for the day of the canonization. These were performed on an extemporized stage in the public square, in the presence of King Philip IV. and his court.

Iversky Virgin. A wonder-working image enshrined in a small chapel at the Iversky gate in Moscow. It is of the usual Byzantine type, dark brown in color, brilliantly dressed and bejewelled, with a crown of precious stones encircling its head. When the Czar visits Moscow, the first thing he does is to go and worship this image. Every day from morning to night there is a throng of people round the door of the chapel, and in front of it a double line of mendicant nuns and beggars of various kinds. The curious thing about the matter is that the picture in the chapel is what theatrical people would call an understudy. And, most curious of all, it is an understudy for a copy. To disentangle this triune personality it should be explained that the Iversky Virgin is a copy made in 1648 from an ikon at Mount Athos which is attributed to St. Luke. The copy was brought to Russia in 1666, when the chapel for its reception was built by

Catherine II. But it grew into such demand as a visitor to the wealthy sick, to great shops, and to monasteries, that it is never at home from early morn till late at night, and the understudy represents it in the chapel to the thousands of prayerful people of all classes who stop to place a candle or utter a prayer. Meanwhile the first copy is travelling about the town in a blue coach adorned with a special device like a coat of arms and drawn by six horses. It occupies the seat of honor. On the front seat are a priest and a deacon, clad in crimson velvet and gold vestments, their heads bare even in the severest weather. The coachman, the footman, and the postilion are likewise supposed to keep their heads perpetually bared during the journey, but when it is very cold they wind woollen shawls of the color of their own hair adroitly around their heads, allowing the fringe to hang and simulate long locks. As the Virgin drives along, passers-by pause, salute, and cross themselves. (ISABEL F. HAPGOOD: *Rambles in Russia*, 1895, p. 321.)

Ivy Day. The Parnellite name for the annual commemoration on October 9 of the death of Charles Stuart Parnell (October 9, 1891). A vast procession goes out from Dublin to visit the grave of the dead chief in Glasnevin Cemetery, two miles to the northeast of the city. It is composed of the Parnellite members of Parliament and other office-holders, of deputations from trade and labor societies and from provincial towns, and of Parnellite citizens generally. Several bands, all with drums draped in black, take part in the proceedings. At the head of the procession is a wagonette loaded down with wreaths and garlands sent from all parts of the country. On arrival at the cemetery these wreaths are deposited on the grave, whilst the assemblage stands uncovered. Then the procession re-forms and marches back to Dublin. The ivy is probably selected as a symbol of Parnell and Ireland because as an evergreen it forms the most appropriate and suggestive foil to Disraeli's primrose. (See PRIMROSE DAY.)

J.

Jackson's Day, or **Old Hickory's Day.** The term popularly given to the anniversary of the battle of New Orleans, which was fought and won by General, afterwards President, Andrew Jackson, on January 8, 1815. It is a legal holiday in Louisiana, and is celebrated by members of the Democratic party throughout the whole country by banquets and speechmaking.

James the Great, St. (Lat. *Jacobus;* Sp. *Iago;* It. *Giacomo* or *Jacopo;* Fr. *Jacques*), patron saint of Spain and of pilgrims to Jerusalem. His reputed death-day, July 25 (A.D. 42), is one of the great national holidays of Spain.

St. James was probably the elder brother of St. John the Evangelist. He was of note among the twelve, being, with Peter and John, one of the three favorite disciples whom Jesus chose to witness the raising of the daughter of Jairus, the transfiguration, and the agony in the garden of Gethsemane. He was put to death by Herod Agrippa I. to please the Jews. To these

MARTYRDOM OF ST. JAMES.

facts of gospel history tradition has added many marvellous details. After the Ascension he is said to have gone to Spain to preach the gospel (see PILLAR, THE), and, having established the faith there, he returned to meet his death in Jerusalem. His disciples placed the saint's body in a ship which angels miraculously guided to Padron, on the coast of Spain. Here the body rested on a stone which hollowed itself out, wax to receive and marble to retain. Some theologians, however, hold that it was in this stone (still extant, and identified by archæologists as a Roman sarcophagus) that the saint floated to Padron. The country was then governed by a wicked queen named Lupa, who ordered saint and stone to be placed on a car drawn by wild bulls. But instead of dashing the relics to pieces, as was expected, the bulls quietly drew the car to the palace of Lupa. Then she was converted, and placed the body and the stone in a cave sacred to Bacchus. Years rolled on, and the burial-place was forgotten. At last, in 800, a hermit named Pelagius, noticing heavenly lights always hovering over a certain spot, made investigations which resulted in the recovery of the body. Thereupon Alonzo el Casto built a church to house it. This gave place to a cathedral consecrated May 17, 899. The city of Santiago or Compostella rose around it. Numerous miracles had already been performed at the shrine, which were capped by the appearance of the saint at the battle of Clavijo in 841, where he killed single-handed sixty thousand Moors. In gratitude for this service, a bushel of wheat from every acre in Spain was annually granted to the shrine at Compostella. This tax was not abolished till 1835.

The shrine at Compostella was frequented even by those Christians who lived among the Moors, and the pilgrims brought back minute reports which are thus incorporated in contemporary Moorish annals (see Moh. D. i. 74, ii. 193): "Their Kabah is a colossal idol, which they have in the centre of the church ; they swear by it and repair to it in pilgrimage from the most distant parts, from Rome as well as from other countries, pretending that the tomb which is to be seen within the church is that of Yakob (James), one of the twelve apostles, and the most beloved of Isa (Jesus), may the blessing of God and salutation be on him and on our prophet!" When the Moorish conqueror Al-Mansur entered Santiago, August 10, 997, he razed the town to the ground, sparing only the tomb of the Spaniards' prophet, before which he trembled with a cognate superstition. Nevertheless the body of the saint disappeared at the advent of the infidel, and has never since been found. There is, indeed, a legend that when Diego Gelmirez erected the modern cathedral of Santiago in 1120 he built the relics into the foundations, in order that they might never be pried into by the impertinent curioso or be removed by the enemy. Certainly St. James lies somewhere, for he was heard clashing his armor when Bonaparte invaded Spain. Pilgrimages were stimulated by fresh indulgences granted by the Popes to sinners who came with offerings, and great was the stream of wealthy guilt which poured in ; kings gave gold. and even paupers their mite. They fell off for a time after the Reformation, when, according to Molina, "the damned doctrines of the accursed Luther diminished the numbers of Germans and wealthy English," and the disorderly scenes which were enacted at the shrine finally caused their prohibition in Spain, save under regulations.

Though the Spanish body of St. James has disappeared, there

are many other bodies of the saint preserved in Europe, One is claimed to have been brought to Toulouse in the fourth century. Another body of St. James is said to have been translated into Italy in the fourth century, and now reposes in the church of Zibili, near Milan. The heads of St. James are very numerous: there is one at Toulouse, while two are at Venice (one in the church of St. George, another in the monastery of SS. Philip and James). There are a skull and a vessel of the saint's blood in the church of the Apostles at Rome, a head at Valencia, another at Amalfi, still another at St. Vaast in Artois, and part of a head at Pistoja. Bones, hands, and arms of the saint are scattered about in great numbers, and are shown at Troyes, in Sicily, on the island of Capri, at Pavia, in Bavaria, at Liége, at Cologne, and in other places. Some bones of the saint are shown in the Escorial.

Nevertheless it was the shrine at Compostella which was famous all over Europe in the Middle Ages. The distinguishing badge of pilgrims to this shrine was a scallop-shell worn on the cloak or hat. The adoption of this badge is accounted for by the old legend on the ground that when the miraculous ship bearing St. James's body arrived at Padron it was encrusted with scallop-shells. Erasmus, however, in his "Pilgrimages" suggests a less miraculous reason.

One of his interlocutors meets a pilgrim, and says, "What country has sent you safely back to us, covered with shells, laden with tin and leaden images, and adorned with straw necklaces, while your arms display a row of serpents' eggs?"

"I have been to St. James of Compostella," replies the pilgrim.

"What answer did St. James give to your professions?"

"None; but he was seen to smile, and nod his head, when I offered my presents; and he held out to me this imbricated shell."

"Why that shell rather than any other kind?"

"Because the adjacent sea abounds in them."

Curiously enough, a scallop-shell is borne at the present day by pilgrims in Japan; and in all probability its origin as a pilgrim's badge, both in Europe and in the East, was derived from its use as a primitive cup. dish, or spoon. This idea is corroborated by the crest of Dishington, an old English family, being a scallop-shell,—a punning allusion to the name and to the ancient use of the shell as a dish. And we may add, as a proof of the former popularity of pilgrimages to Compostella, that seventeen English peers and eight baronets carry scallop-shells in their arms as heraldic charges.

Another curious popular survival in England connects oysters with St. James. It is still customary in London to begin eating oysters on his day. Churchill says,—

> July, to whom, with Dog-star in her train,
> St. James gives oysters, and St. Swithin rain.

And a local proverb asserts that "He who eats oysters on St. James's Day will never want money," which may mean that only the wealthy can afford them on this the opening day. But what is more immediately to the point is the fact that in the course of the few days following upon the introduction of oysters for the season the children of the humbler class employ themselves diligently in collecting the shells which have been cast out from taverns and fish-shops, and of these they make piles in various rude forms. By the time that old St. James's Day (the 5th of August) has come about, they have these little fabrics in nice order, with a candle stuck in the top, to be lighted at night. As you thread your way through some of the denser parts of the metropolis, you are apt to find a cone of shells, with its votive light, in the nook of some retired court, with a group of youngsters around it, some of whom will be sure to assail the stranger with a whining claim, "Mind the grotto!" by which is meant a demand for a penny wherewith professedly to keep up the candle. It cannot be doubted that in the grotto thus made we have a memorial of the world-renowned shrine of St. James at Compostella, which may have been formerly erected on the anniversary of St. James by poor persons, as an invitation to the pious who could not visit Compostella to show their reverence to the saint by alms-giving to their needy brethren. (*Book of Days*, vol. ii. p. 122 ; *Notes and Queries*, First Series, vol. i. p. 6.)

Januarius, St. (It. *Gennaro ;* Fr. *Janvier*), patron saint of Naples and its protector from the eruptions of Mount Vesuvius. He is said to have been a native of Naples, to have become Bishop of Benevento, and to have been martyred with several companions in the amphitheatre at Pozzuoli, near Naples, on September 19, A.D. 305. September 19, therefore, is his day in the Roman Martyrology. Among the Greeks the feast of St. Januarius and his companions is celebrated both on that date and on April 21. In Naples besides the great festival on September 19 a minor feast in honor of the translation of St. Januarius is celebrated on the first Sunday in May, and another on December 16.

Various fables have clustered around the acts of this martyr. A furnace is said to have been heated red-hot for three days, into which St. Januarius was thrown. But he escaped unhurt. Then he and two companions were exposed to the beasts in the amphitheatre; but none would touch them. The people, amazed, imputed their preservation to magic, and the martyrs were condemned to be beheaded. This sentence was executed outside the walls of Pozzuoli. A pious woman collected St. Januarius's blood in two vials; in one of them the blood was pure and unmixed, in the other it was mixed with earth. Under the Emperor Constantine, the bones of the martyr were translated to Naples and deposited in a church built in his honor outside the city walls. The woman who had preserved his blood brought the vials to Bishop St. Severus, and when they were placed in contact with the saint's skull the congealed blood liquefied. In the ninth century Sico, Prince of Benevento, took Naples and removed the body of St. Januarius to Benevento, where it remained until May 2, 1497, when King Ferdinand of Aragon brought it back to Naples with great pomp. The skull and the blood, however, had always remained in the latter city.

In 1608 a magnificent chapel dedicated to St. Januarius was constructed in the Neapolitan cathedral. Thither the head and blood of the saint were transferred. They still remain there. The ordinary exposition of the blood is made on the first Sunday in May and daily through the octave of May 2, the anniversary of the translation, on the 19th of September and daily through its octave, and again on December 16, in commemoration of the saint's deliverance of the city from a terrible eruption of Vesuvius in 1631.

Extraordinary expositions are made whenever Naples is threatened or visited with disaster, pestilence, or volcanic eruption. Perhaps the earliest mention in general literature of the miracle of the liquefaction occurs in the "Pandectæ Medicinales Matthæi Silvatici," a book published in 1474 in Naples by the king's surgeon, Angelo Cato. In the dedicatory preface to King Ferdinand he uses these words: "What ought I to say of the blood of that holy martyr which is preserved at Naples with the greatest respect? Is there, among the miracles which in our day take place under the eyes of faithful Christians, one more evident, more undeniable? At a distance from the skull the blood remains in a solid state; when brought near to it, it becomes as liquid as on the day on which it was shed." The Rev. P. N. Lynch, Bishop of Charleston, South Carolina, published five articles on the subject (afterwards gathered into book form) in the *Catholic World* of September, 1871–January, 1872, and has covered the whole ground of fact and argument from the Roman point of view. He maintains that this phenomenon, which during the last two hundred and fifty years has taken place at Naples at least four thousand times, cannot be accounted for by any natural cause, and must therefore be miraculous.

At rare intervals the blood refused to liquefy. Great was the attendant agony of the spectators, great the shock that ran through Naples. Some terrible calamity was believed to be impending over city or kingdom. "In order that everything should go well at Naples," says the Abbé Richard, author of a "Voyage en Italie" (1766), "it is necessary that the liquefaction of the blood of St. Januarius should occur twice a year, in September and May. The hour when this miracle should occur is approximately known. A great crowd presses into the chapel, and demands of the saint, with confused cries, sighs, and beatings of the breast, that he should perform the miracle. When it does not occur with sufficient expedition, a thousand voices are raised with impatient and angry cries of ' *San Gennaro, fa dunque presto !*' which is to say, ' St. Januarius, hurry up !' If unhappily the miracle does not occur, and the crowd catches sight of some stranger whose looks displease them, they believe him to be a heretic whose presence has prevented the liquefaction of the blood, and the stranger runs great risk of his life. Indeed, several cases are recorded of the assassination of strangers under such circumstances."

When General Championnet at the head of a French army took possession of Naples in 1799, he heard that the clergy, hoping to stir the populace against the invaders, had decided that the miracle of St. Januarius should not be performed that year. On September 19 he appeared in the cathedral. The hour arrived. The blood remained congealed. The populace grew restive. The republican general sent one of his aides to the officiating priest with this message: "Tell his reverence that if the blood does not liquefy in five minutes I will order the bombardment of Naples." Long before the five minutes were up, the miracle was performed, amid the enthusiastic plaudits of the crowd.

January. The first month of the year according to the Gregorian calendar. This position is justified by meteorological fact, so far at least as the Northern hemisphere is concerned. Inasmuch as its beginning is near the winter solstice, the year is thus made to present a complete series of the seasonal changes and operations, beginning with the first movements of spring, and ending in the death of all vegetation with winter. Yet it does not hold that position universally. Numa, indeed, who is credited with having introduced it, made it the first month and named it after Janus, the deity presiding over doors, hence appropriately giving title to the opening of the year.

In the Jewish calendar the year began with March 25, and most of the nations of Christendom followed this arrangement until they adopted the Gregorian calendar. (See CALENDAR.) In England the year began on Christmas till the accession of

JANUARY. PLOUGHING.
(From an eleventh-century MS.)

William the Conqueror, when the date was changed to January 1. The Anglo-Saxons called this *Wulfmonath*, because hunger then drove the wolves down into the settlements.

Jerome, St. (Lat. *Hieronymus ;* It. *Geronimo* or *Girolamo ;* Sp. *Gerónimo ;* Fr. *Jérôme, Hiérôme,* or *Gérosme ;* Ger. *Hieronimus*), patron saint of scholars and students, and one of the four Latin Fathers of the Church. His festival is celebrated on September 30.

St. Jerome was born in Stridon about the year 342. He went to Rome to complete his studies, and became a lawyer. At the age of thirty he was baptized, and went to the East to visit the scenes of the life of Christ. He then retired to a desert in Arabia, where he passed several years in study and in doing penance. He returned to Rome, where he preached for three years against the luxury of the Roman clergy and laity. He then retired to a monastery at Bethlehem, and here he died in 420. It was in this monastery that he made his famous translation of the New Testament into Latin, which has ever since been known as the Vulgate. The attributes of St. Jerome in art are books, illustrative of his writings, and a lion, emblematic of the boldness of the saint. There is also a legend that accounts for the association of the lion with this saint. It is related that while at the monastery at Bethlehem the saint saw a lion limping as if in pain. All others fled in terror, but Jerome approached the lion and extracted a thorn from its paw. The grateful lion refused to leave the saint, who made the beast guard an ass which brought wood from a forest. One day a caravan of merchants passed, and they stole the ass while the lion slept. The lion returned to the convent with an air of shame, and Jerome, who believed that the lion had eaten the ass, set the beast to work in the ass's place. At length the caravan passed by again, and the lion, recognizing his old companion, drove the ass and all the camels into the monastery. Whereupon the merchants acknowledged their theft and were pardoned.

St. Jerome was buried at Bethlehem, but his body was said to have been translated to the church of Santa Maria Maggiore at Rome in the thirteenth century. A head of the saint is shown at Nepi, part of the chin at the Vatican, part of a thigh in the church of St. Cecilia, and an arm in the Jesuit church. A jaw and an arm are shown at Florence, at Bologna part of a shank, a finger, and a thumb, part of the skull at Cluny, a finger at Paris, an arm at Malines, two bones at Tournai, a finger at Prague, part of the spine at Cologne in the church of St. Pantaleon, and in the Carthusian church a rib. The head entire is preserved at the Escorial; the tongue is shown on the island of Samos; and various other relics are scattered about.

The fête of San Gerónimo is the harvest festival of the Pueblo Indians in New Mexico. It is celebrated annually at the Pueblo de Taos with ceremonies that are a strange mixture of Catholic ritual and ancestral pagan superstitions. Indians from all the Pueblos, as well as a considerable number of Apaches and Utes from their more distant reservations, and a sprinkling of Mexicans, meet together this day. Many different stories are told of the origin of the feast. One is that hundreds of years ago a chief of the tribe wandered away into the mountains and never returned, and in memory of this all absent Pueblos come home on this day. But it is possible that the Indians have mixed up their own traditions with the priestly legend of St. Jerome's wandering and fasting in the desert. At all events, the image of St. Jerome forms a prominent feature. Early in the morning all who can spare the time from the preparations for the day's sports meet in the village church, where the image is blessed, and then borne forth, by girls chosen for the honor, to the judges' stand. There are three judges, one from each clan and the third selected from among the Apache visitors. The contestants, lightly clad and with gayly painted bodies, line up in front of the judges, and move past sideways, chanting a wild, gay air. A half-dozen medicine-men follow the runners of each clan, groom them, pat their muscles, and cheer them with predictions of success. The men march in this fashion past the pueblo buildings crowded with spectators. At a signal all the young athletes take their places, fifteen from each side being at either end of a course of about seven hundred yards. When all are ready, the judges give the word. Two men dart from the end of the course nearest the pueblo and run swiftly down to the other end. The instant the leader reaches the stone post marking the end of the course, another runner from his side, who has nicely calculated his exact time, rushes past him on the homeward stretch, followed at the distance between the first two runners by another athlete from the competing clan. Thus the race is kept up until all have had a trial, the final victory being the glory of the clan and not of the individual runner. The result shows which side shall bear the statue of San Gerónimo into its pueblo. (*Harper's Young People*, October 3, 1893, p. 829.) Other games of less imminent interest occupy the intervals during the day. A lamb with its legs tied together is hoisted up a pole sixty feet in the air and left to hang there for some hours as an offering, it is said, to Montezuma. The Mexicans practise their favorite game of riding after and trying to catch chickens without dismounting. A hundred horsemen dash madly up and down before the Pueblo after one poor chicken, and if three or four riders seize it at the same time it is instantly torn to pieces amid the shouts of the crowd. Masked Indians run around playing tricks upon spectators, sousing boys into the streams, stealing fruit from the stands of the traders, and throwing dust.

John the Baptist, St. (Fr. *Jean;* It. *Giovanni;* Ger. *Johann*), patron saint against convulsions and epilepsy, which are called in France and Belgium *le mal St.-Jean.* The day of his beheading by order of Herodias, which is ecclesiastically known as the Decollation, is commemorated in the Western calendar on August 29, in the Eastern on September 26. But the great festival of the saint, both East and West, is that of his nativity, on June 24, or Midsummer Day.

This festival has been celebrated by the Church from a remote age. In the fifth century St. Augustine wrote, " This day of the nativity is handed down to us and is this day celebrated. We have received this by tradition from our forefathers, and we transmit it to our descendants to be celebrated with like devotion." He observes that the birthday in lieu of the death-day of the saint is chosen because this saint was sanctified in his mother's womb.

A mystical significance and an infinite number of pagan survivals have crystallized around this holiday from its position in the calendar. For in the months of June and December occur the solstices. With the summer solstice the days reach their maximum of length, and thenceforth decrease until the minimum is reached with the winter solstice, when they once more increase. In connection with this fact the words of the Baptist, " He must increase, but I must decrease," acquire a new and fanciful meaning. St. Augustine says, " At the Nativity of

Christ the days increase in length, on that of John they decrease. When the Saviour of the world is born, the days lengthen; but when the last prophet comes into the world, the days suffer curtailment."

But long before the dawn of Christianity the period of the summer solstice was almost universally associated with the rites of sun-worship. Pagan customs survived in the Christian festival. Some of these customs were the subjects of ecclesiastical prohibition. St. Augustine forbade the inhabitants of Libya from bathing on the eve of St. John's Day, as a pagan custom. Petrarch in a letter addressed to Cardinal Colonna describes how in 1330 the women of Cologne were wont at sunset on the eve of St. John to wash their arms and feet in the Rhine, thinking that thus they washed off all the potential ills of the year to come. This custom still survives in the Walloon country. St. Eligius forbade those whom he had converted in Gaul to celebrate St. John's Eve with round dances and other pagan customs, and the fourth canon of the Council of Leptines, or Lestines, in 743, prohibited the pagan custom of making new fire on this day by rubbing two sticks together. The usage of burning Beltane fires (see MAY-DAY) has continued from paganism to the present day, and is observed on Midsummer Eve nearly all through Europe. But the solar origin of the custom is forgotten, and the practice is justified by the text "He was a burning and a shining light," words used by Christ to qualify the Baptist.

In France La Saint Jean was formerly celebrated both in town and in country. It did not disappear from Paris until the Revolution. On the Place de Grève a tree was raised, and royalty itself came in solemn state to set fire to "St. John's tree." Louis XIV. was the last king who took part in this ceremony, and he did so only once. When the tree was burnt out, the people carefully gathered up the ashes and brought them home as harbingers of good fortune. A cruel practice that lasted until the eighteenth century was to hang up a sack or basket full of cats in the branches of the burning tree. In the register of the city of Paris may be read this memorandum: "Paid to Lucas Pommereux, one of the commissaires of the quays, 100 sous for having furnished during the three years ending on St. John's Day, 1573, all the cats that were needed for the fire, according to custom, and also for having furnished, last year, when the king assisted, a fox to give pleasure to his majesty, likewise for having furnished a large cloth sack wherein the said cats were gathered."

In Brittany the Baalfires blaze on every hill on the eve of La Saint Jean. All night the peasants dance around them, clad in their holiday clothes, to the sound of the binion (a sort of rustic hautboy) and the shepherd's horn. The girl who dances round nine St. John's fires before midnight is sure to be married within the year. In many parishes the curate himself goes in procession with banner and cross to light the sacred fire.

In England and Scotland, and even in Ireland, the Beltane fires, where they survive at all, are usually lighted on May-Day, rather than on Midsummer Eve. But in Wales midsummer is preferred.

In remote and primitive districts the people still believe that dancing in a ring around a bonfire or leaping through its flames is calculated to insure good luck to the performers, and to serve as a protection from witchcraft and other malign influences during the ensuing year.

In Servia the people believe that out of respect to the memory of St. John the sun three times stands still in the sky on the feast of his nativity.

The shepherds at this time of the year go round their sheep-folds and enclosures, carrying torches formed of the resinous bark of the birch-tree; then they go up to the hills, where they allow the torches to burn themselves out, while they give them-selves over to frolic and amusement.

Bonfires are still lighted in many parts of Germany on Mid-summer Eve. On either side of the bonfire poles are erected, the tops of the poles being joined by a wire or rope, from which are suspended prizes,—hams, sausages, neckties, pipes, etc. The young men of the neighborhood assemble in numbers to compete for the prizes. Each competitor, mounted on a horse, must ride at the bonfire, and while the horse is in the act of jumping over it, his rider has to try to snatch a prize from overhead. The sport is kept up until late at night, when the feast is concluded with a carouse at the village inn.

In Spain, as John Hay tells us, St. John's Eve is celebrated with noisy festivities by the light of moon and stars and gas. A feature of the occasion are the buñuelos, or fritters, which are cooked and consumed on this night to the number of hundreds of thousands in Madrid alone. All over the Prado may be seen the buñuelo-stands. A great caldron of boiling oil is hung over a fire, beside it is a mighty bowl of dough. "The buñolero with the soft precision of machinery dips his hand into the bowl, and makes a delicate ring of the tough dough, which he throws into the bubbling caldron. It remains but a few seconds, and his grimy acolyte picks it out with a long wire and throws it on the tray for sale. They are eaten warm, the droning cry continually sounding, 'Buñuelos! Calientitos!' It is like a vast gitano-camp. The hurrying crowd which is going nowhere, the blazing fires, the cries of the venders, the songs of the majos under the great trees of the Paseo, the purposeless hurly-burly, and, above, the steam of the boiling oil and the dust raised by the myriad feet, form together a striking and vivid picture." (JOHN HAY: *Castilian Days*, pp. 107, 108.)

John the Evangelist, St. The Church commemorates the death-day of this saint on December 27, and fixes the year

ST. JOHN RECEIVED AT THE TEMPLE.
(From " Historia S. Joannis Evangelistæ," Holztafeldruck, 1465.)

at A.D. 101. According to the traditions which supplement the New Testament story, he remained at Jerusalem until the death of the Virgin, and then preached the gospel in Asia Minor, living chiefly at Ephesus. In the persecution of Domitian he was taken to Rome. He was plunged into a caldron of boiling oil, but received no injury. On the scene of this miracle, which is just outside the Latin gate, stands the chapel of San Giovanni in Olio. He drank a cup of poison at the command of the Emperor, but the poison likewise had no effect. This cup is exhibited on great occasions in the church of Santa Croce at Rome. Then he was sent to labor in the mines at Patmos, where he is believed to have written his Revelations, which are traditionally said to have been manifested to him on a Sunday in the year 96. With Nerva's accession he was set at liberty, and returned to Ephesus, where he died. An ancient tradition asserted that he never died in the ordinary sense, but was assumed into heaven. This belief was ably confuted by St. Jerome and St. Augustine, and is now rejected by the Church. The received opinion is that he was buried on a mountain just outside the walls of Ephesus. Enthusiastic pilgrims gradually carried away his dust, which was found to be efficacious for various diseases. Butler informs us that a "stately church stood formerly over this tomb, which is at present a Turkish mosque."

Jordan, Fête of the, or **Benediction of the Waters** of the Neva, in St. Petersburg. An imposing ceremony at which the Czar of Russia officiates with his court on the Epiphany (January 6). Religious pomp joins with military glory to enhance its brilliancy. A pavilion, richly decorated, is built on the frozen river. A hole is bored through the ice to admit of the cross being dipped into the waters, which are solemnly blessed· by the metropolitan ·and his clergy with prayers that they may be beneficial to man and fertilizing to the earth during the ensuing year. These prayers are accompanied by liturgical hymns sung by the choirs of the Winter Palace. Up to the end of the reign of Nicholas I. tradition demanded that the Emperor should follow the procession bareheaded and without cloak, the members of his household all following his example. Even the ladies in the palace used to go down into the snow *décolletées,* their delicate arms and bosoms exposed to the rigorous temperature. At present the old usages have become modified, and cloaks are tolerated. There was even a time when the ceremony gave occasion to explosions of fanaticism. As soon as the priest had plunged his crucifix in the river, mujiks would break holes in the ice and throw themselves into the sanctified waters, with the persuasion that they had acquired the power of washing away their sins and curing all their bodily ills.

The Don, the Volga, and minor streams are likewise blessed on the same day by the local clergy of the river-side towns, and at many places the custom of bathing in the icy waters still survives in all its original fury. The London *Lancet* in 1896 published a description of such a scene in the town of Sviaga, on the Volga : " From ten until one o'clock there was an endless succession of bathers of all ages, some even bringing children as young as seven and dipping them into the river through the broken ice. They all undressed and dressed on the banks, or on the ice in the centre of the river, where some enthusiasts bored a hole through the ice and plunged in, with the additional risk of being carried away by the current."

Joseph, St. (Lat. *Josephus;* It. *Giuseppe;* Ger. *Josef.*) His festival is celebrated on March 19.

But little is related of St. Joseph in the Gospel. He was of the lineage of David and the tribe of Judah, and dwelt in Nazareth, where he followed the trade of a carpenter. Legends add that he was old and a widower when he married Mary, and assert that there were many suitors for her hand, who assembled at the call of the priest Zacharias and deposited their staves or wands in the temple for a night. For it had been revealed to Zacharias that God would show a sign as to who should be the husband of Mary. In the morning it was discovered that Joseph's wand had budded into leaves and flowers, and a white dove issued from it, showing him to be the chosen one. The other suitors broke their wands in despair, and one of them, Agabus, fled to Mount Carmel and became an anchorite. In many pictures the espousals took place in the open air, outside the temple, for with the Jews marriage was a civil contract rather than a religious ceremony.

The next appearance of St. Joseph in the legends is on the journey to Bethlehem, when looking back Joseph saw that the face of Mary betokened weariness and pain, but when he looked again she smiled. When they came to Bethlehem Joseph sought a midwife, but when they came to the stable Mary was sitting with her infant on her knees, and the place was filled with light brighter than the day. Four times angelic messengers appeared to guide St. Joseph in his mission. A dream assured him of the purity of Mary; another dream commanded him to flee into Egypt; the third vision told Joseph to return to Judæa, and a fourth guided him on his journey. After the return to Nazareth Joseph is associated only with a quiet domestic life. The time of his death is a disputed point. Some assert that it occurred when Jesus was nine years old, while others make it nine years later. The 20th of July had been observed in the East as the anniversary of Joseph's death before he became popular in the West. In art he is represented as the caretaker and guide during the journey into Egypt, and in pictures of the Holy Family he is generally in an attitude of quiet and contemplative admiration.

Jubilee. This word, generally used at present to denote the semi-centennial celebration of some important event, does not come from the Latin *jubilare*, "to shout for joy," though etymologists have frequently fallen into this not unnatural pitfall, but from the Jewish *yobel*, meaning literally the blast of a trumpet, and, by extension, the year of jubilee which was announced by this blast. According to the law in Leviticus xxv., this was a semi-centennial epoch of general restoration and emancipation, when liberty was to be proclaimed through the

PROCLAIMING A PAPAL JUBILEE.
(From Picart.)

land with the blowing of trumpets in the synagogue. The year of jubilee was the fiftieth year, each being separated from its predecessor by seven sabbaths of years,—*i.e.*, $7 \times 7 = 49$. During the jubilee year the land was not tilled, all lands that had been sold were restored to the original owners or their heirs, and all bondsmen of Hebrew blood were liberated.

The design is supposed to have been the maintenance of a kind of balance between different tribes and families, to prevent the growth of a few rich land-owners amidst a generally impoverished community, and to increase alike the growth of population and the fertility of the soil. The system is known to have been adopted for a time; but commentators differ in opinion alike as to the period of its practical adoption and the period when it fell into disuse.

The Christian Church adopted the term jubilee from the Jewish, and the jubilee in two forms, the ordinary and the extraordinary, is still an institution in the Roman Church as a period of remission from the penal consequences of sin. Extraordinary jubilees are proclaimed on specially important occasions. The ordinary jubilee is now granted once in twenty-five years. The institution dates from the pontificate of Boniface VIII., who in 1300 issued a bull in honor of the new century, granting a plenary indulgence to all pilgrim visitors of Rome during that year on condition of their penitently confessing their sins and visiting the church of St. Peter and St. Paul fifteen times if they were strangers and thirty times if residents of the city. Boniface's plan was that of a centennial celebration, but the period was shortened successively to fifty, forty-three, and twenty-five years, where it remains at present. For the pilgrimage to Rome have now been substituted certain works of charity and devotion.

The bull announcing a jubilee is published on the Ascension Day preceding the beginning of the jubilee year. The publication takes place in the Sistine Chapel after the Pope has celebrated the Benediction of the Blessed Sacrament. An apostolical subdeacon reads the Latin bull to the Papal court, and another subdeacon reads the Italian translation to the people. As soon as the reading is over, the twelve trumpeters in ordinary to the Pope commence to blow a blast, and a few minutes later twelve hunters join in with the ringing of their silver bugles, and simultaneously the artillery of the castle of St. Angelo discharges a salute.

On the fourth Sunday of Advent the apostolical subdeacons again publish the bull of the jubilee, and on the three days immediately preceding the Christmas festivals the bells of the city announce from all sides the solemn jubilee season which is to open on the morrow.

The 24th day of November in the Holy Year all the secular and regular clergy assemble in the Apostolic Palace, and thence go in procession to St. Peter's Church. But when the clergy have arrived in the great square facing the church they find the doors of this church closed, and all the entrances to the portico occupied by guards who prevent the crowds from entering.

DEPARTURE OF THE CARDINALS.

Meanwhile the Pope, the cardinals, and the bishops in white vestments with their mitres on their heads assemble in the Sistine Chapel, where his Holiness intones the " Veni Creator Spiritus," holding in his hand a lighted wax taper. He then names three cardinals as Legates *a Latere* and despatches them to open the doors of St. John Lateran, Santa Maria Maggiore, and St. Paul Outside the Walls. These cardinals, after having received on their knees the command of his Holiness, go in state to these churches, preceded by trumpeters, oboe-players, and troops of people armed, if one might say so, half in the panoply of war and half in that of religion. (Picart, vol. i. p. 171.)

But they do not take their departure until the Pope has opened the Holy Door of the Sistine Chapel which leads into St. Peter's. A prelate presents him with a golden hammer, which he takes in his right hand. Followed by his clergy, he approaches the door and strikes it three times, saying, " Aperite mihi portas jus-titiæ" (" Open for me the doors of justice"), to which the clergy respond, " This is the eternal door which the just shall enter." Meanwhile the master masons set to work in removing the little wall which has temporarily closed the Holy Door. When this has been torn down and the bricks have been distributed as relics among the spectators, the Penitents of St. Peter's sweep the doorway clean with their brooms. Then the Pope and the clergy march singing into St. Peter's Church, where the immense crowds have by this time been admitted. The jubilee ends by the closure of the Holy Doors. They are walled up again, in the presence of the Pope, the cardinals, and the clergy, on Christmas Eve one year after the jubilee opening. His Holiness lays the first stone in its place.

From Jews and Catholics the term jubilee passed into general use to indicate celebrations which had nothing to do with either Jerusalem or Rome, but commemorated the completion of some important historical, literary, or religious cycle, usually of fifty years, but sometimes more and sometimes less, and was subsequently extended to any monster celebration, independent of dates.

The royal jubilees in England are examples of the use of the word in its more legitimate sense. Only four of England's monarchs have lived to rule for fifty years: Henry III., who sat on the throne for fifty-six years; Edward III., who lived for six months after completing his jubilee; George III., who ruled for fifty-nine years; and Queen Victoria, who has outstripped all her predecessors.

Respecting the celebration of Henry's fifty years' rule very little is recorded; but concerning that of Edward we learn that "he laid hold of that era as the occasion of his performing many popular acts of government; that he had given orders to issue out general and special pardons without paying any fees, for recalling all exiles, and setting at liberty all debtors to the crown and all prisoners for political matters." The Parliament, on their parts, not to be wanting in gratitude, having presented their petitions, on the day of their rising voted the king a duty of twenty-six shillings and eightpence on every sack of wool for three years, besides continuing the former duties upon wools, fells, and skins. The whole jubilee year (1377) was spent by the nobility in hunting through the great forests of England and in other magnificent diversions on which the king laid out an immense sum.

Particulars as to how George III.'s jubilee was celebrated are necessarily more plentiful. How best to commemorate it caused no little preliminary concern to his majesty's subjects. The occasion was indeed an auspicious one, for a like occurrence had not taken place in England for nearly four and a half centuries.

George III. himself pointed the way by many gracious acts. He was the chief subscriber to a fund for liberating all persons confined for debt in the United Kingdom, he granted free pardon to all deserters from the army or navy and to all prisoners of war save only the French, and granted brevet promotions to officers in the army and navy.

Strictly speaking, the actual day of the jubilee ceremonies was at the end of forty-nine years, not fifty. The reign began October 25, 1760, and the jubilee was held October 25, 1809, the day that completed the forty-ninth and commenced the fiftieth year of his reign. This corresponded so far with the ancient Hebrew period.

At Windsor, on this occasion, the morning was ushered in by the mustering of troops, the firing of cannon, and the sound of trumpets and drums. The king, the queen, and other members of the royal family attended divine service; and congratulations afterwards poured in from various quarters.

At one o'clock the queen, with a brilliant retinue, and the mayor and corporation of Windsor, walked to the Bachelors' Acre,—a large piece of vacant ground near the centre of the town,—where an ox and some sheep were roasting whole, the former having been put on the spit at two o'clock in the morning, so that it might be cooked by one in the afternoon. The royal party were received by fifty bachelors, who conducted them to the fire at which the ox was roasting, after which they inspected the culinary arrangements. The butchers who had charge of the cooking of the ox and sheep, the latter of which were put on the fire at nine o'clock, and were stuffed with potatoes, were (shade of Beau Brummel!) dressed in blue frocks and silk stockings. When the animals were ready, they were distributed among the crowd in the presence of the royal party, who were offered and graciously accepted the first slices, the same being served up to them on silver plates by the butchers and bachelors.

At Frogmore an entertainment of brilliant gayety was given by the queen in the evening. The gardens were lighted up with lamps innumerable; the walks and avenues were thronged with the nobility and gentry; transparencies and tiny temples were visible at various points; fireworks blazed up with great splendor; and on a small lake or piece of water in front of the house two triumphal cars drawn by two sea-horses each, one car containing a figure of Neptune and the other a figure of Britannia, moved majestically on the bosom of the waters, followed by four boats filled with persons dressed to represent Tritons, etc. These last were to have been composed of choristers, who were to have sung "God Save the King" on the water, but, unfortunately, the crowd assembled was so immense that those who were to have sung could not gain entrance.

Like celebrations took place in the various towns throughout the country, the proceedings in each instance to a great extent necessarily resembling each other. The day was generally observed as a national holiday; and in almost all corporate towns a civic procession to the church or cathedral was one of the chief features of the occasion; whilst in those places in which military were stationed, numerous volleys were fired by the soldiers in honor of the event. Feasting was indulged in to an enormous extent by all classes, the poor being entertained by their more wealthy neighbors; and the inauguration of charitable institutions and benevolent societies was a characteristic of the jubilee. In keeping with the custom of the times, ox-roastings took place all over the country; and "good old ale" was distributed with the greatest lavishness. In rural districts, most of the nobility and gentry kept open house and provided entertainments for their poorer neighbors; employers feasted their servants, and "The King, and long life to him," was toasted with the utmost enthusiasm throughout the land. Dancing was carried on upon the village green; and balls, bonfires, and pyrotechnic displays concluded the rejoicings of a day on which high and low, rich and poor, had vied with one another in showing loyalty to their sovereign.

The jubilee in honor of Queen Victoria's semi-centennial was celebrated on June 20, 1887, and was an even more triumphant success than that of George III. As the *Saturday Review* said on the succeeding June 25, " Never in modern times has there been in this country a court pageant to compare in splendor and stateliness with that of last Tuesday; and no less indisputable is it that London, the London which we know, or our fathers remember, has never adorned and illuminated her league-long thoroughfares with anything like the abundance of decoration and the glory of gaslight with which they have been glowing daily and blazing nightly throughout the week. Above all, it is a fact as completely and much more importantly beyond question that the great ceremonial in the Abbey, after Corinthian eloquence has done its worst on the historical, political, and poetic aspects of the scene, stands out before us still with all its majesty unimpaired. The Queen receiving the homage of her children and grandchildren on the most historically venerable spot of English ground, and after solemn investiture in the royal robes which she assumed half a century ago to enter upon the happiest and, for her own share in it, the most beneficent reign in our history, —this we feel to be a spectacle which still appeals with undiminished force to our pride of patriotism, to our reverence for antiquity, to our respect for faithfulness in the discharge of the highest of national duties, and, lastly, to that combination of all these instincts with the added feeling of personal regard which goes to make up the modern and, so to say, 'rationalistic,' but none the less powerful, enduring, and politically valuable, sentiment of loyalty to the crown."

The Diamond Jubilee of 1897 celebrated the completion of the sixtieth year of Queen Victoria's reign,—the longest in English history.

Where is the thing to end? Not a day but might be made out by adventurers in chronology, especially by the students of M. Comte's calendar, to be the fiftieth, or one-hundredth, or five-hundredth anniversary of somebody's birth or somebody's death who has won his place in the Valhalla of Memory. There is no single year in the eighteenth century in which some eminent individual will not be found to have been born, to have died, or, at the worst, to have flourished.

Judas in Effigy. The burning, hanging, or scourging of effigies of Judas Iscariot was once a common practice during Holy Week in certain portions of Spain, and still survives in Mexico, as well as in Portugal and all countries where Portuguese blood predominates. It is also practised by Portuguese sailors in whatever port they may happen to be at the appropriate date. This is sometimes Good Friday and sometimes Holy Saturday, while sometimes the agony is prolonged through both days. The *Cork Examiner* in 1868 described a scourging publicly administered to Judas on Good Friday. The traitor was led through the streets in a solemn procession, twenty men marching in front singing an "epithalamium," as the reporter has chosen to call it. The effigy of Judas was laid upon an open bier arranged in the blue shirt and long boots of a stevedore. On returning to the ship the effigy was hung to the yard-arm and fired into with pistols.

The following extract is taken from the *London Times* (April 5, 1874): "At daybreak of Good Friday a block of wood, roughly carved to imitate the Betrayer, and clothed in an ordinary sailor's suit, with a red worsted cap on its head, was hoisted by a rope round its neck into the fore-rigging; the crews of the various vessels then went to chapel, and on their return, about eleven A.M., the figure was lowered from the rigging, and cast into the dock, and ducked three times. It was then hoisted on board, and after being kicked round the deck was lashed to the capstan. The crew, who had worked themselves into a state of frantic excitement, then with knotted ropes lashed the effigy till every vestige of clothing had been cut to tatters. During this process the ship's bell kept up an incessant clang, and the captains of the ships served out grog to the men. Those not engaged in the

flogging kept up a sort of rude chant intermixed with denuncia-
tions of the Betrayer. The ceremony ended with the burning
of the effigy amid the jeers of the crowd."

In Lisbon itself the ceremony is kept up with infinite gusto.
Good Friday is there a day of silence and mourning. The hundreds of bell-towers hold their brazen tongues, military bands,
church organs, and pianos are stilled. The whole city sinks into
penitential silence.

With sunrise on Saturday things stir outside. A mysterious
activity begins on the streets, and the Portuguese street-urchin
offers to contribute his last ten reis towards the universal pleasure.
"Judas" is the order of the day, and the Betrayer appears in
thousands of varieties in effigy. There is scarcely a house in
front of which there is not a grotesquely attired figure, of life
size, with a hideous face and a long beard, set upon a funeral
pile. And not only at houses and gardens do we find them, but
also high up in the air on ropes drawn across the streets hang
the fantastical images and caricatures of the lost one. Here and
there some pitiful soul has added a woman for company, so that
he shall not be alone in the dread hour which is in store for him.

The multitude crowd each other in the streets; rich and poor,
old and young, are crushed together. With impatience they
await the great moment. At last the bell of the Se, the beautiful, grand cathedral, rings forth a warning of the approach of
Easter, and then arise an unexampled noise, a shouting, a rejoicing, a laughing, and a cannonade which mocks that of Metz
and Sedan.

The bodies of the unfortunate Judases are filled with powder
and straw; they explode with dreadful noise, and immediately
all the Judases are consumed by the flames. In a few minutes
the whole city is naturally enveloped in the thickest smoke, and
those possessing the sense of smell quickly flee homeward, or
possibly out as far as the blue sea to breathe fresh air again.
When the fun is over the streets are in great disorder, and it is
difficult work during the few remaining afternoon hours to give
the city a holiday air.

In the island of Madeira, a Portuguese dependency, Judas was
officially abolished in 1889, because it had become more and more
the custom to make the effigy resemble some official upon whom
the people had ceased to smile. When it was a foreign consul
that was caricatured the government smiled, when it was the
mayor of Funchal it frowned, and finally when the august dignity
of the governor of Funchal was subjected to contumely it suppressed the custom altogether.

Judas is hanged and burnt all over South America. The only
place in North America where the custom survives is Mexico.

On Good Friday the effigies make their appearance. The apostle is held up to public loathing in an infinite variety of ways. In all the plazas of the city booths are erected, where grotesque figures, usually made of pasteboard and attired in gaudy-colored paper costumes, are hung on a line awaiting purchasers. They are designed to represent the man who betrayed Christ. The more hideous the physiognomy and shape the more certain that particular Judas is to find a purchaser. There are also sold numerous children's toys, about which there is always some grim suggestion of the fate that befell the recreant apostle. The most common of these are crudely made little wagons, to be drawn by the child through the street, to the axles of which are attached flexible strips of wood, that strike against the wheels in such a way as to give out a loud, clacking sound. This is intended to represent the cracking of the bones of Judas in eternal torment.

On Holy Saturday morning in Mexico city your eyes are kept even busier than your ears. Whichever way you may walk you see in all the streets much the same strange sights. In every block a line is stretched across the street from house to house, and a hideous effigy is hanging there like a lynched felon. It is Judas again,—Judas everywhere! He hangs there limp and ugly, swaying in the breeze, and groups of women and children shout defiance at him from below, while waiting impatiently for the signal of the poor wretch's final doom. It comes instantaneously in all parts of the city. The first stroke of twelve on the big cathedral clock consigns the thousands of swinging figures to the flames.

All Mexico turns out to witness the wild scenes that ensue on the moment of noon. The biggest throngs are always gathered in front of the Jockey Club, on San Francisco Street, the principal thoroughfare of the city. Here the ceremony consists of something more than the simple burning of a paper effigy. Judas himself is accorded the distinction of more elaborate paraphernalia. He is represented sitting astride a horse. His steed is only pasteboard, but its accoutrements are real. There is a real bridle on the horse's head, and a handsome Mexican saddle, ornamented with silver trappings, holds the cavalier, who is himself dressed in a genuine charro costume, with a stripe formed of silver dollars on his trousers. He wears handsome riding-boots mounted with silver spurs, and on his head is a gorgeous sombrero with a silver band. Nor is this all that entitles the brilliant Judas to the attention of the waiting crowd below. He and his horse have been fed on silver coins until they are fat with the diet.

No wonder the shouting and struggling multitude are impatient for the coming of noon! At last a servant comes out of the big door of the Jockey Club, carrying a lighted taper on the end of a long pole. He is greeted with a cheer of welcome by the waiting crowds. Then the shouting gives place to absolute silence, the silence of keen expectancy. In all the huge throng every individual assumes an attitude of listening. Finally the signal comes. Away over all the city roars the big bell in the cathedral tower. Before the first stroke has exhausted its reverberations a mighty shout and a sound as of a thousand cannon burst upon the air. The man with the lighted taper ignites the fuse that hangs from the pendent effigy. The little spark dashes quickly up the thread, and in an instant reaches the deposit of gunpowder inside the equestrian effigy. There is a thunderous explosion, and poor Judas is scattered to the winds. His sombrero falls here, his saddle is hurled there, and wherever his dismembered anatomy or trappings land, a mad, impetuous rush ensues, and men with torn garments and bruised bodies are piled on top of one another, a struggling mass, on the pavement. And steadily continues the downfall of silver coins from the burning débris overhead, encouraging other fierce combats among the Indians. When the last shred has fallen from the rope and the lucky ones have pocketed their spoils, or made off with them through the crowd, those that are left of the huge throngs on the street turn to the crowds at the windows and petition for more of the silver rainfall. For quite an hour the people at the windows continue to toss coins of all values to the ragged mobs. Then, little by little, the multitude grows less on the streets, and the celebration is over.

Juggernaut, Car of. Juggernaut, more properly Jaganâtha, the Lord of the World, is an alternative title for Krishna, one of the avatars or incarnations of Vishnu. The famous temple of Juggernaut is in the town of Puri, which is situated on the Bay of Bengal in the province of Orissa. The whole province of Orissa has for twenty centuries been the holy land of the Hindoos. Its happy inhabitants live secure of a reception into the world of spirits; and even those who visit it and bathe in its sacred rivers obtain remission of their sins. Every town is filled with temples, every village has its monastery, every hill-top far up the mountain sides is crowned with a shrine. But Puri is its Holy of Holies. Its thirty thousand citizens hold their ground rent-free, upon condition of the performance of certain services in and about the temples.

The temple of Juggernaut stands in a spacious square area enclosed by a lofty wall. The enclosure is shared by one hundred and twenty other temples of all sizes, dedicated to various gods. Over them all towers the great pagoda in a tapering elliptical curve to the height of two hundred feet from the ground. The pagoda is properly dedicated to Krishna, but Siva and his wife and sister Subhadra (which is but another name for Kali) are objects of almost equal adoration. The three idols representing these deities are rude logs coarsely fashioned from the waist up in human form,—the same carved by Vishnu himself. On certain festivals golden hands are fastened to the short stumps which project from the shoulders of Juggernaut. The priests give a spiritual significance to the lack of limbs. "The Lord of the World," they say, "needs neither hands nor feet to work his purposes among men."

The service of the temple consists of a daily round of oblations, and of sumptuous ceremonies at special seasons of the year. The offerings are only fruits, flowers, and simple articles of food, such as rice, pulse, butter, milk, salt, vegetables, cocoanuts, and ginger, which are offered up to the images and then eaten by the priests. The entire value of them is put down at £4 8*s.* 4*d.* a day, or £1572 a year. Four times a day the gates are closed while the god is at his meals, attended by a few of his most favored servants. At the door stand a group of ascetics singing his praises, while in the pillared hall the dancing-girls amuse him with voluptuous gyrations.

There are twenty-four high festivals in the year, each occupying several days, or even weeks. At the Red Powder Festival, occurring about Easter, and lasting three weeks, a boat procession is formed on the sacred lake. At the Bathing Festival the images are brought down to the lake, and a proboscis is fastened to their noses, so as to give them the appearance of Ganesa, the elephant-god of the aboriginal tribes. But the Rath Jatra, or Car Festival, is the great event of the religious year. This falls in the month of June or July, according as the months of the Hindoo calendar fall. Its object is to convey Juggernaut, with his brother and sister, from the temple to his country-house, a mile distant.

For weeks before the time the pilgrims come trooping to Puri at the rate of thousands a day. The temple cooks have made their calculations for feeding ninety thousand mouths; for the doctrine is studiously inculcated that no food must be cooked except in the temple kitchen. Each image has a separate car. That of Juggernaut is thirty-five feet square, with wheels sixteen feet in diameter; the others are smaller. When the sacred images are placed in their chariots, the multitude fall on their knees and bow their foreheads in the dust. Then they lay hold of the ropes, and drag the heavy cars down the broad street. Before and behind drums beat and cymbals clash, while from the platforms of the cars the priests shout obscene songs and stories, accompanied by lascivious gestures, amid the shouts and applause of the multitude.

And so the dense mass, tugging, sweating, singing, praying, and swearing, drag the cars slowly along. The journey is but a mile, yet it takes several hours to accomplish it. Once arrived at the country-house, the crowds return to the vicinity of the temple, to spend their time in riot and debauchery. After eight days the ceremony of the Volta rath, or the bringing back of the cars and the idols, takes place. But Lord Juggernaut finds no willing hands among the exhausted debauchees who were erstwhile his coursers. Indeed, he would probably never get back at all, but for the aid of the professional pullers, a special body of forty-two hundred peasants of the neighboring region.

All this is bad enough. But there appears to be no foundation for the oft-repeated story of thousands of pilgrims throwing themselves under the wheels of the car of Juggernaut in the hope of attaining bliss. It is obvious, of course, that in a closely packed, eager throng of a hundred thousand men and women, many of them unaccustomed to exposure or hard labor, and all of them tugging and straining to the utmost under the blazing tropical sun, deaths must occasionally occur. There have, doubtless, been instances of pilgrims throwing themselves under the wheels in a frenzy of religious excitement. But such instances have always been rare, and are now unknown. At one time several unhappy people were killed or injured every year, but they were almost invariably cases of accidental trampling. The few suicides that did occur were for the most part cases of diseased and miserable persons who took this means to put themselves out of pain. The official returns put this beyond doubt.

But in another aspect the victims of Juggernaut far exceed the numbers ascribed to them by fiction. Puri is perhaps the filthiest city on earth. It contains about seven thousand houses. These furnish poor accommodations for a hundred thousand pilgrims. In dry weather, indeed, the spiritual army can sleep out in the open air. But the Car Festival usually falls at the beginning of the rainy season, when the water pours down in almost solid sheets. Every lane and alley becomes a torrent or a stinking canal. The pilgrims must seek the lodging-houses, and five houses out of six are lodging-houses compared with which our poorest tenement-houses are palaces of health and comfort.

One of the most beautiful institutions in Puri also becomes a means of death. This is the almost sacramental ceremony of eating the sacred rice. Portions of cooked rice are sanctified by being brought into the presence of Juggernaut. This food is so holy that it wipes away all distinctions of caste or sect. The highest may eat it with the lowest. A priest will not refuse it from a Christian. This is the common food of all pilgrims. When freshly cooked, it is not unwholesome; but only a small part of it is eaten fresh, and not a grain of it must be thrown away. In twenty-four hours putrefactive fermentation sets in, and in forty-eight hours it becomes a loathsome mass of putrid matter unfit for human use,—dangerous to a person in robust health, and deadly to the wayworn pilgrims.

What wonder that the cholera makes its regular appearance! And even when the disease does not become epidemic the mortality is fearful, especially on the return journey. The estimates of the number of deaths among the pilgrims to Juggernaut vary from twelve thousand to fifty thousand a year.

(See "Orissa," by W. W. Hunter, London, 1872; Bruce's "Scenes and Sights in the East," 1857.)

Julian Hospitator, St. (It. *Giuliano Ospitale;* Fr. *Julien l'Hospitalier*), the patron of hospitals, and (erroneously) of ferrymen, boatmen, travellers, and wandering minstrels. In the most ancient calendars his festival is marked for January 6, which is held to be the probable date of his martyrdom, but, owing to the concurrence of the Epiphany, it was deferred in different churches to different dates. At present January 9 is the date generally agreed on.

St. Julian was born of noble parents at Antinoe, in Egypt. When he was eighteen years old his parents wished him to marry, but Julian was averse to the idea, as he wished to devote himself to a religious life. But it is related that Christ appeared to him in a dream and bade him accede to the wishes of his parents, telling him that he and his wife would live in chastity and enter into the kingdom of heaven as virgins. Thereupon Julian married a maiden named Basilissa, who was noted for her piety. On the night of their marriage the pair, according to old chroniclers, enjoyed celestial visions and saw their names written in the Book of Life, which further strengthened them in their determination to live in chastity. They devoted their revenues to relieving the poor and sick, and turned their house into a hospital. From this circumstance Julian is known as the Hospitaller. Basilissa died first, and some years afterwards Julian met his death during the persecution of Maximin II., A.D. 313. The skull of St. Julian, said to have been brought out of the East into France during the popedom of Gregory the Great, is his only extant relic. A part is preserved in the monastery of Morigny, near Etampes, and part in the church of St. Basilissa, at Paris. In art St. Julian and St. Basilissa are represented holding the same lily-stalk, or looking on the Book of Life wherein their names are written. Certain legends repeated by St. Antoninus but rejected by the Church have given occasion to the Italian painters to represent St. Julian as a sportsman, with a hawk in his hand, and to the French painters to represent him as a boatman in a barge. In France, therefore, ferrymen, bargemen, and postilions kept his feast as that of their principal patron.

July. As the fifth month in the old Roman year, this was called Quintilis, or fifth. It was the birth-month of Julius Cæsar, and after his death Mark Antony named it Julius in his honor. In the old Alban calendar it had thirty-six days. Romulus reduced the number to thirty-one, and Numa to thirty, but Julius

JULY. HAYMAKING.

Cæsar again made it thirty-one. The early Saxons called it *Hegmonath*, it being the month in which they usually mowed and made their hay-harvest. They also knew it as *Mædmonath*, the meads being then in bloom.

July the Fourteenth. (Fr. *Le Quatorze Juillet*.) The anniversary of the taking of the Bastille by a Parisian mob in 1789, and to-day the national festival of the French Republic. The name Bastille is a general one for a fortress flanked by bastions, but is applied specifically to a huge structure which, originally a castle for the defence of Paris, became in later times a famous prison. Here partly in the towers and partly in the cellars below the level of the ground were confined the victims of political, ecclesiastical, or family hate, often so effectually removed from the outside world that when they came to die their very names and the reasons for their incarceration had been forgotten.

The Bastille commanded by its guns the workingmen's quarter in the Faubourg St.-Antoine, and its lofty walls, surrounded by a deep moat, seemed almost impregnable. Yet on July 14, 1789, it was attacked and taken by a mob with twenty cannon, after a feeble defence by the governor Delaunay and his small garrison of eighty-two old soldiers and thirty-two Swiss. Only seven prisoners were found and released, a fact which has thrown some suspicion of exaggeration on the legends of the Bastille, and this suspicion has been confirmed by recent researches.

Next day the destruction of the building was begun by the exasperated multitude, amid the thunder of cannon and the pealing of the Te Deum. The greater part of the stones were used in the building of a new bridge known as the Bridge of the Revolution, the Jacobin feeling a glorious thrill in trampling them under his feet. Others were preserved as relics and exhibited intact at all public festivals, or were broken into small pieces, set in gold, and worn as jewelry by men and women.

The news of the taking of the Bastille shook all Europe, and was everywhere hailed by radical sentiment as the beginning of a new era for humanity. Even at St. Petersburg, we are told, men of all nations flung themselves into one another's arms and wept for joy. The amiable Cowper had already assured his readers that there was not an English heart that would not leap to hear that the horrid towers of the Bastille had fallen. The Bastille was in the eyes of liberal Europe as well as of revolutionary France the symbol of all the iniquities and of all the misdeeds of the kings of France.

Louis XVI. himself accepted the event as a sign that all resistance to the popular demands was useless. He re-entered Paris in the novel character of a submissive and patriot king amid the applause of the populace that had just captured his prison. The fervor of Paris quickly spread to the provinces, and became so intense and so potent that the Assembly was fired with a new spirit, and only three weeks after the Bastille was captured there took place the famous sitting of the Fourth of August, when the nobles and clergy solemnly renounced all their privileges and the reign of equality was started in France. In short, the destruction of the Bastille meant much more than the razing of one stronghold of regal tyranny. It not only started the French Revolution, but impressed a special character on the Revolution. It went far to make it republican, and it tended to create an association of equality with liberty.

The first anniversary of the taking of the Bastille was celebrated by the so-called Feast of Federation in the Champ de Mars in Paris. The people had eagerly with their barrows and pickaxes made the gigantic amphitheatre from which three hundred thousand spectators watched the proceedings. All was love, concord, and fervent hope. A bishop—perhaps the most extraordinary bishop ever known, His Eminence of Autun, he who was soon to become famous as Prince Talleyrand—officiated at the improvised altar. When the unfortunate Louis XVI. ascended the steps and meekly swore fealty to the Revolutionary constitution, the public excitement ran to fever-heat.

In the evening the crowd assembled on the site of the destroyed Bastille, where amid the still extant ruins an artificial forest of eighty-three trees—typical of the eighty-three departments—had been planted and were brilliantly garlanded and illuminated.

In 1792 it was decided to raise a column composed of the remaining stones of the old fortress in the Place de la Bastille. The foundation was laid with great public rejoicing on July 14 of that year.

But it was not until 1880 that the position of July Fourteenth in the French political calendar was assured. In that year an act was passed making it a solemn national feast-day. It went off with tremendous *éclat*. "It excited great enthusiasm," says the correspondent of the London *Saturday Review* (July 17, 1880), "it occupied and absorbed the public mind, it gave great satisfaction to those who planned, and great enjoyment to those who watched. The great event of the day was the distributing of the new flags to the army by the President [at Longchamps] and the march past of the troops that followed. President Grévy, with M. Léon Say on his right and M. Gambetta on his left, represented France such as France now is, and the trio went through their task with as much gravity and dignity as could have been displayed by the three great Emperors of Europe. In the evening there were illuminations, as Paris alone of all cities knows how to manage them. Flags, fountains, clusters and festoons of lamps, combined to dazzle and delight the eye. But what was most striking was the ardor of the people to make the fête their own. They seem to have been carried away with the idea that they would show they were not having a fête given them, but were giving it themselves. They were engaged in paying a solemn tribute, not to a dynasty or a family, but to themselves. The dingier the street, the gayer it was with flags and bunting. Hero-worship never dies out, and something of a personal character was imparted to the spectacle by the exhibition of little wooden effigies of M. Gambetta dressed in evening clothes,—perhaps the quaintest form of mob idolatry ever devised by man. But there was not very much of M. Gambetta or any one else in the festivity. To sing the Marseillaise hour after hour, to look at colored lamps, and to feel that there was a republic broad as the sun above to guide and bless them, was all that the happy and simple population of Paris seemed to need."

Year by year since its institution in 1880 the fête follows much the same routine. Society, in the main, goes out of town, frowning on the Republican anniversary, but a yearly increasing minority of the smart set who have accepted the new order linger behind and join with the official world and the rich people of the foreign colony in lending a show of bravery to the scene, while the general public gives itself up to unrestrained rejoicing. Shops and government offices close, flags adorn the streets, outdoor concerts, balls, fireworks, theatrical representations, and other entertainments provide public amusement in plenty. The great feature of the day is the military review at Longchamps under the eye of the President. Deputies and senators, who close the political see-saw of their session just in time, are besieged by demands for tickets to the official tribune. It is the last event of the expiring season. After this, until late in September, Paris is left to the common people and the casual tourists.

July, the Fourth of (known also as **Independence Day**). The greatest secular holiday of the United States. Its observance has the statutory sanction of every State in the Union.

Yet it may not be generally known that no less than three dates might reasonably compete for designation as the natal day of American Independence and for the honors of the anniversary of that event.

On the 2d of July, 1776, was adopted the resolution of independence, the sufficient legislative act; and it was this day that Mr. Adams designated as the anniversary in the oft-quoted letter written on his desk at the time, prophesying its future celebration by bells, bonfires, cannonades, etc. On the 4th of July occurred the Declaration of Independence. On the 2d of August following took place the ceremony of signature, which has furnished to the popular imagination the common pictorial and dramatic conceptions of the event.

The history connecting these three dates may be intelligently told in a brief space. On the 15th of May, 1776, a convention in Virginia had instructed its delegates in the General Congress " to propose to that body to declare the United Colonies free and independent States, absolved from all allegiance to or dependence on the Crown or Parliament of Great Britain, and that they give the assent of this Colony to such declaration, and to whatever measures may be thought proper and necessary by the Congress for forming foreign alliances and a confederation of the Colonies." The motion thus ordered was on the 7th of June made in Congress by Richard Henry Lee, as the oldest member of the Virginia delegation. It was to the effect that " these United Colonies are, and of right ought to be, free and independent States; that they are absolved from all allegiance to the British Crown;

and that all political connection between them and the state of Great Britain is, and ought to be, totally dissolved." The resolution was slightly debated for two or three days, but from considerations of prudence or expediency the discussion was intermitted. As texts for the action of Congress there were the resolution referred to, and the more formal, or at least more lengthy, document which the committee of five—Jefferson, Adams, Franklin, Sherman, and Livingston—had been instructed on the 11th of June to prepare. This document was draughted by Jefferson and presented under the title of "A Declaration by the Representatives of the United States of America in General Congress assembled."

On the 1st of July there was again called up in Congress the resolution proposed by Mr. Lee. On the 2d of July it passed. Two days later (the 4th of July) was adopted, after various amendments, the "Declaration" from Mr. Jefferson's pen. The document was authenticated, like the other papers of the Congress, by the signatures of the president and the secretary, and, in addition, was signed by the members *present*, with the exception of Mr. Dickinson of Pennsylvania, who, as Mr. Jefferson has testified, "refused to sign it."

But it did not then bear the names of the members of Congress as they finally appeared on it. A number of these still opposed it, and had voted against it; it was passed unanimously only as regarded States. Thus, a majority of the Pennsylvania delegation had persistently opposed it, and it was only the absence of two of their delegates on the final vote that left a majority for this State in its favor. Some days after the Declaration had thus passed, and had been proclaimed at the head of the army, it was ordered by Congress that it be engrossed on parchment and signed by every member; and it was not until the 2d of August that these signatures were made, and the matter concluded by this peculiar and august ceremony of personal pledges in the autographs of the members. It is this copy or form of the Declaration which has, in fact, been preserved as the original: the first signed paper does not exist, and was probably destroyed as incomplete.

If the natal day of American Independence is to be derived from the ceremony of these later signatures, and the real date of what has been preserved as the legal original of the Declaration, then it would be the 2d of August. If derived from the substantial, legal *act* of separation from the British Crown, which was contained rather in the resolution of Congress than in its Declaration of Independence, it would be the 2d of July. But common consent has determined to date the great anniversary from the apparently subordinate event of the passage of the

Declaration, and thus celebrates the Fourth of July as the birthday of the nation.

July the Nineteenth. The anniversary of the declaration of the war of 1870–71, between Germany and France.

In conformity with an order of the Imperial Cabinet dated January 27, 1895, the ceremony of decorating the colors carried by the regiments of the Prussian Guards is annually celebrated in Berlin on this date. The colors, twenty-four in number, are escorted from the court-yard of the Old Castle to the Hall by a squadron of the Cuirassiers of the Guard and a battalion of the Emperor Alexander Regiment. Then, in the presence of a member of the Imperial family, the general staff, and a deputation of officers representing the regiments of the Guard, the commander of the cavalry division of the Guards reads the Imperial Cabinet order and delivers a speech at whose conclusion three cheers are given for the Emperor. Two sprigs of oak are then fastened with a gold band at the top of the staff of each flag, and the colors are escorted back to the castle.

Festivities including parades and speeches are also celebrated by the Berlin University in the Hall of the Singing Academy, closing with a stirring chorus by the students.

June. The sixth month of the year in the modern or Gregorian calendar. Ovid in the "Fasti" indicates that it was named after Juno, but a more likely etymon derives it from Juniores, the lower branch of the original Roman legislature, as that of May was from the higher branch. In the old Latin or

JUNE. CUTTING WOOD.

Alban calendar the month of June had but twenty-six days. Romulus gave it thirty. This was reduced to twenty-nine by Numa, and restored to thirty by Julius Cæsar, a number it has ever since retained.

Among the old Romans June was a lucky as May was an unlucky month for marriages, the especially favorable seasons being at full moon and at the conjunction of the sun and moon.

June the Fourth. Since the abolition of Eton Montem this is the great annual holiday of Eton College, England. It is the trysting-day which attracts all her sons, old and young, from far and wide. Instituted in commemoration of a visit of King George III., it is celebrated on his birthday. The proceedings include "speeches" delivered in the upper school at twelve noon before a large audience, elaborate luncheons, a full choral service in chapel at three o'clock, and at six P.M. the famous Procession of the Boats to Surly Hall, a public house on the right bank of the Thames, some three and a half miles from Windsor. The procession is headed by a quaint old-fashioned boat (an Eton racing boat of primitive days), rowed by watermen and convoying a military band. Every boat is decorated with flags, and the boys all wear gay costumes.

Before outriggers came into vogue, and when the long boats were "tubs," each boat used to carry a "sitter" to dine with the crew. The sitter was some old Etonian of generous and festive disposition (generally an old "oar"), who signified to the captain of a boat his intention of presenting the crew with a certain quantity of champagne. In return he was entitled to be rowed up to Surly in the boat to which he presented the wine; he occupied the coxswain's seat, who knelt or stood behind him.

It is recorded that George Canning, the famous prime minister, went up as "sitter" in the *Monarch* ten-oar, in the year 1824.

Opposite to Surly Hall, a liberal display of good things, spread on tables on shore, awaits the arrival of the crews,—the sixth form alone being accommodated with a tent. After a few toasts, and as much champagne as can be fairly disposed of in a short time, the captain of the boats gives the word for all to re-embark, and the flotilla returns to Eton in the same order. This order, however, is by no means such as would delight the eye of a critical first lieutenant in her majesty's navy: singing, shouting, racing, and bumping, all go on together in the most harmonious confusion.

Before disembarking, the boats row three times round the eyot near Windsor Bridge, while a brilliant display of fireworks is let off from the college.

Justina of Padua, St. (It. *Giustina*), one of the patrons of Padua and Venice. Her festival is celebrated on October 7, the reputed anniversary of her death. St. Justina was a daughter of King Vitalicino, who was a Christian. After the death of her father she was denounced as a Christian before the Emperor Maximian, in the year 303, and was condemned to be slain with a sword. She opened her arms joyfully to receive the sword, and fell pierced through the bosom. She is represented in art with a sword through her bosom, and sometimes a unicorn, the emblem of chastity, appears in her pictures. A church was built at Padua in her honor, and in 1177 her skeleton was supposed to have been discovered under the altar of the church; it was placed in a shrine, and is still exhibited to the veneration of the people. There is another famous church of St. Justina in Venice. On the day of the saint's festival the Senate makes a solemn procession in thanksgiving for the victory of Lepanto, gained over the Turks on October 7, 1571.

K.

Kado, St. A saint who does not appear in the hagiologies, but whose memory is preserved in the local traditions of Brittany. On one occasion he wished to have a bridge thrown over an ill-conditioned river, and, after appealing in vain to the Virgin and the Trinity, was compelled to turn to the devil, who had always been considered an excellent mason. Satan drew an admirable bridge on red paper, and stipulated that he was to have the first soul that crossed over the bridge in payment for his labors. But the saint cheated him by driving a black cat over the bridge as soon as it was finished.

Kali, Festivals of. Kali is the chief goddess in the Hindoo mythology. Her idols are therefore surpassingly hideous, and the festivals in her honor are celebrated with the most frightful exhibitions of devotional self-torture. She is usually represented as a black or dark-blue female, with blood-streaked countenance and dishevelled hair, dancing on the prostrate body of her husband Siva. One of her arms (she has four) holds a sword, another grasps by the hair a human head; all her three eyes (she has one in her forehead) are full of wrath; human victims dangle as ornaments from her ears, and her necklace and girdle are composed of skulls. Yet, however ferocious the appearance of the idol, it represents her fresh from the beneficent deed of slaying the giants, whose blood she has drunk; and the lolling of her tongue is emblematic of her shame on discovering that, in her blind fury, she is trampling on her husband. The autumn worship of Doorga (*q. v.*), one form of Kali, celebrates her as the creative principle in splendid, expensive, and indelicate festivities. The general character of her worship, however, is of a different kind. It is in her honor that the Saiva sect perform

38

the Churruk Poojah (*q. v.*), when self immolated victims swing in the air on hooks fastened into the flesh of their backs. But to understand the hideousness of the Kali worship one must witness the proceedings which during the Churruk Poojah festival take place in her temple at Calcutta, the celebrated Kali Gat.

On entering the precincts of the temple (which has no attractions of an architectural kind), Brahmins are seen standing to receive the free-will offerings of the people, who flow past in eager crowds, receiving in return for their money consecrated flowers. Within is the hideous image of the goddess; and hard by the shrine some men stand with iron spikes, canes, rods, etc. Groups of devotees—ten or a dozen at a time—come up to these men to be operated on. One man is pierced through in either side; a couple of canes are then inserted, and, their ends being held by two of his companions, he dances away as if in a frenzy. Another has his tongue pierced, and passes through the aperture a living snake; another has his arm perforated, and passes through it an iron rod; and another passes an iron rod through his protruded tongue. Group after group press forward to be thus treated. At length, all the groups being conspicuously arranged on a platform, the goats for the sacrifice are decapitated, and the court swims with blood. Strange ingredients are then thrown on the fire. As the smoke and flame ascend, discordant instruments clash forth uproarious music; and in the midst of the din, the chief actors commence their gesticulations, and heighten their voluntary inflictions, by pulling the rods, canes, spikes, snakes, to and fro in the lacerated flesh, till streams of blood pour forth afresh; and the crowd become frantic with excitement, and shout, " Victory to Kali! victory to the great Kali!" Afterwards they leave the temple to parade in similar fashion in the streets; and nothing can be more unearthly than to witness these hideous processions, accompanied by a horrid din of trumpets, gongs, drums, fifes, and cymbals, parading in the chief thoroughfares of Calcutta. (See Bruce's " Scenes and Sights in the East," 1857.)

Kenelm, St. The son of Kenulph, King of Mercia. In 819, at the age of seven, he succeeded his father on the throne; but at the instigation of his sister, the cruel Quindride, he was put to death a year later. His head was cut off, and he was buried under a thorn-tree, but a miraculous light shining over the place revealed the presence of the remains. Naturally so signal a proof of divine favor made them a desirable possession. The Canons of Gloucestershire and Worcestershire contended for them. The dispute grew hot, and the weather was hotter. At last a wise man proposed that the men of the two shires should go to sleep at the same time, and whichever God should first awake should take the body and go their way. Now, the Abbot of Winchcombe and the Gloucestershire men, who perhaps slept with one eye open, awoke first, and quietly levanted with the very profitable body of St. Kenelm. They enshrined it in the abbey of Winchcombe, which became a great resort for pilgrims.

St. Kenelm is commemorated on his death-day, December 13, and also on the day of the translation of his remains, July 17. At the latter date a fair was held in his honor at Clent, in Staffordshire, where he was murdered, and where there was a famous spring called St. Kenelm's well, to which extraordinary virtues were attributed.

Even more famous was St. Kenelm's wake, held on the Sunday after the fair, " on which day," says Brand, " within the memory of persons now living, it was the annual practice to crab the parson." The manner was for the villagers to lie in ambuscade along the route which the clergyman must take on his way to church and pelt him with crab-apples. Brand informs us on the testimony of eye-witnesses that on one occasion there were two sacks of crabs, each containing at least three bushels, emptied in the church field, besides large store of other missiles provided by other parties; and it also appears that some of the more wanton not unfrequently threw sticks, stakes, etc., which probably led to the suppression of the practice.

"Long, long ago, an incumbent of Frankley, to which St. Kenelm's is attached, was accustomed, through horrid, deep-rutted, miry roads, occasionally to wend his way to the sequestered depository of the remains of the murdered saint-king, to perform divine service. It was his wont to carry some provisions with him, with which he refreshed himself at a farm-house near the scene of his pastoral duties. On one occasion, however, having eaten up his store of provisions, he was tempted (after he had donned his sacerdotal habit, and in the absence of the good dame) to pry into the secrets of a huge pot, in which was simmering the savory dish the lady had provided for her household ; among the rest, dumplings formed no inconsiderable portion of the contents. The story runs that the parson poached sundry of them, hissing hot, from the caldron, and, hearing the footsteps of his hostess, he with great dexterity deposited them in the sleeves of his surplice. She, however, was conscious of her loss, and, closely following the parson to the church, by her presence prevented him from disposing of them, and, to avoid her accusation, he forthwith entered the reading-desk, and began to read the service, the clerk beneath making the responses. Ere long a dumpling slipped out of the parson's sleeve and fell on the clerk's head ; he looked up with astonishment, but, taking the matter in good part, proceeded with the service. Presently, however, another dumpling fell on his head, at which he with upturned eyes and ready tongue responded, ' Two can play at that, master,' and, suiting the action to the word, he immediately began pelting the parson with crabs, a store of which he had gathered, intending to take them home in his pocket to foment the sprained leg of his horse, and so well did he play his part that the parson soon decamped, amid the jeers of the old dame, and the laughter of the few persons who were in attendance." (BRAND: *Popular Antiquities*, 1849, vol. i. p. 344.)

Key of Death. (It. *Chiave della Morte.*) A large key preserved in the arsenal at Venice. It is so constructed that the handle may be turned around, revealing a small spring, which, being pressed, drives a very fine needle with considerable force from the other end. This needle is so delicate that the flesh closed over the wound immediately, leaving no mark. It was invented by Tebaldo, a stranger, who established himself as a merchant, in Venice, about 1600. Becoming enamoured of the daughter of an ancient house, he sought her hand in marriage, but was rejected, as she was already affianced. Enraged and seeking revenge, he waited at the church door as the maiden of his choice passed in to her marriage, and then, unperceived, he sent the needle into the breast of the bridegroom. The latter, seized with a sharp pain, fainted, was carried home, and died soon after, his strange illness baffling the skill of the physicians. Tebaldo again asked for the maiden's hand, was again refused, and in a few days both her parents died in the same mysterious manner. Upon examination of their bodies, the small steel instrument was found embedded in the flesh. The young lady went into a convent during her mourning, and here Tebaldo pressed his suit, but, with an instinctive horror of the man, she declined his offer, whereupon he contrived to wound her. Upon her return to her room she felt a pain in her breast, saw a single drop of blood, and when surgeons were hastily summoned, with ready intuition, they cut into the wounded part, extracted the needle, and saved her life. Suspicion immediately falling upon the right culprit, his house was searched, the key was discovered, and Tebaldo was executed.

Keyne or **Keyna, St.** The daughter of Braganus, Prince of Garthmatrim, or Brecon. Her sister, Melaria, was the mother of St. David. Keyna refused all offers of marriage and vowed herself to virginity. She retired to a spot near the Severn, and by her prayers turned the serpents with which the place abounded into Ammonites. She afterwards took up her abode at Mount St. Michael, and there she caused a spring of healing waters to burst from the earth. The legend runs that whoever drinks first of this water after marriage becomes the ruling power in the house. Southey in his poem "The Well of St. Keyne" versifies the following story: A Cornishman took his bride to church, and the moment the ring was on ran up the mount to drink of the mystic water. Down he came in full glee to tell his bride; but the bride said, "My good man, I brought a bottle of water to church with me, and drank of it before you started."

Khalig, Cutting of the. A yearly ceremony in old Cairo at the rising of the Nile, when the Khalig canal dam that closes the river's mouth is cut, so as to allow the waters free egress to the Red Sea. The date depends, of course, upon the height of the river, but is generally about the 10th of August. The attendant festivities attract enormous crowds. On the preceding evening the booths on the shore and the boats on the river are filled with merrymakers, while the Nile itself is a blaze of fireworks. About eight o'clock on the 10th the city's governor arrives with his troops and attendants. He gives a signal, and a score of peasants cut the dam with their hoes, letting the water rush into the bed of the canal. Into the middle of the dam is cast a pillar of mud, called Arooset é Neel, "the bride of the Nile," and its gradual disintegration by the angry waters is eagerly watched. Meanwhile the governor throws a lot of copper coins into the canal, to be scrambled for by boys of all ages, whose quick motions and strategic tricks in the water that threatens to carry them off as it rushes through the openings of the dam are watched with lively interest. As soon as sufficient water has entered the canal, boat-loads of spectators ascend it with loud rejoicings.

The festival dates back to ancient Egypt, when it was performed to propitiate Isis as the goddess of agriculture, and a live virgin was sacrificed as the bride of the Nile. The Arab writers claim that this part of the rite survived under the Coptic Christians until the Saracenic conquest. They assert that the Copts told Amru, the first Moslem ruler, that on the thirteenth day of their month Baonnèh they were accustomed to search for a young and handsome maiden, tear her from her home by force, and, dressing her as a bride, throw her into the Nile at Rhoda. Amru stopped the custom as a wilful waste of scarce women, and ordered the present mud statue to be substituted.

Time was when the Caliph himself got up early to witness the ceremony and spent a matter of a quarter of a million of dollars on the festivities. Even within the memory of men now living, the Cutting of the Khalig was celebrated with a spirit unknown in these days of increased cares and diminished incomes. The old Turkish costumes, the variety in the dresses of the troops, and the Oriental character that formerly pervaded the entire assemblage are sadly missing in the tamer spectacle of to-day.

Kilian, St., Martyr. His festival is celebrated on the reputed anniversary of his death, July 8 (689). A minor festival in honor of the translation of his remains occurs on February 14. Born in Ireland about the middle of the seventh century, of Christian parents, Kilian was early filled with a desire to carry the gospel to infidel lands. Accordingly in 685 he crossed over with two companions, Diethman and Colman, to Franconia, where the people had no gods save a few which the Romans had left behind them. Kilian and his friends lived for years in Würzburg, in a low dark room, with a spring of water welling up in one corner. The Duke Geswert and numbers of his people were converted. But it happened that Geswert had married Geila, his brother's widow, and Kilian obliged him to give her up, whereupon she caused the three men of God to be secretly murdered and buried in their dark room. Slowly and softly the chains of old habits and associations wound round the prince, who forgot his vows and relapsed into idolatry. But God's vengeance only slumbered for a while. The murderers died by strange and horrible deaths, accusing themselves of their crime; and Geswert was left alone in his desolate old age, children and grandchildren all dying before him, till at his own death the line became extinct, and the fief reverted to the Empire. Pepin le Bref, in expiation of the sin, gave the lands to Boniface, the great apostle of Germany, and thus was the see of Würzburg founded in 750. Burkhard, the friend of Boniface, and like him a monk from the shores of Britain, was the first bishop. The relics of Kilian were discovered about a century after his death. The secret was revealed in a vision to the blind abbot of a distant monastery, who groped his way to Würzburg and down into the dark cell and pointed out the exact spot where the three bodies were found; and, in order that a miraculous seal might be set upon his revelation, he bathed his eyes in the fountain and recovered his sight. So the bones were encased in a shrine of carved stone, and a cathedral was built over them.

This cathedral was destroyed by fire, and the present one was built at a little distance from the old site. As years passed, a wish arose to show more honor to Kilian's shrine, and a large church was built over the crypt, called the New Minster, to distinguish it from the cathedral. It has suffered much during nine centuries, and little grandeur or beauty is to be found in it now. Not a vestige remains of its cloister, in which, among other celebrities, was interred Walter von der Vogelweide, the sweetest of Minnesingers. But the shrine of St. Kilian still remains intact.

A quaint custom was observed in Würzburg for centuries on St. Kilian's Day : a herald in gaudy attire rode through the town announcing the approach of an army of beggars, and all the outcasts of the country round came trooping in after him, filling the suburbs on the southern bank of the Main, and for three days the townspeople, for charity and the love of St. Kilian, lodged and fed them and ministered to their wants, till, on the evening of the third day, the herald collected his motley troop and led them out at the south gate. The custom gave rise to such frequent scandals that it was at last suppressed ; but the fountain still rises in the dark crypt by St. Kilian's shrine, and the faithful still believe that weak eyes will be cured by its waters.

Kirmess, or Kirmis. (Dutch *kirk*, German *kirche*, "a church," and *mis* or *messe*, respectively Dutch and German for a feast or church service.) A popular festival throughout Germany, Belgium, and Holland. In 1883 the name and some of the features of the Dutch Kirmess were borrowed by the Lady Managers of the New York Skin and Cancer Hospital for a sort of fair held for the benefit of that hospital in Delmonico's. This was so successful that the experiment was repeated on a larger scale for several years at the Metropolitan Opera-House. The idea was copied elsewhere, and thus the word Kirmesse obtained permanent lodgement in the language.

In South Germany the Kirmess is known as a Kirchweihe, or church consecration. This strengthens the common explanation that the festival was once the anniversary of the dedication of the parish church. Yet it existed even in pagan times, and only changed its name and its external characteristics with the advent of Christianity. The "court days" of the ancient Teutons, when all the inhabitants of a district assembled and wandered from one sacred grove to another, were combined with sacrifices and holiday-making. Christianity adopted these festivities, baptized them with new names, and transferred them from the groves to the churchyard. Thus the Venerable Bede quotes a letter from Pope Gregory the Great to the Anglo-Saxon bishops in which the following passage occurs : "As they"—*i.e.*, the recently converted Anglo-Saxons—" are accustomed to slaughter many oxen and horses on the festivals of devils" (the ancient deities), " it is necessary to allow these festivals to exist, but to substitute some other object. Therefore on the anniversaries of the consecration of the church, and on the commemoration days of the martyrs whose relics are preserved in those churches which have been erected on the sites of the former sacrificial groves, a similar festival shall be held. The spot shall be marked out with green boughs, and a Christian entertainment shall be given. Animals shall no longer be sacrificed in honor of Satan, but to the glory of God and the satisfying of men's appetites, in order that due thanks may be rendered to the Giver of all Good." It was on the principle thus expressed by Pope Gregory that the church ale or wake was established in England (see ALE), and the Kirmess in Germany and the Low Countries.

As years went on, however, the Kirmess, like the church ale, gradually lost its religious characteristics, and sometimes even gave rise to brawls and other excesses. Hence in the fifteenth century the Church festival was separated from the secular holiday. In the Low Countries the latter was transferred to the spring-time; in Germany it is usually celebrated in September or October.

In Holland and Belgium the Kirmess is simply a gala time, in which the peasants give themselves up to several days of festivity. Leaving their homes in holiday attire, they flock to the towns, which they make into a great playground, rushing through the streets to the cry of " Hossen! Hossen!" The Kirmess proper is established in some public square, which is occupied by booths and tents of every description, belonging to wandering theatrical companies, acrobats, astrologers, variety shows, and restaurants. The grounds are made beautiful with flags and bright draperies of every color, and the booths, where articles of food are offered for sale, are in the charge of pretty girls in Old Holland costume. These girls are the very prettiest that can be found, and are dressed in the piquant and attractive costume of the Netherlands peasant girls. A great feature of the Kirmess is found in the various dances executed by groups of peasants from different sections, each vying with the other in their picturesque scenes or in the perfection of the execution of their different dances.

In Germany the festival opens with the joyous disinterring of the symbol of the Kirmess at the place where it had been buried with mourning the previous year. On the eve of the initial day (the latter being usually a Sunday) the village youth march to the spot, accompanied by music. The Kirmess symbol, usually a horse's skull, is dug up, placed on a pole decked with flowers and ribbons, and borne to the village amid loud rejoicings. In many places on the Lower Rhine a figure of Zacchæus (he who did climb a tree our Lord to see) is substituted for the horse's skull. Zacchæus is everywhere the patron saint of the Kirmess, but why, when, or where he became so is unknown. The symbol, crowned with the Kirmess garland of flowers and eggs, is set up in the dancing-hall of the village inn.

Around it gather all the young men and the maidens. The former solemnly bind themselves to make holiday for three or more days, to keep a joint score, and to celebrate the feast jointly, as well as to stand by one another in the event of possible fighting.

In ratification of the compact, each in turn with a heavy wooden cudgel strikes a post fixed in the ground for the purpose. The number of strokes denotes the amount of holidays each will take. Generally three are deemed sufficient, but sometimes four or six strokes are given. It is considered a good omen when the stake is finally driven quite into the ground. The girls, whose business it is to manufacture the Kirmess crown, and in some places to deck the Kirmess tree, are present during the process just described, and they fasten a red ribbon on the breast of every youth, which may not be discarded until the prescribed Kirmess days are over.

On Sunday, as the last chords of the organ die away, the dance-music strikes up, often under the shadow of the village linden. The Kirmess has now begun. It is characterized by all manner of rural sports. The favorite beverages are beer and aniseseed brandy with sugar. On Tuesday the revellers go to church, headed by a band. Formerly they proceeded thither in masquerading guise, and were fetched by the priest himself. The musicians performed during the mass, but the tunes were not always of an edifying description. After service, the party either betake themselves to the dancing-room, or else visit distant farms, where the young men are regaled with cakes baked for the occasion. By Wednesday it is the turn of the married men to take the lead, and the youths retire. Frequently the wildest revelry occurs under the new auspices, and extends over the whole week, so that the Kirmess is not buried until Saturday. Then the horse's skull or the effigy of Zacchæus is carried on a bier through the village with the usual funeral melodies. The erstwhile revellers walk beside it with chalked faces and covered with white cloths. There are also the usual masks, reminiscences of the ancient heathen gods,—such as the Faithful Eckhart, Hakelberend the Wild Huntsman, Knecht Ruprecht, and Frau Berchta,—although they are now made to assume a merely demoniacal aspect. Thus they proceed to the spot whence the Kirmess is to be resuscitated the following year. This is generally a secluded and dismal place, and the flickering torches lend it a still more uncanny appearance. The Kirmess symbol is then laid in the deeply dug grave, and the bones and skulls of animals are also cast in. Whilst the hole is being filled up, a hideous din is created by those present, howling, shrieking, and beating pots and pans. With wild shouts the company return to the village, and the festival is at an end.

The ceremony varies slightly in different parts of Germany, though its main features remain the same. In Suabia and in Baden the symbol of the Kirmess is a bottle of wine. The hat-dance is performed in several Suabian villages on the Sunday succeeding the burial. A hat is drawn up to the top of a long pole by a cord fastened at the bottom, whereto a long piece of lighted tinder is affixed. The young men dance in turn round the pole to an appointed goal, where each delivers up the deco-rated sprig in his hand to his successor. Lots determine the order in which each shall come. He who happens to be dancing when the hat falls from the burnt cord wins the hat.

In that part of Bavaria called the Lechfeld it is usual on the Monday morning after the Kirchweihe to have a solemn mass said for the repose of the souls of all the parish dead. The women appear dressed in black. In the morning before mass the musicians go round to the house of every well-to-do peasant and play a dance, in return for which they expect to be regaled with meat, cakes, and beer.

Kiss of Peace. The kiss of peace, or holy kiss, originally formed an element of every act of Christian worship. No sac-rament or sacramental function was deemed complete without it. Tertullian calls it the seal of prayer, and asks, "What prayer is complete where the holy kiss is absent? What kind of sacri-fice is that from which men depart without the kiss of peace?" At first it was given promiscuously, but gradually the rule was introduced that men should kiss only men, and women women. After the thirteenth century a mechanical substitute was intro-duced in the Western Church. A small wooden tablet, or metal plate, bearing a representation of the crucifixion, was first kissed by the priest and his assistants and then handed to the com-municants to be pressed to their lips. A trace of the kiss of peace lingers in the Episcopalian service, in the final benediction, which begins, "The peace of God." In the Eastern Churches the custom is still in a measure retained. The Russian clergy kiss one another during the recital of the Nicene Creed. In the Coptic Church the custom remains in all its pristine vigor. "Travellers now living," says Dean Stanley, in his "Christian Institutions," "have had their faces stroked and been kissed by the Coptic priest in the cathedral at Cairo, while at the same moment everybody else was kissing everybody throughout the church."

Kissing the Pope's Toe. Among the Oriental nations it was customary to kiss the hands or the feet or the hem of the garment of a person whom the kisser desired to honor. The Egyptians had this custom of the Assyrians, the Greeks of the Egyptians, the old Romans of the Greeks, and the modern Romans of the old, whose Pontifex Maximus had his toe kissed under the Empire. The penitent Magdalene kissed the feet of our Lord. At the present time it is no uncommon thing for a Mohammedan to wash and kiss the feet of a guest who has trav-

KISSING THE POPE'S TOE.
(From Picart.)

elled a long distance to pay him honor. Nay, the Pope himself, as well as Roman Catholic and Greek sovereigns and primates, washes and kisses the feet of pilgrims on Maundy Thursday (*q. v.*). It is related of St. Susanna, a virgin who suffered martyrdom in the year 294, that she kissed the feet of Pope Caius. Therefore it is not necessary to accept the explanation of Matthew Paris that before the eighth century the Popes gave only their hands to be kissed, but that a certain misguided woman, not content merely to kiss the Pope's hand, gave it an affectionate squeeze, which so scandalized His Holiness that he straightway cut off the member which had vicariously offended. Ever after that, continues Matthew, he was forced to present his foot instead,—a practice which has continued for all time. As squeamishness succeeded to the original simplicity, the Pope encased the foot in a slipper, and over the place where the great toe is housed a cross is now decorated, so as to refer the homage to Christ crucified.

On the other hand, the toe of the Sultan is kissed at Constantinople *in puris naturalibus.* Only officials of the most exalted rank are admitted to this treat. Others may but touch the fringe of his scarf with their lips, whilst the lowest of all must content themselves with a simple obeisance. All through the ceremony the Sultan sits immovable, like a statue that sees and hears nothing, the while his subjects defile before him with every mark of the most servile respect.

Kite-Flying Festival. (Chinese, *Chung-Yang-Chieh* or *Téng Kao,* literally, "ascending high.") On the ninth day of the ninth month in the Chinese calendar the Celestials of all ages repair to suburban hills to drink and amuse themselves, and to fly curious kites of extraordinary shapes and gaudily painted. Centuries ago, the legend runs, a certain man was warned in a dream that a misfortune was about to overtake his household on a given day. So he took his family out for the day, and amused himself with flying kites on a lofty hill. On returning in the evening to his homestead he found that his house had fallen in, and that his pigs and dogs had been buried in the ruins. Every year witnesses the flight of millions of kites on the hills of China in memory of the circumstance. In some mysterious way the kites are supposed to carry aloft the evils which may be impending over the households of the fliers, and when the strings are cut the kites, like the scapegoat of old, are believed to bear away into the wilderness the evils incurred by wrongdoings.

Kosher. (Hebrew, "clean," in contradistinction to *trepha,* "unclean.") The name given by the Jews to meat which is killed in the manner authorized by Moses. The *schochat,* or killer, must be cool, wary, experienced, well grounded in religion, and of good moral character, and he must have passed a satisfactory examination before the chief rabbi and received a license. The *schechita,* or killing, is so conducted as to insure the complete effusion of blood ; for the Israelites are forbidden to eat blood. The ox or other quadruped is bound fast, and the windpipe is cut through with a long and very sharp-edged knife. No unnecessary pressure on the throat is allowed. The upper end of the knife is first put to the throat, it is then pushed over to the lower part of the blade, and the knife is drawn back and then forward. No stoppage must occur during the operation. Now comes the *bedigah*, or examination of the instrument and the victim. If there be the slightest nick in the edge of the knife the meat cannot be eaten, as the cut would not be clean, the nick would cause a thrill to pass through the beast, and consequently repel the blood again through the veins. Lungs, liver, heart,— the whole animal, in short, is carefully looked over. Any organic lesion, any inflammation or fracture, condemns the whole as *trepha*. If the examination be satisfactory, a tag attached to each half of a beef is proof of its gastronomic value. This tag gives the name of the killer and the date of the killing.

Kwanyin, Feast of. In Chinese mythology, Kwanyin is the goddess of mercy and fecundity. Sometimes she holds an infant in her arms in an attitude which irresistibly reminds a Christian of the conventional pictures of the Madonna and Child, sometimes she is represented standing on a lotos-flower, pouring the water of plenty upon the thirsty earth. Tradition says she was born on the 19th of the second month (see CALENDAR): hence that is the annual date of her festival. It is especially celebrated by married women who desire offspring or whose husbands and children are ailing. They flock to her temples to prostrate themselves before her shrine. A band usually plays in the vestibule of the temple, while within the sanctuary Buddhist priests conduct a weird and erratic service. The women place their offerings upon two tables and either sit or kneel before them. The priests march around them, chanting prayers in harmony with the music. At first the measure is slow and solemn, but gradually the time is quickened, until at last the priests in an ecstasy dance and whirl around the devotees. When thoroughly exhausted, but still thrilling with excitement, they approach the women and announce that their prayers have been heard.

L.

Labor Day. An annual holiday in honor of workingmen and workingwomen, which in the United States is celebrated on the first Monday in September, and in several European countries on May 1.

The idea of the American holiday seems to have been born in

Boston. But the credit for the first formal movement belongs to New York. In 1882 Matthew Maguire, secretary of the Central Labor Union in that city, with the approval of the Union, corresponded with the various labor organizations in the State with a view to setting aside one day in the year as their own holiday. The proposition was well received. The first Monday in September was chosen. Maguire was made chairman of the committee to arrange for the first Labor Day celebration in that year.

This was so successful that it was determined to continue the holiday annually, and in 1883 the New York Central Labor Union corresponded with similar organizations throughout the country with a view to having celebrations elsewhere. A number of cities responded. The holiday now began to assume a national character. It was endorsed as the official labor holiday by both the Knights of Labor and the American Federation of Labor. Then the work of obtaining legal recognition began. The legislature of New York, by an act passed April 27, 1887, took the initiative.

Massachusetts, and then other States, speedily followed suit. Meanwhile a measure to make the holiday a national one hung fire in Congress until 1894. Then Representative Amos Cummings took hold of the matter in the House, and Senator Kyle, of South Dakota, introduced a bill making Labor Day a holiday throughout the Union. The latter was immediately reported from the Senate Committee by Mr. Kyle without amendment. It was passed without opposition, and was signed by the President and became a law on June 28, 1894.

In point of fact, this declaration of Congress has legal effect only within the District of Columbia and among government employees in the States; but the moral effect was to bring about a general observance of the day in nearly all the States of the Union. Up to 1894 monster parades were held in New York and other cities in honor of the day, but these proved so expensive that they have been abandoned almost everywhere. The festival is now marked mainly by the closing of shops and warehouses, by the cessation of mechanical labor (many labor unions impose heavy fines on members found at work this day), and by picnics, excursions, and public games which are expected to fill the coffers of the Unions rather than deplete them.

The American Socialists take no part in the celebration of the September Labor Day, choosing rather to cling to an unofficial holiday on May 1, which has been chosen by the labor men and socialists in Europe as the occasion for their annual demonstrations. In New York the evening of May Day witnesses a parade through the streets and a mass meeting in Union Square of the various socialistic Unions. The mass meeting is addressed by prominent orators of their faith. Similar demonstrations occur in other large cities. But the rioting and bloodshed that have too often signalized the day in Europe have found no repetition in America.

Lago di Piazza Navona. (It., "Lake of the Piazza Navona.") A curious Roman holiday custom which used to be performed on every Sunday in August. In the centre of the Piazza Navona is a large fountain, adorned with an obelisk and four colossal reclining figures, which represent the four principal rivers of the world. From the urns of these river-gods the water is allowed to stream abundantly, until a third of the piazza, which inclines towards the fountain, is about two feet deep in water. "The dry portion of the piazza," says an eye-witness in *Blackwood's Magazine* for March, 1829, "was covered with booths and spectators; the surrounding windows, and the broad steps of the church of St. Agnes, were occupied with gazers; and every eye was fixed upon the lake, which was crowded with numerous groups in vehicles of every class, from the state coach to the hay-cart, besides equestrians, led horses, and donkeys innumerable. In or out of this dirty puddle the company ride and drive round the piazza until sunset; the horses neigh with delight in this cooling foot-bath, and the scene is varied and enlivened by the festive attire of the more opulent peasants and farmers, who bring their families in large hay-wagons to partake of this illustrious refreshment in the company of princes and nobles. Such is this festive inundation, in which some worshippers of the antique see the relics of a Roman Naumachia. For this motley scene the Corso is deserted, and not a soul remains on Monte Pincio, except perhaps some hypochondriacal Englishman."

Lamb Ale. A festival formerly celebrated at Kidlington, in Oxfordshire, on Whit Monday. A fat lamb was provided. The maidens of the town, having their thumbs tied together, were permitted to run after it, and she who caught the lamb with her mouth was declared the Lady of the Lamb. The lamb, killed and cleaned, was carried on a long pole before the lady and her companions to the green, attended with music and morris-dances of men and women. Next day it was served for the Lady's feast, and the solemnity ended.

Lammas Day. Some suppose that the appellation comes from Lamb Mass, as the feudatories of the cathedral of St. Peter in Vinculis at York (so called, like the Church of St. Peter Outside the Walls of Rome, in memory of St. Peter's chains and imprisonment) were in the habit of bringing each a lamb to the cathedral at the time of high mass upon the 1st of August; others, that it comes from the Saxon Hlafmaesse, "Loaf Mass," because it was usual then to make an offering of the first-fruits or new bread of the Arnmonath.

Properly this is the 1st of August. But the Act of George II. which established the New Style in England excepted the days for the commencement of Lammas rights from the operation of the statute. Therefore Lammas Day at present is August 13. It is a day full of antique survivals, but the one great custom which marks it as a link with a very remote past is the removal of the fences from many lands throughout the country, and the throwing open to common pasturage of lands which till this day from the end of last Lammastide had been used as private property. "Wherever," says Mr. G. Laurence Gomme, "we find Lammas customs in England we may take it for granted that it is the last remaining link of a whole group of customs which together make up the history of the primitive village community. It is curious to observe with what various degrees of integrity customs have lived in various parts of the country. In some places, for instance, we find only the bare mention of Lammastide, and the throwing down of fences and the consequent opening of the land to common. In other places there is much more at the back of this single Lammas custom; there is sufficient to enable us to open the great book of comparative politics, and to take our studies back to that ancient Aryan land, India, or even still further back in the history of primitive society, the native savages of Africa."

Lamprey Pie at Christmas. The lamprey has been associated with royalty ever since the time of Henry I. of England, who was inordinately fond of the fish and is said to have brought on his last sickness by indulging too copiously despite the advice of his physicians. It has been an intermittent custom of the city of Gloucester to present to the sovereign at Christmas a lamprey pie with a raised crust. As Henry I. frequently held his court at Gloucester during the Christmas season, it may have originated in his time. In 1530 the prior of Llanthony at Gloucester sent "cheise carp and baked lampreys" to Henry VIII. at Windsor, for which the bearer received twenty shillings. It was also customary at the commencement of the fishing season to send to the sovereign the first lamprey caught in the river.

During the Commonwealth it appears from the following entry in the corporation minutes that the pie was sent to the members for the City:

" *Item.* Paid to Thomas Suffield, cook, for lamprey pies sent to our Parliament men, £08 00s. 00d."

In 1752 it seems to have been the custom to present a lamprey pie to the Prince of Wales, as appears by Mr. Jesse's book " George Selwyn and his Contemporaries" (vol. i. p. 153), where is printed the following letter from Mr. Alderman Harris to George Selwyn, then M. P. for Gloucester:

"GLOUCESTER, 15th January, 1752.

" SIR,—At the request of Mr. Mayor, whose extraordinary hurry of business will not afford him leisure to direct himself, I am desired to acquaint you that by the Gloucester waggon this week is sent the usual present of a lamprey pie from this Corporation to His Royal Highness the Prince of Wales. It is directed to you; and I am further to request the favour of you to have the same presented with the compliments of this body, as your late worthy father used to do.

" Sir, your most obedient humble servant,

" GAB. HARRIS.

" P.S.—The waggoner's inn is the King's Head, in the Old Change." (*Notes and Queries*, Second Series, vol. ix. p. 184.)

The custom of presenting the sovereign with a lamprey pie was revived in 1893, not at Christmas, but in May, when a beautiful pie with finely moulded paste, and enamelled silver skewers that also served as spoons, was sent to Queen Victoria by the city of Gloucester.

Lavanda, La. (It., " The Washing.") This term is applied ecclesiastically to two ceremonies in the Catholic Church. One is the washing of the pilgrims' feet on Maundy Thursday (*q. v.*; also PILGRIMAGE), the other the washing of the altars on the same day. At St. Peter's in Rome the latter ceremony is performed with special solemnity. There the lavanda of the high altar occurs after the Tenebræ (*q. v.*), at seven o'clock in the evening. Only a few huge candles placed in candelabra at some distance from one another relieve the darkness. The sacristans of the chapter begin by divesting the altar of the cloths which usually cover it, then on a table by its side they place seven crystal vases filled with wine and water, and two silver basins, one of which contains seven sponges, the other seven towels. Then the canons approach the altar, bearing aspersories of boxwood or yew. They are followed by acolytes and clerics. Last of all comes the dean.

Arriving at the foot of the altar, they kneel and say a silent prayer. The dean then mounts the altar with six assistant canons. Vases are presented to the dean and each of the canons.

The latter sprinkle a few drops over the marble top of the altar and yield their places to the other canons, who come up in successive companies of six to go through the same operation.

When the altar has been well washed, the six assistant canons return to the side of the dean and dry the altar, first with sponges and then with towels.

In old Catholic England the cross after its adoration on Good Friday used to be washed with wine and water, and the ablution given to the priests and people to drink after the communion, in memory of the blood and water which flowed from the side of the crucified Redeemer.

A curious survival of this washing was practised at Glentham Church, Lincolnshire, until about 1830. A large recumbent effigy lies in the western end of the church, with a wooden staircase leading to a gallery erected over a portion of it. It is locally known as Molly Grime,—a possible corruption of the Malgraen, or Holy Image, of an ancient local dialect. Seven elderly ladies were wont to receive a shilling each, every Good Friday, as a payment for washing this figure with water from Newell's Well, in the same parish. Anciently the washing of an effigy of the dead Christ on Good Friday, and strewing his bier with flowers, previous to a mock entombment, formed a special observance here. The ceremony was performed by virgins, clad in mourning, with water carried in procession from the adjacent well.

Lawrence, St., patron Saint of Nuremberg, Genoa, and the Escorial. His festival is celebrated on August 10.

Historically little is known of this saint, and the time and place of his birth are matters of doubt. But legends are plentiful. According to these, he was born in Aragon, and when young went to Rome and served Sixtus II. as deacon. When this Pope was led to martyrdom St. Lawrence begged to be allowed to suffer with him. Sixtus told him that he would follow him in three days, and bade him distribute the treasures of the Church to the poor. The prefect, having heard that the treasures were in the care of Lawrence, ordered him to deliver them up, but the saint collected a crowd of the poor among whom he had divided the treasures, and said that the poor people were the treasures of the Church. After suffering various tortures, he was stretched on an iron bed made of bars like a gridiron, and roasted over a fire kindled beneath. His remains were buried in the Via Tiburtina. In the reign of Constantine the Great a church was built in honor of St. Lawrence over his tomb. A great number of churches have been dedicated to him. He is called by the Roman people " Il Cortese Spagnuolo" ("the courteous Spaniard"), because it is related that, two hundred years after his death, when his sarcophagus was opened to receive the relics of St. Stephen, the skeleton of St. Lawrence courteously moved to the left and gave the place of honor on the right to St. Stephen. St. Lawrence is usually painted in the dress of an archdeacon, and bears a palm and a gridiron. Sometimes he carries a dish full of money, and the cross, to signify his office of treasurer to the Church. The gridiron varies in size, and is sometimes embroidered on his robe, and sometimes borne in his hand or suspended around his neck; and again he puts his foot on it in sign of triumph.

The church of St. Lawrence Jewry, London, erected to his name, bears a gridiron on the steeple. Robinson says, "Philip II. of Spain, having won a battle on the 10th of August, the festival of St. Lawrence, vowed to consecrate a palace, a church, and a monastery to his honor. Accordingly he built the Escorial, the largest palace in Europe. This immense quarry consists of several courts, all disposed in the shape of a gridiron. The bars form several courts, and the royal family occupy the handle. Gridirons are met with in every part of the building. There are sculptured gridirons, painted gridirons, iron and marble gridirons; there are gridirons over the doors, in the windows, in the galleries, and in the yards. Never was an instrument of martyrdom so multiplied, honored, and celebrated."

The gridiron on which St. Lawrence suffered is preserved in the church of San Lorenzo in Lucina, Rome. Two churches in the same city preserve portions of his melted fat, a pot full of which was likewise presented to the Escorial by Pope Gregory XIII. Ribs, arms, and shoulder-blades of the saint are scattered through many Roman churches.

Leap-Year. This was known as the Bissextile year, for reasons explained under CALENDAR. The origin of the English name is harder to trace. Many theories have been framed. None is quite satisfactory. Some look on it as a reference to the fact that the gentleman whom we are enjoined to take by the forelock,—Old Time himself, in short,—instead of passing over his accustomed ground during that period, takes an extraordinary leap to the extent of a day more.

Another hypothesis makes the name a misnomer. If the fourth year had consisted of three hundred and sixty-four days, if the difference had been one of defect instead of excess, a day would really have been leaped over. As it is, the three ordinary years would more properly be denominated leap-years. Or we may suppose the fourth year had been denominated leap-year on the principle *lucus a non lucendo*. Probably the most worthy supposition as to the origin of the term is that, at first, the extra day in the fourth year and the one before it were one in the eye of the law. Accordingly, the regular day was considered that one, and the additional day, though civilly held as a day, was legally not so. It was missed or leaped over altogether. So that the legal year as opposed to the civil was in reality a leap-year.

What is the origin of the gallant and delicate privilege which is extended on leap-year to the fairer half of creation? Myth and history both have something to say on the matter. Myth refers it to no less a personage than St. Patrick. And this is the story :

As St. Patrick was perambulating the shores of Lough Neagh, after having driven the frogs out of the bogs and the snakes out of the grass, he was accosted by St. Bridget, who with many tears and lamentations informed him that dissension had arisen among the ladies in her nunnery over the fact that they were debarred the privilege of "popping the question."

It will be remembered that in Bridget's day celibacy, although approved by the Church as the proper life of a religious, and consequently made binding upon the individual by a private vow, was not enforced as a general and absolute rule for the clergy.

St. Patrick—a sternly single man himself—was yet so far moved that he offered to concede to the ladies the privilege of proposing one year in every seven. But at this St. Bridget demurred, and, throwing her arms about his neck, exclaimed, " Arrah ! Pathrick, jewel, I daurn't go back to the gurls wid such a proposal. Mek it wan year in four."

To which St. Patrick replied, " Biddy, acushla, squeeze me that way again, and I'll give you leap-year, the longest one of the lot."

St. Bridget, thus encouraged, bethought herself of her own husbandless condition, and accordingly popped the question to St. Patrick herself. But he had taken the vow of celibacy : so he had to patch up the difficulty as best he could with a kiss and a silk gown.

" And ever since then," concludes the legend, which, it is needless to say, is not found in Butler's " Lives of the Saints" or in any other work of hagiological authority, " if a man refuses a leap-year proposal he must pay the penalty of a silk gown and a kiss."

So much for legend. And now for history. In the year 1288 the following law is said to have been passed in Scotland :

" It is statut and ordaint that during the rein of hir maist blissit Megeste, for ilk yeare knowne as lepe yeare, ilk mayden

ladye of bothe highe and lowe estait shall hae liberte to bespeke
ye man she likes, albeit he refuses to taik hir to be his lawful
wyfe, he shall be mulcted in ye sum ane pundis or less, as his
estait may be; except and awis gif he can make it appeare that
he is betrothit ane ither woman he then shall be free." A few
years later a similar law was passed in France and received the
approval of the king. It is also said that before Columbus sailed
on his famous voyage a similar privilege was granted to the
maidens of Genoa and Florence. There is no record of any fines
imposed under the Scotch law nor any trace of statistics of the
number of spinsters who took advantage of it or of the French
enactment.

According to a curious little book, entitled " Love, Courtship,
and Matrimony," published in London in 1606, the English did
not need to have the leap-year privilege forced upon them by
statute, but allowed it to become a part of the *lex non scripta:*
" Albeit it nowe become a part of the common lawe in regard to
social relations of life, that as often as every leap yeare doth
return, the ladyes have the sole privilege during the time it
continueth of making love, either by wordes or lookes, as to them
it seemeth proper; and, moreover, no man will be entitled to
benefit of clergy who doth in any wise treat her proposal with
slight or contumely."

Up to within a century ago it was another unwritten law of
leap-year that if a man should decline a proposal he should
soften the disappointment which his answer would bring about
by the presentation of a silk dress to the unsuccessful suitor for
his hand.

A curious leap-year superstition is still to be met with in some
parts of New England, and that is that in leap-year the " beans
grow on the wrong side of the pod."

Rossini, the musical composer, was born on February 29, 1792.
On the 29th of February, 1864, when he was seventy-two, he
celebrated what he called his eighteenth birthday, and in the
pleasant companionship of mutual friends declared his deliberate
purpose to " turn over a new leaf and disregard the frivolities of
youth, and the indiscretions of his teens." Oddly enough, Rossini's jesting enumeration of his birthdays was not correct. He
had forgotten that the year 1800 was not a leap-year. Consequently his first birthday was in 1796 and his second not till
1804, making February 29, 1864, the seventeenth and not the
eighteenth birthday.

Lent. A fast of forty week-days enjoined by the Roman,
Greek, and English and some other Protestant Churches as a
preparation for Easter. The English word comes from the Anglo-

Saxon *Lencten,* "spring." The Italian *Quaresima* and the French *Carême* are corruptions of the Latin *Quadragesima, i.e.,* forty, while the German *Fastenzeit* and the Dutch *Vasten* denote the fast by pre-eminence, like ἡ νηστεία in the Greek calendar. It is probable that a fast of some duration previous to the commemoration of the resurrection was kept from very early times, but it was not till the year 840 that the date was definitively fixed for all Catholic Christendom from Ash Wednesday to Holy Saturday inclusive. As Sundays are not days of fasting, this makes the full complement of forty days, and therefore establishes an analogy between Lent and the forty days' fast of Christ, the forty days spent by Moses and Elias in the wilderness, and the forty days' grace given in the preaching of Jonah to Nineveh. But the term Quadragesima adopted for the forty days originally meant forty hours, the early Christians apparently keeping a rigid fast for that space of time from the afternoon of Crucifixion Day to the morning of the feast of the Resurrection.

The Greek Church has always kept four Lents, distributed quarterly throughout the year. These are kept with the utmost strictness. There are no lapses of meat-eating, party-giving, or diversions of any kind through the entire Lenten season.

But strictness in diet is perhaps easier for the Greeks than for other nations less abstemious. There are hundreds of families who never taste meat during the entire year except on New Year's Day and at Easter. The foods they deny themselves, therefore, especially on their holiest days, Mondays, Wednesdays, and Fridays, are just those the Catholics permit themselves,—fish, eggs, milk, and even cheese.

In the early Church Lent was a season in which the faithful begged God's mercy for themselves and were therefore expected to show mercy to others. The money spared by fasting was given in alms, the Imperial laws forbade criminal processes, the Church reconciled penitents at the altars and imposed public penalties in expiation of their guilt, the Emperors released prisoners, masters pardoned their slaves, and enemies became friends. It was a season of mourning. Hence the Church has always discountenanced festivities of all kinds during Lent, and forbidden marriages.

The ladies wore friars' girdles at this season. Camden relates that Sir Thomas More, "finding his lady scolding her servants, endeavored to restrain her. 'Tush, tush. my lord,' said she: 'look, here is one step to heavenward,' showing him a friar's girdle. 'I fear me,' said he, 'that that one step will not bring you one step *higher.*'"

The use of flesh meat, eggs, and milk during Lent was forbidden in England, not only by ecclesiastical but also by statute law, even

into the time of William III. Any violation of the law was
followed by dire penalties. There is the case of the landlady of
the Rose Tavern, St. Catherine's Tower, London, in whose house
during the Lent of 1563 was found a quantity of raw and cooked
meat. She and four other women who were proved to have partaken of the forbidden viands were put in the stocks all night.
In 1570 was passed a statute making the penalties for violating
the Lenten laws sixty shillings and three months' imprisonment.

The chief Lenten food from very early days was fish. In the
thirty-first year of the reign of Edward III. the following sums
were paid from the Exchequer for fish supplied to the royal
household: Fifty marks for five lasts red herrings (a last was
9000); £12 for two lasts white herrings; £6 for two barrels of
sturgeon; £21 5s. for 1300 stockfish; 13s. 9d. for eighty-nine
congers; and 20 marks for 320 mulwells. Herring pies were
considered a great delicacy. Yarmouth by ancient charter was
bound to send annually to the king during Lent one hundred
herrings, baked in twenty-four pies or pasties, while in Edward
I.'s reign Eustace de Corson and two others held thirty acres of
land in copartnership on the tenure of supplying annually for
the king's use on their first coming into season twenty-four
pasties of fresh herring. The queerest of the food eaten in
Lent were undoubtedly the whale, porpoise, grampus, and sea-
wolf, which in those days were held to be fish.

The Church granted dispensations to the sick and infirm whose
physicians certified that they required flesh meat during Lent.
A curious formal record of such dispensation occurs in the parish
register of Wakefield:

"To all people to whom these presents shall come, James Lister, Vicar of Wakefeld, and preacher of God's word, sendeth
greeting: Whereas Alice Lister wife of Richard Lister clerke
who now soiourneth wth her sonne Willm Paulden of Wakefeld,
by reason of her old age & many years & state, and long-con-
tynued sickness is become so weake, and her stomack so colde,
not able to digest colde meates & fish, who by the counsell of
Physicions is advised to absteine from and to forbeare the eateng
of all manner of fruits, fish and milke meates: Know yee therefore for the causes aforesaide and for the better strengthening &
recovery of her health, I the saide James Lister do hereby give
& grant libertie and licence to her the saide Alice Lister att her
will and pleasure att all tymes, as well during the tyme of Lent,
as upon other fasting daies and fish daies (exhibiting by the laws
to eate flesh) to dresse and eate such kind of fleshe as shal be
best agreing to her stomach & weake appetite. In witnes
hereof I the saide James Lister have hereunto sett my hand the
eight day of ffebuary in the sixt year of the Reine of our Sover-

aigne Lord Charles by the grace of God King of England Scotland ffrance and Ireland Defender of the Faith &c. and in the yeare of our Lord god 1630. JAMES LISTER Vicar."

The Puritans defied both law and custom in the matter of Lenten fare. " I have often noted," writes Taylor, in his " Jack a Lent," "that if any superfluous, feasting or gormandizing, paunch-cramming assembly do meet, it is so ordered that it must be either in Lent, upon a Friday, or a fasting: for the meat doth not relish well except it be sauced with disobedience and contempt of authority. And though they eat sprats on a Sunday, they care not, so that they may be full gorged on the Friday night."

James II. in 1687 by public proclamation in the *London Gazette* enjoined abstinence from meat, adding that, under certain conditions of almsgiving to the poor, licenses to eat meat might be obtained from an office in St. Paul's Churchyard. Next year the Revolution occurred. The statutes enforcing Lenten fare remained a dead letter on the books until so recently as 1863, when they were repealed by the Statute Law Revision Act.

By the Anglican Church, and the other Episcopal Churches affiliated with it, Lent at present is observed in a modified way. Moderate abstinence in the use of food is recommended, and an intermission of gayety and pleasure, that more time may be devoted to religious reflection, to contemplation, and to more extended public devotions,—the churches being constantly open for the latter purpose.

In Rome at the present day Lent is full of movement and of interest to the spectator who allows himself no stomachic vacation from the foods he likes best. Dancing is indeed eschewed by the orthodox, but evening receptions are more plentiful than ever. If theatres are closed, concert-rooms are open all the more; and every day there is a "station" at some church or other which is indicated in the "Diario Romano." For many a little church which is perhaps shut up almost all the rest of the year this Lenten station is the gayest day of the three hundred and sixty-five. The street near it is strewed with sand and boxwood; the unfailing beggars line the approach and take up their position on the steps; carriages are seen before the door, and the pavement within is crowded with kneeling people, among whom the visitor who is led by curiosity rather than by devotion winds in and out in search of what is to be seen.

In Spanish countries Lent was represented as an old woman, and in places the children would go about the streets dressed fantastically. beating drums, shaking rattles, and crying,—

Saw down the old woman;
Saw down the old woman.

At midnight the commonalty, taking up the cry, would march
about the streets and knock at every door, shouting,—

> Saw down the old woman ;
> Saw down the old woman,

concluding the ceremony by sawing in two the figure of an old
woman representing Lent.

In Naples there still lingers obsolescently a custom which was
once extremely popular. This is the making of the Quaresima
(literally, "Lent"), an effigy symbolical of the Lenten season,
a small rag doll wearing a black gown and a white head-dress,

LENTEN PREPARATIONS.
(From a mediæval German print.)

which seem to be a rough imitation of the conventual garb. In
her hand she carries a distaff heavily laden with flax, and a
spindle. She has no legs, but where they ought to be is a pointed
stick, one end of which is thrust into her body, while the other
supports an orange. Seven quills are stuck into the fruit, to
denote the seven weeks of Lent. Below the orange is suspended
an osier hoop, to which are hung specimens of the various kinds
of food permitted during Lent, as well as two small bottles, one
filled with wine and the other with spirits. On Ash Wednesday
she is either hung from a single window or more usually dangled
from the middle of a rope whose ends are fastened to opposite
windows across the street. Every Saturday in Lent one of the
seven quill feathers is pulled out, amid great rejoicing.

On Holy Saturday La Quaresima is lowered from her high
position and placed upon her pyre. A packet of gunpowder is

fastened under the rough gown, which by this time has become sadly shabby and weather-worn, and the little bonfire is lighted. Then, when the puppet flies blazing through the air, squibs and crackers are let off, and every one rejoices that the fast is almost at an end. No meat must be eaten for this one day more, it is true, but cakes and confectionery afford a dainty foretaste of the coming feast.

Two popular legends give conflicting accounts of the personality of La Quaresima. In one she is represented as an aged and shrivelled personage who on midnight of Shrove Tuesday at the time when the good Carnival was at the height of his jollity appeared to interrupt the festivities. Carnival asked his old enemy why she had left her nunnery to trouble the world, since she brought only the things that everybody disliked and the things everybody hated, to which she replied that Carnival himself was a good-for-nothing prodigal and spendthrift, who would soon ruin the world if she did not come to set matters right. Finally Carnival fled before her eloquence. But the men and women who loved him and hated her fell upon the old witch and finally beat her to death.

In the other legend Quaresima is no nun, but the wife of Carnival, who is greatly provoked at his riotous living and the good things he demands and devours day by day, and the quarrel ends by the husband thrusting the distaff into the wife's hands and bidding her spin on and remain as lean as she has always been.

The Sundays in Lent are known theologically as First, Second, and so on. An old rhyme thus gives their popular names:

> Tid, mid, and misera,
> Carling, Palm, Pase-Egg Day.

The meanings of the first three words are hopelessly lost, though probably connected with obsolete services for the days.

Carling Sunday is now better known as Mid-Lent or Mothering Sunday. Pase-Egg Day is Easter.

On the first Sunday in Lent many German rural districts held their burning-wheel celebrations, which have now been transferred to St. John's Eve. In the Eifel Mountains of Rhenish Prussia a great wheel was made of straw and dragged by three horses to the top of a hill. Thither the village boys marched at nightfall, set fire to the wheel, and sent it rolling down the slope. In the Rhön Mountains of Bavaria the people would march to the top of some eminence. Children and lads carried torches, brooms daubed with tar, and poles swathed in straw. A wheel wrapped in straw was kindled and rolled down the hill, and the young people rushed about the fields with burning torches and brooms, till at last they flung them in a heap, and, standing around them, struck up a hymn or a popular song. Sometimes the object was explained to be "to drive away the wicked sower," sometimes as a propitiation of the Virgin, that she might preserve the fruits of the earth throughout the year and bless them. (FARRAR: *The Golden Bough*, vol. ii. pp. 248, 249.)

Leonard, St. (Lat. *Leonardus;* It. *Leonardo;* Fr. *Léonard* or *Liénard;* Bavarian, *Leonhart*), patron saint of prisoners and slaves, and in Bavaria of cattle. His festival occurs on the 6th of November.

Brought up at the court of King Theodebert of France, St. Leonard took a great interest in prisoners and did all in his power to relieve them. Weary of court life, he finally retired to a wilderness near Limoges and became a hermit. One day the king and queen with a retinue rode by to the chase. The queen was taken with the pains of childbirth near the saint's retreat; he appeared and prayed for the queen, who was safely delivered. The king in gratitude gave the saint a portion of the forest, which he cleared, and founded a religious community. He would never accept a higher office in the Church than that of deacon. He died about 560. In a list of holidays published at Worcester in 1240 St. Leonard's festival is ordered to be kept as a half-holiday, and all labor save that of the plough is prohibited. In the Bavarian highlands and other portions of the German Alps he is especially reverenced as the patron of cattle. His portrait hangs in front of each stable door, and displays the saint with uplifted crosier; at his feet, a ewe; to the right, a foal; and to the left, a sick ox. For these as patients St. Leonard is summoned as physician in ordinary, but, as nowadays all are specialists, his assistance is not so much required. He has multiplied by himself, and is adored in many localities with a different object: in one place he is especially famed as a healer for horses, in another for cows, and in still other places (as child-doctor) for calves.

His festival, known as the Leonhartsfahrt, is celebrated everywhere in the highlands, and with especial ceremony in the little church of Fischhausen, which lies at the end of the Schliersee, in Prussia. Unless it falls on the Sabbath it is postponed to the succeeding Sunday, when wagons crowned with plaits of pine branches and harnessed with powerful horses approach the church from all sides. Above their collars waves a red cloth. In the wagon itself sits the master, with his mate, in Sunday attire. Those who cannot produce a four-in-hand come with a pair, or a simple one-horse vehicle wherein there is room enough for both man and wife. The servant drives neighing horses; others approach mounted, and amicably call upon their stallion not to obstruct the ancient rite. The cattle, also, returned from the pastures, are in many parts brought to the Leonhartsfahrt, and the shepherdess, in trim bodice, who drives them, wears an extra bunch of flowers to-day on her pointed hat.

Before the procession marches, there is held a solemn mass. The clear voices of the children and the full tones of the organ swell from the little church, while the crowd stands before the open door in quiet devotion.

After divine service, the course commences : each wagon drives around three times at a rapid trot ; vehicles and postilions are mixed up pell-mell; the arches of leaves which are erected over each carriage, and which enframe the passengers, shake with the commotion; the variegated pennants which adorn the two sides of the wagon flutter in the breeze, and many a passing word, many a greeting, flies among the motley throng.

The stalls, also, which are to-day erected under the lime-trees, filled with all sorts of pretty trifles, have plenty of visitors, and the fair peasants purchase here their silken neckerchiefs, and also take sugar-drops for the children. At last the strange crowd disperses. There is a dance in the " Neuhaus." Every festival ends with a frolic. Old and young are collected, and none but the most feeble rest. They go and sit with folded hands near the sunny wall. Their grandchildren are in the dance. They listen. The melodies are the same that they themselves danced to forty and fifty years before. Most of those that then were gay are dead, only the hills and the valleys and the customs remain, and they gaze and weep inward tears, while upon their withered faces there rest smiles that belie themselves, and are not happy, but only sad and mournful. (*The Bavarian Highlands and the Salzkammergut*, by HERMAN SCHMID and KARL STIELER. London: Chapman and Hall, 1875.)

Liberalia. An ancient Roman festival, celebrated on the 17th of March, in honor of the Roman deity Liber, who was identified by the Romans of classical times with the Greek Dionysos, the god of wine. But wine was placed by the ancient Romans under the special protection of Jupiter, the god of the atmosphere and weather; they had no special god of wine ; and Liber, as the name indicates, was associated with the idea of freedom. On this day the boy who had reached a suitable age (usually seventeen) was formally admitted to manhood. He laid aside his boyish toga with purple border—*toga prætexta*—and assumed that of a man, the plain robe of unbleached wool,—*toga virilis ;* the *bulla*, or ornament worn about the neck of the child, was consecrated to the *lares*, or household gods, after which the young man was conducted by his father or guardian to the

Forum, where he appeared as a citizen. The day ended with a sacrifice and a banquet, and now for the first time he bore a name of his own. This was the celebration of the day for young men coming into manhood. The citizens at large offered on this day little sweet cakes to Liber, which were sold in the streets by old women crowned with ivy, who had with them portable hearths or altars for the use of the votaries.

Lich- or Corpse-Gate. The word *lich* means " corpse," and the fundamental idea of the lich-gate is that of a resting-place at the entrance to the churchyard, where the coffin may be set down. This was primarily for the benefit of the pall-bearers, as most of the old English churches are set well back from the street. It is also customary to set down the coffin while the bier is brought from the church. The coffin is placed on the bier and carried into the church. This has been long the custom at the Church of the Transfiguration. The rubrical direction in the Prayer Book now in use says that the priest and clerks are to meet the body at the entrance to the churchyard, but Prayer Books printed in the sixteenth century direct that the body shall be met at the church stile or lich gate. The gate also serves as a general entrance to the churchyard.

It is known that lich gates existed in England thirteen centuries ago, but comparatively few remain, and hardly any of these are more than four hundred years old. The explanation is that at first most of the gates were built entirely of wood. These have disappeared by decay. Most of the older remaining lich-gates are found in wide-spread parishes and mountainous districts. They are most common in Devon, Cornwall, and Wales. In olden times the body was borne to its burial by friends or neighbors, and where the distances were great the time of arrival was somewhat uncertain, and the lich gate, being roofed, afforded shelter on rainy days and a waiting-place at all times.

The most common form of the lich-gate is a simple shed composed of a roof with two gable ends, covered with either tiles or thatch, and supported by strong timbers, well braced together. Frequently, however, they are built of stone, and they vary greatly in the manner of construction. At Berry Harbor is a lich-gate in the form of a cross. At Troutbeck, in Westmoreland, there are three lich-gates in one churchyard. Some of the gates have chambers over them. At Tavistock there is a small room on each side of the gate, having seats on three sides and a table in the centre. In this, as in some other cases, provision is made either for the distribution of alms or for the rest and refreshment of funeral attendants. It was once a common custom at funerals, especially in Scotland, to hold a feast at the church gate. These feasts sometimes led to great excesses. The custom has been discontinued, but it may afford an explanation of the purpose for which the lich-gate rooms were built.

In some gates lich-stones are found. Frequently such stones are found without the gate. The lich-stone is used as a rest for the coffin. It is either oblong, with the ends of equal width, or in the shape of the ancient coffin, narrower at one end than at the other, but without any bend at the shoulder. It stands at the centre of the entrance, and has on each side stone seats on which the bearers rest while the coffin remains on the stone. Very rarely lich-stones are found at a distance from the churchyard, being doubtless intended as rests for the coffin on its way to burial. It is thought the several beautiful crosses erected by King Edward I. at the points where the body of his queen, Eleanor, rested on its way from Herdeby, in Lincolnshire, to Westminster were built over the lich-stones on which her coffin was placed.

Life-Boat Saturday. The third Saturday in May is devoted under this name to the exploitation of the Life-Saving Service in many of the inland and other provincial towns of Great Britain. On May 16, 1896, the observance extended for the first time to London, the hall and the gardens of the Imperial Institute being surrendered for the purpose. Members of the National Life-Boat Institution and of the Ambulance Brigades, and other coast-guard institutions, give exhibitions of their prowess, and there are processions by the guardsmen boys from the training-ships and by the boys and girls of the orphan asylums supported by the Life-Boat Institution. The proceeds of the various celebrations all over the kingdom, which in individual cities have often run up to thousands of pounds, are devoted as far as possible to making provision for men injured, disabled, or superannuated, and for the widows and orphans of those who die in the service.

Lilies of Nola. (It. *Gigli di Nola.*) The little city of Nola, near Naples, on every June 24 (the feast of its patron, St. Paulinus) is the scene of a curious annual ceremony known by this name. Originally these lilies may have been merely pyramids of flowers carried in a procession in honor of the saint. To-day they are huge turreted structures, eighty or ninety feet high, adorned with statues, ornamental friezes, bass-reliefs, and emblems, and built on movable platforms which are borne on the shoulders of some twoscore *facchini*, or porters, who carry them through the streets of the town. Not only that, but the facchini actually dance the steps of the tarantella in the Square of St. Paulinus around the statue of the saint prior to the start of the parade. A *fanfara*, or band of trumpeters, snugly ensconced in the first-floor balcony of each lily, sets the proper pace.

These lilies are built at the expense of the eight town guilds,—tailors, carpenters, shoemakers, blacksmiths, grocers, butchers, bakers, and agriculturists. The ensign or emblem of the particular guild is displayed above each: a man's waistcoat for the tailors; an adze for the carpenters; a last for the shoemakers; an iron anvil for the smiths; a flask of wine and a cheese for the grocers; a horned ox-head for the butchers; a loaf of bread for the bakers; a sheaf of wheat for the agriculturists. Small boys infest the rigging, and a triumphal female sits in state under the central arch. Each lily weighs about three tons and costs about three hundred dollars. The filigree ornaments are all done in paste and papier-maché. Hence they must be done in a hurry, else an accidental shower might melt them back into paste.

But on June 24, if that be a fine day, these Aladdin structures, these births of a single night, present a most decorative appearance. They are borne in solemn procession behind the image of the saint, and all Nola goes wild with delight.

Lincoln's Birthday. Abraham Lincoln was born in Kentucky on February 12, 1809. He was shot in Washington on April 14, and died on the morning of April 15, 1865. Twenty-two years after his death (on February 12, 1887) the Republican Club of New York city gave its initial Lincoln dinner, with Benjamin F. Harrison, Chauncey M. Depew, Frank Hiscock, and others among the orators. The Lincoln dinner has ever since been celebrated by the club on the recurring anniversary, and has proved the parent of many similar commemorations. In Illinois, of which State Lincoln was a resident when elected to the Presidency, a movement was initiated to make his birthday a legal holiday. In 1892 the legislature acceded to the popular wish. In 1896, New York, Minnesota, New Jersey, and Washington followed in the wake of Illinois. An unsuccessful attempt was made in the Fifty-Third Congress to have the holiday declared national.

Lion Sermon. An annual sermon preached on the 16th of October in every year at the church of St. Katherine Cree, Leadenhall Street, London, in commemoration of the miraculous deliverance of Sir John Gayer, whilom mayor of London.

Sir John Gayer was a merchant venturer, and accompanied an

expedition to the East, when, getting separated from the caravan at night, he found himself confronted by lions, prayed the prayer of Daniel for deliverance, and his life was saved. That night was the 16th of October,—the date commemorated by this annual sermon. Another notable episode in the life of Sir John Gayer as lord mayor was his committal to the Tower, with four aldermen, for refusing to comply with the demand which Parliament, in 1647, when it no longer represented the nation, made upon the Corporation of London for a subsidy for the troops. That incarceration probably hastened Sir John's death. He died in the good old faith in which he had lived, and left money for the maintenance of the "Lion Sermon," which records his memory and his wonderful deliverance.

Llechllafar. (Welsh, "Speaking Stone.") A famous slab of marble, described by Giraldus as ten feet in length, six feet in breadth, and one foot in thickness, which anciently formed a stepping-stone across the little river Alan opposite the west front of the cathedral of St. David's in Wales. Its place is now taken by a bridge of rugged stone, built probably in the fifteenth century. The stone was regarded with peculiar reverence from the circumstance that it occasionally exercised the faculty of speech, and it was held unlawful to pollute it by the presence of a dead body. Once, in violation of the prohibition, a corpse was carried across it. It broke out into indignant remonstrance; but the exertion was too much for it, and it split in consequence. Merlin foretold that on this stone a king of England, returning from the conquest of Ireland, was destined to die, wounded by a red-handed man, a prediction applied to Henry II. by a woman whose petition he had rejected. The king stopped, made an oration to the stone, and, according to Giraldus (*Itin. Cambr.*, ii. 1), passed over undaunted and scathless, to make his orisons at the shrine of St. David.

The following note of one John Hooker, alias Vowell, on Holinshed's "Chronicle of Ireland," p. 25, is interesting:

"The writer hereof (of veré purpose), in the year 1575, went to the aforesaid place to see the said stone, but there was no such to be found; and the place where the said stone was said to be is now an arched bridge, under which fleeteth the brook aforesaid. . . . And for the veritie of the foresaid stone there is no certaintie affirmed, but a report is remaining amongst the common people of such a stone to have been there in times past."

Loch-mo-Naire. A lake in Strathnavon, Sutherlandshire, Scotland, famous for its supposed miraculous healing qualities.

Tradition, as usual, has its easy explanation as to the manner in which the loch obtained its peculiar virtues and the name which it now bears. A woman had somehow become the possessor of bright crystal stones which when placed in water had the power of rendering the liquid an infallible cure for all "the ills to which flesh is heir." The fame of the wonder-working pebbles soon spread far and wide. As it spread it excited the cupidity of a member of the neighboring clan Gordon, who determined to secure the miraculous crystals for the exclusive use of himself and his kin. To make sure of his purpose, he feigned sickness. As soon, however, as he presented himself, the woman divined his intention and fled. But escape was impossible, as she was advanced in years and her pursuer had youth and swiftness on his side. Yet rather than surrender her charm-stones she threw them into the first lake to which she came, exclaiming, as she did, *Mo naire!*—*i.e.*, "shame!"—and declaring that its waters should heal all who dipped in them or drank of them, excepting such as belonged to the accursed Gordon tribe.

This tradition, like many a similar one, is evidently very much more recent than the superstition connected with the lake. Loch-mo-Naire does not really mean "the loch of shame," but "the serpent's loch,"—the word for serpent, *nathair*, being pronounced exactly in the same way as *naire*, "shame." This manifestly points to the great archæological fact that almost everywhere the serpent is represented as the guardian of waters supposed to possess curative virtues. It is also the recognized emblem of Æsculapius, the god of the healing art, who himself sometimes appeared in the form of a serpent.

Loch-mo-Naire used to be visited regularly on the first Monday (Old Style) of each season of the year, but especially during May and August, which were considered the most favorable months. Those who went in order to be cured had to be there before midnight. When the hour of twelve arrived, the voices that till then were loud in conversation became at once silenced, and the ceremonies began. The candidates for healing—the paralytic and the halt, the nervous and the insane—had first to go, sunwise, thrice round a well which springs up in a small belt of sand that fringes the north end of the lake, and to drink a copious draught of its clear, cooling water. After this preliminary rite, it was further necessary that they should strip and be led out backward into the lake. They had then to be dipped three times, to drink some of the water, to throw behind them a silver coin as a thank-offering to the spirit of the loch, and to be away from the spot before the break of day. It not unfrequently happened that while this part of the observance was being enacted very painful sights were witnessed.

40

A spectator, writing in August, 1871, gives the following sad picture of what he saw on that occasion : " About twelve stripped and walked into the loch, performing their ablutions three times. Those who were not able to act for themselves were assisted, some of them being led willingly, and others by force, for there were cases of each kind. One young woman, strictly guarded, was an object of great pity. She raved in a distressed manner, repeating religious phrases, some of which were very earnest and pathetic. She prayed her guardians not to immerse her, saying that it was not a communion occasion, and asking if they could call this righteousness or faithfulness, or if they could compare the loch and its virtues to the right arm of Christ. These utterances were enough to move any person hearing them."

Loggan or **Logging Stone.** The most famous of the rocking stones in Great Britain. It is situated on a peninsula of granite near Land's End, in Cornwall. The stone is poised upon a pyramid of rock, very near the edge of the precipice, down which it seems to threaten, every instant, to fall. A very small force, or even a strong wind, will put this stone, though computed to weigh upward of eighty tons, into a state of vibration, which continues for some minutes. Yet it is believed in the neighborhood that the stone has lost some of its elasticity of vibration since 1824. In that year it is said that a certain lieutenant in the royal navy commanding a cutter stationed off the south coast of Cornwall was told of an ancient proverb that no human power should ever succeed in overturning the Loggan stone. In a youthful spirit of bravado he determined to falsify the saying. With the aid of a body of picked men from his crew, he succeeded in dislodging the stone, but it luckily got caught in a crevice in the rocks immediately below the pyramidal rock on which it had been balanced, and so was saved from falling down the sheer precipice into the sea.

The news of the outrage was soon communicated throughout the district, and thence throughout all Cornwall. The indignation of the whole country was aroused. Antiquaries who believed the Loggan stone to have been balanced by the Druids, philosophers who held that it was produced by an eccentricity of natural formation, ignorant people who cared nothing about Druids or natural formations, but who liked to climb up and rock the stone whenever they passed near it, tribes of guides who lived by showing it, innkeepers in the neighborhood, to whom it brought customers by hundreds, tourists of every degree, who were on their way to see it,—all joined in one general clamor of execration against the overthrower of the rock. A full report of the affair was forwarded to the Admiralty ; and the Admiralty acted vigorously for the public advantage, and mercifully spared the public purse.

The lieutenant was officially informed that his commission was in danger unless he set up the Loggan stone again in its proper place. The materials for compassing this achievement were offered to him gratis from the dockyards, but he was left to his own resources to defray the expense of employing workmen to help him. Being by this time awakened to'a proper sense of the mischief he had done, and to a tolerably strong conviction of the disagreeable position in which he was placed with the Admiralty, he addressed himself vigorously to the task of repairing his fault. Strong beams were planted about the Loggan stone, chains were passed round it, pulleys were rigged, and capstans manned. After a week's hard work and brave perseverance on the part of every one employed in the labor, the rock was pulled back into its former position, but not into its former perfection of balance; it has never moved since as freely as it moved before.

Longchamps. The annual cavalcade of Parisians to Longchamps, in the Bois de Boulogne, arose during the reign of Louis XVI. from a visit which certain exalted ladies were in the habit of paying on Good Friday to the Longchamps nunnery, where the choral service in the chapel, conducted by young ladies selected for their good voices and carefully trained, was one of unusual attractiveness. By degrees the visitors brought their friends with them, then gentlemen; then the court came; then the press of visitors became so large that special choral services were held on the Saturday of Holy Week, on Easter Sunday, and on the two following days; until at length the cavalcade to Longchamps became as a yearly fair. Booths were erected, strolling players and dancing dogs congregated; instead of returning to Paris immediately after the service, the fashion arose of stopping to lunch rustically in the open air. During the Revolution the Longchamps nunnery vanished, but the Longchamps fair continued, and it flourishes to this day, no longer as a thing for booths and picnics, but as a three days' drive to the Bois de Boulogne, in which the new spring fashions are worn for the first time, and everybody possessed of a barouche and horse airs them.

Loreto, Holy House of. (It. *Santa Casa di Loreto.*) A famous pilgrimage shrine, reputed to be the veritable house wherein the Virgin Mary lived in Nazareth, which is now preserved in the Chiesa della Santa Casa in Loreto, near Ancona, Italy. The church itself is a beautiful late-pointed building. The Santa Casa, which stands under the central dome, is forty-four feet long, twenty-nine and a half wide, and thirty-six high : it is encased in marble, with columns, and niches, and panels whereon Sansovino has sculptured scenes from the life of the Virgin. The interior is disposed as a chapel, and displays the rough masonry of the original structure. At the eastern end of the Casa stands an altar, and behind the altar is a niche enshrining an image of the Virgin and Child, which is said to have been carved by St. Luke out of olive wood. It is now black with age and smoke. Precious crowns of gold are on each head, and the Madonna is covered from head to foot with a blaze of diamonds and jewelry.

According to legend, it was the Empress Helena who discovered the Santa Casa, as well as the true cross (see CROSS, INVENTION OF THE), on her famous pilgrimage to the sacred places of Palestine. She identified the house at Nazareth partly by its narrowness and meagre appointments, but chiefly by a certain holy dread that it inspired. She caused a basilica to be built over it, which was visited and revered by countless thousands, until its destruction in the final conquest of Palestine by the Saracens. The Holy House, however, was not allowed to perish with its enclosing shrine. During the night of the 10th of May, 1291, it was miraculously severed from its foundations and borne through the air by angels to the hill of Tersatto, in Illyria. Here its divine origin was immediately recognized (1) by St. Luke's sculpture of the Virgin and Child, (2) by an altar at which St. Peter had said mass, (3) by various relics of the Holy Family and of more recent piety, (4) by the same nameless dread that had convinced the Empress Helena, and (5) by the fact that, unsupported by any foundation, it still stood firm and level on uneven ground. The identity of the house was finally established by a commission which went to Palestine and found by careful measurements that the original foundations tallied exactly with the dimensions of the structure at Tersatto.

It is said that Tersatto attracted a large number of pilgrims, who were generous with their offerings and lavish with their devotions. Yet after three years the Virgin seems to have grown dissatisfied. On the night of the 10th of December, 1294, the angels again took up their precious burden, and deposited it in a wood not far from the present Loreto. The wonders and verifications of Tersatto were repeated. But this site was even worse chosen than the last. The wealth of the pilgrims attracted robbers, who murdered and pillaged with impunity under the protecting shadows of the wood. A third miraculous translation, a mile farther inland, made on a morning in August, 1295, resulted in a deadly feud between two brothers, joint owners of the land, and the sacred shrine, being in danger of defilement through fratricidal bloodshed, was a fourth time supernaturally borne in air and finally planted in the middle of a public road belonging to the commune of Recanati, crushing down in its descent, as was discovered in 1751, a certain prickly bush by the roadside, and covering over some acorn-shells, a snail-shell, and a dried nut. Almost immediately the authorities hastened to surround the Holy House with a brick wall for purposes of support, inasmuch as it had no foundation, but the sacred walls would never adhere to the new ones, and broke asunder so far that a little child could pass between with a light in his hand, to show the people, when necessary, the truth of this separation. A number of porticos were soon erected around the house, in which the pilgrims might be sheltered from the weather, and above these porticos some rooms which served as a lodging to the priests were attached to the House. In the course of time the church which contains the Holy House under its dome was erected. It seems to have been begun about the year 1468 by Pope Paul II., and was greatly added to and beautified by Clement VII. Then followed the exquisite setting to the House itself, in which Bramante, Sansovino, and other famous artists were engaged.

Hither have come pilgrims from all climes. Their knees have hollowed the marble base that surrounds the holy shrine. Their kisses have polished the bricks of the wall. The greatest saints of the Church, Popes, sovereigns, the noble and the good, have been among the throng. Fine ladies left here their diamonds, the rich made offerings of gold and precious stones, until a treasury of immense value was accumulated, which, dissipated in 1797 when the French soldiers under Napoleon pillaged the shrine, has in our century grown again to wonderful proportions. Upon the room and the cases which contain these gifts Cardinal Anton Maria Gallo spent more than a quarter of a million dollars. The superb church with its beautiful bronzes, its altar-piece of mosaic, its rare marbles, and the growth of the entire city of Loreto, must also be accounted tributes to the shrine.

Clement VII. allowed the festival of the translation of the Holy House to be celebrated at Loreto on December 10. Urban VIII. extended the feast to all the churches of the neighboring marches in 1632. Innocent XII. approved a special office for the festival in 1669; and in 1724 Benedict XIII. extended the celebration to the States of the Church. By a decree of August 31, 1669, the congregation of Sacred Rites added, with Papal confirmation, to the Roman Martyrology the following notice on December 10: "At Loreto in the Marches the Translation of the House of St. Mary Mother of God, in which the Word was incarnate."

Louis, St. (Lat. *Ludovicus;* It. *Luigi.*) His festival is celebrated on the day of his death, August 25.

St. Louis was born at Poissy in 1215, and was the son of Louis VIII. and Blanche of Castile. He succeeded his father as King of France in 1226. In 1247 he was taken very ill, and made a vow that if he recovered he would go to the Holy Land. He sailed for Egypt with an army of fifty thousand men. After many disasters, he was made prisoner, but was finally ransomed, and returned to France. In 1270 he embarked on another crusade, but fell a victim to the plague at Tunis, and died on August 25, 1270. Some of his relics were taken to Palermo, and the remainder were laid in the church of St. Denis at Paris. These were mostly destroyed during the Revolution. A jaw-bone and one of the saint's shirts are exhibited at Notre-Dame. His attributes in art are a crown of thorns, his kingly crown, and his sword. St. Louis was canonized by Boniface VIII. in 1297.

Lourdes, Our Lady of. (Fr. *Notre-Dame de Lourdes.*) A cave or grotto in Lourdes, a village in the south of France, which is now the most famous Catholic shrine in all Christendom. Its fame dates from the year 1858, when the Virgin Mary is said to have appeared in this grotto to a young girl named Bernadette Soubirous. At that time Lourdes was a simple mountain town, proud of a castle rich in historical memories, and rejoicing in its fertilizing river Gave and its mountains, which, courtesying aside, allow it to peep up the lovely Pyrenean valley. The world forgetting, it had been forgotten by the world. Now everything is changed. The streets are thronged with strangers from all parts of the world. At the great annual pilgrimage which occurs in September during the octave of the Feast of the Nativity of the Virgin as many as forty thousand people pour in on railway-cars, in carts and wagons, and even on foot. Hotels, shops, and booths are everywhere. A magnificent basilica dedicated to Our Lady of Lourdes has risen over the holy grotto. The sleepy little town has opened its eyes to a new and wonderful life.

And a girl of fourteen wrought this marvellous transformation!

Bernadette Soubirous was a peasant, a native of the place, ignorant, pious, and by all accounts utterly guileless and simpleminded. Though too weakly to attend school, she was not in bad health. She was so attached to her beads that her playfellows used to say, "She is no good save to say her rosaries" (Celle-là n'est bonne que pour dire ses chapelets").

Now, just outside of the city there was a cave or grotto, called La Grotte de Massabielle,—*massabielle* meaning, in the patois of the country, "old rocks,"—situated in an unfrequented locality on the banks of the Gave, one among many similar formations.

It happened that on the 11th day of February, 1858, little Bernadette, with her sister and another girl, came hither to gather wood for burning. Her two companions had preceded her a few steps, and had partly filled their aprons with sticks gathered near the rocks, when, glancing backward, they saw Bernadette on her knees in the attitude of prayer, with her gaze fixed intently upon the interior of the cave.

What had happened was this. While her companions were at work she had heard a sound as of a sudden gust of wind. She had looked around. All was still. The poplars and bushes on the banks of the river were motionless. Surely, she thought, she had been mistaken. But once again the sound arose, louder now, and unmistakably proceeding from the cave. Turning her head again quickly, her startled eyes encountered a vision that made her tremble in all her limbs and fall half swooning to her knees.

A woman of surpassing beauty stood at the entrance of the cave, surrounded by an aureole of ineffable brightness, not like sunlight, but rather like a bundle of rays, softened by a gentle shade, which irresistibly attracted the gaze, and on which the eyes reposed with ecstatic delight.

Bernadette tried to make the sign of the cross, but failed. The vision smiled a smile of gracious kindliness, and, with a mild gesture, made the mystic passes herself. Then the child was able to do the same, and even as she was uttering the final words of the Hail Mary the vision disappeared.

Her two companions had seen nothing of the apparition. This she learned by questioning them. She kept her own counsel. With two other friends she returned to the cave next day. Not to them, either, had she mentioned her reasons for wishing to seek the cave of the Massabielle. Again the lady appeared. Again Bernadette was the only one who could see the apparition. But, though her companions saw nothing, they afterwards testified that Bernadette's face and figure became suddenly transfigured as she dropped on her knees before the grotto, and acquired a nobleness and grandeur that seemed almost superhuman. This time the apparition spoke, asking Bernadette to return to the cave for fifteen consecutive days.

And now Bernadette thought she could safely consult her family. The report of what she had seen and heard spread with lightning-like rapidity through the city and surrounding country, and during the visits which the child afterwards made to the grotto she was followed by crowds of curious spectators.

The time had come when these manifestations were to reach their climax. It was the feast of the Annunciation, the day when the angel Gabriel had communicated her destiny to the Virgin Mary. The village priest, sceptical and scornful, had asked Bernadette to exact a sign from the vision. " On the spot where she appears," he said, " there grows a wild rose-bush. Tell her to cause the roses to bloom at once, as if it were spring. If before your eyes and the eyes of all present that prodigy occurs, you may promise her, on my part, that a handsome chapel shall be built on the spot."

Thousands of people, who had poured in from the neighboring villages, accompanied Bernadette to the cavern. Of course they saw nothing. To their eyes the consecrated cave was but a common cavern, the holy niche wherein the vision appeared only a plain, ivy-grown rock. One thing, however, they did see, and that was the little maiden so lost in ecstasy at what she saw that she seemed not to feel the flame of a burning candle. When she rose she repeated the words she had heard from the vision, which were, in brief, that the Virgin wished the people to be happy, and bade them eat the herb of that place and wash in the water. When Bernadette had besought her for her name, she had answered, " I am the Immaculate Conception." Straightway water flowed from the cave, and, although this was not the sign which the incredulous priest had told the child to require as the condition of his belief, it is the water and the words that have made the Lourdes of to-day.

But Lourdes was not made without considerable opposition, both from the ecclesiastical and from the civil authorities. At first they did all they could to check popular manifestations, fearing that superstitious excesses might be fatal to the interests of religion, as well as dangerous to the public peace. The prefect of police, regarding Bernadette as insane, ordered her to be confined in a madhouse ; this, however, was avoided by her friends, who placed her under conventual guardianship. The grotto was enclosed with a strong palisade concealing the spring, and people were warned away by a notice to commit no trespass. Votive offerings, such as bouquets of natural or artificial flowers, pieces of money of all sorts and in great quantities, and wax tapers, were removed.

Finally the story of the miraculous apparitions reached the ears of Napoleon III., who forthwith sent an imperial order restoring Bernadette to liberty and commanding the prefect to allow free access to the grotto, and not to obstruct the people in the manifestations of their religious faith.

Since that time manifestations have gone on increasing. and that in most substantial forms. A handsome new bridge leads to the scene of the visions. The surrounding hills are crowned or dotted with buildings, clerical and lay, of all dimensions,— convents, hospitals, calvaries, crosses, chapels, shrines.

A basilica of hewn stone crowns the hill above the grotto.

Beneath the church is a spacious crypt, known as the Chapel of the Rosary, redolent of incense, and hung with ruby-colored lamps and banners invoking Notre-Dame de Lourdes to pray for Rome and France.

The grotto itself, small and enclosed with an iron palisade, is all but filled with burning candles on iron stands, renewed as they burn out.

As one faces the grotto the natural niche in which the vision of the Virgin appeared to Bernadette is above and to the right. In it has been placed a statue of the Virgin as Bernadette described her, and over its head the words " I am the Immaculate Conception." Beneath this statue and again in a great mass at the grotto's left are hung the implements of illness which have been discarded by the people who have been miraculously cured at the shrine. There are five thousand crutches; there are iron frames for twisted limbs ; there are parts of invalids' chairs; there are trusses. Some of them are new, others smoked by the candles or worn by the weather give mute testimony of the Virgin's goodness to pilgrims of years gone by.

The place where Bernadette knelt on the 11th of February, 1858, is marked by a slab with due inscription, and is therefore a favorite praying station.

The water that sprang so suddenly out of the rock no longer trickles down the mossy bank, for the great rush of pilgrims and the absolute impossibility of restraining their impatience and putting a curb upon their rapture, which led them into such indiscretions as throwing themselves headlong into the waters, years ago rendered primitive arrangements impossible. The waters from the grotto are now received in a reservoir covered with steel plate, and only through perforated holes in the coverings can the pilgrims see them. From this reservoir the water is carried in pipes some thirty yards to the left, where a score of spigots are running night and day. Here the pilgrims drink, and lave their travel-stained foreheads. Through other conduits, and perhaps from the overflow of the spigots and the laving operations, the water is carried to the baths, which are situated twenty yards farther to the left.

The baths, improperly called *piscines*, are small private cabinets or closets like those found in ordinary public bath establishments. The bathing and its results are consequently unseen, except by the attendants. Miraculous and sudden cures are occasionally announced; but Notre-Dame de Lourdes has a debtor as well as a creditor account. The waters of her phe-nomenal spring can kill as well as cure. Not very long ago, an ailing and elderly Breton gentleman, yielding to the urgency of religious advisers, was plunged into the frigid bath, and died sud-denly and unexpectedly on the spot.

At all points whence the water issues it is allowed to be taken gratuitously; but there is for sale a large choice of flasks and cans for carrying away the holy water, of various sizes, plain, and engraved with views of the shrine.

It may perhaps be well to say here that though the present Pope has sent his papal benediction to the shrine, and though very many cardinals visit it yearly, there are many princes of the Church who dispute the authenticity of the vision and the con-versations and occurrences which Bernadette reported. As a general thing, the pilgrimages to Lourdes are encouraged, but implicit belief in the apparition and in the miraculous origin of the fountain is not enforced as an article of faith.

No doubts, however, assail the minds of the devotees who come here day after day or join in the great September pilgrim-age. The French government makes special arrangements on the latter occasion for the transportation of the sick in what are known as the White train and the Blue train. Reduced rates are offered to those whose priests and doctors certify that they are fit subjects for the miraculous powers of the Virgin Mary. Only the sick and their friends can buy railroad-tickets by these trains. Therefore only those whose appeals to human power have been wholly useless are permitted to ride on them.

To the Gare St.-Lazare and the Gare de Lyon in Paris and to the other stations along the road, when these trains are booked to start, comes an awful procession of the afflicted, some limping on canes, some hobbling on crutches, some writhing with pain on carefully swung litters lifted by the tender hands of relatives or priests. In each car is a Sister trained to nurse, binding with gentle fingers horrid sores, and cleansing from the floors and seats the disgusting evidences of hopeless sickness with her ever-present sponge and basin.

Even the ordinary express, on which the charges are high, is not without its quota of painful sights and sounds. Here is a description given by a journalist, Edward Marshall, who attended the pilgrimage of 1896 for the *New York Journal :*

"We left Paris at seven-fifty P.M., and reached Lourdes at about three on the following afternoon. Nearly every carriage in the train had its invalid or invalids, and many of the passen-gers were pilgrims of one sort or another. Many, whose bodies were whole, evidently intended to ask the Virgin to ease some sorrow. During the hour of waiting at Toulouse my neighbors at breakfast were a couple of very respectable French people, who told me frankly that they were on their way to Lourdes to beg the Virgin to grant a baby to them. Hundreds of childless couples beg this boon of the Virgin every year.

"The journey was rendered weird and strange by the devotional chants which rang solemnly out from a hundred open car-windows whenever we stopped at a station, and whenever we slowed enough so that the sound of the singing was not drowned by the roar of the train itself.

"At four o'clock the first division of the White train arrived. If the scene at the station when our train gave up its passengers was startling, the scene when the cars of the White train vomited forth their cargo of unfortunates was not less than awful. These were the poorer pilgrims,—those who took advantage of the reduced railroad fares of the national pilgrimage. Most of them came in the third-class carriages. Exhausted by the long journey, they looked even more dreadful in their curiosities of misery than they had looked at the station in Paris before they embarked. I am told that seven unhappy creatures died on the train, and it is true, I know, that one corpse was left lying on the seat of one of the third-class carriages when it was switched away from the station platform.

"The hospitallers were out in force to meet this train, and they did their work wonderfully well. There were litters and stretchers and wheeled beds, and chairs enough for the whole vast number of helpless ones. Sisters of Mercy and nuns were everywhere with basins and sponges. At least a hundred priests passed in and out through the throng, praying, comforting, exhorting the sufferers to have faith, to believe, to believe, to believe.

"At night—and each night during my stay—there were the superb processions. Starting from in front of the Basilica, whose towering outlines were vividly marked against the darkness by more than five thousand electric lights, not less than twenty thousand pilgrims marched in two widely separated lines, each one bearing a blessed candle shaded with paper on which the image of the Virgin was printed, up a broad path, through the Basilica Park to where a towering cross of fire flamed its holy signal in the night, and back again to the great stone steps of the Rosary Chapel, where, in the glow of innumerable vestas, eloquent addresses were made by French and foreign priests and a terrific out-door devotional service was held.

"At intervals in this long line of pilgrims were groups of priests and choristers, who each ten minutes started the 'Ave Maria,' in which the pilgrims joined with voices trembling but wonderfully tuneful. No effort was made to have the whole procession chant in unison, so there was never a moment when from half a dozen points in the long, blazing line the solemn singing did not come,—now near, now distant,—'Ave Maria, Ave Maria.'

"Up towards the beginning of the line were the bedridden, wheeled slowly in all manner of nondescript conveyances. Everywhere, scattered along the lines, were the lame, the halt, and the blind, some of them assisted by sturdier pilgrims, others hobbling along on crutches, with canes, in iron frames. The night processions at Lourdes are spectacles such as are not to be seen elsewhere in the whole world.

"But of course the interest centres most about the grotto. There was never a moment during my eleven days in Lourdes when there were not many people at the grotto. In the day the crowds of course were vast, and midnight came before the mass of the pilgrims had withdrawn to go to the hospital,—a truly dreadful place, without modern sanitary appliances; to the shelter where the very poorest can sleep on stone benches and the floor; to the hotels. The night after the arrival of the White train, the horrible coughing of a consumptive who was my room-mate made sleep impossible at my hotel, and at two o'clock I returned to the grotto.

"The plaza was comparatively deserted. From the grotto came the soft glow of its thousand candles, which reaching upward made the white-robed statue of the Virgin stand out from the black niche of rock with a living distinctness which was startling. Gathered about, half in and half without the soft radiance of the vestas, were a score of devout sufferers. The priests were gone. The Sisters were gone. These mute, adoring pilgrims were alone in the night with their Virgin. For the first time the silence made the musical murmur of the near-by river Gave audible. Aside from that there was no sound save the low whisperings of prayer, the faintest rustling of the tree-leaves, and the occasional clinking of a metal rosary's beads. Five pilgrims were in their litters, seven were in invalid-chairs, three or four who were able to walk about, to kneel, and to wander off sometimes under the trees to the right, were there. The silent devotion of these night worshippers keeping their vigil in the darkness before the shrine was not the least impressive episode of Lourdes." (*New York Journal*, October 18, 1896.)

Low or **White Sunday.** The first Sunday after Easter. The author of "Christian Sodality," a collection of discourses, 1652, says, "This day is called White or Low Sunday because in the primitive Church those neophytes that on Easter Eve were baptized and clad in white garments did to-day put them off,

with this admonition, that they were to keep within them a perpetual candor of spirit, signified by the *Agnus Dei* hung about
their necks, which, falling down upon their breasts, put them in
mind what innocent lambs they must be, now that of sinful,
high, and haughty men they were by baptism made low, and
little children of Almighty God, such as ought to retain in their
manners and lives the Paschal feasts which they had accomplished."

This is ingenious, but it is more likely that the day was called
Low Sunday by contrast to its predecessor Easter, which is the
highest or greatest Sunday in the year. The name White or
Whit Sunday is now monopolized by Pentecost.

Seymour in his "Survey of London" (1734, book iv. p. 100)
tells us that the aldermen used to meet the lord mayor and
sheriffs at St. Paul's in their scarlet gowns, furred, without their
cloaks, to hear the sermon.

Lucy, St., patron saint of Syracuse, of the laboring poor,
and against diseases of the eye. Her festival is celebrated on
December 13, the reputed anniversary of her martyrdom, A.D.
304. Until the Reformation the day was kept in England as a
holiday of the second rank, in which no work but tillage and the
like was allowed. Born in Syracuse in the third century, St.
Lucy was betrothed to a pagan youth against her will. Her
mother, Eutychia, was afflicted with a grievous malady, and was
persuaded by St. Lucy to visit the shrine of St. Agatha, to pray
that she might be healed. While at the shrine St. Lucy beheld
a vision of St. Agatha, who assured her of her mother's recovery.
Eutychia was cured, and in joy at her recovery gave her consent
to St. Lucy's dedicating herself to a religious life and to the cure
of the poor. This so enraged St. Lucy's lover that he denounced
her as a Christian. Pascasius, the governor before whom she was
taken, ordered her to sacrifice to the idols, and upon her refusal
he commanded her to be dragged away to a house of prostitution.
It was found, however, impossible to move her. Oxen, ropes,
and the spells of magicians were all in vain. Then a fire was
kindled, but this harmed her not. Finally a soldier pierced her
neck with a poniard, and she died. A later legend, probably
originating in the endeavor of painters to express her name—
Lucy, "light"—by placing an eye near her, relates that, in order
to discourage the suit of a youth who was haunted by the beauty
of her eyes, she plucked them out and sent them to him on a
dish. This cured the youth, and converted him to Christianity.
St. Lucy's sight was restored by a miracle. Her body, it is said,
remained at Syracuse for many years, but was at length translated into Italy and thence to Metz, where it is exposed to public

veneration in a rich chapel of St. Vincent's Church. A portion of her relics was carried to Constantinople, and brought thence to Venice. Her attributes in art are a light and a poniard. She is often represented with the balls of her eyes laid in a dish, and sometimes light proceeds from a wound in her neck. Again she is represented as being pulled by men and oxen without effect.

Ludi Romani or **Circenses.** Ancient Roman games in honor of Jupiter, Juno, and Minerva, celebrated from the 4th to the 19th of September.

The Circensian games (*Ludi Circenses*), according to legends, were instituted by Romulus in order to attract the Sabine population to Rome for the purpose of furnishing the Romans with wives. These were first called Consuales, in honor of the god Consus. After the construction of the Circus Maximus the games were called indiscriminately Circenses, Romani, or Magni.

The games began with a grand procession, in which all those who were about to exhibit in the Circus, as well as persons of distinction, bore a part.

The Circus Maximus was in the valley south of the Palatine, and was nearly half a mile long.

The horse-races, either in two-horse—*bigæ*—or four-horse chariots,—*quadrigæ,*—were the earliest form of games; but others were added from time to time,—wrestling, boxing, foot-races, evolutions of trained companies of horsemen,—the *Ludus Trojæ,* described in the fifth book of Virgil's "Æneid," was one of these,—animal-hunts, and, in the latter part of the republic, gladiatorial combats. For all of these, except the races, the form of the Circus was ill suited, and in the course of time the amphitheatre was devised, which was precisely adapted to these purposes.

Originally the games occupied a single day, and often not the whole of that; by degrees they were lengthened, until, in the time of the Empire, they lasted a week or more, and scenic games, *ludi scenici,*—that is, theatrical performances,—were added to those in the Circus. The Circensian games regularly came last. Of the sixteen days of the Ludi Romani only the last five were in the Circus.

Ludmilla, St., patron saint of Bohemia. Her festival is celebrated on September 16.

St. Ludmilla was Queen of Bohemia, and was converted to Christianity by St. Adalbert. She converted her grandson, afterwards St. Wenceslaus. This aroused the anger of his mother and his brother Boleslaus, and a civil war broke out between the Christian and pagan parties in Bohemia. Ludmilla was strangled by hired assassins as she was praying in her oratory. Wenceslaus was slain by his brother. Ludmilla was the first martyr saint of Bohemia. Her martyrdom took place about the year 920. Her remains were translated to Prague by St. Wenceslaus, and are preserved in St. George's Church. The head, separate, in a silver shrine, is now in the cathedral.

Luke, St., patron saint of painters. His festival is celebrated on October 18. Beyond what can be gathered in the New Testament, little is known of St. Luke. He was probably not converted until after the ascension of Christ. He became a devoted disciple of St. Paul, and was with him until his death. That he was a physician is inferred from the fact that Paul speaks of him as " Luke, the beloved physician ;" but the general belief that he was an artist rests on Greek traditions, which can be traced back only to the tenth century. A picture of the Virgin found in the Catacombs and inscribed as painted by Luca is regarded as a confirmation of the Greek legends. Legends also relate that he carried with him pictures of the Saviour and the Virgin painted by himself, by means of which he made many converts. He is often represented in the act of painting the Virgin. His attributes in art are the ox, the emblem of sacrifice, because Luke wrote of the priesthood of the Saviour, a book, signifying his writings, and a portrait of the Virgin placed in his hand. In the church of San Domenico and San Sisto at Rome is preserved a picture of the Virgin by Luke by means of which, it is related, St. Gregory the Great dispelled a pestilence at Rome. Another picture in the Ara Cœli claims to be the one which was thus honored. Accounts differ as regards the manner of St. Luke's death : according to some, he died peacefully ; according to others, he was crucified with St. Andrew at Patræ. The bones of St. Luke are said to have been translated from Patræ in 357 to the church of the Apostles at Constantinople, together with those of St. Andrew and St. Timothy. On the occasion of this translation some distribution was made of the relics of St. Luke. St. Gaudentius procured a portion for his church at Brescia; St. Paulinus got a portion for St. Felix's Church at Nola, and enshrined a part in a church which he built at Fondi. When the church of the Apostles at Constantinople was repaired by order of Justinian, it is said that three coffins, bearing the bodies of St. Luke, St. Andrew, and St. Timothy, were found. Baronius mentions that the head of St. Luke was brought by St. Gregory to Rome and laid in the church of St. Andrew. Some of his relics are shown in the Grecian monastery on Mount Athos.

The most famous of the Madonnas ascribed to St. Luke is preserved at the Monte della Guardia, just outside Bologna, in Italy. According to tradition, this picture was painted at Jerusalem in the year 34. In due time it found its way to the church of St. Sophia, in Constantinople. In the twelfth century a pilgrim named Eutemio, gazing at the picture, heard a voice within crying, "Take the holy picture to the Monte della Guardia!" He mentioned the matter to the custodians, and they cheerfully agreed that he should heed the heavenly monitor. So he travelled all over Europe searching for the Monte della Guardia. Finally at Rome an alliterative Senator named Pascipovero Pascipoveri, a Bolognese by birth, informed him that the mount in question was just outside of his native city. On the top of the mount was a hermitage presided over by two ladies, Azzolina and Beatrice, who were duly appointed guardians of the picture on May 8, 1160. The faithful flocked to the new shrine. Many cures were wrought among them. Then some evil-minded Venetians stole the picture one night, and put to sea with all speed; but the sacrilegious rascals gained nothing by this crime, for before their ship was out of sight of land their prize had disappeared and was safe back in its chosen abode.

Well was it for Bologna that the abduction was frustrated. An earthquake, a pestilence, an inundation, a disastrous war, these are a few of the catastrophes which the Madonna di San Luca warded off. The grateful citizens in the eighteenth century built a new and grander minster on the old site. It was completed March 25, 1765.

For nearly six days every year—that is, from the evening of the Saturday before the Feast of the Ascension to the night of Holy Thursday itself—the Bolognese keep high holiday, not so much in celebration of that religious festival as to manifest their devotion to the picture. This is in obedience to a senatorial decree dating as far back as 1435.

On the Saturday named a priest appears at the sanctuary and formally demands the delivery of the painting, that it may be carried in solemn procession along the grand arcade, nearly three miles in length, stretching from the sanctuary to the Saragozza gate, its arrival there being hailed with shouts of joy from citizens arrayed in their best attire and country-people in holiday dress and holiday spirits, intent upon escorting the Madonna to the cathedral and seeing her safely lodged therein. There she stays, to feast adoring eyes, until sunset on Ascension Eve. Then, placed on a litter as fine as velvet, precious cloths, embroidery, and gilding can make it, she is borne through the streets to the church of San Petronio, carried through the church, and set down on the steps in front of it. All Bologna's bells ring out, the priests raise their voices in a hymn of praise, every head in the thickly packed square is bowed, every knee bent, as the Madonna is moved gently backward and forward and from side to side, so that none in the vast assemblage may depart unblessed. The same ceremony is repeated at the Meloncello bridge the next day, as the Madonna slowly wends her way back to the sanctuary, entering the crowded fane, all ablaze with light, to the music of pealing bells, swelling organ, and well-attuned voices, and Bologna's annual "festa" is over.

In Charlton, England, a great fair was formerly held on St. Luke's Day. One of its quaint features was an elaborate display of horns, the booths not only being decorated with them, but most of the articles offered for sale having representations of this emblem. For a long time antiquaries were much divided as to what connection there could be between horns and Charlton Fair, and many conjectures were started without any satisfactory result. At last, however, light was thrown on this much-disputed question by an antiquary who pointed out that a horned ox is the old mediæval symbol of St. Luke, the patron of the fair. In support of this explanation it was added that, although most of the painted glass in Charlton Church was destroyed in the troublous times of the reign of Charles I., yet fragments remained of St. Luke's ox "with wings on its back and goodly horns on his head." As an additional illustration on this point, we may quote the following extract from Aubrey's "Remains of Gentilisme and Judaisme:" "At Stoke-Verdon, in the parish of Broad Chalke, Wilts, was a chapel dedicated to St. Luke, who is the patron saint of the horn beasts and those that have to do with them; wherefore the keepers and foresters of the New Forest come hither at St. Luke's tide with their offerings to St. Luke, that they might be fortunate in their game, the deer, and other cattle." Many of those, also, who visited Charlton Fair wore a pair of horns on their heads, and the men were attired in women's clothes,—a mode of masquerading thus described by a writer of the last century: "I remember being there upon Horn fair day; I was dressed in my landlady's best gown and other women's attire." Referring to St. Luke's Day, Drake tells us in his "Eboracum" that a fair was annually kept up at York for all sorts of small wares, and was popularly known as "Dish fair," from the large quantity of wooden dishes exposed for sale. It was also characterized by an old custom of "bearing a wooden ladle in a sling on two stangs about it, carried by four sturdy laborers; this being, no doubt, in ridicule of the meanness of the wares brought to the fair."

Luke the Styrites, usually known as St. Luke, though he appears in the Greek hagiologies as only ὅσιος, or "blessed," not ἅγιος, the patron of the famous church and monastery of St. Luke at Styris, near Delphi, in Greece. His festival is kept on February 7, the anniversary of his death. Of Cretan origin, he was born at Costorum, in Phocis, about 890. At eighteen years of age he retired to Mount Ionnitza, where he received the monastic habit from two monks passing there on their way to Rome. After many wanderings, he finally reached Styris, where he established himself in a cell and died about 945. The people from all the surrounding country flocked to his death-bed through a blinding snow-storm that made the roads well-nigh impassable. By his direction, his body was buried on the spot, and attracted a number of monks, who built cells here and finally formed themselves into a community. Luke had prophesied that his country should be delivered from the Saracens by an Emperor named Romanus. When in 961 Crete was reunited to the Empire under Romanus II., that Emperor, in acknowledgment, built this convent and church and dedicated them to the friendly prophet. The reputed tomb of Luke is in one of the side-aisles of the church. It is empty. Local tradition assigns the removal of the relics to the Franks after the Latin conquest of Constantinople. Some relics, however, purporting to be those of the hermit are preserved at Mount Athos.

Lupercalia. An ancient Roman festival, celebrated on the 15th of February. This was one of the most ancient of Roman festivals, and was celebrated in honor of Lupercus, the god of fertility. The day was called *dies februatus,* or " day of expiation."

The traditions of this festival, its localities, and its rude, strange rites, belong to the most primitive times, when Rome was a half-savage community of shepherds. The Lupercal—" wolf's grotto"—was a cave on the western slope of the Palatine Hill, and close by it was the *ficus ruminalis,* or fig-tree under which the twin infants Romulus and Remus had been stranded by the Tiber, when they were found and nursed by the wolf which had its home in the cave. The Luperci, who celebrated this festival yearly, were young men of noble birth, who formed two brotherhoods, the Fabian and Quintilian Luperci, belonging respectively to the Sabine and Latin parts of the city. A third brotherhood, the Julian, was afterwards added in honor of Julius Cæsar. The number of the Luperci is uncertain. The festival commenced with the sacrifice of goats and a young dog at the Lupercal. Then two young men were brought in and their foreheads touched with the bloody knife ; another of the brotherhood wiped the blood away with wool dipped in milk, upon which the young men broke into a laugh. Then followed the sacrificial banquet of the brotherhood, after which the Luperci, clothed in nothing but pieces of the hides of the slaughtered goats, and holding in their hands thongs cut from the same hides, ran up and down through the city, striking everybody that they met. Women would come forth voluntarily to be struck, since they believed that the ceremony rendered them fruitful and procured them an easy delivery. It was as leader of the Luperci Julii, a month before Cæsar's assassination and the very year of the establishment of this brotherhood, that Mark Antony,

> On the Lupercal, . . .
> Thrice did offer him a kingly crown.

The act of running about with thongs of goat-skin was a symbolic purification of the land, and that of touching persons a purification of them.

The festival of Lupercalia, though it necessarily lost its original import at the time when the Romans were no longer a nation of shepherds, was yet always observed in commemoration of the founders of the city. The festival kept its ground even after the triumph of Christianity, and was the last of the pagan festivals to be given up.

M.

Macaire, St. (Lat. *Macarius.*) There were two saints of this name, known respectively as the older (300–390) and the younger (335–395). Both are commemorated together by the Greeks on January 19, but the Latins commemorate the elder on January 15 and the younger on January 2. The first was born in Upper Egypt, the second at Alexandria. Both were hermits who practised great austerities and built themselves huts in deserted places. After the year 375, when both were exiled from Alexandria by the Arian patriarch, they lived much together. In art the younger is represented with wallets of sand on his shoulders, and sometimes with a hyena and its young. The sand is a reference to the fact that he used to walk over the hot desert bowed down under this burden in order to conquer the flesh. The other symbol refers to a legend that a hyena once brought her young one and laid it at the feet of the hermit. He looked at the animal and saw it was blind, therefore he pitied the poor whelp and prayed to God; then he touched its eyes and they were opened. Next day the hyena brought to him a sheepskin and laid it at his feet. The relics of this St. Macaire are preserved in the cathedral of St. Bavon in Ghent. Here only once in a century takes place a great procession in honor of St. Macaire the younger. The last time it was celebrated was May 19, 1867, when the intercession of the saint was invoked to protect Belgium from the cholera, the typhus fever, and the cattle disease, which had visited it in 1866. The Cardinal of Malines, all the bishops of Belgium, the Nuncio, and Bishop Mermillod of Geneva, who preached the Jubilee, assisted. The city was crowded with over one hundred thousand visitors from all parts, even from France, Germany, England, and America. On this occasion the cathedral of St. Bavon was decorated with flowers, flags, and ribbons. The solid silver shrine of St. Macaire, a present from the city of Mons two hundred years ago, was placed upon a temporary altar erected in the middle of the transept, surrounded by thousands of lights. A canopy of evergreens and flowers overshadowed it. The procession took place at five o'clock in the afternoon. Its most notable feature was an historical group accurately reproducing the courts of the King of France and the Comte de Flandre, with their soldiers, archers, chaplains, standard-bearers, and pages, as they assisted at the translation of the relics of St. Macaire in 1067.

Maio, or **Calendi Maggio,** a May-Day festival still surviving in rustic Italy, especially in Tuscany and the Roman provinces, as a relic of the old Roman custom of celebrating the kalends of May. Songs called *maggiolate* are composed, or at least sung, by the peasantry on this occasion, trees are festooned with ribbons and garlands and windows decorated with branches, the adornments being known as the Maio. In the heyday of Florentine glory these festivals were celebrated in the city, and dignified by songs, dances, and feastings, which lasted several days; as, for instance, the grand banquet of the 1st of May given in the Portinari palace, where Dante fell in love with Beatrice. Evidence of the former prevalence of these festivals exists in the numerous maggiolate composed by different authors. and among others by the magnificent Lorenzo dei Medici, whose poems are not at all worse than those of a common citizen. One of his songs commences thus:

> Ben venga Maggio
> El gonfalon salvaggio:

and in another he thus alludes to these festivities:

> Se tu v appicare un maggio
> A qualcuna che tu ami.

One of the latest celebrations of this festival in Florence was in 1612, when a Maio was planted and sung before the Pitti palace in honor of the Archduchess of Austria.

In Rome it was customary for children on the 1st of May to place upon a chair before the house door a puppet of the Madonna, crowned with a garland. Every passenger was then applied to for a donation in the following verse, which was sung by the little beggars:

> Belli, belli giovanotti,
> Che mangiate pasticiotti
> E bevete del buon vino,
> Un quattrin' sull' altarino.

This custom suggests a curious parallel in the past. On the kalends of May the foundation festival of the altars of the *lares prœstites* was celebrated in all the houses of ancient Rome. The *lararium*, bearing the small household gods, was decked on this occasion with fresh garlands of flowers and foliage, and modern antiquarians believe that the custom of the Roman children is a relic of the ancient festival.

Mallard Night. The 14th of January was formerly celebrated under this name at All Souls College, Oxford, in commemoration of the discovery of a very large mallard or drake in a drain when digging for the foundation of the college; and though this observance no longer exists, yet on one of the college "gaudies" there is sung in memory of the occurrence a very old song called "The swapping, swapping mallard," which begins,—

> Griffin, bustard, turkey, capon,
> Let other hungry mortals gape on,
> And on the bones their stomach fall hard,
> But let All Souls' men have their mallard.

Malo, or Maclou, St., patron of the city of St. Malo, in France. His festival is celebrated on the anniversary of his death, November 15 (A.D. 627). Born in Wales, he was brought up by St. Brendan at the latter's monastery at Aleth, in Brittany, the place now known as St. Malo. His virtues exciting the jealousy of the other monks, St. Brendan took St. Malo with him in search of some solitary islet where they might serve God unmolested. But an angel bade them return, and Malo eventually became Bishop of Aleth. He died at Archambray, where his relics remained until the seventh century. A young native of Aleth taking refuge with the sacristan of Archambray plotted to betray the latter and steal the relics. Encouraged by the Bishop of Aleth and fortified by the sacraments of confession and communion, the youth packed up the body when his host's back was turned, and ran away with it to Aleth. Here the relics were received with great pomp by bishop, clergy, and people. One portion was given to the monastery of the Isle of Aron, the other was kept in the cathedral. In 975 they were taken to Paris. They were lost during the Revolution. The only relic that remains is a shoulder-bone at St. Maclou-de-Moiselles, near Versailles.

Mannekin of Brussels. A curious little bronze figure in the Rue de l'Etuve, Brussels, representing a naked boy, which has attained notoriety from its peculiar impropriety of attitude. It stands in a niche carved into the wall, and water passes through it to a basin beneath. On great festival days the water is turned off and wine is substituted. The origin of this sculptural jest is unknown, but it is attributed to Duquesnoy. The citizens of Brussels take great pride in this image, call it "the oldest burgess in Brussels," and dress it up on fête-days and, detaching it from its pedestal, carry it around in all street processions. Mannekin enjoys a yearly income of two hundred francs, bequeathed to him many years ago by an old maid of Brussels, which serves to keep up his very varied wardrobe: he is by turns an old nobleman, a civic guard, a burgess, etc. He possesses eight different costumes in all, the richest having been presented to him by Louis XV., together with the cross of St. Louis. During the Revolution he mounted the red cap of liberty. Napoleon conferred on him a chamberlain's key. At present he is always on the side of the dominant party.

March. From Mars, the god of war, and the reputed father of Romulus, who is traditionally believed to have compiled the first calendar and to have made March the first month in the year. With the 25th day of this month, the approximate date

MARCH. BREAKING UP SOIL—DIGGING—SOWING—HARROWING.

of the vernal equinox, the legal year began with many Christian nations until a quite recent period. It still does so with the Jews.

The Anglo-Saxons called the month *Lenctenmonath*, or Length Month, in reference to the rapid lengthening of the day at this period of the year.

March 25 in the Greek calendar (which is April 6 in ours) is celebrated with great enthusiasm by the Greeks as their Independence Day. It commemorates the raising of the standard of the Cross against the Crescent on April 6, 1821 (N. S.), beginning the war against the Turks which resulted in the independence of Greece.

Marches, Riding the. A ceremony not unlike the English custom of beating the bounds (see Bounds) which still survives in some Scottish towns. The object is to ride the marches or commons of the town's land in order to protect them from the encroachments or thieving propensities of neighboring lairds. The Selkirk Common-Riding is the most famous of these survivals. On the eve of the last Friday of May, Old Style, the senior burgh officer, attended by a piper and a drummer, marches through the town and announces to the lieges that on the morrow the historic ceremonies will be observed. At four o'clock next morning the air is pierced with the music of fife and drum as a summons to the participants. A procession is then formed, consisting of mounted constables, the brass band, the Bailies and members of the Town-Council, the Hammermen with the flag, the Merchant Company, Standard-Bearer carrying the flag of the town, Provost, Town-Clerk, Burleymen, and others, all mounted, to the number of about a hundred. The Common-Riding Choir sing appropriate melodies. Then the riders proceed on their gallop round the marches, and not unusually several "spills" occur among the inexperienced equestrians. Refreshments are served at different places during the journey, and the lease of one farm obliges the tenant to regale the horsemen at the Common-Riding. Races are run for switches amidst wild excitement, and then the company return to the town, where a picturesque ceremony takes place commemorating the noble achievements of the famous Selkirk Souters at Flodden Field. The Hammermen and the Souters cast the colors to the tune of " Up wi' the Souters o' Selkirk," and the ceremony is concluded with tumultuous cheers. The Selkirk Common-Riding is the great festival of the year in the town, and does much to foster local *esprit de corps*, and to preserve the historical and legendary lore of this beautiful Border district. (DITCHFIELD : *Old English Customs*, p. 119.)

Another famous riding occurs in the parish of Hawick, Roxburghshire. The honor of carrying the standard of the town devolves upon the cornet, a young man previously elected for the purpose ; and he and the magistrates of the town on horseback, and a large body of the inhabitants and the burgesses, set out in procession for the purpose of riding round the property of the town and making formal demonstration of their legal rights.

Lanemar or Landmark Day is still observed in June of every year in Lanark, Scotland, by beating the marches of the town lands. One of the march stones is in the river Mouse, and formerly those who shared in the march for the first time were ducked in the river, to impress the event on their memories and give the town the benefit of their immemorial recollection.

Margaret, St. One of the tutelar saints of Cremona, and patroness of women in childbirth. Her festival is celebrated by the Roman Church on July 20, the reputed anniversary of her martyrdom, which is said to have occurred in the last general persecution. The Greeks, however, make the date July 17. The legend represents her as a native of Antioch in Pisidia, who was converted by a Christian nurse, was persecuted by her own father, a pagan priest, and was beheaded after many torments. While in prison awaiting death she was visited by the devil in the form of a dragon, who swallowed her, but instantly burst asunder, leaving her unhurt. On her way to the place of execution she prayed that, in memory of her having been delivered unhurt from the dragon, she might aid all women who called on her in the pains of childbirth. Her cult spread from the East to England, France, Germany, and Italy during the eleventh century, and in the thirteenth her anniversary was made a holiday of obligation in England, all manual labor being forbidden. Her body is shown entire at Monte Fiascone, in Tuscany. Another body, equally authentic, is in the monastery of St. Catherine at Mount Sinai. In addition, half a dozen heads and other relics are exhibited in various European churches. In art, St. Margaret is represented with a cross in her hand and a dragon by her side, and sometimes as rising from a dragon.

Mariazell. A little village in the duchy of Styria, Austria, containing the most famous shrine in Austria. The object of veneration is a miracle-working image of the Virgin, carved in lime-tree wood and about eighteen inches high. It was found in the ninth century on the plateau where the village now stands, and after many vicissitudes came into the possession of a priest of the Benedictine order, who in 1157 built a shrine for it. Henry I., Marquis of Moravia, replaced the shrine by a chapel in 1200, and Ludwig I., King of Hungary, after recovery here from a painful attack of gout, transformed the chapel into the present large church in 1363. The towers on either side of the Gothic spire are, however, of much later origin. The treasure-chamber is reported to possess valuables to the extent of over a million dollars. Many pilgrims come as mere holiday-makers, but still more in search of miraculous cures. Over a hundred thousand men, women, and even children pass yearly over the roads that converge towards this town,—chiefly peasants from all parts of the dual monarchy, from Northern Bohemia, from Southern Hungary, from as far off as Croatia,—peasants dressed in different national costumes, and speaking languages of equal variety. The entire population of a village may march out under the leadership of the village school-master, carrying a banner. In summer they can easily cover a distance of fifty miles, and they sing hymns for spiritual stimulation when bodily weariness sets in. In fine weather they sleep in the woods, in the meadows, or by the roadside. On wet nights they find shelter in wide spaces specially provided for them under the rafters of wayside taverns. The tariff per head is about a dime in our money. The poorer pilgrims, however, are glad to enjoy a "twopenny doss" on the dusty floors of the passages.

For pilgrims from Vienna the journey to and from takes four days. Their point of departure is the old cathedral of St. Stephen. They divide themselves into troops and walk in the wake of a banner. Each pilgrim carries a garland in his left hand and sticks ornamented with flowers in his right. The men wear large straw hats; the women don their holiday attire, including a lace bonnet. Many pilgrims, both male and female, make the pilgrimage in bare feet. Hymns are sung or prayers chanted all the way. At the approaches to the sacred city the various bands of pilgrims from all points of the compass mingle into one common stream. The climbing of the mountain, owing to the narrow roadway, can be accomplished only in couples. On reaching the summit the pilgrims hasten to prostrate themselves before the sacred image. All day long crowds of people fill the church. At night-time all who cannot afford or who fail to find shelter in the hotels sleep under improvised tents in the neighborhood of the sanctuary. When the pilgrimage is finished the pilgrims return home laden down with souvenirs of Mariazell in the shape of images, prayer-books, and rosaries purchased at the booths in the village.

Maries, Feast of the Holy. (Fr. *Fête des Saintes Maries.*) A festival celebrated in Provence, France, on April 24. The Provençal legend tells how during the persecution that arose shortly after the death of Christ certain of his intimates—viz., Lazarus and his two sisters Martha and Mary (the latter being identified by the legend with Mary Magdalene), Mary mother of James the Less, Mary Salome, Sara, their handmaiden, Trophimus, Saturninus, Maximin, and others—were forced into an unseaworthy boat and set adrift in the Mediterranean. The crazy bark, miraculously preserved from destruction, was guided to the shores of Provence, and the involuntary missionaries, landing at the extremity of the Camargue, devoted themselves to the evangelization of the country. Trophimus converted Arles; Saturninus, Toulouse; and Martha, Tarascon. But the three Maries lived and died on the Mediterranean coast, the Magdalene in her famous grotto, and the two others with their handmaiden Sara at the original landing-place, where they built themselves a cell. Sometimes fishermen passed by that lonely coast, and to them the saintly women preached the true faith and won them to Christ. Sometimes from Arles Trophimus came and administered the sacraments to his sisters in the Church. And the fame of the holiness of the three women went abroad, and when, after they died they were buried where they had lived, people journeyed from far and near to visit and pray at the tomb, and many miracles were worked, so that their renown grew ever greater and greater. Before many years it had become a well-known place of pilgrimage,—one of the most ancient in France,—and a mighty church was built over their lowly altar, and many and strange were the wonders wrought.

But Saracens and Danes reduced the church to ruins, and it was eventually rebuilt by William I., Count of Provence. So runs the local legend. Authentic history is silent as to the origin of the ancient church, but affirms that in 1448 the good King Réné discovered three bodies here which he decided were the remains of the two Maries and of Sara. He enclosed the Maries in a richly adorned casket, and built for its reception the curious little chapel on the roof of the church where they now repose and whence they are let down by pulleys once a year on the Maries' fête-day into the cavernous choir below. The relics of St. Sara were placed in the crypt, and are specially reverenced by the gypsies, who claim her as having been of their own race.

The feast of the Holy Maries, which is celebrated annually on the 23d, 24th, and 25th of May, attracts thousands of pilgrims, mostly farmers, peasants, and gypsies. The 24th is the great day when the relics are lowered into the choir. The scene is thus described by Joseph J. Pennell in the *Century :*

" By three o'clock the church was nearly full; by four it was jammed. Around each door outside was a great crowd; inside there was not an empty seat. The long ray of light which streamed in through the broken rose-window at the western end was momentarily shut out by the people who had climbed even away up there. Every one in nave and gallery held a lighted candle, which twinkled and flickered and waved with the great volume of the singing. ' We are in heaven, and the stars are

under our feet,' Gounod said when, one 24th of May, he looked
down upon the same scene. In the raised choir the sick still
waited, their friends and a few priests still prayed and chanted.
'The church was like a wind-swept wood' with the mighty voice
of their supplication.

"Suddenly there was a cry of 'They come!' The people
around the altar fell on their knees; for from the airy chapel,
high above the choir, a great double ark hung suspended, and
now began to move downward, though almost imperceptibly.
As it came slowly nearer the sick and infirm were raised toward
it in the arms of the strong. Women fairly wrestled together,
each seeking to be the first to lay her hand upon the holy relics.
When it was a few feet from its resting-place a solemn procession
of white-robed clergy passed from the sacristy to the choir, and
one priest, springing upon the altar, seized and kissed the relics.
At the same moment he was surrounded by the sick, who, as
though the longed-for miracle had already been worked, pushed
and struggled to touch and be healed. The priest held the
relics, and the people, pressing closer and closer, fell upon them,
touching them with their hands, their eyes, and even their crippled limbs, kissing them passionately, clasping them with frenzy.
It seemed as though the priest's vestments must be torn to
shreds, the relics broken and scattered in a thousand fragments,
from the very fervor of the faithful. But finally the last kiss was
given, the last petition uttered, the ark was set at rest upon the
altar, the sick were placed all around it, and the chants rose
louder and sweeter than ever,—' Vivent les Saintes Maries!'"

On the morning of the 25th a long procession marched from
the church to the sea-shore. It was headed by the banners
given by the various towns of Provence. Then came the Archbishop of Aix, attended by clergy and acolytes; next the sick
and ailing, some hobbling on crutches, some borne on mattresses,
others dragged along by their friends. "Last of all a struggling
crowd of gypsies carried aloft the rude figures of the two Maries
in their little boat, and on every side devout pilgrims strove to
kiss, or at least to touch, the holy bark. Across the sands to the
sea they went, to the water's edge, and then right into the
water, gypsies, people, and even priests. For a moment the
boat was set afloat upon the waves, there where at the dawn of
Christianity the wind had driven the saints from Jerusalem.
And the gypsies again raised it aloft, and waded to land; the
procession, with banners waving, candles flickering dimly in the
sunshine, hymns loudly chanted, turned again across the sands,
through the shadowy streets, and brought back their beloved
Maries to the church. The sick were placed once more about
the altar, and shouts of ' Vivent les Saintes Maries!' echoed

through the church, until, toward evening, the ark rose slowly to its airy chapel, while the faithful watched it with loving eyes."

On the foundation of the ruined château of Les Baux, in Arles, are carved three figures in Roman drapery with an almost effaced Latin inscription, which are held to be portraits of the Maries. These are visited by the neighboring peasantry on May 24 and decorated with flowers. Nevertheless, there are rationalists who hold that the three figures were made to represent the great general Marius (who was encamped near by for many months during his Gallic campaign, 100 B.C.), his wife Julia, and Martha, a Syrian prophetess, by whom Plutarch tells us that he was always accompanied.

Mark, St., patron saint of Venice. His festival is celebrated on the anniversary of his death, April 25 (68).

St. Mark the Evangelist was not an apostle, but a convert. He was the beloved disciple of St. Peter, who converted him. He journeyed with St. Peter to Rome, and there wrote his Gospel, according to some authorities, at the dictation of St. Peter. He afterwards went to Egypt, where he founded the Church of Alexandria, becoming bishop of the diocese. On account of the many miracles that he wrought, St. Mark was accused of being a sorcerer, and he was seized and dragged through the streets with cords until he died, A.D. 68. It is related that as soon as he expired a terrible storm of hail and lightning arose which destroyed his persecutors. The Christians buried his remains in Alexandria, where they were highly venerated.

Centuries passed. The great and growing city of Venice cast envious eyes upon the tomb of the Evangelist. She believed, though the legend was never received by the Church universal, that St. Mark had been sent by St. Peter as apostle to Aquileja, and that on his return to Rome his bark, driven by the wind, came to a landing on the low island which was the first site of the city of the lagoons. Here, while he was rapt in ecstasy, an angel of the Lord appeared to him and said, " Pax tibi, Marce. Hic requiescet corpus tuum." (" Peace be with thee, Mark. Here shall thy body rest.") The angel went on to prophesy that a devout and faithful people would here, after many years, build a marvellous city (*mirificam urbem*), and would deserve to possess the body of the saint, and that through his merits and prayers they would be greatly blessed.

Early in the ninth century two Venetian merchants, visiting Alexandria and finding that the Church authorities were fearful lest the shrine of St. Mark should be desecrated by the Saracens, succeeded in obtaining the coveted remains. The voyage to

Venice witnessed many miracles which gave assurance of the willingness of the saint to be transferred to his destined abode. On the vessel's arrival the Doge himself, accompanied by all the clergy, came down to the landing-place and bore the holy relics to the ducal chapel, where they were deposited until a more fitting resting-place could be prepared for them.

That resting-place was the church of St. Mark's, erected about 829, but destroyed by fire in 976 and rebuilt in 1042–1071. When the second church was finished the consecration was delayed. Ever since the fire of 976, for now a hundred years, the body of St. Mark had disappeared. This was occasion, says the Doge Andrea Dandolo in his chronicle, " of lamentation to the clergy, and of great depression to the laity." It was not to be believed that the sacred treasure, the palladium of the city, destined for it by the decree of Heaven, had perished. Without it the new church must remain vacant of its chief dignity. It could not be the divine will that Venice should be deprived of her own special saint. Now that at length the church was finished and adorned worthily to contain such a treasure, it was resolved, in June, 1094, to keep a fast throughout the city, and to make a most solemn procession through the church, with devout supplication to the Almighty that he would be pleased to reveal the place of concealment of the sacred relics. And, lo! while the procession was moving, of a sudden a light broke from one of the piers, a sound of cracking was heard, bricks fell upon the pavement, and there, within the pier, was beheld the body of the saint, with the arm stretched out, as if he had moved it to make the opening in the masonry; and on one finger was a ring of gold, which, after others had tried in vain, was drawn off by Giovanni Dolfino, one of the counsellors of the Doge.

The joy of the people was now as great as their grief had been before. The miracle quickened their devotion and excited their fancy, and on the 8th of October following, " the church being dedicated to God, the reverend body was laid away in a secret place, the Doge, the primate, and the procurator alone knowing where."

There was another body of St. Mark, however, at Constantinople, whence the head was brought to Soissons. Arms of the saint are shown at St. Mark's Church in Rome, at Marolles, Cambrai, and other places.

On the feast of St. Mark the Catholic Church sings her great litanies to beg that God will avert the scourges due to sin, a custom said to have originated with Gregory the Great. Hence in old calendars the feast is known as Litania Major. Anciently solemn processions of covered crosses were held on this day. These were frequently confounded with the Rogation processions, which, depending upon the movable feast of the Ascension, might occasionally fall as early as April 26.

In England, during the rule of the Roman Church, St. Mark's Day was a great fast. Vaughan says, "I remember, in 1589, being then a boy, that an ale-wife, making no exception of days, would brew upon St. Mark's Day. While she was thus laboring the chimney took fire and her house was burnt. Surely a gentle warning to them that violate forbidden days." Another writer observes "that though there was not anciently any fast-day between Easter and Whitsunday, the Popes had devised a monstrous fast on St. Mark's Day." St. Mark, it appears, was made an exception, and "had his day fasted."

At Alnwick, in Northumberland, England, a ridiculous custom called the Freeman's March (*q. v.*) was kept up till a recent date on St. Mark's Day.

Marriage. Originally man appears to have been a polygamous animal. The Jews of the earlier Old Testament period were polygamous, but later changed their ways, possibly through the influence of their Roman conquerors. Jews since then and Christians from the time of the foundation of their religion have been ostensibly monogamous. The Catholic and Greek Churches make marriage a sacrament, and most other Christian creeds hold that the presence of an officiating clergyman, if not actually obligatory, is, what is more awe-inspiring, "correct." Nevertheless many of the social customs that surround the Christian ceremony have their roots in the pagan past.

In that past marriage was first intertribal, and then exogamous, or outside of the tribe. The first form of exogamous marriage was marriage by capture. The bridegroom simply went out on the war-path, accompanied by a doughty friend or two, seized upon such damsel as had strayed away from parental covert, and carried her away to his home.

In our modern marriage rite the very name of that now useless appendage the "best man" suggests that he is a relic of marriage by capture. He was the strong-armed warrior who assisted the would-be groom to carry off his bride. The wedding-ring symbolizes the fetter with which the bride was bound; the jocose slipper thrown after the departing couple adumbrates the angry missiles hurled by the outstripped pursuers of the past. The honeymoon itself symbolizes that space of time when the captor had to hide his prize from her kinsmen until their consent had been gained.

More obvious survivals are found in all primitive neighborhoods. Among the Irish mountaineers a marriage is considered but a tame affair unless the bridegroom run away with the bride.

In Cardiganshire, Wales, the relatives of the bride assemble and offer a mock resistance to the entrance of the groom, and after a good deal of scuffling and horse-play a dialogue (chiefly in verse) is carried on by two persons,—one on either side. After this the bridegroom is admitted, and sets about seeking the bride, who is commonly disguised in some manner,—as an old woman, for instance, with a male infant, a symbol of good luck and promise of sons, upon her lap. On arriving at the church door the bride is seized by her relatives, who ride off with her, the bridegroom and his party in pursuit. On being overtaken the bride is at once handed over, and whoever caught her is certain to be married within a year.

Marriage by purchase succeeded marriage by capture. Indeed, the two gradually merged together in the latter days of the capture period. The pursuing father gradually learned to mitigate his wrath in the presence of cash or other equivalent. The bridegroom might offer in lieu of cash his own sister, or horses, or cattle, or land. This kind of marriage is still prevalent among semi-civilized as the other among barbarous nations. For example, it exists among the Chinese and various Mohammedan tribes.

Perhaps the most perfect system of marriage by purchase was that of the Babylonians and Assyrians. They assembled all girls of marriageable age in the space before the temple twice a year, and sold them. The handsome girls brought high prices, and the sums so received were turned over to the homely ones as a counter-attraction. Thus every girl caught a husband, some by beauty and some by money.

Marriage by purchase was prevalent among the Anglo-Saxons at the time when Christianity first reached them. Every woman was under the care of some man, who was termed her *mundbora*, or guardian; and no one could marry her without having paid a sum of money as a compensation to him. The father was the guardian of his unmarried daughters; the brother, if the father died; and the next to him the nearest male relative. If, however, the female was friendless and alone, she found in the king her legal guardian. The maid was estimated according to her rank in life. The first step in courtship, therefore, was to buy the consent of the *mundbora*; the lover was then admitted into the society of his mistress, and allowed to claim her in due course as his wife. If, however, her personal charms or her disposition proved, on better acquaintance, unsatisfactory to her suitor, and he failed to complete the bargain, he immediately became amenable to the law. If a man ventured to marry without first having bought and paid for his wife, he was guilty of the crime of *mundbreach*, the consequences of which were both vexatious and disastrous. The husband in such a case possessed no legal authority over his wife; he was a husband, in fact, without a wife; he had no right to her property. By the same law a maiden and a widow were of separate value; the latter could be purchased for one-half the sum which the guardian of a maid was entitled to demand; the man, therefore, who could not afford to purchase a maid might perhaps be able to purchase a widow.

Thrupp, in his "Anglo-Saxon House," gives a full account of a wedding in those days. Not till the ninth or tenth century did women obtain the privilege of choosing or refusing their husbands. Often they were betrothed when children, the bridegroom's pledge of marriage being accompanied by a security, or "wed," whence comes the word. Part of the wedding always consisted of a ring placed on the maiden's right hand and there religiously kept until transferred to the other hand at the later nuptials. Then, also, were repeated the marriage vows and other ceremonies, out of which those now prevailing have grown. The bride was taken "for fairer or fouler, for better or worse, for richer or poorer," and promised to be "buxom and bonny" to her future husband. At the final ceremony the bridegroom put the ring on each of the bride's left-hand fingers in turn, saying at the first, "in the name of the Father;" at the second, "in the name of the Son;" at the third, "in the name of the Holy Ghost;" and at the fourth, "Amen." Then also the father gave to his new son one of his daughter's shoes, in token of the transfer of authority which he effected, and the bride was at once made to feel the change by a tap or a blow on the head given with the shoe. The husband on his part took an oath to use his wife well. If he failed to do so, she might leave him, but by the law he was allowed considerable license. He was bound in honor "to bestow on his wife and apprentices moderate castigation." An old Welsh law decides that three blows with a broomstick on "any part of the person except the head" is a fair allowance, and another provides that the stick be no longer than the husband's arm nor thicker than his middle finger. Prior to the seventh century a wife might at any time be repudiated on proof of her being either barren, deformed, silly, passionate, luxurious, rude, habitually drunk, gluttonous, very garrulous, quarrelsome, or abusive.

Even after the triumph of Christianity marriage for a long time continued to be a purely secular matter. But slowly and gradually the Church encroached upon the State until she finally arrogated to herself the control of marriage as a department of life lying within the province of sacerdotal duty. She drew her precedents from the past. Under the Roman republic marriage was a solemn religious ordinance. Under the Empire, when religion fell into contempt, it came to be virtually a civil contract.

Christianity gave back to marriage its religious character, but only by slow degrees. At first Christian couples pairing off together asked for the blessing of their pastor. In mediæval times the priest was even called in to bless the marriage bed.

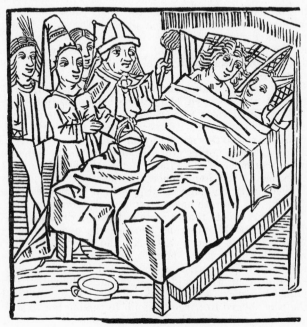

BLESSING THE MARRIAGE BED.
(From an old German print.)

The custom of an ecclesiastical marriage became more and more general. Finally, in 1563, at the Council of Trent, it was made binding.

Though the Protestants rejected the sacramental idea of marriage, they none the less looked upon it as a divine institution, and its celebration in church grew to be indispensable.

The ancient usage was for the priest to join the hands of the man and woman after their consent to the marriage, with such words as " Et ego vos conjungo," etc. Then he laid the ends of his stole upon the hands so joined. It is ordered in some early Roman Sacerdotalia, but disappeared from the Roman Rituale at or before the revision of Paul V. It was, however, retained in the local books of many Continental dioceses.

At Liége the hands were bound together with the ends of the stole, and the practice was the same elsewhere. But it would seem that the usage was not followed in England. Indeed, the ceremony with which it is connected is absent from most English books, probably because in the English forms of the service the joining of hands took place at the time when the man and woman gave their troth to each other. The later joining of their hands by the priest after the delivery of the ring was introduced into England in 1549. It is a ceremony analogous to but distinct from that with which the action with the stole is sometimes conjoined.

To mark the importance and validity of a betrothal, the Council of Trent also declared clandestine betrothals to be null and void. It required them to be celebrated before the curé, in the presence of two or three witnesses at least. Greater weight was afterwards given to this article by an *ordonnance* of Louis XIII., which forbade any notary (that is, any civilian) to sanction or receive any promise of the kind. Before the first French Revolution, such was the importance attached to this pious custom that, except with an express dispensation from the bishop, a priest could not betroth and marry a young couple in the same day. It was requisite that a certain lapse of time, as a test of their fidelity, should intervene between the one ceremony and the other. The old French canon law had provided for the case in which a faithless *fiancé* should marry any other than his betrothed bride. The marriage consecrated by a sacrament was more binding than the simple engagement of betrothal; but if the culprit became a widower, and his first love required it of him, he was obliged to purge his guilt by taking her to wife.

Another way in which the Church had marked its authority long before the Council of Trent was by the prohibition of marriage during certain periods, as the seasons of Advent, Lent, and Whitsuntide. The old register of Cottenham, Cambridgeshire contains this triplet in doggerel Latin:

> Conjugium Adventus prohibet, Hilarique relaxat,
> Septuagena vetat, sed Paschæ octava remittit,
> Rogamen vetitat, concedit Trina potestas.

Similar lines in English are inserted in the register of Everton, Nottinghamshire:

> Advent marriage doth deny,
> But Hilary gives thee liberty.
> Septuagesima says thee nay,
> Eight days from Easter says you may.
> Rogation bids thee to contain,
> But Trinity sets thee free again.

The close time was restricted to Advent and Lent by the Council of Trent (*Concil. Trident.*, 24. Sessio, cap. x.), but this decree had no force in England, and the canons of the Anglican Church still forbid marriages to be celebrated between Rogation Sunday and Trinity Sunday. Such prohibitions, however, have ceased to be regarded in England, and Lent has become, during the present reign, the favorite season for royal marriages.

And now a glance at marriage customs the world over.

In the Greek Church the rites are more elaborate than in any other Christian denomination, if the contracting parties be of any social influence.

Fashion demands for the celebration of the ceremony the chapel of some private house, if the couple have not sufficiently lofty relations to secure the chapel of the palace. A family that respects itself ought to have at its wedding as honorary father and honorary mother, if not the Emperor and the Empress, at least a grand-duke and a grand-duchess. The honorary father gives the holy image, which some little child related to the families carries in front of the *fiancés*. They enter the church, followed by all their friends in gala uniform. The ceremony begins; it is very long, and complicated with many symbolic rites; a small table—a sort of movable altar—is placed in the middle of the oratory; the couple are separated from it by a band of rose-colored satin; when the priest calls, they must advance, and the first who sets foot on the band, whether husband or wife, will be the one who will impose his or her will on the household. This is an article of faith for all the matrons, who watch them at that moment. On the table are placed the liturgical formulary, the candles which they must hold, the cross which they will kiss, the rings which they will exchange, the cup of wine in which they will moisten their lips, and which is called in the Slavonic ritual "the cup of bitterness." Pages relieve each other to carry with outstretched arms two heavy crowns, which must be held above the heads of the *fiancés* while the ceremony continues. At the decisive moment, when the priest is pronouncing the words that bind them together, the couple walk three times around the altar, followed by the crown-bearers; until the third turn is completed there is time to turn back; after that the die is cast, the couple are united for life. Thereupon the singers strike up in their most strident voices the joyous hymn "Let Israel rejoice."

The bride and groom then go and prostrate themselves before a picture of the Virgin, after which they pass into the salon, where champagne is opened and the guests are presented with boxes of sweetmeats marked with the monograms of the young couple.

To eat maize pudding from the same plate, or to eat in any way together, is a widely distributed marriage ceremony. In Brazil a couple may be married by drinking brandy together ; in Japan, by so many cups of wine ; in Russia and Scandinavia it used to be one cup for both. The joining of hands among the Romans and Hindoos is common to many parts of the world. In Scotland it is called " hand-fasting," and couples live together after. To sit together on a seat while receiving friends, or to have the hands of each tied together with grass, or to smear with each other's blood, or for the woman to tie a cord of her own twisting around the naked waist of the man, constitutes marriage in one part or another.

In Australia a woman carries fire to her lover's hut and makes a fire for him. In America she lays a bundle of rods at the door of his tent. A Loango negress cooks two dishes for him in his own hut. In Croatia the bridegroom boxes the bride's ears, and in Russia the father formerly struck his daughter gently with a new whip—for the last time—and then gave the weapon to her husband. Down to the present, it is a custom in Hungary for the groom to give the bride a kick after the marriage ceremony, to make her feel her subjection. Even with all civilized peoples the servitude of the bride is clearly indicated.

The Jewish ceremony is picturesque. The bride dresses in pure white satin, and faces the bridegroom under the *chuppah,* or matrimonial baldacchino. The ritual is read, and a cup of consecrated wine is presented to bride and groom to be sipped. Then comes the address from the officiating rabbi, who closes by taking a glass of wine in his hand and pronouncing the seven prescribed benedictions. Again bridegroom and bride taste the cup; after which the groom places it on the floor and crushes it to atoms under his feet, as a symbol that the marriage must last until the fragments can be united. The first kiss under the new relation is given, and the newly wedded man escorts his wife from chuppah to entrance and then home to the marriage-feast.

Martha, St., of Bethany, patron saint of cooks and housewives. Her festival is celebrated on July 29, the reputed anniversary of her death (A.D. 84). She figures in the Gospels as the sister of Lazarus and the friend of Christ. (For the legend of her adventures after the crucifixion see MARY MAGDALENE, whom tradition makes her sister ; also MARIES, THE THREE.) She is specially honored in Tarascon, the city built on the spot where she captured a terrible dragon called Tarasque which was devastating the neighborhood, and which she bound fast with her girdle so that the people could come up and slay him. The famous Miracle Play of Sainte-Marthe.et el Tarasque, instituted, it was said, by King Réné in 1400, was one of the last Provençal *coronlas* to disappear, as in its day it was one of the most popular. Louis XI. came down to see it in 1444, when he was still dauphin. At all events, he solemnly protested that he came for the play alone, though unfriendly critics accused him of wishing to spy out the land and estimate his chances of succeeding to his uncle King Réné, whose only daughter Margaret was the hapless wife of Henry VI. of England.

LA TARASQUE.

Even after the Mystery Play was itself abandoned, a remnant of it lingered on until the middle of the nineteenth century, in the annual procession of La Tarasque celebrated on July 29 not only at Tarascon but also at Beaucaire. The main feature was a huge figure of a dragon, made of wood and canvas, eight feet long, three feet high, and four feet broad in the middle. The head was small, there was no neck, the body, which was covered with scales, was shaped like an enormous egg, and at the nether extremity was a heavy beam of wood for a tail. Sixteen mummers gayly caparisoned and known as the Knights of la Tarasque were among its attendants. Eight of the knights concealed themselves within the body to represent those who had been devoured, and furnished the motive power, besides lashing the tail to right and left, at imminent risk to the legs of the spectators. The other eight formed the escort, and were followed by drummers and fifers and a long procession of clergy and laity. The dragon was conducted by a girl in white and blue, the leading-string being her girdle of blue silk. When the dragon was especially unruly and frolicsome she dashed holy water over it.

A continuous rattle of torpedoes and musketry was kept up by those who followed in the dragon's train.

The merrymaking was often emphasized by practical joking of a rude sort which frequently led to violent affrays. It was these scenes of disorder which caused the suppression of the spectacle. But the Tarasque itself is still preserved.

St. Martha's attributes in art are a dragon and a pot of holy water, the latter distinguishing her from St. Margaret, who bears a cross. A cooking-utensil is sometimes substituted for the pot.

The body of St. Martha, miraculously discovered in the thirteenth century at Tarascon, is still preserved in a splendid subterraneous chapel of the collegiate church of St. Martha in that town. The head is kept in a rich bust of gold presented by Louis XI.

Martin, St. Bishop of Tours, patron of that city and generally of beggars, tavern-keepers, and vine-growers. His principal festival, famous under the name of Martinmas, occurs on November 11, the day of his burial. A minor feast in honor of his ordination and the translation of his relics is celebrated locally in France on July 4, and another in honor of their return from Auxerre to Tours, called Relatio, on December 13.

The son of a Roman military tribune, born at Sabaria, Hungary, about 316, and bred a soldier, St. Martin forsook the army to retire into monastic seclusion, whence he emerged in 371 to become Bishop of Tours. It was during his military career that he divided his cloak with a poor beggar shivering at the gate of Amiens. Both before and during his bishopric he proved an earnest preacher of the gospel, converting the entire province to Christianity, destroying many pagan temples, and beating back the inroads of Arianism. He recalled to life, for the purpose of baptism, two people who had died without that sacrament, and performed many other wonders. The Emperor Maximus, when he established his capital at Treves, invited the saint to a royal banquet. Wishing to pay him a special mark of honor, Maximus offered him the wine cup before drinking himself, whereupon Martin passed it to a humble priest who stood behind him, to show that he accounted the least of the servants of God before the greatest rulers of earth,—an action that was loudly applauded by the Emperor and all his court. St. Martin died on the 8th of November, probably in 397. Poitiers warmly disputed the possession of his body, but the people of Tours carried it off and buried it in a neighboring grove amid a vast concourse, among whom were two thousand monks and a great concourse of virgins. Here St. Brice, his successor in the bishopric, built a chapel, and later St. Perpetuus founded the great church and monastery of St. Martin, a sumptuous tomb at the back of the high altar being erected for the remains, which were translated hither on July 4. The shrine became so great a place of pilgrimage for all Europe that in mediæval times it was called a second Jerusalem, and the fame of its riches tempted the Saracens to press northward to the plains of Touraine, but, fortunately, to be forever crushed in Gaul by Charles Martel. In the sixteenth century the Huguenots rifled the tomb and scattered the relics, but the church recovered a bone of his arm and a part of his skull. Before this dispersion certain churches had obtained small portions, which they still preserve. Thus, the priory of St. Martin's-in-the-Field in Paris possessed a part, and two teeth are shown at St. Martin's at Tournay. The cloak which St. Martin divided with the beggar was for many centuries preserved in an oratory near the church in Tours, and was carried as a banner in war. It is said that the word chapel,— French *chapelle,*—derived from *chape* or cape, was first applied to this oratory, and that chaplain or *chapelain* was originally the person intrusted with the care of it.

As the feast of Martinmas occurs at the genial period of the year when the harvest is in, and cattle are slain for the winter season, and new wine is first opened and tasted, it followed that Martin became the embodiment of good cheer and inherited some of the characteristics of the ancient Bacchus. There is certainly a strong resemblance between the Vinalia of the ancients and the Martinalia of the mediæval period. Brand quotes an ancient ecclesiastical calendar which under the head of November 11 expressly says, "The Vinalia, a feast of the ancients removed to this day, Bacchus in the figure of Martin." The Danes and the Saxons made St. Martin's Day the occasion of a special carouse which evidently borrowed some of its details from the Roman original.

In continental Europe, the fat goose which in England is most appropriate to Michaelmas was eaten on St. Martin's Day and washed down with copious draughts of wine. A fatted ox, sometimes called a mart, was substituted in England. That is one reason why the saint and his feast became so popular with beef-eating Britons. No less than seven churches were named after him in London. A more emphatic mark of popular approval was blazoned in the hall of the Vintners' Company, where Bacchus and St. Martin divide the pictorial and statuary honors.

When Sir Samuel Dashwood, a vintner, became lord mayor in Queen Anne's time, he had the soldier saint in full armor in his show, preceded by Roman lictors, and followed by a troop of beggars "howling lamentably." At St. Paul's Churchyard he who personated the saint cut his scarlet velvet cloak in many pieces, which he distributed among them, much to the edification of her majesty, who thereafter graciously condescended to dine with the lord mayor at the Guildhall, and to eat and drink a great deal, as became Martinmas, and as was that red-faced woman's habit.

In the North Riding of Yorkshire it was formerly customary for a party of singers, mostly consisting of women, to begin at the feast of St. Martin a kind of peregrination round the neighboring villages, carrying with them a small waxen image of our Saviour adorned with box and other evergreens, and singing at the same time a hymn which, though rustic and uncouth, was nevertheless replete with the sacred story of the Nativity. " The custom is yearly continued till Christmas Eve, when the feasting, or, as they usually call it, ' good living,' commences ; every rustic dame produces a cheese preserved for the sacred festival, upon which, before any part of it is tasted, according to an old custom, she with a sharp knife makes rude incisions to represent the cross. With this, and furmity made of barley and meal, the cottage affords uninterrupted hospitality." (*Gentleman's Magazine*, 1811, vol. lxxxi. pt. i. p. 423.)

At St. Peter's, Athlone, Ireland, "every family of a village," says Mason, in his "Statistical Account of Ireland" (1819, vol. iii. p. 75), "kills an animal of some kind or other : those who are rich kill a cow or a sheep, others a goose or a turkey ; while those who are poor and cannot procure an animal of greater value kill a hen or a cock, and sprinkle the threshold with the blood, and do the same in the four corners of the house, and this ceremonious performance is done to exclude every kind of evil spirit from the dwelling where this sacrifice is made, till the return of the same day in the following year."

If St. Martin's Day be bright and sunshiny there will be a cold winter, or if the trees and vines still retain their foliage the same will follow. But if there be frost before Martinmas the winter will be mild. If the goose slips on the ice at Martinmas she will stick in the mud at Christmas.

Martinmas in some places is rent-day, and debts are paid and cancelled ; the servants also change places on that day, and they say of any one who is changeable and flighty, "He'll eat no Martin's kail," meaning that he'll not stay a year in the same place.

The European association of goose with the saint's day has been variously explained.

Sulpicius Severus, who lived at the beginning of the fifth century and who wrote a book on the life of St. Martin, says, "The feast of St. Martin is set for the 11th of November. This day the Christians observe by drinking and stuffing themselves with roast goose; they do this, it is said, because a goose betrayed St. Martin by her cries while he was concealed in the stall; others say that having eaten the whole of a goose at one meal he died from the effects of it. These are but legends, as the custom is traced to the people of the Northern countries, who are as fond of goose as we are of partridge."

Another writer has it that it was and is customary among the clergy to prepare for fasting by feasting. About the middle of the fifth century Perpetuus, Bishop of Tours, ordered a fast to be observed three times a week from Martinmas to Christmas, and, as geese are supposed to be particularly fine eating at this time of the year, the goose came to be the bird of the day.

A third legend relates that a goose so sadly disturbed St. Martin, when he was preaching, that he retired to a cave to be out of the goose's way; but even there the bird pursued him; and finally the saint made a too hearty dinner of goose, which proved his death. The association is so firmly established that on Martinmas in some parts of France no one dares to drive his geese to pasture, as the goose is then common property and every one may help himself.

If you have roast goose at Martinmas you must ask St. Martin to dine with you, otherwise the goose may not be forthcoming in the following year. There is a superstition that if the farmer has not finished his field-work by Martinmas he will bury his wife before the winter is over.

In France it was for a long time the custom to hang up a goat by the legs and then slowly torture it to death. Clearly this was a survival of an ancient pagan practice.

On Martinmas the first new wine was tasted, and this often gave rise to carousals and drunken feasting, so that poor St. Martin soon came to be in bad repute, and any one who was particularly given to dissipation was called a " Martinsman."

The French call feasting at this time of year " faire le Saint-Martin," and a spoiled stomach is known as " mal de Saint-Martin."

In Germany the proverb says that

> The hog that's killed at Martinmas
> Must be eat up by Candlemas.

This is quite the reverse of another old proverb, which warns people against using up more than half of their provisions before Candlemas (February 2), Martinmas being considered the beginning of winter and Candlemas about the middle of it. The French say, " A la Saint-Martin l'hiver en chemin."

Before the Christian era the people of the North sacrificed to their god Odin, or Wodin, after the harvest, and the little cakes baked all over Germany on this day are in the shape of a horn or a horseshoe, one of the symbols of Wodin.

Along the banks of the Rhine they build immense fires on the hill-tops, and when their red glow illumines the landscape all join hands and dance merrily in a circle around the fires, singing and shouting to their hearts' content.

They have a pretty custom in Suabia of giving presents to the school-master on this day. About a week before Martinmas the older pupils begin secretly to collect gifts from the other children and their parents. When the day arrives the school-master is presented with a fine fat goose, gayly decked with ribbons. They also give him plenty of corn to feed it with, in addition to wine and grapes, and an immense cake in the form of a wreath, that is often three feet in diameter. In some places the children go about in the evening singing and soliciting gifts of apples, nuts, and cakes. When they are successful they reward the giver by telling him that

> Martin is a good man,
> He'll repay you if he can.

But when they receive nothing they cry,—

> Codfish, codfish,
> You always give us an empty dish.

In Halle the children of the Halloren—men who work in the salt-mines there—firmly believe that St. Martin has the power to change water into wine. They therefore fill their jugs with water and kick them, singing,—

> Martine, Martine,
> Change the water to wine.

The parents then secretly take the jugs, empty the water, and refill them with wine; then a martin's horn—a cake baked in the shape of a horn—is laid on top, and the jugs are returned to their hiding-places. The children, after having prayed to St. Martin, hunt for the jugs, and great is their satisfaction at finding that the good saint has answered their prayers.

What Americans call Indian summer (*q. v.*) is in England known as St. Martin's summer, and in France as L'été de Saint-Martin.

But the most curious ceremonial practised in honor of St. Martin is at Dunkerque. A local legend thus explains it. About the year 386, St. Martin, on his travels through Gaul, happened to arrive one evening at Dunkerque, or rather the spot where Dunkerque now stands. He was riding leisurely on donkey-back. Stopping at a little chapel near the Dunes, he left his ass waiting at the gates. There are doubts whether such a chapel existed then, but legends do not scruple at anachronistic details. St. Martin entered some chapel or house. While he was saying his prayers within-doors, the animal strayed away to search for the prickly eringo, or sea-holly, which had caused his mouth to water along the road. His master, missing him, begged the neighboring fishermen to lend their aid to recover him. The worthy fellows started at once, regardless of its being night: some, with resin torches in their hands; some, with the lanterns belonging to their fishing-boats; while others blew the horn which still announces the arrival of a boat at the beach, and which may be made to give a not bad imitation of a donkey's bray when it tries to sing small. At last the gluttonous ass was found, and brought back to the village under the escort of a troop of children, who, as they travelled along the road, were treated, by St. Martin's intervention and the donkey's keep, with an unexpected supply of exquisite spice-bread.

In modern times, on the evening of St. Martin's Day at Dunkerque—and at Dunkerque only—the whole population claims the privilege of going mad from five o'clock till seven in commemoration of the finding of St. Martin's ass. The next day, at the same hour, a second paroxysm returns; and then the town remains sane for a twelvemonth. The professed actors in the farce are all the children of the place, little and big, boys and girls, from babies at the breast to overgrown boarding-school masters and misses. But as the youngsters do not turn out alone, and the old folks enjoy the fun as thoroughly as their juniors, it is hardly an exaggeration to say that the whole city makes a good-natured fool of itself. A writer in *Household Words*, vol. vii. p. 332, thus describes the scene: "Fancy the streets crowded with children, from three to a hundred and eighty months old, and every one of them carrying in his hand a paper lamp of some fashion. Flowers of all colors and shapes, churches, houses, and fantastical figures, are illuminated by a candle's-end that is stuck on a save-all at the extremity of a stick. The usual gas-lights are perfectly unnecessary; for the rays sent forth by the thousands of lanterns produce a brilliant substitute; and by way of musical accompaniment to the scene there are hundreds of penny trumpets, which are expressly prepared for this occasion only.

"As soon as the juvenile orgy begins, no carriage is permitted to pass through the streets; nor *could* it, without committing a Juggernautian slaughter of innocents. The crowd, which eddies and flows in all directions, treads so closely and compactly on one another's heels that a pin could not fall to the ground between them. It is one of the many things of which it may be truly observed that to be believed it must be seen and heard.

"But as all the principal performers are children, and as children go to bed at an early hour, at seven o'clock the throng begins to thin; at half-past seven it is thoroughly ashamed of itself; at eight the town is as sober as usual. The gas is lighted, the vehicles roll along, and the young rogues munch their *croquandoules*, or donkey-nuts, while they undress themselves and jump into bed."

"This country having no patron saint, a contributor to the *Holy Cross Magazine*, the organ of the extreme Catholic party of the Episcopalians, suggests that the omission be supplied by the selection of St. Martin of Tours.

"His reasons for the suggestion are the coincidence that the great festival in commemoration of St. Martin occurs on the Fourth of July, the anniversary of the transportation of the saint's remains, and the circumstance of ' his association with our national colors.' His ordination also is commemorated on the Fourth of July, and his relations to the French, with whose aid we conquered our independence, together with the distinguishing qualities of his character, recommend him peculiarly to Americans, in the opinion of this writer. It is true that St. Martin was not an American, having lived more than a thousand years before the time of Columbus, but that does not constitute a valid objection, to the thinking of the *Holy Cross* writer, ' since Wales, with St. David, is almost alone in possessing as patron a countryman.' If England has St. George of Cappadocia and Ireland St. Patrick of France, why, he asks, should not this country have St. Martin of Tours ?

"The democratic simplicity of the life and the strength of the character of St. Martin, his independence, and his rugged virtues, seem to the *Holy Cross Magazine* writer to make him a very fitting and congenial patron saint for the American people. ' Moreover, the bedesman supported by a royal French endowment wore, in commemoration of the saint, a mantle of red and white, while the cappa of St. Martin, before it was superseded by the oriflamme as the standard of France, was a blue banner of three points.' The variety of his experiences as soldier, exorcist, hermit, monk, and bishop seems also to this writer to be ' a passport to the affections of a people whose avocations are apt to have nearly as wide a range.' St. Martin, too, appears to him especially qualified to be the patron saint of a country whose population is made up of so many nationalities, for, a Hungarian by birth, he was educated in Lombardy, was a soldier in Cisalpine and Transalpine Gaul, a hermit near Genoa, and a bishop between Tours and Treves, a town which is now in Germany.

"The suggestion is interesting, but so long as the present religious disagreement between Roman Catholics and Protestants continues it is not likely to be adopted by popular consent, for of course there must be such consent if we are to have a patron saint generally acknowledged. Moreover, there will be strong objection to importing a saint for the purpose. This country is growing more and more patriotic, jingoistic, as the Mugwumps call it, more self-sufficient, and a patron saint not native to its soil and not associated with its history is not likely to appeal to popular sentiment." (*New York Sun*, July 7, 1896.)

Martyrs for the Holy Scriptures. The 2d of January is specially set apart in the Roman calendar to honor, under this name, the Christians throughout the Roman provinces who, when Diocletian in 303 commanded all copies of the Scriptures to be seized and burned, chose rather to suffer tortures and death than to surrender the sacred writings to the enemies of God. This festival was in Catholic times observed with much ceremony in Lichfield, England, whose very name is derived from Like-field, the "field of corpses," because it is traditionally held that many Christians suffered there during the Diocletian persecution. The arms of Lichfield are a plain strewn with corpses. History, however, is silent on this event.

Mary Magdalene, St. (so called because she was a native of Magdala, in Galilee), patroness of Provence and Marseilles, and of penitent fallen women. Her festival is celebrated on July 22, the traditionary date of her death.

Catholic legend has insisted on identifying as one person Mary of Bethany (the sister of Lazarus), the unnamed "woman which was a sinner" who in Simon's house anointed Christ's feet (Luke vii. 37, 38), and "Mary called Magdalene," who was delivered by our Lord of seven demons (Luke viii. 2) and thereafter followed him from place to place, was present at the crucifixion (John xix. 25) and the burial (Mark xv. 47), came on Easter morning with other women to embalm his body (Mark xvi. 1), and, finding the tomb empty, informed Peter and John, but lingered after they had gone, and was honored with the first appearance of the risen Lord (John xx. 1–18). Modern Biblical critics generally look upon these as three different individuals, and few Catholic theologians accept the identity of Mary of Magdala and Mary of Bethany, though they generally lean to the opinion that the former was one with the penitent woman of Luke vii.

The ancient legends, however, are insistent in their details.

The Magdalene with them was the sister of Lazarus and Martha of Bethany. Martha was virtuous, but Mary, giving herself up to vice, came to be known to all as "the Sinner." Martha in pitiful distress begged her to call on Jesus. Mary obeyed, was stricken with penitence, and was forgiven, the seven demons cast out of her being the seven deadly sins to which she had become a slave. After the Ascension the legend tells how Lazarus and his sisters and many of their friends were placed by their persecutors in an open boat, rudderless and sailless, which was miraculously landed at Marseilles (see MARIES, THE THREE), and how most of the little company dispersed to preach the gospel throughout Provence. But Mary decided to retire into the wilderness, to bewail her sins in solitude. While wandering in the forest known as *la forêt de la Baume,* or forest of the cavern, a few miles from Marseilles, a flock of angels swooped down and carried her to the cave high up in an inaccessible rock. Here, with only her hair to hide her nakedness, and a psalter and a crucifix for furniture, she lived for thirty years. When she felt the approach of death, her old friends the angels flew with her to St. Maximin's oratory. He had just time to give her the last sacraments when she breathed her last, and her soul was seen to fly up to heaven in the form of a dove, July 22, A.D. 86. As to her body, Maximin placed it in a fine marble sepulchre and built over it a church.

Church and sepulchre passed away. In the thirteenth century a lot of bones supposed to be the remains of the Magdalene and others of her band were found at the little town of St. Maximin. On this spot was built in 1279 the basilica of St. Maximin, which still possesses a blackened skull encased in gold, shown as the Magdalene's, and also a pair of rude sarcophagi in its very ancient crypt, which are held to be those of the saint and her maid Marcilla. But another body of the Magdalene, supported by another legend, was shown as early as 1146 at Vézelay, which according to Fleury was visited by St. Louis in 1267. A third body now in St. John Lateran's at Rome, and a third legend, complicate matters considerably. This legend makes the Magdalene accompany John and the Virgin to Ephesus, where she died and was buried in the year 90. In 869 her remains were translated to Constantinople, and in 1216 to Rome.

The chief shrine, however, of the repentant Magdalene is La Sainte Baume, the Holy Cave, in which, according to the Provencal legend, she spent thirty years. No spot was more famous in the Middle Ages. There were few kings of France from St. Louis to Louis XIV. who did not visit it and enrich it. Even in our own time some fifteen thousand pilgrims come here every year.

The Dominican convent is practically the only inn in those parts, and every visitor has to put up with the severely plain accommodation provided by a monastic cell and simple but clean food.

The convent contains about one hundred beds ; the lady visitors are served by nuns, the gentlemen by monks. The convent, which looks almost as ancient as the grotto, is situated on the edge of a vast rocky chain of hills, and almost opposite the monastery, half-way up the steep incline, is the famous grotto cut into the solid rock. There a wide platform is hewn out, partly occupied at present by a second convent.

The grotto is about twenty-five yards square, eight yards high, and, to all intents and purposes, a chapel. The principal altar is surmounted by a fine statue representing Mary Magdalene praying.

Matze. A large round biscuit made of unleavened flour which the orthodox Jew eats during the sacred season of the Passover (*q. v.*). In chapters xii. and xiii. of Exodus the manner of celebration on the first night of the feast is partly told, and there it is commanded that unleavened bread be eaten on the first night and no leaven be kept in the house at any time during the week. This is in remembrance of the fact that the Jews in their hurry to leave Egypt were forced to take along unleavened bread, which they had to bake in the sun. In Europe, when they happen to have any bread or other sort of leaven in the house the housewife locks the pantry and hands over the key to some old Christian friend of hers to keep till the feast is over.

The flour from which the dough is made is ground in a mill by Jews, and is from wheat which has been selected with the greatest care. Especial pains are taken to prevent any impurity from getting into the wheat. The flour is then placed in clean, new barrels, selected expressly for this purpose.

When the work of manufacturing matzes is begun, two men knead the dough in wooden dishes, while another brings the flour, and still another the water, from opposite corners. One man ladles the flour from a bin into a wooden dough-tray, and another, after a short interval, pours a cup of water into the tray.

Two men are always employed at this work, for if only one were at work some of the flour might get into the water, or the reverse. This would make the flour sour and spoil all.

The greatest caution is exercised regarding the water, which must be free from all impurities. In order to have it so, it is carried in the previous evening and allowed to settle. When it is being used, the utmost care is taken, so as not to stir it and thus cause the impurities to rise from the bottom of the vessel.

Like pains are taken when the dough is being prepared, in order that it may be free from all impurity. It is kneaded hard into a big roll, which weighs ten pounds. After this it is cut in pieces by a man specially engaged for the purpose, and is then carried to the women by another man. The women take the pieces and roll the dough flat. Next this flat piece of dough is rolled over two sets of wheels, which make diamond-like impressions on the cakes. Then they are baked.

The latter process can be done only in daylight, work beginning at sunrise and ending at sunset. After the work of preparing the matzes for the oven, a man removes all specks of dough from the rolling-pins with sandpaper and glass.

These matzes are always ordered in advance, but are not delivered until the homes into which they go have undergone a thorough cleaning and after every crumb of leavened bread has been taken from the apartments. If they should, by some mischance, come in contact with ordinary bread, it would render the matzes unfit for use in the festival.

For the very devout among the Hebrews a special matze is baked. This comes much higher than the other varieties, costing eight or ten times as much.

Maundy or **Shere Thursday,** known in the Catholic ecclesiastical calendar as **Holy Thursday.** The day before Good Friday, commemorating Christ's Last Supper, and also, both in the Greek and in the Western Church, his washing of the disciples' feet on that day. The word Maundy comes through old French *mandé* from the Latin *mandatum,* "a command," the reference being to the words of Christ in his discourse at the Last Supper: "Mandatum novum do vobis, ut diligatis invicem" ("A new commandment I give unto you, that ye love one another"). (John xiii. 34.) The word sheer, shere, or chare comes from the Middle English *shere* or *sheere,* meaning "pure," "unalloyed," "clear," (still surviving with a modified meaning in *sheer*), and is an allusion to the physical purity acquired by the ablutions of the day.

In the early Christian ages the chief religious rite performed on this day was the washing of the feet of poor persons or inferiors by a priest, prelate, noble, or sovereign. The custom still has its local survivals both in the Roman and in the Greek Church. In the former the most notable instances are at Rome itself, at Vienna, and at Munich. In the second, ecclesiastical dignitaries perform it at Moscow, St. Petersburg, and Constantinople. In the Anglican Church the custom has been obsolete since 1754.

Naogeorgus, in "The Popish Kingdom," alludes to the universality of the feet-washing ceremonies in mediæval monasteries. This is Barnaby Googe's translation:

And here the monkes their Maundie make, with sundrie solemne rights,
And signes of great humilitie, and wondrous pleasant sights:
Ech one the others feete doth wash, and wipe them cleane and drie,
With hatefull minde, and secret frawde, that in their heartes doth lye.

In England high ecclesiastics and royalty itself unbent to this imitation of Christ's humility. At Durham Cathedral until the sixteenth century every charity-boy had a monk to wash his feet, and every monk then kissed the feet of a boy, and gave him thirty pence, seven red herrings, three loaves, a wafer cake, and some drink.

WASHING THE PILGRIMS' FEET IN ROME.
(From Picart.)

We read of Cardinal Wolsey, at Peterborough Abbey, in 1530, making "his maund in Our Lady's Chapel, having fifty-nine poor men whose feet he washed and kissed; and after he had wiped them he gave every of the said poor men twelve pence in money, three ells of good canvas to make them shirts, a pair of new shoes, a cast of red herrings, and three white herrings." The King of England used formerly, on Maundy Thursday, to have brought before him as many poor men as he was years old, whose feet he washed with his own hands, and then distributed

43

meat, clothes, and money. Queen Elizabeth performed this ceremony, the paupers' feet, however, being first washed by the yeomen of the laundry with warm water and sweet herbs. After washing each foot, the queen marked it with the sign of the cross above the toes and kissed it. This ceremonial was last performed in its full extent by James II. King William left the washing to his almoner, and such was the arrangement for many years: for example, in 1731 we read of the Archbishop of York, lord high almoner, washing the feet of a number of poor people. Latterly the feet-washing has been abandoned, and an additional sum of money has been given in lieu of provisions and clothing.

Since the beginning of Queen Victoria's reign it has been an established rule to present to twice as many aged and deserving poor men and women as there are years in her majesty's life a donation in money known as the Maundy Pennies. A special service, formerly held at the Chapel Royal, Whitehall, has since the abolition of that chapel been transferred to Westminster Abbey. A procession is formed in the nave, consisting of the lord high almoner, representing her majesty, attended by his officials, the yeomen of the guard, and the clergy of the Abbey. During the course of the service two distributions of alms are made to a company of old men and women, the number of each sex corresponding to the age of the sovereign. The prescribed minimum of age is sixty years. The first distribution in lieu of clothing consists of thirty-five shillings to each woman and forty-five shillings to each man. The second distribution is of red and white purses, the red containing one pound, and one pound ten shillings, in gold,—an allowance in lieu of provisions formerly given in kind. The white purses contain as many pence as her majesty is years of age, the amount being furnished in silver pennies, twopences, threepences, and fourpences. These purses are carried in baskets on the heads of the yeomen of the guard in procession, and then distributed by the lord high almoner. Some of the officials wear white scarves, in memory of the linen towel with which our Lord girded himself when he stooped to perform his lowly act of washing his followers' feet.

The Maundy pennies were first coined in the reign of Charles II. They come to the recipients fresh from the mint. Each coin bears on one side the effigy of the queen, with her name and titles, and on the other the denomination of the coin, the crown, and the date, enclosed in a wreath. The edges of the coin are not milled, as it is not expected that they will circulate, and the precaution of milling against the coin-clippers is unnecessary. A full set of Maundy pennies for the reign of Victoria is worth a very handsome sum.

What are known as the minor bounty, discretionary bounty, and Royal Gate alms are, according to old usages, distributed at the Royal Almonry, Craig's Court, on the preceding Saturday, Friday, Monday, and Tuesday, to over one thousand aged, disabled, and meritorious poor of both sexes, recommended to the Almonry by the clergy of the selected parishes of England and Wales.

While this modified and modernized form of the ancient rites of Maundy Thursday takes place in Westminster Abbey, the Roman Catholic cardinal archbishop observes the full ritual of the Catholic Church at the pro-cathedral. Clothed in his episcopal robes, he himself washes the feet of thirteen acolytes garbed in white. The prelate, kneeling before each, pours out the water, and then wipes it away with a linen cloth.

The Footwashings celebrated at Vienna by the Emperor of Austria and at Munich by the King of Bavaria are held in the royal palaces of the respective sovereigns. Here is a description of the former by an eye-witness:

"Shortly after ten o'clock the floor began to fill with score upon score of officers in full uniform, from the different regiments of the kingdom, making a brilliant and imposing scene. In the assemblage were many of the most distinguished members of the Austro-Hungarian court, including ministers of state, archdukes, generals of infantry and cavalry, and vice-admirals of the war-fleet. Chatting with officers in gold-embroidered blue and scarlet uniforms were knights of Malta with white cross on sleeve and breast, Hungarians with high yellow boots and a leopard's skin thrown over the left shoulder, and in marked contrast to these the Polish aristocrats in flowing robes of black mourning for their lost kingdom. In the royal box above were the ladies of the court. At half-past ten the clergy entered the room, followed by the twelve oldest poor men of Vienna (for whom the service is performed), dressed in old German costume,—black, with white cape collars and knee-breeches.

"Many of the aged men were quite feeble, and were assisted to their chairs by their relatives, who stood behind them during the service. Earlier in the morning the Emperor, Francis Joseph I., accompanied by his suite, attended high mass in the royal chapel, and upon his return entered the hall, followed by his cousin, nephews, and a large cortége. The Emperor wore the uniform of a general of infantry, and took his place at once at the head of the table, making the number thirteen, while in the rear stood thirteen of his body-guard. Then appeared from an anteroom twelve of the nobility, each carrying a tray containing the first course of a feast to be served to the Kaiser's guests. The dishes were all placed upon the table by the Emperor himself, but no sooner had he done this than, with the assistance of his brother and the archdukes, he replaced them upon trays held by the thirteen guards, who removed them. It seemed a little hard on the old men to see the tempting viands so quickly taken away, but we learned later that each one received at his home the food and dishes as well, which were made for this occasion, as it had been found that the dinner was much more enjoyed in this way than before such a grand assemblage. The repast was beautifully prepared and handsomely garnished, served in four courses, each presented and removed in the manner described, after which the tables were taken away.

" Footmen then removed the shoes and stockings from the old men and spread over their knees a long white linen roll, after which the chaplain began the Gospel for the day. At the words ' et cœpit lavare pedes discipulorum' the Emperor knelt and began the ceremony of the ' foot-washing,' one prelate holding a basin while another poured the water. The Emperor continued kneeling until he had performed this service of humility for each of the twelve, after which he took from a salver silken bags, each containing thirty pieces of silver, and hung one about the neck of each of the old men. This ended the service ; but we lingered long enough to see these honored guests assisted to the royal carriages to be sent home in the care of members of the Kaiser's body-guard, carrying the sizable wooden chest of provisions and a large flask of wine. When the Empress is at home she performs a similar service for the twelve oldest poor women of Vienna, but in case she is not, as happened this year, they are not present at the ceremonial, but receive at their homes an equal share of the royal bounty. It is not uncommon later to find these royal gifts in an antiquarian's shop,—the original recipients frequently desiring the florins they will bring more than the distinction of possessing the gifts themselves.

"The men and women who can count more than one hundred years are annually included in this royal invitation, but the majority of them receive this honor but once. This year the oldest was ninety-six and the youngest eighty-eight years of age." (*Correspondence of the Springfield Republican*, April, 1895.)

The feet of thirteen pilgrims used to be washed by the Pope. They were chosen from among visiting priests and deacons of diverse nationalities. The ceremony was performed in the right corner of the transept of St. Peter's. The Pope washed successively the right foot of each of the pilgrims, which he dried and kissed. Then he gave to each a bouquet of fresh flowers. He then made ready to celebrate the ceremony of the Cena, or Supper, which took place in the large hall just below the vestibule of the basilica. The thirteen " apostles," all dressed in white, silently ranged themselves around a table covered with cloth of gold and decorated with flowers.

Soon His Holiness appeared, surrounded by distinguished guests, and escorted by the Noble Guards. Amid these brilliant uniforms and variegated costumes the Pope's vestments were distinguished by their extreme simplicity. A prelate of his household presented him a linen apron embroidered with lace, and held up to him a vermilion basin from which the Pope poured water on the hands of the apostles.

After the table had been blessed by His Holiness the dishes were brought by prelates who came in single file and kneeling handed them to the Pope. He in turn placed them in front of each of the "apostles," and poured wine and water into their glasses. Then His Holiness retired, and the apostles, having eaten and drunk their fill, swept the remains of the feast off from the table into huge valises. Frequently the contagion spread to the spectators, who brushed past the guards and gleaned the harvest-field for relics, if only a leaf or a flower.

This ceremony has been discontinued for many years. But the washing of pilgrims' feet by prelates and by the nobility is still performed in various other churches and monasteries.

Another time-honored custom is still celebrated in the afternoon of Maundy Thursday. The Cardinal Grand Penitentiary appears at his post near the pillar of St. Veronica, where he is met by the Minor Penitentiaries. He doffs his cardinal's hat and assumes the beretta. A long rod is brought him, with which he lightly raps the heads of the different prelates of his suite and all other penitents who press forward to gain the indulgence of one hundred days which is attached to this act of humility. (See LAVANDA.)

The feebleness and failing health of Leo XIII. compel him to select a deputy for the task he has accomplished so many years, but nothing is changed in the ceremonial observed in the palace of Madrid, where the chapel is filled by the most exalted persons and the dignitaries of court and state, all, like the queen, arrayed in full court costume. Everybody goes to church on this day, and to as many churches as possible. The fact that all carriages and vehicles are forbidden to pass through the streets of Madrid on Holy Thursday adds a picturesque element to this function, as for that day alone from dawn to dusk may be seen women in gala dress and men in brilliant uniforms coruscating with dazzling orders picking their way on the pavement from church to church, and investing a mass in one at least and an Ave and a Pater Noster in the others.

A silence like that of Venice falls on the rattling capital. With three hundred thousand people in the street, the town seems still. In 1870 a free-thinking cabman dared to drive up the Calle Alcala. He was dragged from his box and beaten half to death by the chastened mourners, who yelled as they kicked and cuffed him, " Qué bruto ! He will wake our Jesus."

Dr. Clarke, author of " Travels in Russia" (1810), gives a description of the Maundy Thursday festivities as practised by the Archbishop of Moscow, which is as true of the present day as it was of his own time :

" The second grand ceremony of this season takes place on Thursday before Easter, at noon, when the Archbishop of Moscow washes the feet of the apostles. This we also witnessed. The priests appeared in their most gorgeous apparel. Twelve monks, designed to represent the twelve apostles, were placed in a semicircle before the archbishop. The ceremony is performed in the cathedral, which is crowded with spectators. The archbishop, performing all and much more than is related of our Saviour in the thirteenth chapter of St. John, takes off his robes, girds up his loins with a towel, and proceeds to wash the feet of them all, until he comes to the representative of St. Peter, who rises, and the same interlocution takes place as between our Saviour and that apostle." (Vol. i. p. 55.)

In a court in front of the church of the Holy Sepulchre the Greek Patriarch of Jerusalem annually washes the feet of twelve of his bishops. It is one of the great sights of the Holy City. Frank G. Carpenter, who witnessed it in 1889, has presented us with an excellent description. In the centre of the court, he says, stood an oval rostrum, about four feet above the stones. Around its floor ran an iron railing enclosing a space about eight feet wide and twelve feet long. Inside the railing and running around it were seats, and at the back was a gold-and-white arm-chair cushioned with red satin. This stage was for the ceremony, and the chair was the stone of the patriarch. The other seats were for the bishops. When all had taken their places, a priest brought to the rostrum a large golden pitcher in a basin of gold as large as a foot-bath, and placed it in front of the patriarch.

All rose amid solemn prayer. The patriarch divested himself of his grand gown and stood forth in a white silk robe girt with a gold and white girdle. He twisted a long Turkish bath-towel about his loins, and then, stooping over, poured the water from the gold pitcher into the basin. " The twelve bishops, in the mean time, were busy getting their feet out of their English congress gaiters and in pulling their white cotton socks off for the washing. Each has one foot bare as the patriarch comes around with the basin, and each holds out his bare foot to be washed. This the patriarch does very quickly, rubbing the foot with water and drying it with a towel. As he finished he bent over and kissed the foot he had washed, and then went on to the next apostle. The last bishop represented St. Peter, and, after the example of Peter of the past, he objected to having his feet washed by his Lord ; he rose and gesticulated violently, but the patriarch opened the Bible and read to him the admonition which Christ made to Peter; he shook his hand at Peter as he did so, and a moment later Peter sat down humbly and submitted to the washing.

" At this moment the bells of the Greek churches all over Jerusalem burst out in a chorus of rejoicing. The patriarch descended, the bishops followed, and in double file they marched out through the crowd, with the kavasses clearing the way. As they did so, a priest carried a vase of the holy water in which the feet had been washed, in front of the patriarch, and into this His Blessedness dipped a great bouquet of roses and sprinkled the water over the crowd. The people held their faces up to catch the purifying rain, and they rushed to the platform and wiped up the drops that had fallen on the floor, with their handkerchiefs, passing them over their faces."

Maurice, St., patron saint of Austria, Savoy, Mantua, and of foot-soldiers. His festival is celebrated September 22. The legend of St. Maurice and the Theban legion is one of the most ancient of all the legends of the saints. St. Maurice was the leader of the Theban legion, which was composed entirely of Christians. When the Emperor Maximian was about to enter Gaul, he ordered a general sacrifice to the gods, and made known that the purpose of his expedition was the extermination of the Christians. A part of the Theban legion had gone on in advance, but the section that remained refused to sacrifice, and was decimated by order of the Emperor. At Cologne and other places many more who belonged to the Theban legion suffered martyrdom. Savoy, Piedmont, and parts of Germany abound in these soldier saints. The name Maurice signifies a Moor, and as such he is represented in some pictures. He is dressed in armor and bears a standard and a palm. In Italian pictures he bears a red cross on his breast, which is the badge of the Sardinian order of St. Maurice. The site of the martyrdom of St. Maurice is pointed out at Veriolez, where a slab of stone is shown upon which the martyr is said to have knelt. Relics such as the bones and blood of St. Maurice are preserved in the abbey church. Relics of St. Maurice and his companions are shown throughout Switzerland.

In Quimperlé, in Lower Brittany, a famous festival called the Pardon des Oiseaux begins on St. Maurice's Day and is appropriately celebrated in the forest of St. Maurice. It is essentially a bird festival, for all kinds of birds, not only fowls, but orioles, woodpeckers, larks, and various woodland songsters, are brought in cages and purchased as presents by lovers for their sweethearts or by parents for their children. The day itself is sacred to religious observances, but the morrow, when national traits and customs inherited from pagan times have full play, is devoted to merrymaking, thus described in *Harper's Magazine* for July, 1875 : " Wrestling matches between the champions of villages or districts, and games established by long traditions, arouse the interest and passions of the assembled multitude to a pitch which prepares them for the dances, in which every one, of high or low degree, of character good, bad, or indifferent, joins without reserve. The musicians, already well moistened, are placed in the centre of the arena, armed with the binion, or bagpipe, and bombardo, and with a barrel of cider within arm's-length. The music proceeds with an energy truly astonishing, and the dance goes round with ever-increasing vivacity. The variety of costume and the enthusiastic performances of these pious bacchanals render the scene very entertaining, and toward the close peculiar to a degree. ' L'on peut dire que le champ de la fête n'est lui-même qu'un immense cabaret,' says a writer whose church predilections and strong advocacy of the *fêtes de pardon* would lead him to avoid exaggeration. Notwithstanding the religious character of the festival, it often terminates in an orgy where scenes are enacted that will hardly bear allusion. ' Mais il n'en prouve pas moins la foi vive dont le Bas-Breton est animé,' says another writer."

May. This month ranked second in the old Alban calendar, third in that of Romulus, fifth in that of Numa. In the first-

MAY. WATCHING SHEEP.

named calendar it was twenty-two days in length, thirty-one in that of Romulus, thirty in that of Numa, and thirty-one again in that of Julius Cæsar. The name of this month is supposed by some to have come from Maia, the mother of the god Hermes, or Mercury. This, however, is based solely on the similarity of the two words, and the name of May was much more probably given in honor of the Majores or Maiores, the original Roman Senate, as June was in honor of the Juniores, the lower branch of the Roman legislature. The Saxons called this month Tri-Milchi, the improved condition of the pastures now enabling the cows to give milk three times a day.

In all ages there has been an antipathy to marrying in May. Eighteen centuries ago, Ovid wrote,—

> Nec viduæ tædis eadem, nec virginis apta
> Tempora. Quæ nupsit non diuturna fuit.
> Hac quoque de causâ, si te proverbia tangunt,
> Mense malas maio nubere vulgus ait.

On the morning of the marriage of Mary Queen of Scots to Both-well, on May 16, 1567, the last line of the above quotation was found fixed upon the gates of Holyrood Palace. In the north of England there is an old proverb,—

> Marry in May,
> And rue the day.

In Scotland they vary the wording, though retaining the same idea:

> Marry in May,
> Rue for aye.

And, to give emphasis to the superstition, the same people assert,—

> From marriages in May
> All bairns die and decay.

An old Scotch clergyman told his young congregation that "The girls are all stark mad that wed in May." Soothsayers predicted all manner of evil to those who defied the superstition. So we find it recorded that

> Married in May and kirked in green,
> Baith bride and groom won't long be seen.

In all soberness and sincerity we are told that women disobeying the rule would be childless; or, if they had children, the first-born would be an idiot or have some physical deformity; or that the married couple would not live happily together in the new life, but would soon quarrel. Even Sir Walter Scott was not free from this fear, for we read how he hurried away from London that his daughter's wedding might take place before the opening of the inauspicious month.

May marriages are considered unlucky in France, and there is a common rhyme,—

Si le commun peuple dit vrai,
La mauvaise s'épouse en Mai.

There is an old English proverb, "Who marries between the
sickle and scythe will never thrive." Sir John Sinclair, in his
"Statistical Account of Scotland," says, "That day of the week
on which the 14th of May happens to fall is esteemed unlucky
through all the remainder of the year; none marry or begin any
business upon it. None choose to marry in January or May, or
to have their banns proclaimed in the end of one quarter of the
year and to marry in the beginning of the next."

May-Day. The First of May. In the Church calendar this
is the combined day of St. Philip the Apostle and St. James the
Less. Throughout Great Britain and to a lesser extent in France
and Germany it was formerly celebrated with festivities which
still have their local but much attenuated survivals. They are
direct descendants of the ancient Roman Floralia (*q. v.*), and of
the Druidic feasts in honor of the god Bel,—the Apollo or Orus
of other mythologies, the Baal of the Scriptures. But their remoter ancestry must be found in the phallic festivals of India and
Egypt, which in those countries took place upon the sun's entering Taurus, and celebrated the renewed fertility of nature. The
Maypole itself is a phallic emblem, the word φάλλος meaning
primarily "a pole," and in the precession of the equinoxes and
the changes of the calendar we shall find an easy solution of
any apparent inconsistencies arising from the difference of
seasons.

The Druids celebrated the feast of Bel on the 1st of May, by
lighting immense fires in his honor upon the various cairns.
Now, even to this day similar customs survive among the Irish
and the Scotch Highlanders,—both remnants of the Celtic stock.
Still more significant is the fact that the festival is known among
them as Beltine or Bealtaine,—that is, "the day of Bel's fire;"
for in the Cornish (a Celtic dialect) the verb to *tine* means "to
light the fire."

Some of the rites of Moloch-worship still survive in several
districts of the Scottish Highlands. These superstitions are
receding before the invasion of the railway and the English
tourist, but it is not so very long since the following customs
might have been witnessed on May-Day even as far south as
Perthshire. All the youths of a township or village met on the
nearest moor. They cut a round table or altar in the green sod,
and in the trench thus formed about the altar the whole company stationed themselves. Here they kindled a fire and dressed
a repast of eggs and milk, of the consistency of a custard. At

the same time they kneaded a cake of oatmeal, which they baked on the embers. After the custard was eaten they divided the cake into as many portions as there were persons in the company. One of these portions was blackened over with charcoal. Then all the pieces were thrown into a bonnet. The company, blindfolded, drew out each a piece, the holder of the bonnet took the last bit, and the drawer of the black bit was made to leap three times through the flame of the bonfire. In the real Baal ceremony the person who took the blackened piece was literally sacrificed as a propitiatory offering to Baal for the productiveness of the ensuing autumn.

The Irish still retain the Phœnician custom of lighting fires at short distances and making the cattle pass between them. Fathers, too, taking their children in their arms, jump or run through them, thus passing the latter as it were through the flames. This custom appears to have been only a substitute for the atrocious sacrifice of children practised by the elder Phœnicians,—that "abomination of the heathen" denounced in II. Kings xvi. 3. The god Saturn—that is, Moloch—was represented by a statue bent slightly forward and so placed that the least weight was sufficient to alter its position. Into the arms of this idol the priest gave the child to be sacrificed, when, its balance being thus destroyed, it flung, or rather dropped, the victim into a fiery furnace that blazed below. If other proofs were wanting of Eastern origin, we might find them in the fact that Britain was called by the earlier inhabitants the island of Beli, and that Bel had also the name of Hu, a word which we see again occurring in the Huli festival of India. (DYER: *British Popular Customs*, p. 224.)

If Druidism survives most obviously in the Celtic portions of the United Kingdom, it is Roman paganism which has left its firmest traces upon the May-Day celebrations in the Anglo-Saxon regions. There the occasion is rather a feast of flowers than of sacrifices, a reminiscence of Flora rather than of Baal and Moloch. And curiously engrafted on Roman paganism is Roman Christianity.

This latter fact is most evident in the May-dolls which, once common throughout England, are still paraded on May-Day in Devonshire, and may even be found in Cornwall and other parts of Wales. The May-doll is remotely a survival from the images of Flora which graced the Floralia, but more immediately from the figures of the Virgin and her Son of Catholic times. In the latter light it may be looked upon as another form of the vessel-cup (*q. v.*). Mr. Ditchfield tells us that at Edlesborough, Buckinghamshire, the girls dress up a doll, sometimes with a small doll in its lap, with many ribbons and flowers, and carry it about in a small chair. This in its origin was evidently intended as a representation of the Virgin and Child. The parish church is dedicated to St. Mary the Virgin, which seems to afford another link of association. A similar custom, almost defunct, prevails at Brightwalton, Berkshire, where the Virgin and Child in the guise of the Queen of the May with a doll in a basket are borne round the parish.

Did the May-dolls suggest the Queen of the May, who, sometimes with a consort, the King, presided over the May-Day festivities until a comparatively recent period, not only in England, but also in certain portions of New York and New England? The suggestion is plausible. Douce, however, holds the opinion that "the introduction of Robin Hood into the celebration of May probably suggested the addition of a king or lord of May." If Robin Hood was the original king, then his Maid Marian, who, with Friar Tuck, Little John, and other merry members of Robin Hood's band, appeared in the same mummeries, was the original Queen of May.

The date of the institution of May-games in England during the Middle Ages cannot be traced. A poem of the fourteenth century, "The Romance of Kyng Alisaunder," says,—

> Mery time it is in May;
> The foules syngeth her lay;
> The knighttes loveth the tornay;
> Maydens so dauncen and thay play.

In "The Court of Love" (about 1450) we read,—

> Thus sange they alle the service of the feste,
> And that was done right early, to my dome [as I judged];
> And fourth goeth al the court, both moste and leste,
> To fetch the floures freshe, and braunche, and blome;
> And namely [especially] hawthorn brought both page and grome,
> With fresh garlandes party blew and white;
> And than rejoysen in their grete delight,
> Eek eche at other threw the flowers bright,
> The primerose, the violete, and the gold [marigold].

This extract shows that the king and queen mingled with their subjects in these fine old English customs. Henry VIII. and Catherine of Aragon once came from their palace of Greenwich to meet the heads of the corporation of London, who had been into the woods of Kent to gather May. The custom seems to have been for people to go into the woods in the night, gather branches of trees, flowers, etc., and return with them at sunrise to decorate their houses.

Other observances were gradually added. The May Queen

was crowned and held one day's sway over her court, consisting of morris-dancers, of Robin Hood and his band, and generally of the villagers or townspeople. A pasteboard hobby-horse ridden by a man was sent around among the spectators to collect contributions in a ladle stuck in its mouth. Everybody who wished to might dance around a Maypole.

The Maypole was usually made of birch, and adorned with flowers and ribbons. In the villages it was often set up for the occasion on May-Day Eve, but in London and elsewhere there were Maypoles permanently standing in the streets. It was only natural that the May revels should invite the condemnation of the Puritans. (See CHRISTMAS.) Stubbes in his "Anatomy of Abuses" (1583) amiably characterized the Maypole as a "stinckyng idol" which the people bring from the woods, "followyng it with greate devotion." And when they have set it up they "leape and daunce aboute it, as the heathen people did at the dedication of their idolles."

Maypoles were forbidden to be erected by the Roundhead Parliament in 1644; but they returned on the restoration of Charles II., and in 1661 the famous Maypole in the Strand was reared with much ceremony and rejoicing. This pole, which stood near where Catherine Street joins the Strand, was of cedar, and was raised by twelve seamen, commanded by the Duke of York, who was then Lord High Admiral of England. It was one hundred and thirty-four feet high. Pope thus alludes to it:

> Where the tall Maypole once o'erlooked the Strand.

It was taken down about 1717, and purchased by Sir Isaac Newton, who had it removed to Wanstead in Essex, to use as a support to the great telescope (one hundred and twenty-four feet in length) which had been presented to the Royal Society by the French astronomer M. Hugon.

In New England, as in Old, the Puritan attacked the Maypole. In 1630 Governor Endicott of Massachusetts marched a posse to Merrymount, where the profligate Morton had established a Maypole, hewed down the pole itself in God's name, and solemnly dubbed the place Mount Dagon, in memory of the Philistine idol that fell before the ark of the Lord.

In England the resuscitated May-Day games gradually fell out of fashion, and now they survive only in rural localities. In London the celebration was abandoned first to the milkmaids and then to the chimney-sweeps. From about the middle of the seventeenth century it grew to be the custom for milkmaids to dress themselves up in their best and call on all their customers, from whom they received some trifling gratuity. Later the chimney-sweeps made it a practice on the same day to parade the streets togged out in tawdry finery, ribbons, and green boughs. Hence the London name for the 1st of May is Sweeps' Day. "Jack-in-the-Green," with "Dusty Bob" and "Black Sal," the latter being usually a man dressed in woman's attire (probably a relic of the milkmaids), would go dancing and capering through the streets, the centre of an admiring rabble. "Jack-in-the-Green" was a man enclosed in a bower made in the shape of a pyramid about ten feet high. Sweeps' Day is not yet entirely extinct in London.

Mr. Ditchfield has made an interesting collection of May-Day survivals in rural England. He tells us that in Cheltenham the chimney-sweeps "hold high revels on May-Day. The dancers have their faces blacked, and their band consists of a fiddle and tin whistle. The centre of the group is formed by a large bush, or hollow cone bedecked with leaves, out of which peers the face of Jack-i'-the-Green. The dresses of the attendants are red, blue, and yellow, and they dance around the bush. The leader of the party is the clown, who wears a tall hat with a flapping crown, and a fantastical dress, and 'fancies himself' greatly. There is also a man with a fool's cap, and black figures fastened on his white pinafore, and the representation of a gridiron. Two boys complete the group, one wearing a girl's hat adorned with flowers. They levy contributions by holding out iron ladles or spoons, and strike the by-standers with bladders fastened to a stick. Their performance consists in dancing and roaring. The Cambridge sweeps evidently used to have a similar festival, as the children still go round with a doll, hung in the midst of a hoop wreathed with flowers, singing the ditty—

> " The first of May is garland day,
> And chimney-sweepers' dancing day;
> Curl your locks as I do mine,
> One before and one behind.

" In Hawick a few of the young people still go a-Maying, and rub their faces in the morning dew, whereby they secure twelve months of rosy cheeks; but year by year the number of the devotees of 'May Morning' are becoming less, and probably the next generation will know little of the secrets of how rosy cheeks were sought for on early May mornings, and perhaps seek less simple and wholesome ways for producing the much-desired bloom.

" Mrs. Pepys knew the virtues of May-dew, as we gather from her husband's diary: ' My wife away to Woolwich in order to a little ayre, and to lie there to-night, and so to gather May-dew to-morrow morning, which Mrs. Turner hath taught her is the only thing in the world to wash her face with.' "

A writer in *Once a Week* for September 24, 1870, gives an account of the May-Day ceremonies celebrated in many a Cornish town. These include the carrying of May dolls by the children and a local practice known as dipping.

Early on May morning, he informs us, every one repairs to the country to pluck a sprig from the "narrow-leaf" elm-tree. This is worn in some conspicuous part of the dress. It is known as "May." It is not obligatory that the wearer should have gathered it himself: all that is insisted on is that it should actually have been gathered on May-Day, and that it is "narrow-leaf" elm. Should it be known to have been gathered the day before, it is indignantly torn from the wearer as being April-May. The broad-leaf elm is denounced as "horses'-May." April-May is a sham in the way of religion, and horses'-May is a blunder in botany. Each is punished by dipping.

In many Cornish towns an open stream of water flows through the principal streets. As soon as the "May" has been secured, and breakfast hurried through, all the boys of the town assemble at this stream or "gutter," each being furnished with his "dipping-horn," which is thus manufactured: the point of a bullock's horn is sawn off, and the end of a stout stick, about four feet long, is firmly inserted into the aperture, which is made water-tight.

Few of the inhabitants were so thoughtless as to appear without the correct May-Day sprig. Wayfarers happening into the town were the usual victims.

As soon as a non-conformist appeared, whether inhabitant or stranger, male or female, the guardians of the rites shouted in chorus, and in tones not to be misinterpreted, " Ha'penny or a penny, or a good wet back ;" and, if the coppers of commutation were not instantly forthcoming, the unfortunate wayfarer was drenched without delay or mercy, and the baptism was mercilessly continued until his or her greater speed had left the pitiless pursuers hopelessly behind.

In Sweden May-Day is still celebrated in a manner derived from its heathen origin. On the previous evening huge bonfires are built in every hamlet, around which the young people dance, while the older ones draw various auguries from the appearance of the flames. On May-Day a sort of sham fight takes place between two parties, one representing Winter and the other Summer. Winter, however, always gets the worst of it in the end. He is buried in effigy, and ashes are strewn over the grave. This was formerly a custom in England also. The children on this day make a point of wandering into the woods for the purpose of robbing the nests of the magpies. The eggs and young are put in a basket and borne to every house, the children singing a song which runs thus:

> Best loves from Master and Madam Magpie,
> From all their eggs and all their fry.
> Oh, give them alms, if ever so small!
> Else hens and chickens and eggs and all
> A prey to the magpies will surely fall.

Every housewife gives them something for a May banquet. May-Day is really the only gala-day of the Swedish children. On this day, also, the Easter witches are wont to send their "Troll hares" to suck the neighbors' cows. The cattle are usually confined in the cow-houses, which are fumigated with brimstone. In the evening they are carefully inspected; and if any injury is found upon them it is put down to the account of the witches, and a light is made by striking two flints over the creature, which is held to be a sure preventive of any further evil consequences. (See MOVING-DAY.)

Mayo, Dos de. (Sp., "the Second of May.") A national festival of the Spaniards commemorating the uprising of the citizens of Madrid against Murat. Murat had entered Madrid as commander-in-chief of the victorious French armies in Spain on March 25, 1808. On May 2 the citizens showed their detestation of their conquerors by murdering all the isolated or wounded Frenchmen they could find. Murat put down the riot vigorously, but not cruelly, for only one hundred and fifty-eight Spaniards fell to five hundred Frenchmen.

Every 2d of May the city of Madrid gives up the day to funeral honors to the dead of 1808. The city government, attended by its maceros, in their gorgeous robes of gold and scarlet, with silver maces and long white plumes, the public institutions of all grades, with invalids and veterans and charity children, and a large detachment of the army and navy, form a vast procession at the town hall, and, headed by the Supreme Government, march to slow music through the Puerta del Sol and the spacious Alcalá Street to the granite obelisk in the Prado which marks the resting-place of the patriot dead. Here mass is celebrated, and then the Church leaves the field clear to the secular power. It is the only purely civic festival in Spain.

Mayor's Day, Lord. In London the 9th of November, the feast of the inauguration of the mayor for the next twelvemonth. A giant parade attends the newly elected official to the Law Courts, where he takes the oath of office. This pageant is colloquially known as the Lord Mayor's Show. All the streets are gayly decorated, especially on the line of march. At present the parade leaves the Guildhall at noon, and proceeds by way of Gresham and Princess Streets to the Mansion House; thence through Cornhill, Leadenhall Street, St. Mary's Avenue, Houndsditch, St. Paul's Churchyard, Ludgate Hill, and Fleet Street, to the royal courts of justice. Returning, the procession reaches the Guildhall by way of the Strand, Northumberland Avenue, Victoria Embankment, Queen Victoria Street, and King Street. The Lord Mayor's Dinner at the Guildhall concludes the festivities of the day. The following account of the pageant as it looks in these days is from a letter by the London correspondent of the *New York Tribune,* dated November 9, 1895:

"To-day's procession marked in nearly every detail the survival of mediæval customs and institutions. It was headed, after the mounted police and the Royal Artillery band, by representatives of eight of the worshipful companies or guilds. First came the Makers of Playing Cards, with banners borne by horsemen representing the four knaves in costumes shown upon the earliest pack of cards which has been preserved. Then followed the Coach Makers and Coach Harness Makers, with their beadle and clerk on foot and their master and wardens in a four-horse coach. Behind them, in characteristic antique uniforms, were the Pattern Makers and the Farriers, with their banners flying and their officials in four-horse coaches. Next came the Fruiterers, with a car of mysterious symbolism, in which the forbidden tree and the serpent were conspicuous objects. The Barber Surgeons interposed a few feeble files of costumed men between the Fruiterers and the Leather Sellers, who appeared in stronger force, with a canopied car illustrating branches of the trade, conspicuous figures being a leather-shaver at his beam, a finisher graining, a shoemaker pegging at his last, and a harnessmaker stitching at his saddle. Behind this hideous car, with its crocodile heads and festoons of hides, marched the Broiderers, with their ancient banners, arms, and standards.

"These eight guilds were the companies with which the Lord Mayor and the Sheriffs were officially connected, and their presence in the procession, with their banners and antique tunics and trappings, was a personal tribute to the three heroes of the civic pageant. Historically the representatives of the famous old companies belonged in this mediæval exhibition, and their power as political and municipal agencies has survived generations of progressive government.

"Besides the representatives of the worshipful companies, there were many other details of the Lord Mayor's Show which were of historical significance. The fire-brigades, perhaps, were not suggestive of old-time municipal life, especially as they ap-

44

peared with steam-engines and modern appliances, and with contingents recruited from twenty cities outside London; but the presence of the Epping Forest Keepers was a token that the corporation of London had preserved those beautiful woods; and the banners of Burnham Beeches, Highgate Woods, and Coulsdon Common had a message of similar import for those who could read it. Six Lord Mayors of different epochs ranging from 1406 to 1814 were represented by cavaliers in appropriate costumes, each with five attendants and an armor-bearer with standard. St. George on horseback followed these worthies, with nothing resembling a dragon close at hand, although the crocodiles had passed on the Leather Sellers' car, and a mysterious beast, unknown to any modern zoo, was to follow on the roof of the South Africa car. The warlike saint was accompanied by twelve mounted knights in armor, and two esquires,—familiar figures in mediæval London. The India car, with Sir Thomas Smyth, the founder of the famous Company, and with a rajah in native costume, with soldiers in the uniform of the East India volunteers and with old-time merchants and other figures, symbolized the connection of the historic city with a great trading enterprise which involved the founding of an empire. The South Africa car was either a special tribute to the benevolence of the daring mining operator, Mr. Barnato, whose services in supporting the market and incidentally aiding his own holdings had been commemorated two nights before by the outgoing Lord Mayor; or else it was an official attempt to identify the strongholds of finance in the Old City with the most remarkable speculative bubble which has been blown since the days of Law.

"But here at last are the banners of the Aldermen and the officers of the Corporation, with the band of the Duke of York's military school to announce with a flourish of trumpets the coming of the three heroes of the show. First in order is the glittering state carriage of Mr. Sheriff Cooper, drawn by four spirited horses, with footmen and coachmen in astonishing liveries of buckskin breeches, purple velvet tunics, heavy gold lace, and cocked hats. To moderate his pride in the grand equipage in which he is seated, and to teach him humility, the Sheriff has with him his worshipful chaplain. Behind him, in another splendid state coach drawn by four richly caparisoned horses and attended by coachmen and footmen in green and gold, is Mr. Sheriff Pound, with his pious chaplain. The Aldermen, who have not passed the chair, are preceded by state trumpeters of the Household Cavalry, and followed by the Recorder and the former Lord Mayors. With one military band in front and another behind him, the retiring Lord Mayor, Sir Joseph Renals, has his final hour of triumph with his liveried men above and below. Then follow the city trumpeters, the mounted band of the Royal Horse Guards, and the Lord Mayor himself, preceded by the Marshal and the servants, with liveries of crimson velvet richly embroidered in gold. The famous Cipriani gilt chariot, which has been seen once a year for a century on Lord Mayor's Day, has been oiled in the axles and varnished and gilded without; but it sways and rumbles as it is drawn along by six horses, and seems destined on some unlucky 9th of November to meet the doom of sudden dissolution which finally overwhelmed Dr. Holmes's well-known vehicle. The Lord Mayor is inside, with scarlet cloak and gold collar, and the traditional attendants are all in their places,—the sword-bearer, the mace-bearer, and the chaplain. Behind them is an escort of the Queen's Hussars, and the procession is at an end."

Time was when the lord mayor went all the way to Westminster to be presented to the King, the Lord High Chancellor, and the Barons of the Exchequer. At first he either rode or walked there or went by boat with no great ceremony. It was Sir John Norman who in 1453 set the fashion of the Lord Mayor's Show by making the journey in a barge, with considerable state and a large number of followers. Thereafter succeeding mayors vied with one another as to which should make the annual show grander and more impressive. A cavalcade through the streets of the city wound up with a procession of barges to Westminster. For a long time it was the custom to take part in the land parade on horseback. But it happened that, in the reign of Queen Anne, Sir Gilbert Heathcote (the original of Addison's Sir Andrew Freeport) was thrown into the gutter by his horse, a spectacle so unseemly that thereafter steps were taken to prevent its recurrence. Next year, 1712, a coach was provided for the use of the chief magistrate. In 1757 this was superseded by a gilded and elaborately decorated equipage built at a cost of £10,065, which remained in use until 1896.

Once, it is related, a lord mayor ventured so far as to discard the coach, shrewdly suspicious, perhaps, that ridicule rather than respect attached to that magnificent but cumbrous vehicle. On this head, however, he was judged to be, for a lord mayor, too much in advance of the current of public opinion. His reform was accounted suicidal. It was perceived that if the state coach were to be driven to limbo, there was real danger lest the civic potentate himself should be constrained to be its inside passenger on that lethal journey. The fates of the man and the conveyance were bound up together, and conterminate. If the laws of strict reason and common sense were to be invoked, then the mayor could be as easily dispensed with as his state coach. So the gilded carriage still wheezed westward every year, growing more and more uncomfortable and anachronistic, until in 1896 a new one was built.

In the sixteenth and seventeenth centuries the City Poet, appointed at a regular salary by the citizens of London (in order to be sure of his services whenever occasion might demand), was intrusted with the duty of preparing the pageants, of superintending their presentation, and of subsequently celebrating them in verse. The list of these poets ends with the name of Elkanah Settle in 1708, after which time the printed descriptions cease. The earliest of these that has come down to us is that by George Peele, in 1585, when Sir Wolstan Dixie was installed. It would appear that a prominent feature of the early pageants was a number of little children appropriately dressed to represent abstract qualities like Magnanimity and Loyalty and concrete objects like the Thames, London, etc. These recited complimentary verses as the mayor passed, or gave him good advice. The quality of the poetry may be inferred from these lines put into the mouth of "one apparelled like a Moor:"

> This now remains, right honourable lord,
> That carefully you do attend and keep
> This lovely lady, rich and beautiful,
> The jewel wherewithal your sovereign queen
> Hath put your honour lovingly in trust,
> That you may add to London's dignity,
> And London's dignity may add to yours.

The inventive faculty of the City Poet was especially taxed to make the pageants in some way representative of the individuality or the vocation of the mayor who was its *raison d'être*. In 1616, for example, Sir John Leman of the Fishmongers' Company was elected. The City Poet was Anthony Munday. He set his wits to work to good purpose.

The first pageant was a fishing-boat, with fishermen "seriously at labour, drawing up their nets, laden with living fish, and bestowing them bountifully upon the people." These moving pageants were placed on stages, provided with wheels, which were concealed by drapery, the latter being painted to resemble the waves of the sea. This ship was followed by a crowned dolphin, in allusion to the mayor's arms, and those of the company, in which dolphins appear; and "because it is a fish inclined much by nature to musique, Arion, a famous musician and poet, rideth on his backe." Then followed the king of the Moors, attended by six tributary kings on horseback. They were succeeded by "a lemon-tree richly laden with fruit and flowers," in punning allusion to the name of the mayor; a fashion observed whenever the name allowed it to become practicable. Then came a bower adorned with the names and arms of all members of the Fishmongers' Company who had served the office of mayor; with their great hero, Sir William Walworth, inside; an armed officer, with the head of Wat Tyler on one side, and the Genius of London, " a crowned angel with golden wings," on the other. Lastly came the grand pageant drawn by mermen and mermaids, "memorizing London's great day of deliverance," when Tyler was slain; on the top sat a victorious angel, and King Richard was represented beneath, surrounded by impersonations of royal and kingly virtues.

The great civil war and the triumph of Puritanism interrupted these pageantries for a period. The Restoration brought them back in all their old-time splendor. In 1660 the principal feature was the Royal Oak, in compliment to Charles II., and thereafter humorous songs and merry interludes, suited to Cavalier tastes, enlivened the festivities. Another interregnum occurred when the quarrel broke out between King Charles and the city, which ended in the temporary abrogation of the city charter and the nomination of mayor and aldermen by the king.

Hogarth has left on record probably the most vivid representation of the show as it appeared in the early part of the eighteenth century. It is one of the series of "The Industrious and Idle Apprentice," a picture too well known to call for any detailed account; but it is worthy of note that the locality chosen by this very faithful artist is the west end of Cheapside, and that the balcony projecting from the house at the end of Paternoster Row provided accommodations for Frederick, Prince of Wales, and the Princess Augusta.

A famous contemporary of Hogarth's, no less a person than Alexander Pope himself, has in the first book of the "Dunciad" thus succinctly satirized a Lord Mayor's Show as presented by Elkanah Settle:

> 'Twas on the day when * * rich and grave,
> Like Cymon, triumphed both on land and wave:
> (Pomps without guilt, of bloodless swords and maces,
> Glad chains, warm furs, broad banners, and broad faces:)
> Now night descending, the proud scene was o'er,
> But lived, in Settle's numbers, one day more.

Mayors, Mock. In many English rural towns and districts these were formerly elected with burlesque ceremony, and in a few of them the custom still survives. Thus at a curious country fair, known locally as the Guild, and held in Rockland, Norfolk, on May 16, a "Mayor of the Guild" is elected, usually some half-witted fellow, who is clothed fantastically, plied with liquor until he is drunk, and then chaired and carried through the parish.

In Newbury, Berks, in a part of the town called specifically "the City," a "Mayor of the City," known also as "Mayor of Bartlemas," was until recently annually elected, together with a "Justice." The burlesque dignitaries, after an official banquet where bacon and beans formed the principal dish, headed a procession through the streets. In lieu of a mace the "Mayor" carried a cabbage on a stick. St. Anne's Day (July 26) was formerly the day of the election, but it was more recently changed to November 9, in compliment perhaps to the mayor of another city somewhat greater than that of Newbury. Though the ceremony has been discontinued for a few years past, it is believed to be rather in a state of suspended animation than actually moribund.

In Tenby, Wales, it was formerly the custom for the fishermen, sometimes before and sometimes after Christmas, to confer upon one of their number the dignity of "the Lord Mayor of Pennyless Cove." Dressing him in a covering of evergreens, with a mask over his face, they would seat him in a chair and carry him around with flags flying and a couple of violins playing before him. In front of every house the mock mayor would address the occupants, wishing them a merry Christmas and a happy New Year. If his good wishes were responded to with money his followers would give three cheers, and he would himself give thanks to an accompaniment of more cheers.

Mayor's Sunday. The Sunday following the 9th of November is so called in the English provincial towns. The newly elected mayor, clothed in his official robes of scarlet and ermine, then rides with his lady and with certain civic dignitaries from the town hall to the parish church through a mob of spectators who line the way. The party is escorted to the state pew in the church with a vast deal of ceremony. "It is, of course, in a manner, a special service. His Worship the Mayor, more than any man present, is the subject of the prayers and the butt of the sermon. The hundreds of men and women in the congregation know it as well as himself. He cannot lift his eyes from his book without being reminded of it. Either the preacher in the pulpit is bending toward him and exhorting him and no one else, or the people are repeating Amen on his behalf or singing hymns which seem to have been composed solely to do him honor. Small wonder his lordship is relieved when the service is over and he may drive home in his crested coach."

Mecca, Pilgrimage to. Mecca, in Arabia, the birthplace of Mohammed, is emphatically the holy city of the Moslem world. An annual pilgrimage called the Hajj takes place thither in the last month of the Mohammedan calendar, hence known as Dhu'l Hajj, or Pilgrimage Month.   As the Mohammedan year is a purely lunar one, with no intercalary month, and contains only three hundred and fifty four days, the Hajj in its annual returns makes the complete round of all the seasons.   Every devout Moslem, wherever his habitation may be, is obliged to join in the pilgrimage to Mecca at least once in his lifetime.   He is then supposed to become as pure from sin as on the day when he was born, and gains for the rest of his life the honorable title Hajji. Besides this greater pilgrimage, Moslems of more than usual devotion may at any time perform an *omra*, or individual pilgrimage to the Holy City.

THE KAABA.
(From a sketch by Sir Richard Burton.)

Mecca was a sacred spot long before the time of Mohammed. Lying on the great trade route from Southern Arabia and India, and possessing in its well Zemzem (*q. v.*) an inexhaustible supply of water, it early became a halting-place for the caravans and the seat of an annual fair.   Once a year, in autumn, the pagan Arabs came in pilgrim guise to worship at the Holy House, known from its shape as the Kaaba, or Cube, which contained the famous black stone said to have fallen from heaven.   As the latter may be an aerolite, science might endorse the traditional belief of a celestial origin.

When Mecca, after a long and painful struggle, accepted the new religion, Mohammed adopted the Kaaba as the centre of religious worship, and turned to account the hoary traditions connected with the ancient city.   Whether they then existed in the form now current, or whether they took that form through his teaching, the Arabs came to believe that Zemzem was a well miraculously created to quench the thirst of the perishing Ishmael in the desert, and that the Kaaba was built by Abraham and Ishmael, to whom the archangel Gabriel presented the black stone, but that its worship had been perverted in the days of ignorance until at last Mohammed arose to restore the true religion of Abraham and the prophets.

Upon the potentate who for the time is accepted as the legitimate successor of Mohammed devolves the duty of maintaining the Kaaba and of equipping a caravan to make the annual pilgrimage in an imposing manner. The Caliphs of Bagdad were wont to perform the journey in person at the head of enormous bands of the faithful. The Sultan of Turkey is at present the acknowledged Caliph, and head of the Moslem world. Though neither he nor his Ottoman predecessors have ever made the journey in person, the most imposing caravan to Mecca is that which starts from Constantinople, escorted by imperial troops under the command of a high Turkish official. Travelling all the way overland by Damascus and through the desert of Arabia, it collects various streams of pilgrims on its way. When to this vast caravan we add the smaller ones from all parts of the Moslem world, we get some idea of the number and varied nationalities of the pilgrims and the pomp with which the great annual festival is celebrated. Nowadays, however, many of the devotees lessen the fatigues of the journey by availing themselves of steamboats for a portion of the way. But the nearest seaport is Jiddah, some sixty-five miles from Mecca. Caravans, travelling very slowly, make the distance in two nights and a day. By the strict law of Islam, every believer on approaching the sacred city must assume the *ihram*, or pilgrim dress. This consists of two seamless pieces of white cloth, which may be of wool, cotton, or linen. One piece is wound round the loins, the other thrown over the neck and shoulders so as to leave the right arm partly bare. The pilgrim's head must be uncovered. If he does not walk barefooted, the instep of the foot must at least be bare. Female pilgrims wear a veil enveloping the whole figure.

On reaching the city the pilgrim must at once proceed to the Kaaba. This is now enclosed in a large mosque. Though cubic in shape, as its name implies, the sides of the Kaaba are not of equal dimensions, the length being about forty-five feet, the breadth thirty, and the height forty. According to Arab authorities, one angle of the building points to the pole-star, so that the front or face would be the northeast wall.

On first gaining sight of the Kaaba the pilgrim gives thanks for his safe arrival. He then passes under an insulated arch called Bab-el-Salam, reciting certain prescribed prayers, and so reaches the Kaaba. He finds his way to the eastern angle, in front of which he performs two rekas, and then kisses the black stone, or, if the crowd be too great, touches it with his fingers. The stone is a small, dark, shapeless mass, suggesting volcanic, or more probably meteoric, origin. Mohammedan tradition says that it was originally white, but was blackened by the kisses of sinful men. It was broken by fire in the siege of A.D. 683, and the pieces are kept together by a silver setting. According to Moslem myth, it was presented by the archangel Gabriel to Abraham.

In fact, it was originally a fetich, the most venerated among a multitude of idols and sacred stones, which stood all round the sanctuary in pagan times and were destroyed with this one exception by Mohammed. The stone is built into the wall, about four feet nine inches from the ground. On the north side of the Kaaba are two slabs of verd antique which are believed to be the graves of Hagar and Ishmael and are appointed places for prayer.

The pilgrim must make the circuit of the sacred cube seven times, stopping at the end of every round to kiss or touch the black stone. These circuits are called the *tawaf*, and are a relic of pre-Mohammedan paganism. On their conclusion he comes close up to the house, at the space between the black stone and the door (the Multazam), and here prays with outstretched arms and breast pressed against the wall.

He next visits the Makam Ibraham, or standing stone of Abraham, whereon the patriarch rested his feet while building the Kaaba, leaving prints that are still visible. This is enclosed in a small building just outside the door to the left.

Thence he goes to the well Zemzem, still farther to the left, where he recites more prayers and drinks of the sacred waters.

Zemzem is a deep shaft enclosed in a massive vaulted building. According to the Mohammedans, this is the spring from which Hagar drew water for her son Ishmael. (See Genesis xvi. 14.) The water is drawn up by buckets, and is eagerly drunk by the pilgrims, or poured over the body.

Every family in Mecca is anxious to use the water for religious purposes, and it is exported in barrels, or carried home by the pilgrims for its supposed miraculous virtues.

Not yet are the pilgrim's duties ended. He must walk seven times between Safa and Merwa, a distance of about six hundred paces, and on that or a succeeding day make a journey of an hour and a half to Omra.

For all these ceremonies no stated day is fixed. They are necessary incidents both of the great pilgrimage and of the private ones made in pursuance of a vow. But on the ninth day of the month Dhu'l Hajj, during the course of the great pilgrimage, there occurs a ceremonial which is its distinguishing and indispensable feature. Without its observance no man is entitled to call himself a Hajji. This is the visit to Arafat, a bare eminence six miles out from Mecca. Here the pilgrims encamp over-night, and at the hour of afternoon prayer on the 9th they gather upon and around the hill, shouting " Labbeyka !" reciting prayers and texts, and listening to a sermon until nightfall. The sermon is usually delivered by the Kadi of Mecca, who stands on the side of the hill.

Before sunrise next morning (the 10th) a second stand like that on Arafat is made for a short time around the mosque of Muzdalifa, but before the sun is fairly up all must be in motion for the village of Mina, four miles on the way back to Mecca. Here is celebrated the day of sacrifice, whose ceremonies are threefold :

1st. Each pilgrim pelts with seven stones a cairn in West Mina. The stones are thrown in the name of Allah, and are generally thought to be directed at the devil. Mohammedans explain that when Adam returned from Arafat he met Satan in the valley of Mina. The latter attempted to bar his passage. But Adam, instructed by Gabriel, repelled him with stones. The fact is that stone-throwing is a rite older than Islam. It was performed during the annual pagan fair, and not unlikely is connected with the old Arab method of closing a sale by the purchaser throwing a stone.

2d. The slaughter and sacrifice of animals, associated with the offering of Ishmael (not Isaac, say the Moslems) by Abraham. The victims are either sheep or goats. Every pilgrim who can afford it slays an animal, and on this day every Moslem through-out the world likewise offers up an animal in whatever place he may be. If the pilgrim be too poor, he must at some future time make up for the deficiency by fasting. The offerer consumes a portion of his victim, dries and salts other parts, and gives the remainder to the poorer pilgrims.

3d. The shaving of the pilgrim and his resumption of ordinary dress, thus completing the Hajj.

The pilgrim may, if he chooses, remain at Mina for three more days, which are devoted to a fair and a feast. No further ceremony is enjoined on him, save that on the 11th and 12th he must repeat the stone-throwing practised on the 10th.

If he remains in Mina, however, he will miss the ceremony of investing the Kaaba with its new covering, which occurs on the 10th Dhu'l Hajj. This covering is a veil or drapery (*kiswa*) of black figured brocade, adorned with a broad band embroidered with golden inscriptions from the Koran. Every year a new covering is forwarded in the Sultan's caravan. The old covering is removed on the 25th of the preceding month and cut into pieces, which are sold as holy relics to the pilgrims. Thus for two weeks the Kaaba remains bare. (PROFESSOR JAMES ROBERTSON, in *Sunday Magazine*, December, 1890.)

Medard, St. (sometimes abridged to **St. Mard**) (457–545), French prelate. His festival is celebrated on June 8, the anniversary of his death. He was Bishop of Vermand, and afterwards of Noyon, the latter being his birthplace. He was a great friend of King Clotaire I. The latter was one of his pall-bearers. He had promised to build a new church at Soissons as a suitable monument to the saint. When the procession reached Crouy, which is about three miles from Soissons, the bier became wholly immovable. The king then promised to give half the borough of Crouy to the new church. On trying again to lift the bier, it was found that the half facing the part given to the church was loose and could be moved, but the other half was as fast as ever. Clotaire now promised the whole borough to the church. The bier instantly became so light that it could be lifted and carried without any trouble to its final destination. The church and abbey of St. Medard were built over the tomb, which is still a celebrated shrine.

St. Medard is the St. Swithin—*i.e.*, the rainy saint—of France. An old proverb says,—

> S'il pleut le jour de Saint-Médard
> Il pleut quarante jours plus tard.

> ("If it rains on the day of Saint-Medard
> It will rain forty days afterward.")

St. Medard's Day is still watched with anxiety in the rural districts of France. (See ROSIÈRE.)

Medina, Pilgrimage to. Medina, in Arabia, is, next to Mecca, the holiest city of the Moslem world. Thither Mohammed fled when Mecca disowned him. In its most important building, the Mosque of the Prophet, is still shown the tomb of Mohammed, as well as the tombs of his principal followers and of his daughter Fatima. The European fable of the coffin of Mohammed suspended by magnets within the mausoleum is unknown to the Mohammedans. Indeed, it is not certain that either coffin or body has been preserved. The feeling which regards the tomb as the great glory of the mosque and as the central object of the pilgrimages does not seem to have sprung up until a century or more after the Prophet's death. But Mohammed left on record the saying that one prayer in the mosque is of more avail than a thousand in any other place except the Kaaba at Mecca. The great annual pilgrimage immediately follows that of the pilgrimage to Mecca; but as it is not obligatory, and as the journey consumes eleven days, barely a fourth of those who visit Mecca during the month Dhu'l Hajj continue their devotions at Medina. Nor are the observances of the latter pilgrimage as fixed and elaborate as at the former.

Mescal Ceremony. The Indian tribes of the Sierra Madre are accustomed to meet at regular intervals to eat the dried tops of the mescal plant with solemn religious ceremony of song, prayer, and ritual. The mescal plant is a small variety of cactus native to the lower Rio Grande region and about the Pecos River in Eastern New Mexico. The local Mexican name for the plant is *peyote*, a corruption of the original Aztec name, from which it would seem that the plant and ceremony were known as far south as the Valley of Mexico at a period antedating the Spanish conquest. Owing to its agreeably stimulating and medicinal properties, the Indians regard the plant as the vegetable incarnation of the Deity.

Meshhed, Mashhad, or Meshed. (Per., "The Place of Martyrdom.") The capital of Khorassan in Persia, and the sacred city of the Shiite sect of Mohammedans, held in as much veneration by them as Mecca is by the Sunnite Moslems. It is visited every year by nearly one hundred thousand pilgrims, the chief attraction being the splendid mosque built over the tomb of Iman Riza, a follower of Ali, and one of the greatest saints in the Shiite calendar. A pilgrimage to this shrine gives to the pilgrim the coveted privilege of styling himself a Meshedi, just as a pilgrimage to Mecca imparts the title of Hajji. Mohammedans alone may enter the mosque; even the outer gate is inaccessible to Christians and four-footed animals. Every pilgrim carries home with him a little tablet of stone or hardened clay made from the sacred soil of Meshed and inscribed with a text from the Koran. Thereafter, when he prostrates himself the orthodox five times a day towards Mecca, he places the little Meshedi tablet before him on the ground and touches his forehead to that instead of to the commonplace soil of his native village. (*A Visit to Holy Meshed*, by Thomas Stevens, *Cosmopolitan*, February, 1889.)

Michael, St. (His name means in Hebrew, "Who is like God?") According to Jewish and Christian teaching, the chief of the archangels and the head of the celestial militia. He is also, though in a minor capacity to that of St. Denis, the patron of France. As such he is believed to have been the direct inspirer of Joan of Arc.

St. Michael is mentioned in the book of Daniel, in the epistle of Jude, and in the book of Revelation, and each time as a warrior and hero of battles.

Milton, following Biblical authority, makes him the leader of God's loyal angels, who vanquished Lucifer and his legions and consigned them to the dark pit. He is represented with a halo around his head, a spear in his hand, and trampling on the fallen Lucifer, and at times he has a banner suspended from a cross; this representation is a reminder of the prayer in the Litany " to beat down Satan under our feet," and typifies the spiritual triumph of good over evil.

Two festivals are celebrated in his honor by the Catholic Church. One, the Apparition of St. Michael, occurs on May 8; the second and greater festival, recognized also by the Anglican Church, and known in England as Michaelmas, in ecclesiastical calendars as the feast of St. Michael and All Angels, or the feast of the Dedication of St. Michael, occurs on September 29. Among the Greeks the chief festival of St. Michael and All Angels is on November 8. Another feast, in memory of an apparition at Colossæ, is celebrated by the Greeks and Copts on September 6. The dedication of a church to St. Michael in a suburb of Constantinople by Constantine the Great is commemorated on June 8 by the Copts and Abyssinians, the Greeks also celebrating the last day in honor of a miracle wrought at Alexandria. By the Abyssinians the twelfth day of every month is observed in memory of St. Michael.

According to Catholic legend, in the year 492 a rich Italian named Gargan, who fed his cattle upon a hill known after him as Mount Gargano (now Monte Sant' Angelo), missed one of his bulls. It was found in a cavern wounded by an arrow. When one sought to remove this arrow, straightway it flew out of its own accord. Gargan told this marvel to the Bishop of Siponto. The latter thereupon fasted for three days, and on the night of the last was visited by an apparition of St. Michael, who explained that the cavern was his favorite resort and that he wished a church to be erected there. So the bishop and the clergy went in reverent procession to the awful cave and celebrated mass there until a noble church was erected above it and dedicated to the archangel. Now, the date of the apparition was May 8, and that of the dedication September 29, whence these days have ever since been set apart for St. Michael.

Many subsequent apparitions of St. Michael are recorded, and in every case a church has been built upon the site. Many of these churches being on hills, St. Michael has come to be looked upon as the patron of mountains.

Among others are Mont St. Michel, a steep fortified rock off the coast of Normandy, which strikingly resembles St. Michael's Mount in Cornwall. Mont St. Michel has an abbey founded in the eighth century, and a church built by the Normans. It was once believed that a "red velvet-covered buckler" exhibited in this church was the identical one won by Michael in his war with Lucifer. This was exhibited until 1607, when the Bishop of Avranches forbade it.

St. Michael's chair is on the Mount in Cornwall, and tradition asserted that any woman who sat in this chair would ever after rule her husband. St. Michael was said to have appeared on this mount in the sixth century, and the place, thenceforth holy, became the seat of a body of monks, and received a charter from Edward the Confessor. On the promontory of Maler is a chapel built to St. Michael, and the superstitious sailors think that a wind blowing from that quarter is caused by the violent motion of St. Michael's wings. Therefore when they sail by that headland they pray to St. Michael to keep his wings still.

When the Emperor Otho III. had, contrary to his word, put to death the rebellious Roman senator Crescentius, his confessor, St. Romuald, enjoined on him to walk barefoot to Mount Gargano. This was in the year 1002. Similar pilgrimages in expiation of sin are not infrequent even in our day. A continuous stream of penitents, some coming singly, some in crowds, have ever poured towards the various shrines of St. Michael in Catholic countries. The favorite date at Monte Sant' Angelo in Italy is May 8. From the church of St. Michael at the top of the mount pilgrims descend by fifty-five steps to the grotto, which was once a desolate cavern.

The feast of St. Michael is alluded to in the ecclesiastical laws of the English king Ethelred in the year 1014, it being there prescribed that every Christian who is of age shall fast on the three days previous and then go to confession and to church barefoot: "Let every priest with his people go in procession three days barefoot, and let every one's commons for three days be prepared without anything of flesh, as if themselves were to eat it, both in meat and drink, and let all this be distributed to the poor. Let every servant be excused from labor these three days, that he may the better perform his task, or let him work what he will for himself. These are the three days, Monday, Tuesday, and Wednesday next before the feast of St. Michael. If any servant break his fast, let him make satisfaction with his hide, let the poor freeman pay thirty pence, the king's thane a hundred and thirty shillings, and let the money be divided to the poor." But these preliminary austerities did not long prevail.

Indeed, the date of Michaelmas carried with it too many associations with the old heathen day of rejoicing when the harvest was gathered in. It was in the very heart of the season of ripened wheat, of fattened fowl and cattle, of vinous possibilities. Necessarily it became an occasion of good cheer and mental and bodily refreshment. In England the custom of having a goose for dinner is almost universal:

> September when by custom (right divine)
> Geese are ordained to bleed at Michael's shrine.
>
> (CHURCHILL.)

According to historical authority, Queen Elizabeth was eating her Michaelmas goose when she received the tidings of the defeat of the Spanish Armada. Some writers urge that this was the origin of the custom. But it existed long before Elizabeth. Blount's "Tenures" notes the fact that so far back as the tenth year of Edward IV. one John de La Hay was bound, among other services, to render to William Barnaby, Lord of Lastres, in Herefordshire, for a parcel of the demesne lands, " xx^d and one goose fit for his lord's dinner on the Feast of St. Michael the Archangel."

Blount adds that probably no other reason can be given for this custom than that Michaelmas Day was a great festival, and geese at that time were most plentiful.

Yet a plausible suggestion is that the custom arose from the practice among the rural tenantry of bringing, when paying the Michaelmas rent, a fine goose to the landlord to gain his favor. The goose was then at its best, owing to the benefit derived from stubble-feeding, and of course the great number of such presents made it a general custom to have a goose for dinner, as the landlord would have so many given him that he could share them with his friends.

This suggestion is supported by George Gascoyne, who wrote in 1575,—

> And when the tenantes come to paie their quarter's rent,
> They bring some fowle at Midsummer, a dish of fish in Lent,
> At Christmasse a capon, at Michaelmasse a goose,
> And somewhat else at New-yere's tide, for feare their lease flie loose.

Moreover, a superstition prevailed that eating goose at Michaelmas guaranteed prosperity for the coming year, and no lack of money. In Lincolnshire and Yorkshire especially such old beliefs and customs were prevalent, though now abandoned. Bonfires were made, stories told, and ballads sung on Michaelmas Eve. A handful of each sort of grain that the farmer had grown was given that night to his cattle for their supper, and some of the grain scattered in the court for the wild birds to pick up; this was intended to bring luck to the homestead.

Many old customs now extinct have been noted by English antiquarians in the past. Brand tells us that " at this season village maidens, in the west of England, go up and down the hedges gathering crab-apples, which they carry home, putting them into a loft, and forming with them the initials of their supposed suitors' names. The initials which are found, on examination, to be most perfect on *Old* Michaelmas Day are considered to represent the strongest attachments and the best for choice of husbands." (*Popular Antiquities*, 1849, vol. i. p. 356.)

Brand also gives an account of a curious septennial custom observed at Bishop Stortford and in the adjacent neighborhood on old Michaelmas Day. He quotes from a London newspaper of the 18th of October, 1787:

On the morning of this day, called Ganging Day, a great number of young men assemble in the fields, where a very active fellow is nominated the leader. This person they are bound to follow, who, for the sake of diversion, generally chooses the route through ponds, ditches, and places of difficult passage. Every person they meet is bumped, male or female, which is performed by two other persons taking them up by their arms and swinging them against each other. The women in general keep at home at this period, except those of less scrupulous character, who, for the sake of partaking of a gallon of ale and a plum-cake, which every landlord or publican is obliged to furnish the revellers with, generally spend the best part of the night in the fields if the weather is fair, it being strictly according to ancient usage not to partake of the cheer anywhere else.

Martin in his "Account of the Western Isles of Scotland" (1703) speaks of the cavalcades that were a feature of the old-time Michaelmas festivities in those regions. At Lingay, for example, both sexes met on horseback at a designated place on the sea-shore where the ground was hard and firm. Here they exchanged presents, ran races, and performed feats of horsemanship. Ancient custom made it lawful for any of the inhabitants to steal his neighbor's horse the night before and ride him all next day, provided he returned him safe and sound after the races.

In Macaulay's "History of St. Kilda" (1764), p. 22, we read, " It was, till of late, an universal custom among the islanders, on Michaelmas Day, to prepare in every family a loaf of cake of bread, enormously large, and compounded of different ingredients. This cake belonged to the archangel, and had its name from him. Every one in each family, whether strangers or domestics, had his portion of this kind of shew-bread, and had,

of course, some title to the friendship and protection of Michael."
He adds, " In Ireland a sheep was killed in every family that
could afford one, on the same anniversary; and it was ordained
by law that a part of it should be given to the poor. This, as
we gather from Keating's General History of Ireland, ii. 12, and
a great deal more, was done in that kingdom to perpetuate the
memory of a miracle wrought there by St. Patrick through the
assistance of the archangel. In commemoration of this, Michaelmas was instituted a festal day of joy, plenty, and universal
benevolence."

There is a pretty and delicate fancy still prevalent in some
parts of England, that at midnight on Michaelmas Eve the
bracken puts forth a small blue flower, which withers and falls
before the dawn. In many sections of England, and also in Ireland, a superstition exists that at Michaelmas Day the devil
puts his foot on the blackberries, or throws his club over them;
people will not gather them after that day, believing that the
devil has made them poisonous.

In addition to its festive features, Michaelmas is one of the
four quarter-days when tenants pay their rent in England, and
a favorite season for the election of magistrates. Chambers's
" Book of Days" says, " Local rulers were esteemed in some respects analogous to tutelar angels in so far as they presided over
and protected the people. It was therefore thought proper to
choose them on the day of St. Michael and All Angels."

In the parish church of St. James, Clerkenwell Green, London,
an annual sermon is preached on Michaelmas Day as well as All
Saints' Day. A certain resident of the parish, named Pierson,
dying many years ago left £50 to the parish on condition that
£3 be spent annually as follows : " Minister, for sermon concerning the preparation for death, in the afternoon of St. Michael's
and All Saints' Day in every year forever (except Michaelmas
Day happen to fall on a Sunday, then on the following Monday)
and the prayers of the Church of England to be there read in
the same church, 15s.; reader, 2s. 6d.; clerk, 1s. 6d., and sexton
1s., for their attendance; and £1 for forty poor people of the
parish attending such service, 6d. each; the residue, £1, to be
devoted to a collation for the parson, churchwardens, and over-
seers after such service."

Michael's Tree, St., or Suicide Tree. An ailantus which
formerly stood in what was known as Mulberry Bend in New
York city. It was destroyed in 1896, when the Bend disappeared
to make room for the present Park. According to tradition, the
tree was planted in 1826 by Henry Passman, whose homestead
at 45 Mulberry Street became in later years the very heart of

the Bend. Of all the trees that grew in his rear-yard this was the only one left when the tenements sprang up and the old residents of Mulberry Street fled before the invasion of Italian and other immigrants. Legend asserts that during the draft riots in 1863 dozens of negroes were hanged on its spreading branches, and that in more recent times it had served as a convenient hanging-place for people who were tired of life. Hence the name Suicide Tree. These legends are almost without foundation. For a full score of years before its destruction, however, the Italians of the neighborhood had dedicated the tree to St. Michael. On the two holidays devoted to the archangel (May 8 and September 29) the Italian societies, civil and religious, don brilliant uniforms and parade around New York. The day's ceremonies end up with a mass-meeting in the night. The rear-yard where the old tree stood used to be the most convenient place in the neighborhood for these meetings. From the little Italian church around the corner, an image of St. Michael was taken in procession and set up directly under the shadow of the ailantus. All around it were placed lighted candles, while lanterns swung from the branches. The night would be spent in merrymaking and in raffles for sheep, watches, chains, and trinkets. In the early morning St. Michael would be returned to his altar.

Middle Kingdom, Feast of the. A festival celebrated by the Chinese about the middle of the second month. (See CAL-

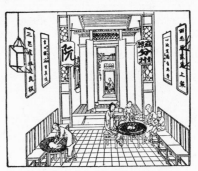

FEAST OF THE MIDDLE KINGDOM.
(By a Chinese artist.)

ENDAR, CHINESE.) The women hang leaves of the sago-plant, with a bulb of garlic and a branch of the cactus tree, over their front doors to ward off evil spirits, and then devote themselves to the preparation of certain cakes a component part of which is a plant which is looked upon as an antidote to all poisons. This is known as the poison-fish plant, because when thrown into the water it is believed to kill everything living therein. Various superstitions attach to the cakes. If eaten while sitting on the threshold of doors they are held to be especially efficacious as mascots. They are distributed as presents throughout the length and breadth of the land, and are even sent by friends to emigrants in California, Australia, and other parts of the world.

Mid-Lent. (Fr. *Mi-Carême;* It. *Mezza Quaresima.*) In most Catholic countries it has been found popularly necessary to break in upon the austerities of the Lenten season by a temporary relapse into holiday festivities. In old Catholic England the occasion was seized on Mid-Lent Sunday (*q. v.*). Here there was no relaxation of Church rules, inasmuch as Sundays in Lent are ecclesiastically *dies non* and are exempt from the obligation of fasting. In France, however, the decay of faith at about the beginning of the eighteenth century led to the establishment of the feast of Mi-Carême, on the third Thursday of Lent. It is believed to have commenced as a sort of return festival given on this date by the young women of the country towns to the young men, in acknowledgment of the ball tendered by the latter to the young women on the preceding Mardi-Gras (*q. v.*). The custom spread to Paris, where it has been taken up by the washerwomen. Four weeks before the appointed date the divinities of the wash-tub in every one of the metropolitan districts meet together to elect a queen, and these queens in turn assemble and choose from their number the queen of queens, who constitutes the principal feature of a great procession that stops for a time all the traffic of the streets. Each district wash-house has a triumphal car decorated in the most gorgeous style, drawn by richly caparisoned horses, escorted by knights in armor and musicians in historical costumes, while perched aloft is the district queen, surrounded by her courtiers and ladies-in-waiting. The great centre of attraction is, of course, the queen of queens, who sits on a golden throne about thirty feet high, her chariot being drawn by Russian horses and surrounded by a burlesque court.

The queen of queens selects a partner, formerly known as the écuyer, or squire, but more recently raised to royal rank as the king of the occasion. The festivities wind up with a ball which is opened by the queen.

The washerwomen's ball was a fruitful theme for the caricaturists in the early part of this century. Two may be found among Cham's works. The legend under one is as follows:

CUSTOMER.—" Can you give me my linen next week?"

WASHERWOMAN.—" Impossible. I have to study the step of the lancers. Next Thursday is our ball."

The other represents a stout washerwoman who says to her assistant, " Go at once and get the countess's linen, so I may wash it. I need an embroidered chemise to wear at the washerwomen's ball."

The following advance notice of the specially gorgeous fête held in 1896 appeared in the *New York Journal* on February 23 of that year:

" Extraordinary preparations are being made this year for the Mid-Lenten masquerade in Paris, and according to the promises and projects it is likely that these fêtes will come nearer to the glories of a Neapolitan Carnival than anything that has been seen in Paris these many years.

"The show of 1896 is to take place on March 12, with its greatest ceremony, the triumphal passing through the streets of the French capital of the queen of queens and her retinue, amid all the magnificence of a triumphal car and the honor of being reviewed by France's Chief Executive himself.

" There is one particular reason why these fêtes will be notable. The shopkeepers have engaged to back the carnival strongly, and the students are entering more heartily into it than usual. But this is not so much the point. The event will be peculiarly notable because there is to be this year a particularly stunning ' Reine des Reines,' the very prettiest of the latter-day Trilbys of Paris.

" For, in accordance with old custom, the queen of this day is selected from the ranks of the blanchisseuses, or laundresses, of the Parisian capital, and in this trade beautiful women are never lacking. The honor has fallen this year upon Henriette Defoulloy, who is one of the ' clear-starchers' of a famous establishment out at Belleville, in the suburbs, an establishment which has already provided several queens and maids of honor for this festival.

" Mlle. Defoulloy is a dark-eyed, entrancing, and slim brunette of seventeen. Her selection as queen is even a greater compliment than is usually implied in the choosing, for this year an entirely new system of picking out a queen has been adopted. In former years the candidates themselves used to gather together and choose one of their number. This winter the candidates, of whom there were thirteen, were ordered to select five of their number, and these five afterwards appeared before the male organizers of the fêtes, who looked over them carefully and pronounced judgment, finally picking out Mlle. Defoulloy. The new system is a better one, for it does away with the traditional wire-pulling that there used to be when the girls themselves had the elective power.

" To be a queen of queens in these Mid-Lent festivals means a great deal to a Parisian laundress. She not only has the enormous public honor of being carried along the streets on a throne, and of having a popular verdict upon her charms, but she is also presented to the President of the Republic. Her emoluments, besides, are very considerable. The Carnival Committee gives her one hundred dollars, and other golden perquisites come to her from the chief police officials of her district, from the municipal councillors, and from others. Last year the queen received a splendid bracelet from President Faure. She is also given gala robes, and these include a garment that she can afterwards use as a wedding-dress. But the requirements of being a royal personage during the fête are hard for a Parisian girl to meet, for she must not only be beautiful and shapely, but she must also be clever, a perfect mistress of her trade, and of unblemished character.

" What has become of the former queens of these pageants is a subject that is interesting to pursue. The queen of the Mid-Lent festivities of 1891 has been found to have recently married, and to be still a working laundress. Her gala togs have been completely worn out, and the only souvenir she possesses of her past glories is the diadem that once adorned her brow, now kept in her little parlor under a glass shade. The queen of 1893 has had a hard road to travel, for her marital life has been unfortunate, and she is now taking proceedings for a divorce. Mlle. Bonhomme, the queen of 1894, has recently been obliged to pawn her crown as well as her robes, and even the bracelet that Carnot, then President, clasped upon her arm on the fête-day. For Bonhomme's father has become a bankrupt.

" Last year's queen is still washing cheerfully away, with a fair outlook of becoming an 'old maid,' for, though she has had many offers of marriage, because of her royal honors she has refused them all. Her laundry specialty is pocket-handkerchiefs and the bosoms of shirts."

In 1896 there was inaugurated on the same day by the Parisian artists of the Montmartre a counter-celebration which went by the name of the Procession of " the Mad Cow" (*la vache enragée*). This was held on the Butte Sacrée, or Sacred Hill.

The " Butte-Sacrée" is a peculiar place. Every stranger who wishes to know Paris must visit that colony of artists, painters, and writers, just as he must go to the top of the Arc de Triomphe or the July column. There at the opposite end of the town a new Latin quarter has been created, in which, however, a man may remain young till he is sixty with impunity, and whose gayety, though fully as noisy as that of the students' quarter, at times assumes an interesting and fascinating artistic coloring.

This was shown especially on this occasion, for while the students followed the Queen of the Washerwomen, exhibiting in their disguises only gayety and even vulgarity, on Montmartre, under the direction of the poet Emile Godeau, who is also a humorist, and of the painter and caricaturist Willette, fun was made of poverty, the usual companion of artists and thinkers.

" A popular phrase," says the Paris correspondent of the *New York Sun*, under date of March 14, 1896, " gave the key-note to the masquerade: *Manger de la vache enragée* means to be reduced to eat meat of poor quality, and, by extension, not to get enough to eat, the fate for long years and often forever of those who remain true to art. In the procession, in front of the celebrated cow whose hoofs were stained red with the blood of poets, but who was securely bound with strong ropes, marched the Anti-Landlord League, bearing on a bed M. and Mme. Pipelet, the types of the Paris concierges created by Eugène Sue. These squirm on the bed in an extraordinary fashion to the sound of a wooden bell incessantly clapping above them; for *déménager à la cloche de bois* means to move out silently without attracting the attention of the landlord's agent and without paying the rent.

" Next came Pegasus, held by two deputy sheriffs for the debts of the poet on his back, followed by the chariot of Poetry, and by floats representing the works of the principal artists of Montmartre, Willette and Faverot with their clowns, Pelez and his poor, Pille and his soldiers, and, to crown all, the reproduction of Puvis de Chavannes' beautiful panel, the Sacred Wood. Some characters belonging to the history of Paris or to legend, such as St. Denis carrying his head under his arm, and the patron saints of the city, closed the procession.

" At the head marched a corps of café waiters, in the place of the sappers who lead regiments, bearing newspaper files instead of axes, followed by a tall woman very much décolletée as a drum-major with a band of little drummers. There was a great deal of fun, but the rain fell steadily and Puvis de Chavannes' Muses had to hold umbrellas up."

In Florence there used to be celebrated a quaint popular ceremony in the Piazza Padella at Mid Lent. A large wooden doll dressed up as a nun and known as La Monica was first sawed in two and then burnt on a funeral pyre amid loud rejoicings. The story ran that this figure was Mezza Quaresima, a sister of the Befana (see EPIPHANY), who had been caught in the middle of Lent eating a Bologna sausage. This heinous crime was pronounced unpardonable, and Mezza Quaresima was condemned (by whom is not stated) to the punishment of being sawn in two, the only remission granted being the privilege of dying incognita in the garb of a nun.

Mid-Lent Sunday. The fourth Sunday in Lent, called Lætare Sunday in the Roman calendar, and popularly known as Mothering Sunday in England. This latter title is explained by the pretty custom which obtained among the young men and women of England who were bound out as apprentices or servants, or who lived at some little distance from their first homes, to return on this Sunday and visit their parents, carrying with them some trifling presents. This was called "going a-mothering." Behind this custom lay a long history reaching back into pagan times. Among the ancient Romans a festival of the Hilaria, or "Mother of the Gods," was held on the Ides of March, when the people made offerings in the temple which became the property of the priests. After the triumph of Christianity the festival was adapted to the new order, and it became the custom on Mid-Lent Sunday for the faithful to visit their "Mother Church,"—*i.e.*, the church in which they were baptized and brought up,—bearing gifts for the altar.

In Shropshire, Yorkshire, and Herefordshire it has long been the custom to make during Lent a cake called a simnel, which is deemed especially appropriate as a "mothering" present. As far back as Herrick we find this quatrain:

To Dianeme.

A ceremonie in Glocester.

I'll to thee a Simnell bring,
'Gainst thou go'st a-mothering,
So that when she blesseth thee,
Half that blessing thou'lt give me.

The inside of a simnel cake was like a rich fruit-cake, but it had an outer crust made of flour and water. Boiled first in water, it was subsequently baked. When done, the crust was as hard as wood, insomuch that it is reported that people unfamiliar with the cakes have mistaken them for footstools. The crust is colored yellow with saffron and ornamented with more or less art. Professional etymologists refer the word simnel to the Latin *simila*, meaning the finest sort of flour. But folk-etymology has far more picturesque origins to suggest. Some pretend that the baker-father of Lambert Simnel, pretender to the throne in the reign of Henry VII., was the first to make these cakes, thence called after his own name. Others say that the cake was the invention of an old man and an old woman named Simon and Nelly, who tried to make a cake for their children out of some old materials which they happened to have. They quarrelled about whether it should be boiled or baked, and after Nelly had broken a broom by way of chastisement over Simon, and

Simon had dislocated a stool by throwing it at Nelly, they agreed that it should be boiled and then baked: so they used the stool for fuel under the pot and the broom for fuel under the oven, and the cake was called by a combination of both their names.

Another dish thought to be appropriate to this day was frumenty, composed of wheat grains boiled in milk sugared and spiced.

Mid-Lent Sunday is occasionally known as Dominica Refectionis, the Sunday of Refreshment, " the reason of which, I suppose," says Wheatley in his book on the Common Prayer, " is the Gospel for the day, which treats of our Saviour's miraculously feeding five thousand; or else, perhaps, from the first lesson in the morning, which gives us the story of Joseph's entertaining his brother."

In mediæval England, as Hone informs us, the boys in the country used to go about on the fourth Sunday in Lent with a figure of Death made of straw. The villagers would either drive them away or purchase their departure with small sums of money. Hone adds that this was only a survival from a more elaborate ceremony of still more remote date, conducted by a larger number of boys, from whom the Death-carriers were a detachment, and who bore two figures to represent Spring and Winter. These two figures were made to fight with each other. Spring invariably won the victory, "and thus was allegorized the departure or death of the year and its commencement or revival as spring." A similar custom has existed in many other countries, and doubtless has its source in pagan antiquity. Thus, a seventeenth-century German, Johann Wilhelm Storch, in his "Description of the Town of Eisenach," mentions the Sommer-Gewinn, or departure of summer, which he similarly surmises to be designed as a celebration of the end of winter and the beginning of summer:

"This feast was always held on the Sunday called Lætare, in the long fore-town, outside the George's Gate, where booths were erected for the sale of confectionery, cakes, and toys. A large multitude of the citizens, with their children, visited, in the afternoon of this day, their friends and acquaintances dwelling in that part of the town, for the purposes of enjoyment and purchasing fir-boughs decorated with sweetmeats, toys, and other fancy articles. Laden with these same decorated boughs, to which the name of 'Summer' was given, they returned towards evening, with their joyful children, to their houses. Formerly two different customs have been known to be connected with this feast. The grown-up lads then were wont to make a wheel, to which a popanz, or figure of straw, was fastened, and to let this run burning down from the top of the

Mädelstein into the fore-town. In the Lausitzer and Meiss-
nischen countries it was customary in many places to carry
round such a dressed-up straw man with songs and rejoicing on
the so-called Dead Sunday, or Lætare, and then to cast the figure
into the water. On the same day Johannisfeuer was lighted up
on every hill-top round about. This Johannis' or John's fire was
literally the summer's-fire, for what we call Midsummer's Day
goes by the name of Johannis-Tag in Germany." According
to Grimm, the straw figure represented the dead Winter, and
was generally associated with the wheel when that article was
employed as part of the spring festival.

Misericordia. (A Latin and Italian word signifying "pity"
or "mercy.") A semi-religious brotherhood in Florence, Italy,
which devotes itself to attendance on the sick and dying. It
took its rise in 1244, when the plague ravaged Europe. The
artisans of Florence, moved by the contagions that desolated
their city and left multitudes of sick without succor and of dead
without burial, were the first to conceive the idea, which was at
once sanctioned by the Church and aided by the aristocracy. At
present the brotherhood is under the direction of seventy-two
members, called Capi di Guardia ("Chiefs of Watch"), and composed of ten prelates, fourteen nobles, twenty priests, and twenty-
eight artisans. Under their immediate orders are two hundred
"giornanti," or journeymen, secular and ecclesiastical. Forty
of these are always on service. There are besides inscribed upon
their lists the names of a thousand or more volunteers (*buone-
voglie*) whom they can call upon at any moment to assist in their
charitable labors. The secret of all these names is kept inviolate
by the Capi di Guardia, partly that the incognito of charity
recommended by Christ may be preserved, and partly because
many of the members are penitents engaged in the expiation
of sin.

"The office of the Misericordia is in the Piazza del Duomo.
Each brother on duty keeps there, marked with his name, a box
containing his black robe, which covers him from head to foot.
They are such as penitents formerly wore, with openings only
for the mouth and eyes, in order that the incognito of charity,
recommended by Christ, shall be strictly preserved. As soon as
the signal is heard that their services are required, the members
on duty assemble at their office, assume their mournful habits,—
which no one can see for the first time without being strangely
affected,—receive their orders, and proceed to the scene of their
duties. Some are required to carry the diseased or wounded to
the hospitals, or other places, as need may be. Others devote
themselves to nursing in the homes of the ill and infirm poor.

They often pass days and nights at their bedsides, bestowing upon them those attentions which try even the constancy of friendship and the affinities of blood. In every place, at any hour, wherever an accident calls, a groan is heard, or there are misery and suffering to be relieved, the Brothers of Pity are required, by their voluntary bond of good deeds, to bestow their alms and their offices. It matters not what may be the origin of the poor victim, or whether he confesses Christ, Moses, or Mohammed. Their charity blesses alike all men, without distinction of race or religion. They bury the unknown dead, carrying themselves the corpse to its sepulchre. The scaffold even does not repel them from fulfilling, in its broadest extent, the spirit of their vows. They are to be found at the latest moment beside the criminal, consoling and preparing him for his doom; and, after his head has fallen under the axe of the guillotine, gathering up his mangled remains, to bestow upon them a Christian burial. Priest and layman, noble and mechanic, unknown to each other, and unrecognizable by their nearest relatives, bear upon their shoulders the same litter, containing, it may be, a poor cripple abandoned by all the world besides." (*Harper's Magazine*, April, 1854.)

Misrule, Lord of. A noted functionary, known also by various other names, who was formerly appointed in every great household in England to direct the revels of the Christmas season and preside over its ceremonies. The custom began with royalty, but became so popular that every nobleman and person of position had a Lord of Misrule. In the more ancient days his rule began at Halloween and ended with Candlemas; but latterly it was restricted to the Twelve Days of Christmas, with occasionally a revival for the nonce at Candlemas.

The performance of this lord during the days of his license of disorder recalls in many points the Roman Saturnalia. The master and all his household must obey the Lord of Misrule as the Romans obeyed the masters of the feasts of Saturn, and there was the same equality of servants with their masters. "Christmas," says Selden, in his "Table-Talk," "succeeds the Saturnalia,—the same time, the same number of holy days; then the master waited on the servant like the Lord of Misrule."

An idea of the authority exercised by this Christmas potentate is given by the articles of appointment of Owen Flood, trumpeter, to be Lord of Misrule for twelve days in the Mansion House of Richard Evelyn, of Walton, in Surrey, High Sheriff of Surrey and Sussex in 1634. The document said, " I give free leave to said Owen Flood to command all and every person or persons whatsoever, as well servants and others, to be at his command whenever he shall sound his Trumpet or Musick, and to do him good service, as though I were present myself, at their perils."

Every person was commanded to appear in the hall at seven A.M. and attend prayers, on pain of such punishment as the lord saw fit to impose. To swear on the precincts, to come into the hall and sit at dinner or supper more than once, to be drunk, or to drink more than is fit, or to offer to sleep, was to incur punishment; while if a person did not drink up his bowl of beer, but flung away his snuffe (that is, his second draught), he should drink two and afterwards be excluded. Drinking too little was as perilous as drinking too much. To quarrel or use ill language within the twelve days was to incur the lord's displeasure: "Item: If any one shall come into the kitchen whiles meat is a-dressing, to molest the cooks, he shall suffer the rigor of his lordship's law. Item: If any man shall kisse any maid, widdow, or wife, except to bid welcome or farewell, without his lordship's consent, he shall be punished as his lordship shall think convenient." And finally, "I give full power and authority to his lordship to brake up all lockes, bolts, barres, doores, and latches, and to flinge up alle doores out of hendges, to come at all those who presume to disobey his lord's commands. God save the king!"

Mr. Philip Stubbes, the morose Elizabethan Puritan whose "Anatomie of Abuses" was published in 1583, has a good deal to say about these "hell-hounds," as he genially denominates the Lord of Misrule and his complices. He tells us that in the rural districts "the grand captaine of mischief," on being crowned and adopted as king by the wild heads of the parish, selects threescore or so lusty attendants "lyke himselfe." These he invests with his liveries, green, yellow, or some other light wanton color. "And as though that were not gaudie enough I should saie, they bedecke themselves with scarfes, ribbons, and laces, hanged all over with golde rynges, precious stones, and other jewelles: this doen, they tye about either legge twentie or fourtie belles, with rich hande-kercheefes in their hands, and sometimes laied across their shoulders and neckes, borrowed for the most parte of their pretie Mopsies and loovyng Bessies for bussyng them in the darcke. Thus thinges sette in order, they have their hobbie-horses, dragons, and other antiques, together with their baudie pipers and thunderyng drommers, to strike up the Deville's daunce withall: then marche these heathen companie towardes the churche and churcheyarde, their pipers pipyng, drommers thunderyng, their stumppes dauncing, their belles jynglyng, their hand-kercheefes swynging about their heads like madmen, their hobbie-horses and other monsters skyrmishyng amongst the throng: and in this sort they goe to the churche (though the minister bee at praier or preachyng) dauncing and swingyng their hand-kercheefes over their heades in the churche, like devilles incarnate, with such a confused noise that no man can heare his own voice. Then the foolishe people they looke, they stare, they laugh, they fleere, and mount upon formes and pews to see these goodly pageauntes solemnized in this sort. Then, after this, aboute the church they goe againe and againe, and so forthe into the churche-yarde, where they have commonly their sommer haules, their bowers, arbours, and banquettyng houses sett up, wherin they feaste, banquet, and daunce all that daie, and (peradventure) all that night too. And thus these terrestrial furies spend their Sabbaoth daie."

In the year 1637 some Lincolnshire farmers came up before the Commissioners for Causes Ecclesiastical on the charge of carrying their Christmas revelries too far. Not content with a Lord of Misrule, they determined he should have a lady or Christmas wife. Probably there was no harm in this, but only in the method by which the lady was assigned to the lord. Eliza Pitto, daughter of the hogherd of the town, was brought in as bride. A farmer named Saunders received her. He was disguised as a parson, wearing a shirt or smock for a surplice. He then married the Lord of Misrule to the hogherd's daughter, reading the whole of the marriage service from the Book of Common Prayer. All the after ceremonies and customs then in use were observed with all the license of the times. The parties had time to repent at leisure in prison.

In the University of Cambridge the functions of the Lord of Misrule were performed by one of the Masters of Arts, who was regularly elected to superintend the annual representation of Latin plays by the students, besides taking a general charge of their games and diversions during the Christmas season, and was styled the Imperator or Præfectus Ludorum. A similar Master of Revels was chosen at Oxford, under the title of Christmas Prince. But it seems to have been in the Inns of Court in London that the Lord of Misrule reigned with the greatest splendor, being surrounded with all the parade and ceremony of royalty, having his lord-keeper and treasurer, his guard of honor, and even his two chaplains, who preached before him on Sunday in the Temple Church, gravely saluting him as they ascended the pulpit, as was the custom in Chapel Royal on preaching before the king. On Twelfth Day he abdicated his sovereignty. In the year 1635 this mock representative of royalty expended in the exercise of his office about two thousand pounds from his own purse, and at the conclusion of his reign was knighted by Charles I. at Whitehall. The office, indeed, seems to have been regarded among the Templars as a highly honorable one, and to have been generally conferred on young gentlemen of good family.

In 1666 Evelyn saw this solemn foolery at Lincoln's Inn, when the mock king was gloriously clad and attended: at this revel the king (Charles II.) and the Duke of York were present. On the 6th of January his majesty opened the revels himself by throwing the dice in the Privy Chamber, and lost at the play one hundred pounds; but he could afford it, for the year before he won fifteen hundred pounds. The ladies also played very deep. As late as the times of Kings George I. and II. the revels remained, and these gracious kings played in public at the hazard-table.

In Scotland, previous to the Reformation, the monasteries used to elect a functionary of a similar character for the superintendence of the Christmas revels, who was known as the Abbot of Unreason. A graphic description of one of these mock ecclesiastics may be found in "The Abbot," by Sir Walter Scott. An ordinance for suppressing this annual burlesque, with other festivities of a like kind, was passed by the Scottish legislature in 1555. The Scotch Abbot is probably an offshoot from the French Abbé de Liesse or Abbas Stultorum who conducted the festivities at the Feast of the Ass.

Mistletoe. In scientific language the mistletoe is a species of *viscum*, of the natural order *Loranthaceæ*, which grows as a parasite both on deciduous and on evergreen trees and shrubs, but mainly on the poplar, the hawthorn, the pear, and the apple, —preëminently, indeed, on the latter. It forms an evergreen bush, about four feet in length, thickly crowded with (falsely) dichotomous branches and opposite leaves.

It grows in a very peculiar manner; unlike all other plants, its shoots extend downward as well as upward, giving the tree an odd general appearance with these tufts sticking below and above the bare branches in winter, lumpy clusters of sprigs, dividing and multiplying at their extremities, in color the darkest green, which look almost black against a clear sky. The leaves and flowers spring from the knotty points of bifurcation, which are added yearly, on the slender stems. There are two leaves, of a dull leathery complexion, at each knot, and a very small yellowish flower, hardly perceptible to the careless eye, at the base of the leaves. Towards the month of November these flowers change into the fruit, the little round whitish berries with which Anglo-Saxon nations become familiar at Christmas in our festive household parties. The berry is filled with a semi-fluid viscous substance as sticky as birdlime. But it is not until the fourth year of its growth that the plant yields these berries, and it is in the fifth or sixth year that it is worth while to take it for their sake.

So much for the hard, dull prose of its biography, which may be gleaned from any encyclopædia. But were this prose all that could be said of the mistletoe there would be small reason for its popularity. It is because that prose is intertwined with poetry and mystery, it is because the mistletoe has become the centre of more than one cycle of legendary and traditional lore, it is because it was connected with the heathen Saturnalia and was adopted into the Christian festivities which transformed the soulless license of the past into the pretty and harmless indecorum of the present,—it is for all these reasons that the very word mistletoe greets the fancy pleasantly and appeals to the latent superstition and mysticism of even the best-balanced minds.

In Scandinavian mythology the mistletoe figures as the material of the arrow with which Balder, the sun-god, was slain. And this is the story. When Balder was born, his mother, Frigga, invoked all the elements, all animals and all plants, and obtained an oath from all that they would do Balder no hurt. One plant only she forgot, on account of its insignificance,—the parasitic mistletoe. When Balder grew up and took his part among the combats of the gods, all weapons glanced harmlessly away from him and all the powers of nature proved innocuous. But Loki, his enemy, determined to learn the secret of his invulnerability. Dressing himself up as an old woman, he wheedled the secret out of Frigga, including the fact that mistletoe had been overlooked. Then Loki made an arrow of mistletoe wood. Entering the assembly of the gods, he said to the blind Höder, " Why do you not contend with the arrows of Balder?" " I am blind and have no arms," returned Höder. Then Loki presented him with the arrow and said, " Balder is before thee." Höder shot, and Balder fell dead.

Among the ancient Druids the mistletoe was the object of special veneration, but only when it grew upon an oak. Pliny, who is our earliest authority on Druidism, furnishes an explanation,—viz., that, as oaks were their sacred trees, whatever was found growing upon one they regarded as sent from heaven, and as a mark that that tree was set apart for special veneration. Hence, he says, they called the parasite *omnia sanitatem* ("all-heal"), and looked upon it as a cure for sterility and an antidote for poisons.

Alas for the rarity of Christian charity among historians and archæologists ! It is hinted that even in Druidic times the parasite rarely if ever grew on oaks, but that the wily priests would furtively transplant their mystic shrub from apple-trees, where it was sure to grow, to oaks, where otherwise it would be unlikely to be found. It is known that the apple-tree was held by the Druids to be the next sacred tree to the oak, and that apple orchards were shrewdly planted by them in the vicinity of their oak groves. At the present moment it is estimated that in all England there are not half a dozen oak-trees on which the parasite is growing. That in the elder days mistletoe oaks were even rarer seems to be proved by an ancient manuscript in the British Museum, from which the following paragraph is quoted: "Heare my Lord Frescheville did live [in Derbyshire], and heare grows the famous misseltoe tree, the only oake in England that bears misseltoe."

At the time of the winter solstice, which was almost universally looked upon in Europe as a festival period, the Druids gathered the mistletoe with great ceremony. Five days after the new moon a grand procession was formed. First came the bards, then a herald, who bore the cutting implement usually described as a golden scythe, though sometimes as a reaping-hook of the same metal, or even a golden knife-blade or hatchet attached to a shaft. The priests came next, with the Prince of the Druids in their wake. All were clad in white. Then followed the people, male and female.

When the oak was reached on which the mistletoe grew, two white bulls were bound to the tree, and the prince, taking the knife from the herald, climbed up the tree and cut the mistletoe, which was caught in a white mantle held by the inferior priests. The bulls, and sometimes even human victims, were then sacrificed. The mistletoe thus gathered was divided into small portions and distributed on the first day of the new year to the people, amid cries of "The mistletoe for the new year!"

In their turn the people hung up the sprays over the entrances to their houses, as a propitiation and an offer of shelter to the sylvan deities during the season of frost and cold. These various rites and ceremonies were kept up throughout the Roman dominion in Britain, and down even to the Anglo-Saxon period. They were also celebrated among the Druids in Northern and Western France.

Bellini in his opera of "Norma" refused to take this historical account of the Druidic ceremony, and substituted an invention of his own, which has gained a certain tolerated acceptance in literature and art. Norma is a Druidic prophetess. At the head of two other Druidesses and of a company of children, all clad in white, she marches into the sacred groves. A gong is attached to an old, fine fellow of an oak, which might lead the uninitiated to suppose that the Druids were up to the manufacture of bell-metal. Norma, stretching forth her white left arm, strikes three strokes, and the other Druids, men and women, come filing in. Then Norma, having two baskets and a reaping-hook brought to her by two of the damsels of the temple, proceeds to cut the sacred mistletoe, which, with the hook, she deposits in the basket still held by the damsels, who then retire.

But let us pass to modern times. Mistletoe was abandoned in the Christmas decking of churches, together with kissing at the services, because both were found to set the young ladies and gentlemen a-reading the marriage service. Holly and unkissed kisses were substituted, to indicate to them the dark monotony of matrimony and the numerous thorns with which it abounded. But, though banished from the churches, mistletoe and the kissing under it flourished apace in the servants' halls at the Christmas period. "In the kitchen," says Brand, "it was hung up in great state, and whatever female chanced to stand under it, the young man present either had a right, or claimed one, of saluting her and of plucking off a berry at each kiss." Nares makes it ominous for the maid not so saluted, inasmuch as this indicated that she would not be married that year.

The mistletoe did not long remain exclusively in the kitchen. It speedily invaded the parlor and the drawing-room, without, however, reducing the quantity of kissing in the lower regions.

Kissing under the mistletoe, as already indicated, is undoubtedly an innocent survival from the Saturnalia of the ancients, when riot and license ran loose.

In England all classes and ages deliver themselves up willing victims to long-established custom. In many old-fashioned houses the elderly gentleman, with long waistcoat and frilled and ruffled shirt, advances to the object of his immediate devotion and makes a low bow. The elderly lady rises and achieves a stately courtesy. Then the pair walk hand in hand to beneath the mistletoe, and the old gentleman delicately touches with his not yet withered lips the cheeks of the elderly lady. Then there is another bow and courtesy, and a third, when the gentleman conducts the lady to her seat. How different all this from the joyous freedom of the younger people! What romping, what slight, pretty screaming, what tittering, what make-believe running away, and what bold standing under the mistletoe! The small fry of short-frocked misses and jacketed masters are never tired of kissing one another, while another class of determined osculators are the rather scrimp and running-to-seed young ladies of thirty-five, who are getting desperate, and the jolly, bald-headed bachelors, who kiss every girl that comes in their way.

French society manners have never approved of kissing games, hence the mistletoe has never in France enjoyed any special significance. As a Christmas decoration the holly, the pine branch, the ivy, the laurel, and other evergreens, with the flower called *rose de Noël*, are found more suitable for artistic arrangement. Yet it is a noteworthy fact that the larger part of the mistletoe sold in England at Christmas comes from the apple orchards of Normandy.

In America a species of mistletoe called the phoradendron grows all along the temperate belt from New Jersey to California. It differs in many points from the foreign variety. The true mistletoe is frequently imported at Christmas-time, but the holly is the favorite evergreen for decoration, and often carries with it the osculatory privileges accorded in England to the mistletoe alone.

Mohammed, Moolid or **Birthday of.** The Prophet's birthday is one of the greatest festivals of the Moslem world, and is celebrated with dances of dervishes, performances of the Aïssaoui (*q. v.*), music, illuminations, the roasting of sheep and bullocks, and general rejoicing. The most famous function of the day is that known as the Doseh, or Trampling, which occurs in the Esbekiyeh Gardens in Cairo. Thousands gather to see this performance. About ten A.M. the two or three hundred dervishes who are to submit to the Doseh make their appearance. Two by two in a long file, the near hands of each pair clasped together, and the off hands resting on the shoulders of the men in front, down they come rushing through a narrow lane made for them through the heaving and struggling multitude. As they come they sway from side to side with a uniform automatic movement, gasping out, "Allah!" They are all pale and bathed with sweat, drunk with fanaticism, possibly with something else. Arriving at the open space in the avenue where the Doseh is to take place, they all stop, fall flat upon their faces, and arrange themselves side by side to form a living pavement, a sort of corduroy road of men.

Busy officials running to and fro fit all the human logs together neatly, by adjusting here an arm and there a leg. The logs, however, are not bound to lie quite still, but, on the contrary, they are expected to keep up, and do keep up, a convulsive twitching motion through their bodies, while at the same time these miserable men are all at work rubbing their noses violently in the dust from side to side, and grunting out the name of God in swinish accents. Some believing bystanders are infected with the fierce plague of fanaticism, and go down among the grovellers. There is a murmur, a shout, and a dead silence, while the crowd sways eagerly forward. A stout man, on a powerful horse, surrounded by about a dozen attendants, moves at a quick walking pace over the prostrate bodies. Each dervish receives the horse's tread over his loins; some throw up their heads and feet when the weight falls, writhing like worms. The sheik rides on and away. The friends of the dervishes run forward to pick them up, and whisper in their ears, "Wahed," which means, "Declare the Unity of God." Some can only groan, some are in a swoon, some respond to the appeal with foaming or with bleeding lips. A few have evidently passed through fanaticism into fits.

Each dervish is entitled to two horse-hairs from the sheik's horse, one from the fore-leg and one from the hind-leg. Those who are injured during the Doseh are thought saintly according to the extent of the damage received. The others—there is a superstitious belief that no one is permanently maimed— are scarcely congratulated; the seal of the Prophet is not on them; they may return to the world and the flesh.

Monday, St., or Cobblers' Monday. It is humorously asserted in the folk-lore of both England and continental Europe that cobblers and shoemakers, not satisfied with their annual

ST. MONDAY.
(From a French lithograph of the eighteenth century.)

outing on St. Crispin's Day, require a weekly holiday every Monday. Hence the personification of St. Monday, or Saint-Lundi. The further explanation is offered in Belgium that the shoemakers do not know exactly on what day St. Crispin's festival rightly falls, save that it should be on a Monday; they therefore celebrate every Monday, so as to be sure of not letting the day slip by unhonored. Popular imagination has even gone so far as to produce a St. Monday in caricature. He is represented as a shoemaker surrounded by people of various trades and squatting on a barrel; his slippers are torn and tattered, his sleeves are rolled up to the elbows, and in his right and left hands respectively he holds a pitcher and a glass of wine. In one of these caricatures, published at Epinal in 1835, the following verses are put in his mouth:

> Vous qui commencez la semaine
> Au troisième jour seulement,
> De Pompe à Mort, dit Long-Haleine,
> Gai savetier, buveur ardent,
> Et de plus votre président,
> Ecoutez tous un avis sage
> Que ma prudence va dicter:
> Abandonnez votre menage
> Et venez tous rire et chanter.

> (" You who begin the week
> Only with the third day,
> From Pomp-in-Death, called Long-Breath,
> A gay cobbler, an ardent drinker,
> And, above all, your president,
> Listen to this wise advice
> Which my prudence dictates to you :
> Quit your households
> And come all to laugh and sing.")

A folk-song which is current with variations in both France and Belgium pictures the shoemaker's life as one continual round of pleasure:

> Les cordonniers sont pires que des évêques.
> Tous les lundis ils en font une fête.
> > Tirez fort, piquez fin !
> > Coucher tard et lever matin.
> Et le mardi ils vont boire la chopinette,
> Le mercredi ils ont mal à la tête,
> Et le jeudi ils vont voir leurs fillettes.
> Le vendredi ils commencent la semaine,
> Et le samedi les bottes ne sont pas faites.
> Le dimanche ils vont trouver leur maître.
> Leur faut l'argent, les bottes ne sont pas faites.
> " Tu n'en auras pas, si les bottes ne sont faites."
> " Si je n'en ai pas je veux changer de maître."

> (" Shoemakers are worse than bishops.
> Every Monday they make a holiday.
> > Pull hard ! Prick lightly !
> > Late to bed and early to rise.

> On Tuesday they drink,
> On Wednesday they have a headache,
> On Thursday they go to see their girls.
> On Friday they begin the week,
> And on Saturday the shoes are not made.
> On Sunday they seek their masters.
> They want money, the shoes are not made.
>   ' You shall have none, if the shoes are not made.'
>   ' If I don't get any, I will change my master.' ")

In Spain the same idea is put more tersely :

> Lunes y Martes de chispa;
> Miércoles la estan durmiendo;
> Jueves y Viernes mala gana;
> Y el Sabado entra el estruendo.

> (" Monday and Tuesday days of wine;
> Wednesday they spend in sleep;
> Thursday and Friday they are sick,
> On Saturday the noise recommences. ")

Month's Mind. An ancient solemn commemorative service in the Catholic Church held one month after the death of the person for the benefit of whose soul it was celebrated. His (or her) name was wont to be written on a tablet and kept on the altar, and was read out at the proper point in the mass. This was called " mynding" the dead. The ceremony might be repeated each month for a year, in which case it was called "a year's mind." The phrase is still retained in Lancashire, England, an exceptionally Catholic county, but elsewhere the " Mind Days" are called "Anniversary Days." In what esteem this "month's mind" was formerly held is shown by the elaborate directions for the conduct of it found in the wills of sundry persons of consequence. Thus, Thomas Windsor, Esq. (1479), wills that at his " Moneth's Minde" " there be a hundred children within the age of sixteen years, to say for my soul." Also, " that against my month's mind candles be burned before the rood in the parish church ; also, that my executors provide twenty priests to sing Placebo, Dirige, etc." Fabyan (born 1450), one of the historians of early Britain, also gives instructions in his will for his " Month's Mind." "I will that myne executrice doo cause to be carried from London xii newe torches to burne in the tymes of the said burying and *monethes minde.* Also, I will that breade, ale and chese for all comers to the parish church be ordered as shall be thought needful against a *monethes mind.*" " In Ireland," we are told by an authority, "after the death of great personages they count four weeks ; and four weeks from that day all priests and friars, and all the gentry far and near, are invited to a great

feast, usually termed the *month's mind.* The preparations for
this feast are masses said in all parts of the house at once for
the soul of the departed. If the room be large, there are three
or four priests celebrating together in the several corners of the
room. The masses done, they proceed to their feasting, but
after all the others each priest and friar is discharged with
his largess."

Montyon Prize of Virtue. This is the most popular and
famous of four foundations of ten thousand francs each established in their present form by the will of the French philanthropist Jean-Baptiste Antoine Auget, Baron of Montyon (1733–
1820). In his own lifetime so far back as 1780 he had established
similar prizes, but they had been interrupted by the Revolution.
By the terms of the will the respective sums were to be put out
at interest, the yearly incomes being given as prizes in the following fashion:

1. For an improvement decreasing the sanitary risks of any
mechanical employment.

2. For the discovery or invention of any medical or surgical
improvement.

3. For an act of virtue performed by a French citizen.

4. For the most moral and useful book written by a French
citizen.

The first two prizes are in the keeping of the Academy of
Sciences, the latter in that of the French Academy. The third,
as already stated, has become the most popular, so that by successive endowments the one original prize of virtue has been
increased to ninety-eight.

Fortunately, the academic discourse which accompanies their
bestowal remains limited to the half-hour prescribed by M. de
Montyon. He also wished that the virtuous actions rewarded
should have endured for a period of at least two years. But
with the present affluence of demands it is oftener a devotedness
of twenty or forty years that is singled out for recompense. As
M. Ludovic Halévy, the orator of 1894, took pains to declare
pleasantly, " The Academy rewards only virtues that are chronic,
inveterate, incurable, and even hereditary."

All the departments and even the colonies of France have the
right to present candidates, the memorials in each case being of
necessity signed by persons of weight in the place, who are responsible for the truth of the statements made. The cases are
required to be presented with the most minute detail, and no
effort is spared to prevent deception. They are then examined
by a committee of the Academy, and proportionate sums are
awarded.

Among the prizes bestowed in the pre-Revolutionary days were some for courage in helping the shipwrecked at the risk of life, for the fidelity of servants who had taken on themselves the support of their masters when these had fallen into poverty, for certain children who had honored themselves by their filial " sensibility." It was the age of Rousseau's sentimentalism. This had its consequence and commentary in the unique and most enthusiastic demonstration made in 1790 over a woman of Paris, a seller of silks and cloths, who received the Montyon prize of virtue of that year for "having broken the fetters of a prisoner of the Bastille."

Here are examples of the class of heroes who in recent years have carried off the highest of the Montyon prizes, twenty-five hundred francs. They are taken from contemporary reports.

1. The curé of the little village of Loigny. "This good priest, then thirty-six years old, on the night of the 2d of December, 1870, saved from massacre in the bloody battle between French and Prussians over five hundred of the wounded of both sides, whom he dragged with his own hands from the confusion of the snow-covered field of combat to the shelter of his house and church. After a day and night spent in hard labor in the midst of the fight, he lay down to rest on a bundle of straw in the cellar,—the only place he had left for himself. After the war he took up again his ordinary life of obscure ministrations. Thanks to Mme. MacMahon and M. Jules Simon, who was then minister of the interior, all the dead of the plain of Loigny were intrusted to his care. With unwearied efforts he has collected two hundred and forty thousand francs, which he has used in building a mortuary chapel where twelve hundred of the fallen soldiers are buried. The twenty-five hundred francs of the Montyon prize are all that is needed to pay off the last bills."

2. Pierre Crouzillat, captain of the life-boat at Sables-d'Olonne. " He has saved from wreck upward of forty barks, schooners, and fishing-boats, the crews of merchant-vessels, English, German, and Norwegian, having borne their testimony, time after time, to his daring courage and extraordinary devotion. Thirty-two years ago he rescued two persons from the midst of a burning house at Brest. Since then he has saved eighteen others from drowning, not only imperilling his own life,—that is taken for granted,—but venturing into circumstances of such extreme danger that even those who knew best his strength and wonderful powers of endurance gave him up for lost. His own belief is that a special providence protects those who risk their lives for the sake of others, and certainly thus far events have justified his theory. Ingratitude he never has met with, or want of ap-

preciation on the part of his superiors. He has received diplomas, medals, even the decoration of the Legion of Honor. But the Montyon prize holds a position in popular favor above and beyond all others, and Pierre Crouzillat is this year made happy by receiving its highest medal."

3. The Abbé Brassier, of Saint Georges de Raimtembault. " Another in the long list of French curés who have given themselves up to the task of reclaiming outcast children. But before undertaking this special work he had already shown himself possessed of the most noble qualities. When the war of 1870 broke out, he left Montfort, where he was vicaire (or assistant priest), and as volunteer chaplain accompanied the troops of his department. Opportunities were not wanting for the display of courage and self-sacrifice, and on more than one desperate occasion his conduct so aroused the enthusiasm of the battalion that, at the request of the officers, the cross of the Legion of Honor was bestowed upon him. At the close of the war he was sent to his present parish, St. Georges, where he has gathered around him, one after another, fifteen vagrant and orphan boys, not only providing them with food and shelter, but having them taught honest and useful trades. Not content with this one orphanage, he has lately opened another for girls. Sixty children constitute his present adopted family,—sixty hungry, growing boys and girls! It is a difficult matter for a poor curé to provide even daily bread for so many; but his faith is strong, he loves his work and his children, and believes that God will never forsake those who care for the orphan. The twenty-five hundred francs of the Montyon prize will lighten, for a time at least, his heavy burden of anxiety."

Mop, Runaway Mop. The word mop, or mapp, is an abbreviation of the Latin *mappa*, applied to some of the old Roman games from the fact that a sort of napkin so named was called into frequent use. It survives in England only in the term a " runaway mop," a second or subsidiary fair or hiring. " Occasionally such a fair is held shortly after the first, and this is termed a runaway mop from its having run away from its usual course and collected the runaways from the regular mops. Although these mops and statutes have in some places dwindled to a shadow of what they were, yet in many parts they still flourish, like weeds of evil growth, despite the efforts made by the clergy and laity in the establishment of servants' registration offices. The Yorkshire Martinmas Statutes, this last November, were as largely attended as usual, and marked by the same riotous drunkenness and·profligacy. Of course the secret of the popularity of such evils is to be found in their affording

to the agricultural laborers and their friends that revelry and
merrymaking from which their lack of holidays deprives them.
If their rational amusements were extended, they would not
find so much pleasure in noxious excitement." (*Once a Week*,
January 15, 1870.)

Moving-Day. This name was formerly given in New York
and Boston to May-Day because the great majority of leases
made of flats in these cities dated from May 1 to May 1. At
present, however, the yearly lease is becoming less common, and
the moving anniversary has consequently lost its universality.
Something of the dolors that have passed away with the occasion may be gathered from Mr. George W. Curtis's wail made in
Harper's Magazine in 1855:

" May-Day is a serious matter. If ' Pa' doesn't own his house,
woe to him. It is as if the world were ending. It is a mael-
strom of furniture, and distracted people carrying mirrors and
fragile articles. It is the grand unveiling of a thousand household economies. You see the state of your neighbor's pots and
pans. You detect his broken pitchers and patched tureens. All
the domestic subterfuges come to light, and are publicly carried
by the window. It may rain, or blow, or snow, or freeze—but
the work goes on. It is the Exodus of Gotham. Unhappy
ones, who pay rent, and who will not rise into ruinous rates, you
must trudge. Behold the *charette* at the door. Bundle! bundle!
And away go the unhappy, tumbling over those who go out as
they come in, and, O Cloacina! they sit down in the dirt of
Mrs. Margery Daw's household, which custom does not require
that housekeeper to remove.

" There is no day more dreary and disgusting than Moving-
Day. And why there should be this insane conspiracy of every
man against his neighbor's convenience, why every lease should
begin and expire upon the same day, does not appear. It might
be more pleasantly arranged, more wisely, and more profitably.
But, we repeat, great is the force of bad habit. And great is
the misery of moving our households, as we do everything else,
in the most awkward, shiftless, and expensive manner. But
there is one thing that an American will not do ; and that is—
learn. He will bungle his way out, if he can. If not, he will
be apt to call his way the best. The Italians, when they wish
to saw wood, rub the log against the saw. But it is not the
best way."

In Paris April 15 is the *terme*. Those who wish to continue
on in their apartments, and are able to pay the rent, remain.
Those who do not, move. Hence it is the moving-day. In Scotland the " Flitting-Day" (*q. v.*) is on May 22.

Mummers. (Dan. *mumme*, Dutch, *momme*, " a mask.") Parties of masqueraders who disguised themselves in masks after the manner of the ancient Romans in the Saturnalia. Christmas was the grand scene of mumming, and some mummers were disguised like bears, others like unicorns, bringing presents. Those who could not procure masks rubbed their faces with soot, or painted them. In the Christmas mummeries the chief aim was to surprise by the oddity of the masks and the singularity and splendor of the dresses. Everything was out of nature and propriety. They were often attended with an exhibition of gorgeous machinery. Besides the set and formal mummings, the members, guests, and servants of a household would put on masks, and, thus disguised, practise rude jests on one another. So many evils grew out of the habit of general masquerade at the holiday season, and so many murders and robberies were committed in London and other large cities by disguised ruffians, that Henry VIII. issued a proclamation declaring the wearing of a mask a misdemeanor; but it does not appear that hilarity of this kind was in any degree repressed by the royal edict. The mummers had their songs, one of the best known being a madrigal to the words

> To shorten winter's sadness
> See where the folks with gladness
> Disguised all are coming
> Right wantonly a-mumming.

In Scotland the mummers are called guisards. The evenings on which these personages are understood to be privileged to appear are those of Christmas, Hogmanay, New Year's Day, and Handsel Monday. Dressed up in quaint and fantastic attire, they sing a selection of songs which have been practised by them some weeks before. Some of their doings are of a theatrical character. There is one rude and grotesque drama (called "Galatian") which they are accustomed to perform on each of the four above-mentioned nights, and which in various fragments or versions exists in every part of Lowland Scotland. The performers, who are never less than three, but sometimes as many as six, having dressed themselves, proceed in a band from house to house, generally contenting themselves with the kitchen for an arena, whither, in mansions presided over by the spirit of good humor, the whole family will resort to witness the scene of mirth. (See Chambers's " Popular Rhymes," p. 170.)

Even now, in the country districts of Wales, mumming is far from uncommon. A party of singers will procure a horse-skull, place it on a pole as a sort of standard, disguise themselves in masks, and, thus rigged out, visit the houses of the gentry and sing before the closed door. The gentleman thus honored has usually taken care to provide a Welsh singer, who, within the house, responds in verses supposed to be extemporaneous to the singers outside, and the contest goes on until the singer inside is unable to continue the versification further, or judiciously acknowledges himself vanquished, when the doors are thrown open, and all enter and are properly entertained. It is said by those conversant with the language and customs of this remarkable people that the rejoinders of these peasant poets often show great brilliancy of wit and wonderful power of versification.

N.

Nativity, Church of the. A church in Bethlehem in Judea, built, according to ancient tradition, on the precise spot where the stable stood in which Christ was born. The spot was determined by St. Helena (*q. v.*) in her pilgrimage to the Holy Land. The original church was built by Constantine in the year 330. The stable itself is a cave beneath the church. It does no violence to our knowledge of the times to believe that a cave may have been used for stabling purposes. Part of the masonry of Constantine's church is still extant, but most of the older work dates from the time of Justinian, about 550. Additions and alterations have been made from time to time since then until the church as it stands is practically a mediæval structure. In 1482, for example, King Edward IV. of England contributed the lead to make a new roof. The lead roof lasted for two centuries, and then was melted down by the Mohammedans to make bullets. However, another roof was soon provided.

In any case the church is a venerable building, and has witnessed some stirring scenes. In it Baldwin the Crusader was crowned King of Jerusalem.

The grotto of the Nativity is reached by a flight of steps from the chancel. Originally it was simply a natural cave in the limestone rock. Now little of the native rock is seen. Marble slabs cover the floor and line the walls. The ceiling, which is about ten feet high, is resplendent with thirty-two brass lamps. Their light enables us to examine the many pictures, portraying scenes in the life of Jesus, which the devotion of Christians has hung about the walls; but these pictures are generally very poor as specimens of art. At the east end of the cave there is a small recess in the rock, before which hang fifteen lamps. In the floor of this recess a bright silver star is inlaid; it is nearly all worn away by the constant kissing it receives. Around the star is an inscription in Latin, which tells us that "Here, of the Virgin Mary, Jesus Christ was born."

Turning just a little to the right from this Place of the Star, and descending a few steps, we are in a small chamber called the Grotto of the Manger. A brilliant silver star marks the spot where Christ is said to have been born. On a neighboring altar the Wise Men are said to have presented their gifts. The spot where the manger stood is also marked by a marble monument. But the original manger is said to have been transported to Rome. (See PRESEPIO.)

The church of the Nativity draws numerous pilgrimages at the Christmas season. Catholics, Greeks, and Armenians all worship here, under the supervision of the Turkish guardians. Luckily, the Greeks and the Armenians, following the Old Style, have a different date for Christmas from the Catholics. On Christmas Eve (New Style) the Christians in Jerusalem gather together and flock out of the city with their faces set for Bethlehem, five miles away. As they reach the end of their march the people of Bethlehem will come out to meet them, and then, preceded by gayly attired wand-bearing heralds, and followed by an immense throng of men, women, and children, they march towards the church of the Nativity.

There midnight mass will be celebrated, while armed Turkish soldiers in full uniform of red fezzes, blue jackets, and baggy trousers stand on guard beside the altar.

With this visit and mass in the grotto the Christmas Eve ceremonies end. On Christmas Day the regular Roman Catholic service is held in the same church, and the remainder of the day is spent in merrymaking.

The Turkish soldiers who guard the holy relics during the ceremonies are not mere figure-heads. That the members of the various Christian sects in the East are not over-friendly to each other is well known, and the soldiers are considered absolutely essential to guard against an outbreak of fanaticism.

The trouble lies in the fact that each sect claims possession of the holy places, and naturally regards any other sect which worships in them as an interloper. Thanks, however, to the vigilance of the soldiers and the other authorities, no serious outbreaks have ever arisen at this season, and as the years ·pass there are many indications that an amicable understanding will be finally arrived at.

Nativity of the Blessed Virgin. A feast kept by both the Greeks and the Latins on September 8. It is also one of the black-letter days of the Anglican calendar. The exact date of its institution cannot be fixed, but it was known in the ninth century, and it had come into general use by the twelfth. It is the least important of all the feasts in honor of Mary, partly because birthdays are not as a rule held to be as sacred as death-days, and partly because, as the Church acknowledges, there is really nothing authentic preserved as to either the date or the place of her birth. That she was the child of St. Anne and St. Joachim is, however, generally agreed. (See ANNE, ST.)

New Year's Day. (Fr. *Le Jour de l'An,* or *Le Jour d'Etrennes;* It. *Capo d' Anno;* Ger. *Neujahr.*) In all Christian countries this is now nominally celebrated on the 1st of January. But the 1st of January in the Gregorian calendar (see CALENDAR) occurs twelve days earlier than in the Julian: hence Russia and Greece, which still retain the latter, celebrate January 1 on our January 13. Even this comparative uniformity among civilized nations was not attained at a bound.

The ancient Egyptians, Phœnicians, and Persians began their year at the autumnal equinox, September 22, and the Greeks of the time of Solon at the winter solstice, December 21. But in the time of Pericles, in B.C. 432, the Greeks changed the date to the summer solstice, June 21.

The Romans reckoned the beginning of the year from the winter solstice until Julius Cæsar in his reform of the calendar changed it to the 1st of January. The Jews began and still begin their civil year with the 1st of the month Tisri, which roughly corresponds to our September. But in their ecclesiastical reckoning the year dates from the vernal equinox, March 22. As this is astronomically the beginning of spring, the date is a logical one, and that or the 25th of March (twenty-five being a more fully rounded number) was accepted generally by Christian nations in mediæval times.

In England, December 25 was New Year's Day until the time of William the Conqueror. His coronation happened to occur on January 1. Hence the year was ordered to commence on that day. But the English gradually fell into unison with the rest of Christendom and began the year with the 25th of March. The Gregorian calendar in 1582 restored January 1 as the gate-way of the year. Catholic countries adopted the change immediately. Protestant countries were recalcitrant. It was not until 1752 that England acquiesced.

Among the Romans, after the reformation of the calendar, the first day of January, as well as the entire month, was dedicated to the eponymic god Janus. He was represented with two faces, one looking forward, the other backward, to indicate that he stood between the old and the new year, with a regard to both.

Throughout January the Romans offered sacrifices to Janus upon twelve altars, and on the first day of that month they were careful so to regulate their conduct that their every word and act should be a happy augury for all the ensuing days of the year.

Ovid and other Latin writers of the Empire allude to the suspension of all litigation and strife, the reconciliation of differences between friends, the smoking altars and the white-robed processions to the Capitol, upon the first day of Janus, or New Year's Day as we now call it. They also tell of the exchanging of visits, the giving and receiving of presents, or *strenœ*, the masquerading and the feasting, with which in their time the day was celebrated throughout the Roman Empire.

The *strenœ* were not only exchanged between relatives and friends, but were exacted by the Emperors from their subjects. Eventually they became so onerous a burden to the people that Claudius limited their cost by a decree.

It was on account of the orgies which accompanied the recurrence of the winter solstice not only among the Romans but among the Teutonic races that the early Christians looked with scant favor upon the whole season. By the fifth century, however, the 25th of December had become a fixed festival commemorative of our Lord's Nativity, whereupon the 1st of January assumed a specially sacred character as the octave of Christmas Day and the anniversary of Christ's circumcision. As such it still holds a place in the calendars of the various branches of the Eastern and Western Churches, but only as a feast of subordinate importance.

The first mention of the feast in Christian literature occurs in Canon 17 of a Council which met at Tours in 567. "In order," so the canon runs, "to tread under foot the customs of the heathen, our fathers ordained that private litanies should be held at the beginning of January, psalms sung in the churches, and, at the eighth hour on the first of the month, the Mass of the Circumcision, pleasing to God." From this canon it appears that the feast was already an established one. Other authorities show that it was originally kept as a fast, evidently as a protest against the immoral excesses of the heathen.

The custom of exchanging presents on New Year's, though in Anglo-Saxon countries it has been largely superseded by the giving of Christmas-gifts, is still retained in France and the Latin countries. It is one of the oldest and was one of the most universal observances of the season.

The Persians celebrated the beginning of the year by exchanging presents of eggs. The ancient Druids distributed, as New Year's gifts, among the early Britons, branches of the sacred mistletoe cut with peculiarly solemn ceremonies on the previous night from the oak-tree in a forest dedicated to the gods. (See MISTLETOE.) Among the Saxons of the Northern nations the new year was ushered in by friendly gifts.

According to Matthew Paris, Henry III. followed the imperial Roman precedent of extorting New Year's gifts from his subjects. The fashion, once set, continued until the reign of Charles I. By the time of Henry VII. the reception of the New Year's gifts presented by the king and queen to each other and by their household and courtiers to the royal pair had become reduced to a solemn formula.

Agnes Strickland, in her "Lives of the Queens of England" (1864, vol. ii. p. 83), quotes the following extract from a manuscript of Henry VII.'s Norroy herald, in possession of Peter Le Neve, Esq.: "On the day of the New Year, when the king came to his foot-sheet, his usher of his chamber-door said to him, 'Sire, here is a New Year's gift coming from the queen;' then the king replied, 'Let it come in.' Then the king's usher let the queen's messenger come within the *yate*" (meaning the gate of the railing which surrounded the royal bed, instances of which are familiar to the public in the state bedrooms at Hampton Court to this day, and it is probable that the scene was very similar), "Henry VII. sitting at the foot of the bed in his dressing-gown, the officers of his bed-chamber having turned the top sheet smoothly down to the foot of the bed when the royal personage rose. The queen, in like manner, sat at her foot-sheet, and received the king's New Year's gift within the gate of her bed-railing. When this formal exchange of presents had taken place between the king and his consort, they received, seated in the same manner, the New Year's gifts of their nobles. 'And,' adds the herald, assuming the first person, 'I shall report to the queen's grace and them that be about her, what rewards are to be given to them that bring her grace New Year's gifts, for I trow they are not so good as those of the king.'"

There is in the possession of the Marquis of Bath, at Longleat, a manuscript, which contains a list of moneys given to King Henry VIII. in the twenty-fourth year of his reign, as New Year's gifts. They are from archbishops, bishops, noblemen, doctors, gentlemen, etc. The amount which the king's grace complacently pocketed on this occasion was £792 10s. 10d. (*Notes and Queries*, Fourth Series, vol. xi. p. 8.)

Honest old Latimer, however, says Hone ("Every Day Book," 1836, vol. i. p. 7), instead of presenting Henry VIII. with a purse of gold, put into the king's hand a New Testament, with a leaf conspicuously doubled down at Hebrews xiii. 4, which, on reference, will be found to have a certain appropriateness to the monarch's domestic failings.

Good Queen Bess, as that very designation implies, knew the way to the hearts of her subjects, and, taking it, had her reward. Their voices, their swords, and their purses were alike at her command. Presents came to her in a profusion unknown to any of her predecessors. Every New Year's Day saw the royal purse replenished with gold, the royal wardrobe enriched with articles of ladies' gear, from embroidered gowns and mantles, to petticoats, stockings, garters, and smocks, and the royal larder stocked with fat oxen and sheep, geese and turkeys, swans and capons, fruit and preserves, marchpanes and sweetmeats; while the gem-loving queen's eyes were gladdened with the sight of necklaces and bracelets, rings, chains, and all sorts of dainty devices in jewellers' ware.

King James had no cause to complain of his new subjects' illiberality for the first two or three years of his reign, at least so far as New Year's gifts went; but after a few years' acquaintance their generosity waned, for Carleton complains that even the accustomed purse of gold was hardly to be had without asking for it. The Earl of Huntingdon, however, stood by the old custom, and put upon record the proper manner of presenting a New Year's gift to his majesty. "You must buy," he says, "a new purse of about five shillings price, and put thereunto twenty pieces of new gold of twenty shillings apiece, and go to the presence-chamber, where the court is upon New Year's Day, in the morning about eight o'clock, and deliver the purse and the gold unto my Lord Chamberlain. Then you must go down to the jewel-house for a ticket, to receive eighteen shillings and sixpence as a gift for your pains, and give sixpence to the boy for your ticket. Then go to Sir William Veall's office and show your ticket, and receive your eighteen shillings and sixpence. Then go to the jewel-house again, and take a piece of plate of thirty ounces' weight, and mark it; and then in the afternoon you may go and fetch it away, and then give the gentleman who delivers it you one pound in gold, and give to the boy two shillings, and to the porter sixpence." At this annual give-and-take game the crown got the advantage.

The custom of presenting the sovereign with New Year's gifts went out with Oliver Cromwell, and did not come back with the Restoration.

The passing around and drinking of the wassail cup (see WASSAIL), after the manner of the more modern loving-cup, had gone out of fashion at court before the time of Queen Elizabeth, and had been succeeded by the cleanlier one of individual cups. But wassail was still drunk, and indeed New Year's Day has never dropped its convivial aspect.

On the eve of New Year it was long a general custom to

unbar the house-door with great formality to "let out the Old and let in the New." English dissenters and certain evangelical sects favor a midnight service at their places of worship. But the custom of widest extension is that of ringing the church bells.

> Ring out, wild bells, to the wild sky,
>   The flying cloud, the frosty light;
>   The year is dying in the night;
> Ring out, wild bells, and let him die.
>
> Ring out the old, ring in the new,
>   Ring, happy bells, across the snow :
>   The year is going, let him go ;
> Ring out the false, ring in the true.

In Scotland, as in France, New Year's Day lords it over Christmas as the most important festival of the year. Its eve is known as Hogmanay, and the two days together are often called the Daft (or Crazy) Days.

The meaning of the word Hogmanay has been a sad puzzle to antiquarians, and its etymology is still an undecided question. According to some authorities, the word is derived from the phrase *Au qui menez* ("To the mistletoe bring"), which the mummers formerly cried in France. Another derivation is from Hoggunott, Hogenat, or Hoggnight, the old Scandinavian term for the night preceding the feast of Yule, and so called in allusion to the animals that were slaughtered on the occasion for sacrificial and festive purposes. Some consider it to be a corruption of *Au gueux menez*,—that is, "Bring to the beggars;" and a further explanation combines the word with another sung along with it in chorus, and suggests that "Hogmanay, trollolay," are a corruption of the French *Homme est né, trois rois allois* ("A man is born, three kings are come"), in allusion to the birth of Christ and the visit of the wise men to Bethlehem, who in mediæval times were known as the Three Kings. All these derivations, however, are equally pure conjecture ; and it is to be hoped that at some time or other the question will be satisfactorily answered.

In retired and primitive towns of Scotland it is customary, says Mr. Chambers, in his "Popular Rhymes," for the children of the poorer class of people on the morning of the last day of the year, or Hogmanay, to get themselves swaddled in a great sheet, doubled up in front so as to form a vast pocket, and then to go along the streets in little bands, calling at the doors of the wealthier inhabitants for a dole of wheaten bread. Each child gets one quadrant section of oat cake (sometimes, in the case of particular favorites, improved by an addition of cheese), and this is called their "hogmanay." In expectation of the large

demands thus made upon them, the housewives busy themselves
for several days beforehand in preparing a sufficient quantity of
cake. As soon as the children arrive at the door of a house they
immediately cry out as loudly as they can, "Hogmanay," which
is in itself a sufficient announcement of their demands. There
are, however, other exclamations which are frequently used.
One of these is "Hogmanay, trollolay." A favorite rhyme, too,
used on the occasion is—

> Rise up, gude-wife, and shake your feathers,
> Dinna think that we are beggars;
> We are bairns come to play
> And to seek our hogmanay.

Another visitor whom every family expects on this night is
the First-Foot (*q. v.*), a name given to the person who first sets
foot over the threshold after the clock strikes twelve. First-
footers often go out in parties, and are welcomed to the fun
within even if they have been anticipated by some prompter
visitor.

Hence in Edinburgh and other large cities the streets in old
days were crowded on New Year's Eve and until the sma' hours
of New Year's morning. The noise was tremendous, particularly
in the great thoroughfares, moving lanterns glared everywhere
as parties of first-footers pressed up or down, carrying a het-pint,
or bowl of hot toddy, which each offered the other with "A gude
New Year!" Any girl caught out in the streets, even if she had
an escort, might be kissed by any youth. Good-natured—even
if not always sober—revelry prevailed everywhere. But these
New Year's Eve rejoicings got a check in Edinburgh on December 31, 1811. A large band of toughs seized the opportunity to
waylay and rob the better class of citizens. Every well-dressed
person was surrounded by parties of this band and knocked
down unless he surrendered. Two men, including one policeman, were killed, and several others wounded. The savage band
managed to keep possession of the streets in defiance of the civil
power till four o'clock in the morning, and reaped a rich harvest
of spoils. The ringleaders were subsequently arrested, and three
of them were publicly executed on April 22, 1812. But good
citizens became scarcer on the streets on ensuing Hogmanay
nights.

Another New Year's Eve custom is said to linger around
Bromyard, in the Worcestershire border of Herefordshire. As
the hour of midnight is on the strike on the 31st of December,
and the last carol is dying away, a promiscuous rush is made to
the nearest spring to snatch the "cream of the year," the first
pitcherful of the new year, and with it the prospect of the best

luck.   The same excitement goes on in the dwellings of South Scotland at the same hour, when, as the poet hath it,—

> Twal struck—twa neebor hizzies raise
> And lilting gaed a sad gate;
> The flower of the well to our house gaes,
> And I'll the bonniest lad get.

"Burning out the old year" is a custom that still has its survivals in Lanarkshire and elsewhere.   For this purpose, during the last day of the year, a large quantity of fuel is collected, consisting of branches of trees, brushwood, and coals, and placed in a heap at the "cross," and at about nine o'clock at night the lighting of the fire is commenced, surrounded by a large crowd of lookers-on, who each think it a duty to cast into the flaming mass some additional portion of material.

New Year's Day itself is spent in visiting and feasting.   The Christmas dinner of English folk is eaten on this day by their Scotch compatriots; the master brews a bowl of punch or toddy, and passes glasses around to the servants, and all unite in drinking and pledging good health and happiness to one another.   In the evening dances, balls, and raffles are the popular amusements.   One of the songs always heard on these festive occasions begins,—

> Here's to the year that's awa'!
> We'll drink it in strong and in sma',
> And to each bonnie lassie that we dearly lo'ed
> In the days o' the year that's awa'.

Scotland has well been called the "Land o' Cakes," for nowhere else, Germany excepted, is there such a variety of confectionery and pastry as in Scotch bakers' shops.   The short-bread, often known as "Pitcaithly bannocks," is highly ornamented with sugar and iced mottoes, "A Happy New Year" and "A Merrie Auld Yule;" then the rye loaves, popular in the Thrums district, black and rich, filled with fruit and peel, and the Scotch bun, composed entirely of eggs, chopped fruit, and peel, encased in a crust which is not eaten, much like the English simnel cakes. Fancy tarts and pastries of all kinds are bought in the greatest profusion.

It is said in Scotland that those who desire to learn what fate or fortune the new year has in store for them may do so by consulting the Bible on New Year's morning before breakfast.   The sacred book must be laid upon a table, and those who wish to consult it must open it at random and place a finger upon one or other of the chapters at which it is opened.   This chapter is read, and is believed to describe, in some way, the happiness or misery during the ensuing year of the person making the trial.

Among many other old superstitions associated with New Year's is a belief that if a lamp or a candle be taken out of a house on that day some member of the family will die within a twelvemonth, while to throw out dirty water, ashes, or anything whatever, no matter how worthless, is regarded as certain to bring ill luck during the whole of that year.

From old Dutch times to the middle of the nineteenth century New Year's Day in New York was devoted to the universal interchange of visits. Every door was thrown wide open. It was a breach of etiquette to omit any acquaintance in these annual calls, when old friendships were renewed and family differences amicably settled. A hearty welcome was extended even to strangers of presentable appearance.

The following is an entry in Tyrone Power the actor's Diary for January 1, 1834: "On this day from an early hour every door in New York is open and all the good things possessed by the inmates paraded in lavish profusion. Every sort of vehicle is put in requisition. At an early hour a gentleman of whom I had a slight knowledge entered my room, accompanied by an elderly person I had never before seen, and who, on being named, excused himself for adopting such a frank mode of making my acquaintance, which, he was pleased to add, he much desired, and at once requested me to fall in with the custom of the day, whose privilege he had thus availed himself of, and accompany him on a visit to his family.

"I was the last man on earth likely to decline an offer made in such a spirit; so, entering his carriage, which was waiting, we drove to his house on Broadway, where, after being presented to a very amiable lady, his wife, and a pretty, gentle-looking young girl, his daughter, I partook of a sumptuous luncheon, drank a glass of champagne, and, on the arrival of other visitors, made my bow, well pleased with my visit.

"My host now begged me to make a few calls with him, explaining as we drove along the strict observances paid to this day throughout the State, and tracing the excellent custom to the early Dutch colonists. I paid several calls in company with my new friend, and at each place met a hearty welcome, when my companion suggested that I might have some compliments to make on my own account, and so, leaving me, begged me to consider his carriage perfectly at my disposal. I left a card or two and made a couple of hurried visits, then returned to my hotel to think over the many beneficial effects likely to grow out of such a charitable custom, which makes even the stranger sensible of the benevolent influence of this kindly day, and to wish for its continued observance."

At the period of which Power speaks there were great feasts

spread in many houses, and the traditions of tremendous Dutch eating and drinking were faithfully observed. Special houses were noted for particular forms of entertainment. At one it was eggnog; at another, rum punch; at this one, pickled oysters; at that, boned turkey, or marvellous chocolate, or perfect Mocha coffee, or, for the select *cognoscenti,* a drop of old Madeira as delicate in flavor as the texture of the glass from which it was sipped. At all houses there were the New Year's cakes, in the form of an Egyptian cartouch, and in later and more degenerate days relays of champagne-bottles appeared,—the coming in of the lower empire.

Then followed the gradual breaking down of all the lines of conventionality into a wild and unseemly riot of visits. New Year's Day took on the character of a rabid and untamed race against time. A procession each of whose component parts was made up of two or three young men in an open barouche, with a pair of steaming horses and a driver more or less under the influences of the hilarity of the day, would rattle from one house to another all day long. The visitors would jump out of the carriage, rush into the house, and reappear in a miraculously short space of time. The ceremony of calling was a burlesque. There was a noisy and hilarious greeting, a glass of wine was swallowed hurriedly, everybody shook hands all around, and the callers dashed out and rushed into the carriage and were driven rapidly to the next house. But more serious than this was the manner in which society women found their houses invaded by people with whom they had very slight and sometimes no acquaintance whatever on the first day of the year. The humblest employee of a great commercial house felt at entire liberty to call upon the wife of the head of the firm, assuming that his salary entitled him to the acquaintanceship. Politicians of all ranks and degrees looked in upon people who they thought could be useful to them. The great army of social upstarts and snobs utilized the day for furthering their claims to recognition. Enough complications and embarrassments, in fact, were woven on the first day of the year to employ the tact and resources of society leaders for several months afterward in the work of undoing.

A reaction naturally began, which, gathering force with every succeeding year, ended by practically abolishing the custom of New Year's calls.

The Old World custom of sitting up on New Year's night to see the old year out and the new year in is perhaps more general in the United States than anywhere. In many large cities the new year is rung in from some famous local belfry,—that of Independence Hall, for example, in Philadelphia, and of Trinity

Church in New York,—attracting huge crowds that blow tin horns and roar and shout, the din being increased by whistles from steam-engines, afloat and ashore.

Nowhere is New Year celebrated with greater solemnity than at the courts of the various rulers of continental Europe. True, in some instances—as, for instance, at Berlin and at Vienna—Christmas-trees and distributions of gifts are arranged for the royal children a week earlier. But this in no sense diminishes the importance of the New Year's Day solemnities, and if Christmas has gradually become the annual festival of the family, New Year's Day continues to remain the principal feast of the year at court, as well as in political, military, and administrative service.

It speaks well for these monarchs of the Old World that with the solitary exception of King Leopold, who holds religion in very small esteem, there is not one of them that does not commence the new year with an appeal to the Almighty for strength, guidance, and blessing. In England, however, the queen is the only member of the royal family who ever dreams of attending divine service on New Year's morning.

At the courts where what is known as the Orthodox Greek faith is professed, and where, consequently, the old calendar is still in force, New Year's Day is celebrated a fortnight later.

King Humbert, who owing to the ban of the Church is unable to indulge in a high pontifical mass, begins New Year's Day by attending a low mass said by his chaplain in the chapel that has been arranged at the Quirinal. After mass is over, king and queen stand on the dais under the canopy in front of their chair of state in the throne-room, to receive with due formality the various parliamentary, military, judicial, and administrative delegations commissioned to lay at the feet of their majesties the good wishes of the various bodies which they represent. Later the king begins to stroll about the various apartments, and a good deal of freedom and abandon prevails until the supper-hour is announced. The royal party then march in procession to a small supper-room and with the ambassadors and their wives take their places at tables adorned with that magnificent golden plate for which the house of Savoy is so famous, while the remainder of the guests rush pell-mell and in a very undignified fashion to the buffets, which are literally taken by storm and quickly devastated, so far as everything in the nature of food or drink is concerned.

At Paris, in spite of the overthrow of the monarchy, the principal features of the ancient celebration of the New Year have been retained. True, there is no divine service, since the President does not claim to be " the anointed of the Lord ;" but he compromises the matter by receiving first and foremost the

Papal Nuncio, who, at the head of the diplomatic corps, presents the congratulations and good wishes of the latter in a formal address, to which the President makes an equally ceremonious response. As soon as the foreign envoys, all of whom are in full uniform, have taken their departure, the Presidents of the Senate and of the Chamber of Deputies arrive, their carriages escorted by squadrons of cavalry. Then follow the heads of the judiciary, the principal officers of the army and navy, and delegations from the Academy, from the clergy, and from all the various branches of the political and administrative system. As soon as this is over, the President, who has been in full evening dress ever since the early morning, drives off with the military officers of his household to return the calls of the Presidents of the Senate and the Chamber of Deputies, these being the only two visits that he is called upon to pay to members of his own nationality throughout the entire year.

Such is the official recognition of the day. In the popular eye New Year's Day is the greatest festival of the year. It is in France what Christmas is in England and America, the day for giving and receiving presents (known as *étrennes*, from the Latin *strenæ*). The abuse of this practice is far more deplorable than at the Anglo-Saxon Christmas. The *étrennes* have nearly reached the climax of representing nothing more than such a conventional sense of duty as the leaving of a card betokens here. It is even said that they are constantly transferred from hand to hand till at last they may circulate back into the hands of the original givers, having performed precisely the same formal office in discharging the debts of social convention that a five-franc piece performs when it likewise, after passing through a number of different hands, returns to the coffers of the bank which issued it.

Nevertheless accidental abuses do not prevent this from being one of the most poetical and beautiful anniversaries in the French calendar. It is the great family day. In the morning the children jump up and (after examining their stockings to see what St. Nicholas has brought them) rush off to the chamber of their parents to salute them and offer their good wishes for the new year. If a member of the family has died during the year, all the near relatives assemble at the grave early in the morning, renewing flowers and ornaments. After the mid-day meal the younger members of the family call upon the older ones, and in the evening they all meet for dinner at the home of the oldest member, who is considered the head of the family. When the French speak of their family it is in a broad sense, and includes all the relatives.

While few, if any, presents are given at Christmas, friends

and servants are remembered with gifts at New Year's. Gifts of flowers and confectionery are received by the ladies. Young men in society are expected to call at the homes of their lady friends, and hither to bring or send flowers or confectionery. For the young man with a small salary this is a great demand; still, if he has been receiving hospitalities all the year here is an opportunity to show his appreciation. The French people do not give their children much candy, but at New Year children and older people indulge in this luxury, and there are few ladies who do not receive one or more *bonbonnières* filled with candy, largely chocolate, for the French run to this kind of confectionery.

All day long Paris is noisy with crowds going to and fro. The fashionable parts of the city are a forest of carriages, buggies, and hacks, standing at every door, and whirling back and forth in feverish haste. The children, gayly decked out with ribbons and flowers, wander with their mothers or their nurses along the streets, and gaze with loud delight into the dazzling windows of the shops. And, indeed, nothing can be more brilliant than the shop-windows of Paris on this day, especially those of the confectioners, the toy-sellers, and the jewellers.

While all these excitements are going on in one part of Paris, over the river the students are having the jolliest of holidays. They are dancing and singing in little halls arranged for the purpose; they are partaking of sumptuous dinners and wines at the restaurants; they are promenading on the boulevard with their sweethearts; they are up in rooms in the top stories of the high old-fashioned houses of the Latin Quarter, playing on fiddles, and telling stories, and singing songs, and acting laughable farces.

On New Year's Day the beggars swarm out from every nook and corner of Paris, for it is the one day of the long year when they may beg in freedom. Most of them catch the merry spirit of the day, and gayly sing their petitions in your face, or dance a jig for a sou, with a cheerful good humor and forgetfulness of trouble which only a hardened heart could resist. Ragged little fellows, scarcely large enough to walk, toddle up, and, with a pert swing of their torn caps, demand a gift as if such a thing as a refusal had never repulsed them; and if, perchance, they do not get the sou-piece they ask for, off they scamper, singing a street-ditty, and carolling up to the next comer with unchilled impudence.

The hardest-working of the Paris people on New Year's Day, and for some days thereafter, are the post-office clerks. It is the universal custom in France to embrace the occasion of this anniversary to send cards of compliment to all one's friends, in whatever part of the country they may be. Thus, a gentleman or lady in Paris is deluged with hundreds of cards, sometimes, from country brothers and sisters, uncles, aunts, and cousins, old neighbors, and absent acquaintances, and sends out to each and all cards in return. So it is that the post-offices are choked up for a long time, and regular letters become very irregular indeed.

New Year's Eve, or St. Sylvester's Night, is celebrated in many German cities, especially in Berlin, by a curious bit of horse-play. Everybody is privileged to bonnet with a blow of the fist any citizen who ventures into the street after dark with a high silk hat.

The unfortunate visitor from the provinces, or the stranger ignorant of the peculiar customs of the day, strolls blithely down the street, clad in the garments usual to elegant civilization, on his head the silk hat. Suddenly a cry reaches his ears, "Hut ab!" Who can be shouting for the removal of a hat? The shout is repeated. From here and there men are hurrying towards him. Pshaw! surely they cannot be telling him to take off his hat. But now from all about comes the sound of voices, crying, "Hut ab! Hut ab!"

The cry becomes a roar, as voice after voice joins its volume to the chorus, "Hut ab! Hut ab!" In an instant a crowd has gathered, a mob of shrieking, laughing, gesticulating ruffians, yelling, "Hut ab! Hut ab! Hut ab!" And before the astonished stranger can begin to understand what all this awful din may betoken, to give point to the words sticks and fists rain blows upon his head. The offending hat is hammered down over its owner's ears farther and lower, until its rim bursts and its crown flies off, and it dangles, a bedraggled collar, on his shoulder. Then the exultant mob, with no more occasion for howling "Hut ab!" howls in applause of its own success.

The stranger, not knowing what catastrophes may follow on a beginning so frightful, enraged, amazed, full of fears, flees to the shelter of the policeman near by. When the assaulted wretch has told his tale, with many a gesture indicating the mangled remains of his hat, the guardian of the peace offers him as the only consolation, "Wesshalb gehen Sie denn aus?" In other words, "Do not wear a silk hat in the street on St. Sylvester's Day."

In his boyhood, and even in his earlier monarchial manhood, Emperor William II. used to sally out incognito on New Year's Eve to take part in this popular diversion. But he has abandoned it since he encountered an old gentleman who, with the view of getting even with the young men who had destroyed his top hats in previous years, had equipped himself with a sort of leather skull-cap studded with nails, points upward. The conse-

quence was that when the imperial fist came down with crushing force on the inviting-looking hat it encountered the nails,
which lacerated his hand in so serious a manner as to necessitate
the attendance of a surgeon.

This custom of the demolition of high hats has been traced
back to 1848. It had its origin in a commemoration of the riots
on St. Sylvester's Day in that year, the lower classes having at
that time resorted to this forcible method of expressing their
hostility to the *bourgeoisie,* of whom the high hat was distinctive.

Happily, in other parts of Germany there are customs which
mark St. Sylvester's Day more courteously. One most pleasant
one is found in the Rhenish provinces. A gentleman is walking
in the street, when suddenly he hears spoken closely to his ear
the words "Prosit Neujahr!" the greeting of the day. By the
law of the day he is thus made captive and must pay ransom.

The friend who has marked the unsuspecting one on the
street, himself unobserved, has followed cautiously, and has approached stealthily on tiptoe until so close that the salutation
can be distinctly heard, although softly spoken. The one thus
saluted unawares must answer by the word "Meister," and acknowledge the other's sovereignty of the moment by the gift of
a cigar, a bottle of champagne, or something else conducive to
the social enjoyment of the occasion. With them, as with us,
all strive to be first in giving the greeting of the season, but they
have emphasized the importance of not being tardy by a genial
system of forfeits to be paid by the unwary or laggard.

The most charming of the German New Year's customs is one
observed from time immemorial in Frankfort-on-the-Main. There,
at the same moment, the whole city salutes itself,—wishes itself
a happy New Year.

On the night of December 31 all the city keeps the festival,
watching the old year out and the new year in. Family parties
or gatherings of friends are to be found in every house. Games,
stories, music, and kindred diversions, with an honorable attention to eating and drinking, serve to speed on the last hours of
the dying year.

Suddenly, at the exact moment when from the great dome of
the cathedral the first stroke of midnight sounds its warning,
every house throws wide open its windows. Forth from the
casements lean all the dwellers in the town, old and young together, each with glass in hand. The glass is raised on high,
and the words of the toast burst on the astonished air of night
in one massive tone, born of more than a hundred thousand
voices, joined in the cry, "Prosit Neujahr!" ("Happy New
Year!")

The whole city thus salutes itself with the greeting of the

season, invoking a blessing for the coming year in its first moment. The sonorous majesty of the sentiment sends out its echoing clamors for a few brief seconds, then ceases. Before the last clang of the twelve from the cathedral's dome has melted into silence the toast of the hour has been drunk, the windows have been closed, and the hush of midnight settles once more over the deserted streets of the city.

The Emperor of Germany invariably begins New Year's Day by attending service with his wife and children in the chapel of the Old Castle at Berlin at about ten o'clock. Then, at the head of all the princes of the blood, and escorted by his generals and staff, he marches on foot to the Main Guard, which turns out, of course, on his arrival. It is composed of the very finest and smartest-looking men of the Seventh Regiment, especially selected for the occasion. Having received the customary reports from the officer in command, he gives the pass-word of the day, and then returns to the palace, where a reception of all the principal personages of the realm takes place with great pomp and ceremony. The first to pay their respects and to present their good wishes for the New Year to the Emperor and Empress, who stand on the dais, under a canopy, just in front of their thrones in the White Hall of the Old Castle, are their relatives, headed as a rule by their mother.

The imperial couple always descend the steps of the dais to greet the illustrious widow, and then invite her, as well as the other princes and princesses of the blood, to take her place beside them on the *estrade*. Next come the foreign ambassadors with their ladies and suites, the dean or senior of the diplomatic corps remaining at the foot of the throne to present his colleagues as they pass before the Emperor. The latter usually addresses to the heads of the various missions a few words, which, while sometimes trivial, are often of such importance as to disturb the financial equilibrium of the whole of Europe for the following week.

After the diplomatic corps come the great dignitaries of the Church, the army, the navy, the judges of the supreme court, the rectors of the universities, the ministers of state and the heads of their various departments, and finally those who are possessed of no office, but merely form part and parcel of the court. The scene is brilliant, for, although the reception takes place by day, the curtains and blinds are drawn, and the vast state apartments are lighted by myriads of wax candles and electric globes ; the ladies are all in court dress with long trains, and the men in full uniform, the gorgeously colored mediæval costume of the university rectors being especially picturesque. A grand banquet at court brings the day to a conclusion.

At Vienna on New Year's Day the Emperor and the arch-duchess, representing the Empress, hold what is known as a " cercle." Each class of visitors who call to present their good wishes for the new year is assigned to a particular apartment, the diplomatic corps being relegated to one, the judiciary to another, the navy to a third, and so on. The Emperor, escorted by the grand officials of his household, enters each apartment in turn with the archduchess, and immediately on his being announced by the grand master of ceremonies all the ladies take up their positions on one side of the room and the men on the other.

The Emperor, with one of his chamberlains, then passes slowly along the side of the room where the men are stationed, and says a few words to each, while the archduchess, escorted by the mistress of the robes to the Empress, does the same on the other side. On reaching the farther end the Emperor returns along the front rank of the ladies, while the archduchess passes in front of the men. As a rule, there is no state banquet at Vienna on New Year's Day, the Emperor generally finishing up the festival at the palace of one of his numerous kinsmen.

In Belgium, on St. Sylvester's Day, or New Year's Eve, the children strive to secure a " sugar uncle" or " sugar aunt," as the relative who falls a victim to their wiles is technically termed. On that day all the children of the household enter into a solemn conspiracy for the mutual good at the expense of the unwary adult whom they may entangle in the meshes of their intrigues.

They employ every artifice to get one of the older members of the household under lock and key. Early on that day the keys of all the doors in the house have mysteriously disappeared. They have been secreted by the children, who retain them, ready for instant use whenever the occasion shall occur. Then strictest watch is maintained, to the end that some unsuspecting one may be alone in a room. An uncle enters a room to search for the paper which he has mislaid. Presto! There comes a pattering rush of feet in the hallway, the door is slammed, the key rattles in the lock. The alarmed uncle springs to the door.

Woe betide him now if he be in a hurry, and if he be ungen-erous, for he must yield to the terms of these youthful brigands before he can escape. He must solemnly covenant with them that he will pay to them whatsoever ransom they may demand ere the prison door will swing open. When the prisoner has promised all that is asked, the triumphant company restore him to liberty.

New Year's Day is made a happy and merry festival in the gloomy old royal palace at Madrid. The queen regent takes care that all, down to the humblest of the servants, get a share in the so-called "aguinaldos," or New Year's bounties, to enable them to have their rejoicings and feastings. It is on New Year's Eve, however, that the young king and his sisters receive their presents beneath a huge Christmas-tree, the tables loaded with gifts being arranged by the queen's own hands, while each one of the gentlemen and ladies in waiting, and the palace dignitaries present, are remembered with some costly token of the regent's appreciation of their services. New Year's Day itself begins with high mass, celebrated with all the pomp and solemnity characteristic of the Catholic Church.

As soon as that is over, a goodly portion of the day is devoted to the reception of an interminable procession of dignitaries, ambassadors, and representatives of the great administrative and political elements of the kingdom, who arrive from all parts of Spain in order to offer to the little king and his estimable mother their good wishes. This little king, who wears the uniform of the Royal School of Cadets, with the Order of the Golden Fleece around his neck, gets very tired of the ceremony long before it is all over, and in past years his mother used to experience the greatest difficulty in preventing him from relieving what appeared to him the dreary monotony of the occasion by tweaking the queue of the Chinese ambassador, or from seating himself astride of the great gold lions that constitute so notable an ornament of his throne.

In rural Russia New Year's begins as pre-eminently a juvenile festival. The boys rise with the sun, fill their pockets with dried peas and wheat, and go in bands from house to house. As doors are never locked, it is easy for them to effect an entrance. They use the dried peas upon their enemies, the gentler wheat upon their friends, hurling the first and sprinkling the latter upon all whom they find asleep.

After breakfast the handsomest horse in the village, its trappings gayly decorated with evergreens and berries, is led to the house of the nobleman, followed by the pea- and wheat-shooters of the early morning. The lord admits horse and guests to the parlor, where all his family are gathered. This is the greeting of the peasants, old and young, to their lord and master. The origin of this custom is shrouded in mystery, but it is supposed to date from Biblical times. The persons who enter the house with the horse are rewarded with small silver coins, which are usually bestowed by the children of the household.

Next comes a procession of real animals, such as the ox, cow, goat, and hog, led by children. These quadrupeds, like the horse, are decorated with evergreens and berries. They do not enter, but pass slowly in front of the house, that the master and his family may view the strange procession from the windows.

Then old women appear, bringing the different barn-yard fowls, which are also decked with evergreens and berries. These are intended as presents for the master.

The peasants believe that the miracle of the feast of Cana of Galilee can be repeated, if the people only have faith, as the old year ushers in the new. At precisely the midnight hour, or as nearly as the clocks of the village reckon that time, men, women, and children stand around a large jar filled with water which they anxiously watch to see if it will turn into wine. Year after year the same performance is enacted, and always with the same result. This superstition is current also in many parts of Germany.

The second day of the new year is devoted to paying visits, a pleasure which the children share with their parents. The visiting over, parents and children separate, the older people to enjoy themselves in their own way, and the young people to follow their example,—both parties usually indulging in sleigh-riding.

The young folks always try to get beyond the reach of the older people. During the attempt many ludicrous scenes occur. For instance, the village youths and maidens, in their wild efforts to get beyond the reach of parental control, frequently have their sleighs upset, when a general scramble ensues, and the vehicles are righted amid much merriment. This amusement concludes the holiday season.

In China and Japan it is the universal rule that all debts must be paid and accounts settled with the ending of the old year. Japan among its recent adoptions of European customs numbers the Gregorian calendar, wherefore its year begins when ours does. The Chinese, however, reckon it from the first moon after the sun enters Aquarius. This happens not earlier than January 21 nor later than February 19. The holiday is a legal one for three days only, but its celebration actually continues much longer. Many shops are closed for a fortnight.

During the three days of legitimate holiday-making the cities assume a very gay appearance. The houses are decorated with fanciful lanterns, large sprays of artificial flowers, and strips of red paper with mottoes on them which are pasted around and above the doors. Here and there one sees blue papers among the red ones, which denote that during the past year there has been a death in the house.

The streets are thronged by a gorgeously dressed crowd, most of them attired in brightly colored silks and satins; for the rich don their best, and even the very poor, who are in miserable rags all the rest of the year, generally contrive to hire or to take out of pawn fine clothes for this occasion. If it is quite impossible for them to do this, they remain hidden away in their homes.

The fashion of paying New Year calls, now dying out with us, is still in vogue in China, but there it is men who receive as well as who pay the visits, Chinese women taking no part whatever in social life. Every Chinaman, except among the very lowest classes, expects to receive visits from his inferiors, and to pay them to those who are above him in station. In some cases sending a card is deemed sufficient. These cards consist of thin strips of scarlet paper with the name of the sender written on them in black characters. Sometimes good wishes are added.

People meeting in the streets salute each other by crying, " Kung-hi! Kung-hi!" ("I humbly wish you joy") or "Sin-hi! Sin-hi!" (" May joy be yours"), so that it seems possible that our custom of saying " Happy New Year" as well as that of paying New Year visits may come to us from the Chinese. (*New York Evening Post*, December 31, 1892.)

The Japanese New Year, though legally limited like the Chinese to three days, stretches over a much longer time, and, save for the matter of date, is practically identical with the Chinese in its general features.

A curious attribute of the period in Japan, China, and Corea is the fact that it is a common birthday for the community. From the moment a child makes his appearance he is spoken of as a year old, and this same age he continues to be considered till the beginning of the next calendar year. Then he is credited with another year.

Nicholas, St., Archbishop of Myra, in Lycia, in the fourth century. A holy personage of many and various attributes. He is patron of Russia, and especially of serfs and serfdom, because he protected the weak against the strong, the oppressed against the oppressor, the poor against the rich; of Venice, Freiburg, and other seaport towns, as well as of mariners and travellers, because he stilled a storm when journeying to the Holy Land; of thieves, because he forced a gang to restore their plunder (in the Middle Ages robbers called themselves Knights or Clerks of St. Nicholas); of boys, especially scholars, because he resuscitated three school-boys whom a wicked innkeeper had murdered and salted in a tub; and of young girls, because, out of compassion for a distressed nobleman about to sacrifice his three daughters to a life of infamy, he cast three purses of gold through the nobleman's window under cover of night, to enable the girls to marry honorably. He is supposed to have died on December 6, 342, and his festival on the anniversary of that date is celebrated in Roman and Greek Catholic countries with especial reference to his patronage of youth. In England it was formerly made memorable by the mummeries of the Boy-Bishop (*q. v.*).

But at present in most Protestant countries St. Nicholas, usually under the German diminutive of Santa Claus, is connected with Christmas as the supposed dispenser of gifts, while his own feast is entirely neglected.

In France, St. Nicholas's Day is the grand fête-day of children in general. Even before its arrival they are accustomed to put up their petitions in these words:

> St.-Nicolas, mon bon patron,
> Envoyez-moi quelque chose bien bon.

> ("St. Nicholas, my good patron,
> Send me something very good.")

The incantation is generally effective in the way of bringing something. But whether that something shall be *bon*, or the reverse of *bon*, depends upon the conduct of the child during the past twelve-month. It is rare, indeed, that St. Nicholas risks his popularity so far as to present his petitioners with nothing at all. It might lead to scepticism in the infant mind. On the eve of his day, expectant children hang up their stockings in the chimney-corner, and then retire to rest. If they have been good during the previous year, toys and bonbons are next morning found to have been miraculously concealed within the stocking; but if naughtiness has been the rule, the stocking is discovered full of old paper, or coals, or refuse, and hidden therein are a rod and a cane. In general, however, even the pleasant things are accompanied by an emblematic rod—half a dozen little birch twigs tied together with an end of pink ribbon—to be kept and looked at from time to time, as a hint that St. Nicholas has his eyes open upon what is going on in nurseries and schools.

In many of the southern provinces of Germany, where Catholics predominate, St. Nicholas's Day is celebrated as a preliminary to Christmas. But there St. Nicholas does not sneak into the house at night. He boldly presents himself just after supper on the eve of his festival. The door-bell rings, and he stalks into the parlor, where the family with all the children have assembled to greet him. His merry round face, encircled by cottony hair and beard, his rubicund nose, his fat and jovial figure, are much like the pictures of our own St. Nick. On his back he bears a bag stuffed with things both good and bad. Rubbing his hands, he greets the company, and then calls each child by name and questions him in regard to his actions in the past year and his promises for the future. If the record is good and he can recite a bit of a verse or jingle, it pleases St. Nicholas mightily, and elicits some reward in the shape of fruit or cakes, with a promise of further remembrance on Christmas Day. St.

Nicholas then departs, with many flourishes and much tinkling of bells, to continue his round of visits. On Christmas Day the Christ-Child appears, and brings the promised gifts for good behavior.

Sometimes the mummery is varied. St. Nicholas appears dressed as a bishop, mitre on head, crook in hand, with long white robes trailing to the ground. After the customary recital of verses and bestowal of gifts, he gives a lecture to the parents on their duties to children, admonishes the children to obey their parents and be good, and asks them what they would like the Christ-Child to bring them for Christmas.

In South Austria, where there is no Christmas Day in our sense of the word, but only a church festival, the eve of St. Nicholas's Day is the great season for gift-making. A young man, well versed in the Church catechism, assumes the part of the bishop-saint. He is accompanied by two angels, dressed much like choir-boys, each carrying a bag or a basket, while in his train follow a lot of devils with blackened faces, tooting on tin horns and furiously rattling the chains that bind them together. He enters the house with his angels, leaving his devils at the threshold.

A great silence falls upon the assembled company, and the children are called up and examined religiously. This is carried out with great seriousness. If the trial is passed successfully, the angels step forward and give the child gifts and nuts and cakes of fantastic forms; if he fails, he has to stand aside.

"When the inquisition is over, the devils are allowed to enter and frighten the children, but not to touch them, and amuse them with their strange dances and antics. Their whole appearance is farcical, and for the evening they are allowed great license and fun in the village. After St. Nicholas has departed the children go to their homes, with the expectation that St. Nicholas will visit each house separately and be more generous and bring them more gifts. So, after saying their prayers with more than usual earnestness, they put baskets and dishes on the window-sills and go to bed. The parents later put their simple gifts in these places.

"The 6th of December, the real day of the feast, is celebrated in the churches alone. The celebration of this day in this way does not seem at all out of keeping with the lives of the simple people." (KATHERINE FARRAND REIGHARD, in *The Outlook*, December 28, 1895.)

Among the old Dutch burghers of New York, New Year's Eve was the date on which fat jolly roistering St. Nicholas made his appearance, sometimes accompanied by his good-natured vrouw, Molly Grietje. Then the children gathered round the immense fireplace, singing in muffled voices their evening hymns to the good saint:

> Santa Klaus, goedt heilig man!
> Knopyebest van Amsterdam,
> Van Amsterdam aan Spanje,
> Van Spanje aan Oranje,
> En brang deze kindjes eenige graps;

> ("Santa Claus, good holy man!
> Go your way from Amsterdam,
> From Amsterdam to Spain,
> From Spain to Orange,
> And bring these little children toys;")

or,

> Sint Nicolaas, myn goden vriend,
> Ik hab u altyd wel gediend;
> Als gy my nu not wilt geben,
> Zal ik dienen als myn leben.

> ("Saint Nicholas, my dear good friend,
> To serve you ever was my end;
> If you me now something will give,
> Serve you I will as long as I live.")

From an ecclesiastical point of view, however, the festival of St. Nicholas is nowhere celebrated with more splendor and earnestness than at Bari, a seaport on the southeastern coast of Italy. Here, in a subterranean building of Saracenic architecture beneath the superb church of St. Nicholas, are treasured the bones of the saint. Legend relates that these were originally buried in his own cathedral at Myra. In the eleventh century they were stolen by certain merchants of Bari, who landed with them at that town on May 9, 1087, and handed them over to the archbishop. On the very day when they were reburied in what was then the church of St. Stephen, thirty persons were cured of various distempers by the intercession of the saint. Since that time the tomb of St. Nicholas of Bari has been famous for pilgrimages. To this day the 6th of December draws hither pilgrims to the number of many thousands, all with staves bound with olive and pine, many of them barefooted; all of them fed, if they will, at the priory gates; all of them clad in their picturesque ancient costumes, devoted, earnest, fiery, and observing a rite that has been known from time immemorial.

A novel and interesting part of the ceremonies is seen when the sailors of the port, in memory possibly of some old rites in honor of Neptune, take the saint's image from the care of the canons, and bear it through the streets and far out to sea, only returning with it at nightfall, when, with bonfires and rockets and torches, the whole population intoning chants and litanies, they carry it about from shrine to shrine, and at length restore it to its keepers under the late stars with solemn earnestness, and with all the wild but half-suppressed religious excitement possible only to the high-wrought Southern temperament.

A contributor to Chambers's "Book of Days" (vol. ii. p. 664) who was present at St. Nicholas's feast in Bari adds some interesting particulars:

"The clergy composing the chapter of St. Nicholas are not slow to maintain the thaumaturgic character of their patron, and seem to believe in it. The bones of the saint are deposited in a sepulchre beneath the magnificent crypt, which is in itself a sort of subterranean church, of rich Saracenic architecture. Through the native rock which forms the tomb, water constantly exudes, which is collected by the canons on a sponge attached to a reed, squeezed into bottles, and sold to the pilgrims, as a miraculous specific, under the name of the ' Manna of St. Nicholas.' As a proof of its supernatural character, a large bottle was shown to me, in which, suspended from the cork, grew and floated the delicate green bladder of one of the Adriatic *ulvæ*. I suppose that its growth in fresh water had been extremely slow, for a person, whose word I did not doubt, assured me that he remembered the bottle from his childhood, and that the vegetation was then much less visible. ' This,' said the grand vicar, a tall aquiline-featured priest, who looked as if he watched the effect of every word upon a probable heretic,—' this we consider to be conclusive as to the character of the water. If vegetation takes place in water that you keep in a jar, the water becomes offensive. This bottle has been in its present state for many years. You see the vegetation. But it is not putrid. Taste it, you will find it perfectly sweet. *Questa è prodigiosa.*' I trust that all the water that was sold to the pilgrims was really thus afforded by St. Nicholas, if its efficacy be such as is asserted to be the case; but on this subject the purchasers must rely implicitly on the good faith of the canons, as mere human senses cannot distinguish it from that of the castle well."

Nigger 'Lection Day. In Boston this was the name given in early times to the day when the name of the newly elected governor was formally announced. The black population were then allowed to throng the Common and join in the festivities of their white brethren. But on the White Election Day, or Artillery Day (*q. v.*), which occurred in the same week, no black man dared to be seen in the places of public resort. In other localities, notably on the Massachusetts coast, in Connecticut, and in Narragansett, the term Nigger 'Lection was applied to the election of a black governor whom the negroes chose to hold sway over them. The authority which this governor wielded over his brethren frequently made him a man of some importance in the community, and his master was glad to pay for the feasting which attended his election and inauguration. Occasionally Nigger 'Lection had a deep political significance and influence. (See Hinman's "American Revolution.")

Noche triste. (Sp., "Sad or Disastrous Night.") The name given by the Spanish under Cortés to the night of July 1–2, 1520, when they were almost cut to pieces by the Mexican natives. Cortés had reached the city of Mexico with his army in the previous November. He was hospitably received, but, fearing treachery, he seized Montezuma in his own house and confined him in the Spanish quarters as a hostage. The Aztecs rose in arms and attacked the quarters. Montezuma, sent by Cortés to the walls to expostulate with them, was received with a shower of stones, and died June 30, 1520. Cortés immediately resolved to leave Mexico city in secret. The movement was discovered, and the natives set upon the Spaniards in the narrow causeway of Tlapoca. The latter finally escaped, with the loss of four hundred and fifty of their small force, besides four thousand of their Indian allies and all their plunder.

November. This name signifies the ninth month (see SEP-TEMBER and OCTOBER), which position it occupied in the ten-month calendar ascribed to Romulus. The name was retained when two additional months were added. The Emperor Tibe-rius was born in this month. Hence the Senate wished to give

NOVEMBER. GROUP ROUND A FIRE.

it his name, following the precedent set by Augustus, but he declined the honor, saying, "What will you do, conscript fathers, when you have thirteen Cæsars?"

It was the *Windmonath*, or Wind Month, of the Saxons, who knew it also as *Blotmonath*, or Sacrifice Month, in consequence either of the sacrifices then performed, or of the custom of slaughtering the cattle for their winter supply of meat.

O.

Oak-Apple Day, Royal Oak Day, or Restoration Day.

A festival which still survives locally in England on May 29 in double commemoration of the birthday of Charles II. and of his return to London after the rebellion, May 29, 1660. The allusion is to his concealment in an oak-tree near Boscobel House, Shropshire, after his defeat by Cromwell at the battle of Worcester on September 3, 1651. John Evelyn in his Diary under date of May 29, 1665, records that this " was the first anniversary appointed by Act of Parliament to be observed as a day of General Thanksgiving for the miraculous restoration of His Majesty; our vicar preaching on Psalm cxviii. 24, requiring us to be thankful and rejoice, as indeed we had cause." A special form of prayer suited to this day remained in the Common Prayer Book until it was abolished by Act of Parliament in 1859 (22 Vict. c. 2). On this day it was also customary for the chaplain of the House of Commons to preach in St. Margaret's Church, Westminster, before " the House," usually represented by the Speaker, the sergeant-at-arms, the clerks and other officers, and some half-dozen members. This observance has been discontinued since 1858. (TIMBS: *Something for Everybody*, 1861, p. 74.)

The circumstances of Charles's flight after the battle of Worcester are full of romantic adventure, and an account of them is necessary to a full understanding of the Oak-Apple Day festivities. Boscobel House had been built in the time of James I. by a Catholic gentleman named John Gifford, who had caused various places of concealment to be constructed for the purpose of affording shelter to proscribed persons of his own religion. Hence it was deemed a safe place for the royal fugitive. There was no one at home save William Penderel, the housekeeper, his wife, and his four brothers. Later Charles was joined by the brave Cavalier, Colonel Carlis, who had been the last man to retreat from Worcester. An alarm reaching Boscobel that the Roundhead troopers were on the track of the fugitives, it was determined by the faithful brothers to conceal them in a thick spreading oak in the adjoining woods. This plan was hit upon none too soon, for the Roundheads soon appeared. Miss Agnes Strickland in *Harper's Magazine* for December, 1850, has preserved a curious tradition of the search that followed. " Pope's popular but long-suppressed line," she says,—

" Angels who watched the royal oak so well,

always makes me think that he must have been familiar with the following incident which my father's mother, Elizabeth Cotterel, who was the grand-daughter of a cadet of the old loyal family of that name in Staffordshire, and maternally descended from one of the honest Penderel brothers, was accustomed to relate as a fact, derived from family tradition, connected with the perils and hairbreadth escapes of Charles II. at Boscobel.

"'The Roundhead troopers,' she said, 'having tracked the king, first to Whiteladies, and then to Boscobel Forest, were led, by the keen scent of their bloodhounds, just at the twilight hour, to the very tree in which he and Colonel Carlis were hidden. The traitors, a sergeant and five others of the same company, made a halt under the Royal Oak, and began to reconnoitre it, while their dogs came baying and barking round about the trunk. Suddenly the leaves began to rustle, and one of the villains cried out,—

"'"Hallo! some one is surely hidden here!—look how the branches shake."

"'"It will be worth a thousand pounds to us if it be the young king," said another.

"'Then the sergeant asked who would volunteer to ascend the tree, and earn a larger share of the reward by taking the supposed prize alive; but, as no one appeared willing to risk the chance of encountering a clapperclawing from the royal lion, dealt from a vantage height, he was just giving the word for them to fire a volley into the tree, when, by the grace of God,' the old lady would add with impressive solemnity, 'a white owl flew out from the thickest covert of the branches and screeched " fie upon them !" as well she might; whereupon the false traitors hooted out a curse as bitter as that of Meroz on the poor bird, and growled to each other that it was she that had misled their dogs, and had stirred the leaves withal, to mock themselves; howsomever, they would have a shot at her, to teach her better manners than to screech at the soldiers of the Lord. But though five of the sorry knaves banged off their musketoons at the harmless bird, not one of them was marksman enough to hit a feather of her. Lastly, the sergeant took out a printed copy of the proclamation, promising " the reward of a thousand pounds for the apprehension of the young man, Charles Stuart, eldest son of the late King Charles," and fastened it on the trunk of the Royal Oak where his majesty was sitting in the branches above them, hearing all they said, and an eye-witness of their treason.'"

After numerous other adventures, the royal fugitive succeeded towards the end of October in securing passage in a little bark from Shoreham to Dieppe, where he landed in safety. More than forty persons, some of them in very humble circumstances, had been instrumental in his escape, not one of whom could be induced to betray him by the large reward offered by the Parliament.

On the 8th of May, 1660, Charles II. was proclaimed king in London and Westminster and subsequently throughout his dominions. On the 16th he came to the Hague, on the 23d embarked with his two brothers for England, and on the 25th landed at Dover, where he was received by General Monk at the head of a portion of the army, who escorted him to Canterbury. On the 29th, his birthday, he made his triumphal entry into London.

On the 13th of June, 1661, Charles summoned the five Shropshire brothers to attend him at Whitehall, when his majesty was pleased to acknowledge their faithful services, and signified his intention of notifying his gratitude by a suitable reward, inquiring if they had any particular favor to ask. They only asked an exemption from the penal laws, with liberty for themselves and their descendants to enjoy the free exercise of their religion, being members of the Catholic Church. This request was granted, and their names, together with those of their kinswoman Mrs. Yates, Mr. Huddleston, and Mr. Whitgreave, were especially exempted in the statute from the pains and penalties of recusancy.

King Charles granted a moderate pension to them and their descendants forever.

"The Oak," says a contemporary, whose pleasant little chronicle of Boscobel was published in 1660, the year of the restoration, "is now properly called ' The Royal Oake of Boscobel,' nor will it lose that name while it continues a tree: and since his majesty's happy restoration that those mysteries have been revealed, hundreds of people for many miles round have flocked to see the famous Boscobel, which. as you have heard, had once the honor to be the palace of his sacred majesty, but chiefly to behold the Royal Oake, which has been deprived of all its young boughs by the visitors of it, who keep them in memory of his majesty's happy preservation."

Dr. Stukeley in his "Itinerarium Curiosum," 1724, vol. iii. p. 57, makes this mention of the tree: " A bowshot from Boscobel House, just by a horse-track passing through the wood, stood the Royal Oak, into which the king and his companion, Colonel Carlis, climbed by means of the hen-roost ladder. when they judg'd it no longer safe to stay in the house; the family reaching them victuals with the nuthook. The tree is now enclosed in with a brick wall, the inside whereof is covered with lawrel, of which we may say, as Ovid did of that before the Augustan

palace. 'mediamque tuebere quercum.' Close by its side grows
a young thriving plant from one of its acorns. Over the door
of the inclosure, I took this inscription in marble : ' Felicissimam
arborem quam in asylum potentissimi Regis Caroli II. Deus O.
M. per quem reges regnant hic crescere voluit, tam in perpetuam
rei tantæ memoriam, quam specimen firmæ in reges fidei, muro
cinctam posteris commendant Basilius et Jana Fitzherbert.
Quercus amica Jovi.' "

The tree and its enclosure have long since disappeared, but
the inscription is still preserved in the farm-house at Boscobel.
Burgess in his "Eidodendron" tells us that the Royal Oak
" succumbed at length to the reiterated attentions of its votaries, and a huge bulk of timber, consisting of many loads, was
taken away by handfuls." Saplings were raised in different
parts of the country from its acorns. Several were sown by the
king himself. Making a pilgrimage to the scene of his former
troubles, he visited the Royal Oak, and was observed to gather
a handful of the acorns. Some of these he planted with his
own hand in St. James's Park. A promising young tree, which
sprang from one of these acorns, which Charles had planted in
the queen's pleasure garden, within sight of his bedchamber, in
St. James's Palace, and was accustomed to water and tend with
great pleasure, was called the King's Royal Oak, and had become an object of interest to the people as a relic of that popular sovereign, but was destroyed by Sarah, Duchess of Marlborough, as soon as her husband obtained the grant of the ground
on which it stood, for the site of Marlborough House. This
was regarded as an outrage on popular feeling.

Two others stood on the north side of the Serpentine in Hyde
Park, but were blighted by a severe frost at the beginning of
the present century. One was entirely removed. The stem and
a few branches of the other still remain, covered with ivy and
protected by an iron fence.

In the Bodleian Library is preserved a fragment of the original
tree, carved in the form of a salver for a tankard. The inscription records that it is a gift from Mrs. Letitia Lane, a member
of the Penderel family. The Barber-Surgeons' Company of
London possesses a curious memorial in the form of a silver cup
presented to it by Charles II., the stem and body of which represent an oak-tree from which hang acorns fashioned like little
bells, which ring as the cup passes from hand to hand around
the festive board of the company on great occasions.

Oak-Apple Day was formerly universally commemorated in
England by the people wearing oak-leaves or oak-apples in their
hats, which were sometimes covered with leaf-gold. In London
it was also usual on this anniversary to decorate the monument

of Richard Penderel in the churchyard of St. Giles with oak branches and to pay a similar tribute to the statue of Charles I. at Charing Cross. These customs survived the Revolution of 1688, even in the army, for Brand records that "two soldiers were whipped almost to death and turned out of the service for wearing boughs in their hats on the 29th of May, 1716." Brand, writing in 1849, also says,—

"I remember the boys at Newcastle-upon-Tyne had formerly a taunting rhyme on this occasion, with which they used to insult such persons as they met on this day who had not oak-leaves in their hats:

> "Royal Oak,
> The Whigs to provoke.

"There was a retort courteous by others, who contemptuously wore plane-tree leaves, which is of the same homely sort of stuff:

> "Plane-tree leaves;
> The Church-folk are thieves."

Even to this day May 29 is known as Shitsack or Shickshack Day in Wiltshire and Berkshire, the young people carrying shit-sack, or sprigs of young oak, in the morning, and powder-monkey or even-ash (ash-leaves with an equal number of leaflets) in the afternoon. "Those who wear these emblems of loyalty have the privilege of pinching or otherwise ill-treating those who do not don the oak-leaf." (P. H. DITCHFIELD: *Old English Customs extant at the Present Time,* London and New York, 1886.) In Nottinghamshire, also, according to the same authority, the anniversary is known as Oak and Nettle Day. The boys arm themselves with oak sprigs and bunches of nettles. The latter they use to strike the hands and faces of all who cannot "show their oak." Rotten eggs, says Mr. Ditchfield, were used as instruments of punishment twenty years ago.

The workingmen of Basingstoke and other towns in Hampshire arise early on the 29th of May to gather slips of oak with the gall on; these they put in their hats or anywhere about their persons. They also hang pieces to the knockers, latches, or other parts of the house doors of the wealthy, who take them in to place in their halls, etc. After breakfast these men go round to such houses for beer, etc. If they do not receive anything, the following verses should be said,—

> Shig-shag, penny a rag
> (Bang his head in Croommell's bag),
> All up in a bundle,—

but fear often prevents them. However, the lads have no fear, and use it freely to any one without an oak-apple or oak-leaf visible on some part of his person,—ill-treating him for his want of loyalty. After noon the loyalty ceases, and then if any one be charged with having *shig-shag,* the following verses are said:

> Shig-shag's gone past,
> You're the biggest fool at last;
> When shig-shag comes again,
> You'll be the biggest fool then.

And the one who charges the other with the oak-leaf receives the ill-treatment. (*Notes and Queries,* First Series, vol. xii. p. 100.)

At the villages of Wishford and Barford, near Salisbury, the inhabitants who claim certain rights in Grovely Woods assert them by meeting here on May 29, when they gather boughs and carry them in procession, with the cry of "Grovely, Grovely, Grovely!"

Hone (1826, vol. i. p. 618) has the following entry:

"At Tiverton, on the 29th of May, it is customary for a number of young men, dressed in the style of the seventeenth century, and armed with swords, to parade the streets and gather contributions from the inhabitants. At the head of the procession walks a man called 'Oliver,' dressed in black, with his face and hands smeared over with soot and grease, and his body bound with a strong cord, the end of which is held by one of the men to prevent his running too far. After these come another troop, dressed in the same style, each man bearing a large branch of oak; four others, carrying a kind of throne made of oaken boughs, on which a child is seated, bring up the rear. A great deal of merriment is excited among the boys at the pranks of 'Master Oliver,' who capers about in a most ludicrous manner. Some of them amuse themselves by casting dirt, while others, more mischievously inclined, throw stones at him, but woe betide the young urchin who is caught; his face assumes a most awful appearance from the soot and grease with which 'Oliver' begrimes it, whilst his companions who have been lucky enough to escape his clutches testify their pleasure by loud shouts. In the evening the whole party have a feast, the expenses of which are defrayed by the collection made in the morning.'

The *Illustrated London News* for May 30, 1857, p. 515, describes Oak-Apple Day as being anxiously looked forward to by old and young: "Early in the morning ropes are stretched across the street, upon which are hung garlands composed of all such flowers as are in bloom. The garlands are also ornamented with colored ribbons and handkerchiefs, and all the teaspoons which can be collected are hung in the middle. Maypoles, which are less common, and large boughs of oak, are pressed into service. Many are the penn'orths of gold leaf sold the day before, with which to gild the oak-apple for the button-hole. A benefit club meets on this day, and walks in procession with bands and flags to church, after which they make a progress through the town with bands playing and colors flying, finishing up with a dinner."

The town of Northampton still preserves a grateful memory of Stuart generosity. A fire nearly destroyed the town in 1675. Charles II. contributed one thousand tons of lumber out of Whittlewood Forest, to enable the citizens to rebuild their houses, and also remitted the duty of chimney money for seven years. Formerly all the citizens placed a large branch of oak over the doors of their houses on May 29. The oak boughs are rapidly disappearing, but Ditchfield (p. 121) assures us that the corporation still attend All Saints' Church, and march thither in procession, followed by all the school-children in the town, the boys having gilt oak-apples in their caps. The statue of the king, near the church, is also decorated with oaken boughs on this day, and many of the houses are similarly adorned.

The same authority mentions the continuance of the custom at Durham for the cathedral choir to ascend the tower of the cathedral on May 29 and sing three anthems from the three sides of it. This custom is as old as the battle of Neville's Cross, which Queen Philippa fought with David I. of Scotland in the year 1346, when the monks chanted masses from the summit of the tower on behalf of the queen. Tradition states that a choir-boy once overbalanced himself and fell from the tower, and was killed. Hence the choir sing their anthems only on the three sides.

At Chelsea Royal Hospital, London, the anniversary is kept every year with military rites and a patriotic consumption of beef and pudding by the aged pensioners, who sport their brightest coats and badges. Chelsea Hospital, it will be remembered, was founded by Charles II. at the suggestion of Nell Gwynn, who probably remembered pityingly the wounded and useless soldiers she used to meet at Whitehall and Westminster in her professional rounds as an orange-girl.

October. This month was so named because it was the eighth month in the primitive Roman calendar ascribed to Romulus. It became the tenth month in the calendar as revised by Numa, who added January and February, but it retained its original name, the more readily, perhaps, because it once more became the tenth month when the year commenced, as it did in early Christendom, with March. Julius Cæsar in his revision of the calendar gave it thirty days, which number was changed to thirty-one by Augustus. As was the case with September, many Roman Emperors sought to change its name in their own honor. It was successively Germanicus, Antoninus, Tacitus, and Herculeus, the latter a surname of the Emperor Commodus. But none of these names clung. The Roman Senate had no better luck when they renamed it Faustinus, in honor of Faustina, wife of Antoninus.

The Anglo-Saxons called October *Winterfylleth,* a name which indicated that winter approached with the full moon of the month. In old almanacs the sport of hawking is adopted as

OCTOBER. HAWKING.

emblematical of this which was accounted the last month of autumn. On October 23 the sun enters the sign Scorpio, the astronomical emblem said to typify, in the form of a destructive insect, the increasing power of cold over nature. In the same manner the equal influences of cold and heat are represented by Libra, or The Balance, the sign of the preceding month of September.

> Hedge-crickets sing; and now, with treble soft,
> The redbreast whistles from a garden-croft.
> (KEATS.)

> The warm sun is failing; the bleak wind is wailing;
> The bare boughs are sighing; the pale flowers are dying.
> (SHELLEY.)

> The rivers run chill; the red sun is sinking,
> And I am grown old, and life is fast shrinking.
> (HOOD.)

> Yet for ever and aye I will bless his name,
> While his winds blow fresh and his sunsets flame,
> This prince of months,—October.
> (HAYNE.)

Oils, Holy. Three oils are used in the sacred services of the Catholic Church: oil for the sick, employed in the sacrament of extreme unction; oil of the chrism, used after baptism, during confirmation, at the consecration of bishops, and of paten and chalice, and in the blessing of bells; and oil of the catechumens, so called because employed on the candidates for baptism before they are brought to the sacred font, but used also in the ordination of priests and the blessing and coronation of kings and queens.

Prior to the fourth century no particular day was fixed for the ceremony of blessing these oils, though from the earliest times

BLESSING THE HOLY OILS (1723).
(From Picart.)

the power of performing the function has been limited to the bishops. The present custom of the Roman Church is to bless the holy oils once a year, on Maundy Thursday. They are immediately distributed among the pastors of the several parishes, who must keep them under lock and key in vessels of silver or alloyed metal. The oils of the past year must not be used, but common oil, in lesser quantity, may be added to the blessed oils if necessary.

In Rome the ceremony of blessing is publicly performed at the church of St. John Lateran. Twelve priests and seven deacons assist the officiating bishop. The bishop and priests

BLESSING THE HOLY OILS.

breathe three times upon each of the oils, meaning by this action that the power of the Holy Spirit is about to descend on the oils ; and after the consecration is complete they salute the oils with the words " Hail, holy oil ! hail, holy chrism !"

The Greek Church differs from the Latin in that the former blesses the oils only once in three years, at Easter time. The ceremony takes place at Moscow or Kief.

On Monday morning the metropolitan goes to the sacristy of the patriarchs, lights a fire, and pours into a caldron a gallon of myro, or chrism, reading meanwhile the Gospel of the day.

The oil is kept boiling for three days and nights, monks attending in relays and stirring the contents of the caldron with silver ladles. Olive oil mixed with white wine of Lisbon and perfumes make up the myro. The final ceremony takes place when the mixture is put into two silver receptacles upon a porcelain stove and stirred by six deacons in vestments of silver and black.

The Empress Catherine II. gave to the church a silver vase, which is still used as the final receptacle into which the oil is poured, with a benediction. The people attend in thousands, as they are permitted, and dip bits of cotton into the holy mixture. On the afternoon of Thursday the vases are carried in a procession to the cathedral, where the metropolitan says mass.

Olaf, St., or **Olaf II.** (995–1030), patron of Norway, and, since the union, of Sweden. His festival on July 29, the day of his death, is still celebrated in the joint kingdom. Descended from the ancient royal line, he was educated in exile as a Christian, and in 1015 succeeded in wresting the crown from the usurper. For fifteen years he devoted himself to the evangelization of his new subjects. In 1030 he was slain in battle against the invader Canute, King of England and Denmark. A year later his remains were found in a miraculous state of preservation, and were buried with great state in a chapel he had erected at Trondhjem. The marvels enacted at his shrine attracted so many pilgrims that the city speedily grew to be the largest and most important in the land, and the chapel gave place to a cathedral, in which the saint's bones still repose. Though he was never canonized, the Church has bowed to popular acclamation and never disputed his saintship.

Ommegang, Procession of the. A famous ceremony which was formerly celebrated in Brussels on the Sunday before Pentecost. It was held in honor of a miraculous statue of the Virgin that had been carried in 1348 from Antwerp to Brussels by a poor woman named Beatrice Soctkens and presented to the church of Notre-Dame des Victoires. The commemoration of the incident was made a municipal one. All the city magistrates, the guilds and corporations, the companies of archers and crossbowmen, joined in a grand cavalcade specifically known as the Ommegang, which accompanied the floats bearing representations of Old and New Testament scenes, together with animals, giants, etc. The image itself was carried in a miniature ship. (See URSULA, ST.)

Ordensfest. (Ger., "Feast of Orders.") A ceremony peculiar to Berlin. On some appointed day in the last week of March all who during the preceding year have received any kind of distinction from the German Emperor—the only source of such honors—are invited to a service in the cathedral, followed by a dinner at the castle. From one to two thousand persons are thus brought together, ranging from the select few who have obtained the order of the Red Eagle to the hundreds who have been decorated with the simplest Hohenzollern house order. Most of the latter are, as a rule, members of the civil service, or of fire-brigades, or non-commissioned officers, or even lackeys, who value such decorations as testimonials and hand them down to their children as heirlooms. All these are called to Berlin, where the excellence of the dinner in the castle fully compensates for the length of the sermon in the church. The guests are seated at a series of tables, each of which is set apart for one particular grade, according to the decoration conferred. The system of orders, which are always announced as coming direct from the king, is undoubtedly of great value in creating a numerous body of loyal adherents.

Ouen or **Ouine, St.** (Lat. *Audoenus*), patron of Rouen, France (595–683). He was bishop of that city for forty-four years. His death-day, August 24, was formerly celebrated with a great fair at St. Malo, in Brittany. This was known as the Saint-Ouine, and alternatively as the Periwinkle Fair,—from the bowlfuls of periwinkles that were sold at it,—or the Whistle Fair, because of the innumerable whistles and trumpets and horns which children bought there four centuries ago as they still buy them to-day. It then took place within the walls of St. Malo. After the great fire in the sixteenth century, which burned half the town to the ground, the site of the fair was changed to the island of the Grand Bey, where there was then a chapel dedicated to the saint, about which the wives of St. Malo sailors prayed for fair winds to bring their men home, turning the chapel cross towards the quarter whence the wind should come, so that the saying arose, " As changeable as the cross of St. Ouine." Lastly, about the middle of the nineteenth century, long after the last ruins of the chapel on the Grand Bey had been swept away or overgrown, the Saint-Ouine was transferred to the broad quays outside the town, where it is now held every year on the fifth Sunday in Lent. But its importance has gone from it: from its ancestor the great Whistle Fair it has inherited only one quality, and that is noise.

P.

Palio. The annual horse-race run in Siena in honor of the Virgin Mary, patron of the city, on August 15. The horses are the stout little nags put to every-day use by butchers, green-grocers, and tradesmen. Each of the seventeen wards of Siena selects its champion, a survival from the old party feuds between the wards, and an attendant company of ten men dressed in mediæval costumes. A few hours before the race, horses and men are blessed with much ceremony in their particular parish, and then proceed to the Campo, the chief square in the city, where they form part in a gorgeous procession headed by the town band and closed by a modern fac-simile of the Carroccio, or battle-car, taken from the Florentines at Monteaperto (1260) by the victorious Sienese. Then come the races, which are run barebacked, the jockeys having a cruel whip of ox-sinew called a *nerbo*, which they are privileged to use not only on their own but also on the rival horses, and on the rival jockeys as well. The winner is escorted back in triumph to the parish church by his own company and their adherents. There the prize banner is hung up among a host of similar trophies, some of them dating back many centuries, for the Palio has been run ever since the fourteenth century.

Pallium. (Lat., "a cover," "a mantle.") A band of white wool adorned with four purple crosses, which is worn by the highest dignitaries of the Catholic Church on the most solemn occasions. It is woven especially for the Pope and sent by him to patriarchs, primates, archbishops, and occasionally to bishops as a sign that they possess " the fulness of the episcopal office." Its origin and early history are obscure. Pallium was the Latin name for the loose upper garment of the Greeks which among the Romans was especially affected by philosophers and among the Christians by ascetics. But no doubt the ecclesiastical pallium had some connection with the shoulder-band of the Jewish high-priest, which being adopted by Christian prelates came to symbolize the Lord seeking after the lost lamb and carrying it, when found, on his shoulder. From the East it was early transferred to the West, where it became the custom for the Bishop of Rome to present it to the metropolitans connected with his see. The "Catholic Dictionary" thus sums up the prob-

ARCHBISHOP RECEIVING THE PALLIUM.
(From Picart.)

able evolution of the pallium: "It was an ornament of metro politans, given to them perhaps from early times by the patriarchs and by the Pope in that comparatively narrow district which was under his most immediate supervision. Then the Pope gave it to his vicars in distant parts, then as a mark of special honor to some bishops, then he required all Western metropolitans to ask it from him before exercising their functions as archbishops, and finally the rule was extended even to patriarchs."

The wearing of the pallium is a matter of much ceremony. First two chosen lambs are on St. Agnes' Day (January 21) brought to the church of St. Agnes at Rome by the apostolic subdeacons, while the Agnus Dei is being sung. These lambs are presented at the altar, received by two canons of the Lateran church, and solemnly blessed. After mass the lambs are taken

in charge by the nuns of St. Agnes until shearing-time, when
their wool is spun and woven into pallia by the nuns of Torre
de' Specchia. On the vigil of the festival of SS. Peter and Paul
the newly made pallia are carried on gilded trays to St. Peter's,
where they are blessed by the Pope and laid by the subdeacons
upon the tomb of St. Peter. Here they remain all night. Next
day they are locked up in a silver coffer close to the relics of St.
Peter, where they remain until required. An archbishop cannot,
strictly speaking, assume the title or the functions of the archiepiscopate until he has received the pallium from Rome. In case
he is elected to a see of metropolitan or higher rank, he must
beg the pallium " instanter, instantius, instantissime," within
three months after his consecration or from his confirmation if
he was already a bishop and has come to the metropolitan see
by translation. He receives it from the hands of another bishop
deputed by the Pope. He cannot transmit it to his successor,
and if translated he must beg for another pallium. The pallium
or pallia, if he has received more than one, are buried with him
when he dies.

Palm Sunday. The Sunday before Easter, commemorating
the triumphant entry of Christ into Jerusalem, when, mounted
upon an ass, he rode into the city, and " a very great multitude
spread their garments in the way; others cut down branches
from the trees, and strewed them in the way. And the multitudes that went before, and that followed, cried, saying, Hosanna
to the Son of David : Blessed is he that cometh in the name
of the Lord; Hosanna in the highest." (Matt. xxi. 8, 9.)

Their enthusiasm, however, speedily cooled, and He whom
they had delighted to honor on the Sunday was on the following
Friday put to a cruel and lingering death amid the applause of
the populace. From a very early date, accordingly, of the
Christian era (from the tenth century at least, if not from the
fifth), the Sunday before Easter was called Palm Sunday, because
on this day the Church ordained that boughs of palm-trees should
be carried in procession, in imitation of those strewed before our
Saviour when he rode into Jerusalem. The palms were consecrated by the priests. A portion of them were (and still are)
preserved to be burned for holy ashes to lay on the heads of the
people on Ash Wednesday in the following year. The rest were
distributed first among the assistant priests and next the congregation. Then the procession took its way from the church
through the streets of the town, and back in procession again.

To represent the Christ, a priest used to ride in the procession
on an ass, carrying the host. Sometimes a wooden ass was used
instead of a real one, and then the figure on its back, representing

49

the Saviour, was also of wood. The whole was mounted on a platform with wheels, and was drawn through the streets by a rope. The people threw down their palm-branches before this car, as it passed, and eagerly picked them up after the wheels had been over them, guarding them afterwards as charms against storms and lightning. In countries where real palms were not to be had, other kinds of branches and boughs were used instead. In England, for instance, willow boughs were the favorite substitute. In some places, after the procession of the wooden ass was over, boys were allowed to hire the ass and its image rider from the sexton, to drag about the streets, while they begged for pennies. Half of all they got was the pay of the sexton. Before England became Protestant these processions were extremely popular through the country, and when King Henry VIII. broke with the Church of Rome he specified the carrying of palms on Palm Sunday as one of the customs that were not to be discontinued. The formal observance of the feast was carried on till some time in the reign of Edward VI., and after that it gradually fell into disuse.

The Pax or Peace Cake was formerly distributed on Palm Sunday in many English churches, the intention being that those who had quarrelled should break the cake together and say, " Peace and good will," thus making up their differences in preparation for the Easter communion. A survival of this custom occurs in the united parishes of Sellack and King's Chapel, Herefordshire, where cakes are distributed on Palm Sunday, the cost of which is defrayed by a rent-charge on a farm in the parish. At one time glasses of ale were handed round with the cakes. Ditchfield informs us that the present vicar (1896) remembers seeing this part of the ceremony.

In some places the priests used to make little crosses of the palms, and these were supposed to protect those who obtained them against lightning. There was a curious little local observance in Cornwall. The people there used to take their crosses of palm to the shrine of Our Lady of Nantswell, and when they had paid small fees to the priest in charge they were allowed to throw the palms into the well. If a cross floated, it meant that its owner would live through the year; if it did not, it meant that he would die. As the crosses must have been reasonably light and generally sure to float, it is easy to see how this would become a popular form of divination. It was also said in Cornwall that if anybody did not have a palm in his hand on Palm Sunday he would some time have his hand cut off.

On Palm Saturday the boys of the grammar-school at Lanark used to parade the streets with a tree of the willow kind (*Salix caprea*) in blossom, ornamented with daffodils, mezereon, and box-tree. It is still customary, too, for those who make excursions into the country surrounding London to bring home some reminiscence of the day, by gathering branches of the willow or sallow with their gray shining velvety buds. With these they ornament their hats, their bonnets, and their breasts, or carry the branches in their hands.

It seems likely at first glance that this custom did not originally belong to Palm Sunday or Saturday at all, but was an adaptation of the more familiar and important May-Day observance.

At Rome the palms used are genuine palms, not boxwood- or olive-branches, as elsewhere, and these palm-leaves are many of them woven into all sorts of graceful shapes and adorned with interleaved lilies, roses, and tulips. The latter are for the well-to-do, who purchase them from the traffickers crowding the steps of the basilica, and are fetched into the church to be blessed at the appropriate moment. The poorer classes content themselves with the plainer leaves that are handed out by the priests in the sacristy.

The little village of San Remo near Genoa has for centuries enjoyed the prescriptive right of furnishing all the palms that are used in St. Peter's Church. The right is said to date from the pontificate of Sixtus V. This Pope had conceived the idea of transporting the obelisk which formerly ornamented the circus of Caligula and Nero to the middle of the piazza of St. Peter's. He publicly announced that the death-penalty would be inflicted upon any one who should, during the ceremony, disturb the silence that was necessary for overhearing the commands of the architect Fontana. Now, it happened that just as the obelisk was being raised in the piazza the hauling-ropes caught fire from friction. What was to be done? Nobody seemed to know. Then above the solemn silence rang out a voice,—

"*Acqua alle funi!*" ("Water to the ropes!")

The advice was good, and was taken at once. The obelisk was saved. But the sbirri arrested the owner of the voice. He was brought before Sixtus V.

"What is your name?" asked the Pope.

"Bresca of San Remo."

"You know that my ordinance punishes your action with death?"

"I know that at the peril of my own life I have saved the lives of hundreds of workmen whom the obelisk would have crushed in its fall."

"Very well. What reward do you wish for your service?"

"Nothing for myself, but for my fellow-countrymen of the Genoese riviera, where superb palms grow, I ask that they be allowed to furnish the palms which are used during Holy Week in the solemn procession at the basilica of St. Peter's."

"Granted," said the Pope, "not only in my pontificate, but in perpetuity under all my successors."

And the promise of Sixtus V. has ever since been respected.

After the palms have been blessed and distributed, a procession follows. The choristers in violet-colored soutanes and surplice lead. Then follow the seminarists, the beneficiaries of the basilica of St. Peter, the canons in surplice and rochet, the cardinal archpriest in a white chasuble embroidered with gold. Each holds a palm-leaf in his hand.

At a given signal the procession moves out of the basilica and makes the tour of the portico, chanting songs of joy. This is the "triumphal march." When the procession seeks to re-enter the church the door is found to be closed. It does not open until a subdeacon knocks against it with the handle of his cross, saying,—

"Attollite portas principes vestras: et elevamini, portæ æternales."

Then the door swings open, and the procession moves up the aisle to the grand altar, where mass is celebrated.

The closing and opening of the door not only symbolized the entry of Christ into Jerusalem, but also the larger truth of the assurance of salvation opened through the expiation of man's sins by the Redeemer. It is repeated, in a less imposing manner, in all the Catholic churches in the world.

In Spain Palm Sunday preserves all its picturesque mediæval characteristics. The chief people in every town, as well as the middle and lower classes, take part in the ceremony. Each bears real palm-leaves and olive-branches. First the clergy go through a little performance intended to represent the reception of Christ at Jerusalem. They go out of the church by a side door, form in procession, make a tour around the building, and come to the main porch, called the Door of the Apostles. This, when they arrive, is closed. The priest knocks three times, the door is flung open, and the clergy enter, followed by all the crowd, the principal people coming first, bearing the palms. In the course of the service these are blessed by the priest in the presence of the archbishop.

On the eve of Palm Sunday in Servia the young girls gather together upon a hill and sing ballads on the resurrection of Lazarus. On Palm Sunday itself before sunrise they repair to the well or fountain whence they draw water. Here they dance in a ring and sing in chorus songs wherein the poet tells how the horns of the stag disturb the water while its eye renders them pure and clear.

Palmknopen Festival. A popular preliminary to the marital ceremony among the Netherlanders. Two days before a wedding, young people of both sexes meet at the house of the bride and weave garlands out of leaves of gold and silver, inter-

PALMKNOPEN FESTIVAL.
(From Picart.)

spersed with natural flowers, or entirely out of natural leaves and flowers. The festival is attended with kissing and other games. On the wedding day these garlands are thrown around among the guests.

Panagia. (Gr. πανάγιος, "all-holy.") In the Greek Church, the distinctive title of the Virgin Mary, as well as of her ikons, or effigies. The most famous of the latter is the Panagia attributed to St. Luke and preserved in the monastery of Sumelas in the Peloponnesus. It is said to have been found in a huge cavern by the holy shepherdess Euphrosyne in the fifth century, and to have been acknowledged by St. Luke as his workmanship in a vision. A monastery was raised on the spot, the cavern itself being turned into the church. For centuries this has been a favorite pilgrim-bourn of members of the Greek religion, who flock to the shrine of the Panagia on the yearly recurrence of her great festival day, the 27th of August in our calendar, the

15th in theirs. At other seasons her visitors are comparatively few ; indeed, snow, rain, and mist render the convent almost inaccessible for full eight months of the 'twelve. The image is a rude alto-rilievo in wood. " A blackish outline," says W. Gifford Palgrave, "chiefly defined by the gold-leaf ground that limits head and shoulders, indicates the figure. Close beside it hang, obliquely from the ceiling, like masts in slings, two huge wax tapers, wrapped in some material, costly, but now undistinguishable through its dingy encrustments. Near the tapers is also suspended an enormous circular chandelier of silver gilt, with a quantity of little ex-votos, silver boats, gold filigree ornaments, coins, and the like, dangling from its rim. We deposit the offering that courtesy requires in the all-receiving platter before the Panagia, and are next called on to revere the special object of devout pilgrimage, a small silver rocking-cradle, of pretty but not ancient workmanship, consecrated to the goddess of the shrine. Into this cradle a piece of money (the more precious the metal the greater its efficacy) is to be laid ; after which the pilgrim, having thrice raised and lowered the toy and its contents on the palm of his or her hand before the unveiled Panagia, deposits it on the plate of offerings. Should the cradle when thus set down continue to rock, the happy votary will infallibly become before long a father or a mother, as the case may be ; its immobility, on the contrary, is a sad but conclusive presage of married sterility. Now, barrenness is at the present day no less an opprobrium in the East than it was in the age of Hannah and Pheninnah ; and its prevention or cure is the motive of far the greater number of pilgrimages to Mariamana ; even newly married Mohammedans, not to mention Armenians, Latins, and other unorthodox Christians of either sex, prove by their frequent visits to the cradle of Sumelas how catching a thing is superstition. The residue of the pilgrims are mostly petitioners for the recovery of a sick child, or relative, or self, and for them also the cradle obligingly extends the subject-matter of its oracles. The origin of this particular observance probably does not go back farther than Comnenian times ; though the monks refer it, like the foundation of the convent itself, to the fifth century." (*The Monastery of Sumelas : Fraser's Magazine.*)

The Greeks look upon the image as their especial patron. During the Saracenic wars she is alleged to have caused the guns of Sultan Murad IV., pointed against the convent walls, to spin round and begin firing upon the Sultan's own troops. Nor did she lose interest in her beloved country during the war of Grecian independence (1821–27). She is then reported to have spoken words of encouragement to the Greeks, to have rejoiced at every victory, and to have shed tears over every defeat. Her emotions during the war of 1897 have not yet found a chronicler.

Panch-Kosi, or circumambulation of the city. The most solemn ceremony practised by the pilgrims to Benares. No pilgrim returns from the holy city without taking advantage of this soul-purifying ceremony. As the circuit is fifty miles and has to be performed on foot, it takes six days to get back to the starting-point, the Manikarnika Ghat, which is close to the burning-places. The circuit being performed sunwise is in effect a pradakshina (*q. v.*). On the last day the pilgrim scatters on the ground grains of barley which he carries in a bag made for the purpose. This curious custom is in honor of Siva. On the theory that the pradakshina has a solar symbolism, and the circle gone over represents the yearly cycle, the barley may possibly mean the results of the sun's power, the food that is annually produced and scattered over the earth for the good of all mankind. (SIMPSON: *The Buddhist Praying-Wheel*, p. 80 ; SHERRING: *The Sacred City of the Hindus*, p. 178.)

An imitation of the Panch-Kosi is performed at Bhuvaneswar, in Orissa. This is called *Kshetra parikramana*, or "Going the Round of the City." Dr. Râjendralâla Mitra (*Antiquities of Orissa*, vol. ii. p. 60) tells us that the circuit takes several days to accomplish. The Ekráma Purāna, however, does not insist upon this large circuit ; it assigns the inner circle formed by a radius of one mile round the Great Tower as the proper boundary of the circumambulation ; but it recommends the operation to be repeated three times, and gives directions how it is to be performed, and what mantras should be repeated when starting on the journey. The religious merit of the operation is even greater than the performance of ten thousand horse sacrifices. All sins that might be contracted in other places are wiped away in visiting Svarnakúta (Khandagiri), but what are contracted in the last-named place can be destroyed only by making the circumambulation of the sacred city.

Pantaleon, St. (It. *Pantaleone*), patron saint of physicians. His festival is celebrated July 27.

St. Pantaleon flourished in the fourth century, and was a native of Nicomedia. On account of his medical skill he was made physician to the Emperor Galerius Maximian. His mother was a Christian and had brought him up in that faith, but amid the pleasures of the court he did not practise his religion. At length a priest called Hermolaus brought him back to the fold. He went about ministering to the poor and needy, and was accused of being a Christian and condemned to be beheaded. He was bound to an olive-tree, and legend relates that as soon as his blood flowed to the roots of the tree it burst forth into leaves and fruit.

In art he is represented as young, beardless, and handsome. He is often painted in the act of martyrdom and bound to an olive-tree. As a patron saint he wears a physician's robe and bears the olive or palm, or both.

The body of St. Pantaleon was shown at Constantinople in 970. The church of St. Gregory at Rome claims to possess part of the body, and the church of St. Pantaleon at Rome exhibits the skull of the saint, some bones, and a bottle of his blood which liquefies on his festival. At Ravello the same claim regarding a bottle of the saint's blood is made. In the Dominican Church at Naples an arm of the saint and a bottle of his blood are shown. The church of the Apostles and the church of the Conception at Naples exhibit some of the bones of the saint and vials of his blood. Also San Ligorio at Naples claims to possess an arm of the saint. At St. Mark's, Venice, a hand and two bones of the head are shown; in the church of St. Pantaleon, Venice, a foot, leg, arm, part of the skull, and a finger, and in the church of St. Mary Magdalene, Venice, a leg-bone and part of an arm. The entire skull of the saint and a bottle of his blood are preserved at Lucca. The body of the saint is shown at La Bureba; an arm at Brindisi; part of the skull at Crema; a jaw at Ravenna. The entire body, however, is at Genoa; and a number of bones are scattered about at Milan, Bruges, Luxemburg, Cologne, and other places. The head of the saint is shown at Lyons, and the rest of the body at St. Denis, near Paris.

Pantheon Madonna, or Santa Maria della Rotonda. A miraculous image in the Pantheon at Rome. Until the beginning of the nineteenth century she had remained inactive and unimportant, only one small lamp shining dimly before her altar, which now blazes with the light of innumerable tapers, and not even a single votive offering adorning her person, which is now loaded with hearts, crowns, bracelets, and necklaces. One day the custos of the Pantheon had forgotten to feed the Madonna's lamp with oil, and towards evening after the doors were closed the sacred flame expired. Suddenly the people in the piazza heard from within the church a loud complaining cry for "Oglio! oglio!" The hearers hastened to the custos. the doors of the sanctuary were opened, the want of oil was discovered, and the miracle proclaimed to the world. The custos narrowly escaped from the violence of the crowding worshippers, and on that same night tapers were lighted round the altar of the insulted image, which ever since has healed the sick and worked all sorts of miracles.

Paray-le-Monial. A town in the French department of Saône-et-Loire. The chapel of the Convent of the Visitation is a famous pilgrim shrine as containing the tomb of a nun named Marguerite Marie Alacoque (1647–1690), who saw visions in a neighboring grove of nut-trees. She claimed that Christ appeared to her, bestowed on her the tenderest names, offered her his bleeding heart, and took her own. Extraordinary colloquies passed between the nun and the vision : " What shall I do ?" she asked one day. " My will is stronger than I am." " Place it," said the Divine Spouse, " in the wound in my heart, and it will there find the force to triumph over itself." " O my God," cried the maiden, in transport, " put it there indeed and enclose it so firmly that it will never come out." (ABBÉ CUCHERAT : *Popular History of the Beatified Marguerite Marie Alacoque*, p. 349.) The Society of Jesus exploited the revelations of this enthusiast, but at first they met with considerable opposition from the hierarchy of the Church. She was finally beatified in 1864. In 1873 she was accepted as a sort of tutelar patroness of the Catholics and royalists, and the colossal pilgrimages organized in July and August of that year marched to wild shouts of " Long live the Pope-King," and " Long live Henry V. !" A canticle had been composed for the occasion, of which the following was the refrain :

Dieu de clémence,
O Dieu vainqueur,
Sauvez Rome et la France,
Au nom du Sacré-Cœur !

("God of clemency,
O God the Victor,
Save Rome and France,
In the name of the Sacred Heart !")

The legitimist deputies, with M. de Belcastel at their head, invaded Paray. There they were met by M. de Charette and the Papal Zouaves. Pilgrims flocked from every diocese in France, many accompanied by their bishops. Even Belgium, Germany, and England sent their devotees. Every band of pilgrims brought rich banners, which they left upon the tomb of Marie Alacoque in the convent chapel. Daily and nightly processions were held. If all these ceremonials did not succeed in restoring Henry V., they at least made the fortune of the church and the village. Even the pre-eminence of Lourdes has not yet entirely eclipsed the pilgrimages to Paray-le-Monial.

Parentalia. Among the ancient Romans the public festival in honor of deceased relatives, which lasted from the 13th to the 21st of February. During these days all the temples were closed, marriages were prohibited, and the magistrates had to appear in public without the tokens of their office. The last day had the special name Feralia. Other festivals in honor of the dead were celebrated on August 24, October 5, and November 8, when the Manes or souls of the dead were believed to rise to the upper world. On these occasions the graves were decked with roses, violets, and other flowers.

Pasch, Pace, or **Pase Egg,** more familiarly known in English-speaking countries as **Easter Egg,** an egg, real or artificial, prepared for Easter by being dyed or decorated. If a real egg, it is always hard-boiled. From the remotest ages the egg has been looked upon as a symbol of creation or new birth. According to the Persians, the world was hatched from an egg at that season of the year which corresponds to the vernal equinox. Hence the Parsees still exchange gifts of colored eggs at the New Year festival, which they celebrate on this date. Among the Jews, the egg entered into all the mysterious ceremonies called apocalyptic, and occupied a prominent position on the household table during the paschal season. Christianity invested the paschal egg with a new significance, namely, that of the resurrection of Christ, and it was colored red in allusion to his blood shed for sinners on the cross. A curious custom in mediæval churches for priests and choristers to join in a game of ball at Eastertide took its rise from the Pasch egg, which was thrown from one to the other of the choristers in the nave of the church while an anthem was being sung. As a missed egg meant a smashed egg, the more durable hand-ball was substituted.

Formerly at the approach of Easter all the hen-roosts of France were ransacked for the largest eggs, which were brought as a tribute to the king. At the conclusion of the Easter high mass in the chapel of the Louvre, lackeys brought into the royal cabinet pyramids of gilded eggs, placed in baskets adorned with verdure; and the chaplain, after having blessed them, distributed them in the presence of His Most Christian Majesty to all the persons about the court.

In some remote districts of France the priest still goes round among his parishioners to bless their homes at the Easter season. In return he receives eggs both plain and painted. In many places it is also believed that the bells which are silent during Passion Week have set out for Rome to get the Pope's blessing. They return on Easter Eve to welcome the Resurrection with a joyous peal. People do not come back from so long a journey without bringing presents to good children. And in fact the joy-bells, which came first, bore with them eggs dyed scarlet like the cloak of a Roman cardinal, which they gave to the heads of families for distribution among the children. The death-bells, which came last, brought nothing.

In Anglesey, North Wales, the children go from house to house from Monday until Saturday in Easter week, announcing

EASTER EGG CEREMONY IN RUSSIA.

their presence by means of a clapper so that the door may be opened to them. If no eggs be in the house, the children are glad to receive the coppers of commutation. This custom was formerly prevalent not only all over Wales but also in many portions of England and Scotland. At Wilmslow an old rhyme was used:

Please, Mr. Smith,
Please give us an Easter egg.
If you do not give us one,
Your hen shall lay an addled one,
Your cock shall lay a stone.

In Northumberland, when a man asks a woman for an egg and is refused, he takes off her boots until she pays a penalty. If a man refuses a Pasch egg to a woman, she snatches away his cap, and will not restore it until he pays a money-forfeit.

Nowhere is the Easter egg more in evidence than in Russia. Here people carry a number of eggs with them when they stir out on Easter Sunday. These they present to their friends, saying, "Christ is risen!" the recipient replying, "He is risen indeed!" In the churches, after the service is over, priests and laymen click eggs together in the same way that we touch glasses, as a ceremonial indication of kindly feelings.

In many parts of rural England and continental Europe various Pasch egg contests survive. A popular game consists in hitting one egg against another, the egg that survives uncracked winning for its owner the weaker antagonist, and so on until an entire basket of eggs may have changed ownership. Another game is to trundle eggs down a hill or slope, those which reach the bottom uncracked being similarly victorious over the others. A survival of the latter custom occurs in America at Washington, where from the beginning of the century it has been the custom for children to gather on the White House grounds every Easter Monday and trundle Easter eggs down the slope.

The use of artificial eggs made of sugar or filigree and enclosing quantities of bonbons or other more sumptuous gifts has for the past half-century been encroaching upon the true Easter egg. In all the large cities of Christendom the confectioners' stores rival one another in their efforts to turn out the daintiest and most attractive Easter eggs. Sometimes these are of mammoth size and cost.

Paschal Candle. A huge torch of wax which in ancient times was used to give light during the watchings of the congregants on Easter Eve or Holy Saturday. Its origin goes at least as far back as the time of Zosimus, who was made Pope in 417, and the "Exultet" or triumphal song which the deacon still sings in the act of blessing the candle is hardly less ancient: Martene attributes it to St. Augustine. The blessing is now performed on Holy Saturday by the deacon, who fixes in the candle five grains of blessed incense in memory of the wounds of Jesus and the precious spices with which he was anointed in the tomb. From Easter until Whitsunday the Paschal candle appears on the Gospel side of the altar during mass and vespers, as a symbol that Christ, the light of the world, has risen from the grave. Anciently this torch was a huge affair. In 1457 that

BLESSING THE PASCHAL CANDLE.
(From Picart.)

at Canterbury weighed three hundred pounds, and the height of the one at Norwich was so great that it was lighted by means of an orifice in the roof of the choir.

Passing or **Soul Bell.** A bell that was rung or tolled for a person who was dying,—*i.e.*, who was passing from this life to the next,—to bespeak the prayers of all good Christians for the soul about to leave its mortal body. The bell was also popularly believed, says Grose, "to drive away the evil spirits who stood at the bed's foot and about the house, ready to seize their prey, or at least to molest and terrify the soul in its passage, but by the ringing of the bell (for Durandus informs us evil spirits are much afraid of bells) they were kept aloof, and the soul, like a hunted hare, gained the start, or had what is by sportsmen called law. Hence, perhaps, exclusive of the additional labor, was occasioned the high price demanded for tolling the greatest bell of the church, for. that being louder, the evil spirits must go farther off to be clear of its sound, by which the poor soul got so much more the start of them; besides, being heard farther off, it would likewise procure the dying man a greater number of prayers."

After the Reformation and until the time of Charles II. the passing bell was still retained. In the "Advertisements for due Order" passed in the seventh year of Queen Elizabeth occurs the following: "Item, that when anye Christian body is in passing, that the bell be tolled, and that the curate be speciallie called for to comforte the sick person; and after the time of his passinge to ring no more, but one shorte peale, and one before the buriall, and another shorte peale after the buriall." Bishop Hall thus apologized for the preservation of the custom: "We call them soul bells, for that they signify the departure of the soul, not for that they help the passage of the soul."

The number of strokes of the passing bell was usually so regulated that hearers might determine the sex and social condition of the dying or dead person. Thus, the bell was tolled once for a child, twice for a woman, and thrice for a man.

Passion Play. The Oberammergau Passion Play is the most celebrated, although by no means the sole, survival of the mediæval Mysteries now existing in Christendom. In the Middle Ages the clergy endeavored to give to religious rites, especially to those connected with Easter and the other great festivals of the Church, a highly dramatic character, and did not hesitate to add to the popular interest in these sacred representations by all kinds of buffoonery and burlesque, in which the devil and his imps played the part of clowns. There were performances called "Diableries," in which only devils in the garb of harlequins appeared, and which bore about the same relation to the ordinary Mystery that the ballet in the modern theatre does to what is called the legitimate drama.

The jests which these histrionic troupes from the infernal regions indulged in and often improvised, and in which the peccadilloes of priests were not spared, were óften very obscene, but always amusing to the multitude. Indeed, in the more serious plays the conversations in heaven were coarse and unseemly. In 1210, Pope Innocent III. tried in vain to suppress the performances, and forbade the use of churches and ecclesiastical vestments for such purposes; the only result of this prohibition was that they were held out of doors in temporary buildings erected in front of the churches and attracted larger throngs than ever before.

Even the Reformation did not abolish them. Both Luther and Melanchthon favored the dramatization and representation of Biblical subjects. "These spectacles," says the Reformer in his "Table-Talk," "strike the imagination of the people through their eyes and move them far more powerfully than public preaching." He then adds, "If Christians avoid the theatre on account of the coarse jests and indecencies which the plays contain, the same scruple should prevent them from reading the Bible."

Hans Sachs, the friend of Luther and the poet of the Reformation, in his "Comedy of Eve's Unequal Children" is guilty of as gross incongruities and anachronistic absurdities as can be found in any Papal Mystery.

As is well known, the Passion Play of Oberammergau originated in vows taken by the pious villagers in 1633 that if the pestilence then devastating the mountain valley should be stayed, they would give, every ten years, a representation of the Passion of our Saviour "for the grateful reverence and edifying contemplation of the public." The chronicler relates that, in consequence of this solemn pledge, "no more died of the plague, albeit the plague-marks were upon many when the vow was made." Such sacred plays were at that time still quite common, and were regarded as highly meritorious acts of piety, like building a church, founding a cloister, endowing an altar, or going on a pilgrimage to the shrine of some saint. That the vow of the Oberammergauers took this form was due to an impulse of artistic feeling developed and transmitted through many generations in a community of wood-carvers.

With the growth and diffusion of the spirit of modern civilization these relics of mediævalism gradually withdrew from the lowlands into the highlands, like rude aborigines taking refuge in the mountains from the advance of a superior invading foe. It was not uncommon for these Passion Plays to last two or three days, and one was given in 1514 at Botzen, in the Tyrol, the representation of which took a whole week. Early in the present century an earnest effort was put forth by the ecclesiastical authorities in Southern Germany to suppress what was regarded as the scandal of the Passion Plays. When, in 1810, a deputation from Oberammergau came to Munich to obtain the usual permission to give such representation, the Bavarian government refused to grant it. As this request had been hitherto considered a mere form, the peasants were taken by surprise, and after vainly beseeching the highest dignitaries of the Church to revoke their decision, and meeting only with rude rebuffs, they applied directly to the king, the good-natured and paternal Max Joseph, who received them graciously, and finally acceded to their desire, on condition that the play should be purged from everything that might be an occasion of offence.

The old mediæval text was accordingly subjected to a thorough revision by a Benedictine monk, and later another priest gave it its present unity of design and of religious doctrine, as well as its present perfected form of dramatic action,—the latest adapter avowing that " the labor was performed for the love of the divine Redeemer, and with but one object in view, the edification of the Christian world." Edward Devrient, a well-known German actor and critic, was the first to call public attention to the play in Germany in 1851, and the general reading public of America first heard of its existence six or eight years later, when the novel of " Quits," by the Baroness Tautphœus, published in 1857, devoted an entire chapter to Oberammergau and its sacred drama.

Until about 1830 the performances were given in the open air and in the village churchyard, but now they take place in a vast theatre and upon a platform which is partly covered by a roof; beyond and about this artificial stage the on-lookers get occasional glimpses of natural scenery, which, when the weather is favorable, add greatly to the interest and realism of the play. " During the entire representation," wrote Hans Christian Andersen in 1860, " we had had alternate rain and wind, all the while cloudy weather; but by chance, just as the Christ was lowered into the grave, the sun broke forth, and illumined the stage, the spectators, the whole surroundings. Birds sang and flew, here and there, over us. It was a moment one never forgets."

An especially curious variant of the old Mystery Plays still recurs annually in the Roman Campagna during Holy Week. The whole population of every village takes part. In the first place a despairing woman is seen wandering about the streets crying, in tones of agony, " My Son! my Son!" and covering her face with her blue mantle. She is followed by the crowds in the streets, who ask, " What is it?" " The Madonna has lost her Son," comes the answer. As the multitude pass down every street and alley of the place, all the windows of the houses along the road are thrown open, and questions and answers are exchanged between those within and those outside. Then those inside the houses wring their hands, tear their clothes, and untie their hair, while the Madonna's cry of " My Son! my Son!" fills the air. The Madonna stops at every house, and asks, " Have you seen him? Oh, if you are mothers, answer me." Sometimes an answer comes, " Yes, I am a mother; bless my children!" and the Madonna kisses them on the forehead. Sometimes, in her despair, she falls on her knees and prays aloud, while those around her kneel, beat their bosoms, and recite the Lord's Prayer.

By and by a boy runs to the Madonna from afar. His face is dirty, his feet are muddy, and he wears a long white robe, with paper wings tied to his shoulders. He is an angel, and has come from above to tell the Madonna that he has seen the Saviour. "He was alone, talking to himself, and had a gold hoop on his head. There he is!" says the boy. "There he is! He is coming here!" The Saviour kneels to his mother, who raises him and clasps him in her arms. Jesus wears a red tunic and a blue mantle. His hair is long, and he has a beard. A crown of gold paper encircles his head. After this comes the death of the Madonna, who is carried into the little church on a carpet of herbs and flowers. Four tapers burn round her, and she has lilies in her hand and a golden crown upon her head. At dawn two angels descend from heaven and stand by the altar. They wear helmets of gold paper, and are dressed in white robes. Their feet are bare, and they carry wooden swords and tin shields.

Then the young girls of the place raise the body, which is an image made of straw, with the head, hands, and feet of stucco. The eyes are of glass, and the hair is red and curled in several rows. The body is covered with a white satin robe embroidered with gold; the feet are covered with silk stockings and satin shoes, and a blue mantle, bestarred with silver, falls from the shoulders. Thus attired, the image is placed in a crystal coffin, and before this is closed every one whispers a wish in the Madonna's ear, and the children promise her that they will be good.

Every day during Passion Week the Christ is being tormented and persecuted. But during the few moments' peace which his persecutors grant him he goes about comforting those who are suffering. He is accompanied by St. John the Baptist, who wears a goat's skin and carries a stick in the shape of a cross. At the corner of every street Jesus stops and tells a parable in the dialect of the place. He also gives little sermons in dialect. He educates, advises, and comforts all who go to him. (*London Vanity Fair*, April, 1897.)

The most extraordinary of all Passion Plays is performed in certain remote parts of the Territory of New Mexico by an order of Indian converts which is an offshoot from Spanish Catholicism but is now looked at askance by the Church. This is known as The Penitent Brothers (Los Hermanos Penitentes). They make their head-quarters at the little village of Taos, New Mexico.

All during Holy Week they inflict cruel self-torture upon themselves. On a hillock at some distance from the "morada," or brotherhood house, is planted a cross to represent Calvary. Day after day processions march thither and back again, the members doing penance before the cross by lashing their backs and applying thorny cactus to their bare flesh. The crowning event occurs on Good Friday. From many applicants a victim is selected to represent Christ. The parts of Peter, Pontius Pilate, Mary, and others are assigned to other applicants. At two o'clock a procession starts slowly on foot for "El Calvario." All are barefoot. Many are naked from the hips up. Half-way up the hill the "Christ" joins the procession. His only garment is a cotton or muslin sheet draped around his body. A crown of cactus thorns is pressed around his bleeding forehead. A cross of huge timbers is placed upon his back, and, bowed low under his burden, he takes his place at the head of the procession. The man pants and gasps at times, but never looks up or speaks. On the way a pathway of broken stones has been made, and the most devout Penitentes walk over these with bare feet and never flinch. The counterfeit Christ is spit upon by any and all. Little boys and girls run ahead that they may more deliberately spit in his face and throw stones upon his bending form.

When El Calvario is reached, the great, clumsy cross is laid upon the ground and the actor of Christ is seized and thrown upon it. The assemblage joins in a chorus of song while several Penitentes lash the man's arms, hands, and legs to the timbers with cords of cowhide. The bands are made as tight as the big muscular vaqueros and ranchmen can draw them. The ligaments sink into the flesh, and even cut so that blood runs out. The arms and legs become blue and then black under the awful binding, but not so much as a sigh escapes the lips of the actor. He repeats in a mixed dialect of Spanish and Indian the words uttered by Christ at Calvary, and bids his brothers to spare him not.

When all is ready a dozen men lift the cross and its human burden, and, carrying it to an excavation near at hand, they drop the base in the earth. The hole is quickly filled, and the Penitentes gather about the foot of the cross with uplifted faces. The women weep, and the children look on dumfounded. Some of the men mock and jeer the man on the cross; others throw clods of sunbaked earth at him, and still others, feeling that they must have some part in the physical agony of the afternoon, call upon the multitude to lash and beat them. The invitation is never in vain, for there are strong arms and hands ever glad to lay the lash on the backs of the fanatics and to provide leaves of cactus to apply to the swollen and bleeding flesh.

In several localities in Colorado and New Mexico it was once the practice to nail the hands of the acting Christ to the timbers of the cross, but the Catholic priests of this generation put a stop to that.

After the first half-hour of noise and flagellation about the cross at El Calvario the excitement dies away. The crucified man, whose arms and legs are now black under the bands, must be suffering indescribable pain, but he only exclaims occasionally in Spanish, "Peace, peace, peace," while the Penitentes, who have had no part in the self-abnegation and punishment, prostrate themselves silently about the cross. A motion of the hand from the Pietro, and the spectators bow their bared heads in reverential attitude.

Save for the hysterical sobbing, moaning, and suppressed sobs of the women, there is now not a sound.

At sunset the procession is re-formed, and slowly wends its way back to the village. Some twenty of the leading Penitentes remain behind, and when the spectators and others have gone away they lift the cross from the earth and lower its burden. The cords of cowhide are removed, and the pseudo-Christ, who is now probably unconscious from long and dreadful bondage, is lifted from the timbers.

Then, following the narrative of the scenes on Calvary, the body of the actor is wrapped about with a mass of white fabric and is carried to a dug-out cave in the hill-side near at hand. Several women, who have been appointed to impersonate Mary and Martha, follow some distance behind, all the time violently weeping and lamenting.

In the cave the bleeding and tortured body of the chief actor is rudely nursed to strength.

But it has sometimes happened that it never gives any sign of life and is never seen in public after it is carried into the "morada."

Passover, or **Pesach,** known also as the **Feast of Unleavened Bread.** The first and one of the most important of the festivals in the Jewish ecclesiastical year. It begins on the 14th of the first month, Nisan (roughly corresponding to portions of March and April in the Christian year), and lasts for eight days. It commemorates the deliverance of Israel through the tenth and last plague, when God destroyed the first-born of Egypt (Exodus xii.). In Biblical times all males were bound to go up to Jerusalem to keep the Passover and make their offerings to God in the temple.

The first day is given to preparation. All leaven and leavened bread is banished from the house, and the matzes (*q. v.*) are substituted. To insure the removal of every kind of fermented food or liquor, the master of the house is in duty bound to make a strict search throughout the house on the eve of the 14th of Nisan. This is therefore called the Eve of Searching for Leaven.

THE FIRST PASSOVER.

Strict silence must be maintained during the search. After the master has gathered every crumb he can see, he declares that if any leaven remain it shall be null and accounted dust of the earth. About ten o'clock on the following morning all the leaven that was gathered must be burned.

On the 14th the Paschal lamb is slain, in commemoration of the lamb which God commanded the Israelites to slay when about to deliver them out of bondage and whose blood they sprinkled on the door-posts of their houses to protect their first-born from the destroying angel. In allusion to the latter fact, the first-born male child if he be above the age of thirteen fasts for twenty-four hours before the great meal of the 14th of Nisan.

This begins at nightfall, and marks the real beginning of the season, inasmuch as the Jewish day is measured from nightfall to nightfall. The table is set with three matzes, or passover cakes of unleavened bread, placed on a dish, each covered separately; a dish containing part of the shank-bone of the lamb, roasted, symbolical of the Paschal offering; a dish containing a roasted egg, the symbol of creation and fecundity, the usual festival sacrifice; a dish of charosheth, or chopped-up apples, almonds, and other fruit, representative of the mortar used by the Israelites in Egypt; and a cup of vinegar or salt water, and the green tops of horseradish or other bitter herb, which are eaten with charosheth in commemoration of the bitter oppression suffered by the Israelites. Our roast lamb with mint sauce, it may be added in parenthesis, is the direct descendant of the Paschal lamb and its attendant bitter herbs.

Four cups of wine must be drunk at special parts of the service, each draught having its own symbolism; the cup must have at least the capacity of an egg and a half. At a solemn moment, the tallest goblet is filled to the brim, the doors are thrown open for the prophet Elijah, who may appear to announce the coming of the Messiah, and the words are said, " Blessed is he that cometh in the name of the Lord." Historians have traced this custom of opening the doors to the necessity of asking non-Jews to look in and see for themselves that no blood of Christian child was used in the ceremonial,—a monstrous charge which was often made. (See HUGH, ST.) The Jews believe that they are specially under the care of God at Passover. Some leave their doors open at night, as a token of trust in the Divine guardianship.

At this time every Hebrew father is a king in his household; he reclines on a throne, sometimes an easy-chair with pillows on the arms. As a sign of freedom, the celebrants lean on the left side when they drink the wine or take anything to eat from the Seder dish. One-half of the middle cake in the plate is broken by the father; the other half, the " Afikuman," is reserved until

after supper. Sometimes the mother or one of the children pre-
tends to steal the "Afikuman," and surrenders it to the father
when he promises to grant whatever is desired.

When every member of the household touches the dish containing the lamb bone and the egg, all recite together, "Lo, this
is the bread of affliction which our ancestors ate in the land of
Egypt; let all those who are hungry enter and eat thereof, and
all who are in distress come and celebrate the Passover. At
present we celebrate it here, but the next year we hope to celebrate it in the land of Israel."

After the removal of the lamb bone, the youngest son asks
the reasons for the celebration, and he is answered by a recital
of the Haggadah, or Agadah, an account of the slavery under
Pharaoh and the deliverance from Egypt, with digressions concerning Haman, Daniel, and the wise men of Bona Berak. In
the homes of the wealthy this is often read from illuminated
manuscripts; the poor usually have printed books with quaint
wood-cuts representing the miracles in Egypt, Moses burying
the Egyptian, and other incidents of the narrative. At the
mention of each plague the finger is dipped in wine and the
drops sprinkled over the shoulder, in repudiation of the ten
plagues of Egypt, which have been cabalistically magnified to
two hundred and fifty.

On the 15th of Nisan the counting of Omer (see SHEBUOTH)
begins, and is continued for forty-nine days. The first two and
last two days of the festival are kept by all Jews as strictly as
the Sabbath, but on the four intervening days urgent business
may be attended to. On the seventh day of the festival the
description of the passage of the Red Sea is read from Exodus,
together with the song chanted by Moses and the children of
Israel on that occasion.

In Biblical times the 14th day of the month Yiar was observed as the Second Passover by such as were unable to keep
the proper date on account of sickness or of unavoidable absence
from home.

Patrick, St. (Lat. *Patricius;* Fr. *Patrice*), patron of Ireland,
whose festival on March 17 is celebrated by Irishmen wherever
they may happen to be. There is no other great saint in the
Catholic hagiology about whom so much uncertainty exists. It
is not even known whether March 17 is the date of his death or
of his birth, though it is sometimes said to be both. The year
and the place of his nativity are matters of dispute. Indeed, so
many conflicting legends have been woven into his story that it is
now generally assumed there were two or more St. Patricks who
have been rolled into one. Patricius, the Latin name, simply

means a patrician, and may have then been the *sobriquet* of any Christian apostle of aristocratic lineage. Nevertheless that there was some one commanding personality towards whom all the myths naturally gravitated is evident. This was probably the author of two brief fifth-century tractates, — one entitled his "Confession," the other his "Letters to Coroticus." According to the best authorities, this Patrick was born about A.D. 386 in the village of Nemphthur, just outside of Glastonbury, England. His father was a decurion, or town councillor. The favorite legend, however, makes him a native of Tours, in France, and a nephew of St. Martin. From the Confession itself we learn that in his sixteenth year he was carried away by pirates and taken to the north of Ireland, where he was sold as a slave. That he eventually became a noted Christian evangelist to the heathen in Ireland and rose to the rank of bishop is certain, but that he is the same person who helped to Christianize the west of Scotland and the Isle of Man is improbable.

Opinions differ as to the exact time when Bishop Patrick began his ministrations in Ireland, but as to his immediate success there is abundant testimony offered by the old legends and more modern historians.

He was a statesman as well as a priest, and addressed himself first of all to the chiefs, and through them reached the people. He understood, as did most of the early Christian missionaries, how to adapt the superstitions and the pagan rites which he found existing to the teachings of the Church, and one of his first doings was to light a Paschal fire on the Hill of Slane in opposition to a Druidical fire on the Hill of Tara, and the light from Slane eclipsed the light on Tara forever. His work in Ireland may be summed up by saying that he founded three hundred and sixty-five churches and planted a school by the side of each; that he organized at least one archiepiscopal see, that of Armagh, consecrated two or more bishops, established one or two colleges, and civilized the people generally.

The most popular of the legends regarding St. Patrick is that which gives him credit for driving all the snakes and similar vermin out of Ireland. Not only has it maintained its vitality better than many a sober truth could have done, but it has been strengthened and improved by successive generations of story-tellers and miracle-mongers. The story as current to-day is told in one of the most popular of Irish songs, from which the following is an extract:

> There's not a mile in Ireland's isle where the dirty vermin musters;
> Where'er he put his dear forefoot he murdered them in clusters.
> The toads went hop, the frogs went flop, slap dash into the water,
> And the beasts committed suicide to save themselves from slaughter.

Nine hundred thousand vipers blue he charmed with sweet discourses,
And dined on them at Killaloo in soups and second courses.
When blindworms crawling on the grass disgusted all the nation,
He gave them a rise and opened their eyes to a sense of the situation.

The Wicklow Hills are very high, and so's the Hill of Houth, sir;
But there's a hill much higher still—ay, higher than them both, sir;
'Twas on the top of this high hill St. Patrick preached the sarmint
That drove the frogs into the bogs and bothered all the varmint.

It seems that St. Patrick, wherever he went, was always preceded by a drum, and the noise thus made attracted the people. In this the example of the saint appears to have been imitated by the modern Salvation Army. As Patrick was terribly in earnest, so was his drummer,—if he had a drummer, for the chronicles are rather vague as to this point, and sometimes we might infer that he whacked away at the instrument himself. At all events, just before going up to the hill to preach the sermon that was to finish the snakes the drum was beaten so vigorously that it burst. The theme and object of the discourse had been announced to the people, so they had assembled in great multitudes to see the miracle performed. As they had an idea that a good deal of Patrick's power lay in his drum, they were sadly disappointed at the accident, especially as a big black snake was seen gliding down the hill with his jaws distended, a leer in his ugly eyes, and a tremor in his whole body as if it were convulsed with laughter. But, as the story goes, an angel came down and patched up the drum, the sermon proceeded, and all the reptiles vanished as if by magic.

St. Patrick died at Saul, a place not far from Downpatrick, and in the abbey of the latter town his body was buried, amid the sorrow of the whole people. He had long looked forward to death as a release from care and as a reward for his labors and trials. He had become blind and feeble. The saint's age at the time of his death has been the subject of very many intricate and ingenious calculations, and the estimates have run anywhere between eighty-eight and one hundred and twenty-one years.

It is impossible to say when the 17th day of March in each year began to be set apart as St. Patrick's Day and observed as the popular holiday of Ireland. But, whatever may have started it, there can be no doubt that the day is a national holiday in Ireland and is observed with much enthusiasm, and that it renews and intensifies the patriotism of the people. In most of the large cities of America it is celebrated by a parade through the streets of the Irish national societies and other citizens of Irish birth or blood.

In Ireland itself the celebration is less formal, but more universal. The shamrock is worn everywhere, in commemoration of the fact that when St. Patrick was preaching the doctrine of the Trinity he made use of this plant bearing three leaves upon one stem as a symbol of the great mystery. In every household a plateful of the herb is placed upon the breakfast-table of the "master" and the "mistress," who are expected to "drown the shamrock" in generous draughts of whiskey and then send the bottle down into the kitchen for the servants. In Dublin the higher classes conclude the festivities of the day by attending a great ball in St. Patrick's Hall, Dublin Castle. None can be admitted who have not been presented and attended the viceroy's drawing-room; and of course every one must appear in court dress or full uniform. In the smaller hamlets the local inn used to be a place of universal resort for young men. A "Patrick's pot" of beer or whiskey and a small allowance of oaten bread and fish to each were benevolently contributed by the host. All additional orders had to be paid for. "The majority of those who sought entertainment at the village inn were young men who had no families, whilst those who had children, and especially whose families were large, made themselves as snug as possible by the turf fire in their own cabins. Where the village or hamlet could not boast of an inn, the largest cabin was sought out, and poles were extended horizontally from one end of the apartment to the other; on these poles, doors purposely unhinged, and brought from the surrounding cabins, were placed, so that a table of considerable dimensions was formed, round which all seated themselves, each one providing his own oaten bread and fish. At the conclusion of the repast they sat for the remainder of the evening over a 'Patrick's pot,' and finally separated quietly." (HONE: *Every Day Book*, vol. ii. p. 386.)

Patrick, Purgatory of St. According to mediæval legend, there was an entrance to purgatory in a cave on the island of Lough Derg, Ireland. This was widely known as the Purgatory of St. Patrick, because it was to that saint that Christ revealed its existence, informing him that any one might go down into it who had the courage, and it should be for him as if he had passed through purgatory after death. The saint is said to have built a monastery about the entrance and to have secured the way with a strong iron gate. The fame of this spot was largely owing to a poem by Henry of Saltrey (*circa* 1153), which described the adventures of a certain Sir Owayne Miles, who took this opportunity of expiating his crimes and saw many and wonderful sights in the course of his pilgrimage to the nether world. The poem was translated into nearly all European languages, and it may have furnished Dante with a hint for his great work. Other visits to the cave are recorded at rare intervals. A few of the visitors published accounts of what they had seen and heard, which bore a great resemblance to the poem of Henry of Saltrey; others confessed that they had seen nothing wonderful with their waking eyes, but on falling asleep had been visited with wonderful dreams, " different from those they were accustomed to in their chambers." At last, in 1496, a monk from Holland visited the place and reported to the Pope that it differed in no respect from an ordinary cavern, whereupon the Pope ordered it to be destroyed, and the order was carried out on St. Patrick's Day, 1497. The myth of St. Patrick's Purgatory undoubtedly owes its origin to the hell-descents prevalent among all heathen nations.

Patron Day. In Ireland and formerly in Catholic England the day of the saint to whom the parish church had been dedicated was called the Patron Day. This anniversary was one of the most important of all the festivals within the parish. Clergy and laity would meet within the church to implore the continual protection of the patron saint. In the churchyard the graves were cleared of weeds and adorned with flowers, the funeral dirge was renewed, and the worthy actions of the dead were recounted. Booths were erected here also, from which provisions were distributed by the charitable to those who had come from a distance to attend the services. The celebration was often extended over two or even three days. But after the Reformation in England the exercises of devotion at such meetings gradually gave way to profane amusements, and at last the Patron Day (or wake, as it was often called) was abolished in that country. In Ireland it continued with ever diminishing importance until 1846, when the first great failure of the potato crop and the consequent immigrations from Ireland commenced a revolution in the traditionary customs of the Irish peasantry. At present there are only a few parishes where the Patron Day is observed.

An interesting description of a Patron Day, or, as it is there called, a Consecration Feast, in the Bavarian Highlands is thus given by an eye-witness: "In the morning mass is read in the chapel. Gayly adorned, the little procession winds up the narrow steps, a red flag flutters among them, and every one wears his holiday attire. Of course but a few enter the low portal, which is hung with garlands; the rest remain grouped in the open air, and listen to the tones of the 'Agnus Dei' or the words of the sermon. When the host arrives, the people fall on their knees. These are calmly joyful moments; the brook rolls itself more gently, the beeches themselves cease their murmurs.

"Thus ends the spiritual portion of the affair. But after mass come the pleasures of the world, with the joyful voice and the insolent strength of youth. The musicians lead the little procession, which descends from the little church; the lads pull their hats waggishly on one side, and the lasses come down with a lighter step than they went up. All sorts of things are going on below, for the entrance of the house has become a bar; great casks stand ready, and are broken open with the hammer; forms of lofty stature, carrying their jackets upon their shoulders, watch the operations with satisfaction; and, in reality, there is no time to be lost for the first draught; the dance may commence at any minute; for the latter a flooring of planks has been laid down. Only a slight tap on the shoulder, and the fair maid follows her lad into the tumult with joyful mien. Between approving glances and aggressive hobnail shoes she steers skilfully; but, when a daring youth snatches at the scarlet flowers she wears in her bodice, she quickly casts down her eyes, and vanishes before he is aware of it.

"As consecration comes but once a year, dancing is kept up pretty late; when the stars begin to pale, then return home is first mentioned; most of the girls ascend the same night to the pastures from which they came, and the wood-cutters go straight away from the feast to their work at four o'clock in the morning."

In many Italian villages, especially in those within the limits of the old Papal States, the feast of the local patron saint is the event of the year, and is chosen not only as a day of prayer but also as one of family rejoicing. The "military" turn out and bring their band to church with them; petards are fired off in quick and deafening succession during the most solemn parts of the mass; the fair outside the church doors deals largely in devotional mementos of the patron saint, and the lemonade-and fruit-stalls are besieged in proportion as the beads and fruits are sold. At night a general illumination takes place; Bengal fires are lit in every open place, and turn fitful colored gleams upon the rickety structure of church and cottage, while the peasants dance and sing in harmless glee, making this day a holiday for the body as well as for the soul.

Paul Pitcher Day. The eve of St. Paul's Day, or January 24, is thus called by the tinners of Cornwall from a custom they have of setting up a water-pitcher and pelting it with stones until it is broken. The men then leave their work and adjourn to a neighboring ale-house, where a new pitcher bought to replace the old one is successively filled and emptied, and the evening is given up to merriment and misrule.

On inquiry whether some dim notion of the origin and meaning of this custom remained among those who still keep it up, it was found to be generally held as an ancient festival intended to celebrate the day when tin was first turned into metal,—in fact, the discovery of smelting. It is the occasion of a revel, in which there is an open rebellion against the water-drinking system which is enforced upon them whilst at work.

The boys of Bodmin used to parade the town with broken pitchers, and into every house where the door could be opened or had inadvertently been left so, they would hurl a "Paul's pitcher," exclaiming,—

> Paul's Eve,
> And here's a heave.

According to custom, the first heave could not be objected to, but a repetition brought just punishment down upon the offender, if he could be caught.

Paul, St. According to tradition, the great apostle to the Gentiles was beheaded on the same day that St. Peter was crucified, June 29, and the day is known as that of St. Peter and St. Paul. But whether it was the same year, A.D. 64, or the next, is a matter of dispute. Paul has a separate feast on January 25, the anniversary of his conversion.

The church of San Paolo delle tre Fontane, near Rome, is built over three fountains which are said to have sprung up at the three places where the head of St. Paul fell and bounded after being cut off by the executioner. It is said that the waters vary in warmth, the first, where the head fell, being hottest, while the two others, commemorating successive bounds, are cooler and cooler. The body of St. Paul was originally interred on the spot where now stands the church of San Paolo fuori le Mura, between the Ostian Gate and the Aqua Salvia, but according to one legend it was removed with that of St. Peter to the Catacombs and laid in the same tomb during the reign of Heliogabalus. Two hundred years later the Oriental Christians endeavored to secure them, but the Roman Christians contended for them with success and removed them to the church of the Vatican, placing them together in a magnificent shrine which still remains in St. Peter's.

The feast of St. Paul's Conversion, January 25, was formerly kept in London as a great processional occasion, especially during the reign of Queen Mary, who saw in it a symbol of the conversion of the realm back to the true faith. In the "Chronicle of the Grey Friars of London" we are told that on January 25, 1555, "there was a general procession, with the children of

all the schools in London, with all the clerks, curates and parsons and vicars, in copes, with their crosses, also the choir of
St. Paul's ; and divers bishops in their habits, and the Bishop of
London, with his pontificale and cope, bearing the sacrament
under a canopy, and four prebends bearing it in their grey
amos : and so up into Leadenhall, with the mayor and aldermen
in scarlet, with their cloaks, and all the crafts in their best
array; and so came down again on the other side, and so to St.
Paul's again. And then the king, with my lord Cardinal, came
to St. Paul's, and heard masse, and went home again, and at
night great bonfires were made through all London, for the joy
of the people that were converted likewise as St. Paul was
converted."

Among agriculturists all over Great Britain and Western
Europe the feast had especial significance as a prognosticator of
the weather for the entire ensuing year. This fact is the more
remarkable as the day was ranked among the old almanac-
makers as a *dies Ægyptiacus,* or unlucky day. The special
knowledge of the future which it was believed could be derived
from it was thus laid down in monkish Latin :

> Clara dies Pauli bona tempora denotat anni ;
> Si nix vel pluvia, designat tempora cara ;
> Si fiant nebulæ, pereunt animalia quæqua ;
> Si fiant venti, designat prœlia genti.

There are several extant translations of these lines into French
and English. Here is one of the English versions :

> If St. Paul's Day be fair and clear,
> It does betide a happy year;
> But if it chance to snow or rain,
> Then will be dear all kind of grain ;
> If clouds or mist do dark the sky,
> Great store of birds and beasts shall die;
> And if the winds do fly aloft,
> Then war shall vex the kingdom oft.

Peer, Swearing in a New. This is one of the drollest customs connected with Parliamentary usage. In the House of
Commons when a new member is to take his seat everybody is
cognizant of the matter and may be on hand to see and to congratulate. But a new peer drops into the House of Lords with
a pretty air of accident, though the presence of Garter King-
at-Arms and the bringing forth of the red cloaks slashed with
ermine testify to a certain amount of preparation. The first
intimation of the event that strangers receive is to behold passing under the doorway to the left of the throne a little procession. Spiritual peers are usually escorted by the Primate and

the Bishop of London, lay peers by the Prince of Wales and the Duke of Norfolk, hereditary Earl Marshal. In all cases behind them walk Black-Rod and Garter King-at-Arms. Lay peers wear their scarlet gowns, their precise rank being indicated by the varying number and disposition of the bars of ermine.

The sponsors of the new peer lead him up in the first place to the woolsack, whereon is seated the Lord Chancellor in full-bottomed wig and gown, staring at vacancy. When addressed the latter gives a little start of surprise, receives from the new peer a document purporting to be his summons to sit as a peer in Parliament, and waves him over to a table where a clerk stands ready to swear him in.

Then Garter King-at-Arms takes the lead of the procession. Supposing, as most frequently happens, the new-comer is a baron, he is led to the barons' seats, situate near the bar, remote from the woolsack. The ordinary way there is straight enough. But Garter King-at-Arms knows better than to violate all precedent. Leading the procession towards the bar as if making straight for the barons' seats, he suddenly takes a turn to the right at the cross benches, the new peer immediately behind him, his sponsors following in single file, Black Rod bringing up the rear. Having made the full circuit of the benches in this part of the house, Garter King now heads for the barons' benches, the red-cloaked pack close behind him, as if the game were follow-my-leader. Skipping up the gangway, Garter King stops short of the topmost bench, passing along in front of it. In nine cases out of ten the new peer, however well drilled, attempts to follow him. But that is the wrong turn, and Garter King, knowing what would happen, is ready to direct the novice to take the next turn higher up, which lands him on the topmost seat. All this is in dumb show. Safely seated, the peer and his sponsors turn their heads, which they have covered with their three-cornered hats, towards the woolsack. Three times a mutual salute of solemn hat-lifting passes between the Chancellor and the noble trio. Then the latter move back to the woolsack, the new peer is formally introduced to the Chancellor, kisses the latter's hand, and so passes out of the doorway, presently to reappear in every-day clothes.

Penny Hedge, Planting the. A curious custom still observed in Whitby, Yorkshire, on the eve of Ascension Day. It is thus described in an extract from the *Whitby Gazette* of May 28, 1870, quoted in Dyer's "British Popular Customs." "The formality of planting the penny hedge in the bed of the river Esk on Ascension Eve was performed on Wednesday last by Mr. Isaac Herbert, who has for fifty years discharged this onerous duty. The 'nine stakes,' the 'nine strout-stowers,' and the 'nine gedders' have all been once more duly 'planted.' The ceremony was witnessed by a number of ladies and gentlemen, and that highly important functionary, the bailiff of the lord of the manor, Mr. George Welburn, of Fylingdales, was present, and blew the usual malediction, 'Out on you! Out on you! Out on you!' through the same identical horn which seventeen centuries ago roused with its lugubrious notes, on Ascension Eve, our ancestors from their peaceful slumbers. Whether the wood was cut at the 'stray head,' and with a 'knife of a penny price,' we are not able to say, but a good hedge was planted; and although each stake may not be quite 'a yard from another,' the hedge will doubtless be of such strength as to withstand the effect of the prescribed number of tides."

Peter, St. The chief of the apostles, and, according to the claims of the Catholic Church, the first Bishop or Pope of Rome. His martyrdom, together with that of St. Paul, is celebrated on June 29. But his great feast is in August, known as the feast of St. Peter's Chains. Another festival, the Feast of the Chair of St. Peter, takes place on January 18 in honor of his formal establishment of the episcopate in Rome.

To the gospel story tradition adds that St. Peter confounded Simon Magus, a famous magician among the Jews, by miracles far excelling all his sorceries. Simon endeavored to buy from the apostle the secret of how these were done. Peter indignantly spurned him. Then Simon destroyed his books and fled to Rome, where he became a favorite of Claudius and again of Nero. Peter also came to Rome, and afterwards Paul. Again rivalry broke out between the magician and the apostles. At last Simon attempted to fly to heaven. He launched himself from a tower, and for a time was supported by a demon, but Peter knelt and commanded the fiend to release his hold, when Simon fell to earth and was dashed to pieces. In the church of St. Francesca Romana at Rome there are two stones let into the wall bearing a double depression said to be the marks of Peter's knees made on this occasion. During the first persecution the Christians besought St. Peter to save himself by flight, which at first he consented to do. As he was leaving Rome by the Appian Way in the early dawn, he met Jesus Christ. Casting himself at the feet of his Master, he asked him, "Domine, quo vadis?" ("Master, whither goest thou?"). To which the Lord replied, "Venio iterum crucifigi" ("I am coming to be crucified again"). Penitent and ashamed, Peter returned to the city and met his fate. The chapel of Domine quo Vadis, on the Appian Way, commemorates the scene and preserves the legend.

St. Peter and St. Paul were both thrown into the Mamertine prison. Here the centurions who guarded them and many prisoners were converted. A miraculous fountain, still extant, sprang up at Peter's prayer to furnish water for the baptism. There is also still shown in the prison the impression of St. Peter's head made in the wall when a jailer struck him. The chains with which the saint was bound are preserved in the church of San Pietro in Vincoli in Rome in a bronze tabernacle, and are exhibited on the festival of St. Peter in Vinculis on August 1. The reputed date of the martyrdom both of St. Peter and of St. Paul is June 29, A.D. 64.

Paul, as a Roman citizen, was beheaded. But Peter, because he was of low degree, was led out and across the Forum and over the Sublician bridge, up to the heights of Janiculus. He was then very old and weak, so that he could not carry his cross, as condemned men were made to do. When they had climbed more than half-way up the height, seeing that he could not walk much

farther, they crucified him. He said that he was not worthy to suffer as the Lord had suffered, and begged them to plant his cross with the head downward in the deep yellow sand. The executioners did so. The Christians who had followed were not many, and they stood apart, weeping.

When he was dead, after much torment, and the sentinel soldier had gone away, they took the holy body, and carried it along the hill-side, and buried it at night close against the long wall of Nero's circus, on the north side, near the place where they buried the martyrs killed daily by Nero's wild beasts and in other cruel ways. They marked the spot, and went there often to pray.

ST. PETER'S MARTYRDOM.

Thirty years later, Anacletus, a Pope who had been ordained priest by St. Peter, built a little oratory over the grave. That, it is said, was the beginning of St. Peter's Church. But Anacletus died a martyr, too, and

the Popes after him all perished in the same way up to Eutychi-
anus, whose name means something like "the fortunate one" in
barbarous Greek-Latin, and who was indeed fortunate, for he
died a natural death. But in the mean time certain Greeks had
tried to steal the holy body, so that the Roman Christians carried
it away for nineteen months to the Catacombs of St. Sebastian,
after which they brought it back again and laid it in its place.
And again after that, when the new circus was built by Heliogabalus in 219, they took it once more to the same Catacombs,
where it remained in safety for a long time.

Then came Constantine, who is said to have laid the foundations of the old church of St. Peter's, which afterwards stood
more than eleven hundred years until it was replaced by the
present basilica. He built it on the site of Nero's circus and
over the little oratory of Anacletus. It was not till the days
of Honorius, however, that the body of St. Peter was taken
from the Catacombs and brought back for the last time, with
great concourse and ceremony, and laid where its dust still rests
in a brazen sarcophagus.

The famous bronze seated statue of St. Peter in the great
basilica at Rome, whose great toe is now nearly worn out by the
reiterated osculations of centuries, has been a subject of much
antiquarian dispute. Assertions have freely been made that it is
a statue of Jupiter Capitolinus, and much heavy fun has been
excited by ringing the changes on *Punch's* Punch-like pun of
Jew Peter. But Mr. F. Marion Crawford, an excellent authority
himself, claims that the weight of modern authority and artistic
judgment is to the contrary:

"The work cannot really be earlier than the fifth century,
and is therefore of a time after Honorius and the disestablish-
ment. Any one who will take the trouble to examine the lives
of the early Popes may read the detailed accounts of what each
one did for the churches. It is not by any means impossible
that the statue may have been made under St. Innocent I., a
contemporary of Honorius, in whose time a Roman lady called
Vestina made gift to the Church of vast possessions, the proceeds of which were used in building and richly adorning numerous places of worship. In any case, since it is practically
certain that the statue was originally intended for a portrait
of St. Peter, and has been regarded as such for nearly fifteen
hundred years, it commands our respect, if not our veneration."

The practice of dressing up this statue in magnificent robes
on the feasts of St. Peter is connected with the ancient Roman
custom which required the censors, when entering upon office,
to paint the earthen statue of Jupiter Capitolinus a bright red.
But the connection lies in the Italian mind and character, which

cling desperately to external practices for their hold upon inward principles. It is certainly not an inheritance of uninterrupted tradition, as Roman church music, on the contrary, most certainly is; for there is every reason to believe that the recitations now noted in the Roman missal were very like those used by the ancient Romans on solemn occasions.

On St. Peter's Day (August 1) the services are similar to those of Easter. But the congregation is different. Instead of the irreverent Easter tourists, rushing, pushing, laughing, and talking as if entering an opera-house, the seats are thinly occupied by a sprinkling of men and women, habited mostly in black, and of peasants in gaudy attire, all of whom show by their respectful demeanor that they have come to pray and not to stare.

Perhaps there is nothing more beautiful than the illuminations and fireworks with which St. Peter's Day is celebrated at Rome. Chief is the illumination of St. Peter's. "The whole of this immense church—its columns, capitals, cornices, and pediments, the beautiful swell of the lofty dome towering into heaven, the ribs converging into one point at top, surmounted by the lantern of the church, and crowned by the cross—all are designed in lines of fire; and the vast sweep of the circling colonnades, in every rib, line, mould, cornice, and column, is resplendent with light. On the cross of fire at the top waves a brilliant light, as if wielded by some celestial hand, and instantly ten thousand globes and stars of fire roll along the building as if by magic, and blaze into a flood of glory. It seems the work of enchantment. One would suppose the illumination to be complete, but ten thousand lamps are still to be illumined. Their vivid blaze harmonizes beautifully with the milder light of the lanterns; while the brilliant glow of the whole illumination sheds a rosy light upon the fountains, whose silver fall and ever-playing showers accord well with the magic of the scene. Viewed from Trinità de' Monti the effect is unspeakably beautiful; an enchanted palace seems to be hung in the air, called up by the wand of some invisible spirit. The *girandola* or fireworks from the castle of St. Angelo are equally magnificent. They begin with a tremendous explosion, representing the eruption of a volcano. Red sheets of fire seem to blaze upward into the glowing heavens, and then to pour down their liquid streams upon the earth. This is followed by a complicated display of every varied device that imagination can figure, one changing into another, and the beauty of the first effaced by that of the last. Hundreds of immense wheels turn round with a velocity that almost seems as if demons were whirling them, letting fall thousands of hissing snakes, scorpions, and fiery dragons, whose long convolutions, darting forward as far as the eye can reach in every direction, at length vanish into air. Fountains and jets of fire throw up their blazing cascades into the skies. The whole vault of heaven shines with vivid fires, and seems to receive into itself innumerable stars and suns, which, shooting up into it in brightness almost insufferable, vanish like earth-born hopes. The reflection in the calm, clear waters of the Tiber is scarcely less beautiful than the spectacle itself; and the whole ends in a tremendous burst of fire that almost seems to threaten conflagration to the world." Such is the account of the celebration of St. Peter's Day at Rome given by the author of "Rome in the Nineteenth Century." Apart from these illuminations there are religious ceremonies, which are conducted with all the pomp which marks the ceremonial of the Roman Church in her chief seat.

" One of the most remarkable incidents which occurred during my long residence in Rome," says a contributor to *Blackwood's Magazine* in May, 1829, "was the refusal of Naples, in 1788, to yield the accustomed annual homage to the vicegerent of Christ. In 1787, on the festival of St. Peter, I had seen this ceremony performed with all its accustomed pomp. The papal guards paraded in the piazza of St. Peter's; the white horse, the representative symbol of Naples, was led into the church by Prince Colonna; the Pope was borne in an elevated throne to the great nave, where the well-trained horse bent his knees before him in homage, while a purse of ducats, the yearly tribute of the kingdom of Naples, was humbly offered to the Holy Father.

" On this occasion, however, the scene was widely different. The King of Naples had refused to acknowledge any longer his subjection to the Pope, offering at the same time to pay him the value of a horse, that he might purchase one, but declaring that never again should a white horse, in behalf of the kingdom of Naples, bend its knees to him in homage.

" Notwithstanding this mortifying refusal, the papal guard paraded as usual in the piazza, and the Pope was carried on his lofty throne into St. Peter's; but, alas! no white horse appeared to do him homage. When the Holy Father arrived at the spot where the horse had formerly knelt before him, a formal protest was read against this insulting refusal of the King of Naples, followed by a declaration that, notwithstanding this refusal, the Pope reserved all his rights and claims to the accustomed homage, &c., &c.

" It was truly a piteous spectacle to see the head of the Romish Church returning, in his throne, for the first time, without the homage of horse and man, so long annually offered to him on St. Peter's Day. The Holy Father, who had previously exhausted himself by a speech in the Consistory of Cardinals, looked unusually pale and infirm. There was, I thought, an air of mortified humility about him as he dispensed the benediction, and it appeared to me that he sought to excite, by his mien and gesture, a popular feeling for his insulted dignity. The Romans, however, evinced no sympathetic indignation, nor indeed any feeling but mortification that the evening fireworks, always hitherto given on this occasion, would be discontinued."

In England June 29 is known as St. Peter's Day, and local survivals of ancient Catholic customs are not uncommon. The most peculiar of these is at Nun-Monkton, in Yorkshire. It is thus described by a correspondent of *Notes and Queries*, Fourth Series, vol. i. p. 361:

"The feast-day of Nun-Monkton is kept on St. Peter's Day, and is followed by the 'Little Feast Day,' and a merry time extending over a week. On the Saturday evening preceding the 29th a company of the villagers, headed by all the fiddlers and players on other instruments that could be mustered at one time, went in procession across the great common to 'Maypole Hill,' where there is an old sycamore (the pole being near it), for the purpose of 'rising Peter,' who had been buried under the tree. This effigy of St. Peter, a rude one of wood, carved no one professed to know when, and in these later times clothed in a ridiculous fashion, was removed in its box-coffin to the neighborhood of the public house, there to be exposed to view, and, with as little delay as possible, conveyed to some out-building, where it was stowed away and thought no more about till the first Saturday after the feast-day (or the second if the 29th had occurred at the back end of a week), when it was taken back in procession again, and re-interred with all honor, which concluding ceremony was called 'Buryin' Peter.' In this way did St. Peter preside over his own feast. On the evening of the first day of the feast, two young men went round the village with large baskets for the purpose of collecting tarts, cheese-cakes, and eggs for mulled ale, all being consumed after the two ceremonies above indicated. This last good custom is not done away with yet, suppers and, afterwards, dancing in a barn being the order while the feast lasts."

Peter's Chair, St. It was an ancient custom observed by churches to keep an annual feast of the consecration of their bishops, and especially of the founding of the episcopate in them. The Feast of the Chair of St. Peter is found in ancient martyrologies, and is celebrated on January 18, because St. Peter is said on this day to have taken the throne of his episcopate in Rome. An ancient wooden seat, said to be that of St. Peter, is preserved in the Vatican.

On this solemn festival, which is celebrated in the church of

St. Peter at Rome, the Pope used to be borne in his pontifical chair of state on the shoulders of twelve men, attired in vestments of gold and wearing the tiara. On each side of the Pope was carried a large fan of ostrich feathers into which were set the eye-like portions of peacocks' feathers, symbolical of vigilance and universal supervision.

Peter's Pence, or **Rome-Scob.** (Lat. *Denarius Sancti Petri.*) The tax formerly paid annually to the See of Rome, now collected as a voluntary offering in every church of Catholic Christendom. The date, following the ancient precedent, is usually on the feast of St. Peter in Vinculis. The earliest documentary evidence of it seems to be the letter of Canute (1031) sent from Rome to the English clergy and laity. Among "the dues which we owe to God according to ancient law" the king names "the pennies which we owe to Rome at St. Peter's [denarii quos Romæ ad Sanctum Petrum debemus], whether from towns or vills." Hence the tax must have been one of ancient standing in the time of Canute. But its exact origin is a matter of dispute. Matthew Paris in his "Two Offas" ascribes the grant to Offa, King of Mercia, who reigned from 755 to 796, and says that it was paid for the support of the English school and hostel at Rome. He adds that it was one silver penny for every family occupying land worth thirty pence a year. On the other hand, Layamon the poet ascribes the institution to Ina, King of Wessex, who abdicated in 728. Eventually it became general throughout England, being imposed on any family possessing twenty pence' worth of goods of any kind. It was extended to Ireland under the bull granted by Pope Adrian to Henry II., and was subsequently introduced into Poland, Prussia, and Scandinavia, though the Papal legates could never succeed in getting it paid regularly. Gregory VII. failed in his attempt to exact it from France and Spain. In England it seems to have been paid more or less regularly till the reign of Henry VIII., but for some time previously it had been regarded as only a charity and was not enforced from the people. The Peter's Pence of modern days is a purely voluntary offering, made by the faithful and taken up under the direction of their bishop for the maintenance of the Holy See.

Philip, St. (It. *Filippo.*) Patron saint of Brabant and Luxemburg. His festival is celebrated on May 1 by the Roman and on November 14 by the Greek Church. St. Philip was born at Bethsaida. Little is told of him in the Gospels, but legend relates that after the Ascension he preached in Scythia and then travelled to Hierapolis in Phrygia. Here he found the people worshipping a huge dragon as a personification of Mars. He held up the cross and bade the dragon to disappear, whereupon it crawled out from beneath the altar and sent out such a frightful odor that many persons, among them the king's son, fell dead. Philip restored them to life, and the dragon disappeared. The priests of the dragon were so enraged that they bound Philip to a cross and stoned him to death.

Polycrates states that he was buried at Hierapolis in Phrygia. An arm of St. Philip, it is said, was brought from Constantinople to Florence in 1204. His body is said to be in the church of SS. Philip and James in Rome. In art St. Philip is represented as a man of middle age with a scanty beard and a benevolent face. His attribute is a cross, or a staff with a small cross at the top.

Philip Neri, St. (It. *Filippo Neri*), founder of the Oratorians. His festival is celebrated on the day of his death, May 26 (1595).

St. Philip Neri was born in Florence in 1515. When eighteen years old he went to Rome as tutor in a noble family. He became the friend and almoner of St. Charles Borromeo, and was influential in the religious movements of his time. He gathered about him young men of family and learning who devoted themselves to charity, and from them he founded the order of Oratorians. They were bound by no vows, and did not seclude themselves from the world. The son and heir of the Massimi family, in which St. Philip was tutor, fell ill, and the saint asked him if he was willing and resigned to die. The boy replied that he was. "Go in peace," said St. Philip, and the boy, it is said, immediately expired. On the 16th of March of each year the Palazzo Massimi at Rome is decorated for a festival in honor of this event, and the Pope sometimes officiates at the services. St. Philip died in 1595, after a long life devoted to the poor and the sick. He is buried in a chapel at Florence, and many miracles are reported as having taken place at his tomb. He was canonized by Gregory XV. in 1622.

Pilgrimage. In the Catholic Church, a religious discipline which consists in making a journey to some place in order to adore the relics of a saint or to visit the scene of some event in sacred history. Among the ancient Romans pilgrimages were made to pagan shrines, such as that of Jupiter Tyrius at Gades, of Jupiter Capitolinus at Rome, of Apollo at Delphi, and of Diana at Ephesus. The pilgrimages of the Jews to Jerusalem at the time of the great festivals were matters of precept and obligation. Pilgrimages are still performed by Mohammedans to Mecca, Medina, Jerusalem, etc., and by Hindoos to a large number of sacred places.

Catholic authorities carefully differentiate Christian from pagan pilgrimages. As Arnold and Addis point out in their "Catholic Dictionary" (*s. v.*), the latter usually proceed on the assumption that the power of the divinity whose help is sought is locally circumscribed, but that within the limits of his own jurisdiction it is indefinitely great. The Christian creed, according to which " God is a spirit," to be sought and found " not specially on this mountain, nor yet at Jerusalem," but wherever the true worshippers approach him in spirit, might seem at first sight to afford little encouragement to pilgrimages. " Nevertheless, so certain is it that religious impressions, blunted and weakened by the daily business of the market-place and the street, require in most minds to be often graven afresh (and that by means of impulses from without, for it would be vain to trust to the sufficiency of those coming from within), that the Church has from the first, while admitting the danger of abuses and taking measures to prevent them, approved the use of pilgrimage to holy places as a very potent help and incentive to a holy life. She also favors the practice, because she recognizes the undoubted fact that God has often granted, and still grants, interior and exterior favors, graces, and miracles, at particular places or shrines, to honor certain mysteries, saints, etc."

The first recorded pilgrim is St. Alexander, who in the third century is said to have visited Jerusalem in fulfilment of a vow. But from the letters of Paula and Eustochium (included among those of St. Jerome) it would appear that from the date of the Ascension to their own time a continual stream of pilgrims had resorted to the Holy Places.

The custom reached its height about the eleventh and twelfth centuries, when it was followed by all classes of society from kings to peasants. The Church granted privileges and indulgences to those who visited certain places of devotion, and many made it their calling in life to go from one shrine to another.

The more famous shrines towards which the currents of pilgrimage have set strongly are the Holy Places in Palestine (see Church of the Holy Sepulchre and Church of the Nativity), the various shrines of the Blessed Virgin, as Walsingham in England, Einsiedeln in Switzerland, Chartres, Fourvières, and Lourdes in France, Mariazell in Germany, Loreto in Italy, Guadalupe and Montserrat in Spain, and Guadalupe in Mexico, and the shrines of saints and angels, such as St. Michael's at Monte Gargano, Italy, and in France, the English St. Thomas of Canterbury, St. Andrew in Scotland, St. James at Compostella, and many others.

Despite the vigilance of the Church, abuses undoubtedly crept into the mediæval pilgrimages. A curious example came out during the examination for heresy of William Thorpe by the Archbishop of Canterbury in 1407.

" Ungracious lousel!" said the archbishop, addressing his victim, " thou favorest no more truth than an hound. Since, at the road at the north door at London, at our lady at Walsingham, and many other divers places in England, are many great and praisable miracles done, should not the images of such holy saints and places be more worshipped than other places and images where no such miracles are done ?"

Thorpe was accused by Archbishop Arundel of having asserted that " those men and women who go on pilgrimages to Canterbury, to Beverley, to Walsingham, and to any other such places, are accursed and made foolish, spending their goods in waste." Thorpe, in effect, admits such to be his opinion, and in justifying himself is led into the following lively description of what the fashionable pilgrimages of the time really were.

" Examine," he says, " whosoever will, twenty of these pilgrims, and he shall not find the men or women that know surely a commandment of God, nor can say their *Pater-noster* and *Ave-Maria*, nor their *Credo*, readily in any manner of language. The cause why that many men and women go hither and thither now on pilgrimages, is more for the health of their bodies than of their souls; more to have riches and prosperity of this world than to be enriched with virtues in their soul; more to have here worldly and fleshly friendship than for to have friendship of God and of his saints in heaven."

He contends that such persons as these, who spend much money and time in seeking out and visiting the bones or images of this or of that saint, do that which is in direct disobedience to the commands of God, inasmuch as they waste their goods partly upon innkeepers, many of whom are women of profligate conduct, partly upon rich priests, who already have more than they need.

" Also, sir," he concludes, " I know well that when divers men and women will go thus after their own wills, and finding out one pilgrimage, they will ordain with them [arrange with one another] before to have with them both men and women that can well sing wanton songs, and some other pilgrims will have their bagpipes; so that every town they come through, what with the noise of their singing, and with the sound of their piping, and with the jangling of their Canterbury bells, and with the barking out of dogs after them, they make more noise than if the king came there away with all his clarions and many other minstrels."

" Lewd wasel!" replied the archbishop, determined at all risks to defend all this unseemly merriment, " thou seest not far enough in this matter. I say to thee that it is right well done that pilgrims have with them both singers and also pipers, that when one of them that goeth barefoot striketh his toe upon a stone and hurteth him sore, and maketh him to bleed, it is well done that he or his fellow begin then a song, or else take out of his bosom a bagpipe, for to drive away with such mirth the hurt of his fellow. For with such solace the travel and weariness of pilgrims is lightly and merrily brought forth."

The archbishop was evidently of the mind of the host in Chaucer:

> Ye gon to Canterbury—
> The blissful martyr quitte you your meeds;
> And wel I wot, as ye gon by the way,
> Ye shapen you to talken and to play;
> For truely comfort ne mirth is none
> To riden by the way dumb as the stone.

Pilgrimages to Rome are still kept up with many of the old usages by the inhabitants of Italy and the neighboring countries. These are generally made at Easter, but sometimes on St. Peter's Day or the anniversary of the Pope's election, when the illumination of St. Peter's is repeated as on Easter Sunday.

The great hospital of the Holy Trinity is thrown open for a week to the pilgrims, who are there fed and housed by thousands. A confraternity of ladies and gentlemen, both Roman and foreign, have the management of this charity, and wear a distinctive costume while engaged in these hospitable duties. This consists of a scarlet apron of common twill with a cross on the shoulder, the garment covering the figure entirely in its spreading folds, and resembling a dressing-gown in shape and amplitude. Men and women alike wear this, and so arrayed serve their guests in separate wards of the vast building. During the day they may be seen guiding them to the different shrines of the city, and in the vast and gloomy recesses of St. Peter's.

Every evening the scene at the hospital is the same, but only the newly arrived pilgrims are admitted to the Lavanda (*q. v.*), or "washing of the feet." This custom is very ancient, and used to be much more extensively carried out than at present. Even in our day, at least during Holy Week, its observance involves no sinecure. The pilgrims of course have made all or the greater part of their journey on foot, and the *chaussure* of many of them is extremely primitive, such modern improvements as shoes and stockings being replaced by long linen bands swathed about the feet in coils full twenty or thirty yards long, until a sufficient thickness is reached to protect the flesh against the inequalities of Italian mountain roads. Still these mummy-like swathings are not wholly proof against the continued friction of stones and sticks, so that when the wayfarers arrive at the hospital these rags are often soaked in blood and clotted dust. The pilgrims are immediately led to a basement room furnished with a low continuous wooden settle skirting the wall, and numberless wash-basins with coarse soap and strong towels to each. The members of the confraternity accompany them, and, removing their bandages, carefully wash their sore and bleeding feet in warm water.

This washing of the feet is continued throughout the evening by some portion of the members, as there are always enough pilgrims to refill the basement room as fast as it is emptied. Those whose feet have been washed are then conducted to a long refectory full of deal tables with coarse white table-cloths, where an ample supper of bread and meat is provided. After the meal the remnants are thus disposed of: every pilgrim cuts open a small loaf, and, taking out the greater part of the crumb, eats it at once, thus making room for the remainder of his or her portion of meat, which is kept over and serves for breakfast in the morning. When all have been cared for, a procession is formed of the total number of guests, and the members of the confraternity lead them to the vast, airy dormitories, where they help the old and infirm to bed. Litanies and hymns are sung in the mean while, and a more peaceful, orderly scene can hardly be imagined. This institution, though not so old as some other hospitals, yet brings to one's mind the similar but probably ruder establishments of the early Middle Ages. The hospital built by good King Ina of the West Saxons in the seventh or eighth century, and served by himself in person, was one of these, and was specially devoted to the Saxon pilgrims who in those ages of faith readily undertook the toilsome journey to Rome. This pilgrimage would sometimes be made as an act of expiation for violence done to a neighbor, sometimes as a pledge of future good conduct or a thanksgiving for some boon obtained by prayer. When pilgrims began to fail, scholars took their place, and young and needy boys were collected in the hospital and lodged gratis, while they picked up an education hap-hazard at the lectures of the different colleges of Rome. Gradually the hospital itself was transformed into a college, and, though destroyed in one of the ruinous invasions of Rome by pagan and undisciplined hordes, nevertheless survived as an institution, being rebuilt by the Saxons and becoming the germ of the present English College. All other nations had the same national hospitals for pilgrims, all under the special protection of their respective sovereigns; and most of these underwent the same wise transformation into colleges when the needs of the age made learning the *summum bonum* in the eyes of the rising generation.

Religious pilgrimages are much in vogue among the Hindoos. Besides the ordinary festivals observed in most of the temples, to which all the pious of the adjoining districts flock, there are special festivals at particular places—such as the great festivals at Ramisseram, held at intervals of twelve and sixty years respectively—to which pious Hindoos flock from a great distance. Attendance at the car-festival at Juggernaut is thought to emancipate the soul at death from the evils of future birth. Sacred spots and places are likewise made the objects of pilgrimage. Such is Hurdwar, where the Ganges emerges from the Himalaya into the plains; such are the holy cities of Benares and Allahabad; such also is the spot in Southern India where Sita, the consort of Rama, went through the ordeal of fire to test her conjugal purity. At this latter spot multitudes flock together from every part of India, on the auspicious occasions, to bathe in the sea, in the full belief of attaining special favor from heaven. There is a temple at Gungotri, far up in the Himalayas, to which pilgrims resort, though they find there no other shelter than a few wooden sheds, and caves in the adjoining cliffs. Kedernath, in the same snowy locality, is also visited by pilgrims; and here a score of devotees annually sacrifice their lives, either by precipitating themselves from a certain precipice, or by proceeding into the snowy mountain-wastes until they perish from cold and hunger. Still higher in the mountains, and consequently deserted for half the year, is another goal of pilgrimage, the lonely temple of Badrinath,—standing with its glittering gilded spire and balls amidst the snows, with the icy peaks of Roodroo Himala towering above it to the height of twenty-three thousand feet. The great object of all Hindoo pilgrimages is to obtain purification from past sins and exemption in the future life from transmigration. These pilgrimages often occupy months in the performance, and to meet their expenses the Hindoo sometimes borrows money at high interest, pledges his jewels, etc., and becomes impoverished for life. Thousands never return, perishing by the way, and leaving their bodies to be devoured by the vulture and the jackal. But their fate deters no one,—so great is the glory of those who return in safety. Shaving all the hair off their heads and bodies, and rubbing themselves with holy ashes, the returned pilgrim devotees march stark naked through the town, accompanied by flags and music, and followed by crowds of admiring young people of both sexes, who offer to them incense and presents, say prayers to them, and regard them as superior beings. To the Hindoos, it has been truly said, immortality is not so much a belief as a *certainty*. In consequence, the present life appears a smaller thing to them than to any other people in the world; and what is it to risk the fleeting breath of earthly life in pilgrimages, when the spiritual recompense is believed to be so great, and when the personal ovation upon return is so excessively flattering and so full of worldly advantages?

Pillar, The. (Sp. *El Pilar.*) The name popularly given to one of the cathedrals in Saragossa, Spain, on account of the holy pillar preserved here. According to legend, the apostle James (*q. v.*), when preaching the gospel in Spain, fell asleep on the site of this church, October 12, A.D. 40. During his sleep the angels caught up the Virgin Mary, then dwelling in Palestine, transported her to Saragossa on a jasper pillar, and carried her back again, after she had desired him to raise a chapel on the spot. St. James awoke, and, lo! the pillar stood before him as an evidence that his dream was true. The chapel was built, and to it the Virgin often came afterwards to mass.

The holy pillar is kept covered up with a casing in a chapel in the centre of the cathedral. At the back there is a hole in the casing, through which the faithful may, kneeling, peep at and kiss the sacred marble. Here a large dent is worn by multitudinous labial devotion. The marble steps are also foot- and kiss-worn. An image of the Virgin and Child carved in dark wood surmounts the pillar. All around the shrine are suspended votive offerings, mostly models in wax or silver of afflicted members healed by the intercession of the Virgin. October 12, the anniversary of her descent, is the greatest festival of Saragossa. Then pilgrims of all ages and both sexes crowd in from the neighboring country and even from the remotest parts of Spain. The battle-hymn of the Aragonese soldiers used to run as follows:

> La Virgen del Pilar dice
> Que no quiere ser Francesca,
> Que quiere ser capitana
> De la gente Aragonesa.

("The Virgin of the Pillar says that she does not wish to be a Frenchwoman, that she wishes to be a captain of the Aragonese people.")

Pinkster Day. (From Dutch *Pinkster,* "Pentecost," or Whit-sunday.) A holiday, or often a series of holidays, celebrated at Whitsuntide in Colonial and early New York, and to some extent in Pennsylvania and Maryland. Nowhere was it a greater festival than in Albany, especially among the negro population, to whom it was eventually abandoned by the whites. Capitol Hill, which was the centre of the celebrations, was then universally known as Pinkster Hill. Here the booths and sports were opened on Whitsun Monday, white curiosity-seekers being on that day the chief visitors. On Tuesday the blacks all appeared. Great was the consumption of gingerbread, cider, and apple-jack. But the chief feature was the dancing, an evident importation from Africa. Munsell tells us that for nearly fifty years the leader was a darky known as Old King Charley, said to have been a prince in his own country and to have survived to the age of one hundred and twenty-five. "On those festivals, old Charley was dressed in a strange and fantastical costume; he was nearly barelegged, wore a red military coat trimmed profusely with variegated ribbons, and a small black hat with a pompon stuck on one side. The dances and antics of the darkies must have afforded great amusement for the ancient burghers. As a general thing, the music consisted of a sort of drum, or instrument constructed out of a box with sheepskin heads, upon which old Charley did most of the beating, accompanied by singing some queer African air. Charley generally led off the dance, when the Sambos and Phyllises, juvenile and antiquated, would put in the double-shuffle heel-and-toe break-down." From other authorities it seems that the dance was called the Toto Dance, and partook so largely of savage license that it gradually came to be shunned by respectable whites. In 1811 the Common Council of Albany prohibited the erection of booths, as well as all dancing, gaming, and drinking, on Pinkster Day. The enforcement of this statute eventually drove the holiday out of existence.

Cooper in his "Satanstoe," a tale of Colonial New York, calls Pinkster the great Saturnalia of the blacks. "Although this festival is always kept with more vivacity at Albany than in York, it is far from being neglected, even now, in the latter place." He tells us that it lasted three days, the negroes flocking for miles around to what is now City Hall Park. In Brooklyn, it seems, they gathered around the old market near the ferry.

"On Long Island," says Alice Morse Earle in her "Colonial Days in New York" (1896, p. 199), "the Dutch residents also made the day a festival, going to pinkster fields for pinkster frolics, exchanging visits and drinking schnapps, and eating 'soft-wafels' together. About twelve years ago, while driving through Flatlands and New Lots one beautiful day in May, I met a group of young men driving from door to door of the farm-houses, in wagons gayly dressed with branches of dogwood blossoms, and entering each house for a short visit. I asked whether a wedding or a festival were being held in the town, and was answered that it was an old Dutch custom to make visits that week. I tried to learn whence this observance came, but no one knew its reason for being, or what holiday was

observed.   Poor Pinkster! still vaguely honored as a shadow, a
ghost of the past, but with your very name forgotten, even
among the children of those who gave to you in this land a
name and happy celebration!"

Plough Monday.   The first Monday after Epiphany (*q. v.*)
is still celebrated under this name in some parts of rural England and Scotland.   Anciently it marked the farmer's resumption of the severer arts of husbandry after the Christmas dissipa-
tions, just as St. Distaff's Day marked his good wife's return to
her domestic vocations.   In Catholic times the ploughmen kept
lights burning before images in the churches, so as to secure a
blessing upon their work, and went about in procession from
door to door begging money ostensibly for the support of their
plough-lights.   The Reformation put a stop to the lights, but
not to the collection, which was now frankly and openly spent
in the tavern.   New details had been added year by year to the
Plough procession, as it was called, until by the sixteenth and
seventeenth centuries, when the festivities reached their final
development, they formed quite an elaborate affair.

A plough called the Fool Plough, bedizened with ribbons and
other decorations, was dragged through the streets or roads by
thirty or forty ploughmen similarly decorated, and with their
shirts over their jackets.   In front strode one of their number
fantastically attired as an old woman, who was known as Bessy.
A fool with his fool's-cap, a masker wearing a fox's skin over
his head, and a band of morris-dancers or other mummers, occasionally attended the vanguard.   Then followed a procession of
as many ploughmen as cared to join, and frequently threshers
carrying their flails, reapers bearing their sickles, and carters
with long whips.   Bessy, jumping and dancing, rattled a box as
a stimulus to votive offerings, and the rest followed, making all
the noise they could.   At the larger farms ale and other refreshments would be given, as well as money.   Even the smaller cottagers threw a few pence into Bessy's box.   Woe to any substantial householder who refused.   The ground in front of his house
would be ploughed up by the angry yokesmen and left brown,
bare, and ridgy.

Tusser's "Five Hundred Points of Husbandry" alludes to a
rivalry on this day between ploughman and servant-maid which
still has its local survivals.   Tusser's words are,—

> Plough Munday, next after that twelf-tide is past,
> Bids out with the plough ; the worst husband is last.
> If plowman get hatchet or whip to the skrene,
> Maids loseth their cocke, if no water be seen.

Which are thus explained in "Tusser Redivivus" (1744, p. 79): "After Christmas (which formerly, during the twelve days, was a time of very little work), every gentleman feasted the farmers, and every farmer their servants and task-men. *Plough Monday* puts them in mind of their business. In the morning, the men and the maid-servants strive who shall show their diligence in rising earliest. If the ploughman can get his whip, his plough-staff, hatchet, or anything that he wants in the field, by the fire-side, before the maid hath got her kettle on, then the maid loseth her Shrovetide cock, and it wholly belongs to the men. Thus did our forefathers strive to allure youth to their duty, and pro-vided them with innocent mirth as well as labor. On this Plough Monday they have a good supper and some strong drink." (See also *Every Day Book*, 1826, vol. i. p. 71.)

In the northern counties of England a custom formerly pre-vailed on Plough Monday that if a ploughman came to the kitchen-hatch and could cry, "Cock in the pot," before the maid could cry, "Cock on the dung-hill," he was entitled to a cock for Shrove Tuesday. (*Notes and Queries*, Second Series, vol. i. p. 386.)

In Northamptonshire, according to Baker's "Northampton-shire Words and Phrases" (1854, ii. 1257), there used to be a custom on this day that when the ploughman returned from his labors in the evening the servant-maid would meet him with a jug of toast and ale; and if he could succeed in throwing his plough-hatchet into the house before she reached the door, he was entitled to a cock to throw at Shrovetide; but if she was able to present him with the toast and ale first, then she gained the cock.

In the city of London the first Monday after the Epiphany was once a great state among the civic dignities, as being the day on which was held "the Great Court of Wardmote," for the purpose of receiving presentments from the several wardmote inquests and of swearing in constables. The aldermen were summoned to attend at the Guildhall in their scarlet gowns, and the lord mayor came in state from the Mansion House, accom-panied by the sheriffs. In the evening his lordship entertained the officers of his household. The great silver bowl was intro-duced at the end of the banquet filled with punch, and "pyra-mids" of cakes and sweetmeats placed on the table with the dessert. Such as were not eaten by the guests were removed and divided into parcels for them to take home, in addition to which there was formerly given a piece of twelfth cake in a separate parcel. The custom of dividing the sweetmeats and cakes was continued down to the mayoralty of Samuel Wilson in 1839, but the twelfth cake was frequently omitted, and in that year the division of the sweetmeats, etc., was also done away with. The practice, however, both as to the sweet cakes and the slice of twelfth cake in a separate parcel, appears to have been again in force ten years later.

"At the present day," says the *London Athenæum*, January 5, 1889, " the Great Court of Wardmote continues to sit for the purpose of receiving returns of elections of members of the Common Council for the various wards of the City (the election itself having taken place on St. Thomas's Day, viz., December 21 preceding), for hearing objections to any election, and for swearing in ward beadles, the city marshal, and extra constables not under the jurisdiction of the commissioner of police. All presentments of nuisances, etc., have ceased to be made to this court. The lord mayor still entertains the officers of his household, but extends his hospitality to a large number of clerks employed in the various offices of the Corporation. In place, however, of the twelfth cake and sweetmeats, each guest is presented with a box containing biscuits or preserved fruit, the box itself being sufficiently handsome, according to the taste and liberality of the lord mayor, to be afterwards converted to some useful purpose. A bowl of punch is always a conspicuous feature at this entertainment."

Plymouth Rock. A famous rock or ledge on which the Pilgrims are believed to have landed when they first stepped from their boats in the harbor of what is now Plymouth, Massachusetts. (See FOREFATHERS' DAY.) The tradition that this is the identical rock was handed down from father to son. In 1741 Elder Thomas Faunce, then an old man of ninety, came to make public protest against any injury to the rock from the building of a wharf, mentioning that it had been pointed out to him by some of the original Pilgrims.

A circumstance which adds force to the tradition is that, in spite of Mrs. Hemans and her description of "the stern and rock-bound coast" of Plymouth Bay, this stepping-stone of the Forefathers is almost the only rock of any size to be found on these sandy shores. It is uncertain whether Elder Faunce and his forebears had in mind the landing of the exploring expedition of seventeen men which took place December 21, or that of the entire party from the Mayflower on January 4, 1621. But the former date is the one generally accepted, and the two events have become mingled into one in the popular imagination.

In 1774 the rock was a passive, but none the less an important, factor in a stirring scene. British oppression had aroused the spirit of the old colony. The descendants of the Pilgrims determined to consecrate anew the stone which their forefathers had hallowed. On October 5 five thousand freemen assembled in Plymouth with the intention of removing the Rock to the centre of the Town Square. But while they were raising it in its bed it split in two. The colonists paused in dismay. Then a quick-witted whig hailed the omen as a sign of a speedy sundering of the British Empire. The suggestion was hailed with enthusiasm. The upper half was dragged by twenty yoke of oxen, amid thunders of applause, to the square in front of Pilgrim Hall. There it remained until 1880, when it was replaced on the original boulder in what is now Water Street. Over the reunited fragments rises a canopy of dressed stone supported by four columns. In the top of this are the bones of some of the original settlers, removed from Coles's Hill.

Polycarp, St., Bishop of Smyrna. His festival is celebrated on January 26.

St. Polycarp was converted to Christianity in the year 80, when quite young. He was a pupil of St. John, and was consecrated Bishop of Smyrna by him in the year 96. In the sixth year of the reign of Marcus Aurelius that Emperor ordered a persecution of the Christians throughout his dominion. The Christians of Smyrna were made to fight with wild beasts for the amusement of the populace. Polycarp was advised to withdraw from the storm, and he concealed himself for a time at a short distance from the city. The officers bribed one of his servants to reveal his hiding-place, and horsemen were sent by night to capture the saint. He received the soldiers with great courtesy, and set out refreshments for them with his own hand. On the way back to Smyrna the soldiers tried in vain to get him to recant. He was given another chance by the proconsul while the soldiers were preparing the stake at which he was burnt alive. But Polycarp steadfastly refused to recant, and so expired at the stake. The martyrdom occurred in the year 167. Soon after his death one of his followers, Irenæus, wrote an account of his life and death, and some of his congregation met together to settle as to how they should commemorate his memory. They agreed that they should solemnly keep the day of his martyrdom every year, which they called his " birthday." This is probably the origin of keeping saints' days. St. Polycarp's tomb is still shown near Smyrna.

Pope Ladies. A species of buns sold in Hertfordshire, England, on the feast of the Annunciation. This is a custom that dates from a remote antiquity. A legend thus accounts for their origin. A noble lady and her attendants were benighted while travelling on the road to St. Albans. Lights in the clock tower at the top of the hill guided their steps to the monastery, and the grateful lady gave a sum of money to provide an annual distribution to the poor on Annunciation or Lady Day of cakes baked in the form of ladies. As this bounty was distributed by the monks, the Pope Ladies probably thus acquired their name. At the time of the Reformation the dole came to an end, but the local bakers continued to bake and sell buns made on the same pattern.

Popinjay, Festival of the. (Fr. *La Fête du Papegai*, the latter word being probably a corruption of the Italian *pappagallo*, "a parrot.") The papegai was generally a pigeon roughly carved in wood and set up on some high tower or other eminence. He who shot it away needed considerable skill, whether he used bow or arrow, as in the early days, or later a clumsy gun resting upon a high stand. He received the title of King of the Papegai, which he bore during the year, together with a silver chain from which hung medals of all the former kings of the Papegai, as well as a more substantial reward in the shape of an allowance for the year of his royalty.

The festival of the Papegai was until quite a recent period celebrated at St. Malo in Brittany on the first Sunday in Lent. It was introduced there by the good Duchess Anne herself.

Early in the fifteenth century it was no empty honor to be King of the Papegai and decorated as such by the duchess, for the town granted him an allowance varying in value from three hundred to five hundred dollars, a very considerable sum in those days.

The festival of the Popinjay was one of the many importations which the French alliance brought into Scotland. Readers of "Old Mortality" will remember with what ceremony Lady Margaret Bellenden went to attend the festival in the county of Lanark on a May morning in the year 1679, and of the shock her pride received at the discomfiture of Goose Gibbie. Sir Walter says that the custom prevailed in Ayrshire down to his own time.

Pradakshina. A ceremony of almost universal use in Brahminical as well as in Buddhist ritual. This means going round with the right shoulder to the centre, which is the same turn as that given to the prayer-wheel (*q. v.*). Towns and fields and smaller objects are circumambulated in this manner, with blessing both to the devotee and to the object of his devotion. The great pilgrimage of the Panch-Kosi at Benares, one of the most important observances of the Hindoos, is simply a long pradakshina performed around that city. Here the circuit lengthens out about fifty miles. As an every-day instance Mr. Simpson in " The Buddhist Praying-Wheel" cites the case of a Hindoo whom he saw making a pradakshina around a tulsi plant, which is held sacred to Vishnu. " It was growing on a mud pedestal carefully prepared for it, and around this he walked a number of times, with his right hand to the centre."

CIRCUMAMBULATING THE TULSI PLANT.
(From Simpson's " The Buddhist Praying-Wheel.")

He found that to go round in the opposite direction, or with the left hand to the centre, was the rule at death-ceremonies. It was on other occasions productive of evil.

Now, it puzzled him to find that among the Semites, both Moslems and Jews, the custom is generally that of going round with the left side turned to the centre. He gives a tentative explanation that as in India the left hand to the centre is the rule in connection with the dead, the Semitic custom may have become the stereotyped rule from the practice of worshipping at tombs, which is known to be still a marked feature of Moslem faith. The Kaaba at Mecca, for example, is built in the semblance of a huge tomb, and the Moslem performs his pradakshina around it in the reverse direction.

From the East Mr. Simpson turned his attention to the West. He found an extraordinary parallel to the pradakshina in the

Highlands of Scotland, where there is a custom now well-nigh extinct, but once extremely prevalent, known as the deisul (*q. v.*) or deasil.

The bonfires which in many parts of Great Britain and the European continent are still lighted on St. John's Eve and other occasions furnish more analogies. It is frequently the custom for the celebrants to dance around them in a sunwise direction. Torches are revolved rapidly, so as to give the appearance of a circle of fire. Burning disks are whirled into the air. Wheels and barrels are eagerly sought for, lighted, and rolled down-hill as globes of fire. Blazing torches, barrels, or disks are carried around a field or a town in order to bless it and keep it from harm during the ensuing season.

Nay, may we not find another survival in the custom, well-nigh universal among gamblers, of turning a chair or walking around it in order to bring about a change of luck? It may be noted that this turning is always from left to right.

Prayer-Wheel. An instrument used chiefly among the Lamaist Buddhists for the purpose of offering prayers by mechanical means. Prayer-wheels are of various shapes and sizes, from small cylinders turned by the hand to huge ones driven by water or wind. Long strips of paper with a written or printed formula repeated hundreds or even thousands of times are wrapped round these cylinders, and as the cylinders revolve the paper rolls uncoil, and so the prayer is said.

Sometimes the wheels are monster cylinders worked with string and crank by a monk, sometimes a long row of small cylinders, ranged along the wall at such a height as to be within reach of passers-by, who give them a twirl and go on rejoicing in the consciousness of having earned the blessing of Providence. Sometimes prayer-tubs are propelled by water-wheels. In other parts windmills perform the like service, while the smaller domestic prayer-wheels are often caused to revolve by the heated air over the fireplace. In short, it makes no difference what is the propelling force, the Karma can be realized if only the circular motion be produced. The more rapid the revolution the greater the merit of the devotee.

Most European writers have looked upon the prayer-wheel as a strange freak of superstition, an exceptional form of ritualism. Carlyle contemptuously alludes to it as the " Rotatory Calabash." Travellers have generally spoken of the grinding of prayers in a mill as an excellent subject for jokes. In 1896, however, Mr. William Simpson, in his " Buddhist Praying-Wheel," as he prefers to call it, set himself to show that it is but one offshoot from the common centre of an infinite variety of myths and ceremonies, whose ramifications reach even into the Christian ritual. His conclusion is that the circular movement is symbolical of the solar motion, or, it may be, of the great revolving circle of the heavens, in which the sun is a subordinate traveller. The virtue of the wheel lies in its being turned sunwise,—*i.e.*, from east to west,—or, to make matters more plain, in the direction which a man would· take if he perambulated it, keeping the object always on his right. The reverse action brings evil and undoes any merit previously acquired by turning the machine in the orthodox direction. (See PRADAKSHINA and DEISUL.)

Presepio. (Gr. *Krippe;* Fr. *Crèche,*—all three words meaning "a manger.") The Latin and Italian and therefore the original name for a representation of the infant Christ lying in a manger, to which were subsequently added all sorts of accessories in the way of members of the Holy Family and other scriptural characters, both human and animal. The presepio is exhibited in churches or in the private houses of the wealthy at Christmastime. It is said to owe its origin to St. Francis of Assisi, who, beginning with 1223, was wont to decorate a stable at Christmastime with the principal scenes of the Nativity. In that stable so transformed he celebrated mass and preached to the people until the holy season was over.

Subsequently the presepii spread throughout Italy and to Spain, Portugal, France, the Netherlands, and Germany. They vary in size and expensiveness from the rude wooden figures of the Alpine goatherd, cut out with his own hands during the long winter evenings for domestic use, to the pretentious representations of the larger churches, with their elaborate carving and gilding, velvet drapery, and cloth of gold. In many parishes of Catholic Europe everybody contributes to the expense of fitting up the presepio. Moribund misers and others anxious to purchase their way into the next world frequently leave considerable sums for the further embellishment of the village presepio.

A presepio in a Capuchin church in Rome is thus described. The Holy Family occupy the foreground. In the manger reposes the Bambino, or infant Christ, over whom St. Joseph, holding a bouquet, and the Virgin, dressed in satin or lace, with blue veil and silver crown, bend admiringly. Around kneel sundry shepherds in the act of adoration, while overhead angels with golden wings float among the clouds, chanting the Gloria in Excelsis. A silver star with its comet-like trail directs the approach of the Eastern Magi, who, with their brilliant retinue of horsemen and attendants, dazzle the eyes of the juvenile spectators with their Oriental pomp and pageantry. Here a ragged beggar stretches out a beseeching palm, and there a devout hermit kneels before a rustic chapel. In the background rise the mountains, dotted with villas and chalets, with flocks of sheep and goats grazing here and there upon their grassy slopes, while peasants are everywhere seen approaching, bearing the products of the farm, the dairy, and the chase as their simple offerings to the new-born Child.

PROCESSION OF THE MANGER.

In some places in Bohemia the Krippe is used in private families as the receptacle of the toys and sweetmeats which the Christ-Child is fabled to bring in his chariot drawn through the air by four milk-white horses. Thus in a measure the Krippe takes the place of the Christmas-tree of the North. Dramatic performances, styled Krippenspiele, or "manger plays," are frequently indulged in by the members of the family.

The original wooden presepio or crib wherein Christ was born in the Bethlehem stable is believed to be preserved in the church of Santa Maria Maggiore in Rome.

According to tradition, the stone manger contained within it another of wood, which was used as a cradle for the infant Christ. That of stone still exists at Bethlehem, not in its primitive state, but decorated with white marble and enriched with magnificent draperies. The wooden one was in the seventh century, at the time of the Mohammedan invasion in the East, transported to Rome and placed in the basilica of Santa Maria

Maggiore. Here it still reposes in a magnificent crystal shrine, mounted on a stand of silver enamelled with gold and precious stones, the splendid offering of Philip IV., King of Spain. The shrine itself is preserved in a brazen coffin. Once a year, on Christmas Day, it is carried around the church in procession on the shoulders of the officiating clergy, and then exposed to the veneration of the faithful on the grand altar.

Primrose Day. The anniversary of the death of Benjamin Disraeli, Earl of Beaconsfield, April 19 (1881), is observed throughout England under this name. Conservatives everywhere appear decorated with primroses, and the statue of the former premier opposite the Houses of Parliament in London, as well as his tomb at Hughenden, is profusely decorated with primrose, laurel, and ivy, contributed by his admirers. Her majesty annually sends to Hughenden a large wreath of primroses, which are placed at the head of Lord Beaconsfield's grave by his nephew, Mr. Coningsby Disraeli, M.P. The Conservative clubs throughout the country are also decorated, the primrose being especially conspicuous everywhere. Yet there is no evidence that primroses played any important part in either the public or the private life of Lord Beaconsfield. Nor does he appear to have had any fondness for them. "Primroses?" exclaims Lord Aldegonde, in "Lothair:" "I believe they are good to make salad of." The *Pall Mall Gazette* in the days when it was a liberal organ made public the following explanation of the anomaly:

"Apropos of Primrose Day and the very uncomplimentary allusions in Lord Beaconsfield's books to that flower, it may be worth while to recount the origin of the myth. When Lord Beaconsfield was buried, the queen sent a wreath of primroses, and wrote, on a card attached to the wreath, '*His* favorite flower.' Her majesty referred, of course, to the late Prince Consort; but her words were misunderstood to mean that the primrose was Lord Beaconsfield's favorite flower. Hence the newspaper allusions to 'the flower he loved so well,' and the annual celebration of Primrose Day. The explanation of the myth has long been current among Lord Beaconsfield's colleagues, but for obvious reasons they did not care to make it public."

Processions. Ecclesiastical processions are of early origin in the Latin and Greek Churches. They were introduced into Constantinople by Chrysostom in A.D. 398 to counteract the effect produced by the Arians, who, being forbidden to use any churches in the city, were accustomed to assemble about the porches and march to their meeting-houses without the walls, singing anthems. By the fifth century processions had come into general use by the Church. Processions may be classified as extraordinary, ordered by ecclesiastical authority for some special cause, and ordinary, prescribed by the common ritual of the Church. To the latter class belong the processions on Candlemas, Palm Sunday, St. Mark's Day, three Rogation days, and Corpus Christi. (See these entries.) In Catholic countries these are elaborate parades through the streets of the city. In countries where Protestantism prevails they only make the circuit of the church, or at most of the churchyard.

Processions are very frequent in Italy, Spain, and other Catholic countries. Besides those on the days already mentioned, every church has processions in honor of the Madonna or some saint specially reverenced in that particular church. They make the circuit of the parish limits, passing through all its principal streets, and every window and balcony is decorated with yellow and crimson hangings and with crowds of dark eyes. The front of the church, the steps, and the street leading to it are spread with yellow sand, over which are scattered sprigs of box. After the procession has been organized in the church, they "come unto the yellow sands," preceded by a band of music, which plays rather jubilant and what the unco guid would call profane music, polkas and marches, and airs from the operas. Next may follow great lanterns of strung glass drops, accompanied by soldiers; then an immense gonfalon representing the Virgin at the Cross, or the local saint, which is borne by the *confraternità* of the parish, with blue capes over their white dresses, and all holding torches. Then follows a huge wooden cross, garlanded with golden ivy-leaves, and also upheld by the *confraternità*, who stagger under its weight. Next come crucifixes followed by the *frati* of the church in black, carrying candles and dolorously chanting a hymn. Then mayhap comes the bishop in his mitre, his yellow stole upheld by two principal priests (the curate and subcurate), and to him his acolytes waft incense, as well as to the huge figure of the Madonna which follows. This figure is of life-size, carved in wood, surrounded by gilt angels, and so heavy that a dozen or so of stout *facchini*, whose shabby trousers show under their improvised costume, are required to bear it along. With this the procession comes to its climax.

The Hindoos have celebrations of a not dissimilar sort. Processions of the idol-gods are the main features of the festivals in various holy cities of Southern India. The idols, decked with flowers, are carried about in gorgeously painted cars, generally with two priests fanning them, preceded by dancing-girls, a band of noisy musicians, bareheaded Brahmins walking hand in hand and singing hymns in honor of the god, and the elephants of the temple, gay with crimson and orange trappings, their very trunks elaborately painted for the occasion. Sometimes cannon fire at intervals; and as the idol-god, thus escorted, approaches, the people shout, and in long lines throw themselves down before him in reverence. Half festival and half fair, it is a curious scene that spreads around. Toys, luscious sweetmeats, and betel are sold at the stalls; numerous go-rounds and swinging boats perform their evolutions, filled with beautiful and artistically dressed children; dancing-girls in their peculiar costume mingle in the crowd or dance before the idol; youths leap past you with towers of flowers on their heads, and boys, dressed up like tigers, go springing about, the crowd rushing to and fro as if threatened by the actual animal. Self-torturing fakirs abound. Some have shoes stuck full of nails, but sing lustily and play on the vina; others dance about, extinguishing torches on their bare breasts; others swing to and fro aloft with a rope around their waist. Beggars and deformed or diseased children roam through the crowds, hideously painted to attract shuddering attention. At night fireworks are let off. Rockets course through the air. Pyrotechnic devices showing the figure of the god blaze in front of the temple where the idol reposes. The little temples in the middle of the tank are illuminated as the god is carried, amid the clash of cymbals, in nocturnal procession around the basin of flashing waters; while the glare of innumerable torches, and the blaze of Indian lights,—white, blue, orange, and green,— change darkness into almost insufferable light. (See *The Land of the Vedas*, by Rev. R. P. Percival.)

Pulgen, or Crowning of the Cock. A simple Christmas ceremony which until the middle of the nineteenth century was commonly observed in Wales and still has a few local survivals in out-of-the-way districts. About three o'clock on Christmas morning the people would assemble in church, and, after prayers and a sermon, continue there, singing psalms and hymns with great devotion, until daylight. If through age or infirmity any were disabled from attending, they did not fail to say prayers and sing carols at home.

Pumpkin, Festival of King. (Fr. *Fête du Roi Potiron.*) In September of every year a grotesque scene occurs in the Halles Centrales or Great Markets of Paris. A monster pumpkin, decorated with a crown of paper and tinsel and borne upon a board which serves for a throne, is carried in state through the airy corridors and along the wide outer pavements. The market-people gather around and pay obeisance to the royal vegetable, and afterwards King Pumpkin is mercilessly dissected, sold in slices at auction, and made into succulent soup which is eaten amid much Gallic merriment.

Purdan. In Wales an ordeal through which unfaithful wives were obliged to pass. Covered with a white sheet, they were made to walk up the aisle of the parish church with their paramours during the hours of divine service. This custom obtained in certain parts of South Wales till the middle of the present century.

Purim (or "Lots"), **Feast of.** This occurs on the 14th day of the twelfth month (Adar) of the Jewish ecclesiastical year, and lasts forty-eight hours. It is immediately preceded by the Fast of Esther, on the 13th of Adar. The origin of both these observances is explained in the book of Esther. When Ahasuerus, King of Persia, put away his wife Vashti and took in her place the Jewish maiden Esther, who had been brought up by her cousin Mordecai, the latter together with his entire race excited the jealous animosity of Haman, the king's minister. Haman obtained from the weak-kneed king permission to wreak the full measure of his wicked will. He cast lots to decide the date, and, as the lot fell to the month of Adar, he issued orders that all the Jews in Persia should be put to death on the 14th of Adar, without regard to age or sex. In this extremity Mordecai entreated Queen Esther to intercede for her own people. Now, according to a law of the Persian monarchy, any person who entered uninvited into the king's presence was at once put to death, unless the king held out to the visitor his golden sceptre as a token of forgiveness. Esther determined to brave the king's displeasure. But first she ordered that all the Jews in Shushan, the Persian capital, should hold a solemn fast. Then she approached the king. He extended his sceptre, listened to her pleadings, and in response ordered that Haman and his ten sons should be hanged, and that the Jews should have liberty to defend themselves against their enemies. Hence the Fast of Esther on the 13th of Adar and the Feast of Purim on the 14th, the latter being the date when the Jews of Shushan turned the tables upon their enemies. It is a time of great rejoicing, of balls, amateur theatricals, and tableaux, the proceeds of which are devoted to hospitals and other charities. The great Hebrew charity ball which is an annual feature of all the leading American cities occurs on this day. At the synagogues, the Megillah, a parchment scroll on which the book of Esther is written, is read both morning and evening. The 15th of Adar is also a day of rejoicing, of exchanging presents, and of giving alms to the poor.

Push-Penny. Under this title a curious custom was until recently sanctioned by the dean and chapter of Durham Cathedral, England. On Oak-Apple Day and Guy Fawkes's Day—respectively the 29th of May and the 5th of November—the senior verger of the cathedral would cast thirty shillings in copper pieces into the college yard to be scrambled for. The pupils of the Blue Coat schools were on these two dates drawn up in rank and file in the nave of the cathedral, for the inspection of the prebends, who minutely examined their new scholastic garments, after which the children were ushered into the choir. At the end of the service a pell-mell rush would be made for the cloister doors, in order to be present at push-penny. The germ of the custom dates to an unknown antiquity. In the old monastic period pennies used to be thrown to the citizens who were wont to assemble in the vicinity of the prior's mansion. At Bishop-Auckland the bishop was accustomed to throw away silver pennies at certain times of the year, and it is even said that so much as a peck of copper was in earlier times scattered broadcast among the people. The Reformation, however, swept these and many other old customs away, but after the Restoration of Charles II. the dean and chapter no doubt considered that the 29th of May and the 5th of November ought to be kept as days of rejoicing, and as one means of doing so caused one of their officials to throw a bagful of pennies to the people who met in the college. The custom survived until the middle of the nineteenth century. (THISELTON DYER: *British Popular Customs*, p. 303.)

Pussy-Willow Fair. (Russian, *Vérbnaya Yármarka*.) An annual fair held in the week preceding Palm Sunday at the Nevsky Prospekt in St. Petersburg. Its ostensible object is to provide the public with twigs of pussy-willow (the only plant showing a vestige of life at that season), which are used in lieu of palms on Palm Sunday. But it is now utilized for the sale of all sorts of cheap goods suitable for the coming Easter season,—paper roses for the Easter cake, confectionery, toys, imitation eggs, and the pascha, or Easter cake, made of cream and other delicacies tabooed in Lent, with which the long fast will be broken after the Easter matins. Finches and other song-birds are exposed in cages, and it is a pretty custom to buy them and set them free. The sites for the booths are the special privilege of soldiers' widows, who draw them by lot and may either use them or sell them as they elect.

Pyx, Trial of the. The annual testing of the standard of gold and silver coins in the English mint. It is a very ancient custom, and derives its name from the pyx, or chest, in which the coins to be examined are kept. The mint-master was in former time simply a person under contract with the government for the manufacture of the coinage, and periodical examinations were consequently necessary to see that the terms of the contract had been complied with. Though he is now an officer of the crown, the manner of conducting the ceremony is substantially unchanged. The finished coins are delivered to the mint-master in weights called journey-weights,—*i.e.*, 15 pounds troy weight of gold, containing 701 sovereigns, or 1402 half-sovereigns; of silver, 60 pounds troy. From each journey-weight a coin is taken, and placed in the pyx for the annual trial. The examination of the coins is made by the Goldsmiths' Company, under the direction of the crown, in the presence of the " queen's remembrancer," who administers the oath to the jury and presides over the proceedings. The coins are compared with pieces cut from trial-plates of standard fineness, in the keeping of the " warden of the standards." If the coins are found to be of standard fineness and weight, within certain limits, a statement to that effect is testified to by the jurors, and handed over to the treasurer. The coins to be tested are kept in the ancient chapel of the pyx, at Westminster Abbey, in joint custody of the Lords of the Treasury and the Comptroller-General. This custom was first ordered during the thirty-second year of the reign of King Henry II. (1154–1189), and took place occasionally in subsequent reigns, whenever royalty chose to order it. King James was present at one of these ceremonies in 1611. There was one held at the Exchequer Office July 17, 1861, and the next, February 15, 1870. During the year 1870 a coinage act was passed by Parliament, providing for an annual trial of the pyx, and the ceremony has been observed each year since then.

In the United States the trial of the pyx is made at the mint in Philadelphia, on the second Wednesday of February annually, before the judge of the district court of the United States for the Eastern District of Pennsylvania, the comptroller of the currency, the assayer of the New York Assay Office, and such other persons as the President of the United States shall from time to time designate for the purpose. A majority of the commissioners constitutes a competent board. Their examination is made in the presence of the director of the mint. The number of coins reserved for the assay from each delivery made by the chief coiner is prescribed by the director, and the reserved pieces, after being sealed up and labelled, are deposited in the pyx, kept under the joint care of the superintendent of the mint and the assayer, each of those officers securing it by an independent lock. The reserved coins from the coinage of other mints besides that at Philadelphia are transmitted quarterly to the Philadelphia mint, and, in addition to these, the director may at his pleasure take any other pieces for test. The commissioners are not sworn for the ceremony as in England, but after the examination they prepare a certified report of the trial, which, if the coins are within the limit of tolerance in fineness and weight, is satisfactory, and is simply filed; but if not, the fact is certified to the President of the United States, and if on a view of the circumstances of the case he shall so decide, the officer or officers implicated in the error are thenceforward disqualified from holding their respective offices.

Q.

Quietus, St. This saint is memorable in the annals of the Catholic Church of America because the enshrinement of his bones in the church of Our Lady of Grace in Hoboken (Archbishop Bailey officiating) on June 1, 1856, was the first ceremony of the kind ever performed in the United States. The innovation provoked a lively newspaper discussion as to the devotional value of the bones themselves or the religious gain of the ceremony attending their translation. Otherwise the saint has slight hagiological importance. He has not even a day set apart in the calendar. Almost nothing is known about him. His bones, together with a vase containing his blood and an epitaph recording his name (spelled Quetus) and his age, five years, were found in the cemetery of St. Pretextatus at Rome in January, 1849. It is presumed that he was one of a family of Christian martyrs, and that he himself was massacred for the faith. In July, 1850, Pope Pius IX. gave the relics to Rev. Father Cauvin, who was then pastor of the Hoboken church. The church was torn down and a new one erected in 1890–1, which necessitated a new translation of the relics on August 2, 1891. A procession of one thousand children, wearing white dresses, typical of the saint's unsullied childhood, and red sashes, typical of the blood he is presumed to have shed for the faith, accompanied the relics to the new sanctuary.

Quinquagesima. (Lat., "Fiftieth.") The first Sunday before Ash Wednesday, so named because it was fifty days before Lent. The two Sundays preceding Quinquagesima—*i.e.*, the second and third Sundays before Lent—are respectively known as Sexagesima and Septuagesima Sundays, possibly because they were looked on as being in round numbers sixty and seventy days before Easter. That the custom of so naming them is ancient we know, for we find them mentioned in the writings of Gregory the Great; but the practice of keeping them as a preparation for Lent has always been confined to the Western Church.

R.

Ramadan. The ninth lunar month in the Mohammedan calendar. It may be called the Mohammedan Lent. Every day from sunrise to sunset is kept as a strict fast. Not a morsel of food or a drop of drink is tolerated. Tobacco and snuff are forbidden. But the day fasting is made up for by night feasting. The moment the sun has set, a carnival begins which lasts well on until sunrise. In the great cities the restaurants and cafés are lighted, and the streets are full of revellers making up for the austerities of the day. The wealthy keep open house. But the mosques are open too, and are crowded night and day. On the 15th day of Ramadan the Sultan goes in grand procession from the Yildiz palace in Pera across the Bosporus to Stamboul to kiss Mohammed's coat (see COAT OF MOHAMMED). This is the one day of the year in which the Sultan appears in Stamboul. If Ramadan be the Mohammedan Lent, BAIRAM (*q. v.*) is the Mohammedan Easter. This is the season which ends the great fast.

"When the moon of Ramadan has set and that of Bairam has risen, all Constantinople puts on its new clothes and the people come out and rejoice over the day. There are bands of music everywhere through the streets. Calls are made among friends and neighbors. The boats on the Bosporus are decorated with flags, and everything and everybody goes wild with joy. The watching for the moon is a great occasion, and the Turk who brings the first news of its rising to the Cadi of Constantinople gets a reward of ten thousand piasters, or four hundred and fifty dollars. The competitors station themselves on the hills about Constantinople, and as soon as they see the thin band of light which marks the new moon's coming in the sky, they rush for the office of the judge, and the first one in gets the prize. The cadi is waiting for them, and he fixes the next morning as the beginning of Bairam." (FRANK G. CARPENTER: *Lent among the Mahometans*, in the *Cosmopolitan*, April, 1893.)

Red-Letter Days. A term now extended to any gala occasion or memorable day in the life of an individual or a nation. But originally and specifically the term is an ecclesiastical one, used to characterize the more important festivals and saints' days of the Church, which appear in red letters instead of black in the calendar. In ordinary cheap prayer-books both of the English and of the Roman Church, where two colors are not used in the printing, these days are characterized by italics or Gothic capitals, and the black-letter days (*q. v.*) or minor festivals by lower-case Roman type. The practical difference in the public worship of the English Church is that black-letter days have no collect, etc., as the others have.

Relics. (Lat. *reliquiæ*, "remains.") In its Catholic use this word includes the bodies of saints and martyrs, or fragments of the same, or any objects with which in life the person was associated.

The old Romans and Greeks had their holy relics,—for instance, the egg of Leda. The Hindoos waged bloody wars over the monstrous supernatural tooth of Buddha. The Mohammedans preserve the standard, arms, clothes, beard, and two teeth of their Prophet. In the Catholic Church St. Helena was the first great relic-hunter.

The Second Nicæan Council ordered that no church should be consecrated unless it enshrined some relics, and imputes a disregard for them to the opponents of images. So encouraged, relic-hunting became a favorite pastime, in which earth and heaven joined their forces. Numerous saints revealed the whereabouts of their bodies in dreams and visions, some of them being so eager in the cause that they pointed out more than one. Miraculous lights settled over the resting-places of other holy men. Indeed, at every critical moment relics were sure to be discovered. They often came down from heaven in answer to devout prayer. A woman at St.-Maurin, for instance, who had chosen St. John for her patron, importuned him daily for three years for some little bit of his body for which he had no further use. He turned a deaf ear until at last the woman got desperate and vowed that she would not touch food till her prayer was heard. She kept her vow for seven days, and was nearly at her last gasp, when she found on the altar the thumb of the saint. Three bishops wrapped this holy relic very reverently in linen, and three drops of blood fell from it,—one drop per bishop.

When the Empress Constantine petitioned Pope Gregory I. to send her the head of St. Paul, he replied that it was not the custom at Rome to lay violent hands on the remains of the martyrs. He added that many persons who had presumed to handle the bodies of St. Peter and St. Paul had been struck dead in consequence, and that he could send her only a cloth which had touched the apostle's body. Such cloths, he reminded her, possessed the same miraculous power as the relics themselves. The practice of removing relics, he said in conclusion, gave rise to fraud, as in the case of some Greek monks, who, when detected in digging up dead bodies by night at Rome, had confessed to an intention of passing them off in Greece as relics of martyrs.

At the time of the Crusades Europe was overflowed with relics. Whenever a town in the Holy Land was conquered the Crusaders looked first for relics, as more precious than gold or gems. St. Louis made two unfortunate crusades, but he comforted himself with the relics he brought home. Chief among these was the holy crown of thorns, one of the ornaments of the Imperial Chapel at Constantinople. The court of France advanced as far as Troyes, in Champagne, to meet with devotion this inestimable relic. It was borne in triumph through Paris by the king himself, barefoot, and in his shirt. Among the other treasures secured by the same simple-minded monarch were a portion of the true cross, part of the baby linen of the infant Jesus, and various other relics of the Passion. To house them all properly St. Louis built the Sainte-Chapelle of Paris, where many of them may still be seen.

Among relics of a painfully grotesque character whose description we meet with in mediæval authorities may be reckoned a portion of the melted fat of St. Lawrence; the bones of Moses; the sigh which St. Joseph heaved when he was splitting wood; feathers from the wings of the archangels Gabriel and St. Michael; the thorn in the flesh which troubled St. Paul; a beam of the star which conducted the Wise Men from the East; the perch whence the cock crew its reproach to Peter; the bones of the ass on which the entry into Jerusalem was made; the staff with which Moses parted the Red Sea; manna from the desert; and a piece of the rock from which Moses drew water.

What has become of many of these relics and of the jewel-incrusted caskets, reliquaries, and shrines in which they were preserved? It is certain that only a limited number have been preserved. The greater portion were swept away in the wars which at various epochs have devastated the face of Christendom. In England and Northern Europe very few survived the iconoclasticism of the Reformation.

First in the estimation of the faithful come, of course, all personal relics of Christ. Most of these were found by St. Helena (*q. v.*) during her famous pilgrimage to Jerusalem. Of the cross and other instruments associated with the Passion some details are given under the head of CROSS, INVENTION OF THE.

A small portion of Herod's staircase is at the Escorial, and the remainder is at Rome. (See SCALA SANTA.) The column at which the scourging took place is also at Rome, in the church of St. Praxede, with the exception of some fragments which are at Venice. The present whereabouts of the rope, whip, and sceptre is not quite clear. All we learn is that the rope was at Carlstein in 1515, that the whip was treasured at Constance, and that Soissons, Courtrai, and the Sainte-Chapelle in Paris held the sceptre for a long time. The crown of thorns, which was given to St. Louis by the Emperor of Constantinople, is now in Notre-Dame at Paris. Thorns have been taken from it, and are objects of veneration in many places. Of the purple vestments, some are in the church of Bucoleon at Constantinople, and others are at the Sainte-Chapelle in Paris.

Of the actual person of Christ all that remains are some drops of the blood (see BLOOD, PRECIOUS) and a few hairs. The latter are dispersed among the churches at Corbie, Namur, and St. Denis.

Other relics comprise, first, the clothes worn by Christ, the sandals, the tunics, the swaddling-clothes, the manger, etc.; second, the relics of the Lord's Supper, such as the bread, the communion-cup, the cloth, the dish, the table, the basin for washing the feet, and the linteum.

Fragments of the sandals are at Corbie, Treves, and Alberstadt; the swaddling-clothes are at the Sainte-Chapelle in Paris, Clermont, Courtrai, Namur, Toledo, Vizille; the tunics are at Argenteuil, Treves (see COAT, HOLY), and Aix-la-Chapelle, and there are also fragments of them at Corbie and Toledo; and a portion of the manger is at St. Denis, though Rome claims to have it almost entire (see PRESEPIO). The cup used at the marriage of Cana, known as the Sacro Cattino (*q. v.*), is at Genoa.

Remedios, Virgen or **Nuestra Señora de los.** (Sp., "Virgin or Our Lady of Succor.") A famous image preserved in the little historic church of Los Remedios on the hill of Totoltepec, about twenty miles from the city of Mexico. Being looked upon as a rival of the Virgin of Guadalupe (see GUADALUPE) and more than suspected of Spanish leanings, she has become much discredited since Mexico achieved her independence. Indeed, she is even derisively spoken of as La Gachupina ("the little Spanish woman"). The image is a wooden doll a foot high, holding in its arms a tiny infant Jesus. Both faces are carved with a rough penknife. Two holes represent the eyes, and another the mouth. "No Indian idol," says Madame Calderon de la Barca, "could be much uglier. She has been a good deal scratched and destroyed in the lapse of ages. C——n observed that he was astonished they had not tried to restore her a little. To this the padre replied that the attempt had been made by several artists, each one of whom had sickened and died." (*Letters.*)

Tradition asserts that this image was brought to Mexico by Juan Villafuerte, a soldier of Cortez's army. Now, the hill of Totoltepec, at the coming of the Spaniards, was an Otomi stronghold. On its rugged, lava-seamed heights was a great building, half temple, half fortress, which was dedicated to the worship of Otomcapulco, who is more generally known by his Aztec name of Tlaloctlamacazqui, the god of the rains, and his royal sister, Chalchiuhtliycue, the spirit of the waters. The former held dominion over the water that came from the heavens, and the latter ruled the running streams and the tides of the sea. In pre-Spanish times a great feast lasting a whole month was held in honor of these two gods, at which hundreds of human sacrifices were offered. This worship extended to the sea-coast on both sides of the mountains.

Cortez persuaded Montezuma to allow him to set up an altar in the city of Mexico, and there Villafuerte's image was installed. There it remained until the Spaniards were driven from the city on the night of June 30, 1520 (see NOCHE TRISTE). Throughout all the horrors of that night, so the legend says, the good Villa-fuerte carried the precious image in his bosom, and throughout the subsequent attacks upon the fortress of Totoltepec, during which he was sorely wounded. At last, finding himself about to die, he hid the image under the great leaves of a maguey plant.

Twenty years afterwards, Cequahutzin, a famous chief of the Otomi nation, who had lately become a Christian, happening to be out hunting upon the hill, saw a vision of the Virgin, who, in her own person, directed him to search under the maguey for her image. This he did, and, having found it, he took it to his home; but the same day it returned to its place under the maguey. Again he carried it to his house and set before it, in a gourd dish, the most tempting food that he possessed, but again the image fled to the hill. Once more he went for it and carried it back with him, and, to make sure of it this time, he locked it securely in a strong box, upon the top of which he made his bed for the night. But when he awoke in the morning the image had again fled to its place under the maguey plant. Cequahutzin went that very day to the holy fathers of San Gabriel in Tacuba and told them what had happened. They divined that the Virgin desired a temple to be erected to her service upon the hill of Totoltepec. Accordingly a little church was immediately built upon the spot where the image had been discovered, and some thirty-five years later the present building was completed (1575).

In time the shrine of Totoltepec became the richest and most famous throughout the land. Gifts of immense value were showered upon the image. Her jewels and ornaments alone were valued at one million dollars. The railings that enclosed the main altar were carved from massive bars of silver. Before the altar itself stood a massive maguey plant in pure silver. A treasurer was appointed to take charge of her jewels, a camarista to superintend her rich wardrobe. In seasons of drought she was brought in from her mountain dwelling and carried in procession through the streets of Mexico. The viceroy himself, on foot, used to lead the holy train. A dignitary of high rank drove the carriage in which she was seated. She visited the principal convents in succession, the nuns bowing in humble adoration as she passed.

It happened that in the revolution of 1810 the patriot Hidalgo took as his standard an image of the Virgin of Guadalupe. The Spanish sympathizers answered by appealing to the patronage of the Virgin of Los Remedios, and her image was conducted to Mexico, dressed as a Spanish general. On the triumph of the revolutionists, she was stripped of her military dress, her church was despoiled of its treasures, and her passport was signed, with an order for her to leave the republic. But calmer counsels prevailed. She was allowed to remain, was eventually restored to her honors, and still retains her treasurer, a small portion of her treasures, and a semi-suspicious hold upon the reverence of the Mexicans.

But, though the lustre of the glory of Our Lady of Succor is dimmed, she has still many strong admirers, chief among whom are the remnants of the old imperialist party; and every good Catholic in Mexico is willing to admit her wonderful power over the rivers and the rain, which she usurped from the ancient Aztec gods of the floods and the storms. And so she still continues to inhabit the bare, damp-stained, smoke-colored walls of the ancient, half-ruined sanctuary on the hill of Totoltepec.

A correspondent of the *New York Sun* who dates his letter Mexico, June 29, 1896, writes as follows: " A special service to pray for rain at the shrine of Nuestra Señora de los Remedios has been followed by a plenteous downpour, and so the fame of the shrine is proportionately greater. Yesterday the sun rose over the Valley of Mexico with a clear, keen, steady brightness that caused the old people to shake their heads. It was a day that made the weather-prophets hide themselves in despair; a dawning that once more painted on the steel-blue sky the words of which all the land had weeks ago grown weary,—'No rain.' Everywhere the pulque-fields and the corn-lands lay cracked and seamed with the long, steady, scorching heat of the tropical sun.

" But all this time a curious ceremony was going on in the little old historic church of Los Remedios. Thousands of people from all over the republic sent up their prayers to the little image of Our Lady of Succor that she would remember them as she had done in the past and send them the rain to gladden their parched fields; for such a drought as there has been upon the land for the past eight months has not been felt in Mexico for many years. Until yesterday hundreds of petitions and pilgrimages had been made to Our Lady of Succor without avail. Finally the authorities of the Church gave notice that there would be a special service at the shrine. The service commenced at ten A.M. with the celebration of low mass by Canon Pedro de Verona Gutierrez. This was followed by solemn high mass, which was sung by Father Flores of San Miguel.

"At the conclusion of the mass the little image of Our Lady of Succor was carried around the churchyard (for the laws do not permit any public procession of a religious character outside the walls of the churchyard). The 'Little Lady' stood erect under a blue and silver canopy, from which she looked serenely forth upon a long procession of the faithful, each carrying a lighted taper.

"When the procession was over, the sun looked down as pitilessly into the court-yard of the church as it had continued to do for weeks past, but during the evening rain fell in torrents, and the faith of the believers is proportionately strengthened."

Rhyne Toll. An annual tax collected between October 30 and November 7 in the parish of Chetwode, a small village about five miles from Buckingham, England, by the lord of the manor, who ever since Saxon times has been the head of the Chetwode family. Tradition asserts that in ancient times the parish formed part of a forest which was infested by a destructive wild boar. The inhabitants were never safe from his attacks, and strangers who heard of his ferocity were afraid to visit or pass through the district, so that traffic and friendly intercourse were seriously impeded, as well as much injury done to property, by this savage monster. The lord of Chetwode, bent on ridding his neighborhood of this pest, sallied forth into the forest, and, as the old song has it,—

> Then he blowed a blast full north, south, east, and west—
> Wind well thy horn, good hunter;
> And the wild boar then heard him full in his den,
> As he was a jovial hunter.
>
> Then he made the best of his speed unto him—
> Wind well thy horn, good hunter;
> Swift flew the boar, with his tusks smeared with gore,
> To Sir Ryalas, the jovial hunter.

Then the wild boar, being so stout and so strong—
   Wind well thy horn, good hunter;
Thrashed down the trees as he ramped him along
   To Sir Ryalas, the jovial hunter.

Then they fought four hours in a long summer day—
   Wind well thy horn, good hunter;
Till the wild boar fain would have got him away
   From Sir Ryalas, the jovial hunter.

Then Sir Ryalas he drew his broadsword with might—
   Wind well thy horn, good hunter;
And he fairly cut the boar's head off quite,
   For he was a jovial hunter.

Matters being thus settled, the neighborhood rang with the praises of the gallant deed of the lord of Chetwode, and the news thereof soon reached the ears of the king, who "liked him so well of the achievement" that he forthwith made the knight tenant *in capite*, and constituted his manor paramount of all the manors within the limits and extent of the royal forest of Rook-woode. Moreover, he granted to him, and to his heirs forever, among other immunities and privileges, the full right and power to levy every year the "Rhyne Toll" on all cattle found within the district between the 30th of October and the 7th of November. The commencement of the toll, which is proclaimed with much ceremony, is thus described in an old document of Queen Elizabeth's reign:

"In the beginning of the said drift of the common, or rhyne, first at their going forth, they shall blow a welke-shell, or horne, immediately after the sun rising at the Mansion-House of the manor of Chetwode, and then, in their going about, they shall blow their horne the second time in the field between Newton Purcell and Barton Hartshorn, in the said county of Bucks, and also shall blow their horne a third time at a place near the town of Finmere. in the county of Oxford, and they shall blow their horne the fourth time at a certain stone in the market of the town of Buckingham, and there to give the poor sixpence ; and so, going forward in this manner about the said drift, shall blow the horne at several bridges called Thornborough Bridge, King's Bridge, and Bridge Mill. And they also shall blow their horne at the Pound Gate, called the Lord's Pound, in the parish of Chetwode. . . . And also (the lord of Chetwode) has always been used by his officers and servants to drive away all foreign cattle that shall be found within the said parishes, fields, &c., to impound the same in any pound of the said towns, and to take for every one of the said foreign beasts twopence for the mouth, and one penny for a foot for every one of the said beasts." All cattle thus impounded at other places were to be removed to the pound at Chetwode, and if not claimed and the toll paid within three days, "then the next day following after the rising of the sun, the bailiff or officers of the lord for the time being shall blow their horne three times at the gate of the said pound, and make proclamation that, if any persons lack any cattle that shall be in the same pound, let them come and shew the marks of the same cattle so claimed by them, and they shall have them, paying unto the lord his money in the manner and form before-mentioned, otherwise the said cattle that shall so remain shall be the lord's as strays." This toll was formerly so rigidly enforced that if the owner of cattle so impounded made his claim immediately after the proclamation was over, he was refused them, except he paid their full market price.

Though the custom is still regularly observed, it has undergone some changes since the date of the above document. The toll now begins at nine in the morning instead of at sunrise, and the horn is first sounded on the church-hill at Buckingham, and gingerbread and beer are distributed among the assembled boys, the girls being excluded. The officer then proceeds to another part of the liberty on the border of Oxfordshire, and there, after blowing his horn as before, again distributes gingerbread and beer among the assembled boys. The toll is then proclaimed as begun, and collectors are stationed at different parts to enforce it, at the rate of two shillings a score upon all cattle and swine passing on any road within the liberty, until twelve o'clock at night on the 7th of November, when the "Rhyne" closes.

The occupiers of land within the liberty have long been accustomed to compound for the toll by an annual payment of one shilling. The toll has sometimes been refused, but has always been recovered with the attendant expenses. It realized about twenty pounds a year before the opening of the Buckinghamshire Railway; but now, owing to Welsh and Irish cattle being sent by trains, it does not amount to above four pounds, and is let by the present lord of the manor for only one pound five shillings a year. (CHAMBERS: *Book of Days*, vol. ii. p. 516.)

Roche, St. (Fr. *Roch* or *Roque;* It. *Rocco*), patron of prisoners and the sick, especially the plague-stricken. In England his festival on August 16 used to be celebrated as a general harvest home, with dances in the churchyard in the evening, and was known as the great harvest festival. (FOSBROOKE: *Dictionary of Antiquities.*)

Born about 1280, at Montpellier, France, of a noble family, left an orphan at twenty with a vast patrimony, St. Roche distributed the latter among the poor and started on a pilgrimage to Rome. There and in other Italian cities he devoted himself to tending the sick in the hospitals, for a great plague was then raging. At Piacenza he took the infection himself. He crawled into a wood without the city. His little dog, who had accompanied him, tenderly nursed him through the illness that followed. Every day the dog went back to the city and returned in the evening with a loaf of bread in his mouth. The legend relates that an angel appeared and dressed his wounds, but others explain this by saying that it was a kind-hearted man named Gothard, who, not knowing who he was, took compassion on him, proving, as it were, his " good angel." When he had recovered sufficiently, St. Roche turned his steps towards his old home, but when he arrived he was so changed by suffering that, not recognizing him, the officers arrested him as a possible spy, and threw him into prison. Even his own uncle, who was the judge, did not know him, and the saint, believing that it was the will of God, did not reveal himself, but quietly endured the hardships of confinement for five years.

At the expiration of that time, the jailer entering the cell one morning was dazzled by a brilliant light which filled the whole room. The prisoner was dead, and beside him lay a paper which contained his name and these words : " Ceux qui sont frappez de peste, et imploreront la faveur de Sainct Roche, seront guéris." (*Les Fleurs des Vies des Saints.*) When his uncle and the people learned who he was, they were filled with grief and remorse ; and he was buried amidst the tears and prayers of the whole city.

Nearly a century passed after this event (which is generally believed to have occurred about 1327) before the memory of St. Roche was revived outside of his native city. But at the time of the great Church Council held in 1414 at Constance (the same that condemned Huss) the plague broke out, and the clergy and laity were in great consternation, when a young German monk, who had heard of St. Roche in France, proposed that his aid should be invoked on behalf of the plague-stricken people. Acting upon this advice, the Council ordered that the effigy of that saint should be carried in procession through the streets ; and no sooner was this done, accompanied by prayers and litanies, than the plague suddenly ceased.

The cupidity of the Venetians was now aroused. Owing to their extensive commercial relations with the East, they were peculiarly exposed to infection. Who could need more than they the pestilence-defying bones at Montpellier ? In 1485 was formed an alliance of holy buccaneers. Under pretence of performing a pilgrimage, they landed at Montpellier, stole the relics, and carried them away to Venice, where the Doge received them in state. The splendid church of San Rocco was built for their reception under the auspices of a community which had already been formed for the purpose of caring for those ill with infectious disease. This community still exists, under the title of the Brotherhood of San Rocco (a society analogous to that of the Misericordia in Florence), wherein many of the nobility and gentry of Venice enroll themselves for shorter or longer periods as a penance for sin or as a step in the quest for the higher life.

It may be mentioned, however, that Arles contains a rival body of St. Roche. Certain relics of the saint are also shown at Rome, Antwerp, and other places.

In art St. Roche is usually represented as a man in the prime of life, dressed as a pilgrim, with a cockle-shell in his hat and a wallet at his side. In one hand he holds a staff, in the other he lifts his robe to show the plague-spot, and his dog stands near. The events of his life have been depicted by some of the most celebrated artists of Italy and Germany, Carracci, Guido, Tintoretto, Bassano, and Rubens, the most famous work being the altar-piece in the church at Alost, which was completed in eight days, and for which Rubens received eight hundred florins from the Brotherhood of St. Roche.

Rogation Days. The Monday, Tuesday, and Wednesday before Ascension Thursday, so called because in the Roman Church the Litany of the Saints is chanted in the procession which takes place on each of the three days. Rogatio (from *rogare*, " to pray") is the Latin equivalent for the Greek word λιτανεία, " litany." These litanies are called lesser by comparison with the more ancient and solemn chanting of the litany on St. Mark's Day.

Litanies sprang from the early Christian processions to martyrs' tombs, which gradually developed in a general custom of supplications for the appeasing of God's wrath and the averting of public evils. These were called Litanies by the Greek Church and Rogations by the Latin. St. Chrysostom is said to have introduced the custom of singing litanies in procession at Constantinople. The usage was brought into more regular and definite shape by Mamertus, Bishop of Vienne, in Gaul, about the middle of the fifth century, when the province suffered from earthquake and other troubles. In 511 the First Council of Orleans appointed the Rogation Days before the Ascension to be observed with fasting and solemn processions, and directed that all slaves should be exempted from work, that they might be able to attend the public services on those three days. Gregory the Great, a century later, collected and arranged the various litanies in a common form very much as they are now used in the Latin Church,

under the name of "Litanies of the Saints," which are still sung
on the Rogation days, either in church, or, in many Catholic
countries, in procession about the streets. But Gregory only
enjoined their use on St. Mark's Day, and left it to Leo III.
(who died in 816) to introduce the Rogation days at Rome.
Leo omitted the obligation of fasting. It was in the time of Pope
Gregory, however, that St. Augustine introduced the custom into
the English Church. He had learned the usage on his way
through Gaul, and availed himself in this matter of Gregory's
wise advice to adopt for the newly-formed Church such liturgical
observances prevalent elsewhere as he might find most suitable,
even though not used at Rome. It was, in fact, to the chant
of the rogations or litanies that Augustine and his monks
came in procession, with silver cross and banner borne before
them, to their first meeting with Ethelbert in the Isle of Thanet.
And in the same order and with the same solemn chant—borrowed from the use of the Church of Lyons—they soon afterwards made their entry into Canterbury on one of the Rogation
days in the Ascension week of 597. It was natural, therefore,
that when Augustine was organizing the Church he had founded
he should include in its ritual these Gallic "Rogations." Hence
we find the Council of Clovesho in 747 enjoining the Litany and
the processions on Rogation days to be kept up in England,
"according to the way of our fathers," besides directing the
Litany to be used on St. Mark's Day for the future as at Rome.
The season continued to be observed with fasting, solemn processions, and litanies until the Reformation, and perhaps in some
places still later. The Rogation Fast is still prescribed in the
Rubrics of the Reformed English Prayer Book.

Gradually the perambulations deteriorated. First the minister
ceased to make the tour. Then the beadle and churchwarden
failed to attend. Finally the constable was left to lead the processions. Thus they took on an entirely secular aspect, which
they have retained even in the parishes which have revived the
old custom or never quite relinquished it. In that part of London called the City the bounds of every parish are still beaten
with long staves by a motley crowd of old and young, generally
under the leadership of a policeman. (See BOUNDS, BEATING OF
THE.)

Romain, St., patron of Rouen, in France. He is commemorated on October 23, the anniversary of his death in 639. He
is styled the Apostle to Normandy, because he established Christianity in that province, becoming Bishop of Rouen. Among
the marvels related of him was that of commanding the waters
of the river Seine to recede when an inundation threatened the

city. No sooner had they obeyed than a dragon rose from the slime, which the good bishop with the aid of a murderer succeeded in overcoming. Hence it was that until the Revolution the chapter of Rouen on the annual recurrence of the saint's day possessed the privilege of pardoning a criminal condemned to death.

Romuald, St. (956–1027), founder of the monastery of Camaldoli, about thirty-six miles from Florence, Italy. He died June 19, but February 7, the day of his translation, was ordered by Clement VIII. to be kept in his honor. His most famous act was to force the Emperor Otho III. to perform barefoot a pilgrimage from Rome to Mount Gargano, as a public penance for having treacherously slain Crescentius, governor of Tivoli, whom he had lured away from sanctuary in the castle of St. Angelo in Rome under promise of indemnity. Southey has a humorous poem upon one of the legends of this saint. Having as a hermit acquired a great reputation for sanctity, the country-folks in the neighborhood, unwilling to run the risk of having so eminent a saint buried among strangers, determined to strangle him one night. But the saint got wind of the project, and, being unambitious of so much worldly honor, quietly stole away from the place.

St. Romuald was buried in his own monastery of Val di Castro. On February 7, 1481, his relics were translated to the church of St. Blaise in the town of Fabri, where they remain to this day.

In art he is represented as holding his finger to his lips in token of silence, and often with a ladder by his side. The latter is in reference to a dream wherein he saw a ladder set up between heaven and earth, which his monks ascended clad in white habits. Hence he ordered that they should always wear white in lieu of the gray originally indicated.

Roncesvalles, Our Lady of. (Sp. *Nuestra Señora de Roncesvalles;* Fr. *Notre-Dame de Roncevaux.*) A miraculous image of the Virgin which is preserved at Roncesvalles, or Roncevaux, a village on the borders of Spain and France famous for the legendary achievements of Roland. The ruined chapel in which it is kept is said to have been founded by Charlemagne, and among its other relics is the Bible on which the ancient kings of Navarre took the oath of allegiance.

The shriving of penitent pilgrims at this chapel is an annual ceremony performed with much curious detail. The pilgrims come from the neighboring valleys, generally on the Spanish side of the Pyrenees. They arrive about dawn.

Their bodies are covered with a black blouse drawn tight at the waist with a cord, and their heads with a sombre cowl. On their shoulders they carry a heavy cross, formed of two weighty branches nailed together, supposed to resemble the cross which Christ bore to Calvary. They advance slowly, preceded by the mayors of their commune, attired in a long municipal robe. When they have reached the monastery, some of the pilgrims have travelled, crosses on back, ten, twenty, and even thirty miles.

After half an hour's rest they form ranks again in two files, between which walk the clergy, with the wives, sisters, or mothers of the penitents. They pass before the tomb which is fabled to contain the remains of Roland's companions, enter the chapel, and there hear mass, confess, and take communion. Then to breakfast at the neighboring inn,

PILGRIM OF RONCESVAUX.

after which the line reforms, and the pilgrims, shouldering their crosses once more, march home ten, twenty, or thirty miles across the Pyrenees.

Rosa di Lima, St., the only canonized female saint of the New World. Her festival is on August 30. She was born at Lima, Peru, in 1586. From her infancy she gave great evidence of piety, and began mortifying herself at a very early age. She destroyed her beautiful complexion with quicklime in order to disenchant her lovers. She supported herself and her aged parents by toiling in a garden, and by working at night with her needle. She died August 24, 1617, and was entombed at Lima. She was canonized by Clement X. in 1671. It is related that this Pope at first refused to canonize her, but a shower of roses fell all about him and continued until he felt assured of her sanctity.

Rosalia, St., patron of Palermo, in Sicily, which was her birthplace. Her feast is celebrated on September 4, the anniversary of the translation of her body. Of noble parentage, she forsook all worldly vanities in her youth and made herself an abode in a cave on Monte Pelegrino, three miles from Palermo.

Here she died in 1160. In 1625, the jubilee year of Pope Urban VIII., a body supposed to be hers was found buried in a grot under the mountain, and was translated to the metropolitan church of Palermo, which was dedicated to her. A pestilence raging in that year ceased at once. It used to be the annual custom on her feast-day for the priests to take the relics in solemn procession around Monte Pelegrino. It must be added that Dean Buckland positively identified the remains as those of an unusually large and venerable he-goat. Nevertheless St. Michael's Church in Brooklyn, New York, prides itself on the possession of five fragments of her "forearm," which were brought over as a gift from the Cardinal of Palermo in 1893. They are encased in a small silver box of oval shape.

Roses, Tribute of. (Fr. *Baillée des Roses.*) A graceful ceremony which existed in France up to the end of the sixteenth century and consisted of a tribute of roses from the peers of France to parliament, and was rendered in the months of April, May, and June on a day when the sitting was held in the great hall. The peer whose turn it was to pay the tribute had to see that on the appointed day all the rooms of the palace were strewed with roses, flowers, and sweet herbs : before the sitting commenced he was bound to enter every chamber with a large bowl of silver borne before him containing as many crowns of roses and bouquets as there were members of parliament and officers attached to its service ; and when the roses had been distributed to the various claimants of the homage and the audience was ended, he gave a great feast to the presidents, councillors, clerks, and ushers of the court. The origin of this custom is quite unknown. It not only existed at the parliament of Paris, but was maintained at all the other parliaments of the kingdom, especially that of Toulouse ; and the tribute was obligatory on the children of the king, princes of the blood, dukes, cardinals, and other peers. There is said to have been an edict of Henry III. relating to it.

Rosh Hashanah. The Jewish New Year, being the first day of the secular year. The Jewish calendar really has two New Year's Days. One, Rosh Hashanah, is held by tradition to be the anniversary of the day on which God created the earth. It falls in either September or October of the Christian calendar, being reckoned by the new moon of the seventh month, Tisri. It ushers in the civil year. Abib (see PASSOVER) is the first month in the religious year. Abib, or Nisan, corresponds with parts of March and April, the year dating from the moon after the vernal equinox. The prophets speak of the sacred year, while those in secular employments reckon by the civil. The number of months is the same as in the Christian calendar, but they are all lunar, and the discrepancies are remedied by the introduction of a thirteenth intercalary month every third year.

The celebration of Rosh Hashanah was established by Mosaic precept. In the book of Leviticus, twenty-third chapter, twenty-fourth and twenty-fifth verses of the English version, it is written, "Speak unto the children of Israel, saying, In the seventh month, in the first day of the month, shall ye have a Sabbath, a memorial of blowing of trumpets, a holy convocation. Ye shall do no servile work therein : but ye shall offer an offering made by fire unto the Lord."

Business is generally suspended in Hebrew commercial circles during the New Year's celebration, and the Jewish temples and synagogues are thronged with worshippers. Among the orthodox Hebrews the festival lasts for two days, but the Reformed Jews confine the celebration to one day.

Like all the other festivals in the Jewish calendar, Rosh Hashanah lasts from sunset to sunset. As the succession of the priesthood has been lost, sacrifice can be offered no longer, and the Biblical decree ordering an offering cannot be obeyed. The trumpets, however, remain. These with the more conservative synagogues are the shofars or rams' horns of traditional antiquity. The Reformed Jews substitute brass instruments. Experts are employed for the express purpose of producing the inharmonious notes that serve to arouse the worshippers to a full sense of their religious duties to God and their fellow-men. There are three or four distinct blasts, one of which is quite prolonged, as if the blower was bound to expend every particle of breath in his body, another is short and tremulous, and a third is broken or disconnected. The latter has been defined as a reminder of the many broken vows and religious precepts. These various blasts are repeated at frequent intervals during the day, and are always succeeded by short melodies, some of which are sung with great zest by the members of the congregation.

On the New Year two scrolls of the law or five books of Moses are taken from the ark or sanctuary and borne amid impressive ceremonies to the reading-desk, where one is unrolled and sections read to six members of the congregation who are "called up" to the reading desk. From the second scroll a single section is read to a single member. The passages read from both scrolls are appropriate to the day. The reading-desk and the ark are on New Year's Day covered with a rich white material trimmed with silver and gold fringe, and present a very fine appearance.

With the close of the synagogue and the return of the worshippers to their homes they refresh themselves and exchange visits of greeting, after the style of the Christian New Year. The rest of the day is given up to good cheer.

The Day of Atonement (Yom Kippur, *q. v.*) falls ten days after New Year, and the intervening period is known as the penitential days. During this period strict Jews abstain from all frivolity or pleasure, for again tradition says that the judgment which was rendered by the Almighty on the New Year is not finished until the expiration of the Day of Atonement, when the decision is sealed and irrevocable. Rabbis throughout the Talmud are very careful to impress upon the minds of their disciples that expiation for sins is practicable between man and God, but between man and man there must be absolute reparation.

It is believed that on Rosh Hashanah three books are opened. One is for the righteous, who are immediately inscribed for life; one for the wicked, who are instantly inscribed for death; and one for the nondescript, who are left on probation. If the latter repent during the ten penitential days, their names are written in the book of life; if not, in that of death. As the Day of Judgment Rosh Hashanah is alternatively known as Yom Hardin, and as the Day of Memorial as Yom Hazikkaron.

Rosière, Fête de la. A festival celebrated in many villages of France, notably in Salency, Nanterre, Surennes, and Sanssouci-des-Fleurettes, in which the essential feature is the crowning with white roses of a maiden who has preserved an unsullied reputation for virtue, and the presentation to her of a sum of money. A Sunday in late May or early June is usually chosen for the beginning of the festival, which in some localities lasts three days.

The first rosière is said to have been established at the beginning of the sixth century by St. Medard at Salency, of which place he was seigneur. He charged his family estate with a sum of money to be given annually, together with a crown of white roses, to the most virtuous girl in the village. The first crown, by the unanimous vote of the village, is said to have gone to St. Medard's own sister, and in a picture above the altar in the chapel of St. Medard at Salency he is represented as crowning her. According to the terms of the original foundation, not only must the girl be irreproachable, but her ancestors for four generations before her must have stood well in the community. The seigneur of Salency had the right to choose the rosière out of three girls, natives of the village, presented to him. When he had named her the parish was informed of it from the pulpit on the following Sunday, and all who had any just cause or impediment to advance were bidden to do so. On the feast of St. Medard, June 8, at two o'clock in the afternoon, the rosière, dressed in white, attended by twelve girls in white with blue sashes, and twelve boys, her father and mother and relations, went to the castle of Salency, where the procession was met by the seigneur or his bailiff, who conducted the procession to the church to vespers.

Vespers over, clergy and people went in procession to the chapel of St. Medard. Here on the altar was the garland of roses, bound by a blue ribbon and ornamented in front with a silver ring. After blessing it the officiating priest placed it on the brows of the kneeling rosière, and presented her with twenty-five livres in presence of the seigneur and the village officials. Thus crowned, the rosière with the rest returned to the parish church, where the Te Deum and a hymn to St. Medard were chanted, while outside the village youths fired salutes from guns and muskets. On finally emerging from the church the rosière was led to the middle of the great street of Salency, where a table had been spread with six plates, six napkins, two knives, a salt-cellar, two quarts of claret, two glasses, a quart of fresh water, two loaves of bread, a cheese, and a dish of nuts. The seigneur, the mayor, the village priest, and two other dignitaries seated themselves at this frugal banquet with the heroine of the occasion. At the end thereof the maiden was presented with an arrow, two tennis-balls, and a whistle made of horn, upon which one of the dignitaries blew three times before presenting it. This beautiful ceremony, interrupted by the Revolution, was re-established in 1812, and takes place now every year, but it has undergone certain modifications. The rosière now receives three hundred francs, of which sum the municipal council gives half.

Meanwhile, during the eighteenth century, under the influence of Rousseau and his continuous appeals for a return to nature and simplicity, it had become fashionable for wealthy persons, whose acquaintance with virtue, mayhap, was rather one of hearsay than of personal experience, to establish rosière prizes in their neighborhood and leave endowments to carry them on in the future. This was done at no less than fifty places throughout France.

Nanterre, the birthplace of St. Genevieve, was one of the first. Whitsunday is here the appointed time. The rosière is supposed to be the girl of the village who has most virtuously followed in the footsteps of the gentle maiden who was born there in 422, but she is generally the prettiest or the most popular girl, and is chosen from among the daughters of influential citizens. She is the queen of the three days' fête, which on the first day has a religious meaning; on the second there is a mock civil marriage at the mairie, and on the third occurs the usual French fête, with roller-skates, travelling theatrical troupes, and a good patronage for cafés and gingerbread-booths.

If the rosière live to be ninety, the name given to her at her baptism will be forgotten in favor of a graceful *sobriquet* which will ennoble her like a title, and men, women, and children will call her Madame la Rose. At first the parish priest and a quorum of village notables selected the rosières, but it was contended that the organ of the confessional might know too much about parish virtues and the notables too little, so the matter is now in most places left to the municipal council.

Every Saturday for June 28, 1873, copies from an amusing description of the fête as witnessed at Sanssouci-des-Fleurettes:

" A Sunday sun sheds its gilding over the village and brightens a double row of spectators packed close as corn, and forming a lane between the rosière's house and the church. Three weeks have elapsed since the election, and animosities have had time to be smoothed away and melt. Like other sovereigns, this Queen of Roses rules by accomplished fact; so it is better to smile on her and seem proud of her, in order that strangers may not go away with the impression that tongues are forked and envious at Sanssouci-des-Fleurettes. Twelve o'clock is pealed musically from the church belfry; the bell-pullers ring out the chimes; the corps of communal firemen with brass helmets gleaming in the sun draw up as a guard of honor outside the rosière's door, and the mayor, glorious in a white cravat, his sash, and a pair of new white cotton gloves, is descried coming in the distance with the *garde champêtre*, in cocked hat and dirk, stalking in front, and the councillors all trooping behind. The band of the firemen takes up its position, the fireman captain unsheathes his sword, and now the mayor, who has gone into the rosière's house, emerges with her leaning on his hand; the firemen present arms, the band struts off filling the air with martial music, the firemen wheel round and follow at the quick march; then comes the rosière in white, and with a veil of muslin; the rosière of last year walks by her side to the left, and nothing can exceed the enthusiasm of the on-lookers as they wave their hats or handkerchiefs, shower flowers on the road, and then rush off one on the top of another to try and jam themselves into the church. But the church porch is guarded by that trusty French beadle with glittering halberd, silver baldric, and tapering sword. The seats are all filled, and he would not let his own uncle slip in: so make way, messieurs et dames, for the firemen, who stream up the nave like a loud-sounding sea; make way for the rosière, who looks a little pale and nervous at the cheering; and step aside for M. le Maire, whose face is as a fine new brick just out of the kiln. The gracious lady—duchess, countess, or prefète—who is to bestow the crown is already in her seat near the altar rails; the rosières of preceding years shine in a row in their special pew up the chancel; the choristers, thurifers, and clergy are arrayed in gorgeous vestments, each at his proper post, and the beadle brings down his halberd with a noise of thunder on the stone flooring to bid the organist strike up a triumphal march. Then when this has been played out and died away under the vaulted roof, mass begins; then ensues the sermon, from which let us draw the comforting moral that life is ever strewn with roses for the virtuous, or at least ought to be, which is the same thing. Then of one accord we all rise on our legs to see the rosière led up to the altar and kneel to receive the crown of white roses together with the other incentives to continued purity. The rosière is generally pretty; and if the prating of evil tongues were listened to, we might go to bed with a notion that she is selected rather with a view to her personal attractions than to other points, seeing how painful it would be for any village that respected itself to exhibit to those Parisians, who laugh at everything, a countenance of passing ugliness as the only specimen of local virtue. But let us take things gratefully as they come, without inquiring into causes. Enough for us that the rosière is fair; enough that the crown fits her well, and that the plates handed round among the congregation are soon filled with gold and silver sufficient to form a pleasant supplement to the thousand-franc note which the foundress has bequeathed. Let us only hope that the watch and chain, the pair of ear-rings, and the bracelet—which are the kind though hazardous gifts of the municipality, the neighboring gentry, and the lady patroness respectively—will not imbue the amiable young peasant girl with the belief that perseverance in virtue will help her to complete her stock of jewelry in after-life. Nor let her be persuaded, by and by, as she banquets with the authorities off roast chicken and champagne, which the rate-payers will afford, that mankind is always ready thus to honor with fermented beverages those who distinguish themselves by a display of modest qualities. If the rosière's experience of life could only cease at the moment when the cloth is removed from the banqueting-board, this globe might indeed seem to her, as she floated upwards, the Elysium of the Just. Unfortunately to-morrow lies beyond, and who knows what shocks may await the trusting rosière who has imagined that bands of music, eighteen-carat trinkets, and the vintage of Mme. Clicquot are institutions kept alive by, and for the sole use of, the virtuous?"

Something analogous to the French rosière exists in the grimiest part of London. Early in the seventeenth century there flourished on the north bank of the Thames, among the sailors of Wapping, Shadwell, and Poplar, a brewer named Henry Raine, who founded in St. George's parish a school for boys and girls, fifty of each, with salaries for master and mistress. This done, and the school well started, he presently built and endowed an asylum for girls, to be taken out of the school, trained for four years in the duties of domestic service, and then put out into good places. The girls were not necessarily to be orphans, but they were to remain under some sort of surveillance for four years after leaving the asylum. If during that time they kept their good character for virtue, and found a lover also of good character, who must be a native of St. George's or an adjoining parish, and a churchman, they might at the age of twenty-two draw lots with other girls who fulfilled the same conditions for a marriage portion of one hundred pounds. The drawing of lots, the marriage ceremony, and the ceremony of presentation are all regulated by custom and order supposed to have been arranged by Raine himself.

The lots are drawn in May. The marriage and presentation of the purse take place on the succeeding November 5, the former in the church of St. George's and the latter in the vestry hall. A feature of the presentation is the singing of an anonymous ode in honor of Henry Raine, with this chorus :

> Proclaim his worth, fulfil the plan
> Of this unrivalled friend of man.

Rough Music. The English equivalent of the French charivari (*q. v.*). In many of the southern counties of England it is or was until recently the fashion for the villagers to express a neighborly contempt for individual weaknesses or errors by gathering together for the infliction of what is known as rough music upon the offender. If a husband beat his wife or suffer himself to be henpecked, if either be unfaithful to the other, a mob of men, women, and children march to the culprit's house, each provided with some instrument for aural torture, a pan or a kettle, for example, drummed on by a huge key; fire-shovels and tongs rattled together; iron pot-lids used as cymbals; a cowhorn or a marrow-bone used as a trumpet, or anything else that experience or imagination may suggest as combining the most noise with the least harmony. Above the din of the infernal concert rise shouts of "Shame! Shame! who beat his wife? [or what not.] I say, John Doe, come out and show yourself!" After an hour or so spent in this amusement, the procession moves off through the village streets, proclaiming in all the

most public places the name and the crime of the unwilling
hero or heroine of the occasion. The piquancy of the accusa-
tions is often greatly enhanced by some village humorist, who,
grotesquely arrayed and with his face rouged or blacked, acts
the part of herald. In the northern counties this herald is carried astride of a stang or pole. Hence the ceremony is there
known as Riding the Stang (*q. v.*).

Rousing Staff. A long stick or pole which was anciently
used by beadles in churches to prod inattentive or dozing members of the congregation and bring them to a proper sense of
reverence for their surroundings. At the palace of the Bishop
of London at Fulham another sort of rousing stick is still used,
in accordance with time-honored custom, for the purpose of
knocking up certain of the servants at successive hours, beginning at about half-past five in the morning. This is a slender
rod some fifteen feet in length, with which the palace lodge-
keeper raps on the antique casements of the servants' bedrooms
in the quadrangle within the massive wooden gates of the large
western archway, and he continues the attention until the
sleeper gives a more or less grateful answer.

In the earlier years of the nineteenth century, at Holy Trinity Church, Warrington, a masculine bit of womanhood named
Betty Finch held the office of sluggard-waker, which was there
known as the bobber. She is described as walking majestically
along the aisles during the service, armed with a long stick like
a fishing-rod, which had a "bob" fastened to the end of it, and
when she caught any one speaking or talking she gave him a
"nudge." Her son was engaged in the belfry, and often truth-
fully sang,—

> My father's a clerk,
> My sister's a singer,
> My mother's the bobber,
> And I am a ringer.

Andrews, in his "Curiosities of the Church," gives a description of an official who used to be employed as sluggard-waker.
He was a respectable-looking man, with a churchwarden air, who
carried a long stout wand with a fork at the end of it. "At
intervals he stepped stealthily up and down the naves and aisles
of the church, and whenever he saw an individual whose senses
were buried in oblivion, he touched him with his wand so effectually that the spell was broken, and in a moment he was recalled
to all the realities of life. I watched as he mounted, with easy
steps, into the galleries. At the end of one of them there sat in
the front seat a young man who had very much the appearance
of a farmer, with his mouth open and his eyes closed, a perfect

picture of repose. The official marked him for his own, and, having fitted his fork to the nape of his neck, he gave him such a push that, had he not been used to such visitations, it would probably have produced an ejaculatory start highly inconvenient on such occasions. But no; every one seemed to quietly acquiesce in the usage, and, whatever else they might be dreaming of, they certainly did not dream of the infringement upon the liberties of the subject, nor did they think of applying for the summons on account of the assault."

Rumald or **Rumbald, St.,** patron of Brackley and Buckingham, England. The regular festival of this saint is on November 3, the anniversary of his death, but at Brackley it used to be celebrated on August 28 (probably the date of the translation of his bones), while in Kent Christmas Eve is known as Rumbald Night. Hasted in his "History of Kent," vol. iii. p. 380, mentions a singular custom used of long time by the fishermen of Folkestone. They chose eight of their largest and best whitings out of every boat when they came home from the fishery, and sold them apart from the rest. Out of the money arising from them they made a feast every Christmas Eve which they called a Rumbald. The master of each boat provided this feast for his own company. This custom, now fallen into disuse, might anciently have been instituted in honor of St. Rumald, being originally designed as an offering to him for his protection during the fishery.

This saint, whose legend is not accepted in its entirety by careful hagiologists, was an instance of rare precocity. Son of the King of Northumbria by a Christian woman, and born at Sutton in Northamptonshire, he came into the world crying three times, "I am a Christian!" He expressed a desire for immediate baptism, chose his own name and his godfather's, directed that a large hollow stone should be brought in as the font, immediately after the ceremony walked to a well near Brackley which still bears his name, there preached for three successive days, and then died. According to his own request, his body lay buried for one year in Sutton, for the second year in Brackley, and at the beginning of the third it was translated to Buckingham and deposited in a shrine in an aisle of the church which afterwards bore his name. Richard Fowler, chancellor to Edward IV., undertook to rebuild this aisle, but died in 1477, before its completion, leaving the following directions in his will: "Item, I wolle that the aforesaid Isle [aisle] of St Rumwold, in the aforesaid church prebendal of Bucks, where my body and other of my friends lyen buried, the which isle is begonne of new to be made, be fully made and performed up perfitely in all things att my costs and charge; and in the same isle that there be made of new a toumbe or shrine for the said saint where the old is now standing, and that it be made curiously with marble in length and breadth as shall be thought by myn executors most convenient, consideration had to the rome, and upon the same tombe or shrine I will that there be sett a coffyn or a chest curiously wrought and gilte, as it appertaynith for to lay in the bones of the same saint, and this also to be doan in all things at my cost and charge." Hence it appears that in the fifteenth century the relics of this infant saint were already held in high veneration. They continued to be the object of pilgrimages till the middle of the sixteenth century. Foxe in his Martyrology tells of certain Lollards who having renounced their errors were required in expiation to walk to Buckingham and present an offering at the shrine of St. Rumald. There was also a famous image of the saint at Boxley, in Kent, small and hollow and apparently very light, yet only a chaste woman could move it. Fuller explains this paradox in a quaint passage. "The moving hereof," he says, "was made the condition of women's chastity. Such who paid the priest well might easily remove it, whilst others might tug at it to no purpose. For this was the contrivance of the cheat,—that it was fastened with a pin of wood by an invisible stander behind. Now, when such offered to take it who had been bountiful to the priest before, they bare it away with ease, which was impossible for their hands to remove who had been close-fisted in their confessions. Thus it moved more laughter than devotion, and many chaste virgins and wives went away with blushing faces, leaving (without cause) the suspicion of their wantonness in the eyes of the beholders; whilst others came off with more credit (because with more coin) though with less chastity."

Rush-Bearing. An ancient religious ceremony which still has local survivals in England. Formerly the floors of churches and dwelling-places consisted of the hard dry earth, which was covered over with rushes to render it grateful to the feet. Even in the royal palaces, rushes and straw, sometimes mixed with sweet herbs, formed the sole carpeting. In the household roll of Edward II. is an entry of money paid to John de Carleford for going from York to Newcastle to procure straw for the king's chamber. Hentzner in his "Itinerary" says of Queen Elizabeth's presence-chamber at Greenwich, "the floor, after the English fashion, was strewed with hay," meaning rushes. In a little book called "Wits, Fits, and Fancies" (1614) is the following anecdote: "When Henry III., King of France, demanded of Monsieur Dandelot what especial things he had noted in

England during the time of his negotiation there, he answered that he had seen but three things remarkable, which were, that people did drinke in bootes, eate raw fish, and strewed all their best rooms with hay; meaning black jacks, oysters, and rushes." Yet the use of rushes on floors was not unknown in France, for Froissart in his account of the death of Gaston, Count de Foix, relates how the hero's chamber was strewn with rushes and green leaves, and the walls hung with boughs newly cut for perfume and coolness, as the weather was marvellously hot.

Erasmus, in a letter to Dr. Francis, physician to Cardinal Wolsey, complains that as the rushes were seldom thoroughly changed, and the habits of the inmates were not always very cleanly, the smell soon became anything but pleasant. He speaks of the lowest layer of rushes (the top only being renewed) as remaining unchanged sometimes for twenty years, a receptacle for beer, grease, fragments of victuals, and other organic matters. To this filthiness he ascribes the frequent pestilences with which the people of England were afflicted. He recommends the entire banishment of rushes and a better ventilation.

In the churches it grew to be the custom to renew the rushes once a year, usually on the Saturday next after the feast of the patron saint. The parishioners came in procession to strew the floor with newly cut rushes. Long after carpets and matting had taken the place of rushes, the rush-bearing ceremony continued. "In Westmoreland, Lancashire, and districts of Yorkshire," wrote the Rev. G. Miles Cooper so recently as 1857, "there is still celebrated between hay-making and harvest a village fête called the Rush-Bearing. Young women dressed in white, and carrying garlands of flowers and rushes, walk in procession to the parish church accompanied by a crowd of rustics with flags flying and music playing. There they suspend their floral chaplets on the chancel rails, and the day is concluded with a simple feast." (*Sussex Archæological Collections*, vol. ix.)

In Cheshire, at Runcorn and Warburton, fifty years ago, as we are told by a contributor to *Notes and Queries*, First Series, i. 356, the annual rush-bearing wake was carried on in grand style: "A large quantity of rushes—sometimes a cart-load—is collected, and, being bound on the cart, they are cut evenly at each end, and on Saturday evening a number of men sit on the top of the rushes, holding garlands of artificial flowers, tinsel, etc. The cart is drawn through the parish by three or four spirited horses, decked with ribbons, the collars being surrounded with small bells. It is attended by morris-dancers fantastically dressed; there are men in women's clothes, one of whom, with his face blackened, has a belt, with a large bell attached, round his waist, and carries a ladle to collect money from the spectators. The party stop and dance at the public house on their way to the parish church, where the rushes are deposited and the garlands are hung up, to remain till the next year."

Grasmere, in the English Lake district, claims to be the only place where the custom of rush-bearing preserves an unbroken record from a remote antiquity to the present day. The preservation of the ceremony during the middle of the nineteenth century was due largely to the influence of the poet Wordsworth, and more recently to the energy of the late vicar, Mr. Fletcher, and the liberality of a wealthy resident, one Dawson, of Allan Bank, Grasmere. The latter was an admirer of the old custom, and encouraged the children to keep up the procession by presenting a reward to each of the youthful rush-bearers.

Hone gives an interesting account of how rush-bearing was celebrated at Grasmere on July 21, 1827:

"The church door was open, and I discovered that the villagers were strewing the floor with fresh rushes. During the whole of this day I observed the children busily employed in preparing garlands of such wild flowers as the beautiful valley produces for the evening procession, which commenced at nine P.M, in the following order. The children, chiefly girls, holding these garlands, paraded through the village, preceded by the Union Band (thanks to the great drum for this information). They then entered the church, when the three largest garlands were placed on the altar, and the remaining ones in various other parts of the place. In the procession I observed the Opium-Eater, Mr. Barber (an opulent gentleman residing in the neighborhood), Mr. and Mrs. Wordsworth, Miss Wordsworth, and Miss Dora Wordsworth. Wordsworth is the chief supporter of these rustic ceremonies. The procession over, the party adjourned to the ball-room, a hayloft, at my worthy friend Mr. Bell's, where the country lads and lasses tripped it merrily and heavily. The dance was kept up till a quarter to twelve, when a livery servant entered and delivered the following verbal message to Billy (the fiddler): 'Master's respects, and will thank you to lend him the fiddle-stick.' Billy took the hint: the Sabbath was now at hand, and the pastor of the parish had adopted this gentle mode of apprising the assembled revellers that they ought to cease their revelry. The servant departed with the fiddle-stick, the chandelier was removed, and when the village clock struck twelve, not an individual was to be seen out of doors in the village."

Up to 1841 the floor of the church remained unpaved and

was yearly strewn with rushes. Pews and floors were introduced in that year, but the rush-bearing continued to be kept
up with undiminished vigor. Until 1885 it took place on the
Saturday nearest July 20. It is now celebrated on the Saturday next after August 5, the festival of St. Oswald, to whom
the church is dedicated. The children assemble with their garlands, which they arrange along the churchyard wall. At half-
past six o'clock the procession is marshalled in the road in the
following order :

Banner of St. Oswald.

Clergy and Choir in Surplices.

Band.

Queen, with Pages.

Maids of Honor, bearing the Rush-Sheet.

The Rush-Bearers.

The queen and her court and the bearing of the rush-sheet,
which were important features in the old festival, were revived
in 1891. "Arranging the sheet," says Bamford, a Lancashire poet,
" was exclusively the work of girls and women ; and in proportion as it was happily designed and finely put together was the
praise or disparagement meted out by the people,—a point on
which they were not a little sensitive. The sheet was a piece
of white linen, generally a good bed-sheet, and on it were
pretty rosettes and quaint compartments, and borderings of all
colors and hues which either paper, tinsel, ribbons, or natural
flowers could supply. In these compartments were arranged
silver watches, trays, spoons, sugar-tongs, teapots, quart tankards,
drinking-cups, and other fitting articles of ornament and value."
The present sheet was spun in Grasmere by a young woman of
the village.

After the procession has been formed, the hymn for St. Oswald is sung, and the band plays the " Rush-Bearing March"
(said to have been played nearly a century ago), and the procession perambulates the village, the bells ringing and the tower
flag flying. On returning to the church the Rush-Bearers'
Hymn is sung, and the garlands are arranged round the walls.
Full choral evensong follows. The children afterwards receive
gingerbread, and some wrestling-bouts engage the attention of
the young men. The garlands are removed on the following
Monday to a neighboring field, where the Maypole is set up and
a regular gala held for the rush-bearers and all who choose to
share it. The words of the Rush-Bearers' Hymn and that of
St. Oswald have no great distinguishing merit, and two verses
of the former may suffice :

The Rush-Bearers' Hymn.

Our fathers to the House of God,
    As yet a building rude,
Bore offerings from the flowery sod,
    And fragrant rushes strewed.

May we, their children, ne'er forget
    The pious lesson given,
But honor still, together met,
    The Lord of Earth and Heaven.

The rush-bearing with morris-dancing is still kept up at Whitworth, near Rochdale, Warcop, Westmoreland, Haworth and Saddleworth, Yorkshire, and other places. (DITCHFIELD, p. 134 *et seq.*)

Sometimes churches are now strewn with grass or hay in lieu of rushes. Thus, the parish of Clee, in Lincolnshire, possesses an ancient privilege of cutting rushes from a piece of land called "Bescars" for the purpose of strewing the church on Trinity Sunday. A small quantity of grass is annually cut to preserve this right. (EDWARDS : *Old English Customs*, p. 217.)

At Old Weston, in Huntingdonshire, a piece of greensward belongs by custom to the parish clerk for the time being, subject to the condition of the land being mown immediately before Weston feast, which occurs in July, and the cutting thereof being strewn on the church floor previous to divine service on the feast Sunday. (Ibid., p. 220.)

At Braunstone, Leicestershire, the parish church is strewn with hay on the Sunday after St. Peter's Day (June 29). On the Thursday previous the Holme Meadow is mown. On Saturday the parish clerk fetches a small load of hay, which he must spread with his hands on the floor of the church. The portion of the meadow whence the hay is brought is called "The Clerk's Acre," and the rest of the hay belongs to him. (DITCHFIELD, p. 138.)

S.

Sabbath or **Saturday.** The seventh day of the week. The Sabbath of the Jews begins at sunset on Friday. Its advent is noted by the matron of the household, who lights the two long tapers in candlesticks standing on the dining-room table. Then she and the children greet the head of the family with the salutation "Shabbath," or Good Sabbath. At the commencement of dinner, when the males appear with their hats on, the "Kiddush," or sanctification, takes place. First a brief thanksgiving prayer is said, then the house father blesses a vessel of wine, and, after tasting it himself, passes it around as a loving-cup. A double loaf of bread, commemorative of the double portion of manna which fell on the sixth day in the wilderness, is cut into slices, salted, and offered to every one. Every child, in the order of seniority, is next blessed by both parents. Hats are then removed, and the meal commences. At its close the hats are again donned for the closing prayer in Hebrew. No cigars are smoked by the strictly orthodox, as no fire, not imperatively needed, may be kindled on the day of rest. All the Sabbath meals are prepared on Friday. The prohibition against kindling a fire is explained in this way. In their wanderings in the wilderness the only method of the Israelites for kindling a fire was by rubbing two sticks together until a flame was produced. This involved considerable labor, and the commandment against it has been retained so strictly that a Jew is forbidden even to touch a fire when kindled, to lift a lighted candle, or to extinguish a fire or a candle when lit. In other ways the strict Jews carry their Sabbath formalities to excess. A handkerchief loose in the pocket, a superfluous pin in the clothes, is looked upon as a burden unfit for the Sabbath. But if the handkerchief be pinned to the pocket, or tied round the waist like a girdle, there is then no harm, as it may be considered a part of the garments. No fruit may be gathered from the tree, though if they can get at it with their teeth they may bite off as much as they wish. They will not meddle with any tool, nor write, nor sign their names, on the Sabbath, nor ride, nor travel, nor play any musical instrument, nor bathe, nor tear or break anything, even a hair: hence a very strict Jew will not comb his hair on the Sabbath.

The Sabbath closes at starlight on Saturday. Paterfamilias makes ready for the return of weekday duties by providing a wine-cup which he holds in his right hand, a spice-box, beautifully worked in silver filigree, in his left, and a wax taper consisting of several strands braided on the flat, which he places on the table in front of him. Some of the Kabbalists explain the wine-cup, spice-box, and taper as emblems of water, air, and fire. The two former symbolize the Sabbath, the latter the weekday. The family group themselves around the table as their head chants the Habdalah, or prayer of separation between the Sabbath and the secular week. Then his wife lights the taper as he pronounces a benediction, first over the wine-cup and next over the spice-box. He inhales the fragrance of the latter, and his example is followed by every one present. Another benediction follows, during which all raise their hands and look at the fingers, in recognition of the coming duty to devote them to secular work for six days. At the final benediction, Paterfamilias tastes

the wine, applies a little to his eyes, saying, "The commandment of the Lord is pure, enlightening the eyes" (Psalm xix. 8),
and spills a portion of the remainder into a dish. His wife now
hands him the taper, which he extinguishes in the dish. The
Sabbath is at an end.

Sacrament of the Miracle, Festival of the Most Holy.

(Fr. *Fête du Très-Saint Sacrement de Miracle.*) The Grande
Kermesse or chief holiday of Brussels. It is celebrated on the
first Sunday after July 13, the anniversary of the translation of
three consecrated wafers or hosts from St. Catherine's Church to
St. Gudula, under the following circumstances, as legend states
them. In the year 1370, sixteen hosts were stolen by the Jews
from the tabernacle of St. Catherine and carried to their synagogue. On Good Friday they assembled and derisively stabbed
the hosts with a penknife. Blood flowed. Shocked, but not
converted, they destroyed the bleeding evidences of their sacrilege and intrusted three of the hosts which had escaped un-
scathed to a Jewess who was to carry them to their brethren
in Cologne. Now, it happened that this woman was a secret
convert to Christianity. She carried them to the priest of St.
Catherine's chapel and told the whole story. The Jews were
arrested, the guilty ones executed, and the remainder banished
from Brussels.

St. Catherine's was a chapel of St. Gudula's, so the clergy
went in grand procession, followed by the reigning sovereigns,
nobility, and dignitaries, to escort the consecrated wafers to St.
Gudula's, where they have ever since been kept in a splendid
monstrance. A number of royalties, from Charles V. to Marie
Antoinette, have helped to decorate the chapel and the shrine.
The latter sent her wedding necklace of diamonds to be suspended around the monstrance.

The synagogue where the outrage was committed was converted into a beautiful expiatory chapel, where a community of
ladies, semi-religious, perpetually adore the Blessed Sacrament in
the spot where it was profaned. Here for a week before the
festival a retreat is always given. During the octave there are
sermons by some famous preacher every day at St. Gudula's
itself.

The grand procession leaves St. Gudula's after the high mass,
and wends its way through the streets to military music. It is
composed of soldiers, clerics, and laity, the most conspicuous
features being children strewing flowers and priests swinging
censers before the Très-Saint Sacrement de Miracle, which is
borne under a magnificent canopy by the deacon and subdeacon
of the mass, followed by the dean. Through the kneeling crowds

they march until they reach the Grande Place, and there, on an altar ornamented with the national colors, the three hosts are exposed for adoration.

" At that moment it is superb; the military form the square, the beautifully dressed children kneel in the centre; the clergy are ranged on the high flight of steps leading up to the altar; incense is burning from huge urns; the dean intones the Tantum Ergo, it is taken up by hundreds, and then the bells ring, the drums roll, the soldiers present arms, the dean raises the Très-Saint Sacrement de Miracle, and gives the benediction to the Hôtel de Ville, and in blessing that hall blesses the city." (*Catholic World*, July, 1892.)

Sacramental Fast. The Thursday before the annual or half-yearly Communion Sunday—variously known as the Sacramental Fast, the Summer Occasion, and, among the profane, as all readers of Burns will recollect, the Holy Fair—was at the beginning of the Scotch Kirk observed as a strict fast. Fasting, however, in the ordinary sense of the word was eventually put aside as a relic of Popery, though the old name was retained. The day was kept throughout Scotland as a supplementary Sunday by church services, closing of all public offices and shops, and an entire cessation of all secular business. And this was not only an ecclesiastical but also a civil ordinance, for the Kirk Sessions had legal authority to enforce it. The sacramental fast was intended to serve as a preparation for the approaching communion,—a kind of Puritan substitute for the old sacramental confession. But the religious use gradually declined, the excursion-trains on fast-days were crowded, and the churches all but empty. It was on that account that the several presbyteries of Glasgow abolished the observance about 1880, and that the presbyteries of Edinburgh, as well of the Established as of the Free Kirk and the United Presbyterians, followed suit in 1887. Sacrament Fast now lingers only in the remote Highlands. There it is the prelude to the five days of sacrament-time, which extend over from Thursday, the fast-day so called, until the following Monday.

Salt Water Day. On the second Saturday in August it has long been the custom of the farmers of Northeastern New Jersey to get out their wagons, and, with wives and children decked out in their best, drive down to the sea-shore, where all give themselves up to bathing, picnicking, and general merriment. By far the most popular place of resort has always been on the beach at Wrack Pond, near what is now Sea Girt. South Amboy is a far-away second, and other points along the coast are or have been sparsely visited. But in all these places, even at Sea Girt, Salt Water Day is no longer what it was in the past, the finest, simplest, most jovial of all rustic gatherings known to the Eastern coast, the only parallel in the North to the Southern barbecue. Then none but the farmer class celebrated it. They had no bath-houses, no conventional bathing-suits. Whole families undressed themselves with the utmost innocence in the neighboring woods or in their own wagons (woe to any Peeping Tom who took unfair advantage of his opportunities), and then, arrayed in all variety of unique and astonishing bathing-costumes, sported with boisterous tumult in the sea-waves, emerging later to take part in dancing, in singing, in a round of country games. This was in the good old days before all the coast hereabout had been turned into "resorts," before the influx of city folks, before railroads were. Now the summer boarders and vagrant interlopers from New York and other places thrust their unwelcome presence upon the farmers. The Edenic innocence has been disturbed by bath-houses, the quaint originality in costumes has been levelled to the hideous common-place of the blue flannel bathing-suit, the beach is filled with booths and stands for catchpenny games, the trees are hung with tawdry bunting and drabbled flags, perspiring performers project mechanical music into the atmosphere, and over all there hangs heavily the suggestion of evil days and evil ways, of town vices, of gambling and drinking and uncanny roistering.

Therefore it is good that a sympathetic observer has given us a sketch of the festival as it appeared in 1891, during the period of transition indeed, yet while most of the original features still remained, amid many innovations. Here is an excerpt from Hamlin Garland's article in the *Cosmopolitan* for August, 1892:

" Packed upon the soft, yellow sand were hundreds and hundreds of carriages, as various as the garments of the people around them. Horses were tied to the wheels, eating oats from their boxes,—gaunt, hard-worked horses, whose harnesses hung from the whippletrees or were piled under the wagons. Beyond them were groups of tents and booths, from which came confused cries and those high-pitched, brazen rigmaroles which are heard at a circus; and over and beyond them the sea, pinkish gray, melted into the infinite haze of the sky.

" Swarming around these teams and booths, drinking red lemonade, eating peanuts, courting and visiting, were the blonde and freckled Jerseymen and Jersey-women. The whole scene was like our universal, characteristic, American county fair, only more disorganized, more individual, more sprawling in effect. It was strange to me by reason of the sand under my feet, the sea at my left, and yet it was familiar in its amusements, its types, its atmosphere of determined enjoyment. The fashionable ladies and gentlemen on the Cliff House veranda found it comical. I did not. I knew these people too well to laugh at them.

"But the unfamiliar and most characteristic part of it all, the part to which I hastened with most interest, was the bathing. Down on the glorious sand strolled the young people; girls in polka-dotted cambric dresses, blue and black; others in the blue-ribboned ill-fitting white gowns, common from Maine to Dakota, with wilted lilies at their belts and gay hats upon their heads. Some of the young men sweltered along in heavy wool-len clothing, others carried their coats upon their arms, their hats perched jauntily upon the back of their heads. With them, among them, in unabashed freedom, walked the bathers, in dresses of every sort and length and color; and they were not all young. There were men and women of all ages in suits that were not suits, but rigs,—old men in suits of field clothes, brown denims, and faded hickory shirts, and old ladies in striped squash-figured gowns and blue-checked sunbonnets, all laughingly, tim-orously stepping into the water. The bathers and the on-lookers were inextricably mixed. Lovers walked along hand in hand, he in an ill-fitting blue flannel bathing-suit, she in a self-con-structed sailor gown with awkward pantalets. Children spatted along the smooth wet beach in shoals. Farmer boys who had never known knickerbockers, and who made no change from their usual suits of denims and hickories, with trousers upheld by cord suspenders, screamed and scuffled and threw sand at each other in boisterous play in the sunny edge of the water.

"Gathered into a varied line along the beach rope were scores of these bathers, of all ages and classes, clinging to the rope, desperately in some cases, in all cases shouting in excitement and vast delight as the grass-green foam spread glassily curling waves and broke over their shoulders."

The origin of this great annual celebration is not known. Someway, somewhere, it started without organization; yet it is as certain in its return as the season itself. The common tradition is that it arose among the Indians, with whom it was a very ancient custom.

Sardine, Burial of the. An Ash Wednesday custom which is frequent in Spain and in many countries where Ash Wednes-day is a special feast. The principal feature is the carrying in procession of a small paper-covered coffin containing a small fish or morsel of sausage, which is buried with great ceremony, this being regarded as a symbol of the burial of all worldly pleasures and desires during the impending fast. At Madrid a vast throng turns out to witness the burial of the sardine on the banks of the Manzanares. (See CARNIVAL, KING.)

Saturnalia. An ancient Roman festival in honor of Saturn, celebrated on the 17th of December. Saturn being an ancient national god of Latium, the institution of the Saturnalia is lost in the most remote antiquity. Falling towards the end of December, at the season when the agricultural labors of the year were completed, it was celebrated by the country-people as a sort of joyous harvest home, and in every age was viewed by all classes of the community as a period of absolute relaxation and unrestrained merriment. The festival was extended in later times to three days, and often continued beyond this time.

During the celebration of this holiday no public business could be transacted, the courts were closed, war was suspended, all private enmities were for the time forgotten, and the city was alive with hilarity. On this day the slaves feasted and were waited upon by their masters, as the female slaves were waited upon by their mistresses on the Matronalia. The special feature of the festival was the gift of wax candles and of little images of wax or clay called *sigilla*. The public festival, in the time of the republic, was for only one day; but for seven days the celebration continued in private houses.

Saviour of the Miracle, Our. A life-size figure of Christ on a colossal cross, preserved in the collegiate church at Salta, in the Argentine Republic. Its fame as a wonder-worker draws to its shrine a continual stream of pilgrims from all the surrounding districts, and even from Bolivia, Chili, and Peru. Periodical processions are held in its honor. Jabez Balfour, the famous English forger and impostor, has preserved in his diary a very vivid account of one of these which he witnessed. It is quoted in the *Pall Mall Gazette* for November 23, 1894. "I have seen many street displays," he says, "in England and abroad, but none so picturesque and none so truly popular. Nearly the whole population of the city turned out either as participators in the procession or as spectators. The only element conspicuously absent was the well-dressed male element, which stood ostentatiously aloof. The procession seemed to be largely self-organized and arranged. It was preceded by a promiscuous crowd of men and boys carrying lighted colored candles. These moved along without any attempt at order, as the skirmishers or forerunners of the regular procession, which was headed by three ecclesiastics carrying a silver cross and two long silver staffs. They were followed by some hundreds of men walking in two single files, one on each side of the roadway. Nothing could be more picturesque than the appearance of these men. Each one carried a lighted candle. The greater number were evidently country-folk of Indian extraction, there being a great preponderance of tall men with copper-colored skins, aquiline features, shaggy beards, and jet-black eyes and hair; but the salient feature, which invested the scene with indescribable picturesqueness, was the brilliant coloring of the ponchos. Every man was dressed in his best, and doubtless many had bought new ponchos for the occasion. The bright reds, blues, yellows, greens, and browns of the ponchos produced the most striking effects,—none the less striking, indeed, because they were obviously accidental and undesigned and were changing every moment as the men passed slowly on. The combinations of colors were as varied as if produced by the shifting of a kaleidoscope. After the long files of men came the highly reverenced Image itself, borne aloft on the shoulders of a great number of men, and surrounded by an enormous quantity of lighted candles and lamps. As the image passed, nearly every spectator uncovered and knelt. It was followed by long files of young girls prettily dressed in white, and with either bright red or bright green sashes, and then by ladies in black gowns, with black shawls thrown over their heads like hoods. This is the strictly conventional go-to-church dress of Salta ladies. All carried lighted candles in their hands and had rosaries hanging from their waists. The number of ladies was enormous, and must have included nearly all the female population of Salta, besides a numerous contingent which had come here on a pilgrimage for the occasion from the city of Cordoba and consisted of members of a sisterhood or association known as the ' Daughters of Jesus.' After the ladies came a life-size figure of the Virgin clad in beautiful bridal attire, and standing on a gilt platform or stage, also borne shoulder-high. This was followed by the governor of the province, who, bareheaded, looked remarkably handsome, in evening dress, with white waistcoat and white gloves. He was accompanied by his ministers and the intendente of police in a splendid uniform. After these personages came the band and two or three weak companies of local troops, and then a confused crowd of men, women, and police. A curious and rather pretty feature in the crowd was the number of little boys, children from three to six years of age, who could just toddle along, and who were clad by their fond parents in perfect sacerdotal garb, with little white lace surplices over black skirts, and five-cornered black caps such as are worn by priests when in full canonicals. Nothing could exceed the good order of the procession, or be better than the general decorum of all, rich and poor alike, who took part in it. The weight of the platforms or stages which bore the cross and the Virgin must have been considerable, but there was always a keen competition among the men for the privilege—which is, indeed, considered a very great privilege—of assisting in transporting the sacred and mystic emblems through the streets of the city. Of course the bishop and some ecclesiastics formed part of the procession, but they were by no means conspicuous, and certainly, in spite of governor, bishop, and soldiers, the whole ceremonial was distinctively popular, and not official nor ecclesiastical. The occasion of the procession was the conclusion of a ' Novena' in honor of the image of our Saviour, to whose miraculous intervention is attributed the immunity from serious shocks of earthquake which Salta has latterly enjoyed. The fame of this miraculous image is by no means local, but is spread throughout a large part of South America. It is known as ' Our Saviour of the Miracle,' and is almost as great a local institution and power here as Our Lady of Lourdes is to the faithful of France."

SCALA SANTA IN 1723.

Scala Santa. (It., "Holy Staircase.") A cherished relic preserved in Rome and said to be the identical staircase in Pilate's house which Christ mounted and descended several times on the morning of the day of his passion, and which was empurpled with his blood when after the flagellation he descended for the last time to take his way to Mount Calvary.

At the top of the Scala Santa the pilgrim comes face to face with a dark chapel, which none may enter, but which can be looked into through a barred gate. Pope Leo III. deposited herein four large caskets full of saintly relics. The chapel is known as the Sancta Sanctorum (" Holy of Holies"), and an inscription over the gateway reads, " *Non est in toto sanctior orbi locus*" (" There is no holier spot in the whole earth").

Scambling Days. The ancient English name for the Mondays and Saturdays in Lent, when no regular meals were provided, and the members of the great families scambled. In the old household-book of the fifth Earl of Northumberland there is a particular section appointing the order of service for these days, and so regulating the licentious contentions of them. Shakespeare, in his play of " Henry V." (Act v. Scene 2), makes King Henry say, "If ever thou be'st mine, Kate, I get thee with *scambling*, and thou must therefore needs prove a good soldier-breeder."

The word scambling is conjectured to be derived from the Greek σκαμβός, " oblique," " indirect."

> The scambling and unquiet time.
> (*Henry V.*, Act i. Sc. 1.)

(*Med. Ævi Kalend.*, vol. ii. p. 350; *Antiq. Repert.*, 1809, vol. iv. pp. 87, 91, 305.)

Scholastica, St. The sister of the great St. Benedict, near whose monastery at Monte Casino she founded and governed a nunnery. She visited her holy brother once a year, and, inasmuch as she was not allowed to enter his monastery, he went out with some of his monks to meet her at some distance. Once she begged him to stay all night and converse with her. He refused. Thereupon she appealed to the Almighty, who sent a storm of thunder and lightning so great that it was impossible for any one to venture out in it. " God forgive you, sister," said Benedict, " what have you done?" She answered, " I asked of you a favor, and you refused it to me : I asked it of Almighty God, and he has granted it me." Three days later, February 10 (*circa* 543), she died.

At Monte Casino it is claimed that, although the original monastery and the nunnery were both destroyed by the Lombards in the seventh century, the relics of brother and sister still remain, and they are shown in the new monastery.

On the other hand, it is asserted that the relics were translated into France and deposited in a rich silver shrine, still extant, in the collegiate church of St. Peter, in Mans. The festival of the translation is kept on July 11 in Mans.

At Oxford the feast of St. Scholastica, February 10, is memorable in collegiate annals as being the anniversary of the most furious of all Town and Gown (*q. v.*) rows in the year 1355. The townsmen had the best of it, and there is little doubt that they abused their victory unmercifully. Forty scholars are said to have lost their lives. Some of those taken prisoners are said to have been scalped in mockery of the clerical tonsure. Crucifixes and holy vessels were torn from the churches and profaned by a drunken mob. The better part of the citizens were ashamed of the excesses which had been committed, and shocked at the number of the victims. The sheriff of Oxfordshire was dismissed from his office. An interdict laid upon the city was only removed by the consent of the authorities to an indenture under the university and city seals, by which the mayor, bailiffs, and chief citizens to the number of sixty-two bound themselves to appear annually at mass in St. Mary's Church on the fatal day of St. Scholastica and offer there each a penny, and also to pay a yearly fine of a hundred marks, which latter obligation was subsequently relaxed on condition of the due fulfilment of the former. The citizens always chafed sorely against this ordinance, under whatever modification. It came at last to a simple attendance at the reading of the Litany. But, though thus modified by consent of the university from time to time, it continued actually in force until the present century. In 1800, the hundred marks were sued for and recovered from the Mayor of Oxford for making default. At last, in 1825, the university, at the request of the town council, gracefully consented to waive a ceremony which only served to keep up the memory of an unhappy feud of ages past, and could not but be regarded by the citizens in the light of a humiliation.

Scoppio del Carro. (It., "Explosion of the Car.") An Easter Eve ceremony peculiar to Florence, Italy. At about eleven o'clock in the morning of Holy Saturday the huge and clumsy vehicle which for centuries has been used at this function is drawn into the Piazza del Duomo by four white oxen gayly decorated with scarlet sashes and bunches of flowers. The body of the carro is festooned with rows of green, red, and white fireworks. After the oxen have been unhitched and led away to a side-street, a wire is attached to the carro, the other end being fastened to the high altar of the Duomo. Then a procession of priests files out from the baptistery and crosses over into the Duomo to officiate at the services. Just at twelve o'clock an artificial dove, known as the Colombina, dashes along the wire from the altar to the carro, bearing in its beak a spark of fire from the sacred flame which burns there continually. It is a popular superstition that if the dove succeeds in lighting the fuse of the fireworks and returns safely to the altar a good harvest will follow. Hence thousands of peasants crowd into the square and the cathedral on the fateful day. In former times the Colombina occasionally missed the mark, and then the peasantry were so overwhelmed with pessimistic fears that their own lack of energy brought about only too surely the fulfilment of the prophecy. But modern improvements in pyrotechnic mechanism make disappointment practically impossible. With much crackling and sputtering and then with report after report, like toy pistols, the red, white, and green fireworks go off amid the joyous shouts and cheers of the people. The oxen are brought back and reharnessed, and then the old car lumbers off with a stream of spectators behind it to the Palazzo Pandolfini. Here it is again brought to a halt, and the last row of fireworks is set off according to time-honored custom. For it was a Pandolfini who in the crusading ages brought the sacred flame from Jerusalem to Florence. Legend says that he rode backward all the way, to protect it from the possibility of extinguishing draughts.

Scramble Feast. The name given by foreigners to a ceremony that takes place yearly in the Rajpoot town of Ajmeer on the anniversary of the local saint, and in front of his shrine. Two huge caldrons, each containing many thousand pounds of rice and butter, are filled to the brim, and this gigantic mess is then served out broadcast amid the myriads of native beggars that always assemble for the occasion, many for want of any other receptacle extending their clasped hands for the scalding rice. After this the keepers of the shrine, and the inhabitants of a favored part of the town who have enjoyed the prescriptive right from time immemorial, swathe themselves in thick shawls as a protection against the heated metal, and, scrambling into the caldrons, scrape them clean.

What are known as Scrambling Charities or Scrambling Doles (see DOLE) are not uncommon in England. The most remarkable is one at St. Briavel's, Gloucestershire. It is thus described in the *Gentleman's Magazine* for 1816: " On Whit Sunday several baskets full of bread and cheese cut into small squares of an inch each are brought into church ; and immediately after divine service is ended, the churchwardens, or some other persons, take them up into the galleries, whence their contents are thrown among the congregation, who have a grand scramble for them in the body of the church. This occasions as great a tumult and uproar as the amusements of the village wake, the inhabitants being always extremely anxious to attend worship on this day. The custom is holden for the purpose of preserving to the poor of St. Briavel's and Hewelsfield the right of cutting and carrying away wood from three thousand acres of coppiceland, for which each housekeeper is assessed twopence to buy the bread and cheese which are given away."

The most recent endowment of the sort seems to be at Wath, near Rotherham, where one Tuke, dying in the year 1810, left, among other strange bequests, forty dozen penny loaves to be thrown from the church leads at twelve o'clock on Christmas Day forever.

Sebald, St. The legend of this saint describes him as the son of a Danish king, who in the eighth century settled in England and accompanied St. Boniface on his mission to Germany. Many miracles and conversions are ascribed to him. He is said to have changed stones into bread and water into wine with which to feed his fellow-missionaries. One day he came into a hut where a poor family was perishing with cold, and turned the icicles on the roof to fuel. He lived the greater part of his life near Nuremberg. His remains are interred in a magnificent bronze shrine, the work of Peter Visscher and his five sons, which stands in the elegant church dedicated to the saint in that city. The shrine encloses the oaken chest encased with silver plates which contains the saint's body.

Sebastian, St., patron of Chiemsee, Mannheim, Oetting, Palma, Rome, Soissons, of makers of military laces, of archers and makers of fencing-foils. His festival is celebrated on January 20.

St. Sebastian was born at Narbonne, in Gaul, but his parents were natives of Milan, and he was brought up in the latter city. He was secretly a Christian, although he served in the Roman army. He was placed in command of the first cohort by the Emperors Diocletian and Maximian. He used his power to the utmost for the protection of his fellow-Christians, and converted many of his companions. Two brothers, Marcus and Marcellianus, were suspected of being Christians and were put to the torture. They were expecting execution in prison, and their relatives and friends, who were admitted to see them, implored them to save their lives by denying the Christian faith. Sebastian heard of this, and immediately went to the prison, when he not only succeeded in holding the two young men true to their faith, but converted the relatives and friends. St. Sebastian was finally denounced as a Christian, and was ordered by Diocletian to be shot to death with arrows. He was taken to a field and pierced with many arrows by archers and left for dead. But a devout widow named Irene, who came to bury the body, found that he still lived, and took him to her home, where she tended him until he recovered. Sebastian determined to confront Diocletian, and one day, hearing the trumpet notes which told of the Emperor's approach, he went out and addressed Diocletian, pleading for the persecuted Christians and rebuking him for his sins. The Emperor was amazed at the sight of Sebastian, whom he thought dead, and was enraged at his words. He caused the saint to be beaten to death with clubs, and his body to be thrown into a sewer, whence it was rescued by a Christian woman named Lucina, who buried it in the Catacombs. From his connection with arrows, St. Sebastian came to be regarded as the especial patron saint against pestilence, which is symbolized by arrows. There is a tablet in San Pietro in Vincoli in Rome recording a notable instance of the deliverance by St. Sebastian of that city from the plague.

The relics of the saint were translated to Soissons, in France, in 826, and are scattered in various places, some at Soissons, the head at Ebernach, in Luxemburg, and other portions at Mantua, Malaga, Seville, Toulouse, Munich, Paris, Tournay, Antwerp, and Brussels.

In art the saint can always be recognized as a young man transfixed with arrows.

MARTYRDOM OF ST. SECUNDUS.

Secundus, St., patron of Asti, in which Italian city he was martyred on March 30, 119, by having his head cut off. The anniversary of his death is celebrated there with much pomp. His relics are preserved in the church dedicated to him.

Sementivæ, Feriæ. ("Feast of Sowing.") An ancient Roman festival celebrated in January.

The Feriæ Sementivæ was a movable feast, and was held on two days in January a week apart. This was the first of the long series of agricultural festivals, the number and antiquity of which are the best proofs that Rome was at first a community of peasants. Sacrifices were made to Tellus, the earth, and Ceres, goddess of agriculture; and all the minor deities who presided over the several operations of tillage were invoked to be propitious: Vervactor, the god of breaking up fallow land; Reparator, of renewing its powers; Obarator, of ploughing; Occator, of harrowing; Imporcitor, of drawing furrows; Insitor, of grafting; Sarritor, of hoeing; Subruncinator, of weeding; Messor, of harvesting; Convector, of gathering in; Conditor, of storing up; Promitor, of bringing out for use. So minute were the Romans in their religious observances; and, for fear that any divine power had been overlooked, they were wont to add in their prayers, *sive deo, sive deæ* ("any unknown god, male or female"); but always Janus was called upon first. On the same day with the Sementivæ the Paganalia were celebrated in the country,—the feast of the townships,—*pagi,*—when the seed was all in the ground, the plough was laid away until spring, and the cattle rested in the stall.

Separation of the Waters. (Fr. *La Séparation des Eaux.*) A festival celebrated annually at Avignon in honor of a miracle that occurred there November 30, 1433, during a general inundation of the valley from the overflow of the Rhône, the Durance, and the Sorgue. The water had risen to so great a height around the church of the Gray Penitents at Avignon that the brethren, fearing it might reach the niche containing the eucharist, went thither in a boat, but found the waters parted, leaving a dry passage to the altar, as between two crystal walls. This was attested by twelve Penitents, three doctors of theology, and many lay persons. Cardinal Fieschi witnessed it, and Théophile Raynaud speaks of it as a well-known fact. This occurrence has been celebrated in several hymns in the Latin and Provençal tongues, and in a famous epigram:

> Suspendit Jordanis aqua cum permeat Arca;
> Ad te, Christe, viam pensilis unda dedit;
> Quæ quondam Domini cognoverat unda vel umbram,
> Non nosset Dominum quem videt illa suum?

("The water of Jordan parts while the Ark passes through. To you, O Christ, the overhanging wave yields a way. That element which once had recognized the mere symbol of the Lord, would it not know him when it saw him in person?")

Besides the anniversary a jubilee celebration takes place every twenty-five years to commemorate both the Separation of the Waters and the historic procession instituted by Louis VIII. (See CROSS, EXALTATION OF THE.) The last of these occurred in 1876. "All the Gray Penitents in the south of France take part. The procession begins at the church of the Holy Cross. There are six or seven hundred Gray Penitents alone, some with great golden bâtons curiously wrought, some with tall girandoles, the branches set with burning tapers, and others with torches of all sizes, from one pound in weight up to fifty, and adorned with silver shields covered with religious devices. Mingled with them are bands of musicians, with trumpets, viols, rural pipes, or strange instruments like the Set Gau,—the Seven Joys,—used in many country churches of Provence, consisting of a wheel with seven bells that gayly ring out every note of the gamut:

> Et les Sept Joies au timbre clair
> Carillonnaient joyeusement.
>
> (MISTRAL.)

There are white-winged choristers with clear, flute-like voices; white-robed priests chanting some angelic hymn, like the 'Sacris Solemniis,' or, clad in silvery copes, bearing the rich Gremium, or carrying feretories, and coffers, and golden busts, and silver hands and arms, containing relics of the blessed saints, or beautiful statues of Our Lady and the saints popular at Avignon, such as St. Agricol, invoked in every public calamity, and St. Martha, dear to every housewife. There are dignitaries with silver maces, magistrates *en grande tenue*, Swiss guards with halberds on their shoulders, and companies of foot-soldiers and cavalry with stirring martial music. Bands of children are scattering flowers,—the golden gorse, the sweet roses of Provence, roses first brought from the East by the Crusaders, leaves of the fennel, the *ferigoulo*, and other aromatic plants that grow profusely on every cliff of this region. The ways are carpeted with them and embowered with arches of verdure. There are lamps at every Madonna shrine at the corners or before the houses. The narrow, sunless streets are hung with tapestries and gay cloths and floating banners, and aflame with long lines of tapers, borne by the procession, looking like the aisles of some vast cathedral. The bells of the Ville Sonnante are in full peal.

"In the midst of all this grandeur appears the divine host—O

Salutaris Hostia!—borne by priests in spotless robes, with a look of awe on their faces, attended by a band of levites, some swinging smoking censers, others with baskets of flowers they are scattering in the air. Around blaze huge torches of four wicks, bearing silver shields, on which, in *repoussé* work, is a glittering cross, the sun-like emblem of the Blessed Sacrament, or the watchword of the Penitents,—*Gloria, Laus et Honor!*

"Here and there on the way are *reposoirs* as beautiful as flowers and lights can make them; everywhere the church doors are open, the convent gates wide spread, with monks kneeling at the entrance,—monks now banished from their peaceful homes, —or abbesses at the head of their nuns, or pious confraternities, to hail the coming of the Lord. There are looks and attitudes of devotion on every side. At every hand there is a fresh salute, a new outburst of music, more clouds of incense, a fresh rain of flowers, a more joyous frenzy of bells.

"At length the procession winds up to the Rocher des Doms. It ascends the sacred *escalier du Pater* to the cathedral, which is once more to be divinely blessed. There in the broad portal stands the venerable archbishop, attended by the canons in their robes. The prelate lays aside his mitre and crosier at the appearance of the host. He raises it on high. The whole city, in movement an instant before, is now silent and prostrate. A thousand lights blaze on the heights of the Doms. The 'Pange, lingua' is sung by thousands of voices. There is a display of fireworks, and a salute of cannon from the ramparts, as, from the verge of this lofty terrace overlooking Avignon, the divine benediction is solemnly given to the kneeling crowd." (*Catholic World*, July, 1886.)

September. The name comes from the Latin *septimus*, "seventh," because under the ten-month calendar, and afterwards under the reckoning which made March the beginning of the year, September was the seventh month. After July and August (originally Quintilis, "fifth," and Sextilis, "sixth") had been so named in honor of Julius Cæsar and Augustus, several Roman Emperors sought to give their names to September, but in this case the innovation did not survive. Julius Cæsar gave September thirty-one days in his revision of the calendar, but it was subsequently reduced to thirty days by Augustus, who changed the length of all the months after August in order to give his titular month the same length as July.

The Saxons called September *Gerstmonath*, or Barley-Month, this crop, from which their favorite beverage was brewed, being then gathered. It is still called *Herbstmonat*, or Harvest Month, in Switzerland. The harvest-moon comes in this month, being the full moon nearest the autumnal equinox. For several evenings the moon rises near sunset, thus enabling the harvesters to

SEPTEMBER. HUNTING—PASTURING SWINE.

extend their day's work,—a phenomenon less noticed in the United States than in England and Northern Europe. The autumnal equinox occurs about September 24.

September, Sixteenth of. This is the Independence Day of Mexico, when every city, town, and village puts on its gayest attire and gives itself up to merriment. Not with the boom of cannon or the crackling of fire-crackers is the day ushered in, but with the music of military bands stationed in the "portales" or the plaza. Cock-fights and bull-fights fill up the daytime. In the evening the plaza, gayly decorated with bunting and lanterns, becomes the general meeting-ground. The band is stationed under the canopy of a kiosk in the centre, around which circles a constant stream of humanity. Women walk in one direction, and men in the other.

Hidalgo, the Washington of Mexico, only proclaimed independence: unlike his prototype, he did not achieve it. It was on Saturday night, September 15, 1810, that this patriotic Mexican priest with a few chosen followers liberated a few prisoners in Dolores and armed them. The next morning from his pulpit he declared the independence of Mexico, and made a passionate appeal to his parishioners to follow his leadership and fight to free the country from the hated Spaniard. This was Sunday, September 16.

A new Viceroy—Don Francisco Xaver Venegas—had just taken up the reins of government in Mexico when this movement occurred. The imperial troops were sent against the priest, and were completely routed at Monte de las Cruces, near the city of Mexico. Hidalgo, instead of immediately pressing forward into the city with his victorious patriots, withdrew to the city of Querétaro. A new force of Spanish troops was massed in the mean time, and the independents were disastrously routed at Aculco. But one more stand was made by Hidalgo at Puente de Calderón, near Guadalajara, and, again meeting defeat, the patriots fled towards the northern frontier.

At Las Norias de Baján, near the Rio Grande, they were captured, and Hidalgo, Allende, Aldama, and Jimenez, the four leaders, were shot in the city of Chihuahua, on June 26, 1811. Thus ended the first effort made by Mexico for freedom. But the cause lived. The Mexicans were aroused. The country was but a sleeping volcano. Spain knew it well, but still continued the system of misgovernment, which had but the one result,— independence. The heads of the patriots were exposed for days on poles at Guanajuato. In later years they were buried with great pomp in the cathedral at the city of Mexico.

September, Twentieth of. The anniversary of the final union of Italy under Victor Emmanuel through the downfall of the temporal power of the Papacy. The Papacy virtually fell with the second Napoleonic Empire. For many years the bayonets of France had alone upheld it against the wishes of the majority of Italians. With his first reverses in the Franco-Prussian war Napoleon III. saw that he would need all his available forces to oppose the formidable foe into which Prussia had developed. Only a remnant of Zouaves were left in Rome, the larger part of the French forces being withdrawn from Civita Vecchia shortly after the outbreak of the war. Victor Emmanuel was not slow to seize the opportunity thus presented. He acted immediately on receiving news of the great French defeat at Gravelotte. But his first appeal was to diplomacy and not to force. A revolution was imminent in Rome itself. The Italian king notified the Pope that the duty of maintaining order in the peninsula and the security of the Holy See had devolved upon himself, and that in the despatch of this duty his army must enter the Pontifical States. He begged the Pope to yield to the will of the people and accept a guarantee of his income and of his own personal independence. To these demands the Pope returned a spirited refusal. Thereupon the Sardinian troops crossed the frontier. They were met everywhere with enthusiasm by the Pope's own subjects.

On September 20, 1870, they arrived before the walls of Rome. General Cadorna summoned the garrison to surrender. Only a feint of resistance was made. Hardly had the invaders opened a bombardment when the white flag of surrender was displayed upon the ramparts. Next day the Zouaves, nine thousand in number, were massed in the square of St. Peter's to receive the Papal blessing, and after the conclusion of the ceremony marched out of Rome. With their departure the temporal power of the Pope ceased to exist.

On October 2 a plébiscite was held. The numbers are significant: for the King, 40,788; for the Pope, 46. But though the work was thus accomplished in the autumn of 1870 it was not until January 2, 1871, that the king made his triumphant march into the new capital of united Italy.

The 20th of September is one of the great secular holidays of Italy, observed with especial ceremony. But many Catholics keep it as a day of fasting and humiliation.

Septuagesima. The third Sunday before Lent. (See Quinquagesima.) It was formerly distinguished in England by a strange ceremony denominated the Funeral of Alleluia. On the Saturday of Septuagesima, at nones, the choristers assembled in the great vestiary of the cathedral, and there arranged the ceremony. Having finished the last *benedicamus*, they advanced with crosses, torches, holy water, and incense, carrying a turf in the manner of a coffin, passed through the choir, and went howling to the cloister as far as the place of interment; and then, having sprinkled the water and censed the place, they returned by the same road. (Fosbroke: *British Monachism*, 1843, p. 56.)

Sepulchre, Church of the Holy. This most sacred of all the holy places in the world, "in comparison of which," as Dean Stanley says, "all the rest sink into insignificance if it is genuine, the interest of which even if not genuine stands absolutely alone in the world," stands in the northwestern part of Jerusalem and encloses within its walls the site of Calvary as well as the tomb of Christ, these holy spots being only about sixty feet distant from each other. According to tradition, the Romans under Hadrian, with the deliberate intention of insulting the Christian religion, filled the Holy Sepulchre with earth and built an idolatrous temple on the spot. This was in 137. Two centuries later Constantine, after the Council of Nice, determined to rescue from profanation the places consecrated by the life and death of Christ. The Holy Sepulchre was his first care. He directed that a magnificent church should be built over it in honor of our Lord's Resurrection. This was consecrated in 335. (See Cross, Invention of the.) The church maintained its grandeur until the beginning of the seventh century. Then began a series of vicissitudes which culminated in 1187, when the church, after captures and recaptures, passed definitively into the hands of the Saracens under the Sultan Saladin. It is now part of the possessions of his successor the Sultan of Turkey.

Though the earlier part of the tradition has been assailed, there is no possible doubt that since the time of Constantine the church of the Holy Sepulchre has been revered by the larger part of the Christian world " as the scene of the greatest events in the world's history, and has itself in time become for that reason the centre of a cycle of events of incomparably less magnitude, indeed, but yet of an interest in the highest degree romantic." (DEAN STANLEY: *Sinai and Palestine.*)

The Turkish government suffers the presence of Christians within the sacred edifice, both as spectators and as resident guardians.

The central body of the church, answering to the nave, as the rotunda, which contains the Holy Sepulchre, answers to choir and apse, is the Greek chapel, and the most magnificent in the building. The portion of the church set apart to the Latins, opening also out of the rotunda, is merely a small chapel. The Armenians have still more contracted accommodations, and the poor Copts and Syrians enjoy but a closet apiece.

Each of the rival sects, under regulations imposed by the Turks to preserve peace and order, has access to the various Holy Places and other objects of general reverence. There are in all thirty-seven of these. The most important are the following:

The Stone of Unction, a rectangular mass of rose-colored marble about eight feet long and four feet wide, whereon tradition asserts that the body of Christ was laid when it was anointed for burial.

The tombs of Nicodemus and of Joseph of Arimathea.

The spots where the Virgin stood at the crucifixion and at the anointment of the body respectively.

The spots at which Christ appeared respectively to Mary Magdalene and to the Virgin Mary.

A fragment of the column of flagellation.

The tomb of Melchizedek.

The chair in which Helena sat when the cross was found. The spots marking the successive stages in the Invention or finding of the cross are duly tabulated.

The tomb of Adam.

Various spots where Christ stood at different stages of the passion.

The tomb of Christ, or Holy Sepulchre. This, the most important of all Christian relics, is in the centre of the rotunda. It is a marble structure, about thirty feet high, twenty-five feet long, and seventeen feet wide. It is more like a chapel than a tomb. Candles cover the front and sides. Curious brass lamps with glass globes of different colors hang like a frieze around its alabaster top, and between these are oil-paintings with scriptural scenes upon them. In its front, in gold pillars as high as a man, are columns of painted wax, each six inches thick and twelve feet long, and at the top of each of these a flame trembles.

A low door admits you to a vestibule. In its centre stands a column three feet high supporting a piece of the stone that was rolled from the door of Christ's tomb. From the vestibule you pass into the tomb itself. The room is so small that it will hold only four persons. It is dimly lighted with candles, and a Greek priest in cap and gown is always on guard. At the right of the room, set into the wall, there is a marble slab of the purest white, which rests upon another slab about four feet high, forming a box or ledge, which fills one side of the room. This is the box wherein Christ's body is said to have lain.

The daily religious functions and ceremonies are of a unique character, combining the splendors of both the Eastern and Western Churches. The sacred liturgy is celebrated daily at midnight by the three recognized communities, the Greeks officiating first. The Greeks have preserved the old Oriental liturgical chant, which is similar to that of the Eastern nations. They make no use of the organ for accompaniment, as the instrument cannot well be adapted to the strange modulations of their voices. About one o'clock they begin their mass, and this ceremony varies in length and solemnity according to the feasts. The patriarch and the bishops wear gorgeous vestments, and on these occasions use crowns instead of mitres.

The Armenians celebrate after the Greeks. Their liturgy is more grave, the chant being uneven and mournful, and being accompanied by the sound of little bells attached to disks which are carried on long stems by acolytes. Church-bells are not in favor with them. They use instead, as in early times, a wooden or metallic plank, upon which they strike with hammers. The noise thus created is deafening and disagreeable.

With the Latins day begins at midnight, when the Franciscans repair to the choir to say the matins, which last until about half-past one. After this they take a short rest and then say their masses. The greater part of the day is occupied by various offices and meditations. Their spare time is devoted to the spiritual wants of the pilgrims, to study. or to literary work. The meals are sent from the convent of St. Saviour, which is about five minutes' walk from the Holy Sepulchre. When the basilica is closed the food is passed in through an aperture in the main door.

The influx of pilgrims and tourists to Jerusalem increases with every year. The French have organized an annual pilgrimage, which generally takes place about Pentecost, and have built a special pilgrim-house called Notre-Dame de France. The pilgrims, as a rule, remain about two weeks. The Germans and

Austrians have also their pilgrim-houses in the Holy City. The Austrian house is situated on the Via Dolorosa, and has been honored by the presence of the Emperor, his unfortunate son Rudolph, and other members of the imperial family. Spain organizes an occasional pilgrimage, and so does Italy. The first English Catholic pilgrimage took place in 1890, when, for the first time since the Crusades, the halls of the basilica resounded with English hymns. It was headed by the Duke of Norfolk and the late Bishop Clifford. America had its pilgrimage in 1889. It was headed by the Very Reverend Charles A. Vissani, and numbered about one hundred persons. A beautiful silk banner from the United States was deposited at the Holy Sepulchre and is displayed there on great festivals.

Russia sends the greatest contingent of pilgrims to the Holy Land. During Lent all the streets are crowded with them. They lead a very frugal life, and visit all the holy places on foot, often walking for days at a time. Many of them never see their homes again, but find a resting-place in Palestine. Nearly all of them buy their shrouds in Jerusalem, which they rub over the stone of unction for sanctification. They generally leave on the Holy Saturday of the Greeks, immediately after witnessing the ceremony of the Holy Fire.

Both the movable and the immovable festivals of the Greeks, Armenians, etc., being founded on the old calendar, differ in date from those of the Latins,—a lucky circumstance, because, even as it is, the struggles between the rival sects to obtain precedence at the great ceremonies of the year sometimes lead to disgraceful and even bloody scenes.

The ceremony of the Holy Fire, therefore, which takes place on the Greek Holy Saturday, and which is the most remarkable ceremonial performed within the church, is not participated in by the Latins. They have not taken part in it for three centuries, and the Pope protests against it. The Greeks claim that it has been celebrated ever since the time of the apostles. They hold it to be an annually recurrent miracle. The fire, they maintain, comes down from heaven. This occurs precisely at two o'clock in the afternoon of Holy Saturday in the tomb of the Holy Sepulchre.

On the previous night hundreds of pilgrims sleep in the different chapels and in the rotunda, in order to hold good places for the morrow. In the morning all the lights in the church are put out. Every one has a bunch of unlighted candles in his hand. Shortly after one the ceremonies begin. The Greek patriarch and his bishops in gorgeous dresses march three times round the sepulchre behind a flag and a cross. They pray God to send down the fire. There are chanting and crossing, and then the Copts follow their Ethiopian patriarch, gorgeous in his gold cap and gown.

"Now there is silence. The Greek patriarch has entered the sepulchre, and every one is waiting for the fire. There is nothing to prevent the holy man from lighting it with a surreptitious lucifer match. But to suspect this would be blasphemy.

DISTRIBUTING THE HOLY FIRE.

"There are holes in the sepulchre through which suddenly the crowd sees a faint light shining out. There is a mighty shout. The Turkish soldiers struggle to keep the crowd back. Men with whips run this way and that, making roads through the mass, which the soldiers try to keep clear. The priests stand at the holes in the walls, and great bunches of candles are passed in. They are handed out lighted, and fleet-footed runners seize them and run to the various chapels. The Copt chapel, at the back of the sepulchre, blazes with lights, and in less time than it takes me to write this sentence, the whole of the mass below me is a blaze of fire. Every man, woman, and child has his or her candle lighted, and the lights are hauled up by strings from one gallery to the other. Fleet-footed messengers, emerging from the church, carry the holy fire all over Palestine, to Bethlehem and to Nazareth, to the Sea of Galilee, and to the different parts of the earth from which the pilgrims come. The interest in this ceremony is as great as that which surrounds the Passion Play of Oberammergau." (FRANK CAR-PENTER : *Easter in Jerusalem,* in the *Cosmopolitan Magazine.*)

Setsubun. A movable Japanese festival celebrated at the beginning of the natural year, when winter first softens into spring. On this day occurs the ceremony of Oni-yarai, or casting out of devils. The exorcist wandering through the streets crying, " Devils out! Good fortune in !" is eagerly welcomed into native houses to perform his feat, which consists in the recitation of certain prayers and the rattling of a wand called a shakujō. Then dried peas are thrown about the house in four directions. Japanese devils have a loathing for dried peas such as Satan in Europe is fabled to cherish for holy water. The peas, having accomplished their function of expelling the devils, are swept up and carefully preserved until the first clap of spring thunder is heard, when it is the custom to cook and eat some of them.

In order to prevent the devils from returning, a small piece of stick perforating a leaf of holly and crowned with a fish's head is affixed to every doorway. No one appears to know the origin of these superstitions, and they are now merely accepted as giving occasion for merrymaking.

Shakespeare Celebrations. William Shakespeare was born on April 23, 1564, and died on his birthday in 1616. But the first Shakespeare Jubilee so called was held in a year and at a season not associated in any way with those dates. In 1769, the erection of a new town-hall at Stratford-on-Avon, and the presentation to David Garrick of the freedom of the borough, enclosed in a box made from the wood of Shakespeare's mulberry-tree, suggested a further holiday to the townsmen in association with their great poet. A temporary amphitheatre was constructed ; cannon, fireworks, and illumination lamps were sent down from London ; Birmingham produced a " Shakespeare medal," and Coventry a " Shakespeare ribbon." On the 6th of September serenaders awakened the townsmen and visitors at an early hour in the morning ; a public breakfast took place at nine o'clock, with Garrick officiating as one of the stewards ; the corporation and principal visitors went to hear Arne's oratorio of " Judith" performed in the parish church ; all went then in procession, headed by choralists and instrumentalists, to the amphitheatre, purposely taking a route by the front of Shakespeare's house ; and at three o'clock a grand banquet was given. Allowing themselves a few hours' rest after so much hard sight-seeing, the guests reassembled in the amphitheatre, where a ball was held; while the humbler folk were amused with illuminations and fireworks out of doors. Thus ended the first day. On the second day, a downpour of rain checked a grand out-door display, and therefore the amusements were confined chiefly to a public breakfast, recitations and musical accompaniments, a public banquet, a dinner, a concert, and a masquerade. The third day was as unpropitious as the second; heavy rain spoiled all the plan for a grand theatrical procession and pageant through the town, in which a hundred actors and actresses from London were to take part, dressed for various characters in Shakespeare's plays.

Pageants and festivals in years really associated with the anniversaries of Shakespeare's birth and death have not been numerous. One was held by the Shakespeare Club at Stratford-on-Avon on the birthday of the poet in 1827, and the two following days, during which a pageant, something like that devised by Garrick fifty-eight years before, was performed.

So much money was realized from the visits of the twenty thousand strangers that local speculators got up a similar affair in 1830,—very gay, but very unpoetical. Minor rejoicings were held at Stratford in 1836 and later years, but in 1864 an attempt was made to celebrate the real tricentenary of Shakespeare's birth. Stratford-on-Avon had many days' rejoicing, and in London there was a little ceremonial at the Agricultural Hall, a little at the Crystal Palace, and the planting of a Shakespeare Oak on Primrose Hill.

Shebuoth. (Heb., "Feast of Weeks.") One of the three great festivals of the Jewish ecclesiastical year. It was the feast of the ingathered harvest (hence sometimes known as Chag Haggatsir, or Feast of Harvest), but the later Jews have given it a deeper significance as the anniversary of the proclamation of the Ten Commandments on Mount Sinai. It is kept on the sixth and seventh days of the third month, Sivan, the former being the fiftieth day after the beginning of the Passover. Hence the Greek name πεντηκοστὴ, or pentecost, "the fiftieth," under which it is mentioned in the New Testament. (See WHITSUNDAY.) The title Feast of Weeks indicates that it marks the completion of seven weeks, counting from the second day of Passover, when the Jews of Palestine presented their omer of newly reaped barley in the temple. As the second day of Passover was the celebration over the barley crop, so Shebuoth is the rejoicing over the wheat, the first ears of which were then offered up in the temple. But as among the Western nations the holiday does not occur during the wheat harvest, but when the flowers are in full bloom, it is made a sort of floral festival, the synagogues being decorated with flowers and shrubs. Strict Jews sit up on the first night to read the law and the prophets.

Among the Reformed Jews this is the chosen day for the confirmation of youth, when boys and girls over the age of thirteen are submitted to a public catechising, and if deemed sufficiently instructed are solemnly admitted to church membership. Emerging from the underlying school, they march up the aisles of the synagogue to the platform occupied by the rabbi, make avowal of their belief, and pledge themselves to live in accordance with their faith. The rabbi then throws open the doors of the ark behind the pulpit, revealing the sacred scrolls, and between him and the ark pass long strings of catechumens. On each head in succession his hand rests in blessing. Then they slowly wend their way to the family pews. The ceremony is not approved of by orthodox Jews.

Sheelah's Day. The Irish celebrate the 18th of March, the day after St. Patrick's, under this name. Who Sheelah was is uncertain. Some assert that she was Patrick's wife, others that she was Patrick's mother, but " all agree," says Hone, " that her immortal memory is to be maintained by potations of whiskey. The shamrock worn on St. Patrick's Day should be worn also on Sheelah's Day, and on the latter night be drowned in the last glass. Yet it frequently happens that the shamrock is flooded in the last glass of St. Patrick's Day, and another last glass or two, or more, on the same night deluges the over-sodden trefoil. This is not ' quite correct,' but it is endeavored to be remedied the next morning by the display of a fresh shamrock, which is steeped at night in honor of ' Sheelah' with equal devotedness." (*Every Day Book*, vol. ii. p. 387.)

Shorne, Master John. A famous personage of the thirteenth century, who was rector of North Marston and achieved so great a reputation for sanctity as to overshadow in the popular mind many duly canonized saints. It is reported of him that he conjured the devil into his boot and kept him there, allowing him to emerge only at intervals as a sort of diabolical jack-in-the-box. At death Master Shorne's body was enclosed in a shrine which became a favorite object of pilgrimage until the Reformation. His claims seem to have been endorsed by the local clergy, for Fox tells us in his Martyrology that repentant heretics were sometimes compelled to make pilgrimages " some to the Rood at Wendover, some to Sir John Schorn." A Protestant ballad has these lines :

To Maister John Schorn, that blessed man born,
For the ague to him we apply,
Which jugeleth with a boot, I beshrew his herte-rote
That will trust him, an it be I.

Near North Marston Church there is still extant a well, known as Master John Shorne's well, whose waters were in Catholic times believed to have great curative powers over the ague and kindred diseases. Its reputation is now entirely gone. The body and the shrine of John Shorne were destroyed at the Reformation, but there is preserved an ancient screen in the church of Gateley in Norfolk, bearing a representation of the pseudo-saint with Satan peeping out of the top of a boot in his left hand.

Shrove Tuesday, known in Scotland as **Fastens-Een.** (Fr. *Mardi-Gras.*) The Tuesday before Ash Wednesday, hence the last day previous to Lent, and in Catholic Europe the concluding and culminating day of the Carnival festivities. In England it was a chosen holiday for the apprentices and working classes generally. Yet the very title Shrove Tuesday indicates a penitential date when it was the custom of the faithful to apply to the priest to shrive or absolve them in the confessional before entering on the holy Lenten season of fasting and prayer. That none might plead forgetfulness of this duty, the great bell was rung at an early hour in every parish, and in after-times this ringing was still kept up in some places, though the cause of it ceased with the Reformation, when it became merged into the Pancake Bell. After confession the people were allowed to indulge in merrymaking, which in the later days of Catholicism and the earlier ones of Protestantism degenerated into unbounded license.

The association of pancakes with Shrovetide is an ancient one. The most plausible explanation is that offered by a Catholic ecclesiastic in *Notes and Queries*, Eighth Series, vol. i. : " When Lent was kept by a strict abstinence from meat all through the forty days, it was customary to use up all the dripping and lard in the making of pancakes. To consume all, it was usual to call in the apprentice-boys and others about the house, and they were summoned by a bell. which was naturally called pancake bell." Eventually the functions of the pancake-bell and of the shriving-bell were combined, and, as the pancake-bell, the church signal survived the Reformation.

John Taylor the Water Poet in his " Jack-a-Lent" (*Works*, 1630, vol. i. p. 115) attacks this and other Shrovetide customs extant in his day with great vigor:

" Always before Lent there comes waddling a fat, grosse

groome, called *Shrove Tuesday*, one whose manners show he is
better fed than taught, and indeed he is the only monster for
feeding amongst all the dayes of the yeere, for he devoures more
flesh in fourteene houres than this old kingdom doth (or at least

SHROVE TUESDAY PREPARING TO DO BATTLE WITH LENT.

should doe) in sixe weekes after. Such boyling and broyling,
such roasting and toasting, such stewing and brewing, such baking, frying, mincing, cutting, carving, devouring, and gorbellied
gurmondizing, that a man would thinke people did take in two
months' provision at once. Moreover it is a goodly sight to see
how the cookes in great men's kitchins doe frye in their master's
suet, that if ever a cooke be worth the eating, it is when Shrove
Tuesday is in towne, for he is so stued and larded, basted, and
almost over-roasted, that a man may eate every bit of him and
never take a surfet. In a word, they are that day extreme
cholerike, and too hot for any man to meddle with, being monarchs of the marrow-bones, marquesses of the mutton, lords high
regents of the spit and kettle, barons of the gridiron, and sole
commanders of the frying-pan. And all this hurly-burly is for
no other purpose than to stop the mouth of the land-wheale,
Shrove-Tuesday, at whose entrance in the morning all the whole
kingdome is in quiet, but by the time the clocke strikes eleven—
which, by the help of a knavish sexton, is commonly before nine,
—then there is a bell rung called the *Pancake-Bell*, the sound
whereof makes thousands of people distracted and forgetful
either of manners or humanitie. Then there is a thing cal'd

wheat'n flowre, which the sulphory, necromanticke cookes doe mingle with water, eggs, spice, and other tragicall, magicall inchantments, and then they put it little by little into a frying-pan of boyling suet, where it makes a confused dismal hissing—like the Lernean snakes in the reeds of Acheron, Stix, or Phlegeton —until at last by the skill of the cooke it is transformed into the forme of a *flap-jack*, which in our translation is call'd a *pancake*, which ominous incantation the ignorant people doe devoure very greedily—having for the most part well dined before—but they have no sooner swallowed that sweet candied baite, but straight their wits forsake them, and they runne starke mad, assembling in routs and throngs numberlesse of ungovernable numbers, with uncivil civil commotions."

In spite of Taylor and other assailants, the pancake on Shrove Tuesday and even the pancake-bell still survive in England, though the latter has only local avatars. In some places it is known as Fritters-bell or Panburn-bell. Jingling rhymes in connection with this custom are still current among the peasantry of Northamptonshire. The following are the most current:

> Pancakes and fritters,
> Says the bells of St. Peter's.
> Where must we fry 'em?
> Says the bells of Cold Higham.
> In yonder land thurrow [furrow],
> Says the bells of Wellingborough.
> You owe me a shilling,
> Says the bells of Great Billing.
> When will you pay me?
> Says the bells at Middleton Cheney.
> When I am able,
> Says the bells at Dunstable.
> That will never be,
> Says the bells of Coventry.
> Oh, yes, it will,
> Says Northampton Great Bell.
> White bread and sop,
> Says the bells at Kingsthrop.
> Trundle a lantern,
> Says the bells at Northampton.

That the bells of the churches of Northampton used also to be rung on this day may be inferred from the following similar doggerel:

> Roast beef and marshmallows,
> Says the bells of All Hallow's.
> Pancakes and fritters,
> Says the bells of St. Peter's.
> Roast beef and boil'd,
> Says the bells of St. Giles'.

> Poker and tongs,
> Says the bells of St. John's.
> Shovels, tongs, and poker,
> Says the bells of St. Pulchre's.
> (BAKER: *Northampton Words and Phrases*, vol. ii. p. 92.)

At Apsley Old Hall in Nottinghamshire, butter and lard, fire and frying-pans, were formerly provided for all the poor families of Wollaston, Trowell, and Cossall who chose to come and eat their pancakes at this mansion. The only conditions attached to the feast were that no quarrelling should take place, and that each wife and mother should fry for her own family, and that when the cake needed turning in the pan the act should be performed by tossing it in the air and catching it again in the pan with the uncooked side downward. And many were the roars of laughter which took place among the merry groups in the kitchen at the mishaps which occurred in the performance of this feat, in which his Honor and Madam joined.

In addition to the pancakes, every man was allowed a quart of good ale, every woman a pint, and every child a gill. (SUTTON: *Nottingham Date Book*, 1852, p. 75.)

The children of Berkshire have still their rhymes which they sing on this day and receive their accustomed perquisites. At Purley they say,—

> Knick-knock, pan's hot,
>   I'm come a-shroving;
> Bit of bread and a bit of cheese,
>   That's better than nothing.
> Last year's flour's dear,
> That's what makes poor Purley children come shroving here.
>   Hip, hip, hurrah!
> Up with the pitcher and down with the pan,
> Give me a penny and I'll be gone.

In Oxfordshire similar rhymes are sung :

> Knick, knock, the pan's hot,
> And we be come a-shroving :
> A bit of bread, a bit of cheese,
> A bit of barley dompling,
> That's better than nothing.
> Open the door and let us in.

These rhymes have many variants, which may be heard in all the southern and midland counties. In Dorsetshire and Wiltshire the children have unpleasant ways of manifesting their displeasure if the accustomed gift be withheld. Laying in a stock of bits of broken glass, crockery, and other rubbish, and with a captain at their head, they go round in parties from house to house. The captain knocks at the door, and when it is opened sings this truculent rhyme:

> I'm come a-shroving
> For a piece of pancake,
> Or a piece of bacon,
> Or a little truckle cheese,
> Of your own making.
> If you give me a little I ask you no more ;
> If you don't give me nothing I'll rattle your door.

If the request be denied, the captain gives a signal, and the door is straightway bombarded with the mutilated remains of plates, mugs, jugs, and basins. The practice is known as Lent Crocking.

Before the pancakes were eaten there was always a great deal of contention among the revellers to see which could most adroitly toss them in the pan. Hone tells us that it was customary to present the greatest slut or lie-abed in the party "with the first pancake, which commonly falls to the dog's share at last, for no one will own it their due." Hence Tusser's allusion,

> Maids, fritters and pancakes enough see you make ;
> Let Slut have one pancake, for company's sake.
> (*Five Hundred Points of Good Husbandry*, 1620.)

In parts of Lancashire and Cheshire the tossing of pancakes with its ancient accompaniments is still a source of Shrovetide mirth. In some places fritters are substituted.

> It is the day whereon both rich and poor
> Are chiefly feasted on the self-same dish ;
> When every paunch, till it can hold no more,
> Is fritter fill'd, as well as heart can wish;
> And every man and maide doe take their turne,
> And tosse their pancakes up for feare they burne,
> And all the kitchen doth with laughter sound,
> To see the pancakes fall upon the ground.
> (*Pasquil's Palinodia*. HARLAND AND WILKINSON,
> *Lancashire Folk Lore*, 1867, p. 218.)

An interesting survival of "tossing the pancake" exists at Westminster School, and is accompanied with several quaint observances. The cook, bearing a frying-pan with a pancake, is conducted by a verger carrying the silver mace from the college kitchen to the great school-room, where all the boys are assembled. The cook tries to toss the pancake over an iron bar which runs across the school-room from one wall to another. If the pancake goes clear over, the boys make a rush and try to catch it whole. The boy who gets it whole receives a guinea from the dean on showing it in an unbroken condition. The cook also receives ten shillings if he does his part properly. Nowadays, only so many boys join in the struggle for the pancake as there are forms in the school. Each form names a representative. Formerly the whole school made a rush, which was rather a dangerous sport, and very wisely the number of competitors for the prize has been limited.

In 1864, the cook, who had failed for several years to elevate the pancake right over the bar, so exasperated the boys by again depriving them of their fun—for there was no scramble if the pancake did not go over the bar—that they hurled at his head a shower of books, dictionaries, as being heaviest, by preference. He retaliated by flinging his frying-pan into the midst of the boys, and, in fact, there was a pretty quarrel, which was eventually adjusted by the dean.

At Charterhouse, Shrove Tuesday, as at Westminster, brings its annual excitement in the shape of an institution known as the "lemon fight." Each boy at dinner is provided with half a lemon, wherewith to flavor the customary pancake; but it is a point of honor not to use the lemon for this very ordinary purpose, but to save it up for the spirited warfare which follows. "Gown Boys" range themselves against "The Rest," and each side pelts the other with vigor and persistency.

But fiercer sports than these were known to the Shrove Tuesday of the past. The underlying instinct of brutality in the Anglo-Saxon seems to have found free vent at this time, for the inhuman sports of cock-fighting and throwing at cocks were well-nigh universal. School-boys were allowed to bring cocks to school with them, and masters and scholars alike forgot the rod and books and became eager spectators of the cruel sport. Cock-fighting was countenanced in many of the schools of Scotland as late as the beginning of this century, and the teachers enjoyed the privilege of claiming the runaway cocks, called fugees, as their perquisites.

But among the masses no other diversion could vie with the allurements of throwing at cocks. Fortunately this barbarous pastime was never indulged in at any other time of the year, and finally was suppressed altogether early in the nineteenth century. Some say that the custom took its rise from St. Peter's memorable experience when he denied the Saviour. Sir Charles Sedley, in the *Monthly Miscellany* for January, 1692, has this couplet:

> May'st thou be punished for St. Peter's crime,
> And on Shrove Tuesday perish in thy prime.

Others assert that it must have originated at the time of Henry the Fifth's victories over the French, the cocks being symbolical of the conquered Gauls. In Blenheim Castle there is a curious carving in stone over one of the portals representing a lion tearing a cock to pieces.

However, an explanation given in *The British Apollo* for 1708 seems the most rational of all, particularly as cock-throwing is known to have been practised both in England and in France long before the battle of Agincourt. This authority says that in

COCK-THROWING: THE TRIUMPH OF THE VICTOR.

the days of Danish oppression the people of a certain city had formed a plan to massacre their tyrants in the early morning of Shrove Tuesday, but the sleeping Danes were aroused by the crowing of the cocks and defeated the plot, wherefore revenge was taken on the fowls every Shrove Tuesday.

Hogarth gives a graphic picture of cock-throwing in his "Four Stages of Cruelty." The animals were carefully trained by their owners for weeks beforehand, sticks and other missiles being thrown at them untiringly until they acquired skill in dodging. In the game the cocks were tied to a stake in an open space, the throwers standing about twenty-two yards distant; twopence procured the privilege of three shies, and whoever knocked the cock down and caught him before recovery won the bird as a prize. The feat being difficult to accomplish, the owners sometimes made a great deal of money.

A satirical old song of 1679 thus tells the story of the "Shrovetide Martyr:"

> Cock-a-doodle-doe, 'tis the bravest game,
> Take a cock from his dame
>   And bind him to a stake;
> How he struts, how he throwes,
> How he swaggers, how he crowes,
>   As if the day newly brake.
>
> How his mistress cackles
> Thus to find him in shackles,
>   And tied to a packe-thread garter.

> Oh, the beares and the bulls
> Are but corpulent gulls
> To the valiant Shrovetide Martyr.

Hens were also used for this purpose. The *Gentleman's Magazine* for 1749 tells of a hen that spoke and delivered an excellent sermon (which is given in full) just before she met her death in this way. Threshing the fat hen was another custom akin to this, and probably derived from it, but with a better element of sport, though scarcely less cruelty. A hen was tied upon the back of one of the men, who also wore a string of horse-bells, while the others were blindfolded and armed with boughs, with which they tried to hit the hen, being guided by the sound of the bells. Naturally they often hit the man who carried the hen, and naturally, too, they often hit one another. The hen was afterwards boiled with bacon and eaten with pancakes:

> Come, go to the barn now, my jolly ploughmen,
> Blindfolded, and speedily thresh the fat hen;
> And if you can kill her, then give her thy men,
> And go ye on fritters and pancakes dine then.
> (TUSSER: *Five Hundred Points of Husbandry.*)

It was customary in Cornwall to take any hen which had not laid eggs before Shrove Tuesday and lay it on a barn floor to be thrashed to death. A man hit at her with a flail; and if he succeeded in killing her therewith he got her for his pains.

Hone, writing in 1820, speaks of the custom of throwing at cocks as still existing in some remote districts of England. At present it has only phantom reminiscences, as at Norwich, where the bakers exhibit at Shrovetide a small currant-loaf called a coquille, which the boys also cry in the streets. A notice at the shops runs as follows: "Hot coquilles on Tuesday morning at eight o'clock, and in the afternoon at four o'clock." Possibly the word is derived from its shell-like shape (Fr. *coquille*, "a shell"), but more probably it may be connected with cockerel or cock, and is a descendant from the old cock-throwing days. A more evident survival is in Wales, where it is still the custom to make thin lead figures of birds and animals. Whatever the shape, these are known as birds. They are set up on Shrove Tuesday, and boys are invited to throw chunks of lead at them. If the "bird" be knocked down it becomes the property of the thrower, but every chunk of lead that misses its aim is claimed by the owner of the "bird."

Foot-ball was one of the chief pastimes of Shrovetide in old England and Scotland, and it still has many local survivals. At Alnwick the contest used to take place in the street, but the Duke of Northumberland instituted an annual match which now takes place in "the Pasture" every Shrove Tuesday between the two parishes of St. Michael and St. Paul. The committee receives the ball at the barbican of the castle from the porter, and marches to the field headed by the duke's piper. After the contest a fierce struggle takes place for the possession of the ball. At Chester-le-Street the game retains possession of the street, all the windows being carefully barricaded. A burn lies in the course of the players, who have a fine scrimmage in the waters. At Dorking also the street is the scene of the game. A collection is made during the morning throughout the streets, nominally to defray the cost of damages. The foot-ballers first parade the streets clad in grotesque costumes and attended by bands of music. The foot-ball is kicked off in the centre of the High Street at two o'clock, and all who wish join in the game. The play is furious, and the ball is kicked everywhere, sometimes reaching the fields at the outskirts of the town. During four hours the contest lasts, and towards the end of the struggle there are much excitement and vigorous kicking, extremely dangerous to the limbs of the competitors.

In Scotland the streets of Duns are enlivened by a game of hand-ball on Fastens-Een. The ball is started in state by the lord of the manor. The goals are the kirk and the mill.

Nowhere was Shrovetide foot-ball carried to greater excesses than in mediæval Florence. Early in the morning the young Florentines of the better classes disguised themselves, and, forming parties, set out to scour the city. Each party was provided with a large foot-ball, and every individual was armed with a mop well bedaubed with soot, grease, pitch, and other such matter. The ball was kicked through the streets; if a shop happened to be open, in it bounded, and the players after it, upsetting everything. A like fate befell such stalls as chanced to stand in their way. The passengers, too, were hunted, even into the churches, and belabored with mops; for these subjects of Momus considered it high treason to their king for any one to pursue his vocations on such a day. When two parties encountered, a battle with mops ensued, which frequently warmed into a real fight. Indeed, the day seldom passed without several serious affrays.

Perhaps the most singular of all Shrovetide ceremonies was one that used to be celebrated yearly in the now demolished cathedral of St. Lambert at Liége. It seems that at some unknown period the unlucky peasants of Nomale, in the Hesbaye, had ventured to take liberties with the geese belonging to the canons of St. Lambert, and, what was worse, had contrived to be found out. In consequence thereof, they were compelled to do penance every Shrovetide as follows. Early that morning all the villagers who were not bedridden gathered on the village green. Having picked out the most repulsive-looking old woman among them, they dressed her with appropriate absurdities and stuck a live goose under her arm. Then, forming in procession, they posted the hag in front, and, cackling and hissing the while like so many lunatics, they marched to the cathedral, where the canons awaited them. The villagers formed round the church, while the canons stood in a group in the centre. Up to this group went the old woman and presented her goose with an appropriate speech ; then, hobbling from one churchman to another, she bestowed a hideous grimace upon each. " And," adds the annalist, " when she happened to repeat the same gesture twice over, the canons, who were connoisseurs in that kind of thing, made her begin again."

Sicilian Vespers. The name given to a sanguinary massacre of the French, who under Prince Charles of Anjou were then masters of Sicily, begun at Palermo on Easter Monday, March 30, 1282. Charles's rule was tyrannous and galling. Obnoxious to the Sicilians from his nation, the people had as well to bear the presence of a licentious and brutal alien soldiery, to whom nothing was sacred. Under such oppression, it was little wonder that the hot fire of Italian wrath should be smouldering, and waiting but for some slight fanning to leap into devastating flame. The occasion arrived. On Easter Monday a procession of the people of Palermo was formed to attend vespers at the church of the Holy Ghost, just outside the walls. The French rulers made this a pretext for searching for arms. To a brutal, licentious soldiery this supplied an opportunity for offering gross insults to the females, one of whom was a young married lady of great beauty and position. Her screams aroused the multitude ; the spark was laid to the train ; and, led by the lady's father and husband, the people rose in tumult. Arms were seized, and an indiscriminate slaughter of all the French in the city was the result.

This was but the alarm-note for a general rising. In town after town massacres took place, until Messina, the last stronghold of the French, fell into native hands. Every person of French blood was massacred with relentless fury. Even Christian burial was denied them, but pits were afterwards dug to receive their despised remains ; and tradition still points out a column surmounted by an iron cross, raised by compassionate piety in one of those spots, probably long after the perpetration of the deed of vengeance. Tradition, moreover, relates that the sound of a word, like the Shibboleth of the Hebrews, was the test by which the French were distinguished in the massa-

cre, and that if there were found a suspicious or unknown person, he was compelled, with a sword to his throat, to pronounce
the word *ciceri*, and the slightest foreign accent was the signal
for his death. Forgetful of their own character, and as if
stricken by fate, the gallant warriors of France neither fled, nor
united, nor defended themselves; they unsheathed their swords
and presented them to their assailants, imploring, as if in emulation of each other, to be the first to die; of one common soldier only is it recorded that, having concealed himself behind a
wainscot, and being dislodged at the sword's point, he resolved
not to die unavenged, and, springing with a wild cry upon the
ranks of his enemies, slew three of them before he himself
perished. The insurgents broke into the convents of the Minor-
ites and Preaching Friars and slaughtered all the monks whom
they recognized as French. Even the altars afforded no protection; tears and prayers were alike unheeded; neither old men,
women, nor infants were spared; and, as a last refinement of
cruelty, Sicilian wives who were pregnant by French husbands
were ripped open and the fruit of the mingled blood of the
oppressors and the oppressed was dashed against the stones.

Simeon, a prophet mentioned in the New Testament. According to Luke ii. 25–35, he was enlightened by the Spirit to
appear at the temple when Christ was presented. For the
Holy Ghost had revealed to him that he should not see death
before he had seen the Lord's Christ. "And when the parents
brought in the child Jesus, to do for him after the custom of the
law, then took he him up in his arms, and blessed God, and
said, Lord, now lettest thou thy servant depart in peace, according to thy word: for mine eyes have seen thy salvation, which
thou hast prepared before the face of all people; a light to
lighten the Gentiles, and the glory of thy people Israel." The
feast of Candlemas (*q. v.*) is sometimes known as Festa Simeonis,
and in the Greek Church, especially, Simeon's words are the
key-note of the celebration. Tradition has enlarged upon the
Biblical narrative. According to the legend, Simeon was nearly
three hundred years old at the time of the Presentation. When
Ptolemy Philadelphus wanted a Greek version of the Hebrew
Scriptures for the library at Alexandria, about 260 B.C., he sent
to Eleazar at Jerusalem for scribes. Among those who undertook the work was Simeon, and he translated the book of Isaiah.
When he reached the prophecy, "Behold, a virgin shall conceive,
and bear a son," he was afraid that it might cause his religion
to be looked upon as foolish by the Greeks, and so rendered the
passage by using a Greek word meaning simply "young woman."
Then an angel came and erased the word and put down the

proper one, and twice repeated the alteration. After this Simeon had a vision and received a promise that he "should not see death before he had seen the Lord's Christ:" so he lived on, and was at the temple on the day when the Virgin came to present the Child, and, embracing him, gave his prophecy.

St. Gregory of Tours says that Simeon was buried on Mount Olivet. In the sixth century Justin the Younger translated his relics to Constantinople. Portions were given to Charlemagne, and were by him placed at Aix, where the arm on which the infant Saviour rested when the "Nunc Dimittis" was first said is shown. The head is in the Jesuit College at Brussels. Arms or parts of arms are shown at Périgueux, Palermo, and Harzburg, and two entire bodies are extant, one at Andechs, in Bavaria, the other at Zara, in Dalmatia.

Sin-Eater. A functionary who, within the memory of living men, officiated at funerals in Wales. A relative—usually a woman—would place a quantity of bread and cheese and beer on the bosom of the corpse. Then the Sin-Eater would be summoned to consume them. It was believed that thus he appropriated to himself the delinquencies symbolized by the viands and prevented them from disturbing the rest of the sinner.

Snapdragon, or Flapdragon. A favorite Christmas pastime in old England, little known outside of that country, and now obsolescent even there. Some small inflammable body is set on fire in a glass of spirits, and the courage of the players is tested by their willingness to snatch it out with the fingers and put it blazing into the mouth. Raisins in brandy were the commonest snapdragons. They might be safely seized by a quick motion, put in the mouth, and swallowed after the flames were extinguished by closing the lips. A correspondent of *Notes and Queries*, Second Series, vol. vii. p. 277, suggests as a derivation the German *schnapps*, "spirit," and *drache*, "dragon," and deems it equivalent to "spirit-fire."

Shakespeare alludes to the sport under the name of flapdragon:

> And drinks off candles' ends for flapdragons.
> (*Second Part of Henry IV.*, Act ii. Sc. 4.)
> Thou art easier swallowed than a flapdragon.
> (*Love's Labor's Lost*, Act v. Sc. 1.)

Stang, Riding the. A stang, or cowl-staff, is nothing more nor less than a stout pole used in the southern counties of England for carrying a cowl or water-vessel, which is suspended from the middle, while each end of the stang rests on the shoulders of a carrier. Hence Riding the Stang is the same as the American Riding a Rail. In the eighteenth century it was one of the customary New Year features of rural England. The method is thus described in the *Gentleman's Magazine* for 1791, p. 1169: "Early on the morning of the first of January the Fæx Populi assemble together, carrying stangs and baskets. Any inhabitant, stranger, or whoever joins not this ruffian tribe in sacrificing to their favorite saint-day, if unfortunate enough to be met by any of the band, is immediately mounted across the stang (if a woman, she is basketed), and carried shoulder high to the nearest public-house, where the payment of sixpence liberates the prisoner."

In Yorkshire and some other counties a ceremony called Riding the Stang still survives among the lower orders as a method of vicarious punishment for any frailty on the part of man or wife. Some "good-natured friend" is selected; he bestrides the stang, and is borne through the streets in the dusk of the evening on the shoulders of two men, preceded by another carrying a lantern. At every fifty yards or so the procession makes a halt, and the rider declaims these verses, *mutatis mutandi* to suit the occasion:

> Good neighbors attend while I you harangue.
> 'Tis neither for your sake nor my sake
> That I ride the stang,
> But it is for the wife of John Smith
> That I ride the stang.

Then all the mob hurrahs. The procession winds up before the house of the sinner, where, after a chorus of hoots and jeers, it disperses. Sometimes the vocal discord is supplemented by an instrumental pandemonium, in which pots, pans, and kettles are utilized to assail the offender with what is known as rough music (*q. v.* See also CHARIVARI).

Stephen, St. (Fr. *Étienne;* Ger. *Stefan.*) The protomartyr, or first Christian martyr, patron of horses. He is commemorated on December 26. The New Testament (Acts vii.) tells the story of his death by stoning at the hands of the Jewish people just outside of the gate at Jerusalem now called by his name. A legend relates that nothing was known of the martyr's relics until four hundred years later, when Gamaliel appeared in a vision to Lucian, a priest living in Jerusalem, and revealed to him that they had been buried in Gamaliel's own garden with those of Nicodemus and other holy men. The relics were found December 26, 417. Their genuineness was attested by many miracles, and they were placed in the church of Sion at Jerusalem. They were carried from Jerusalem to Constantinople by

Theodosius II. about 439, and obtained for Rome more than a century later by the legates of Pope Pelagius. They now lie in the church of St. Lawrence, side by side with the bones of the latter saint, who, it is said, courteously moved to the left of his sarcophagus, thus giving the place of honor on the right to St. Stephen. For this act of politeness Lawrence has been dubbed by the Roman populace " Il Cortese Spagnuolo" (" The Courteous Spaniard"). There is a curious and anachronistic legend giving an account of the translation of St. Stephen's remains which has been painted in the newly restored church of St. Lawrence Outside the Walls in Rome. According to this story, the Empress Eudoxia, wife of Valentinian III., Emperor of Rome, had been invited to Constantinople by her father, Theodosius II., that she might be delivered, by touching the relics of St. Stephen, from the torments of a devil who afflicted her. But the demon gave her to understand that she could never be cured unless the saint himself came to Rome. It was arranged, therefore, that the relics of St. Lawrence should be given in exchange for those of St. Stephen, and on the latter reaching Rome the Empress was healed. But when the Greek emissaries tried to remove St. Lawrence they fell down as dead, and, though restored at the moment by the prayer of Pope Pelagius, they died within ten days. All the Romans who had counselled the exchange were struck with madness, but were healed at the joint intercession of the two martyrs when laid side by side in the marble sarcophagus where they still repose. The legend would have been more credible but for the facts that Theodosius II. died in 450 and that Pope Pelagius reigned from 555 to 560. St. Stephen is represented as young and beardless, in the dress of a deacon. His special attributes are the stones with which he was murdered.

A bone of the saint is shown at Longpont, near Paris, others at Metz, at St. Etienne in Paris, at St. Mark's in Venice, and in the island of Minorca. Stones said to be reddened with the blood of the martyr are preserved at Metz and at Ancona.

St. Stephen's being the day after Christmas, it was formerly the custom for the poor to go round begging the broken victuals left over from the holiday feast. Hence perhaps arose the practice in many English parishes of distributing bread and cheese and other doles to the poor. This meal was known as St. Stephen's Breakfast. Southey in his " Common-Place Book" mentions that the three vicars of Bampton used in his time to give beef and beer on the morning of St. Stephen's Day to those who chose to partake of it. Bread and cheese and ale was the offering made by the rector of the parish of Drayton-Beauchamp. Here the usage gave rise to so much rioting that it was discontinued, and an annual sum was distributed instead in proportion

to the number of claimants.   About the year 1827, however, the
compromise itself was dropped.

According to the *Gentleman's Magazine* for May, 1811, the
inhabitants of the North Riding of Yorkshire celebrated the
feast of St. Stephen by making large goose pies, "all of which
they distribute among their needy neighbors except one, which
is carefully laid up and not tasted till Candlemas."   On this day
also sword-dances were performed in the same locality.   (See
SWORD-DANCE.)

But in old England St. Stephen's Day is chiefly celebrated
under the name of Boxing Day,—not for pugilistic reasons, but
because on that day it was the custom for persons in the humbler
walks of life to go the rounds with a Christmas-box and solicit
pecuniary gifts from patrons and employers.   Hence the word
Christmas-box came eventually to signify gifts made at this
holiday season by superiors to inferiors, and retained this meaning
even after the boxes themselves had been abolished.   These boxes
were of heathen origin, and carry us back to the Roman Paganalia, when earthen boxes in which money was slipped through
a hole were hung around for contributions at these rural festivals.

Aubrey in his " Wiltshire Collections" (1670, p. 45) describes a
trouvaille of Roman relics: "Among the rest was an earthen
pot of the color of a crucible, and of the shape of a Prentice's
Christmas-box, with a slit in it, containing about a quart, which
was near full of money.   This pot I gave to the Repository of
the Royal Society at Gresham College."

The Church, which at first denounced these pagan institutions,
finally ended by adopting them, if we are to believe Mr. John
Dunton, the ingenious editor of "The Athenian Oracle" (1703,
vol. i. p. 360), a periodical that was the first forerunner of the
modern *Notes and Queries.*   Here are his question and answer:

" *Q.* From whence comes the custom of gathering of Christmas-box money?   And how long since?

" *A.* It is as ancient as the word *mass*, which the Romish
priests invented from the Latin word *mitto*, to send, by putting
the people in mind to send gifts, offerings, oblations; to have
masses said for everything almost, that no ship goes out to the
Indies but the priests have a box in that ship, under the protection of some saint.   And for masses, as they cant, to be said for
them to that saint, etc., the poor people must put in something
into the priests' box, which is not to be opened till the ship
return.   Thus the mass at that time was *Christ's-mass*, and the
box *Christ's-mass-box*, or money gathered against that time, that
masses might be made by the priests to the saints, to forgive the
people the debaucheries of that time; and from this, servants
had liberty to get *box-money*, so that they might be enabled to

pay the priest for masses—because, *No penny, no paternoster*—for though the rich pay ten times more than they can expect, yet a priest will not say a mass or anything to the poor for nothing; so charitable they generally are."

Whatever their origin and evolution, there is no doubt that the Christmas-box was a recognized institution in the England of the seventeenth century. In the British Museum several specimens are preserved,—small and wide bottles of thin clay, from three to four inches in height, surmounted by imitation stoppers, covered with a green baize. On one side is a slit for the introduction of money. The box must be broken before the money can be extracted. Thus, Mason's "Handful of Essaies" (1621) says of a miser that, "like a swine, he never doth good till his death; as an apprentice's box of earth apt is he to take all, but to restore none till he be broken." The same simile is used in Blaxton's "English Usurer" (1634):

> Both with the Christmas Box may well comply;
> It nothing yields till broke, they till they die.

At a dinner on St. Stephen's Day in the Inner Temple, among a great deal of dreary mummery and solemn tomfoolery was this "merry disport," which may or may not have been typical of the lawyers' practice in those days. When the company was seated at the chancellor's table "a huntsman cometh into the hall with a fox and a purse-net with a cat, both bound at the end of a staff, and with these nine or ten couple of hounds, with the blowing of hunting-horns. And the fox and cat are set upon by the hounds, and killed beneath the fire." There is a quatrain of an old spiritual song that probably refers to this ceremony:

> The hunter is Christ that hunts in haist,
> The hunds are Peter and Pawle,
> The paip is the fox, Rome is the Rox
> That rubbis us on the gall.

A curious superstition was formerly prevalent regarding St. Stephen's Day,—that horses should then, after being first well galloped, be copiously bled in order to insure them against disease in the course of the following year. In Barnaby Googe's translation of Naogeorgus the following lines occur:

> Then followeth Saint Stephen's Day, whereon doth every man
> His horses jaunt and course abrode, as swiftly as he can,
> Until they doe extreemely sweate, and then they let them blood,
> For this being done upon this day, they say doth do them good,
> And keepes them from all maladies and sicknesse through the yeare,
> As if that Steven any time tooke charge of horses heare.

The practice appears to be very ancient, and Douce supposes that it was introduced into England by the Danes. In one of the manuscripts of John Aubrey occurs the following record : " On St. Stephen's Day the farrier came constantly and blouded all our cart-horses." (*Remains of Gentilisme*, Lansdowne MSS., 226.) Very possibly convenience and expediency combined on the occasion with superstition, for in "Tusser Redivivus," a work published in the middle of the last century, we find this statement : "About Christmas is a very proper time to bleed horses in, for then they are commonly at house, then spring comes on, the sun being now coming back from the winter solstice, and there are three or four days of rest, and if it be upon St. Stephen's Day it is not the worse, seeing there are with it three days of rest, or at least two."

But the custom may have reference to the fact that St. Stephen was the patron of horses. The Germans call his day *der grosse Pferdstag.* In Rome it was formerly the custom to celebrate it by physicking and bleeding the Pope's stud, for the sake of the blood, which was supposed to be a specific in many disorders.

St. Stephen's Day was formerly called Straw Day in the south of France, because of the benediction of the straw which some rituals then appointed. In Denmark it is sometimes known as Second Christmas Day. (See also WREN, HUNTING THE.)

Stone of Infamy. (It. *Pietra d'Infamia.*) In many Italian cities a stone so called, formerly used for the purpose of punishing bankrupts, is still extant. In Venice it stands near St. Mark's Church, in Verona and in Florence it is placed in the old markets. On a certain day of the Carnival all traders who had failed during the preceding twelvemonth were led to this stone. Around them gathered a vast mob, the school-boys being accorded the foremost rank, as likely to learn from the ceremonial an important lesson in commercial morality. One by one the bankrupts were placed on the centre of the stone to hear the reading of their balance-sheet and to endure as many reproaches as their creditors could cram into a limited time. When time was up, the presiding official touched his bell, and the storm of interjection was instantly hushed. Then the bankrupt was solemnly divested of a necessary portion of his dress, after which three stout public officers laid hold of his shoulders, and three others of his knees, and, raising him every time as high as they could, bumped him deliberately twelve times, " in honor of the twelve apostles," against the cold stone. An old writer states that the creditors crowed like cocks during the bumping, but that when it was over few of them entertained animosity against the bumpee. In proof whereof, he avers that not one of them could look at him with dry eyes as he sneaked through the crowd.

Stray Sale Day, or **First Monday,** in Texas. By an unwritten law of Texas, the first Monday in every month is set apart as the day on which all the stray horses and cattle that have been duly " taken up," " posted," and " kept" shall be taken down to the public square in the capital of every county throughout the State, there to be auctioned off or exchanged. Early in the morning men begin coming into town, jogging along on horseback through the black mud, and leading strings of from two to ten ponies of all conceivable degrees of disreputableness of appearance. Not all of these are really strays. Most of them, indeed, are brought in for sale or for trade along with the strays. By eight o'clock the square presents a lively appearance. By ten o'clock the whole space is covered with a densely packed mass of struggling, squirming, kicking, fidgeting Texas ponies. A little after ten the auction begins, and continues until every horse has been disposed of.

Not only is " first Monday" the day for stray sales and for general horse-trading, but it is also the day for getting and giving information about lost stock. But for it there would be far more stray stock in Texas than there is. It is wonderful to notice the degree of system which exists in regard to the matter. Every honest stock-man in Texas is a self-appointed committee of one to note any stray animals he may see, and to give accurate information concerning them whenever asked for it. Fences in Texas are rarely ever proof against the jumping or breaking force of the average Texas pony. When a pony gets out, he has all Texas to hide in, and the task of finding him would seem about as difficult as that of finding the proverbial needle in the proverbial haystack. He is almost sure to be found sooner or later, though, and "first Monday" is one of the principal devices used to aid in finding him.

Sunday. The first day of the week, named after the sun, and therefore an evident relic of sun-worship. In French it is *Dimanche,* in Italian *Domenica,* both from *Dominus,* " the Lord." Christians, with the exception of the Seventh-Day Adventists, have substituted it as a day of rest and prayer in lieu of the Jewish Sabbath.

According to the New Testament, the early Christians were in the habit of assembling in the evening of the first day of the week for worship. They met to break bread in remembrance of Jesus, because on that day he rose from the dead. But in the texts of the New Testament, as well as in the earliest ecclesiastical history, we find nothing that goes to show that the early Christians had any idea of keeping a Sabbath or that on that day they discontinued their ordinary vocations. In thousands of instances it would have been impossible for the Christians of those days to rest on the first day of the week, inasmuch as they were the servants of Jewish or heathen masters, who would not have permitted to them a day of idleness for the sake of the Man of Nazareth.

Irenæus is the first of the early fathers who speaks of cessation from labor on Sunday. He says that reaping and gathering into barns are then forbidden. Tertullian (A.D. 202) also says, " On the Lord's day of resurrection we ought to abstain from all habit and labor of anxiety, putting off even our business, lest we give place to the devil." But he also calls it a day "on which we allow ourselves to be joyous." A decree of Constantine commanded that all business and employment except agriculture should cease on "the honored day of the sun." The Emperor Leo, in 469, included agriculture in the prohibition.

During the Middle Ages Sunday grew into more and more importance as a holy day, deriving its sanction, however, not from the fourth commandment, but from the Church ordinances. It was on this account that the early Reformers protested against it as against other Church feasts. Luther, though he allowed that the appointment of one day in the week for rest and for attending divine worship was salutary, added that " If anywhere this day is made holy for the mere day's sake, . . . then I order you to dance on it, and feast on it, to do anything that shall remove this encroachment on Christian liberty." Calvin agreed with Luther. He conformed his practice to his precept. It is incidentally related that when John Knox once visited the Genevan Reformer on Sunday he found him playing at bowls. Knox was not shocked. He was no more of a Sabbatarian than Calvin. But the English Reformers retained the Catholic Sunday, as they did the vestments and national hierarchy of the old Church, and indeed enforced it with a severity unknown to Rome.

In all these controversies the word Sabbath as applied to Sunday does not make its appearance until about the year 1573, in the second edition of Bullein's " Dialogue against the Fever Pestilence," published at Frankfort. It holds up to admiration an ideal " Keepinge of the Saboth Day," but finds it necessary to explain that the Saboth "is the seventh daie, that is sondaie." And this is the manner in which Bullein (or possibly some interpolator) describes the " keepinge of the Saboth" in his imaginary Utopia: "There were no people walking abroad in the service tyme; no, not a Dogge or catte in the streate, neither any Taverne doore open that daie, nor wine bibbyng in them, but onely almose, fasting and praier."

Bullein called his imaginary city Nodnol, an anagram of London. And in fact it was in London, the head-quarters of Puritanism, that his ideal was first to be realized. The very adoption of the word Sabbath, which soon became general, showed which way the brain in the Roundhead was trending. If Sunday were to be treated as identical in all save its position in the week with the Jewish Sabbath, then the severest of the Old Testament ordinances would apply to the Christian holy day. So early as 1580 the magistrates of London secured from Queen Elizabeth the prohibition of theatrical entertainments within the limits of the city on Sunday. The Puritan mode of Sunday-keeping already existed among the chosen few. " The Sabboth daie of some is well observed," says Stubbes, " namely, in hearing the blessed worde of God read, preached, and interpreted ; in private and publique praiers ; in reading of godly psalmes ; in celebrating the sacraments ; and in collecting for the poore and indigent, which are the true uses and endes whereto the Sabbaoth was ordained."

Nor was the innovation at first unwelcome to the stricter English divines, who saw with alarm that Sunday after the morning services was entirely given up to out door games, to the brutally cruel sports of bull- and bear-baiting, to merry morris-dances, in which the performers were gayly decked and hung with jingling bells in different keys, as well as to coarse farces called interludes, which were played on stages under booths and sometimes in the churches.

Unfortunately, in its austere reaction against this license and frivolity Puritanism pushed Sabbath-keeping to its extreme, reprobating even the most innocent and domestic recreations, and changing a day of rest and refreshment into one of alternate periods of application to religious devotion and of scrupulous vacuity. The theory of a Sunday-Sabbath, which from the first was not confined to the Puritans, permeated English and American thought and life. But from that time forward the Puritans made rigid Sabbath-keeping the very mark and password of the faithful. From England the theory spread northward to Scotland, where it found a congenial soil.

In New England Puritanism reduced the ascetic Sunday to its logical absurdity. As the Jewish Sabbath was from sunset to sunset, so the New England Sunday began on Saturday afternoon. Everybody must cease from labor at three o'clock, and spend the rest of the day in such preparation for the morrow " as the ministers shall direct." All good people occupied some part of these hours in teaching their children the Shorter Catechism of the Westminster Assembly of Divines,—and not only their children, but their servants. One perplexed parson wrote back to England of the difficulty of getting servants who " enjoyed catechising and family duties,"—" family duties" meaning prayers.

Thus prepared, the Puritans awoke on Sabbath morning. The

Sabbath was a day of rest and religion. Whatever did not agree with these purposes of the day was an offence, punishable by law. In 1670 John Lewis and Sarah Chapman, lovers, were set on trial for "sitting together on the Lord's day under an apple-tree in Goodman Chapman's orchard." An old soldier in Dunstable for "netting a piece of old hat to put in his shoe," to ease a sore foot, was fined forty shillings. Captain Kemble, of Boston, sat two hours in the public stocks for his "lewd and unseemly behavior" in kissing his wife on his own door-step, he having on a Lord's day morning returned from a three years' cruise. The New Haven Sabbath laws set forth that "Profanation of the Lord's day shall be punished by fine, imprisonment, or corporal punishment; and if proudly, and with a high head against the authority of God, with death."

Relics of the old "blue-law" legislation exist on the statute-books of nearly all the States of the Union, but only as dead letters. The sternest magistrate would not dare to enforce them.

Suttee. A voluntary death by fire once common among Hindoos of both sexes. The earliest European travellers mentioned it as well-nigh universal in the parts of India they knew. Thus, Benjamin of Tudela observes, "Some of the great of this country take a vow to burn themselves alive. When he declares his intention, all applaud him, and say, ' Happy shalt thou be, and it shall be well with thee.' " Other travellers of the same early date tell the same story, but those who visited the country later speak only of the widow's self-immolation on her husband's funeral pyre. It would appear that this horrible limitation of the rite was established between the twelfth and fifteenth centuries. When the English acquired India they for a long time refrained from any prohibition of the custom, on

A WIDOW ON THE FUNERAL PYRE.

the ground that it would be an interference with the religious prejudices of the natives. In the early part of the nineteenth century, however, it was ordered that when a suttee was about to take place the official persons on the spot should inquire whether the act was voluntary on the part of the widow, and that they should attend at the funeral pyre and see that no force was used. This only increased the evil. It at once authorized suttees, and by requiring the presence of the magistrate or his representatives gave the sacrifice a consequence which it had not previously enjoyed. As no European could witness such a scene without trying, by gentle means at least, to prevent it, unavailing interference gave the victim the air of a martyr, and natural vanity and pride were called in to the aid of superstition.

Swan-Upping, Swan-Hopping, or Swan-Marking. At a very early date it was a high privilege, granted only by the sovereign to certain companies and individuals, to keep and preserve swans on the English lakes and rivers. Each proprietor had his own peculiar swan-mark, which was cut in the skin or on the beak of the young bird with a sharp knife or other instrument. The marking was generally performed in the presence of all the swan-herds on that stream, and on a particular day, of which all had notice. Cygnets received the mark found on the parent bird, but if the old swans had no mark the whole were seized for the king and marked accordingly. No swan-herd was allowed to affix a mark except in the presence of the king's swan-herd or of his

SWAN-UPPING.

deputy. The king's swan-herd kept a book of swan-marks, and no new marks were permitted to interfere with the old ones.

The marking was usually attended with much festivity, and, though no longer obligatory, the Dyers' and Vintners' Companies in the City of London, who have uninterruptedly enjoyed the privilege of keeping swans on the river Thames from London to some miles above Windsor, still keep up the old custom of going with their friends and acquaintances, accompanied by the royal swan-herds and assistants, on the first Monday in August in every year, for the purpose of catching and marking all the cygnets of the year, and also renewing any marks on the old birds that may have become obliterated. The struggles of the swans when caught by their pursuers, and the duckings that the men get in the contests, form amusing episodes.

The practice of swan-upping still survives in Stratford-on-Avon. *The Antiquarian* for November, 1884, has this note: "The old custom of swan-upping was observed at Stratford-on-Avon in September last, and was attended by the mayor and a distinguished party of visitors from Clopton House. A fleet of about forty boats, including a few canoes, well manned and provided with ropes and crooks, put off from the Clopton Bridge about half-past three o'clock in quest of the young birds. After an amusing chase up the river of from two to three miles, the cygnets were captured one by one, and subjected to the marking process, which consists of punching a hole in the web of the foot, whilst to prevent the birds flying any considerable distance it was thought advisable to cut the pinions."

Swastika, or **Fylfot.** (The first term comes from the Sanskrit *sv,* "good," or "well," and *asti,* "to be," or "being;" the second is the Anglo-Saxon for "four-footed.") A species of pre-Christian cross of peculiar shape which is found widely distributed throughout the globe. It is the oldest of all Áryan symbols. Other symbols which are found in archæological investigations, the straight line, the circle, the cross, the triangle, are simple forms easily made, and might have been invented and reinvented in every age of primitive man and in every quarter of the globe, each time being an independent invention, meaning much or little, and meaning different things among different peoples, or even at different times among the same people. But the Swastika was probably the first symbol to be made with a definite intention and a continuous or consecutive meaning, the knowledge of which passed from person to person, from tribe to tribe, from people to people, and from nation to nation, until, with possibly changed meanings, it has finally circled the globe.

A description of some of these early crosses and the differences between them and the Swastika is interesting. The Latin cross is the one found on coins, medals, and ornaments anterior to the Christian era. It was on a cross of this shape that Christ is said to have been crucified, and thus it became accepted as the Christian cross. The Greek cross differs from the Latin cross in that the arms are of equal length. The St. Andrew's cross is the same as the Greek cross, but turned to stand on two legs instead of one. The crux ansata, according to Egyptian mythology, was the emblem of Ka. The other crosses, which are variations of these forms, with some modifications, are the Tau cross, the Monogram of Christ, the Maltese cross, and the Celtic crosses. But of all these many forms of the cross the Swastika is the most ancient. The bars of the normal Swastika are straight, of equal thickness throughout, and cross each other at right angles, making four arms of equal size, length, and style. The peculiarity of the Swastika and the form which makes it perfectly recognizable, because so different from any other cross, lies in the fact that all the ends of the bars are bent at right angles in the same direction, be it either to the right or to the left. There are several varieties of cross probably very nearly related to the Swastika, which have been found in almost every part of the globe. These consist in spiral forms of the turned ends.

Archæologists differ as to the origin and meaning of the Swastika. They believe it to have been the emblem of Zeus, of Baal, of the sun, of the sun-god, of Indra, the rain-god, of the sky, and finally the deity of all deities, the great God, the maker and ruler of the universe.

The theory now most generally accepted is that the Swastika is a form of the wheel (*q. v.*) and a symbol of the solar motion. As Max Müller says, " it is an abbreviated emblem of the solar wheel with spokes in it, the tire and the movement being indicated by the crampons." On the bust of Apollo in the Kunsthistorisches Museum of Vienna there is a large and prominent Swastika, which goes far to show its solar significance. But in ancient usage the most important of its attributes seems to have been its character as a charm or amulet, as a sign of benediction, blessing, long life, or good luck. This character has continued into modern times, and, while it is to-day recognized as a holy and sacred symbol by at least one Buddhistic religious sect, it is still used by the common people of India, China, and Japan, to whom it has been naturally handed down from their forefathers as a sign of long life and good fortune. It had great extension, having spread itself practically over the known world, largely, if not entirely, in prehistoric times. Many specimens of it were found in excavations on the site of ancient Troy, on the hill of Hissarlik.

As it has also been found in North and South America, the Swastika furnishes almost conclusive evidence that the early peoples of the Eastern hemisphere were in constant communication with the early peoples of the Western.

Swithin or **Swithun, St.,** patron of Winchester, of which diocese he was bishop from 852 till his death, July 2, 862. He shared with St. Neot the glory of educating King Alfred, and was chancellor under Egbert and Ethelwolf. But at present his chief popular fame arises from the fact that he is a sort of

Jupiter Pluvius in the Protestant calendar of England. The common belief is that according as it rains or shines on St. Swithin's Day—which is celebrated on July 15, the anniversary of the translation of his relics—the next forty days will be either rainy or bright:

> St. Swithin's Day, if thou dost rain,
> For forty days it will remain :
> St. Swithin's Day, if thou be fair,
> For forty days 'twill rain nae mair.

This tradition is founded on a legend that, before dying, the humble-minded saint had begged to be interred in the open churchyard, and not in the chancel of the church, as was usual with bishops. Here he remained for over a century, when the monks, thinking it disgraceful that so great a saint should have so lowly a burial-place, resolved to move the body into the choir. The 15th of July was appointed for the purpose. But on that day a mighty rain-storm burst forth, and continued without intermission for the next forty days. The monks took this as a sign of heavenly displeasure, and instead of removing the body they built a chapel over it where it lay.

Unfortunately for the legend, however, it happens that the formal translation of the relics of St. Swithin from the grave in the churchyard to a magnificent shrine within the cathedral was in fact effected on July 15, 971, only one hundred and nine years after his death, without any meteorological interference. Many legends were set afloat at the time to prove that this was done by the saint's wishes as expressed in visions. A few years afterwards the church, which had originally been dedicated to the apostles Peter and Paul, changed these guardians for St. Swithin, who in turn had to yield to Henry VIII.'s substitution of the Holy Trinity.

It may be added that Swithin was never regularly canonized by the Pope,—a practice not introduced until two hundred years after his translation, which is the only ceremony on which he rests his claim to the title.

One of the earliest literary allusions to the saint's powers as a weather-prophet is in Ben Jonson's " Every Man out of his Humor," where Sordido, sarcastically critical of an almanac, cries, " 'Slid, stay, this is worse and worse. What says he of St. Swithin's? Turn back, look : St. Swithin's, the xv day—variable weather, for the most part rain, good. For the most part rain ; why it should rain forty days after now, more or less ; it was a rule held afore I was able to hold a plough, and yet here are two days no rain ; ha! it makes me muse !"

In " Poor Robin's Almanac" for 1697 are the following verses:

In this month is St. Swithin's Day,
On which if that it rain, they say
Full forty days after it will,
Or more or less, some rain distil.
This Swithin was a saint, I trow,
And Winchester's bishop also,
Who in his time did many a feat,
As Popish legends do repeat;
A woman, having broke her eggs,
By stumbling at another's legs,
For which she made a woful cry,
St. Swithin chanced for to come by,
Who made them all as sound or more
Than ever that they were before.
But whether this were so or no
'Tis more than you or I do know;
Better it is to rise betime,
And to make hay while sun doth shine,
Than to believe in tales and lies
Which idle monks and friars devise.

The satirical Churchill also mentions the superstitious notions concerning rain on this day:

July, to whom the dog-star in her train,
St. James gives oisters, and St. Swithin rain.

Hone's "Every Day Book" tells the story of an old lady who when St. Swithin's Day opened bright and fair expressed her belief in an approaching term of fine weather, but, a few drops of rain having fallen in the evening, changed her tune and announced that the next six weeks would be wet. Her prediction failed, the weather having been remarkably fine. "No matter," she would say; "if there has been no rain during the day there certainly has been during the night."

The shrine of St. Swithin early sprang into great repute. Worshippers, sick folk, the maimed and the halt, flocked hither and left behind them substantial signs of gratitude. For centuries Swithin was the most popular healing saint in England. He entirely overshadowed the rival St. Josse or Jodocus long previously established in the neighboring minster of St. Grimbald, and finally drove his competitor out of Winchester. Wulfstan records an interesting instance of this rivalry: "There was a poor man so sick that he despaired of life. His friends bore him to the city, and were for taking him to St. Josse; but as they drew nigh to the gate of the new minster, one met them who asked them what they did. St. Swithin's bones, he said, were far more potent in the old minster hard by. To this advice they listened, and so laid the sick man under the relics of the holy St. Swithin; and there they kept watch with him, praying and dozing, through the night. Towards daybreak they all fell off to sleep, and to the sick man in his dreams it seemed as if the shrine above him rocked and swayed mightily, and some one was tugging at his shoes. And he awoke in fear, and lo! he was healed; but one of his shoes was gone, and, though men sought diligently for it, to this day it has never been found."

Sword Dance. This name was anciently given to a curious ceremony annually performed in the North Riding of Yorkshire on St. Stephen's Day which survived until the beginning of the nineteenth century. It is thus described in "Time's Telescope" (1814, p. 315): "Six youths clad in white and bedecked with ribbons, with swords in their hands, travel from one village to another. They are attended by a fiddler, a youth whimsically dressed, named 'Bessy,' and by one who personates a physician. One of the six youths acts the part of a king in a sort of farce, which consists chiefly of music and dancing, when the Bessy interferes while they are making a hexagon with their swords, and is killed."

Symphorosa, St. A Jewish martyr, better known as the mother of the Maccabees. Her festival is celebrated by the

MARTYRDOM OF ST. SYMPHOROSA'S SONS.

Greek Church on July 18. She and her family belonged to that noble army of Palestinian martyrs who suffered persecution under Antiochus Epiphanes. She beheld her seven sons, one after another, suffer a most excruciating death rather than violate the law of God; and, after encouraging them with a fortitude unexampled to endure unto the end, she at last died herself, the mother and her seven sons in one day winning the crown of martyrdom. The authentic history of their torture, endurance, and death will be found in the seventh chapter of the second book of Maccabees, one of the Apocryphal books of the Bible, the account beginning, "It came to pass also that seven brethren with their mother were taken, and compelled by the king against the law to taste swine's flesh, and were tormented with scourges and whips. But one of them that spake first said thus: What wouldest thou ask or learn of us? We are ready to die, rather than to transgress the laws of our fathers."

St. Symphorosa is frequently confounded with the Christian martyr St. Felicitas. She is accepted as a saint by the Greek Church only, who reject St. Felicitas, the latter saint having a place in the calendar of the Eastern Church. Baring-Gould suspects that the saints are really identical.

T.

Tammany Hall, St. Tammany. The famous Tammany Society, which has always proved one of the most formidable organizations of the extreme wing of the Democratic party in the city of New York, was formally organized on May 12, 1789, just twelve days after the first installation of Washington as President of the United States. Its germ existed further back. During the Revolution the British troops had St. George for their patron and his name for their war-cry. The Americans, or some of them, not to be outdone, invented a patron saint of their own. They took for his legendary personality one Tamanend, a famous chieftain of the Delaware Indians, who probably lived at about the time of Columbus's discovery of America, and had his favorite hunting-grounds in what is Eastern Pennsylvania, especially around the Delaware Water Gap. A mountain-peak there now bears his name. There are many legends of him, mostly imaginative. Fenimore Cooper has drawn a fine picture of him in "The Last of the Mohicans" (chaps. xxviii., xxix.). A story of his personal battle with the devil is widely known, which relates that the Indian vanquished the fiend and drove him from the Pennsylvania mountains to Manhattan Island, where he has since made his home.

The Pennsylvania troops took to inscribing his name upon their banners and speaking of "Saint" Tamanend or Tammany as their patron saint. They fixed upon May 12 as his birthday, and celebrated it each year with great festivities, marked by such use of fire-water as at length led to their suppression by the authorities, as tending to debauch the army. Forts were named after him, and in every camp a wigwam was built in his honor, adorned with tomahawks, wampum, and painted totems. There the soldiers would gather from time to time, themselves decked with feathers, paint, and a buck's hide with the tail hanging down behind, to listen to a harangue from one of their number personating a sachem and to indulge in a grand powwow. After the war was ended these observances were carried into civil life. Tammany wigwams were built in many towns, Tammany societies were formed, and St. Tammany's Day, May 12, was a formidable rival of July 4 as a public holiday.

Such was the state of affairs when Aaron Burr conceived the plan of forming a secret political club. To insure its success, he must himself, at least in the beginning, not appear to be identified or at all concerned with it. In point of fact he never became an actual member. He put forward his friend and most obedient servant William Mooney to be its ostensible founder. This latter was an upholsterer, an ardent patriot, of Irish parentage, with a hatred of the British and of all things aristocratic, and a love for the mysterious and spectacular. Mooney borrowed the general scheme of the Tammany societies, called the meeting-place of the new organization a Wigwam, its head the Great Father, its council of twelve Sachems, its master of ceremonies a Sagamore, and its door-keeper a Wiskinkie. He wanted to discard the name Tammany, however, and call it "The Columbian Order." But it was deemed desirable to compromise the matter. The "Great Father" was transformed into "Grand Sachem," and the name finally adopted was "The Tammany Society, or Columbian Order." As such it was formed at the date named above, and soon grew into importance and influence. It celebrated both May 12 and July 4 as national holidays, and on the former date in 1790 was introduced to the public in *The New York Daily Gazette* in these terms:

"The Society of St. Tammany, being a national society, consists of Americans born, who fill all offices, and adopted Americans, who are eligible to the honorary posts of warrior and hunter. It is founded on the true principles of patriotism, and has for its motives charity and brotherly love. Its officers consist of one grand sachem, twelve sachems, one treasurer, one secretary, one door-keeper; it is divided into thirteen tribes, which severally represent a State; each tribe is governed by a sachem, the honorary posts in which are one warrior and one hunter."

Its legal incorporation was effected on April 9, 1805, the Legislature granting to " William Mooney and other inhabitants of the city of New York" a charter " for the purpose of affording relief to the indigent and distressed members of the association, their widows and orphans, and others who may be found proper objects of their charity." The first Wigwam was in Barden's City Hotel, on Broadway, the second in a Broad Street tavern, and the third, which was used until the first Tammany Hall was erected, in " Martling's Long Room," a drinking-place and dance-hall, commonly known as the " Pig-Pen." The character of the meetings was afterwards well described by Halleck:

> There's a barrel of porter in Tammany Hall,
> And the Bucktails are swigging it all the night long.

The society began the collection of a museum of patriotic relics, of which it presently got tired, and which it turned over to P. T. Barnum, to become the nucleus of his famous museum. One of its most notable early performances, in 1790, was to save the nation from an Indian war. The Creeks were about to go on the war-path, when a delegation of them was induced to visit New York, then the Federal capital. If the delegates were pleasantly impressed, war might be averted. So the Tammany Society invited them to its Wigwam; all the Tammany men were arrayed in paint and feathers, and fire-water was abundant. The result was that the Creeks reported to their tribe that it would never do to go to war with their own hospitable brethren: so the peace was kept.

In 1811 Tammany became rich enough to leave the Pig-Pen and put up a hall of its own. This was a three-story brick building on the southeast corner of Nassau and Frankfort Streets. It contained what was then the finest public ball-room in the city. This building was afterwards enlarged and improved, and served the society as its head-quarters until 1868, when the present building in Fourteenth Street was occupied, the corner-stone having been laid on July 4, 1867, with an oration by Gulian C. Verplanck.

Tenebræ. The name given to the matins and lauds sung in Roman Catholic churches on the afternoon or evening of Wednesday, Thursday, and Friday in Holy Week. At the beginning of the office thirteen candles are placed on a triangular candelabrum, and at the end of each psalm one is put out, till only a single candle is left lighted at the top of the triangle. During the singing of the Benedictus the candles on the high altar are likewise extinguished, and at its close the single candle left alight is taken from the candelabrum and hidden at the Epistle corner of the altar, to be brought out again at the close of the service.

TENEBRÆ,—EXTINCTION OF THE LIGHTS.

This extinction of lights (whence probably the name *tenebræ*, or "darkness") symbolizes the growing darkness of the time when Christ, the light of the world, was taken. The last candle, Benedict XIV. explains, is hidden, not extinguished, to signify that death could not really obtain dominion over Christ, though it appeared to do so. The clapping of hands after the singing of the Miserere symbolizes the confusion consequent on Christ's death. In Rome and other Italian cities the entire congregation joins in clapping, stamping on the floor, and other noisy demonstrations. Children go to the churches carrying sticks entwined with colored ribbons, which are exposed for sale in every street-stall in the city. These are beaten violently and with a deafening clatter against the floor, walls, or pillars of the church. The juvenile explanation makes this the flagellation of the devil,—apparently a curious evolution from the flagellation of Christ.

Tenures, Curious. The law-books are full of cases of singular tenures by which estates used to be or are still held, so that, in the quaint language of Blount, one can but "smile at the inoffensive mirth both of our kings in former times and lords of manors in creating them." Here is an out-of-the-way instance. One Solomon Attfield held lands at Repland and Atterton, in Kent, upon condition that, as often as the king should cross the sea, the said Solomon and his heirs should accompany him, in order that they might "hold his head" if his gracious majesty were unfortunately visited with sea-sickness. Take another example. In the reign of Edward III. one John Compes had the manor of Finchfield given to him as a reward for his arduous services at the king's coronation,—which services consisted in turning the spit in the royal kitchen.

Many noble lords held manors by the service of carving for the king at annual feasts, or serving him, or bearing a rod before him, or guarding his person (as at Shrewsbury when he lay there). The lord of the manor of Houghton, Cumberland, was obliged to hold the stirrup of the king when he mounted his horse in Carlisle Castle, and the lord of Shirefield had the unpleasant duty of being master of the king's *meretrices*, or laundresses, as well as of dismembering condemned malefactors and measuring the gallons in the king's household. To carry a hawk for his majesty, to present him with a gray hood or cap or a white ensign whenever he warred in Scotland, to attend with proper arms, a horse, sword, lance, or simple bow and arrows, whenever their services were required, such were the duties incumbent upon other manor lords. The service of cornage or blowing horns was very common, especially in the Border counties, where Scottish invasions were frequent. The owner of Kingston Russell, Dorset, was obliged to count the king's chessmen and to put them in a bag when the king had finished the game.

The tenant of a large farm at Broadhouse, near Langsett, Yorkshire, England, holds the right to the property as long as he shall pay a yearly rental of "a snow-ball at midsummer and a red rose at Christmas" to the landlord. A red rose at Christmas in these days of hot-houses is easy enough to obtain. But a snow-ball at midsummer? At first sight it would appear that an utterly disproportionate trouble and expense must be entailed upon the owner of the Broadhouse property. In point of fact, whatever may have been the original intent of the donor, from time immemorial the midsummer rent has been received in the form of a Guelder rose, which is called a snow-ball in the neighborhood.

One of the dukes of Scotland relinquishes his rights to his lands if it should ever get warm enough to melt the snow from the highest peak of the highest mountain in Scotland.

William de Albemarle holds the manor of Leaston "by the service of finding for our lord the king two arrows and one loaf of oat bread when the sovereign should hunt in the forest of Eastmoor." Although the forest is no longer a hunting ground, and arrows have long since given place to rifles and shot-guns of the best make, still the heirs of Albemarle keep the arrows and the oat bread ready for any stray king that may happen that way, thus holding good the title to their estates.

Geoffrey Frumbrand and heirs hold sixty acres of land in Suffolk, England, on condition that they pay the sovereign a yearly rental of two white doves.

Not many of these ancient tenures have survived. But for over seven hundred years the Corporation of London has annually discharged two quaint ceremonies as quit-rents to the reigning sovereign for certain lands in the counties of Salop and Middlesex of which the Corporation are tenants in capite to the crown. The actual site of the property itself has been lost in the mists of antiquity. But the ceremony has never been omitted. It now takes place in the office of the Queen's Remembrancer, but anciently before the Cursitor Baron of the Exchequer, an office which was abolished forty years ago. Here is how the *London Daily Chronicle* describes the ceremony in 1896:

"Many visitors—mostly ladies—were present to see the ceremony, which dates back to A.D. 1211. The first rental was rendered after the following proclamation had been made, viz.: 'Tenants and occupiers of a piece of waste ground called the Moors, in the County of Salop, come forth and do your service.' Whereupon the city solicitor cut a fagot with a hatchet and another with a bill-hook. On this occasion, by desire of the queen, the implements used will be sent to her majesty. The second rental rendered was after the following proclamation: 'Tenants and occupiers of a certain tenement called the Forge, in the Parish of St. Clement's Danes, in the County of Middlesex, come forth and do your service.' The city solicitor came forward again, and counted on the table six horseshoes and sixty-one hobnails, which the Queen's Remembrancer declared to be 'good numbers.' This brought the ceremony to a close. During her majesty's reign of sixty years, four Queen's Remembrancers have taken part in the ceremony, Mr. Pollock being the fourth."

Terminalia. An ancient Roman festival celebrated on February 23 in honor of Terminus, the god of boundaries and frontiers. The neighbors on either side of any boundary gathered round the stones (*termini*) which marked territorial limits and crowned them with garlands. Cakes and bloodless sacrifices were offered up. In later times, however, a lamb or sucking pig was sometimes slain and the stone sprinkled with the blood. In conclusion the whole neighborhood joined in a general feast.

Teufelstisch. (Ger., "Devil's Table.") The name given to a large flat rock lying near Graefenberg, Bavaria. Here, it is popularly believed, a glass palace, invisible to mortal eyes, springs up just after midnight on May 1. The devil's table occupies the centre of the banqueting-hall in this palace, and a ghostly crew, including Gambrinus, the inventor of beer, and the shades of the ancient kings of France, hold high revelry around the big flat rock.

Thanksgiving Day. A holiday now observed in all the United States. Custom prescribes that the date shall be set by special proclamation of the President, and adds that the date shall be the last Thursday in November. The proclamation would appear to stamp the feast with a sort of official character possessed by no other holiday in America. But that character is only apparent. It is not for the Federal government to tell the people of the United States when they shall quit business and take to pleasure. The President's proclamation only recommends that the people, ceasing from their ordinary occupations, observe the day with proper ceremony. It only makes it a legal holiday in those States which provide for its legality by special statute. Thanksgiving, though observed in all the States, is not a legal holiday in all of them.

The celebration has a long and curious history. Days set apart for special thanksgiving to the Lord were known to the Israelites, and are mentioned throughout the Bible. They were not uncommon in England before the Reformation and among Protestants afterwards. So recently as 1872 a day of thanksgiving was appointed on February 27 for the recovery of the Prince of Wales from typhoid fever.

The first thanksgiving held in North America was conducted by an English minister named Wolfall, in the year 1578, on the shores of Newfoundland. The reverend gentleman accompanied the expedition under Frobisher which brought the first English colony to settle on these shores. The records of this day's observances are thus preserved in the ship's log: "On Monday morning, May 27, 1578, aboard the Ayde we received all the communion by the minister of Gravesend and prepared as good Christians toward God and resolute men for all fortunes and toward night we departed toward Tilberry Hope. Here we highly praysed God and altogether upon our knees gave Him due humble and hearty thanks, and Maister Wolfall, a learned man appointed by her Majesty's council to be our minister, made unto us a godlye sermon, exhorting all especially to be thankful to God for His strange and miraculous deliverance in those dangerous places," etc. This was perhaps the first Christian sermon preached and the first celebration of the Holy Communion in North America.

The earliest record of any observance of a similar service within the present territory of the United States was held by the Popham colony settled at Sagadahoc, on the coast of Maine, in August, 1607.

But these were mere thanksgiving services, which only consumed a few hours and did not color the whole day. The real origin of Thanksgiving as a day specially set apart for prayer and rejoicing must be attributed to Governor Bradford, the first governor of Massachusetts Colony. In gratitude for the plenteous harvest of 1621, following upon a period of great depression, he proclaimed a day of thanksgiving to be observed on December 13 (Old Style) of that year.

In practical furtherance of his proclamation, he at once sent out four men in search of game. Thus early in the history of the day does our good friend the turkey make his appearance; for, successful in their quest, the four sportsmen returned, struggling under a burden of wild fowl, principally turkeys, sufficient to meet the wants of the little colony for a week. Then the thrifty housewives took the matter in hand and made all the goodies possible from their somewhat limited supply of material.

At the first gray dawn of that first Thanksgiving Day, one of the cannon that crowned the hill-top thundered forth a salute. A solemn procession to the meeting-house was formed, the men marching three abreast, Elder Brewster, in his long preacher's camlet coat, walking beside them, bearing with a gravity befitting the occasion the great Bible, while the Sergeant in Counsel and Governor Bradford brought up the rear. After the service followed the dinner, whose savory odors seem to have penetrated the forest's fastnesses, for in the midst of the festivities an Indian shout was heard, and ninety friendly red men, under King Massasoit, appeared as if by magic, bearing as an addition to the feast huge haunches of venison. The day of Thanksgiving lengthened into three, the mere bodily feastings being varied with the singing of psalms and songs, with war-dances by the savages, with exhibitions of military drill by Captain Standish's well-trained soldiery, and with such sports and pastimes as characterized the recreations of the middle class of English people in those times at home.

The festival proved the prelude to frequent days of thanksgiving in the following years throughout the New England colonies. Sometimes it was appointed once a year, sometimes twice, sometimes a year or two were skipped,—according as reasons for giving thanks presented themselves or not. Now the reason was a victory over the Indians, then the arrival of a ship with supplies or " persons of special use and quality," and yet again a bountiful harvest. The frequent appointments for the last cause finally made August the customary month. Beginning with 1684, the festival became a formal and annual one in Massachusetts. Her example was soon followed by all the New England colonies.

One of the potent influences which aided its general acceptance in these colonies was the Puritanic hatred of Christmas as a relic of "Popish mummery." Such "superstitious meats" as baron of beef, boar's head, plum-pudding, and mince pie, all redolent of memories of the ancient feast, were eschewed in favor of the indigenous turkey, Indian pudding, and pumpkin pie.

In pioneer Thanksgiving times in Rhode Island and Connecticut, however, venison or bear's meat rather than turkey was the centre of the festal board. In a newspaper published in Connecticut, in colonial times is to be found an account of the feast spread before the Governor and Her Majesty's Commissioners on Thanksgiving Day, 1713, from which it appears that, before the company fell to, the announcement was made that the venison had come from a deer which had been shot " on ye Lord's Day." Thereupon the entire company refused to eat, and it was decided that the Indian who had shot the deer should receive thirty-nine stripes and should restore to the purchaser the price paid for the meat. Then, having inflicted a "just and righteous sentence on ye sinful heathen," the company (with the exception of one member, whose conscience was not satisfied) fell upon the venison and devoured it.

During the Revolutionary War Thanksgiving lost some of its local New England character. The Continental Congress recommended no less than eight days of Thanksgiving. They fell in April, May, July, and December. The appointments were made in the form of recommendations to the heads of the various colonial governments. With one exception, Congress suspended business on the days appointed.

Washington issued a proclamation for a general thanksgiving by the Continental Army, Thursday, December 18, 1777, and again at Valley Forge, May 7, 1778. A few days before the adjournment of Congress in September, 1789, Representative Elias Boudinot moved in the House that the President be requested to recommend a day of thanksgiving and prayer in acknowledgment of the many signal favors of Almighty God, and especially his affording them an opportunity of establishing a constitution of government for their safety and happiness. Roger Sherman, of Connecticut, supported the motion. Ædanus Burke, of South Carolina, did not like "this mimicking of European customs," and Thomas T. Tucker, of Virginia, intimated that it might be as well to wait for some experience of the efficiency of the Constitution before returning thanks for it. In spite of these objections, the motion was carried, and President Washington issued a proclamation appointing as Thanksgiving Day November 26.

The original manuscript of this proclamation, interesting as the first ever issued by a President of the United States, is now (1897) in the hands of the Rev. J. W. Wellman, who had it as an heirloom from his grandfather, William Ripley, of Cornish, New Hampshire.

Following Washington, several Presidents issued general proclamations on special occasions; but usually it was left to the governors of the States to determine whether there should be a day of Thanksgiving and what that day should be.

Now, it happened that Mrs. Sarah J. Hale, coming down from Boston to Philadelphia to edit *Godey's Lady's Book*, realized as she had not done while in her New England home how limited was the observance of the day. Wherefore she sat down and wrote letters to the governors of all the States and Territories, suggesting that they should, by proclamation, appoint the last Thursday of November as a day for thanksgiving, so that the celebration might be given a national character. This she did year after year, and was so far successful that in 1859 the governors of all the States but two yielded to her request. But as yet there was no very wide-spread attention from the people invited to keep the day. During the war the custom lagged in those States in which it had not firmly intrenched itself, especially in the South, where indeed it has always had to combat the suspicion of being a Puritan substitute for Christmas. But most of the Northern governors continued to issue their proclamations, which were generally followed by great devastations among the flocks of turkey-gobblers. Immediately after the battle of Gettysburg, in July, 1863, Mrs. Hale wrote to President Lincoln, enclosing a copy of Washington's Thanksgiving proclamation issued from New York in 1789, and suggested that he, too, should proclaim a day of National Thanksgiving. Her suggestion was followed on July 15, when the President issued a proclamation "for the observance of Thursday, August 6, as a day for national thanksgiving, praise, and prayer." Since then (with only one exception of date) the Presidents have appointed the last Thursday of November, exchanging the local and variable observance of early days for one truly national.

The Thanksgiving of the present is built upon the Thanksgiving of the past, but has incorporated into itself many of the genial features of Christmas, and this in its turn has among Americans borrowed something from the modern holiday. There has been an unconscious unification of the two feasts in certain material aspects. The Thanksgiving turkey has driven the Christmas goose from all tables; and on the other hand the mince pie of Christmas shares the honor of completing the Thanksgiving indigestion with the pumpkin pie which once monopolized the work.

A correspondent of the *New York Evening Post* (November 25, 1891) has given a pleasant account of how Thanksgiving was celebrated about the middle of the century in New England. Many of the old forms are still retained, yet some have been so modified or so nearly lost that it is well to keep a record of them.

"The old country Thanksgiving," this authority tells us, " then as now had its threefold character,—sportive, festal, and religious, —but two of its sportive elements have now almost faded away. One was the 'raffle,' always held on Thanksgiving Eve. Sometimes it was held at a farm-house, sometimes at the country store, more often at the local butcher's shop. Each turkey, goose, or chicken, all usually the relics of the earlier Thanksgiving sales and therefore tough and adamantine, had its number of chances ticketed upon it in sprawling figures. A fair-sized fowl had ten chances of sixpence each; a fat goose ran up to a dozen sixpences, and a turkey, if fat, fair, and not forty, to thirty sixpences or fewer ninepences. A dice-box, two dice, and three throws, with their maximum of thirty-six points, a crowded room in the flickering glow of 'taller dips' or camphene lamps, and a jolly crowd of rustics, fringed with small boys, were the other components of the picture. The 'banker,' if such the proprietor of the raffle may be called, had little tricks of his own. Sometimes he loaded up a turkey, fair to the eye but sinewy in flesh, with many high-priced chances. Geese, rotund in figure but rank and fishy from self-fattening on the minnows of their natal pond, were another form of his deceit; and he had a true Yankee trick of watching keenly the gambling fervor of his patrons and disposing of his toughest fowls when the frenzy ran highest. Human nature cropped out in those ancestral turkey-raffles as clearly as in Wall Street nowadays.

"Another of the sportive features of the Yankee Thanksgiving Day, now almost extinct, was the shooting-match, usually held in the morning, and therefore not viewed with favor by the Church, because of its tendency to entice the youth from the Thanksgiving service. In an open field a base-line was marked on the turf. From this were laid off certain shooting-distances.

Eight rods, about, was 'chicken distance;' about nine rods, turkey distance; while for rifle-shooting, with a turkey as target and prize, the distance was more arbitrary, but not often more than twenty rods. There were at each distance ' stools' of block and nail to tie the doomed fowls to, and twenty feet back of the base-line a ' rest' of a dry-goods box, on which shooters so desiring could place their guns under penalty of the longer range. The match was more between the fowls and the gunner than between the shooters. The chickens and turkeys chosen by the shrewd master of the Yankee Schützenfest were ever of the most archaic type, with flesh of iron, and so long as they could 'stand up or fly a rod' the fusillade had to continue. They seemed to absorb shot like cornmeal, and occasionally survived fifteen or twenty of the cruel firings.

"In its religious character the old Yankee Thanksgiving was a curious hybrid. On the one side was the severe ancestral orthodoxy and a religion which has been aptly described as a brooding sense that something awful was always going to happen; and on the other hand the official Church order to rejoice and give thanks on the day, even though the pit yawned on the day before and the day after. To the severely pious, therefore, the day was a sort of paradox, and to the youngsters of the congregation, pent up in the pew, a veritable Sunday, only diluted by the single service and by the aroma of the coming turkey. The wives often stayed at home to prepare the dinner; and this absenteeism was sometimes made the object of severe reproach from the pulpit, aimed at preference for the flesh-pots over spiritual things. Nevertheless even the Yankee pulpit 'cheered up' perceptibly on Thanksgiving. Not seldom it turned, as on 'fast day,' towards secular topics, local, State, or national; and it was on a Thanksgiving that one of our stanch Federalist pastors of Connecticut prayed, ' And, O Lord, endow the President [Jefferson] with a goodly portion of thy grace, for thou, O Lord, knowest that he needs it.'

"But the festal trait of the old Yankee Thanksgiving was the prime mark of the day. It was the one time of the year when into the hard-fisted home life and its deep religious gloom the sunlight fairly entered, and it was proportionally made much of, with preparations begun many days before the feast, and the feast itself looked forward to with an excitement of which our later Yankee generation knows nothing. Its reunions, its vacant chairs, its yearly story of profit or of pain, touched the inner chords of those stern old Yankee souls and made them vibrant. The table fare was graded downward on a sort of barn-yard scale: for the squirearch the stall-fed turkey, specially fattened and sometimes rising twenty pounds, at one end of the board, chicken pie at the other; for the well-to-do farm household, a turkey of minor degree, without the pie; and for the poorer farmers, the pie without the turkey. But every table, rich or poor, had its cider and its mince pie, which, with a fowl of some kind, were the trinity of the feast. They survive still until our time; but from the modern board one very common side-dish of the old Thanksgiving is missed,—pigeon pie. In those days the wild pigeons lighting by hundreds on the buckwheat-fields were enticed by a decoy bird within range of a spring net and taken in multitudes. Kept alive in enclosures and fattened on grain, they entered at last the dish to whose savory quality our ancestors could render no higher tribute than by their daring mutilation of a favorite hymn:

> " When I can read my title clear
> To mansions in the skies,
> I'll bid farewell to every fear
> And live on pigeon pies.

"In the hospitable glow of the season, no tramp went unfed, and even the town poor-house had its turkey; old enemies chose the time for 'making up' their feuds; and the day, as a rule, infinitely more than now under our sunnier creeds, turned men for a while from the darksome theory of retribution towards the gentle humanities. In our days of liberal theology, expanding Christian unities, and organized charities, we of a later Yankee generation can never fully know how to our ancestors that old and single Thanksgiving Day of the year was worth the whole fifty-two Sundays, and how it tempered the fierce doctrinal heats of a hundred and four sermons."

In the State of New York the first Thanksgiving proclamation was issued by Governor John Jay in 1795. It was announced as an expression of gratitude for the cessation of the yellow fever plague of that year, and was appointed for Thursday, November 26. Political opponents, on the alert for fault-finding, bitterly censured this act as another evidence of the governor's aristocratic or federal notions of government and in excess of his due prerogatives as an executive officer.

In the middle of the century it was fashionable, and therefore customary, to make calls. Thanksgiving Day rivalled New Year's Day in this respect. Society folk dined at noon, drove to Kingsbridge and back, and then held receptions. It is recorded that in the days when Ward McAllister and Peter Marie were young beaux and Bond Street was a fashionable promenade they never missed a Thanksgiving afternoon call upon a gentleman whose name has come down to posterity only as "Turner the generous."

Mr. Turner lived in lower Fifth Avenue, and his Thanksgiving afternoons were famous. He kept open house, as did many other New Yorkers, and dispensed a peculiarly seductive eggnog, which was sipped through a straw. A box of cigars was offered as a prize to the guest who could drink three of these eggnogs, and tradition says that Mr. McAllister was a prize-winner.

Another and somewhat strange way of observing the holiday in New York has been, up to very recent years, to dress one's self in the most fantastic costume imaginable and parade the streets. This was undoubtedly a survival of the old Pope Day or Guy Fawkes's Day (*q. v.*) mummeries translated to a later day in the same month. Hundreds of companies of these motley persons, under some such name as the "Square Back Rangers," the "Slenderfoot Army," or the "Original Hounds," and dressed chiefly, as an old account says, as "clowns, Yankees, Irishmen, kings, washerwomen, and courtiers," thronged the streets all day. These "ragamuffin parades" have fallen into disuse except for a few small boys, but as recently as 1885 they were in full swing, as the following paragraph, printed in the *Sun* on November 27, 1885, testifies:

"Fantastic processions burst out all over the town in unusual abundance and filled the popular eye with a panorama that looked like a crazy-quilt show grown crazy and filled the popular ear with the din of thumping drums and blaring trumpets. Thirty-six companies of fantastics had permits to march around making an uproar, and they did it with great success. Local statesmen went around with the down-town paraders and helped them whoop things up. There were lots and lots of fantastics who hadn't any permit, and who didn't care either. They were the thousands and thousands of small boys who put on their sisters' old dresses, smeared paint on their faces, pulled on red, yellow, brown, black, and indiscriminate wigs, and pranced round their own particular streets, without the least fear of police interference."

These fantastic parades sometimes attained the dignity of a political demonstration. In 1870 the chief feature of Thanksgiving Day observances in New York was a parade of the Shandley Legion. The route was from Essex Market to Irving Hall, and the whole town turned out to see it. The newspapers the day before announced that "Senator Tweed will review the troops from the parlor windows of the Blossom Club, and not from the balcony of his residence at Forty-First Street and Fifth Avenue."

Prizes worth over ten thousand dollars were distributed among the paraders. The list of those contributing towards the prizes makes rather interesting reading at this time. Here are a few

extracts from the list: Senator William M. Tweed, $500 in gold;
Assistant District Attorney Fellows, a diamond ring, worth $75;
James Timoney, of Wallack's, silver, $20; E. D. Bassford, set of
crockery, worth $175; the Hon. Tim J. Campbell, check for $50;
Mr. William Edelstein (law partner of young Tweed), $50; a
friend of Commissioner Shandley, a set of harness; General
Miles, president of the Sixpenny Savings Bank, gold, $100; the
Stable Gang, bills, $100; W. J. Florence, the comedian, check
for $50. The *Sun*, in concluding its list of these donations, says,
"And so on to an almost interminable length," the list comprising
everything from a piano to a shirt-stud."

Theresa, St. (It. *Santa Teresa;* Fr. *Sainte-Thérèse;* Sp.
Santa Teresa), patron saint of Spain. Her festival is celebrated
on the day of her death, October 15.

St. Theresa was born at Avila, in Old Castile, on the 28th of
March, 1515. She was of a noble family, and was very piously
brought up. Her mind was probably unbalanced by her emotional nature, and when she was but nine years old she set off
with her brother into the country of the Moors, in the hope
of becoming a martyr. The children were brought back, and
then resolved to become hermits, but were not allowed to carry
out this idea. At the age of twenty St. Theresa entered the
Carmelite convent at Avila, where she was in great stress of
mind for a number of years. She has left behind a history of
her struggles and temptations, from which it appears that she
derived much comfort and consolation from the "Confessions"
of St. Augustine. She became active in deeds of charity, and
threw herself into the task of reforming the Carmelite order.
She began with eight nuns only in a small convent, but by the
time of her death she had founded thirty convents and had
established her rule in a number of monasteries as well. Her
main idea was that those who followed the rule should possess
absolutely nothing and subsist on charity. Besides the history
of her life she wrote many devout works. She died at Alva in
1582. Philip III. declared her to be the second patron saint of
Spain. She was canonized by Gregory XV. in 1622. Her body
was buried at Alva, but was removed to Avila in 1585. The
following year, however, it was moved back to Alva by an order
from Rome obtained by the Duke of Alva, where it remains to
the present day. Many miracles are recorded as wrought by her
relics and through her intercession. The body of the saint is
not now entire at Alva, and some of her relics have been scattered. Her left arm is at Lisbon. Fingers of her right hand
are at Seville, Rome, Avila, Paris, and Brussels. Her right foot
is in Rome, together with a slice of her flesh. A wooden cross

with which the saint is said to have combated devils is at Rome, and another at Brussels. Her slippers are shown at Avila, and also her staff and rosary; her veil is at Cagliari; a piece of flesh and a tooth are preserved in the Carmelite church of Venice. At Piacenza a napkin stained with the blood of the saint is exposed on the day of her festival. At Milan a slice of her heart and a tooth are shown; at Naples are a lump of flesh and the saint's scapular, and another lump of flesh is at Paris. Two large slices of flesh are at Cracow. St. Theresa is represented in art with a flaming arrow penetrating her heart, or with Christ presenting a nail to her. Sometimes she appears in a biretta with book and pen, and with the Dove whispering in her ear, as a doctor of the Church.

Thomas à Becket, St. (1117–1170), or **St. Thomas of Canterbury,** as he is better known to the hagiologists. The most popular saint of Catholic England. His memory was formerly commemorated not only on the anniversary of his murder or martyrdom, December 29, but also and more particularly on the anniversary of the translation of his relics, July 7 (1223). The latter was and is still known in Great Britain as St. Thomas's Day. Its eve was kept as a strict fast by the clergy and pilgrims to his shrine. The pilgrimages to Canterbury are especially famous in literature through the "Canterbury Tales" of Chaucer. For upwards of three centuries after the translation, pilgrims from every nation, rank, and class thronged to the martyr's tomb on St. Thomas's Day. Up to a comparatively recent time, a faint survival of the festivities of this day was retained in Becket's Fair, held on July 7 at Canterbury. It may also be noted that according to "Time's Telescope" (1822, p. 192), quoted in Dyer's "British Popular Customs," the Sunday after St. Thomas's Day formerly went by the name of Relic Sunday in some parts of Northamptonshire. (See also Bodmin Riding.)

The details of Becket's life are too well known to need any but the briefest recapitulation. He commenced life as a gay companion of Henry II., who loaded him with favors and finally conferred on him the archbishopric of Canterbury. From that time Thomas's character underwent a complete transformation. The former worldly-minded courtier now became the devout and ascetic priest, who walked alone in the cloister bewailing his past sins, who washed the feet of pilgrims and beggars, and whose sole aim was the exaltation of the power of Church over State. We need no longer look at the great prelate through the spectacles of his posthumous Protestant opponents. With all its faults, the Church of Becket's day was the only possible helper of the people. The Bishop of Rome was just then a less dangerous shepherd than Henry, the Angevin king. Becket may not have become consciously a champion of the people when he turned an opponent of the king, nevertheless he proved a mighty agent in winning that long battle for English liberty which was by no means closed on the scaffold of King Charles, five hundred years later.

Henry, stung by repeated acts of contumacy, one day let fall the angry expression, "Of the cowards that eat my bread, are there none that will relieve me of this upstart priest?" Four Norman knights accepted the unwary remark as a hint. The result was the murder of the archbishop on the very steps of his altar.

The news filled all Christendom with horror. King Henry, in sackcloth and ashes, bewailed the crime which he had unwittingly instigated. "He shut himself up three days in his closet," says good Bishop Butler, "taking almost no nourishment and admitting no comfort, and for forty days never went abroad, never had his table or any diversions as usual, having always before his eyes the death of the holy prelate. He not only wept, but

SHRINE OF ST. THOMAS À BECKET.

howled and cried out in the excess of his grief." He assured the Pope of his absolute innocence in intention. He voluntarily made all the concessions which St. Thomas had demanded. The martyr was canonized two years after his death by Alexander III., and there was an immediate outbreak of miracles at his shrine, which long continued to be the most popular pilgrimage place in England, while his cult spread rapidly throughout every country in Europe.

Among the first of these pilgrims came Henry II. to do a second penance in expiation of his unwitting crime and sacrilege.

After having lived upon bread and water for some days, and after walking barefooted to the cathedral, he knelt in the transept, where the martyrdom had occurred, and then in the crypt, where à Becket's tomb then was. Upon this he bowed his head, and, his lower garments having been removed, the King of England, a Plantagenet, received five strokes from the rod of each bishop and abbot who was present, and three from each of the eighty monks! After this he stood the whole night barefooted upon the ground, resting only against one of the rude stone pillars of the crypt.

St. Thomas's fame now extended throughout Europe. Even to this day his hair shirt is preserved in a reliquary in the English college at Douay; a small part in the abbey of Liesse; a bone of his arm in the church of St. Waltrude, at Mons; his chalice in the nunnery of Bourbourg; his mitre and linen, dipped in his blood, at St. Bertin's, in St. Omer, and other relics at Rheims, at Rome, at Florence, at Verona, at Lisbon. There is a chapel dedicated to him at Lyons, and a house with an inscription bearing his name at Lille; his figure may still be seen in the church of Monreale at Palermo, and his story is blazoned in the beautiful windows of Chartres, of Sens, and of St. Ouen, while his martyrdom is elaborately embroidered on a cloth still kept in the cathedral of Anagni. The Crusaders founded a church and cemetery in his honor at Acre.

In England, of course, the tokens of devout homage were more conspicuous and universal. It is hence that the name of Thomas became so common among Englishmen, and that so many of the English ancient bells, like that of Christ Church, Oxford, rejoice in the name " Great Tom."

It is obvious that the unfeigned and abiding homage which for nearly four centuries was paid to his name marks something in his character and career which awoke a national response in the national heart. In the first half-century after his death the monks kept the door of his vault in which the body lay under lock and key, but on Friday in Easter week and on the Nones of April the door was opened and all persons were permitted to perform their devotions at the tomb.

On July 7, 1223, the relics were translated from the crypt to a sumptuous shrine in the east end of the cathedral, amid a splendid assemblage of the highest prelates and potentates of England, headed by the primate and by the sovereign himself, Henry III., then a boy of thirteen.

The shrine is thus described by John Stow in his Annals: " It was built about a man's height of stone, then upward of plain timber, within which was an iron chest, containing the bones of St. Thomas, as also the skull, with the wound of his death, and the piece cut out of the skull laid in the same wound. The timber work of this shrine on the outside was covered with plates of gold, damasked and embossed, garnished with brooches, images, angels, chains, precious stones, and great Oriental pearls." Chief among the jewels was the royal diamond given by Louis, King of France. The marble stones before the place remain to this day, much worn and hollowed by the knees of the pilgrims who resorted thither.

In 1520, Henry VIII., with his guest the Emperor Charles V., came to pay his devotions at St. Thomas's shrine. Fifteen years later, on July 6, the eve of the great feast of the Translation of St. Thomas, and therefore, as he touchingly expressed it, "a meet day and very convenient for me," Sir Thomas More was executed for denying the royal supremacy.

Two years later, that same day, which had always hitherto been observed by the English primates as a strict fast, was ostentatiously kept as a festival at Lambeth Palace, the archiepiscopal residence, by Archbishop Cranmer, who "ate flesh, and did sup in his hall with his family, which was never seen before." Next year the blow fell. With a ludicrous parody of the forms of justice, the dead archbishop was formally summoned before the Privy Council to answer charges of "treason, contumacy, and rebellion," and was, of course, convicted; whereupon his name was stricken from the reformed calendar, his bones were ordered to be burned, and the treasures of his shrine forfeited to the crown. A royal commission under the notorious Dr. Leyton was sent down to Canterbury to carry out this order, but unfortunately no authentic record is extant of the proceedings, and hence the doubts which have since arisen about the disposal of the body. Dean Stanley says that "the bones were either scattered to the winds, or, if interred, mingled indiscriminately with others." And he quotes in proof of it a passage from Harpsfield's Life of Sir Thomas More: "We have of late unshrined him, and buried his holy relics."

An examination of the text, however, reveals the fact that "burned," and not "buried," was the word used by Harpsfield, and this is now the prevalent belief. Nevertheless, in 1888, the despoiled shrine was opened with much ceremony and some bones were discovered. The controversy which raged over the genuineness of these bones as relics of the great saint has ended in their general rejection by historical experts and by the Catholic Church.

St. Thomas's Day was never restored, even as a black-letter day, to the English Common Prayer Book. It is, however, found in the calendar of Queen Elizabeth's Præces Privatæ (1564), and was often inserted in ordinary almanacs and in calendars published by the Stationers' Company, under the authority of the Archbishop of Canterbury, down to 1832.

On a recent visit of the Archbishop of Canterbury to the cathedral of his diocese a very ancient and very pretty custom was revived. His grace was "received" by an assembly, one and all of whom wore lilies of the valley. The custom is said to date from Thomas à Becket, who was so fond of the flower that he filled his gardens adjoining the cloisters with it. For years after his death and canonization bouquets of his lilies used to be placed upon his shrine, and in time the flower came to be worn in the season by all who attended upon the primate. Even the casual visitor to Canterbury cannot fail to have been struck by the millions of lilies which lend grace to all the gardens in the vicinity of the minster. (*London Graphic*, March 23, 1892.)

Thomas Didymus, St., apostle, and patron saint of Portugal and of Parma. His festival is celebrated on December 21.

Besides what is known of St. Thomas from the New Testament, tradition avers that after the Ascension he travelled into India, where among others he baptized the three Magi, and founded the Christian sect which is still known by his name in India. According to one legend, when the apostle was at Cæsarea it was revealed to him that he should go to Gondoforus, King of the Indies, and undertake the building of a splendid palace which the king desired. He accordingly went to the king, who intrusted him with the building of the palace and gave him much treasure. The king himself went away for two years, and meantime Thomas distributed the treasure to the poor. When the king returned he was enraged and threw the saint into a dungeon. But just then the king's brother died, and four days afterwards he appeared to the king and told him of a glorious palace of gold and silver that Thomas had built for him in heaven. Then Gondoforus released Thomas. Another legend, known as that of the "Madonna della Cintola," relates that when Mary ascended into heaven Thomas was not present with the rest of the apostles; and, as he was of a sceptical turn of mind, he would not believe the narrative of his brother apostles. Her tomb was therefore opened, and found to be empty; moreover, so the legend runs, the Virgin dropped her girdle to Thomas from heaven to assure him of the truth of her ascension. A girdle which is said to be the one the Virgin threw to Thomas is still preserved in the cathedral of Prato. Tradition relates that St. Thomas suffered martyrdom at Meliapor, now called St. Thomas, on the banks of the Ganges, being pierced with a lance at the foot of a cross he had erected. His body is supposed to have been entombed at Edessa. In 1523 his tomb is said to have been discovered at Meliapor by John III. of Portugal, and the remains were deposited at Goa. Relics are shown at Goa and at Ortona. The Latins keep the feast of St. Thomas on the 21st of December, the Greeks on the 6th of October, and the Hindoo Christians

MARTYRDOM OF ST. THOMAS DIDYMUS.

on the 1st of July. When St. Thomas is represented in art as an apostle his attribute is a builder's rule or square; as a martyr he bears a lance.

In England St. Thomas's Day is still commemorated by old women who perambulate many of the towns in the expectation of receiving small gratuities. This is usually called "going a-goodening" or "a-gooding." But it is locally known in Yorkshire as "mumping," and in Cheshire as "going a-Thomassing." The last term is obvious enough. The word "gooding" may be derived from "goody," the name given to old widows, though it also may be a corruption of "hodening" and therefore refer to Woden or Odin, the presiding deity of the ancient Yule-tide rites. The word "mumping" comes to us from the Dutch, and signifies to mumble or mutter, the mumpers being usually old and toothless people.

The following rhyme for this day is taken from the *Bilston Mercury*, Staffordshire:

> Well-a-day, well-a-day,
> St. Thomas goes too soon away;
> Then your gooding we do pray,
> For the good time will not stay.
> St. Thomas Grey, St. Thomas Grey,
> The longest night and the shortest day,
> Please to remember St. Thomas' Day.

Three Kings of Cologne. This is the name under which the Wise Men of the East (Matt. ii.) are popularly known. (See EPIPHANY.) Although there is no Biblical sanction for this attribution of royalty, legend has endowed them with specific kingdoms and given them names which were unknown to the Evangelists. According to these authorities, the Wise Men were Caspar, or Jaspar, King of Tarsus, the land of myrrh; Melchior, King of Arabia, where the soil is ruddy with gold; and Balthasar, King of Saba, where frankincense flows from the trees. They were wise and learned men, for in those days kings and princes were not as they are to-day.

When they beheld the wondrous star, they arose joyfully and mounted their dromedaries and set forth on their long and perilous journey, the star going before, and arrived at length in Jerusalem. And they asked, " Where is he who is born King of the Jews? We have seen the star, but we have lost it."

For, indeed, it had disappeared when the kings reached Jerusalem. This was done in accordance with the will of God, who desired that the nativity of his precious Son should be made known throughout Jerusalem.

It soon came to the ears of Herod that these Three Kings were making inquiries concerning a child whom they called the King of the Jews. So he summoned all his learned men and asked them where the prophets had said that the Messiah should be born. And they answered, " In Bethlehem." Herod was grievously troubled. He summoned the Three Kings and feasted them, and told them to go to Bethlehem, and if they found the child they should return and tell him, " that I may come and worship him also."

So the kings departed, and when they were out of Jerusalem the star reappeared as before in the heavens and guided them to Bethlehem. When Mary heard the tramping of their dromedaries' feet, she was much alarmed, and took Jesus into her arms, fearing that he would be taken from her; and it was in this attitude the kings found the mother and the child. They threw themselves on their knees with the utmost reverence, and adored Jesus as God and the Saviour of the world. Then they offered him rich gifts. Caspar gave gold, to signify that the babe was king; Melchior gave frankincense, to show that he was God; and Balthasar offered myrrh, as a reminder that he was man, and doomed to die.

In return, the Saviour bestowed upon them gifts of more matchless price. For their gold he gave them charity and spiritual riches; for their incense, faith; and for their myrrh, truth and meekness. And the Virgin, his mother, also bestowed on them a precious gift and memorial,—namely, one of those linen bands in which she had wrapped the Saviour; for which they thanked her with great humility and laid it among their treasures.

When they had performed their devotions and made their offerings, the Three Kings, having been warned in a dream to avoid Herod, turned back again to their own dominions. And, arriving there, they laid down their earthly state and distributed their goods to the poor, and went about in mean attire preaching to their people the Child-King, the Prince of Peace.

About forty years later, St. Thomas, travelling in India, found the Wise Men there, and he baptized and ordained them. Later still they were martyred for their faith, and were buried together. Divers great and glorious miracles were performed at their tomb. Thither came the devout Empress Helena and found their bones, which she carried to Constantinople and laid in the church of St. Sophia, but at the time of the first Crusade they were transported to Milan. Thence Barbarossa took them at the siege of Milan, and deposited them in the cathedral of Cologne. The shrine of the Three Kings became so popular a place of pilgrimage that it was soon felt that the old cathedral was not a fitting shrine for them. A providential fire destroyed the old cathedral, and a new one was built on its ruins.

And in that marvellous old church the bones of the Three Kings are shown to this day, laid in a shrine of gold and gems, and surrounded with other relics of like interest and authenticity.

Thump. A local name in Lancashire for a feast held on the Sunday after a village wake (*q. v.*). The name is said to have arisen from the rude custom of "thumping" any one who entered an inn on such an occasion and refused to pay for liquor. "At a recent Halifax wake," says Ditchfield, "an offender of this description was laid face downward and beaten with a heated fire-shovel. The ringleader of this frolic nearly suffered a month's imprisonment on account of his strict adherence to old customs." (*Old English Customs*, p. 131.) The same authority mentions as still extant the Queensbury Thump, and the Clayton,

Thornton, Denholme, and Allerton Thumps, when the natives who reside elsewhere make a rule to visit their old home, and the reassembling of scattered families causes much social happiness. " At Great Gransden the feast is held on the Monday after the feast of St. Bartholomew, the patron saint of the village, when stalls are erected near the Plough Inn, and the villagers indulge in dancing. At West Houghton, Lancashire, a huge pie is made in the shape of a cow's head, which is eaten on the day of the wake, the Sunday after St. Bartholomew's Day."

Tichborne Crawls, The. During the reign of Henry II. the Lady Mabella Tichborne, who had been bedridden for years, and was then at death's door, besought her husband, Sir Roger, to bestow upon her such means as should enable her to leave a bequest of a loaf to all applicants on the festival of the Annunciation (March 25) forever. In reply her husband promised her the produce of so much of his property as she could go round while a brand which he caused to be lighted should burn. He fancied that by reason of her great age and infirmity she would get over very little ground, but, being borne to a corner of the park, she made a vehement effort, hobbled round twenty-three acres of very rich land, known to-day as " the Crawls," and was then carried back to her bed. Presently she called her household around her, and prophesied that the Tichborne family would prosper so long as the dole was continued to the poor, but that if it was neglected the family name would be lost for want of male issue, and that in such case the baronet of the day would have seven sons, but that the next heir would have seven daughters and no male children. In 1796, a great crowd of gypsies, thieves, and other lawless characters having behaved in a very unruly manner during the distribution of the dole, the neighbors made an outcry, and it has never been given regularly since. Strange to say, a partial fulfilment of Lady Mabella's prophecy followed. In 1803 the then head of the family died and left seven sons, the eldest of whom succeeded to the baronetcy, but he died leaving seven daughters, whereupon that branch of the family took the name of Doughty, so that the Tichborne name was actually merged for a time.

Touching for King's Evil. An old English superstition which survived even to the eighteenth century attributed to the British sovereign the power of curing disease by touching the part affected. Especially was this the case in regard to the disease known as scrofula, or king's evil, which eventually monopolized the supposititious royal curative powers. Edward the Confessor is thought to have commenced the practice, the first

mention of which is found in William of Malmesbury, who wrote
about eighty years after his reign. Some French writers, however, have sought to trace the gift of healing virtue to Clovis, as
conferred upon the first Christian sovereign of France with the
holy chrism, and preserved by his successors, asserting that the
kings of England exercised it only by some collateral right. It
was a custom to bestow upon the sick person some slight gift as
a substantial token of the exercise of this healing power. This
gift was in the time of Edward I. a small sum of money, probably as alms; but in later times a gold coin was given, and perforated for suspension to the neck. Henry VII. gave the angel
noble, the smallest gold coin in circulation; and the angel was
the piece distributed at the ceremony of the Royal Touch during
the succeeding reigns. Charles I. had not always gold to bestow,
and he sometimes substituted silver, or even brass. After the
Restoration the applicants for the healing were so numerous that
small medals were struck for the special purpose of such distribution. These touch-pieces were themselves looked upon as pana-
ceas against king's evil. Charles II. is recorded to have touched
not less than ninety thousand seven hundred and ninety-eight applicants, according to the registers which were constantly kept.
James II. on one occasion healed three hundred and fifty persons.
William III. scoffed at the superstition, and did his best to discourage it. When he heard that his palace was besieged by a
crowd of sick people towards the close of Lent, he exclaimed,
" It is a silly superstition; give the poor creatures some money,
and send them away." On another occasion, to escape from the
importunity of a sick man, he laid his hand upon him, with the
prayer, " God give you better health and more sense." Under
Queen Anne, however, the ceremony was restored to all its
ancient dignity. A Church-of-England prayer-book published
in her reign gives a service "At the Healing," in which the following instructions appear: "Then shall the infirm persons, one
by one, be presented to the queen upon their knees; and as
every one is presented, and while the queen is laying her hands
upon them, and putting the gold about their necks, the chaplain
that officiates, turning himself to her majesty, shall say the
words following: 'God give a blessing to this work, and grant
that these sick persons, on whom the queen lays her hands, may
recover, through Jesus Christ our Lord.'" Here the touch is at
once a royal and a religious ceremony. An old man, witness at
a trial, averred that when Queen Anne was at Oxford she
touched him (then a child) for the evil; he added that he did
not believe himself to have had the evil, but "his parents were
poor, and had no objection to a bit of gold." Queen Anne was
the last sovereign of England who performed the rite, and

among the latest occasions was that when Samuel Johnson, at three years of age, was brought from Lichfield to be touched with two hundred others. Meanwhile the Pretenders successively claimed that as the rightful rulers of England they possessed the only genuine touch. "James III." and "Henry IX." both had silver touch-pieces struck for them.

A singular anecdote is recorded of George I., who soon after his accession was applied to by a gentleman in behalf of his son. The king referred him to the Pretender, as possessing the hereditary gift of the Stuarts. The result was this, that the son was touched and recovered, and the father became a devoted partisan of the exiled family. The gift was claimed by the kings of France as well as by the British sovereigns, and the ceremonial, long observed, appears to have been established by St. Louis. A great number of persons were healed by Henry IV., and the inherent virtue was undiminished in Louis XIV. and Louis XV. The ceremony of the touch was even prescribed in the authorized ceremonial for the coronation of Charles X.

Tower Hill. The hill overlooking the Tower of London, made memorable as a former place of execution for political offenders. The members of the Guild of Our Lady of Ransom (a Catholic organization of clergy and laity whose hope is the final conversion of the English people to Catholicism), besides paying an annual visit to the tombs of British martyrs at Canterbury and Westminster, make a pilgrimage to the gardens on the brow of Tower Hill every May 8, seeking out the spot where Sir Thomas More and Bishop Fisher were executed. Formerly these pilgrimages were made with much pomp and pageantry. But the antagonism of No-Popery Protestantism was aroused, and since 1894 they have been conducted more quietly. Here is the account of the affair in that year as given by the *Daily Graphic* on May 10:

"The gates of the Tower close at half-past four, and shortly after that time little groups of pilgrims began to gather round the square place in the grass where the scaffold once stood, and lilies and lilac and iris, in wreaths and crosses and loose bunches, began to bloom vividly upon the gray granite stones. A few children loitering about the garden came up wonderingly to watch, and outside the palings of the garden the Tower Hill proletariat, rather draggle-tailed and down at heel, looked on at the curious ceremonies with feelings which hesitated between amusement and disapproval. The ceremony was brief,—a few short addresses by Father Dalton and Father Fletcher setting forth the reasons why the saints and martyrs, Blessed John

Fisher and Blessed Thomas More, should be honored in their deaths as in their lives, and, following this, a space for silent prayer. The pilgrims, gentle and simple, went down on their knees upon the stones and remained so in prayer for some moments. When the prayers were over, the little gathering of the faithful stooped down and kissed the stones, and a few of them threw single flowers upon the heap which already bloomed there. A few words were spoken by Mr. Drummond, the secretary of the Guild of Ransomers, and then the meagre assembly went away. In the evening a triumphal service was held at the Church of the Martyrs in Great Prescot Street."

Towers of Silence. The burying-places of the Parsees in Bombay, India.

"Thou shalt not defile the earth," was one of the teachings of Zoroaster. Therefore no dead Parsee is laid into mother earth, to taint her with his corruption. His body is exposed in the open air to vultures, ravens, or even dogs. In the Towers of

TOWERS OF SILENCE.

Silence, just outside Bombay, this method of burial reaches its most elaborate form. There are six in all. Five are placed together. One stands apart, for here the bones of notorious criminals lie crumbling in eternal separation from those of their fellow-believers who have died in good repute. The word "tower" is perhaps a misnomer. Though four hundred and fifty yards in diameter, they are not more than eighteen or twenty in height. They are made of carefully joined blocks of granite, plastered all over with a white cement. Each is surrounded by a shallow, dry moat. There is one narrow stone bridge or causeway, which leads from the ground to the small square door through which the body is taken.

The top of the tower, forming the platform on which the bodies are laid, is quite hidden by a parapet that surrounds it.

And on this parapet, motionless themselves as stone, with their bare heads sunk in their bodies, perch the vultures, in one close, unbroken rank. Facing inward, there they rest, silent and still as is all around them, till the white-robed bearers of the dead place the corpse upon the floor before them. Then all swoop down.

The arrangement of the platform is curious. The surface is divided into three concentric circles of shallow receptacles for the dead; between each circle and between each receptacle is a narrow pathway for the bearers, and in the centre is the grated opening to the well, down which are thrust the dry bones of the dead. These three rings represent the three maxims of Zoroaster, "Good acts, good words, good thoughts." The outer ring, that lies next the parapet, is for the bodies of men, representing "good acts;" the next, those of women, "good words;" and the last, the smallest circle round the well itself, is for the little children, who represent "good thoughts."

No other persons than the duly appointed bearers of the dead ever enter the building. Neither priest nor layman may approach nearer than a distance of ten or fifteen yards.

When a body is brought for burial the mourners accompany it to the house of prayer, an old stone building, surrounded by open colonnades, in the garden outside the towers. Within all is dim and still. The cool air is heavy with the scent of sandalwood, for here the sacred fire forever burns, tended day and night by a watchful priest, whose mission it is to feed the holy flame with perfumed precious woods. Solemn prayers are said over the deceased, and the body is then taken out by two carriers to be laid on the platform on the tower.

Meanwhile the mourners must remain in the fire temple, with heads devoutly bent in prayer, until the skeleton lies bleaching on the sunny summit of the tower.

Thus they do not see the sudden swoop of the birds upon the corpse, the tearing of the flesh by bloody beaks, the entire sickening details.

A fortnight later the same men that carried in the corpse revisit the tower, and, with a kind of tongs, place the dry and separated bones in the large central well.

This well is filled with chemicals, to kill any impurity that may arise from the incessant flow of blood and for the destruction of osseous matter. Furnished with subterraneous passages, it is supposed to communicate mysteriously with the other world and afford an easy transit to the regions of the blessed.

Town and Gown Rows. Quarrels and fights between the undergraduates of Oxford College and the townspeople of Oxford still occur periodically under this name, the favorite time being November 5 (Guy Fawkes's Day), but they are very mild survivals from the bloody brutalities of the past. It might be supposed that, inasmuch as the wealth and prosperity of the city arose out of and depend upon the presence of the university within its walls, the citizens would regard the gownsmen as their most substantial friends. But it has never been so at any period. Class jealousy has been stronger even than self-interest; and not even the danger, more than once imminent, of the whole scholastic body migrating to Northampton or to Stamford, and condemning the streets of Oxford to a perpetual long vacation, could suffice to make the municipal body regard their guests in any other light than as an alien army of occupation, whose money it was good to take, and whose presence, therefore, must be endured. Not that the fault lay altogether with the citizens. There is an insolence inherent, it would seem, in the student-life, whether English, Spanish, or German.. The German *bursch* terms the whole non-academic world Philistines, and his fellows at Oxford or Cambridge regard it in much the same light; a feeling which the other party is not slow to detect, and does not fail to return in its own fashion. For this reason, perhaps, more than any other, when the University of Oxford clung to what was left of Romanism, the town was Puritan; when the university was in arms for the king, the townsmen were almost unanimously Roundheads; when the university pronounces for Conservatism, the town feels it a point of honor to return two Radicals.

In mediæval times the ill will between the two classes was fomented by the claim of the students to be exempted as clerks from trial before the ordinary tribunals. This was intolerable to the townsmen, who thought that the gownsmen would find more lenient judgment in the court of the chancellor than in that of the mayor.

Now and again a tavern row between scholars and townsmen widened into a general broil, and the academical bell of St. Mary's vied with the town bell of St. Martin's in clanging to arms. The rustics from the villages round would flock in to help the citizens against the detested scholars, the latter in their turn would pour out fully armed into the streets, and the affrays frequently ended in many wounded and a few killed on both sides. (See St. Scholastica.)

Trafalgar Day. The anniversary of the great naval victory won in Trafalgar Bay by Lord Nelson over the combined French and Spanish fleets, October 21, 1805. This effectually blasted all Napoleon's hopes of invading England. In the heat of the conflict Nelson on the deck of his flagship received his death-wound, and lived just long enough to know that he had gained his last and greatest victory. Trafalgar Day was long celebrated at the Portsmouth dockyard and other naval stations of Great Britain by dinners and speeches and by decorating all the Trafalgar ships afloat with wreaths of laurel at the mast-head, bowsprit-points, and yard-arm ends. On the Victory the spot where Nelson fell and the place in the cockpit where he died were similarly decorated, and over the steering-wheel were inscribed on a scroll the words of Nelson's signal to his fleet: "England expects every man to do his duty." But even these local celebrations had fallen into desuetude when in 1896 the Navy League of Liverpool and Canada revived the commemoration on a larger scale. They obtained permission to decorate the Nelson column in Trafalgar Square, London, by encircling it from capital to base with a monster roping of laurel and bay leaves. On the main ledge at the base of the pillar was a twelve-foot wreath, and numerous other wreaths were grouped around, offerings from the commander-in-chief, officers, and men of the old Victory, also from the Foudroyant, the Neptune, and the Excellent, from the Navy League of Liverpool and Canada, from the Malta Branch of the Navy League, and from descendants of Nelson's officers and men. The square and its neighborhood were thronged all day long, and after nightfall were uncomfortably packed. Crowds also visited St. Paul's Cathedral, where during the morning wreaths were placed on Nelson's tomb in the crypt, and the Museum of the United Service Institution, where a special display of Nelson's relics was made during the day. A large number of lectures on the navy and on the necessity of preserving its efficiency were delivered in various parts of London by members of the League, this being one of the practical measures included in the celebration of the day. Naval clubs and naval men generally celebrated Trafalgar-Day dinners in London and elsewhere. All through the country Nelson's monuments were decorated, and at Portsmouth the old Victory was hung more elaborately than ever before with garlands and festoons of laurel and boughs of evergreen. A large cross was deposited in the place in the cockpit where the hero fell. On board the old Foudroyant, then lying at Cardiff, the famous signal was run up, "England expects every man to do his duty."

At Montreal, Canada, Nelson's monument in the Jacques-Cartier Square was decorated with flowers, amid which were displayed both the Union Jack and the tricolor.

"London, October 24.—Last winter, when everybody in England surrendered himself to blind rage against the German

Emperor, and the memorable step of mobilizing a special service squadron was taken, the people who feel a special interest in strengthening the British Navy took advantage of the popular feeling to arrange that hereafter Trafalgar Day should be celebrated as a national patriotic anniversary. As the date drew near, the government tried all it could quietly to discourage the thing, but the enthusiasts insisted, and, considering the absence of organization and the official cold water, Wednesday's celebrations throughout the island were really very creditable. Unhappily, however, no amount of British protestations could avail to prevent the French from remembering that Trafalgar was their defeat, and, not unnaturally, they asked why on earth, this year of all others, this piece of ancient history should be so violently revived, especially as the English are just now professing an exceptional anxiety to establish cordial relations with France. It has been an up-hill task for the English papers to explain the psychology of this paradox, and Paris still only half accepts their plea that John Bull is really such an ingenuous, simple-minded creature that he blunders into these embarrassing performances through sheer mental awkwardness. As the Continental situation stands, it was undoubtedly the most inopportune thing imaginable, but perhaps its effect in stimulating popular feeling here counterbalances any harm it may have done across the Channel." (HAROLD FREDERIC, in *New York Times*, October 25, 1896.)

Transfiguration, Feast of the. The anniversary of the Transfiguration, when Christ ascended Mount Tabor with his three favorite disciples, Peter, James, and John, and displayed himself to them in his glory, is kept in the Greek and Latin Churches on August 6. It is not set down in the English Church. This festival was probably initiated in the early ages, but it did not obtain much position in the Western calendar until 1457, when Pope Calixtus decreed that it should thenceforth be kept in commemoration of the successful defence of Belgrade, Mohammed II. having abandoned the siege of that place on August 6 and removed a cloud from Europe.

A little chapel dedicated to the Transfiguration caps the highest peak of Mount Athos in Greece, where a great annual service is performed on the recurrence of the festival. The scene is thus described by Tozer: " As we approached from the east we first heard the sound of chanting from within the chapel, and when we came round the platform in front a scene appeared which I shall never forget. Distinctly seen in the moonlight were the weird, ghostly figures of the monks, closely wrapped in their gowns, with long black beards and mushroom

locks, some sitting close to the little window of the chapel, where
the service was going on, some lying about in groups, like the
figures of the three apostles in Raphael's picture of the Transfiguration; and on going about to different points we could see
them lying relieved against the white rocks, or dimly seen in
the dark shadows, themselves a shadowy band.   There were
about sixty of them, besides a number of Russian pilgrims.   At
intervals, as we sat there, the priest came out arrayed in gorgeous vestments and swung the incense about us.   The vigil
lasted the whole night."

Tree, Fête of the.   (Sp. *Fiesta del Arbol.*)   A Spanish holiday devoted to tree-planting, evidently copied from our Arbor
Day.   It is celebrated annually on March 26.   The festival was
instituted in 1896.   The young King Alfonso with the queen
regent and the ladies of the court proceeded to some grounds
lying near the village of Hortaleza, about two miles to the east
of Madrid.   There he planted a pine sapling.   Two thousand
children selected from the Madrid schools followed his example.
Gold medals commemorative of the event were distributed among
them.   The inscription runs, "First Fête of the Tree, instituted
in the reign of Alfonso XIII., 1896."   The school-boys who
planted the saplings are taken periodically by their school-
masters to note the progress of their respective trees, and are
encouraged to foster tree-planting in their country.

Trinity Sunday.   The Sunday after Whitsuntide, or fifty-
seven days after Easter, specially devoted to the commemoration
of the mystery of the Trinity.   The feast is not of very early
origin, and its adoption by the universal Church is still more
recent.   Stephen, Bishop of Liége, about 620 had an office drawn
up relating to the mystery of the Trinity, which made its way
into other churches.   A decretal of Alexander II. in the Corpus
Juris informs us that some churches kept this feast on the Sunday before Whitsuntide, others on the Sunday before Advent, but
that it was not kept at all in Rome, since every day the Trinity
was praised and worshipped.   Nevertheless when the doctrine
of the Trinity was attacked by the Arians the Church thought
it right to fix a special day in its honor.   In 1334 John XXII.
ordered its observance by the whole Church on the Sunday succeeding Whitsunday.   Previous to this time it had been introduced into England by St. Thomas à Becket, and it still retains a
place in the Anglican calendar.

The records of Lambeth, the palace of the Archbishop of
Canterbury, show that great expenses were formerly incurred
for the due celebration of Trinity-tide.   The festivities began on

Trinity Even, and concluded on Trinity Tuesday. "It is still a custom of ancient usage in London," Hone tells us, "for the judges and law-officers of the crown, together with the Lord Mayor and Common Council, to attend divine service at St. Paul's Cathedral and hear a sermon which is always preached there on Trinity Sunday by the Lord Mayor's chaplain. At the first ensuing meeting of the Common Council it is usual for that body to pass a vote of thanks to the chaplain for such sermon, and order the same to be printed at the expense of the corporation, unless, as has sometimes occurred, it contained sentiments obnoxious to their views."

Aubrey mentions in his "Miscellanies" (1714, p. 49) that there was an old custom in Wiltshire upon Trinity Sunday, in remembrance of a donation made by King Athelstan, to ring the bell, and for a young maiden to carry a garland to church, which she gave to a young bachelor with three kisses; he then put the garland upon her neck and gave her three kisses. The ceremony was considered symbolic of the Trinity.

In Carnarvonshire, Wales, "a very ancient custom," says Pennant, "is still observed on Trinity Sunday. The offerings of calves and lambs which happen to be born with the *Nod Beuno*, or mark of St. Beuno,—a certain natural mark in the ear,—have not yet entirely ceased. They are brought to the church (but formerly to the monastery) of Clynnok Vaur on Trinity Sunday, and delivered to the churchwardens, who sell and account for them, depositing the money in a great chest, called Cyff St. Beuno, made of one oak, and secured with three locks. From this, the Welsh have a proverb for attempting any very difficult thing, 'You may as well try to break open St. Beuno's chest.' The little money resulting from the sacred beasts or casual offerings is applied either to the relief of the poor or in aid of repairs." (TENNANT: *Tour through North Wales,* 1781, vol. ii. p. 210.)

Trooping the Colors. A military ceremonial which is witnessed to perfection only in London and on the queen's birthday, May 24. The scene is St. James's Park, to which admission is granted by tickets. About nine o'clock a strong body of the Household troops, infantry, make their appearance on the parade-ground and are posted, at some six paces from one another, all round the vast square, each side of which is nearly a quarter of a mile in length. At half-past nine appear the troops selected to represent each regiment of the brigade of Foot Guards, followed by representative cavalry from the Life-Guards. At a little after ten the Prince of Wales, in his uniform as colonel of the Life-Guards, with other members of the royal family and distinguished army generals, makes his appearance.

After the preliminary saluting, the officer commanding the parade gives a signal to the senior drum-major, who immediately turns round to the bands and gives the command to "Troop!" Three slowly given strokes of the bass drum follow, succeeded by a roll of the side drums, crescendo and diminuendo. As the sound of the rolling dies away, the drum-major, in a loud voice, gives the command, "Slow March;" and the combined bands, playing a stately march, parade slowly from one end of the line to the other, countermarching at the other side of the parade, and, after a brief pause, returning to their original position in quick time.

As they cease playing, the escort for the color is called by a peculiar beat of the drum performed by a drummer standing on the extreme right of the line. Then a captain, a lieutenant, and a company of men advance from the right of the line, and, preceded by the bands playing the "British Grenadiers," proceed to the spot where the State Color is in waiting. Here the escort halts, the sergeant-major takes the color, a handsomely embroidered banner, and advances towards the lieutenant. The escort then presents arms, and, after saluting the color, the lieutenant

TROOPING THE COLORS.

sheathes his sword, and receives the color from the sergeant-major. The latter then draws his sword, and salutes the color also, the bands playing "God Save the Queen," and the prince and the troops also saluting. The salute finished, the line shoulders arms, and the escort marches in slow time, preceded by the bands playing the "Grenadiers' March," to the left of the line. Arrived there, the bands cease playing, and the captain, followed by the lieutenant with the color, proceeds along the front of the line, while the men forming the escort file along the rear. At the same time, the troops once more present arms, and the bands resume playing until the color and its escort reaches its place at the right of the line. When this ceremony is completed, the whole of the troops march past in slow and quick time, and the cavalry trots past, the bands playing the parade march of each corps as it passes the saluting-point. Then the whole line advances in review order, gives a royal salute, and the "trooping" is finished. (*Chambers's Journal*, April 8, 1882.)

Tulabhara. A curious Hindoo ceremony which consists in ascertaining the weight of some important personage in gold or spices or grain and distributing that weight in charity. It is only the very wealthiest persons, of course, who can afford the gold. The ceremony is performed but once in his lifetime. *The Antiquary* for June, 1885 (vol. xi. p. 275), records that the Maharajah of Travancore submitted in the early part of that year to be weighed against a mass of pure gold, which was then dispensed in charity. This custom is one of great antiquity, and is said to be traceable in Travancore to the fourth century. The Maharajah weighed a little over nine stone. The Brahmins, it is said, wished to defer the ceremony, in the hope that the Maharajah might more nearly approach the weight of his father, who did not undergo the rite until forty-seven years old, when he weighed fourteen and three-quarters stone.

Tynwald Day. The great annual holiday and legal day of the Isle of Man, whereon the people and their representatives and governors meet on Tynwald Hill, an artificial mound in the heart of the island, for the promulgation of their laws, the reading of their constitution, and general festivity. Its ancient date was that of Midsummer Day. It is now fixed on July 5, a change that may be accounted for by the difference between Old and New Style. As the direct lineal descendant of the Althing day or days in the valley of the Löberg at Thingvellir, Iceland, Tynwald Day is another connecting link between the little Manx nation and the Sea-kings of the Sagas. The Althing continued in force in Iceland until its legal abolition in 1800. Thingvellir, the meeting-place, is a lava island, surrounded by a narrow stream, bounded by overhanging walls cut deep with fissures, and standing in the heart of a vast amphitheatre of dark hills and great jökulls tipped with snow. There is no such natural mount of laws in the Isle of Man, but, ages ago, an artificial mount was raised, not of the oval shape of the Löberg at Thingvellir, but circular, bounded by a wall and ascended by flights of steps cut into the turf. In all its essentials the ceremony of Tynwald is similar to that of the old Althing, and the constitution of Man is almost identical with that of Iceland.

The Isle of Man is a dependency of the crown of England, and its legislature consists of three estates: the lord, represented by his governor; the council, a sort of house of lords, composed of representatives of both church and state; and the house of keys, consisting of twenty-four delegates elected by the people. The two chambers, council and keys, sit sometimes in joint session, presided over by the governor, and are then known as the Tynwald court. This is the supreme legislative assembly, and when a public measure has received its assent it is called an act of Tynwald. Before the act can become law, however, it is submitted to the crown for formal sanction, and this being obtained it is promulgated on Tynwald Hill in the eve of the day, and in presence of the whole congregation of the people.

Tynwald Hill is the centre of a grass-plat that is now bounded by inns and small houses, but was, no doubt, at one time as solitary as the plains of Thingvellir, which are broken only by the little church that stands near.

The legal ceremony of Tynwald Day is still quite primitive, thanks to the precise instructions which have been handed down in the *lex scripta* of the Isle of Man, as given for law to Sir John Stanley in 1417. "This," says the record, "is the constitution of old time, how you shall be governed on the Tynwald day. First, you shall come hither in your royal array, as a king ought to do, by the prerogatives and royalties of the land of Manne. And upon the hill of Tynwald sit in a chaire covered with a royal cloath and cushions, and your visage unto the east, and your sword before you, holden with the point upward. Your barons in the third degree sitting beside you, and your beneficed men and your deemsters before you sitting, and your clarke, your knights, your esquires and yeomen about you in the third degree; and the worthiest men in your land to be called in before your deemsters, and you will ask anything of them, and to hear the government of your land and your will; and the commons to stand within the circle of the hill, with three clarkes in their surplices. And your deemsters shall make call on the coroner of Glenfaba, and he shall call on all the coroners of Man, and their yardes in their hands, with their weapons on them, either sword or axe; and the moares, that is, to wit, of every sheading. Then the chief coroner, that is the coroner of Glenfaba, shall make affence, upon paine of life and lyme, that no man make any disturbance or stirr in the time of Tynwald, or any murmur or rising in the king's presence, upon paine of hanging and drawing; and then to proceed in your matters,

whatsoever you have to do, in felonie or treason, or other matters that touch the government of your land of Manne."

Such is the ceremony observed down to this day, with only
such changes of procedure as the slight differences of constitution have rendered necessary.

No better authority than that of Hall Caine can be quoted for
a description of the day exactly as it is celebrated nowadays.
The article quoted from appeared in the *London Graphic,* July 5,
1890 :

"Prayer is first said in the church of St. John, which stands
on the east margin of the green, and then a procession is
formed from the church to the mount, beginning with the constables, the coroners, and captains of parishes, succeeded by the
clergy of the island, the members of the house of keys, and
ending with the council, whereof the two deemsters, the attor-
ney-general, the lord bishop, and the governor are a part. On
arriving at the hill, the governor and the bishop take their seats
on the summit, with the council on the first step below, the
keys on the second step, the constables on the third, and the
general assembly of the people in a throng beyond the wall that
bounds the lowest ring. Then, with his face to the east and the
sword of state held before him, the governor begins the Tynwald by calling on the chief coroner of the island to 'fence' the
court, a solemnizing and hallowing ceremony, similar in purpose
to that of the bishop's opening prayer at the Löberg, and promising pains and penalties to such as ' do bawl or quarrel, lye, lean,
or sit.' Then the coroner gives in his wand of office, for his
term expires on Tynwald Day, and his successor is appointed at
the nomination of the governor, and takes an oath administered
by the elder deemster. After that the acts of Tynwald are
read, or their titles recited, by the deemster in English, and by
the senior coroner in Manx. This, with certain other formalities, constitutes the business of Tynwald, which concludes with
the return of the procession to the chapel, where the laws that
have been promulgated are signed and attested by the governor,
council, and keys.

"Thereafter the mount and its green are given up to the
people for their annual fair, and the proceedings are of a mixed
and various sort, for Tynwald Day is not only the little nation's
legal day, but its day of general holiday, and as such is as much
looked forward to and zealously preserved, at least so far as
concerns its recreative functions. The Manx people come to
Tynwald from north, south, east, and west, and there the man
from Andreas meets the man from Malew, and the man from
Braddan meets the man from Michael.

"In old times the powers of Tynwald over life and death appear to have been absolute, and equal in all respects to martial law. No jury was necessary to a capital conviction on a charge of treason ; and in this respect, among others, we recognize the connection which Mr. Gladstone mentioned between the Isle of Man and Scandinavia. Down to comparatively recent times it was within the power of the Lögsögumadur, or speaker of the Althing, to try even capital charges without jury, wheresoever he might be, and under whatsoever conditions,—walking, riding, at home, or on a journey. In like manner no inquest by a deemster was necessary to the death-sentence of a man who rose against the governor on his seat on Tynwald. It was also in old times a common right of the people to present petitions at the Tynwald, a common privilege of persons unjustly punished to appeal against judgment, and a common prerogative of outlaws to ask for the removal of their outlawry. No doubt all these ancient powers still exist, though they are now never exercised, and have rarely, if ever, been asserted since the time of Bishop Wilson, serenest of saints and most despotic of tyrants. Exactly the same powers, privileges, and prerogatives appear to have existed in Iceland down to the abolition of the annual meeting at Thingvellir at the beginning of this century."

U.

Uphalie Day. An ancient festival on January 29, the twenty-fourth night after Christmas (Old Style), which marked the close of the Yule-tide season.

The Antiquary for March, 1889, notes its celebration in that year at Lerwick: "At nine o'clock a large number of masqueraders, representing all sorts of characters, assembled at the Market Cross, at which a great crowd had gathered. Here over a hundred torches were served out, and the masqueraders, falling into procession, marched through the principal thoroughfares of the town."

Urban, St., Pope and martyr. He succeeded Pope Calixtus in the year 223, and reigned about seven years. The exact date and method of his martyrdom are unknown. His festival, May 25, which may be the anniversary of his death, was celebrated in France with particular devotion in the sixth century. His body was found, in 821, with that of St. Cecilia, in an old church dedicated to St. Urban on the Appian Road, near the place of his reputed first sepulture, the cemetery of St. Pretextatus. Pope Paschal translated it into the church of St. Cecilia. The mon-

astery of St. Urban, near Joinville, France, has a body which is
claimed to be this one, sent to the monks of St. Germanus by
Pope Nicholas I. in 862. But Papebrooke is at some pains to
show that this is the body of another saint of the same name.

St. Urban fares ill, especially in Germany, if his festival be
not a fair day. "Upon St. Urban's Day," says Aubanus, "all
the vintners and masters of vineyards sit at a table, either in the
market stand, or in some other open and public place, and, covering it with fine drapery, and strewing upon it green leaves and
sweet flowers, place upon the table the image of the holy bishop ;
and then, if the day be fair, they crown the image with great
store of wine ; but if the weather prove unpleasant and rainy
(believing that the saint has withdrawn his protection), they cast
mire and puddle water upon it, persuading themselves that if
that day be fair and calm, their grapes, which then begin to
flourish, will be good that year ; but if it be stormy and tem-
pestuous, they will have a bad vintage."

St. Paul and St. Vincent Ferrier are also invoked by vintners.
There is an old Latin saying, " Vicenti festo, si sol radiet, memor
esto," which the French translate into a proverb that may be
Englished thus :

> If St. Vincent's Day be fine,
> 'Twill be a famous year for wine.

Ursula, St., patroness of young girls, especially school-girls,
and of educational institutions. Her festival is on October 21,
the date of her martyrdom with eleven thousand companions.
According to the legend, she was the daughter of Dunnat, King
of Cornwall, and was famous for her beauty, her learning, and
her virtue. So when Conan, a Scotch prince, a Christian serving
in the army of Maximus, was appointed by that Emperor King
of Armorica, or Little Britain, he sent deputies to demand
Ursula in marriage, with the further request that she should
bring with her as many young women as would bear her company and become the wives of the Christian Britons who had
followed him to Armorica. So the princess with eleven thousand
other virgins set sail from London. But a storm carried them
towards the Rhine. Opposite Cologne the ships were captured
by the Huns, and as the maidens, incited by St. Ursula, refused
to sacrifice their virginity, they were barbarously massacred.
This was in 383.

Many attempts have been made by sceptics to rationalize the
legend by minimizing the number of the virgin martyrs. According to one guess, this number may have been eleven. Their
massacre, it is conjectured, was commemorated in an inscription
running thus :

VRSVLA ET XI MM VV

which read rightly would signify *Ursula et undecim martyres virgines*, or " Ursula and eleven virgin martyrs." An ignorant translator read *millia* instead of *martyres*, and so multiplied by one thousand the number of victims. This explanation is simple and plausible enough. Nothing prevents the characters MM from meaning *millia* ("thousands") instead of *martyres* ("martyrs"). But it has not met with unqualified approval.

Another suggestion reduces the total number of martyrs to two. It runs in this wise: It was a frequent usage, when the family was numerous, to give to the children a name that should denote the order of their birth. The first was thus called Primus, the second Secundus, and so on. Two of these prænomens have survived. To this day the names of Septimus and Octavius are not rare. Now, Septimus means "seventh" and Octavius "eighth." The eleventh child would then take the name Undecimus, and if it was a girl the form would be Undecima. The eleventh child might be regarded as the pet of the house,—the "baby." Undecima then would become Undecimilla, a diminutive form of the name.

St. Ursula might have had for a companion a young girl of this name. Now, in place of *Ursula et Undecimilla* it would have been easy to read *Ursula et Undecimillia* ("eleven thousand"), whence the legend of eleven thousand virgins could have arisen. As letters were never doubled in writing, the error is easily explained; it becomes altogether probable if the story of the martyr Ursula was handed down by tradition. It would suffice that the narrator, or even the writer, was ignorant of this name of Undecimilla, which was perhaps very rare, and so transformed it into *undecimillia*.

Still a third:

Baring-Gould in " The Lives of the Saints" and in " Curious Myths of the Middle Ages" identifies St. Ursula with the goddess Isis, the Norse Freya, and the Thuringian Hörsel. In Thuringia she was said to live in the Hörselberg, surrounded by her thousand maidens, and by *Märten* and *Seelen*, "spirits" and "souls," which accompanied her everywhere.

Tacitus tells us that a ship was carried about in the festivals of Isis. Now, Hörsel sailed about the blue heavenly seas in her silver ship, seeking her husband. She was, in fact, the moon-deity, accompanied by her train of stars.

Not only is Ursula an obvious corruption of Hörsel, but the names of two of her companions are given as Martha and Saula, which look like less obvious corruptions of *Märten* and *Seelen*. A still more remarkable coincidence kinning Ursula to Isis and

Hörsel is the fact that in the Middle Ages there grew up a curious custom of founding confraternities or guilds in Germany called "the Skiffs of St. Ursula." The symbol of the confraternity was a boat, which was carried about in public processions. But St. Ursula's skiff was a purely imaginary vessel, which every member of the guild had to help load with prayers, masses, penances, and good works for the general good. To this day a relic of the custom survives in the Ommegang at Brussels, and in a similar festival at Boulogne, in which ships are drawn by horses through the town.

Now, it is quite possible that Christian maidens may have been slaughtered by Huns in Cologne. Indeed, the very fact that a church dedicated to virgin martyrs existed here at a very early date seems to indicate that there had occurred some martyrdom of maidens there. But this Mr. Gould thinks is absolutely all that can be said in favor of these saints, whom popular tradition has enveloped with the attributes and even the names of old Teutonic mythological personages.

So much for the virgins. Now for their remains. These to the number of several thousands are preserved in Cologne. They were gathered together in the church of St. Ursula, where the princess lay canonized, with the story of her tragic fate pictured on the walls about her. This queer old twelfth-century church is one great tomb, the walls being filled in with bones, of which glimpses may be had through gratings. In the treasury the walls have been adorned with all manner of fantastic devices wrought with the martyrs' remains, many of their skulls enclosed in silver busts being set in the niches. More of these skulls are preserved in a cupboard and enclosed in velvet cases wrought with gold thread and studded with gems, the cases open at the top to show the blow that cleft or crushed the skull; one of them with wisps of auburn hair still clinging to either side of the gaping wound and a row of superb pearls sewn across the velvet that covers the mouth.

It was in the seventh century that the body of St. Ursula herself was recovered. While St. Cunibert was saying mass in the church of the Holy Virgins, he saw a white dove which rested on a tomb. He opened it and discovered the remains of St. Ursula. He translated them to the abbey of Deutz. January 28 is observed by the Church as the anniversary of this translation. There were no further discoveries till 1106, when the walls of the city were being rebuilt. Near the church of St. Cunibert the workmen came on a considerable number of bones. Visions assured the workmen that these were the relics of the martyred virgins. It is not improbable that the new walls had traversed an old burial-ground belonging to the church of St.

Cunibert. But this explanation was too simple to be received by the credulous populace. And in fact, trading on this credulity, Gerlach, the abbot of Deutz in 1155, made the greatest "invention" of all. "It is perhaps one of the most painful histories of fraud which have ever been recorded," says Mr. Gould. "So preposterous is it, that the Jesuit father, De Buck, waxes wroth and indignant over it."

Gerlach did not content himself with digging up all the bodies he could find, but he connived at the manufacture of inscriptions and tombstones which pretended to give the names of the former tenants of the bodies. He also induced a nun named Elizabeth to see visions in which appropriate legends were devised for each.

V.

Valentine, St. Custom, more potent than any other authority known to man, has decreed that on St. Valentine's Day, which in the Roman and Anglican calendar falls on February 14, young folks of both sexes, and older ones, too, for that matter, should exchange missives and epistles, either comic or sentimental, in which the foibles of the receiver or the love of the sender are set forth in prose, in verse, and in emblematic picture. Now, there is no custom without a reason. But the reason for this cannot be found in the life of the good saint who is made to indorse the custom with his name. He wrote no love-songs. No one rises up to accuse him of casting sheep's eyes on any Roman maiden. He was a bishop or Pope of Rome who stood steadfast to the faith during the Claudian persecutions, and for that faith was cast into jail, where he cured his keeper's daughter of blindness. *Honi soit qui mal y pense.* It is the pleasure of Cupid, blind himself, to bring upon his votaries a similar blindness, not to cure it.

Nor was there anything, either comic or sentimental, in the fate of St. Valentine when the miracle was made known to the authorities. They first beat him with clubs and then beheaded him. What was left of him is preserved in the church of St. Praxedes at Rome, where a gate, now known as the Porta del Popolo, was formerly named, in his honor, Porta Valentini, or Valentine's Gate.

Another Valentine also claims a share in the day, who has as little to do with comedy or sentiment. He was the bishop who healed a son of Craton the rhetorician, and was choked to death by a fish-bone. In Italy and Germany they pray to him to cure epilepsy. Either Valentine would be surprised to find himself a lovers' saint, but he has his compensation. Truly spoke Charles Lamb to the bishop, "Like unto thee, assuredly, there is no mitred father in the calendar; not Jerome, nor Ambrose, nor Cyril; nor the consignor of undipt infants to eternal torments, Austin, whom all mothers hate; nor he who hated all mothers, Origen; nor Bishop Bull, nor Archbishop Parker, nor Whitgift. Thou comest attended with thousands and ten thousands little Loves, and the air is

> Brush't with the hiss of rustling wings.

"Singing Cupids are thy choristers and thy precentors, and instead of the crosier the mystical arrow is borne before thee."

In default of any light thrown upon the custom by biography, etymologists and lexicographers, antiquarians and hagiologists, have drawn more or less satisfactory explanations from their special studies.

Hearken first to the etymologist. He points out that *v* and *g* were frequently interchangeable in popular speech, and as a notable instance produces the words gallant and valiant, which both spring from the Latin *valens.* He then explains that the Norman word *galantin*, a lover of the fair sex, or what in these slangy days might be called a masher, was frequently written and pronounced valantan or valentin. And from these premises he concludes that by a natural confusion of names Bishop Valentine was established as the patron saint of sweethearts and lovers, although he has no real connection, not even an etymological one, with that class of beings.

So far so good. As a guess why St. Valentine became associated with the custom this is plausible, though not convincing. Still, it leaves the origin of the custom as much in the dark as ever.

Try we, therefore, the lexicographer. And, as there is far more amusement to be extracted from the ancient than from the modern lexicon, let us turn to Bailey's, the first of the great English dictionaries (1721). Here we find the following: "Valentines (in England). About this time of the year—month of February—the Birds choose their Mates, and probably thence came the Custom of the Young Men and Maidens choosing Valentines, or special loving Friends, on that Day." Pretty and poetical, but not entirely satisfactory. So let us turn to the antiquary. Francis Douce, in his "Illustrations of Shakespeare" (1807), suggests that St. Valentine's Day is the Christianized form of the classic Lupercalia, which were feasts held in Rome during the month of February in honor of Pan and Juno (hence known as Juno Februata), when among other ceremonies it was customary to put the names of young women into a box, from which they were drawn by the men as chance directed, and that the Christian clergy, finding it difficult or impossible to extirpate the pagan practice, gave it at least a religious aspect by substituting the names of particular saints for those of the women.

He buttresses up his opinion by an appeal to the hagiologist. This is no less a person than the Rev. Alban Butler, who, in his "Lives of the Saints," explains that pastors of the Christian Church, "by every means in their power, worked zealously to eradicate the vestiges of pagan superstition; chiefly by the simple process of retaining the ceremonies, but modifying their significance; and substituted, for the drawing of names in honor of the goddess Februata Juno, the names of some particular saints. But as the festival of the Lupercalia took place during February, the 14th of that month, St. Valentine's Day, was selected for this new feast, as occurring about the same time. The saints whose names were drawn were proposed for imitation to the persons who received the slips of paper whereon they were written, and in many religious houses, where this custom still prevails, each member of the community preserves his billet during the year, as an incitement to imitate the virtues and invoke the special intercession of his holy Valentine."

But see how strong is the old Adam in the hearts of the unregenerate. Wanton youth was not satisfied to imitate these holy fathers and ballot for a ghostly partner in heaven. It longed for tangible flesh and blood here on earth,—flesh and blood of that delightful variety which has a spice of the devil in it (*teste* many holy men who have fled aghast from its witcheries), and is known as woman. So it went back to something like the pagan custom.

This was at least as early as the fourteenth century, for we find these lines in a poem written by John Lydgate in praise of Catherine, the wife of Henry V.:

> Seynte Valentine of custome yeere by yeere
> Men have an usuance, in this regioun,
> To loke and serche Cupides kalendere,
> And chose theyr choyse by grete affeccioun,
> Such as ben move with Cupides mocioun,
> Takyng theyre choyse as theyre sort doth falle;
> But I love oon whiche excelleth alle.

In the latter part of the sixteenth century the Church, in the person of St. Francis de Sales, once more stepped in to sanctify the rites of St. Valentine's Day. Again Butler is our authority. He tells us how St. Francis "severely forbad the custom of Valentines, or giving Boys in writing the name of Girls to be admired and attended on by them; and, to abolish it, he changed it into giving billets with the names of certain Saints, for them to honor and imitate in a particular manner."

But in the end the Boys and the Girls triumphed over the Saint. Nay, the Girls triumphed also over the Boys, wresting from them their exclusive privilege of choosing mates. In France itself it appears that the names of young people of both sexes were written out and put into proper receptacles, and drawings took place, in which each sex could secure a partner from the other, and it was customary for the sentimental bond set up by the selection so made to inure for one year and no longer, unless, as a sarcastic bachelor observes, " terminated by the marriage or death of the parties." During the year each stood to the other in the relation of Cavalier and Lady of Beauty, the knight being bound to the honor and defence of his fair one, for which she repaid him in smiles and silk favors, when silk was obtainable and too much good-natured encouragement was not strictly forbidden by parents and guardians.

The same mutuality obtained across the Channel. Misson, in his " Travels in England", (1698), tells us that on the eve of St. Valentine's Day " an equal number of Maids and Bachelors get together, each writes their true or some feigned name upon separate billets, which they roll up and draw by way of lots, the Maids taking the Men's billets, and the Men the Maids'; so that each of the young Men lights upon a Girl that he calls his Valentine, and each of the Girls upon a young Man which she calls hers. By this means each has two Valentines—but the Man sticks faster to the Valentine that is fallen to him than to the Valentine to whom he is fallen. Fortune having thus divided the company into so many couples, the Valentines give balls and treats to their mistresses, wear their billets several days upon their bosoms or sleeves, and this little sport often ends in Love. This ceremony is practised differently in different Countries, and according to the freedom or severity of Madame Valentine. There is another kind of Valentine, which is the first young Man or Woman chance throws in your way in the street, or elsewhere," on Valentine's Day itself. The latter appears at an early date to have been the manner in Scotland, if Sir Walter is right in his description of the wooing of the Fair Maid of Perth and of Hal of the Wynd. A more notable example is Ophelia's song:

> Good morrow, 'tis St. Valentine's Day,
>> All in the morn betime,
> And I a maid at your window,
>> To be your valentine.

It is evident, therefore, that in Shakespeare's day the custom of challenging your valentine had already commenced. The challenge consisted simply in saying, " Good morrow, 'tis St. Valentine's Day," and he or she who said it first on meeting a person of the opposite sex received a present. Later a gallant custom enacted that the gentleman alone should give the present, but only if he were successfully challenged. This explains good Mr. Pepys's anxiety when early on St. Valentine's Day (1664) he called at Sir William Batten's and would not go in " till I asked whether they that opened the door was a man or a woman, and Mingo, who was there, answered a woman, which, with his tones, made me laugh ; so up I went, and took Mrs. Martha for my Valentine (which I do only for complacency) ; and Sir W. Batten he go in the same manner to my wife, and so we were very merry."

It seems also that some element of choice as well as of chance had now been introduced into the sport, for a person could wilfully close his or her eyes and refuse to open them until an appropriate mate arrived. Thus, on next St. Valentine's Day Mr. Pepys records that Will Bowyer came to be his wife's valentine, " she having (at which I made good sport to myself) held her hands all the morning, that she might not see the painters that were at work gilding my chimney-piece and pictures in my dining-room."

From the same diarist we get the first record of a drawing or illustration as connected with the day. This is under date of February 14, 1667 : " This morning came up to my wife's bedside little Will Mercer to be her valentine, and brought her name writ upon blue paper, in gold letters, done by himself very pretty ; and we were both well pleased with it." Another innovation is mentioned under the same date : " I do first observe the drawing of mottoes as well as of names ; so that Pierce, who drew my wife's, did draw also a motto. Her motto was ' most courteous and most fair,' which, as it may be used for an anagram upon each name, might be very pretty."

And so in the pages of Pepys we trace the hint for the modern valentine. It only remained to join the illustration and the motto, to enlarge the latter into a verse, original or selected, and to give the sender an unlimited choice as to the person or persons whom he should favor. Exactly when this union of qualities was effected we have no later Pepys to inform us. But we know that by the beginning of the present century the new method had fully established itself in popular favor.

In the days of quill pens and dear postage the transmission of valentines through the post was an expensive luxury. The amorous swains of that period had to content themselves and their idolized fair ones with thick sheets of gilt-edged letter-paper,—envelopes had not then come into use, and book postage was still unknown,—the first page of each sheet being adorned with a gilt Cupid, carefully gummed on, surmounting a few lines, the favorite formula announcing in terms still held sacred to St. Valentine that because the rose is red and the violet blue, therefore the sender is as sweet as sugar.

With the reduction of the heavy postal charges printed valentines gradually came into use. They generally consisted of a gaudily colored picture, representing a loving couple seated in a bower, with a church in the distance, and a few lines descriptive of the tender sentiments of the persons forwarding the same. The designers of these amatory

THE FIRST PRINTED VALENTINE.

billets seem to have entertained rather singular notions respecting the proper attire of the ladies and gentlemen of whose feelings they sought to become the interpreters. The lady was invariably dressed in a scarlet gown, with a blue or green shawl; the gentleman was attired in lavender trousers, yellow waistcoat, blue surtout, and green or crimson cravat. The effect thus obtained was, as might be imagined, somewhat striking; but our fathers and mothers were apparently satisfied with these quaint productions. The introduction of the cheap postage of to-day laid the foundation of the present trade in valentines, the manufacture of which now constitutes an important branch of industrial activity, furnishing, directly or indirectly, employment to several thousand persons of both sexes.

Cheap postage is also responsible for the introduction of the comic valentine, that hideous bit of vulgarity sold for a cent in the United States and in Great Britain for a penny or a half-penny, which still remains one of the tribulations of the day. But side by side with this monstrosity grew up the pretty and fanciful cards whose use in a modified form has been extended also to Christmas and to New Year's.

Veiled Prophet. An annual pageant performed in St. Louis, Missouri, on the first Tuesday in October. It consists of a great evening procession through the streets of the city, in which thousands of maskers take part, many of them seated on elaborate floats. The feature of the occasion is Mokanna, the Veiled Prophet himself. He wears a long beard, a crown with wings, and an elaborate Turkish costume of the finest satin, and bears in his hand an incandescent boss. He is surrounded by electric lights, fairies, pages, high-priests, sword-bearers, and maids of honor. The rest of the masqueraders are a quaint mixture of Eastern and Western, modern and ancient, mythology. Comus, the Lord of Misrule, Gambrinus, are mingled together in defiance of chronology and geography. But the general effect is gorgeous, and is enhanced by the fireworks that are let off all along the route from the many floats and by the calcium lights and other illuminations. The procession concludes with a ball at the Merchants' Exchange Hall, where the Veiled Prophet chooses and crowns a queen.

The story of the Veiled Prophet was made familiar to lovers of poetry by Moore's "Lalla Rookh," in which it forms an episode. Mokanna, however, was not a creation of fancy, but a genuine historic character of the eighth century. His name was Hakem ben Allah, but he called himself Al-Mokanna ("the Veiled"). Having lost one eye from an arrow wound, he wore a thick veil to conceal the deformity, and laid claim to be an incarnation of the Deity. He had many followers in Arabia, and soon possessed himself of a large part of that country, and was acknowledged by a number of cities. His influence was retained by many devices, such being his skill in magic and legerdemain that his tricks passed for miracles.

Troops were sent against him by the caliph Almahdi, his armies were defeated in the field, and he was besieged in a small fortress in the south of Arabia. Finding success impossible, and deeming escape hopeless, he poisoned his attendants in a banquet and leaped into a well or cistern which had been partly filled with destructive acids. When the conquerors forced a way into the castle they searched in vain for him or his body, the latter having been entirely dissolved by the corrosive fluids. The secret was discovered by the confession of one who had beheld the preparations for suicide; but in some parts of Arabia there are still persons who believe that Mokanna ascended to heaven.

Veronica, St. Her festival is celebrated on Shrove Tuesday. There are varying accounts concerning this saint. According to some, she was the daughter of Salome and the niece of Herod; according to others, she was the woman who was healed of an issue of blood by touching the hem of Christ's garment. When the Saviour was bearing the cross to Calvary, she handed him her handkerchief to wipe his face, and ever afterwards Christ's features remained impressed on the cloth. The Emperor Tiberius summoned St. Veronica to Rome, that she might heal him of a terrible disease, but he died before her arrival there. She is said to have subsequently suffered martyrdom with St. Peter and St. Paul. Another account makes her go to Europe with Lazarus and his sisters and suffer death in Provence or Aquitaine. A chapel in St. Peter's at Rome is dedicated to St. Veronica, and the face of the Saviour painted on linen is shown there as the veritable handkerchief of the legend. In art St. Veronica is represented holding the napkin.

Vessel-Cup, also known as **Wesley-Cup** and **Wesley Bob.** The name is evidently a corruption of "wassail;" but the thing is a curious admixture of the old Catholic crib (see PRESEPIO) and the semi-pagan wassail customs. As it survives at present in Yorkshire and other parts of rural England, the vessel-cup is made of holly and evergreens, like a bower, inside which are placed either one or two dolls, adorned with ribbons. The whole affair is wrapped in a veil and borne upon a stick during Christmas week by children who go from house to house singing either the well-known strains of "God rest you, merry gentlemen," or a carol beginning,—

> God bless the master of this house,
> The mistress also,
> And all the little children
> That round the table go.

When they come to a house they uncover the cup, in the expectation of some small gratuity. In some localities young girls and women are the bearers, as was formerly the case with the wassail-cup. Up to almost the middle of the nineteenth century the dolls were known as Advent Images, a name which clearly indicated their Catholic origin. They were dressed to represent the Virgin and the infant Christ, and were carried in a box with a glass lid. This was covered over by a white napkin, and carried from door to door in the arms of a woman. On reaching a house the bearer uncovered the box and sang this carol:

> The first good joy that Mary had, it was the joy of one,
> To see her own son Jesus to suck at her breast-bone.
>   It brings tidings of comfort and joy!
>
> The next good joy that Mary had, it was the joy of two,
> To see her own son Jesus to make the lame to go.
>   It brings, etc.
>
> The next good joy that Mary had, it was the joy of three,
> To see her own son Jesus to make the blind to see.
>   It brings, etc.

The next good joy that Mary had, it was the joy of four,
To see her own son Jesus to read the Bible o'er.
  It brings, etc.

The next good joy that Mary had, it was the joy of five,
To see her own son Jesus to make the dead alive.
  It brings, etc.

The next good joy that Mary had, it was the joy of six,
To see her own son Jesus to bear the crucifix.
  It brings, etc.

The next good joy that Mary had, it was the joy of seven,
To see her own son Jesus to wear the crown of heaven.
  It brings, etc.

At every house before which the bearers stopped a halfpenny
was expected, in return for which the giver was allowed to take
a leaf or a flower, which was carefully preserved as a cure for
toothache. That household which was not visited was deemed
in danger of ill luck. An old proverbial expression in Yorkshire
ran, " As unhappy as the man who has seen no Advent Images."
  It was infinitely more unlucky, however, to withhold the halfpenny in case the Advent Images came along.

Viaticum. (Lat., " Provision for a journey,"—hence for the
last journey from this world to the next.) This name is given
to the communion administered to the dying. In countries
where Protestantism prevails the consecrated host is carried to
the bedside by the Catholic priest without public display. But in
Catholic countries a solemn procession escorts it from the church
to the door of the patient. At any hour of the day or night this
procession may be seen traversing the streets. You first hear a
bell in the distance, and as the sound draws nearer lights begin
to appear in the windows, and the passers-by slacken their pace
and presently kneel down. The procession comes by; it is simple
enough, consisting of a priest, bearing the sacred host in a pyx
or golden box, with a sort of umbrella held over him (a *baldacchino*, as it is called), in token of reverence, a few clerics
carrying lighted torches, and a crowd of poorly dressed followers
clustering behind. The crowd swells as it goes, many falling
into the ranks as they pass by, and making, as it were, a guard
of honor about the door of the sick person's house. In Naples
it is customary for any noble or wealthy occupant of a carriage,
who may happen to meet such a procession, to alight upon the
spot and give up his carriage to the priest, following it on foot
himself. At Rome one often sees richly dressed ladies get out of
their carriages and kneel among the crowd, regardless of dust

or mud, as the viaticum is carried past. Similar customs are common in all Catholic countries.

Special state was observed in the older days when the Pope himself carried the viaticum to some great personage.

THE VIATICUM IN PAPAL PROCESSION.

In France until the Revolution, when the viaticum was borne to the sick or dying the priest placed himself under a dais. He was preceded by a lantern-bearer, a bell-bearer, and a deacon. At the tinkling of the bell all the wayfarers knelt down, and horses and carriages stopped in the street. If the patient were a person of quality, all the servants and often the master of the house provided themselves with torches to receive the priest at the threshold. Madame de Sévigné on November 19, 1664, describes how the viaticum was borne to Queen Marie Thérèse, then in danger as the result of a confinement: "It was the most magnificent and the saddest thing in the world to see the king and all his court with tapers and thousands of torches go to seek and bring back the Holy Sacrament." One day Louis XV., returning from the Palais de Justice, met the viaticum at the Pont-Neuf. Descending from his carriage, he dropped on his knees in the mud, and the priest emerging from beneath the dais took his seat in the royal carriage amid the acclamations of the people.

In Madrid on Easter Sunday the host is sent round in one of the royal coaches, preceded by bands of music, and escorted by a body of troops. It stops at the houses of sick persons, and is taken in to them. Three priests alight from the carriage, the centre one wearing a gold and silver robe, and bearing the consecrated wafer, which, in common Spanish parlance, is called Dios, or God. Four assistants carry, by means of four sticks, a silken awning over the priests and their sacred charge. The centre of the awning sinks a little, and on it rest fresh flowers. The royal carriage is of an antique form, of a deep cherry-red, with burnished gildings. It is drawn by six grays, with postilion and coachman. When the host descends from the carriage, the military band plays the Royal March,—played only on such occasions and in the presence of royalty. The people at the windows throw out flowers and little squares of paper of various colors, with grotesque wood-cuts and barbarous verses printed upon them. These *aleluyas*, as they are called, are the invariable accompaniments of processions here, and are thrown out in great quantities, thickly strewing the ground, much to the delight of the street-urchins, who make collections of them.

Victor, St., patron of Marseilles, France. A Roman soldier in the army of the Emperor Maximian who refused to worship heathen gods and with three companions suffered martyrdom at Marseilles. Their bodies were thrown into the sea, but, being cast ashore, were buried by the Christians in a grotto hewn out of a rock.

After Jerusalem and Rome, Marseilles is claimed by the lovers of St. Victor as the earliest place of Christian worship. It is told that at one time as many as five thousand monks lived in the rocks and met in the catacombs for prayer. This was in the time of St. Cassien. Early in the fifth century, after his Oriental wanderings, this remarkable character came to Marseilles, and was allowed by the bishop to establish himself in the grotto. Finally he was surrounded by imitators of his piety and penitence to the number of thousands. In 420 he built a church and a monastery above ground, and also founded a house for women. To this church the greater part of the relics of St. Victor were transferred, the remainder being conveyed to Paris and laid in a chapel dedicated in his honor, which was subsequently enlarged and turned into the royal monastery of St. Victor's.

Saracens destroyed the first abbey of St. Victor in Marseilles. Its successor of 1040 suffered also. The building of 1200 remains, and is a favorite place of pilgrimage for devout Catholics. Besides the relics of its eponymic saint, it contains a number of hagiological "attractions." Among these are the legendary cross on which St. Andrew was crucified, and the equally legendary tomb of Lazarus, who after his resurrection came to Mar-

seilles with his sisters about A.D. 40. (See MARIES, THE THREE.)
The latter is in the chapel of Mary Magdalene in the grotto beneath, where is also preserved a smooth stone known as the seat of Lazarus. Its hollowed end forms a basin where Christians received baptism, and here, "very ancient and respectable tradition" reports, the "sainted bishop and friend of the Saviour of men" used to hear confession and administer the sacrament to his converts.

The magnificent tomb of Pope Urban V., which was one of the former glories of the place, disappeared in the Revolutionary year 1793. Urban in 1361 was head of the abbey, and after death he was buried within its walls. His tomb was the shrine of the upper church, and had to be protected by an iron grating from the indiscreet piety of pilgrims. Many lords, kings, and princes have heaped treasure there, and sought intercession for their sins. In the Revolutionary turmoil this monument suffered with others. Recently its remains have been discovered, but not the bones.

The Revolutionists used the crypts of St. Victor as a prison, and confined there their convict galley-slaves. With this century restoration began, and in 1804 the upper church was purified and restored to sacred use, while in 1822 worship was resumed in the poor shorn catacombs.

In the chapel of Notre-Dame de la Confession is preserved the famous Black Virgin, an image vulgarly attributed to St. Luke, but evidently of mediæval date. It has a child on its knee, and is darkly stained. The peculiar color, or the uncanny fact that the bluest skies darkened and rain fell in torrents whenever the Virgin was carried out of doors, or similarly good reasons, protected her in the Saracen raids, while during the Revolutionary assaults some faithful monk managed to secrete her in a cottage. Crutches and other mementos of the miraculously healed hang about her shrine.

The stories of the Black Virgin's power are voluminous and characteristic. One of the most popular legends is that of the green candles. A devout maid of the early ages worshipped at this shrine until her constancy became proverbial. Arriving home in the crypts one morning before four o'clock, the mass began and proceeded with her as the only attendant. Coming to the next mass, she met grieved and wondering reproof for her neglect of the morning service from the priests, who, in turn, were amazed by her assurance that she had attended. Hurt by their disbelief, she told them to look for her offering, and surely there was a ring she had left on the altar. But they were yet only half convinced, until she reminded them that at the mass green candles had replaced the usual white ones. They again visited Notre-Dame de la Confession, and, lo! the candles were all green. And then they knew that the Black Virgin, about whom the lights blinked so sleepily, had recognized the piety of the earthly virgin and had caused to be celebrated for her solely this miraculous mass.

The Black Virgin is now taken from her underground home but one day in the year, the first of the great "Chandeleur" (Candlemas) week or "octave" which affects Marseilles life so picturesquely during the early days of February. It is a medi-æval time of cakes and candles and priests and white-robed virgins, with nineteenth-century pilgrims swarming the narrow streets that meet at the broad earth platform overlooking the glorious sea and port and "Old Town" views, and surrounding the dark walls of the sacred fortress with its blocked and secretly wrought windows, and its flag-decked towers, where great black bells turn and swing in the openings against the blue sky.

"The church entrance, where every species of pitiful deformity begs, is approached through an avenue formed by booths for the selling of cakes, candles, and souvenirs, and presided over by comfortable white-capped old women or beribboned young ones. Inside, the church is rapidly filled with chairs, of which every comer receives one, in return for a sou, from more smiling gran-nies. Forward where the crowd presses about the Black Virgin little can be seen but burning tapers and the white gowns of the young girls who that morning bore her from the crypts. At four o'clock in the morning the initial service of the Chandeleur is held amid suffocating crowds, and then is formed the priestly procession, which, accompanying the Virgin, winds through the subterranean ways and up the staircase to the church above, where all day the people throng about their Lady in solicitation and adoration, and where services are held at intervals until six o'clock, when the Virgin is returned to her chapel.

"The services in the crypts during the remaining days are most interesting,—the soft taper lights, the altar richly dressed in green, white, and gold, the kneeling multitude, the passing costumes of various religious orders, the tapping response of the stone pavement, and, above all, the associations of saints, monks, sovereigns, and martyrs, imparting a peculiar fascination. Amid such scenes the nineteenth-century bonnets seem incongruous and emphasize the sweet propriety of the peasant's native cos-tume, when the eye rests on some placid Arles woman in her folds of black and white, or an Italian girl from the fishers' quar-ter, in nondescript garb, gracefully resting against a pillar, or a type from the Catalans, some scarfed Spanish contour poised by a happy instinct in one of the balcony-like openings, which forms a stone frame. Many of the Chandeleur candles are specially blessed to be burned at sea to allay tempests, and among the thousands sold are many green ones in memory of the old legend. And a yet older custom still is kept, whereby on departing from the church every one buys one of the little boat-shaped cakes called 'navettes,' which probably originated in commemoration of the voyage of Lazarus to Provence." (M. K. B., in *New York Evening Post*, April 17, 1897.)

Vincent, St., patron saint of Lisbon, Valencia, Saragossa, Milan, and Châlons. His festival is celebrated on January 22. At the age of twenty he was an ordained deacon. He was denounced as a Christian together with his bishop, Valerius. St. Vincent proclaimed his faith and defied torture, whereupon the proconsul gave him over to terrible tortures. Legend has it that angels came down and strengthened him, and that his jailers heard their songs and beheld the prison filled with light, and were converted. As his spirit could not be conquered by torture, the proconsul had him placed on a bed of roses, and everything was done to ease his pain, in order that he might be seduced by luxury. But he expired on his bed of roses, and, according to legend, angels bore his soul to glory. His body was thrown to wild beasts, but it was untouched and was guarded by a raven. Then it was attached to a millstone and thrown into the sea. But when the boatmen who had taken the body out returned to the shore they found that the body had preceded them. They ran away in terror, and the waves hollowed out a grave for the corpse. Here it lay for many years, when it was revealed to some Christians, who took the remains to Valencia and interred them. Some of his relics found their way to Saragossa. It is related that when Childebert laid siege to this city he raised the siege on condition that the stole of St. Vincent should be given to him. He carried it to Paris and placed it in a church which he built. In the year 885 some of the bones of St. Vincent were translated from Valencia to France and deposited in the abbey of Castres. The greater portion of the bones of the saint was taken from Valencia by the Christians when driven out by the Moors, and deposited on a promontory since called Cape St. Vincent. Here ravens are said to have guarded the remains. In 1147 Alonzo I. removed these relics to Lisbon and placed them in the cathedral. This translation is annually commemorated by the Portuguese; the feast was confirmed by Sixtus V. St. Vincent is represented in art as a handsome young man, and his proper attribute is a crow or a raven.

Vincent de Paul, St., founder of the order of the Sisters of Charity. His festival is celebrated on July 19.

St. Vincent de Paul was born in Gascony in 1576. At the age of twenty he entered the Franciscan order. On a voyage from Marseilles to Narbonne he was captured by pirates and was sold into slavery at Tunis, but he finally converted his master and his wife, and together they made their escape, landing in France in 1607. Thence he went to Rome, where he was intrusted with a mission to the French court, and became almoner of Queen Marguerite de Valois. He then set himself to work for the relief of prisoners, as well as for the poor and outcasts in general, thus gaining the title of the Father of the Poor. He died at St. Lazare on the 27th of September, 1660, and was buried in the church of that name. The saint was canonized in 1737 by Pope Clement XII. Many miracles are reported as having been worked at his shrine.

Vine of the Lord. (It. *Vigna di Dio;* Fr. *Vigne du Seigneur.*) A vine in a corner of the Vatican gardens which for generations has been tended by the Pope himself and his vicar. It produces annually one or two tuns of wine, white in color, with a faint rosy tinge, and of a most choice and exquisite bouquet. The first pressing is the best. This virgin juice, the cream of the entire crop, is sedulously preserved for a special purpose. Every Tuesday morning, in accordance with a noble old custom, His present Holiness celebrates divine service in his private chapel, and this service is " for the benefit of the enemies of the Church." There and then the holy Father prays earnestly for the souls of the most militant sceptics and most outspoken radicals, as also for the souls of Freemasons and all others who in any way make war or try to cast discredit on the Roman Catholic Church. And at this service the only wine used is the first juice of the Lord's vine.

The second pressing is used at the Pope's table, just as it has been used for centuries at the tables of his predecessors. The Pope, indeed, is in a sense bound to use it, for it is his duty to care for the vine and to hand it down unharmed to his successor.

The origin of this great vine is lost in the night of time. A legend says that it first blossomed and bore fruit in the earthly Paradise in company with other delicious fruits and other food, and that Adam in his blindness did not discover its virtue and potency until it was too late for him to enjoy it. As all the world knows, our first father preferred apples. So the vine, called into being by the Lord, remained undiscovered until the patriarch Noah passed by one day and leisurely ate a few of the luscious grapes. He at once cherished the goodly plant and warmed his heart with the wine. On one occasion, indeed, he indulged a trifle over-much, thereby setting a bad example to his sons, Shem, Ham, and Japheth.

Subsequently the vine passed into the possession of many celebrated personages, and was coveted by all the kings of Israel. Many deadly contests were waged on account of it, and often was it sorely injured. But in adversity as in prosperity it flourished ever the same, producing beautiful grapes and delicious wine. Its fame spread throughout the world on one memorable occasion, for when Christ turned water into wine at the wedding feast at Cana of Galilee, the story went abroad that wine from the Lord's vine was used.

The vine has seen many evil days since then. It has seen the Papacy disturbed and the temporal power shorn away from the hands of its masters. It has heard the sound of battles, and has often come near to death for want of nourishment. It has even more than once seen its wealth of grapes scattered on the ground and trampled underfoot. A happy season came when it went with the Popes to Avignon. A little vineyard was planted there, and, from the Popes down to the humblest peasants, all took pleasure in tending the vines. When the Popes went back to Rome these young vines were transplanted to the Vatican, and in due time wine was again made and carefully stored away in a cellar.

Vine-Growers' Feast. (Fr. *Fête des Vignerons.*) A pageant performed at irregular intervals at Vevay by the members of the Swiss confraternity of wine-growers. It is believed that the society was born about the year 1536, but this fact cannot be positively ascertained, because its records were unfortunately destroyed by fire in 1688. The festival, however, may be of much earlier date; indeed, it is not impossible that it is a direct survival from the Cerealia of pagan times. In 1688 the society consisted of only thirty members. Their duty was to superintend the culture of the vines. They visited and inspected the vineyards at fixed periods, and had authority to dispossess any proprietor or tenant who neglected his vines for other forms of horticulture. At that time the fête was a very modest affair, hardly more than a parade in costume through the village to the blare of trumpets.

By the eighteenth century the membership had increased into the hundreds, Christian and pagan mythology were represented among the paraders, and the concluding banquet was attended by civic and even national dignitaries. The latest performance was in August, 1889. The festivities were kept up for an entire week, but the processions in the amphitheatre took place only on Monday, Tuesday, Thursday, and Friday, leaving Wednesday and Saturday for the participants to rest from their labors and enjoy themselves in a general merrymaking holiday, finishing with a grand illumination in the town and on the lake at night.

Two thousand performers took part in the processions. These consisted of Swiss guards in their red and white uniforms; the members of the confraternity, some in Louis Quinze costumes and others in green hats and small clothes, with white waistcoats and stockings; figures of Pales, Ceres, and Bacchus, with their followers, each headed by a high-priest and accompanied by a band dressed in ancient Roman costumes, but in colors suited to the season they represented.

After the procession the followers of each divinity took part in turn in characteristic dances and ballets. Pales was personified by a handsome brunette, arrayed in light blue and crowned with flowers, occupying a decorated throne, drawn by white oxen with gilded horns and hoofs. In her train were little boys and girls dressed in blue, white, and pink, named the children of spring, shepherds and shepherdesses in blue and pink, gardeners in blue and white, mowers, rakers, alpine yodlers, milkers, and cheese-makers.

Ceres, the goddess of corn, was a blonde, with golden hair, dressed in red and occupying a similar throne drawn by red oxen. Her attendants were reapers and binders, threshers and gleaners, and lastly the miller and his wife, with their mill in full operation grinding out the flour.

Bacchus and his cortége were of course the most important features of the occasion. Bacchus was a young man crowned with ivy leaves sitting on a throne drawn by four gray horses. Wine-growers, grape-gatherers, tun-makers, and wine-makers, all engaged in the practice of their vocations, gave way finally to the clown of the occasion, Silenus on his donkey, so full of sack that he had to be supported by a negro slave on each side, ushering in a merry rout of satyrs, fauns, and bacchanals in tights and leopard-skins. The programme in the amphitheatre concluded by the two thousand figurantes gathering in front of the president's platform and singing the Hymne finale. Then all filed out in the order of their *entrée* and marched in grand procession through the principal streets.

Vitus, St., patron saint of Bohemia, Saxony, and Sicily, and of dancers and actors.

St. Vitus was born in the third century, in Sicily, of a noble family. His father was a pagan, but the saint was converted by his nurse, and declared his faith in Christianity when a mere boy. His father, in a rage, threw him into a dungeon, but legend relates that angels came and danced in the dungeon in the midst of a dazzling light. When the father looked in to the prisoner he was struck blind, but was cured by the intercession of his son. The father continued to persecute the son, and he fled into Italy. There he was denounced as a Christian and thrown into a caldron of boiling oil. After his death, it is related, a wolf kept guard over his body until it was found and buried by the Christians. In art St. Vitus is represented as a beautiful boy, and has many attributes,—a palm, a caldron of oil, a wolf, a lion, and a cock.

Votive Offerings. These are now known in ecclesiastical Latin as *offerta ex-voto.* Among the ancient Romans similar offerings to the gods, known as *votiva paries*, were hung up in temples as tributes of gratitude for divine aid in emergencies. Models of arms and legs with records of their cure once decorated the temple of Æsculapius on the Tiber island, as they do now the images of wonder-working saints and Madonnas. The heathen Romans, after escape from shipwreck, hung pictures of the tempest and sometimes also their sea-drenched apparel in the temple of Neptune, or made the votive offering of a miniature marble galley to Jupiter Redax. The same practices are now continued under Christian forms. In all the famous shrines of Europe and in a large number of churches there may be seen a greater or less number of waxen or silver representations of bodily members that have been healed, crutches that restored patients have discarded, and rude drawings of dangers escaped, while the bushes in the vicinity of holy wells (see WELLS, HOLY) are hung with rags and the beds of the waters are lined with pins.

Hindoo and Buddhist temples in the East are decorated in similar fashion. In Japan the offerings assume a peculiarly grotesque mixture of the ancient and the modern. At the great shrine of Kompira, for example, may be seen a life-preserver bearing in English letters the name of the ship, Tosa, to which it belonged; and there, also, among old-fashioned ex-voto pictures of junks saved from wreck by divine power, are new pictures of steamers and modern schooners similarly rescued by the god. At nearly all of the greater temples, and at many of the smaller ones, are spoils of the war with China. Among these are Gatling and Armstrong guns, canister shot and 32-centimetre shells, Männlicher rifles and Martinis, Colt revolvers and Winchester repeaters, as well as Chinese banners, uniforms, and lances,—a vast part of the captured armament having been disposed of in this manner.

W.

Waits, Christmas. (Old Fr. *waite, gaite,* "a guard," "sentinel," "watchman.") At present these are unorganized bands of boys and men who on the nights preceding Christmas, and especially on Christmas Eve, parade the streets of towns and villages in England, singing carols and accompanying themselves on simple instruments of music, expecting in return to receive a gratuity from the houses in front of which they stop. In their origin, which may be dated back to the fourteenth or fifteenth century, they were probably musical watchmen who were required to give practical evidence of their vigilance by playing on the hautboy or flageolet at stated times during the night. In the household of Edward IV. there is made mention in the "Liber Niger Domus Regis" of "a Wayte, that nyghtely from Mychelmas to Shreve Thorsdaye pipe the watch within this courte fowere tymes; in the Somere nightes three tymes, and maketh bon gayte at every chambre doare and offyce, as well for feare of pyekeres and pilfers [pickers and stealers]."

These "Waytes" afterwards became organized bands of musicians, who held themselves in readiness to play at weddings, banquets, etc. Almost every city and town had its corporation waits. In London they earned a small stipend for playing before the lord mayor in his inaugural procession, and eked out a living by performing at private festivities. Their regular uniform in the sixteenth and seventeenth centuries was blue gowns, red sleeves and caps, and a silver collar about the neck.

The dedication of Morley's "Consort Lessons" (1599) to the lord mayor and aldermen of London seems to indicate that these waits were no mean musicians:

"As the ancient custom of this most honorable and renowned city hath been ever to retain and maintain excellent and expert musicians to adorn your Honor's favor, feasts, and solemn meetings—to these your Lordships' Wayts, I recommend the same—to your servants' careful and skilful handling."

Wake. (Originally *lyke-wake* or *liche-wake,* from the Anglo-Saxon *lic,* "a corpse," and *wœcce* or *wake,* "to watch," "to keep vigil.") An all-night watch of friends and relations over the remains of the dead before the funeral. The custom is of unknown origin and antiquity. Although at present it is almost entirely confined to Ireland and to Irish communities in foreign lands, it flourished at one time in many parts of Great Britain and later in colonial New England.

How that the liche-wake was yholde
Al thilke night.
(CHAUCER: *Knight's Tale*, 1. 2100.)

It may have originated from a superstition that the body would be carried away or defaced by evil spirits, or from a more rational idea of injury to it from rats or from wild beasts. Christianity introduced the idea of making it an occasion for offering prayers for the repose of the soul of the deceased. Usually the corpse was deposited under a table with a plate of salt on its breast, and the table was covered with various kinds of liquor to revive the flagging energies of mourners and watchers. But it was found in very early days that, in Miss Edgeworth's words, the presence of liquor turned these meetings "held professedly for the indulgence of holy sorrow into orgies of unholy joy." Church and State both made efforts to regulate the wake and to weed out its objectionable features, though both were unwilling to abolish it altogether. The tenth canon of the provincial synod held in London during the reign of Edward III. warned the faithful that the design of people's meeting together upon such occasions was to join their prayers for the benefit of the dead person; that this ancient and serviceable usage was overgrown with superstition and turned into a convenience for theft and debauchery; therefore for a remedy against this disorder it was decreed that upon the death of any person none should be allowed to watch before the corpse in a private house excepting near relations and friends of the deceased and such as offered to repeat a number of psalms for the benefit of his soul. The penalty annexed was excommunication. This may have been one of the factors which worked towards the abolition of the custom in England. The Reformation and the consequent disuse of prayers for the dead gave it its death-blow.

That some sort of funeral feasts not entirely unlike wakes were practised at a remote antiquity is evident from frequent allusions in the Old Testament and other ancient writers. "Delicates poured upon a mouth shut up are as messes of meat set upon a grave," says Ecclesiasticus. "Pour out thy bread upon the burial of the just," says the book of Tobit; and Jeremiah, foretelling the calamities that shall befall the Jews, predicts that "they shall not be buried, . . . neither shall men give them the cup of consolation to drink for their father or for their mother." At the present day a feast in honor of the dead is practised by the Albanians and the Abyssinians which is almost identical with the Irish wake. This fact is frequently used as an argument for the common origin of the Oriental races and the Celts.

Something very like a wake was observed by the Puritans in colonial New England. Hawthorne has recorded the jollity that was usual at a funeral among these otherwise stern and sober folk: "They were the only class of scenes, so far as my investigation has taught me, in which our ancestors were wont to steep their tough old hearts in wine and strong drink and indulge in an outbreak of grisly jollity. Look back through all the social customs of New England in the first century of her existence and read all her traits of character, and find one occasion other than a funeral feast where jollity was sanctioned by universal practice."

Miss Alice Morse Earle, in "Customs and Fashions of Old New England," p. 310, quotes a bill for the mortuary expenses of David Porter of Hartford, who was drowned in 1678, which shows how universally liquor was served to all who had to do with a funeral:

By a pint of liquor for those who dived for him	1s.
By a quart of liquor for those who bro't him home	2s.
By 2 quarts of wine & 1 gallon of cyder to jury of inquest .	5s.
By 8 gallons and 3 qts. wine for funeral	£1 15s.
By barrel cyder for funeral	16s.
1 coffin	12s.
Windeing sheet	18s.

Not only at a gathering held on the night before the funeral, but also at the funeral itself, copious draughts of liquor were consumed. Even town paupers had two or three gallons of rum or a barrel of cider given by the town to be drunk at their burial. The liquor at the funeral of a minister was usually paid for by the church or the town. An experienced committee was appointed to superintend the mixing of the grog or punch which was the ceremonious tap of the occasion and to see that it was liberally dispensed among the mourners.

Sargent tells us that in his boyhood a table with liquors was always provided at country funerals: "Every one, as he entered, took off his hat with his left hand, smoothed down his hair with his right, walked up to the coffin, gazed upon the corpse, made a crooked face, passed on to the table, took a glass of his favorite liquor, went forth upon the plat before the house, and talked politics, or the new road, or compared crops, or swapped heifers or horses, until it was time to lift. A clergyman told me that when settled at Concord, New Hampshire, he officiated at the funeral of a little boy. The body was borne in a chaise, and six little nominal pall-bearers, the oldest not thirteen, walked by the side of the vehicle. Before they left the house a sort of master of ceremonies took them to the table and mixed a tumbler of gin, water, and sugar for each."

Something resembling a wake was practised among the early Knickerbockers. Both in New York and in Albany each house had its *dood-kamer*, or dead-chamber, where the dead were placed until the funeral. Dutch ladies were famous for their attendance on such occasions, and, if the deceased were of their sex, burnt wine was served them in silver tankards. The funeral was always a great event, and the good vrouw's skill was spent to the utmost to load her table with choicest delicacies for the *dood-feest*, the most prominent dish being the *dood-koecks (q. v.)*. They were thick disks about four inches in diameter and similar in ingredients to our New-Year cakes, and were kept for years as mementos of the departed. "Each burgher had a pipe of wine spiced in reserve for his funeral, and I regret to say the mourners were often in a mournful condition after the event; and in this connection we recall an incident. A familiar name in the old Dutch times in Albany was Wyngaard. Skipper Block, in his cruise of discovery, called an island he came across Martin Wyngaard's Island, *Martin Vineyard's Island*, corrupted to Martha's Vineyard; and likewise Wyngaard's Point is now known as Vineyard Point. The last in the male line was one Lucas Wyngaard, who died about 1756, unmarried, and leaving estate. The invitations to the funeral were general,—a custom still kept up among old Dutch families in Albany,—and all relatives and friends received a written invitation to be present. Of course the attendance was large, and those who attended returned, as was the custom, to the house, not leaving till morning's light. In the course of the night a pipe of wine was drunk, dozens of pounds of tobacco consumed, grosses of pipes broken, not a whole decanter or glass left in the house, and finally the pall-bearers ended the debauch by kindling a fire with their scarfs." (*A Glimpse of an Old Dutch Town: Harper's Magazine,* vol. lxii. p. 54.)

Walburga, St., also called **Walpurgis, Walbourg, Val-purge, Gualbourg,** and **Avangour.** Her festival is celebrated on February 25, the anniversary of her death, and on May 1, that of the enshrinement of her relics at Furnes.

St. Walburga was born in the kingdom of the West Saxons in England, and was educated in the monastery of Winburn, where she took the veil and remained for twenty-seven years. She accompanied her uncle St. Boniface and her brother St. Willibald to the continent, and went with ten other nuns to Mayence. She afterwards was made abbess of the convent of Heidenheim. After the death of Willibald she also governed a community of monks which he had founded at Eichstädt. She had studied medicine, and is reported to have made some wonderful cures.

She died about the year 778, and was entombed in a rock near Eichstädt which exuded a bituminous oil. It was believed by the people that this oil came from the remains of the saint, and that it had remarkable curative powers: it was called Walpurgis oil. The rock became a place of pilgrimage, and a church was built on the spot. On the eve of her festival, Walpurgis Night, the witches are supposed to hold their orgies on the summit of the Blocksberg. A considerable portion of the remains of the saint was translated to Furnes, and enshrined on May 1, on which day her chief festival is celebrated in the Belgic martyrologies. From Furnes small parts of the relics were distributed to Antwerp, Brussels, Thiel, Arnhem, Würtemberg, Cologne, Hanover, and other places. Christ Church at Canterbury received some of the relics. The saint's festival, on account of various translations of her relics, is marked on several days of the year, but is kept in most places on the day of her death. She is represented in art in the Benedictine habit with a crosier and a flask, the latter a symbol of the Walpurgis oil.

Walsingham, Our Lady of. A wonder-working image of the Blessed Virgin which in old Catholic days was preserved in the church at Walsingham, Norfolk, which thence became one of the chief objects of pilgrimages in England.

Erasmus informs us that Walsingham was almost entirely supported by the vast numbers of persons who came to make their offerings to the Virgin. In the church in which the image stood was a little chapel of wood, into which the pilgrims were admitted from each side by a narrow door. There was scarcely any light, except that of the gratefully odorous wax tapers; but a person looking in would say that it was an abode of the gods, so bright and resplendent was it all over with jewels, gold, and silver.

To show what constant tribute was paid to "Our Lady of Walsingham," a few extracts may be given from the "Household book of the Earl of Northumberland:" "Sect. 43. Item: My lord useth yearly to send afore Michaelmas for his lordship's offering to our lady of Walsingham—4*d.* Item: My lord useth and accustometh to send yearly for the upholding of the light of wax which his lordship findeth burning yearly before our lady of Walsingham, containing eleven pounds of wax in it after— 7*d.* Ob. For the finding of every pound ready wrought by a covenant made with the channon by great, for the whole year, for the finding of the said light burning—6*s.* 8*d.* Item: My lord useth and accustometh to send yearly to the channon that keepeth the light before our lady of Walsingham, for his reward for the whole year, for keeping of the said light, lighting it at all service times daily throughout the year—12*d*. Item: My lord useth and accustometh yearly to send to the priest that keepeth the light, lighting of it at all service times daily throughout the year—3*s*. 4*d*."

Royalty as well as the nobility delighted to do honor to the Walsingham shrine. In May, 1469, Edward IV. and his queen made a pilgrimage thither, as we read in a letter from James Hawte to Sir John Paston: "As for the king, as I understand, he departs to Walsingham upon Friday com sev'night, and the queen also, if God send her health."

In 1538 Henry VIII. stripped the magnificent shrine of all its treasure, and dissolved the religious house of which it was the pride and the support. The wonder-working image, and those of Ipswich, Worcester, and many others, were all taken away at the instance of Cromwell; those of Walsingham and Ipswich were brought up to London, "with all the jewels that hung about them," and along with the rest were burned at Chelsea. (See also PILGRIMAGES.)

But though the shrine has disappeared, the holy wells which it sanctified still remain,—two circular stone pits filled with water, enclosed with a square wall, where the pilgrims used to kneel and throw in a piece of gold, whilst they prayed for health. These waters formerly had the reputation of curing disorders of the head and stomach. This property, however, has been replaced by another of a more comprehensive character,—the power of accomplishing all human wishes. In order to attain this desirable end, writes Mr. Glyde in the *Norfolk Garland*, "the votary, with a due qualification of faith and pious awe, must apply the right knee bare to a stone placed for that purpose between the wells. He must then plunge to the wrist each hand, bare also, into the water of the wells, which are near enough to admit of the immersion. A wish must then be formed, but not uttered with the lips, either at the time or afterwards, even in confidential communication to the dearest friend. The hands are then to be withdrawn, and as much of the water as can be obtained in the hollow of each is to be swallowed. This silent wish will be accomplished within the following twelve months."

Washington's Birthday, February 22. It was the most natural thing for our forefathers to choose Washington's Birthday as a time for general thanksgiving and rejoicing, and it is interesting to note that the observance was not delayed until after the death of Washington. Washington had the satisfaction of receiving the congratulations of his fellow-citizens many times upon the return of his birthday, frequently being a guest at the banquets given in honor of the occasion. In fact, after the Revolution, Washington's Birthday practically took the place of the birthday of the various crowned heads of Great Britain, which had always been celebrated with enthusiasm during colonial times. When independence was established, all these royal birthdays were cast aside, and the birthday of Washington naturally became one of the most conspicuous in the calendar of America's holidays.

It may be interesting at this time to look back upon those early days of the republic and see how the newly liberated citizens attested their admiration for their great general and the first President of their country. But the people did not wait until Washington was raised to the highest position his country could give him before honoring his birthday.

The first recorded mention of the celebration is said to be the one in *The Virginia Gazette* or *The American Advertiser* of Richmond: "Tuesday last being the birthday of his Excellency General Washington, our illustrious Commander-in-Chief, the same was commemorated here with the utmost demonstrations of joy." The day thus celebrated was February 11, 1782, the Old Style in the calendar not having then been everywhere and for every purpose abandoned. Indeed, the stone placed as late as in 1815 on the site of his birthplace in Westmoreland County, Virginia, had the following inscription: "Here, the 11th of February, 1732, George Washington was born."

Twelve months later the 11th was commemorated at Talbot Court-House in Maryland. On the same day a number of gentlemen met in a tavern in New York. One had written an ode. Another brought a list of toasts. All, before they went reeling and singing home, agreed to assemble in future on the same anniversary and make merry over the birth of Washington.

Next year they had an ampler opportunity. In the previous October the British troops had evacuated New York city, which was gradually recovering from the distresses of the long war. The demonstrations were not very elaborate, but they were intensely patriotic. In a newspaper of February 17, 1784, we find an interesting account of this first public celebration in New York:

"Wednesday last being the birthday of his Excellency, General Washington, the same was celebrated here by all the true friends of American Independence and Constitutional Liberty with that hilarity and manly decorum ever attendant on the Sons of Freedom. In the evening an entertainment was given on board the East India ship in this harbor to a very brilliant and respectable company, and a discharge of thirteen cannon was fired on this joyful occasion."

A club called a "Select Club of Whigs" assembled in New York on the evening of February 11, and a brief account of the proceedings at its meeting was sent to the *New York Gazette*, with an amusing song, written, it was stated, especially for this occasion. The following stanzas will serve as a sample of this effusion of poetical patriotism:

> Americans, rejoice;
> While songs employ the voice,
>   Let trumpets sound.
> The thirteen stripes display
> In flags and streamers gay,
> 'Tis Washington's Birthday,
>   Let joy abound.
>
> Long may he live to see
> This land of liberty
>   Flourish in peace;
> Long may he live to prove
> A grateful people's love,
> And late to heaven remove,
>   Where joys ne'er cease.
>
> Fill the glass to the brink,
> Washington's health we'll drink,
>   'Tis his birthday.
> Glorious deeds he has done,
> By him our cause is won,
> Long live great Washington!
>   Huzza! Huzza!

The following is also an interesting example of newspaper editorial patriotism which appeared in the *New York Gazette* at the same time: "After the Almighty Author of our existence and happiness, to whom, as a people, are we under the greatest obligations? I know you will answer, 'To Washington.' That great, that gloriously disinterested man has, without the idea of pecuniary reward, on the contrary, much to his private danger, borne the greatest and most distinguished part in our political salvation. He is now retired from public service, with, I trust, the approbation of God, his country, and his own heart. But shall we forget him? No; rather let our hearts cease to beat than an ungrateful forgetfulness shall sully the part any of us have taken in the redemption of our country. On this day, the hero enters into the fifty-third year of his age. Shall such a day pass unnoticed? No; let a temperate manifestation of joy express the sense we have of the blessings that arose upon America on that day which gave birth to Washington. Let us call our children around us and tell them the many blessings they owe to him and to those illustrious characters who have assisted him in the great work of the emancipation of our country, and urge them by such examples to transmit the delights of freedom and independence to their posterity."

It is also interesting to know that New York city was not the only place in the country remembering Washington's Birthday in this year 1784. The residents of Richmond, Virginia, were not forgetful of the day, and in the evening an elegant entertainment and ball were given in the Capitol Building, which, we are informed, were largely attended. So late as 1796, Kentucky and Virginia persisted in preserving the Old Style date. But we have documentary evidence that in 1790 the Tammany Society of New York celebrated the day on February 22. The society had been organized less than a year, and it is interesting to see that it did not allow the first Washington's Birthday in its history to pass by without fitting expressions of regard for the man who was then living in the city as President of the United States. Washington, at that time, lived in the lower part of Broadway, a few doors below Trinity Church. Congress was in session in the old City Hall, on the corner of Wall and Nassau Streets, now occupied by the Sub-Treasury. New York was the capital of the country, but it was the last year that it enjoyed that distinction, for before the close of 1790 the seat of government was removed to Philadelphia, where it remained until 1800, when permanent governmental quarters were taken up at Washington. It may be of interest to know how the founders of this famous political organization commemorated Washington's Birthday. Fortunately, the complete account of this first Tammany celebration has been preserved. It was published in a New York newspaper, a day or two after the event, as follows:

"At a meeting of the Society of St. Tammany, at their wigwam in this city, on Monday evening last, after finishing the ordinary business of the evening, it was unanimously resolved: That the 22d day of February be, from this day and ever after, commemorated by this society as the birthday of the Illustrious George Washington, President of the United States of America. The society then proceeded to the commemoration of the auspicious day which gave birth to the distinguished chief, and the following toasts were drank in porter, the produce of the United States, accompanied with universal acclamations of applause:

"1. May the auspicious birthday of our great **Grand Sachem**, George Washington, ever be commemorated by all the real sons of St. Tammany.
2. The birthday of those chiefs who lighted the great Council Fire in 1775.
3. The glorious Fourth of July, 1776, the birth of American Independence.
4. The perpetual memory of those Sachems and warriors who have been called by the Kitchi Manitou to the Wigwam above since the Revolution.

5. The births of the Sachems and warriors who have presided at the different council fires of the thirteen tribes since 1776.

6. Our Chief Sachem, who presides over the council fire of our tribe.

7. The 12th of May, which is the birthday of our titular saint and patron.

8. The birth of Columbus, our secondary patron.

9. The memory of the great Odagh 'Segte, first Grand Sachem of the Oneida Nation, and all his successors.

10. The friends and patrons of virtue and freedom from Tammany to Washington.

11. The birth of the present National Constitution, 17th of September, 1787.

12. The Sachems and warriors who composed that council.

13. May the guardian genius of freedom pronounce at the birth of all her sons—Where Liberty dwells, there is his country.

"After mutual reciprocations of friendship on the joyous occasion, the society adjourned with their usual order and harmony."

In Washington ever since the first President was inaugurated it had been the practice of the House to adjourn for half an hour to congratulate him on the happy return of his natal day. But this observance was dropped in 1796, on account of the animosities excited by the Jay Treaty.

The Philadelphians, always patriotic, never allowed Washington's Birthday to go by without due celebration. In 1793 a number of old Revolutionary officers belonging to the First Brigade of Pennsylvania Militia had a "very splendid entertainment at Mr. Hill's tavern in Second Street, near Race Street." According to a Philadelphia newspaper account, the company was numerous and truly respectable, and among the guests on that occasion were the Governor of Pennsylvania, Thomas Mifflin, and Mr. Muhlenberg, Speaker of the House of Representatives. At all these patriotic banquets it was customary to give as many toasts as there were States in the Union, so that during the early years we invariably find that thirteen toasts was the rule. As new States were added, however, extra toasts were added to the list. Just when this custom died out can perhaps not be definitely determined, but probably the rapid increase of the States may have had something to do with it, as the diners probably saw that it was taxing their drinking abilities too heavily with the addition of each new State. However, at this Philadelphia celebration the toasts were fifteen, as two new States had recently been added, and among some of the most interesting are the following:

The people of the United States—May their dignity and happiness be perpetual, and may the gratitude of the Nation be ever commensurate with their privileges.

The President of the United States—May the evening of his life be attended with felicity equal to the utility and glory of its meridian.

The Fair Daughters of America—May the purity, the rectitude, and the virtues of their mind ever continue equal to their beauty and external accomplishments.

The Republic of France—Wisdom and stability to her councils, success to her armies and navies, and may her enemies be compensated for their defeats by the speedy and general diffusion of that liberty which they are vainly attempting to suppress.

May Columbia be ever able to boast a Jefferson in council, a Hamilton in finance, and, when necessary, a Washington to lead her armies to conquest and glory.

The Day—May such auspicious periods not cease to recur till every day in the year shall have smiled on Columbia with the birth of a Washington.

Our Unfortunate Friend, the Marquis de Lafayette—May America become shortly his asylum from indignity and wrong, and may the noon and evening of his life be yet honorable and happy in the bosom of that country where its morning shone with such unclouded splendor.

In conclusion, the newspaper account of this celebration states that "the afternoon and evening were agreeably spent in social pleasures and convivial mirth, and the conduct of the whole company was marked by that politeness, harmony, and friendship which ought ever to characterize the intercourse of fellow-citizens and gentlemen."

Balls and banquets, it will be seen, were the chief methods employed in celebrating the day, and there was hardly a town so small that it could not manage to have at least one of these functions in honor of George Washington. The early newspapers for a month, and often longer, after the 22d of February, were filled with brief accounts of these celebrations from different localities. Many of them are very interesting, showing, as they do, the patriotism of the people, as well as their customs and habits in their social entertainments. For instance, when Washington's Birthday was celebrated in Alexandria, Virginia, in 1791, the *Baltimore Advertiser* gives us the following amusing account of a ball held at Wise's tavern:

"The meeting was numerous and brilliant. Joy beamed in every countenance. Sparkling eyes, dimpled cheeks dressed in smiles, prompted by the occasion with all the various graces of female beauty, contributed to heighten the pleasure of the scene. At an interesting moment a portrait of the President, a striking likeness, was suddenly exhibited. The illustrious original had been often seen in the same room in the mild character of a friend, a pleased and pleasing guest. The song of 'God bless great Washington, Long live great Washington,' succeeded. In this prayer many voices and all hearts united. May it not be breathed in vain."

Wassail. (Anglo-Saxon, *wes hāl*, "be whole," "be well," equivalent to "here's to your health.") Originally a pledge drunk between friends. The word is now applied especially to a festive occasion or meeting where drinking and toasting are the order of the hour, and also to the liquor used thereat. The wassail bowl which still survives locally was a prominent feature of the mediæval English Christmas festivities, making its appearance not only on the day itself, but on New Year's and Twelfth Night or Epiphany. This bowl was often of massive silver, and was frequently decked with ribbons and sprigs of rosemary. The component parts of its good cheer were ale, sugar, nutmeg, and roasted apples, a mixture which also went under the name of "lamb's-wool." It is evident that crab-apples were often used in the wassail bowl, as frequent allusions are made in old English poetry to "turning a crabbe in the fire," and Shakespeare makes Puck say,—

> And sometimes lurk I in a gossip's bowl,
> In very likeness of a roasted crab,
> And when she drinks, against her lips I bob,
> And on her withered dewlap pour the ale.

One of the earliest mentions of the wassail bowl in England is that well-known scene when Rowena, the daughter of Hengist, presented to her father's guest, King Vortigern, a bowl of wine, with the words, "Louerd King Wass-heil!" to which he replied, "Drinc Heil!" The American New Year's toasts of health and happiness seem the legitimate successors of these ancient pledges. In the early part of the nineteenth century the mistress of many an American home was wont to rise before daybreak and with the help of her maids prepare a huge bowl of eggnog, of which each member of the family drank, servants as well, and to which each chance guest of the Christmas or New Year's morn was invited.

In a collection of ordinances for the regulation of the royal household in the reign of Henry VII. on Twelfth Night the steward was enjoined, when entering with the spiced and smoking bowl, to cry "Wassail" three times, to which the royal chaplain had to respond with an appropriate song, whether he was in voice or not.

The custom of wassailing at New Year's obtained in monasteries as well as in private houses. The mighty bowl called "Poculum Caritatis" was placed at the upper end of the refectory table at the front of the abbey, and from it the Superior drank to all, and all drank in succession to one another.

A custom much like this is still kept up in the Corporation feasts of London. A double-handled flagon, full of sweetened and spiced wine, is handed to the master, who drinks, standing, to the general health as announced by the toast-master, then passes it to his neighbor on the left, who drinks, standing, to his next neighbor, also standing, and so on until all have drunk. This is the popular ceremony of the "loving-cup."

While the wealthier classes were pouring down their copious libations, young women of the poorer classes went from house to house with wassail bowls adorned with ribbons, and singing carols calculated to beguile even the hard heart of a Midas into giving. If, however, the combined efforts of song and wine failed to elicit a sufficient pecuniary recognition, the carol speedily terminated in malignant anathemas. Here is a good old wassail song :

> A Jolly Wassail Bowl,
>   A Wassail of good ale ;
> Well fare the butler's soul
>   That setteth this to sale—
>   Our jolly Wassail.
>
> Good Dame, here at your door
>   Our Wassail we begin ;
> We are all maidens poor,
>   We pray now let us in
>   With our Wassail.
>
> Our Wassail we do fill
>   With apples and with spice ;
> Then grant us your good will
>   To taste here once or twice
>   Of our good Wassail.
>
> But here they let us stand
>   All freezing in the cold.
> Good Master, give command
>   To enter and be bold
>   With our Wassail.
>
> Much joy into this hall
>   With us is entered in.
> Our Master, first of all,
>   We hope will now begin
>   Of our Wassail.

If songs like the above met with no immediate acknowledgment, the singers followed them up with verses like these :

> Give way, give way, ye gates ! and win
> An easy blessing to your bin
> And basket by our entering in.
>
> Oh, may your dairies prosper so
> As that your pans no ebb may know ;
> But if they do, the more to flow,

> Like to a solemn sober stream
> Banked all with lilies, and the cream
> Of sweetest cowslips filling them;
>
> Last, may your harrows, shares, and ploughs,
> Your stacks, your stalls, your sweetest mows,
> All prosper by our virgin vows.
>
> Alas! we bless, but see none here
> That brings us either ale or beer:
> In a dry house, all things are near.

On St. Stephen's Day it was the fashion, in the early part of the century, to exhibit a " merry disport," or pageant, which perhaps had something to do with the Reformation, in the hall of the Inner Temple in London. Mr. Hone describes it in his " Year Book." Revelling appears to have formed an important part of the scene, if we may judge from one of the stanzas chanted by the " ancientest of masters :"

> Bring hither the bowle,
> The brimming brown bowle,
> And quaff the rich juice right merrilie;
> Let the wine-cup go round
> Till the solid ground
> Shall quake at the noise of our revelrie.
> Let wassail and wine
> Their pleasures combine,
> While we quaff the rich juice right merrilie;
> Let us drink till we die,
> When the saints we relie
> Will mingle their songs with our revelrie.

The custom of drinking wassail in Scotland prevailed even into the early part of the nineteenth century. As the clock struck the knell of the departing year, it was accompanied by a cordial shaking of hands, and a decorous dance around the table, and the following song:

> Weel may we a' be;
> Ill may we never see.
> Here's to the King
> And the gude companie!

The elders of the family would then sally forth, bearing the hot bowl and a generous supply of buns and short-cake or bread and cheese, to interchange cordial greeting with their neighbors. So general was this custom that in Edinburgh the principal streets were more densely thronged between the hours of twelve and one A.M. than at mid-day.

An unlucky circumstance, however, on January 1, 1812, put an end to this national custom. A party of young ruffians decided to turn this custom of their elders to account for purposes of personal aggrandizement. No sooner had the thrifty well-meaning people come abroad with their refreshments than these rascals sallied forth in small bands and began their attack. Their previous agreement was to "strike for" the white neck-cloths, astutely reasoning that the highly respectable wearers of those immaculate cravats would be most likely to carry property worth the taking.

Wassailing the Orchards. An old English custom was that of wassailing the fruit-trees on Christmas Eve, New Year's, or Epiphany. Herrick says,—

> Wassail the trees, that they may beare
> You many a plum, and many a peare:
> For more or less fruits they will bring
> As you do give them wassailing.

This custom differed in date and in ceremonial detail according to the locality. In Devonshire and other cider counties the farmer with his family, his friends, and his servants would march out in the evening of Twelfth Night. One of the party bore a large pitcher filled with "cyder" and roasted apples hissing therein. The procession encircled the biggest and most productive tree, as a representative of the rest, and drank the following toast three times :

> Here's to thee, old apple-tree,
> Whence thou mayst bud, and then mayst blow!
> And whence thou mayst bear apples enow!
> Hats full! Caps full!
> Bushel, bushel, sacks full!
> And my pockets full, too, huzza!

They then sprinkled the tree with cider, or dashed a bowl of cider against it. In other places only the farmer and his servants assembled on the occasion, and after immersing cakes in cider hung them on the apple-trees. They then sprinkled the trees with cider, pronounced their incantation, and went home to feast.

In the western counties of England and some parts of Wales it is the regular practice to salute the apple-trees on Christmas morning. The inhabitants of a village turn out about seven o'clock, while it is yet dark, and gather at a rendezvous previously decided upon. There they are joined by the parson of the village church, the beadle, parish clerk, and school-master. A procession is then formed and marches around the adjacent district, visiting each large orchard in turn. On arriving at an orchard the people are received by the owner and admitted. Then they are conducted to one of the best trees, which is considered a representative of all the others in the orchard, and around it they gather. The beadle or a well-known man in the village produces a large bottle of cider and sprinkles the tree with the beverage. Meanwhile all the other people remain silent, and the officiating villager addresses the tree in a quaint fashion something like this :

" O tree! O tree! O tree! Bear fruit and flourish. Thy owner nourish. Give wealth and plenty."

The people repeat these words, and then, accompanied by the owner, the procession re-forms and marches to another orchard, where a like ceremony is performed. It is supposed that every plantation treated in this way will be a fruitful source of income to its owner during the coming year.

Horsfield in his "History of Sussex" tells us that in his time the wassailing or, as it is locally termed, the worsting of the fruit-trees is considered a matter of great importance there, and its omission is believed to bring ill-luck, if not the loss of the entire year's crop. Those who engage in the ceremony are called " howlers."

The farm-laborers or village boys assemble under the lead of a trumpeter equipped with a cow's horn. After gaining the owner's consent, which is rarely denied, they proceed to the orchard, and, encircling the representative tree, chant in a low voice some variant of the rhyme already quoted. This ended, the trumpeter blows a loud blast, and all shout in chorus. Then they go from tree to tree, rapping each with their sticks, and after wassailing the whole orchard return to the owner and sing at his door a song which obtains them admission. Ranging themselves around the kitchen fire, they are treated to ale and join in various in-door amusements.

In the neighborhood of the New Forest the following lines are sung at the wassailing of the trees :

> Apples and pears, with right good corn,
> Come in plenty to every one ;
> Eat and drink good cake and hot ale,
> Give earth to drink, and she'll not fail.

Analogous customs are found in many parts of Continental Europe. In Southern Germany during the Christmas season the table-cloths are shaken over the roots of the fruit-trees as an offering. A more ancient custom was for some one to go in a state of nudity at midnight on Christmas Eve and bind the fruit-trees with ropes of straw. In the Tyrol the fruit-trees are violently beaten with clubs and staves. A like custom prevails in Bohemia, where all of the household, at the hour of midnight on Christmas Eve, go about the orchard shaking the trees. In some agricultural sections, during the night preceding Christmas Day lighted torches are carried in procession through the orchards, and hymns are sung which contain prayers for a large harvest. In others the fruit-trees are regaled with the remains of the Christmas supper, to which they have been previously and specially invited.

These Teutonic customs all point to the mysterious influences attributed by the ancient Germans to the Twelve Nights as the origin of the wassailing customs.

Well-Dressing. A ceremony which still survives in England and is probably an adaptation to Christian usage of the ancient Roman Fontinalia, or annual flower-festival of the spirits of the streams and fountains. Derbyshire with the adjacent counties is the home of the custom. The most famous of all the well-dressings occurs at Tissington on Ascension Day. Derby and Wirksworth select Whitsuntide; Goulgrave, St. John's Day; Barton, the Thursday nearest to the latter date; Endon, in Staffordshire, Royal Oak Day.

The origin of the Tissington custom is popularly attributed to a great drought that occurred in 1615, when the people for miles around drove their cattle to drink at the five wells or springs of Tissington and a thanksgiving service was appointed for every succeeding Ascension Day. But the custom is probably far more ancient.

The five springs are rather fountains or cascades, the water descending from above, and not rising, as in a well. These are decorated for the occasion with flowers arranged in the most beautiful devices. Boards are cut into arches, pediments, pinnacles, and other ornamental forms, and are covered with moist clay to the thickness of about half an inch; the flowers are cut off their stems and impressed into the clay as closely together as possible, forming mottoes, borders, and other devices; these are then placed over the wells, and it is impossible to conceive a more beautiful appearance than they present, the water gurgling from beneath them, and overhung by the fine foliage of the numerous evergreens and forest trees by which they are surrounded. There is one particular variety of the double daisy, known to gardeners as the Tissington daisy, which appears almost peculiar to the place, and is in much repute for forming the letters of the texts and mottoes with which the wells are adorned. The day is observed as a complete holiday, and the festival attracts a considerable number of visitors from all the neighboring towns and villages. Divine service is performed in

the church, and on its conclusion the minister and congregation
join in procession and visit each well.

The three Psalms appointed for the day are read successively
at the first three wells, and a hymn is sung. The Epistle and
Gospel are read at the last two wells.

At Endon there are two wells, one very ancient and almost
dried up, the second comparatively modern, which supplies the
village with water. The proceedings are under the personal
guidance of the vicar of the parish, and at two o'clock a procession of school-children is formed at the new well. headed by a
band of music. The children wave flags vigorously, and the procession marches to the old parish church, where a solemn service
is held and the villagers attend in large numbers. Hymns and
psalms applicable to a thanksgiving service for water are sung,
and at the conclusion of the service the procession is re-formed
and marches back to the new well. Then the clergy and choir
walk slowly round the well, singing " Rock of Ages" and " A
living stream so crystal clear." The well is adorned, as at Tissington, with a large wooden framework erected in front of it,
covered with a surface of clay, and thickly studded with flowers
of every kind of hue. "O ye wells, bless the Lord!" was the
text that garnished the summit. Maypole dances, including the
crowning of the May Queen, occupy the greater part of the
afternoon, and in the evening the band plays for dancing, and
the Maypole dances are repeated. After dusk there is a display
of fireworks. (DITCHFIELD: *Old English Customs,* p. 187 ; DYER :
British Popular Customs, p. 211. See also *Chambers's Book of
Days,* vol. i. p. 595.)

Wells, Holy. Water-worship was an element of all primeval
faiths. It still survives in the superstitious reverence accorded
to wells and springs not only by Christians of the more primitive
type, but by Jews and Mohammedans, by savages and semi-
savages. The Pool of Bethesda and Zemzem (*q. v.*), the Holy
Well of Mecca, find their counterparts all over Europe and Asia,
and wherever the aboriginal races dominate in the New World.

Mr. Dorman, in his "Origin of Primitive Superstitions," tells
us how the tribes of Central America, Mexico, and New Mexico
had their sacred springs, and mentions the various sacrifices
offered to them. The Indians of Colorado regard springs that
bubble up from the ground with awe and reverence, and bring
their sick thither to be cured. The bubbling of the water is
supposed to be due to spirits breathing into it, the healing power
being ascribed to these supernatural agents. In New Mexico,
near the thirty-fifth parallel, Lieutenant Whipple found a spring
which from time immemorial " had been held sacred to the rain-

god." Some idea of the respect paid to this spring may be gathered from the fact that no animal may drink of its waters, and it must be annually cleansed "with ancient vases, which, having been transmitted from generation to generation by the caciques, are then placed on the walls, never to be removed." Dr. Bell also, in the *Ethnological Journal*, informs us that in New Mexico, not far from Zuñi, there is a sacred spring about eight feet in diameter, walled around with stones, of which neither man nor cattle may drink. Once a year the cacique and his attendants perform certain religious rites at this spring, offerings being presented to it.

Again, in the Deccan and in Ceylon, trees and bushes near springs and wells are of common occurrence, and may frequently be seen covered with votive offerings. Atkinson, in his "Oriental and Western Siberia," speaking of the Bouriats, informs us that they have their sacred lakes or wells. In one of his rambles, he says, "I came upon the small and picturesque lake of Ikeougoun, which lies in the mountains to the north of Sanghin-dalai and is held in veneration. They have erected a small wooden temple on the shore, and here they come to sacrifice, offering up milk, butter, and the fat of animals, which they burn on the little altars. The large rock in the lake is with them a sacred stone on which some rude figures are traced; and on the bank opposite they place rods with small silk flags having inscriptions printed on them." In Northern Asia, writes Sir John Lubbock, in his "Origin of Civilization," the Tunguses and Votyaks worship various springs; and in the tenth century a schism took place in Persia among the Armenians, one party being accused of despising the holy well of Vagarschiebat.

In Northern Europe almost every village has its sacred spring, and Danish folk-lore tells us of the traditionary origin of many of the wishing wells still regarded with so much superstitious reverence. Thus, near Harrested, in Seeland, is the far-famed St. Knud's Well, which is much visited by persons afflicted with bodily ailments, and also by those anxious to gain an insight into futurity,—it having suddenly gushed forth, runs the legend, on the spot where Duke Knud Lavard was treacherously murdered by the king's son Magnus, in the year 1129. In the same locality is Helen's Well, which has acquired a wide-spread celebrity on account of its miraculous virtues. On St. John's Day pilgrimages are made to it by the sick and crippled, many travelling from distant parts to visit it. According to one traditionary account, given by Thorpe in his "Northern Mythology," Helen was a Scanian princess, and much famed for her beauty. A king fell in love with her; and, as he could not win her affection, he resolved on violence. In her distress, Helen fled from place to place, pursued by the king; and when, on reaching the sea-shore, the king was about to seize her, she plunged into the deep. But she did not perish, for a large stone rose from the bottom of the ocean and received her, on which she floated over to Seeland. On the spot where she first set her foot there sprang forth a fountain, which still bears her name.

Sir John Lubbock also adds that in the Scotch islands are many sacred wells, and that he himself has seen the holy well in one of the islands completely surrounded by the little offerings of the peasantry, consisting principally of rags and halfpence. One may further quote the testimony of Mr. Campbell, who in his " Popular Tales of the West Highlands" writes thus: " Holy healing wells are common all over the Highlands, and the people still leave offerings of pins and nails and bits of rag, though few would confess it. There is a well in Islay where I myself have, after drinking, deposited copper caps among a hoard of pins and buttons and similar gear placed in chinks and trees at the edge of the Witches' Well. There is another well with similar offerings freshly placed beside it in Loch Maree." Among further illustrations, he informs us how a small well in the Black Isle of Cromarty has miraculous healing powers, and adds, " A country-woman tells me that about forty years ago she remembers it being surrounded by a crowd of people every first Tuesday in June, who bathed in and drank of it before sunrise. Each patient tied a string of rag to one of the trees that overhung it before leaving."

The same custom obtains at various holy wells in Ireland. Indeed, it survives in all countries where Roman Catholicism flourishes, which is not surprising when it is borne in mind that the Roman Church had a special prayer for blessing clouts used for the cure of diseases. At Wierre-Effroy, in France, where the water of St. Godeleine's Well is esteemed efficacious for ague, rheumatism, gout, and all affections of the limbs, a hetero-geneous collection of crutches, bandages, rolls of rag, and other rejected adjuncts of medical treatment is to be seen hanging upon the surrounding shrubs. These are intended as thank-offerings and testimonies of restoration. Other springs, famous for curing ophthalmia, abound in the same district; and here, too, bandages, shades, guards, and rags innumerable are ex-hibited.

The most famous of these sacred places in England are the wells at Tissington in Derbyshire (see WELL-DRESSING), and St. Winifred's well at Holywell.

Cornwall boasts of the well of St. Madron, near Penzance, and another at Gulval. The latter is thus described in Gilbert's " Parochial History of Cornwall:" " To this place numbers of people, time out of mind, have resorted for pleasure and profit of their health, as the credulous country-people do in these days, not only to drink the waters thereof, but to inquire after the life or death of their absent friends; where, being arrived, they demand the question at the well whether such a person by name be living, in health, sick, or dead. If the party be living and in health, the still quiet water of the well-pit, as soon as the question is put, will instantly bubble or boil up as a pot; but if it remain quiet it is an indication that the party is dead."

Throughout the British isles there are numerous holy wells where the passer-by has but to breathe a wish and drop a pin or other valueless offering into the water to obtain what he wants. Such is St. Helen's well, near Sefton, Lancashire, the bottom of which, says Mr. Hampson, in his " Medii Ævi Kalendarium," " I have frequently seen almost covered with pins, which must have been thrown in for this purpose." It seems that young ladies have still continued up to recent times to throw pins into this well, and to draw conclusions as to the fidelity of their lovers, the date of marriage, and so forth, from the turning of the pin to the north or any other point of the compass.

Wëpebôrt. (Ger., " Willow Wheel.") An apparatus that forms part of the rural German festivities on St. Sylvester's Day, or New Year's Eve. This consists of a wheel made of willow, in the centre of which there is a gilded ornament that flashes like a star. At the extremity of the spokes on the exterior of the rim there is a succession of spikes, upon which apples are stuck. Just after midnight the bearer throws it into the house of his lady-love, demanding a token in return. He then fires a pistol, and runs away at the top of his speed, pursued by the inmates of the house, who, if he is caught and brought back, compel him to drink *rothwasser* and ride astride of the pot-hanger.

Werburga, St., patron saint of Chester. Her festival is celebrated on the day of her death, February 3.

St. Werburga was the daughter of a king of Mercia, and flourished in the seventh century. She was abbess of Repandum, and founded many convents. She died in 708, and her body was interred at Hamburg. In the reign of King Alfred her remains were translated to Chester. The cathedral of Chester was dedicated to her in 800. Her relics were scattered in the reign of Henry VIII., but her shrine was converted into the episcopal throne of the cathedral. The monument is of stone, embellished with antique images of the kings of Mercia. Many miraculous cures and preservations of the city of Chester from assaults and fire are attributed to St. Werburga's intercessions. In 1180 a fire broke out which threatened to consume the city; but it is related that the shrine of the virgin was carried in procession, and that immediately the fire was extinguished.

Wheel. In many modern ceremonies which survive as relics of ancient paganism, a wheel itself or some rotary motion suggests solar symbolism. Grimm's "Teutonic Mythology" has shown a curious analogy between the very words sun and wheel. After explaining that the sun was likened to a wheel of fire and the element blazing out of him was represented in the shape of a wheel, he continues:

"The Gothic letter ☉ [= HV] is the very symbol of the sun, and plainly shows the shape of a wheel; we must therefore suppose it to have been the initial of a Goth. *hvil* = AS. *hweol*, ON. *hvël*. From 'hvel' was developed the Icel. *hiol*, Swed. Dan. *hjul*, O. Swed. *hiughl*; and from ' hweol, hweohl' the Engl. *wheel*, Nethl. *wiel*, and Fris. *fial*. In view of all these variations, some have even ventured to bring in the ON. *jol*, Swed. Dan. *jul* [Yule], the name of the winter solstice, and fasten upon it also the meaning of wheel; on that hypothesis the two forms must have parted company very early, supposing the Gothic name of November, *jiuleis*, to be cognate. The word *wheel* seems to be of the same root as *while*, Goth. *hveila*, OHG. *huîla*, *i.e.*, revolving time."

In many parts of Germany it is customary to wrap straw around an old cart-wheel, set it on fire, and send it rolling down a hill. Barrels are sometimes substituted. Elsewhere lighted torches are carried round in a sunwise movement (see PRADAK-SHINA). The burning of the Clavie (*q. v.*) is an analogous British custom, one of the few that have survived, though they were once very common in England and Scotland as well as Ireland. Originally it is more than probable that these ceremonies were part of the Midsummer rites (see JOHN THE BAPTIST, ST.), but when their solar origin had been forgotten they naturally attached themselves to the feasts of the principal local saints or other chief holidays. Thus, in Northern Germany Easter is generally the favored day, as St. John's Eve is in Southern. Germany also yields us examples of burning wheels on St. Michael's Day (September 29) and St. Martin's Day (November 11). On St. Peter's Day (February 22) the children in Westphalia are wont to go begging from door to door, and as they beg they turn an old wheel round and round.

Although the wheel figures also in the *fêtes* on French soil, there are no accounts of its being rolled down the side of a hill as in Germany. Still in both countries the ceremonies were supposed to be a propitiation of fortune. In Germany at several places along the Moselle, notably at Konz, if the wheel rolled down burning to the river an abundant vintage was expected. In France, in the former province of Poitou, a burning wheel is carried around the fields at midsummer in the expectation of securing a blessing on the crop. M. Gaidoz in " Le Dieu Gaulois du Soleil" quotes an old document which shows that burning wheels figured among the ceremonies at one time in Lorraine. The transaction took place in 1565 between Madame Iolande de Bassompierre, an abbess of Epinal, and the magistrates of that place, in which that lady transfers to the town a portion of the forest, so that in future she might be free from the obligation of furnishing " la roue de Fortune et la paille pour la former." As Epinal is near the German frontier, the celebration at that place would probably be the same as at Konz; and the two towns not being far distant from each other helps to confirm this suggestion. There is a further confirmation in the fact, which at the same time gives importance to these customs, that in both places the civic authorities took part in them. At the Konz ceremonies the maire of Sierk officiated, and received a basket of cherries, "according to ancient custom," for so doing. At Epinal it was the magistrates that entered into the negotiations with the abbess about the wheel and the straw, showing that they took some part in the affair as a public business. In Paris, at the bonfires on St. John's Day, the king attended and was an important actor in the rite. These details are evidence that the customs were no children's pastimes, but were serious performances.

Whitebait Banquet at Greenwich. Properly speaking, there is no such fish as whitebait. The popular *entrée* served at London or Blackwall dinners and which bears that name, and the similar dishes offered in American restaurants, consist of whatever mess of " fry" fishermen are able to catch. When first the attention of naturalists was turned to whitebait it was generally held to be the young of the shad, until it was proved that the shad is not common enough in English waters nor prolific enough to furnish forth the vast quantities of whitebait eaten in England. Then Yarrell, in 1828, proclaimed that the fish was a distinct member of the herring family, and baptized it *Clupea alba*. It is singular that it should not have occurred to so practical a naturalist as Yarrell to look for an example of *Clupea alba* containing eggs or milt, because every fish, no matter what its size, must spawn at some time. No one has ever seen an example of whitebait with spawn in it. Dr. Gunther's conclusion may be accepted that five-sixths of the fish which are served under the name of whitebait are the young of either the sprat or the herring.

It is sometimes asserted that whitebait was first brought to public notice in 1780 by one Richard Conner, a fisherman of Blackwall. But so far back as 1612, at the general feast of the founder of the Charterhouse, given on May 28 in Stationers' Hall, London, we read that among the delicacies were "six dishes of whitebait." It is even conjectured that the savory fry was not unknown to Henry VIII. and to Queen Elizabeth at their banquets in the palace of Greenwich. In the early part of this century Lovegrove's "Bait-Kitchen" at Blackwall was a favorite resort of Londoners. But whitebait is especially famous through the annual dinner of English cabinet ministers at Greenwich.

The history of the dinner is involved in some antiquarian doubt. But all accounts agree that it was originally celebrated at Dagenham, a village in Essex. On December 17, 1707, an extraordinarily high tide in the Thames broke down a part of the sea-wall that protected the neighboring marshes. About one thousand acres of land were flooded. After many unsuccessful efforts, the breach was closed in 1721. The land was all drained, save sixty acres, still known as Dagenham Breach, or Dagenham Lake, and constituting a large sheet of reedy water well stocked with pike, carp, roach, and eels. So important was deemed the maintenance of the restored embankment that a commission was appointed by Parliament to make a periodical inspection. This inspection, in course of time, became little more than an excuse for an annual holiday. The commissioners, mostly City magnates, with Sir Robert Preston, M.P. for Dover, as president, and some members of the Admiralty, went down in state just about the time when Parliament broke up in the autumn. After the official inspection, a dish of freshly caught whitebait was served up in the board-room,—the latter being situated in a building erected for the accommodation of the superintendents, close to the flood-gates, and usually known on the river as the Breach House. One year Prime Minister Pitt, who was always a great favorite with the City men, was invited by the commissioners to partake of their annual fish dinner. He was so highly pleased that next year some of his political colleagues and private friends were included in the invitation. And so every year the dinner became more sumptuous and acquired more and more the character of a ministerial banquet. Even after the inspection was given up Sir Robert Preston continued to send out the annual invitations until his death in 1834, when the dinner was transferred to Greenwich and became strictly ministerial.

Such is one account of the Whitebait Dinner. Another, equally circumstantial, differs somewhat in detail. According to this, Sir Robert Preston had a cottage on the banks of Dagenham Lake. He called it his fishing cottage, and often in the spring retired thither with a friend or two, to forget the cares of state and of business. His most frequent guest was George Rose, Secretary to the Treasury. One day Mr. Rose intimated to Sir Robert that Mr. Pitt, of whose friendship they were both justly proud, would no doubt much delight in the comfort of such a retreat. Sir Robert cordially accepted the suggestion. A day was named, and the Premier was accordingly invited, and received with great cordiality at the fishing cottage. He was so well pleased with his visit and the hospitality of the baronet —they were all considered two if not three bottle men—that, on taking leave, Mr. Pitt readily accepted an invitation for the following year, Sir Robert engaging to remind him at the proper time. For a few years, Mr. Pitt, accompanied by " Old George Rose," was a regular visitor at Dagenham Breach. But the distance was great for those days. Railways had not yet started into existence, and the going and coming were considered somewhat inconvenient.

But Sir Robert—hearty Briton as he was—was equal to the occasion. Why not dine near London? Greenwich was suggested as the new meeting-place, and the suggestion was accepted.

The party was now changed from a trio to a quartette, Mr. Pitt having requested to be allowed to bring Lord Camden. The ice thus broken, a fifth guest was soon added to the number,— namely, Mr. Long, afterwards Lord Farnborough. All still were the guests of Sir Robert Preston ; but, one by one, other men of position—all of the Tory school—were invited, until at last Lord Camden reasonably remarked that, as they were all dining at a tavern, it was only fair that Sir Robert should be released from the expense. It was then arranged that the dinner should be given as usual by Sir Robert Preston,—that is to say, at his invitation,—and he insisted on still contributing a buck and champagne ; but the remaining charges were to be defrayed by the other guests, and on this arrangement the dinners continued to be held annually till the death of Mr. Pitt. Sir Robert Preston was requested, in the following year, to summon the several guests, the list of whom by this time included most of the cabinet ministers. The time for meeting was usually after Trinity Monday, a short period before the end of the session.

Whatever the exact origin of the Whitebait banquets, they continued to flourish at Greenwich, whether Whig or Tory were the head of the feast, until 1870, when they were discontinued, but were revived by the Disraeli ministry in 1874.

Some of the corporations of London indulge in a similar

annual festivity, and the town council of Exeter likewise celebrates an annual dinner of which whitebait is the distinctive feature.

White Horse of Berkshire. A colossal representation of a galloping horse cut in outline on the side of a steep hill, known as White Horse Hill, near Great Faringdon, Berkshire. The cutting is done in the form of trenches eighteen feet wide and six deep hollowed out in the yellowish-white clay soil, but seen from a distance against the dark background of herbage the outlines appear to be delicately traced in chalk crayons. The figure is five hundred and ten feet long, the horse's ears alone measuring forty-five feet, and its eye six feet, and the space it occupies is about two acres. It can be seen at a distance of fifteen miles across country on a clear day.

No exact evidence can be adduced regarding the origin of this remarkable figure. Thomas Hughes, in his "Scouring of the White Horse" (1857), is inclined to accept the popular tradition that it was carved to commemorate the victory of King Ethelred and his brother Alfred, afterwards Alfred the Great, over the Danes at Ashdown, in the year 871. The actual site of this great battle is not known, and has been the subject of some discussion; but the balance of probability is in favor of its having been fought in the neighborhood of White Horse Hill, on the summit of which, at the height of eight hundred and ninety-three feet above the sea, is an ancient encampment, consisting of a plain of more than eight acres in extent, surrounded by a rampart and ditch. This enclosure is called Uffington Castle, and immediately beneath it is the stupendous engraving of the White Horse.

Once every three years in September the peasantry used to assemble and carefully remove any of the turf that had encroached upon the figure, a ceremony known as "Scouring the White Horse." Since Mr. Hughes renewed attention to both the Horse and the ceremony, the latter has occurred every year. These meetings form a sort of rural carnival to the people for fifty miles around. After the trenches have been carefully cleaned and scoured, the participants engage in rustic and athletic games of various kinds, and prizes are distributed to the most successful. The festival lasts for two days, and, according to immemorial usage, the lord of the manor entertains the participants at his own expense.

White Thursday. (Welsh, *Jeu-nhydn.*) In Cornwall this was the name given to the last Thursday that was one clear week before Christmas Day. According to tradition, this was the annual recurrence of the period when black tin or ore was first melted or turned into white tin or metal in these parts. Hence until quite recently the tinners claimed a holiday on this day.

Whit Monday or **Whitsun Monday.** The day after Whit-sunday. It is now one of the English Bank holidays (*q. v.*) which owe their being to the efforts of Sir John Lubbock. This and Whitsun Tuesday were anciently semi-holidays in England.

Southey, in his "Common-Place Book" (1849, Second Series, p. 336), gives the following extract from Mrs. Fienne's MSS.:

"At Lichfield they have a custom at Whitsuntide, ye Monday and Tuesday, called the Green Bower Feast, by which they hold their charter. The bailiff and sheriff assist at the ceremony of dressing up babies with garlands of flowers and greens, and carry them in procession through all the streets, and then assemble themselves at the market-place, and so go in a solemn procession through the great street to a hill beyond the town, where is a large green bower made, in which they have their feast. Many smaller bowers are made around for company, and for booths to sell fruits, sweetmeats, gingerbread," etc.

In Lancashire the Whitsun fairs were held on Whit Monday, and Hiring Fairs (*q. v.*) are still kept up in this county and else-where. At Hinckley in the same county until the beginning of the nineteenth century the custom was kept up of millers riding in procession dressed in ribbons, with what they called the King of the Millers at their head.

A writer (in 1787) describing one of these fairs says, To the old ceremony of riding millers, many improvements were made upon a more extensive and significant plan,—several personages introduced that bore allusions to the manufacture and were con-nected with the place. Old Hugo Baron de Grentemaisnel, who made his first appearance in 1786, armed in light and easy paste-board armor, was this second time armed cap-a-pie in heavy sinker plate, with pike and shield, on the latter the arms of the town. The representative baron of Hinckley had the satisfac-tion of being accompanied by his lady, the Baroness Adeliza, habited in the true antique style, with steeple hat, ruff-points, mantle, etc., all in suitable colors, each riding on nimble white steeds properly caparisoned; they were preceded by the town banner, and two red streamers embroidered with their respective names. Several bands of music gave a cheerful spirit to the pageant, but more particularly the militia band from Leicester. The framework knitters, wool-combers, butchers, carpenters, etc., had each their plays, and rode in companies bearing devices or allusions to their different trades. Two characters well supported were Bishop Blaise and his chaplain, who figured at the head of the wool-combers. In their train appeared a pretty innocent young pair, a gentle shepherd and shepherdess, the latter carrying a lamb, the emblem of her little self more than of the trade. Some other little folks, well dressed, were mounted on ponies, holding instruments the marks of their fathers' businesses, and ornamented with ribbons of all colors waving in the air. (See NICHOLS : *History of Hinckley*, 1813, p. 678.)

A correspondent of the *Gentleman's Magazine* (1783, vol. liii. p. 578) says there seems to be a trace of the descent of the Holy Ghost on the heads of the apostles in what passes at Whitsuntide Fair in some parts of Lancashire, where one person holds a stick over the head of another, whilst a third, unperceived, strikes the stick, and thus gives a smart blow to the first.

The *London Graphic* for May 19, 1894, thus describes the Whit Monday bank holiday of that year : " London was a wonderful sight. Every place with a pretence to providing entertainment was full, and yet all day long people seemed to be getting somewhere. Every omnibus was full on top ; the parks, but for the absence of banners, might have been the scene of demonstrations in favor of more Whit Mondays, and every restaurant made hay while the sun shone or the money lasted. Even the museums—those curious places in which to seek amusement—kept their turnstiles moving all day long, and the National Gallery held quite a reception. But this ability to be easily amused is one of the pleasantest and perhaps it is also one of the most pathetic sights of London taking a holiday. Go where you would on Monday, there you would see people upon whom 'toil had left a furrowed trace on every feature of their face,' sitting down in the sun and doing nothing but ' doing nothing.' Sometimes they carried babies, venerable-looking little creatures who had yet to learn the difference between Bank Holidays and other days ; and sometimes they eat fragments of stodgy-looking lunch out of baskets or pieces of newspaper. But mostly they simply sat there, perhaps beating time to the tune of any band within hearing, or perhaps vaguely conscious that it was a very pleasant thing to have, for once in a way, nothing much to bother them. In the places just outside London—Greenwich, Richmond and the River, Happy Hampton and Chingford—the people saw the country as sweet as English spring could make it. Besides, the entrepreneurs had provided special entertainments for Monday's visitors. In Epping Forest, as on Hampstead Heath, the donkeys had been for weeks in training, and for days before the proprietors of ' Aunt Sally' and other games of skill had been selecting carefully deceptive places in which to set up this form of amusement. Their ingenuity met with an abundant reward during the latter part of Monday, and all day long in the cocoa-nut groves of Epping Forest natives might have been seen gathering fruit. At Hampton Court the boat-builders had prepared for the occasion by putting up their prices, a precaution for which they will not be very much blamed by those who have been privileged to observe the experimental methods by which the Bank holiday waterman propels his craft ; and at Greenwich, where the amusements are not so varied, consisting mainly of rolling down Greenwich Hill and comparing watches with the Observatory clock, the restaurateurs of the neighborhood had risen to the occasion by providing unusual quantities of ' tea and s'rimps.'

" In the great places of entertainment—the emporiums of amusement we might almost call them—a new era has set in, an era which began with the tropical summer of last year and to which a day like Whit Monday was eminently favorable: the era of the cigarette and the small table. Earl's Court was perhaps the first to begin it ; the Crystal Palace has been the latest to adopt it. It arose from the disposition, which Earl's Court was the first to discover, of the public to enjoy itself after the Continental fashion,—which is to sit at a small table in company with a cigarette and coffee and the music of a first-class band. If the first-class band can first accompany a first-class dinner at a reasonable price, so much the better, but the small table and the music and the illuminations, and the presence of hundreds of other couples enjoying them in the same way as ourselves, these are the essentials."

On Whitsun Monday a curious sight was formerly to be seen in St. Petersburg. Mothers belonging to the merchant class arrayed their marriageable daughters in their best attire, hung about their necks the jewelry and silver-ware which formed a part of their dowry, and took them to the Summer Garden to be inspected and proposed for by the young men.

Whitsunday, or **Pentecost.** An annual feast of the Eastern and Western Churches instituted in commemoration of the day upon which the Holy Ghost descended upon the apostles and when the three thousand were baptized. It occurs exactly fifty days after Easter Sunday. The entire fifty days, known as Whitsuntide or Pentecost, was an especial season in the early Church for the administration of adult baptism. On Whitsunday the catechumens, and those who had been baptized in the course of the season, presented themselves in *albs*, or white garments. Hence the name Whit- or White-Sunday. Another etymon is suggested in a poem of the fourteenth century, which assumes that *whit* is a corruption of wit or wisdom :

> This day Whitsonday is cald,
> For wisdome and wit sevenfald
> Was goven to the Apostles on this day.

Pentecost means "fiftieth." The feast was alternatively so called because the first Whitsunday occurred on the Jewish Pentecost, or Shebuoth (*q. v.*), which is exactly fifty days after Passover. Hence the Christian Pentecost bears the same numerical relation to Easter that the Jewish Pentecost does to the Passover.

Whitsunday was kept as a Christian festival from very early times. It is mentioned by Origen and in the canons of the Council of Elvira (A.D. 306). Benedict XIV. mentions many customs which formerly prevailed on this day in some places, as the blessing of the candle, the blowing of trumpets at the "Veni, Sancte Spiritus" in the Whitsunday mass, the discharge of fire from the roof, the letting doves loose in the church, and the scattering of roses. Doves are a symbol of the Holy Ghost : hence they frequently reappear in the popular customs associated with the day. In Holland, according to Picart, children used to go to church with doves in their hands. Naogeorgus has these lines :

> On Whitsunday whyte pigeons tame in strings from heaven flie,
> And one that framed is of wood still hangeth in the skie.
> Thou seest how they with idols play, and teache the people too,
> None otherwise than little gyrls with puppets used to do.

The allusion here is to the dramatization of the descent of the Holy Ghost which was common both in Germany and in England in Roman Catholic times. Lambarde says that "when a child he saw in St. Paul's the descent of the Holy Spirit performed by a white pigeon let fly out of a hole in the midst of the roof of the great aisle, with a long censer, which, descending from the same place almost to the ground, was swung up and down at such length that it reached with one sweep almost to the west gate of the church, and with the other to the choir stairs, breathing out over the whole multitude a most pleasant perfume."

A Puritan writer mentions as an historical fact that in 1640, on Whitsunday, in Cornwall, during service the church was struck by lightning, there being an awful storm, and that many were injured, which he regarded as a "fearfull judgment" upon ceremonies. But these "judgments" do not seem to have been general. Fosbroke remarks that Whitsunday was formerly "celebrated in Spain with representations of the gift of the Holy Ghost and of thunder from engines which did much damage. Wafers or cakes, preceded by water, oak leaves, or burning torches, were thrown down from the roof of the church ; small birds with cakes tied to their legs, and pigeons, were let loose; sometimes there were tame ones tied with strings, or one of wood, suspended."

Similar scenes used also to be enacted in Ireland. The Irish often kept the feast with milk, like the Hebrews, and with cakes and bread made with hot water and wheaten bran. Whitsun ales (see ALES) were long in vogue in England.

In Rome Whitsunday is celebrated with great effect, like all the other leading feasts of the Church. The ceremonies are chiefly religious.

Whitsuntide was also noted once for the ceremony of font-hallowing. This was done in anticipation of the christenings which were to take place. The following is from Strutt's "Manners and Customs," iii. 174: "Among many various ceremonies, I find that they had one called the 'Font hallowing,' which was performed on Easter Even and Whitsunday Eve; and, says the author of a volume of Homilies in Harl. MS. 2371, 'in the begynnyng of holy chirch, all the children weren kept to be crystened on thys even, at the Font hallowyng; but now, for enchesone that in so long abydynge they might dye without chrystendome, therefore holi chirch ordeyneth to crysten at all tymes of the yeare; save eyght dayes before these Evenys, the chylde shalle abyde till the Font hallowing, if it may savely for perrill of death, and ells not.'" It was usual also in some places to strew the church floors with grass, and everywhere to give alms to the poor.

A superstitious notion appears anciently to have prevailed in England, that "whatsoever one did ask of God upon Whitsunday morning at the instant when the sun arose and play'd, God would grant it him." See Arise Evans's "Echo to the Voice from Heaven; or, A Narration of his Life," 1652, p. 9. He says "he went up a hill to see the sun rise betimes on Whitsunday morning," and saw it at its rising "skip, play, dance, and turn about like a wheel."

Whitsuntide in England was long a semi-holiday season, especially among the young folk, who used to indulge in various games and amusements. Drop-handkerchief was played in Greenwich Park as late as 1825. Many marriages in humble life have had their origin in the games of this season. The gayeties were continued through Whit Monday and Whit Tuesday, and were all of a similar character.

In the Kennet Valley, near Newbury, Whitsuntide is the great village holiday. Decked out in their best clothes, adorned with ribbons and banners, the men parade the lanes preceded by a band, and march to the church, where a special service is held.

Then they adjourn to a barn and have dinner, and later in the day go to one or two of the principal houses in the neighborhood, where dancing takes place on the lawn or drives, while the band plays vigorously. " Village sports, running, and racing are not uncommon at these club feasts, and at Brindle, near Preston, Lancashire, we have seen a most graceful company of morris-dancers, consisting of about sixteen young men, dressed in tight-fitting purple knickerbockers and stockings, with football 'sweaters' of the same color. They had staves in their hands, and danced up the village street, striking their staves together in rhythmic time, while a band played stirring melodies. It was a graceful and pleasing spectacle, and may still be seen in the neighborhood of Preston and Chorley." (DITCHFIELD : *Old English Customs*, p. 128.)

The Irish peasants believe that on a particular day at Whitsuntide all those who have been drowned in the sea come up and ride over the waves on white horses and hold strange revels. A fisherman who remained on the water on the night of this ghastly pageant saw a crowd of the dead on white horses making their way towards him. Their faces were pale with the hue of death, and their eyes burned with fire. They stretched out thin long arms to lay hold on him, but he managed to escape from their fearful grasp. As he landed, however, one of the horsemen rode close to him, and he saw the face of a friend who had been drowned the year before, and heard a voice calling to him to escape. Accordingly he fled at full speed, never daring to look back to see whether he was pursued.

A mild variation of the Feast of Fools (*q. v.*) was in ancient times performed on Whitsunday in Châlons-sur-Saône and other French cities. This was known as the Dance of the Canons. Immediately after complines the dean, the canons, and the minor priests went in procession from the church to the refectory or other large room in the monastery. There, holding on to the ends of one another's surplices, two by two they made the circuit of the apartment, chanting the responses of the feast. Though the pastime was an innocent one, it shared the general condemnation of the Church against the Feast of Fools, and was finally abolished through the efforts of Cyrus de Thiard, Bishop of Châlons-sur-Saône.

At Whitsuntide the Servians celebrate the Feast of the Kralitze, or Queen. The young girls assemble ; one represents the standard-bearer, another the king, and a third the queen herself, who, her face veiled, and attended by a maid of honor, stops to dance and sing before each house in the village. The subject of these songs is generally marriage, the choice of a husband, the happiness of married life, or the cares of maternity.

At the end of each stanza they repeat the refrain "Lelio," the name of the divinity who presided over love among the ancient Slavs, and who seems to be the same as the Lado of the Russians and the Selum of the Poles.

They also repeat in procession symbolical chants in honor of the Vila, or nymphs of the forest, whom they represent as dancing under the trees where the fruit is ripening; or of the Radischa (elves), who delight in shaking the dew from the flowers and leaves, and who, pursuing some nymph, try to entice her into the shade of the forest by the promise that she shall there, by her mother's side, spin precious silk with a golden distaff.

On Whitsunday the churches in Russia are decorated with birch-tree boughs, and young birch-trees are stood up in every corner, brought thither by the peasantry. The tradition is that one must shed as many tears for his sins as there are dew-drops on the birch bough which he carries if he have no flowers. In spite of a recent law which forbids the destruction of young trees, this Pentecostal custom is winked at by the authorities. But the well-to-do classes, and indeed many poor people who make a special effort, bring a bouquet of flowers with them to church. Every one is clad in white or light colors, as at Easter, even those who are in mourning having donned the bluish-gray which serves them for festive garb.

DUTCH CHILDREN'S WHITSUNDAY FESTIVAL.

In Naples the festival of Monte Vergine begins on Whitsunday and lasts for three days. The central feature is the pilgrimage to a church on Monte Vergine, near Avellino. This being a day's journey from Naples, all sorts of vehicles are called into requisition, which on the return journey are decorated with flowers and boughs of trees. A donkey and a bullock, gayly bedecked with ribbons, frequently form the driving-team. Numerous bands of merrymakers bearing sticks with flowers and pictures of the Madonna dance untiringly alongside.

But it is in Holland that Whitsuntide, under the name of

Pinkster (*q. v.*), is most ceremoniously observed. Sunday, Monday, and Tuesday exceed even the Christmas season in importance. Processions of children carrying doves in their hands appear in all the streets. Formerly it was also the custom for maidens in cities and villages to bear one of their number on a plank upon their shoulders and collect offerings of money from the passers-by in the streets or the dwellers in the houses.

Whit or **Whitsun Tuesday.** The Tuesday after Whitsunday. Formerly the Whitsun festivities were kept up until this day in England, as they still are in many Catholic countries. The Eton Montem originally held on Innocents' Day was later transferred to Whit Tuesday.

For a long time in England Whit Monday and Whit Tuesday were reproductions of May-Day, except in the matter of marriage, for it was deemed unlucky to marry in May, while it was considered fortunate to marry during Whitsuntide. But the revelries were reproduced. Thus, poles were erected and adorned with flowers and flags, and merry meetings were held around them with games and dances. Even clubs were instituted for the maintenance of these amusements. At Necton, Norfolk, his seat, a Major Mason established a guild for rural sports upon these days.

William, St., patron of Bruges. His festival is celebrated on January 10, the anniversary of his death. William Berruyer was born in the twelfth century of an illustrious family, and was educated by his uncle, Peter the Hermit, Archdeacon of Soissons. He was made canon of Soissons and afterwards of Paris. He entered the Cistercian order, and was made abbot of Challis. In the year 1200 he was consecrated Archbishop of Bruges. He was about to start on a mission among the Albigenses when he died on January 10, 1209. His body was interred in his cathedral, and his relics were preserved until 1562, when they were burnt by the Huguenots. A bone of his arm is shown at Challis, and a rib in the College of Navarre at Paris. The saint was canonized by Pope Honorius III. in 1218.

In art St. William is represented holding a monstrance, or in adoration before one, to show his great devotion towards the host. He is also represented with tears on his cheeks, for he is said to have wept whenever he heard of some scandal in his diocese or some oppression of the poor.

Willibrod, St., Dancing Festival of. An annual ceremony performed on the first Tuesday after Whitsunday at Echternach, a small village near Treves, in the grand duchy of Luxemburg.

St. Willibrod, who lived in the seventh century, was to the Netherlands and the Flemish and Lower Countries what St. Patrick was to Ireland. He carried thither the Christian faith, and finally, after a lifetime of missionary work, sought rest for his last days in Echternach, where he founded an abbey. Tradition says that his return to the village was celebrated by the sacred dances which are renewed every year. Only during the French Revolution was the custom interrupted. The festival now attracts thousands of pilgrims from the neighboring provinces, as well as curious spectators from all parts of the world. Most of the former come on foot, camping wherever they can in the open air or in barns. Those who are musical bring their instruments with them. In the morning all this crowd form themselves on the German territory beyond the bridge across the Sure, which is the river frontier between Germany and the grand duchy. A priest, who must be a native of Echternach, makes a short address and then places himself at the head of the pilgrims and leads the procession across the bridge to the old church. The advance guard sing the litany of the saint in a calm, dignified, religious tone which strangely contrasts with the clamors of the thousand instruments and the extraordinary dances in the rear. These are nothing but repeated jumps. The higher the jump the greater the evidence of devotion. Arriving at the old church, the priests bless the many articles which the pilgrims wish to place under the saint's patronage. Mass is celebrated, everybody partakes of communion, and the pilgrims spend the rest of the day in the streets of the village, where a fête something like the Flemish Kermesse is celebrated.

Wilmington Giant. A rude figure of a man, colossal in proportions, cut in outline on a hill of the South Downs, near Wilmington, Surrey, England, the slope being so steep that the figure appears almost upright, and by its size and altitude brings to mind the Colossus of Rhodes.

Until recently, few comparatively were aware of its existence, for it had been so nearly obliterated by the turf that it required a peculiar light to be easily traced; and those who looked on the "Long Man," as it was locally called, were not likely to recognize the interest of the inquiry which it had the power to awaken. At length the figure became known as the Wilmington Giant, and as such it has undergone some restoration. The Giant is two hundred and forty feet in length, while the head is above twenty-one feet in diameter. In each of the outstretched arms is a club or staff.

These clubs are sometimes supposed to have a gnomonic character,—that is, they may indicate the hours of the day, according to the shadows that are thrown upon the surface. At noon the sun is exactly over the Giant's head, and the whole figure is then seen in its restored outline; while the most casual observer can easily trace by the shadows, as they lessen or deepen in tone, the hours before or after noon. If the whole surface were kept clean, as is the case with the White Horse of Berkshire (*q. v.*), this power would be intensified; realizing which, we are the better able to understand the part it would play in regulating and directing the movements of the ancient Britons. It has indeed been calculated that, with the chalk fully exposed to view, it could have been used as a day-signal and made the means of communicating over a vast area.

WILMINGTON GIANT.

Another suggestion is worth considering. Cæsar in his notice of the painted savages whom he found at his first landing in Britain refe ʼs to their habits and religious ceremonies, wherein sacrificial rites had a prominent place. "They have," he says, "figures of a vast size, the limbs of which are formed of osiers; they fill these with living men, which being set on fire, the men perish in the flames." This terse and simple statement appears to have been the foundation for the belief that wicker-work idols of the human form were the recognized deities of the Britons. This idea has been introduced into ballad literature and popularized by pictorial illustrations. But recent researches have made plausible the belief that on sacrificial days such figures as the Wilmington Giant and the White Horse of Berkshire had hurdles of osiers placed around them as enclosures. The whole district over which the Giant towered was formerly occupied by an enormous wood, sacred to two deities known as Andred and Andras,—in other words, the powers of nature; and probably there is some connecting link between the remaining monument and the departed forest-like feature of the country.

Winifred, St. A noble British maiden of the seventh century. Repulsing the dishonorable advances of a certain Prince

Cradocus, he cut off her head, and was straightway swallowed up by the earth. As to his victim, her head rolled down the hill, and where it stopped a miraculous spring or well gushed forth. St. Beuno picked it up and skilfully reunited it to the body, after which St. Winifred lived a life of sanctity for fifteen years. Her festival is celebrated on November 3.

St. Winifred's miraculous well is still extant in Holywell, Flintshire, and is the most famous of all the holy wells in the United Kingdom, but the statues of the Virgin Mary and of St. Winifred herself which decorated it seem to have disappeared with the Reformation.

Even up to the seventeenth century the well was a constant resort for the sick and the devout, both Catholic and Protestant. Pennant found the roof of the vault hung with the crutches of grateful cripples. But he says that the number of pilgrims had much decreased in his day : " In the summer still a few are to be seen in the water, in deep devotion, up to their chins for hours, sending up their prayers, or performing a number of evolutions round the polygonal well, or threading the arches a prescribed number of times."

The fountain is enshrined within a perpendicular Gothic building. The enormous quantity of water that bubbles up (one hundred tons a minute), the coloring of the stones by the red moss, attributed to the blood of the saint, the singular fact that, although intensely cold, the water never freezes, are all features worth notice in themselves.

M. de Montalembert has a pleasant passage about this well : " At the spot where the head of this martyr of modesty struck the soil, there sprung up an abundant fountain, which is still frequented and even venerated by a population divided into twenty different sects, but animated by one common hatred for Catholic truth. This fountain has given its name to the town of Holywell. Its source is covered by a fine Gothic porch of three arches, under which it forms a vast basin, where from morning to evening the sick and infirm of a region ravaged by heresy come to bathe, with a strange confidence in the miraculous virtue of these icy waters." Some two or three years ago, however, the well passed into the hands of the Jesuits.

A writer in *The Senate* gives this account of Holywell and its pilgrims as he saw them under the new conditions in 1895 :

"The flooring of the chapel is damp with the water, the prayers echo with a hollow mournful sound in the chill air of the autumn ; the very water we know flows away, a force carefully stored, to turn some flannel-works at the bottom of the hill ; but over all a sentiment of fervor, a wonderful warmth of faith, a desire to be healed and to live, with the unspoken acknowledgment of weakness and sin alone in the way, give to the place a strange personality, growing upon one curiously as one watches the poor thin white figures slip into the green water, the fingers that take tremblingly the iron rails and for a moment are endowed with wonderful strength to retain their hold, the quick-moving lips that mutter prayers alone to be heard in the silence; these are the things that seize for a moment upon one, for they are, and have always been, the working machinery of miracles.

"It is amazing what the priests have done for the place, how well they have understood the possibilities of their new acquirement. Twenty years ago the name was scarcely known or unregarded, a few cases of cures there are on record, a few stray visitors in the summer-time of the year, but now almost throughout the whole year the gates are open, prayers and hymns are chanted, while in the warmer days excursions bring hundreds of sufferers up the steep hill in conveyances, and some there are of them who have finished the ascent to the town, walking alone, who had not looked to walk again. There are many besides who go for a pilgrimage. Two bicycles leaned prosaically outside against the outer wall of the chapel. Inside, their owners, shivering in the cold waters, muttered quickly their devotions, kissed, standing in the water of the inner well, the stone now smooth with many lips, and finished by plunging into the water head first. Afterwards I watched them slowly wheel their bicycles down the hill. The bicycles looked strangely prosaic, with their fat, vulgar pneumatic tires. It was incomprehensible as a dream. It was above all essentially Roman Catholic.

"As to the miracles, are they real?

"Yes, I think so: false miracles do not pay; and there are every year cases of semi-paralysis and nervous disorders cured upon dipping in the icy waters. I had myself the pleasure of conversing with a little child cured by the waters, as she told me, of hip-disease. She was certainly able to walk up the hill with a gait that showed but small traces of her former malady; and I can believe there are several who have received temporary benefit, and not a few who have been more permanently restored to natural vigor and use of limb, by the power of faith developing a state of auto-suggestion, the groundwork and basis of all curative miracles."

Wren, Hunting the. A custom which survives locally in the Isle of Man, in Essex County, England, and in Ireland, though the Society for the Prevention of Cruelty to Animals has stamped out its general observance. It consisted in killing wrens with stones and carrying them about on furze bushes from house to house. It sometimes occurred on Christmas or on New Year, but most frequently on St. Stephen's Day. Hence a connection has been fancied between it and the stoning of the martyr. An Irish legend is to the effect that one of St. Stephen's guards was awakened by a wren just as the prisoner was about to escape. The popular Manx legend, however, explains that once there lived on the island a beautiful elf or lorelei, who by her charms and songs lured many of the young men into the sea, where the waves, rising at her spell, swept them away to death. At last the people rose in a rage and attacked the sorceress, who fled in fear, and, being close pressed, took the form of a wren and so escaped. But from a higher power a decree went forth that every year on St. Stephen's Day she must appear as a wren, until it should come to pass that she perish by man's hand. For this reason the people of the Isle of Man devoted the hours between sunrise and sunset to the effort of extirpating the fairy. All wrens that showed themselves on this fatal day were pursued, pelted, fired at, and destroyed without mercy. Their feathers were preserved by fishermen as a preventive from death by shipwreck. When the chase ceased, one of the little victims was affixed to the top of a long pole with its wings extended, and carried in front of the hunters, who marched in procession to every house, chanting the following rhyme:

> We hunted the wren for Robin the Bobbin,
> We hunted the wren for Jack of the Can,
> We hunted the wren for Robin the Bobbin,
> We hunted the wren for every one.

After making the usual circuit and collecting all the money they could obtain, they laid the wren on a bier and carried it in procession to the parish churchyard, where, with a whimsical kind of solemnity, they made a grave, buried it, and sang dirges over it in the Manx language, which they called its knell. After the obsequies were performed, the company, outside the churchyard wall, formed a circle and danced to music which they had provided for the occasion.

At present the custom is followed only by boys, who are satisfied with a far less promiscuous slaughter. A "bush," consisting of two hoops crossed, sometimes with a wren suspended by the legs in the centre, and sometimes minus the bird, is carried around to the singing of the quatrain already quoted. They collect money, and in return present each donor with a feather, which is supposed to avert the danger of shipwreck. Afterwards the bird is buried on the sea-shore (no longer in the churchyard) with much solemnity.

In Ireland groups of young villagers used to bear about a holly-bush adorned with ribbons and having many wrens depending from it. "This is carried from house to house with some ceremony, the 'wren-boys' chanting several verses, the burthen of which may be collected from the following lines of their song :

> "The wren, the wren, the king of all birds,
> St. Stephen's Day was caught in the furze.
> Although he is little, his family's great,
> I pray you, good landlady, give us a treat.

> "My box would speak if it had but a tongue,
> And two or three shillings would do it no wrong ;
> Sing holly, sing ivy—sing ivy, sing holly,
> A drop just to drink, it would drown melancholy.

> "And if you draw it of the best,
> I hope in heaven your soul may rest ;
> But if you draw it of the small,
> It won't agree with the wren boys at all ; etc.

A small piece of money is usually bestowed on them, and the evening concludes in merrymaking with the money thus collected." (CROKER : *Researches in the South of Ireland*, 1824, p. 233.)

Ditchfield in "Old English Customs," p. 32, informs us that a wren-box was sold at Christie's a few years ago which used to be carried in procession in some parts of Wales on St. Stephen's Day. It is about seven inches square, and has a glass window at one end. Into this box a wren was placed, and it was hoisted on two long poles and carried round the town by four strong men, who affected to find the burden heavy. Stopping at intervals, they sang,—

> "Oh, where are you going?" says milder to melder ;
> "Oh, where are you going?" says the younger to the elder.
> "Oh, I cannot tell," says Festel to Fose ;
> "We're going to the woods," says John the Red Nose.
> We're going, etc.

> "Oh, what will you do there?" says milder to melder ;
> "Oh, what will you do there?" says the younger to the elder.
> "Oh, I do not know," says Festel to Fose ;
> "To shoot the cutty wren," says John the Red Nose.
> To shoot, etc.

And so on for eight more verses, taking the form of question and answer, as in the ballad of "Cock Robin," and describing the method of shooting the wren, cutting it up, and finally boiling it.

Y.

Yeomen of the Guard, familiarly known as **Beef-Eaters.**
A corps organized by Henry VII. for his own protection on the
day of his coronation, October 30, 1485, which has served as a
body-guard of the English sovereign ever since. In the reign
of Henry VIII. there were two hundred of them, half of whom
were mounted. In that reign they acquired the name of Beef-
eaters,—a name generally supposed to be a corruption of *buffe-
tiers,* but the etymology is doubtful, as the Yeomen never had
charge of the royal buffet or sideboard. Preston ("History of
the Yeomen of the Guard," 1885) suggests that they may have
received their name from a bird called beef-eater, whose strong
thick bill bore some resemblance to their partisans. Indeed,
the Yeomen were often referred to as "billmen" because they
carried a weapon with a hook like the beak or bill of a bird.

At the Restoration their number was reduced to one hundred.
The corps was reorganized in 1861, purchases of officers' commissions abolished, and future vacancies directed to be given to
officers of the army of long and good service. The captain is
always a peer, and goes out with each ministry; the lieutenant
must be, or have been, a colonel or lieutenant-colonel in the
army; the ensign and clerk of the cheque, lieutenant-colonels
or majors; the exons, or exempts, captains; and the privates,
non-commissioned officers not below the rank of sergeant.

The "Yeomen Warders of the Tower," whose duty it is to
keep watch over the historic Tower of London, are honorary
members of the Yeomen of the Guard. They are appointed,
forty in number, by the constable, and are recruited from the
retired non-commissioned officers of the army.

The ceremony of closing the Tower gates every night is full
of antique quaintness. A few minutes before the clock strikes
the hour of eleven—on Tuesdays and Fridays, twelve—the Head
Warden or Yeoman Porter appears at the Main Guard and applies for the "Escort for the Keys." This consists of a party
of six privates, commanded by a sergeant, who accompany the
porter to the outer gate and assist him to close it. Having
locked both the gate and the wicket, the Yeoman Porter returns, bearing the keys, and followed by the escort. As he
passes the sentries, on his way back to the Main Guard, each of
them challenges, and in reply to "Who goes there?" is answered,
"The keys." The sentry rejoins, "What keys?" to which the
reply is given, "The Queen's keys," and the escort passes on till
it arrives at the Main Guard, which now turns out, and after the

same questions and answers as to the "keys" and what keys they are, the officer opens the ranks, and presents arms to "the Queen's keys," which are then carried by the Yeoman Porter to the Governor's house and placed in his office. All this ceremony and precaution may seem superfluous, but it is a remarkable fact, and not less so from the late Duke of Wellington having caused much inquiry to be made on the subject, at the Home Office and elsewhere, that there has never been any riot or serious disturbance in London without some plan being laid by the ringleaders for the attack and seizure of the Tower.

An annual inspection of the Yeomen of the Guard is held in the gardens of St. James's Palace on June 14. The friends and relatives of the Yeomen, as well as persons of distinction, are privileged to be present. Here is the *Daily Graphic's* account of the inspection of 1895 : "Field-Marshal Sir Donald Stewart was received on his arrival at midday by Lord Kensington, captain of the Yeomen of the Guard, and was conducted to the parade ground. Sir Donald Stewart's inspection of the men was one which was more than merely formal, for as he made his way down the lines there was not one of the veterans with whom he did not stop for a moment to ask a

ANNUAL INSPECTION OF THE YEOMEN.

question, to examine a medal, or to pay a kindly compliment. When the inspection was over the old soldiers were drawn up in square, and were addressed in a few well-chosen soldierly words by the Field-Marshal. They were the flower of the British army, he told them ; and he hoped that their long and brilliant services to their country would be an incentive to young men of the present day to follow their example."

Yom Kippur (Heb., "The Day of Atonement"), also known as a day of prayer and fasting in the Jewish calendar, based upon the command in Leviticus xvi. 29–34. Falling on the tenth day of the month Tisri, it is the concluding ceremonial in the New Year observances. On Rosh Hashanah (*q. v.*), or New Year's Day, there were praise and prayer, but no afflicting of the flesh. Then the fate of the pious was merely inscribed in the great book which lies open for changes during ten days; but after Yom Kippur the register is closed and sealed, and what is written is written. So the greeting for the first day is "Chaihivoh Tovoh," the short for "May you have a good inscription," while that of Yom Kippur is "Chatimoh Tovoh," "a good seal."

As the Jewish day lasts from sunset to sunset, the ceremonies begin on what we should call the preceding evening.

Every family purchases a cock. The eldest male, taking it by the legs, swings it nine times over the heads of the others, praying God to transfer their sins into the body of the fowl. The bird is then either killed as a sacrifice or given to the poor.

The last meal for twenty-four hours is taken just before the first dark hour. Until sunset next day not a drop of water, not a mouthful of food, can pass the lips of the fasters. All are now in readiness to start for the synagogue, which has been strewn with straw. The anxious mothers and wives question the men eagerly about the state of their souls. Have they forgiven all transgressions against them? If they have not, theirs may not be forgiven them.

Though unprescribed in the laws, this domestic ceremony, which may be called the parting for the synagogue, is often a most harrowing and touching scene, especially among the sterner believers of orthodox Jewry. The mother, with tears in her eyes, embraces her son and beseeches him to purify his soul, and the wife does likewise with her husband. In the tense emotional excitement, with the dark, obscure dread of atonement upon them, the men sometimes make up quarrels they had thought too bitter ever to be settled. Brothers and sisters are reconciled, and not infrequently husbands and wives, who have separated in anger, rush into each other's arms in this hour.

In the basement of the synagogue are arranged dozens of long narrow boxes filled with sand. Each worshipper brings with him a candle, sticks it in the sand, lights it, and in a brief prayer beseeches God to let the light of his mercy shine upon the candle and by making it burn long and clear indicate a long and happy life for the supplicant.

The men remove their shoes and take their places in stocking-feet on the floor of the synagogue. The women are usually in the gallery. Many of the men wear the kittel, or burial-robe of white trimmed with black stripes, and the talith, or white satin death-cap. The ceremonies commence with the Kol Midre, or service for the absolution of all vows, which is thrice repeated. Prayers and readings break the spell of it, and the Jews believe, as the name implies, that they are absolved from all the vows of the previous year, and that those made on New Year's

Day are satisfactory and are inscribed with a good omen for the twelve months.

After the Kol Midre most of the Jews go home and sleep. But the more devout remain in the synagogues all night, and all return early in the morning, at five or six o'clock, to resume their devotions. The morning service is the Shachvith. It includes the reading of the Torah, or scroll, and lasts till ten or eleven o'clock. The second service, from eleven till one or two o'clock, is the Musoph. Then comes in the afternoon the Minchah, which continues till the closing hour, when the Neeloh supersedes. This ceremony must be continued till three stars are out. Sometimes all the Psalms are read, but if the day is not yet over, the reading begins again, or some other book of the Bible is taken up and is painfully repeated by the reader till at last the stars are announced and the ram's horn sounds the glad tidings. The Book of Life is closed, the seal is affixed, the judgment is set.

Yue-Ping (Chinese, " Moon-Cakes"), **Feast of.** The Chinese Thanksgiving, held at the full moon in the eighth month of their calendar. A clear sky is always eagerly prayed for, as a sight of the moon on this occasion is held to be of happy augury. It is a very old festival, and is chiefly commemorated by an abundance of good things to eat. They have no turkeys in China, or if they have them they prefer pigs, and hence the proper dish on this day is a porker of eight pounds' weight, roasted to a rich brownish red and seasoned with many sweet-smelling herbs. With this as the main dish come the moon-cakes, which in point of complexity and number of ingredients put the plum-pudding of our English sires to the blush. They are round, are served with a sweet sauce, and are stuffed with a hash of minced pork, watermelon-seeds, nuts, ginger, and spices. So far as their appearance goes, they are supposed to resemble a full moon ; but, it may be said with emphasis, the resemblance is a conventional one, and a Chinese convention at that.

Not only are moon-cakes eaten at home, but friends and relatives pay visits to present them to one another, with many protestations of affection and with a preliminary pouring out of libations to the moon. It is very remarkable that a verse of one of the Jewish prophets should be explained by this Chinese custom. " The children gather wood," said the seer, " and the fathers kindle the fire, and the women knead their dough to make cakes to the queen of heaven."

Yule Doughs or **Doos.** A peculiar sort of cake made at Christmas in many parts of Northern England for distribution among the young people. They are from six to twelve inches long, roughly fashioned in the shape of a human figure, doubtless representing the infant Jesus. Raisins are inserted for the eyes and nose. There are various other cakes peculiar to the season, as in Cornwall, where each household makes a batch of currant cakes on Christmas Eve. A small portion of the dough in the centre of each top is pulled up, and this small head-piece to the cake is called "the Christmas." Each member of the family has his own special cake; but every one ought to taste a small piece of every other person's cake. In Alnwick a custom existed of giving sweetmeats to children at Christmas time. These were called Yule Babies. Ben Jonson's "Masque of Christmas" has a character called Baby Cake, but this is explained to refer to the Twelfth Night cake.

Yule-Log. The name given by the ancient Goths and Saxons to the festival of the winter solstice was *Jul*, or *Yule*. The latter term is still preserved by the Scotch, and obsolescently by the English, and it survives everywhere in English-speaking countries in the compound Yule-log. The etymology of the word is uncertain. The Greek ουλος or ίουλος, the name of a hymn in honor of Demeter, the Latin *jubilum*, "a time of rejoicing," and the Gothic *ol* or *oel*, a feast as well as the favorite liquor used at the feast, namely our ale,—all these have been suggested. But a more probable derivation is from the Gothic *giul* or *hiul*, "wheel,"—the wheel being everywhere a symbol of the turning-point of the year, or the period when the sun made a revolution in his annual circuit and entered on his northern journey.

Now, the burning of the Yule-log or Yule-clog, known by other names in Continental Europe, was an ancient Christmas ceremony descending from the Scandinavians, who at their feast of Jul used to kindle huge bonfires in honor of their god Thor. Similar bonfires were kindled in Europe and elsewhere at the summer solstice (see JOHN THE BAPTIST, ST.), whence it is surmised that all these customs have their source in sun-worship.

The English ceremony of bringing in and burning the Yule-log on Christmas Eve, which still has its local survivals, was full of picturesque detail. The log was a massive piece of wood, frequently the rugged and grotesquely marked root of an oak. It was drawn in triumph from its resting-place amid shouts and laughter, every wayfarer doffing his hat as it passed. On its entrance into the baronial hall the minstrels hailed it with song and music, or in the absence of the minstrels each member of the family sat upon it in turn and sang a Yule song. A favorite Yule song began with—

> Welcome be thou, heavenly King,
> Welcome born on this morning,
> Welcome for whom we shall sing
> Welcome Yule.

Meanwhile Yule doughs (*q. v.*) were eaten and washed down with draughts from the mighty wassail bowls (see WASSAIL) and tankards of spiced ale.

The sport of "Dun in the Mire" was often played ere the final conflagration. The Yule stock, drawn into the middle of the floor, became "Dun, the cart-horse," for the nonce; the cry was raised that he had stuck in the mire:

> If thou art Dun, we'll draw thee from the mire,
> Of this (save reverence) love, wherein thou stick'st
> Up to the ears.

Two of the company, with or without ropes, advanced to extricate Dun; after various real and feigned exertions, they called for more help, until all present were mixed up in the rough-and-tumble exertion; the fun rose from the horse-play of the revellers, falling about, and contriving to roll or drop the log on each other's toes; this was kept up with hearty enjoyment until, the fun being exhausted, "Dun was drawn out."

In "Romeo and Juliet," Mercutio observes to Romeo,—

> Tut, Dun's the mouse, the constable's own ward:
> If thou art Dun, we'll draw thee from the mire.

After the endless amusement afforded by the Yule games, the log was kindled to cheer up the hearts of the revellers and to defy the cold. The firing was to be accomplished, according to traditional usage, from a portion of the charred Yule block carefully preserved from the preceding Christmas for this purpose:

> Kindle the Christmas brand, and then
> Till sunneset let it burne;
> Which quencht, then lay it up agen,
> Till Christmas next returne.

> Part must be kept, wherewith to teend
> The Christmas log next yeare;
> And where 'tis safely kept, the fiend
> Can do no mischief there.

It was believed that the preservation of last year's Christmas log was a most effectual security to the house against fire. We are further informed that it was regarded as a sign of very bad luck if a squinting person entered the hall when the log was burning, and a similarly evil omen was exhibited in the arrival of a barefooted person, and, above all, of a flat-footed woman. As an accompaniment to the Yule-log, a candle of monstrous size, called the Yule Candle, or Christmas Candle, shed its light on the festive board during the evening. Brand, in his " Popular Antiquities," states that in the buttery of St. John's College, Oxford, an ancient candle-socket of stone still remains, ornamented with the figure of the Holy Lamb. It was formerly used for holding the Christmas Candle, which during the twelve nights of the Christmas festival was burned on the high table at supper.

In Provence the analogue of the Yule-log of the Northern nations is called the Cachofio. Every household has one, which is burned from Christmas Eve to January 1. Naturally it must be a good stout log some five feet long. The head of the family— grandfather, father, or eldest son—must make the first incision in the tree, which is usually an olive or an almond, though any fruit-bearing tree will do. The log when cut is borne home in triumph on the shoulders of the two sturdiest members of the family, the father and the eldest son, or the husband and wife, while the children caracole around them or lend little helping hands. Already, because destined for the Christmas rites, it has acquired a sacrosanct character, so that it would resent any unduly rough handling or disrespect. But when treated reverently and burned with fitting rites, the log brings a blessing on the household, and its very ashes are potent for good.

Formerly when the Counts of Provence lived and ruled in Aix it was customary for the magistrates of the city to carry in solemn procession a huge cachofio to the palace and formally present it to the sovereign or his seneschal as a free-will and good-will offering. And after the ceremony of presentation the city fathers were served with a collation in the great hall of the palace and enabled to drink the health of the count in his own good wine.

The Servians also have their Yule-log. On Christmas Eve the father of the family goes to the wood and cuts down a straight and well-grown young oak. He brings it in, saying, " Good-evening, and a merry Christmas ;" to which all present reply, " May God grant both to thee, and mayest thou have riches and honor." Then they throw over him grains of corn. Presently the young tree is placed upon the coals, where it remains until the morning, which is saluted by repeated pistol-shots. When a neighbor pays a visit he first throws grains of wheat through the open door, crying, " Christ is born !" Those upon whom the grain has fallen answer, " He is born indeed !" The visitor then enters, and, striking the log with a piece of iron, adds, " For as many sparks as come out of you, let there be as many oxen, horses, sheep, goats, pigs, and bee-hives." At length the mistress of the house throws a veil over all the assembled guests, and the remains of the log are carried out into the orchard. The ashes are retained, as they are believed to bring good luck.

Z.

Zemzem. (So called, by obvious onomatopœia, from the murmuring sound of its waters.) A holy well in Mecca, one of the most sacred objects within the precincts of the Kaaba. (See Mecca.) According to Moslem legend, when Hagar and the infant Ishmael were abandoned by Abraham for domestic reasons which every family man must approve, they wandered into the valley of Mecca, or rather where Mecca was afterwards founded, and Hagar, oppressed by the heat, began to search for water to relieve the thirst from which she and the child were suffering. She ran backward and forward between the hills of Safa and Marwa, seeking in vain, but, returning to the spot where she had left the infant, found that Ishmael had himself discovered the spring they both needed by a simple expedient, familiar to babies of all nations and all periods. Kicking out against the ground, his infantile efforts had laid bare one of those springs which in Arabia are frequently concealed by a light layer of sand. This was the well Zemzem.

It is certain that Zemzem, like the Kaaba, is one of the most ancient of the antiquities of Arabia. Both were connected with the oldest rites of the pagan Arabs, and existed in very much their present form and were applied to very much their present uses before the time of Mohammed. It was the Prophet's grandfather who reopened the well, of the position of which he had been informed in a dream, whilst he was trying to devise some convenient means of fulfilling his special duty and privilege of supplying water to the tribes who flocked annually to worship at the Kaaba. Digging in the appointed spot, he found the remains of an ancient piece of masonry enclosing a copious and never-failing spring, which was at once accepted as the traditional well of Hagar. It is probable at least that the masonry dated from the old days of the mercantile prosperity of Mecca, perhaps even from pre-Christian times. Ever since this rediscovery of the well, Zemzem has held a prominent place among the holy things of the Arabian temple. The millions of pilgrims to Mecca do not leave the "Haram esh-Sherif" without washing in, or at least tasting, the water of the well Zemzem, and most of them carry away a flask of the holy water. No more valuable present can be offered by a returned hajji to his friends than a bottle of this miraculous, though admittedly brackish, fluid. Its properties are quite unique in the eyes of the faithful. It can cure diseases ; sprinkled on grave-clothes it produces the most salutary results in the future state of the deceased ; while a single sip is the best cordial that a host can offer to his most distinguished guest. One famous traditionist, whose memory was proverbial, ascribed his retentive powers entirely to the copious draughts he had taken of the water of Zemzem, which Sale gravely remarks appears to be really as efficacious in its own province as the spring of Helicon has proved to the inspiration of poets. But from what one knows of the sanitary methods of the East there is nothing surprising in the discovery that the well of Zemzem is as foul as a good many other saintly springs. The water in the fountains of mosques never strikes the eye or nose with any very pleasing impression, and Zemzem is in the midst of a thickly built city, where drainage is of a peculiarly primitive description, and the well is almost necessarily affected by the drainings from the countless carcasses of beasts which are annually sacrificed by the pilgrims in the neighboring valley of Mina.

THE END.